CASES & PROBLEMS IN CRIMINAL LAW

CASES & PROBLEMS IN CRIMINAL LAW

Sixth Edition

Myron Moskovitz
Professor of Law
Golden Gate University

ISBN: 978-1-4224-7675-8

Library of Congress Control Number: 2011927986

Library of Congress Cataloging-in-Publication Data
Moskovitz, Myron.
Cases & problems in criminal law / Myron Moskovitz. -- 6th ed.
p. cm.
Rev. ed. of: Cases and problems in criminal law / Myron Moskovitz. 5th ed. c2003.
Includes index.
ISBN 978-1-4224-7675-8
1. Criminal law--United States--Cases. I. Moskovitz, Myron. Cases and problems in criminal law. II. Title. .
KF9218.M67 2011
345.73--dc23   2011039434

> ### NOTE TO USERS
> To ensure that you are using the latest materials available in this area, please be sure to periodically check the LexisNexis Law School web site for downloadable updates and supplements at www.lexisnexis.com/lawschool.

Editorial Offices
121 Chanlon Rd., New Providence, NJ 07974 (908) 464-6800
201 Mission St., San Francisco, CA 94105-1831 (415) 908-3200
www.lexisnexis.com

MATTHEW◊BENDER

(2012–Pub.3513)

PREFACE

Most criminal law casebooks focus on the philosophy of criminal law. While this book delves into those issues on occasion, its main focus is more practical: it teaches students how to analyze problems the way a lawyer who practices criminal law would.

Suppose a client comes to a lawyer with a difficult legal problem, involving a complex set of facts. The lawyer then researches the legal issues, finding a cluster of cases and statutes — almost all from the jurisdiction in which the problem arises. In order to advise the client (and — if necessary — to litigate the case), the lawyer must analyze, distinguish, reconcile, and interrelate the authorities in the cluster, seeing them as a group indicating the direction of that state's law as well as seeing them separately.

This book is an attempt to recreate that experience for the law student, and to help the student learn how to handle it. To learn to do something practical, one needs 3 things: a task, some tools, and a teacher. This book supplies the task and the tools. The task is the Problem at the outset of each chapter. The tools are the statutes and cases which follow. To make the experience more realistic, each statute and case in the chapter is from the jurisdiction in which the Problem arose. Following each case is a note giving the student a hint as to how the case might be used to help analyze the Problem.

I have tried to select cases which have interesting facts, raise issues that tend to be central to the topic of the chapter, and which contain readable — though not always "correct" — analyses by the courts. I have edited the cases severely to make them even more readable. In most chapters, the main cases are all from a single jurisdiction (the jurisdiction in which the Problem takes place) and presented chronologically. A practicing lawyer will focus on cases in the jurisdiction the case is to be tried, trying to understand and reconcile them. I want my students to do the same.

This book is primarily a tool for learning skills, rather than for learning all the intricacies of each doctrine of criminal law. While the materials should enable the professor to explore many basic principles of criminal law, greater breadth of coverage can be obtained from a good treatise or hornbook. I usually suggest that my students read LaFave & Scott, Criminal Law (West), which I consider the best of its kind. The LaFave and Scott, Criminal Law material appearing throughout this work has been reproduced with the permission of the authors and West Publishing Company.

While I believe that the approach taken by this book is pedagogically sound, I have another, more selfish reason for using this approach in my teaching: it is fun to play lawyer. My students usually agree, and I think this in itself enhances their learning. This approach does demand more work from them. Not only must they read the cases, but they must try to apply them to the Problem. I also ask them to prepare an outline of an analysis of the Problem, based on the authorities in the chapter. All this takes more time and effort, but they do it and seem to enjoy doing it. They know that they are reading the cases as a lawyer would, for a specific purpose: to answer the Problem. I hope you enjoy it too.

Many thanks to James Upp and Rory Hodgson for their research assistance on this Sixth Edition.

Myron Moskovitz

CONTENTS

CONTENTS

CONTENTS

CONTENTS

CONTENTS

CONTENTS

INTRODUCTION

I. AN OVERVIEW OF THE CRIMINAL PROCESS

This book is about "substantive criminal law" — the definitions of certain basic crimes and defenses, and the underlying reasons why we define certain conduct and mental states as "criminal." You will learn about "criminal procedure" in a separate course (using a separate book) which will deal with the various constitutional restrictions on police arrests, searches, and interrogations, and with the several stages of the criminal case as it proceeds through the courts.

Nevertheless, to help you follow procedural matters which appear in the cases in this book — and to set the substantive issues in their procedural contexts — here is a brief overview of the whole process in felony cases, as it usually operates in federal courts and most state courts.[1]

Suppose the police believe that Dan has committed a series of four bank robberies. They arrest Dan and "book" him (write the charges and biographical data about Dan in a book), and they send a report of the case to the prosecutor's office ("United States Attorney" in the federal system, "District Attorney" in most states). The prosecutor considers the strength of the evidence against Dan and other factors in determining what charges to file, and then files a *complaint* against Dan in court. The complaint is similar to a complaint in a civil case. Each count (i.e., each separate charge) in the complaint states that on a certain date, Dan committed certain acts which violated a specified penal statute, at a location within the jurisdiction of the court.

Within a few days, Dan will be *arraigned* before a magistrate of the court (who does not have as much authority as the judge who will later preside at the trial of the case). At the arraignment, the magistrate will read the charges to Dan and ask him to enter a *plea* of guilty, not guilty, not guilty by reason of insanity, or *nolo contendere* (i.e., a default), to each charge. If Dan does not have a lawyer with him to advise him on what plea to enter, the magistrate will usually give Dan some time to hire one, or, if Dan is indigent, time to arrange for the services of a public defender. If Dan pleads guilty to any charge, the magistrate will sentence him or refer him to a judge for sentencing.

Suppose that, after consulting with counsel, Dan pleads not guilty to all charges. The magistrate will then set a date for a *preliminary hearing* (sometimes called a *preliminary examination*), to be held before the magistrate, unless Dan waives his right to a preliminary hearing. The magistrate will also consider whether Dan should be released on *bail* (or on his "own recognizance"), pending the preliminary hearing.

---

[1] This overview is taken from Moskovitz, *Cases & Problems in Criminal Procedure: The Courtroom.* Copyright 1998 by Matthew Bender & Co., Inc. Reprinted with permission. All rights reserved.

The preliminary hearing is intended to permit the magistrate to decide whether there is "probable cause" to hold Dan for trial on each count. This is a screening device, meant to save Dan the expense and anxiety of a trial on a weak case, and meant to save the courts the expense of a trial which is unlikely to lead to a conviction. At the preliminary hearing, the prosecutor will put on a somewhat skeletal case, with a minimum of witnesses — enough to show probable cause but not enough to let defense counsel see the whole prosecution case. The defense will seldom put on witnesses of its own, but will cross-examine prosecution witnesses in an effort to undermine probable cause and to try to "discover" as much of the prosecutor's case as possible, in preparation for trial.

The magistrate's decision may take several forms. She may dismiss some or all charges against Dan. She may also reduce some or all charges to "lesser-included" crimes. (For example, she may find probable cause to believe that Dan stole the money, but no probable cause to believe that he used force or threats — so a robbery charge should be reduced to larceny.) If the magistrate finds probable cause as to any charge which is a felony, she will "hold the defendant to answer" the charges at trial, and she will order the defendant "bound over" to the court for trial on these charges. The prosecutor will then file an *information* in the trial court. The information is similar to the complaint, setting out the remaining charges.

In federal court and in a few states, the prosecutor must obtain an *indictment* from a grand jury (unless Dan waives indictment, in which case an information may be filed). The grand jury may indict only if it finds probable cause to believe that Dan committed the crimes, based on evidence presented in secret by the prosecutor to the grand jury. (Defense counsel is not present before the grand jury, and no cross-examination of witnesses occurs.) Usually, if the prosecutor obtains the indictment before the date set for the preliminary hearing, the preliminary hearing will not be held, as the purpose of the preliminary hearing — to determine "probable cause" — will already have been served.

After the indictment or information is filed, Dan will be arraigned before a trial court judge, and Dan will enter a plea of guilty or not guilty to the remaining charges. If Dan pleads not guilty, the judge will set a date for the trial. The judge may also decide whether Dan should be released on bail pending trial. Before trial, both the prosecutor and defense counsel may be given certain rights to *discover* each other's case — although these rights are much more limited than discovery rights in civil cases.

Before trial, defense counsel may file certain *pretrial motions*, such as motions for discovery and motions to suppress evidence which is the result of an illegal search or interrogation.

At any point in this process, but usually before the trial begins, the parties may engage in *plea bargaining*. Each defendant has a right to a *speedy trial* (i.e., a trial which begins fairly soon after the arrest or indictment), but the prosecutor and the court do not have the resources to give a speedy trial to every defendant. So the prosecutor must induce most defendants to plead guilty. This is done by offering to dismiss or reduce some charges or to recommend certain sentences. Before accepting a guilty plea, the judge will make sure that the defendant knows what he has been promised and not promised, and that he is giving up the right to trial by jury on the charges. At trial, if both parties agree, the case may be tried by the judge. Usually, however, the defendant demands a jury trial, as it is generally assumed that a group of lay people is less likely to convict than a "case-hardened" judge. In most cases, the jury's verdict must be unanimous, which makes it less likely that the prosecutor will obtain a guilty verdict from a jury. The case begins with *voir dire*, the questioning of prospective jurors by the two lawyers and/or the judge. If any prospective juror displays improper bias, a lawyer may challenge that person "for cause," and if the judge finds improper bias, that person will be dismissed. Each lawyer also has a limited number of *peremptory challenges*, allowing the dismissal of several prospective jurors for any (almost) or no reason.

After the jury is selected and sworn, each lawyer may make an *opening statement* to the jury, summarizing the evidence to be presented. Then the prosecution puts on its witnesses, who are subject to cross-examination by the defense. When the prosecution rests its case, defense counsel may move for a *directed verdict* of acquittal, on the ground that the prosecution evidence, even if believed by the jury, does not show all of the elements of the crime(s) charged in the information or indictment. If such a motion is denied or not made, the defense then puts on its case, and its witnesses are subject to cross-examination by the prosecutor. The defendant has a constitutional right not to testify, but if he does testify, he too is subject to cross-examination by the prosecutor. When the defense rests, the prosecutor may introduce rebuttal evidence, and sometimes the defense may introduce surrebuttal evidence. After each side rests its case, each attorney submits to the judge proposed *jury instructions*, containing the rules of law which apply to the case. Some of these instructions will be standard instructions taken from appellate court opinions and form books, and others will be devised by the lawyers. After hearing and ruling on any objections to proposed instructions, the judge will inform the lawyers as to which instructions will be given. Each lawyer then delivers a *summation* (sometimes called *closing argument*) to the jury. Because the prosecutor has the burden of proof (beyond a reasonable doubt), she will go first, then the defense lawyer will argue, and then the prosecutor is allowed a final rebuttal. Since each lawyer then knows what instructions the judge will give the jury, the lawyers will usually argue that the law contained in the instructions, when applied to the evidence heard by the jury, dictates a result favorable to that side.

After the summations, the judge reads the jury instructions to the jury. The jury then deliberates and returns with its verdict. If the jury is unable to decide any of the charges by the required majority (usually unanimity), the judge will declare a *mistrial* as to those charges and, if the prosecutor so requests, set the case for re-trial before a new jury. If the jury acquits the defendant, the defendant will be released and case is over — the prosecutor has no right to appeal an acquittal. If the jury convicts the defendant on any charge, the jury is then discharged, in most cases. Usually, the jury plays no role in the next phase — sentencing — unless the jury convicted the defendant of a capital crime and the prosecutor is seeking the death penalty. Statutes control what the judge may consider in sentencing the defendant. Some statutes set low and high limits on the sentence, but allow the judge wide discretion as to any sentence within these limits (e.g., "2 to 10 years"). Such statutes often allow the judge to consider just about any factor in choosing the sentence. Other statutes confer the authority to select the actual sentence on some other board or agency. Some statutes set the sentence at specific terms of years, depending on certain factors the judge must find (e.g., 2 years for a robber with no criminal record and who injured no one, 6 years for a robber with a record who injured someone, and 4 years for an in-between robber). Before sentencing the defendant, the judge will usually request a *pre-sentence report* from the court's probation department or similar agency. These officials will investigate the defendant's background and recommend a sentence to the judge. At the sentencing hearing, defense counsel may object to all or parts of the presentence report, and may present evidence on the appropriate sentence. The sentence may also include a fine. In some cases, the judge may grant *probation* to the defendant, perhaps on condition that the defendant serve a few months in a local jail.

After selecting the appropriate sentence for the defendant, the judge will enter a *judgment*, which states both the conviction and the sentence. From this judgment, defendant may file a *notice of appeal* to the appellate court which oversees the trial court. Filing this notice does not stay the sentence, and the defendant will have to seek a stay of the sentence and bail on appeal in order to avoid incarceration during the appeal.

A defendant will often obtain a new attorney on appeal, one who specializes in appellate work. The prosecutor often does the same. Copies of the pleadings and other documents are compiled (usually into a volume called the "clerk's transcript"). A court reporter's transcript of all of the oral testimony and argument is also prepared. Using these transcripts and any exhibits submitted as evidence at trial, the defendant's lawyer writes and files an "Appellant's Opening Brief," the prosecutor's attorney writes and files a "Respondent's Brief," and the defendant's lawyer then writes and files an "Appellant's Reply Brief." The appellate court then sets the case for oral argument, the case is argued, and it is submitted for decision. The appellate court then decides the case, usually issuing a written opinion, which may or may not be published in the official reports. The court may affirm the trial court judgment, reverse it (usually for retrial, but sometimes with instructions to dismiss certain charges), or modify it (e.g., by reducing the sentence). If either side is unhappy with the appellate court's ruling, that party may seek review from the next highest court (usually the state supreme court or United States Supreme Court), but that court usually has discretion to grant or deny a hearing in the case.

An appeal must be based on the *record* — the transcripts and exhibits from the trial court — and no other evidence will be considered by the appellate court. If a defendant claims that evidence outside of these transcripts and exhibits warrants relief, he must file a petition for a writ of *habeas corpus*. For example, if Dan claims that one of the jurors who convicted him was threatened during jury deliberations, evidence of this claim is unlikely to appear in the trial transcripts, and Dan must prove it by submitting affidavits attached to his petition for writ of habeas corpus. If Dan claims that a state court denied him his constitutional rights, he may sometimes seek habeas corpus relief in federal court.

If all else fails, Dan must pay his debt to society.

II.   ON PROBLEM ANALYSIS

Each chapter of this book begins with a Problem, which is meant to simulate a case which a lawyer might be called on to analyze, in order to advise a client or to prepare some litigation document.

Analyzing these Problems is not easy, even if you think you know "the law" in the chapter. Just as cases in real life are seldom simple, one-issue cases, each Problem raises several issues. The key to analyzing these Problems is good *organization* of the issues. Once you arrange the issues into a proper framework for analysis, the rest is — well, not easy, but manageable. Organization of the issues is done by preparation of an *outline*. A typical outline will break down something like this:

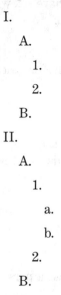

I.

  A.

    1.

    2.

  B.

II.

  A.

    1.

      a.

      b.

    2.

  B.

What goes into these blank spaces? The following two principles usually work pretty well:

> *Principle Number 1:* The issues in the "first level" of the outline (i.e., the roman numerals, I, II, etc.) come from *the question* raised by the Problem. You do not need to know *any* law to write in these issues — just read the Problem, find the question, and read it carefully.[2]

> *Principle Number 2:* The issues in the lower levels of the outline (the As and Bs, 1s and 2s, etc.) come from *the rules of law* which appear in the cases and statutes in the chapter. To write in these issues properly, you will have to learn the rules of law — in some detail.

Let's apply these principles to a sample Problem.

Problem X

---

[2] You might try this out by turning to almost any Problem in the book — now, before you have even read any of the chapters. Knowing no law, you should nevertheless be able to write out the major issues for an outline of a memo on the Problem — simply by finding the *question* in the Problem.

To: My law clerk

From: Mary Mason, Esq.

Re: *State v. Woods*

My client, Don Woods, has been charged with forcible rape and statutory rape of Susan Carr. At trial, the sole witness for the prosecution was Ms. Carr, who testified as follows:

> Q. Ms. Carr, what happened when you went out with Mr. Woods?
>
> A. We went out to dinner last month. Then he took me to his apartment and we had a few drinks. We started to kiss and hug. He said, "When I want sex, I get it, or else." He then just got on top of me and started to have sex with me, without even asking. I did not want to have sex with him.
>
> Q. Did you protest in any way?
>
> A. No. I was too drunk or scared, I guess. I did push him once or twice.
>
> Q. How old are you?
>
> A. I just turned 18. My birthday was last month.

Based on this evidence, I would like to move for a directed verdict of acquittal on each of the two charges. The judge will grant the motion if she finds that the above testimony, even if believed by the jury, does not contain evidence of all the elements of a charge. Please read the attached authorities and advise me as to the best arguments I can make and how the judge is likely to rule on them. (I will probably use your memo as a basis for the brief I write, so please do a good job.)

Penal Code § 123

"Forcible rape is an act of sexual intercourse accomplished against a person's will by means of force or fear."

Penal Code § 124

"Statutory rape is an act of sexual intercourse accomplished with a female not the wife of the perpetrator, where the female is under the age of 18 years."

State v. Twitt

[This case holds that the prosecutor has the burden of presenting evidence which a reasonable jury could believe shows all elements of the charged offense. The case also holds that if the prosecutor fails to do this, the judge should grant a defense motion for a directed verdict of acquittal.]

State v. Dweeb

[This case holds that the words "against a person's will" in § 123 mean "without consent, where the lack of consent has been expressly or impliedly communicated to the defendant."]

State v. Twerp

[This case holds that the word "fear" in § 123 means "a reasonable apprehension of immediate bodily injury or death."]

State v. Dripp

[This case holds that one does not violate § 124 unless the female is under 18 years old at the time of the act of sexual intercourse.]

After reading the above material, you have probably spotted a few issues which should be discussed in your memo to your employer. Does the evidence show that Ms. Carr was over 18 at the time of the act? Did she impliedly communicate lack of consent? Did Woods use "force"? There is no evidence that they were not married.

Good issues, but how do you present them? As they occur to you? In the order in which they appear in the testimony? Unless you find some coherent way to organize your issues, your presentation will be less effective and persuasive than it should be, and it might even descend into an incoherent mess. Preparing an outline pursuant to the two principles mentioned above may help you write a good memo. Also, it should help you to see *all* of the relevant issues.

Let's begin our outline. First, specify the major issues — the Roman numerals. These come directly from the *question*, which appears somewhere in the Problem. Here, you'll find it in the last paragraph, where lawyer Mason says she wants to move for a directed verdict on each of the 2 charges, and asks you for arguments and predicted rulings on the motion. Since there are 2 charges, the motion will consist of 2 parts:

I. Motion for Directed Verdict on *Forcible Rape* Charge

II. Motion for Directed Verdict on *Statutory Rape* Charge

Usually, the major issues should be discussed in the same *order* that they arose in the facts, chronologically. This will minimize the need for repetition and allow you to refer back (rather than ahead) to facts or issues discussed elsewhere, producing a more readable memo. In Problem X, however, the events relating to the two charges occurred simultaneously, so it does not really matter which charge we discuss first.

Next, fill in the "submajor" issues, where they belong. This requires us to learn the *definition* of each of the charges. Because we must determine whether the evidence shows "forcible rape," we must find out what "forcible rape" means, i.e., the *elements* of this crime (and then "apply" these elements to the facts, i.e., examine Ms. Carr's testimony to see if she supplied facts showing each of these elements). These elements will become our submajor issues under Issue I, and the elements of "statutory rape" will become the submajor issues under Issue II.

We get these definitions and elements from the statutes and cases. Thus, an examination of Penal Code § 123 tells us that "forcible rape" consists of the following elements: (1) an act of sexual intercourse, (2) accomplished against a person's will, (3) by means of (a) force or (b) fear. After breaking down § 124 the same way, we now have:

I. Motion for Directed Verdict on *Forcible Rape* Charge

A. Act of sexual intercourse

B. Accomplished against a person's will

C. By means of:

   1. Force

   2. Fear

II. Motion for Directed Verdict on *Statutory Rape* Charge

A. Act of sexual intercourse

B. With a female

C. Not the wife of defendant

D. Where female is under 18

Now, examine the *cases* which *interpret* some of these terms, to see if they add more subissues which must be considered. Thus:

I. Motion for Directed Verdict on *Forcible Rape* Charge (For each element, discuss whether testimony would permit reasonable jury to find that element. *State v. Twitt.*)

A. Act of sexual intercourse

B. Accomplished against a person's will (see *State v. Dweeb*)

   1. Was lack of consent *expressly* communicated to defendant?

   2. Was lack of consent *impliedly* communicated to defendant?

C. By means of:

   1. Force

   2. Fear of bodily injury or death (*State v. Twerp*)

II. Motion for Directed Verdict on *Statutory Rape* Charge (For each element, discuss whether testimony would permit reasonable jury to find that element. *State v. Twitt.*)

A. Act of sexual intercourse

B. With a female

C. Not the wife of defendant

D. Where female is under 18 at time of sexual intercourse (see *State v. Dripp*)

Now the outline is almost complete. But it is *too* complete. Some of these "issues" are not *live* issues, because you have no reasonable argument that these elements are not present. For example, you would look pretty silly if you advised your employer to argue to the judge (who saw Ms. Carr testify) that the evidence did not show that Ms. Carr was a "female." So we must now go through our outline and *cull out* "issues" which turn out to be "nonissues" — because of our facts.

I. Motion for Directed Verdict on *Forcible Rape* Charge (For each element, discuss whether testimony would permit reasonable jury to find that element. (See *State v. Twitt.*)

    A. Accomplished against a person's will (see *State v. Dweeb*)

        1. Was lack of consent *expressly* communicated to defendant?

        2. Was lack of consent *impliedly* communicated to defendant?

    B. By means of:

        1. Force

        2. Fear of bodily injury or death (*State v. Twerp*)

II. Motion for Directed Verdict on *Statutory Rape* Charge (For each element, discuss whether testimony would permit reasonable jury to find that element. See *State v. Twitt.*)

    A. Where female is under 18 at time of sexual intercourse (see *State v. Dripp*)

    B. Not the wife of defendant

We have one more job to do. Our memo will include not just a report on the *law*, but also how that law *applies* to the *facts* of our case, so we can then do the final job of predicting how the judge will rule. Therefore, at the lowest level of the outline, we should briefly note the facts which are relevant to each legal issue. Thus, our final outline might look like this:

I. Motion for Directed Verdict on *Forcible Rape* Charge (For each element, discuss whether testimony would permit reasonable jury to find that element. (See *State v. Twitt.*)

    A. Accomplished against a person's will (see *State v. Dweeb*)

        1. Was lack of consent *expressly* communicated to defendant? No facts show this.

        2. Was lack of consent *impliedly* communicated to defendant?

            a. C pushed W.

            b. Unclear how hard she pushed.

    B. By means of:

        1. Force

            a. W got on top of C.

            b. No evidence of relative weights or strengths.

        2. Fear of bodily injury or death (*State v. Twerp*)

            a. C said, "When I want . . ."

            b. "Or else" is unclear.

II. Motion for Directed Verdict on *Statutory Rape* Charge (For each element, discuss whether testimony would permit reasonable jury to find that element. See *State v. Twitt.*)

    A. Where female is under 18 at time of sexual intercourse (see *State v. Dripp*)

        1. Incident occurred "last month."

        2. C turned 18 "last month."

    B. Not the wife of defendant
No evidence C & W were not married.

Now our outline is about as good as we can make it. Our *assignment* is not done yet — we still have to write the memo. Our memo will carefully *apply* each of the above issues to the *facts*. But we have laid the groundwork for a well-organized memo which covers all of the relevant issues. When you come to each new chapter of this book, you might write an outline for the Problem in that chapter. This may seem difficult at first, but it should become easier as you gain some experience with it. The skills you learn from doing this may prove useful to you when taking exams — and when practicing law.

After writing the outline, you might wish to finish the job and write the memo. In writing the memo, try to follow the following principles:

- Focus on the *question* posed by the Problem

- Stay organized, following your outline

- Discuss each issue and subissue in something like an "IRAC" format: state the *Issue* (I), briefly state the correct legal *Rule* (R), *Apply* (A) that rule to the *facts*, and end the discussion of each issue and subissue with a *Conclusion* (C) — a prediction of what the court will rule and why — before moving on to the next issue

- Spend more time on issues and subissues on which reasonable people might disagree, presenting all reasonable arguments on *both* sides before reaching a conclusion

For Problem X, the final memo might look something like this. Note that except for brief introductory and conclusory paragraphs, every other paragraph follows the IRAC format:

To: Mary Mason, Esq.

From: Your law clerk

Re: *State v. Woods*

I. Motion for Directed Verdict on *Forcible Rape* Charge To prove forcible rape, the prosecutor must show that Woods had sex with Carr against her will, and by means of either force or fear. Penal Code § 123. If he fails to present evidence of these elements which would permit a reasonable jury to find each of them, our motion for directed verdict of acquittal as to this charge should be granted. *State v. Twitt.*

Was there sufficient evidence that the sex act was against Carr's will? At first glance, it would seem so, as she testified that she did not want to have sex with Woods. But, according to *State v. Dweeb*, the act is not against one's will unless the lack of consent is expressly or impliedly *communicated* to the defendant.

Was there evidence that Carr *expressly* told Woods that she did not want to have sex with him? There is no evidence of this in the record. As the prosecution had the burden of proving the elements of the crime (*State v. Twill*), the absence of such evidence must be taken to mean that she did not expressly communicate her lack of consent.

Was there evidence that Carr *impliedly* communicated her lack of consent to Woods? She did testify that she pushed Woods once or twice, and I believe that a reasonable jury could find that Woods should have construed this as lack of consent. We should argue that the prosecution failed to show how hard Carr pushed Woods, or when she did so, and therefore the "communication" might have been weak, ambiguous, or untimely. But I conclude that the judge will rule that the jury could find that the pushes were an implied communication here, despite our arguments (which should be made to the jury in our closing argument).

Was there evidence that Woods used *force* to have sex with Carr? Carr testified that Woods just got on top of her and had sex. From this, a reasonable jury might infer that Woods was stronger and heavier than Carr and was thereby able to overcome her pushes. Carr also testified that she did not want to have sex with Woods. The jury could infer that if she did not want to, then Woods would have been unable to have sex with her unless he used force. We should argue that there is no evidence of the relative weights, ages, or strengths of the two people, so that Carr's testimony is too skimpy to show force. But I conclude the judge will rule that the jury could find from Carr's testimony that Woods used force, for the above reasons (and once again we may point out the weaknesses in her testimony in our closing argument to the jury). Was there evidence that Woods used *fear* to have sex with Carr? In *State v. Twerp*, the court defined "fear" as a "reasonable apprehension of immediate bodily injury or death." Carr testified that Woods said, "When I want sex, I get it, or else." This statement seems to threaten something, but the "or else" is very unclear as to just what is being threatened. The "or else" *could* be some type of physical attack, perhaps resulting in physical injury or death, perhaps not. "Or else" could also mean something non-physical, such as rejection, i.e., Woods would not date Carr any more. Because "or else" is so ambiguous, I conclude that the judge will hold that a reasonable jury could not find that these words would create a reasonable apprehension of bodily injury or death, and therefore Woods did not use "fear."

Based on the above analysis, I conclude that the judge will deny our motion for directed verdict on the forcible rape charge. Nevertheless, the issues are close enough that we should pursue the motion, as there is a reasonable chance that we might succeed.

II. Motion for Directed Verdict on *Statutory Rape* Charge

For Woods to be convicted of statutory rape under Penal Code § 124, the evidence must show that Carr was under 18 when the act was committed. *State v. Dripp*. If the prosecution failed to present evidence of this fact which a reasonable jury could believe, our motion for directed verdict of acquittal should be granted. *State v. Twitt.*

Carr testified that she had sex with Woods "last month," and also that her 18th birthday occurred "last month." Since these 2 events occurred during the same month, and she gave the exact date of neither event, a reasonable jury could not find on this evidence that she had sex with Woods before her 18th birthday. For this reason, I predict that the judge will grant our motion for directed verdict on the statutory rape charge.

Penal Code § 124 also requires the prosecution to show that Carr and Woods were not married at the time of the act. There is no express evidence of this in Carr's testimony. Could absence of marriage be *inferred*, from her testimony that they went to "his" apartment, rather than "their" apartment? Possibly, but this inference is not strong. Married people sometimes separate and have separate residences. So I conclude that the judge will grant our motion for directed verdict on the statutory rape charge on this ground also. One final suggestion: when you work on these Problems, try to separate your emotions from the characters, the events, and the charges described. Criminal law involves issues (such as rape and murder) which are often very disturbing to law students and lawyers. You might find yourself hating the defendant, the legislators who wrote the statutes, or the judges who authored the cases. This is understandable. Despite claims (and jokes) to the contrary, lawyers are just as human and emotional as other people. But lawyers have a job to do, and they cannot let their emotions interfere with good job performance. You would not want to be operated on by a surgeon who is trembling with emotion. Likewise, clients do not want your emotions to interfere with your best judgment as an advocate or advisor.

Sometimes, however, your emotional reactions may *help* you to find or understand the law. Judges are human too, and their emotions (which might be similar to yours) might have affected how the law developed. If you were working on Problem X, for example, and became outraged at what Woods did or became sympathetic to Carr's plight, you should look to see if your concerns are reflected some way in the policies underlying the applicable rules of law — as explained in the statutes and cases. If they were, you might mention these concerns as a way of strengthening your legal arguments. But do *not* let your concerns dictate the *result* you *want* to reach *before* you do your legal analysis. Such "result-oriented prejudging" usually leads to a weak analysis and poor representation for your client.

When you begin practicing law, you might decide not to take cases like those described in this book. Clients in criminal cases (and many civil cases) often have done things which are not very nice. But once you take a case, you have an ethical duty to do your best for your client — no matter how you feel about him or her.

While you are doing these Problems, pretend that you have taken the case, and do your best for the client. This will help you to develop the skills needed to help the clients you *want* to represent. (It might help to remind yourself that none of the characters or events in these Problems are real. They are purely figments of the author's rather bizarre imagination.)

III. ABOUT THE MODEL PENAL CODE

In the back of this book is an Appendix which contains several selected sections of the Model Penal Code. That Code was drafted by a team of scholars and judges working for the American Law Institute. The Institute also adopts "uniform" codes, where uniformity among state laws is desirable for enterprises which cut across state lines. There is no particular need for a *uniform* penal code, but the Institute saw a need for a *model* penal code, which would reflect the best modern thinking on crime and punishment, and state the rules in clear language.

The Model Penal Code was adopted by the Institute in 1962. The Institute has no power to require any state legislature to adopt the Code, but several states have chosen to adopt parts of the Code. In addition, where a statute is unclear and a court has room to interpret the statute as reflecting the best policy, the court might use the policy expressed by a particular section of the Code as authority for interpreting the statute. We will see some examples of this in Chapter 18, Attempt.

The Institute prepared "commentaries" for each section. These have not been included in the Appendix, but you may find them in your law school library.

Each Chapter will refer you to sections of the Model Penal Code for comparison to the state statutes you will be working with. Ask yourself whether the Code provision is indeed clearer and a better policy choice than the state statute.

Part I

Mental States — In General

Every crime requires both a proscribed mental state — the *mens rea* — and a proscribed act — the *actus reus*. And many crimes also require a specified *harm*. Thus, suppose a statute defines *arson* as "the intentional burning of a dwelling house." The *mens rea* of this crime would be "*intent*" to burn a house — as contrasted with a *negligent* burning. The *actus reus* would be some act that causes a fire to start in a house, e.g., lighting a match to some gas-soaked rags. And the *harm* required by "burning" would be some fire damage to a house.

What *mens rea* is required varies from crime to crime — and might even vary for different elements of the same crime.

Suppose Dan shoots his gun, and the bullet hits and kills Vic. Has Dan committed murder? This depends on the definition of murder. The *actus reus* of murder is the act (here, Dan's firing of the gun) that causes the specified *harm* (the death of a human being), but what *mens rea* is required for murder, i.e., what mental state must a jury find in order to convict Dan? There are several possibilities, including:

1. *Intent* to kill. If this is the standard, then Dan is guilty only if there is evidence that Dan intended to kill Vic. (What evidence? Well, maybe Wally will testify that Dan told her he planned to kill Vic, or told her after the killing that he meant to kill Vic.)

2. *Negligence*.[1] If this is the standard, than Dan *might* be guilty, but we need to know more facts. (Did Dan know that Vic was nearby? Did Dan know that the gun was operable and loaded?)

---

[1] There are several degrees of negligence used in various torts and crimes, including "simple" negligence, "gross" negligence (sometimes called "criminal" negligence), recklessness, and extreme recklessness (sometimes known as "depraved heart").

3. *Strict liability.* Under this standard, where one voluntarily does a certain thing, he is responsible for all injuries he causes — even those he did not intend and was not negligent in causing. If this is the standard (i.e., if the law were to provide "anyone who fires a gun is guilty of murder for all deaths caused thereby"), then Dan would be guilty.

Note that if a crime has more than one element — as most do — it is quite possible that different mental states will be required for different elements. Murder requires the killing of a *human being.* Suppose, in the above example, Dan believes (erroneously) that Vic is a deer, and Dan shoots at the "deer" with intent to kill. It is conceivable that a legislature or court might define murder to allow *gross negligence* to suffice for the "kill" element of murder, but require *intent* (or "actual knowledge") regarding the "human being" element. If this were the rule, then Dan *would* be guilty of murder if Dan *knew* Vic was human and was grossly negligent in killing him, but would *not* be guilty if he believed Vic were a deer.

How do you determine which mental state is required for an element of a crime? Today, in most jurisdictions, crimes are set out in *statutes* enacted by state legislatures and by Congress. So your first stop should be the statute. Sometimes the statute will clearly indicate what mental state is required. Often, however, the statute will say nothing about this,[2] or it will use some word (such as "willfully" or

---

[2] The notion that a statute's silence regarding mental state means strict liability was suggested by lawyer W.S. Gilbert, in *The Mikado* (Act II). When the Mikado (the emperor) learns that Ko-Ko, Poobah, and Pitti-Sing had apparently killed Nanki-Poo (the son of the Mikado) without realizing who he was, the Mikado indulges in a bit of statutory construction:

MIKADO: I forget the punishment for encompassing the death of the Heir Apparent.
KO-KO, POOBAH, & PITTI-SING: Punishment?
MIKADO: Yes. Something lingering, with boiling oil in it, I fancy. Something of that sort. I think boiling oil occurs in it, but I'm not sure. I know it's something humorous, but lingering, with either boiling oil or melted lead. Come, come, don't fret - I'm not a bit angry.

KO-KO [in abject terror]: If your majesty will accept our assurance, we had no idea -
MIKADO: Of course.
PITTI-SING: I knew nothing about it.
POOBAH: I wasn't there.
MIKADO: That's the pathetic part of it. Unfortunately, the fool of an Act says "compassing the death of the Heir Apparent." There's not a word about a mistake -

KO-KO, PITTI-SING, & POOBAH: No!
MIKADO: Or not knowing -
KO-KO: No!
MIKADO: Or having no notion -
PITTI-SING: No!
MIKADO: Or not being there -
POOBAH: No!
MIKADO: There should be, of course -
KO-KO, PITTI-SING, & POOBAH: Yes!
MIKADO: But there isn't.
KO-KO, PITTI-SING, & POOBAH: Oh!
MIKADO: That's the slovenly way in which these Acts are always drawn. However, cheer up, it'll be all right. I'll have it altered next session. Now, let's see about your execution - will after luncheon suit you? Can you wait till then?

KO-KO, PITTI-SING, & POOBAH: Oh yes - we can wait till then.

MIKADO: Then we'll make it after lunch.
POOBAH: I don't want any lunch.

"knowingly") which is subject to different interpretations. Then, the court will attempt to divine the intent of the legislative body — or it will simply assume that the legislature intended to conform to principles or policies which the court believes to be fair.

When you read each case in the following chapter, try to discern from the court's opinion (1) *which* mental state it chose, (2) *why* it chose that mental state, (3) *which element(s)* of the crime are governed by that mental state, and (4) whether the court's ruling and/or rationale could help — or hurt — your client in Problem 1.

MIKADO: I'm really very sorry for you all, but it's an unjust world, and virtue is triumphant only in theatrical performances.

Chapter 1

MISTAKE

No area of the substantive criminal law has traditionally been surrounded by more confusion than that of ignorance or mistake of fact or law. It is frequently said, on the one hand, that ignorance of the law is no excuse, and, on the other, that a mistake of fact is an excuse. Neither of these propositions is precisely correct, and both are subject to numerous exceptions and qualifications. * * * * In actuality, the basic rule is extremely simple: ignorance or mistake of fact or law is a defense when it negatives the existence of a mental state essential to the crime charged.

LaFave & Scott, *Criminal Law* (West)

The law of *mistake* raises some interesting issues regarding *mens rea*. Going back to our example of Dan shooting Vic, consider the following possibilities:

Dan *mistakenly* but reasonably believed that Vic was a deer.

Dan *mistakenly* but unreasonably believed that his gun was unloaded.

Dan *mistakenly* but reasonably believed that it was lawful to shoot Vic because Vic was a shoplifter.

Should Dan be punished in *all* of these situations? *Any* of them? Why (not)? What *purposes* of punishment might be served or disserved by punishing or releasing Dan in any of these situations?

This chapter will address these troublesome questions of *mistake*.

PROBLEM 1

To: My Law Clerk

From: Wanda Walkem

Re: *People v. Rea*

My client, Manny Rea, got into a dispute with his neighbor in Berkeley. As a result, Manny has been charged with a violation of California Penal Code § 418, which provides:

> Every person using or procuring, encouraging or assisting another to use, any force or violence in entering upon or detaining any lands or other possessions of another, except in the cases and in the manner allowed by law, is guilty of a misdemeanor.

Misdemeanors are punishable by up to 6 months in county jail or a fine of up to $1,000, or both — although the maximums are seldom given to first offenders.

Manny's version of what happened appears in the attached transcript of my interview with him. I'd like him to tell his story to the jury at trial. As you can see, howewver, he was mistaken about some of the things he believed about the situation. I'm not sure, however, whether the judge will allow the jury to hear his testimony about these mistakes. The deputy district attorney prosecuting the case — Roger Righteous — will probably object on the ground that these mistakes are irrelevant under the applicable rules of law. The trial judge, Judge Stickler, will sustain any objection supported by the law.

I found some authorities which seem to be pertinent here, though none mentions Penal Code § 418. Please read them and be prepared to advise me regarding the relevance of the various parts of Manny's testimony; including the best arguments Righteous can make, our best responses, and how Judge Stickler is likely to rule on this issue.

Transcript of Interview With Manny Rea

WW: So, what happened?

MR: My next-door neighbor, Al Airhead, is really a creep. He drinks too much, plays loud music, and has too many parties. He recently put in an outdoor hot tub, and I thought that about a foot of it was over the property line onto my property. I thought I knew where the property line was, because when I bought my house last year, the real estate agent told me that the telephone wire to the house was right over the property line.

WW: Did you tell this to Airhead?

MR: Sure, and I told him to get the hot tub off my property. But he said that the property line was 2 feet farther over. My daughter, Minnie, is a law student, so I asked her what to do. She went to City Hall and asked to see the subdivision map on file. She told me that it showed the telephone wire easement right on the property line. She also told me that a city ordinance required that you have a valid permit before installing a hot tub. She looked up Airhead's permit, and saw that it was not signed by the head of the city's building department. The city clerk then told Minnie that because of this, the permit was not valid. I went and told Airhead what Minnie had said. He called me a liar and walked away.

WW: So then, of course, you consulted a lawyer about your legal remedies, right?

MR: Not exactly. Lawyers cost too much, and besides, I know how to take care of myself. That night, I went out with my flashlight, tape measure, and a saw, and I cut off a foot of the hot tub. It was on my property, and Airhead wouldn't remove it, so I removed it myself.

WW: I take it Airhead wasn't too pleased when he saw what you did.

MR: He was furious — especially when I told him he could still take half a bath. He complained to the District Attorney's Office. The DA checked with City Hall. They found another file, which showed that 3 years ago the phone company had been granted an easement to move the phone line over 2 feet. So Airhead was right about the property line, and the hot tub was actually on his property. When I saw the phone wire, it had been moved 2 feet from the property line, and I didn't know it.

WW: How come Minnie hadn't seen this file?

MR: I guess she didn't know enough to look for it. She had told the clerk that she wanted to know how to find the property line, and he just gave her the subdivision map. He didn't tell her about any other file. Oh, by the way, it turns out that the city ordinance on permits does not require the permit to be signed by the head of the building department. The city clerk was mistaken when he told Minnie otherwise.

WW: Were you surprised when the DA filed the complaint against you?

MR: Yes. I thought Airhead might sue me for shortening his hot tub a bit, but I had no idea that this might be a crime. I never heard of this Penal Code section 418.

WW: If Airhead were to sue you, he'd probably win. In civil law, if you go on someone else's property without permission, it's considered a trespass — even if you made a reasonable mistake — and he could collect for any damages you caused. You are considered "strictly liable" for a civil trespass. In criminal law, however, the rule *might* be different. Various criminal statutes require various states of mind.

MR: So, do I have any defense?

WW: Maybe. I just hired a bright new law clerk who might be able to give me some help on this. Let's talk about my retainer . . .

California Penal Code

§ 20: In every crime or public offense there must exist a union, or joint operation of act and intent, or criminal negligence.

§ 26: All persons are capable of committing crimes except those belonging to the following classes:

One - Children under the age of 14, in the absence of clear proof that at the time of committing the act charged against them, they knew its wrongfulness.

Two - Persons who are mentally incapacitated.

Three - Persons who committed the act or made the omission charged under an ignorance or mistake of fact, which disproves any criminal intent.

Four - Persons who committed the act charged without being conscious thereof.

Five - Persons who committed the act or made the omission charged through misfortune or by accident, when it appears that there was no evil design, intention, or culpable negligence.

Six - Persons (unless the crime be punishable with death) who committed the act or made the omission charged under threats or menaces sufficient to show that they had reasonable cause to and did believe their lives would be endangered if they refused.

NOTES FROM WANDA:

(1) I pulled out these statutes because they deal with the mental states required for crimes in California. Read them carefully. Do they tell us whether Manny is guilty? § 20 mentions "intent," but does it indicate *what* intent is required? What is "criminal negligence"? Was Manny acting under "an ignorance or mistake of fact," under § 26(3)? Didn't Manny commit the act "by accident," under § 26(5)? When you read the following cases, note what use *they* made of these statutes.

(2) Compare these statutes with Model Penal Code § 2.04, in the Appendix.

PEOPLE v. O'BRIEN
Supreme Court of California
96 Cal. 171 (1892)

PATERSON, J.

In May, 1886, J. H. Derevan conveyed to the defendant a tract of land in Modoc County. The defendant erased his own name, "Denis," from the deed, and inserted therein "Mary," his wife's name, thus making the deed purport to convey the property to Mary O'Brien, instead of to himself. In this form the deed was, at the request of the defendant, recorded in the office of the county recorder. Thereafter the defendant called upon T. B. Reese, the county recorder, before whom the deed had been acknowledged by Derevan, informed him of the change which he, the defendant, had made, and requested him to change the deed and the record so that both would speak the truth with respect to the transaction. Reese refused to make the changes unless Derevan and Mrs. O'Brien consented thereto. Their consent having been obtained, Reese erased the name "Mary" in the deed and also in the record, and inserted in lieu thereof the name "Denis" in each place.

The defendant was convicted of the crime of altering a public record, and was sentenced to serve a term of two years in the state prison. From the judgment, and from an order denying his motion for a new trial, he has appealed.

It is conceded that the case is prosecuted under §§ 113 and 114 of the Penal Code. Section 113 provides that "every officer having the custody of any record filed or deposited in any public office, or placed in his hands for any purpose, who is guilty of stealing, willfully destroying, mutilating, defacing, altering the whole or any part of such record is punishable," etc. Section 114 provides that "every person not an officer such as is referred to in the preceding section, who is guilty of any of the acts specified in that section, is punishable," etc. The language of the indictment is: "The said Denis O'Brien, not being an officer such as referred to in § 113 of the Penal Code, did then and there willfully alter and procure to be altered a certain deed record of real estate."

It is urged with much earnestness that no offense could have been committed by the defendant, because there was no intention on his part to do an unlawful act, his object being simply to rectify a wrong already done. It is admitted that the defendant was not excusable for procuring the deed to be recorded in its altered form, but it is insisted that his subsequent attempt to rectify the error cannot be deemed a crime. The attorney-general admits that the evidence fails to show any fraudulent intent on the part of defendant, and the question presented is, whether it is necessary, in making out the offense, for the prosecution to show that the act was done for some sinister purpose.

It is an emphatic postulate of both civil and penal law that ignorance of a law is no excuse for a violation thereof. Of course it is based on a fiction, because no man can know all the law, but it is a maxim which the law itself does not permit any one to gainsay. It is expected that the jury[1] and the court, where it is shown that in fact the defendant was ignorant of the law, and innocent of any intention to violate the same, will give the defendant the benefit of the fact, and impose only a light penalty. 1 Bishop's Crim. Law § 2961.

The rule rests on public necessity; the welfare of society and the safety of the state depend upon its enforcement. If a person accused of crime could shield himself behind the defense that he was ignorant of the law which he violated, immunity from punishment would in most cases result. No system of criminal justice could be sustained with such an element in it to obstruct the course of its administration. The plea would be universally made, and would lead to interminable questions incapable of solution. Was the defendant in fact ignorant of the law? Was his ignorance of the law excusable? The denser the ignorance the greater would be the exemption from liability.

The absurdity of such a condition of the law is shown in the consummate satire of Pascal, where, speaking upon this subject, he says, in substance, that although the less a man thinks of the moral law the more culpable he is, yet under municipal law "the more he relieves himself from a knowledge of his duty, the more approvedly is his duty performed." It is a familiar rule, that to constitute crime there must be a union of act and intent; but our code provides that "the word 'willfully,' when applied to the intent with which an act is done or omitted, implies simply a purpose or willingness to commit the act or make the omission referred to. It does not require any intent to violate law, or to injure another, or to acquire any advantage." Pen.Code § 7.

It has been held that one who marries a second time under an honest but erroneous belief that a decree of divorce which had been granted was valid is afforded no protection by the invalid decree, and that evidence of his good faith will be excluded. 2 Wharton's Crim. Ev., 8th ed., § 1695a. The same principle is applied to many cases, such as selling intoxicating liquors to minors, abducting girls under a certain age, usurping an office under the belief that the usurper was truly elected, illegal voting under the belief that the voter is a qualified elector, publishing a libel in ignorance of its contents, storing gunpowder, and the like. 1 Wharton's Crim. Law, § 88; *Hill v. State*, 62 Ala. 170.

Sections 7, 112, and 113 of the Penal Code, when read together, clearly establish the proposition that it was not necessary in making out the offense to prove any fraudulent intention on the part of the defendant.

---

[1] Editor: Today, in California and most other states, the jury plays no role in selecting the penalty - except where the prosecutor seeks the death penalty.

No hardship will result from the administration of the law as thus construed. The legislature has wisely given the court a wide latitude in fixing the penalty, evidently with the idea of meeting just such cases as this. The penalty fixed is "imprisonment in the state prison not exceeding five years or in a county jail not exceeding one year, or by a fine not exceeding one hundred dollars, or by both." Thus are provided appropriate penalties for all degrees of offenses committed under this act.

[Ed.: The court then considered some additional arguments presented by Defendant: that the trial court had erroneously overruled his objections to the admissibility of certain evidence, and that the trial court had incorrectly instructed the jury. Accepting these arguments, the court reversed the judgment and remanded for a new trial.]

NOTES FROM WANDA:

1. Didn't the court overlook Penal Code §§ 26(4) and 26(5)? Can you find some language in those sections that might have helped O'Brien?

2. This case seems to hurt us. How much? Does it knock out *all* of our possible arguments?

PEOPLE v. SNYDER
Supreme Court of California
32 Cal.3d 590 (1982)

RICHARDSON, J.

Defendant Neva Snyder appeals from a judgment convicting her of possession of a concealable firearm by a convicted felon (Pen. Code § 12021), based upon her 1973 conviction for sale of marijuana, a felony (former Health & Saf.Code § 11531). Defendant contends that the trial court erred in excluding evidence of her mistaken belief that her prior conviction was only a misdemeanor. We will conclude that defendant's asserted mistake regarding her legal status as a convicted felon did not constitute a defense to the firearm possession charge. Accordingly, we will affirm the judgment.

At trial, defendant offered to prove the following facts supporting her theory of mistake: The marijuana possession charge resulted from a plea bargain not involving a jail or prison sentence. At the time the bargain was struck, defendant's attorney advised her that she was pleading guilty to a misdemeanor. Believing that she was not a felon, defendant thereafter had registered to vote, and had voted. On one prior occasion, police officers found a gun in her home but, after determining that it was registered to her husband, the officers filed no charges against defendant.

The trial court refused to admit any evidence of defendant's mistaken belief that her prior conviction was a misdemeanor and that she was not a felon. The court also rejected proposed instructions requiring proof of defendant's prior knowledge of her felony conviction as an element of the offense charged.

Penal Code § 12021, subdivision (a), provides: "Any person who has been convicted of a felony under the laws of the State of California who owns or has in his possession or under his custody or control any pistol, revolver, or other firearm capable of being concealed upon the person is guilty of a public offense . . ."

The elements of the offense proscribed by § 12021 are conviction of a felony and ownership, possession, custody or control of a firearm capable of being concealed on the person. *People v. Bray* (1975) 52 Cal.App.3d 494. No specific criminal intent is required, and a general intent to commit the proscribed act is sufficient to sustain a conviction. With respect to the elements of possession or custody, it has been held that knowledge is an element of the offense.

Does § 12021 also require knowledge of one's legal status as a convicted felon? No case has so held. Penal Code § 26 provides that a person is incapable of committing a crime if he acted under a "mistake of fact" which disproves criminal intent. In this regard, the cases have distinguished between mistakes of fact and mistakes of law. As we stated in an early case: "It is an emphatic postulate of both civil and penal law that ignorance of a law is no excuse for a violation thereof. Of course it is based on a fiction, because no man can know all the law, but it is a maxim which the law itself does not permit any one to gainsay. The rule rests on public necessity; the welfare of society and the safety of the state depend upon its enforcement. If a person accused of a crime could shield himself behind the defense that he was ignorant of the law which he violated, immunity from punishment would in most cases result." *People v. O'Brien* (1892) 96 Cal. 171. Accordingly, lack of actual knowledge of the provisions of Penal Code § 12021 is irrelevant; the crucial question is whether the defendant was aware that he was engaging in the conduct proscribed by that section.

In the present case, defendant was presumed to know that it is unlawful for a convicted felon to possess a concealable firearm. Pen. Code § 12021. She was also charged with knowledge that the offense of which she was convicted (former Health & Saf. Code § 11531) was, as a matter of law, a felony. That section had prescribed a state prison term of from five years to life, and the express statutory definition of a "felony" is "a crime which is punishable with death or by imprisonment in the state prison." Pen. Code § 17(a).

Thus, regardless of what she reasonably believed, or what her attorney may have told her, defendant was deemed to know under the law that she was a convicted felon forbidden to possess concealable firearms. Her asserted mistake regarding her correct legal status was a mistake of law, not fact. It does not constitute a defense to § 12021.

None of the California cases relied on by defendant is apposite here. *People v. Hernandez* (1964) 61 Cal.2d 529 and *People v. Mayberry* (1975) 15 Cal.3d 143, each involved mistakes of fact, not law. In *Hernandez*, the mistake concerned the age of the alleged victim of a statutory rape. In *Mayberry*, defendant erred in assuming that the adult victim of forcible rape consented to his acts. *People v. Vogel* (1956) 46 Cal.2d 798, involved the good faith belief of a defendant charged with bigamy that he is free to remarry. We were careful to explain that defendant's mistake was a factual one: "We have concluded that defendant is not guilty of bigamy, if he had a bona fide and reasonable belief that *facts* existed that left him free to remarry."

Moreover, *Vogel* characterized bigamy as a crime which "has been regarded for centuries as involving moral turpitude." Obviously a bona fide belief that one is free to remarry nullifies the moral opprobrium attached to the charge. On the other hand, being an ex-felon in possession of a concealable firearm, while illegal, hardly stamps the person charged as a moral leper. His belief that he is not a felon thus does not affect the criminality of his conduct.

Defendant relies primarily upon *People v. Bray*, supra, but that case is distinguishable. There defendant pleaded guilty in Kansas to being an accessory after the fact and was placed on two years' summary probation, which he successfully completed. When he subsequently sought to register to vote, he filled out an explanatory form referring to a Kansas offense, and indicating that he was uncertain whether he had been convicted of a felony. He was permitted to vote. Seeking employment as a security guard, he stated that he had not been convicted of a felony but described the circumstances of his arrest and probation. The Bureau of Collection and Investigative Services registered him as a guard. On several other job applications he indicated his uncertainty as to his status while fully setting forth the circumstances of his arrest and probation.

In *Bray*, the court concluded that under these unusual circumstances the trial court erred in refusing to instruct on mistake or ignorance of fact and knowledge of the facts which make the act unlawful. The court cautioned, however, that its decision "should not be interpreted to mean instructions on mistake or ignorance of fact and knowledge of the facts are required every time a defendant claims he did not know he was a felon. It is only in very unusual circumstances such as these that the giving of these instructions is necessary."

In the present case, unlike *Bray*, defendant made no attempt to inform government officials of the circumstances of her conviction or to seek their advice regarding her correct legal status. (Some authorities have suggested that reliance upon the erroneous advice of governmental authorities might constitute an exception to the general rule that a mistake of law is no defense. See Perkins on Criminal Law (2d ed. 1969) p. 938; A.L.I. Model Pen. Code (Proposed Official Draft 1962) § 2.04(3)(b).)

We conclude that the trial court properly excluded evidence of defendant's asserted mistake regarding her status as a convicted felon.

The judgment is affirmed.

BIRD, C.J., MOSK, J. and KAUS, J. concurred.

BROUSSARD, J.

I dissent.

In determining whether a defendant's mistaken belief disproves criminal intent pursuant to Penal Code § 26, the courts have drawn a distinction between mistakes of fact and mistakes of law. Criminal intent is the intent to do the prohibited act, not the intent to violate the law. 1 Witkin, Cal.Crimes (1963) § 148. "It is an emphatic postulate of both civil and penal law that ignorance of a law is no excuse for a violation thereof. Of course it is based on a fiction, because no man can know all the law, but it is a maxim which the law itself does not permit any one to gainsay. The rule rests on public necessity; the welfare of society and the safety of the state depend upon its enforcement. If a person accused of a crime could shield himself behind the defense that he was ignorant of the law which he violated, immunity from punishment would in most cases result." *People v. O'Brien* (1892) 96 Cal. 171, 176. Accordingly, lack of knowledge of the provisions of Penal Code § 12021 is irrelevant; the crucial question is whether the defendant was aware that he was engaging in the conduct proscribed by that section.

While mistake as to whether the conduct is violative of a statute is not a defense, a mistaken impression as to the legal effect of a collateral matter may mean that a defendant does not understand the significance of his conduct and may negate criminal intent. When the victim's status is an element of the crime, a mistaken belief as to the status has been held a defense in several decisions by this court. In *People v. Hernandez*, supra, it was held that a reasonable and honest belief that the prosecutrix was 18 years or more of age would be a defense to a charge of statutory rape, negating the requisite mental intent. Similarly, in *People v. Atchison* (1978) 22 Cal.3d 181, 183, it was held that a reasonable and honest belief that the victim was 19 years of age was a defense to charges of annoying or molesting a child under age 18 and of contributing to the delinquency of a minor. And in *People v. Mayberry*, supra, it was held that a mistaken belief that the prosecutrix had consented would be a defense to a charge of forcible rape and kidnapping.

This court has also held that criminal intent may be negated by defendant's reasonable and bona fide but erroneous belief as to his status. In *People v. Vogel*, supra, the defendant was prosecuted for bigamy, and it was held that the defendant's bona fide and reasonable belief that his first wife had divorced him and remarried would be a good defense. The court reasoned in part that it would not be reasonable to hold "that a person is guilty of bigamy who remarries in good faith in reliance of a judgment of divorce or annulment that is subsequently found not to be the 'judgment of a competent court' (Pen. Code § 282), particularly when such a judgment is obtained by the former husband or wife of such person in any one of the numerous jurisdictions in which such judgments can be obtained. Since it is often difficult for laymen to know when a judgment is not that of a competent court, we cannot reasonably expect them always to have such knowledge and make them criminals if their bona fide belief proves to be erroneous." The court also pointed out that at common law an honest and reasonable belief in circumstances which, if true, would make the act for which the person is indicted an innocent act, has always been held to be a good defense.

People v. Flumerfelt (1939) 35 Cal.App.2d 495, also illustrates the distinction between mistake of fact and mistake of law. In that case, the defendant was charged with selling corporate securities without a permit. The defendant claimed that before she sold the securities, her attorney told her that a permit to sell had been obtained, and it was held that her honest but mistaken belief that a permit to sell had been issued constituted a defense. However, the court distinguished the situation where counsel erroneously advises that the instrument to be sold is not a security, pointing out that a mistake as to the legal consequences of the act which constitutes a violation of the statute would not be a defense.

The *O'Brien, Hernandez, Atchison, Mayberry, Vogel* and *Flumerfelt* cases, read together, make clear that a mistake of law is one premised on ignorance of the terms of the statute which the defendant is charged with violating. However, when the defendant reasonably and honestly believes that the statute is not applicable to him or that he had complied with it, there is a mistake of fact. There is a mistake of fact even though the matter as to which the defendant is mistaken is a question of law. The questions of age in *Hernandez* and *Atchison* were matters resolved as a matter of law as was marital status in *Vogel* and the nonissuance of a permit in *Flumerfelt*.

The Court of Appeal has held that a mistaken belief that a conviction was not a felony conviction could negate criminal intent in a prosecution for violation of Penal Code § 12021. *People v. Bray*, supra. *Bray* graphically illustrates the injustice which results from holding that a reasonable and good faith belief of lack of felony status is not a defense. Bray pled guilty in Kansas to being an accessory after the fact and was placed on two years summary probation which he successfully completed. When he subsequently sought to register to vote, he filled out an explanatory form referring to the Kansas offense, indicating he was uncertain whether he had been convicted of a felony. He was permitted to vote. Seeking employment as a security guard, he stated he had not been convicted of a felony but set forth the circumstances of his arrest and probation. The Bureau of Collection and Investigative Services registered him as a guard. On several other job applications he indicated his uncertainty as to his status setting forth the circumstances of his arrest and probation. At Bray's trial for violation of § 12021, the prosecutor recognized "'in even our own jurisdiction, let alone a foreign jurisdiction such as the State of Kansas, it's extremely difficult to determine whether a sentence was a felony or a misdemeanor.'"

In *Bray*, it was concluded that in the circumstances the trial court erred in refusing to instruct on mistake or ignorance of fact and knowledge of the facts which make the act unlawful.

The Court of Appeal stated that its decision should not be interpreted to mean instructions on mistake or ignorance of fact or knowledge of the facts are required every time a defendant claims he did not know he was a felon. Relying on that statement, the majority concludes that *Bray* should be limited to situations where a state agency has misled the defendant. The statement relied upon merely reflects that only in rare cases will there be a basis for a reasonable belief that a felony conviction was a misdemeanor conviction. The reasoning in *Bray* applies to any case where there is a reasonable and good faith mistake and is in accord with the common law and our statutory rule. The source of the reasonable and good faith mistake does not affect the existence of criminal intent.[1]

Had the trial court in the instant case admitted the offered evidence and given the requested instruction, the jury could properly have concluded that defendant had a reasonable and good faith belief that her conviction was not a felony

---

[1] I am perplexed by the majority's apparent limitation of the mistake doctrine to would-be "moral lepers." The more heinous the crime the more reason to limit defenses, and the majority's suggested limitation appears to turn the usual relationship between law and morality upside down.

conviction. She was granted probation without jail or prison sentence. Her attorney had advised her that the offense was a misdemeanor,[2] and there were additional circumstances reflecting a good faith belief.

The errors in excluding the offered evidence and refusing the offered instructions denied defendant the right to have the jury determine substantial issues material to her guilt and require reversal of the conviction.

I would reverse the judgment.

NEWMAN, J., and REYNOSO, J., concurred.

NOTES FROM WANDA:

(1) *Snyder* gives us some excellent examples of how cases can be used (or distinguished) when making (or rebutting) an argument. The process of "distinguishing" cases is very important to the practicing lawyer (or judge). By this process, you can deflect the impact of a case which would otherwise be a binding or persuasive precedent against your position.

When a lawyer cites another case, she is saying: "Judge, our courts must be *consistent*, in order to be fair among different parties and to give the rules some stability. In a prior case, our courts held X. The present case involves essentially the same facts, so you must apply the rule of X here too." Her opponent might say, "Judge, that prior case involved facts that are different from the present case in a way that is significant under the rule of X. Therefore, the prior case is *distinguishable* and the rule of X does not apply here."

To *distinguish* a case, it is not enough merely to identify some difference between the facts of that case and the facts of your case. You must show how the factual difference affected the rule or reasoning of the judges in the prior case (or how it *might* have affected their rule or reasoning, had they been confronted with your facts instead of the facts they had before them).

For example, suppose the majority opinion in *Snyder* were to distinguish *Bray* on the ground that there, the defendant's last name started with the letter B, while Snyder's last name begins with S. Intuitively, you know that this "distinction" is absurd, but see if you can articulate *why* it is absurd.

In *Snyder*, the dissent invokes *Mayberry*, but the majority attempts to distinguish *Mayberry*. (Which does a better job of persuading you?) The dissent invokes *Vogel*, but the majority attempts to distinguish *Vogel* - and the dissent, in footnote 2, attempts to rebut the majority's proposed distinction! (Which is more persuasive?) The dissent invokes *Bray*, but the majority attempts to distinguish *Bray*. (Which is more persuasive?)

---

[2] It has been held that advice of counsel that prohibited conduct is lawful is not a defense because it would place the advice of counsel above the law. See 1 Witkin, Cal. Crimes, supra, § 150. Counsel's advice in the instant case is relevant to establish good faith; it does not in and of itself establish a defense.

(2) After I read *O'Brien*, I thought I had a pretty good handle on the distinction between a mistake of law and a mistake of fact. After reading *Snyder*, however, I'm not so sure where the line is. If, as the majority in *Snyder* held, the defendant is "charged with knowledge that the offense of which she was convicted . . . was, as a matter of law, a felony," does this mean that Manny is "charged with knowledge" that Airhead's permit to build the hot tub was valid? Does it also mean that Manny is "charged with knowledge" that the legal property line meant that the hot tub was on Airhead's land, not Manny's? I need your prediction as to how the California courts would decide these issues.

(3) In *Miller v. Commonwealth*, 25 Va.App. 727, 492 S.E.2d 482 (1997), Miller was both a convicted felon and an avid hunter. He knew that it was a crime for a convicted felon to possess a firearm, but thought that a muzzle-loading rifle was exempt from this statute. Before buying such a rifle, however, he did some research:

> Miller testified that he "talked to everyone who he thought might know the answer." He spoke with his probation officer, who told him he could have a muzzle-loading rifle. He also inquired of the Federal Bureau of Alcohol, Tobacco and Firearms (ATF) and the Virginia Department of Game and Inland Fisheries (VDGIF), and representatives from each, who knew Miller was a convicted felon, told him he could have a muzzle loader. Miller acknowledged that no one told him he could possess a "firearm" and that a muzzle loader was "in a sense" a firearm because "it fires." Relying on the interpretation provided by the government officials contacted, Miller purchased a muzzle loader and obtained a license to hunt with it. In short, Miller, a convicted felon, knowingly and intentionally possessed a muzzle-loading rifle.

The trial judge believed Miller, but nevertheless convicted him for "knowingly and intentionally possessing a firearm after having been previously convicted of a felony, in violation of Code § 18.2-308.2." But the appellate court reversed, holding that — even assuming that a muzzle-loading rifle *is* a "firearm" — the conviction violated the Due Process Clause of the 14th Amendment of the U.S. Constitution:

> The due process argument is, in essence, that the criminal statute under which the defendant is being prosecuted cannot constitutionally be applied to the defendant without violating due process of law, where government officials have misled the defendant into believing that his conduct was not prohibited. See *People v. Studifin*, 504 N.Y.S.2d 608, 610 (N.Y.Sup.Ct.1986). ("For the state to prosecute someone for innocently acting upon such mistaken advice is akin to throwing water on a man and arresting him because he's wet.").

> The ultimate due process inquiry is whether a defendant's conviction, for reasonably and in good faith doing that which he was told he could do, is fundamentally unfair in light of the content of the information he received and its source. The cases addressing the defense demonstrate that the defendant must establish, as a threshold matter, the legal sufficiency of the content and source of the information received. The application of the defense then requires a factual determination whether the defendant's

reliance upon the information received was reasonable and in good faith. The defendant bears the burden of establishing the affirmative defense.

With respect to content, the defense is available only where the information upon which the defendant has relied is an affirmative assurance that the conduct giving rise to the conviction is lawful. In the absence of such an affirmative assurance, the due process concerns that the defense is designed to protect are not implicated, and the defense fails

As to the source of the information, it must be established that the information was received from a "government official." See *U.S. v. Clark*, 986 F.2d 65, 69 (4th Cir. 1993) (taxidermist not government official); *United States v. Indelicato*, 887 F.Supp. 23, 25 (D.Mass.1995), (private attorney not government official). Compare *Howell*, 37 F.3d at 1206 (private firearms dealer licensed by government not government official), with *United States v. Tallmadge*, 829 F.2d 767, 774 (9th cir. 1987) (firearms licensee is government official). Indeed, this is necessary as a matter of constitutional law because the Due Process Clause is limited to "state action."

However, a government official's status as "state actor" has not alone been sufficient to invoke the defense in cases recognizing its availability. The issue is not whether an "agent" of the state has bound the government by his or her word. The issue is whether convicting an individual who has reasonably relied on the advice of a state actor is so fundamentally unfair as to raise due process concerns. Such concerns are implicated only when the source of the information is a public officer or body charged by law with responsibility for defining permissible conduct with respect to the offense at issue. * * * *

In the present case, the trial court found that Miller's probation officer and representatives from ATF and VDGIF told Miller that he could possess a muzzle-loading rifle. The trial court concluded that Miller had established the legal sufficiency of the content of the information he received, *viz.*, an affirmative assurance that certain conduct — his possession of the muzzle loader — was lawful.

Moreover, there can be no doubt that the sources upon which appellant relied — a federal ATF agent, a VDGIF agent, and his probation officer — were "state actors." The determinative issue, therefore, is whether these sources were legally sufficient to invoke the due process defense, *viz.*, whether the sources were charged by law with responsibility for defining permissible conduct with respect to offense for which Miller was convicted.

We hold that Miller's case fails as a matter of law with respect to the ATF agent and the VDGIF agent. Neither of those agents was charged by law with responsibility for defining permissible conduct under Code § 18.2-308.2. The ATF agent, although arguably charged with such responsibility under federal firearms laws, has no such duty with respect to Virginia law. The ATF officer's opinion as to whether Miller could possess a muzzle loading rifle under Virginia law simply does not invoke due process concerns in the Commonwealth of Virginia's bid to prosecute Miller.

Likewise, the Commonwealth of Virginia has not charged the VDGIF with the duty of defining permissible conduct under Code § 18.2-308.2. The VDGIF exists to provide public, informational and educational services related to Title 29.1, which concerns Game, Inland Fisheries and Boating. See Code § 29.1-109. It is the agency responsible for the administration and enforcement of all rules and regulations of Title 29.1 and related acts, but it is not charged with defining what conduct Code § 18.2-308.2 proscribes. Thus, the opinion of VDGIF with respect to the permissibility of Miller's possessing a muzzle loader does not implicate due process concerns.

By contrast, however, Miller's probation officer was charged by the Commonwealth with responsibility for defining Miller's permissible conduct with respect to Code § 18.2-308.2. The legislature granted the probation officer supervisory responsibility for Miller's conduct and treatment during the course of his probation (see Code § 53.1-145), including the responsibility for arresting him for a violation of his probation. Violation of the law regarding the possession of a firearm by a convicted felon was surely one. It follows that a probation officer, statutorily required to supervise, assist, and provide a probationer with a statement of the conditions of his release from confinement, as well as to arrest a probationer for a violation of the terms of his release, is, *a fortiori*, charged by law with defining a probationer's permissible or impermissible conduct. The authority to enforce the law and effect an arrest, of necessity, requires an interpretation of what constitutes permissible conduct. For these reasons, we hold that the trial court erroneously concluded that Miller's probation officer was not a source legally sufficient to invoke the Due Process Clause as a bar to his prosecution and conviction.

It remains only to be determined whether, based on the totality of the circumstances, Miller's reliance on the advice of his probation officer was reasonable and in good faith. Upon review of the uncontradicted evidence in this case, we find, as a matter of law, that it was.

Question: *Miller* is not a California case. Is a California judge "bound" by it? (What does it mean to be "bound" by a case? What will happen to a judge who does not follow a "binding" case? Will the judge be fired?) If *Miller* is not "binding" in California, is it totally irrelevant to our case? Is there any way it might be used to help *persuade* a California judge to rule for one side or the other?

(4) In *U.S. v. Morton*, 999 F.2d 435 (9th Cir. 1993), defendant was charged with assaulting a federal officer. The officer chased Morton, yelling "police" and "stop". Morton refused to stop, and fought the officer when he was caught. Morton testified that although he heard the officer, he did not believe he was a policeman, because the officer was in plain clothes and this occurred in a high-crime area. He did not see a police badge on the officer's belt. The court held that defendant's evidence was sufficient to show that he made a reasonable mistake as to the officer's authority, and the trial court erred by refusing to submit this issue to the jury.

Question: How may *Morton* be reconciled with *Snyder*?

(5) In *U.S. v. Fletcher*, 634 F.3d 395 (7th Cir. 2011), Fletcher was convicted of production of child pornography (and sentenced to 480 months in prison!). The court read the federal statute under which he was convicted not to require proof that he knew the victim was underage. Fletcher then argued that the statute violated his right to Equal Protection of the laws, because statutes criminalizing *possessing* child pornography *do* require proof of knowledge of the victim's age. The court disagreed:

> Those statutes requiring knowledge of a victim's age — receiving, distributing, or possessing child pornography — are all readily distinguishable from the production of child pornography, where the perpetrator confronts the underage victim personally and may reasonably be required to ascertain that victim's age. * * * * The compelling nature of the interest in protecting children from exploitation supports putting the risk of error on producers.

(6) In *In re Jennings*, 34 Cal.4th 254 (2004), the court held that the misdemeanor crime of purchasing alcoholic beverages for a minor is a strict liability offense, so the prosecution need not introduce evidence that the defendant knew the victim was underage. Does this also mean that the defendant cannot be acquitted if he proved that he was reasonably mistaken about the victim's age? On the one hand:

> A mistake of fact defense is not available unless the mistake disproves an element of the offense. *People v. Parker* (1985) 175 Cal.App.3d 818, 822. Thus, in *Parker*, the defendant illegally entered a structure, allegedly believing it was a commercial building. Because the building was in fact a residence, he was charged with and convicted of first degree burglary. On appeal, the appellate court rejected his argument that the trial court had erred by failing to instruct the jury that his mistaken belief the building was an uninhabited structure constituted an affirmative defense. The appellate court reasoned that because the prosecution was not required to prove a defendant knew the building entered was a residential one in order to convict of burglary, "ignorance concerning the residential nature of a building does not render a defendant's unlawful entry into it with a felonious intent innocent conduct."

But on the other hand, the court noted that the Legislature had provided that persons holding a liquor license could defend by proving that they demanded and relied on a minor's identification showing age:

> Does section 25660 suggest the Legislature's intent to permit a similar defense to nonlicensees? We hold that it does. A contrary conclusion would lead to an absurd result, to wit, while licensees, who may serve alcoholic beverages to dozens or even hundreds of customers in a single night, can demand, check and act in reliance on bona fide evidence of identity and age and thereby enter a safe harbor, protected from criminal liability, a nonlicensee who serves alcoholic beverages only occasionally and to just a few persons, and who similarly demands, checks and acts in reliance on bona fide evidence of identity and age, and may honestly and reasonably believe the person for whom he or she purchased alcohol was over 21 years old, would absent a mistake of fact defense be subject to criminal liability,

punishable by a minimum of six months in jail. The Legislature could not have intended this disparity of treatment.

(7) Sometimes, when a statute (such as California Penal Code § 418) is not clear on a certain point, a sensible interpretation can be gleaned by determining which interpretation best serves the *purposes* of the statute - where its purpose is obvious or can be learned from legislative history. Where, however, the purpose of a particular criminal statute *cannot* be learned this way, then one might examine how various interpretations of the statute tend to serve the *general* purposes of punishment for crime.

A good summary of these purposes is set out in LaFave & Scott, *Criminal Law*:

There are a number of theories of punishment, and each theory has or has had its enthusiastic adherents. Some of the theories are concerned primarily with the particular offender, while others focus more on the nature of the offense and the general public. These theories are:

(1) *Prevention.* By this theory, also called *intimidation,* or when the deterrence theory is referred to as general deterrence, *particular deterrence,* criminal punishment aims to deter the criminal himself (rather than to deter others) from committing further crimes, by giving him an unpleasant experience he will not want to endure again. The validity of this theory has been questioned by many, who point out the high recidivism rates of those who have been punished. On the other hand, it has been observed that our attempts at prevention by punishment may enjoy an unmeasurable degree of success, in that without punishment for purposes of prevention the rate of recidivism might be much higher. * * * *

(2) *Restraint.* The notion here, also expressed as *incapacitation, isolation,* or *disablement,* is that society may protect itself from persons deemed dangerous because of their past criminal conduct by isolating these persons from society. If the criminal is imprisoned or executed, he cannot commit further crimes against society. Some question this theory because of doubts that those who present a danger of continuing criminality can be accurately identified. * * * *

(3) *Rehabilitation.* Under this theory, also called *correction or reformation,* we "punish" the convicted criminal by giving him appropriate treatment, in order to rehabilitate him and return him to society so reformed that he will not desire or need to commit further crimes. It is perhaps not entirely correct to call this treatment "punishment," as the emphasis is away from making him suffer and in the direction of making his life better and more pleasant. * * * * [M]uch of what is done by way of postconviction disposition of offenders is not truly rehabilitative, which is perhaps why the theory of reformation has not as yet shown very satisfactory results in practice. * * * *

(4) *Deterrence.* Under this theory, sometimes referred to as *general prevention,* the sufferings of the criminal for the crime he has committed are supposed to deter others from committing future crimes, lest they suffer the same unfortunate fate. The extent to which punishment actually

has this effect upon the general public is unclear; conclusive empirical research on the subject is lacking, and it is difficult to measure the effectiveness of fear of punishment because it is but one of several forces that restrain people from violating the law.

It does seem fair to assume, however, that the deterrent efficacy of punishment varies considerably, depending upon a number of factors. Those who commit crimes under emotional stress (such as murder in the heat of anger) . . . are less likely than others to be deterred. * * * * The magnitude of the threatened punishment is clearly a factor, but perhaps not as important as the probability of discovery and punishment.

(5) *Education.* Under this theory, criminal punishment serves, by the publicity which attends the trial, conviction and punishment of criminals, to educate the public as to the proper distinctions between good conduct and bad - distinctions which, when known, most of society will observe. While the public may need no such education as to serious *malum in se* crimes, the educational function of punishment is important as to crimes which are not generally known, often misunderstood, or inconsistent with current morality.

(6) *Retribution.* This is the oldest theory of punishment, and the one which still commands considerable respect from the general public. By this theory, also called *revenge* or *retaliation*, punishment (the infliction of suffering) is imposed by society on criminals in order to obtain revenge . . . . Typical of the criticism is that this theory 'is a form of retaliation, and as such, is morally indefensible.'

However . . . it is claimed that retributive punishment is needed to maintain respect for the law and to suppress acts of private vengeance. * * * *

Although retribution was long the theory of punishment least accepted by theorists, it is suddenly being seen by thinkers of all political persuasions as perhaps the strongest ground, after all, upon which to base a system of punishment.

If we apply these theories of punishment to § 418, which mental state is most appropriate? For example, can we argue that the "prevention" theory of punishment does not favor a strict liability standard here, because if Manny is punished now for going onto what he thought was his own land, this is not likely to deter him from trespassing on some later occasion where he mistakenly believes that the land is his own? Or, can the prosecution argue that the "prevention" theory *does* favor a strict liability standard, because punishing Manny now will make him super-careful about boundary lines in the future, and this serves the purposes of § 418?

Courts seldom discuss issues of criminal law on such a fundamental level, and there is not much discussion in this vein in the cases I've given you. In a case where the law is not clearly established, however, the courts might be receptive to this approach. Please see what you can do with it in analyzing our case.

Part II
Property Crimes

This Part considers what are often called "the three common law property crimes": larceny, embezzlement, and false pretenses. This description is not totally accurate, however. "Common law" suggests that they were created by judges, rather than by legislators. This is true of larceny, but not true of embezzlement and false pretenses. And it is questionable whether larceny was really meant to protect property.

But these are quibbles. These three crimes are called "the three common law property crimes" because they have ancient origins and because they form the basis for the modern law of theft, and courts today often begin any theft case by looking for the elements of these crimes.

Chapter 2

LARCENY

Larceny at common law may be defined as the (1) trespassory (2) taking and (3) carrying away of the (4) personal property (5) of another (6) with intent to steal it. American statutes dealing with larceny as a discrete offense have generally left the six elements of this crime unchanged . . .

LaFave, *Criminal Law* (West)

Today, we consider larceny a "property" crime: it protects a person's interest in personal property. This was not always so. In the early days of the common law, when the government's ability to punish crime was very limited — there were no police forces, as we know them, and no public prosecutors — larceny was punished primarily in order to prevent the fights which were provoked by thefts. The most the government could do was to protect the public against violence. That purpose had its effect on how the early common law courts chose the above definition of "larceny." (Note that larceny was invented by common law judges, not by legislators, as England had no viable Parliament at that time.)

But times have changed. We now have police forces, district attorneys, United States attorneys, and FBI agents — the means to do more for people than merely protect them from violence. Does this mean that the definition of larceny also should change? If so, who should make the change: the courts or the legislatures?

If the courts make the change, should they do so *openly* — by creating a new crime, or by changing or deleting some of the six elements of larceny? Or should they instead leave the written definition of larceny alone but change its meaning by creating "legal fictions" which stretch the meaning of those words beyond their common usages?

And if courts do change the law, shouldn't they do so only *prospectively*, so that defendants who relied on the old definition are not unfairly punished under the new definition? (Does a criminal defendant *rely* on the definition of a crime before he commits his *actus reus*?)

The above definition of larceny has six specified elements. As you consider this definition and how the cases in this Chapter interpret the six elements of that definition, ask yourself whether it does a very good job of protecting property. As you will see, a defendant might commit an act which you might view as "stealing" — and yet the courts might not deem this to be larceny. Why? Why should the courts limit themselves to the six specific elements of an ancient common law crime — rather than simply punish someone who acts and thinks like a "thief"? And even if the courts should be limited to the six specific elements, shouldn't they read those elements *broadly* (perhaps using a few "judicial fictions"), rather than *narrowly*, in order to lock up as many "thieves" as possible? Courts often say that criminal laws are to be "strictly construed in favor of the defendant", i.e., any doubts about meaning are to be resolved in favor of the defendant. Why? Why let crooks off on "technicalities"?

PROBLEM 2

To: My Law Clerk

From: Rhonda Bout, Deputy District Attorney, Borough of Manhattan

Re: *People v. Goniff*

I have been assigned to prosecute defendant Gloria Goniff on 2 charges of larceny, in violation of New York Penal Law § 155.05. Attached is a copy of the police report prepared by New York City Police Sergeant Peter Preston. Sergeant Preston is a good, thorough investigator, so I don't think we will be able to get much more evidence than what appears in his report.

Please read the attached authorities and let me know whether this evidence is sufficient to get the case to a jury on either charge.

The above excerpt from LaFave states the common law definition of larceny. Start with this definition, and then check to see if the New York statutes and cases have modified it.

Police Report

This morning I was on mounted patrol in Central Park, near the riding stables. At 10:10 a.m., Mr. Paul Omino ran up to me. Omino is the manager of a concession at the stables which rents out horses to the public for $20 an hour. He said that there was a young woman in his stable fooling around with the horses, and Omino wanted me to do something about it.

I rode over to Omino's stable. A sign outside the stable said, "Horses for Rent - See Office. Do Not Enter Without Permission." Omino said that the young woman had not come to the office. I looked inside the stable and saw 4 horses. All had saddles, but none were tied up. Omino told me he keeps them that way so they are ready to go at any time.

I then saw a young woman (the suspect) in the back of the stable. She came to the stable door, opened it, and looked around, but she did not see Omino or myself. She left the door open, went back into the stable, and got on an old brown horse named Sam. Omino whispered to me that Sam usually would not go unless you first gave him a sugar cube. Sam stood still while the suspect got on. The suspect held the reins, but left her feet out of the stirrups. She pulled on the reins and Sam lifted his head. Before Sam could move from where he was, I entered the stable and told the suspect that she was under arrest for larceny. She said her name was Gloria Goniff, that she liked horses, and just wanted to sit on the horse for a while. I took her to the station, booked her, and released her on $500 bail.

Later that afternoon, I was back on mounted patrol in Central Park. I went by Omino's stable to say hello to him. He said that one of his employees, Tex, had been putting a saddle on Nellie, a gray roan, when a young woman came up to him. She asked if she could sit on Nellie for a minute, and if she liked the horse, she would rent her for an hour. Tex said OK, and then he turned away to help some other customers. When he turned around, the woman and Nellie were gone. Omino was particularly upset because that afternoon he had more potential customers than he had horses, and he was losing rental money he could be making on Nellie.

I went back on patrol. On a trail near the stable, I saw a teenage girl riding a gray roan. I stopped her and asked her where she got the horse. She said her name was Jamie West. She had been walking in the park when she saw a young woman riding the roan, at about 3:30 p.m. She loved horses and all the horsemen knew her. She spoke to the woman, who offered to let Jamie ride the horse for an hour for $10. Jamie gave her the $10, and the woman got off the horse and left. I had with me a photo of Goniff which I had taken at her booking, and I showed the photo to Jamie. She said that was the woman who rented the horse to her. At 4:30 p.m., I brought the roan to Omino, who identified it as Nellie. I then went to Goniff's home and arrested her for a second charge of larceny.

Sgt. Preston, Mounted Police, NYPD.

New York Penal Law

Section 155.00: Larceny; Definition of Terms

The following definitions are applicable to this title:

1. "Property" means any money, personal property, real property, computer data, computer program, thing in action, evidence of debt or contract, or any article, substance or thing of value, including any gas, steam, water or electricity, which is provided for a charge or compensation.

2. "Obtain" includes, but is not limited to, the bringing about of a transfer or purported transfer of property or of a legal interest therein, whether to the obtainer or another.

3. "Deprive." To "deprive" another of property means (a) to withhold it or cause it to be withheld from him permanently or for so extended a period or under such circumstances that the major portion of its economic value or benefit is lost to him, or (b) to dispose of the property in such manner or under such circumstances as to render it unlikely that an owner will recover such property.

4. "Appropriate." To "appropriate" property of another to oneself or a third person means (a) to exercise control over it, or to aid a third person to exercise control over it, permanently or for so extended a period or under such circumstances as to acquire the major portion of its economic value or benefit, or (b) to dispose of the property for the benefit of oneself or a third person.

5. "Owner." When property is taken, obtained or withheld by one person from another person, an "owner" thereof means any person who has a right to possession thereof superior to that of the taker, obtainer or withholder.

A person who has obtained possession of property by theft or other illegal means shall be deemed to have a right of possession superior to that of a person who takes, obtains or withholds it from him by larcenous means. * * * *

Section 155.05: Larceny; Defined.

1. A person steals property and commits larceny when, with intent to deprive another of property or to appropriate the same to himself or to a third person, he wrongfully takes, obtains or withholds such property from an owner thereof.

2. Larceny includes a wrongful taking, obtaining or withholding of another's property, with the intent prescribed in subdivision one of this section, committed in any of the following ways:

> (a) By conduct heretofore defined or known as common law larceny by trespassory taking, common law larceny by trick, embezzlement, or obtaining property by false pretenses * * * *

> (d) By false promise. * * * *

[Ed. - These statutes were enacted in 1965, with subsequent amendments.]

NOTES:

(1) Compare these statutes with Model Penal Code § 223.0 through § 223.9, in Appendix II

(2) The old common law rules of pleading were very technical and strict. If a prosecutor charged the defendant with larceny, and the defendant was able to prove that he committed embezzlement instead of larceny, the jury was required to acquit him. To cure this problem, many modern statutes *consolidate* several theft crimes into one crime. In California, for example, the prosecutor is permitted simply to charge the defendant with "theft." If the prosecutor proves at trial that the defendant committed larceny, embezzlement, or obtaining property by false pretenses, the defendant may be convicted of "theft." California Penal Code sections 484, 490a.

New York Penal Law § 155.05(2) does the same thing, by defining "larceny" to include not only common law larceny, but the other major theft crimes as well.

PEOPLE v. ALAMO
New York Court of Appeals,[*]
34 N.Y.2d 453, 315 N.E.2d 446 (1974)

GABRIELLI, JUDGE.

The Westchester County Grand Jury charged defendant with grand larceny, second degree for theft of an automobile, and with criminal possession of burglary

---

[*] [Ed. New York's highest court is called the "Court of Appeals" — while its major trial courts are called "Supreme Courts".]

tools and a hypodermic instrument which were found with defendant in the automobile. Defendant was found guilty after a jury trial on all charges. The Appellate Division has unanimously affirmed the convictions. The point raised on this appeal with which we are chiefly concerned is whether it was error for the Judge to charge the jury that they might find a completed larceny even though they found defendant to have started the car, but not to have moved it.

The People's case insofar as it relates to the larcenous act was proved through the two police officers who made the arrest. Officer Davis testified that at approximately 1:00 a.m. on December 14, 1971 in the Town of Greenburgh he and fellow Officer Downey were cruising and spotted defendant in an automobile near the curb; that they felt the situation warranted a routine check whereupon the police cruiser was parked alongside the subject car to block its exit from the curb. Defendant, who was behind the wheel, was unable to produce a proper registration. Upon ascertainment that the true owner of the car was Stephen Solomon, a nearby resident, defendant was placed under arrest. The burglar tools and hypodermic needle were found in the car with defendant.

Officer Davis testified that "we noticed a vehicle on the right-hand side, in a curb lane, with its headlights on, the motor running, and a person operating this vehicle. The wheels were cut to the left and the vehicle was inching out into the roadway." Officer Downey rendered approximately the same account of these events and stated: "As we approached the intersection of Hillside Avenue and Virginia Road, we noticed a vehicle to our right parked facing north with the engine running with the lights on just starting to pull out of a parking space." There was additional evidence that the side vent window of the car had been forced. The only inroad which was made on the evidence that the car was in motion was Officer Davis' Grand Jury testimony that when he saw the car it was "parked" at the curb. The defense produced no witnesses and introduced no proof.

The Judge instructed the jury on the larceny count, reading to them subdivision 1 of § 155.05 of the Penal Law, i.e., that larceny consists of the wrongful taking, obtaining or withholding of property. He also told them that if they found that defendant had forced the window, removed the ignition switch, started the automobile and exercised control over the automobile by any act, then they could find him guilty of larceny. After some deliberation, the jury returned for further instruction on the meaning of control and whether movement of the vehicle was required to effectuate control. The Judge answered as follows:

> Control would be a proprietary act, any act which constituted appropriating the automobile to the defendant's own use, exercising some degree of jurisdiction over the automobile, taking an affirmative act. In this case, the entering of the car, the closing of the door, turning the lights on, and starting the vehicle may be considered acts of control. You have asked further the question: "Does control require movement of the vehicle?" I would say to you that control in the sense as creating a larceny and as I included in my original charge would not require movement of the vehicle.

Although defendant argues that it was error for the Judge not to allow the jury to find an attempt, this is welded to the argument that there can be no completed larceny until the vehicle is moved by the would-be thief. The argument has to be that not only was it error not to charge attempt, but that it was error to tell the jury they could find a completed larceny even though they might find the vehicle not to have been moved.

All the testimonial evidence on the point was that the car was beginning to move out from the curb after the officers spotted it. There is no affirmative proof that the car was not moving. Officer Davis' prior statement that the car was "parked" may to some small degree have affected his credibility on the question of the movement of the car, however. It may be argued that the jury may have doubted the officers' testimony on this matter and this theory is supported by the fact they asked for more specific instructions as to what they should do depending on whether the car was moved.

The Judge not only refused to charge attempt; he told the jury that there could be a completed larceny without movement of the car. We must, therefore, also deal with the question whether that was a correct instruction.

It is woven into the fabric of the common law that asportation is an element of a completed larceny. Indeed, these cases involve automobiles, the courts searching for the asportation element in all three. There does not appear to be, however, any authority which approximates the facts in the instant case, i.e., where an automobile is entered, where the culprit positions himself behind the wheel, starts the engine, turns on the lights and starts to move the car or is about to do so.

The authoritative case in this jurisdiction on the essential elements of larceny is *Harrison v. People*, 50 N.Y. 518. There a pickpocket grasped the victim's wallet and lifted it no more than several inches and not all the way out of the pocket when the victim, having become aware, grabbed at the wallet and thrust it back down to the bottom of the pocket. The court held that a completed larceny had been committed. The temporary possession by the thief, even though for a moment, was sufficient, as was the slight movement accompanying the possession. While it is to be conceded that the element of movement was a consideration in the court's reasoning, critical analysis of that reasoning discloses that the elements of possession and control were the paramount elements sought and that the fact of movement merely tended to support the idea of control. Thus, it was stated:

> To constitute the offence of larceny, there must be a taking or severance of the goods from the possession of the owner. But possession, so far as this offence is concerned, is the having or holding or detention of property in one's power or command.

There ensued discussion concerning instances where the object of the theft was connected to the owner by a string or chain and where, therefore, there could be no completed larceny because of the continued connection to the owner even though there was limited asportation. It was then stated concerning the wallet: "It was in his possession. He directed, and, for the instant of time, controlled its movements."

The actions needed to gain possession and control over a wallet, including movement of the wallet which, in itself, is merely an element tending to show possession and control, are not necessarily the actions needed to gain possession and control of an automobile. A wallet, or a diamond ring, or a safe are totally inert objects susceptible of movement only by physical lifting or shoving by the thief. An automobile, however, is itself an instrument of transportation and when activated comes within the total possession and control of the operator. In this situation movement or motion is not essential to control. Absent any evidence that the vehicle is somehow fastened or immovable because of a mechanical defect, the thief has taken command of the object of the larceny. He has, in the words of subdivision 1 of § 155.05 of the Penal Law, wrongfully "taken" the property from its owner surely as much so as had the thief in *Harrison*.

Consistency is always desirable in the application of the various laws and such would not be achieved were we to hold that on these facts defendant had not gained possession and control of the car. An established line of authority in New York and elsewhere holds that for purposes of offenses for driving while intoxicated under the Vehicle and Traffic Law, Consol. Laws, c. 71, operation of the vehicle is established on proof that the defendant was merely behind the wheel with the engine running without need for proof that defendant was observed driving the car, i.e., operating it so as to put it in motion.

It would be difficult to understand how a person who is operating a car, as defendant was under the authority just discussed, could be said nevertheless not to be in possession and control of that car. It is further to be noted that where the Legislature has specifically addressed itself solely to automobile taking, a person is guilty of unauthorized use where he "takes, operates, exercises control over, rides in or otherwise uses a vehicle." Penal Law § 165.05, subd. 1. Although it might be argued that the unauthorized use statute is not a larceny statute and thus utilizes lesser criteria, the distinction meant by the Legislature between the two kinds of offenses lies in the intent of the taker, not in the means used to effect the taking. Thus, the unauthorized use statute contemplates only a borrowing and not a complete appropriation. If operation of the automobile can effect a taking under the unauthorized use statute, then operation ought also to suffice under the larceny statute.

Finally, we do not, as stated in the dissent, "disregard" the relative constancy of the statute under which defendant was convicted. It is to be noted that not since 1942 have we in this jurisdiction been strictly bound to the ancient common-law concepts of larceny. At that time the first unnumbered paragraph of former § 1290 was enacted. That was the forerunner of current subdivision 1 of § 155.05 of the Penal Law which was charged to the jury in the instant case and which in very broad terms prohibits wrongful appropriation, taking, obtaining or withholding of another's property with the requisite intent.

There is nothing in the definitions section which states that asportation is in all cases an essential element of such taking or obtaining (§ 155.00). Subdivision 2 of § 155.00 defines "Obtain" as follows: " 'Obtain' includes, but is not limited to, the bringing about of a transfer or purported transfer of property or of a legal interest therein, whether to the obtainer or another." Surely a person transfers an instrument of transportation to himself when he commences to operate the instrument for its intended purpose. At that point it comes under his sole dominion and control and, assuming requisite intent, amounts to the completed taking as envisioned under our broadened statutory concepts. To require that the vehicle be moved by the operator is to slavishly adhere to the auxiliary common-law element of asportation which is simply not necessary to the finding of the primary elements of dominion and control where an activated automobile is concerned.

The order appealed from should be affirmed.

JONES, WACHTLER, SAMUEL, RABIN and STEVENS, JJ. concur.

BREITEL, CHIEF JUDGE (dissenting).

I dissent and vote to reverse and order a new trial because defendant was entitled to his requested charge that on the evidence the jury could conclude that only an attempt rather than a consummated larceny had been committed.

There is no significant disagreement in the court whether the jury was properly instructed on the issue of a completed larceny, if there had been a movement of the vehicle for which there was available evidence. There was, indeed, ample evidence to establish movement of the vehicle by defendant. The only issue which divides the court is whether the jury could be instructed, as it was, that no movement was required to establish a completed larceny.

Disregarded by the majority is that the 1967 statute under which defendant was tried and convicted is in its operative language substantively identical with the predecessor statute. Moreover, the law of this State has always been, and indeed, the unanimous Anglo-American view insofar as discoverable is, that some movement, albeit slight, is required before a conviction for a completed larceny may be had (*Harrison v. People*, 50 N.Y. 518, 523-524).

A person may be guilty of operating a motor vehicle while intoxicated although the vehicle was observed only as stationary. Even if that principle be legally sound, it has no application to a larceny prosecution. The statutory proscription against persons operating a motor vehicle while intoxicated is directed at a different evil involving a lesser degree of turpitude and a special problem of proof hardly applicable to larceny. Moreover, an attempt to commit the crime of operating a motor vehicle while intoxicated most often would be inconceivable.

Indeed, the majority helpfully cites automobile larceny cases, every one of which holds that movement of the automobile is necessary, and that possession with control, but without movement, constitutes only the attempt rather than the completed larceny (cf. LaFave and Scott, *Criminal Law*, p. 632 (1972)). Hence, these authorities demonstrate that on the evidence in this case the jury could have found either an attempt or the completed crime. Consequently, defendant was entitled to the requested charge on attempt.

The evidence was equivocal whether the automobile had been moved at all from its parking place. Merely sitting in the driver's seat, motor running, and with the lights on was not a taking of possession and control by defendant. This is not to say that the jury was not entitled to find on the other evidence of movement, if believed, that the completed larceny had occurred.

In the concrete instance of automobile larceny it is particularly important to distinguish between seating one's self in the driver's seat, as children often do, and some child-like adults do, "controlling" the vehicle, and, whether when the acts extend no further than that, there has been a taking. It is not a close legal question, as the majority analysis would show, but is an inescapable issue of fact for any fact-finder, when considering the tinkering and dallying habits of human beings. A trespass or even an attempt there may be, on any view, but a larceny is another matter. As with the wallet in the *Harrison* case, discussed in the majority opinion, control and possession to the exclusion of the owner is not shown without some movement, any more than it could be shown in the shoplifter case if the alleged larcenist did no more than put his fist around a bauble. In short, asportation under the applicable statute is, inevitably because definitionally, an element of larceny, and it may not be analyzed away (in contrast see American Law Institute, Model Penal Code, art. 223, especially § 223.2; American Law Institute, Tentative Draft No. 1 (1953), Comment D, at pp. 65-66)

JASEN, J. concurred with BREITEL, C.J.

NOTES FROM RHONDA:

(1) In *People v. Rembert*, 562 N.Y.S.2d 356 (1990), a transit policeman riding a subway saw Rembert put his hand in a woman's handbag and begin to lift a change purse. Before he could remove the change purse from the handbag, the woman pulled the handbag away. Citing *Harrison* and *Alamo*, the judge rejected Rembert's claim that he had committed no more than attempted larceny. "Since the defendant herein possessed the complainant's change purse and held it in his power and command albeit briefly until the moment when the complainant became aware of his action and forcibly regained possession, the defendant's act would be legally sufficient as to permit the court to submit to the jury the change of grand larceny . . ."

(2) In *People v. Zombo*, 813 N.Y.S.2d 624 (2006), Zombo was convicted of robbery, which consists of "forcibly stealing" property.

> Defendant approached the victim at a gas station while she was pumping gas into her vehicle. He pressed an object against her back and ordered her to give him the keys to her vehicle. The victim pleaded with defendant to allow her five-year-old daughter to leave the vehicle, and defendant agreed. After retrieving her daughter, the victim gave defendant the keys, and defendant instructed her to leave.

> While walking away from the gas station, the victim observed defendant enter her vehicle. A short time later, defendant again approached the victim. He grabbed her and asked her how to work the alarm on the vehicle. The victim testified that her vehicle has an anti-theft system requiring the operator to press a button inside the vehicle in order to start the vehicle. Instead of so informing defendant, however, the victim told him that the alarm was not activated and that the vehicle should be operable.

> After defendant returned to the gas station, the victim approached a passerby for assistance. Upon going to the gas station, the passerby was approached by defendant, who asked whether he knew how to operate a

remote control vehicle. The passerby accused defendant of stealing the vehicle, and a scuffle ensued. The police arrived and arrested defendant, and the victim identified him as the perpetrator.

On appeal, Zombo argued that the evidence was insufficient to prove that he "stole" the car. The court disagreed:

> The "taking" element of a larceny is satisfied where the defendant exercised dominion and control over the property for a period of time, however temporary, in a manner wholly inconsistent with the owner's continued rights. In the event that the stolen property is a vehicle, "movement or motion is not essential to establish the element of control" *People v. Alamo*, 34 N.Y.2d 453, 458, 358 N.Y.S.2d 375.

> Here, in addition to testifying that she observed defendant enter her vehicle, she further testified that her cell phone jack was missing from the vehicle, and the People presented evidence that the cell phone jack was found in defendant's possession after defendant's arrest. The victim also testified that she found a cell phone in her vehicle that did not belong to her. The People therefore presented evidence establishing that, after defendant entered the vehicle and had unsuccessfully attempted to start it, he was compelled to ask both the victim and the passerby how to start the vehicle. Thus, the evidence is legally sufficient to establish that defendant began to "operate the vehicle for its intended purpose," thereby bringing the vehicle under his sole dominion and control *Alamo*, 34 N.Y.2d at 460.

(3) *Alamo* was considered in *State v. Donaldson*, 663 N.W.2d 882 (Iowa 2003), where a police officer interrupted defendant's attempt to "hot-wire" a car. The Iowa Supreme Court affirmed his conviction for theft:

> Is a person guilty of theft if he breaks into another's car and engages the entire electrical system, save the engine? Specifically, the question on appeal is whether Dean Lester Donaldson possessed or controlled another's van when he broke into it, dismantled the steering column, and manipulated the ignition switch, turning on the radio and lighting the "check engine" sign on the dashboard. * * *

> The State charged Donaldson with second-degree theft pursuant to Iowa Code § 714.1(1). This statute provides "a person commits theft when" he or she "takes possession or control of the property of another, or property in the possession of another, with the intent to deprive the other thereof." Iowa Code § 714.1(1). At the end of the State's case, Donaldson moved for a judgment of acquittal. He argued the State failed to prove the elements of theft and, at most, showed Donaldson was guilty of attempted theft. Counsel argued the "starter must be engaged for there to be actual control over that vehicle." The court disagreed and overruled Donaldson's motion. * * * *

> The Iowa theft statute is modeled after the Model Penal Code, with slight variation. Model Penal Code § 223.2 cmt. 2, at 165 (1980). Our terms "possession or control" of another's property replace the common law larceny requirements of "caption" and "asportation." "Caption," or taking,

occurred when the actor secured dominion over the property of another. The element of "asportation," or carrying away, was satisfied with even the most slight change in position of the stolen object. At common law, to prove a theft, the State had to show a defendant took the property of another, i.e., secured dominion over it, and carried the property away.

The asportation requirement was important at common law because if a defendant's actions fell short of causing the object of the theft to move, the defendant was guilty of attempt only. Because a completed larceny was generally a felony whereas attempt was a misdemeanor, significant differences in "procedure and punishment turned on the criminologically insignificant fact of slight movement of the object of theft." In modern criminal law, however, the penal consequences between attempt and a completed theft are so minimal that it has become less important to draw a bright line between the two actions. As such, the element of asportation is no longer necessary.

Iowa, like many other states following the Model Penal Code, has abandoned the common law asportation requirement.[2] Our definition of "theft" under Iowa Code § 714.1 is based on the Model Penal Code. We now define theft as the possession or control of another's property with intent to deprive the owner thereof. The key to our statute is the words "possession or control." In determining the meaning of "possession" and "control," we look to the Model Penal Code for guidance as our statute is modeled after it. The Model Penal Code contemplates "control" of the object to begin when the defendant "uses it in a manner beyond his authority." The method of exerting control over the object of the theft is important only insofar as it "sheds light on the authority of the actor to behave as he did." Our statute replaces the common law element of "taking" with "possession." The Model Penal Code provides a person commits theft if he or she "unlawfully takes, or exercises unlawful control over" the property of another. A taking in this sense concerns whether the offender exerted control over the object "adverse to or usurpatory of the owner's dominion." *State v. Victor*, 368 So.2d 711, 714 (La.1979). That is, one possesses an object if he or she secures dominion over it. *See* Model Penal Code § 223.2 cmt. 2, at 164. To summarize the above concepts, "possession or control" begins and a theft is completed when the actor secures dominion over the object or uses it in a manner beyond his authority.

Donaldson argues his conduct, at most, is sufficient to prove attempted theft, not a completed theft. We acknowledge the issue before us is complicated because all theft partakes of the character of attempt. The line between attempt and a completed theft is a thin one. The thief proposes to make the property his own more or less permanently; but he is nonetheless a thief if, shortly after he exerts his dominion over the property of another,

---

[2] Other jurisdictions following the Model Penal Code are Alabama, Arizona, Arkansas, Colorado, Delaware, Hawaii, Illinois, Indiana, Kansas, Kentucky, Maine, Minnesota, Missouri, Montana, Nebraska, New Hampshire, New Jersey, North Dakota, Ohio, Oregon, Pennsylvania, Texas, Utah, Washington, Wisconsin, Michigan, Oklahoma, and West Virginia. *See* Model Penal Code § 223.2 cmt. 2, n. 3, at 165.

he is prevented from making off with it. It is not necessary that the actor have gone far enough to gain unhindered control.

The question before us concerns whether the defendant possessed or controlled the object of the theft. The critical issue, as the statute dictates, is *not* whether the defendant used or operated the object of the theft. As to Donaldson's conduct, we must determine whether he exercised wrongful dominion or unauthorized control of the van. Bearing in mind the definitions of "control" and "possession" as contemplated by the Model Penal Code, we turn to the facts.

The undisputed facts of the case are the following. At approximately 1:30 a.m., Donaldson entered a van owned by Combined Pool & Spa. The owner of the van did not give Donaldson authority or permission to take possession or control of the van. The officer spotted the van located in the parking lot of Combined Pool & Spa and noticed the van's sliding door was partially open. As the officer walked toward the van, he saw the brake lights flash suggesting someone was inside the van. As the officer approached, Donaldson got out of the driver's side and ran away. The officer called after Donaldson, identified himself as a police officer, and ordered him to stop. Donaldson kept running. When the officer checked the van, he saw the steering column had been forcibly dismantled; there were wires hanging from the column. The ignition switch had been removed. The radio was operating. The "check engine" sign on the dashboard was lit. At trial, one of the officers testified Donaldson had engaged all of the electric systems. After turning on the electric accessory systems in the car, according to the officer, all Donaldson had left to do was engage the starter.

There is no evidence in the record to suggest Donaldson's tearing apart the steering column was intended for any purpose other than to deprive the owner of her possession of the van. Donaldson argues he did not possess or control the van because he did not have the "ability to readily move or remove" it. This, however, is not the test for possession or control. Because we have abandoned the common law asportation requirement, movement or motion of the car is not essential to finding a defendant had possession or control of the car. *See, e.g., People v. Alamo*, 34 N.Y.2d 453 (1974) (where defendant was charged with grand larceny of an automobile, movement or motion was not essential to find defendant exerted control sufficient to support conviction). Our theft statute does not state possession or control is tantamount to "operation" of the object of the theft. To interpret our statute in this manner is to restrict the definition of theft more narrowly than the legislature intended. Given a strict interpretation of the statute, the State only had to show Donaldson had control of the van, i.e., he had dominion over it in a manner inconsistent with his authority. *See* Model Penal Code § 223.2, at 166. We are unwilling to imply an "operation" requirement for certain kinds of property that are normally operated by its possessor.

The mere fact that Donaldson was interrupted by the police officer before he engaged the starter motor does not remove this case from the realm of a completed theft. It is not necessary that the engine was running and the van could have been moved. *Alamo*, 358 N.Y.S.2d at 380.[4] That is, technical operation of the van is not necessary to find Donaldson exercised wrongful dominion or unauthorized control over the van.

Certainly, Donaldson's acts were sufficient to set into motion the steps necessary to power the van. It was not necessary that the engine was actually running. Rather, at the moment Donaldson began to manipulate the electrical wires for the purpose of starting the engine, he exerted complete control over the vehicle.

In sum, the facts before us show Donaldson was using the van owned by another person. He had the power and intention at the given time to exercise unfettered dominion over the van. Donaldson was in a position to exclude all others from the van, for example, by locking it. No one else could have hot-wired the van or started it with a key while Donaldson had control over it. Moreover, he used the van without the owner's consent and in a manner beyond his authority. Donaldson entered the company's van around 1:30 in the morning. He tore apart the steering column. The ignition switch had been removed; wires protruded from the ignition. The brake lights flashed. The radio worked. The "check engine" sign was lit. When the officer approached the van, Donaldson got out of the driver's side and ran away. All of these facts together are sufficient to show Donaldson controlled the van within the meaning of Iowa Code section 714.1(1). As such, the trial court properly denied Donaldson's motion for judgment of acquittal. We affirm.

(4) How does *Alamo* affect our first larceny charge against Goniff? Must we prove "asportation?" Does the evidence show that Goniff had "control" of Sam, under *Alamo's* analysis?

PEOPLE v. OLIVO
New York Court of Appeals
52 N.Y.2d 309, 420 N.E.2d 40 (1981)

COOKE, CHIEF JUDGE.

These cases present a recurring question in this era of the self-service store which has never been resolved by this court: may a person be convicted of larceny for shoplifting if the person is caught with goods while still inside the store? For reasons outlined below, it is concluded that a larceny conviction may be sustained,

---

[4] We note the facts in *Alamo* are not the same as the ones before us. In *Alamo*, the defendant started the engine, turned on the lights, and appeared to be about to move the car. The *Alamo* court found this conduct constituted control over the car sufficient to justify the conviction of grand larceny in the third degree. Nothing in the opinion indicated the court would have found to the contrary if the engine had not been running. Rather, the court considered this fact, together with all of the other circumstances of the case to find the defendant controlled the car. As we quoted above, any act that alone or one that sets into motion the actions necessary to power the car is sufficient to find control. *Alamo*, 358 N.Y.S.2d at 380.

in certain situations, even though the shoplifter was apprehended before leaving the store.

I.

In *People v. Olivo*, defendant was observed by a security guard in the hardware area of a department store. Initially conversing with another person, defendant began to look around furtively when his acquaintance departed. The security agent continued to observe and saw defendant assume a crouching position, take a set of wrenches and secret it in his clothes. After again looking around, defendant began walking toward an exit, passing a number of cash registers en route. When defendant did not stop to pay for the merchandise, the officer accosted him a few feet from the exit. In response to the guard's inquiry, he denied having the wrenches, but as he proceeded to the security office, defendant removed the wrenches and placed them under his jacket. At trial, defendant testified that he had placed the tools under his arm and was on line at a cashier when apprehended. The jury returned a verdict of guilty on the charge of petit larceny. The conviction was affirmed by Appellate Term.

II.

In *People v. Gasparik*, defendant was in a department store trying on a leather jacket. Two store detectives observed him tear off the price tag and remove a "sensormatic" device designed to set off an alarm if the jacket were carried through a detection machine. There was at least one such machine at the exit of each floor. Defendant placed the tag and the device in the pocket of another jacket on the merchandise rack. He took his own jacket, which he had been carrying with him, and placed it on a table. Leaving his own jacket, defendant put on the leather jacket and walked through the store, still on the same floor, by passing several cash registers. When he headed for the exit from that floor, in the direction of the main floor, he was apprehended by security personnel. At trial, defendant denied removing the price tag and the sensormatic device from the jacket, and testified that he was looking for a cashier without a long line when he was stopped. The court, sitting without a jury, convicted defendant of petit larceny. Appellate Term affirmed.

III.

In *People v. Spatzier*, defendant entered a bookstore on Fulton Street in Hempstead carrying an attache case. The two co-owners of the store observed the defendant in a ceiling mirror as he browsed through the store. They watched defendant remove a book from the shelf, look up and down the aisle, and place the book in his case. He then placed the case at his feet and continued to browse. One of the owners approached defendant and accused him of stealing the book. An altercation ensured and when defendant allegedly struck the owner with the attache case, the case opened and the book fell out. At trial, defendant denied secreting the book in his case and claimed that the owner had suddenly and unjustifiably accused him of stealing. The jury found defendant guilty of petit larceny, and the conviction was affirmed by the Appellate Term.

IV.

The primary issue in each case is whether the evidence, viewed in the light most favorable to the prosecution, was sufficient to establish the elements of larceny as defined by the Penal Law. To resolve this common question, the development of the common-law crime of larceny and its evolution into modern statutory form must be briefly traced.

Larceny at common law was defined as a trespassory taking and carrying away of the property of another with intent to steal it (e.g., La Fave & Scott, *Criminal Law* § 85; see 4 Blackstone's Commentaries, at pp. 229-250). The early common-law courts apparently viewed larceny as defending society against breach of the peace, rather than protecting individual property rights, and therefore placed heavy emphasis upon the requirement of a trespassory taking (LaFave & Scott, *Criminal Law*, § 85). Thus, a person such as a bailee, who had rightfully obtained possession of property from its owner, could not be guilty of larceny (see, e.g., *Carrier's Case*, Y B Pasch 13 Edw. IV, f.9, p. 1 5 (1473)). The result was that the crime of larceny was quite narrow in scope.[1]

Gradually, the courts began to expand the reach of the offense, initially by subtle alterations in the common-law concept of possession (e.g., American Law Institute, Model Penal Code (Tent Draft No. 1), art 206, app. A, p.101). Thus, for instance, it became a general rule that goods entrusted to an employee were not deemed to be in his possession, but were only considered to be in his custody, so long as he remained on the employer's premises (e.g., 3 Holdsworth, *A History of English Law* (3d ed, 1923), at p. 365).[2] And, in the case of *Chisser* (83 Eng.Rep. 142), it was held that a shop owner retained legal possession of merchandise being examined by a prospective customer until the actual sale was made. In these situations, the employee and the customer would not have been guilty of larceny if they had first obtained lawful possession of the property from the owner. By holding that they had not acquired possession, but merely custody, the court was able to sustain a larceny conviction.

As the reach of larceny expanded, the intent element of the crime became of increasing importance, while the requirement of a trespassory taking became less significant. As a result, the bar against convicting a person who had initially obtained lawful possession of property faded. In *King v. Pear* (168 Eng.Rep. 208), for instance, a defendant who had lied about his address and ultimate destination when renting a horse was found guilty of larceny for later converting the horse. Because of the fraudulent misrepresentation, the court reasoned, the defendant had never obtained legal possession. Thus, "larceny by trick" was born (see Hall,

---

[1] One popular explanation for the limited nature of larceny is the "unwillingness on the part of the judges to enlarge the limits of a capital offense" (*Commonwealth v. Ryan*, 155 Mass. 523; Hall, *Theft, Law and Society* (2d ed), at p. 118 et seq.). The accuracy of this view is subject to some doubt (see Fletcher, *Metamorphosis of Larceny*, 89 Harv.L.Rev. 469).

[2] In 1529, a statute was passed subjecting employees to the law of larceny as to all valuable property entrusted to them by their employers (21 Hen. VIII, ch. 7).

Theft, Law and Society (2d ed), at p. 40). Later cases went even further, often ignoring the fact that a defendant had initially obtained possession lawfully, and instead focused upon his later intent (e.g., *Queen v. Middleton*, LR 2 Cr.Cas.Res. 38 (1873)). The crime of larceny then encompassed, not only situations where the defendant initially obtained property by a trespassory taking, but many situations where an individual, possessing the requisite intent, exercised control over property inconsistent with the continued rights of the owner.[3] During this evolutionary process, the purpose served by the crime of larceny obviously shifted from protecting society's peace to general protection of property rights (Fletcher, *Metamorphosis of Larceny*, 89 Harv.L.Rev. 469, 519-520).[4]

Modern penal statutes generally have incorporated these developments under a unified definition of larceny (see e. g., American Law Institute, Model Penal Code (Tent Draft No. 1), sec. 206.1 (theft is appropriation of property of another, which includes unauthorized exercise of control)). Case law, too, now tends to focus upon the actor's intent and the exercise of dominion and control over the property (see, e.g., *People v. Alamo*, 34 N.Y.2d 453). Indeed, this court has recognized, in construing the New York Penal Law, that the "ancient common-law concepts of larceny" no longer strictly apply (*People v. Alamo*, supra, 34 N.Y.2d at p.459).

This evolution is particularly relevant to thefts occurring in modern self-service stores. In stores of that type, customers are impliedly invited to examine, try on, and carry about the merchandise on display. Thus, in a sense, the owner has consented to the customer's possession of the goods for a limited purpose. That the owner has consented to that possession does not, however, preclude a conviction for larceny. If the customer exercises dominion and control wholly inconsistent with the continued rights of the owner, and the other elements of the crime are present, a larceny has occurred.[6] Such conduct on the part of a customer satisfies the "taking" element of the crime.

It is this element that forms the core of the controversy in these cases. The defendants argue, in essence, that the crime is not established, as a matter of law,

---

[3] Parliament also played a role in this development. Thus, for example, in 1857 a statute extended larceny to all conversions by bailees (20 & 21 Vict., ch. 54).

[4] One commentator has argued that the concept of possessorial immunity — i.e., that one who obtains possession of property by delivery from the owner cannot be guilty of larceny - stems from a general reluctance of the early common law to criminalize acts arising out of private relationships (Fletcher, *Metamorphosis of Larceny*, 89 Harv.L.Rev. 469, 472-476). Thus, although an owner deprived of property by a bailee could seek a civil remedy in detinue and later trover (Maitland, *Equity and the Forms of Action at Common Law*, at pp. 356-357, 365), the harm was deemed private and not a matter for societal intervention. Over time, the public-private dichotomy waned and the criminal law increasingly was viewed as an instrument for protecting certain interests and controlling social behavior (Fletcher, at pp. 502-504). As a concomitant development, the criminal law changed its main focus from the objective behavior of the defendant to his subjective intent (id. at pp. 498-518).

[6] Also, required, of course, is the intent prescribed by subdivision 1 of § 155.05 of the Penal Law, and some movement when property other than an automobile is involved (see *People v. Alamo*, 34 N.Y.2d 453, 458-460, supra). As a practical matter in shoplifting cases, the same evidence which proves the taking will usually involve movement. The movement, or asportation, requirement has traditionally been satisfied by a slight moving of the property (see *Harrison v. People*, 50 N.Y. 518). This accords with the purpose of the asportation element, which is to show that the thief had indeed gained possession and control of the property (*People v. Alamo*, supra, 34 N.Y.2d at pp. 458, 460; see *Harrison v. People*, supra).

unless there is evidence that the customer departed the shop without paying for the merchandise.

Although this court has not addressed the issue, case law from other jurisdictions seems unanimous in holding that a shoplifter need not leave the store to be guilty of larceny (e.g., *State v. Grant*, 135 Vt. 222; *Groomes v. United States*, 155 A.2d 73 (D.C.Mun.App.), supra; *People v. Baker*, 365 Ill. 328; *People v. Bradovich*, 305 Mich. 329). This is because a shopper may treat merchandise in a manner inconsistent with the owner's continued rights — and in a manner not in accord with that of prospective purchaser — without actually walking out of the store. Indeed, depending upon the circumstances of each case, a variety of conduct may be sufficient to allow the trier of fact to find a taking. It would be well-nigh impossible, and unwise, to attempt to delineate all the situations which would establish a taking. But it is possible to identify some of the factors used in determining whether the evidence is sufficient to be submitted to the fact finder.

In many cases, it will be particularly relevant that defendant concealed the goods under clothing or in a container. Such conduct is not generally expected in a self-service store and may in a proper case be deemed an exercise of dominion and control inconsistent with the store's continued rights. Other furtive or unusual behavior on the part of the defendant should also be weighed. Thus, if the defendant surveys the area while secreting the merchandise or abandoned his or her own property in exchange for the concealed goods, this may evince larcenous rather than innocent behavior. Relevant too is the customer's proximity to or movement towards one of the store's exits. Certainly it is highly probative of guilt that the customer was in possession of secreted goods just a few short steps from the door or moving in that direction. Finally, possession of a known shoplifting device actually used to conceal merchandise, such as a specially designed outer garment or false bottomed carrying case, would be all but decisive.

Of course, in a particular case, any one or any combination of these factors may take on special significance. And there may be other considerations, not now identified, which should be examined. So long as its bears upon the principal issue - whether the shopper exercised control wholly inconsistent with the owner's continued rights - any attending circumstance is relevant and may be taken into account.

V.

Under these principles, there was ample evidence in each case to raise a factual question as to the defendants' guilt.[7] In *People v. Olivo*, defendant not only concealed goods in his clothing, but he did so in a particularly suspicious manner. And, when defendant was stopped, he was moving towards the door, just three feet short of exiting the store. It cannot be said as a matter of law that these circumstances failed to establish a taking.[8]

---

[7] In analyzing the proof to determine legal sufficiency, the evidence must be viewed in the light most favorable to the prosecution.

[8] As discussed, the same evidence which establishes dominion and control in these circumstances will

In *People v. Gasparik*, defendant removed the price tag and sensor device from a jacket, abandoned his own garment, put the jacket on, and ultimately headed for the main floor of the store. Removal of the price tag and sensor device, and careful concealment of those items, is highly unusual and suspicious conduct for a shopper. Coupled with defendant's abandonment of his own coat and his attempt to leave the floor, those factors were sufficient to make out a prima facie case of a taking.

In *People v. Spatzier*, defendant concealed a book in an attache case. Unaware that he was being observed in an overhead mirror, defendant looked furtively up and down and aisle before secreting the book. In these circumstances, given the manner in which defendant concealed the book and his suspicious behavior, the evidence was not insufficient as a matter of law. * * * *

VII.

In sum, in view of the modern definition of the crime of larceny, and its purpose of protecting individual property rights, a taking of property in the self-service store context can be established by evidence that a customer exercised control over merchandise wholly inconsistent with the store's continued rights. Quite simply, a customer who crosses the line between the limited right he or she has to deal with merchandise and the store owner's rights may be subject to prosecution for larceny. Such a rule should foster the legitimate interests and continued operation of self-service shops, a convenience which most members of the society enjoy.

Accordingly, in each case, the order of the Appellate Term should be affirmed.

NOTES FROM RHONDA:

(1) I had some trouble identifying which *element* of the crime of larceny was at issue in *Olivo*. Please help me out on this, as it will affect our analysis how *Olivo* applies to Goniff's case.

(2) Is *Olivo* consistent with *Alamo*? In *Olivo*, the court says that "If the customer exercises dominion and control wholly inconsistent with the continued rights of the owner, and the other elements of the crime are present, a larceny has occurred." But *Alamo* said that if defendant enters a car which has a mechanical defect and will not run, he has *not* committed larceny - even though it would seem that he has done something "wholly inconsistent with the continued rights of the owner." Can these cases be reconciled, or does *Olivo* overrule *Alamo*?

(3) Exactly *when* did the defendants in *Olivo* commit the "taking" of the property? Suppose a defendant took an item from the shelf with the intent to pay for it, but on the way to the check-out stand, he changed his mind and decided to smuggle it out of the store. When would the "taking" have occurred? I think this might be important, because of the following general rule, and its possible impact on our case:

---

often establish movement of the property. And, the requisite intent generally may be inferred from all the surrounding circumstances. It would be the rare case indeed in which the evidence establishes all the other elements of the crime but would be insufficient to give rise to an inference of intent.

With larceny, as with other crimes requiring both specified physical conduct and a specified state of mind, the defendant's conduct and his mental state must coincide. So the taking and carrying away (the physical conduct in larceny) and the intent to steal (larceny's state of mind) must concur. * * * * As an aid in finding that the taking-and-asportation and the intent to steal coincide, the law of larceny under some circumstances makes use of the fictional notion of *continuing trespass*, under which the original trespassory taking, although not coinciding with an intent to steal (for the taker originally has no such intent), continues until the taker does form such an intent. [LaFave, *Criminal Law* (West)]

PEOPLE v. JENNINGS
Court of Appeals of New York
69 N.Y.2d 103, 504 N.E.2d 1079 (1986)

TITONE, JUDGE.

On December 13, 1982, the Sentry Armored Courier Corp. warehouse in Bronx County was burglarized and robbed of some $11 million by individuals unconnected to Sentry, who were later apprehended and prosecuted. In the aftermath of the robbery, the Bronx County District Attorney's office focused its attention on Sentry's own business practices. A series of indictments charging Sentry and its principals with various counts of larceny and misapplication of property ensued. The question presented for our consideration is whether the indictments' allegations concerning defendants' handling of the money entrusted to their care would, if proven, support convictions for the crimes charged.

The six indictments presently before us collectively charge defendants John Jennings, Angela Fiumefreddo, John Finnerty, Sentry Armored Courier Corp. and Sentry Investigations Corp. with several counts of grand larceny in the second degree and misapplication of property. At the time the indictments were issued, Sentry was principally engaged in transporting and storing large sums of cash and performing related services on behalf of its clients. Defendant Jennings was the president of the Sentry Armored Courier Corp., defendant Fiumefreddo was the senior vice-president of that corporation, and defendant John Finnerty was the vice-president and cashier of the Hudson Valley National Bank, which played a role in one of the alleged misappropriation "schemes."

* * * *

IV. *The Repurchase Agreement Plan*

Indictments Nos. 4379/83, 4380/83 and 370/84, on which the named defendants are John Jennings, John Finnerty, Sentry Armored Courier Corp. and Sentry Investigations Corp., all concern a business practice that the People have dubbed the "Repurchase Agreement Scheme." All of the counts in these indictments were dismissed by the trial court, and the dismissals were upheld on the People's appeal to the Appellate Division. We agree with the Appellate Division that the facts presented to the Grand Jury were legally insufficient to support the charges of second degree grand larceny and misapplication of property that were contained in these indictments.

Taken in the light most favorable to the People, the evidence before the Grand Jury showed that Sentry had an agreement with its client, Chemical Bank, under which Sentry was to pick up from Chemical's Water Street offices certain "bulk deposits" that Chemical had received from its commercial customers. Sentry was to "fine count" this money in its warehouse and then deliver it within 72 hours to Chemical's account at the Federal Reserve Bank in lower Manhattan, reporting any overages or shortages discovered in the counting process.[3] In fact, Sentry was able to perform the "fine counting" task in approximately 24 hours, considerably less time than the 72 hours its agreement with Chemical allowed.

Reluctant to retain all of the cash on Sentry's premises for the full 72-hour period, defendant Jennings met with defendant Finnerty, an officer of Hudson Valley National Bank, and arranged for the "fine counted" money to be delivered to Hudson's account at the Federal Reserve Bank, with the funds to be credited to Sentry's newly created escrow account with Hudson. Once the funds were delivered, an employee of Sentry was to call Hudson and specify the amount that was to be used to buy "repurchase agreements" from that bank.

Under these "repurchase agreements," which were analogous to loans or bonds, Hudson was given the right to invest the money, while Sentry's account was debited in an appropriate amount. The loan was secured by A-rated bonds held in Hudson's Federal Reserve Bank vault. At the conclusion of the 72-hour period Sentry had to deposit Chemical's money in its Federal Reserve account, Hudson would "repurchase" the bonds from Sentry by crediting Sentry's escrow account with the principal amount plus a portion of the interest Hudson had earned on its investments. On telephone orders from Sentry's employee, Hudson would then wire transfer the principal amount to Chemical's account at the Federal Reserve Bank, leaving Sentry's account enriched by the amount of the interest payment. The "repurchase agreement" plan was implemented in July of 1981.

By late August, Chemical had noticed that its funds were being routed through Hudson and demanded an explanation. Although an officer of Sentry told Chemical's representative that the rerouting had been initiated for "insurance purposes," Chemical was evidently unsatisfied and directed Sentry, both orally and in writing, to deliver the "fine counted" money directly to Chemical's account at the Federal Reserve Bank. Despite this admonition, Sentry continued its practice of routing the money through Hudson until November of 1981, when Chemical decided it could "fine count" its bulk deposits internally.

During the period when its arrangement with Hudson was in effect, Sentry gained a total of nearly $17,000 in interest earned on over 40 "repurchase

---

[3] Before Sentry picked up the deposits, Chemical would complete a "bulk count" by verifying the numbers of bundles its customers had deposited. Sentry would then "fine count" the deposits by counting the individual bills within each bundle. The agreement required Sentry to deliver to Chemical's Federal Reserve Bank account the amount that was necessary to satisfy Chemical's deposit requirements; the remainder of the cash, if any, was to be returned directly to Chemical.

agreements." The full amount of the principal belonging to Chemical, however, was always returned to its owner within the allotted 72-hour time frame.

The People have advanced several theories in support of their larceny charge, including a "breaking of the bale" and an unlawful "separation of the value of the money from its engraved ink and paper container." None of the theories the People have proffered, however, would support a larceny conviction under our modern statutes defining that crime. While Sentry's conduct may have provided a basis for civil liability in some form, that conduct did not constitute criminal larceny.

The crime of larceny consists of an unauthorized taking, coupled with the "intent to deprive another of property or to appropriate the same" (Penal Law § 155.05(1)). The terms "deprive" and "appropriate" are specifically defined in Penal Law § 155.00:

> 3. "Deprive." To "deprive" another of property means (a) to withhold it or cause it to be withheld from him permanently or for so extended a period or under such circumstances that the major portion of its economic value or benefit is lost to him, or (b) to dispose of the property in such manner or under such circumstances as to render it unlikely that an owner will recover such property.

> 4. "Appropriate. To "appropriate" property of another to oneself or a third person means (a) to exercise control over it * * * permanently or for so extended a period or under such circumstances as to acquire the major portion of its economic value or benefit, or (b) to dispose of the property for the benefit of oneself or a third person.

As one commentator has noted, the concepts of "deprive" and "appropriate," which "are essential to a definition of larcenous intent," "connote a purpose to exert permanent or virtually permanent control over the property taken, or to cause permanent or virtually permanent loss to the owner of the possession and use thereof." Hechtman, *Practice Commentaries*, McKinney's Cons.Laws of N.Y., Book 39, Penal Law § 155.00, p. 103.

The intent element of larceny is therefore very different in concept from the "taking" element, which is separately defined in the statute (Penal Law § 155.05(1),(2); see Penal Law § 155.00(2)) and is satisfied by a showing that the thief exercised dominion and control over the property for a period of time, however temporary, in a manner wholly inconsistent with the owner's continued rights (see *People v. Olivo*, 52 N.Y.2d 309; *People v. Alamo*, 34 N.Y.2d 453). Indeed, in *People v. Olivo*, where we discussed the principles underlying the "taking" element at length, we noted that "the intent prescribed by [Penal Law § 155.05(1)]" must be separately considered.

The "taking" element of the crime of larceny was established prima facie here, since for certain periods, however temporary, defendants exercised dominion and control over Chemical's funds in a manner that could be found to be wholly inconsistent with Chemical's ownership (see, *People v. Olivo*, supra, at pp. 316-318; *People v. Alamo*, supra, 34 N.Y.2d at pp. 457-458). Such a finding could be based on the facts that defendants used Chemical's money for their own purposes and continued to do so even after Chemical specifically directed them to stop. What is lacking here from the People's proof is evidence demonstrating an "intent to deprive * * * or to appropriate" (Penal Law § 155.05(1)).

The gist of the People's claim is that by investing Chemical's money for periods up to 48 hours, defendants evinced an intent to deprive its true owner of the money's "economic value or benefit," that is, the interest that the money was capable of generating. The *mens rea* element of larceny, however, is simply not satisfied by an intent temporarily to use property without the owner's permission, or even an intent to appropriate outright the benefits of the property's short-term use.

The problem presented in this case is similar to that presented in "joy-riding" cases, in which it was held that the intent merely to borrow and use an automobile without the owner's permission cannot support a conviction for larceny (e.g., *Van Vechten v. American Eagle Fire Ins. Co.*, 239 N.Y. 303, 305).[4] An analysis of the evidence before the Grand Jury in this case indicates only that defendants exercised control over Chemical's money to the extent of using it to make short-term, profitable investments and, as a result, appropriated some portion of its economic benefit for themselves. However, in light of the fact that their unauthorized use of Chemical's money extended over no more than a series of discrete 48-hour periods, the proof was insufficient to show that they intended to use Chemical's money "for so extended a period or under such circumstances as to acquire the major portion of its economic value or benefit."[5]

Moreover, the "economic value or benefit" to be derived from the money was the interest or other financial leverage that could be gained by the party who possessed it. Inasmuch as Chemical had ceded possession of its money to Sentry for various 72-hour periods, it had no legal rights during those periods to the money's "economic value or benefit," which is an incident of possession. Thus, to the extent that defendants intended to appropriate to themselves the "economic value or benefit" of Chemical's money, it cannot be said that their intentions were unlawful or even inconsistent with the terms of the bailment. Significantly, the People did not place the agreement between Sentry and Chemical before the Grand Jury. As a consequence, not only was there no proof of any express restrictions on Sentry's disposition of Chemical's money during the 72-hour period allotted for "fine counting," but there was not even proof that Chemical had a right to expect early return of its money if the "fine counting" process were completed before the expiration of that period.

For similar reasons, it cannot be said that defendants committed larceny by

---

[4] It was because larceny was held to include the element of an intent permanently to deprive or appropriate that the Legislature enacted Penal Law § 1293-a (since replaced by Penal Law §§ 165.00, 165.05, 165.06 and 165.08) to bring intentional temporary misuse of another's property within the purview of the criminal law.

[5] Although a person who "borrows" a vehicle without the owner's consent unquestionably appropriates its entire economic benefit during the time he is using it, our case law does not recognize such conduct as larceny if it was accompanied by an intention to return the vehicle to its true owner. Thus, contrary to the dissent's view, we do not deem defendants' conduct larcenous because they "acquired all the economic benefit of (Chemical's money) for the time they held it." Indeed, if that proposition were true, there would be no distinction between the crime of larceny and the crime of misapplication of property under Penal Law § 165.00.

intentionally and permanently stealing the interest earned on Chemical's money, as distinguished from the money itself. First, absent proof of an agreement to the contrary, Chemical cannot be deemed the true owner of the interest earned while its money was in defendants' custody pursuant to the parties' "fine counting" agreement. Indeed, there is really no practical difference between the contention that defendants stole the interest on Chemical's money and the contention that they stole the money itself by intentionally appropriating its "economic value or benefit."

Second, it would be inconsistent with the statutory design to treat defendants' concededly permanent taking of the interest earned on Chemical's funds as a larceny within the meaning of Penal Law §§ 155.00, 155.05 and 155.35. It is clear that an individual who "joy-rides" and thereby deprives the automobile's owner of the value arising from its temporary use is not liable in larceny for stealing that intangible "value" under article 155 of the Penal Law. By parity of reasoning, an individual who temporarily invests another's money and thereby gains interest or profit cannot be deemed guilty of larceny for appropriating that interest or profit. Consistent with our long-held view that criminal liability "cannot be extended beyond the fair scope of the statutory mandate" (*People v. Gottlieb*, 36 N.Y.2d 629), we hold that in these circumstances the statute must be read to apply only to a taking of the property itself and not to a permanent taking of what is, in essence, only the economic value of its use during the short time the property has been withheld.

Finally, we note that neither Sentry's patently false response to Chemical's inquiry concerning the rerouting of its money through Hudson nor Sentry's disobedience when ordered by Chemical to deliver the money directly are sufficient to establish that Sentry was acting with the larcenous intent required by Penal Law § 155.00(3),(4) and § 155.05(1). At worst, Sentry's conduct demonstrates its unwillingness to relinquish what was obviously a profitable short-term use of Chemical's money. It does not, however, alter the inescapable and uncontradicted inference that Sentry was merely emulating the behavior of many reputable financial institutions by taking advantage of the "float" on the temporarily idle money in its possession.

* * * *

WACHTLER, C.J., and KAYE and HANCOCK, JJ., concur with TITONE, J.

SIMONS, JUDGE (dissenting in part).

I cannot concur in the majority's remarkably indulgent determination that defendants were merely emulating the practices of "reputable financial institutions," and that Sentry's use of Chemical Bank's money for esoteric investment schemes or to secure favored loan conditions for itself amounted to little more than a noncriminal financial "joy-ride." Investing the "float" may be legal in a debtor-creditor relationship, but a bailee for hire undertakes to protect and preserve the bailor's property with only such use of the property as the parties to the bailment agree upon. The bailee does not have carte blanche to risk the bailor's property for its own gain.

There is no dispute in this case that Chemical Bank bailed its property to Sentry intending that Sentry securely store the funds on is premises, safely transfer them to the bailor's customer, Waldbaum, or perform related services for Chemical, such as coin counting, before depositing the funds in Chemical's account at the Federal Reserve Bank. Defendants not only performed those services badly, but while doing so they lost thousands of dollars of Chemical's funds and risked the loss of millions more by these illegal schemes and use of their bailor's insurance funds. I agree with the two Grand Juries that found sufficient evidence that defendants' conduct was criminal, and I would sustain the indictments.

Turning first to the larceny counts, the majority concedes, as to the repurchase agreement scheme and compensatory balance scheme, that the evidence supports the Grand Jury's finding that defendants wrongfully took substantial sums of money from Chemical Bank, the rightful owner, by depositing them in Hudson Valley National Bank and Citibank. Defendants did so by exercising "control over property inconsistent with the continued rights of the owner" (*People v. Olivo*, 52 N.Y.2d 309, 316; *People v. Alamo*, 34 N.Y.2d 453, 457-458). However, the majority does not find sufficient evidence before the Grand Jury of defendants' larcenous intent in those takings.

The statute provides that the requisite intent for the crime of larceny is an "intent to deprive another of property or to appropriate the same to himself or to a third person" (Penal Law § 155.05(1)). The charges involving the repurchase agreements and the compensatory balance scheme rest on the second statutory alternative. The intent to appropriate is defined in several ways, but includes the intent to exercise control over property "under such circumstances as to acquire the major portion of [the] economic value or benefit [of the property]" (Penal Law § 155.00(4)).

I disagree with the majority's analysis of what constitutes "an intent to appropriate," because it fails to differentiate between a property's economic value and its economic benefit, and because it mistakenly construes the statutory definition to require a permanent or near permanent appropriation. The majority finds it necessary that the People show defendants intended to appropriate the economic value of the property although the statute clearly provides a legally sufficient alternative: the appropriation of "a major portion of its economic * * * benefit," i.e., its ability to make more money. There can be little doubt that defendants intended to use Chemical's money to their own financial advantage; they invested it with Hudson Valley National Bank, and earned $17,000 in the process, and they also used it to collateralize a loan with Citibank. This evidence was more than sufficient to establish defendants' intent to acquire the economic benefits of Chemical Bank's funds within the literal language of Penal Law §§ 155.00(4), 155.05(1).

The majority also claim that the necessary *mens rea* for the larceny was lacking because any intent to appropriate the economic benefit of the funds was only the intent to deprive Chemical of its property temporarily or "short term." The statute does not specify how long a defendant must intend the appropriation to last, it merely requires, *inter alia*, an intent to appropriate "for so extended a period or under such circumstances" as to acquire a major portion of its economic benefit (Penal Law § 155.00(4)). Regardless of the limited time involved in diverting the funds involved in the repurchase agreement or the compensatory balance schemes, the defendants appropriated the property "under * * * circumstances" in which they acquired all the economic benefit of the property for the time they held it. That being so, the time and/or the circumstances were sufficient to establish the crime. The majority finds little difference between defendants' "short term" use of the bank's money and "joy-riding" in an automobile. There is a cognizable distinction, however, between using another's property with the intent to return it and appropriating property to acquire a major portion of its economic benefit - which may never be returned - even if the appropriation is for a short time.

The conclusory assertion of the majority, based upon the Practice Commentary, that there must be a "purpose * * * to exert permanent or virtually permanent control over the property taken" is not only without legal support, it is contrary to our decisions (see *People v. Shears*, 143 N.Y.S. 861 (construing Penal Law of 1909 § 1302, now incorporated in Penal Law § 155.05(2)); *People v. Meadows*, 199 N.Y.1,7), and to the clearly manifested broad sweep of the statute which does not limit the intent to appropriate in terms of the time involved. Rather, the statute defines the crime as an appropriation "under such circumstances" as to acquire the economic benefit of the property.

The general nature of the repurchase agreements is set forth in the majority opinion, but it has not delineated the five discrete steps taken on each of the more than 40 occasions when defendants transferred Chemical Bank's money to Hudson Valley. According to the plan between Sentry and Hudson Valley: (1) Sentry would deposit the "fine count" funds into Hudson Valley National Bank's account at the Federal Reserve; (2) Hudson Valley National Bank would credit the amount of such deposit to the newly created escrow account for Sentry Armored Courier Corporation; (3) the principal in the escrow account was then used to buy A-rated bonds owned by Hudson Valley National Bank and stored at the Federal Reserve; (4) Hudson Valley National Bank would later repurchase these bonds and credit Sentry's escrow account for the amount of the principal plus interest, less Hudson Valley National Bank's broker's fee (the interest was then transferred to another account at Hudson Valley National Bank held in the name of Sentry Investigations Corp.); and finally (5) prior to the expiration of the 72-hour period allotted to Sentry for the "fine counting", an employee of Sentry Investigations Corp. would telephone Hudson Valley National Bank and authorize a wire transfer of the principal in the escrow account held by Sentry Armored Courier Corp. to Chemical Bank's account at the Federal Reserve. A wire transfer fee was then deducted from the Sentry Investigations Corp. account.

Chemical had retained Sentry to "fine count" in early 1981; the repurchase agreement scheme started in July 1981 and the contract between Sentry and Chemical was terminated in November of the same year. During the months that the scheme existed, Sentry and Hudson Valley invested approximately $26 million of Chemical's funds in the repurchase agreements. The majority makes the unwarranted assumption that, absent production of the written bailment contract, the Grand Jury could not find that Sentry's acts in these transactions were contrary to its provisions. The speculation is rebutted by testimony not only by the Bank's officers but by that of Sentry's own employees as well. Thus, Chemical's officer, David Williams, testified that when he discovered Sentry was using Chemical's funds contrary to the Bank's wishes, in August 1981, he called Mr. Mead, an officer of Sentry, to inquire about it. When Mead gave a patently pretextual excuse that the transfers were dictated by insurance considerations, Williams instructed him that Sentry was to stop these transactions immediately. After the telephone conversation, Williams wrote a letter to Sentry confirming his demand that Sentry stop using Chemical's money in a manner contrary to the contract.

The Grand Jury could reasonably conclude from all of this not only that Sentry's investment of Chemical's funds was contrary to the bailment agreement but also, because of the false excuse given by Sentry's officers, that Sentry knew that to be so. Moreover, the Grand Jury could reasonably assume that Sentry's confirmed possession of Chemical's funds was conditioned on its acceptance of this direction and that, had Sentry not indicated that it would discontinue the practice, Chemical would have terminated the agreement. Notwithstanding Chemical's instructions given by telephone and letter, however, Sentry continued the repurchase scheme until the coin counting contract was terminated in November.

This evidence was sufficient, prima facie, to establish defendants' larcenous intent to appropriate the economic benefit of Chemical Bank's funds to itself. It is irrelevant that Chemical Bank had no expectation or plan of realizing for itself the interest potential of the moneys during the 72 hours that they were in the hands of Sentry. The statute sets forth no such requirement (see Penal Law § 155.00(4)). Nor is it a defense that Chemical Bank's moneys were intended to be returned - and, in fact, were returned — within the 72 hour time period (see *People v. Kaye*, 295 N.Y. 9, 13).

Similarly, there was more than enough evidence to permit the jury to find defendants possessed the requisite larcenous intent when Sentry improperly took Chemical's funds and deposited them in Citibank to its own credit in its compensatory balance scheme. By so depositing the money, Sentry obtained the major portion of the economic benefit of the funds during the period of the deposit because it, in effect, collateralized its loan from Citibank with Chemical's money and it also received a reduced interest rate on the loan. This improper transfer and deposit notwithstanding, defendant Fiumefreddo claims that the evidence was insufficient to connect her to the crime, or to establish the requisite intent as to her. Fiumefreddo participated in the transfer of Chemical Bank's funds to the Citibank account, however, and she signed the account's signature card. Moreover, she was in charge of Sentry's money room, and its daily audit reports showed falsely that the $100,000 deposited in the Citibank account was located at Sentry. Fiumefreddo was also the Sentry officer who told the independent auditor that $100,000 of the Chemical Bank shortfall in the Sentry money room deposits was located in a Citibank account. Manifestly, such evidence is sufficient to establish Fiumefreddo's knowledge of the crime, her connection with it and her requisite larcenous intent.

In conclusion, it is worth noting the concern other branches of our State government have expressed over the enormous increase in large scale white-collar crimes. Thus, in 1986 the State Executive Department recommended comprehensive efforts to "deter the extraordinary increase in sophisticated, economic crime" by proposing the amendment of five different articles of the Penal Law. The Legislature acted upon these recommendations by enacting several new statutes, including a statute increasing larceny penalties, which expanded, rather than contracted, the methods of fighting white-collar crimes (see L.1986, ch. 514 (computer offenses); and L.1986, ch. 516 (Organized Crime Control Act)). Apparently the Governor's staff and the Legislature found the existing larceny statutes adequate to deter and punish peculations, such as those with which defendants are charged, since substantive changes in the provisions of the larceny statutes were not recommended or enacted. In contrast to this concern over the problem, the majority has trivialized the seriousness of defendants' conduct and interpreted the statutes narrowly, virtually excising important and operative language from them.

MEYER AND ALEXANDER, JJ. concur with SIMONS, J.

NOTES FROM RHONDA:

1. I had some trouble discerning which element of larceny was at issue in *Jennings* too. Try to figure this out before applying *Jennings* to Goniff's case.

2. Take another look at the questions set out at the beginning of this Chapter. Isn't *Jennings* a classic example of a court letting crooks off on a technicality?

3. In *People v. Jensen*, 86 N.Y.2d 248 (1995), the prosecution's case at trial consisted of the following evidence:

> On November 6, 1992, at approximately 3:13 A.M., Cornell University Department of Public Safety Officers Kathy Zoner and Richard Brewer observed defendant carrying a dormitory lounge chair on his head as he crossed a bridge on the Cornell campus. Upon being stopped defendant informed the officers that he had obtained the chair in Donlon Hall, a residence located on the North Campus, and was taking it to the West Campus as a prank. Defendant declined to confirm whether he was a student. He stated that he had no identification on his person and, despite repeated requests, otherwise refused to identify himself in any manner. He was informed, in response to his inquiry, that he would be referred to the Cornell Judicial Administrator if he was a student; if he was not a student, he would be charged with petit larceny in City Court. After approximately 10 minutes of fruitless inquiries, one of the officers expressed impatience with defendant's uncooperative behavior, at which point defendant stated that he did have identification after all, and began reaching into his pocket. Officer Brewer stated that he would remove the identification from defendant's pocket himself and directed defendant to turn and face the police car. When Officer Brewer reached for defendant's pocket, defendant slapped his hands away. Informed that he was under arrest, defendant bolted from the officers and ran toward the gorge under the bridge. He was pursued by Officer Zoner, who caught him . . .

The court held that this evidence was sufficient to show the elements of larceny:

Defendant was stopped at 3:13 A.M. carrying away a dormitory lounge chair he admitted did not belong to him. When appropriately questioned by the officers, defendant offered the explanation that he was involved in a "prank". However, throughout the 10-minute encounter, defendant would not confirm whether he was a student and repeatedly refused to identify himself in any manner. In light of the unusual circumstances and defendant's evasive and uncooperative behavior, there was sufficient proof before the Grand Jury from which it could rationally infer that defendant intended to steal the chair. That other, innocent inferences could possibly be drawn from the facts is irrelevant

JUSTICE TITONE dissented:

Here, the evidence against defendant showed that he was seen on campus carrying a lounge chair apparently belonging to the University. The People did not even adduce proof as to the identity of the chair's owner or the lack of such owner's permission to move the chair from one part of the campus to another. This defect in proof is alone sufficient to nullify the indictment's larceny charge.

He had not removed the chair from the University grounds and, more importantly, he had committed no act that could be construed as an exercise of dominion and control inconsistent with the owner's rights. Nor was there evidence from which such an exercise could be inferred. To the contrary, the *only* evidence before the Grand Jury was that the lounge chair defendant carried was being taken to another part of the University campus for use in a different dormitory. Thus, neither defendant's conduct in carrying the chair away from its usual location nor his stated plan for the chair was inconsistent with its owner's rights. Notably, even if the Grand Jury chose to disregard the exculpatory portions of defendant's statements to the campus police, it could not rationally have drawn an inference that the statutory "taking" element was satisfied, since there was no other evidence in the case to support such an inference.

For similar reasons, the element of larcenous intent was not established. Larceny requires the specific intent to "deprive" another of property or to "appropriate" another's property to oneself or to a third person (Penal Law § 155.05 [1]). "Deprive" and "appropriate" " 'connote a purpose . . . to exert permanent or virtually permanent control over the property taken, or to cause permanent or virtually permanent loss to the owner of the possession or use thereof' " *People v. Jennings, supra,* at 118, quoting Hechtman, Practice Commentaries, McKinney's Cons Laws of NY, Book 39, Penal Law § 155.00, at 103 [1975]). Larceny's intent requirement is not satisfied where the actor's intent was only "temporarily to use property without the owner's permission" *(id. at 119).*

The facts in this case demonstrate, at worst, a temporary misuse by defendant of a lounge chair that had been made available to the students residing in a particular dormitory. There was no basis for inferring an intention to exert "permanent or virtually permanent" control of the chair or to cause its permanent loss to the owner. Accordingly, the intent element of the crime was simply not present.

4. Normally, to satisfy the "intent to steal" element of larceny, the prosecutor must show that the defendant intended to permanently deprive the owner of it, and not merely to use it temporarily. But not always:

> It is not a defense to larceny merely to have an intent to return the property; in addition one must, at the time of taking, have a substantial ability to do so (even though, as events turn out, it may later become impossible to do so). Thus if one takes another's property intending to use it recklessly and then abandon it, the obstacles to its safe return to the owner are such that the taker possesses the required intent to steal. Even without the intent to use recklessly, an intent to abandoned, accompanied by a not-too-well founded hope that the property will find its way back to its owner does not negative the intent to steal. [LaFave, *Criminal Law*]

Chapter 3

EMBEZZLEMENT

> Embezzlement, a statutory crime, is defined somewhat differently in different jurisdictions . . . [I]n general it may be defined as: (1) the fraudulent (2) conversion of (3) the property (4) of another (5) by one who is already in lawful possession of it.

> LaFave & Scott, *Criminal Law* (West)

How does this definition differ from larceny? And why do we need the crime of embezzlement? Isn't larceny broad enough to encompass all thieves? Maybe not. Consider this example.

Mr. Wooster tells his butler, "Jeeves, my silver candlesticks look scruffy. Here. Please polish them." Jeeves accepts the candlesticks and begins polishing them — when he remembers that his favorite horse is running at Ascot. Needing money to place a bet, Jeeves packs up the candlesticks and sells them to a local fence.

Has Jeeves committed larceny? He looks like a thief — but we have a problem. Larceny requires a "trespassory taking." Jeeves didn't "trespass" on the candlesticks or "take" the candlesticks from Mr. Wooster — because Wooster *gave* the candlesticks to Jeeves. When Jeeves formed the intent to steal, he *already had lawful possession* of the candlesticks. If the words "trespass" and "take" are given their normal meanings, Jeeves is innocent of larceny.

This result makes us squirm — it doesn't "feel right." Jeeves is a thief, and he should be punished. On the other hand, the law is the law, and he did not break the law of larceny as written — unless we are willing to play some games with the law, i.e., create a "legal fiction."

And this is exactly what the common law courts did. They held that Wooster did *not* give "*possession*" of the candlesticks to Jeeves. Wooster retained "constructive" possession of the candlesticks, and gave Jeeves only "custody" of them. Jeeves retained this "custody" so long as he used the candlesticks in the way he was told to use them, i.e., he polished them. But once Jeeves violated his trust and left the house with the candlesticks with intent to sell them, Jeeves then "took possession" of them. As all of the other elements of larceny were also present at this moment (asportation, intent to steal, etc.), *voila*: Jeeves has committed larceny!

A satisfactory result, perhaps, though a rather shocking way of reaching it. But the common law judges wanted to do something to protect wealthy people like Mr. Wooster (and, probably, themselves), and the law of larceny was the nearest available tool.

But how far would they stretch the law to encompass new ways of stealing? How many legal fictions may a judge invent and still be able to sleep at night?

England evolved into a merchantile society. Jeeves is now a teller at the Bank of Wooster. A customer comes into the Bank and hands Jeeves 20 pounds for deposit. Jeeves smiles, says goodbye — and puts the money in his pocket. Has he committed larceny? Not from the customer, as the customer *gave* the money to Jeeves. Not from the Bank, as the Bank *never had* possession of the money. Once again, legal fictions might fill in these legal gaps. The courts *might* say that the customer retained "constructive" possession until Jeeves put the money in the cash drawer, *or* that the Bank obtained "constructive" possession through Jeeves as soon as Jeeves received the money — and when Jeeves put the money in his pocket, he "took possession" of it from either the customer or the Bank.

The courts *might* have said these things — but they didn't. "We'll stretch the law, but not that much." Why not? Well, partly because there was now a way to punish Jeeves without stretching the law of larceny out of shape: Parliament. The English legislature was now a strong enough institution to create new crimes. And that is just what happened. Parliament created "embezzlement."

PROBLEM 3

Memo to: My law clerk.

From: U.S. District Court (Wyoming) Judge Jane Justice

Re: *U.S. v. Buck*

Defendant Bob Buck was indicted for embezzlement, in violation of 18 U.S.C. § 654. I am now in the middle of the trial of this case. The prosecution has just finished putting on its case, and the defense counsel has moved for a directed verdict of acquittal, on the ground that the prosecution's evidence (even if believed by the jury) does not show all the elements of embezzlement.

Attached is a transcript of the testimony of the key prosecution witnesses. Also attached are some authorities on embezzlement which might be relevant.

Please advise me as to whether I should grant the motion.

Reporter's Transcript — *U.S. v. Buck*

Q: (by Prosecutor): Please state your name and occupation.

A: I am Walter Wolff. I work for the United States Government, National Park Service. I am the Chief Ranger at Yellowstone National Park. Defendant Buck worked for me as a park ranger last summer.

Q: What were Buck's duties?

A: He had just recently been hired, so I didn't give him a lot of authority. He did not supervise any other rangers. I put him in charge of some college students that we had working for us as trail-workers during the summer. They worked from 9 to 5 each day fixing up our hiking trails.

Q: Did some back-packers leave their cars with you?

A: Yes. Some people back-pack into the mountains for a week or 2 at a time, and some get worried about leaving their cars for this long at the trailhead, where someone might break into them. So we let such people put their cars in our compound, for $2 a day. The compound is surrounded by a chain-link fence, with a gate we keep locked. Buck had a key to the gate, because we also kept the trail-clearing tools in that compound, and Buck needed to get them each day. I kept the keys to each car in my desk drawer, as Buck and every other ranger well knew. The rangers were allowed to come into my office whenever they liked, to look at maps and the like, but they were not allowed to go into my desk. Occasionally I would have Buck or another ranger move one of the cars, and I would tell him to get the car keys from my desk.

Q: Thank you. Next witness, please. Would you state your name and occupation?

A: I'm Felicia Fox, and I'm a law student. Last summer, I worked as a trail-worker at Yellowstone, and Ranger Buck was my supervisor.

Q: On July 5 of last summer, did you see Ranger Buck take a back-packer's car from the compound at Yellowstone?

A: Yes.

Q: How did you happen to see this?

A: Well, that afternoon at about 2 o'clock, I went with Buck to the compound to get some tools. Buck unlocked the gate and we entered. Buck noticed that one of the back-packers' cars was a new Jaguar, and he said that it would be great to use the car on a date he had that night, with a woman camper he wanted to impress. He said that he would get the car back into the compound the next morning before the Chief Ranger got there, so he would never know that Buck had used it. He said he would buy a tank of gas at the end of his date, so the car owner would not lose any gas. So he went into the Chief Ranger's office — the Chief wasn't there — and he opened the desk drawer and took out the key to the car. He got in the car and drove out the south entrance to the park. That night, he took the car out on his date, and he accidentally ran into a deer and ran off the road. The car was pretty much demolished. Boy, was Chief Ranger Wolff mad — and so was the owner of the car.

United States Code, Title 18, § 654

Whoever, being an officer or employee of the United States or of any department or agency thereof, embezzles or wrongfully converts to his own use the money or property of another which comes into his possession or under his control in the execution of such office or employment, or under color or claim of authority as such officer or employee, shall be fined under this title or not more than the value of the money and property thus embezzled or converted, whichever is greater, or imprisoned not more than ten years, or both; but if the sum embezzled is $1,000 or less, he shall be fined under this title or imprisoned not more than one year, or both. [Enacted in 1948, with subsequent amendments.]

UNITED STATES v. TITUS
U.S. District Court, New Jersey
64 Fed. Supp. 55 (1946)

FORMAN, DISTRICT JUDGE.

Harry Mace Titus, Sr., the defendant, was charged with embezzlement of certain personal property of the government at Post Exchange No. 10., Fort Dix, New Jersey, a government reservation; in violation of 18 U.S.C.A. § 468 and R.S.2:124-11 of New Jersey, N.J.S.A. The federal statute provides for the application of state penal statutes to actions committed on government reservations within the territorial limits of the state where they are not made penal by any laws of Congress. The latter statute of New Jersey defines the following offense:

> Any consignee, factor, bailee, agent or servant, intrusted with the care or sale of any personal property, or intrusted with the collection or care of any moneys, who shall fraudulently take or convert the same, or the proceeds of the sale of the same, or any part thereof, to his own use or to the use of any other person whatsoever, except the rightful owner thereof, shall be guilty of a misdemeanor. [R.S. 2:124-11 of N.J., N.J.S.A.]

The indictment, following the latter statute, is in four counts. The first charges him with the embezzlement on November 27, 1944 of two cases of cigarettes of the value of $145. The second count charges him with the embezzlement on November 28, 1944 of 120 cartons of cigarettes of the value of $156. The third count charges him with the embezzlement on November 30, 1944 of 100 cartons of cigarettes of the value of $145, and the fourth count charges him with the embezzlement on December 2, 1944 of 120 cartons of cigarettes of the value of $156.

The defendant, a civilian, was employed as manager of Post Exchange, Branch No. 10. In such capacity he was in possession, custody, and control of various quantities of cigarettes, which were the property of the Army Exchange Service. Defendant, after taking the cigarettes mentioned in the first three counts of the indictment, sold and delivered them to a cigar store operator in Mt. Holly, N.J., at prices respectively in excess of the government sale price. After each sale when he returned to the Post Exchange he deposited an amount of money equivalent to the government sale price of the cigarettes in the cash register and retained the overage. He failed to deposit the money for the cigarettes mentioned in the fourth count of the indictment because he was apprehended by the Military Police on December 2, 1944, as he was leaving the Fort Dix Reservation with the cigarettes.

Defendant's sole defense to the first three counts of the indictment is that he has not defrauded the government of the pecuniary value of the cigarettes.

With respect to the fourth count, the defense is that he intended to put into the cash register of the Post Exchange an amount equivalent to the government sale price of the cigarettes after he had delivered them to his customer.

In this case the defendant had the duty only of delivering merchandise to customers over a counter and to receive the purchase price therefor and place it forthwith in his employer's till. When he removed the merchandise from his employer's place of business to Mt. Holly for sale there to his private profit, his crime under the New Jersey statute was complete.

The authorities all seem to unite in support of the general rule that any subsequent return of the property or its equivalent to the owner does not purge the original offense. 29 C.J.S., *Embezzlement*, § 12. The intent to fraudulently take and convert the cigarettes of the government cannot be affected by the intent to reimburse the government after the sale. The fraud and crime inhere in the act and would not be eliminated therefrom by any mere mental process however amiable or virtuous it may have been.

In *Hancey v. United States*, 10 Cir., 108 F.2d 835, the court in dealing with a similar argument held: "The crime of embezzlement is committed when property belonging to another, rightfully in possession of accused, is feloniously appropriated. Subsequent repayment does not vitiate the crime. The gravamen of the offense is the intent, coupled with its execution. In *National Life & Accident Ins. Co. v. Gibson*, 31 Ky.Law Rep. 101, the court said: 'The gravamen of the offense is the intent. There must be a criminal intent, but this intent must, of necessity, be gathered from the acts of the agent and the circumstances surrounding the particular case, rather than from his express declarations, and if the agent knowingly appropriates money belonging to his principal to his own use, even though at the time he does so he intends to restore it, it is nevertheless embezzlement within the spirit as well as the letter of the law, for when one knowingly appropriates money belonging to another to his own private use, the law presumes a criminal intent."'

A judgment of guilty as charged on all counts of the indictment will be entered against the defendant and he should be arraigned before this court for sentence on Monday morning, February 4, 1946, at 9:30 o'clock.

NOTES FROM THE JUDGE:

(1) When did Titus form an intent to pay for the cigarettes — when he took them, or later? Did the court's ruling turn on this distinction?

(2) How do these facts compare to our facts, as to Buck's intent regarding the car and the gas? If there are factual differences, are they sufficient to warrant my "distinguishing" *Titus*?

GOVERNMENT OF THE VIRGIN ISLANDS v. LEONARD
U.S. Court of Appeals, 3rd Circuit
548 F.2d 478 (1976)

HUNTER, CIRCUIT JUDGE:

Charles Leonard was convicted of aiding and abetting Herbert Williams in embezzling some 49 rolls of chicken wire from the storeroom of the Civil Defense Office on St. Thomas. He appeals from the judgment on the verdict of guilt. For the reasons that follow, we reverse.

I.

On August 4, 1975, one Edmond A. Penn became Director of the Office of Civil Defense and Emergency Services for the Virgin Islands. At that time, the Civil Defense Office also comprised a Deputy Director, two secretaries and a Communication Officer Technician - Herbert Williams. Upon taking over as Director, Mr. Penn was given no inventory of the Office's various emergency supplies. He asked Herbert Williams to conduct an inventory of the Office's storeroom on St. Thomas, and Williams did so during the last week of August, 1975.[1] According to that inventory, the St. Thomas storeroom contained some 62 rolls of chicken wire. Civil Defense kept this wire in case war or other emergency cut the islands off from normal sources of food; Civil Defense would then distribute the wire to local fishermen, who would fashion fish traps and help sustain the islands' population during the emergency.

On some nine or ten occasions in the fall of 1975, Williams entered the Civil Defense Office at night, obtained the keys to the storeroom from the filing cabinet where they were kept,[2] and took from two to four rolls of the chicken wire. He sold the wire to fishermen for $100 a roll, a price far below actual cost. On several occasions, Leonard, together with Williams, left the company of local fishermen and returned to the group in Leonard's taxi with chicken wire. Leonard also participated in several sales to the fishermen.

On November 23, 1975, Williams set fire to the storeroom in an attempt to conceal his misdeeds. The investigation of the fire revealed that many rolls of wire were missing. All of the Civil Defense employees were interrogated regarding the missing wire, and under questioning Williams admitted having taken it and having started the fire.

By information, Williams was charged with arson, grand larceny, and embezzlement. Leonard was charged with aiding and abetting[3] Williams in the commission of grand larceny[4] and aiding and abetting in the commission of embezzlement.[5]

After the Government rested, both defendants moved for a judgment of acquittal on the embezzlement charges, contending that there was no evidence to support the charges. The court denied the motion. The jury found Williams guilty

---

[1] Mr. Penn testified that Williams was "responsible for keeping inventory of our supplies," but there is no evidence that Williams took any inventories before or after the one taken at Penn's express request in August, 1975.

[2] All Office employees, including the secretaries and part-time volunteers, knew where the keys were kept.

[3] Under 14 V.I.C. § 11, an aider and abettor is guilty as a principal.

[4] 14 V.I.C. § 1083, *Grand larceny*: Whoever takes property (1) which is of $100 or more in value; or (2) from the person of another — commits grand larceny and shall be imprisoned for not more than 10 years.

[5] 14 V.I.C. § 1089, *Embezzlement by public and private officers*: Whoever, being an officer of the Virgin Islands or a subdivision thereof, or a deputy, clerk, or servant of such officer, * * * fraudulently appropriates to any use or purpose not in the due and lawful execution of his trust, any property which he has in his possession or under his control by virtue of his trust, or secretes it with a fraudulent intent to appropriate it to such use or purpose, is guilty of embezzlement.

of arson and both Williams and Leonard guilty of embezzlement; no findings were made with respect to the larceny charge. On appeal, Leonard insists that there was no evidence to support the jury's findings of embezzlement.

II.

Title 14, § 1089 of the Virgin Islands Code forbids embezzlement by a public officer of "any property which he has in his possession or under his control by virtue of his trust." Leonard contends that Williams — as principal — and therefore Leonard — as aider and abettor — could not be convicted of embezzlement, because the chicken wire purloined from the storeroom was not "property which Williams had in his possession or under his control by virtue of his trust." Because we agree with Leonard, we must reverse.

Williams obviously did not have the chicken wire in his possession, so the critical question is whether it was under his "control" by virtue of his trust. Mr. Penn testified that Williams was not authorized to place items in or remove them from the storeroom, or to exercise dominion over the contents of the storeroom in any way. Williams had been authorized, on at least one occasion, to enter the storeroom, but only for the purpose of noting the contents, not for disposing of them in any fashion. He knew where the storeroom keys were located, but so did the secretaries and part-time volunteers, who also were not authorized to use the keys without permission. Such knowledge scarcely amount to "control" over the contents of the storeroom. Moreover, Williams came like a thief in the night, entered the storeroom in the same manner as anyone who had accidentally discovered the location of the keys, and removed the wire rolls.

These facts convince us that the elements of embezzlement were not made out. Mere access to the storeroom was not sufficient to invest "control" in Williams. Williams' crime was similar to that of a janitor, entrusted with the key to an office, who takes an item left lying on a desk. And under any statutory system that differentiates between larceny and embezzlement, as does the Virgin Island Code, the janitor's crime is the former. LaFave & Scott, *Criminal Law*, § 89 (1972).

The district court clearly recognized this distinction in its charge to the jury:

> Now, let's make a distinction between embezzlement and larceny. Let us say I work for the Chase Manhattan Bank, I am a teller. Somebody comes in, they deposit with me $100. Now, I have received that $100 only because I am the teller employed by the bank. In this position of trust I am required to make out some notes on the deposit slip, give them a copy, file the bank's copy here, put the money in the drawer. But what I do, I probably write something wrong on the slip, put the money in my pocket. This is embezzlement, because I obtained that money only because it came to me in the course of my employment and I put it to a use and purpose to which it was not supposed to have been put. All right, I am still employed by the Chase Manhattan Bank, I am still the teller, but one of my duties as teller of that bank is to open the vault in the morning. Now, I know it does take two or three persons to open the vault, let's say I can open it alone, I have the key to the door. At night when the bank is closed, I open the bank, I go

into the vault and I take out the $100. Now, I didn't come into possession of that money by virtue of my employment, I am stealing, this is larceny, that is the difference.

It is apparent that the district court's illustration of larceny fits almost perfectly the actions of Williams in this case. Like the court's bank teller, Williams returned after hours and opened the storeroom, taking property out otherwise than "by virtue of his trust." There simply was no evidence that he took the wire from the storeroom in the course of his duties. Hence, the defense motion for a judgment of acquittal on the embezzlement charges should have been granted.

In an era when more and more jurisdictions are consolidating larceny and embezzlement under a single statute forbidding theft, see, e.g., 18 U.S.C. § 659 (punishing anyone who "embezzles, steals, or unlawfully takes, carries away, or conceals, or by fraud or deception" goods moving in interstate commerce), it may appear unfortunate that the result we reach in this case serves to free a defendant who may well be guilty of some sort of wrongful conversion. But the fact is that the Virgin Islands have not consolidated their statutes governing larceny and embezzlement, and we are constrained to observe the traditional procedural strictures with respect to conviction of one crime when the proof shows another. See, e.g., 3 Torcia, *Wharton's Criminal Procedure*, § 509 (12th ed. 1975). Compare *United States v. Petti*, 459 F.2d 294 (3d Cir. 1972) (holding that one charged with embezzlement under 18 U.S.C. § 659 could properly be convicted where facts established larceny, since § 659 covers both). Moreover, this was not a case in which the subtlety of the distinctions between the crimes confused the court; indeed, the court in its charge, quoted above, quite clearly recognized the distinctions, which, on the state of the evidence, were applicable in this case.

For the foregoing reasons, the judgment of conviction will be vacated and the case remanded with instruction to enter a judgment of acquittal on the charge of aiding and abetting embezzlement.

NOTES FROM THE JUDGE:

(1) To understand the distinction *Leonard* makes between larceny and embezzlement, you might find the following helpful:

> [W]here the master (in more modern terminology, employer) puts his servant (employee) in charge of his property, the master still has possession ("constructive possession") while the servant has mere custody. * * * [T]he cases draw a distinction between a caretaker or other minor sort of employee, who has custody only, and one to whom the employer has delegated considerably more authority, who has possession. [LaFave & Scott, *Criminal Law*.]

(2) *Leonard* was discussed in *Carmichael v. Govt. of Virgin Islands*, 46 V.I. 391 (2004).

(3) In *Bruhn v. Commonwealth*, 544 S.E.2d 895 (Va.App. 2001), Bruhn worked as a woodworker for Old World Cabinetry, which built cabinets. Old World did not allow employees to use the shop for "side jobs." Nevertheless, used the shop to refinish

some furniture for Farley, using Old World's supplies. Bruhn delivered the furniture to Farley, who paid Bruhn with a check for $519 made out to Bruhn. Bruhn was convicted of larceny, but the appellate court reversed:

> In Virginia, larceny is defined by its elements at common law as, the wrongful or fraudulent taking of personal goods of some intrinsic value, belonging to another, without his assent, and with the intention to deprive the owner thereof permanently. In every larceny there must be an actual taking, or severance of the goods from the possession of the owner.

> In this case, the Commonwealth alleges the property stolen by Bruhn was the right to receive the $519 payment that Farley owed in exchange for refinishing her furniture. The Commonwealth contends that the payment was owed to Old World, not Bruhn. Even assuming the Commonwealth's contention is correct, because Bruhn never turned the funds over to his employer, Old World never obtained possession of the money. A larceny was, therefore, not committed. Furthermore, were Bruhn found to have wrongfully taken Old World's right to payment, an intangible cannot be the subject of larceny under Code § 18.2-95.

> The Commonwealth argues in the alternative that, if Bruhn's retention of the funds does not constitute larceny, then it constitutes embezzlement, and that proof of embezzlement is sufficient to sustain a conviction on an indictment charging Bruhn with larceny. Assuming, without deciding, Bruhn committed embezzlement, we hold that proof of embezzlement does not support a conviction under an indictment alleging larceny.

Question: Did Bruhn commit embezzlement?

(3) How do the facts of *Leonard* compare to the facts of our case? Did Buck have more "control" over the compound and its contents than William had over the storeroom and its contents? In sum, may I properly distinguish *Leonard*?

UNITED STATES v. WHITLOCK
U.S. Court of Appeals, District of Columbia Circuit
663 F.2d 1094 (1980)

Before ROBINSON, MACKINNON and ROBB, CIRCUIT JUDGES.

Judge Robinson files an opinion in Parts I and IV* of which Judges MacKinnon and Robb concur. Judge MacKinnon files an opinion in which Judge Robb concurs. Thus, Parts I and IV of Judge Robinson's opinion together with Judge MacKinnon's opinion constitute the opinion of the court. The order of the District Court appealed from herein is affirmed.

---

* Ed. — In Part IV, all 3 judges agreed to reject appellant's claim that the evidence was insufficient to show that, due to her alleged "hysterical personality," she lacked the mental capacity to commit the crime.

ROBINSON, CIRCUIT JUDGE

After a bench trial, appellant was convicted in the District Court of embezzling $85,000 from the DuPont Circle Branch of Riggs National Bank in purported violation of 18 U.S.C. § 656.[1] Acknowledging the theft, she contends that the court should have entered *sua sponte* a judgment of acquittal on the ground that the evidence did not demonstrate that she had prior lawful possession of the money, as was required to establish the crime of embezzlement.

I believe the District Court's disposition should be sustained with the exception of the specification of the § 656 offense. I would reverse the conviction of embezzlement and remand the case with instructions to enter a judgment convicting appellant of willful misapplication of bank funds under that section, unless the District Court were to determine that a new trial should be granted in the interest of justice. My colleagues, however, uphold the conviction in all respects.

On the morning of August 11, 1977, Terrence A. Burkett, head teller of Riggs' DuPont Circle Branch, noticed the apparent absence of bundles of currency from the branch's cash reserve vault. He then notified other employees, and an audit revealed that $85,000 was missing. Naturally enough, the ensuing investigation focused immediately upon those with access to the vault.

The door of the vault could be opened only by use of a combination and a key. Only Burkett had memorized the combination, only bank officers — including appellant[8] — held keys; cash was to be put into or removed from the vault by Burkett and an officer together. Officers could, however, obtain a copy of the combination from a staple-sealed envelope in the bank manager's vault in the event that Burkett was unavailable when cash was needed.[10] After a week of probing, bank security personnel had uncovered unusual financial transactions in the personal accounts maintained at Riggs by three of the officers, including appellant.

Resultantly, Melvin L. Chrisman, senior vice president of the bank, conferred with appellant and asked her to elucidate the activity in her accounts, including two recent deposits rather sizable in amount. She tendered an explanation, but about an hour later telephoned Chrisman and requested him to set up a meeting with the chairman of the board to discuss the missing money. At this meeting and at a subsequent one with an agent of the Federal Bureau of Investigation, appellant voluntarily admitted that she had taken the $85,000 and described in detail how she had accomplished the theft.

Approximately two weeks before August 4, she procured from the branch manager's vault the envelope containing the combination to the cash reserve vault.

---

[1] The District Court suspended imposition of sentence and placed appellant on supervised probation for three years with specific conditions, including outpatient psychiatric treatment and medication as prescribed by her physician.

[8] Appellant had the title of assistant manager and assistant cashier. Functionally, she was in charge of the branch's note department.

[10] The combination was changed whenever it became known in this manner to someone other than Burkett.

She then unsealed the envelope, obtained the combination, resealed the envelope and returned it to the manager's vault. Between then and August 4 she entered the cash reserve vault three or four times by using the combination and her key, but did not appropriate any funds on those occasions because she could not "work up the nerve to take the money." Finally, on August 4 she gathered the $85,000, put it in a clothing bag and took the bag back to her desk before leaving for the evening.[17]

At trial, appellant did not undertake to retract or dispute this version of the affair, but sought instead to establish a defense of mental incapacity.

I.

Appellant was indicted, tried and convicted on the specific charge of embezzling bank funds in contravention of § 656. She now insists that the conviction must be set wholly for naught because, she says, the Government did not shown that the bank had ever confided the $85,000 to her care. The Government argues that the evidence portrays her stewardship of the stolen money sufficiently to make out embezzlement. Although the Court agrees with the Government, my view does not coincide completely with either of these positions. 18 U.S.C. § 656 (1976) in relevant part provides:

> Whoever, being an officer, director, agent or employee of, or connected in any capacity with any Federal Reserve bank, member bank, national bank or insured bank, * * * embezzles, abstracts, purloins or willfully misapplies any of the moneys, funds or credits of such bank or any moneys, funds, assets or securities intrusted to the custody or care of such bank, or to the custody or care of any such agent, officer, director, employee or receiver, shall be fined not more than $5,000 or imprisoned not more than five years, or both.

Embezzlement, as an offense, did not exist at common law; consequently, the exact composition of its ingredients depends ultimately upon the statute giving it birth. A seemingly invariable prerequisite of embezzlement statutes is that the accused have received or held the subject property in some particular character before he usurped it. Put another way, embezzlement has become a word of settled technical meaning, connoting that the accused was previously entrusted with possession — either actual or constructive — of the property.[28]

I discern nothing in the text of § 656 rendering the word "embezzlement" ambiguous on this score, or suggesting that Congress envisioned for it anything other than its common meaning. So pervasive in the concept of embezzlement is the need for some type of prior lawful possession that the unmodified use of the word in § 656 constrains me to conclude that it demands a relationship featuring no less.

With this construction of the statutory language, I share appellant's view that the Government's proof cannot support a conviction of embezzlement. The record is

---

[17] Most of the money was recovered from a bag in a closet at appellant's home and from an account in a Maryland bank. The bank was fully reimbursed for the $85,000 taken.

[28] *Moore v. United States*, 160 U.S. 268 (1895).

devoid of evidence indicating that appellant's function as a bank officer extended to any type of possession of cash in the reserve vault. Her assigned domain was the branch's note department, and from all that appears neither she nor the employees whom she supervised had any need for reserve-vault cash in the performance of their duties. To be sure, appellant had a key to the vault door and access to the combination, but their use was authorized only for admission of Burkett and other tellers when they themselves ran low on cash.[32] Appellant thus cannot be deemed to have been entrusted with the missing funds in such a way as to justify a conviction for embezzlement. Mere ability to perpetrate a theft of bank funds is not the possession that embezzlement inexorably demands.[33]

Our inquiry does not halt here, however, for § 656 also makes punishable other kinds of misappropriation of protected bank funds. By its very terms, the section is transgressed not only when a national bank officer "embezzles" but also when he "abstracts, purloins or willfully misapplies any of the [bank's] moneys [or] funds . . ." Notwithstanding the incapability of the evidence to establish embezzlement, the uncontradicted proof of appellant's misdeed established beyond peradventure a willful misapplication of bank funds, and thus an offense necessarily included within the embezzlement charge.

Thus, though I differ with the court in that I find insufficient evidence of prior lawful possession of the $85,000, I would still uphold the § 656 conviction — as one of misapplication rather than embezzlement.

MacKINNON, CIRCUIT JUDGE (Concurring specially).

I concur in Parts I and IV of Judge Robinson's opinion. In my analysis the evidence does support a conviction for embezzlement as well as for the included offense of willful misapplication. In reaching that conclusion I give neither the statute (18 U.S.C. § 656) nor *Moore v. United States*, 160 U.S. 268, 269-70 (1895) the highly restrictive construction that is urged in appellant's brief and adopted by Judge Robinson's opinion. Courts have affirmed convictions of embezzlement where the accused had "control by virtue of a position of trust" as well as where there was actual "prior lawful possession" of the property. The defendant here had all the means for effective access to and control of the money by virtue of a special trust placed in her by her employer. Consequently, when she used her access and control to convert that money to her own use in violation of that trust, she committed embezzlement as well as willful misapplication.

Moore v. United States, supra, defines "embezzle" expansively to include the fraudulent appropriation of property by a person to whom such property has been intrusted or into whose hands it has lawfully come. It differs from larceny in the fact that the original taking of the property was lawful, or with the consent of the owner,

---

[32] My colleagues criticize my position on the ground that I would insist upon actual possession as an essential element of embezzlement. See opinion of Judge MacKinnon. On the contrary, I recognize that constructive possession may suffice. My point is that appellant did not have any lawful possession whatever of money in the reserve vault, but only the means of access thereto.

[33] *Government of Virgin Islands v. Leonard*, 548 F.2d 478, 480-481 (3d Cir. 1977); *United States v. Sayklay*, 542 F.2d at 944.

while in larceny the felonious intent must have existed at the time of the taking. Thus, *Moore* extends embezzlement to those situations where the property has been "intrusted" to the accused's control or custody as well as to those situations where the property "has lawfully come into the accused's hands."

Under the present statute, embezzlement clearly extends to property entrusted to one's "custody" or "care" as well as to property in one's actual lawful possession. That conclusion is fortified by reference to some of the numerous state decisions that have explicitly extended embezzlement to custody and care situations.

These state decisions hold that embezzlement may be committed by one who has control of property by virtue of a trust, even if he lacked actual possession of the property or took possession without authorization. Most of the cases involve state statutes that in effect adopt the trust concept which is set forth in *Moore* and which is also evident in the language of § 656. These statutes, by contemplating that embezzlement may be committed by conversion of property in the control of the accused by virtue of a special trust, do not require actual prior possession. But then neither is such possession required by the Supreme Court's definitional decision in *Moore* or by the present language of § 656.

Illustrative of embezzlement involving a breach of trust without prior actual possession are those cases where an agent who is authorized to administer his principal's checking account makes unauthorized withdrawals and converts the funds to his own use. Although the agent comes into possession of the principal's funds only by an unauthorized act, the majority of these cases hold that the agent has nonetheless embezzled, because he had control over the funds by virtue of his position of trust. See Annot., 88 A.L.R.2d 688, 689 (1963) (cases in which accused made out checks to his own creditor). E.g., *Evans v. State*, 343 So. 2d 557, 560 (Ala. 1977) (employee who had authority to issue and sign checks on his employer's bank account drew check for his personal benefit). *Evans* indicates that money, the disbursement of which is entrusted to the defendant, is in his possession for purposes of embezzlement. The funds in such cases may be considered to be in the agent's constructive possession. It remains, therefore, that actual possession may not be required where funds are entrusted to the accused's care; and it may not be required that the accused come into the possession of the funds by an authorized act.

In *State v. Lamb*, 310 A.2d 102 (N.J.Super.Ct.App.Div. 1973), the receiving clerk never had actual possession of the goods; nor was he authorized to sign false receipts. Yet the court held that he embezzled when he signed false receipts which enabled his friend to collect from the clerk's employer for goods the employer never received: "Even though the goods may still have been on the delivery truck at the time, defendant, nevertheless, was able to exercise a sufficient measure of control over them so as to be in constructive, if not actual, possession of the goods on behalf of his employer." *Id.* at 105. The court followed the *Moore* definition of embezzlement and affirmed the clerk's conviction.

In a Louisiana case, the statute proscribed as embezzlement any state officer's conversion to personal use of public money "he is authorized to collect, or which may be entrusted to safe keeping or disbursement." This statute recognizes the trust theory. Defendant, a sheriff and tax collector, in effect made improper expense reimbursement requests which the parish treasurer routinely honored by issuing the sheriff checks that were drawn on the Sheriff's Salary Fund. Defendant averred he could not embezzle money he did not legally possess. The court answered that although the sheriff lacked physical possession or legal custody of the money in the salary fund, "for all practical purposes he was the legal possessor. He had and exercised exclusive control of it. Upon the presentation of the Sheriff's warrant, regular on its face, a duty developed upon the treasurer to pay it, provided there were funds in the amount sufficient therefor." *State v. Doucet*, 14 So.2d 917, 919 (La. 1943).

Several Arizona decisions support the same theory. In *State v. Roderick*, 448 P.2d 891 (Ariz. App. 1969). Defendant was authorized to buy a plane for resale. He asked the seller to rebate the dealer's discount in the form of a check payable to his order, and then pocketed the money instead of turning it over to his employer. Because defendant acquired the check under "color of authority (claiming to be the buyer's agent in procuring the discount)," he gained the property by virtue of his trust, and by the misappropriation committed embezzlement.

II.

The foregoing representative cases strongly suggest that the common meaning of embezzlement is at least as broad as the *Moore* definition of 1895 and includes the aspect of control by virtue of a position of special trust. This kind of control may exist apart from the element of "prior lawful possession," as witnessed by the statutes specifying "possession or control." Or it may exist as a concept subsumed within "possession," as in those cases which speak of "constructive possession" as a sort of synonym for defendant's control, and in those cases where the defendant is estopped to deny prior possession because he had gained possession under color of authority.

Virgin Islands v. Leonard, 548 F.2d 478 (3d Cir. 1977), and *United States v. Sayklay*, 542 F.2d 942 (5th Cir. 1976) are closest on the facts to the present case. In *Leonard*, the defendant was a civil defense storeroom employee who entered his employer's office at night, took the storeroom keys from a universally known location, and stole chicken wire. The court reversed defendant's embezzlement conviction under a statute covering property in a public officer's possession or under his control "by virtue of his trust." 548 F.2d at 480. The chicken wire was not under defendant's prior control because he had no authority to exercise any dominion over the contents of the storeroom. He was like any other employee (including secretaries and part-time help) in knowing where the storeroom keys were, and he came into the storeroom (not under any color of authority but) like "a thief in the night."

Leonard is distinguishable from the present case because the *Leonard* defendant was like a janitor, as the court noted; he was not in a high position of trust as was Whitlock as an assistant cashier and assistant manager with the special trust powers that gave her access to the keys, the combination and the money. The *Leonard* defendant did not, like Whitlock, act under color of authority in getting access to the converted property. See also *Warren v. State*, 62 N.E.2d 624 (Ind. 1945) (warehouseman who used his key to open warehouse and steal material is guilty of larceny rather than embezzlement; his was not a special position of trust).

In *United States v. Sayklay*, supra, the bank bookkeeper was able to perpetrate a check fraud through her access, as bookkeeper, to a check encoding machine and blank checks. The *Sayklay* court held it was not enough that the defendant is entrusted with all the tools necessary to gain access to the funds; the defendant must be entrusted with the funds themselves, as a bank teller or bank president is. Whitlock differs from the *Sayklay* bookkeeper both in the degree of trust placed in her and in the fact that the bookkeeper had to perform an intervening unlawful act — fraudulent check encoding — whereas Whitlock here got her hands on the money simply by exercising her prerogatives as a bank officer and the access that she was given by virtue of her special trust duties.

III.

This brings us to Whitlock's access to and authority and control over the money. Appellant attempts to play down her role of authority at the bank by terming herself a "note officer." Actually she was much more. She was an "assistant cashier and assistant manager", and necessarily had the authority and access within the bank that goes with those positions. In particular, she occupied a special position of trust along with two other bank officers who had the keys to the reserve vault. Through these keys money could be obtained from the vault in conjunction with the manager who had memorized the combination thereto. Both the keys and the combination were necessary for a person to reach the money. However, the manager also kept the combination in an envelope in a separate "manager's vault" and Whitlock and the other two officers did "know about the combination being in the manager's vault." They were entrusted with such knowledge as part of their special duties. In the manager's absence "they use the combination."

"Any one of the three bank officers had access to that piece of paper inside the manager's vault that had the combination." Thus, although this plan was designed to place the reserve vault cash under "dual control", in practice the plan provided each of the key-bearing officers with single access and control: any one of the three could exercise his or her access to the combination and combine it with use of the key. Under such circumstances the district court was clearly entitled to find that Whitlock was effectively entrusted with the combination to the safe as well with the keys.

It therefore appears that, by virtue of Whitlock's position of trust as Assistant Cashier and Assistant Manager, and the special access she was given to the key and the combination, the funds in the vault were under her effective control. Upon such undisputed facts it must be concluded that Whitlock was one of the "persons to whom such money had been intrusted . . ." and she committed an embezzlement in converting it to her own use. This conclusion follows from the meaning of embezzlement current at least since the decision in *Moore* and is enforced by the amended present language of the statute, which precisely, if redundantly, covers the situation of a bank "officer . . . [or] employee [who] . . . embezzles . . . moneys . . . intrusted . . . to the custody or care of such . . . officer [or] . . . employee."

For the foregoing reasons it is my opinion that Whitlock was guilty not only of the included offense of willful misapplication but also of embezzlement.

Judge Robb joins in this opinion affirming the conviction of embezzlement.

NOTES FROM THE JUDGE:

(1) I had a bit of trouble reading this case. Which comes first, the majority opinion or the dissent?

(2) How did the second opinion distinguish *Leonard*? Is our case closer to *Leonard* or to *Whitlock*?

UNITED STATES v. SELWYN
U.S. Court of Appeals, 8th Circuit
998 F.2d 556 (1993)

Lay, Senior Circuit Judge.

Calvin A. Selwyn appeals from his conviction under 18 U.S.C. § 1709 for embezzling a package entrusted to the United States mail. He contends that the prosecution presented no evidence that he came into possession of the package lawfully, one of the elements of embezzlement. We agree and reverse the judgment of conviction.

Selwyn worked at the downtown Minneapolis post office as a maintenance control clerk. He was responsible for handling paperwork for the maintenance department and had no authority or responsibility for handling mail. While working a night shift in January 1992, Selwyn apparently entered a loading dock area near his office and removed a package. The package contained a cocktail dress that a mail order customer was attempting to return to a store in downtown Minneapolis. A few days later, Selwyn brought the dress to the store and sought to return it for a cash refund. He explained that his wife had received the dress as a gift but did not like it. Because Selwyn did not have a receipt, the store could not give him an immediate refund. Store employees became suspicious and ultimately their inquiry led to Selwyn's arrest and conviction.

In this appeal, Selwyn does not challenge the government's proof that he removed the package from the mails without proper authority. Rather, Selwyn claims that the government failed to present any evidence on one of the elements of embezzlement — that he secured possession of the package lawfully. He argues that, therefore, his conviction cannot stand because it is at variance with the indictment.

Section 1709 creates two distinct offenses of postal theft. The first clause of the section makes it a crime for postal employees to embezzle mail; the second clause makes it illegal to steal the contents of mail.[1] The indictment against Selwyn,

---

[1] The statute states: "Whoever, being a Postal Service officer or employee, embezzles any letter, postal card, package, bag, or mail, or any article or thing contained therein entrusted to him or which comes into his possession intended to be conveyed by mail, or carried or delivered by any carrier,

however, accuses Selwyn only of embezzlement.[2] It is well settled that the crimes of embezzlement and stealing are inconsistent in that "embezzlement presupposes lawful possession and theft does not." *Id.*; 2 Wayne R. LaFave & Austin W. Scott, Jr., *Substantive Criminal Law* § 8.6 (1986).

In rejecting Selwyn's motion for judgment of acquittal, the district court determined that the government satisfied the lawful possession requirement by presenting evidence that Selwyn violated a position of trust as a postal employee. It observed that the statute is cast in the alternative, making it a crime for a postal worker to embezzle mail "entrusted to him or which comes into his possession intended to be conveyed by mail." The district court reasoned that although this package was not entrusted to Selwyn, it did come into his possession intended to be conveyed by mail.

We believe this interpretation ignores § 1709's threshold requirement that the conduct be embezzlement and thus the initial possession be lawful. Lawful possession is not created by "mere access" to an item to be taken. *Government of Virgin Islands v. Leonard*, 548 F.2d 478, 480 (3d cir. 1977); *United States v. Sayklay*, 542 F.2d 942, 944 (5th cir. 1976). The government failed to produce evidence at trial that Selwyn had any authority over the mail; all it showed was that he had access to the mail. For this reason, Selwyn's conviction must be reversed.

Congress has enacted consolidated statutes that treat the separate, non-overlapping crimes of embezzlement, false pretenses, and larceny as a single crime.[3] See, e.g., 18 U.S.C. § 659 (whoever "embezzles, steals, or unlawfully takes, carries away, or conceals, or by fraud or deception" removes goods from interstate or foreign freight); see also *United States v. Petti*, 459 F.2d 294, 296 (3d cir. 1972) (holding that "fine distinctions between common-law larceny and embezzlement are inapplicable to the consolidated statutory offense"). However, Congress has not consolidated the theft offenses under § 1709.[4] Unlike the consolidated statutes cited above, § 1709 creates different requirements for embezzlement and stealing of mail by post office workers. "It is to be noted that the first offense under the statute is that of embezzlement and includes (1) letters or (2) articles contained therein. The second offense is that of stealing articles removed from any such letter

---

messenger, agent, or other person employed in any department of the Postal Service, or forwarded through or delivered from any post office or station thereof established by authority of the Postmaster General or of the Postal Service; or steals, abstracts, or removes from any such letter, package, bag, or mail, or article or thing contained therein, shall be fined not more than $2,000 or imprisoned not more than five years, or both."

[2] The indictment states: "On or about the 25th day of January, 1992, in the State and District of Minnesota, the defendant, CALVIN A. SELWYN, a Postal Service employee, did knowingly and willfully embezzle a package, or anything contained therein, which was entrusted to him or which came into his possession, and which was intended to be conveyed by mail, or forwarded through a post office or station thereof established by the authority of the Postal Service; all in violation of 18 United States Code § 1709."

[3] Many states have similarly enacted consolidated statutes. See, e.g., Ark.Code Ann. § 5-36-102 ("Conduct denominated theft in this chapter constitutes a single offense embracing the separate offenses heretofore known as larceny, embezzlement, false pretense, extortion, blackmail, fraudulent conversion, receiving stolen property, and other similar offenses."); Minn.Stat. § 609.52 (1992); see also 2 Wayne R. LaFave & Austin W. Scott, Jr., *Substantive Criminal Law* § 8.8 (1986) (discussing the trend toward consolidation).

as distinguished from the letter itself." *Trevino*, 491 F.2d at 75. Because the government did not indict Selwyn for stealing from the mail, proof that Selwyn did so is at variance with the indictment and cannot support his conviction.5

There appears to be no doubt that Selwyn is guilty of wrongfully converting property entrusted to the United States mail. However, as the Fifth Circuit said in another embezzlement case:

> "Embezzlement" is a technical term imbued with a specific meaning. To uphold a conviction for embezzlement under these facts would confuse the distinction that Congress clearly drew between embezzlement and other forms of conversion. More is at stake here than convicting a wrongdoer of something: fidelity to Congress' clear purpose and refusal to convict anyone of a crime of which he has not been — and cannot be, on the facts — proved guilty. This is a hard case, but the bad law (if such it be) was made when Congress chose to carry forward the technical and antediluvian elements by which the Supreme Court long ago distinguished embezzlement from similar crimes. [*Sayklay*, 542 F.2d at 944.]

In this case, the problem, however, lies not only with Congress, but also with the government's indictment. The Eighth Circuit's Manual of Model Criminal Jury Instructions reminds prosecutors that a "postal employee, who does not, by nature of his duties, originally have lawful possession of certain mail matter, can be charged and convicted under the stealing provisions in the second clause of § 1709." Manual of Model Criminal Jury Instructions for the District Courts of the Eighth Circuit § 6.18.1709 (committee comments). Such was not done here.

For the foregoing reasons, the judgment of conviction will be vacated and the case remanded with instruction to enter a judgment of acquittal.

LOKEN, CIRCUIT JUDGE, dissenting.

I respectfully dissent. In denying Selwyn's post-verdict motion for judgment of acquittal, the district court explained: The court instructed the jury, as requested by defendant, according to the Eighth Circuit Manual of Pattern Instructions § 6.18.1709:

The crime of embezzling mail as charged in the indictment has three essential elements which are: One: the defendant was a United States Postal Service employee at the time stated in the indictment; Two: in his position with the Postal Service, the defendant had possession of a package which was intended to be conveyed by mail; and Three: the defendant took from that package a dress with the intent to convert it to his own use.

The court instructed the jury that to embezzle means "willfully to take, or convert to one's own use, another's money or property, of which the wrongdoer acquired possession lawfully, by reason of some office or employment or position of trust." The court also gave the standard possession instruction, Devitt & Blackmar § 16.07, which defines actual and constructive, and joint and sole, possession:

> The statute is specifically cast in the alternative: that defendant em-
> bezzled an article in a package "entrusted to him or which comes into his

possession intended to be conveyed by mail". Although the package with the dress may not have been intended to pass through defendant's hands in the course of its conveyance by mail, the evidence showed that it did come into his actual or constructive possession in his position as a postal employee. He violated his position of trust as a postal employee with regard to the package. This is sufficient to support his conviction under § 1709.

In my view, this is a correct construction of the statute that is factually supported by the trial record. I would affirm.

Chapter 4

FALSE PRETENSES

False pretenses, a statutory crime, * * * consists in most jurisdictions of these five elements: (1) a false representation of a material present or past fact (2) which causes the victim (3) to pass title to (4) his property to the wrongdoer, (5) who (a) knows his representation to be false and (b) intends thereby to defraud the victim.

LaFave & Scott, *Criminal Law* (West)

Larceny is a crime usually committed by strangers — "sneak thieves" and the like. Embezzlement is committed by people who were given temporary possession of property — employees, bailees, and the like.

Neither of these crimes seems to fit very well with the *marketplace*, where a buyer or seller tells lies in order to obtain *title* to property from the other party. As England became a commercial power, a need to deal with this problem arose. The common law judges might have done so by adopting new legal fictions to stretch either larceny or embezzlement to encompass this situation. (Just for fun — and to test your creative abilities — think about how this might have been done!)

But the judges refused to go that far. Instead — just as they did with embezzlement — the courts left this problem to Parliament. And Parliament responded with a new crime: false pretenses.

PROBLEM 4

To: My law clerk

From: Mary Goround, Esq.

Re: *United States v. Mann*

My client, Congressman Cornelius ("Conn") Mann, has been indicted on 2 counts of theft, in violation District of Columbia Code § 22-3811. The first count arises from an alleged theft on June 6 of last year, and the second count arises from an alleged theft on August 28 of last year. A copy of the grand jury transcript is attached.

I would like to file a motion to dismiss each count of the indictment, on the ground that the evidence before the grand jury did not show each essential element of the crime, on either count. Please advise me on what to argue and whether I am likely to win. Attached are some authorities which you might find helpful.

Transcript of Grand Jury Hearing in *U.S. v. Mann*

Q (by Prosecutor): Please state your name and where you worked last year.

A: My name is Diane Diaz. Last year, I was an aide to Congressman Mann. I helped him with his work as a member of the House Commerce Committee.

Q: Tell us what happened at a meeting you attended on June 6.

A: A man named Buzz Bird came to see Conn, and I sat in on the meeting. Bird said that he manufactured toy airplanes, and cheap foreign imports were hurting his business. He asked Conn to sponsor a bill putting an import quota on toy airplanes.

Conn said it would be difficult to introduce a new bill so late in the session, but he would try. He said even if he introduced it, he could not get it out of committee unless the Chairman approved, and the Chairman did not like import quotas. He said the Chairman was being challenged in the next Congressional election and needed campaign funds. He said that if Bird gave Conn a check for $10,000, Conn would pass the money along to the Chairman and tell him that it came from a source who wanted an import quota on toy airplanes. Bird then gave Conn a check for $10,000, made out to Conn. Bird thanked Conn and left.

Conn then turned to me and laughed. He said that the Chairman had already introduced a trade bill that put import quotas on *all* toys, including toy airplanes, and the bill was sure to get out of committee. Conn put the Bird's check in his pocket and said, "The Chairman does need the money, but I need it more. Bird wouldn't mind. He'll get his import quota."

The bill did get out of committee. In fact, it passed both houses of Congress, and it became law.

As a young attorney, I was quite upset with Conn's ethics, so I quit working for him. Then I called Bird and told him what Conn had done.

Q: Thank you, Ms. Diaz. Next witness, please. Your name?

A: Buzz Bird.

Q: Mr. Bird, after Ms. Diaz told you what Congressman Mann had done to you, what did you do?

A: On August 28, I went to Mann's office with a tape recorder hidden in my briefcase and turned on. I confronted Mann with Ms. Diaz' story, and Mann admitted that he had lied to me, because he needed the money for his alimony payments. I demanded by $10,000 back, but he said he didn't have it.

I then showed Mann the tape recorder, and I said that he could have the cassette I had just used, for $10,000. His face went red and he swore, but he said OK. He gave me 2 checks, one for $5,000 drawn on Riggs Bank and another one for $5,000 drawn on First National Bank. I gave him the cassette.

The next day, I went to the Riggs bank to cash the first check, but they refused to cash it, saying that Mann had not had more than $200 in the account for the past 3 months. I then went to First National, but I had no better luck there. They said that Mann did have over $5,000 in the account for the past month, but Mann had been in the bank that morning and drawn all the funds out of the account. So I got nothing from the 2 checks.

Q: Thank you, Mr. Bird. That concludes our evidence.

District of Columbia Code, 1982, § 22-3211 - Theft

(a) For the purpose of this section, the term "wrongfully obtains or uses" means:

    (1) taking or exercising control over property;

    (2) making an unauthorized use, disposition, or transfer of an interest in or possession of property; or

    (3) obtaining property by trick, false pretense, false token, tampering, or deception. The term "wrongfully obtains or uses" includes conduct previously known as larceny, larceny by trick, larceny by trust, embezzlement, and false pretenses.

(b) A person commits the offense of theft if that person wrongfully obtains or uses the property of another with intent:

    (1) To deprive the other of a right to the property or a benefit of the property; or

    (2) To appropriate the property to his or her own use or to the use of a third person. * * * *

[Enacted in 1982].

CHAPLIN v. UNITED STATES
U. S. Court of Appeals, District of Columbia Circuit
157 F.2d 697 (1946)

CLARK, ASSOCIATE JUSTICE.

This is an appeal from a conviction under the first count of an indictment charging appellant and his wife with obtaining money by false pretenses.[1]

[The indictment charged] that appellant and his wife, co-defendant below, "with intent to defraud, feloniously did pretend and represent to one Violette McMullen, then and there being, that they, the said Sydney A. Chaplin and the said Dorothy Chaplin, were engaged in the wine and liquor business in Alexandria, Virginia, and that if she, the said Violette McMullen, would advance certain money, they would purchase certain liquor stamps with said money and would return any money so advanced." It is charged that the defendants "would not purchase such liquor stamps and would not return the money advanced as they well knew."

It appears from the indictment that the prosecution's case was necessarily founded on the defendants' intention, at the time of acquiring the money, not to do

---

[1] D.C.Code 1940, § 22-1301.

two things promised: (1) buy stamps, and (2) repay the money. Both of these promises relate to things the defendants were to do in the future. The prosecution did not prove that the defendants misrepresented their business connection. On the contrary, it appears from the record that the appellant and his wife were in the liquor business, that they did own a large quantity of wine for which state stamps were required, and that they did buy some small amount of tax stamps.

The question for our decision comes down to whether the "present intention" of the defendants not to return the money and not to buy the stamps, as they said they would, relates to a "present or past existing fact" such as will support a conviction for the crime of false pretenses.

The rule stated in *Wharton's Criminal Law*, 12th Ed., § 1439, is that: "A false pretense, under the statute, must relate to a past event or existing fact. Any representation with regard to a future transaction is excluded. Thus, for instance, a false statement, that a draft which the defendant exhibits to the prosecutor has been received from a house of good credit abroad, and is for a valuable consideration, on the faith of which he obtains the prosecutor's goods, is within the law; a promise to deposit with him such a draft at some future time, though wilfully and intentionally false, and the means of prosecutor's parting possession with his property, is not. So a pretense that the party would do an act that he did not mean to do (as a pretense that he would pay for goods on delivery) was ruled by all the judges not to be a false pretense under the Statute of Geo. II., and the same rule is distinctly recognized in this country, it being held that the statement of an intention is not a statement of an existing fact." We think the great weight of authority sustains this statement of the rule and compels us to answer the question in the negative.

A majority of the courts having this problem placed before them have not subscribed to the theory that "intention", as manifest by false and misleading promises, standing alone, is a fact in the sense required for a conviction on the charge of false pretenses.

Not only is the rule deeply rooted in our law, but moreover, we think the reasons upon which it is founded are no less cogent today than they were when the early cases were decided under the English statute cited by Wharton, supra. It is of course true that then, as now, the intention to commit certain crimes was ascertained by looking backward from the act and finding that the accused intended to do what he did do. However, where, as here, the act complained of - namely, failure to repay money or use it as specified at the time of borrowing - is as consonant with ordinary commercial default as with criminal conduct, the danger of applying this technique to prove the crime is quite apparent. Business affairs would be materially incumbered by the ever present threat that a debtor might be subjected to criminal penalties if the prosecutor and jury were of the view that at the time of borrowing he was mentally a cheat. The risk of prosecuting one who is guilty of nothing more than a failure or inability to pay his debts is a very real consideration. It is not enough to say that if innocent the accused would be found not guilty. The social stigma attaching to one accused of a crime as well as the burdens incident to the defense would, irrespective of the outcome, place a devastating weapon in the hands of a disgruntled or disappointed creditor.

The business policy, as well as the difficulties and dangers inherent in a contrary rule are illustrated by the earlier English cases. In *Rex v. Goodhall*, 1821, Russ. & R.C.C. 461, the accused was found to have obtained a quantity of meat, promising to pay for it but not so intending. In reversing the jury's verdict of guilty the court said: "It was merely a promise for future conduct, and common prudence and caution would have prevented any injury arising from the breach of it."

In *Reg. v. Woodman*, 1879, 14 Cox C.C. 179, the prosecution advanced precisely the same argument that is urged here, contending that the defendant's intention was the existing fact about which the misrepresentation had been made. To this the court responded: "How can you define a man's mind? It is a mere promissory false pretence."

If we were to accept the government's position, the way would be open for every victim of a bad bargain to resort to criminal proceedings to even the score with a judgment proof adversary. No doubt in the development of our criminal law the zeal with which the innocent are protected has provided a measure of shelter for the guilty. However, we do not think it wise to increase the possibility of conviction by broadening the accepted theory of the weight to be attached to the mental attitude of the accused.

Reversed.

EDGERTON, ASSOCIATE JUSTICE (dissenting).

The court holds that "the great weight of authority compels us." This is a new rule and an important one. I think it is erroneous.

Usually there are good reasons for a doctrine which is widely accepted, and uniformity itself has some value even in criminal law. Accordingly we should consider the weight of authority elsewhere for what it may be worth. But we should not determine our action by a count of foreign cases regardless of logic, consistency, and social need. "The social value of a rule has become a test of growing power and importance".[1] We should decide the question before us in accordance with present-day standards of wisdom and justice rather than in accordance with some outworn and antiquated rule of the past which was never adopted here. To let judges who lived and died in other times and places make our decisions would be to abdicate as judges and serve as tellers.

This court, like every other American court, overrules its own decisions when need arises. Decisions of other courts are not more binding on us. We may as well disregard the overwhelming weight of authority elsewhere and start with a rule of our own, consistent with practical experience. This court's new rule against new rules appears to mean that this court must take no part in the development of the law.

Considered without regard to the foreign cases on which the court relies, the indictment is plainly valid. No doubt a promise is commonly an undertaking, but it

---

[1] Cardozo, *The Nature of the Judicial Process*, p. 73. "Perhaps the most significant advance in the modern science of law is the change from the analytical to the functional attitude".

is always an assertion of a present intention to perform. "I will" means among other things "I intend to". It is so understood and it is meant to be so understood. Intention is a fact and present intention is a present fact. A promise made without an intention to perform is therefore a false statement about a present fact. This factual and declarative aspect of a promise is not a new discovery. It has come to be widely recognized in civil actions for deceit.

In criminal cases, most courts and text writers have clung to an old illusion that the same words cannot embody both a promise and a statement of fact. But this tradition that in a criminal case "the statement of an intention is not a statement of an existing fact" has begun to break down. It is an obvious fiction. The meaning of words is the same whether their author is prosecuted civilly or criminally or not at all. The fiction that a promise made without intent to perform does not embody a misrepresentation conflicts with the facts, with the deceit cases, and with the interest of society in protecting itself against fraud. An Act of Congress makes it a crime in the District of Columbia to obtain money "by any false pretense, with intent to defraud."[8] Congress did not exempt, and the court should not exempt, a pretense conveyed by words which also convey a promise. As a matter of plain English there could be no clearer case of false and fraudulent pretense than a borrower's pretense that he intends to repay money which he actually does not intend to repay.

The old illusion that a promise states no facts is not the only source of the old tolerance of falsehoods regarding intention. That a fool and his money are soon parted was once accepted as a sort of natural law. In 1821 the fact that "common prudence and caution would have prevented any injury" seemed to an English court a good reason for refusing to penalize an injury which had been intentionally inflicted by a false promise. The fact that common agility in dodging an intentional blow would have prevented any injury would not have seemed a reason for refusing to penalize a battery. Fools were fair game though cripples were not. But in modern times, no one not talking law would be likely to deny that society should protect mental as well as physical helplessness against intentional injuries.

Though the court decides the case on the basis of authority, the opinion concludes with a defense of the prevailing rule. But to justify this rule it would be necessary to show that false pretenses regarding intention are a harmless way of obtaining money, or else that intention cannot be proved in prosecutions for false pretenses as it is constantly proved in other criminal prosecutions and in civil actions for deceit.

Difficulties of proof are seldom greater in criminal cases than in civil, except that the prosecution must prove its case beyond a reasonable doubt. No peculiar difficulty of proof distinguishes this crime from others. Intentions of one sort or another must be proved in most criminal cases. They are usually proved by conduct. It is inherently no more difficult to prove an intent not to perform a promise than, for example, an intent to monopolize, to commit a felony, or to receive goods knowing them to be stolen.

Appellant's conduct showed his intent. After getting $375 from a nurse by

---

[8] D.C.Code 1940, § 22-1301.

promising to buy liquor stamps and repay the money, he made the same promise a few days later and got $700 more. He said he needed the money to get the stamps. Yet he bought less than $40 worth of stamps, if any, during the next six weeks, and there is no evidence that he bought any stamps at any later time. Meanwhile he continued to borrow money from the woman. He made no repayments at any time. The jury might well conclude, as it did, that the difference between his promises and his performance was not accidental but was part of his original plan. The court does not suggest that the proof of his original intention was insufficient. If it were thought to be insufficient, the conviction should be reversed on that ground. The rule which the court adopts will make prosecutions impossible even when admissions or other evidence make guilt obvious.

No peculiar danger to innocent men distinguishes this crime from others. No honest borrower who fails to repay a loan, or changes his mind about the use which he intended to make of the money, is likely to be charged with obtaining it by false pretenses. Prosecutions are not undertaken without evidence and convictions do not withstand attack unless they are supported by sufficient evidence. The danger of a counter suit for malicious prosecution is always present to discourage unfounded charges. The court's picture of a flood of indictments against honest business men is unconvincing. No such flood has been observed in the few jurisdictions which have adopted the modern rule. It is true that innocent men are sometimes accused of crime. Innocent men have been convicted of murder. Since it is impossible to prevent occasional miscarriage of justice, every criminal statute jeopardizes innocent people in some degree.

The court suggests that the law should not jeopardize legitimate business. But this is the unavoidable price of public protection against illegitimate business. If the suggestion is sound the anti-trust law, the pure food law, the child labor law, the law against receiving stolen goods, and many others should be repealed, for malicious and damaging charges and erroneous convictions are possible under all of them. If the suggestion is sound the entire law of false pretenses and not merely a part of it should be repealed, for legal machinery is fallible with respect to the making, the falsity, and the maker's knowledge of the falsity, of representations of every kind.

There is, as the court says, a vast difference between criminal penalties and civil redress. It is the more unfortunate to hold, as the court does, that a common sort of fraud is not a crime. Since civil redress is not punitive but compensatory, the decision means that the law of the District of Columbia offers no deterrent to this sort of fraud. If a swindler has property which can be taken in execution on a civil judgment, he may not always win by practicing this fraud. But he cannot lose. If he perseveres he will win in the long run, for he will not always be sued to judgment. And one who has no property on which execution can be levied is bound to win as often as he can find a victim.

NOTES FROM MARY:

(1) In other jurisdictions, the "modern prevailing view" — by case law and the Model Penal Code — is more in accord with the dissent in *Chaplin* than with the majority. Model Penal Code § 223.3 goes on to caution, however, that evidence of

mere failure to perform a promise shall not alone be sufficient to prove that the promisor never intended to perform. See also *People v. Ashley*, 42 Cal.2d 246, (1954); *People v. Norman*, 85 N.Y.2d 609 (1995).

(2) *Chaplin* might help us, but I'm not sure how much. Look very carefully at the representations Mann made (express and implied) to see which relate to the future and which relate to the present or past.

NELSON v. UNITED STATES
U.S. Court of Appeals, District of Columbia Circuit
227 F.2d 21 (1955)

DANAHER, CIRCUIT JUDGE.

This is an appeal from a conviction for obtaining goods by false pretenses in violation of D.C.Code § 22-1301 (1951).[1] The trial court entered judgment of acquittal on a second count charging grand larceny.

Evidence was offered to show that appellant from time to time over a period of months, for purposes of resale, had purchased merchandise from Potomac Distributors of Washington, D.C., Inc. By September 18, 1952, his account was said to be in arrears more than thirty days.

Late that afternoon, appellant sought immediate possession of two television sets and a washing machine, displayed his customers' purchase contracts to support his statement that he had already sold such merchandise and had taken payment therefor, and told one Schneider, secretary-treasurer of Potomac Distributors, "I promised delivery tonight." Appellant was told no further credit could be extended to him because of his overdue indebtedness in excess of $1,800, whereupon appellant offered to give security for the desired items as well as for the delinquent account. He represented himself as the owner of a Packard car for which he had paid $4,260.50, but failed to disclose an outstanding prior indebtedness on the car of $3,028.08 secured by a chattel mortgage in favor of City Bank. Instead, he represented that he owed only one payment of some $55 not then due.

Relying upon such representations, Potomac Distributors delivered to appellant two television sets each worth $136[2] taking in return a demand note for the entire indebtedness, past and present, in the total, $2,047.37, secured by a chattel mortgage on the Packard and the television sets. Appellant promised to make a cash payment on the note within a few days for default of which the holder was entitled to demand full payment. When the promised payment was not

---

[1] In pertinent part the section provides: "Whoever, by any false pretense, with intent to defraud, obtains from any person anything of value, or procures the execution and delivery of any instrument of writing or conveyance of real or personal property . . . shall, if the value of the property . . . so obtained . . . is $50 or upward, be imprisoned not less than one year nor more than three years . . ." [Ed. This section was repealed in 1982, when it was replaced by § 22-3811.]

[2] and a washing machine valued at $77.50 which, for some reason not shown, was not otherwise included in the transaction, although delivered to appellant.

forthcoming, Schneider, by telephone calls and a personal visit to appellant's home, sought to locate appellant, but learned be had left town. The Packard about that time was in a collision, incurring damage of about $1,000, and was thereupon repossessed in behalf of the bank which held the prior lien for appellant's car purchase indebtedness.

Appellant argues that Potomac Distributors could not have been defrauded, for the car on September 18, 1952, "had an equity of between $900 and $1,000 and roughly five times the value of the two television sets." That fact is immaterial.

He urges that the chattel mortgage to Potomac Distributors, as to the two television sets, must be construed as a conditional sales contract, and since on that account appellant never received title to them, he could not have committed an offense within the language of the Code. Such circumlocution is irrelevant, for the Code reads: "Whoever, by any false pretense, with intent to defraud, obtains from any person anything of value . . ." is guilty. Besides, appellant need not have received absolute title. *Whitmore v. State*, 1941, 238 Wis. 79.

He argues that it was error to admit evidence to show that there was a valid prior outstanding chattel mortgage in favor of City Bank to secure an indebtedness of more than $3,000 of the purchase price of the car, and that such evidence varies the terms of a written instrument. It amounts to an argument that the appellant by deceit and willful prevarication may obtain delivery of two television sets and convert them to his own use, but when his victim has relied upon his misrepresentations and has believed them, the truth may not be shown if the fraud has culminated in a written instrument at variance with the facts. Such a position is untenable.

This appellant has sold two television sets, and apparently had taken payment therefor, although he had no television sets to deliver to his customers. He could not get the sets from Potomac Distributors without offering security for his past due account as well as for his present purchase. In order to get them, he lied. He represented that his car, acquired at a cost of more than $4,000, required only one further payment of $55. He now complains because his victim believed him when he lied. He argues that the misrepresentations were not material although the victim testified, and the jury could properly find, that he would not have parted with his goods except in reliance upon appellant's statements.

> No one can be permitted to say, in respect to his own statements upon a material matter, that he did not expect to be believed; and if they are knowingly false, and willfully made, the fact that they are material is proof of an attempted fraud, because their materiality, in the eye of the law, consists in their tendency to influence the conduct of the party who has an interest in them and to whom they are addressed. [*Claflin v. Commonwealth Ins.Co.*, 1884, 110 U.S. 81.]

He argues that there was no proof of an intent upon his part to defraud his victim. "Wrongful acts knowingly or intentionally committed can neither be justified nor excused on the ground of innocent intent. The color of the act determines the complexion of the intent. The intent to injure or defraud is presumed when the unlawful act, which results in loss or injury, is proved to have been knowingly committed. It is a well-settled rule, which the law applies in both criminal and civil cases, that the intent is presumed and inferred from the result of the action." This quotation from a challenged charge was found by the Supreme Court to be "unexceptionable as matter of law" in *Agnew v. United States*, 1897, 165 U.S. 36, 53.

Affirmed.

WILBUR K. MILLER, CIRCUIT JUDGE (dissenting).

When the essential ingredients of the crime of false pretense have been accurately ascertained, and when irrelevant facts in the evidence have been identified as such and eliminated from consideration, I believe it will be apparent that the Government failed to make out a case for submission to the jury. It will then also appear, I think, that the trial judge erroneously refused to direct a verdict of acquittal, only because he mistakenly attributed significance to the fact that appellant's automobile was damaged in a collision which occurred "early in October" — at least two weeks after September 18, the day he purchased the two television sets and the washing machine from Potomac Distributors.

As to the ingredients of the offense. While our false pretense statute does not in express language require that the person from whom the property is obtained should be defrauded thereby,[1] nevertheless the crime is not complete unless he is in fact defrauded. In order to convict under the statute, the Government must therefore prove that in making a false pretense the defendant intended to defraud the person from whom he obtained property, and that he did thereby defraud him. The trial judge recognized this, and charged the jury accordingly.

Nelson did make a false representation; but the question is whether there was evidence from which the jury could properly be permitted to infer that he intended to defraud, and to conclude that Potomac was thereby defrauded.

As to the relevant evidence, which required acquittal. During the first eight and one-half months of 1952, Nelson had been a substantial and constant customer of Potomac. In that period, his purchases amounted to more than $25,000 and he had always paid within the permitted 30-day credit period. But on September 18, his account, which then amounted to $1,697.87, included for the first time some charges more than 30 days old.

When on that day Nelson wanted to buy on credit two television sets at $136 each, and a washing machine at $77.50, Potomac refused to make the sale unless he would give security for the total purchase price of $349.50, and would also secure the pre-existing indebtedness of $1,697.87. Nelson agreed to give a lien on the articles being purchased and on his Packard automobile as well, and signed a note for $2,047.37. He executed a chattel deed of trust on the two television sets and the automobile, Potomac having purposely omitted the washing machine in preparing

---

[1] Title 22, § 1301, D.C.Code (1951), as amended in 1953, provides: "Whoever, by any false pretense, with intent to defraud, obtains from any person anything of value * * * shall, if the value of the property or the sum or value of the money or property so obtained * * * is $100 or upward, be imprisoned not less than one year nor more than three years * * *." [Ed. This section was repealed in 1982, when it was replaced by § 22-3811, set out at the beginning of this chapter.]

the instrument. He told the Schneider brothers, principal proprietors of Potomac, that he owed a balance of only $55 on his car, when in fact he owed a lien debt of $3,028.08 to a local bank. This is the false pretense upon which the indictment and conviction were based.

Of course it was very wrong of Nelson to make this false statement. But whether it was felonious or not depends on two questions: (a) did he intend thereby to defraud, and (b) even if he did so intend, was Potomac actually defrauded?

Differing definitions of the word "defraud" probably cause the difference in opinion between the majority and me. They seem to think it means, in connection with a purchase, to make a false pretense in the process of obtaining goods even though the purchase price is well secured. I think the word means, in connection with a purchase, to make a false pretense as a result of which the seller is deprived of his goods or of the purchase price. The difference is particularly important in a case like this one where a purchaser is charged with defrauding a seller. A purchaser can be said to have defrauded the seller of his goods only if he intended to defraud him of the purchase price for which the seller was willing to exchange them. It seems to me to follow that a purchaser who makes a false statement in buying on credit has not defrauded the seller of his goods if he nevertheless amply secures the debt.

In considering the criminality *vel non* of the false statement, it must be remembered that the past due indebtedness of $1,697.87 is to play no part. That credit had already been extended generally, and with respect to it Potomac parted with nothing on September 18. Nelson was only charged with defrauding Potomac by obtaining through false pretense the articles then delivered, which had a total value of only $349.50.

What was the actual value on September 18 of the property upon which Potomac took a lien, on the strength of which it parted with property worth $349.50? The bank collection manager, testifying for the Government, said that although on September 18 Nelson still owed the bank $3,028.08, he had on that day an equity in the car worth from $900 to $1,000. The mortgaged television sets were, I suppose, worth their price of $272. Adding to this the minimum equity in the automobile proved by the prosecution, it appears that Potomac had a lien on property worth at least $1,172 to protect a debt of $349.50. The proportion was more than three to one.

Such is the evidence as to what happened September 18, from which the jury was permitted to infer that Nelson then intended to defraud, and to conclude that he then did fraudulently obtain from Potomac the three articles purchased. As to intent, I suggest that it is wholly irrational to presume or infer that one intends to defraud when he buys goods on credit and safeguards that credit by giving more than triple security for it - no matter if he does falsely pretend that the security is even greater. It is equally illogical to conclude that the creditor was thereby defrauded. For that reason, my opinion is that the proof I have outlined - which was the only pertinent proof - did not warrant the trial court in submitting the case to the jury.

As to the irrelevant evidence, which produced conviction. Why then did the trial judge let the case go to the jury? He knew an actual defrauding was necessary to conviction and, as I have said, so instructed the jury. And why, in the light of that instruction, and under Government proof which clearly showed Potomac was not defrauded, did the jury convict? Principally, I think, because of a subsequent fortuitous circumstance which Nelson could not have anticipated on September 18, and which of course was not the result of his deliberate act.

This circumstance was that some two weeks or more after the goods had been obtained, the mortgaged automobile was damaged in a collision to an extent estimated at about $1,000. If the damage was not compensated for by insurance or otherwise, the accident practically destroyed Nelson's equity in the car. The bank seized the damaged automobile and disposed of it to a transferee, who evidently saw some equity still in it, as he paid the bank's debt. Potomac seems to have stood idly by while this was going on, without taking any steps to protect its lien, which was or should have been then of record. If damages were collected by or for Nelson from a tortfeasor, Potomac's lien attached thereto. The record does not show whether such damages were or should have been recovered. It should be noted also that Potomac made no effort to enforce its lien on the television sets.

Aside from all that, however, the salient point is that the reduction in the value of the automobile caused by the collision could not properly be considered by the jury; the question was as to its value September 18, for it was that value which should have been considered in deciding whether Potomac had been defrauded. Had the trial judge observed this distinction, he would have directed a verdict of acquittal, since he was aware of the necessity that there be actual defrauding. The judge made this clear when he said in a bench colloquy: "Until I heard that there had been a wreck and the car had been repossessed I thought maybe there was sufficient equity there to cover the loss sustained; and if that were the case there would be no defrauding." I have demonstrated there was more than sufficient equity September 18 to cover the credit then extended, so there was no defrauding, even though an accident later impaired the margin of protection.

In addition to the irrelevant proof of the collision damage, which should not have been received and without which an acquittal would have been directed, there was another irrelevancy in evidence which may well have played a part in moving the jury to its verdict: the preexisting indebtedness. Because of Nelson's misrepresentation of his equity in the car, Potomac did not get, as it thought it was getting, security for both old and new debts with a margin of more than two to one. But, as has been shown, Potomac did get more than triple security for the goods which the indictment said were fraudulently obtained. It was therefore of first importance that the jury be told to disregard Potomac's failure to get the security for the pre-existing debt which it had been led to believe it was getting, and to consider only whether Potomac had been defrauded out of goods worth $349.50. The jury should also have been told the reason for the distinction, for without it the lay jurors might have concluded — as apparently they did — that on September 18 Nelson defrauded Potomac with respect to the pre-existing indebtedness.

As I have said, Nelson was guilty of a moral wrong in falsely and grossly misrepresenting his debt to the bank, but in the circumstances he should not have been indicted and convicted because of it. The District of Columbia statute under which he was prosecuted does not make mere falsehood felonious; it only denounces as criminal a false pretense which was intended to defraud and which in fact had that result. Even a liar is entitled to the full protection of the law. I am afraid a grave injustice has been done in this case.

NOTES FROM MARY:

1. I'm not sure how *Nelson* bears on our case, but I have a feeling that it might. Didn't Bird get everything he wanted for his $10,000, as he did get his import quota?

2. In *Darwish v. State*, 937 So.2d 789 (Fla. 2006), after Hurricane Charley devastated Charlotte County, Florida, relief officials at a fire station distributed cases of bottled water free to people in need. Darwish owned a local convenience store. He went to the fire station, where fireman Burrell gave him several cases of bottled water. Darwish said to the fireman, "It's not like I'm going to go and sell out of my store, ha, ha, ha." Darwish then took the cases to the store and sold the bottles to customers. His conviction for obtaining property by false pretenses was reversed:

> The water was distributed for free. The bottles were not marked to indicate that they were not intended for resale. Persons requesting relief supplies were not asked to sign an application form or to identify themselves to receive water. Although recipients of quantities of water greater than two cases were sometimes asked to explain their intended use of the water, Mr. Burrell did not direct any such inquiry to Mr. Darwish. Thus Mr. Darwish was not required to state his plans for the use of the water before he received it.

> In addition, the testimony about the timing of Mr. Darwish's comment was vague. Mr. Burrell was not specific about when Mr. Darwish made the comment in relation to the receipt of the water. We do not know if Mr. Darwish made the comment before he received the water, while it was being loaded into his van, or just before he drove away with the cases of water already loaded. Most important, Mr. Burrell did not testify that Mr. Darwish obtained the water by representing to Mr. Burrell that he would not resell it. Mr. Burrell never said that he would have refused to give Mr. Darwish the water - or more than a normal distribution of two cases - absent the comment.

> Based on these facts, the State did not prove that Mr. Burrell was induced to part with the water in reliance on Mr. Darwish's comment. Thus the State failed to prove an essential element of the offense of cheating by false pretenses.

> We do not condone the conduct of Mr. Darwish that is at issue in this case. Nevertheless, the State failed to carry its burden of proving that he was guilty of cheating by false pretenses.

LOCKS v. UNITED STATES
District of Columbia Court of Appeals
388 A.2d 873 (1978)

FERREN, ASSOCIATE JUDGE:

On June 7, 1976, appellants Anthony and Carl Locks were each indicted on five counts of grand larceny (D.C.Code 1973, § 22-2201) and five counts of uttering a check with intent to defraud (D.C.Code 1973, § 22-1410). The jury found Anthony Locks guilty on three counts of each offense charged and convicted his brother, Carl Locks, on two counts of each charge. The trial court sentenced Anthony Locks to concurrent prison terms of three to nine years on each count of grand larceny and to consecutive terms of one to three years on each count of uttering. Carl Locks was sentenced to concurrent prison terms of two to six years for each grand larceny count and to consecutive terms of one to three years on each uttering count. As to both appellants, the sentences for grand larceny and uttering were to run concurrently.

Appellants maintain that the trial court should have granted their motions for judgment of acquittal as to grand larceny. They claim, more specifically, that the government's factual allegations - while perhaps warranting indictments charging false pretenses - did not permit indictments for the more severely punishable offense, grand larceny, given the elements of that particular crime. We agree with appellants and accordingly must reverse their grand larceny convictions.

The indictment alleges that appellants carried out an elaborate scheme to steal goods from various retail stores. Anthony or Carl Locks, using an alias, would get acquainted with a young woman, develop an intimate relationship to gain her confidence, and eventually reveal a tantalizing plan guaranteed to win at a local numbers game because of access to inside information. He would then take her to a local retail store, select an expensive consumer product (such as a television or stereo set), and induce her to pay for it with her own, worthless check. He would promise, however, to cover the check, as well as provide her with substantial profit, out of immediate winnings to be generated by numbers tickets acquired with the products from the store (after conversion to cash proceeds).

Appellants contend, basically, that because the various store owners intended unconditionally to sell (i.e., part with title to) the various goods acquired with the personal checks of Ms. Green and Ms. Douglas, appellants' scheme could subject them, at the worst, to indictment under the false pretenses statute, with a three-year limitation on imprisonment.[1] Indictment for grand larceny, they argue, with

---

[1] D.C.Code 1973, § 22-1301: False pretenses. "Whoever, by any false pretense, with intent to defraud, obtains from any person any service or anything of value * * * shall, if the value of the property or the sum or value of the money, property, or service so obtained, procured, sold, bartered, or disposed of is $100 or upward, be imprisoned not less than one year nor more than three years; or, if less than that sum, shall be fined not more than $1,000 or imprisoned for not more than one year, or both."

The crime of false pretenses accordingly has five elements: false representation; knowledge of falsity; intent to defraud; reliance by the defrauded party; and obtaining something of value through a false representation.

its heavier penalty (up to ten years), is available only when one feloniously takes away property which, at the time of the taking, remains the property of the victim - which is not the case here.[2]

In *Great American Indemnity Co. v. Yoder*, D.C.Mun.App., 131 A.2d 401 (1957), we noted this distinction:

> The common-law distinction is acknowledged in this jurisdiction that where one gives up possession of a chattel to another who converts it to his own use, the wrongdoer is held to have committed a trespass and the taking is by larceny. However, where one, although induced by fraud or trick, actually intends that title shall pass to the wrongdoer, the crime is that of false pretenses.

According to its brief, the government has "no quarrel" with this line of cases, involving "a lone individual who made a false representation and who was erroneously convicted for larceny"; but it argues that the present case is distinguishable because of "the use of third persons as agents to commit the larcenies upon the stores . . . . The Locks brothers were principals who stole merchandise through a scheme employing others for the initial acquisition of goods." It follows, according to the government, that "appellants' entire argument as to passing of title really begs the more fundamental question of whether they can be held accountable for the natural results of their scheme. Without question, they were thieves; their clear intent was to steal."

The intent to steal, of course, does not distinguish larceny from false pretenses; the fact that appellants feloniously obtained property does not in itself provide a basis for holding that they can be indicted under any statute whatsoever involving misappropriation, without regard to the particular elements of crime specified by statute and supporting case law. Furthermore, in stressing appellants' use of agents, the government offers no cogent reason why appellants, as principals, should be convicted of larceny for the false pretense actions of their agents. There is no support in the D.C. Code, case law, or logic for the proposition that felonious principals, such as appellants, may be subject to greater criminal liability than their agents for the false pretense crimes they jointly commit. Whether the individual who passes a bad check is acting alone or as an agent, the crime for which any participant, principal or agent, will be chargeable is premised on inducement of the seller to transfer title - the classic indicator of false pretenses.

The government cites two cases, however, in urging us to conclude that an overriding criminal intent, coupled with a theft facilitated by a false pretense, can be sufficient to bring an accused within the grand larceny statute - the pretense being, as the government puts it, merely a "first step in the overall crime." In *Fowler v. United States*, D.C.App., 374 A.2d 856 (1977), we affirmed the defendant's

---

[Ed.: § 22-1301 was repealed in 1982, when § 22-3811 was enacted.]

[2] D.C.Code 1973, § 22-2201: Grand larceny. "Whoever shall feloniously take and carry away anything of value of the amount or value of $100 or upward, including things savoring of the realty, shall suffer imprisonment for not less than one nor more than ten years. The crime of larceny presupposes the intent to appropriate the property to a use inconsistent with the owner's rights."

[Ed.: § 22-2201 was repealed in 1982, when § 22-3811 was enacted.]

convictions for grand larceny and false pretenses. He had utilized a "flimflam" scheme to obtain money from women for an alleged business venture in which he told them they would receive an interest. Similarly, in *Skantze v. United States*, 288 F.2d 416, the defendant, a cashier at the Swedish Embassy, was convicted of both grand larceny and false pretenses. He had presented checks on the Embassy account, payable to cash, to one of his superiors for signature, saying that the Embassy's petty-cash fund needed replenishing. He then pocketed the money and, to cover the thefts, made false entries on Embassy records showing payments to various firms.

It is important to note that in *Skantze* the Embassy official who signed the check did not intend to give the defendant/employee a personal claim to the money; he intended to entrust the money to the employee for use of the Embassy. Similarly, under the scheme in *Fowler*, the victims explicitly were told that their funds would be converted into a business interest; the defendant essentially took the money as a fiduciary. *Skantz* and *Fowler*, therefore, fit within a subspecies of larceny cases - called "larceny by trick" — in which the victim, while fraudulently induced to surrender money or other property, does so for a "special purpose," such that restricted possession rather than title is delivered to the wrongdoer.

In classic terminology, "the distinction drawn by the common law is between the case of one who gives up possession of a chattel or money for a special purpose to another who by converting it to his own use is held to have committed a trespass, and the case of one who, although induced by fraud or trick, nevertheless actually intends that title to the chattel shall pass to the wrongdoer." *Graham v. United States*, 187 F.2d 87 (1950).[5]

In the present case, the first count of the indictment does state that after appellants had "caused the women to write bad checks the defendants would not give the women the money promised." However, the thrust of the indictment — the articulation of the crimes — is directed solely at thefts from retailers; no count can be characterized as a charge of theft from the women who took title (and were financially responsible for the checks appellants caused them to bounce). This case, therefore, is fundamentally distinguishable from *Fowler*, *supra*, where the women conned by the accused were also the victims of the larceny. Here, in contrast, the women were participants in criminal frauds against third parties; their own losses, if any, were not a subject of Anthony and Carl Locks' indictment.

Were we to uphold the grand-larceny convictions in the present case, we would eliminate altogether a fundamental distinction between grand larceny and false pretenses. We would have to be saying either (1) that in any unconditional sale of merchandise in exchange for a check, the seller shall be deemed to retain a proprietary interest for criminal-law purposes,[6] or (2) that the traditional distinc-

---

[5] There is still another subspecies of larceny represented by cases in which banks have mistakenly credited too much money to the account of a depositor, who thereupon has converted it. In *United States v. Posner*, 408 F.Supp. 1145, 1151 (D.Md.1976), the court noted that the rationale justifying a larceny conviction, despite the bank's apparent transfer of title to the money, "seems to be that the owner has no intent to consent to the transfer of title where he is under a mistake, and therefore, retains constructive possession of the goods and title does not pass."

[6] In accordance with the Uniform Commercial Code, appellants' agents acquired title at the time they

tion between larceny and false pretenses, turning on the passage of title, is not meaningful and accordingly is abandoned. We conclude that as a practical matter in today's commercial world, our acceptance of the first alternative would be tantamount to adopting the second. As a result, every acquisition of property by means of deceit would be punishable as grand or petit larceny (D.C.Code 1973, §§ 22-2201 and 2202), without regard to whether the owner had intended to part with title, and the crime of false pretenses (D.C.Code 1973, § 22-1301) - unless newly defined as a lesser included offense - would become an additional means of punishing the act of deceit itself.

We do not believe we can go that far, given not only the traditional distinction between larceny and false pretenses embedded in our case law — and acknowledged by the government - but also because the Congress has imposed a lesser maximum penalty for false pretenses.[8] We do not believe that we should judicially reform the penalty for false pretense thefts by expanding the scope of grand larceny, despite the manifest illogic of a lesser-than-grand-larceny penalty for the present case.[9] The "nice hairline distinctions" we have been making here point up the wisdom of legislative reconsideration of the crimes against property — how defined and how punished.

The convictions for uttering a check with intent to defraud are affirmed; the convictions for grand larceny are reversed.

NOTES FROM MARY:

(1) Doesn't *Locks* get Mann off the hook on the first count? It looks great. Tell me if you see any problem with this.

(2) In *People v. Lorenzo*, 64 Cal.App.3d Supp. 43, 135 Cal.Rptr. 337 (1976), the manager of Von's market saw Lorenzo switch price tags on some gloves, take the higher-priced gloves (with the lower price tag now on them) to the check-out counter, pay the lower price for them, and take them to the parking lot, where the manager arrested him. Lorenzo was convicted of theft by false pretenses. The appellate court modified the conviction:

---

took delivery of the goods, D.C.Code 1973, § 28:2-401(2), and could transfer the title to good faith purchasers even though voidable by the original sellers because of the bad checks. D.C.Code 1973, § 28:2-403(1).

[8] Indictments based on false pretenses, rather than on larceny by trick, would have reduced the maximum potential sentence for each count from ten to three years, compare D.C.Code 1973, § 22-2201, with D.C.Code 1973, § 22-1301 (quoted at notes 2 and 3, supra), and also would have turned the uttering counts into lesser included offenses.

[9] It has been said that the "artificial and illogical" significance of whether title has - or has not - passed to the wrongdoer in determining whether a crime is larcenous may have been "evolved by judges in a humane search for legal methods for saving defendants from the consequences following conviction upon a charge of larceny, which at the time many of the cases were decided was a capital offense." *United States v. Patton*, 120 F.2d 73, 76 (3d Cir. 1941). In addition, our court once noted that a defrauded party had "had every opportunity in the course of this [used automobile] transaction to demand cash or payment by certified check," *Great American Indemnity Co. v. Yoder*, *supra* at 403, suggesting that the victim of a fraud at least has some degree of control over his or her fate that the victim of a larceny does not. If that rationale were used to justify a lesser penalty for false pretenses than for larceny, however, one might be hard pressed to reconcile that judgment with the higher penalty for larceny by trick.

It is apparent to us that the crime of theft by false pretenses was not committed here. The victim of the crime was alleged to be Von's market. The manager of the market at all times was aware that defendant had switched the price labels and merely allowed defendant apparently to consummate his scheme in order to be able to arrest him in the parking lot. The manager at no time relied upon defendant's conduct. Since the manager is the agent of the victim-market owner and his knowledge is that of the victim, we cannot hold on these facts that theft by false pretenses was established.

The People argue, nevertheless, that another species of theft, larceny by trick, was established. Aside from the fact that the jury was never instructed on this theory, a considerable obstacle in the way of our adopting it, that crime is not established either for the same reason — lack of reliance. While our attention has not been called to any cases dealing with the element of reliance in the case of theft committed in the guise of larceny by trick, it is apparent that reliance is as much an element of this kind of theft as it is in the case of theft committed by the use of false pretenses. The only difference between larceny by trick and false pretenses is that in the latter both title and possession to the property in question is acquired by fraudulent means, whereas larceny by trick consists of the fraudulent acquisition of possession only and not title. It is basic law that reliance on a false representation is an element of fraud; since fraudulent means are required in order for larceny by trick to be committed, a lack of such reliance must be equally fatal to the commission of that offense.

We are of the view, however, that the evidence amply establishes defendant's attempt to commit theft. Reliance is not an element of that offense. The successful consummation of the offense was prevented only by the manager's alertness. But for the manager's observations defendant would have carried the actual theft to its completion. Accordingly, we hold that the verdict and judgment must be modified to show that defendant is guilty of attempted theft only and not theft.

Compare *Lorenzo* with *State v. Hauck*, 190 Neb. 534, 209 N.W.2d 580 (1973), where clerks at a sporting goods store saw Hauck switch price tags on two rifle scopes and bring the more expensive rifle scope to the cash register and offer to pay the lower price for it. At that point, he was arrested. He was convicted of larceny, but the Nebraska Supreme Court reversed:

The necessary elements of larceny which are critical here require that the property must be taken and carried away with the intent to steal it and it must be without the consent of the owner.

The determination of what constitutes a taking and carrying away of property with the intent to permanently deprive the owner of possession and whether that taking is with or without the consent of the owner involves issues of intent which are often difficult of determination. Where merchandise in a store is involved, those issues are vitally affected if the store is operated on a self service basis. The cases appear to be in agreement that in a self service store, where customers select and pick up articles to be paid for at the checkout counter, the mere picking up of an article in the display area does not constitute asportation.

Under the self service method of store operation, the owner of the property authorizes a conditional temporary possession by customers between the display area and the checkout counter, at least where the possession is not clearly adverse to that of the store. The cases indicate that concealing the goods in a fashion sufficient to place them under the complete and exclusive control of the defendant may be sufficient asportation to constitute larceny, no matter what part of the store it occurs in. See *Groomes v. United States*, 155 A.2d 73 (D.C.Mun.App., 1959). In any event, carrying of concealed articles past the checkout stand of a self service store constitutes a sufficient asportation to support a conviction for larceny.

In the absence of concealment we have found no case, nor have we been cited to any, which holds that openly carrying an article to the checkout counter of a self service store is sufficient to support a conviction for larceny, whether the price tag has been altered or not.

Under the facts stipulated here, the defendant not only carried the carton with the rifle scope to the checkout counter, but he offered to pay for it as well. It is quite obvious that he intended to purchase the scope but to pay only the lesser price shown on the changed price tag and by the misrepresentation to defraud the owner of a part of its value. Nevertheless, that is not larceny. The defendant was charged with stealing a single rifle scope. On the stipulated facts it cannot be said that taking one rifle scope from the shelf and carrying it to the cashier's stand and offering to pay for it was partly lawful and partly criminal, nor that he intended to purchase part of a rifle scope and steal part of a rifle scope. Such distinctions are wholly illogical and will not support a conviction of the crime of larceny. Evidence that the defendant changed the price tag on a carton containing a rifle scope on a display shelf in a self service store, and openly and without any attempt to conceal or hide the carton, picked it up and carried it to the checkout counter and offered to pay for it, is insufficient to establish the essential elements of larceny necessary to sustain a conviction for stealing the rifle scope.

The defendant clearly intended to defraud the store by changing the price tag and by that act or device, persuade the owner to transfer both the title and possession of the property to him for less than its value. If the defendant had been successful in carrying out and completing the transaction as intended, he would have been guilty of obtaining property by false pretenses in violation of § 28-207, R.R.S.1943.

The statutes dealing with the two crimes of larceny, and obtaining property under false pretenses, belong to the same family of crimes, but in the ordinary case are readily distinguishable. The basic distinction between larceny and obtaining money or property under false pretenses lies in the fact that in the latter crime, the false pretenses result in securing the consent of the owner to part with the title as well as the possession of the property. In the case of larceny the defendant does not obtain any title or property interest but only possession. While such distinctions may well rest in the subjective intent of the victim, this is generally a sound and reliable test.

It is quite clear that had the defendant been successful in his attempt to defraud the store and purchase the rifle scope for a fraction of its true value, he would have obtained title as well as possession and would have been guilty of obtaining property under false pretenses. We have held, however, that an essential element of obtaining property under false pretenses is that there be reliance upon the representations made. The pretense must be an effective cause in inducing the owner to part with his property, and if the owner has knowledge of the truth, the offense has not been committed. In the case before us the store was aware of the truth, did not rely on the misrepresentations created by defendant by the false price tag, and did not part with its property. The crime of obtaining property under false pretenses was not completed, even if it had been charged.

In this state there is no statutory crime of attempted larceny nor of attempting to obtain property under false pretenses. Neither is there a general criminal attempt statute such as that contained in § 5.01(1)(a), Tentative Draft No. 10 of the Model Penal Code. Neither the changing or alteration of price tags, nor an attempt to obtain property by false pretenses, nor an attempt to commit larceny is a crime under any legislative enactment of the State of Nebraska or the City of Scottsbluff.

JUSTICE SPENCER dissented:

I understand "larceny" to include obtaining another's property by trick or artifice with the intent to convert it. That is what is involved in this case.

Defendant admittedly exchanged price tag stickers with the intent to obtain the more expensive rifle scope at the lower price. He then took possession of the item and carried it to the checkout counter. He was apprehended when he attempted to pay the lower price.

This court said in *McIntosh v. State* (1920), 105 Neb. 328, 180 N.W. 573: "One of the elements of larceny is asportation. It is not necessary, however that the property stolen be retained in the possession of the thief. To remove it with the requisite felonious intent from one part of the premises to another, or from the spot where it is found is a sufficient asportation."

Questions:

1. Can you reconcile *Lorenzo* with *Hauck*?

2. Can you reconcile *Lorenzo* and *Hauck* with *People v. Olivo* (in Chapter 1)?

(3) In *State v. Hogrefe*, 557 N.W.2d 871 (Iowa 1996), the court stated:

When there is an understanding between the parties that a check is not cashable [no money in the account to cover the check] at the time it is received, but will be made so at some time in the future, the representations made are only promises, there is no deception and, thus, no criminal liability results under § 714.1(6) [theft by check]. If, however, the surrounding circumstances at the time a check is given, including the statements made, are representations that sufficient funds exist at the time to cover the check, then criminal liability may result even though a check is postdated. Our focus remains on the representations made at the time a check is delivered.

Under our approach, a postdate is only evidence that a check was intended as a promise of future payment and does not alone relieve a defendant of criminal responsibility. It must also be established that both parties understood that a check was not cashable when delivered before criminal liability is precluded as a matter of law. Where both parties do not understand that a postdated check is not cashable until a future date, the question of guilt should be submitted to the fact finder. It is then up to the fact finder to determine whether the maker deceived the party receiving the check by presenting a check that the maker knew, at the time of delivery, would not be paid when presented to the bank it was drawn upon.

Chapter 5

ROBBERY

Robbery consists of all six elements of larceny — a (1) trespassory (2) taking and (3) carrying away of the (4) personal property (5) of another (6) with intent to steal it - plus two additional requirements: (7) that the property be taken from the person or presence of the other and (8) that the taking be accomplished by means of force or putting in fear.

LaFave & Scott, *Criminal Law* (West)

Does the above definition of robbery look familiar? It should. You've already seen most of it — when you studied larceny, in Chapter 2. So robbery appears to be "larceny plus" some additional elements which involve threatened or actual harm to the person of the victim. As such, it is more harmful than larceny, and should call for a punishment greater than that for larceny. And that is exactly what the law calls for. But how clear a threat and how much harm should be present before we impose this higher punishment?

If robbery is "larceny plus," then it would seem to follow logically that any defense that defeats a larceny charge will also defeat a robbery charge. But should such "logic" dictate how we treat people who use improper threats or force to obtain property?

This Chapter will address these questions.

PROBLEM 5

To: My Law Clerk

From: Gordon Getum, Deputy District Attorney

Re: *Commonwealth v. Turpin*

Dick Turpin was arrested for robbery last week, although we haven't filed formal charges against him yet. This guy is a bad actor, and we've wanted him off the streets for a long time, but we haven't been able to nail him yet. I'd like to put him away for as long as possible.

Attached is a transcript of an interview Philadelphia Police Detective Fred Friday conducted with Willie Woods, who will be our key witness in the case. Also attached is our state robbery statute (note that it provides for several degrees of robbery, with differing penalties), and some other authorities. Turpin has a smart lawyer, who will try to distinguish these cases if he can. Please advise me how to make the most of these materials and rebut any arguments Turpin's lawyer can come up with.

Transcript of Interview with Willie Woods

FF: What happened last night?

WW: My friend Mike Moss and I were sitting at a table in Joe's Bar, drinking and talking. I noticed that Mike had a nice new watch on, and he said that Turpin had loaned it to him. A little while later, Turpin came in and sat down with us. He asked Mike for his watch back, but Mike said he wanted to keep it for a few more days. We kept drinking and talking, and pretty soon Mike got sort of drunk and spaced out.

FF: What do you mean, spaced out?

WW: Well, he was awake, but he stopped talking with us and just stared straight ahead. Turpin banged his fist on the table and said to me, "If he doesn't give me that watch, I'll make him wish he had." Mike kind of jumped a bit when Turpin hit the table, but he didn't say anything.

FF: Then what?

WW: Turpin and I talked for another 20 minutes or so. Mike was still spaced out, and his hands were on the table. Turpin reached over, lifted Mike's left hand a little, and slipped off the watch. I said, "Hey. Leave him alone." Turpin shook his fist at me and said, "You stay out of this." Turpin got up and walked toward the door. Mike called out to him, "Hey, I'm still using that." But Turpin kept walking and left. Mike put his head down on the table for a few minutes, and then got up and walked out. Turpin was sitting in his car, which was parked in front of the bar. Turpin was talking to some ladies. Mike went over to him and said, "Give me my watch." Turpin pushed Mike, who fell down on the sidewalk. Turpin then drove off.

Pennsylvania Statutes, Title 18

§ 3701. Robbery

(a) Offense defined. —

> (1) A person is guilty of robbery if, in the course of committing a theft, he: (i) inflicts serious bodily injury upon another; (ii) threatens another with or intentionally puts him in fear of immediate serious bodily injury; (iii) commits or threatens immediately to commit any felony of the first or second degree; (iv) inflicts bodily injury upon another or threatens another with or intentionally puts him in fear of immediate bodily injury; or (v) physically takes or removes property from the person of another by force however slight.

> (2) An act shall be deemed "in the course of committing a theft" if it occurs in an attempt to commit theft or in flight after the attempt or commission.

(b) Grading. — Robbery under subsection (a)(1)(iv) is a felony of the second degree; robbery under subsection (a)(1)(v) is a felony of the third degree; otherwise, it is a felony of the first degree.

Note: Compare Model Penal Code § 222.1, in the Appendix.

COMMONWEALTH v. ENGLISH
Supreme Court of Pennsylvania
446 Pa. 161; 279 A.2d 4 (1971)

Before BELL, EAGEN, O'BRIEN, ROBERTS, POMEROY, JONES & BARBIERI, JJ.

Opinion by MR. CHIEF JUSTICE BELL

On January 8, 1968, William English, defendant, appellee, was tried for murder of Roosevelt English (no relation to defendant), which took place on May 31, 1967. After four days of trial, the jury found the defendant guilty of voluntary manslaughter. On May 6, 1969, defendant's motion for a new trial was granted, and the Commonwealth has taken the present appeal.

From the evidence produced at trial, it is apparent that as the defendant and the deceased (hereafter referred to as Roosevelt) emerged from a tavern, they were arguing about a $10 debt which Roosevelt owed the defendant. The defendant hit Roosevelt in the face with his fist and knocked him down with such force that he struck his head on the pavement. While Roosevelt was unconscious, defendant went through his pockets and removed Roosevelt's wallet, which was empty. Eight days after being struck by defendant, Roosevelt died. The cause of death was cranial-cerebral injuries resulting from Roosevelt being punched, knocked down and striking his head on the pavement.

Throughout the trial, the Commonwealth maintained that the death occurred during the commission of a felony, i.e., attempted robbery, and therefore the killing was a felony murder and consequently murder in the first degree. Defendant contended and attempted to establish that there was no robbery, because he was merely making an effort to collect the $10 which Roosevelt owed him.

Defendant requested the trial judge to charge the jury that, in order to find a felony murder the jury must first find that the defendant intended to rob Roosevelt and that the homicide occurred while defendant was perpetrating a robbery. At various places throughout the charge, the trial Judge did instruct the jury in accord with defendant's requested point for charge, but the Court went on to say: "Even if the defendant believed that the decedent owed him money, if he tried to take the money by force or violence, it would still be robbery." Although defendant took no specific exception to this portion of the charge, and indeed no general exception to the charge, it effectively negated defendant's only defense, and if incorrect it would constitute basic and fundamental error. It is this portion of the charge which the trial Judge considered to be error, and this was his sole reason for granting defendant's motion for a new trial.

The law is well settled that the grant or denial of a motion for a new trial will not be reversed by this Court, unless the lower Court's Order was a clear abuse of discretion or an error of law which controlled the grant or denial of the new trial.

In these days when crime is rampant and disobedience and defiance of Law and

Order are so widespread, it would be folly to permit a person who has an adequate remedy at law to take the law into his own hands and attempt to recover his property or his property claims by force or violence or by any other violation of the law. No matter how worthy a defendant's or any person's objective may be, Law and Order must be preserved. To allow a creditor to resort to violence or force to recover a debt would be an unwarranted procrustean stretch of a creditor's legal rights.

We expressly hold that a "claim of right" does not entitle a creditor to resort to violence or to justify a forcible robbery of his debtor in order to collect his debts, nor can it create a defense to a felony, such as robbery, or to murder or manslaughter.

It is clear that the grant of a new trial was based upon an error of law, and it therefore must be reversed.

Concurring Opinion by MR. JUSTICE EAGEN:

Robbery is a larceny from the person or presence of another by means of violence or threat of violence. *Commonwealth v. Simpson*, 436 Pa. 459 (1970). One of the elements of larceny is a felonious intent to steal, i.e., the *animus furandi*. It is not larceny where one takes property from another under a claim of right. *Commonwealth v. White*, 133 Pa. 182; 3 Wharton's Criminal Law, § 1097.

Hence, the charge of the trial court was erroneous in part in the instant case. However, since there was more than ample evidence to establish that the accused Committed an unlawful killing and was therefore guilty of voluntary manslaughter, the error, in my view, was harmless.

I concur in the result.

MR. JUSTICE JONES, MR. JUSTICE O'BRIEN and MR. JUSTICE POMEROY join in concurring opinion.

Concurring Opinion by MR. JUSTICE ROBERTS:

I concur in the result because neither a specific nor even a general exception was taken to the charge of the trial court. * * * *

NOTES FROM GORDON:

(1) What is the rule of this case? Which opinion is the *Supreme Court's* opinion?

(2) Chief Justice Bell says that "claim-of-right" should not justify a *creditor's* resort to violence to collect a *debt*. I'm afraid that Turpin's lawyer might use this to try to distinguish Bell's opinion. How can we deal with such an argument?

COMMONWEALTH v. SLEIGHTER
Supreme Court of Pennsylvania
495 Pa. 262, 433 A.2d 469 (1981)

Before Justices O'Brien, Roberts, Nix, Larsen, Flaherty, Kaufman, &
Wilkinson. Justice Roberts filed a concurring opinion in which Justices O'Brien,
Nix and Wilkinson join.

Mr. Justice Flaherty

In the early morning hours of September 19, 1978, William Paul Walters met his
death as a result of a severe beating inflicted upon him in the lobby of the Madden
Hotel in Chambersburg and in the alley adjacent to the hotel. Appellant herein and
co-defendant, James Harmon, were charged as a result of this incident. Harmon
was convicted in a non-jury trial of murder of the second degree and robbery.
Appellant entered a plea of guilty to the charge of murder generally in exchange
for the Commonwealth's agreement to *nolle pross* all other charges against him. A
degree of guilt hearing was held on March 5, 1979. On March 7, 1979 the lower
court found that the degree of appellant's guilt rose to second degree, and on that
date sentenced the appellant to life imprisonment. This is a direct appeal from the
lower court's judgment of sentence.

Viewing the evidence in a light most favorable to the Commonwealth, the
following facts evinced at the degree of guilt hearing.

Appellant and Harmon were in the lobby of the Madden Hotel along with the
victim, Mr. Walters. Earlier in the evening, there had been some discussion
concerning a gambling debt Mr. Walters allegedly owed appellant. Appellant
became upset with Walters, at which time he hit him and demanded that Walters
surrender his rings to appellant. Upon Walters' refusal to do so, Harmon and
appellant began to kick and hit Walters. After appellant threw Walters to the floor,
he took Walters' rings. About this time, Harmon was going through the victim's
pants pockets, from which he removed change and a wallet containing $25.00 or
$30.00 in cash. The wallet was handed to appellant by Harmon. Harmon also
removed the victim's watch, put it in his pocket and later gave it to appellant, who
attempted to hide it in a police cruiser.

It was apparently at this time that Mr. Harold Keith entered the lobby of the
Madden to observe the appellant standing over the victim, whose face had been
bloodied by this time. Mr. Walters left the lobby of the Madden and proceeded
down the alley adjacent to the Madden. Appellant and Harmon followed the victim
into the alley whereupon they proceeded to hit and kick him until he was
unconscious. After the victim lost consciousness, appellant and Harmon dragged
him to the rear of the hotel, placed him in an automobile and locked the doors. The
autopsy reported revealed that the victim died as a result of the blows inflicted by
Harmon and appellant.

At the degree of guilt hearing, the Commonwealth proceeded on the theory that
appellant was guilty of murder of the second degree due to the application of the
felony murder doctrine, because Walters was the victim of robbery and the death

occurred while appellant was engaged as a principal or accomplice in the commission of that robbery. Appellant argues that he cannot be found guilty of murder of the second degree because there was no robbery due to the fact that no theft was committed. Likewise, he argues that accomplice liability cannot be based on the actions of Harmon because Harmon did not commit theft.

Appellant relies on the fact that the decedent owed him $30.00 as a gambling debt, and that appellant took the rings from the victim under a "claim of right" as payment for that debt. There is no factual ground set forth by which it could be said that Harmon did not commit theft. Only the bare assertion is made.

Appellant cites *Commonwealth v. English*, 446 Pa. 161 (1971) in support of this argument. The facts in *English* are substantially the same as those of the instant case. There occurred a beating, resulting in the eventual death of the victim, in the collection of an alleged gambling debt. The jury found the defendant guilty of voluntary manslaughter, not murder of the second degree. In any event, the court's charge regarding robbery as the underlying felony was challenged on appeal.

In a concurring opinion joined by three members of the court, Mr. Justice Eagen, reasoning that the mental element of larceny has been negated where one takes property from another under a "claim of right," concluded that the trial court erred in instructing the jury that "even if the defendant believed that the decedent owed him money, if he tried to take the money by force or violence, it would still be robbery." This four man majority concluded that while the instruction was in error, it was harmless because the defendant was not convicted of murder of the second degree but of voluntary manslaughter. It is upon this concurring majority opinion that appellant herein relies, asserting that he took the property from the victim under a claim of right and therefore, there was no underlying felony.

We disagree. Thus, we reject and overrule the instantly discussed concurring opinion of *Commonwealth v. English*, which broadly and confusingly serves to exonerate a criminal defendant of liability under an easily asserted claim of right.

However, the opinion of *English* authored by Mr. Chief Justice Bell and joined by one member of the court reaches an opposite and meritorious conclusion. We adopt the view stated therein.

Mr. Chief Justice Bell concluded that "a 'claim of right' does not entitle a creditor to resort to violence or to justify a forcible robbery of his debtor in order to collect his debts, nor can it create a defense to a felony, such as robbery, or to murder or manslaughter."

While there exists case law which provides that under certain isolated circumstances a good faith claim of right will negate the requisite mental element for theft, certainly where there is violence or threat of violence in the assertion of that claim of right, the law does not excuse the actor who so asserts his claim. Only a peaceful taking under a good faith claim of right, where there is no breach of the peace, can even begin to approach the threshold of excusable conduct. And even then, the party asserting the claim of right has the burden of proving that there existed at the time of the taking a bona fide and reasonable claim of right.

Additionally, a gambling debt is an illegal obligation in the eyes of the law. For the law to approve the collection of an illegal obligation would serve only to encourage the use of violence in the collection of such debts, the collector safe in the knowledge that there is only the sanction of a prosecution for assault, as opposed to robbery. Accordingly, we adopt the quoted language of Mr. Chief Justice Bell in *Commonwealth v. English*. To the extent that that case is inconsistent with the result reached today, it is overruled.

Affirmed.

ROBERTS, J., concurring:

Although I agree with the opinion of Mr. Justice Flaherty that judgment of sentence must be affirmed, I cannot join that opinion, for the facts of this case simply do not warrant a reexamination and overruling of this Court's holding in *Commonwealth v. English*. It is not and had never been this Court's practice to render advisory opinions. Our function is to decide cases upon facts of record, not to pose and decide hypothetical issues in order to change a previous holding which some members of the Court may now consider unwise.

In denying appellant's motions in arrest of judgment, the trial court expressly stated that it did not find credible appellant's testimony that the decedent owed him a debt. Moreover, the court went on to observe that, even if the decedent had owed appellant a sum of money, appellant had no arguable claim of right to the rings which the decedent was wearing. Thus, under either of the views expressed in *Commonwealth v. English, supra*, appellant was guilty of robbery in taking by force that to which he had no claim of right. Manifestly, consideration of when and whether the existence of a bona fide claim of right may serve as a defense to a charge of robbery should await a case in which the defendant does, in fact, have such a claim. I therefore concur only in the result.

MR. CHIEF JUSTICE O'BRIEN, MR. JUSTICE NIX AND MR. JUSTICE WILKINSON join this concurring opinion.

NOTES FROM GORDON:

(1) I suppose I have the same question about *Sleighter* that I had about *English*: which opinion is the *Court's* opinion?

(2) In *State v. McMillen*, 925 P.2d 1088 (Hawaii Supreme Court, 1996), the court held:

> While most jurisdictions apparently still follow the common law rule that a forcible taking of property is not robbery where the taker has a good faith belief that she is the owner, the modern trend is in the other direction. "The proposition that a claim of right negates the felonious intent in robbery 'not only is lacking in sound reason and logic, but it is utterly incompatible with and has no place in an ordered and orderly society such as ours, which eschews self-help through violence.' " *People v. Hodges*, 496 N.Y.S.2d 771, 773-74 (1985) (quoting *State v. Ortiz*, 124 N.J.Super. 189 (App.Div.1973)). Given that the legislature has enacted specific statutes defining separate

defenses depending on whether or not force was used, we hold that the
§ 708-834 claim of right defense to theft does not apply in a prosecution for
robbery.

(3) *People v. Butler*, 65 Cal.2d 569 (1967), involved the following facts:

Defendant was accused of felony murder based on the underlying crime
of robbery. At trial, the defendant testified he had been employed by the
victim, who had not paid him for some work. The defendant, armed with a
gun, went to the victim's home one evening to collect payment. Although the
victim had at one point agreed to pay the defendant, he subsequently
changed his mind and approached the defendant with a pistol. During the
ensuing scuffle, the defendant shot and killed the victim, and also shot
another person present in the victim's home. After quickly searching the
home for money and finding none, the defendant grabbed a wallet and ran
from the house. In recounting the events, the defendant claimed he did not
intend to commit robbery when he went to the house, but intended only to
recover the money he was owed. Over the defendant's objection, the
prosecutor was permitted to argue to the jury that a robbery had been
committed even if the defendant honestly believed the victim owed him
money. The jury convicted the defendant of first degree felony murder and
fixed the penalty at death.

The California Supreme Court reversed:

Although an intent to steal may ordinarily be inferred when one person
takes the property of another, particularly if he takes it by force, proof of
the existence of a state of mind incompatible with an intent to steal
precludes a finding of either theft or robbery. It has long been the rule in
this state and generally throughout the country that a bona fide belief, even
though mistakenly held, that one has a right or claim to the property
negates felonious intent. A belief that the property taken belongs to the
taker, or that he had a right to retake goods sold is sufficient to preclude
felonious intent. Felonious intent exists only if the actor intends to take the
property of another without believing in good faith that he has a right or
claim to it.

However, in *People v. Tufunga*, 21 Cal.4th 935 (1999), the court held that the
Butler holding went too far. Claim-of-right is a proper defense to robbery only when
the defendant seeks to recover the specific property he gave the victim, and not
where he seeks to collect a debt. The court note that cases from other jurisdictions
(including *Commonwealth v. Sleighter*) "have rejected *Butler's* expansive holding
that a good faith belief by a defendant that he was entitled to the money or
possessions of the victim to satisfy or collect on a debt is a defense to robbery." The
court quoted one of these cases, *Edwards v. State*, 49 Wis.2d 105 (1970):

The distinction between specific personal property and money in general
is important. A debtor can owe another $150 but the $150 in the debtor's
pocket is not the specific property of the creditor. One has the intention to
steal when he takes money from another's possession against the possess-
or's consent even though he also intends to apply the stolen money to a

debt. The efficacy of self-help by force to enforce a bona fide claim for money does not negate the intent to commit robbery. Can one break into a bank and take money so long as he does not take more than the balance in his savings or checking account? Under the majority rule [as it then existed, allowing a claim of right defense to any robbery] the accused must make change to be sure he collects no more than the amount he believes is due him on the debt. A debt is a relationship and in respect to money seldom finds itself embedded in specific coins and currency of the realm. Consequently, taking money from a debtor by force to pay a debt is robbery. The creditor has no such right of appropriation and allocation.

COMMONWEALTH v. BROWN
Supreme Court of Pennsylvania
506 Pa. 169, 484 A.2d 738 (1984)

MR. JUSTICE PAPADAKOS

This is the appeal of Gregory Brown from the Superior Court's Order affirming a Philadelphia County Common Pleas Court's Order, finding Appellant guilty of Robbery, a Felony in the Third Degree, and sentencing him to one and one-half to five years of confinement.

Appellant now argues that insufficient evidence was presented at trial to establish that he committed a robbery "by force however slight" * * * *.

Our review of the record indicates an uncomplicated factual pattern which can easily be summarized. The victim had just cashed a check for $221.00, which she placed in her purse. She left her bank, visited a doctor in a nearby clinic, and as she left from the doctor's office heard running steps behind her. The purse slung over her arm was grabbed and she saw Appellant run away from her with the purse. No one else was adjacent to her. She began screaming.

Appellant argues that this is insufficient to establish "force however slight" and that the robbery conviction against him cannot stand. We disagree.

The crime of robbery is currently defined in the Crimes Code, Act of December 6, 1972, as amended, June 24, 1976, 18 Pa.C.S. § 3701, and provides as follows:

§ 3701. Robbery

(a) Offense defined. —

(1) A person is guilty of robbery if, in the course of committing a theft, he: (i) inflicts serious bodily injury upon another; (ii) threatens another with or intentionally puts him in fear of immediate serious bodily injury; (iii) commits or threatens immediately to commit any felony of the first or second degree; (iv) inflicts bodily injury upon another or threatens another with or intentionally puts him in fear of immediate bodily injury; or (v) physically takes or removes property from the person of another by force however slight.

(2) An act shall be deemed "in the course of committing a theft" if it occurs in an attempt to commit theft or in flight after the attempt or commission.

(b) Grading. — Robbery under subsection (a)(1)(iv) is a felony of the second degree; robbery under subsection (a)(1)(v) is a felony of the third degree; otherwise, it is a felony of the first degree.

Prior to the Enactment of the 1972 Crimes Code, our statutes did not define the crime of robbery, and we defined it by its common law definition:

Robbery is the felonious and forcible taking from the person n of another of goods or money to any value by violence or putting in fear. [*Commonwealth v. Darcy*, 362 Pa. 259]

The degree of force (actual or constructive) used was immaterial, so long as it was sufficient to compel the victim to part with his property. The 1972 Crimes Code significantly changed the force requirement needed to commit a robbery by defining robbery as follows:

(1) A person is guilty of robbery if, in the course of committing a theft, he: (i) inflicts serious bodily injury upon another; (ii) threatens another with or unintentionally puts him in fear of immediate serious bodily injury; or (iii) commits or threatens immediately to commit any felony of the first or second degree. [18 Pa.C.S. § 3701(a)(1).]

By defining robbery in terms of "serious bodily injury," the Legislature abandoned the common law "force no matter how slight" requirement for robbery and created a new, less severe, "bodily injury" standard which it applied in defining the crime of theft by extortion at 18 Pa. C.S. § 3923. That section, in pertinent part, stated:

(a) Offense defined - A person is guilty of theft if he intentionally obtains or withholds property of another by threatening to: (1) inflict bodily injury on anyone or commit another criminal offense.

Distinguishing between a "serious bodily injury" and a "bodily injury" standard was certainly within the Legislature's prerogative and represented its recognition that the amount of force used or threatened on a person deserved separate treatment and penalty.[3] Distinguishing between robbery and theft by extortion, however, proved harder than expected and in reaction to the problem of determining the amount of force needed to sustain a robbery charge, the Legislature removed the references to bodily injury in subsection (1) of § 3923(a)(1) and amended § 3701 by adding subsections (iv) and (v).

Subsection (iv) provides that a robbery occurs when in the course of committing a theft the defendant "inflicts bodily injury upon another or threatens another with or intentionally puts him in fear of immediate bodily injury" (18 Pa. C.S. § 3701(a)(i)(iv)), and is graded as a felony of the second degree with a penalty of up to ten (10) years imprisonment. Under Subsection (v), a robbery occurs where in the

---

[3] The maximum sentence for robbery was twenty years and the maximum penalty for theft by extortion was five years, 18 Pa.C.S. §§ 3923, 3924(b), 1104.

course of committing a theft the defendant "physically takes or removes property from the person of another by force, however slight," 18 Pa. C.S. § 3701 (a)(1)(v), and is graded as a felony of the third degree with a penalty of up to seven (7) years imprisonment.

By including subsections (iv) and (v) under the Robbery Section of the Crimes Code, both force standards were once again merged under one crime, thus reinstating the common law standard. In so doing, our Legislature has eliminated the vexing problem of determining the amount of force required to commit a robbery. The amount of force used is relevant only when grading the offense as a first, second, or third degree felony, and is in keeping with the legislative directive to punish robbers according to the amount of violence they inflict on their victims.

It is clear to us that any amount of force applied to a person while committing a theft brings that act within the scope of robbery under § 3701(1)(a)(v). This force, of course, may be either actual or constructive. Actual force is applied to the body; constructive force is the use of threatening words or gestures, and operates on the mind. *Commonwealth v. Snelling*, 4 Binn. at 383.

The degree of actual force is immaterial, so long as it is sufficient to separate the victim from his property in, on or about his body. Any injury to the victim, or any struggle to obtain the property, or any resistance on his part which requires a greater counter attack to effect the taking is sufficient. The same is true if the force used, although insufficient to frighten the victim, surprises him into yielding his property.

The victim's testimony reveals that she left her doctor's clinic and apprehended the presence of a man who came up from behind her and took from her person a pocketbook hanging from her left arm.[4] The force used in taking the purse from the victim's arm was a harmful touching of the person, accompanied with sufficient force to compel the victim to part with the conscious control of her property, and supports a robbery conviction under § 3701. This conduct substantially differs from the case of the thief who merely takes the property of another with intent permanently to deprive him thereof, using no force or threat of force on the victim — like the pickpocket (Chapter 39 of the Crimes Code). Such conduct is non-violent, poses no threat to the victim who is unaware of the taking, and is accordingly graded less severely than robbery. A victim who is aware of the taking of property from his person is apt to use reflex action to protect himself and his property and thus may be injured by the felon.

For this reason, robbery has always been considered a greater harm against society because violence is caused or threatened. The ordinary citizen has the right to go about his way free from the fear of attack to his person from those who would deprive him of control over his goods. That right is violated even by the slight tug on the arm by the purse thief who must use force to wrench the purse from the arm of the victim without regard to her safety. Accordingly, we find that the evidence

---

[4] While the victim did not actually testify that appellant took the purse from her, there is no question from reading all her testimony at the September 19, 1979 suppression hearing and drawing all reasonable inferences in favor of the Commonwealth as verdict winner that he did, indeed, snatch the purse from her and that she immediately screamed at him to retrieve her purse and money.

was sufficient to establish robbery under § 3701 (a)(1)(v).

JUSTICE ZAPPALA

I dissent from the majority's finding that the evidence was sufficient to support the conviction of robbery. I would reduce the degree of guilt to theft and remand for resentencing.

The complainant's testimony of the events was limited:

Q. Briefly describe to his Honor what happened to you that day.

A. Well, I was coming from the bank to cash my check. I went into the clinic to see the doctor that day. I came out, and the guy was coming in back of me, running. I had this same pocketbook on this side (indicating) -

THE COURT: On what side, please?

THE WITNESS: On this side [indicating].

THE COURT: On her left arm.

THE WITNESS: I was screaming out, hoping that he would give me the pocketbook back and the money.

The majority's attempt to distinguish the factual circumstances of this case from a pickpocket "who merely takes the property of another . . . using no force or threat of force on the victim" must necessarily fail. Because the record is devoid of any evidence of force, the majority itself is compelled to supply the evidence of an essential element of the crime.

The majority underscores the fact that the complainant had the purse on her arm. Based upon that fact, it finds that force was used. It has effectively concluded that a taking from the person involves force per se. The weakness of this reasoning is demonstrated by its own example of a pickpocket. It is necessary to establish that a modicum of force was used. That goes beyond showing a mere taking from the person. The evidence would have been sufficient if it showed that Appellant engaged in a struggle to get the purse away from the complainant. This is distinguishable from a victim screaming and pursuing the perpetrator after the fact. The evidence would be sufficient also if the complainant had been holding the purse in her hand, in which case Appellant would have had to use at least a slight degree of force to remove it, *Commonwealth v. Frison*, 301 Pa. Super. 498 (1982).

In the instant case, the evidence clearly establishes only that the complainant had the purse on her arm. Emphasizing the fact that the complainant was aware of the Appellant's presence, the majority abruptly alters the concept of force by substituting a state of mind for a physical act to satisfy the elements of robbery. Do we now venture into an unprecedented legal concept that the removal of personal possessions from one's person without more is "robbery"? * * * *

Mr. Justice Larsen joins in this dissenting opinion.

NOTE FROM GORDON:

(1) If Brown is guilty of robbery, why isn't the pickpocket, according to the court?

(2) Under the majority opinion in *Brown*, what is the significance of the fact that Mike was "spaced out" when Turpin took the watch?

(3) In *People v. Davis*, 935 P.2d 79 (Colo. Supreme Court, 1996):

> The 68-year-old victim was walking away from a shopping mall carrying some paint she had purchased. She carried a purse by a strap looped over her left arm between her elbow and wrist. Defendant followed her surreptitiously until he was directly behind her. Then, he grabbed the purse and, with a quick jerking motion, caused the strap to break. The victim testified that she had felt a "very slight" tug as the strap broke. Defendant then ran away with the purse, but was later stopped by a passerby.

The Court affirmed the robbery conviction:

> There are no Colorado appellate decisions that clearly articulate the nature and extent of the force needed to constitute a robbery in a "purse snatching" case. However, other courts and commentators have examined the meaning of "force" in cases involving facts similar to those presented here. And, as noted in 2 W. LaFave & A. Scott, Jr., *Substantive Criminal Law*, § 8.11(d)(1): "The line between robbery and larceny from the person (between violence and lack of violence) is not always easy to draw. The 'snatching' cases, for instance, have given rise to some dispute. To remove an article of value, attached to the owner's person or clothing, by a sudden snatching or by stealth is not robbery unless the article in question (e.g., an earring, pin or watch) is so attached to the person or his clothes as to require some force to effect its removal." * * * *
>
> Thus, we hold that robbery includes the snatching of an object attached to the person of another if force is used to tear or break the attachment.

In *People v. Thomas*, 133 Cal.App.4th 488 (2005):

> Carol Ippolito was with her husband and daughter in the parking lot of an Albertson's store in Lancaster. She was loading groceries into the family truck. Her purse hung down to her waistline and was secured by a strap around her left shoulder. She "felt something hot against [her] arm, and then the strap, something grabbed it. And I was holding on to it, and the strap broke or pulled right out of my hand, so the strap was broken." The hot object was a knife. She tried to hang onto her purse. It started going off her arm, and she held on to it, but the strap, then broken, slipped through her hands — "it just pulled right through. I couldn't hold it" although she tried to do so with both hands.
>
> Prior to this incident the strap was in good condition, not broken. It was connected to the purse with loops and sewn leather, which also were in good

condition. She got a good look at the person who took her purse, and described him. She saw his hands, which were gripping the purse, and she felt it pulling away.

The entire episode took only seconds, and after getting the purse, the man ran to a white Nissan and dove into the back open window with his feet remaining outside the car, and the car sped away. Mrs. Ippolito got the license plate numbers with the assistance of a man who drove up and wrote them down as she called them off. Her credit card, which was in the purse, was used twice within the next 15 minutes; some $150 was charged on the card.

Thomas had driven the getaway car. The jury convicted Thomas of being an accomplice to robbery. On appeal, she argued that the evidence showed only theft, not robbery. The court disagreed:

Defendant's companion grabbed Mrs. Ippolito's purse and tried to pull it away from her; she pulled back, trying to prevent her purse from being taken. The thief succeeded by cutting or breaking the strap that was over the victim's shoulder and pulled on the strap with enough strength to defeat efforts to hold on to the purse. That description perfectly fits the force provision of the crime of robbery.

(4) In *Commonwealth v. Williams*, 550 A.2d 579 (Pa.Super. 1988), the victim was drunk and passed out when Williams rolled him over onto his side and removed his wallet from his pants pocket. Williams was convicted of robbery, but — citing *Brown* — the appellate court reversed:

If the victim in this case had been aware of this force [rolling him over], a robbery conviction might have stood based upon the possible distinction between the force used to roll the victim over, and the force used to remove the wallet. However, the victim was not aware of any force in this case; consequently, we find the appellant cannot be found guilty of robbery.

Judge Cavanaugh dissented: "The robbery statute does not require among its elements that the victim be aware of the taking or that he part with conscious control of his property."

(5) In *People v. Jackson*, 128 Cal.App.4th 1326 (2005), the victim found Jackson in the victim's apartment and tried to stop Jackson from fleeing. Jackson fought back and then left. Later, the victim discovered that Jackson had stolen his watch from the apartment. Jackson appealed his robbery conviction, arguing that he cannot be convicted of robbery unless the victim knew at the time force was used that his property was taken. The court disagreed:

Defendant's position is incorrect, for it is settled that a victim of robbery may be unconscious or even dead when the property is taken, so long as the defendant used force against the victim to take the property. *People v. Frye*, 18 Cal.4th at 956 [murder victims were robbed where defendant formed intent to take their property, killed them, and then took it]; *People v. Dreas* (1984) 153 Cal.App.3d 623 [unconscious victim was robbed when defendant drugged him in order to take his property].) There is no requirement that the victim be aware that his property is being taken from his presence by force or fear.

COMMONWEALTH v. ROZPLOCHI
Pennsylvania Superior Court
561 A.2d 25 (1989)

BECK, JUDGE:

The principal issue presented by this case is whether a defendant commits one robbery or two if he threatens to kill two employees of a business establishment during the course of a single theft from the business establishment. We find that under these circumstances, a defendant may be punished for two independent violations of the robbery statute.

This is an appeal by Albino Rozplochi from a judgment of sentence consisting of consecutive terms of imprisonment for two counts of robbery and a further consecutive term of imprisonment for the offense of former convict not to own firearm. Appellant contends that his trial counsel was ineffective for failing to challenge the sufficiency of the evidence of one of the counts of robbery . . .

On September 18, 1985, at approximately 8:45 A.M. Barbara Cavaliere and Elizabeth DeJesse, manager and employee, respectively, of the Financial Exchange Company, were inside the company office preparing to open for the day's business. The company is located at 1130 Chester Pike, Sharon Hill, Pennsylvania, and is situated inside of an ACME food store at that address.

While preparing to open, Ms. Cavaliere heard a knock on the office door and proceeded to look out of a window located near the door to determine the identify of the person seeking entry. She saw the Defendant standing outside the door and inquired as to how she might help him. Defendant answered that he had a package from her superior, "Bobby Louisa", and held up a picture identification card and a manila envelope which resembled the envelopes she received daily from the Department of Public Welfare. Ms. Cavaliere again asked the Defendant to state his business and he replied that he was "on-route" and was in a hurry. Ms. Cavaliere started to admit the Defendant but asked for a closer inspection of his identity card. However, when she opened the door, she saw that Defendant had pulled a revolver from the manila envelope and, upon seeing this, both she and Ms. DeJesse attempted to push the door closed in order to keep the Defendant out. Unfortunately, they were forced to relent in their efforts when Defendant, while brandishing the gun, threatened to "blow them away".

Once in the office, Defendant pushed Ms. DeJesse against a wall in front of the company safe and pushed Ms. Cavaliere up to the safe. At gunpoint, Ms. Cavaliere emptied the safe of approximately $22,000.00 in cash and food stamps which Defendant stuffed into the manila envelope. When the envelope could hold no more, Defendant grabbed a company money bag and began filling it.

At some point there was a knock at the door. In response, Defendant cocked the gun, held it to the back of Ms. Cavaliere's head and demanded that she hurry stating "if I don't get out of here you aren't either". Ms. Cavaliere noted that the gun was loaded and, indeed she was so close to it that she could see the bullets inside. Moments later, Defendant left the store with the money and food stamps. The entire incident took approximately ten minutes during which time the Defendant was in full view of his victims for almost the entire time.

In her trial testimony, Ms. DeJesse specified that appellant pointed his gun at her and directed his threats at her as well as at Ms. Cavaliere.

Appellant was apprehended and charged with numerous offenses including one count of robbery based upon his conduct toward Ms. Cavaliere and one count of robbery based upon his conduct toward Ms. DeJesse. Following a jury trial, he was found guilty of both counts of robbery . . . . He was sentenced to consecutive sentences of ten to twenty years for the first robbery count, ten to twenty years for the second robbery count, and one to five years for former convict not to own firearm. * * * *

I.

Appellant first argues that his trial counsel should have challenged the sufficiency of the evidence as to one of the counts of robbery. He emphasizes that the assets which he stole belonged exclusively to the Financial Exchange and that he did not at any time attempt to confiscate the private property of either Ms. Cavaliere or Ms. DeJesse. He further notes that although he threatened both employees, only Ms. Cavaliere was compelled to hand him cash belonging to the Financial Exchange. He therefore reasons that only one robbery took place and that the victim of that robbery was the Financial Exchange, rather than either of the women he held at gunpoint.

Whether a defendant commits multiple robberies if he threatens two people while attempting to steal the property of their common employer is a question of first impression for the appellate courts of Pennsylvania. To answer this question, we must examine the section of the Pennsylvania Crimes Code which defines the offense of robbery. That section provides in relevant part:

(1) A person is guilty of robbery, if, in the course of committing a theft, he:

. . . .

(ii) threatens another with or intentionally puts him in fear of immediate serious bodily injury;

. . . .

(2) An act shall be deemed "in the course of committing a theft" if it occurs in an attempt to commit theft or in flight after the attempt or commission.

18 Pa.Cons.Stat.Ann. § 3701.

During the course of committing a theft from the Financial Exchange, appellant threatened Ms. Cavaliere with immediate serious bodily injury. This was sufficient to constitute robbery. During the course of committing a theft from the Financial Exchange, appellant also threatened Ms. DeJesse with immediate serious bodily injury. This was also sufficient to constitute robbery. Thus, the text of the statute indicates that appellant committed two robberies when he threatened two individuals during the course of a single theft. * * * *

Our conclusion is supported by the general purposes of the Crimes Code. Among those purposes are that of insuring that punishment is proportionate with criminal liability, 18 Pa.C.S.A. § 104(3), and that of differentiating among offenders based on the seriousness of their offenses, 18 Pa.C.S.A. § 104(5). An offender whose unlawful act harms or is likely to harm many people is more culpable, and thus deserving of more severe punishment, than an offender whose unlawful act harms only one person.

By defining the crime of robbery as threatening another during the course of a theft, the legislature intended to permit separate punishments for threatening more than one person. If the legislature had intended to preclude multiple punishments, it could have defined robbery as threatening *another person or persons* during the course of a theft. Just as appellant could have been convicted of two counts of recklessly endangering another person by waving a gun at both Ms. Cavaliere and Ms. DeJesse, he may be convicted of two counts of robbery for threatening to harm both Ms. Cavaliere and Ms. DeJesse while stealing from the Financial Exchange.

In arguing for the opposite conclusion, appellant cites *Commonwealth v. Lockhart*, 223 Pa.Super. 60 (1972). His reliance on that case is misplaced. In *Lockhart*, the defendant forced the victim to hand over both $800 of his own money as well as additional funds belonging to his employer. The Superior Court held that a defendant commits only one robbery if he takes property belonging to different owners from the same person at the same time. As the appellant notes, the *Lockhart* case states that "a separate robbery may be found to have occurred each time another individual is put in fear, and from whom goods or money is taken." 223 Pa.Super. at 62. From this, appellant would conclude that separate robberies *cannot* be found to have occurred *unless* more than one individual is put in fear and goods or money are taken directly from each of those individuals. *Lockhart* does not stand for this principle. Instead, *Lockhart* is consistent with the view that the number of robberies that results from a single course of conduct depends upon the number of persons who have been threatened with physical harm.

We conclude that where only one person is threatened, only one robbery occurs even if the defendant makes off with goods that belong to two owners. However, where more than one person is threatened, more than one robbery may occur even if the defendant makes off with goods that belong to only one owner.

We further note that *Lockhart* was decided under the common law of robbery and before the adoption of section 3701 of the Pennsylvania Crimes Code. Section 3701, the current robbery statute, was derived from the Model Penal Code. The commentary to the Model Penal Code states that "the primary concern of the robbery provision is with the physical danger or threat of danger to the citizen rather than with the property aspects of the crime." Model Penal Code and Commentaries § 222.1 commentary at 100 (Official Draft and Revised Comments 1985). This language tends to undermine appellant's theory that he is guilty of only one robbery because all of the cash and food stamps that he took were owned by the Financial Exchange. The purpose of the robbery statute was not exclusively to protect the property interests of institutions such as the Financial Exchange. Section 3701 was primarily intended to protect people such as Ms. Cavaliere and Ms. DeJesse by deterring threats against workers who are under a duty to safeguard the financial reserves of their employers.

We are aware that in other jurisdictions, courts have significantly limited criminal liability for multiple counts of robbery. In several states, if a defendant commits a theft from a business enterprise, he can be found guilty of only one robbery regardless of how many people he has forced to hand over the assets of the enterprise. *See, e.g., State v. Collins, 329 S.E.2d 839 (W.Va.1984)* (collecting cases); *State v. Faatea*, 65 Haw. 156, 648 P.2d 197 (1982). In other states, the number of robberies for which the defendant may be prosecuted depends upon the number of people from whose possession property has been taken separately by force or intimidation. *See, e.g., Jordan v. Commonwealth, 2 Va.App. 590 (1986)* (collecting cases). These authorities do not control our interpretation of the Pennsylvania Crimes Code. Moreover, we note that our interpretation of Pennsylvania law is in accord with the decision of the Supreme Judicial Court of Massachusetts in *Commonwealth v. Levia*, 385 Mass. 345 (1982). The *Levia* opinion states:

> So long as the victim of the assault has some protective concern with respect to the property taken from his person or presence, then the defendant may be convicted and sentenced for a separate and distinct robbery as to that person. If the indictments or counts for the robbery of numerous persons are unreasonably multiplied, the judge, in superintending the course of trial and in passing sentence, will act accordingly to prevent oppression. [385 Mass. at 350-351]

In the instant case, both Ms. Cavaliere and Ms. DeJesse were employees of the Financial Exchange and both had a protective concern for the property of the Financial Exchange. We need not decide whether appellant could be convicted of multiple robberies if he had threatened several bystanders who had no connection with the owner of the stolen property. We hold that where a defendant threatens to inflict serious bodily injury on two employees in order to effectuate a theft of property from their common employer, the defendant may be convicted of two counts of robbery.

We conclude that the evidence produced at appellant's trial was sufficient to sustain his conviction for two robberies. Trial counsel cannot be deemed ineffective for failing to assert a meritless claim. Therefore, appellant was not deprived of the effective assistance of counsel by counsel's failure to seek an arrest of judgment on one of the robbery counts.

Judgment of sentence affirmed.

NOTES FROM GORDON:

1. *State v. Bridgers*, 988 A.2d 939 (Del.Super. 2007), involved the following facts:

> Defendants robbed a PNC bank by taking the bank's money from four employees at gunpoint. Defendants also threatened three other bank employees, Johnson, Gleason and Kirk. Defendant Bridgers first ap-

proached Johnson, the branch manager, and told him that Defendants were robbing the bank and he forced Johnson into the vault. Gleason was the assistant branch manager. Bridgers forced Gleason to order her tellers to step back and away from their stations to facilitate the robbery.

As the robbery unfolded, Chrichlow confronted nine customers at gunpoint. Defendants did not take anything from them, but Chrichlow held the customers at bay in order to stifle their interfering. During the robbery, Bridgers also noticed Kirk sitting in Kirk's office. He ordered Kirk out and forced him across the bank to where Chrichlow was holding the customers.

How many robberies did Bridgers and Chrichlow commit?

Under Delaware's law, each employee from whom Defendants took money and the branch manager are separate robbery victims. In Delaware, and other states, a single bank robbery may spawn many robbery victims, typically the bank's tellers whose cash drawers are "cleaned-out." And, no one disputes that threatening a bystander at gunpoint is a felony, aggravated menacing. * * * *

Someone who is merely a threatened bystander has not been robbed. A threatened bystander is a victim of the violent, class E felony specifically meant to apply to armed threats - aggravated menacing - not a victim of robbery. * * * *

Bridgers forced Gleason to participate actively in the theft when he forced her to order the tellers out of his way. Accordingly, the evidence supports the conclusion that Gleason was far more than a bystander. As for Kirk, Bridgers forced him out of his office and frog-marched him across the lobby so that Chrichlow could hold him at gunpoint with the customers. Although neither employee gave anything to Defendants, Gleason actively participated in the theft, and they both had a custodial interest in the bank's money. They had to watch and do nothing as Defendants took their employer's money, intimidated their co-workers and frightened the bank's customers. Thus, the character of the threats toward them was different, as was, perhaps, the way they perceived those threats. In theory, a jury could find that neutralizing employees during a bank robbery by threatening them is causally related to the theft.

2. In *People v. Scott*, 45 Cal.4th 743 (2009), Scott and two associates entered a McDonald's restaurant.

The three men entered the restaurant at approximately 6:15 a.m., shortly after it opened. Each wore dark clothing and ski masks; one had a gun, and another had a rifle.

Ms. Guillebeau was working at the restaurant's drive-through window. When she saw two masked men, one with a gun, she immediately hid under the grill and remained there for the duration of the robbery. Ms. Salazar was working in the kitchen area, preparing food, when she saw the men. She observed that one of the men stood in front of the counter, holding a rifle. She hid under a table and remained there for the duration of the episode.

Ms. Wong, the manager, was working at the drive-through window. She heard Ms. Guillebeau scream, turned around, and saw a man holding a handgun. This individual directed Wong to the back of the store toward the safe. She brought him to the office and opened the safe using the combination, which she had memorized. She placed money in a bag, along with an electronic tracking device that she had been trained to place with the money in case of a robbery. Later, through the activation of the tracking device, the police located both defendants at an apartment building where defendant Scott resided.

Ms. Wong was the only employee working at the restaurant during the robbery who had access to the safe. As the shift manager, she was responsible for directing the work of others, taking care of any customer complaints, and generally overseeing the operation of the restaurant. Ms. Guillebeau's responsibilities included taking customers' orders, presenting food to customers, and working one of the cash registers. Ms. Salazar's duties involved food preparation. She did not handle money or work at a cash register.

The jury convicted Scott of 3 robberies — one for each of the three employees. The California Supreme Court affirmed, overruling prior cases that held that whether an employee "constructively possesses" the employer's property depends on the particular responsibilities of that employee:

A person from whose immediate presence property was taken by force or fear is not a robbery victim unless, additionally, he or she was in some sense in possession of the property. * * * *

A person who owns property or who exercises direct physical control over it has possession of it, but neither ownership nor physical possession is required to establish the element of possession for the purposes of the robbery statute. The theory of constructive possession has been used to expand the concept of possession to include employees and others as robbery victims. Two or more persons may be in joint constructive possession of a single item of personal property, and multiple convictions of robbery are proper if force or fear is applied to multiple victims in joint possession of the property taken. * * * *

Although not every employee has the authority to exercise control over the employer's funds or other property during everyday operations of the business, any employee has, by virtue of his or her employment relationship with the employer, some implied authority, when on duty, to act on the employer's behalf to protect the employer's property when it is threatened during a robbery. * * * *

The employee's relationship with his or her employer constitutes a "special relationship" sufficient to establish the employee's constructive possession of the employer's property during a robbery.

Furthermore, it is reasonable to infer that the Legislature intended that all on-duty employees have constructive possession of the employer's property during a robbery, because such a rule is consistent with the culpability level of the offender and the harm done by his or her criminal conduct. As a matter of common knowledge and experience, those who commit robberies are likely to regard all employees as potential sources of resistance, and their use of threats and force against those employees is not likely to turn on fine distinctions regarding a particular employee's actual or implied authority. On-duty employees generally feel an implicit obligation to protect their employer's property, and their sense of loss and victimization when force is used against them to obtain the employer's property is unlikely to be affected by their particular responsibilities regarding the property in question. * * * *

In the context of the crime of robbery, the policies served by the element of possession are obviously quite different, because possession itself is not the unlawful act. The crime of robbery may be committed against any person who is in possession of the property taken, because such a person may be expected to resist the taking, and — in order to achieve the taking — the robber must place all such possessors in fear, or force them to give up possession. By requiring that the victim of a robbery have possession of the property taken, the Legislature has included as victims those persons who, because of their relationship to the property or its owner, have the right to resist the taking, and has excluded as victims those bystanders who have no greater interest in the property than any other member of the general population. It would not further the purposes of the robbery statute to require that the robbery victim have the same level of custody or control over the property that is required in order to establish that the perpetrator is guilty of possessing contraband.

3. I just got a call from Turpin's lawyer, who said he found a Rhode Island case which really helps him. Here it is. How should I deal with it?

STATE v. HOLLEY
Rhode Island Supreme Court
604 A.2d 772 (1992)

KELLEHER, JUSTICE.

The defendant, Julio Holley, appeals his conviction by a Superior Court jury in which he was found guilty of robbery and conspiracy to commit robbery. Subsequently the trial justice imposed a sentence of forty-five years. For reasons set forth herein, we modify Holley's conviction and remand the case to the Superior Court for the entry of a judgment of conviction of assault with the intent to rob.

For forty-three years Melkon Varadian (Varadian) and his wife owned and operated, six days a week, the Public Street Market, a neighborhood grocery store in Providence. Varadian testified that on the morning of February 6, 1987, two men entered his store. One man, whom Varadian immediately recognized as a previous customer, wore a blue jumpsuit and a blue hat with gold braid. The other man, whom Varadian did not recognize, was of shorter stature. The familiar, taller man, later identified as Zachary Spratt (Spratt), meandered his way about the market, approached the meat counter and began to recite a list of various meats Varadian was to fetch for him. Meanwhile Holley paced between the meat counter and another aisle, a distance of approximately three feet. Although Varadian commented that the price of hamburger was too high, Spratt insisted on ordering three pounds of the meat. Spratt next requested pork chops and began again to stroll about the store. While Varadian prepared the chops, he carefully eyed the wandering taller man and testified later that Spratt put two cans of tuna fish into his jacket pocket. Spratt returned to the counter and ordered two slices of cheese and followed this request with another, for two slices of bologna. Varadian testified that at this point he knew he was "in trouble." Finally Spratt asked for some hot sausage, then changed his mind and canceled that portion of the order.

Frustrated with this tedious exchange, Varadian rang up the two men's purchases, which totaled $16, whereupon Spratt complained of the high price and began removing certain packages of meat from the grocery sack. Varadian explained that he had simply prepared the foods Spratt himself had ordered, then asked him to take the two cans of tuna fish out of his pocket and "to get the hell out" of his store.

At that moment, Spratt nodded to Holley, who also was standing at the counter. Responding to the signal, Holley moved towards Varadian and pushed a gun into the proprietor's belly. Varadian reacted by swinging at Holley's chin. Holley hit Varadian back, dragged the sixty-five-year-old proprietor fifteen feet up an aisle of the store, threw Varadian to the floor, and began beating him across the face with the barrel of his gun.

In the meantime Spratt was attempting to open the cash register and succeeded only in breaking the top of the machine and its keys. No cash was taken. Varadian broke free of Holley and scrambled for a telephone to notify the police. Despite their efforts Spratt and Holley fled with no money, nor did they take away any of the food ordered, save the two tins of tuna. * * * *

The facts of this case have provided us with much food for thought. In his first issue on appeal Holley insists he is wrongly sentenced to forty-five years for his cohort's taking of two cans of tuna fish. Specifically Holley contends that the tuna fish, having been put into Spratt's pocket prior to any exercise of force, makes unsupportable Holley's robbery conviction. We agree.

As Rhode Island subscribes to the common-law definition of robbery, we define the crime as the "felonious and forcible taking from the person of another of goods or money to any value by violence or putting him in fear." *State v. Pope*, 414 A.2d 781, 788 (R.I.1980), citing 4 Black. Comm. 241). Larceny at common law is essentially a wrongful taking without right and a carrying away of another's personal property with a felonious intent to steal. By definition, robbery includes larceny because the robbery act requires a taking and a carrying away of another's property. 67 Am.Jur.2d Robbery §§ 1, 2 (1985). When a defendant takes possession of another's property, there is a taking; when a defendant exercises dominion and control over the property, there is possession. Finally when a defendant carries away the property, there is an asportation. We note that there cannot be an asportation unless there has first been a taking. 4 Wharton's Criminal Law § 472 (Torcia 14th ed. 1981).

We observe that it is the element of force, violence, or intimidation in the taking of property that distinguishes robbery from larceny. Annot. 58 A.L.R. 656 (1929). Indeed, a seining of case law regarding what constitutes robbery indicates a clear division between force used preceding or contemporaneous with a taking of property and force used subsequent to a taking. The majority of common-law jurisdictions support the conclusion that force used to retain property already peacefully taken, or to attempt to escape, is not the force essential to satisfy the element of force required for robbery. See, e.g., *Eckelberry v. State*, 497 N.E.2d 233 (Ind.1986); *State v. Long*, 234 Kan. 580, 675 P.2d 832 (1984); *State v. Hope*, 77 N.C.App. 338, 335 S.E.2d 218 (1985), rev'd, 317 N.C. 302, 345 S.E.2d 361 (1986). See Annot. 93 A.L.R.3d 643, 647 (1979). By the same token, a robbery has been held to occur when a defendant uses force or fear in resisting an attempt to regain the property or in attempting to remove property from the owner's immediate presence. See *Burko v. State*, 19 Md.App. 645, 313 A.2d 864 (1974).[2]

In order to ascertain whether a robbery conviction is proper, then, we need first to determine whether the taking of property had been completed at the time the force was used by a defendant. The relevant facts indicate that Holley and Spratt had finished their taking of the tuna before Holley bludgeoned Varadian. The force Holley applied to Varadian was not aimed at the taking of the tuna, which was concealed peacefully, albeit wrongly, in Spratt's jacket. Instead the facts show, and the state argued, that the force Holley dealt upon the store owner was directed toward the moneys in the cash register, which Spratt unsuccessfully attempted to open. Consequently, as the requisite elements of common-law robbery are unsustainable, we must vacate the robbery conviction.

We are persuaded that a modification of the judgment of conviction to assault with the intent to rob, and not a judgment of acquittal, is proper in this instance. Although it was legally impossible to sustain a conviction of robbery, there is ample evidence to support a conviction of the lesser included offense of assault with intent to rob, an offense about which the jury was alternatively instructed should the robbery charge be found unsupportable. * * * *

---

[2] A substantial minority of authority exists to support the conclusion that force or intimidation used to retain property nevertheless constitutes the force or intimidation necessary to support a robbery offense. See *Winborne v. State*, 455 A.2d 357 (Del.1982); *Cantrell v. State*, 184 Ga.App. 384 (1987); *Commonwealth v. Boiselle*, 16 Mass.App. 393 (1983). In the same vein, other cases have held that the use of force merely to escape does not supply the element of force needed for robbery. See *Becker v. State*, 298 Ark. 438 (1989); *State v. Hope*, 317 N.C. 302 (1986). The reasoning for this line of demarcation in case law, however, is unclear, because of the uncertainty regarding when a taking is completed. Annot. 93 A.L.R.3d 643, 645 (1979). Whether a particular offense is properly characterized as larceny, robbery, or a related charge is contingent upon the timing at which force is exerted. We note that some states, in predicating robbery upon the use of force to retain possession of the property or to facilitate escape, effectively extend the common-law view by lengthening the thief's "taking" period. This statutory extension is "not necessarily inconsistent with the common-law theory of robbery." 4 Wharton's Criminal Law § 478 at 65 (Torcia 14th ed.1981). Indeed, it is a view with which we conceptually agree. However, Holley may not be punished under a retroactive application of a modification in the law. U.S. Const. Art. I, § 10, cl. 1.

For the foregoing reasons, we vacate the conviction for robbery and remand the case to the Superior Court with directions to enter a judgment of conviction of assault with intent to rob and to resentence Holley upon that charge.

NOTE FROM GORDON:

1. In *People v. Randolph*, 648 N.W.2d 164 (Mich. 2002), a majority of the Michigan Supreme Court held that force used after the taking does *not* convert a larceny into a robbery.

2. In *Hobson v. Commonwealth*, 306 S.W.3d 478 (Ky. 2010), Hobson went to a store, selected items, and brought them to the check-out register. When he tried to pay for them with a stolen credit card, Police Officer Schoch took him to the manager's office, leaving the items at the check-out register. While in the office, Hobson bolted out of the office and fled the store. The officer caught him, and Hobson used force on the officer, who broke his ankle. Hobson's robbery conviction was reversed:

> If, at the time a defendant first uses or threatens force, he has abandoned his intention to accomplish a theft, the plain language of the robbery statutes constrains us to conclude that the elements of robbery are not met. * * * *

> In the present case, it is undisputed that Appellant neither used, nor threatened to use, force against another until his struggle with Schoch in the parking lot after he fled the store. At that juncture, Appellant knew that his purpose had been foiled. The merchandise he intended to steal had long been left at the checkout counter. It is beyond doubt that the attempted theft had ended. It cannot be reasonably disputed that when Appellant fought with Schoch, he had no intention to "accomplish the theft," but, rather, was attempting to avoid arrest and prosecution.

A Note on Extortion

What is extortion? Pennsylvania Statutes § 3923 provides:

Theft by extortion

(a) *Offense Defined.* A person is guilty of theft if he intentionally obtains or withholds property of another by threatening to:

    (1)   commit another criminal offense;

    (2)   accuse anyone of a criminal offense;

    (3)   expose any secret tending to subject any person to hatred, contempt or ridicule;

    (4)   take or withhold action as an official, or cause an official to take or withhold action;

    (5)   bring about or continue a strike, boycott or other collective unofficial action, if the property is not demanded or received for the benefit of the

group in whose interest the actor purports to act;

(6)   testify or provide information or withhold testimony or information with respect to the legal claim or defense of another; or

(7)   inflict any other harm which would not benefit the actor.

(b) *Defenses.* It is a defense to prosecution based on paragraphs (a)(2), (a)(3) or (4) of this section that the property obtained by threat of accusation, exposure, lawsuit or other invocation of official action was honestly claimed as restitution or indemnification for harm done in the circumstances to which such accusation, exposure, lawsuit or other official action relates, or as compensation for property or lawful services.

Compare Model Penal Code § 223.4, in the Appendix.

How does extortion differ from robbery? In *Commonwealth v. Burdell*, 380 Pa. 43, 110 A.2d 193 (1955), the court stated:

> The two have no relation to one another, for they are wholly dissimilar in nature. In robbery the taking of property is against the will by means of force or violence, while in extortion the taking is with the consent of the victim, induced, as it may be, by the threat of some exposure or the making of some criminal charge whether false or otherwise. A person who would be apt to commit the crime of blackmail or extortion is a very different type from the one who would burglarize a house, commit a vicious assault, and rob at the point of a gun.

However, in *Commonwealth v. Froelich*, 458 Pa. 104, 326 A.2d 364 (1974), the court had this to say about the above quote from *Burdell*:

> In *Burdell*, we were merely restating the traditionally accepted distinction between robbery and extortion. This statement, however, is not to imply that for the transfer of possession from the victim to the accused to possess the requisite consent for extortion it must necessarily be free of all compulsion. Extortion and blackmail have always been recognized as embracing an element of coercion or intimidation. However, as has been noted by some text writers, the use of the concept of consent in this context is not necessarily the most informative method of distinguishing between the crimes. "It is sometimes said that robbery differs from statutory extortion in those states which require property acquisition in that in the former the taking of property must be "against the will' of the victim, while in the latter the taking must be 'with the consent' of the victim, induced by the other's unlawful threat; but, in spite of the different expressions, there is no difference here, for both crimes equally require that the defendant's threats induce the victim to give up his property, something which he would not otherwise have done." La Fave & Scott, Criminal Law, 707 (1972).
>
> The historical development of these crimes best explains what may otherwise appear to be an inconsistency. Robbery at common law was a taking from the person accomplished by violence or intimidation and, as a felony, it was punishable by death. Because of the severity of the punishment upon conviction the common law courts were most circumspect, in

robberies by intimidation, in limiting the type of threats to be included therein. Where the threat was of immediate personal violence the earlier courts were satisfied that the punishment provided was appropriate. Later, the lesser crimes of extortion and blackmail evolved to cover other types of intimidation which were apparently viewed as presenting a lesser threat to personal security and thus not requiring the same severe punishment.

"Doubtless because the severe penalty for robbery, long a capital offense, restrained the courts from expanding robbery to include the acquisition of property by means of other effective threats — such as a threat to inflict future rather than immediate bodily harm, or to destroy the victim's property other than his house, or to accuse him of some crime other than sodomy, or to expose his failings or secrets or otherwise damage his good name or business reputation. To fill this vacuum practically all states have enacted statutes creating what is in effect a new crime — in some states called statutory extortion, in others blackmail, and generally carrying a penalty less severe than for robbery." La Fave & Scott, Criminal Law, 705 (1972).

Thus, whether we attempt to distinguish robbery from extortion and blackmail on a theory of "consent" to transfer possession of the property in question or look to the historical development of the crimes, it is evident that the crimes of extortion and blackmail do encompass a degree of coercion or intimidation.

Except where violence is threatened, extortion is a peculiar crime. It is no crime for Dan to accuse Vic of a crime, and it is no crime for Dan to accept $100 from Vic. And yet if Dan tells Vic, "I will publicly accuse you of a crime unless you give me $100," and this causes Vic to give Dan $100, Dan has committed extortion. Why? This conundrum has been explored by several writers. See, e.g., James Lindgren, *Unraveling the Paradox of Blackmail*, 84 Columbia L.Rev. 670 (1984); George Fletcher, *Blackmail: The Paradigmatic Crime*, 141 U.Penna.L.Rev. 1617 (1993); Douglas Ginsburg & Paul Shechtman, *Blackmail: An Economic Analysis of the Law*, 141 U.Penna.L.Rev. 1849 (1993); and Wendy Gordon, *Truth & Consequences: The Force of Blackmail's Central Case*, 141 U.Penna.L.Rev. 1741 (1993).

Chapter 6

BURGLARY

Burglary was defined by the common law to be the breaking and entering of the dwelling house of another in the nighttime with the intent to commit a felony. * * * * Across the intervening centuries these elements have been expanded or discarded to such an extent that the modern-day offense commonly known as burglary bears little relation to its common-law ancestor.

LaFave & Scott, *Criminal Law* (West)

Take a good look at the common law definition of burglary, above. What *purpose* did it serve that was not *already* served by the law of trespass and the law regarding whatever felony the defendant intended to commit after entry?

Once you figure out the answer to that question, answer this one: if we *remove* one of the required elements of common law burglary, does the remaining definition still serve that purpose? If not, what purpose *did* the removed element serve?

In other words, *why have* a "modern-day offense" of burglary that lacks some of the elements of common law burglary? If you have trouble coming up with a satisfactory answer to that question — and yet, like it or not, you must apply such a statute because the legislature has enacted it — would that predispose you to read such a statute *narrowly*?

As you read the cases in this Chapter, consider whether that is what some of the judges are doing.

PROBLEM 6

To: My law clerk

From: Mr. Morris Mumpole, Barrister-at-Law

Re: *Regina v. Tinsel*

My client, Tina Tinsel, is one of the infamous Tinsel family, a clan of minor villains who provide much of my business. Tina was visiting her brother in Brixton the other day, and she got into a bit of a scrape at a local department store. She has been charged with burglary, in violation of § 9 of the Theft Act. Based on the police constable's report (which I believe contains all the evidence the Crown will present), I think we might have a shot at persuading Judge Bullington to instruct the jury that the evidence is not sufficient to support the charge. The Bull would love to send another Tinsel to the Holloway nick, but he is inclined to follow the law on occasion. Please peruse the attached authorities and advise me what chance we might have with the old darling.

Police Report

At 2:00 this afternoon, I received a phone call from Mr. Markson Spencer, manager of a department store in Brixton. Security personnel at the store were holding Ms. Tina Tinsel. I went to the store and interviewed Mr. Spencer. He gave the following statement:

> We were in the midst of our fall clearance sale, and we had large banner in the front window which proclaimed: "FALL SALE - COME ON IN AND SEE WHAT YOU LIKE." To promote the sale, we had a table near the front door at which a saleman was giving out free umbrellas - the small, inexpensive kind - one to a customer. At about noon, I saw Ms. Tinsel come in the front door with a large handbag. I knew she had been arrested for shoplifting at the store before, so I asked her if I could inspect her handbag. She agreed, and I discovered a false bottom in the handbag. I said, "So, out for a bit of morning thievery, are we, Tina?" She replied, "Well, I fancied that cute brolly I saw in the window, so I thought I'd drop in and nip one. But when I got to the front door, I saw the man was giving them away. As one of your valued customers, I am entitled to one. I was about to go over and get one when you so rudely accosted me."

I then placed Ms. Tinsel under arrest for burglary.

R. Peel, P.C.

Theft Act 1968, Chapter 60

Section 9.

(1) A person is guilty of burglary if —

> (a) he enters any building or part of a building as a trespasser and with intent to commit any such offence as is mentioned in subsection (2) below; or

> (b) having entered any building or part of a building as a trespasser he steals or attempts to steal anything in the building or that part of it or inflicts or attempts to inflict on any person therein any grievous bodily harm.

(2) The offences referred to in subsection (1) (a) above are offences of stealing anything in the building or part of a building in question, of inflicting on any person therein any grievous bodily harm therein, and of doing unlawful damage to the building or anything therein.

(3) A person guilty of burglary shall on conviction on indictment be liable to imprisonment for a term not exceeding —

(a) where the offence was committed in respect of a building or part of a building which is a dwelling, fourteen years;

(b) in any other case, ten years.

(4) References in subsections (1) and (2) above to a building, and the reference in subsection (3) above to a building which is a dwelling, shall apply also to an inhabited vehicle or vessel, and shall apply to any such vehicle or vessel at times when the person having a habitation in it is not there as well as at times when he is.

NOTES:

1. In 2003, Parliament deleted the words "or raping any person" from subsection (2).

2. Compare Model Penal Code § 221.0 and § 221.1, in the Appendix.

REGINA v. COLLINS
Court of Appeal, Criminal Division
2 All E.R. 1105 (1972)

EDMUND DAVIES, L.J., delivered the judgment of the court.

This is about as extraordinary a case as my brethren and I have ever heard either on the Bench or while at the Bar. Stephen William George Collins was convicted on 29th October 1971 at Essex Assizes of burglary with intent to commit rape and he was sentenced to 21 months' imprisonment. He is a 19 year old youth, and he appeals against the conviction by the certificate of the trial judge. The terms in which that certificate is expressed reveals that the judge was clearly troubled about the case and the conviction.

Let me relate the facts. Were they put into a novel or portrayed on the stage, they would be regarded as being so improbable as to be unworthy of serious consideration and as verging at times on farce.

At about two o'clock in the early morning of Saturday, 24th July 1971, a young lady of 18 went to bed at her mother's home in Colchester. She had spent the evening with her boyfriend. She had taken a certain amount of drink, and it may be that this fact affords some explanation of her inability to answer satisfactorily certain crucial questions put to her. She has the habit of sleeping without wearing night apparel in a bed which is very near the lattice-type window of her room. At one stage on her evidence she seemed to be saying that the bed was close up against the window which, in accordance with her practice, was wide open. In the photographs which we have before us, however, there appears to be a gap of some sort between the two, but the bed was clearly quite near the window.

At about 3:30 or 4:00 a.m. she awoke and she then saw in the moonlight a vague form crouched in the open window. She was unable to remember, and this is important, whether the form was on the outside of the window sill or on that part of the sill which was inside the room, and for reasons which will later become clear, that seemingly narrow point is of crucial importance. The young lady then realised several things: first of all that the form in the window was that of a male; secondly that he was a naked male; and thirdly that he was a naked male with an erect penis. She also saw in the moonlight that his hair was blond. She thereupon leapt to the conclusion that her boyfriend, with whom for some time she had been on terms of regular and frequent sexual intimacy, was paying her an ardent nocturnal visit. She promptly sat up in bed, and the man descended from the sill and joined her in bed and they had full sexual intercourse.

But there was something about him which made her think that things were not as they usually were between her and her boyfriend. The length of his hair, his voice as they had exchanged what was described as "love talk", and other features led her to the conclusion that somehow there was something different. So she turned on the bed-side light, saw that her companion was not her boyfriend and slapped the face of the intruder, who was none other than the appellant. He said to her, "Give me a good time tonight," and got hold of her arm, but she bit him and told him to go. She then went into the bathroom and he promptly vanished.

The complainant said that she would not have agreed to intercourse if she had known that the person entering her room was not her boyfriend. But there was no suggestion of any force having been used on her, and the intercourse which took place was undoubtedly effected with no resistance on her part.

The appellant was seen by the police at about 10:30 a.m. later that same morning. According to the police, the conversation which took place then elicited these points: He was very lustful the previous night. He had taken a lot of drink, and we may here note that drink (which to him is a very real problem) had brought this young man into trouble several times before, but never for an offence of this kind. He went on to say that he knew the complainant because he had worked around her house. On this occasion, desiring sexual intercourse - and according to the police evidence he had added that he was determined to have a girl, by force if necessary, although that part of the police evidence he challenged - he went on to say that he walked around the house, saw a light in an upstairs bedroom, and he knew that this was the girl's bedroom. What he could see inside through the wide open window was a girl who was naked and asleep. So he descended the ladder and stripped off all his clothes, with the exception of his socks, because apparently he took the view that if the girl's mother entered the bedroom it would be easier to effect a rapid escape if he had his socks on that if he was in his bare feet. Having undressed, he then climbed the ladder and pulled himself in when she awoke. She then got up and knelt on the bed, she put her arms around his neck and body, and she seemed to pull him into the bed. He went on:

> I was rather dazed, because I didn't think she would want to know me. We kissed and cuddled for about ten or fifteen minutes and then I had it away with her but found it hard because I had had so much to drink.

The police officer said to the appellant:

> It appears that is was your intention to have intercourse with this girl by force if necessary and it was only pure coincidence that this girl was under the impression that you were her boyfriend and apparently that is why she

consented to allowing you to have sexual intercourse with her.

It was alleged that he then said:

> Yes, I feel awful about this. It is the worst day of my life, but I know it could have been worse.

Thereupon the officer said to him — and the appellant challenges this — "What do you mean, you know it could have been worse?" to which he is alleged to have replied:

> Well, my trouble is drink and I got very frustrated. As I've told you, I only wanted to have it away with a girl and I'm only glad I haven't really hurt her.

Then he made a statement under caution, in the course of which he said:

> When I stripped off and got up the ladder, I made my mind up that I was going to try and have it away with this girl. I feel terrible about this now, but I had too much to drink. I am sorry for what I have done.

In the course of his testimony, the appellant said that he would not have gone into the room if the girl had not knelt on the bed and beckoned him into the room. He said that if she had objected immediately to his being there or to his having intercourse he would not have persisted. While he was keen on having sexual intercourse that night, it was only if he could find someone who was willing. He strongly denied having told the police that he would, if necessary, have pushed over some girl for the purpose of having intercourse.

There was a submission of no case to answer on the ground that the evidence did not support the charge, particularly that ingredient of it which had reference to entry into the house "as a trespasser." But the submission was overruled, and, as we have already related, he gave evidence.

Now, one feature of the case which remained at the conclusion of the evidence in great obscurity is where exactly the appellant was at the moment when, according to him, the girl manifested that she was welcoming him. Was he kneeling on the sill outside the window or was he already inside the room, having climbed through the window frame, and kneeling on the inner sill? It was a crucial matter, for there were certainly three ingredients that it was incumbent on the Crown to establish. Under § 9 of the Theft Act 1968, which renders a person guilty of burglary if he enters any building or part of a building as a trespasser and with the intention of committing rape, the entry of the appellant into the building must first be proved. Well, there is no doubt about that, for it is common ground that he did enter this girl's bedroom. Secondly, it must be proved that he entered as a trespasser. We will develop that point a little later. Thirdly, it must be proved that he entered as a trespasser with intent at the time of entry to commit rape therein.

The second ingredient of the offence - the entry must be as a trespasser — is one which has not, to the best of our knowledge, been previously canvassed in the courts. Views as to its ambit have naturally been canvassed by the textbook writers, and it is perhaps not wholly irrelevant to recall that those who were advising the Home Secretary before the Theft Bill was presented to Parliament had it in mind to get rid of some of the frequently absurd technical rules which had been built up in relation to the old requirement in burglary of a "breaking and entering." The cases are legion as to what this did or did not amount to, and happily it is not now necessary for us to consider them. But it was in order to get rid of those technical rules that a new test was introduced, namely that the entry must be "as a trespasser."

What does that involve? According to the learned editors of Archbold:

> Any intentional, reckless or negligent entry into a building will, it would appear, constitute a trespass if the building is in the possession of another person who does not consent to the entry. Nor will it make any difference that the entry was the result of a reasonable mistake on the part of the defendant, so far as trespass is concerned.

If that be right, then it would be no defence for this man to say (and even were he believed in saying), "Well, I honestly thought that this girl was welcoming me into the room and I therefore entered, fully believing that I had her consent to go in." If Archbold is right, he would nevertheless be a trespasser, since the apparent consent of the girl was unreal, she being mistaken as to who was at her window. We disagree. We hold that, for the purposes of § 9 of the Theft Act 1968, a person entering a building is not guilty of trespass if he enters without knowledge that he is trespassing or at least without acting recklessly as to whether or not he is unlawfully entering.

A view contrary to that of the learned editors of Archbold was expressed in Professor J. C. Smith's book on *The Law of Theft*, where, having given an illustration of an entry into premises, the learned author comments:

> It is submitted that D should be acquitted on the ground of lack of *mens rea*. Though, under the civil law, he entered as a trespasser, it is submitted that he cannot be convicted of the criminal offence unless he knew of the facts which caused him to be a trespasser or, at least, was reckless.

The matter has also been dealt with by Professor Griew, who in his work on the Theft Act 1968 has this passage:

> What if D wrongly believes that he is not trespassing? His belief may rest on facts which, if true, would mean that he was not trespassing: For instance, he may enter a building by mistake, thinking that it is the one he has been invited to enter. Or his belief may be based on a false view of the legal effect of the known facts: For instance, he may misunderstand the effect of a contract granting him a right of passage through a building. Neither kind of mistake will protect him from tort liability for trespass. In either case, then, D satisfies the literal terms of § 9(1): He "enters . . . as a trespasser." But for the purposes of criminal liability a man should be judged on the basis of the facts as he believed them to be, and this should include making allowances for a mistake as to rights under the civil law. This is another way of saying that a serious offence like burglary should be held to require *mens rea* in the fullest sense of the phrase: D should be liable for burglary only if he knowingly trespasses or is reckless as to whether he trespasses or not. Unhappily it is common for Parliament to

omit to make clear whether *mens rea* is intended to be an element in a statutory offence. It is also, though not equally, common for the courts to supply the mental element by construction of the statute."

We prefer the view expressed by Professor Smith and Professor Griew to that of the learned editors of Archbold. In the judgment of this court, there cannot be a conviction for entering premises "as a trespasser" within the meaning of § 9 of the Theft Act 1968 unless the person entering does so knowing that he is a trespasser and nevertheless deliberately enters, or, at the very least, is reckless whether or not he is entering the premises of another without the other party's consent.

Having so held, the pivotal point of this appeal is whether the Crown established that the appellant at the moment that he entered the bedroom knew perfectly well that he was not welcome there or, being reckless whether he was welcome or not, was nevertheless determined to enter. That in turn involves consideration as to where he was at the time that the complainant indicated that she was welcoming him into her bedroom. If, to take an example that was put in the course of argument, her bed had not been near the window but was on the other side of the bedroom, and he (being determined to have her sexually even against her will) climbed through the window and crossed the bedroom to reach her bed, then the offence charged would have been established. But in this case, as we have related, the layout of the room was different and it became a point of nicety which had to be conclusively established by the Crown as to where he was when the girl made welcoming signs, as she unquestionably at some stage did.

How did the learned judge deal with this matter? We have to say regretfully that there was a flaw in his treatment of it. Referring to § 9, he said:

> There are three ingredients. First is the question of entry. Did he enter in to that house? Did he enter as a trespasser? That is to say, did he - was the entry, if you are satisfied there was an entry, intentional or reckless? And, finally, and you may think this is the crux of the case as opened to you by counsel for the Crown, if you are satisfied that he entered as a trespasser, did he have the intention to rape this girl?

The judge then went on to deal in turn with each of these three ingredients. He first explained what was involved in "entry" into a building. He then dealt with the second ingredient. But he here unfortunately repeated his earlier observation that the question of entry as a trespasser depended on "was the entry intentional or reckless?" We have to say that this was putting the matter inaccurately. This mistake may have been derived from a passage in the speech of counsel for the Crown when replying to the submission of "No case." Counsel for the Crown at one stage said:

> Therefore, the first thing that the Crown have got to prove, my Lord, is that there has been a trespass which may be an intentional trespass, or it may be a reckless trespass.

Unfortunately the trial judge regarded the matter as though the second ingredient in the burglary charged was whether there had been an intentional or reckless entry, and when he came to develop this topic in his summing-up, that error was unfortunately perpetuated. The trial judge told the jury:

He had no right to be in that house, as you know, certainly from the point of view of the girls' mother, but if you are satisfied about entry, did he enter intentionally or recklessly? What the Prosecution say about that is, you do not really have to consider recklessness because when you consider his own evidence he intended to enter that house, and if you accept the evidence I have just pointed out to you, he, in fact, did so. So, at least, you may think, it was intentional. At the least, you may think it was reckless because as he told you, he did not know whether the girl would accept him.

We are compelled to say that we do not think the trial judge by these observations made it sufficiently clear to the jury the nature of the second test about which they had to be satisfied before the appellant could be convicted of the offence charged. There was no doubt that his entry into the bedroom was "intentional." But what the appellant had said was, "She knelt on the bed, she put her arms around me and then I went in." If the jury thought he might be truthful in that assertion, they would need to consider whether or not, although entirely satisfied by such a reception being accorded to him, this young man might not have been entitled reasonably to regard her action as amounting to an invitation to him to enter. If she in fact appeared to be welcoming him, the Crown do not suggest that he should have realised or even suspected that she was so behaving because, despite the moonlight, she thought he was someone else. Unless the jury were entirely satisfied that the appellant made an effective and substantial entry into the bedroom without the complainant doing or saying anything to cause him to believe that she was consenting to his entering it, he ought not to be convicted of the offence charged. The point is a narrow one, as narrow maybe as the window sill which is crucial to this case. But this is a criminal charge of gravity and, even though one may suspect that his intention was to commit the offence charged, unless the facts show with clarity that he in fact committed it, he ought not to remain convicted.

Some question arose whether or not the appellant can be regarded as a trespasser *ab initio*. But we are entirely in agreement with the view expressed in Archbold that the common law doctrine of trespass *ab initio* has no application to burglary under the Theft Act 1968.

One further matter that was canvassed ought perhaps to be mentioned. The point was raised that, the complainant not being the tenant or occupier of the dwelling-house and her mother being apparently in occupation, this girl herself could not in any event have extended an effective invitation to enter, so that even if she had expressly and with full knowledge of all material facts invited the appellant in, he would nevertheless be a trespasser. Whatever be the position in the law of tort, to regard such a proposition as acceptable in the criminal law would be unthinkable.

We have to say that this appeal must be allowed on the basis that the jury were never invited to consider the vital question whether this young man did enter the premises as a trespasser, that is to say knowing perfectly well that he had no invitation to enter or reckless of whether or not his entry was with permission. The certificate of the trial judge, as we have already said, demonstrated that he felt there were points involved calling for further consideration. That consideration we have given to the best of our ability. For the reasons we have stated, the outcome of the appeal is that this young man must be acquitted of the charge preferred against him. The appeal is accordingly allowed and his conviction quashed.

NOTES FROM MR. MUMPOLE:

(1) Which element(s) of the crime of burglary were at issue in *Collins*? Are they at issue in our case?

(2) Precisely where did the trial court err, according to the appellate court?

(3) In *Cooper v. People*, 973 P.2d 1234 (Colorado Supreme Court, 1999), the court held:

> Burglary punishes the defendant who trespasses with the intent to do more harm once on the premises. Thus, to convict a defendant of burglary, a jury must conclude that the defendant had made up his mind to commit some other offense at the point at which he or she becomes a trespasser. If the defendant forms the intent to commit the crime after the trespass is under way, he or she may be guilty of that underlying crime (or attempt) and of trespass — but is not guilty of burglary. Both circumstances reflect criminal acts, but burglary is the more serious. Burglary is the crime that requires that the defendant have a criminal intent to do more than trespass. To hold otherwise would convert burglary into a sentence enhancer for any crime committed in tandem with a trespass.

(4) To constitute an "entry," how much body must cross the threshold? In *Regina v. Brown*, Court of Appeal (Criminal Division), The Times 31 January 1985, the court rejected defendant's argument that his entire body must enter:

> It seems to us to be an astounding proposition that a person can go along the street, break a shop window, put his hand within and steal goods and not be held to have entered the shop as a trespasser.

(5) In *People v. Jackson*, 190 Cal.App.4th 918 (2010), Jackson was on the victim's balcony, "halfway inside the Schipper's apartment and halfway on the balcony." The court found that this satisfied the "entry into a building" element of burglary:

> The definition of burglary has been held to include, for example, a carport and the area between a window screen and the window. Although the parties, the trial court, and this court have been unable to find caselaw addressing a balcony similar to the one at issue here, in determining whether a structure is part of an inhabited dwelling, the essential inquiry is whether the structure is functionally interconnected with and immediately contiguous to other portions of the house. "Functionally interconnected" means used in related or complementary ways. "Contiguous" means adjacent, adjoining, nearby or close.
>
> Schipper's balcony was immediately adjacent to his living room and extended the living room space. In addition, the balcony was separated from Schipper's bedroom by one thin wall. The balcony accordingly was functionally interconnected to and immediately contiguous to the part of the apartment used for residential activities. * * * *

There is no question in this case that Schipper's balcony was accessible only through Schipper's apartment and was intended for the exclusive use of the inhabitants of Schipper's apartment. The balcony accordingly was an element of the building that enclosed an area into which a reasonable person would believe that a member of the general public could not pass without authorization. Schipper clearly held a "possessory interest" in the balcony.

Finally, even had the trial court erred by including the term "balcony" in the definition of burglary, the undisputed evidence is that appellant was halfway inside Schipper's apartment and halfway on the balcony when Monsalud saw him. It has long been settled that any kind of entry, complete or partial, will suffice.

REGINA v. JONES
Court of Appeal, Criminal Division
3 All E.R. 54 (1976)

JAMES, L.J., delivered the following judgment of the court.

On 22nd September 1975 at the Crown Court at Winchester, John Jones and Christopher Smith were convicted of burglary, contrary to § 9(1)(b) of the Theft Act 1968. By leave of the single judge, each appeals against his conviction.

The facts of the matter which gave rise to the charge of burglary were these. Christopher Smith's father, Alfred Smith, lived at 72 Chapel Lane, Farnborough. He was in the course of negotiating a move from that house to other premises. At the material time, in May 1975, in that house, were two television sets, one owned by Mr. Alfred Smith, the other owned by another person but lawfully in the possession of Mr. Alfred Smith. Christopher Smith lived with his own family at Arborfield. The appellant Jones lived in the opposite direction from Chapel Lane, Farnborough to Arborfield, namely in Lakeside Road, Ashvale.

In the early hours of 10th May 1975, a police officer in Ashvale saw a motor car with the two appellants inside and a television set protruding from the boot of the car. Having regard to that which he saw and the time of the morning, he followed the car, which turned into a side road where eventually it was stopped by a gate being in its way. The officer called for further officers to attend, and when another officer went to the car, he saw the appellant Jones sitting on the back seat with a second television set beside him. In the front of the car was Smith. They were told that the police believed that the television sets were stolen and that they were being arrested. Smith responded with the question: "Are they bent?" and Jones made the observation: "You cannot arrest me for just having a ride in a car."

When, at the police station, they were searched, Jones was found to have in his possession a pair of pliers. Another police officer, Detective Sergeant Tarrant, who gave evidence for the Crown, had received a report from Mr. Alfred Smith and, as a result, had gone off to 72 Chapel Lane where Mr. Alfred Smith had pointed out a window in the front bedroom, which window had a hole in it due to an old breakage. The window had been secured with what appeared to be cleanly cut cable tied between the handles of the window. In the living room of the house, the officer found a further quantity of cable which had also been cut and the ends of the cut were clean. That cable was subsequently ascertained to have come from the two television sets that had been in the room. The television sets that had been in the room were the same television sets that were in the car in which the appellants were found, and there was no dispute about that.

The rest of the evidence for the Crown concerned conversations between police officers and the appellants in the course of investigating the alleged theft of the television sets by burglary. Detective Sergeant Tarrant gave evidence of Jones's denial that he had done anything and said also that Smith, in answer to the question: "Where have the television sets come from?" had said: "My dad's, he told me I could take them." When he was asked when he took the television sets he replied: "This morning, we went and got them. We was going to take them to my place for safe keeping." He went on to explain that his father was intending to move house. The officer, according to his evidence, then told Smith that his father had reported them to have been stolen. Somebody had broken into the bungalow and Smith is said to have replied: "No, I went there, the door was open and we went in and took them, we were only going to look after them." Asked, "Why at that time of the morning?" there was no reply. Asked why they drove away when the police tried to stop them, Smith explained that he had got no car tax and no insurance for the use of the motor vehicle. Asked why, if they were taking the sets to Arborfield, they were in fact going in the opposite direction when travelling from Mr. Alfred Smith's house, the explanation was given by Smith that they were just popping to Jones's house for a while.

At the trial, both the appellants gave evidence. It was the case for Smith that he had permission from his father to go into the house of his father. With that permission was a general licence to go there at any time he wanted to. It was the case for Jones at the trial, contrary to what he had said to the police, that he had gone into the house, that he had gone purely as a passenger with Smith and gone in in the belief, honestly held, that Smith had permission to take the television sets from his father and that in taking them, Smith was not stealing them or acting in any dishonest way. He, himself, insofar as he was concerned with the matter, was not acting in any dishonest way.

There was a discrepancy in the evidence of Smith between what he said on oath at the trial and what he had said to the police officers in relation to the situation in which he had gone into his father's house and had not spoken to his father, although his father was present in the house (and admittedly present) to his knowledge. In his answers to the police, he had given the answer that, as he put it, "we", that is the appellants Smith and Jones, thought Smith's father had been drinking and "we" (Smith and Jones) did not wish to disturb him.

He said they had gone in with some degree of noise, they had flushed the lavatory, put on the light, shouted "Hello", received no answer and, from the circumstances, thought his father must be out. I hope that sufficient has been said as to the facts of the matter to enable the argument and the judgment of this court on the argument to be followed.

. . .

The next ground of appeal relied on by counsel for the appellants in his argument is that which is put forward as the first ground in each of the appellant's grounds. It is the point on which counsel had laid the greatest stress in the course of his argument. The argument is based on the wording of the Theft Act 1968, § 9(1), which provides:

> A person is guilty of burglary if . . . (b) having entered any building or part of the building as a trespasser, he steals or attempts to steal anything in the building or that part of it or inflicts or attempts to inflict on any person therein any grievous bodily harm.

The important words from the point of view of the argument in this appeal are "having entered any building . . . as a trespasser".

It is a section of an Act of Parliament which introduces a novel concept. Entry as a trespasser was new in 1968 in relation to criminal offences of burglary. It was introduced in substitution for, as an improvement on, the old law, which required considerations of breaking and entering and involved distinctions of nicety which had bedevilled the law for some time.

Counsel for the appellants argues that a person who had a general permission to enter premises of another person cannot be a trespasser. His submission is as short and as simple as that. Related to this case, he says that a son to whom a father has given permission generally to enter the father's house cannot be a trespasser if he enters it, even though he had decided in his mind before making the entry to commit a criminal offence of theft against the father once he had got into the house and had entered that house solely for the purpose of committing that theft. It is a bold submission. Counsel frankly accepts that there has been no decision of the court since this Act was passed which governs particularly this point. He has reminded us of the decision in *Byrne v. Kinematograph Renters Society Ltd*[1], which he prays in aid of his argument. In that case, persons had entered a cinema by producing tickets not for the purpose of seeing the show, but for an ulterior purpose. It was held in the action, which sought to show that they entered as trespassers pursuant to a conspiracy to trespass, that in fact they were not trespassers. The important words in the judgment are[2]:"They did nothing that they were not invited to do." That provides a distinction between that case and what we consider the position to be in this case.

Counsel has also referred us to one of the trickery cases, R v. Boyle[3], and in particular to a passage in the judgment of that case[4]. He accepts that the trickery cases can be distinguished from such a case as the present, because in the trickery cases it can be said that that which would otherwise have been consent to enter was negatived by the fact that consent was obtained by a trick. We do not gain any help in the particular case from that decision.

---

[1] [1958] 2 All ER 579.

[2] [1958] 2 All ER 579.

[3] [1954] 2 All ER 721, 2 QB 292.

[4] [1954] 2 All ER at 721, 722; 2 QB at 295.

We were also referred to *R v. Collins*[5] and in particular to the long passage of Edmund Davies LJ, where he commenced the consideration of what is involved by the words "the entry must be 'as a trespasser' ". Again it is unnecessary to cite that long passage in full; suffice it to say that this court on that occasion expressly approved the view expressed in Professor Smith's book on the Law of Theft, . . . and also the view of Professor Griew . . . in his publication on the Theft Act 1968 on this aspect of what is involved in being a trespasser.

In our view the passage there referred to is consonant with the passage in the well-known case of *Hillen and Pettigrew v. ICI (Alkali) Ltd*[9] where, in the speech of Lord Atkin, these words appear:

> My Lords, in my opinion this duty to an invitee only extends so long as and so far as the invitee is making what can reasonably be contemplated as an ordinary and reasonable use of the premises by the invitee for the purposes for which he has been invited. He is not invited to use any part of the premises for purposes which he knows are wrongfully dangerous and constitute an improper use. As Scrutton LJ has pointedly said[10]: "When you invite a person into your house to use the staircase you do not invite him to slide down the banisters."

The case of course was a civil case in which it was sought to make the defendant liable for a tort.

The decision in *R v. Collins*[11] in this court, a decision on the criminal law, added to the concept of trespass as a civil wrong only the mental element of *mens rea*, which is essential to the criminal offence. Taking the law as expressed in *Hillen and Pettigrew v. ICI (Alkali) Ltd*[12] and in *R v. Collins*, it is our view that a person is a trespasser for the purpose of § 9(1)(b) of the Theft Act 1968 if he enters premises of another knowing that he is entering in excess of the permission that has been given to him, or being reckless whether he is entering in excess of the permission that has been given to him to enter, providing the facts are known to the accused which enable him to realise that he is acting in excess of the permission given or that he is acting recklessly as to whether he exceeds that permission, then that is sufficient for the jury to decide that he is in fact a trespasser.

In this particular case, it was a matter for the jury to consider whether, on all the facts, it was shown by the prosecution that the appellants entered with the knowledge that entry was being effected against the consent or in excess of the consent that had been given by Mr. Alfred Smith to his son Christopher. The jury were, by their verdict, satisfied of that. It was a novel argument that we heard, interesting but one without, in our view, any foundation.

Finally, before parting with the matter, we would refer to a passage of the

---

[5] [1972] 2 All ER 1105; 2 QB 100.

[9] [1936] AC 65 at 69; [1935] All ER Rep 555 at 558.

[10] The Calgarth, the Otarama [1927] p. 93 at 110.

[11] [1972] 2 All ER 1105; [1973] QB 100.

[12] [1936] AC 65; [1935] All ER Rep 555.

summing-up to the jury which I think one must read in full. In the course of that the recorder said:

> I have read out the conversations they had with Detective Sergeant Tarrant and in essence Smith said, "My father gave me leave to take these sets and Jones was invited along to help." If that account may be true, that is an end of the case, but if you are convinced that that night they went to the house and entered as trespassers and had no leave or licence to go there for that purpose and they intended to steal these sets and keep them permanently themselves, acting dishonestly, then you will convict them. Learned counsel for the prosecution did mention the possibility that you might come to the conclusion that they had gone into the house with leave or licence of the father and it would be possible for you to bring in a verdict simply of theft but, members of the jury, of course it is open to you to do that if you felt that the entry to the house was as a consequence of the father's leave or licence, but what counts of course for the crime of burglary to be made out is the frame of mind of each person when they go into the property. If you go in intending to steal, then your entry is burglarious, it is to trespass because no one gave you permission to go in and steal in the house.

Then the recorder gave an illustration of the example of a person who is invited to go into a house to make a cup of tea and that person goes in and steals the silver and he went on:

> I hope that illustrates the matter sensibly. Therefore you may find it difficult not to say, if they went in there, they must have gone in order to steal because they took elaborate precautions, going there at dead of night, you really cannot say that under any circumstances their entry to the house could have been other than trespass.

In that passage that I have just read, the recorder put the matter properly to the jury in relation to the aspect of trespass and on this ground of appeal as on the others we find that the case is not made out, that there was no misdirection, as I have already indicated early in the judgment, and in those circumstances the appeal will be dismissed in the case of each of the appellants.

Appeals dismissed.

NOTES FROM MR. MUMPOLE:

(1) In *Gonzales v. State*, 905 S.W.2d 4 (Tex.Ct.App. 1995), Krissi's parents disapproved of her relationship with her boyfriend, Gonzales, so Krissi invited Gonzales into the family home in order to kill her parents. Gonzales entered and killed Krissi's mother. Gonzales was convicted of "capital" murder, based on the prosecutor's claim that the murder was committed during a burglary. On appeal, Gonzales argued that he was not guilty of burglary, because a resident of the home — Krissi — had invited him in. The court disagreed.

> We hold that, when an accused has the intent to commit a felony at the time he enters a habitation and the party giving the accused consent to

enter the premises aids and assists the accused in the commission of the offense, the accused does not have "effective consent" from the owner to enter the premises. Texas Penal Code § 1.07(a)(19) expressly provides that consent is not effective if "given by a person the actor knows is not legally authorized to act for the owner." Here, appellant entered the Caldwells' home for the purpose of committing an illegal act with the assistance of a participant to the offense. Appellant knew that Krissi was not legally authorized to give him consent to enter her parents' home to kill them.

The Texas Court of Criminal Appeals affirmed. 931 S.W.2d 574 (1996).

In *People v. Johnson*, 906 P.2d 122 (Colorado Supreme Court, 1995), Johnson's wife (Tina) separated from him and leased an apartment for herself. Tina filed a petition for divorce, but did not obtain an order restraining him from coming into her apartment. While the petition was pending, Johnson entered the apartment with intent to commit certain crimes, and he was convicted of burglary. On appeal, he argued that he was "licensed" to enter the apartment because — as they were still legally married — the lease was marital property in which he had an economic interest. The court held that this did not matter, as "in determining whether the crime of burglary has been committed, the focus is on the possessory rights of the parties, and not their ownership rights." See also *Commonwealth v. Majeed*, 548 Pa. 48, 694 A.2d 336 (1997).

Compare *Commonwealth v. Robbins*, 662 N.E.2d 213 (Mass.1996), where Robbins was separated from his wife but occasionally stayed in her house (with her permission). On one occasion when he was not staying at the apartment, he broke in and killed her. He was charged with felony murder, based on the felony of burglary. The court reversed his conviction, holding that it was not clear whether Robbins had a legal right to enter, and that the trial judge should have instructed the jury that, in order to convict, they must find that "the defendant knew that he had no right to enter that premises."

(2) That banner in the window might help us. Does *Jones* have any bearing on this?

(3) If Tina intended to steal the brolly, I can understand why she should be punished for *attempted larceny*. But why punish her for *burglary*? What additional danger to society does a thief create by entering an open department store in broad daylight in order to ply her trade?

She certainly did not commit burglary under the *common law* definition of burglary. I grant that our *modern* burglary statute has come a long way from the common law definition, but I don't see *why*? What *purposes* were meant to be served by the common law definition? What *purposes* are meant to be served by the modern definition? Here is how one of your American courts handled this troubling question.

PEOPLE v. DAVIS
California Supreme Court, 1998,
18 Cal.4th 712

Defendant was convicted of forgery, receiving stolen property, and burglary, based upon evidence that he presented a stolen and forged check to the teller at a check-cashing business by placing the check in a chute in a walk-up window. Defendant maintains that the burglary conviction must be reversed because he did not enter the check-cashing facility. For the reasons that follow, we agree.

I.

On May 27, 1995, defendant approached the walk-up window of a check-cashing business named the Cash Box and presented a check to the teller by placing the check in a chute in the window. The teller later described the chute as follows: "It has a handle, and it opens out like a flap. It opens out, and they put the check in. They pass the check through." The check was drawn on the account of Robert and Joan Tallman, whose names were imprinted on the check, and was payable in the amount of $274 to Mike Woody, a name defendant sometimes used. The check was signed with the name Robert Tallman.

The teller placed a small white oval sticker on the back of the check, passed the check back to defendant, and asked him to place his thumbprint on the sticker and endorse the check. Defendant placed his thumbprint on the sticker, signed the back of the check with the name Michael D. Woody, and passed the check back to the teller, using the chute.

The teller telephoned Robert Tallman, who denied having written the check. Tallman later discovered that a group of checks, including this one, had been stolen from his automobile. The teller placed Tallman on hold and telephoned the police. An officer arrived within minutes and arrested defendant, who still was waiting at the window. At the police station, the police directed defendant to give several examples of his handwriting by repeatedly signing the name "Robert Tallman."

At trial, Tallman testified that neither the signature nor any of the other writing on the check was his.

Defendant was convicted of forgery (Pen. Code § 470), burglary (§ 459), and receiving stolen property (§ 496, subd. (c)). * * * *

II.

Under § 459, a person is guilty of burglary if he or she enters any building (or other listed structure) with the intent to commit larceny or any felony. We must determine whether the Legislature intended the term "enter," as used in the burglary statute, to encompass passing a forged check through a chute in a walk-up window of a check-cashing or similar facility.

The burglary statutes do not define the term "enter." In the present case, the Attorney General conceded at oral argument that no part of defendant's body entered the building, but it long has been established that a burglary also can be committed by using an instrument to enter a building.

In his Commentaries on the Laws of England, Sir William Blackstone stated regarding the elements of burglary: "As for the entry, any the least degree of it, with any part of the body, or with an instrument held in the hand, is sufficient; as to step over the threshold, to put a hand or a hook in at a window to draw out goods, or a pistol to demand one's money, are all of them burglarious entries." 4 Blackstone's Commentaries 227. But the common law drew a puzzling distinction. An entry by instrument was sufficient for burglary only if the instrument was used to commit the target larceny or felony. Insertion of an instrument for the sole purpose of gaining entry to the building did not constitute burglary.

The common law drew no such distinction if any part of the defendant's body entered the building. As Rollin Perkins observes in his textbook on Criminal Law:

> Where it is a part of the body itself, its insertion into the building is an entry, within the rules of burglary, whether the purpose was to complete the felonious design or merely to effect a breaking. Thus if the miscreant should open a window too small to admit his body, and should insert his hand through this opening merely for the purpose of unlocking a door, through which he intends to gain entrance to the building, he has already made an 'entry' even if he should get no farther. But where a tool or other instrument is intruded, without any part of the person being within the house, it is an entry if the insertion was for the purpose of completing the felony but not if it was merely to accomplish a breaking. If the instrument is inserted in such a manner that it is calculated not only to make a breach but also to accomplish the completion of the felonious design, this constitutes both a breach and an entry.

An illustrative case cited by Perkins is *Walker v. State* (1879) 63 Ala. 49, in which the defendant bored a hole through the floor of a corn crib, caught the shelled corn in a sack as it flowed through the hole, then sealed the hole using a corn cob. The entry of the bit of the auger into the corn crib was held to be a sufficient entry for purposes of burglary, because the instrument was used both to effect entry and to accomplish the larceny.

Although many jurisdictions adhere to the rule that entry by means of an instrument is sufficient for burglary only if the instrument was used to commit the intended larceny or felony the reason for this rule is not clear, and California courts have declined to adopt it. * * * *

In *People v. Osegueda* (1984) 163 Cal.App.3d Supp. 25, burglars were apprehended after they had succeeded in creating a small hole in the wall of an electronics store. It reasonably could be inferred that, in creating the hole in the wall, some portion of the tools had entered the building, but that the entry of these implements was not for the purpose of completing the intended larceny. The Appellate Department of the Los Angeles Superior Court found this was a sufficient entry for purposes of burglary: "We reject the decisions of out-of-state jurisdictions which differentiate between an entry by body and by instrument. We find no plausible reason for holding that an entry by instrument must be for the purpose of removing property. We find no California authority for contrary reasoning." * * * *

We agree that a burglary may be committed by using an instrument to enter a building - whether that instrument is used solely to effect entry, or to accomplish the intended larceny or felony as well. Thus, using a tire iron to pry open a door, using a tool to create a hole in a store wall, or using an auger to bore a hole in a corn crib is a sufficient entry to support a conviction of burglary. But it does not necessarily follow that the placement of a forged check in the chute of a walk-up window constitutes entering the building within the meaning of the burglary statute. * * * *

Inserting a stolen ATM card into the designated opening in an ATM is markedly different from the types of entry traditionally covered by the burglary statute, as is passing a forged check through a chute in a walk-up window. In each situation the defendant causes an object to enter the air space of a building, but it is not apparent that the burglary statute was meant to encompass such conduct. It is important to establish reasonable limits as to what constitutes an entry by means of an instrument for purposes of the burglary statute. Otherwise the scope of the burglary statute could be expanded to absurd proportions. For example, the Attorney General asserted at oral argument that mailing a forged check from New York to a bank in California, or sliding a ransom note under a door, would constitute burglary. A person who mails a forged check to a bank or slides a ransom note under a door causes that forged check or ransom note to enter the building, but it cannot reasonably be argued that these acts constitute burglary. Under the expansive approach to the burglary statute taken by the Attorney General, it is difficult to imagine what reasonable limit would be placed upon the scope of the burglary statute. It could be argued similarly that a defendant who, for a fraudulent purpose, accesses a bank's computer from his or her home computer via a modem has electronically entered the bank building and committed burglary.

The crucial issue is whether insertion of the ATM card was the type of entry the burglary statute was intended to prevent. In answering this question, we look to the interest sought to be protected by the burglary statute in general, and the requirement of an entry in particular.

The interest sought to be protected by the common law crime of burglary was clear. At common law, burglary was the breaking and entering of a dwelling in the nighttime. The law was intended to protect the sanctity of a person's home during the night hours when the resident was most vulnerable. As one commentator observed:

> The predominant factor underlying common law burglary was the desire to protect the security of the home, and the person within his home. Burglary was not an offense against property, real or personal, but an offense against the habitation, for it could only be committed against the dwelling of another. . . . The dwelling was sacred, but a duty was imposed on the owner to protect himself as well as looking to the law for protection. The intruder had to break and enter; if the owner left the door open, his carelessness would allow the intruder to go unpunished. The offense had to occur at night; in the daytime home-owners were not asleep, and could detect the intruder and protect their homes. [Note, *Statutory Burglary - The Magic of Four Walls and a Roof* (1951) 100 U. Pa. L.Rev. 411, 427].

The drafters of the Model Penal Code observed: "The notable severity of burglary penalties is accounted for by the fact that the offense was originally confined to violent nighttime assault on a dwelling. The dwelling was and remains each man's castle, the final refuge from which he need not flee even if the alternative is to take the life of an assailant. It is the place of security for his family, as well as his most cherished possessions. Thus it is perhaps understandable that the offense should have been a capital felony at common law . . . ." Model Pen. Code & Commentaries, com. to § 221 1 [FN4]

In California, as in other states, the scope of the burglary law has been greatly expanded. There is no requirement of a breaking; an entry alone is sufficient. The crime is not limited to dwellings, but includes entry into a wide variety of structures. The crime need not be committed at night. "Of all common law crimes, burglary today perhaps least resembles the prototype from which it sprang. In ancient times it was a crime of the most precise definition, under which only certain restricted acts were criminal; today it has become one of the most generalized forms of crime, developed by judicial accretion and legislative revision. Most strikingly it is a creature of modern Anglo-American law only. The rationale of common law burglary, and of house-breaking provisions in foreign codes, is insufficient to explain it." Note, *Statutory Burglary - The Magic of Four Walls and a Roof*, 100 U. Pa. L.Rev. at 411. * * * *

Inserting a stolen ATM card into an ATM, or placing a forged check in a chute in the window of a check-cashing facility, is not using an instrument to effect an entry within the meaning of the burglary statute. Neither act violates the occupant's possessory interest in the building as does using a tool to reach into a building and remove property. It is true that the intended result in each instance is larceny. But the use of a tool to enter a building, whether as a prelude to a physical entry or to remove property or commit a felony, breaches the occupant's possessory interest in the building. Inserting an ATM card or presenting a forged check does not. Such acts are no different, for purposes of the burglary statute, from mailing a forged check to a bank or check-cashing facility.

By analogy, a person who returns books to a library by depositing them in a book drop, causing the books to slide down a chute into the library, has not entered the library. It would be unreasonable to characterize the books as "instruments" used to enter the library. But if a person reaches his or her hand into the book drop, or uses a tool, in an attempt to steal books, such an act would constitute burglary.[FN6]

[FN4] Blackstone's Commentaries states that burglary "has always been looked upon as a very heinous offense; not only because of the abundant terror that it naturally carries with it, but also as it is a forcible invasion and disturbance of that right of habitation, which every individual might acquire even in a state of nature; an invasion, which in such a state would be sure to be punished with death, unless the assailant were the stronger. But in civil society the laws also come in to the assistance of the weaker party; and, besides that they leave him this natural right of killing the aggressor, if he can, they also protect and avenge him, in case the might of the assailant is too powerful. And the law of England has so particular and tender a regard to the immunity of a man's house, that it styles it his castle, and will never suffer it to be violated with impunity." 4 Blackstone's Commentaries 223.

[FN6] The record in the present case does not disclose whether, or to what extent, defendant reached into the chute of the walk-up window as he passed the check into the facility. As noted above, the Attorney General conceded at oral argument that no part of defendant's body entered the check-cashing facility.

Our conclusion that the limits of the burglary statute should not be stretched beyond recognition does not leave the public without reasonable protection from criminal conduct, for the Legislature has enacted a variety of penal statutes that apply to the activity involved in the present case. The use of an ATM card with intent to defraud, for example, specifically is penalized by § 484g and the Legislature, of course, could enact a similar statute pertaining to check-cashing facilities. Unauthorized entry into a computer system is addressed by sections 502 and 502.01. And in the present case, our reversal of defendant's conviction of burglary does not affect his convictions for forgery and receiving stolen property, or his resulting sentence of four years in prison.

For the reasons discussed above, we conclude that defendant's placement of a forged check in the chute of the walk-up window of the check-cashing facility at issue cannot reasonably be termed an entry into the building for purposes of the burglary statute. Accordingly, the judgment of the Court of Appeal is reversed to the extent it affirms defendant's conviction for burglary, and affirmed in all other respects.

Mosk, J., Kennard, J., and Werdegar, J., concurred.

Baxter, J.

I respectfully dissent. Defendant's act of passing a forged check through the walk-up security window of the check-cashing facility met the statutory and common law requirement of an "entry" sufficient to sustain his conviction of burglary. Defendant used the forged check as an instrumentality to trick the teller into handing him money back through a chute designed to protect this very type of particularly vulnerable business - a check-cashing facility - and its employee-occupants, from persons with criminal designs such as his. Defendant's use of the forged check served both to breach the security system of the business, by tricking the teller into taking the check from him through the security chute, and to gain entry into the premises, insofar as the check was literally used as a paper "hook" to enter the air space of the check-cashing facility and effectuate theft of cash on the spot from the business. Such was no less an act of larceny, and no less a breach of the business owner's "possessory interest" in his business premises accomplished through a burglarious entry, than if defendant had reached through an open window or entered through an unlocked door and grabbed his loot.

The majority suggest that conviction of burglary on these facts would unduly expand the scope of the burglary statutes to "absurd proportions." To the contrary, the majority's holding is patently at odds with the approach courts have been taking since the crime of burglary was codified over a century ago-that of moving the law in a direction away from the inflexible restraints that characterized burglary at early common law, and instead adapting the crime, within the confines of its legislative codification, to meet the security needs of a growing, changing, and

---

We need not, and therefore do not, consider whether a slight entry of a portion of defendant's body into the chute of the walk-up window would be a sufficient entry under the statute defining the offense of burglary.

increasingly crime-ridden modern society. * * * *

Under a straightforward application of the law to the facts of this case, defendant stood at the walk-up window and handed or passed a forged check through the security chute into the check-cashing facility with the intent to steal money from the business. His larcenous intent was a felonious intent. Forgery is also a felony. To the extent defendant passed the check through the chute to perfect and realize gains from his act of forgery, either felonious intent (larceny or forgery) would serve to establish the requisite unlawful specific intent for burglary.

As regards the element of "entry," in this case we are concerned specifically with an entry by tool or instrument wielded by the defendant - to wit, the forged check. When defendant gave the forged check to the teller through the security chute, at the very least, the paper document he "wielded" in his hand crossed through the outer boundary of the business premises as it was received by the teller. Respondent's misleading and imprudent suggestion at oral argument that mailing a forged check from New York to a bank in California would likewise constitute burglary - and the majority's own hypothetically stated concern that a defendant "who, for a fraudulent purpose, accesses a bank's computer from his or her home computer via a modem and has thereby electronically entered the bank building" should not be subject to prosecution for burglary - are red herrings. In neither hypothetical has a tool or instrument been wielded by a burglar to serve as an extension of his hand, arm, or body for the purpose of gaining entry into the premises. Simply put: no burglar at the crime scene, no burglary.

The crux of the matter is simply this: Can the forged check validly be deemed a "tool or instrument" wielded by defendant and placed or passed through the outer boundary of the business premises (the security chute) for the felonious purpose of burglarizing the establishment?

The majority start out by correctly observing that "the early common law drew a puzzling distinction. An entry by instrument was sufficient for burglary only if the instrument was used to commit the target larceny or felony. Insertion of an instrument for the sole purpose of gaining entry to the building did not constitute burglary." In other words, under the early common law, a burglary would have been complete upon the insertion of a hook through a window for the purpose of snagging and pulling out valuables from the burglarized structure. But if the burglary suspect used a crowbar to break through a window or door and then fled before any portion of his body had entered the structure, the insertion of the crowbar into the air space of the building or structure was insufficient to establish a burglarious entry.

The majority further acknowledge, as they must, that unlike several out-of-state jurisdictions, California courts have declined to draw any distinction between the nature or purpose of the "tool or instrument" wielded by the burglar and used to enter the burglarized structure.

In short, it is of no legal consequence in this case that the forged check defendant "wielded" and passed through the check-cashing facility's security chute was not used by him to forcibly break or gain entry into the business premises.

In contrast, it is of legal significance to note that defendant used the forged check both as a tool or instrument to breach the secured premises of the check-cashing facility (i.e., trick the teller into taking it from him through the air space of the security chute through which all of the business's transactions were conducted), and as the means for effectuating his felonious intent to steal (i.e., further trick the teller into cashing the forged check and passing money back out to him through the chute). As Rollin Perkins observes in his textbook on Criminal Law: "If the instrument is inserted in such a manner that it is calculated not only to make a breach but also to accomplish the completion of the felonious design, this constitutes both a breach and an entry." Although either purpose would alone suffice to establish a burglarious entry under California law, here, use of the forged check to gain access into the business premises through the security chute and to steal money from the teller within satisfied both. In short, the forged check in this instance served both as a crowbar and a paper "hook."

The most commonly recognized test for determining whether an entry sufficient to establish a burglary has occurred is to ascertain whether the defendant, or any tool or instrument wielded by the defendant, has crossed the outer boundary of the "air space" of the structure or premises. * * * *

Defendant's act of passing the forged check through the security chute plainly established the requisite entry for burglary. The insertion of a forged check through the chute of a walk-up window is at least as intrusive as inserting an ATM card into a machine. Obviously, the check-cashing facility is a commercial establishment that extends only a conditional invitation to its patrons to transact lawful business through its security chute - i.e., the tendering of valid checks to the teller through the chute for cashing. The facility clearly does not extend an invitation to persons like defendant to pass forged checks through its security chute in an attempt to gain possession of, and thereby steal cash from, the business. * * * *

As the rationale for their "test" or holding, the majority state the following: "Inserting a stolen ATM card into an ATM, or placing a forged check in a chute in the window of a check-cashing facility, is not using an instrument to effect an entry within the meaning of the burglary statute. Neither act violates the occupant's possessory interest in the building as does using a tool to reach into a building and remove property. It is true that the intended result in each instance is larceny. But the use of a tool to enter a building, whether as a prelude to a physical entry or to remove property or commit a felony, breaches the occupant's possessory interest in the building. Inserting an ATM card or presenting a forged check does not. * * * *

From a factual standpoint, defendant's passing of the forged check through the security chute posed an increased danger to the employee-occupants of the check-cashing facility as well as others in the vicinity. A check-cashing business is known by all to have a large amount of cash on hand; the nature of its business operation is to cash checks and hand cash out to its patrons. For this very reason its business is transacted through the walk-up window and security chute - in a sense, the only way for a patron to get "in" or "out" of the facility, i.e., transact business with it, is through the air space of the security chute. In this case, the alert teller sensed crime afoot and summoned police, who were able to arrest defendant at the crime scene without further incident. However, the potential for harm or violence always exists during a burglary and will vary with the circumstances. Although a walk-up window and security chute are specifically designed to discourage theft and robberies, there is no guarantee they will accomplish that end in every instance.

In any event, even assuming arguendo defendant's passing of the forged check through the security chute in actuality posed no direct threat of harm or violence to the business's employee-occupants, that factor was legally irrelevant to the determination of whether a burglarious entry occurred. A shoplifter who surreptitiously enters a store with the intent to steal commits burglary even though his or her clandestine effort to slip merchandise into a jacket does not necessarily threaten anyone's personal safety.

The majority's holding today will further lead to anomalous results. Under the majority's rationale, if a person inserts a stolen ATM card into an ATM machine affixed to the exterior wall of a bank and succeeds in unlawfully withdrawing money from the cardholder's account, such is not burglary because the passing of the ATM card through the ATM machine is not an unauthorized entry of the sort the burglary statute is designed to prevent. But if that same person walks into the bank building with the stolen ATM card in hand, intending to perpetrate the same unlawful transaction at an ATM machine located inside the bank lobby, he has committed burglary at the moment he crosses the threshold of the building, and he can be arrested for that crime once inside the bank even if he never approaches the ATM or attempts the fraudulent transaction. The same anomalous results would obtain in comparing a business that has a walk-up window or security chute affixed to an external wall of the building, and one that admits patrons into a lobby but then requires them to transact business with their employees through openings in a secured or windowed counter area. In the former type of business, under the majority's rationale, the tendering of a forged check or similar fraudulent document through the external security chute is not burglary even if the suspect makes off with the loot, whereas in the latter business setting, a burglary would be complete when the suspect physically enters the lobby premises with felonious intent, without any further action necessary on his part to perfect his burglarious entry.

Yet another anomalous result that will flow from the majority's holding is that an incomplete and unsuccessful attempt at a forcible entry (i.e., inserting a crowbar or other burglar tool into the air space of a window, security chute mechanism, or ATM) will suffice as a legally sufficient entry for burglary, whereas a completed and successful nonforcible entry with a "tool or instrument" such as a stolen ATM card or forged check, by which the suspect nets his loot and makes his getaway, will not. The irony here is that those very businesses which, by their nature, are particularly vulnerable to theft and burglary, and for that reason protect themselves with anticrime devices such as walk-up windows, security chutes, or card access machines requiring passwords, will receive less protection in our courts if the burglar is caught and an attempt made to bring him to justice.

The majority find it significant that "in the present case, our reversal of defendant's conviction of burglary does not affect his convictions of forgery and receiving stolen property, or his resulting sentence therefor." I fail to see the significance of this observation. The statutes proscribing check forgery and receiving stolen property have as their primary underlying purpose protection of the security interests of the original maker of the check and his bank. Defendant did not make the forged check out to himself, endorse it in his real name, or attempt to deposit it into his own bank account. Under such facts, forgery, and perhaps only forgery, would be his crime. Here, in contrast, defendant made the stolen check out to a fictitious payee and endorsed it with that fictitious name. From a practical standpoint, the forged check, as made out, had no value to defendant other than as a "tool or instrument" useable for the dual purpose of breaching the security system of the check-cashing facility (when it was accepted through the air space of the walk-up security chute) and as a paper "hook" to grab the loot (had the teller been tricked into cashing the forged check and handing money out to him through the chute).

Moreover, lest we forget, every burglary by definition has as an integral element the suspect's intent to commit a felony within the targeted premises. It would seem to beg the question to suggest, as do the majority, that conviction of burglary is unnecessary where conviction of the target felony (here forgery and receiving stolen property) is otherwise obtainable. Such circular reasoning would preclude the charging and conviction of burglary in many if not most burglary cases where the target felony (i.e., larceny) has been completed.

In sum, defendant's use of the forged check was no different than if he had "put a hand or a hook in at a window to draw out goods" from the victimized business, a clearly "burglarious entry" even at common law.

CHIN, J., and BROWN, J., concurred.

Part III

Homicide

"Homicide" means the killing of a human being — the most serious harm that may be inflicted. Obviously, it calls for the most severe punishment.

But always?

Suppose five defendants have committed similar *acts*: each drove his car into someone, causing the victim's death. Are all of these defendants equally culpable? They have all committed the same *actus reus*, but they might not have the same *mens rea*. Al was a hired "hit man" who had planned for days to kill Vic. Bob had gotten into an argument with Vic recently, had just seen him crossing the street, and on an impulse decided to kill him. Carl had just learned that Vic had raped Carl's sister yesterday, so he angrily drove into Vic. Don tried to avoid hitting Vic, but could not do so because Don was speeding (and, perhaps, was drunk). Ed was driving safely and had no intent to kill Vic, but Ed was driving away from holding up a liquor store when Vic carelessly crossed the street in front of Ed.

The result in all five cases is the same: a dead Vic and some very distraught relatives. If these relatives sue the driver *in tort* for compensatory damages, the result might be the same for each driver (except, perhaps, Ed). Each is liable, because his wrongful act caused the plaintiffs' loss — and the amount of that loss does not depend on the driver's mental state.

But the criminal law is different. The *actus reus* is important, but the *mens rea* is also very important. We punish people not just for *what* they did, but also for *why* they did it. Al is much more culpable than Don. Al is a greater threat to kill more people in the future, so we need to send a strong message to other people who are inclined to do what he did, and he also stirs in us a greater desire for retribution: unlike Don, he is not merely careless, but evil. Applying the principles of punishment discussed at the end of Chapter 1, we should punish Al much more severely than Don. The culpability of Bob and Carl would seem to fall somewhere in between Al and Don, so their punishments should fall somewhere in between. And Ed? Some people (not all) feel that a robber should be *strictly liable* for any deaths caused by the robbery.

To accomplish these results, we might do the following: charge each defendant with the crime of "homicide," tell the jury to convict if they find *any* wrongful mental state, and later — if the jury convicts — direct *the judge* to take these culpability distinctions into account in sentencing.

But we don't. (Why not?) Instead, we ask *the jury* to make these distinctions by finding which mental state the defendant possessed. The judge instructs the jury on the specific forms of homicide: *murder* (which is broken into two degrees of culpability: first and second), *voluntary manslaughter*, and *involuntary manslaughter*. And there is one more possibility: defendant's mental state might be of such minimal culpability that he should not be punished for *any* homicide crime — even though he might liable in tort to V's relatives.

In this Part, we will examine all of these possibilities. Al, Bob, Carl, Don, and Ed each represent one of the several different types of homicide discussed in the next three Chapters. As you read these Chapters, see if you can figure out which type applies to each defendant.

Chapter 7

MURDER AND INVOLUNTARY MANSLAUGHTER

Though murder is frequently defined as the unlawful killing of another "living human being" with "malice aforethought," in modern times the latter phrase does not even approximate its literal meaning. Hence it is preferable not to rely upon that misleading expression for an understanding of murder but rather to consider the various types of murder (typed according to the mental element) which the common law came to recognize and which exist today in most jurisdictions: (1) intent-to-kill murder; (2) intent-to-do-serious-bodily-injury murder; (3) depraved-heart murder; and (4) felony murder.

LaFave & Scott, *Criminal Law* (West)

Although a few states have held that ordinary (tort) negligence will suffice for involuntary manslaughter, the great weight of authority requires something more in the way of negligence than ordinary negligence. Most of the cases which state that more than ordinary negligence is needed for manslaughter do not clearly articulate what the extra something is; but on principle it must be either one or both of these two things: (1) the defendant's conduct, under the circumstances known to him, must involve a high degree of risk of death or serious bodily injury, in addition to the unreasonable risk required for ordinary negligence; and (2) whatever the degree of risk required (merely unreasonable, or both unreasonable and high), the defendant must be aware of the fact that his conduct creates this risk. (If both are required, then "recklessness" is a more appropriate term than negligence.)

LaFave & Scott, *Criminal Law* (West)

In deciding the culpability of a homicide defendant, one of the key determinants will be how high a *risk* he raised — and whether he knew (or should have known) of this risk. Let's once again assume that each of several defendants drives his car into a victim. Abe intends to kill V because he hates V. Bill did not intend to hurt V, but Bill is in a hurry to get home for dinner and drives through a crowded intersection at rush hour — hoping he will miss everyone, but unfortunately he hits and kills V. Chuck unintentionally hits V because Chuck drives through a red light at a lightly-used intersection in a rural area. And Dave is simply driving 35 miles an hour in a 25 MPH zone when he unintentionally hits V.

Each defendant caused the same result: a dead V. But the *mens rea* of each defendant was different, because the *known risk* raised by each defendant was different. As the culpability of each defendant was different, perhaps they should receive different punishments. And if our categories of homicide are designed to assign different punishments according to culpability, then some defendants might be convicted of murder (high culpability, high punishment) and some might be convicted of involuntary manslaughter (low culpability, low punishment). And perhaps Chuck and/or Dave should not be convicted of any homicide at all.

We have a problem, however. We have more defendants — i.e., more steps on the culpability spectrum — than we have categories of homicide. Assume, for the moment, that our only choices are murder, involuntary manslaughter, and no homicide at all. (As a practical matter, we cannot give a jury an infinite number of homicide crimes to fit an infinite number of levels of culpability.) We have only 3 categories, but we have 4 defendants. Abe is the most culpable, so maybe we should convict him of murder. Chuck is in the middle, sort of, so maybe we should convict him of involuntary manslaughter. What do we do with Bill? Is he more like Abe or Chuck? And what do we do with Dave? Is he enough like Chuck to deserve the same punishment as Chuck, or should we not punish him for homicide at all?

This Chapter will address these tough questions.

PROBLEM 7

From: Natalie Drest

To: My law clerk

Re: Appeal in *State v. Dozer*

My client, Dan "Bull" Dozer, was charged with second degree murder of Jake Jones. The judge properly instructed the jury on the elements of second degree murder and - as a lesser included offense - involuntary manslaughter. The jury brought in a verdict of second degree murder.

The key witness at the trial was George Glass. The transcript of his testimony is attached. On appeal, I would like to argue that his testimony was insufficient to support a verdict of second degree murder or involuntary manslaughter. As an alternative argument, I would like to try to persuade the court to reduce the verdict to involuntary manslaughter (as the court did in *State v. Bolsinger*, attached). Please read the transcript and attached authorities and advise me as to the best arguments on these points I can make on appeal, and whether I am likely to win.

Transcript of Testimony of George Glass

Q: Mr. Glass, what is your occupation?

A: I am a bartender at the Wonder Bar, in Ogden.

Q: Did you see an altercation between Bull Dozer and Jake Jones in the Wonder Bar last April 23?

A: Yes.

Q: Please describe what you saw and heard.

A: It happened around 10 p.m. Bull and Jake had been standing at the bar drinking whiskey and shooting dice, for about an hour. They had a quart bottle of whiskey in front of them which was about half full. All of a sudden they started arguing loudly about their dice game. Jake was yelling that Bull had cheated by turning one of the dice when Jake wasn't looking, and Bull owed him $5 on a bet they made. Bull said he hadn't cheated, and he said that Jake had no right to attack his honor. Then Jake said, "Well, there isn't much honor to attack," and Bull got very angry and said, "It's all over for you, buddy." Bull picked up the whiskey bottle and clobbered Jake over the head with it. Jake just crumbled. Bull said, "I didn't mean to kill him," and he ran out the door. We called a doctor, but it was too late. Jake had died of a brain hemorrhage.

Q: Would you describe the two men?

A: They were both about 5 feet, 10 inches tall. Bull was a little heavier, maybe 180 pounds, while Jake was about 160 pounds. Bull was 35 years old and Jake was 42.

Q: Was Bull drunk?

A: No, but he was a bit high from the whiskey. He's usually a very easy going guy, but when he drinks he tends to get pretty combative. I've told him about this before, and I advised him not to drink too much.

Utah Criminal Code

Section 76-5-203. Murder

* * * *

(2) Criminal homicide constitutes murder if:

   (a) the actor intentionally or knowingly causes the death of another;

   (b) intending to cause serious bodily injury to another, the actor commits an act clearly dangerous to human life that causes the death of another;

   (c) acting under circumstances evidencing a depraved indifference to human life, the actor engages in conduct which creates a grave risk of death to another and thereby causes the death of another;

   (d) [commits certain felonies].

Section 76-5-205. Manslaughter

(1) Criminal homicide constitutes manslaughter if the actor:

   (a) recklessly causes the death of another . . .

[These 2 statutes were enacted in 1953, with subsequent minor amendments.]

NOTES:

(1) In *State v. Standiford*, 769 P.2d 254, 258-259 (Utah, 1988), the Utah Supreme Court noted that "The present Criminal Code has abandoned the common law terminology of malice aforethought and adopted more descriptive and precise language describing the requisite culpable mental states in defining the various crimes. Since the term 'malice aforethought' is a confusing carry-over from prior law and could lead to confusion, if not error, it should no longer be used. * * * * Thus, the culpable mental states included in the second degree murder statute are (1) and intent to kill, (2) an intent to inflict serious bodily harm, (3) conduct knowingly engaged in and evidencing a depraved indifference to human life, and (4) intent to commit a felony other than murder. These terms are comparable to the old malice aforethought, but are much more precise and less confusing."

(2) Compare these statutes to Model Penal Code § 210.0 through 210.5, in the Appendix.

STATE v. OLSEN
Supreme Court of Utah
108 Utah 377, 160 P.2d 427 (1945)

LARSON, CHIEF JUSTICE.

The facts, not disputed, show that defendant was employed as a truck driver at Kearns Army Base. She was ordered to the Union Pacific Station to pick up some soldiers in her truck. Just after leaving Kearns, she became drowsy. She opened the windows for a breeze to combat this feeling, and drove on. She stopped for the semaphore light at 5th West and North Temple Streets, just west of the viaduct where the accident occurred. With the green light, she started to go up the viaduct, and had just shifted into third gear when she fell asleep. Defendant has no recollection of the facts of the accident, but it is not disputed that the truck went up over the right or south curb onto the sidewalk, and went along the sidewalk for some distance, striking and killing a child playing on the sidewalk.

The jury returned a verdict of guilty of involuntary manslaughter, and sentence of one year in the county jail was imposed. Defendant appeals.

* * * *

Defendant's second argument is that denial of the motion to dismiss and to direct a verdict of not guilty was error. The basis of this argument is that the state failed to prove the offense charged in that there is no showing of criminal negligence sufficient to go to the jury. This is purely a question of law.

In *People v. Robinson*, 253 Mich. 507, the court said: "The danger of driving an automobile on the highways by one who is not in possession of his faculties is a matter of common knowledge. This defendant knew that he had been going without sleep, that he had been drinking that which would disturb his faculties, and that he was not in a fit condition to drive a car. An ordinarily prudent man would have known it. An ordinarily prudent man would have known that this or some other accident would probably happen while driving in that condition. So, under the circumstances as shown by his own evidence, the defendant was negligent in falling asleep. He was negligent in trying to drive a car when a man of ordinary prudence would have known it was not safe for him to do so. It was negligent for him to drive when he was weary and sleepy. It was his duty to stop driving until he had overcome his weariness and regained control of his faculties."

This case is followed and cited in *Devlin v. Morse*, 254 Mich. 113, where the court also makes the observation that "the approach of sleep is indicated by premonitory symptoms." To the same effect is *Manser v. Eder*, 263 Mich. 107, wherein the defendant had gone to sleep shortly before the accident, and narrowly missed a collision. After being awakened and told of the incident, defendant insisted he could still drive. The court said: "Thus forewarned, his insistence that he continue driving, and that plaintiff remain with him, constituted such a reckless disregard for the consequences of an obvious danger and the safety of his passengers as amounted to willful and wanton misconduct."

Perhaps the leading case on this subject is *Bushnell v. Bushnell*, 103 Conn. 583, wherein the court said: "In any ordinary case, one cannot go to sleep while driving an automobile without having relaxed the vigilance which the law requires, without having been negligent. It lies within his own control to keep awake or cease from driving. And so the mere fact of his going to sleep while driving is a proper basis for an inference of negligence sufficient to make out a prima facie case, and sufficient for a recovery, if no circumstances tending to excuse or justify his conduct are proven."

And in *Whiddon v. Malone*, 220 Ala. 220, the court merely states: "Without extended discussion, we hold that going to sleep at the wheel while operating a car is evidence of negligence. The dangers of running a car while asleep are so obvious as to need no comment. It is the duty of the driver to keep awake or cease to drive. A failure so to do is prima facie evidence of negligence. The burden passes to the defendant to show some unusual cause of his falling asleep which reasonable diligence could not foresee nor forestall."

The burden of the foregoing authorities is overwhelmingly that the fact of going to sleep at the wheel of an automobile, without more, at least presents a question for the jury as to whether the driver was negligent. We think this a sound and salutary rule, for while one cannot be liable for what he does during the unconsciousness of sleep, he is responsible for allowing himself to go to sleep — to get into a condition where the accident could happen without his being aware of it, or able to avoid it. We think the jury could find such conduct to be negligence manifesting a marked disregard for the safety of others on the highway. Were this not the rule, the negligent driver of an automobile would better sleep while driving and avoid criminal and civil responsibility than remain awake and be responsible for his acts of negligence.

The evidence presented an issue for the jury, and is sufficient to sustain their verdict. Judgment affirmed.

WOLFE, JUSTICE (concurring in part).

I cannot agree that "the fact of going to sleep at the wheel of an automobile, without more, at least presents a question for the jury as to whether the driver was negligent" when such rule is applied to a criminal case such as this. Courts have even refused to apply such a rule to a civil case wherein the plaintiff has been required to show more than ordinary negligence. *Forsman v. Colton*, 136 Cal.App. 97; *Kaplan v. Kaplan*, 213 Iowa 646; *Boos v. Sauer*, 266 Mich. 230; *Devlin v. Morse*, 254 Mich. 113; *De Shetler v. Kordt*, 43 Ohio App. 236.

Under the holding of *State v. Lingman*, 97 Utah 180, the state is required in a case such as this to prove that the defendant was driving in marked disregard for the safety of others. A mere showing that the driver of an automobile went to sleep at the wheel will not by itself show a marked disregard.

When the driver of an automobile falls asleep at the wheel, courts in civil cases have, in addition to the fact of sleep, paid particular attention to the preceding events to determine whether or not the driver was negligent in continuing to operate the automobile. As noted in *Steele v. Lackey*, 107 Vt. 192: "One cannot be held to be negligent for what he does or fails to do in the operation of an automobile after he has involuntarily fallen asleep any more than he could be so held after he had suffered a stroke of paralysis, or epileptic seizure, or had suddenly been stricken blind, because the failure to exercise the requisite degree of care and prudence presupposes that the person sought to be charged is capable of sense perception and judgment. The question is, was he negligent in permitting himself to fall asleep, or in operating the car when he knew, or ought to have known, that sleep might come upon him?"

The focal point of the inquiry then must be whether or not the driver continued to operate the automobile after such prior warning of the likelihood of sleep, so that continuing to drive constituted marked disregard of the safety of others. In this regard see *Boos v. Sauer, supra*, wherein it is stated: "Gross negligence requires willful or wanton misconduct. To constitute gross negligence in falling asleep while driving, there must have been such prior warning of the likelihood of sleep that continuing to drive constitutes reckless disregard of consequences. There must be an appreciation of the danger of falling asleep or circumstances which would cause a reasonably prudent person to appreciate it and proceed in defiance of results."

It has been held in civil cases that the mere fact that the driver of an automobile went to sleep while driving raises a presumption of negligence, which if not rebutted will take the issue of negligence to the jury. The rule is stated in *Diamond State Tel. Co. v. Hunter*, 41 Del. 336, as follows: "There exists a presumption of law, if a person while engaged in the operation of a motor vehicle permits himself to fall asleep, that such conduct on his part constitutes negligence. The reason for the rule creating such a presumption is obvious. However, the rule extends no further than a presumption. It is not conclusive. The burden of proof merely shifts, so to speak, to the defendant to satisfactorily account for his conduct to the jury, and in the event the jury accepts the defendant's explanation of his conduct, and it is found to be sufficient, then the presumption is successfully rebutted and is of no further force and effect."

This so-called presumption of negligence has a natural relationship to the fact proved — to-wit, that the driver of an automobile went to sleep at the wheel. It is a common experience of men that sleepiness does not overtake the driver of an automobile without some prior warning of its approach. Sleep does not necessarily depend upon the length of time the driver has been at the wheel, nor upon the amount of sleep the driver has had in the period immediately prior to the time of the accident, although these matters are important. Circumstances over which the driver has little control may make him sleepy. For example, exhaust fumes may seep into the interior of the car in sufficient quantity to make the driver drowsy. Yet, no matter what the cause of sleepiness, whether from exhaust fumes or complete physical exhaustion, it is not probable that sleep would overtake the driver without him having home prior warning. The jury may take this probability into account.

However, I do not believe that it is correct to say that this raises a presumption of criminal negligence. It is but an evidentiary fact to be submitted to the jury along with all other facts and circumstances. If under all the circumstances the evidence discloses that the driver continued to operate the car without regard to premonitory symptoms of sleepiness, then the jury could find that he was driving in marked disregard of the safety of others. But a mere showing that the defendant went to sleep while driving will not by itself overcome the presumption of innocence or prima facie show criminal negligence sufficient to take the case to the jury.

Regarding the evidence that she was asleep, the defendant's testimony shows that she left Kearns air field at 1 o'clock p.m. immediately after lunch. She proceeded to 33d South and Redwood Road, along Redwood Road to North Temple and then east on North Temple to 5th West Street. The accident happened on the viaduct on North Temple just east of 5th West Street. One witness for the state, a ten year old girl, fixed the time of the accident about 3:30 p.m. Another witness for the state Mr. Peacock, fixed the time at about 1:30 p.m.

Defendant was drowsy just as she left Kearns. She rolled down the window of the truck in an attempt to shake off the drowsy feeling. She claims to have been revived and wide awake as she approached 5th West Street stop light. She saw the light turn green and proceeded through the intersection and remembers shifting into third gear. Yet, she fell asleep immediately thereafter and careened off the highway. An officer from Kearns, who was familiar with the type of truck being driven by the defendant, testified that because of the high, constant humming noise made by the transmission of such trucks, it was difficult to stay awake while driving. Defendant admitted that she knew that this type of truck induced sleepiness.

From this evidence the jury could have concluded that the defendant was asleep at the time of the accident; that she had had at least one prior warning that sleepiness was approaching; that under the circumstances, of her just finishing lunch, driving a truck that induced drowsiness, the warm day, etc., she did not successfully shake off the drowsiness; that she was approaching the business district of Salt Lake City where other people could reasonably be expected to be; that she was driving a heavy truck that could cause serious injury and property damage if it careened out of control. The jury could also conclude that in the common experience of men sleepiness does not suddenly approach without any prior warning; that defendant reacted normally in this regard for she testified that she was forewarned of sleep.

The jury could have refused to believe that she was wide awake when she approached 5th West Street. Whether, under the circumstances, she was guilty of driving in marked disregard for the safety of others in continuing to operate the automobile is probably a jury question.

I therefore concur.

NOTES FROM NATALIE:

(1) Exactly how does the concurring opinion differ from the majority opinion? Does it apply a different standard of care?

(2) I wonder how much relevance *Olsen* has to our case. Is the standard of care adopted by the majority still the proper one, under § 78-5-205?

(3) Compare *Olsen* to *Forbes v. Commonwealth*, 27 Va.App. 304 (1998). Forbes was a diabetic who blacked out while driving. His car then ran into another car, killing an occupant. Forbes was convicted of involuntary manslaughter, but the appellate court reversed:

> Forbes has been a diabetic for "thirty-some" years. At trial, Forbes testified that, on the morning of March 23, 1996, he awoke, took his insulin, and ate breakfast. He checked his blood sugar level at about 5:00 p.m. and found that it was "okay." He then took his insulin, ate supper, and drove from his residence in eastern Richmond to a friend's house on the south side of Richmond.

> Forbes testified that, at about 11:00 or 11:30 p.m., he ate several chicken wings and drank a seven-ounce beer. He fell asleep until about 2:30 a.m., and, when he awoke, he felt "a little woozy." Forbes testified that he ate "a couple of mints," drank a glass of orange juice, and sat down for about fifteen minutes. Forbes stated that he then felt "fine" and entered his car to drive home. As he warmed up his car, his friend, Mozelle Carter, brought him two more mints, which he ate. Forbes again told Carter that he felt "fine," and he started driving toward his home.

> Forbes recalled driving on Jefferson Davis Highway, crossing the James River on the Lee Bridge, and seeing the Second Street exit. He did not recall anything else until after the accident. * * * *

> Dr. Randolph Palmore, Forbes' physician since January 1994, testified that he never instructed Forbes not to drive or advised Forbes that it would be hazardous to drive. Dr. Palmore also stated that he had no record that Forbes told him he had suffered black-outs. He did not know whether Forbes had "any diabetic reactions." Forbes' last visit with Dr. Palmore prior to the accident was on February 21, 1996. At that visit, Dr. Palmore said Forbes' "sugar was stable, and there were no changes made in his

insulin." Dr. Palmore saw Forbes again on March 29, 1996, five days after the accident, and adjusted his insulin at that visit.

Dr. John Nestler treated Forbes on March 25, 1996, when Forbes was in the hospital after the accident. Dr. Nestler said Forbes told him he knew he was having a low blood sugar reaction on March 24, 1996 because he felt "confused" and woozy prior to driving his car. However, Forbes said he felt better after resting and eating mints. Dr. Nestler also testified that most diabetics go through two "stages" when they develop a low blood sugar attack. In the first stage, they release adrenaline, get nervous, have heart palpitations, shakiness and headaches. In the second stage, the patient experiences confusion. Dr. Nestler said that, based on his interview with Forbes concerning his low blood sugar attacks, he "clearly doesn't have that first phase. So he doesn't have those warning signs that most diabetic patients have. He goes straight into confusion, and that's something that's termed hypoglycemia unawareness."

Dr. Nestler also testified that he usually advises his patients to consume mints or drink one-half of a glass of orange juice, wait one-half hour, and check their blood sugar when they experience a low blood sugar episode.

To constitute involuntary manslaughter, the negligence involved must be criminal and not ordinary civil negligence. Inadvertent acts of negligence without recklessness, while giving rise to civil liability, will not suffice to impose criminal responsibility. * * * *

The Commonwealth asserts that the record establishes that Forbes had a history of diabetic attacks, resulting in black-outs. The Commonwealth contends that Forbes continued to drive, knowing that he was susceptible to black-outs and that he drove on March 24, 1996, knowing his blood sugar was low and disregarding the known risk that he posed to other motorists. Thus, the Commonwealth contends Forbes' conduct was criminally negligent.

Forbes argues that, because he took precautionary measures and felt "fine" before he drove on March 24, 1996, the evidence did not prove he acted in a criminally negligent manner. We agree.

Hypoglycemia, or low blood sugar, is seen in the diabetic "who takes too much insulin, too little food, or both or over-exercises." 4B Lawyers' Medical Cyclopedia of Personal Injuries and Allied Specialties 27 (James G. Zimmerly, M.D., J.D., M.P.H. ed.1984). Corrective measures for the condition include "giving the sufferer generous amounts of glucose by mouth in the form of sugar, honey, candy, or a sweetened beverage." *Id.* Dr. Nestler testified that he advises his patients to eat mints or drink one-half of a glass of orange juice, wait one-half hour, and check their blood sugar level when they experience low blood sugar. Further, Dr. Nestler testified that Forbes "clearly" did not have the warning signals that most diabetic patients experience when having a low blood sugar attack. Forbes testified that on one prior occasion he had experienced no warning signs prior to his black-out. On another occasion, he blacked-out before he could "treat himself."

On these facts, we find that Forbes' conduct did not constitute negligence so gross, wanton, and culpable as to show a reckless disregard of human life. For a diabetic to operate a motor vehicle is not negligence per se. Forbes followed the medical directions he had been given to correct an insulin imbalance. The factual findings of the court sitting without a jury will not be set aside unless it is plainly wrong or without evidence to support it. However, a trial court's conclusion based on evidence that is 'not in material conflict' does not have this binding effect on appeal. The trier of fact must determine the weight of the testimony and the credibility of the witnesses, but it may not arbitrarily disregard uncontradicted evidence of unimpeached witnesses which is not inherently incredible and not incon-sistent with facts in the record. A court may not base its findings on a suspicion which is contrary to the undisputed positive testimony.

Forbes checked his sugar level at about 5:00 p.m. on March 23, 1996. He ate breakfast and dinner that day. He took insulin at 5:00 p.m. Forbes also ate a small meal at about 11:30 p.m. on March 23, 1996 before he fell asleep. When he awoke and felt "woozy," Forbes ate "a couple of mints," drank a glass of orange juice, and rested for about fifteen minutes. Forbes stated that he felt "fine" before he drove his car. As he sat in his car, his friend brought him two more mints, which he ate. Carter also testified that Forbes "was driving fine" as she watched him drive away from her house. He had not been advised by his physician to stop operating a motor vehicle.

Therefore, the evidence proved, without contradiction, that Forbes took precautionary measures when he felt "woozy" and suspected he was experiencing a low blood sugar episode. Although Forbes did not check his blood sugar level before he drove, he performed several other acts that are recommended to restore blood sugar level. Further, Forbes testified that he felt "fine" before he drove his car. Moreover, he had experienced black-outs on only two or three occasions in his thirty years as a diabetic, with the last black-out occurring in December 1995. Under these facts, we cannot say Forbes knew or should have known that his conduct created a great risk reasonably calculated to produce injury. Although Forbes' conduct may have been negligent under these circumstances, his negli-gence did not amount to wanton negligence so culpable as to show a "reckless disregard of human life."

For these reasons, we reverse the involuntary manslaughter conviction.

(4) Compare also *Conrad v. Commonwealth*, 29 Va.App. 661 (1999):

At about 9:00 a.m. on May 11, 1997, on Gayton Road in Henrico County, appellant fell asleep at the wheel of his automobile and drove off the road, striking and killing Judy Dahlkemper, a jogger. Officer R.J. Smith re-sponded to the scene. Shortly after 11:00 a.m., after examining the physical evidence, Smith took appellant's statement. Smith described appellant as "extremely tired" and having bloodshot eyes, and he noticed a faint odor of alcohol about appellant's person. Appellant reported to Smith that he had last slept on May 10, the day before the accident, arising at 11:00 a.m. after six hours of sleep. It was not unusual for appellant to stay up for long periods of time because he had been working an irregular schedule at a retail store and playing in a band. On May 10, appellant worked a shift at the retail store, ran errands, practiced with his band, and went to the home of a friend in Richmond. While at his friend's home, between about 11:00 p.m. and 1:30 a.m., appellant consumed about fifty ounces of beer. He remained at his friend's home, awake and watching television, until about 8:45 a.m., at which time he left to return home. Appellant testified that he was not sleepy before he left for home and that it had not occurred to him that he might fall asleep on the drive home.

Appellant traveled about twenty minutes on Interstate 64 to Gaskins Road. As appellant exited Interstate 64, "he really got tired and felt himself going to sleep." Because he was only about five minutes or four-and-one-half miles from home, "he did not really want to stop." He reported to Officer Smith that "he ran off the road only after dozing off for a half second, caught himself drifting four or five times, still nodding, but said he would catch himself and said he would snap out of it." On Gayton Road, a little over one-half mile from his home, he fell asleep and heard a loud noise. He initially thought someone had hit his car with a bottle, but then he saw the body and stopped his vehicle. * * * *

In finding appellant guilty of involuntary manslaughter, the trial court found that appellant had been awake for twenty-two hours and "felt himself just about going to sleep," allowing "his car to drift over to the right on four or five different occasions" as he was "nodding in and out." Although appellant had "previously dozed prior to the accident," observed the court, "he chose to continue to drive to try to make it home." The trial court concluded that appellant "was operating that motor vehicle in a state that he knew very well or should have known very well that he may, in fact, fall asleep" and that his conduct was "gross, wanton, and culpable, and showed a disregard for human life."

But the appellate court reversed:

The evidence, viewed in the light most favorable to the Commonwealth, did not exclude the reasonable hypothesis that appellant became sleepy, as he told Officer Smith, only after leaving Interstate 64, when he was only five minutes from home. In addition, the evidence established that after realizing he had dozed off for "a half second" and run off the road, appellant was able on four or five subsequent occasions to catch himself as the car began to drift and to keep it from running off the road again. Finally, for two-tenths of a mile before the accident, appellant drove without apparent difficulty, maintaining a proper speed and driving within the lines. Under these circumstances, we cannot conclude that appellant knew or should have known that his conduct in proceeding the short distance to his nearby home "probably would cause injury to another" or that he acted mercilessly or inhumanely in failing to stop. That his conduct did, in fact, result in death is tragic and may constitute ordinary or even gross negligence, but it does not, without more, support a finding of criminal negligence.

(5) *Commonwealth v. Fortes*, 712 N.E.2d 104 (Mass.App.Ct. 1999) involved the following facts:

> Early one evening in February, 1992, the defendant and a companion, Westgate, were out walking in New Bedford "seeing what they could get into." They saw a sixty-five year old woman, Lucille Labens, bringing out her household trash and decided to steal her purse, which hung by a strap from her left arm. Westgate walked up behind Mrs. Labens, grabbed the purse strap, and attempted to slide it off her arm. Mrs. Labens caught the strap in her hand and a brief struggle ensued, during which Westgate pushed or pulled her to the pavement, seriously injuring her knee. She continued to hold on, and he freed the purse only after pulling her along the ground. Mrs. Labens underwent surgery the next day to repair her dislocated kneecap. Blood clots developed as a complication of the surgery, which led to her death by coronary embolism six days after the purse snatching. The defendant, charged with unarmed robbery of a person age sixty-five years or older, and involuntary manslaughter, was tried as a joint venturer and convicted on both charges.

The court affirmed the involuntary manslaughter conviction:

> Any robbery from the person, with the possible exception of pickpocketing, involves a substantial likelihood that the victim will resist and that a struggle may ensue. Where the victim is elderly, years removed from the rough and tumble of the playground and contact sports, and with the impaired resilience of bone and sureness of balance that age entails, any resistance will lead predictably to falls and a high likelihood of injury. This is a matter of common experience, that any fall of an elderly person — particularly a rough fall on a hard surface, as here — is a source of serious concern, as are the anxiety of the occasion and the exertion of resistance, which pose dangers to the elderly that might not be expected in younger victims. A robber who subjects an elderly victim to a highly predictable risk of serious injury cannot escape responsibility merely because he hoped that the victim would docilely yield up a purse or wallet without resisting. It is immaterial that the defendant and Westgate might not have anticipated the danger. The legal test is the danger that a reasonably prudent person would apprehend.

(6) The rather severe punishment meted out to the defendant in *Olsen* (a year in jail) for simple negligence raises a fundamental question about involuntary manslaughter: why should we use the criminal law *at all* to punish unintentional homicides? Ms. Olsen had no "evil mind," and we would not punish her (much) if she had not had the bad luck to run into someone. In applying the purposes of punishment (general deterrence, isolation, etc.) to this situation, it seems that the only one which operates is *retribution*: the community is angry about the death, and since the defendant is "at fault" she must pay for it - in jail time, not just civil damages. Is this fair?

In Schulhofer, *Harm or Punishment: A Critique of Emphasis on the Results of Conduct in the Criminal Law*, 122 U.Penna.L.Rev. 1497 (1974), the author considers whether the imposition of a harsher penalty solely because harm results from unintentional conduct serves any of the fundamental purposes of the criminal law. He gives particular attention to vehicular homicide statutes based on drunk driving, as there the *disparity* in penalty is usually the greatest. He concludes that the purpose of *deterrence* is not served, as one who is not deterred by the penalty for driving under the influence *and* the risk of injury or death *to herself* from this particular crime is unlikely to be deterred by the very slight risk (under 5%, studies show) that she will cause another's death and thereby be punished for vehicular manslaughter. Professor Schulhofer also says that "selection of those who cause harm [for a stiffer punishment] is a kind of lottery, just as selection of those born on certain days, determined at random, would be a kind of lottery." While retaliation seems to loom as the dominant motive for a punishment based on results — an eye for an eye — "most American jurisdictions exclude retaliation from the legitimate goals of the criminal law." Regarding vehicular homicide, he states that "emphasis on results seems devoid of support in the arguments considered", and he concludes that "The crime of vehicle homicide or involuntary manslaughter should for practical purposes disappear from the statute books."

Do you agree?

STATE v. JENSEN
Supreme Court of Utah
120 Utah 531, 236 P.2d 445 (1951)

CROCKETT, JUSTICE.

Defendant appeals from a conviction of second degree murder. He asserts that there is not sufficient evidence from which reasonable minds could find beyond a reasonable doubt either (1) that he had the intent necessary to constitute second degree murder or (2) that any act on his part caused the death.

With respect to his intent: It is the established law of this state that in order to make the crime of second degree murder the defendant must have intended to either (a) kill, or (b) do great bodily harm, or (c) do an act which would naturally and probably cause death or great bodily harm to the deceased.

In this case, the jury was instructed to that effect. From their verdict, it must be assumed by us that they found from the evidence beyond a reasonable doubt that the requisite intent was present. If the evidence justifies that finding, it is our duty to affirm the verdict.

From the record, it appears that all of the characters in this drama were a good deal below the moral standard which generally prevails in our Utah communities. They had all been drinking together at a dance on the evening prior to this tragedy; both defendant and deceased were drunk. After the dance, the defendant accidentally dropped and lost his car keys and sent his wife for a taxi. The deceased, Val Gene Steele, offered to drive her and her husband home. She got in his car; he drove on past her husband who was standing by his truck and went on to a public park.

There is evidence that he made an indecent proposal to her and that he may have been a bit rough in trying to force his attentions on her. He being dead, her version of the story is the only evidence available; she stated that after a short struggle he gave up, drove her back and let her off at her husband's truck. Whatever the episode amounted to, the defendant's wife made no mention of it to her husband that night. She first told him about it the next morning at breakfast. There is no evidence that he was then much concerned or upset about it.

At about 8:30 or 9:00 a.m., the defendant left home to see about working that day. On the highway, he met one Sherill Crane who also had a hangover from the previous night; they proceeded to a tavern in Salina to drink beer together. As defendant sat in the tavern drinking beer, he talked volubly about the affront to his wife, telling all the customers about it. This is some indication of what a sensitive creature he must be and how outraged his feelings must have been at the claimed insult to his wife.

Defendant and Crane spent most of the forenoon in the tavern. Defendant boasted several times, referring to Steele, that he was going to "kill the son of a bitch" and "beat him to death". He did this in the hearing of numerous people; the tavern operator told the defendant that he "would not be talking about it in a public place." Sherill Crane, the so-called friend of the defendant, kept urging the defendant on to start some trouble.

It should be remembered that the defendant was a big, strong man, practically in the prime of life. He weighed 180 pounds, was 5'10" tall, and 34 years old. The deceased was a much smaller and considerably older man. He weighed 130 to 135 pounds, was 5'5" tall and was 41 years of age. Even if one tolerated the idea of physical violence as a method of rectifying a wrong, it would have been unsportsmanlike for this larger, younger man to administer a beating to the deceased. But the evidence supports a finding of a more serious determination. Several witnesses testified to hearing the defendant make unconditional threats to kill the deceased.

Finally, just before noon, the defendant told this Crane to go get the deceased and he, the defendant, would kill him. Defendant allowed Crane to take the defendant's truck for that purpose. Crane lied to the deceased, presuming on his friendship to ask him to help Crane move a refrigerator. This deceased readily agreed to do, relayed this information to his wife, got in the truck and went with Crane. The latter then took the deceased to the tavern; parked the truck and got out of it; then went and informed the defendant that Steele was there, thus laying the scene for this crime. One can visualize how proud Crane must be of the part he played in this affair which resulted in the death of deceased, leaving as a widow a trusting wife and mother and causing five small children to be fatherless.

Upon learning that the truck was in front of the tavern - the defendant took off his shirt, went out and tried to get the deceased out of the truck. In doing so, he again expressly threatened to kill the deceased. The deceased only attempted to keep in the truck and avoid being taken out of it by the defendant. The latter got up on the running board and proceeded to flail upon the deceased, who was then lying in the seat trying to keep away from the defendant, the most vicious and violent blows he was capable of.

As the witnesses could not actually see into the cab of the truck, no one was in a position to tell whether defendant was striking Steele with anything but his hands; we assume that all of the blows were struck with his bare fists. After defendant had rained many blows upon the deceased, one Sharp Rasmussen, a bystander, stopped the defendant. As he did so, the defendant was still threatening to kill Steele and continuing to call him names. Ernest Lau, who knew the deceased well, got up on the running board and looked into the truck; the deceased was so bruised and bloody that Lau did not recognize him and inquired who he was; Lau testified that "there was blood all over."

A few minutes later, after deceased had washed and cleaned up as best he could, when Crane let him off at his home, his wife noticed "a deep gash on his mouth," "a large black mark on his temple," "his eyes swollen" and other marks of violence upon him. He seemed not to know what was going on, kept asking the same questions about the World series ball game which was on the radio - walked out into the yard - and within a few minutes one of the children observed him lying on the ground gasping his last. Although there is some uncertainty about the time, his death occurred within two hours of the time of the assault upon him.

Any difference in facts between this and the dissenting opinion is because Mr. Justice Wade is placing some emphasis on certain of defendant's evidence, while we rely on the evidence produced by the State.

Is the foregoing evidence sufficient to meet the requirements of the law as to the intent necessary for second degree murder? The question of intent is practically always one for the jury.

It is true that striking with fists, without more, will not ordinarily imply an intent to kill. See *People v. Crenshaw*, 298 Ill. 412, 15 A.L.R. 671, and authorities cited in connection with the A.L.R. report on that case and note following it. But at p. 676, the annotator says, "It has been held that an assault without a weapon may be attended with such circumstances of violence and brutality that an intent to kill will be presumed."

Under that rule, the violence and brutality of the attack in this case, coupled with the difference in the sizes and ages of the men and the other circumstances, was such that the court may very well have submitted the question of the defendant's intent, even if the defendant had made no threat nor expression of his intention. However, that is a matter which we need not consider nor pass on. Here the defendant not only expressly stated his intent beforehand to kill the deceased, but sent for him for the avowed purpose of carrying out his threat.

It is uniformly held that it is not necessary that a deadly weapon be used in order to justify a finding by the jury that a defendant intended to kill. * * * *

Defendant asks us to theorize that, in threatening to kill Steele, he did so in a manner of "big talk" or "bragging." The jurors saw and heard the witnesses, including the defendant himself. Because they are closer to the actuality, the flesh and blood and drama of the crime and the trial, they are in a much better position than is this court to determine what defendant's intent was. The jury was composed of presumably fair-minded citizens of the locality, properly selected and fully and accurately instructed by a conscientious and careful trial judge. Respecting the matter of the intent, his instruction was:

> Before you can find the defendant guilty of murder in the second degree, you must believe from the evidence beyond a reasonable doubt the following:
>
> * * * *
>
> Sixth: That the killing was the result of the specific intention on the part of the defendant to take the life of said Val Gene Steele or with specific intention of committing the alleged unlawful act with the knowledge that the natural and probable consequences thereof would be to cause death or great bodily harm to said Val Gene Steele.

That instruction correctly states the law as to the intent required in second degree murder.

There could hardly be more direct or certain evidence of the defendant's intent than for him to declare before, during and after the attack, his intention to kill. However, we do not disagree with the idea that the jury could have weighed against it the fact that the defendant (apparently) only used his fists, and if there were any reasonable doubt in their minds as to his intention to kill or do great bodily harm to Steele, then the verdict could not have been for more than involuntary manslaughter.

On the other hand, they were also entitled to consider the evidence of the difference in the sizes and ages of the men; the brutality of the attack and the expressed threats of the defendant to kill the deceased. Under that evidence, the trial court was required to allow the jury to determine what his intent was. If they chose to believe that he meant what he said, and found from the evidence beyond a reasonable doubt that he did intend to kill or do great bodily harm to the deceased, it was their privilege so to do. There was evidence upon which reasonable minds could conclude as they did, and this court will not disturb their verdict.

The conviction is affirmed.

WADE, JUSTICE (dissenting).

I conclude that it is unreasonable under the facts and circumstances of this case as disclosed by the record to find that there is no reasonable doubt of defendant's intention to either kill decedent or do him great bodily harm or to do an act knowing that it naturally and probably would do decedent great bodily harm. I use the phrase "unreasonable to find that there is no reasonable doubt" rather than the conventional phrase "no reasonable mind can find beyond a reasonable doubt" because I think it more accurate.

Our problem is whether the result reached is reasonable not whether the mind which reaches that result should be classified as a reasonable mind. Most minds act reasonably most of the time, very few always so act. Unless the phrase "reasonable mind" means a mind which never acts unreasonably, then its use in describing this concept is inaccurate, for such a mind might act unreasonably in the instant case, although in all other cases it might act reasonably.

I think the picture against the defendant is greatly overdrawn in the prevailing opinion so I make my own version of the facts as disclosed by the record.

On the evening of October 7, 1949, decedent and defendant and his wife were at a ball in Salina, Utah, and decedent and defendant were both somewhat intoxicated. When the dance closed, defendant and his wife went to his truck to drive home, but he accidentally dropped and lost the car key, and while he searched for it, he sent his wife to Mom's Cafe to get a taxi. While she was waiting for one, decedent came in and sat beside Mrs. Jensen, and after some conversation, she accepted his offer to drive her and her husband home in his car. However, when she got in his car he drove past her husband and his truck without picking him up and went on to a public park, where he proposed intercourse which she refused, and he struck her between the eyes with his fist. After a short struggle he gave up and then let her off at her husband's truck, where in the meanwhile defendant had found the keys, and they drove home.

Mrs. Jensen first told her husband of decedent's attack the next morning and he became upset about it. About 8:30 or 9:00 a.m., defendant left home to see if he had work, but on the way he met Sherill Crane, who also had a hangover from the previous night, and they proceeded to Jack's Knotty Pine Inn, in Salina, where they drank beer together. Soon defendant told the people there of decedent's attack on his wife the previous evening, that he deserved a beating and should be made to apologize, and Crane drove defendant's truck to decedent's home and brought him back to the Inn. There defendant told decedent to get out of the car, and there is evidence that he demanded an apology for the attack on his wife, and threatened to beat him to death if one was not forthcoming. Decedent refused to get out of the truck and defendant stood on the running board and proceeded to attack decedent through the open door with his fists. To ward off the blows, decedent drew his feet upon the seat between his face and defendant and his head went partially down on the seat, and defendant grabbed decedent's feet and started to pull him out of the truck, when Sharp Rasmussen, who had been drinking with defendant that morning, took defendant by the arm and said he had been beaten enough.

Thereupon defendant ceased the attack, but continued in a loud voice to demand an apology to his wife and repeatedly said if he did not do so he would kill decedent. At first decedent asked for a little time, but later agreed to go to her home immediately and make the apology. Thereupon, Crane drove him in defendant's truck to defendant's home where decedent apologized to her, and they brought Mrs. Jensen back with them to the Inn where he again apologized to defendant and his wife alone at the truck. Then Crane took decedent back home and on the way they stopped by the road and drank a bottle of beer.

The encounter between defendant and decedent occurred a few minutes after 12:00 in the busiest part of Salina on a Saturday. It was witnessed by customers and waiter of the Inn and a number of people on the street. Before the encounter, decedent was in good health and his face unmarred. After the altercation, he did not appear to be badly hurt although his face had a number of bruises and was bleeding from a laceration on the lower right lip and an abrasion on his right brow, and there was evidence of contusions over his right jaw, the right side of his nose and right cheek and ear and a more severe contusion with swelling on his right temporal region. To me it seems quite probable decedent's injuries resulted from bumping against the sides of the truck cab rather than from direct blows of defendant's fists for in such a small compartment with a steering wheel between them and decedent trying to avoid the blows it would be difficult to do the damage which resulted.

The encounter lasted from less than a minute to possibly a minute and a half. Defendant started the encounter largely at the suggestion of others, and stopped when he was told he had done enough. Defendant was 34 years old, he said he weighed between 155 and 165 pounds, and he was 5 feet 10 inches tall; another witness called by defendant estimated that he weighed about 180. Decedent was nearing 42 years of age, weighed about 135 pounds and was 5 feet and 5 inches tall. Decedent was away from his home less than an hour. When he returned home, there was no evidence he was seriously injured. Shortly after he returned, he began to be restless and said to his wife that he was not well, and appeared to be going to bed, then went outside and before 3:00 o'clock he was found unconscious and was dead before a doctor arrived.

There was nothing about defendant's attack on decedent which indicated an intention to kill or do great bodily harm, nor was his death the natural and probable result thereof. It is true that defendant said he would kill him or beat him to death if he did not apologize, but that was qualified on condition that decedent refused to apologize, and it was said more in a manner of big talk rather than as indicating an intention to carry it out literally. It is not uncommon for people to make such statements without meaning to carry them out. There is nothing to indicate that defendant was particularly violent in his attack on decedent. He seems to have thought, as most husbands would think, that decedent deserved a thrashing. He was a larger and younger man than decedent, but this difference is not so great that it would suggest that this short encounter would result fatally or in great harm to decedent. There is no evidence that he took unfair advantage or that he unduly persisted in punishing decedent or that at any time during the scuffle decedent was in a helpless condition. No one suspected that decedent was badly hurt until he suddenly died.

Under these circumstances, it would be unreasonable to conclude that there was no reasonable doubt that he had the necessary intention to constitute murder in the second degree.

Most courts recognize that in a case of striking only with the hands and fists, without extraordinary circumstances which indicated an intention to kill or do serious bodily harm, the evidence is not sufficient to sustain a verdict of first or second degree murder. *People v. Crenshaw*, 298 Ill. 412; *People v. Munn*, 65 Cal. 211. In the last case, the court said: "In the trial of cases of homicide committed by violence it is almost always important to consider the character of the weapon with which the homicide was committed, and all through the cases great emphasis is laid on the fact that a weapon likely to produce death was used by the accused. If the means employed be not dangerous to life, or, in other words, if the blows causing death are inflicted with the fist, and there are no aggravating circumstances, the law will not raise the implication of malice aforethought, which must exist to make the crime murder."

These cases recognize that the circumstances may be such as to evidence an intention to kill or do great bodily harm even though no weapon other than the fists is used, and there is a line of cases which so hold. See note to 15 A.L.R. 675, and 24 A.L.R. 666, but the facts in those cases are not similar to this case.

In *State v. Cobo, supra*, we held that even voluntary manslaughter requires an intent to kill or do great bodily harm or the doing of an act which will naturally and probably have such effect, and that striking with fists in a fair fight does not have a tendency to show such an intention. In view of this decision, the only crime which defendant could be guilty of under this evidence is involuntary manslaughter. If we mean what the phrase "convinced beyond a reasonable doubt" says, then the evidence must be sufficient to establish defendant's guilt, including his intent, so conclusively that the trier of the facts could reasonably conclude that any doubt thereof would be unreasonable, for as long as a contrary conclusion is reasonably possible under the evidence, then there is a reasonable doubt. See Wigmore on Evidence, 3d Ed., Sections 2497 and 2498.

I think it would be unreasonable to conclude from this evidence that to find that defendant did not intend to kill, cause great bodily harm or do an act knowing that it would probably cause decedent great bodily harm would be unreasonable. I therefore dissent.

NOTE FROM NATALIE:

The majority examined the record for substantial evidence of intent to kill. Did it overlook any *other* possible ground(s) for affirming the conviction?

STATE v. BOLSINGER
Supreme Court of Utah
699 P.2d 1214 (1985)

HOWE, JUSTICE:

Defendant appeals from a verdict convicting him of murder in the second degree.

On March 29, 1980, 33-year-old Kaysie Sorensen was found dead by her boyfriend, Mark Anger, in his apartment when he returned from a 24-hour shift as a firefighter. She was lying spread-eagled on the bed, all but her legs covered with a sheet. The cord of a clock radio resting on the bed was loosely tied around her neck. A catalogue advertising sexual paraphernalia and entitled "Romeo . . . your Source of Sexual Pleasure" was nearby on the floor. "The Joy of Sex" and "Supersex," two books of explicit sexual literature, were in the nightstand by the bed. The living room seemed to indicate that a burglary had taken place. The contents of Kaysie's purse were scattered on the floor, a lamp was knocked over, and Mr. Anger's stereo was missing.

Kaysie had last been seen alive on March 28, 1980, in Bill's Lounge in Magna, where she was a regular customer. She arrived there in a state of intoxication around 8:00 p.m. She sang along with a jukebox, danced by herself on the dance floor and "tried to kiss a lot of guys on the cheek up and down the bar." She finally approached the 23-year-old defendant when he entered the bar around 9:00 p.m., watched him play pool, put her arms around him between pool shots, kissed him on the cheek and finally left with him shortly before 10:00 p.m.

After preliminary investigation, defendant was arrested and booked in the Salt Lake County jail on April 1, 1980, where he made a confession in the early morning hours of April 2.

According to the confession and later undisputed testimony at trial, defendant and Kaysie drove to defendant's home, where they picked up a bottle of whiskey and then continued to Mr. Anger's apartment. They played records on the stereo, danced and drank straight from the bottle for about an hour. Both were quite intoxicated. They went to the bedroom, partially undressed, lay down on the bed, and eventually engaged in sexual intercourse with defendant atop Kaysie.

Thereafter, the statements given in defendant's confession and at trial diverged. At trial defendant testified that after about five minutes he stopped for a moment to rest, started to get up, and Kaysie said "no." He rolled off to the side and she rolled over to pick up the clock radio, setting it down next to her. Neither of them commented about the radio. The couple resumed intercourse, defendant felt Kaysie move around, opened his eyes and saw the cord around her neck. They continued intercourse, and defendant opened his eyes again when he heard Kaysie say "pull." At this time she was holding the cord with her arms extended in a 45-degree upward angle. When questioned why he took hold of the cord, defendant replied, "she asked me to. I heard there was something like that, and I don't know where but I heard something like that." Defendant pulled "like tying your shoes" for about fifteen to twenty seconds, reached a climax and relaxed, still on top of Kaysie, then rolled off to the side.

When he looked at her a few moments later, he noticed that Kaysie's face looked strange, not awake or reacting. He became afraid, got up, picked up his clothes, went into the living room, dressed and walked back into the bedroom. Kaysie was still in the same position. Defendant looked at her for a few moments, could not be sure at trial but thought that he put a sheet over her, picked up his bottle, returned to the living room, dumped the contents of her purse and left the apartment with the stereo.

This testimony paralleled the confession in all but three aspects. Defendant there stated that it was he who grabbed the radio and he who wrapped the cord around her neck after intercourse, but while he was still on top of her; that Kaysie "got kinda weirdlike," indignant; and that it just happened. He was not mad, there was no fight, "she just laid there." The confession ended with the following exchange:

Q: Do you know why it happened?

A: Wish I did.

Q: Have you ever been involved in anything else like this before?

A: Never. Not even close. Never even any, hurt anybody before.

At trial defendant explained that he had lied to the police in his taped confession. He had been told that the scene looked like a rape murder, but that if what he told the police did not happen during intercourse, the charge could be reduced. All he knew at that time was that he wanted to keep himself from being charged with first degree murder and being sentenced to death. He also did not think that anyone would believe the truth.

The State's medical examiner testified that the victim was wearing a vaginal contraceptive at the time of death. Sperm and seminal fluid were present in the vagina. Her alcohol blood level was .22. There was no structural damage to the neck. * * * * There was no evidence of furrowing or any indication that the cord was ever knotted or in a tied position. * * * * Pressure applied to the throat of an intoxicated person would produce death more quickly. This testimony was essentially corroborated by an expert witness for the defense. He testified that a third factor hastening death was the weight of defendant on Kaysie's chest, as evidenced by congestion of the blood vessels across the uppermost portion of the chest of the victim. * * * *

Kaysie's boyfriend, Mark Anger, testified that Kaysie had a drinking problem, that during her drinking sprees she would be very depressed, that she had been drinking shortly before her death, that "she had to have sex all the time" and that she had difficulty achieving sexual gratification. He also admitted that he and Kaysie had explored some of the practices described in the literature but never engaged in "anything like that."

The defendant raises several issues on appeal. We have noted them all, but because of our holding conclude that two of them are dispositive. * * * *

II.

Defendant next contends that the evidence was insufficient to convict him of murder in the second degree under any of the three theories advanced by the State. We shall examine the first two theories together, viz., (1) intentionally or knowingly causing the death of another, U.C.A., § 76-5-203(1)(a) (1978), or (2) causing the death of another while committing an act clearly dangerous to human life but intending to cause only serious bodily injury, U.C.A., § 76-5-203(1)(b) (1978). We review the evidence and all reasonable inferences to be drawn therefrom in the light most favorable to the jury verdict.

According to the State, defendant admitted that when Kaysie acted indignantly, he grabbed the clock radio, wrapped the cord around her neck and "just started pullin' on it." From that admission, the State would infer that defendant intended to kill, or at least cause serious bodily injury to, Kaysie. We have carefully read and analyzed the confession and find that it is incomplete and vague as to the defendant's state of mind. He did not say or even imply in the confession that he put the cord around her neck because she looked indignantly at him. Indeed, he negates that inference by saying that he was not mad and that she did not poke fun at him or talk at all. His questioner did not ask him why he reached for the cord and placed it around her neck. The defendant simply said that he did it. His confession offers no clue or hint as to his *mens rea*. His questioner totally failed to explore that subject.

Nothing in the exchange between defendant and Kaysie can form a basis from which an inference to kill or harm can be drawn. During the entire evening and night they were together, no anger was expressed, no threats were made, and no struggle or violence occurred. He stated he pulled on the cord for what "seemed like a second." The incident was part of a consensual act of intercourse between two intoxicated persons in an atmosphere of tranquility. We thus conclude that the confession does not support an inference beyond a reasonable doubt that the defendant intentionally or knowingly killed Kaysie or intended to cause her serious bodily injury. * * * *

We next focus on the State's third theory. Under § 76-5-203(1), criminal homicide constitutes murder in the second degree if the actor:

> (c) Acting under circumstances evidencing a depraved indifference to human life, he engaged in conduct which creates a grave risk of death to another and thereby causes the death of another.

Section 76-1-501(1) presumes a defendant to be innocent until each element of the offense charged against him is proved beyond a reasonable doubt; the requisite *actus reus* and *mens rea* set out in § 76-1-501(2) constitute the elements of the offense as follows: (a) The conduct, attendant circumstances, or results of conduct prescribed, prohibited, or forbidden in the definition of the offense; (b) The culpable mental state required.

We recently had an opportunity to clarify the apparent hiatus left by the legislative elimination in 1979 of the reckless state of mind previously required to find depraved indifference. In *State v. Fontana*, 680 P.2d 1042 (1984), we held the proper subjective mental state under that subsection to be "knowing," one of four possible categories of *mens rea* required to prove criminal responsibility under § 76-2-101(1).

Section 76-2-103 states: "A person engages in conduct: * * * * (2) Knowingly, or with knowledge, with respect to his conduct or to circumstances surrounding his conduct when he is aware of the nature of his conduct or the existing circumstances. A person acts knowingly, or with knowledge, with respect to a result of his conduct when he is aware that his conduct is reasonably certain to cause the result."

Correlating the conduct, circumstances, and result required under the depraved indifference statute and the *mens rea* of knowledge as promulgated in *State v. Fontana*, supra, we conclude that the following elements had to be present to properly convict the defendant under the State's third theory:

> 1. The defendant engaged in conduct which created a grave risk of death to another and that conduct resulted in the death of another — the *actus reus*.

> 2. The defendant knew that his conduct or the circumstances surrounding his conduct created a grave risk of death to another — the *mens rea*.

3. Defendant acted under circumstances evidencing a depraved indifference to human life — a qualitative judgment to be made by the jury in determining the extent of the defendant's conduct. It is not a description of the *mens rea* involved in the commission of the crime, but an evaluation of the *actus reus*.

There is no question that defendant engaged in conduct creating a grave risk of death and actually resulting in death. It is the degree of culpability as well as the evaluation of the conduct that we question here. As enunciated under *State v. Fontana*, knowledge of one's conduct or the circumstances surrounding the conduct is the cognizance that the conduct or the circumstances surrounding it create a life-endangering risk to another.

We begin with the requisite *mens rea*. At trial the State stressed the discrepancy between the two versions of the defendant's story. That discrepancy is deceiving at best. What emerges instead is an identical *mens rea* under both versions. Both in the confession and at trial, the defendant denied having intended any harm. No words, angry or otherwise, were exchanged by the couple. Defendant was not mad. There was no struggle. He was on top of the victim when he pulled the cord for what may have been no more than thirty seconds. The physical evidence is undisputed with respect to the absence of a struggle and to the position of the defendant when he pulled on the cord.

Given those facts, reasonable minds must perforce entertain reasonable doubt that there was that degree of awareness with respect to the defendant's conduct and surrounding circumstances to impute to him the knowledge that his conduct created a grave risk of killing Kaysie and that he possessed the medical knowledge that compounding factors existed which would hasten her death.

There is, however, sufficient evidence that the defendant was aware of, but consciously disregarded, a substantial and unjustifiable risk that placing and/or pulling a cord around the victim's neck would result in her death. That risk was of such a nature and degree that its disregard constituted a gross deviation from the standard of care that an ordinary person would exercise under all the circumstances as viewed from defendant's standpoint. Such conduct is "reckless" under § 76-2-103(3).

In evaluating the defendant's conduct, reasonable minds must be free from reasonable doubt that the defendant was guilty of depraved indifference to the grave risk of death created by his conduct. To constitute depraved indifference, the act must be one "which has been rather well understood at common law to involve something more serious than mere recklessness alone which has had an incidental tragic result." *People v. Poplis*, 30 N.Y.2d 85, 89 (1972). There must be a knowing doing of an uncalled-for act in callous disregard of its likely harmful effect on a victim, which is so heinous as to be equivalent to a "specific intent" to kill. *Neitzel v. State*, Alaska App., 655 P.2d 325 (1982); *People v. France*, 394 N.Y.S.2d 891 (1977). Depraved indifference to human life is characterized by unmitigated wickedness, extreme inhumanity or acts exhibiting a high degree of wantonness.

In *Neitzel*, *supra*, the court enumerated four determining factors a jury should be asked when it evaluates conduct resulting in death and alleged to be depraved indifference: (1) the utility of the defendant's conduct, (2) the magnitude of the risk, (3) the defendant's knowledge of the risk, and (4) any precautions taken by the defendant to minimize that risk. In differentiating reckless conduct amounting to depraved indifference from conduct amounting to reckless manslaughter, the jury is asked to pay particular attention to the social utility of the defendant's conduct and the precautions he takes to minimize the apparent risks.

Much as the social utility in this case is lacking, it must nonetheless be assessed against the backdrop of a delicate situation which involved only the defendant in the consensual act of intercourse with a sexually sophisticated woman ten years his senior. The physical evidence present in the bedroom, the testimony at trial attesting to her lack of sexual fulfillment and the admission by her lover of two years (a witness for the State) that he and the victim had explored some of the suggestions found in the manuals do not attest to the depraved act of a murderer. Both medical experts were in agreement that the strangulation was accomplished with little force and was enhanced by at least one other factor, the high alcohol content in the blood of the victim. Both medical experts agreed that the ligature marks were light, resulting from momentary pressure. That physical evidence alone confirms the defendant's attempt — albeit ineffective — to take precautions to minimize the risk of harm, and it negates the existence of a depraved indifference to human life.

In sharp contrast to defendant's conduct here, conduct in the following cases was properly held to constitute depraved indifference: *Neitzel, supra* (defendant fired several shots directly at girl friend while she sat on the ground. Some struck the ground within an inch of the victim before the fatal shot entered her head); *People v. Lilly*, 422 N.Y.S.2d 976 (1979) (defendant inflicted vicious and brutal injuries on 6 1/2-pound baby girl over period of one month and sought no medical attention to ease substantial pain); *People v. LeGrand*, 402 N.Y.S.2d 209 (1978) (defendant beat former wife to death, dragged her body down two flights of stairs, chopped her up and stuffed her into plastic bags for easier disposal); *State v. Nicholson*, Utah, 585 P.2d 60 (1978) (defendant neglected and mistreated small son for a period in excess of five months. Victim was found dead of malnutrition and dehydration in garbage, spoiled food and human feces reaching a depth of three feet in some places).

The evidence here simply does not support a finding of depravity in the conduct of the defendant that caused the death of Kaysie. The jury may well have been swayed by the reprehensible conduct of the defendant subsequent to her death. But that conduct is not before us for review. The evidence is undisputed that Kaysie was dead when defendant rose from the bed. He himself covered her face with a sheet, a universal gesture acknowledging death. At that moment the conduct which subjected him to a charge of criminal homicide came to an end.

We hold that there is insufficient evidence to support a conviction for murder in the second degree as charged, but that there is sufficient evidence to support a conviction for the included offense of manslaughter. The jury was given an instruction on manslaughter under § 76-5-205(1)(a) and (c). The defendant requested an additional instruction on that offense, which was refused. The jury necessarily found every fact required for conviction of that included offense. The defendant concedes that his conduct created a grave risk of harm which necessarily includes "recklessness," which is the requisite state of mind for manslaughter. Defendant has thus impliedly consented to the reduction. Accordingly, by authority of § 76-1-402(5), we remand the case to the trial court with directions to set aside the verdict and to enter a judgment of conviction for manslaughter without the necessity of a new trial and to sentence the defendant accordingly.

HALL, CHIEF JUSTICE (dissenting):

I do not join the opinion of the Court because it violates the cardinal rule of appellate review that precludes this Court from substituting its judgment for that of the jury on issues of fact.

This Court will not lightly overturn the findings of a jury. We must view the evidence properly presented at trial in the light most favorable to the jury's verdict, and will only interfere when the evidence is so lacking and insubstantial that a reasonable man could not possibly have reached a verdict beyond a reasonable doubt. We also view in a light most favorable to the jury's verdict those facts which can be reasonably inferred from the evidence presented to it.

The facts of this case, when viewed in a light most favorable to the jury verdict, adequately support defendant's conviction of second degree murder. Defendant admits that he caused the death of Kaysie Sorensen by strangulation. During his initial interrogation by investigating officers prior to his arrest, defendant lied about his involvement in the death of Sorensen, claiming that he simply dropped her off at Mark Anger's apartment without going in. Following his arrest, three days after the killing, defendant made an oral statement that was recorded and thereafter reduced to writing. The statement recites that defendant took Sorensen to Anger's apartment where they listened to music and danced and that each consumed a sufficient amount of whiskey to inebriate them. In his words, he became "pretty high" and Sorensen became "intoxicated." Thereafter, they engaged in a single act of intercourse lasting a "half hour maybe. Maybe less, when we got done she got kinda weird like. I, uh, indignant, I don't know what the word is."

Defendant then pulled the radio cord from the wall and wrapped it around Sorensen's neck once. When asked if Sorensen did anything, he responded: "Nothin', she just laid there, she wasn't really all the way passed out but she was more or less, I guess. I just started pullin' on it, it only seemed like just a second. And then it was over." In response to a question whether defendant thought Sorensen knew what he was doing when he put the electrical cord around her neck, he stated: "I hope not. I don't know. I just hope not." When asked if she fought back, he responded: "No." Defendant then emptied Sorensen's purse on the floor, but found no money; pulled a sheet over her head; stole a stereo set and left the premises.

Defendant's testimony at trial, nearly a year later, materially contradicted his prior written statement in several respects. He testified that they engaged in sexual intercourse about five minutes without climaxing. He stopped to rest, and Sorensen asked him not to stop. She rolled over and picked up the radio and set it down next to her, and they again engaged in intercourse. He opened his eyes and Sorensen had the cord around her neck. She was holding the cord and said, "Pull." While lying on top of Sorensen, he took the cord in his hands, pulled it tight "like tying your shoes" for a period of "fifteen-twenty seconds," all the while continuing the act of intercourse from which he climaxed. This he supposedly accomplished while deprived of the leverage of his arms and hands that were otherwise utilized in pulling on the cord. After climaxing, he relaxed and remained lying atop Sorensen for about a minute. He then rolled off, saw a "strange, weird" look on Sorensen's face, became scared, emptied her purse, took the stereo and left.

Defendant further testified that he lied in his prior written statement in order to avoid the death penalty for rape-murder, he being of the opinion that the truth was so bizarre that it was unbelievable.

An autopsy was performed by the state medical examiner. He testified that he found ligature abrasions encircling the victim's neck, scratches on her right cheek consistent with fingernail scratches, bruises on the back of the left hand and top of the right foot, and hemorrhages in the skin around the eyes, chin and in front of the right ear. His expert opinion was that the cause of death was strangulation by ligature.

The medical examiner described the process of ligature strangulation, explaining that application of pressure cuts off blood to the brain, closes the airways to the lungs, and slows the cardiovascular and respiratory systems. He testified that significant pressure on the ligature would have to be applied continuously for a minimum of 30 seconds to 2 1/2 minutes to cause death if there was no attempt to resuscitate the victim. Unconsciousness would occur 5 to 10 seconds after pressure was applied, and the victim's natural reaction would be to struggle, even after becoming unconscious. He stated that the ligature was applied only once to the victim's neck. He further testified that it is impossible for a person to strangle himself with a ligature because unconsciousness would result before enough pressure to cause death could be exerted. He classified the manner of death as a homicide.

The chief medical examiner of San Francisco County, California, testified on behalf of the defendant. The examiner represented himself as having acquired an expertise in the area of asphyxia during sexual practice, advising that restricting the flow of oxygen and blood to the brain as a means of sexual gratification was not uncommon in California, particularly in the area of San Francisco. He considered the autopsy photographs and the facts as related by the defendant and concluded that Sorensen was accidentally strangled during intercourse. He testified that the amount of pressure applied to Sorensen's neck by use of the cord was not great, but also acknowledged that the degree of pressure applied was not indicative of whether the killing was accidental or intentional. He also testified that the act of placing a ligature around the neck is intentional and that it always poses a danger to life, particularly so when the victim is intoxicated. Sorensen had a blood-alcohol level of .22% at the time of the autopsy.

The factual issue thus presented to the jury for its determination was concise and unambiguous. Did the defendant kill Sorensen intentionally or accidentally? Wherein did the truth lie between defendant's two conflicting accounts of the death?

As was its prerogative as fact finder, the jury chose to accept as truth defendant's initial written statement that clearly depicted an intentional act on his part that caused the death of Sorensen. That statement, coupled with the totality of the evidence, including the testimony of the Utah state medical examiner, the autopsy, and the evidence at the scene of the crime, is wholly consistent with an intentional killing and adequately supports the jury verdict.

I would affirm the conviction and judgment of the trial court.

NOTES FROM NATALIE:

(1) Is *Bolsinger* consistent with *Jensen*, regarding the proper role of an appellate court in reviewing a jury's verdict? How can you reconcile the two cases?

(2) I'm not sure I understand the difference between "depraved heart" murder and involuntary manslaughter, according to *Bolsinger*. Can you explain it, in terms that are useful in analyzing our case?

(3) In *State v. Hales*, 152 P.3d 321 (Utah 2007), the court affirmed Hales's conviction for murdering a 5-month old baby by shaking him:

> Hales next argues that there was not sufficient evidence that he acted with the state of mind necessary to convict him of murder and we should therefore vacate his conviction. We disagree. At trial, the State presented its murder case against Hales on two alternative theories: (1) that "intending to cause serious bodily injury to another, he committed an act clearly dangerous to human life that caused the death of another" or (2) "acting under circumstances evidencing a depraved indifference to human life, he engaged in conduct which created a grave risk of death to another and thereby caused the death of another." The State needed to provide only enough evidence to satisfy either of these tests, and we review the evidence in the light most favorable to the jury's guilty verdict.

> To convict a defendant of depraved indifference murder, which is not as difficult to prove as intentional murder, a jury must find that the defendant (1) engaged in conduct which created a grave risk of death to another and that conduct resulted in the death of another - the actus reus"; (2) *knew* that his conduct or the circumstances surrounding his conduct created a grave risk of death to another - the mens rea; and (3) acted under circumstances evidencing a depraved indifference to human life - an evaluation of the actus reus. *State v. Bolsinger, 699 P.2d 1214, 1219 (Utah 1985)* (emphasis added).

> Viewed in the light most favorable to the jury's verdict, Westerman's testimony that Hales said, "I'm sorry I did it" while driving her to the hospital supports an inference that Hales believed that he had harmed Luther, but it is insufficient to support a reasonable inference that Hales confessed to inflicting the injuries intentionally or with depraved indifference. Therefore, all of the evidence relating to Hales's mental state is circumstantial. When determining whether a mental state is sufficiently supported by circumstantial evidence, we ask (1) whether the State presented any evidence that the defendant possessed the requisite intent,

and (2) whether the inferences that can be drawn from that evidence have a basis in logic and reasonable human experience sufficient to prove that the defendant possessed the requisite intent.

In this case, the evidence regarding the injuries that Luther suffered constitutes the key circumstantial evidence as to Hales's mental state. At trial, Dr. Walker testified that Luther suffered a massive brain injury caused by shaken baby syndrome and that the injury shown on the CT scans must have been caused by "violent force." Further, because Westerman testified that Luther was fine when she put him to sleep and Dr. Walker testimony testified that Luther's brain injuries must have caused immediate unconsciousness, the jury could have inferred that Luther was fine until the 20 to 30 minutes that he spent with Hales on the night of December 5, 1985.

Combining this evidence, the jury could reasonably infer, consistent with logic and reasonable human experience, that Hales injured five-month-old Luther by violently shaking him, an act that created a grave risk of death to Luther and that resulted in Luther's death, that Hales knew his conduct presented a grave risk of death to Luther, and that the circumstances evidenced depraved indifference to human life. Regardless of Hales's degree of knowledge regarding the scientific theory of shaken baby syndrome, reasonable human experience indicates that an adult would know that violently shaking a five-month-old baby with less-developed neck control presents a grave risk of death to the baby. * * * *

The jury was presented with evidence of nonaccidental injuries caused by violent force - evidence from which the jury could have reasonably inferred that the perpetrator knew that his conduct would create a grave risk of death and that he acted under circumstances evidencing depraved indifference to human life.

Further, in addition to the evidence regarding the nature of the injuries, Westerman testified to the following at trial: that Luther was an inconvenience to Hales; that two days prior to Luther's injuries, Hales had an argument with Westerman in which he told Westerman that he would "hurt" her; that Hales was the only person with Luther and that Luther was securely belted into Hales's truck when he sustained the bruising to his face; and that Hales was tired and did not want to be disturbed when he returned home from work on the night of December 5, 1985. Finally, Westerman testified at trial that Hales told her while driving to the hospital that he was "sorry he did it." This additional circumstantial evidence bolsters the physical evidence that Hales acted with knowledge that his conduct presented a grave risk of death to Luther. Accordingly, we hold that Hales's conviction was supported by sufficient evidence,

(4) Under what circumstances (if any) may D be convicted of murder or involuntary manslaughter for failing to restrain her dog, who mauls and kills a neighbor? See *People v. Knoller*, 41 Cal.4th 139 (2007) and 2010 WL 3280200 (2010), and *People v. Noel*, 128 Cal. App. 4th 1391 (2005).

(5) Suppose D fires his gun at A, misses A, but hits and kills B. Is D guilty of murder of B? Yes, according to the common law rule of "transferred intent." D's intent to kill A is "transferred" to B.

> Under the "classic formulation" of the transferred intent doctrine, where a defendant intends to kill a victim but misses and instead kills a bystander, the intent to kill the intended victim is imputed to the resulting death of the bystander and the defendant is liable for murder. However, under the transferred intent doctrine, the defendant's intent is not actually transferred from the intended victim to the unintended victim. Rather, as applied here, the transferred intent doctrine connotes a *policy* - that a defendant who shoots at an intended victim with intent to kill but misses and hits a bystander instead should be subject to the same criminal liability that would have been imposed had he hit his intended mark. [*People v. Concha*, 47 Cal. 4th 653, 666 (2009).]

Is D *also* guilty of *attempted* murder of A? Yes, held the California Supreme Court in *People v. Scott*, 14 Cal.4th 544 (1996). Scott argued that his intent was "used up" once it was transferred to B, so it could not again be used for the attempted murder of A. The court disagreed. The court noted that the "transferred intent" doctrine was "a bare-faced legal fiction."

> Contrary to what its name implies, the transferred intent doctrine does not refer to any actual intent that is "used up" once it has been employed to convict a defendant of a specific intent crime against an intended victim. Rather, the doctrine of transferred intent connotes a policy. As applied here, the transferred intent doctrine is but another way of saying that a defendant who shoots with an intent to kill but misses and hits a bystander instead should be punished for a crime of the same seriousness as the one he tried to commit against his intended victim. * * * * Under such circumstances, the accused is deemed as culpable, and society is harmed as much, as if the defendant had accomplished what he had initially intended, and justice is achieved by punishing the defendant for a crime of the same seriousness as the one he tried to commit against his intended victim.

As Scott committed crimes against two persons by firing a single shot, he was properly charged and convicted of *both* crimes.

Justice Mosk concurred, arguing that "the time has come to reconsider the antique common law rule referred to as 'transferred intent.'" He noted that the doctrine is *unnecessary*, because D would often be guilty of murder of B anyway, under an *extreme recklessness* ("depraved heart") theory — shooting at A when other people are nearby puts the other people in serious danger. Also — as Justice Mosk reads the cases - while an intent to kill is a sufficient mental state for murder, and a death is also required, there is no requirement that the intent to kill be an intent to kill the person who is *actually killed*. "There is no requirement of an unlawful intent to kill an intended victim." For these reasons, Justice Mosk would abrogate the "transferred intent" doctrine.

Chapter 8

FELONY MURDER

At the early common law one whose conduct brought about an unintended death in the commission or attempted commission of a felony was guilty of murder. Today the law of felony murder varies substantially throughout the country, largely as a result of efforts to limit the scope of the felony-murder rule. American jurisdictions have limited the rule in one or more of the following ways: (1) by permitting its use only as to certain types of felonies; (2) by more strict interpretation of the requirement of proximate or legal cause; (3) by a narrower construction of the time period during which the felony is in the process of commission; (4) by requiring that the underlying felony be independent of the homicide.

LaFave, *Criminal Law* (West)

Assume Don holds up Vic, a convenience store clerk, and threatens to shoot him unless he gives Don the money in the cash register. Then one of the following happens:

1. Because Vic refuses, Don shoots him in the heart. Don intended to kill, and he succeeded.

2. Because Vic refuses, Don shoots him in the shoulder. Don intended to seriously injure Vic, but Vic dies from loss of blood.

3. Because Vic refuses, Don decides to shoot near Vic's head to scare him. But Don misses, and the bullet hits Vic in the head and kills him.

4. Vic is so frightened that he suffers a heart attack and dies.

5. Vic gives Don the money, and Don drives away. Pete the policeman drives after Don. Pete speeds around a corner and hits another car, and Pete is killed.

In Cases #1, #2, and #3, Don is guilty of murder under one of the doctrines that you studied in Chapter 7: intent to kill, intent to cause serious bodily injury, and "depraved heart."

But what about Cases #4 and #5? Don has the culpability of a robber, but does he also have the culpability of *a murderer*? Not under the doctrines you studied in Chapter 7. So if we are to convict Don of murder in Cases #4 and/or #5, we must use a new doctrine: the "felony murder" doctrine. Should we? Why?

This Chapter will explore this question.

PROBLEM 8

To: My law clerk

From: Judge Phelanie Merter, Superior Court, Los Angeles County

Re: *People v. Deever*

Defendant Daniel Deever has been charged with committing a felony by violating Penal Code § 136.1, and also with the murder of Tom Tinker and Martha Muffet. I held the preliminary hearing in the case, and at the end of it Deever's lawyer argued that the evidence was insufficient to support either of the murder charges, and that therefore I should not hold Deever for trial on those charges. The key witness at the preliminary hearing was Los Angeles Police Detective Joseph Thursday. Please read the attached transcript of his testimony and the attached authorities, and advise me as to whether either of the murder charges is supported by Thursday's testimony.

Transcript of Testimony of Joseph Thursday

Q: Detective Thursday, were you handling the investigation of the robbery case against Mr. Deever?

A: Yes. Deever had been charged with robbing Nellie Blye, and his trial was set for June 6. On June 1, I went to Ms. Blye's house to speak to her about the case, and as I went up to the door Deever rushed past me. Ms. Blye came out crying and said, "He just said he would kill me if I testify against him."

Q: What happened then?

A: Deever jumped into a car parked nearby. Another man was in the passenger seat. I yelled for them to stop. The car was facing in my direction. Deever started the car and yelled out the window, "I'll get you, copper." He then drove the car very fast toward me. He drove past me without hitting me, though he missed by only an inch or two. I pulled out my gun and fired one shot at the car. Apparently, I hit the other man, who turned out to be Tommy Tinker, a friend of Deever. He was killed.

Q: Did you try to follow the car?

A: No. My car was parked about a block away. There was no way I could get to it in time to find Deever's car in the traffic.

Q: Did you later investigate the death of Martha Muffet?

A: Yes. About a mile from where I was, about 2 minutes after Deever drove off, several witnesses saw Deever driving about 50 miles an hour in a 25 miles per hour speed limit zone and go right through a red light. Miss Muffet was then walking across the street. She was struck by Deever's car and killed.

California Penal Code

Section 17. Felony; misdemeanor; infraction; classification of offenses

(a) A felony is a crime which is punishable with death or by imprisonment in the state prison. Every other crime or public offense is a misdemeanor except those offenses that are classified as infractions.

(b) When a crime is punishable, in the discretion of the court, by imprisonment in the state prison, or by fine or imprisonment in the county jail, it is a misdemeanor for all purposes under the following circumstances:

(1) After a judgment imposing a punishment other than imprisonment in the state prison.

* * *

(5) When, at or before the preliminary examination . . . , the magistrate determines that the offense is a misdemeanor, in which event the case shall proceed as if the defendant has been arraigned on a misdemeanor complaint. * * *

Section 136.1. Intimidation of witnesses and victims.

(a) Except as provided in subdivision (c), every person who does any of the following is guilty of a public offense and shall be punished by imprisonment in a county jail for not more than one year or in the state prison:

(1) Knowingly and maliciously prevents or dissuades any witness or victim from attending or giving testimony at any trial, proceeding, or inquiry authorized by law.

(2) Knowingly and maliciously attempts to prevent or dissuade any witness or victim from attending or giving testimony at any trial, proceeding, or inquiry authorized by law.

* * *

(c) Every person doing any of the acts described in subdivision (a) or (b) knowing and maliciously under any one or more of the following circumstances, is guilty of a felony punishable by imprisonment in the state prison for two, three, or four years under any of the following circumstances:

(1) Where the act is accompanied by force or by an express or implied threat of force or violence, upon a witness or victim . . .

Section 187. Murder defined.

(a) Murder is the unlawful killing of a human being . . . with malice aforethought.

* * * [Enacted in 1872]

Section 188. Malice defined.

Such malice may be express or implied. It is express when there is manifested a deliberate intention unlawfully to take away the life of a fellow creature. It is implied, when no considerable provocation appears, or when the circumstances attending the killing show an abandoned and malignant heart. When it is shown that the killing resulted from the intentional doing of an act with express or implied malice as defined above, no other mental state need be shown to establish the mental state of malice aforethought. Neither an awareness of the obligation to act within the general body of laws regulating society nor acting despite such awareness is included within the definition of malice. [Enacted in 1872. The second paragraph was added in 1981.]

Section 189. Murder; Degrees.

All murder which is perpetrated by means of a destructive device or explosive, a weapon of mass destruction, knowing use of ammunition designed primarily to penetrate metal or armor, poison, lying in wait, torture, or by any other kind of willful, deliberate, and premeditated killing, or which is committed in the perpetration of, or attempt to perpetrate, arson, rape, carjacking, robbery, burglary, mayhem, kidnapping, train wrecking, or [child molesting], or any murder which is perpetrated by means of discharging a firearm from a motor vehicle, intentionally at another person outside of the vehicle with the intent to inflict death, is murder of the first degree. All other kinds or murders are of the second degree. * * *

To prove the killing was "deliberate and premeditated," it shall not be necessary to prove the defendant maturely and meaningfully reflected upon the gravity of his or her act. [Enacted in 1872, with subsequent amendments. The second paragraph was added in 1981.]

PEOPLE v. WASHINGTON
California Supreme Court
62 Cal. 2d 777, 402 P.2d 130 (1965)

Traynor, Chief Justice.

Defendant appeals from a judgment of conviction entered upon jury verdicts finding him guilty of first degree robbery and first degree murder and fixing the murder penalty at life imprisonment. Pen.Code §§ 187, 189, 190, 190.1. He was convicted of murder for participating in a robbery in which his accomplice was killed by the victim of the robbery.

Shortly before 10 p.m., October 2, 1962, Johnnie Carpenter prepared to close his gasoline station. He was in his office computing the receipts and disbursements of the day while an attendant in an adjacent storage room deposited money in a vault. Upon hearing someone yell "robbery," Carpenter opened his desk and took out a revolver. A few moments later, James Ball entered the office and pointed a revolver directly at Carpenter, who fired immediately, mortally wounding Ball. Carpenter then hurried to the door and saw an unarmed man he later identified as defendant running from the vault with a moneybag in his right hand. He shouted "Stop." When his warning was not heeded, he fired and hit defendant who fell wounded in front of the station.

The Attorney General, relying on *People v. Harrison*, 176 Cal.App.2d 330, contends that defendant was properly convicted of first degree murder. In that case, defendants initiated a gun battle with an employee in an attempt to rob a cleaning business. In the cross fire, the employee accidentally killed the owner of the business. The court affirmed the judgment convicting defendants of first degree murder, invoking *Commonwealth v. Almeida*, 362 Pa. 596, and *People v. Podolski*, 332 Mich. 508, which held that robbers who provoked gunfire were guilty of first degree murder, even though the lethal bullet was fired by a policeman.

Defendant would distinguish the *Harrison, Almeida,* and *Podolski* cases on the ground that in each instance the person killed was an innocent victim, not one of the felons. He suggests that we limit the rule of the *Harrison* case just as the Supreme Courts of Pennsylvania and Michigan have limited the *Almeida* and *Podolski* cases, by holding that surviving felons are not guilty of murder when their accomplices are killed by persons resisting the felony. *Commonwealth v. Redline*, 391 Pa. 486; *People v. Austin*, 370 Mich. 12; *see also People v. Wood*, 8 N.Y.2d 48. A distinction based on the person killed, however, would make the defendant's criminal liability turn upon the marksmanship of victims and policemen. A rule of law cannot reasonably be based on such a fortuitous circumstance. The basic issue therefore is whether a robber can be convicted of murder for the killing of any person by another who is resisting the robbery.

"Murder is the unlawful killing of a human being, with malice aforethought." Pen.Code § 187. Except when the common-law-felony-murder doctrine is applicable, an essential element of murder is an intent to kill or an intent with conscious disregard for life to commit acts likely to kill. The felony-murder doctrine ascribes malice aforethought to the felon who kills in the perpetration of an inherently dangerous felony. That doctrine is incorporated in § 189 of the Penal Code, which provides in part: "All murder . . . committed in the perpetration or attempt to perpetrate . . . robbery . . . is murder of the first degree." Thus, even though § 189 speaks only of degrees of "murder," inadvertent or accidental killings are first degree murders when committed by felons in the perpetration of robbery.

When a killing is not committed by a robber or by his accomplice but by his victim, malice aforethought is not attributable to the robber, for the killing is not committed by him in the perpetration or attempt to perpetrate robbery. It is not enough that the killing was a risk reasonably to be foreseen and that the robbery might therefore be regarded as a proximate cause of the killing. Section 189 requires that the felon or his accomplice commit the killing, for if he does not, the killing is not committed to perpetrate the felony. Indeed, in the present case the killing was committed to thwart a felony. To include such killings within § 189 would expand the meaning of the words "murder . . . which is committed in the perpetration . . . [of] robbery" beyond common understanding.

The purpose of the felony-murder rule is to deter felons from killing negligently or accidentally by holding them strictly responsible for killings they commit. *See*

Holmes, *The Common Law*, pp. 58-59; Model Penal Code (Tent.Draft No. 9, 1959) § 201.2, comment 4 at pp. 37-38. This purpose is not served by punishing them for killings committed by their victims.

It is contended, however, that another purpose of the felony-murder rule is to prevent the commission of robberies. Neither the common-law rationale of the rule nor the Penal Code supports this contention. In every robbery there is a possibility that the victim will resist and kill. The robber has little control over such a killing once the robbery is undertaken, as this case demonstrates. To impose an additional penalty for the killing would discriminate between robbers, not on the basis of any difference in their own conduct, but solely on the basis of the response by others that the robber's conduct happened to induce. An additional penalty for a homicide committed by the victim would deter robbery haphazardly at best. To "prevent stealing, the law would do better to hang one thief in every thousand by lot." Holmes, *The Common Law*, p. 58.

A defendant need not do the killing himself, however, to be guilty of murder. He may be vicariously responsible under the rules defining principals and criminal conspiracies. All persons aiding and abetting the commission of a robbery are guilty of first degree murder when one of them kills while acting in furtherance of the common design. Moreover, when the defendant intends to kill or intentionally commits acts that are likely to kill with a conscious disregard for life, he is guilty of murder even though he uses another person to accomplish his objective. *Johnson v. State*, 142 Ala. 70; *see also Wilson v. State*, 188 Ark. 846; *Taylor v. State*, 41 Tex.Cr.R. 564. Defendants who initiate gun battles may also be found guilty of murder if their victims resist and kill. Under such circumstances, "the defendant for a base, antisocial motive and with wanton disregard for human life, does an act that involves a high degree of probability that it will result in death" (*People v. Thomas*, 41 Cal.2d 470, 480), and it is unnecessary to imply malice by invoking the felony-murder doctrine.

To invoke the felony-murder doctrine to imply malice in such a case is unnecessary and overlooks the principles of criminal liability that should govern the responsibility of one person for a killing committed by another. * * *

To invoke the felony-murder doctrine when the killing is not committed by the defendant or by his accomplice could lead to absurd results. Thus, two men rob a grocery store and flee in opposite directions. The owner of the store follows one of the robbers and kills him. Neither robber may have fired a shot. Neither robber may have been armed with a deadly weapon. If the felony-murder doctrine applied, however, the surviving robber could be convicted of first degree murder (*see Commonwealth v. Thomas*, 382 Pa. 639, *overruled by Commonwealth v. Redline*, 391 Pa. 486), even though he was captured by a policeman and placed under arrest at the time his accomplice was killed. (*Commonwealth v. Doris*, 287 Pa. 547.)

The felony-murder rule has been criticized on the grounds that in almost all cases in which it is applied it is unnecessary and that it erodes the relation between criminal liability and moral culpability. *See, e.g.*, Model Penal Code (Tent. Draft No. 9, 1959) § 201.2, comment 4; *Report of the Royal Commission on Capital Punishment*, Cmd. No. 8932 (1949-1953); Packer, *The Case for Revision of the Penal Code*, 13 Stan.L.Rev. 252, 259; Morris, *The Felon's Responsibility for the*

Lethal Acts of Others, 105 U.Pa.L.Rev. 50.[3] Although it is the law in this state (Pen.Code § 189), it should not be extended beyond any rational function that it is designed to serve.

Accordingly, for a defendant to be guilty of murder under the felony-murder rule, the act of killing must be committed by the defendant or by his accomplice acting in furtherance of their common design. *Commonwealth v. Campbell,* 89 Mass.541; *Butler v. People,* 125 Ill. 641; *Commonwealth v. Moore,* 121 Ky. 97; *State v. Oxendine,* 187 N.C. 658.

On his appeal from the robbery conviction, defendant contends that he did not participate in the robbery. He testified that on the evening of the robbery he was with Ball and a man named Johnson. He did not know that they intended to commit robbery. He was "pretty drunk" at the time and fell asleep in the automobile. When he awoke, the automobile was parked near Carpenter's gasoline station, and Ball and Johnson were absent. He left the automobile to look for them. As he approached the station, Johnson ran from the vault. Carpenter shot just as Johnson ducked around a corner and dropped the moneybag. Carpenter's bullet hit defendant who fell wounded near the bag that Johnson had dropped.

Defendant's testimony was corroborated by the testimony of James Johnson, an inmate of the state prison for an unrelated crime at the time of defendant's trial. Johnson testified that he was the man who ran from the vault with the moneybag. Carpenter controverted their testimony, however, by identifying defendant as the man who ran from the vault. The evidence is therefore sufficient to support defendant's conviction of robbery. * * *

The judgment is affirmed as to defendant's conviction of first degree robbery and reversed as to his conviction of first degree murder.

Burke, Justice (dissenting).

I dissent. The unfortunate effect of the decision of the majority in this case is to advise felons:

> Henceforth in committing certain crimes, including robbery, rape and burglary, you are free to arm yourselves with a gun and brandish it in the faces of your victims without fear of a murder conviction unless you or your accomplice pulls the trigger. If the menacing effect of your gun causes a victim or policeman to fire and kill an innocent person or a cofelon, you are absolved of responsibility for such killing unless you shoot first.

Obviously this advance judicial absolution removes one of the most meaningful deterrents to the commission of armed felonies.

In the present case, defendant's accomplice was killed when the robbery victim fired after the accomplice had pointed a revolver at him. In *People v. Harrison* (1959) 176 Cal.App.2d 330, the rationale of which the majority now disapprove, the

---

[3] The felony-murder rule has been abolished in England (English Homicide Act, § 1, 1957, 5 & 6 Eliz. II, c. 11), and has been converted to a rebuttable presumption of malice by the Model Penal Code (Tent. Draft No. 9, 1959) § 201.2.

robbery victim was himself accidentally killed by a shot fired by his employee after defendant robbers had opened fire, and the robbers were held guilty of murder for the killing.

The majority now attempt to distinguish *Harrison* on the ground that there the robbers "initiated" the gun battle; in the present case the victim fired the first shot. As will appear, any such purported distinction is an invitation to further armed crimes of violence.

There is no room in the law for sporting considerations and distinctions as to who fired first, when dealing with killings which are caused by the actions of felons in deliberately arming themselves to commit any of the heinous crimes listed in Penal Code § 189. If a victim or someone defending the victim seizes an opportunity to shoot first when confronted by robbers with a deadly weapon (real or simulated), any "gun battle" is initiated by the armed robbers. In such a situation, application of the felony-murder rule of § 189 of the Penal Code supports, if not compels, the conclusion that the surviving robbers committed murder even if the lethal bullet did not come from one of their guns, and whether it is an innocent person or an accomplice who dies.

Section 187 of the Penal Code declares that "Murder is the unlawful killing of a human being, with malice aforethought." Section 188 states that "Such malice may be express or implied. It is express when there is manifested a deliberate intention unlawfully to take away . . . life . . . . It is implied . . . when the circumstances attending the killing show an abandoned and malignant heart."

Section 189 specifies that "All murder which is perpetrated by . . . any . . . kind of wilful, deliberate, and premeditated killing, or which is committed in the perpetration or attempt to perpetrate . . . robbery [or five other named felonies], is murder of the first degree."

So heinous has the Legislature considered murders in the perpetration of these offenses that it grouped them with murder by means of poison, lying in wait or by torture, and, fundamentally, the law in this respect has remained unchanged for more than one hundred years.

Despite these declared principles long established and effective in their deterrence of crimes of violence, the majority now announce that "When a killing is not committed by a robber or by his accomplice but by his victim, malice aforethought is not attributable to the robber, for the killing is not committed by him in the perpetration or attempt to perpetrate robbery. It is not enough that the killing was a risk reasonably to be foreseen. * * * Section 189 requires that the felon or his accomplice commit the killing, for if he does not, the killing is not committed to perpetrate the felony. To include such killings within § 189 would expand the meaning of the words 'murder . . . which is committed in the perpetration . . . [of] robbery' beyond common understanding."

But § 189 carries not the least suggestion of a requirement that the killing must take place to perpetrate the felony. If that requirement now be read into the section by the majority, then what becomes of the rule which they purport to recognize that an accidental and unintentional killing falls within the section? How can it be said that such a killing takes place to perpetrate a robbery?

Moreover, as already noted, the malice aforethought of the abandoned and malignant heart is shown from the very nature of the crime, here armed robbery, the defendant is attempting to commit. *People v. Milton* (1904), 145 Cal. 169.

A homicide which arises out of an attempt at armed robbery is a direct causal result of the chain of events set in motion by the robbers when they undertook their felony. When a victim fires the lethal bullet, whether or not he fires first, the killing is caused by the act of the felon, and the felon is as responsible therefor as when the firing is by his accomplice or when it is accidental or unintentional. The majority suggest "it is unnecessary to imply malice by invoking the felony-murder doctrine" where the robber "initiates" a gun battle by shooting first. This suggestion by the majority, I respectfully submit, emphasizes the inconsistency of their opinion. First they declare that "When a killing is not committed by a robber . . . but by his victim, malice aforethought is not attributable to the robber, for the killing is not committed by him in . . . robbery." Later they state that "Defendants who initiate gun battles may also be found guilty of murder if their victims resist and kill . . . and it is unnecessary to imply malice by invoking the felony-murder doctrine."

But malice aforethought is an essential element of murder. Pen. Code § 187. If it is not attributable to the robber when a killing is "committed by" his victim rather than by himself in a gun battle initiated by the robber, is the essential malice express or is it to be implied under some doctrine other than the felony-murder rule? Do the majority imply the malice of the abandoned and malignant heart (Pen. Code § 188) only if the robber shoots first, but not if he merely creates the foreseeable risk that "the victim will resist and kill"? And this despite the fact that, as the majority further affirm, "the robbery might therefore be regarded as a proximate cause of the killing"? Even if, as the majority suggest, it is unnecessary to imply malice by invoking the felony-murder doctrine where the robber shoots first, that doctrine can and should be invoked in a case in which, as here, a robber with a gun in his hand confronts a victim who can and does resist by firing the first shot. In such a case, the robber "initiated" the criminal plan, he "initiated" it by willfully, maliciously and wantonly putting the victim in fear of his life, and he "initiated" any resultant shooting, whether by his gun or that of the victim. Where the victim is in a position to shoot first and his bullet kills, the killing should be viewed in law and in fact as having been "committed" by the robber (as it was in *People v. Harrison, supra*), and application of the felony-murder rule to such circumstances is, in my view, exactly the sort of "rational function that it is designed to serve," in the phrasing of the majority.

Extreme examples may be imagined in which the application of a rule of criminal liability would appear manifestly unjust. However, when this court and others have been faced with such an example exceptions have been made to avoid an unconscionable result. To reject invocation of the felony-murder rule here, as do the majority, because of possible harshness in its application in other circumstances, for example, to fleeing robbers who are not armed, dilutes the enforcement of criminal responsibility. The case anticipated and the injustice sought to be protected against by the majority are not before us, and can best be dealt with when and if encountered. It may be observed, however, that robbers are not compelled to flee and thus to be shot at endangering themselves and others. They need only surrender, as many have done, to avoid death, to themselves or others, and the awesome penalties which attach under the felony-murder law.

I agree with the majority that one purpose of the felony-murder rule is to deter felons from killing negligently or accidentally. However, another equally cogent purpose is to deter them from undertaking inherently dangerous felonies in which, as the majority state, a "killing was a risk reasonably to be foreseen. * * * In every robbery there is a possibility that the victim will resist and kill." As declared in *People v. Chavez* (1951) 37 Cal.2d 656, 669, "The statute (Pen. Code § 189) was adopted for the protection of the community and its residents, not for the benefit of the lawbreaker." Why a felon who has undertaken an armed robbery, which this court now expressly notifies him carries a "risk and a possibility that the victim will resist and kill," and which "might therefore be regarded as a proximate cause of the killing" should nevertheless be absolved because, fortuitously, the victim can and does shoot first and the lethal bullet comes from the victim's gun rather than from his own, will be beyond the comprehension of the average law-abiding citizen, to say nothing of that of victims of armed robbery. Nor is such a view compatible with the felony-murder doctrine.

But, say the majority, "The robber has little control over such a killing once the robbery is undertaken," and "To impose an additional penalty for the killing would discriminate between robbers, not on the basis of any difference in their own conduct, but solely on the basis of the response by others that the robber's conduct happened to induce." A robber has no control over a bullet sent on its way after he pulls the trigger. Certainly his inability to recall it before it kills does not cloak him with innocence of the homicide.

The truth is, of course, that the robber may exercise various "controls over" a possible killing from his victim's bullet "once the robbery is undertaken." The robber can drop his own weapon, he can refrain from using it, he can surrender. Other conduct can be suggested which would tend to reassure the victim and dissuade him from firing his own gun. Moreover, the response by one victim will lead to capture of the robbers, while that of another victim will permit their escape. Is the captured felon to be excused from responsibility for his crime, in order not to "discriminate between robbers . . . solely on the basis of the response by others that the robber's conduct happened to induce"?

The robber's conduct which forms the basis of his criminal responsibility is the undertaking of the armed felony, in which a "killing was a risk reasonably to be foreseen" including the "possibility that the victim will resist and kill." If that risk becomes reality and a killing occurs, the guilt for it is that of the felon. And when done, it is murder in the first degree calling for death or life imprisonment. And to say that the knowledge that this awesome, sobering, terrifying responsibility of one contemplating the use of a deadly weapon in the perpetration of one of the listed offenses is not the strongest possible deterrent to the commission of such offenses belies what is being demonstrated day after day in the criminal departments of our trial courts.

I would hold . . . that the killing is that of the felon whether or not the lethal bullet comes from his gun or that of his accomplice and whether or not one of them shoots first, and would affirm the judgment of conviction of murder in the instant case.

NOTES FROM THE JUDGE:

1. According to the court, which California statute provides the source for California's felony murder rule? Read the statute carefully. Does it say that a killing occurring in the course of a felony is felony murder?

2. I am not sure that the evidence in our case is sufficient to show that Tommy Tinker was the defendant's co-felon. Does this matter, under *Washington*?

TAYLOR v. SUPERIOR COURT
California Supreme Court
3 Cal. 3d 578, 477 P.2d 131 (1970)

BURKE, JUSTICE.

Petitioner and his codefendant Daniels were charged by information with the murder of John H. Smith, robbery, assault with a deadly weapon against Linda West, and assault with a deadly weapon against Jack West. The superior court denied petitioner's motion to set aside the information as to the murder count (Pen. Code § 995), and we issued an alternative writ of prohibition.

At the preliminary hearing, the following facts were adduced regarding the murder count: On the evening of January 12, 1969, two men attempted to rob Jax Liquor Store which was operated by Mrs. Linda Lee West and her husband Jack. Mrs. West testified that James Daniels entered the store first and asked Mr. West, who was behind the counter, for a package of cigarettes. While Mr. West was getting the cigarettes, John Smith entered the store and approached the counter. Mrs. West, who was on a ladder at the time the two men entered the store, then heard her husband say something about money. Turning her attention to the counter, she heard Daniels repeatedly saying, "Put the money in the bag," and observed her husband complying with the order.

While Mr. West was putting the money from the register in the bag, Daniels repeatedly referred to the fact that he and Smith were armed. According to Mrs. West, Daniels "chattered insanely" during this time, telling Mr. West, Put the money in the bag. Put the money in the bag. Put the money in the bag. Don't move or I'll blow your head off. He's got a gun. He's got a gun. Don't move or we'll have an execution right here. Get down on the floor. I said on your stomach, on your stomach.

Throughout this period, Smith's gun was pointed at Mr. West. Mrs. West testified that Smith looked "intent" and "apprehensive" as if "waiting for something big to happen." She indicated that Smith's apparent apprehension and nervousness was manifested by the way he was staring at Mr. West.

While Daniels was forcing Mr. West to the floor, Mrs. West drew a pistol from under her clothing and fired at Smith, who was standing closest to her. Smith was struck on the right side of the chest. Mrs. West fired four more shots in rapid succession, and observed "sparks" coming from Smith's gun, which was pointed in her direction. A bullet hole was subsequently discovered in the wall behind the place Mrs. West had been standing, approximately eight or nine feet above the floor. During this period, Mr. West had seized a pistol and fired two shots at Smith. Mrs. West's last shot was fired at Daniels as he was going out of the door. He "lurched violently and almost went down, but picked himself up and kept going." Smith died as the result of multiple gunshot wounds.

The evidence at the preliminary examination indicated that petitioner was waiting outside the liquor store in a getaway car. He was apprehended later and connected with the crime through bills in his possession and through the automobile which was seen by a witness leaving the scene of the robbery.

Under Penal Code § 995, an information must be set aside if the defendant has been committed without "reasonable or probable cause." Of course, the probable cause test is not identical with the test which controls a jury in a murder case. The jury must be convinced to a moral certainty and beyond a reasonable doubt of the existence of the crime charged in the information and of every essential element of that crime. But a magistrate conducting a preliminary examination must be convinced of only such a state of facts as would lead a man of ordinary caution or prudence to believe, and conscientiously entertain a strong suspicion of the guilt of the accused.

The information herein charged petitioner with the crime of murder. "Murder is the unlawful killing of a human being, with malice aforethought." Pen. Code § 187. Except when the common-law-felony-murder doctrine is applicable, an essential element of murder is an intent to kill or an intent with conscious disregard for life to commit acts likely to kill. *People v. Washington*, 62 Cal.2d 777.

Petitioner correctly contends that he cannot be convicted under the felony-murder doctrine, since "When a killing is not committed by a robber or by his accomplice but by his victim, malice aforethought is not attributable to the robber, for the killing is not committed by him in the perpetration or attempt to perpetrate robbery." *People v. Washington, supra,* at p. 781.

However, apart from the felony-murder doctrine, petitioner could be found guilty of murder on a theory of vicarious liability. As stated in *People v. Gilbert*, 63 Cal.2d 690, "When the defendant or his accomplice, with a conscious disregard for life, intentionally commits an act that is likely to cause death, and his victim or a police officer kills in reasonable response to such act, the defendant is guilty of murder. In such a case, the killing is attributable, not merely to the commission of a felony, but to the intentional act of the defendant or his accomplice committed with conscious disregard for life. Thus, the victim's self-defensive killing or the police officer's killing in the performance of his duty cannot be considered an independent intervening cause for which the defendant is not liable, for it is a reasonable response to the dilemma thrust upon the victim or the policeman by the intentional act of the defendant or his accomplice."

Therefore, if petitioner were an accomplice to the robbery, he would be vicariously responsible[1] for any killing attributable to the intentional acts of his

---

[1] "Under the rules defining principals and criminal conspiracies, the defendant may be guilty of murder for a killing attributable to the act of his accomplice. To be so guilty, however, the accomplice must cause the death of another human being by an act committed in furtherance of the common design."

associates committed with conscious disregard for life, and likely to result in death. We must determine whether the committing magistrate had any rational ground for believing that Smith's death was attributable to intentional acts of Smith and Daniels meeting those criteria.

Petitioner relies upon the following language in *Washington*, wherein defendant's accomplice merely pointed a gun at the robbery victim who, without further provocation, shot and killed him: "In every robbery there is a possibility that the victim will resist and kill. The robber has little control over such a killing once the robbery is undertaken as this case demonstrates. To impose an additional penalty for the killing would discriminate between robbers, *not on the basis of any difference in their own conduct*, but solely on the basis of the response by others that the robber's conduct happened to induce."

As indicated by the italicized words in the foregoing quotation, the central inquiry in determining criminal liability for a killing committed by a resisting victim or police officer is whether the conduct of a defendant or his accomplices was sufficiently provocative of lethal resistance to support a finding of implied malice. If the trier of fact concludes that under the particular circumstances of the instant case Smith's death proximately resulted from acts of petitioner's accomplices done with conscious disregard for human life, the natural consequences of which were dangerous to life, then petitioner may be convicted of first degree murder.[2]

For example, we pointed out in *Washington* that "Defendants who initiate gun battles may also be found guilty of murder if their victims resist and kill. Under such circumstances, the defendant for a base, anti-social motive and with wanton disregard for human life, does an act that involves a high degree of probability that it will result in death, and it is unnecessary to imply malice by invoking the felony-murder doctrine." 62 Cal.2d at p. 782.

Petitioner contends that since neither Daniels nor Smith fired the first shot, they did not "initiate" the gun battle which led to Smith's death. However, depending upon the circumstances, a gun battle can be initiated by acts of provocation falling short of firing the first shot. Thus, in *People v. Reed*, 270 Cal.App.2d 37, defendant resisted the officers' commands to "put up your hands," and pointed his gun toward the officers and toward the kidnap-robbery victim. The officers commenced firing, wounding defendant and killing the victim. Although defendant did not fire a single shot, his murder conviction was upheld on the theory that his aggressive actions were sufficient evidence of implied malice, and that "under these circumstance it may be said that defendant initiated the gunplay."

Similarly, in *Brooks v. Superior Court*, 239 Cal.App.2d 538, petitioner had directed "opprobrious language" to the arresting officer and had grasped the officer's shotgun. The officer, being startled and thinking that petitioner was trying to disarm him, yanked backwards and fired the gun, mortally wounding a fellow officer. In upholding an indictment for murder, the court concluded that under the

---

People v. Gilbert, supra, 63 Cal.2d 690, 705. Petitioner does not dispute that the conduct of his confederates set forth above was in furtherance of the robbery.

[2] When murder has been established pursuant to the foregoing principles, Penal Code § 189 may be invoked to determine its degree.

circumstances, the petitioner's act of reaching for and grasping the officer's shotgun was "fraught with grave and inherent danger to human life," and therefore sufficient to raise an inference of malice.

In the instant case, the evidence at the preliminary hearing set forth above discloses acts of provocation on the part of Daniels and Smith from which the trier of fact could infer malice, including Daniels' coercive conduct toward Mr. West and his repeated threats of "execution," and Smith's intent and nervous apprehension as he held Mr. West at gunpoint. The foregoing conduct was sufficiently provocative of lethal resistance to lead a man of ordinary caution and prudence to conclude that Daniels and Smith "initiated" the gun battle, or that such conduct was done with conscious disregard for human life and with natural consequences dangerous to life.[3]

Accordingly, we conclude that the evidence supported the magistrate's finding that reasonable and probable cause existed to charge petitioner with first degree murder. The alternative writ heretofore issued is discharged and the peremptory writ is denied.

PETERS, JUSTICE (dissenting).

* * *

In sum, the instant case — like *Washington* — involves a typical first degree robbery situation without any independently malicious act by the robbers. In the instant case, a gun was pointed at one of the victims and threatening language was used; in *Washington*, a gun was pointed at the victim by a robber appearing suddenly in the victim's office. For such highly unsocial and unjustifiable conduct, appropriately harsh penalties have been allotted. *See, e.g.,* Pen. Code § 213. In each case, solely because the victim killed one of the robbers, the prosecutor attempts to charge the defendant with the additional count of murder. As this court stated in *Washington*, a robber has little control over the response of a victim and to impose an additional penalty when such uncontrollable response results in a death — to discriminate between robbers solely on the basis of the uncontrollable responses of their victims — would deter robbery haphazardly at best. * * *

I would issue prohibition as to the murder count.

---

[3] Petitioner contends that we should ignore evidence regarding Smith's conduct, on the theory that Smith could not have been held responsible for his own death. We rejected a similar contention in *Washington*, stating that "A distinction based on the person killed, however, would make the defendant's criminal liability turn upon the marksmanship of victims and policemen. A rule of law cannot reasonably be based on such a fortuitous circumstance. The basic issue therefore is whether a robber can be convicted of murder for the killing of *any* person by another who is resisting the robbery." 62 Cal.2d at 780. Therefore, the trier of fact may find that Smith set into motion, through the intentional commission of acts constituting implied malice and in furtherance of the robbery, a gun battle resulting in his own death. Since petitioner may be held vicariously responsible for *any* killing legally attributable to his accomplices, he may be charged with Smith's death.

MOSK, JUSTICE (dissenting).

While reserving my views on the soundness of the holding in *People v. Washington*, I agree with Justice Peters that the factual distinction upon which the majority opinion in the present case is based is without legal significance.

In every robbery in which the criminal aims a gun at his victim as he demands his money or property, the very act of pointing the weapon is an implied but unmistakable *conditional* threat that it will be used if the demands are not promptly met.

Under the circumstances, such a deliberate gesture can have no other meaning. Nothing is added, therefore, when the robber makes the threat explicit by concluding his demands with the qualifying phrase, "or I'll shoot" — or any variation on that theme, e.g., "or I'll kill you," "or I'll blow your head off," "or we'll have an execution right here." The latter two formulations were used in the case at bar; dispassionately viewed, however, they are merely vigorous semantic descendants of the classic highwayman's command, "Your money or your life!" Dick Turpin's victims might be shocked by the graphic explicitness of contemporary intimidation, but they would easily recognize its traditional meaning.

Fundamental principles of criminal responsibility dictate that the defendant be subject to a greater penalty only when he has demonstrated a greater degree of culpability. To ignore that rule is at best to frustrate the deterrent purpose of punishment, and at worst to risk constitutional invalidation on the ground of invidious discrimination. We cannot, of course, ascribe such an intent to the Legislature. In my view, a robber who simply articulates one of the foregoing conditional threats is in no way more culpable than one who remains silent while brandishing a gun in his victim's face.

The reason for this is apparent: every such conditional threat — whether express or implied — is inherent in the commission of the robbery itself. Indeed, the crime cannot be committed without making or carrying out a threat of violence: it is code law that "Robbery is the felonious taking of personal property in the possession of another, from his person or immediate presence, and against his will, *accomplished by means of force or fear*." Italics added; Pen. Code § 211. Fear is generated by the menace of such force, e.g., by a threat to commit personal violence upon the victim unless he complies with the robber's demands. The threat thus has no independent significance, no purpose other than to facilitate the commission of the robbery. It is, in short, a necessary incident of the crime.

In this regard the conditional threat is similar to the brief movements which virtually every robber finds it necessary to compel his victims to perform, such as going to the safe or cash register, lying on the floor, or entering a back room while the getaway is in progress. Yet in *People v. Daniels* (1969) 80 Cal.Rptr. 897, we recently held that the statute defining the crime of kidnapping to commit robbery was not intended to include robberies "in which the movements of the victims are merely incidental to the commission of the robbery and do not substantially increase the risk of harm over and above that necessarily present in the crime of robbery itself." By the same token, the conditional threats uttered in the case at bar were merely incidental to the robbery and did not substantially increase the risk of harm to the victims. I cannot square the present majority opinion with the spirit of our decision in *Daniels*.

This is not to maintain that no conduct short of actually pulling the trigger first will support a finding of implied malice aforethought. Thus the true distinction to be drawn in robbery cases is not between an express and an implied *conditional* threat, but between a conditional threat — whether express or implied — and an *unconditional* threat to kill.

For example, after seizing the property the robber might voice an intent to shoot his victims on the spot to prevent their giving an alarm or later identifying him; or, being surprised by the police and having no hope of escape, a desperate criminal might announce that rather than surrender he will take his own life and that of his hostages as well. Manifestly such a threat greatly increases the risk of harm over and above that which is present in the usual robbery situation, and hence demonstrates a greater degree of culpability on the part of the wrongdoer. The consequences of creating this risk are likewise predictable: if one of the victims has access to a hidden weapon, he will be driven to use it in a last-ditch attempt to prevent his assailant from carrying out his unconditional threat to kill. Such a threat, accordingly, may fairly be said to "initiate" the ensuing gun battle just as surely as if the robber had been the first to fire.

Other examples appear in the cases: implied malice has been found, in effect, when the robber used his victim as a shield or hostage (*cf. People v. Reed* (1969) 270 Cal.App.2d 37), or committed some other highly reckless act such as pistol-whipping his victim with a loaded gun (*In re Le Caille*, Crim. 14525), or seizing the barrel of a shotgun held at the ready by a police officer (*Brooks v. Superior Court* (1966) 239 Cal.App.2d 538). These events substantially increased the risk of harm to all present, and may well be deemed "intentional acts . . . committed with conscious disregard for life, and likely to result in death." Majority opinion, *ante*.

To list such examples, however, is vividly to delineate the gulf between them and the traditional commands made in the course of the otherwise uneventful holdup. For the reasons stated, I conclude that a robber who articulates such conditional threats does not, by that act alone, engage in a greater degree of antisocial conduct than his more taciturn companions in arms, nor does he manifest implied malice aforethought as that concept has been defined in our decisions. For lack of that essential element, the murder charge against the defendants in the case at bar should fall.

NOTES FROM THE JUDGE:

1. Was the majority's affirmance based on the felony murder rule?

2. How risky was our defendant's conduct, compared to that of Daniels and Smith?

3. In footnote 3, did the majority hold — in effect — that Taylor might be guilty of murder because Smith murdered Smith?

4. It appears that the felony murder rule has two aspects. First, a *culpability* aspect: it raises accidental or negligent killings to murder, where committed during an inherently dangerous felony, thereby increasing the *culpability* of the felon who causes the killing. For example, where a robbery victim dies of fright, the robber becomes guilty of murder. *See People v. Stamp*, 2 Cal. App. 3d 203 (1969). Second, a *complicity* aspect: the felony murder rule makes accomplices to the felony guilty of murders committed by their fellow-felons.

For example, in *Taylor*, had Daniels shot and killed Mr. West during the robbery, Taylor would have been guilty of murder.

This distinction was noted in *People v. Pulido*, 15 Cal. 4th 713 (1997). Pulido testified that — unbeknownst to Pulido — Aragon robbed and killed a gas station attendant. After this happened, Pulido learned of the robbery and helped Aragon escape. The court held that — assuming the jury believed Pulido — Pulido would not be guilty of felony murder based on the robbery.

The court held that Pulido would be guilty of *the robbery*, because "the robbery continues until the loot has been carried away to a place of temporary safety." The court also noted (citing *Salas*) that had the two men accidentally killed someone *during the escape*, both would be guilty of felony murder of that person. This is due to the "aggravation of culpability" aspect of the felony murder rule. However, under the "complicity" aspect of the felony murder rule, an accomplice to the underlying felony is not guilty of felony murder based on killings committed before the accomplice joined the felony. The court noted that "extension of the felony murder rule's complicity aspect to late joiners would not serve the rule's primary purpose, 'to deter felons from killing negligently or accidentally by holding them strictly responsible for killings they commit' [citing *People v. Washington*]."

In some states (including California), the felony murder rule has a third aspect: it raises murders committed during certain listed felonies to *first degree* murder. *See* California Penal Code § 189. Thus, in the above examples, both Stamp and Taylor would be guilty of *first degree* murder.

PEOPLE v. PHILLIPS
California Supreme Court
64 Cal. 2d 574, 414 P.2d 353 (1966)

TOBRINER, JUSTICE.

Defendant, a doctor of chiropractic, appeals from a judgment of the Superior Court of Los Angeles County convicting him of second degree murder in connection with the death from cancer of one of his patients. We reverse solely on the ground that the trial court erred in giving a felony murder instruction.

Linda Epping died on December 29, 1961, at the age of eight, from a rare and fast-growing form of eye cancer. Linda's mother first observed a swelling over the girl's left eye in June of that year. The doctor whom she consulted recommended that Linda be taken to Dr. Straatsma, an ophthalmologist at the UCLA Medical Center.

On July 10th Dr. Straatsma first saw Linda; on July 17th the girl, suffering great pain, was admitted to the center. Dr. Straatsma performed an exploratory operation and the resulting biopsy established the nature of the child's affliction.

Dr. Straatsma advised Linda's parents that her only hope for survival lay in immediate surgical removal of the affected eye. The Eppings were loath to permit such surgery, but on the morning of July 21st, Mr. Epping called the hospital and gave his oral consent. The Eppings arrived at the hospital that afternoon to consult with the surgeon. While waiting, they encountered a Mrs. Eaton, who told them that defendant had cured her son of a brain tumor without surgery.

Mrs. Epping called defendant at his office. According to the Eppings, defendant repeatedly assured them that he could cure Linda without surgery. They testified that defendant urged them to take Linda out of the hospital, claiming that the hospital was "an experimental place," that the doctors there would use Linda as "a human guinea pig" and would relieve the Eppings of their money as well.

The Eppings testified that in reliance upon defendant's statements, they took Linda out of the hospital and placed her under defendant's care. They stated that if defendant had not represented to them that he could cure the child without surgery and that the UCLA doctors were only interested in experimentation, they would have proceeded with the scheduled operation. The prosecution introduced medical testimony which tended to prove that, if Linda had undergone surgery on July 21st, her life would have been prolonged or she would have been completely cured. Defendant treated Linda from July 22 to August 12, 1961. He charged an advance fee of $500 for three months' care as well as a sum exceeding $200 for pills and medicines. On August 13th Linda's condition had not improved; the Eppings dismissed defendant.

Later the Eppings sought to cure Linda by means of a Mexican herbal drug known as yerba mansa and, about the 1st of September, they placed her under the care of the Christian Science movement. They did not take her back to the hospital for treatment.

Defendant testified that he knew that he could not cure cancer, that he did not represent to the Eppings that he could do so, that he urged them to return Linda to the hospital and that he agreed to treat her only when it became clear that the Eppings would never consent to surgery. He further testified that in administering treatment, he sought to build up Linda's general health and so prolong her life. He insisted that he had never purported to "treat" cancer as such, but only to give "supportive" care to the body as a whole. He variously described his purpose as being "to build up her resistance," "assisting the body to overcome its own deficiencies" and "supporting the body defenses."

As we have noted, the trial court gave an instruction on felony murder; we point out that, although defendant could, of course, be prosecuted for grand theft, such a crime, not an inherently dangerous felony, does not support an instruction on felony murder. The giving of that instruction caused defendant prejudice and compels reversal.

The Instruction on Second Degree Felony Murder

Defendant challenges the propriety of the trial court's instructions to the jury. The court gave the following tripartite instruction on murder in the second degree:

The unlawful killing of a human being with malice aforethought, but without a deliberately formed and premeditated intent to kill, is murder of the second degree: (1) If the killing proximately results from an unlawful act, the natural consequences of which are dangerous to life, which act is deliberately performed by a person who knows that his conduct endangers the life of another, or (2) If the circumstances proximately causing the killing show an abandoned and malignant heart, or (3) If the killing is done in the perpetration or attempt to perpetrate a felony such as Grand Theft. If a death occurs in the perpetration of a course of conduct amounting to Grand Theft, which course of conduct is a proximate cause of the unlawful killing of a human being, such course of conduct constitutes murder in the second degree, even though the death was not intended.

The third part of this instruction rests upon the felony murder rule and reflects the prosecution's theory that defendant's conduct amounted to grand theft by false pretenses in violation of Penal Code § 484.

Despite defendant's contention that the Penal Code does not expressly set forth any provision for second degree felony murder and that, therefore, we should not follow any such doctrine here, the concept lies imbedded in our law. We have stated in *People v. Williams* (1965) 47 Cal.Rptr. 7, that the cases hold that the perpetration of some felonies, exclusive of those enumerated in Penal Code § 189, may provide the basis for a murder conviction under the felony murder rule. We have held, however, that only such felonies as are in themselves "inherently dangerous to human life" can support the application of the felony murder rule. We have ruled that in assessing such peril to human life inherent in any given felony "we look to the elements of the felony in the abstract, not the particular facts of the case." *People v. Williams, supra.*

We have thus recognized that the felony murder doctrine expresses a highly artificial concept that deserves no extension beyond its required application. *People v. Washington* (1965) 62 Cal.2d 777. Indeed the rule itself has been abandoned by the courts of England, where it had its inception. It has been subjected to severe and sweeping criticism. No case to our knowledge in any jurisdiction has held that because death results from a course of conduct involving a felonious perpetration of a fraud, the felony murder doctrine can be invoked.

Admitting that grand theft is not inherently dangerous to life, the prosecution asks us to encompass the entire course of defendant's conduct so that we may incorporate such elements as would make his crime inherently dangerous. In so framing the definition of a given felony for the purpose of assessing its inherent peril to life, the prosecution would abandon the statutory definition of the felony as such and substitute the factual elements of defendant's actual conduct. In the present case, the Attorney General would characterize that conduct as "grand theft medical fraud," and this newly created "felony," he urges, clearly involves danger to human life and supports an application of the felony murder rule.

To fragmentize the "course of conduct" of defendant so that the felony murder rule applies if any segment of that conduct may be considered dangerous to life would widen the rule beyond calculation. It would then apply not only to the commission of specific felonies, which are themselves dangerous to life, but to the perpetration of *any* felony during which defendant may have acted in such a manner as to endanger life.

The prosecution does not deny that the giving of a felony murder instruction engendered the possibility of a conviction of murder in the absence of a finding of malice. It contends, however, that even if the jury acted on the erroneous instruction it must necessarily have found facts which establish, as a matter of law, that defendant acted with conscious disregard for life and hence with malice. The prosecution thus asks us to dissect the jury's verdict, setting the facts of the case against the instructions in an attempt to isolate the facts which the jury necessarily found in reaching its verdict. From these facts it further asks us to infer the existence of others which the jury was never asked to find.

Examination of the record suggests that even this doubtful enterprise would not enable us to overcome the effect of the erroneous instruction. The prosecution urges that the jury could not have convicted defendant under the felony murder instruction without having found that he made representations to the Eppings which he knew to be false or which he recklessly rendered without information which would justify a reasonable belief in their truth. Such a finding does not, however, establish as a matter of law the existence of an "intent with conscious disregard for life to commit acts likely to kill." *People v. Washington, supra,* 62 Cal.2d 777, 780.

In the absence of a finding that defendant subjectively appreciated the peril to which his conduct exposed the girl, we cannot determine that he acted with conscious disregard for life. The record contains evidence from which a trier of fact could reasonably have concluded that although defendant made false representations concerning his ability to cure, he nevertheless believed that the treatment which he proposed to give would be as efficacious in relieving pain and prolonging life as the scheduled surgery.

Of course, the jury could have concluded from some of the evidence that defendant did not entertain any such belief in the relative efficacy of his proposed treatment. We cannot, however, undertake to resolve this evidentiary conflict without invading the province of the trier of fact. We cannot predicate a finding of conscious disregard of life upon a record that would as conclusively afford a basis for the opposite conclusion.

The judgment is reversed.

BURKE, JUSTICE (dissenting).

I submit that here a miscarriage of justice did not result from any error in giving the instruction, in view of the overwhelming evidence that defendant, motivated by mercenary greed, acted in conscious disregard for the life of 8-year-old Linda Epping when he induced her parents to cancel the scheduled cancer operation and place her under his care, thereby shortening her life.

Under the instructions given, the jury was told that malice aforethought was a necessary element of murder, and the instructions permitted the jury to find such malice not only on the basis of the felony murder rule but also if the killing was committed under circumstances that show an abandoned and malignant heart. To be so committed, the defendant must have an intent with conscious disregard for life to commit acts likely to kill. *People v. Washington*, 62 Cal.2d 777. There was ample evidence that defendant, a chiropractor, intended to induce Linda's parents to cancel the operation for her fast-growing eye cancer and place her under his care. Motive was shown by evidence that he was then behind in his rent and that he charged Linda's parents $500 in advance for her treatment and made an additional profit exceeding $100 by selling pills for her at a 100% mark-up.

That defendant was well aware that canceling the surgery and placing the child under his care would endanger her life is apparent from his own testimony. He testified as follows: Before Linda was removed from the hospital he knew the form of cancer she had, and, having taken several semesters of pathology at school, he recognized that her condition was "very, very dangerous." He recalled having read that "early exenteration of the orbit offers the only hope of survival, and that a slender one." He stated he was aware that Linda's case required medical attention, which he was not going to give her. Upon being told that the doctors at UCLA planned to perform surgery on her, he told her mother to listen to the doctors. Later, when Linda's mother informed him that she had removed Linda from the hospital, he told her she had made "a very, very grave mistake" and should return Linda to the hospital.

Thereafter, each time Linda was brought to him for treatment, he stated that she should have surgery. He graduated from a college of chiropractic in 1958 and testified that he knew he could not cure cancer, and that if he had reason to believe that one of his patients had a malignant tumor, he would refer the patient to a surgeon.

In view of the foregoing testimony by defendant, any possibility the jury would have concluded, as suggested by the majority, that he believed the treatment he proposed to give would be as efficacious as the scheduled surgery in prolonging her life, and thus that he did not act with conscious disregard for her life is so remote as to be virtually nonexistent.

The majority note that defendant testified that he understood that Linda's cancer was incurable, but this is not inconsistent with his testimony indicating his belief that surgery offered the best chance of prolonging her life. Moreover, his testimony relating to whether her form of cancer was curable, when the testimony is taken as a whole, merely indicated that he believed that such cancer was ordinarily incurable but that there was a slight chance of survival if there was early exenteration of the orbit.

The majority opinion is misleading in stating that "defendant testified that he . . . understood that surgery might stimulate the spread of the disease to other parts of the body and thus hasten death." Defendant testified that he had read that "after removal there is wasting and death due to metastasis" i.e., a transfer of the disease from one part of the body to another. The quoted matter which defendant said he had read may mean merely that removal does not always prevent death, not that removal might "stimulate" the spread of the disease and thus hasten death.

Defendant was indeed fortunate that he was not tried and convicted of first degree murder for Linda's death. Even if it be assumed that it was error to give the felony murder instruction, the record shows that it is not reasonably probable that a result more favorable to defendant would have been reached had the instruction not been given. Since the giving of the instruction did not result in a miscarriage of justice, I would affirm the judgment of conviction under the mandate of Section 4 1/2, article VI, of the California Constitution.

NOTE FROM THE JUDGE:

It seems to me that, in our case, the way the defendant drove his car towards Thursday was "inherently dangerous." Is this enough to qualify for the felony murder doctrine, under *Phillips*?

PEOPLE v. BURROUGHS
California Supreme Court
35 Cal. 3d 824, 678 P.2d 894 (1984)

GRODIN, JUSTICE.

Defendant Burroughs, a 77-year-old self-styled "healer," appeals from a judgment convicting him of unlawfully selling drugs, compounds, or devices for alleviation or cure of cancer (Health & Safety Code § 1707.1); felony practicing medicine without a license (Bus. & Prof.Code § 2141.5, now § 2053); and second degree felony murder (Penal Code § 187) in the treatment and death of Lee Swatsenbarg. Burroughs challenges his second degree murder conviction by contending the felonious unlicensed practice of medicine is not an "inherently dangerous" felony, as that term has been used in our previous decisions to describe and limit the kinds of offenses which will support application of the felony-murder rule.

We conclude that while the felonious unlicensed practice of medicine can, in many circumstances, pose a threat to the health of the individual being treated, commission of that crime as defined by statute does not inevitably pose danger to human life. Under well-established principles it cannot, therefore, be made the predicate for a finding of murder, absent proof of malice. As a consequence, we must reverse defendant's second degree felony-murder conviction.

The trial court did properly instruct the jury with respect to the unlawful selling of drugs, compounds, or devices for alleviation or cure of cancer, and felony practicing medicine without a license. There was substantial evidence presented from which the jury could have convicted defendant of these crimes. We affirm these convictions. Lee Swatsenbarg had been diagnosed by the family physician as suffering from terminal leukemia. Unable to accept impending death, the 24-year-old Swatsenbarg unsuccessfully sought treatment from a variety of traditional medical sources. He and his wife then began to participate in Bible study, hoping that through faith Lee might be cured. Finally, on the advice of a mutual acquaintance who had heard of defendant's ostensible successes in healing others, Lee turned to defendant for treatment. During the first meeting between Lee and defendant, the latter described his method of curing cancer. This method included consumption of a unique "lemonade," exposure to colored lights, and a brand of vigorous massage administered by defendant. Defendant remarked that he had successfully treated "thousands" of people, including a number of physicians. He suggested the Swatsenbargs purchase a copy of his book, *Healing for the Age of Enlightenment*. If after reading the book Lee wished to begin defendant's unorthodox treatment, defendant would commence caring for Lee immediately. During the 30 days designated for the treatment, Lee would have to avoid contact with his physician.

Lee read the book, submitted to the conditions delineated by defendant, and placed himself under defendant's care. Defendant instructed Lee to drink the lemonade, salt water, and herb tea, but consume nothing more for the ensuing 30 days. At defendant's behest, the Swatsenbargs bought a lamp equipped with some colored plastic sheets, to bathe Lee in various tints of light.

Defendant also agreed to massage Lee from time to time, for an additional fee per session.

Rather than improve, within two weeks Lee's condition began rapidly to deteriorate. He developed a fever, and was growing progressively weaker. Defendant counseled Lee that all was proceeding according to plan, and convinced the young man to postpone a bone marrow test urged by his doctor. During the next week Lee became increasingly ill. He was experiencing severe pain in several areas, including his abdomen, and vomiting frequently. Defendant administered "deep" abdominal massages on two successive days, each time telling Lee he would soon recuperate. Lee did not recover as defendant expected, however, and the patient began to suffer from convulsions and excruciating pain. He vomited with increasing frequency.

Despite defendant's constant attempts at reassurance, the Swatsenbargs began to panic when Lee convulsed for a third time after the latest abdominal massage. Three and a half weeks into the treatment, the couple spent the night at defendant's house, where Lee died of a massive hemorrhage of the mesentery in the abdomen. The evidence presented at trial strongly suggested the hemorrhage was the direct result of the massages performed by defendant.

I.

Defendant's conviction of second degree felony murder arose out of the jury's determination that Lee Swatsenbarg's death was a homicide committed by defendant while he was engaged in the felonious unlicensed practice of medicine. The trial court ruled that an underlying felony of unlicensed practice of medicine could support a felony-murder conviction because such practice was a felony "inherently dangerous to human life."[1] Consequently, the trial judge instructed the

---

[1] Felony practicing medicine without a license violates § 2053 of the Business and Professions Code which states: "Any person who willfully, under circumstances or conditions which cause or create a risk of great bodily harm, serious physical or mental illness, or death, practices or attempts to practice, or advertises or holds himself or herself out as practicing, any system or mode of treating the sick or afflicted in this state, or diagnoses, treats, operates for, or prescribes for any ailment, blemish, deformity, disease, disfigurement, disorder, injury, or other physical or mental condition of any person, without

jury that if the homicide resulted directly from the commission of this felony, the homicide was felony murder of the second degree.[2] This instruction was erroneous as a matter of law.

When an individual causes the death of another in furtherance of the perpetration of a felony, the resulting offense may be felony murder. *People v. Doyell* (1874) 48 Cal. 85. This court has long held the felony-murder rule in disfavor. "We have repeatedly stated that felony murder is a 'highly artificial concept' which 'deserves no extension beyond its required application.' ' *People v. Dillon* (1983) 34 Cal.3d 441. For the reasons stated below, we hold that to apply the felony-murder rule to the facts of the instant case would be an unwarranted extension of this highly "anachronistic"[3] notion.

At the outset we must determine whether the underlying felony is "inherently dangerous to human life." We formulated this standard because "if the felony is not inherently dangerous, it is highly improbable that the potential felon will be deterred; he will not anticipate that injury or death might arise solely from the fact that he will commit the felony." *People v. Williams* (1965) 63 Cal.2d 452, 458, fn. 4. In assessing whether the felony is inherently dangerous to human life, "we look to the elements of the felony in the abstract, not the particular 'facts' of the case." *Id.* at 458, fn. 5; *People v. Phillips*, 64 Cal.2d 574, 582. This form of analysis is compelled because there is a killing in every case where the rule might potentially be applied. If in such circumstances a court were to examine the particular facts of the case prior to establishing whether the underlying felony is inherently dangerous, the court might well be led to conclude the rule applicable despite any unfairness which might redound to the defendant by so broad an application: the existence of the dead victim might appear to lead inexorably to the conclusion that the underlying felony is exceptionally hazardous. We continue to resist such unjustifiable bootstrapping.

In our application of the second degree felony-murder analysis, we are guided

----

having at the time of so doing a valid, unrevoked or suspended certificate as provided in this chapter, or without being authorized to perform such act pursuant to a certificate obtained in accordance with some other provision of law, is punishable by imprisonment in the county jail for not exceeding one year or in the state prison."

[2] Second degree felony murder was defined for the jury as, "The unlawful killing of a human being, whether intentional, unintentional or accidental, which occurs as a direct causal result of the commission of or attempt to commit a felony inherently dangerous to human life, namely, the crime of practicing medicine without a license under circumstances or conditions which cause or create risk of great bodily harm, serious mental or physical illness, or death, and where there was in the mind of the perpetrator the specific intent to commit such crime, is murder of the second degree. The specific intent to commit such felony, i.e., practicing medicine without a license under circumstances or conditions which cause or create risk of great bodily harm, serious mental or physical illness, or death, and the commission of or attempt to commit such crime must be proved beyond any doubt." (CALJIC No. 8.32.) [Ed. — "CALJIC" stands for California Jury Instructions, Criminal — a set of standard jury instructions used in California.]

[3] * * * In *People v. Dillon, supra*, 34 Cal.3d 441, we reaffirmed the first degree felony-murder rule, despite serious reservations as to its rationality and moral vitality, because we regarded ourselves bound by the explicit statutory provision (Pen. Code § 189) from which that rule derived. The second degree felony-murder rule, by contrast, is a creature of judicial invention, and as the Chief Justice's concurring opinion suggests, the time may be ripe to reconsider its continued vitality. We decline to do so here, however, since that issue has not been raised, briefed, or argued.

by the bipartite standard articulated by this court in *People v. Henderson*, 19 Cal.3d 86. In *Henderson*, we stated a reviewing court should look first to the primary element of the offense at issue, then to the "factors elevating the offense to a felony," to determine whether the felony, taken in the abstract, is inherently dangerous to human life, or whether it possibly could be committed without creating such peril. In this examination we are required to view the statutory definition of the offense as a whole, taking into account even nonhazardous ways of violating the provisions of the law which do not necessarily pose a threat to human life.

The primary element of the offense in question here is the practice of medicine without a license. The statute defines such practice as "treating the sick or afflicted."

One can certainly conceive of treatment of the sick or afflicted which has quite innocuous results — the affliction at stake could be a common cold, or a sprained finger, and the form of treatment an admonition to rest in bed and drink fluids or the application of ice to mild swelling. Thus, we do not find inherent dangerousness at this stage of our investigation.

The next level of analysis takes us to consideration of the factors which elevate the unlicensed practice of medicine to a felony: "circumstances or conditions which cause or create a risk of great bodily harm, serious mental or physical illness, or death." That the Legislature referred to "death" as a separate risk, and in the disjunctive, strongly suggests the Legislature perceived that one may violate the proscription against the felonious practice of medicine without a license and yet not necessarily endanger human life. Our analysis of the other two categories of risk delineated in Business and Professions Code § 2053 further supports this conclusion.

"Great bodily harm" is not defined in § 2053, but the closely analogous term "serious bodily injury" is defined in Penal Code § 243 — which establishes appropriate punishments for the crime of battery when committed under various circumstances — as "(a) serious impairment of physical condition, including, but not limited to the following: loss of consciousness; concussion; bone fracture; protracted loss or impairment of function of any bodily member or organ; a wound requiring extensive suturing; and serious disfigurement." Pursuant to this definition, a broken arm or leg would constitute serious bodily injury — and by implication, great bodily harm as well. While painful and debilitating, such bone fractures clearly do not, by their nature, jeopardize the life of the victim.

In addition, we acknowledge that " 'serious bodily injury' and 'great bodily injury' are essentially equivalent elements." *People v. Corning* (1983) 146 Cal.App.3d 83. The term "great bodily injury," defined for purposes of enhancement in Penal Code § 12022.7 as "significant or substantial physical injury," has been held to include a broken jaw (*People v. Johnson* (1980) 104 Cal.App.3d 598) and a broken hand (*People v. Kent, supra*). Obviously these injuries do not rise to the level of being inherently life-threatening.

There is no indication the Legislature intended to ascribe a different meaning to "great bodily harm," as that term is used in § 2053, than is signified by "great bodily injury," or, for that matter, "serious bodily injury," in the Penal Code sections we have discussed. Thus, we must conclude that the risk of great bodily harm under § 2053 is likewise not inherently dangerous to human life.

The statute at issue can also be violated by administering to an individual in a manner which threatens risk of serious mental or physical illness. Whether risk of serious physical illness is inherently dangerous to life is a question we do not reach; however, we believe the existence of the category of risk of serious mental illness also renders a breach of the statute's prohibitions potentially less than inherently dangerous to life.

As with the term "great bodily harm," "mental illness" is not defined in § 2053. We have found no case in which a court of this state has made an attempt at such definition in the context of an adjudication pursuant to that statutory provision. Based on the meaning of "mental illness" in other contexts under California law, however, we are convinced this term encompasses a range of conditions, some of which are not inherently threatening to human life.

* * *

While conceding these definitions contemplate the possibility that mental illness may be inherently dangerous, we note they suggest there are occasions when this need not be the case. It is not difficult, for example, to envision one who suffers from delusions of grandeur, believing himself to be the President of the United States. An individual who purports without the proper license to be able to treat such a person need not be placing the patient's life in jeopardy, though such treatment, if conducted, for example, without expertise, may lead to the need for more serious psychiatric attention.

Consequently, we are disinclined to rule today that the risks set forth in § 2053 are so critical as to render commission of this felony of necessity inherently dangerous to human life. Indeed, were we to interpret either the risk of great bodily harm or serious mental illness as being synonymous with the risk of death for purposes of the felony-murder rule, we would be according those terms a more restrictive meaning than that which the Legislature obviously meant them to have in the definition of the felony itself. Such a reading would require that an unlicensed practitioner of medicine actually perform treatment under circumstances or conditions which necessarily place the very life of the patient in jeopardy before such a practitioner could be susceptible to a conviction for felonious unlicensed practice. We possess grave doubts that the Legislature intended such a result.

Moreover, our analysis of precedent in this area reveals that the few times we have found an underlying felony inherently dangerous (so that it would support a conviction of felony murder), the offense has been tinged with malevolence totally absent from the facts of this case. In *People v. Mattison* (1971) 4 Cal.3d 177, we held that poisoning food, drink, or medicine with intent to injure was inherently dangerous.

The willful and malicious burning of an automobile (located in a garage beneath an occupied home) was ruled inherently dangerous in *People v. Nichols* (1970) 3

Cal.3d 150. Finally, we held kidnapping to be such an offense in *People v. Ford*, 60 Cal.2d 772.

To hold, as we do today, that a violation of § 2053 is not inherently so dangerous that by its very nature, it cannot be committed without creating a substantial risk that someone will be killed, is consistent with our previous decisions in which the underlying felony has been held not inherently hazardous. We have so held where the underlying felony was felony false imprisonment (*People v. Henderson, supra*), possession of a concealable firearm by an ex-felon (*People v. Satchell, supra*), escape from a city or county penal facility (*People v. Lopez, supra*), and in other, less potentially threatening circumstances.

Finally, the underlying purpose of the felony-murder rule, to encourage felons to commit their offenses without perpetrating unnecessary violence which might result in a homicide, would not be served by applying the rule to the facts of this case.

Defendant was or should have been aware he was committing a crime by treating Swatsenbarg in the first place.[5] Yet, it is unlikely he would have been deterred from administering to Lee in the manner in which he did for fear of a prosecution for murder, given his published beliefs on the efficacy of massage in the curing of cancer.

Indeed, nowhere is it claimed that defendant attempted to perform any action with respect to Swatsenbarg other than to heal him — and earn a fee for doing so.

This clearly is a case in which conviction of felony murder is contrary to our settled law, as well as inappropriate as a matter of sound judicial policy. The instruction regarding felony murder was erroneous.

Accordingly, defendant's second degree murder conviction is reversed.

II.

In addition to asserting the felonious unlicensed practice of medicine will not provide the predicate for a felony-murder conviction because felonious unlicensed medical practice is not inherently dangerous to human life, Burroughs claims the trial court erroneously refused to give an instruction, requested by defendant, on the purportedly lesser included offense of involuntary manslaughter. Our conclusion the felony of practicing medicine without a license is not inherently dangerous, of course, obviates the necessity of reaching this alternative basis for purposes of reversal. To provide guidance to the trial court should Burroughs be retried for the death of Lee Swatsenbarg, however, we now consider whether, on the facts alleged, Burroughs could properly be charged and convicted of involuntary manslaughter.

We will conclude that while there was no evidence to suggest Swatsenbarg's demise was the intended consequence of Burroughs' treatment of the decedent, there was substantial evidence that this treatment, the administering of "deep

---

[5] He had been convicted of practicing medicine without a license in 1960.

abdominal massages" in particular, was performed "without due caution and circumspection," and was the proximate cause of Lee Swatsenbarg's death. Thus, on the evidence presented, Burroughs was susceptible to a possible conviction of involuntary manslaughter, and the jury should have been so instructed.

Thus, while Burroughs' second degree felony-murder conviction must be reversed, if the decision again be made to prosecute him he is susceptible to a charge and possible conviction of involuntary manslaughter.

BIRD, CHIEF JUSTICE, concurring.

The majority reverse appellant's second degree felony-murder conviction on the ground that practicing medicine without a license is not an inherently dangerous felony. I agree with that conclusion, as well as with the directions that on retrial appellant may be prosecuted for involuntary manslaughter. However, I would rest the reversal on a broader ground. The time has come for this court to discard the artificial and court-created offense of second degree felony murder.

As Justice Mosk noted for the court in *People v. Dillon* (1983) 34 Cal.3d 441, 462, this court "holds no brief for the felony-murder rule." Felony murder has been described as "a highly artificial concept that deserves no extension beyond its required application." *People v. Phillips* (1966) 64 Cal.2d 574, 582. "The rule is much censured 'because it anachronistically resurrects from a bygone age a "barbaric" concept that has been discarded in the place of its origin' and because 'in almost all cases in which it is applied it is unnecessary' and 'it erodes the relation between criminal liability and moral culpability.' " *People v. Dillon, supra*, 34 Cal.3d at 463. This court is responsible for the legal doctrines which it creates. The second degree felony-murder rule is, as it has been since 1872, a judge-made doctrine without any express basis in the Penal Code. Therefore, the power to do away "with the 'barbaric' anachronism which we are responsible for creating" lies with this court. *People v. Dillon, supra*, 34 Cal.3d at p. 494. Such long overdue judicial surgery would not intrude upon the prerogatives of the other two branches of government.

Accordingly, this court should take the long-overdue step and eliminate the second degree felony-murder rule.[2]

---

[2] This court would not be the first to take such a step. In *People v. Aaron* (1980) 409 Mich. 672, 299 N.W.2d 304, the Michigan Supreme Court, interpreting a statute similar to Penal Code § 189, concluded after an exhaustive and scholarly analysis that the statute did not codify the common law felony-murder rule, but merely elevated any murder otherwise proven to murder of the first degree when committed during the perpetration of one of the named felonies. This interpretive step was not a radical one. Several other state courts had so interpreted similar statutes. The Michigan court went further, however. It reviewed the *common law* doctrine of felony murder and concluded that "it violates the basic premise of individual moral culpability upon which our criminal law is based." 299 N.W.2d at 328. As a result, the court abolished the felony-murder rule in Michigan.

In *Dillon*, a majority of the court declined to follow the *Aaron* court's lead with respect to the first degree felony-murder rule since the rule had been codified by the Legislature. Thus, "however much the court agreed with the reasoning of *Aaron*, it could not duplicate its solution to the problem." 34 Cal.3d at 463. However, no statutory bar appears with respect to the second degree felony-murder rule, so this court may in that context follow the lead of the Michigan Supreme Court.

I.

Many writers and commentators have concluded that the common law doctrine of felony murder is of questionable origin. *People v. Aaron, supra,* 299 N.W.2d at p. 307; *see also* Kaye, *The Early History of Murder and Manslaughter, Part II* (1967) 83 LAW Q.REV. 569, 593 (hereafter Kaye); *Recent Developments, Criminal Law: Felony-Murder Rule — Felon's Responsibility for Death of Accomplice* (1965) 65 COLUM.L.REV. 1496, fn. 2 (hereafter *Recent Developments*). In an attempt to understand the development of the doctrine and the numerous restrictions and limitations which have been imposed by both courts and legislatures, it is necessary to briefly review the common law concept of homicide and its relationship to the felony-murder rule. At early common law, all homicides were criminal[4] without regard to the mental state of the actor. Sayre, *Mens Rea* (1932) 45 HARV. L. REV. 974 (hereafter Sayre). As with every other felony,[5] homicide was punishable by death.[6] Perkins & Boyce, *Criminal Law,* 14; Seibold, *The Felony-Murder Rule: In Search of a Viable Doctrine* (1978) 23 CATH.LAW. 133.

The law soon recognized the need to distinguish between intentional and accidental killings. By the 13th century, it was clear that an accidental killing or killing "by misadventure," while not subject to acquittal, would entitle the person convicted to a royal pardon. Perkins, *A Re-examination of Malice Aforethought* (1934) 43 YALE L.J. 537.

The influence of the Church and canon law also resulted in the addition of certain distinctions to the law of homicide. Ecclesiastic courts had always retained jurisdiction to try clerics accused of felonies. Because the Church refused to impose capital punishment, submission of a case to Church jurisdiction resulted in leniency of the most important sort. *See* Note, *Felony Murder as a First Degree Offense: An Anachronism Retained* (1957) 66 YALE L.J. 427, 429 (hereafter *Anachronism Retained*). "Benefit of clergy," as this practice was known, thus became a means of mitigating the harshness of the common law's meat-axe approach to all homicides, regardless of mental state. The punishment for those felons eligible for benefit of clergy was limited to the branding of a thumb and one year's imprisonment. Focusing on the character of the offender rather than the nature of the offense, the practice was gradually expanded by the use of a presumption that any person who could read and write was a cleric, and thus ineligible for the death penalty. *Anachronism Retained,* 66 YALE L.J. at 429.

As a greater proportion of the society became literate, the injustice of the system became apparent. Moreover, the principle of benefit of clergy conflicted with the fundamental philosophy of canon law, which had always emphasized the

---

[4] The law at this point recognized no distinction between a crime and a tort. Liability for a homicide included both punishment of the offender and payment to the surviving relatives of the deceased.

[5] The common law concept of a felony is, of course, considerably different from the felony as it appears in modern statutory codes. At common law, the term was limited to a few very serious crimes, nearly all involving assaultive conduct or the danger of physical harm. *See* Perkins & Boyce, *Criminal Law* (1982) 14-15.

[6] There is some evidence to believe that while the punishment of death was theoretically possible in the case of all felonies, it was far from uniformly applied, varying principally with the seriousness of the offense. *See* 2 Pollack & Maitland, *The History of English Law* 488.

importance of subjective moral blameworthiness in assessing the degree of criminal culpability.

These factors led to a series of statutes in the 15th and 16th centuries which abolished the benefit of clergy for certain of the more culpable homicides. *Anachronism Retained*, 66 YALE L.J. at 429-430. These more culpable homicides, denominated murder,[8] were distinguished as having been committed with "malice aforethought" or "malice prepensed." All other homicides, for which benefit of clergy was still available, developed into the crime of manslaughter. *Malice Aforethought*, 43 YALE L.J. at 543-544.

It is within this framework that the felony-murder rule was born. The exact origins of the rule, however, are far from clear. The most oft-cited early statement of the rule appears in Lord Coke's Third Institute (6th ed. 1680) page 56. Coke did not propose a rationale but rather illustrated by example:

> If the act be unlawful it is murder. As if A. meaning to steal a deer in the park of B., shooteth at the deer, and by the glance of the arrow killeth a boy that is hidden in a bush: this is murder, for that the act was unlawful, although A. had no intent to hurt the boy, nor knew not of him. But if B. the owner of the park had shot at his own deer, and without any ill intent had killed the boy by the glance of his arrow, this had been homicide by misadventure, and no felony. So, if one shoot at any wild fowle upon a tree, and the arrow killeth any reasonable creature afar off, without any evil intent in him, this is *per infortunium* [misadventure]: for it was not unlawful to shoot at the wilde fowle: but if he had shot at a cock or hen, or any tame fowle of another mans, and the arrow by mischance had killed a man, this had been murder, for the act was unlawfull.

This statement of the rule was refined by Hale and Foster, who limited the murder designation to any killing in the course of a felony. 1 Hale, *Pleas of the Crown* (1847) p. 465, 475; Foster, *Crown Cases* (2d ed. 1791) pp. 258-259; *see Malice Aforethought*, 43 YALE L.J. at 559. The basis for Lord Coke's statement, which went unquestioned for several hundred years, appears dubious. Two 16th century English cases have been suggested as support, but courts and commentators have concluded that each was, in reality, based on an entirely different proposition. Professors Moreland and Perkins, in their respective treatises, analyze in a historical sense the genesis of the rule, but neither theory provides much support for the rationality of the doctrine.

In 1883, Judge Sir James Fitzjames Stephen embarked on an extensive criticism of Coke's conclusion. Stephen termed the felony-murder rule "astonishing" and "monstrous." 3 Stephen at 57, 65, 75. He further stated that the Coke passage is "entirely unwarranted by the authorities which he quotes." Modern writers have

---

[8] "Murder" derives from the term *murdrum* which originally referred to a heavy amercement which was levied against an English village whenever a Norman lord was killed in an ambush. By the mid-14th century, there were no longer any foreign-born Normans left in England and the requirement for an amercement was statutorily abolished. *Murdrum*, however, remained a part of the language as a way of referring to the most serious kind of homicide. *See* 2 Pollack & Maitland, *The History of English Law*, at 486-488.

reached the similar conclusion that Coke's "creation" of the felony-murder rule was totally without legal or rational foundation.

II.

The history of the felony-murder rule is in reality a history of limitation. The path of limitation, as well as the result, has differed depending on the jurisdiction. As early as 1834, an English governmental commission described the felony-murder rule as being "totally incongruous with the general principles of our jurisprudence." First Rep. of His Majesty's Commissioners on Crim. Law (1834) at p. 29.

The statement merely made explicit what was an ongoing process in English common law to limit application of the felony-murder doctrine. A series of cases in the 19th century culminating with *Regina v. Serne* (1887) 16 Cox Crim.Cas. 311 virtually abolished the common law felony-murder rule in England. In *Serne*, Judge Stephen, whose pointed criticism of Coke was noted earlier, stated the law as follows: "Instead of saying that any act done with intent to commit a felony and which causes death amounts to murder, it would be reasonable to say that any act known to be dangerous to life, and likely in itself to cause death done for the purpose of committing a felony which caused death, should be murder."

Stephen's characterization of the law strongly suggests that a reckless *mens rea* is required to prove murder. The actor must know that his act is "likely in itself to cause death." Professor Perkins concluded that Stephen was "inclined to require for murder the same degree of wanton and willful disregard for human life which would constitute malice aforethought if no felony were being attempted." *Malice Aforethought*, 43 YALE L.J. at 559.

Yet Judge Stephen's enlightened view was not long-lived. A series of cases beginning in 1898 and culminating with the House of Lords decision in *Director of Public Prosecutions v. Beard* (1920) App.Cas. 479, re-established the felony-murder rule, albeit with some restrictions.[15] Notwithstanding its renewed existence, the rule was rarely invoked in the 20th century. It was applied, if at all, in cases in which there was ample independent evidence that the defendant possessed at least a reckless mental state. Prevezer, 57 COLUM.L.REV. at 635.

The death knell for the felony-murder rule in England was sounded by the Homicide Act of 1957. Section 1 of the act provided in relevant part: "Where a person kills another in the course or furtherance of some other offence, the killing shall not amount to murder unless done with the same malice aforethought (express or implied) as is required for a killing to amount to murder when not done in the course or furtherance of another offence." Thus by statute, Parliament vindicated the view expressed by Judge Stephen some 60 years earlier that a killing in the

---

[15] In *Beard*, the defendant was charged with murder when he accidentally suffocated his rape victim while trying to quiet her screams. The House of Lords held that if the defendant, in the course of a violent felony, commits a violent act which results in death, he is guilty of murder regardless of how unintended the resulting death was. The attempt to quiet the girl's screams was held in *Beard* to be a sufficiently violent act.

course of a felony is not murder unless the essential element of malice is independently proved.[16]

In the United States, the rule has followed a somewhat similar path. Since the state of English common law in 1776 served as the basis for the development of American jurisprudence, Blackstone's version of the felony-murder rule became an integral part of the common law of the first 13 states. Not surprisingly, the Atlantic separation did nothing to reduce the amount of criticism to which the doctrine has been subjected. As early as 1854, this criticism appears to have resulted in the statutory abolition of the felony-murder rule in Ohio. *See* Model Pen.Code § 201.2, Com. 4 (Tent.Draft No. 9, 1959) 35.

Oliver Wendell Holmes questioned the rule's deterrent effect in 1881.

If a man does an act with intent to commit a felony, and thereby accidentally kills another, the fact that the shooting is felonious does not make it any more likely to kill people. If the object of the rule is to prevent such accidents, it should make accidental killing with firearms murder, not accidental killing in the effort to steal; while, if its object is to prevent stealing, it would do better to hang one thief in every thousand by lot.

[Holmes, *The Common Law* (1881) pp. 57-58.]

Two states, Hawaii and Kentucky, have followed Ohio in abolishing the felony-murder rule by statute. Hawaii Rev.Stat. § 707-701 (1976); Ky.Rev.Stat. § 507.020 (1975). The comment to the Hawaii statute is instructive.

Even in its limited formulation the felony-murder rule is still objectionable. It is not sound principle to convert an accidental, negligent, or reckless homicide into a murder simply because, without more, the killing was in furtherance of a criminal objective of some defined class. Engaging in certain penally-prohibited behavior may, of course, evidence a recklessness sufficient to establish manslaughter, or a practical certainty or intent, with respect to causing death, sufficient to establish murder, but such a finding is an independent determination which must rest on the facts of each case. In recognition of the trend toward, and the substantial body of criticism supporting, the abolition of the felony-murder rule, and because of the extremely questionable results which the rule has worked in other jurisdictions, the Code has eliminated from our law the felonymurder rule. [Hawaii Rev.Stat. § 707-701 (1976) commentary, p. 347.]

The drafters of the Model Penal Code concluded that the felony-murder rule should be abandoned. Model Pen.Code § 201.2, Com. 4 (Tent.Draft No. 9, 1959) p. 33; Wechsler, *Codification of Criminal Law in the United States: The Model Penal Code* (1968) 68 COLUM. L. REV. 1425, 1446. However, concern over possible

---

[16] Criticism of the felony-murder rule and the concept of presumed or constructive malice appears in virtually every country whose legal system, based on the tradition of English common law, is "blessed" with this relic of our medieval heritage. *See, e.g.,* Burns & Reid, *From Felony Murder to Accomplice Felony Attempted Murder: The Rake's Progress Compleat?* (1977) 55 CANADIAN BAR REV. 74, 104-105; Westling, *Manslaughter By Unlawful Act: The "Constructive" Crime Which Serves No Constructive Purpose* (1974) 7 SYDNEY L. REV. 211, 223. India abolished the felony-murder rule by statute in 1951. *See* Model Pen.Code § 201.2, Com. 4 (Tent.Draft No. 9, 1959). None of the nations of continental Europe has a concept of criminal law analogous to the felony-murder rule. *Ibid.*

political opposition to the idea led them to insert a provision in section 201.2(b)'s definition of reckless murder, to the effect that "recklessness and extreme indifference to the value of human life are rebuttably presumed if the actor is engaged or is an accomplice in the commission of, or an attempt to commit or flight after committing or attempting to commit [one of seven enumerated felonies]." *Ibid., see now* Model Pen.Code § 210.2, subd. (1)(b) (Official Draft 1962) p. 13.

While New Hampshire is the only state to have adopted the Model Penal Code formulation,[18] several other states require that the accused exhibit a *mens rea* above and beyond the mere intent to commit a felony. Arkansas requires that the defendant cause death "under circumstances manifesting extreme indifference to the value of human life." Ark.Stat.Ann. § 41.1502. The Texas Penal Code provides that the act causing death must be "clearly dangerous to human life." Tex.Pen.Code Ann. § 19.02(a)(3). The Delaware first degree murder statute mandates that the accused at least have acted with criminal negligence in the course of committing certain enumerated felonies or recklessly in the course of committing nonenumerated felonies. Del.Code, tit. 11, § 636(a)(2), (6) (1979).

Numerous other states have passed legislation modifying the rule or restricting its application. In at least six states, a conviction based on a felony-murder theory can only be punished as second degree murder.[19] Wisconsin treats felony murder as a class B felony,[20] while Maine distinguishes it from any other degree of murder.[21] Perhaps the most objectionable and often criticized feature of the felony-murder rule involves its vicarious application to accomplices who did not participate in the acts which caused the victim's death. Accordingly, legislatures in 10 states have adopted statutes which provide an affirmative defense for such persons in certain limited circumstances.[22]

---

[18] If the presumption of recklessness and extreme indifference is not rebutted, the defendant is guilty of second degree murder. N.H.Rev.Stat.Ann. § 630:1-b(I)(b) (1974).

[19] Alaska Stat. § 11.41.110(a)(3); Louisiana Rev.Stat.Ann. § 14:30.1(2); New York Pen.L. § 125.25(3); Pennsylvania Cons.Stat.Ann., tit. 18, § 2502(b); Utah Code Ann. § 75-5-203(1). Min-nesota classifies a nonsex offense-related felony murder as murder in the second degree. Minn.Stat.Ann. §§ 609.185, 609.19. For an excellent overview of the relationship of the felonymurder rule to statutory criminal law in American jurisdictions, see Alderstein, *Felony-Murder in the New Criminal Codes* (1975-1976) 4 AM. J. CRIM. LAW 249.

[20] Wisconsin requires that the killing be a "natural and probable consequence of the commission or attempt to commit a felony." Wis.Stat.Ann. § 940.02(2). A class B felony in Wisconsin is punishable by a term of imprisonment not to exceed 20 years. § 939.50(3)(b).

[21] Felony murder in Maine can result in a maximum imprisonment of 20 years. Me.Rev.Stat.Ann., tit. 17A, § 202, 1252(2)(A).

[22] The New York statute (N.Y. Pen. L. § 125.25(3)) is typical: "In any prosecution under this subdivision, in which the defendant was not the only participant in the underlying crime, it is an affirmative defense that the defendant: (a) Did not commit the homicidal act or in any way solicit, request, command, importune, cause or aid the commission thereof; and (b) Was not armed with a deadly weapon, or any instrument, article or substance readily capable of causing death or serious physical injury and of a sort not ordinarily carried in public places by law-abiding persons; and (c) Had no reasonable ground to believe that any other participant was armed with such a weapon, instrument, article or substance; and (d) Had no reasonable ground to believe that any other participant intended to engage in conduct likely to result in death or serious physical injury." *See also* Alaska Stat. § 11.41.115(b); Ark.Stat.Ann. §§ 41-1501(2), 41-1502(2); Colo.Rev.Stat. § 18-3-102(2); Conn.Gen.Stat.Ann. § 53a-54c; Me.Rev.Stat., tit. 17-A, § 202; N.J.Stat.Ann. § 2C:11-3(a)(3); N.D.Cent.Code § 12.1-16.01(3); Or-

While some state legislatures have been active in modifying the felony-murder rule, most of the limitations on the doctrine have been imposed by the courts as part of their role in the continuing development of the common law.[23] In 1959 the drafters of the Model Penal Code listed seven major limitations which had been imposed by various state courts. The intervening 25 years have done little to reduce the need for or number of limitations on the rule. The most important of these include requirements that the underlying felony be inherently dangerous (*Wade v. State* (Okl. Cr. 1978) 581 P.2d 914; *Commonwealth v. Bowden* (1973), 456 Pa. 278 (conc. opn. of Nix, J.); *see also* Annot. (1973) 50 A.L.R.3d 397); that the killing be committed by one of the felons (*State v. Canola* (1977) 73 N.J. 206; *Commonwealth ex rel. Smith v. Myers*, 438 Pa. 218; *Commonwealth v. Balliro* (1965) 349 Mass. 505; *see also* Annot. (1974) 56 A.L.R.3d 239); that the duration of the felony be strictly construed (e.g., *People v. Smith* (1974) 55 Mich.App. 184; *State v. Golladay* (1970) 78 Wash.2d 121; *People v. Jackson* (1967) 20 N.Y.2d 440; *see also* Annot. (1974) 58 A.L.R.3d 851); and that the purpose of the underlying felony be independent of the killing. (E.g., *Garrett v. State* (Tex.Cr.App.1978) 573 S.W.2d 543; *State v. Branch* (1966) 244 Or. 97; *see also* Annot. (1971) 40 A.L.R.3d 1341.)

California's approach to the rule mirrors these developments. This court has consistently reiterated that the "highly artificial concept of strict criminal liability" (*People v. Satchell* (1971) 6 Cal.3d 28, 34) embodied in the felony murder rule "should not be extended beyond any rational function that it is designed to serve." *People v. Washington*, 62 Cal.2d at 783. Accordingly, in deciding whether to apply the rule in various factual settings, this court has "sought to insure that the doctrine be given the narrowest possible application consistent with its ostensible purpose — which is to deter those engaged in felonies from killing negligently or accidentally." *People v. Satchell, supra*, 6 Cal.3d at 34.

The reasons for limiting the rule were well summarized over a decade ago in *People v. Satchell, supra*. This court observed that the felony-murder rule is "usually unnecessary for conviction." *Id.* at 33. In almost all cases in which the rule is applied, conviction "can be predicated on the normal rules as to murder and as to accomplice liability. If the defendant commits the felony in a highly reckless manner, he can be convicted of second degree murder independently of the shortcut of the felony-murder rule. Under California's interpretation of the implied malice provision of the Penal Code (§ 188), proof of conduct evidencing extreme or wanton recklessness establishes the element of malice aforethought required for a second degree murder conviction. [In cases where the facts suggested such a theory], the prosecution would be free to prove the extreme recklessness of the conduct. The jury would decide whether the evidence, including the defendant's conduct and inferences rising from it, established the requisite malice aforethought." *Id.* at 33-34. In the "small residuum" of cases where the "normal rules" of murder would not apply, "there may be a substantial question whether the rule reaches a rational result or does not at least distract attention from more relevant criteria." *Ibid.*

In keeping with this view of the rule, the limitations on its application have been

---

e.Rev.Stat. § 163.115(3); Wash.Rev.Code Ann. § 9A.32.030.

[23] It was on this basis that the *Aaron* court abolished the common law felony-murder rule in Michigan.

extensive. This court has "refused to apply the doctrine in cases wherein the killing is committed by persons other than the defendant or an accomplice acting in furtherance of a common felonious design; in cases wherein the operation of the doctrine depends upon 'a felony which is an integral part of the homicide and which the evidence produced by the prosecution shows to be an offense included in fact within the offense charged'; and in cases wherein the underlying felony is not one of the six enumerated in § 189 of the Penal Code and is not inherently dangerous to human life." *People v. Satchell, supra,* 6 Cal.3d at 34.

As to this last limitation, "if the felony is not inherently dangerous it is highly improbable that the potential felon will be deterred; he will not anticipate that any injury or death might arise solely from the fact that he will commit the felony." Maj. opn., *ante.* Thus, California courts have identified several felonies which are not inherently dangerous to human life and have on that basis prohibited conviction on second degree felony-murder principles. Maj. opn., *ante* (practicing medicine without a license); *People v. Henderson* (1977) 19 Cal.3d 86, 93-95 (false imprisonment); *People v. Satchell, supra,* 6 Cal.3d at 35-41 (possession of a concealable firearm by an exfelon), 41-43 (possession of a sawed-off shotgun); *People v. Lopez* (1971) 6 Cal.3d 45 (escape from a city or county penal facility); *People v. Phillips, supra,* 64 Cal.2d at 582-583 (grand theft by false pretenses); *People v. Williams, supra,* 63 Cal.2d at 458 (conspiracy to possess methedrine without a prescription); *People v. Morales* (1975) 49 Cal.App.3d 134 (grand theft person); *People v. Lovato* (1968) 258 Cal.App.2d 290 (possession of concealable weapon by an alien); *see also People v. Houts* (1978) 86 Cal.App.3d 1012 (sodomy).[27]

Even today's majority recognize that appellant would most likely not have been deterred by the possibility that his actions could have subjected him to a murder conviction, since his "published beliefs on the efficacy of massage in the curing of cancer" (maj. opn., *ante*) were firmly entrenched and for well over two decades formed the basis for his "medical practice."

As the list of limitations and modifications grows longer, the California second degree felony-murder rule bears less and less resemblance to Blackstone's simple statement that "when an involuntary killing happens in prosecution of a felonious intent it will be murder." 4 Blackstone's Commentaries, *supra,* at 192-193. As the *Aaron* court noted, "to the extent that these modifications reduce the scope and significance of the common-law doctrine, they also call into question the continued existence of the doctrine itself." 299 N.W.2d at 316. In sum — and particularly in light of the fact that this court has sole responsibility for the creation of the rule — the viability of it is a question that can no longer be ignored.

---

[27] On the other hand, certain felonies have been found to be inherently dangerous to human life. *People v. Mattison* (1971) 4 Cal.3d 177 (poisoning food, drink, or medicine with intent to injure); *People v. Nichols* (1970) 3 Cal.3d 150 (wilful and malicious burning of a motor vehicle); *People v. Kelso* (1976) 64 Cal.App.3d 538 (simple kidnaping); *People v. Calzada* (1970) 13 Cal.App.3d 603 (driving a vehicle under the influence of narcotics); *People v. Taylor* (1970) 11 Cal.App.3d 577; *People v. Cline* (1969) 270 Cal.App.2d 328 (furnishing or administering dangerous drugs); *Brooks v. Superior Court* (1966) 239 Cal.App.2d 538 (forcibly preventing a police officer from performing his duty). In these few cases, as today's majority observe, the felony at issue "has been tinged with malevolence."

III.

The second degree felony-murder rule erodes the important relationship between criminal liability and an accused's mental state. That relationship has been described as "the most basic principle of the criminal law." Gegan, *Criminal Homicide in the Revised New York Penal Law* (1966) 12 N.Y. L. FORUM 565. "It is as universal and persistent in mature systems of law as belief in freedom of the human will and a consequent ability and duty of the normal individual to choose between good and evil." *Morissette v. United States* (1952) 342 U.S. 246, 250. The second degree felony-murder rule, as a strict liability concept, violates this most important principle. Not only does it obliterate the distinction between intended and unintended homicides, but it seeks to apply the same ponderous sanction to any participant in the criminal conspiracy or enterprise from which a death results. Thus, the doctrine has been applied where a codefendant served only in a getaway driver capacity (*People v. Hill* (1967) 66 Cal.2d 536 (first degree felony murder)); where the codefendant was present at the scene of the killing but did not fire the fatal shot (*People v. Kelso, supra,* 64 Cal.App.3d at 541-542); where the victim died from a heart attack precipitated by the fright induced by commission of the felony. *People v. Stamp* (1969) 2 Cal.App.3d 203 (first degree felony murder).

Legal commentators have been virtually unanimous in their condemnation of the felony-murder rule because it ignores the significance of the actor's mental state in determining his criminal liability. As the drafters of the Model Penal Code concluded in 1959, "principled argument in defense [of the felony-murder rule] is hard to find." Model Pen.Code § 201.2, Com. 4 (Tent.Draft No. 9, 1959) at p. 37.

As noted earlier, the rule is perhaps the last vestige of an archaic and indiscriminate philosophy still present in our modern system of criminal law.[30] "The rationale of the doctrine is that one who commits a felony is a bad person with a bad state of mind, and he has caused a bad result, so that we should not worry too much about the fact that the fatal result he accomplished was quite different and a good deal worse than the bad result he intended. Yet it is a general principle of criminal law that one is not ordinarily criminally liable for bad results which differ greatly from intended results." LaFave & Scott, *Criminal Law* (1972) p. 560. Thus, it is difficult to take issue with one commentator's conclusion that "the felony-murder rule, as a hold-over from the days of our barbarian Anglo-Saxon ancestors, has very little right to existence in modern society." Mueller, *Criminal Law and Administration* (1959) 34 N.Y.U.L.REV. 83, 98.

Of course, recognition of the irrationality of the felony-murder doctrine is not novel. This court's pronouncements on the disfavored status that the rule holds in California jurisprudence are numerous. *See, e.g., People v. Henderson, supra,* 19 Cal.3d at 92. Indeed, this court's decisions over the past 20 years may probably best be characterized as an attempt to avoid rather than to apply the rule. Given the court's repeated conclusion that application of the second degree felony-murder

---

[30] As Professor Hall has noted, "the underlying rationale of the felony-murder doctrine — that the offender has shown himself to be a 'bad actor,' and that this is enough to exclude the niceties bearing on the gravity of the harm actually committed — might have been defensible in early law. The survival of the felony-murder doctrine is a tribute to the tenacity of legal conceptions rooted in simple moral attitudes." Hall, *General Principles of Criminal Law* (1947) p. 455.

rule is not mandated by any California statute, a decision to abrogate that rule would be merely a natural extension of our prior holdings.

This court could, of course, leave the decision of whether to apply the second degree felony-murder rule in a given instance to the trier of fact. It is well established that the jury has the power to disregard the law and/or the facts in returning a verdict which is contrary to the evidence, as long as such verdict does not prejudice the accused.

However, the harshness of the rule, which leads some juries to disregard the law and others to follow it only with great reluctance, results in haphazard application of the criminal sanction. *See* Ludwig, *Foreseeable Death in Felony Murder* (1956) 18 U.PITT.L.REV. 51, 62. As the Ohio Supreme Court concluded more than a century ago in deciding to abandon the felony-murder rule, "crime is more effectually prevented by the *certainty* than by any unreasonable *severity* of punishment disproportionate to the turpitude and danger of the offense." *Robbins v. State, supra*, 8 Ohio St. at 170. In my view, it is far preferable to do away with an irrational doctrine than to permit it to be applied in an irrational manner.

IV.

The abrogation of the common law second degree felony-murder rule would not change the result in the majority of homicide cases. In cases other than first degree felony-murders, malice would remain the essential distinguishing element of murder. Pen. Code § 187. As in the past, malice would be established in one of two ways: (1) when the accused "manifest[s] a deliberate intention unlawfully to take away the life of a fellow creature" (Pen. Code § 188), or (2) when he (a) commits an act which is likely to cause death, and (b) consciously and unjustifiably disregards the substantial probability that death will result. *People v. Washington, supra*, 62 Cal.2d at p. 780. In order to establish conscious disregard in this context, the state would still have to show that the accused understood "the duty imposed upon him not to commit [such] acts" and that he acted despite this understanding. *Id.* at 760. If the trier of fact found malice by one of these two theories, § 187 would, as in the past, classify the killing as murder. In such a situation, a killing which occurs in the course of any inherently dangerous felony not enumerated in Penal Code § 189 would be murder in the second degree. No longer would a killing which occurs during the commission of an inherently dangerous felony, standing alone, constitute second degree murder. However, one should not conclude that when death ensues in such a situation, the commission of a dangerous felony is an irrelevant factor in determining whether or not the defendant acted with malice. To the contrary, the circumstances of the crime, including the commission of the felony, may provide strong circumstantial evidence that the defendant intended to kill the victim or that he committed an act in conscious disregard of the substantial probability that death would result.

The jury would be given the opportunity to make an independent determination of each defendant's individual culpability, a determination which would not be reversed on appeal unless unsupported by substantial evidence. Therefore, abolishing the second degree felony-murder rule would not significantly reduce the number of murder convictions.

This conclusion is supported by the experience of jurisdictions which have abolished the felony-murder rule. *See, e.g., People v. Aaron, supra*, 299 N.W.2d at pp. 328-329; Model Pen.Code § 201.2, Com. 4 (Tent.Draft No. 9, 1959) p. 39. Additionally, even if a jury were to find that a killing was without malice, the accused is still liable for the underlying felony as well as any lesser degree of homicide which the evidence may support.

There will be times when a jury is convinced that the accused's mental state does not justify a murder conviction.[33] In the first degree felony-murder context, this court's powers are circumscribed because the rule is a creature of statute. However, where no statutory bar appears, this court should not mandate a murder conviction in the absence of a finding of malice. To do so violates very basic concepts of rationality and proportionality.

As Holmes so eloquently stated, "It is revolting to have no better reason for a rule of law than that so it was laid down in the time of Henry IV. It is still more revolting if the grounds upon which it was laid down have vanished long since, and the rule simply persists from blind imitation of the past." Holmes, *Collected Legal Papers* (1920) p. 187. It is time this court laid this ill-conceived rule to rest.

RICHARDSON, JUSTICE, dissenting.

I respectfully dissent. In my view, the unauthorized practice of medicine "under circumstances or conditions which cause or create a risk of great bodily harm, serious physical or mental illness, or death" (Bus. & Prof.Code § 2053) fully supports application of the second degree felony-murder rule.

Relying on hypertechnical and irrelevant distinctions between great bodily harm, serious physical and mental injury, and the risk of death, the majority ignores the "rational function that [the felony-murder rule] is designed to serve." *People v. Washington* (1965) 62 Cal.2d 777, 783. As we have frequently reiterated, that purpose "is to deter those engaged in felonies from killing negligently or accidentally. *See People v. Washington, supra*, 62 Cal.2d 777, 781-783."

In those cases in which we have found the felony-murder doctrine not to apply, the felony, properly viewed in the abstract, contained by definition elements which did not usually entail any risk of harm to the victim. Thus the possibility of negligent or accidental death did not flow logically from each possible element of the crime. *See People v. Henderson, supra*, 19 Cal.3d 86 (false imprisonment effectuated by "violence, menace, fraud or deceit" with no distinction in the statute between violent and fraudulent or deceitful means); *People v. Lopez* (1971) 6 Cal.3d 45 (escape,

---

[33] Consider the facts in *People v. Dillon, supra*, 34 Cal.3d 441. Dillon was a 17-year-old student who unsuccessfully attempted to rob — and in the process fatally shot — a rural marijuana grower who was guarding his crop. The jury convicted Dillon of first degree murder based on its finding that the killing had occurred during the course of an attempted robbery.

As was clear from their communications with the trial court during and after deliberations, the jurors had serious reservations about applying the felony-murder rule. Nevertheless, on appeal, a majority of this court was compelled by statute to uphold application of the rule. The court found, however, that the life sentence imposed as a result violated the cruel or unusual punishment clause of the California Constitution (art. I, § 17), and accordingly reduced the conviction to second degree murder.

where statute encompassed both violent and nonviolent escapes); *People v. Satchell*, *supra*, 6 Cal.3d 28 (possession of a concealable firearm by a felon); *People v. Phillips* (1966) 64 Cal.2d 574 (grand theft); *People v. Williams* (1965) 63 Cal.2d 452 (conspiracy to obtain methedrine).

In contrast, the statute at issue here explicitly requires a risk of actual harm or "injury" to a person. * * *

In enacting Business and Professions Code § 2053, the Legislature clearly sought to impose a greater penalty in those cases where the unauthorized practice of medicine causes significant risks that may lead to death. The use of the felony-murder rule in this context clearly furthers the goal of deterring such conduct. The underlying conduct proscribed by § 2053 is manifestly "inherently dangerous to life." Viewed in the abstract, improper treatment of the "sick and afflicted" under the dangerous circumstances and conditions specified in that section is almost synonymous with inherently dangerous conduct.

I would affirm the judgment of conviction.

NOTES FROM THE JUDGE:

1. Exactly how did the majority decide that Burroughs's felony was not inherently dangerous? Try to apply that method to our case.

2. In *People v. Patterson*, 49 Cal. 3d 615 (1989), the trial court applied the *Burroughs* test to Calif. Health & Safety Code § 11352, which makes it a felony to furnish any one of several controlled substances (including cocaine) to someone. The trial court held that a violation of this statute, in the abstract, was not inherently dangerous, and dismissed a felony murder charge.

The Supreme Court reversed for a new hearing in the trial court, holding that (1) the court should not ask whether the entire statute involved inherently dangerous activity, but only the part dealing with cocaine (2) the trial court should hear expert testimony on the issue — the Supreme Court would not take judicial notice of the dangerousness of cocaine, and (3) "inherently dangerous to human life" means "a high probability that death will result."

Justice Lucas concurred, noting the anomaly that several felonies listed in § 189 (e.g., burglary, robbery, rape & child molesting) raise a *lower* danger to life than furnishing cocaine, and yet they clearly qualify for *1st degree* felony murder.

Justice Mosk dissented, arguing that the statute should be considered in its entirety.

Justice Panelli also dissented, on the ground that the second-degree felony murder doctrine is unconstitutional. He noted that the California Constitution gives the power to create crimes to the Legislature, not the courts, so the courts have no power to create common law crimes.

3. In *People v. Morse*, 2 Cal. App. 4th 620 (1992), Morse stored a bomb in his garage. When two police officers tried to dismantle it, the bomb exploded, killing the officers. Morse was convicted of felony murder, based on the felony of "reckless or malicious possession of a destructive device." On appeal, Morse argued that "because there are *conceivable* ways of violating the statute that do not necessarily pose a threat to human life," the felony was not "inherently dangerous." The court affirmed the conviction.

Our task is not to determine if it is possible (i.e., "conceivable") to violate the statute without great danger. By such a test no statute would be inherently dangerous. Rather the question is: does a violation of the statute involve a *high probability* of death? *People v. Patterson*. If it does, the offense is inherently dangerous.

We do not regard the question as a close one. To recklessly or maliciously possess a bomb in a residential area, as appellant did, inherently involves a high probability of death. Almost uniquely, bombs have an inherently dangerous nature. They are so dangerous that even when not set to explode, their possession violates the statute. A bomb has special characteristics which obviously differentiate it from all other objects. In the first place, the maker often loses control over the time of its detonation. In the second place, its victims are often unintended sufferers. And finally, considering its vast destructive potentialities, it is susceptible of fairly easy concealment.

Justice Johnson dissented, calling this "a drastic expansion of the felony murder doctrine." He noted that there was no evidence that defendant intended to detonate the bomb or had even built it — he merely stored it with its safety switch on. Justice Johnson insisted that, under *Burroughs*, the proper test was the one the *Morse* majority denounced: whether it was possible to violate the statute without great danger to life. Here, this *was* possible, as cases had held that the statute could be violated even though the bomb was inoperative. He also noted that prior cases had held that mere possession of guns, knifes, and drugs were not considered inherently dangerous felonies, and he was not persuaded that a bomb with the safety catch on was any more dangerous.

4. Suppose Prosecutor Paula charges Dan with murder and presents evidence that Dan went into Vic's house with a gun and shot Vic in the shoulder, and this caused Vic's death. Paula asks the judge to instruct the jury on three traditional forms of "malice": (1) intent to kill, (2) intent to commit serious bodily injury, and (2) "depraved heart" (extreme recklessness). But Paula is worried. Dan testified that he meant to hurt Vic, but not kill or seriously injure him. And "depraved heart" is so vague that the jury might not understand it. Thinking creatively, Paula comes up with an ingenious way to close these escape hatches: she asks the judge to instruct the jury on felony murder. What felony? Well, how about assault with a deadly weapon — which Dan clearly committed even if the jury believes his testimony?

In *People v. Ireland*, 70 Cal. 2d 522 (1969), the court held that the felony murder doctrine may not be applied here.

We have concluded that the utilization of the felony-murder rule in circumstances such as those before us extends the operation of that rule "beyond any rational function that it is designed to serve." *People v. Washington* (1965) 62 Cal.2d 777, 783. To allow such use of the felony murder rule would effectively preclude the jury from considering the issue of malice aforethought in all cases wherein homicide has been committed as a result of a felonious assault — a category which includes the great majority of all homicides. This kind of bootstrapping finds support neither in logic nor in law. We therefore hold that a second degree felony murder instruction may not properly be given when it is based upon a felony which is an integral part of the homicide and which the evidence produced by the prosecution shows to be an offense included in fact within the offense charged.

"All right," says Paula, "how about this one? The evidence would permit the jury to find that Dan entered Vic's house with the intent to commit assault with a deadly weapon (a felony) — and thus Dan committed *burglary*. Burglary clearly qualifies under the felony murder doctrine — indeed, it is expressly listed in Calif. Penal Code § 189." But in *People v. Wilson*, 1 Cal. 3d 431, 462 P.2d 22 (1969), the court rejected this argument too:

> Here the prosecution sought to apply the felony-murder rule on the theory that the homicide occurred in the course of a burglary, but the only basis for finding a felonious entry is the intent to commit an assault with a deadly weapon. When, as here, the entry would be nonfelonious but for the intent to commit the assault, and the assault is an integral part of the homicide and is included in fact in the offense charged, utilization of the felony-murder rule extends that doctrine "beyond any rational function that it is designed to serve." We have heretofore emphasized "that the felony-murder doctrine expresses a highly artificial concept that deserves no extension beyond its required application." *People v. Phillips* (1966) 64 Cal.2d 574, 582.

"The purpose of the felony-murder rule is to deter felons from killing negligently or accidentally by holding them strictly responsible for killings they commit." *People v. Washington* (1965) 62 Cal.2d 777, 781. Where a person enters a building with an intent to assault his victim with a deadly weapon, he is not deterred by the felony-murder rule. That doctrine can serve its purpose only when applied to a felony independent of the homicide.

In *Ireland*, we reasoned that a man assaulting another with a deadly weapon could not be deterred by the second degree felony-murder rule, since the assault was an integral part of the homicide. Here, the only distinction is that the assault and homicide occurred inside a dwelling so that the underlying felony is burglary based on an intention to assault with a deadly weapon, rather than simply assault with a deadly weapon.

We do not suggest that no relevant differences exist between crimes committed inside and outside dwellings. We have often recognized that persons within dwellings are in greater peril from intruders bent on stealing or engaging in other felonious conduct. Persons within dwellings are more likely to resist and less likely to be able to avoid the consequences of crimes committed inside their homes. However, this rationale does not justify application of the felony-murder rule to the case at bar. Where the intended felony of the burglar is an assault with a deadly weapon, the likelihood of homicide from the lethal weapon is not significantly increased by the site of the assault. Furthermore, the burglary statute in this state includes within its definition numerous structures other than dwellings as to which there can be no conceivable basis for distinguishing between an assault with a deadly weapon outdoors and a burglary in which the felonious intent is solely to assault with a deadly weapon.

In *Ireland*, we rejected the bootstrap reasoning involved in taking an element of a homicide and using it as the underlying felony in a second degree felony-murder instruction. We conclude that the same bootstrapping is involved in instructing a jury that the intent to assault makes the entry burglary and that the burglary raises the homicide resulting from the assault to first degree murder without proof of malice aforethought and premeditation. To hold otherwise, we would have to declare that because burglary is not technically a lesser offense included within a charge of murder, burglary constitutes an independent felony which can support a felony-murder instruction. However, in *Ireland* itself we did not assert that assault with a deadly weapon was a lesser included offense in murder; we asserted only that it was "included in fact" in the charge of murder, in that the elements of the assault were necessary elements in the homicide.

In the same sense, a burglary based on intent to assault with a deadly weapon is included in fact within a charge of murder, and cannot support a felony-murder instruction.

We recognize that *Ireland* dealt with a court-made rule while this case involves first degree felony murder, which is statutory. However, the statutory source of the rule does not compel us to apply it in disregard of logic and reason.

5. In *People v. Chun*, 45 Cal.4th 1172 (2009), the court followed *Ireland* and held that the crime of *shooting at an occupied vehicle* could not be used as the basis for a felony murder conviction, because it was an "assaultive" felony that merged with the homicide.

6. Take a look at the purposes of punishment discussed at the end of Chapter 1. Which, if any, of these purposes is served by the felony murder doctrine?

7. Professor Tomkovicz, in *The Endurance of the Felony-Murder Rule: A Study of the Forces That Shape Our Criminal Law*, 51 WASH. & LEE L. REV. 1429 (1994), discusses "one of the more remarkable legal phenomena of our time — the survival of the felony murder rule." He notes that despite overwhelming criticism of the felony murder rule by legal scholars, "scholarly pleas for abolition have met stern resistance and have had little success." Why? He suggests several reasons. First, history gave us the rule, and inertia tends to keep it going (though he doubts that it would be adopted today if it did not already exist). Second,

> The abolition of felony-murder . . . is inconsistent with the law and order current. Consequently, anyone bent on reforming the rule must fight the tide and be prepared to pay a political price. In the world of American politics, logical consistency and fairness to felons are not very potent weapons against the charge that one is soft on crime and hostile to law and order.

Third, scholars' notions of "proportional culpability" do not mesh with those of the public.

A felon's interest in fair, proportional treatment stands in stark contrast to the life of an innocent victim. The decision to favor the latter may not be rationally consistent with culpability premises and may not be empirically supportable in deterrent terms, but it is emotionally compelling. Innocent victims merit our support, our protection, and, when their lives are lost, our affirmation of their value. Denunciation of the killer — who is, after all, a felon — is a way of proclaiming the significance of innocent human life.

He adds that "ordinary citizens place a greater emphasis on harm than the scholarly community."

Do you agree with this assessment of the American public?

Do you feel this way *yourself*? If so, do you agree with the result in *People v. Earl*, 29 Cal. App. 3d 894 (1973)? There, a department store security guard stopped Earl for shoplifting. In the ensuing scuffle, the guard was killed. The prosecutor argued that the jury could convict Earl of first degree murder — and impose the death penalty — even if it did not find that Earl intended to kill. The prosecutor reasoned as follows: (1) while the shoplifting itself was only a misdemeanor, there was evidence that Earl had entered the store with the intent to shoplift (he had no money or charge card when he entered), and therefore he was guilty of burglary under California's "modern" definition of burglary, (2) burglary is a felony, so Earl committed felony-murder, even if he had no intent to kill, (3) because burglary is one of the felonies listed in Penal Code § 189, the murder is raised to first degree murder. The jury convicted Earl and sentenced him to death. While the death penalty was reversed as unconstitutional, the first degree murder conviction was affirmed. The court agreed that it "seems illogical" to draw a distinction between thieves based on *when* they make their decisions to steal, but the distinction was made by the legislature and cannot be changed by the courts.

Similarly, in *People v. Thongvilay*, 62 Cal. App. 4th 71 (1998), defendants committed second degree burglary by going into an automobile to steal a stereo. They drove off, were chased, and ran a red light — colliding with another car and killing the occupant. As burglary is listed in California's first degree felony murder statute (Penal Code § 189), the court upheld their convictions for first degree murder.

While application of the felony-murder rule to this case may seem harsh, we are reminded of the rule's primary purpose, "to deter felons from killing negligently or accidentally by holding them strictly responsible for killings they commit." *People v. Washington*, (1965) 62 Cal.2d 777.

In *People v. Fuller*, 86 Cal. App. 3d 618 (1978), however, the court was reluctant to uphold a first degree murder conviction based on an auto burglary: "Such a harsh result destroys the symmetry of the law by equating an accidental killing resulting from a petty theft with a premeditated murder." But the court upheld the conviction anyway, as "the force of precedent requires the application of the first degree felony-murder rule to the instant case."

PEOPLE v. WILKINS
California Court of Appeal, 4th District, 2011
191 Cal.App.4th 780

It has long been recognized in this state that "the purpose of the felony-murder rule is to deter felons from killing negligently or accidentally by holding them strictly responsible for killings they commit." *People v. Washington* (1965) 62 Cal.2d 777, 781. Defendant committed a burglary of a residence under construction before workers arrived to begin their day. He loaded the back of his pickup truck with numerous boxed appliances and fixtures. He stuffed the cab of the truck to the windows with smaller items. In his haste to leave the scene unnoticed, he left the tailgate on the truck down and did not tie down the loot loaded into the bed of the truck despite the fact that he had ties in his truck. Sixty miles later on his drive home where he would unload the loot, the stove defendant stole fell off the back of his truck, resulting in the victim's death. The jury convicted defendant of first degree murder under the felony-murder rule. He contends that the evidence does not support his conviction and that the court erred when it refused to instruct the jury that a burglary is complete upon the perpetrator reaching a place of temporary safety.

Although defendant was, by all accounts, driving normally and his crime had not yet been discovered, defendant committed the acts that resulted in the death while he was at the scene of, and in the process of committing, the burglary. The acts that caused the homicide — the failure to tie down the load of stolen loot and raise the truck's tailgate — occurred at the scene of the burglary, not 60 miles later when part of the unsecured load fell off the back of the defendant's truck as he drove to where he could unload and hide the haul. As a result, it was not unreasonable for the jury to conclude the homicide and the burglary were part of one continuous transaction, inasmuch as defendant was in flight from the scene with his license plates secreted.

We also reject defendant's argument that the trial court erred in refusing his request to instruct the jury pursuant to CALCRIM No. 3261 [burglary complete upon the burglar reaching a place of temporary safety]. The Supreme Court has held the instruction on the "continuous-transaction" doctrine is sufficient to inform the jury on the duration of a felony for purposes of the felony-murder rule and that the escape rule, which terminates a felony at the point the perpetrator reaches a place of temporary safety, defines the scope of an underlying felony for certain ancillary purposes and not for felony-murder purposes. *People v. Cavitt* (2004) 33 Cal.4th 187, 208[FN1] * * * *

[FN1] The continuous transaction doctrine and the escape or flight rule, which refers to the accused reaching a place of temporary safety, are closely related, but distinct concepts. Cavitt, supra, 33 Cal.4th at p. 208. Cavitt provides the roadmap to successful navigation of the difficulty created by the courts' use of both concepts in connection with the felony-murder rule.

FACTS

Appliances at the Work Site

Defendant lived in Long Beach with Nancy Blake. On one day of the week before July 4, 2006, and one day of the week after, he worked at a home construction site in Menifee, a city in Riverside County. The homeowner had a delivery of major appliances and other items purchased from Home Depot on June 28. Defendant's cell phone records showed he was in the area of the Menifee jobsite on the delivery date. The delivery included a refrigerator, a dishwasher, a stove, a range hood, a microwave and a sink. It also included light fixtures, ceiling fans, door locks and door handles. Most of the items were stored in the kitchen area and some were in the garage.

At the end of the work day on July 6, all of the items were still in the residence when the workers locked the premises. While the owner was having breakfast the next morning, he received a call from the carpenter working at the house telling him all of his purchases were missing. He called the police. Defendant's cell phone records showed he was in the area of the Menifee construction site during the early morning of July 7.

Defendant, Trivich, and Telephone Calls

In September 2005, sometime after their romantic relationship ended, Kathleen Trivich and defendant entered into a business relationship to buy a piece of property in Palm Springs and build on it. Trivich paid for the land and was to pay for the materials to build a house on the property. Defendant said his contribution was to "basically oversee the project." Trivich also bought a Ford F–250 truck for defendant in 2006. The truck was to be used to haul building materials. As of July 2006, no construction "whatsoever" had been completed.

On July 6, 2006, defendant left his home in Long Beach about "8:30 or 9:00" p.m. He was driving his Ford F–250 truck. Trivich was at a speech and acting class at 8:00 p.m. that night, until just after midnight. Sometime thereafter she checked her cell phone and found a message from defendant. He wanted gas money. She called defendant back on his cell phone. She agreed to give him money. She drove to Long Beach, where she put $100 or $200 in an envelope and slid it under the door to his house.

After driving to Long Beach, where Trivich went to an ATM and withdrew the money she left for defendant at his house, she again spoke to defendant on the phone. She told him she dropped the money off at his house, and defendant said he had some news for her. He said, "I've got a surprise for you. I got some really big things for the kitchen." Trivich asked him what he had, but he did not tell her. At the time of this call, defendant's cell phone was using a cell tower along the 91 Freeway.

The Freeway

Calls to the California Highway Patrol began at 5:01 a.m. on July 7, 2006. The callers said there were items in one of the lanes of the westbound 91 Freeway, right before "Kraemer and Glassell in Anaheim." One said he ran into a big box, and that he saw someone else run into it, too. About four minutes after the first call, someone reported that a tanker truck rolled over.

At trial, Danny Lay testified he was westbound on the 91 Freeway somewhere around Kraemer right before a freeway interchange at about 5:00 o'clock in the morning of July 7, 2006. He was in the second lane to the right of the carpool lane. A Ford pickup without a rear license plate was in front of *him. There were "a lot of boxes in the back of the truck." When Lay was 25 to 50 yards behind the truck just east of Kraemer, "a large box fell from the right corner of the truck into the freeway." Lay had a car to his left and a car to his right, so he hit his brakes and tried to stop. He hit the box.

Lay proceeded after the pickup. He turned on his flashing lights, turned his bright lights on and off repeatedly and hit his horn. The truck slowed down and both vehicles pulled off the freeway. Lay pulled up next to the passenger side of the pickup, but there were so many boxes blocking the window, he couldn't see the driver. He thinks the driver looked over at him, saw him and then "accelerated away." Lay kept flashing his lights and honking his horn, and was finally able to pull up alongside the pickup again. The driver of the pickup stopped and threatened Lay, using a vulgarity.

Lay identified defendant as the person who was driving the pickup truck. Defendant and Lay got out of their vehicles, and defendant said he was "going to kick Lay's ass." Lay said, "bring it on, but first something fell from your truck." Defendant looked in the back of the pickup and remarked, "Oh, my God. It's a thousand-dollar stove." Lay saw the tailgate on the truck was down. There were no ropes or tie-downs. He also saw various sized boxes. He remembered seeing ceiling fans and a refrigerator. He asked defendant for identification. Defendant went to the glove box and appeared to look through it. He then said he must have forgotten his license, and that a friend, Kathleen Trivich, owned the truck. He identified himself as Michael Wilkins.

Charles Thomas was also on the freeway that morning, driving behind a white truck. The white truck made a "pretty severe" lane change. Thomas said "as soon as he swerved and I kind of got startled and slowed down, and then all of a sudden, I saw a white box, my headlights shined on this white box." He explained it was dark out and he wanted to move, but "there was cars and a lot of traffic." He was asked if he hit the box, and responded: "It was so fast. Yeah, I hit it. It was so fast. I didn't slam on my brakes, there was nothing I could do." He said he called 911, and that another vehicle hit the box, too, and they both pulled over to the side of the road. The other vehicle suffered a flat tire, and "had a hard time limping off."

Donald Wade was driving behind a big rig truck that morning, and "saw an automobile coming across out of the left lanes across the traffic about, looked like about 90–degree angle and he hit the truck in front of me."

James Davies, also on the freeway at the time, saw a truck as it hit the K-rail.

"When I moved forward in traffic about 50 yards or so, I did see an appliance sitting in the lane." Davies pulled over to the side of the road, called 911 and spoke with a motorcycle officer who arrived at the scene.

Thomas Hipsher was driving "a big truck, tractor with two trailers" carrying a full load of powdered cement that morning as he drove along "the slow lane" at 55 miles per hour. He felt an impact and lost control of his vehicle. He suffered bruised ribs and "a lot of cuts and bruises." He never saw the car that struck him.

The Death

California Highway Patrol Officer John Heckenkemper responded to the scene shortly after 5:00 a.m. on July 7. He described the scene: "Upon my arrival, there was — traffic was obviously in disarray. There was a stove in the middle of the lanes and beyond that, just west of the stove, there was an accident involving a big rig that had overturned."

Captain paramedic John Mark of Anaheim described what he saw: "Upon our arrival, we found a large semi-truck commodity hauler on its side off the shoulder of freeway with the cab extending off the shoulder. And we recognized that there was a vehicle actually trapped between the two trailers." They could not get to the car underneath the truck until the truck was removed. Then "it took a fair amount of time to extricate the victim from the vehicle." The man inside was deceased.

The coroner testified she conducted an autopsy of David Piquette. She described numerous injuries on the body, and said the cause of death was "positional asphyxia. That caused — due to compression of neck and chest, positional asphyxia."

An accident reconstructionist testified "Piquette swerved in an area just shy of where the stove was to hit the big rig where we know he did." His investigation showed the driver of the big rig "steered to the right at about the same time that a driver probably saw Piquette coming from the left, and then that would be a completely natural human reaction." He said that in order to avoid hitting the stove, given the conditions, a driver in Piquette's position would have had to have been driving at 28 miles per hour, and the speed limit in the area was 65 miles per hour. * * * *

California Highway Patrol Officer Joseph Kenneth Morrison drove to the construction. The distance from the construction site to the place where Piquette was killed is a little over 60 miles. The distance from where Lay said he first saw the truck carrying the appliances to the collision scene is approximately 5.6 miles. * * * *

When the felony-murder rule is invoked by the prosecution, the issue of whether the homicide occurred "in the perpetration of" the underlying felony often arises. First degree felony murder does not require a strict causal relation between the felony and the killing. The only nexus required is that both are part of one continuous transaction. The continuous transaction doctrine was adopted "for the protection of the community and its residents." *Cavitt*, supra, 33 Cal.4th at 207.

The *Cavitt* court recognized that the continuous-transaction doctrine and the escape rule are "two related, but distinct, doctrines." In *Cavitt*, Cavitt and Williams plotted with Cavitt's girlfriend McKnight to burglarize the McKnight residence, tie up McKnight's stepmother, Betty, and steal Betty's jewelry. Once they were inside, Cavitt and Williams put a sheet over Betty's head, bound her wrists and ankles, and beat her. They tied up McKnight and left her at the scene to make it look as if she, too, was a victim. Cavitt and Williams then left the scene. Betty died of asphyxiation. The defendants' trial position was that McKnight intentionally killed her stepmother after they left the scene and had reached a place of temporary safety. Unlike the present case, the jury in Williams's trial was not only instructed on the continuous transaction-rule, but was also given an escape/temporary safety instruction. Williams's contention on appeal was that the trial court erred when it added to the temporary safety instruction a paragraph stating perpetrators have not reached a place of temporary safety if the victim of the burglary remains in the control of any of the perpetrators. He argued the law does not require all perpetrators to reach a place of temporary safety before the burglary is deemed completed.

The court held that whereas the "escape rule" defines the duration of the underlying felony, in the context of certain ancillary consequences of the felony the continuous-transaction doctrine, defines the duration of felony-murder liability which may extend beyond the termination of the felony itself, provided the felony and the act resulting in death constitute one continuous transaction. In rejecting Williams's argument, the court stated it "would have been sufficient to have instructed the Williams jury on the continuous-transaction doctrine alone." * * * *

The temporary safety doctrine does not define felony-murder liability. The *Cavitt* court found that limiting the felony-murder rule to only those killings that occur prior to the felon reaching a place of temporary safety would lead to absurd and unintended results.

Reconciling *Cavitt* with cases that have discussed temporary safety as a component of the felony-murder rule, leads us to the following conclusion: for purposes of the felony-murder rule, a robbery or burglary continues, at a minimum, until the perpetrator reaches a place of temporary safety. That is to say a killing, even an accidental killing, committed while the perpetrator is in flight and prior to reaching a place of temporary safety, may be fairly said to be part of one continuous transaction with the underlying felony. But reaching a place of temporary safety does not, in and of itself, terminate felony-murder liability so long as the felony and the killing are part of one continuous transaction. * * * *

Defendant contends the evidence does not support his conviction for first degree murder under the felony-murder rule because (1) the evidence was insufficient to prove he committed the burglary, and (2) the evidence did not prove the burglary and the death were part of one continuous course of conduct. We disagree. * * * *

Burglary falls expressly within the purview of California's first degree felony-murder rule. Any burglary within Penal Code section 459 is sufficient to invoke the rule. Whether or not the particular burglary was dangerous to human life is of no legal import. Although defendant was not charged with burglary, his murder conviction is based upon the felony-murder rule and the felony that triggered the rule in this case was a burglary. Defendant argues that other than the fact he was in possession of property stolen during the burglary, there is little other evidence "to support the element of entry with the intent to steal." However, as we pointed out above in discussing the instruction on the inference permissible from possession of recently stolen property, little more is needed to support a conviction. Here there was substantial corroborating evidence. Defendant worked at a construction site near the site where the items were located before the burglary. His cell phone records show he was in the area at the time the merchandise was delivered to the residence and again around the time of the burglary. The night the appliances were stolen, he called Trivich and told her he "got some really big things for the kitchen." There was also evidence from which an inference could be drawn that he was in a hurry to get away with the stolen items in that he did not take the time to secure them on his truck, even though he had ties in the truck. Additionally, defendant did not have license plates on his truck that night. The plates were inside the passenger compartment. A jury could reasonably infer defendant made an attempt to conceal identification of his truck by driving without the plates on his truck. Plus, he testified he "needed the stuff for the house to be built in Palm Springs." The evidence was more than sufficient to support the jury's determination the loot in defendant's truck was from a burglary he committed.

The burglary took place in Riverside County. The death occurred in Orange County on the 91 Freeway, about 60 miles from the burglary. The incident that claimed Piquette's life was caused by a stolen stove falling from the back of defendant's truck into the lanes of traffic. At the time of Piquette's death, the burglary had yet to be discovered. In support of his argument that the evidence does not demonstrate the death and the burglary were part of one continuous transaction, he asserts that (1) at 1:00 a.m. he told Trivich he had acquired large kitchen appliances and the cell phone records indicate he was traveling west to east (toward Palm Springs) at the time; (2) the death occurred four hours later, when defendant was travelling in the opposite direction, away from Palm Springs; and (3) defendant had reached a place of temporary safety and lingered there before getting on the 91 Freeway and heading back to Long Beach. He contends these facts demonstrate he (1) already had the loot when he spoke with Trivich four hours before Piquette's death; (2) he then drove to Palm Springs with the loot; and, (3) and remained in Palm Springs for some time before bringing the loot back toward Long Beach and arriving in Orange County where the collision occurred. He argues that as a result, there is no evidence to support a conclusion the "the death occurred during efforts to escape the burglary or that the accident resulted from an attempt to conceal the property which was openly on display in the bed of the pickup truck."

In light of the deferential standard of review that applies to this sufficiency of evidence claim, we must reject his interpretation of the evidence. The jury could have reasonably concluded defendant left his residence in Long Beach intending to drive to Menifee to steal the appliances and that he made the telephone call to Trivich for gas money because he would need gas to drive the appliances from Long Beach, where he would get the money from Trivich, to the project in Palm Springs. The cell phone records demonstrate he was driving west to east at the time of the telephone calls. That fact, however, does not mean he was headed to Palm Springs. Menifee is south of the 91 Freeway, off of Interstate 215. Driving from Long Beach, defendant would have taken the 91 Freeway east to Interstate 215 south. The July 7, 4:30 a.m. cell phone record show his phone was pinging a cell phone tower between Interstate 215 and the 91 Freeway. The jury could have concluded he was on his way back from Menifee at that time and rejected defendant's testimony that he went to Palm Springs that morning, just as it rejected his testimony that he bought the stolen property at a Home Depot and did not commit the burglary.

Defendant, in an apparent rush to flee the scene of the burglary, loaded up his pickup truck with the loot and left the tailgate down. He did not tie down the refrigerator, stove, and other appliances although he had ties in the truck. He then fled the scene and while he was on his way back to Long Beach to unload the loot, the stove fell off the back of his truck and Piquette died as a result. The homicide occurred while defendant was in immediate flight from the burglary to the location where he would unload the loot. The burglary and the homicide were part of a continuous transaction. Once a person perpetrates or attempts to perpetrate one of the enumerated felonies, then in the judgment of the Legislature, he is no longer entitled to such fine judicial calibration, but will be deemed guilty of first degree murder for any homicide committed in the course thereof. Here, the act that caused the homicide — the failure to tie down the load of stolen loot — occurred at the scene of the burglary, not 60 miles later when part of the unsecured load fell off the back of defendant's truck as he drove to where he could unload and hide the loot. Accordingly, we find sufficient evidence to support the murder conviction.

Defendant argues that use of the felony-murder rule on the facts of this case denied him due process of law and rendered his trial fundamentally unfair. He argues that because he was not escaping or being pursued by anyone at the time of the killing, the felony-murder rule should not apply and the only conduct being deterred by application of the rule "was a lack of care in securing the load in the bed of the truck." Having found the evidence supports the conviction, we find no due process violation. As stated above, the purpose of the felony-murder rule is to prevent accidental or negligent killings in the perpetration of certain felonies, including burglary, by holding felons strictly responsible for killings them commit. The Legislature has said in effect that this deterrent purpose outweighs the normal legislative policy of examining the individual state of mind of each person causing an unlawful killing to determine whether the killing was with or without malice, deliberate or accidental, and calibrating our treatmentof the person accordingly. Once a person perpetrates or attempts to perpetrate one of the enumerated felonies, then in the judgment of the Legislature, he is no longer entitled to such fine judicial calibration, but will be deemed guilty of first degree murder for any homicide committed in the course thereof. Policy concerns regarding the inclusion of burglary in the first degree felony-murder statute remain within the Legislature's domain, and do not authorize this court to limit the plain language of the statute.

This is not a case where the homicide occurred because defendant committed some minor traffic violation 60 miles from the location where he had earlier committed a burglary and which only coincidentally connected the homicide and burglary together. Piquette's death was caused by defendant's negligent act committed while he was actively engaged in committing the burglary.[FN5] Had he used the ties he had in the truck and/or closed the tailgate on his truck, rather than leaving the scene in a rush to avoid detection, the homicide would not have occurred. To that end, the purpose of the felony-murder rule — to deter accidental or negligent killings is met and application of the felony-murder rule did not deny defendant due process. * * * *

The judgment is affirmed.

WE CONCUR: FYBEL AND IKOLA, JJ.

NOTE FROM THE JUDGE:

Wilkins was a thief, a burglar, and very careless. But was he a "murderer" (in the first degree, no less!) — as we commonly understand that term?

[FN5] Burglaries, may be more appropriate. Considering the amount of items stolen and loaded into his truck, including a refrigerator, stove, fixtures, and the kitchen sink, defendant would have had to have made multiple entries into the house, all with the intent to steal.

Chapter 9

FIRST DEGREE MURDER

Almost all American jurisdictions which divide murder into degrees include the following two murder situations in the category of first degree murder: (1) intent-to-kill murder where there exists (in addition to the intent to kill) the elements of premeditation and deliberation, and (2) felony murder where the felony in question is one of five or six listed felonies, generally including rape, robbery, kidnapping, arson and burglary.

LaFave, *Criminal Law* (West)

This Chapter will focus on the first way to find first degree murder, mentioned above: "premeditation and deliberation."

Not all murderers are equally culpable. But should differences in culpability be considered when deciding on how to punish *murderers* — our worst criminals? Shouldn't we give *all* murderers the *same* penalty: the maximum (as determined by the legislature)?

The law says no. Murderers *do* have different levels of culpability — but not very many. In fact, most states recognize *only two* levels of murder: first degree and second degree (although many states allow juries to distinguish among *first* degree murderers by giving some life imprisonment and some the death penalty).

The question then becomes: on what basis do we place some murderers in the more culpable category: first degree? There are many possibilities. We could place there the most brutal murderers. Or, we could place in that category those murderers who kill people who contribute the most to society. Or we could place there those who plan their murders, and leave to the lower category those who kill without planning.

The law has chosen the last distinction. Does this make sense? Is a person who spends a few hours (or minutes) planning to kill, say, another criminal, more culpable than one who impulsively kills by stabbing an innocent teacher, doctor, scientist, or priest many times? What purpose of punishment (discussed at the end of Chapter 1) is served by drawing the line at "premeditation" — rather than another line?

And what does "premeditation" mean? Planning the crime? How much planning? A few hours? A few minutes? A few *seconds*? If we allow a few seconds to be sufficient for "premeditation," have we forgotten *why we made* the distinction between first and second degree murder?

Consider these issues as you read the cases in this Chapter.

PROBLEM 9

To: My law clerk

From: Molly Balloo

Re: *State v. Dealer*

My client, Dick Dealer, is on trial for the first degree murder of Al Addick.

A toxicologist testified for the prosecution that Addick died from injecting himself with a lethal dose of pure heroin. He also testified that in the heroin trade, the drug is always "cut" — watered down by being mixed with some other substance — before it is used. If taken in usual doses without being cut, it would almost certainly kill the user.

The only evidence regarding Dealer's state of mind was a tape recording of an interrogation of Dealer by Seattle police detectives. A transcript of that interrogation is attached. I would like to file a motion to strike the first degree murder charge — on the ground that there is not sufficient evidence to permit the jury to convict Dealer of first degree murder — and have the judge instruct the jury on second degree murder only. Please read the transcript and the attached authorities and advise me as to what arguments to make and whether they are likely to succeed.

Transcript of Interrogation of Dick Dealer

Q: [Detectives advised Dealer of his *Miranda* rights, which Dealer waived.] So, what happened, Dicky-boy?

A: Al had been one of my customers for the last few months. Sometimes I sold him stuff on credit, but he didn't always pay on time. Last night, he came over to my place to make a buy, but I told him I couldn't sell him any more until he paid me the $200 he owed me. He got mad, and he said, "I'm never going to pay you, man, and I'm taking my business elsewhere." He started to leave.

Q: What did you do?

A: I guess I got pretty mad too. I had just smoked a joint of marijuana, and maybe I wasn't thinking too clearly. I thought to myself, "I'm going to get this guy." I told Al to wait, and I would give him some dope. I went into my kitchen and got some new dope that I had not cut yet. I came out and gave it to Al. He sat down on the couch and rolled up his sleeve. He took a needle out of his pocket, loaded it up, and shot the stuff into his arm.

Q: How long did it take him to do all this?

A: A couple of minutes.

Q: What did you do?

A: I just watched him. I didn't say anything. Look, I think I've said enough about all this. I don't want to talk to you guys any more.

Washington Criminal Code

Section 9A.32.020.

(1) As used in this chapter the premeditation required in order to support a conviction of the crime of murder in the first degree must involve more than a moment in point of time. * * *

Section 9A.32.030. Murder in the First Degree.

(1) A person is guilty of murder in the first degree when:

(a) With a premeditated intent to cause the death of another person, he or she causes the death of such person or of a third person; * * *

[Enacted in 1975]

STATE v. BROOKS
Supreme Court of Washington
97 Wash. 2d 873, 651 P.2d 217 (1982)

STAFFORD, JUSTICE.

The defendant, Steven Brooks, appeals from a judgment and sentence entered on a jury's verdict of guilty of murder in the first degree. RCW 9A.32.030(1)(a). Defendant assigns error to the trial court's refusal to give his proposed instruction on voluntary intoxication and to the trial court's refusal to admit opinion testimony of the defense psychologist concerning premeditation.

I. *Voluntary Intoxication*

The trial court instructed the jury that to convict the defendant of murder in the first degree it must find he acted "with intent to cause the death" of the victim and that "the intent to cause the death was premeditated." The State appears to agree intoxication may be shown for its bearing on both intent . . . and premeditation. The trial court refused, however, to give defendant's proposed instruction bearing on voluntary intoxication asserting there was no evidence that the consumption of alcohol affected defendant's ability to form an intent or impaired his mental state. In so ruling, the trial court stated that premeditation involves the passage of time and is not a mental state. Thus, the court held, voluntary intoxication has no bearing on premeditation. At the time of closing argument the trial court did permit defendant to argue that the consumption of alcohol reduced defendant's ability to premeditate.

Both parties agree there was insufficient evidence of involuntary intoxication to negate specific intent. Further, the State concedes defendant's proposed instruction on voluntary intoxication correctly states the general law.[1] The

---

[1] "No act committed by a person while in a state of voluntary intoxication is less criminal by reason

question, then, is whether the instruction was sufficiently supported by evidence of the effect drinking had on defendant's ability to premeditate an intent to kill rather than on his ability to form the specific intent itself.

Although the defendant's argument relates to proof of intoxication and its effect on premeditation alone, the State suggests the rules governing evidence of voluntary intoxication are the same whether specific intent or premeditation is at issue. Thus, the State argues, it is proper to turn for guidance to those cases involving voluntary intoxication as it relates solely to specific intent. In that regard, then, the State asserts more was needed to support the proposed instruction than evidence of the excessive consumption of alcohol. It contends that additionally defendant must establish the drinking had an effect on defendant's ability to form a specific intent. *State v. King*, 24 Wash.App. 495 (1979). It is the latter requirement the State contends is missing, i.e., an absence of substantial evidence that defendant's drinking interfered with his ability to form a specific intent to kill (and thus, inferentially, his ability to premeditate such an intent).

The State's argument oversimplifies the issue. Intent and premeditation are not synonymous. They are separate and distinct elements of the crime of murder in the first degree. RCW 9A.32.030(1)(a), .050(a). Premeditation is the element that distinguishes first from second degree murder as charged herein. *State v. Shirley*, 60 Wash.2d 277 (1962).

Although intent and premeditation each involve processes of the mind, their impact upon the ultimate decision to be made by a jury is dissimilar. "Intent" involves the mental state of "acting with the objective or purpose to accomplish a result which constitutes a crime." On the other hand, the verb "premeditate" encompasses the mental process of thinking beforehand, deliberation, reflection, weighing or reasoning for a period of time, however short. Thus, the objective or purpose to take human life (sufficient to support a charge of second degree murder) must have been formed after some period of deliberation, reflection or weighing in the mind for the act to constitute first degree murder. One may be capable of forming an intent sufficient to support a charge of second degree murder and still be incapable of deliberation or forming a premeditated intent to take the life of another.

The question before us, then, is whether evidence of the consumption of alcohol was sufficient to permit the jury to consider whether the amount consumed had an effect upon defendant's ability to reflect, reason, deliberate or weigh in the mind an objective or purpose to take human life. We hold there was sufficient evidence, which if believed by the jury, would support a determination that defendant was unable to premeditate an intent to take another's life.

Defendant's proposed instruction 11.

Without question some of the evidence of intoxication is in dispute. Nevertheless, there is evidence, which if believed by the jury, would establish the following: On June 21, 1979, defendant went camping with a friend near the place

---

of that condition, *but whenever the actual existence of any particular mental state is a necessary element to constitute a particular kind or degree of crime, the fact of intoxication may be taken into consideration in determining such mental state.*" (Italics ours.)

where the victim's body was found on June 22. Defendant began drinking beer, whiskey and rum and continued to do so almost constantly from June 21 through the afternoon of the victim's death.

Numerous witnesses described defendant's condition as follows: he was drunk; he was "staggering around drunk, a bottle of whiskey in his hands through the biggest part of the day"; he was offered a grey spider which he ate and washed down with whiskey; his face was blotchy and his eyes were "buggy red"; his speech was slurred; he was trembling; he walked lopsided; he was unsteady on his feet; he swayed back and forth; he stumbled; and, he staggered and fell in the water. * * *

In addition, Dr. Lubach, a psychologist who had done extensive interviewing and psychological testing of defendant, offered to testify about defendant's ability to premeditate or deliberate. The offer of proof indicated the psychologist would testify that assuming the personality disorder revealed by his tests, the excessive usage of alcohol, and the decrease in defendant's ability to control aggressive impulses when under the influence of alcohol, "He would be very probable to act in an unpremeditated impulsive fashion under those conditions." Dr. Lubach indicated he would also testify that his testimony related to the likelihood of *premeditation* rather than *intent*.

The trial court's rejection of Dr. Lubach's testimony has been assigned as error which will be discussed in Part II of this opinion. It is sufficient to say, at this juncture, that the testimony taken as a whole, particularly when coupled with the defendant's offer of proof involving the doctor's testimony, was sufficient to support the requested instruction on voluntary intoxication insofar as it pertained to premeditation. Failure to give the requested instruction constituted reversible error.

II. *Premeditation*

Dr. Lubach did not testify about defendant's *specific intent* at the time the crime was committed. Rather, he sought to testify concerning defendant's ability to premeditate the intent to cause the victim's death. The psychologist declared that, based on reasonable medical probability, defendant had a personality disorder affected by the excessive use of alcohol; that he had a tendency to act aggressively and impulsively when under the influence of alcohol; and, "He would be very probable to act in an *unpremeditated impulsive* fashion under those conditions." (Italics ours.) Later, he sought to testify that defendant's ability to control hostility and aggression was made worse by drinking and that drinking "increases his tendency to resort in kind of an *impulsive, non-premeditated* kind of way, to just react kind of *automatically*." (Italics ours.)

The trial court only permitted Dr. Lubach to testify that defendant had a personality disorder, was an alcoholic, and tended to act in an impulsive manner. He was not permitted to give his opinion on whether defendant was capable of premeditating an intent to kill. Apparently it was the view of the trial court and Court of Appeals that premeditation, unlike intent, is not a mental state and thus the doctor's testimony about the impact of excessive drinking was not relevant. The trial court and Court of Appeals were of the view that it was necessary for the psychologist to connect the claimed mental disorder with defendant's inability to form specific intent to commit the crime charged rather than connect it with premeditation. * * *

As indicated earlier, both intent and premeditation encompass mental processes to be considered by the jury in resolving separate and distinct issues pertaining to elements of the crime charged. Thus, the proffered medical testimony about psychological testing, mental diagnosis, excessive drinking and an expert medical opinion based thereon was relevant to the issue of defendant's ability to premeditate an intent to take the victim's life. The trial court erred by excluding the doctor's testimony in this regard. * * *

If a particular state of mind, i.e., premeditation, is required to establish a degree of crime, the fact of intoxication and its impact upon a defendant's mental process may be shown to demonstrate an absence of premeditation. * * * In the instant case there was considerable lay and medical testimony which, if believed by the jury, would establish that the excessive drinking superimposed upon defendant's mental disorder would interfere with his ability to premeditate. The trial court erred by rejecting this relevant testimony. The trial court and Court of Appeals are reversed and the cause is remanded for a new trial.

NOTES FROM MOLLY:

1. The court found the evidence of intoxication insufficient to negate intent to kill, but sufficient to negate premeditation. How is this possible?

2. I don't quite understand the effect of intoxication on "premeditation." When a drunk driver gets into his car to drive home, doesn't he "premeditate" his decision to drive home? He is usually able to plan his route and destination, and he does so. Maybe he takes even more time on this, *because* he is drunk. So can't a drunk be said to have "premeditated" doing something — like killing Al Addick?

STATE v. LINDAMOOD
Court of Appeals of Washington
39 Wash. App. 517, 693 P.2d 753 (1985)

SCHOLFIELD, Acting CHIEF JUDGE.

Robert W. Lindamood appeals a conviction for aggravated first degree murder while armed with a deadly weapon. He asserts the evidence was insufficient to support a finding of premeditation.

Facts

On December 18, 1982, Lindamood, who was then 18 years of age, discussed with his friend, Dennis, a plan to rob Roy George, a 77-year-old neighbor. Lindamood had heard rumors that George kept several thousand dollars in his house or buried in his yard and testified that he planned to go to George's house, knock him out, take his money, then, with Dennis, buy a car and go to California.

Lindamood went to his mother's house and got a coffee table leg, which he wrapped in a paper sack tied with string. Lindamood then went to George's door, and when George answered his knock, tried to enter, saying that he wanted to discuss something with George. George told him to go away. Lindamood pushed his way into the house and started striking George on the head with the table leg. Lindamood failed to knock him unconscious at first, but after several blows George fell to the floor, where he pleaded with Lindamood not to strike him anymore. Lindamood continued striking George about the head with the table leg, and afterward struck him about the head or chest with a large piece of stove wood. While George was lying on the floor unconscious, Lindamood went through the house looking for money. After taking some cash and silverware, he left.

George died of the injuries inflicted by Lindamood. Dr. Donald T. Reay, the medical examiner for King County, testifying on the basis of his autopsy of George's body, stated that there were fractures of the base of the skull, nasal and facial bones, the sternum and ribs. There was also a tear of the aorta, which caused extensive bleeding. He described the cause of death as "blunt impact-type injuries sustained to the head and to the chest region." He testified that the table leg was capable of causing the described injuries. He also testified that all of the blows were struck while George was still alive and that many of the blows were struck while George was lying flat on his back on the floor. Dr. Reay concluded that the head injuries alone were serious enough to be the probable cause of death (he counted 19 separate blows to the head), and that the chest injuries alone could also have caused George's death.

Lindamood was charged with one count of premeditated murder, aggravated by the fact that it was committed in the course of first degree burglary and first degree robbery, pursuant to RCW 9A.32.030(1)(a) and (c)[1] and RCW 10.95.020(9)(a) and (c).[2] Lindamood was tried by a jury.

---

[1] RCW 9A.32.030 provides, in part:

Murder in the first degree. (1) A person is guilty of murder in the first degree when:

(a) With a premeditated intent to cause the death of another person, he causes the death of such person or of a third person; or . . .

(c) He commits or attempts to commit the crime of either (1) robbery, in the first or second degree, (2) rape in the first or second degree, (3) burglary in the first degree, . . . and; in the course of and in furtherance of such crime or in immediate flight therefrom, he, or another participant, causes the death of a person other than one of the participants . . .

[Ed. — RCW § 9A.32.040 provides that "any person convicted of the crime of murder in the first degree shall be sentenced to life imprisonment."]

[2] RCW 10.95.020 provides, in part:

Aggravated first degree murder defined. A person is guilty of aggravated first degree murder if he or she commits first degree murder as defined by RCW 9A.32.030(1)(a), as now or hereafter amended, and one or more of the following aggravating circumstances exist : . . .

(9) The murder was committed in the course of, in furtherance of, or in immediate flight from one of the following crimes:

(a) Robbery in the first or second degree; . . .

(c) Burglary in the first or second degree . . .

[Ed. — RCW § 10.95.030 provides that anyone convicted of aggravated first degree murder shall be sentenced to life imprisonment without possibility of parole or, if at a special proceeding "the trier of fact

Lindamood testified that his friend, Dennis, provided him with a pair of gloves, which he wore during the commission of the crime for the purpose of avoiding leaving fingerprints. He also testified that he made no effort to disguise himself by the use of a mask, even though he had worked for George in the past and knew George could identify him. Lindamood also testified that he was big and strong enough to have tied up George, gagged him, and thus sufficiently disabled him for the purpose of committing the burglary. Lindamood weighed 180 pounds. The evidence showed that Roy George was 5 feet 8 inches in height and weighed 170 pounds. Lindamood denied any intent to kill George and denied any premeditation of a murder.

The State introduced into evidence Lindamood's written confession to Detective Sanford, Seattle Police Department, on December 21, 1982, in which he made this statement: "Just before going to George's house to kill him, I wrapped it (the table leg) in a brown paper bag and tied it with some string."

Premeditation

Lindamood argues that there was no substantial evidence of premeditation, that the evidence showed nothing more than a plan to rob the victim by getting inside his home, rendering him defenseless or unconscious by striking him over the head with a wooden table leg and then taking the victim's money and fleeing to California.

The fact that Lindamood killed Roy George was not disputed; the sole contested issue at trial was whether the murder was premeditated.

The test for sufficiency of the evidence is whether, after viewing the evidence in the light most favorable to the State, any rational trier of fact could have found the essential elements of the crime beyond a reasonable doubt. *State v. Green*, 94 Wash.2d 216 (1980). Intent and premeditation are separate and distinct elements of the crime of murder in the first degree. *State v. Brooks*, 97 Wash.2d 873 (1982). The premeditation required to support a conviction of murder in the first degree "must involve more than a moment in point of time." RCW 9A.32.020; *State v. Griffith*, 91 Wash.2d 572 (1979). Premeditation is a question for the jury. *Griffith*, at 577.

Prior case law in Washington does not offer a comprehensive articulation of the types of evidence that can be used to prove premeditation. Evidence of planning activity before the murder, however, has been widely accepted as probative of premeditation. *State v. Tikka*, 8 Wash.App. 736 (1973). In *State v. Lanning*, 5 Wash.App. 426 (1971), the court reasoned that the defendant's availing himself of a knife or other sharp instrument capable of nearly severing the victim's neck provided evidence of premeditation. In *State v. Commodore*, 38 Wash.App. 244 (1984), evidence the defendant went to a room where he knew he could find a gun and then returnedto shoot the victim was held to be evidence of planning activity that could support a finding of premeditation. These cases and ordinary logic support the view that any planning activity by the defendant prior to the murder,

---

finds that there are not sufficient mitigating circumstances to merit leniency," to death.]

which relates to the manner in which the murder was accomplished, can be evidence of premeditation.

There was sufficient evidence in this case to support a finding of premeditation. Lindamood discussed with a friend a plan to rob the victim. This planning included arming himself with a table leg, a weapon capable of inflicting lethal wounds. The friend provided Lindamood with gloves, which he wore at the time of the offense. The purpose of the gloves was to avoid leaving fingerprints. George was well acquainted with Lindamood, who had worked for him in the past. The victim could have identified Lindamood had he lived. Lindamood also made no effort to mask his face or his voice. These facts could be interpreted by the jury as evidence that Lindamood did not expect George to survive. His written confession to police that he wrapped the table leg in brown paper "just before going to George's house to kill him" was evidence from which the jury could infer that Lindamood formed the intent to kill well in advance of the crime.

We conclude that a rational trier of fact, after viewing the evidence in the light most favorable to the State, could have found the element of premeditation beyond a reasonable doubt.

Judgment affirmed.

NOTE FROM MOLLY:

In our case, try to identify the types of evidence which tend to prove premeditation, according to *Lindamood*. Do we have enough?

STATE v. BINGHAM
Supreme Court of Washington
105 Wash. 2d 820, 719 P.2d 109 (1986)

GOODLOE, JUSTICE.

In this case, we review the sufficiency of the evidence of the premeditation element in an aggravated first degree murder conviction. The Court of Appeals found the evidence insufficient and reversed and remanded for resentencing for second degree murder. We affirm the Court of Appeals decision.

On February 18, 1982, the raped and strangled body of Leslie Cook, a retarded adult, was found in a pasture in Sequim. Cook was last seen alive on February 15, 1982 with respondent Charles Dean Bingham. The Clallam County Prosecutor, by amended information, charged Bingham with aggravated first degree (premeditated) murder, rape being the aggravating circumstance. The prosecutor also notified Bingham that the State would seek the death penalty.

The evidence presented at trial showed that on February 15, Cook and Bingham got off a bus together in Sequim about 6 p.m. There was no evidence that they knew each other before this time. They visited a grocery store and two residences. Cook was last seen at the residence of Wayne Humphrey and Enid Pratt where Bingham asked for a ride back to Port Angeles. When he was told no, Bingham said they would hitchhike. They left together heading toward the infrequently traveled Old Olympic Highway. None of the witnesses who saw the two heard any argument or observed any physical contact between them. Three days later, Cook's body was found in a field about a quarter mile from the Humphrey-Pratt residence.

At trial, King County Medical Examiner Reay described the results of the autopsy he performed on Cook's body. The cause of death was "asphyxiation through manual strangulation," accomplished by applying continuous pressure to the windpipe for approximately 3 to 5 minutes. Cook had a bruise on her upper lip, more likely caused by a hand being pressed over her mouth than by a violent blow. Tears were found in Cook's vaginal wall and anal ring. Spermatozoa was present. These injuries were inflicted antemortem. Also, there was a bite mark on each of Cook's breasts. Reay testified that these occurred perimortem or postmortem.

Two forensic odontologists testified that the bite mark on one breast matched Bingham's teeth. No conclusive determination could be made with respect to the other bite mark.

The prosecutor's theory, as revealed in both his opening statement and closing argument, was that Bingham wanted to have sex with Cook and that he had to kill her in order to do so. The prosecutor hypothesized that Bingham had started the act while Cook was alive, and that he put his hand over her mouth and then strangled her in order to complete the act. The prosecutor also told the jury that the murder would be premeditated if Bingham had formed the intent to kill when he began to strangle Cook, and thought about that intent for the 3 to 5 minutes it took her to die.

The court instructed the jury on aggravated first degree murder and on the lesser included offenses of first and second degree murder and first degree manslaughter. The court also gave Bingham's proposed instruction on voluntary intoxication.

The jury found Bingham guilty of aggravated first degree murder. The jury also found, in the penalty phase, that the State had failed to prove that there were insufficient mitigating circumstances to warrant leniency. The trial court therefore sentenced Bingham to life imprisonment without the possibility of release or parole. * * *

We must determine whether evidence of premeditation was sufficiently demonstrated in order for the issue to go to the jury and in order to sustain a finding of premeditated killing.

The constitutional standard for reviewing the sufficiency of the evidence in a criminal case is "whether, after reviewing the evidence in the light most favorable to the prosecution, any rational trier of fact could have found the essential elements of the crime beyond a reasonable doubt." *Jackson v. Virginia*, 443 U.S. 307, 319 (1979).

The element challenged in this case is "premeditated intent." Bingham was charged with first degree murder pursuant to RCW 9A.32.030(1)(a), which requires for conviction "a premeditated intent to cause the death of another." The element of premeditation distinguishes first and second degree murder. *State v. Brooks*, 97

Wash.2d 873 (1982). Section (1)(a) of the second degree murder statute, RCW 9A.32.050, requires for conviction "intent to cause the death of another person but without premeditation."

The only statutory elaboration on the meaning of premeditation is found in RCW 9A.32.020(1), which states that premeditation "must involve more than a moment in point of time." Washington case law further defines premeditation as "the mental process of thinking beforehand, deliberation, reflection, weighing or reasoning for a period of time, however short." *Brooks* at 876. We recently approved an instruction which defined premeditation as "the deliberate formation of and reflection upon the intent to take a human life." *State v. Robtoy*, 98 Wash.2d 30, 43 (1982).

Premeditation may be shown by direct or circumstantial evidence. Circumstantial evidence can be used where the inferences drawn by the jury are reasonable and the evidence supporting the jury's verdict is substantial. In this case, the State presented no direct evidence. The issue thus becomes whether sufficient circumstantial evidence of premeditation was presented. Bingham was not charged with felony-murder. To show premeditation, the State relied on the pathologist's testimony that manual strangulation takes 3 to 5 minutes. The State argues this time is an appreciable amount of time in which Bingham could have deliberated. Bingham argues that time alone is not enough and that other indicators of premeditation must be shown. * * *

To allow a finding of premeditation only because the act takes an appreciable amount of time obliterates the distinction between first and second degree murder. Having the opportunity to deliberate is not evidence the defendant did deliberate, which is necessary for a finding of premeditation. Otherwise, any form of killing which took more than a moment could result in a finding of premeditation, without some additional evidence showing reflection. Holding a hand over someone's mouth or windpipe does not necessarily reflect a decision to kill the person, but possibly only to quiet her or him. Furthermore, here a question of the ability to deliberate or reflect while engaged in sexual activity exists.

The position of the State appears to be that, if the defendant has the opportunity to deliberate and chooses not to cease his actions, then it is proper to allow the jury to infer deliberation. They offer three cases for the proposition that premeditation may properly be inferred from evidence of the lapse of time to death. *State v. Harris*, 62 Wash.2d 858 (1963); *State v. Griffith*, 91 Wash.2d 572 (1979); *State v. Luoma*, 88 Wash.2d 28 (1977). While *Harris*, *Griffith*, and *Luoma* do use language regarding reliance on circumstances of the crime to show premeditation, the circumstances showed more action or thought than mere infliction of the fatal act.

In *Harris*, the assailant, after inflicting a terrific head beating, tied a vacuum cleaner cord around the victim's neck and strangled her. The interim time period between the beating and the strangulation, as well as the presence and use of a vacuum cleaner cord in effectuating the victim's death, distinguish this case from the manual strangulation situation with which we are presented.

In *Griffith*, some children were hitting a basketball against the house where defendant lived with his mother. The defendant took the ball from the children. He went to his car, got a gun, and placed it on a table next to the front door. Within 5 minutes, two adults went to the house to retrieve the ball. The defendant, while talking to the adults at the front door, reached for the gun, pointed it at the adults, and shot one of them. The court said: "Although the period of time in which these events transpired was approximately 5 minutes, there was sufficient evidence from which the jury could have found that the defendant formulated an intent and deliberated upon it prior to the shooting." The planned presence of a weapon necessary to facilitate a killing has been held to be adequate evidence to allow the issue of premeditation to go to the jury.

In *Luoma*, the defendant transported the victim to the crime scene, took her down a bank, positioned her and then crushed her head with a large rock. From the facts in *Luoma*, "the jury could properly conclude that the death was not the result of an impulsive, spontaneous act." We note that the language in *Luoma* focuses on intent, not premeditation. As is clear from the statutory requirements and *State v. Brooks*, premeditation is a separate and additional element to the intent requirement for first degree murder.

Here, no evidence was presented of deliberation or reflection before or during the strangulation, only the strangulation. The opportunity to deliberate is not sufficient. As was recognized in *Austin v. U.S*, 382 F.2d 129, 138-39 (D.C.cir. 1967):

> The facts of a savage murder generate a powerful drive, almost a juggernaut for jurors, and indeed for judges, to crush the crime with the utmost condemnation available, to seize whatever words or terms reflect maximum denunciation, to cry out murder "in the first degree." But it is the task and conscience of a judge to transcend emotional momentum with reflective analysis. The judge is aware that many murders most brutish and bestial are committed in a consuming frenzy or heat of passion, and that these are in law only murder in the second degree. The State's evidence suffices to establish an intentional and horrible murder — the kind that could be committed in a frenzy or heat of passion. However the core responsibility of the court requires it to reflect on the sufficiency of the State's case.

Exercising our responsibility, we find manual strangulation alone is insufficient evidence to support a finding of premeditation. We affirm the Court of Appeals decision.

DOLLIVER, C.J., and UTTER, BRACHTENBACH, & PEARSON, JJ., concur.

CALLOW, JUSTICE (dissenting).

I would reinstate the aggravated first degree murder conviction of defendant.

Sufficient evidence was presented on premeditation for that issue to be submitted to the jury. The decision on that issue is the function of the jury; not to be taken away. * * *

The rule announced by the majority seems to be that premeditation must take place before the commencement of the act that results in death. Take the farmer's son who begins to fill the bin with wheat as a joke on his brother sleeping at its bottom. Then, realizing that he will inherit the whole farm if he persists, he does so and causes his brother's death. He had time to premeditate and did so in the middle of the act. He has committed aggravated first degree murder. That a murderer originally commenced an act without intending death does not grant him a carte blanche to persist when he realizes that to do so will kill his victim. * * *

The facts in this case could be found to reflect a deliberated decision to kill Leslie Cook by applying between 3 and 5 minutes of continuous and steady pressure to her neck. The act of strangulation inflicted by the defendant upon the deceased is considerably more than just the "holding of a hand over someone's mouth or windpipe." *See* Majority opinion. The testimony of Dr. Donald Reay, Chief Medical Examiner for King County, who performed the autopsy on Leslie Cook, is illuminating as to what is necessary to effect death by manual strangulation.

Q: Doctor, based upon your examination of the deceased, did you come to an opinion as to her cause of death?

A: Yes, I did.

Q: And what is that opinion?

A: I attributed death to manual strangulation, with injuries to the neck and evidence of spaces of blood and death attributed to asphyxiation through manual strangulation.

Q: Doctor, when you say manual strangulation, you mean the hands?

A: Yes, correct.

Q: Okay, now how long does it take someone to die by manual strangulation, doctor?

A: Ordinarily the process will take three to five minutes.

Q: And what sort of force or what sort of action is required during that three to five minutes period?

A: The requirement is to stop the blood flow to the brain and at the same time prevent a person from breathing. The result is that they become oxygen deficient and the heart is sensitive over a period of time and leads to lack of oxygen that develops an abnormal rhythm which proceeds to death.

Q: Doctor, does unconsciousness come before death in a case of manual strangulation?

A: Oh, yes. Yes.

Q: And how long does it take before someone is unconscious, do you know?

A: If a well placed hold about the neck, it can take a matter of seconds. We have done some tests where a person becomes unconscious in a matter of six to seven seconds, if the vessels are pinched in a very quick fashion.

Q: And death ensues within three to five minutes?

A: Yes, that may be unconsciousness, but if the pressure is released the person will wake up. It's a hold that some times is used by law enforcement, but if the pressure is sustained then the brain goes without oxygen and in addition the airways collapse over the lungs and heart go without oxygen and there are deficits building up which effect the heart and it starts to develop abnormal beats or rhythms and eventually leads to death.

Q: Doctor, does this sort of asphyxiation by manual strangulation in this instance, does it take a steady pressure for that three to five minute period?

A: Yes, the pressure can vary, certainly, but the important thing is to include the airway and the arterial supply. One or the other will effectively do it.

Q: Doctor, how is it that the hyoid bone becomes fractured?

A: The hyoid bone is a "U" shaped, almost a wishbone type of structure in the neck. It's the open part of the "U" is facing rearward and as the front of the neck is squeezed that is caught, pinched, and eventually the wing of it cracks.

Q: Does that fracture of the hyoid have any ramifications with regard to the windpipe?

A: It is part of the structures in the neck. Its real value is because it does represent, or does demonstrate that pressure was applied to the neck. It is in the immediate area of the windpipe and certainly when that is broken that is pretty good evidence that the airway was collapsed.

Q: For a three to five minutes period?

A: Yes. In addition to the airway itself there is also the tongue, which is pushed backwards, rearwards. When that happens the tongue goes back up against the roof of the mouth, in the process of forcing it upwards and that adds to it, so there is the occlusion in addition to the squeezing, there is also the pressure upwards, which occludes it. * * *

Here it can be inferred that the defendant thought about the consequences as he choked his victim. The period of premeditation might not have been during the initial squeeze, but the evidence of premeditation certainly was present in the continued application of force, knowing it would bring about death.

The evidence needed to prove premeditation is likely to be circumstantial and such evidence suffices where the inferences drawn by the jury are reasonable and the evidence supporting the jury's findings is substantial. Although there was no direct proof of intent, premeditation may still be found where intent is logically inferred from the facts of the crime. A review of the pertinent circumstances surrounding Leslie Cook's death is required. The evidence indicates that the defendant and the deceased did not know each other prior to the day of the killing. They met on the bus to Sequim. Later that day the deceased wished to return to Port Angeles. The defendant took the deceased toward the infrequently traveled Old Olympic Highway purportedly to hitchhike to Port Angeles. The defendant took the deceased to a secluded location where he raped her. He then used his bare hands to strangle her. It took between 3 and 5 minutes to effect death. After the killing he bit the breasts of the deceased. He left the body in the secluded location exposed to the winter elements.

There is no evidence of passion, provocation or struggle reflected in the record. Indeed, there is more here than the mere opportunity to deliberate. There is adequate evidence for the jury to find that he did form a design to kill.

We turn to the decisions of other jurisdictions. In *Hounshell v. State*, 61 Md.App. 364, 372 (1985), the court stated:

> Death by strangulation does not in and of itself establish first degree murder. Whether the time required to produce death by strangulation is sufficient for the assailant to reflect upon his actions before death ensues is a matter for the jury to determine.

In *Hounshell*, the facts were similar to the case at bar. The evidence indicated that defendant had been with the deceased on the night of her death, that the deceased had died from manual strangulation, and that the deceased had semen in her mouth. The jury found the defendant guilty of first degree premeditated murder. On appeal the conviction was affirmed.

Logic and common sense dictate that for one person to strangle another person to death, a significant length of time must pass for the victim to die. This time period in which the perpetrator must continuously exert sufficient force on the victim's throat to block the victim's breathing affords the perpetrator a significant opportunity for reflection and a change of heart.

The court specifically stated that strangulation in and of itself does not constitute first degree murder and that the manner of killing was only one circumstance for the jury to consider in reaching its verdict.

In the present case, the jury could have determined beyond a reasonable doubt that appellant made a premeditated decision to commit murder within the interval of time it took him to initiate and then ultimately complete the act of strangulation.
* * *

Regarding the type of circumstantial evidence that is relevant to the issue of premeditation, the court in *People v. Irby*, 129 Mich.App. 306, 323 (1983), listed the following nonexclusive factors pertinent to establish premeditation: (1) A prior relationship showing motive; or (2) a murder weapon acquired and positioned as an indication of preparation; or (3) evidence which supports an inference the killer transported the victim to a secluded location for an illicit or criminal purpose; or (4) circumstances suggesting premeditation and deliberation; or (5) subsequent organized conduct which suggests the existence of a plan. The facts in *Irby* indicate the 15-year-old defendant and the deceased entered into consensual sexual relations.

Following the sexual activity something "came over him" and he strangled the victim to death with his bare hands. Thereafter, he moved the deceased, cleaned up the body and placed it in a garbage can. He later made the statement that some boys in a car dropped the body off at his house for disposal. The court upheld defendant's first degree premeditated murder conviction.

We agree with defendant that the trial court erred in holding that the element of premeditation was prima facie shown by evidence of manual strangulation alone. Nevertheless, the evidence of manual strangulation and defendant's subsequent actions after the victim's death do support a prima facie case of first-degree premeditated murder. * * *

In the case at hand, the evidence is that the defendant left his victim lying exposed in the field in Clallam County in winter and the evidence also supports the inference that the defendant transported his victim to this secluded spot for an illicit or criminal purpose.

The circumstances of Leslie Cook's death are replete with evidence besides the manual strangulation which raise the inference the defendant did premeditate: (1) the defendant took the deceased to a secluded location; (2) the defendant raped the deceased; (3) the time that is necessary to cause death by strangulation; (4) the defendant had plenty of opportunity to desist after the deceased lapsed into unconsciousness, but nevertheless, he chose to continue to strangle Leslie Cook to death; (5) there is no evidence of provocation; (6) the defendant is a large man and there is little sign of struggle; and (7) the defendant bit the breasts of the deceased and left the near-naked body exposed to the winter elements. The jury heard the testimony of Dr. Reay that it takes 3 to 5 minutes to effect death by manual strangulation. Continuous and steady pressure on the victim's neck is required. The amount of pressure required is sufficiently greater than the amount required to keep someone from crying out. The strangulation of Leslie Cook was cruel and brutal. The jury would be justified in concluding from the circumstances of this case that the death was not the result of an impulsive or spontaneous act flowing from an attempt to overcome resistance or to effect sexual contact and that the defendant chose to kill in order to silence his victim and conceal a rape.

The majority seems to suggest that for a jury to find premeditation or deliberation it must have preceded the formation of intent to kill. In other words, it seems to hold, if the intent to kill is formed impulsively there can be no premeditation. Neither logic nor case law leads me to concur with that conclusion. The fact of deliberation for the requisite time is the key ingredient of premeditation. Common sense suggests that premeditation exists as much if one is reflecting on an already formed intent to kill as it does when one is deliberating whether or not to kill. In either case, reflection and deliberation are present, if the deliberation is for an appreciable time. If the killing follows this process of reflection, then it is a premeditated killing.

The time period during which one continuously exerts sufficient pressure on a victim's throat to block breathing which, in turn, causes unconsciousness and then death, affords a person a significant opportunity for a change of heart. If a person consciously rejects the opportunity to lessen the pressure in that period, the person may be found to have deliberated. The more time required, the greater the probability that even a slow thinker had time to reflect. What a person does is often the best gauge of his or her thinking. The fact finder is called upon to determine whether a defendant premeditated from the facts surrounding the killing. Here, the jury concluded, as well they might, that this defendant took this mentally retarded young woman to a secluded area of Clallam County, raped her, strangled her with little difficulty for 3 to 5 minutes until she was dead, and then proceeded to bite her dead body. From this evidence a rational trier of fact could conclude beyond a reasonable doubt that the defendant was capable of reflecting and did reflect on his deed sufficiently to cause him to be guilty of premeditated murder in the first degree.

Premeditation cannot automatically be inferred from elapsed time. Even so, the jury should be permitted to examine the evidence to glean what it can about intent and premeditation. I find the evidence of elapsed time, of the crime scene and other pertinent circumstances compel the conclusion the defendant had ample opportunity to premeditate. Further, the defendant caused Leslie Cook's death by strangulation. What one does is highly indicative of what one intended to do. The jury should not be precluded from considering the method of killing if its very nature provides clues to the mental process of the perpetrator.

If one sits quietly and watches the clock for 3 to 5 minutes, an appreciation of the fullness of that length of time pervades one's thoughts. The jury was entitled to put itself in the shoes of the victim and the murderer. The victim would have gone from apprehension to fear, terror, and then lapsed into unconsciousness. During this time the victim, in all likelihood, would have struggled and the defendant would have watched all of this in the eyes of his victim. As to the defendant, the continued, deliberate exertion of strength required for that length of time was substantial. By the fact of death, we know that not once during all that it took to effect death, did he desist from accomplishing his purpose.

For the element of premeditation in an aggravated first degree murder case to be decided by the jury, there must be (a) proper instructions given defining premeditation and (b) sufficient evidence to support the giving of the instruction and to survive a challenge. The majority finds no fault with the instructions. The sole issue is whether there is evidence that the defendant thought about his act and intended to kill his victim. I find such evidence present and the conclusion as to whether the defendant did, in fact, deliberate and form an intent to take the life of his victim, a matter for the jury, not this court. * * *

ANDERSON, DURHAM, & DORE, JJ., concur.

NOTES FROM MOLLY:

1. Suppose the defendant kills the victim by giving him a small amount of poison each day for 30 days. Would the *Bingham* majority hold that premeditation could occur *before* the 30 days began to run, but not *during* the 30 days? Which result would better serve the *purpose* of separating first degree murder from second degree murder?

2. In our case, what is the relevant time period for premeditation (i.e., when did it start and when did it end), according to the *Bingham* majority? Would the dissent consider a different time period?

STATE v. OLLENS
Supreme Court of Washington
107 Wash. 2d 848, 733 P.2d 984 (1987)

GOODLOE, JUSTICE.

This case involves a brutal killing inflicted by multiple stabs and slashes with a knife. We address whether, as a matter of law, there is sufficient evidence to allow the issue of premeditation to go to a jury. We answer in the affirmative.

Respondent Lawrence C. Ollens was charged with the crime of aggravated murder in the first degree for the November 9, 1985 robbery/stabbing death of William Tyler, a Tacoma taxicab driver. Before trial, respondent moved that the trial court review and dismiss the aggravated first degree murder charge because of lack of evidence to prove the element of premeditation. The State acquiesced to pretrial review. Pretrial review on the element of premeditation took place in Superior Court on May 19 and 20, 1986.

The State relied on the testimony of Dr. Emmanuel Lacsina, the Pierce County Medical Examiner. Dr. Lacsina testified that Tyler died from multiple stab wounds and resulting blood loss. One stab perforated the left lung and the right ventricle of the heart. Dr. Lacsina indicated that this was one of the first wounds inflicted. A second stab perforated the right lobe of the liver and the soft tissues around the right kidney. A third stab entered between Tyler's ribs penetrating the right lobe of the liver. These wounds were not immediately fatal. However, all three wounds were potentially fatal if not treated shortly after their infliction. A fourth stab penetrated Tyler's right thigh.

In addition, Dr. Lacsina testified that Tyler's throat had been slit. More than one slashing motion was needed to complete the 6-inch gash which nearly transected the voice box and jugular vein. This injury was also capable of causing death. Dr. Lacsina testified, however, that Tyler could have been alive and struggling for 2 to 3 minutes after the neck wound.

Dr. Lacsina stated that the stab wounds preceded the slashing of Tyler's throat.

Dr. Lacsina also noted that there were numerous defensive wounds. These wounds were inflicted when the victim was alive and indicate that the assailant and victim struggled.

At the hearing, the defense asserted that the State's main witness, Lawrence Haney, would testify that Ollens supposedly admitted to him that he had killed the victim when the victim made a move as if to reach for a weapon and "Ollens cut the man because he felt it was either the man's life or his."

Citing to *State v. Bingham*, 105 Wash.2d 820 (1986), and *Austin v. United States*, 382 F.2d 129 (D.C.cir. 1967), the Superior Court removed the question of premeditation from the trial and entered an "Order Dismissing Element of Premeditation" and supporting "Findings of Fact and Conclusions of Law — Premeditation." The Superior Court concluded that the "use of a knife to inflict more than one wound, in and of itself, is not probative of premeditation, but can only be probative of intent to kill." The State appealed to this court, seeking review as a matter of right pursuant to RAP 2.2(b)(1). Superior Court proceedings have been stayed pending a further order of this court.

The issue we address is: Given multiple stab and slash wounds, is there sufficient evidence to send the question of premeditation to a jury?

Specific intent to kill and premeditation are not synonymous, but separate and distinct elements of the crime of first-degree murder. *See* RCW 9A.32.030(1)(a), .050(1)(a); *State v. Brooks*, 97 Wash.2d 873, 876 (1982). Premeditation has been defined as "the deliberate formation of and reflection upon the intent to take a human life" (*State v. Robtoy*, 98 Wash.2d 30, 43 (1982)), and involves "the mental process of thinking beforehand, deliberation, reflection, weighing or reasoning for a period of time, however short." *Brooks*, 97 Wash.2d at 876. Premeditation must involve more than a moment in point of time. RCW 9A.32.020(1).

The State argues that *Bingham* is limited to its facts. In *Bingham*, we held that manual strangulation alone shows only an opportunity to deliberate and is insufficient to sustain the element of premeditation. The State points out, however, that *Bingham* recognizes that "the planned presence of a weapon necessary to facilitate a killing has been held to be adequate evidence to allow the issue of premeditation to go to the jury." *Bingham*, at 827. *State v. Lanning*, 5 Wash.App. 426, 439 (1971), in which the victim's neck had been slashed, states: "Some premeditation was necessarily involved in order to have available a knife-edged, lethal instrument capable of nearly severing the victim's neck."

The State argues that Ollens necessarily planned the presence of a weapon, the double-edged knife used to inflict the fatal wounds. The State posits that the evidence suggests that Ollens carried such a knife in another robbery approximately 1 week earlier. The State concludes that the presence of a knife, as distinguished from no weapon, suffices to allow the issue of premeditation to go to a jury.

The State argues that as evidenced by the multiple stab wounds to the chest and heart, respondent intended to kill Tyler. It further argues that the multiple slashing of the victim's neck, which occurred after the stabbings, conclusively demonstrates a deliberation — however short — on the previously formed and demonstrated intent to kill. The State concludes that the physical evidence of manner and method of death, as a matter of law, sustains the element of premeditation.

Ollens disputes that the evidence in this case permits the inference that premeditation occurred. He argues that some time did pass during the struggle, however, this passage of time is inherent in the manner of a multiple stabbing death and is mere passage of time, not evidence of premeditation.

Respondent also asserts that the manner of death, i.e., violence and multiple wounds, does not support an inference of deliberation actually occurring or of a calmly calculated plan to kill which is requisite for premeditation and deliberation. *Austin v. United States*, 382 F.2d 129, 139 (D.C.cir. 1967), provides: "Violence and multiple wounds, while more than ample to show an intent to kill, cannot standing alone support an inference of a calmly calculated plan to kill requisite for premeditation and deliberation, as contrasted with an impulsive and senseless, albeit sustained, frenzy. *See also People v. Anderson*, 70 Cal.2d 15 (1968). Respondent argues that the evidence may indicate an intent to kill in the frenzy of the struggle, but it provides no basis from which a jury could infer that premeditation occurred. Ollens argues that *Bingham* is not limited to manual strangulation, as *Bingham* emphasizes the application of its analysis to other methods of death. Having the opportunity to deliberate is not evidence the defendant did deliberate, which is necessary for a finding of premeditation. Otherwise, any form of killing which took more than a moment could result in a finding of premeditation, without some additional evidence showing reflection. *Bingham*, 105 Wash.2d at 826.

Austin v. United States, supra, which is quoted in *Bingham*, involved a homicide committed with a knife, wherein the victim was stabbed 26 times and the knife left imbedded in the victim's skull. The *Austin* court held this evidence was insufficient to prove the elements of premeditation and deliberation, concluding that: "The Government was not able to show any motive for the crime or any prior threats or quarrels between appellant and deceased which might support an inference of premeditation and deliberation. Thus the jury could only speculate and surmise, without any basis in the testimony or evidence, that appellant acted with premeditation and deliberation." *Austin*, at 139. This is distinguished from the present case where a possible motive is present — that Ollens killed Tyler in order to effectuate the robbery.

We also note that *Bingham* quotes *Austin* solely to caution against letting "the facts of a savage murder generate a powerful drive to crush the crime with the utmost condemnation available." *Bingham*, 105 Wash.2d at 827-28. *Austin* was not quoted as part of *Bingham*'s analysis on the issue of premeditation.

The issue before this court is whether *Bingham* is controlling in this situation such that given the evidence no trier of fact could find premeditation beyond a reasonable doubt. We hold that *Bingham* is distinguishable. First, manual strangulation involves one continuous act. In the case at hand, not only did Ollens stab the victim numerous times, he thereafter slashed the victim's throat. This subsequent slashing is an indication that respondent did premeditate on his already formed intent to kill. Second, a knife was used in the killing. The strangulation in *Bingham* did not involve the procurement of a weapon. Third, from the evidence a jury could find that Ollens struck Tyler from behind, a further indication of premeditation. Finally, as indicated above, a jury could find the presence of a motive and, therefore, it would not be left to speculate or surmise only as to the existence of premeditation.

We hold that there is sufficient evidence to submit to a jury the issue of whether Ollens not only intended to kill the victim, but also premeditated. It is properly the function of a jury to determine whether Ollens deliberated, formed and reflected upon the intent to take Tyler's life in order to effectuate the robbery.

We reverse the Superior Court's dismissal of the premeditation charge and remand for the continuation of proceedings consistent with this opinion.

CALLOW, JUSTICE.

I concur in the result. The majority states that "the planned presence of a weapon necessary to facilitate a killing" is adequate evidence to allow the issue of premeditation to go to the jury. The majority poses the issue as being whether under the evidence no trier of fact could find premeditation beyond a reasonable doubt. The majority distinguishes *State v. Bingham* by stating that (1) *Bingham* involved one continuous act while Ollens involves stabbings and a final throat slashing; (2) the strangulation used in *Bingham* did not involve the procurement of a weapon, while the stabbing in Ollens does; (3) the jury could have found that Ollens struck the defendant from behind as evidence of premeditation; and (4) the jury in Ollens could find a motive which would eliminate speculation as to the existence of premeditation. The majority then concludes that it is the function of the jury to determine whether Ollens "deliberated, formed and reflected upon the intent to take Tyler's life in order to effectuate the robbery."

Premeditated means thought over beforehand. When a person, after any deliberation, forms an intent to take human life, the killing may follow immediately after the formation of the settled purpose and it will still be premeditated. Premeditation must involve more than a moment in point of time. The law requires some time, however long or short, in which a design to kill is deliberately formed. WPIC 26.01.

When the four justifications for finding sufficient evidence for the issue of premeditation to go to the jury set forth in the majority are compared with *Bingham*, we find: (1) both attacks were prolonged, continued for an appreciable period of time and concluded with the death of the victims (2) the absence of a weapon in *Bingham* is more than compensated for by the physical advantage of a man over a retarded female. I recognize that the procurement of a knife is a conscious act, but when a person habitually carries a knife as a tool this may not be evidence of premeditation, while, on the other hand, the physically powerful man who can kill a smaller woman at will without a weapon may well have premeditated. Is the evidence of the first fact evidence of premeditation and of the latter fact not for consideration by a jury on the question of premeditation? I submit the presence of the knife in the first situation might not prove premeditation, while evidence of a dominant, physically strong man with a motive to kill to silence a potential witness reflects a situation which could establish premeditation. I submit that in either situation the evaluation of the totality of the evidence in the light of all of the surrounding circumstances is for the jury.

(3) The jury in Ollens, because they could have found that the defendant struck the victim from behind, is permitted to find that this was evidence of premeditation. The jury in *Bingham* had before it the conclusive evidence that the defendant had violently raped and then strangled his victim. This latter fact is surely as probative as speculation as to which stab wound was inflicted first and from what direction. (4) While the jury in Ollens is permitted to find a motive ("could find") to eliminate speculation as to premeditation, the jury in *Bingham* had before it as strong a reason to find a motive from the evidence as exists in this case.

I do not concur for the purpose of rehashing the result in *Bingham*; I concur to point out that no basis exists to make homicide by strangulation an isolated crime where premeditation cannot be proven. The majority's rationale forces this conclusion when only the defendant and the victim were present in a one-on-one situation, yet allows proof of premeditation in a one-on-one situation when a weapon is present. Sufficiency of the evidence of premeditation to allow the issue to go to the jury is present in this case, and I submit the evidence was sufficient to pass that test in the *Bingham* circumstances.

The only question for this court is whether we can evaluate from the record the sufficiency of the evidence to take the question to the jury.

As stated by the court in *Bingham*, the standard for reviewing the sufficiency of evidence is "whether, after viewing the evidence in the light most favorable to the prosecution, any rational trier of fact could have found the essential elements beyond a reasonable doubt."

The decision of the majority in this case does not violate that standard of review, while the decision in *Bingham* does. A special area has been carved out and removed from jury consideration. This is a dangerous precedent and it is for this reason that I concur in the result.

NOTES FROM MOLLY:

1. The majority says that "the planned presence of a weapon" tends to show premeditation. But shouldn't this depend on *why* defendant had the weapon? Did Ollens bring the weapon in order to *kill* Tyler, or merely to threaten him in order to rob him?

2. The majority also says that the "subsequent slashing" of Tyler's throat was premeditated, as Ollens had already formed an intent to kill, as evidenced by the earlier stabs to the body. But couldn't the same have been said of Bingham's final squeezes of his victim's neck, after his earlier squeezes?

3. In his concurring opinion, Justice Callow favors leaving the issue of premeditation to the jury, in both *Bingham* and *Ollens*. But shouldn't the courts be especially careful before sending the issue of premeditation to a jury? The fine distinctions made in these two opinions would seem to be difficult for lay people to make, and they might not be in much of a mood to do so, having just heard evidence of a vicious crime (whether or not defendant "premeditated" it).

4. *Why should* the line between first and second degree murder be drawn at "premeditation"? Even assuming Bingham and Ollens did not "premeditate," weren't they just as culpable as murderers who *do* "premeditate"? If they were, what language would you put into a first degree murder statute to encompass the conduct of people like Bingham and Ollens? How about "particularly vicious"?

Chapter 10

VOLUNTARY MANSLAUGHTER

Voluntary manslaughter in most jurisdictions consists of an intentional homicide committed under extenuating circumstances which mitigate, though they do not justify or excuse, the killing. The principal extenuating circumstance is the fact that the defendant, when he killed the victim, was in a state of passion engendered in him by an adequate provocation (i.e., a provocation which would cause a reasonable man to lose his normal self-control). * * * * There are four obstacles for the defendant to overcome before he can have his intentional killing reduced from murder to voluntary manslaughter: (1) There must have been a reasonable provocation. (2) The defendant must have been in fact provoked. (3) A reasonable man so provoked would not have cooled off in the interval of time between the provocation and the delivery of the fatal blow. And (4), the defendant must not in fact have cooled off during that interval.

LaFave & Scott, *Criminal Law* (West)

People kill for a reason. Some reasons are very bad — e.g., for money or for racial or religious hatred. Some reasons are pretty good — self-defense, to protect loved ones, and the like — so good that they entirely justify or excuse the act of killing. (These will be considered in later chapters.)

And some reasons are in between. Often the killing is committed in response to something said or done by the victim, which angered the defendant. This might not justify or excuse the killing, but doesn't it make the defendant *less culpable* than a killer who was *not* so provoked? Always? Never? Sometimes — depending on the nature of the provocation? If so, what provocations are sufficient? And should we take into account this defendant's peculiar susceptibility to certain provocations?

Those are the questions posed by the cases in this Chapter.

PROBLEM 10

To: My law clerk

From: District Court Judge Luke Warm

Re: *State v. Berkowitz*

I am in the middle of trial in this case. Defendant Brenda Berkowitz is charged with the second degree murder of Ron Ruiz. The prosecution's evidence showed that Ruiz was killed by a stab wound in the chest, inflicted by Berkowitz.

Berkowitz testified in her own defense. The transcript of her testimony is attached. Her lawyer wants me to instruct the jury that, if they believe her testimony, they may return a verdict of guilty of voluntary manslaughter, instead of murder.

Please review the transcript and the attached authorities, and advise me as to whether I should give such an instruction and, if so, how the instruction might read.

Transcript of Berkowitz's Testimony

Q: Ms. Berkowitz, what was your relationship with Mr. Ruiz?

A: We were lovers for about 2 years, though we did not live together. We had planned to get married next year.

Q: What happened on the evening of May 8?

A: Ron and I were having dinner at his apartment in Santa Fe, and we were drinking wine. Wine doesn't relax me, but usually makes me rather anxious. Over our tomales and chopped liver, Ron told me that he had slept with Joan, my best friend. He also said that he did not want to marry me.

Q: Did he say why?

A: Yes. He said he didn't think our ethnic backgrounds went well together, as Mexicans were hot and Jews were cold. I started to cry and protest, and he called me a "whining Jewish princess."

Q: What did you do then?

A: I am very proud of my Jewish heritage, so I became very upset. I got up and walked out. I walked around the neighborhood for a couple of hours. When I returned to Ron's apartment, he was asleep on the couch, from drinking the wine, I guess. I went into his bedroom and looked in his desk drawers. I found a short letter to Ron from a woman, dated a couple of years ago, saying how much she loved him. I thought it was from Joan. I went back into the living room, and Ron was still asleep. I looked at his face. He seemed so calm, even though he had hurt me so much. This really infuriated me, so I picked up a knife from the kitchen sink and stabbed him. Later, I found out that the letter had been written by Ron's mother.

New Mexico Statutes, 1978, § 30-2-3(A)

Voluntary manslaughter consists of manslaughter committed upon a sudden quarrel or in the heat of passion.

STATE v. NEVARES
New Mexico Supreme Court
36 N.M. 41, 7 P.2d 933 (1932)

SADLER, J.

The appellant was convicted of murder in the second degree and appeals. Under a plea of not guilty, he made the defense of emotional insanity. Conflicting evidence upon the question of appellant's sanity was introduced, and it is not urged that the verdict, necessarily resolving this issue against appellant, is without substantial support in the evidence.

The appellant complains of the trial court's refusal to submit the issue of voluntary manslaughter. The appellant was a young man twenty-one years of age. The deceased, Miss Eva Smith, was a young girl eighteen years of age, a student in the high school at Las Cruces, residing with her mother and stepfather at Tortugas, about two miles below Las Cruces. The stepfather conducted a store at Tortugas in the rear of which the family resided.

For something more than a year prior to the homicide, the young couple had been friendly, and it is evident from the record that appellant was enamored of the deceased. An estrangement between them took place during the Christmas holidays in December, 1929, and had continued to the day of the homicide.

On April 13, 1930, the appellant appeared in a car at the home of deceased about 3 o'clock in the afternoon and requested that she go for an automobile drive with him that evening. She declined, saying she must study, and that she was through with him. He responded by saying he would see whether or not she was through with him. He drove away and about an hour and a half later reappeared and sent in a note to deceased by a younger brother. She received the note, which is in evidence, and sent out to him by this brother a reply, the contents of which were never disclosed. The appellant drove away but reappeared in about ten minutes and through a brother of the deceased asked her to come out to his car, which he had stopped directly in front of the store. The deceased went out to the car, was seen to be talking to appellant for a few moments and was in the act of returning into the store having one hand on the screen door, for opening same, when appellant jumped from his car with a shotgun, rushed rapidly toward deceased and called upon her to turn toward him. As she did so, he fired directly into her left breast and she fell dead at his feet. The appellant then drove rapidly away.

It is difficult to perceive how on this state of facts an instruction on voluntary manslaughter was warranted or permissible. Counsel for appellant predicate the right to the instruction on the testimony of Alejandro Smith, a younger brother of deceased, that at the time of rushing toward her with the shotgun appellant appeared "angry." Also, that by reason of a disordered mentality, following a head injury in an automobile accident, some two years previously, he was peculiarly susceptible to emotional stress or excitation, likely to result from the circumstances immediately surrounding the homicide for which he was on trial. And the testimony of Dr. S.D. Swope, an expert witness for appellant, that such emotional stress might have been the result of sudden anger, "if anger there was in this particular case."

The defense was insanity. The appellant did not testify, but if the jury had accepted the testimony of his witnesses on the issue of insanity, he would have been acquitted. Having been found not to be insane, but capable instead of appreciating and distinguishing between right and wrong in respect to the killing, it remains to be determined whether there is some middle ground between insanity, which will render a homicide excusable, and sanity, which renders its perpetrator accountable, within whose compass its commission will be deemed manslaughter rather than murder.

This brings us to an application of the law to the facts. Mere sudden anger or heat of passion will not reduce the killing from murder to manslaughter. There must be adequate provocation. The one without the other will not suffice to effect the reduction in the grade of the offense. The two elements must concur. And words alone, however scurrilous or insulting, will not furnish the adequate provocation required for this purpose.

The test of whether the provocation was adequate must be determined by considering whether it would have created the passion offered in mitigation in the ordinary man of average disposition. If so, then it is adequate and will reduce the offense to manslaughter. If not, it is inadequate.

Here is shown nothing but words apprising appellant of the fact that the deceased had rejected his suit, except testimony tending to show that by reason of his peculiar, even defective, state of mind, not amounting to insanity, such knowledge likely would result in a state of excitation and anger in him, altogether not to be expected in the ordinary man of average disposition. This circumstance does not alter the rule. Wharton on Homicide (3d Ed.), § 172; *King v. Lesbini* (1914) 3 K.B. 1116.

We agree with the soundness of the rule adopted in England and followed generally in this country, that different degrees of mental ability in prisoners who are sane cannot be taken into account for reducing a homicide from murder to manslaughter. In *King v. Lesbini, supra*, the court had this argument urged upon it. Lord Reading, Chief Justice, speaking for the court, said:

> It substantially amounts to this, that the court ought to take into account different degrees of mental ability in the prisoners who come before it, and if one man's mental ability is less than another's it ought to be taken as a sufficient defense if the provocation given to that person in fact causes him to lose his self-control, although it would not otherwise be a sufficient defense because it would not be provocation which ought to affect the mind of a reasonable person. We agree with . . . the principles enunciated in *Reg. v. Welsh* (1869) 11 Cox C.C. 338, where it is said that "there must exist such an amount of provocation as would as would be excited by the circumstances in the mind of a reasonable man, and so as to lead the jury to ascribe the act to the influence of that passion." We see no reason, therefore, to dissent in any way from the principle of law on which this case was tried. On the contrary we think it is perfectly right. This court is

certainly not inclined to go in the direction of weakening in any degree the law that a person who is not insane is responsible in law for the ordinary consequences of his acts.

So in the case at bar, the appellant's peculiar susceptibility to excitation, anger, or passion, even though resulting from a defective mentality, which still left him capable of distinguishing between the right and the wrong of the offense with which he stood charged, cannot aid him. He must have applied to him, for determining the adequacy of provocation relied upon, the test of its effect on the ordinary man of average disposition.

Measured by this test, the correctness of the trial court's refusal to submit voluntary manslaughter is readily apparent. The appellant importuned deceased, his former sweetheart, to go driving with him. She refused and informed him she was through with him. He went away, evidently brooded, and, returning a few minutes later, slew her. It was murder, and the court properly declined to submit voluntary manslaughter.

We conclude that the judgment of the lower court is based upon a record free from error and should be affirmed.

NOTES FROM THE JUDGE:

(1) *Nevares* used the term "reasonable man." If I instruct the jury on voluntary manslaughter, should I use this term — where the defendant is a woman?

(2) In *State v. Cooley*, 19 N.Mex. 91, 140 P. 1111 (1914), the court held:

> Intoxication of the defendant at the time of the killing, while a proper subject of inquiry in determining whether the deliberate premeditation necessary to constitute murder in the first degree was present, cannot be said to furnish the provocation required to reduce murder in the second degree to voluntary manslaughter. If, by reason of intoxication, the mind of the defendant was incapable of that cool and deliberate premeditation necessary to constitute murder in the first degree, but the killing was unlawful, and the act was not done under circumstances which would make the killing only voluntary or involuntary manslaughter, necessarily it would be murder in the second degree, as malice would be implied. Between the two offenses, murder in the second degree and voluntary manslaughter, the drunkenness of the offender forms no legitimate matter of inquiry; if the killing is unlawful and voluntary, and without deliberate premeditation, the offense is murder in the second degree, and malice will be implied from the killing, unless the provocation were of such a character as would reduce the crime to manslaughter, for which offense a drunken man is equally responsible as a sober one.

Question: Don't the cases on first degree murder [in Chapter 9] hold that intoxication is relevant to the issue of premeditation? Why should the rule be different for voluntary manslaughter?

STATE v. CASTRO
New Mexico Court of Appeals
92 N.M. 585, 592 P.2d 185 (1979)

SUTIN, JUDGE.

Defendant John Castro was convicted of voluntary manslaughter and aggravated burglary. The victim was Linda, his divorced wife. John appeals. We reverse on voluntary manslaughter and affirm on aggravated burglary.

Linda and John had been married for approximately eight years and were divorced in either August or September, 1977. The homicide was committed on October 6, 1977. John was off work at about 3:00 p.m., went home, drank two bottles of beer and had supper. While John was watching a baseball game on television, Linda called and wanted money for rent. He told her to let him alone and she said she didn't have to. Linda then used abusive language. Subsequently, John went to the store and purchased a gun and ammunition. This transaction took about ten minutes and John appeared calm. He went back home, loaded the gun, walked around for about a half hour and then walked to Linda's house. He planned on shooting her in the spine to prevent her from dancing.

John saw Linda sitting on the couch watching television and knocked on the door. Linda became scared, called the police, hollered and ran toward the back bedroom. John broke the lower left hand window, unlocked the door, and from a distance of five feet shot Linda three times and killed her.

John was charged with first degree murder and aggravated burglary. The jury returned a verdict of guilty of voluntary manslaughter and aggravated burglary, both with the use of a firearm.

A. *No evidence supported submission of voluntary manslaughter.*

Section 30-2-3(A), N.M.S.A. 1978 reads: "Manslaughter is the unlawful killing of a human being without malice. (a) Voluntary manslaughter consists of manslaughter committed upon a sudden quarrel or in the heat of passion."

Smith v. State, 89 N.M. 770 (1976) says: "It follows logically and obviously from the definition that, in order to convict of voluntary manslaughter, the jury must have evidence that there was a *sudden quarrel* or heat of passion *at the time of the commission of the crime* (in order, under the common law theory, to show that the killing was the result of provocation sufficient to negate the presumption of malice; see, e. g., R. Anderson, Wharton's Criminal Law and Procedure § 242 (1957))."

U.J.I. Crim. 2.20 was submitted to the jury. It contained the definition and meaning of "sufficient provocation" and reads:

> The difference between second degree murder and voluntary manslaughter is provocation. In second degree murder the defendant kills without having been sufficiently provoked, that is, without sufficient provocation. In the case of voluntary manslaughter, the defendant kills after having been sufficiently provoked, that is, as a result of sufficient

provocation. Sufficient provocation reduces second degree murder to voluntary manslaughter. Sufficient provocation can be any action, conduct or circumstances which arouse anger, rage, fear, sudden resentment, terror or other extreme emotions. *The provocation must be such as would affect the ability to reason and cause a temporary loss of self control in an ordinary person of average disposition. The provocation must be such that an ordinary person would not have cooled off before acting.* (Emphasis added.)

The State claims that the provocative telephone call from Linda put into motion the series of events that led to Linda's death. The State contends that it showed conclusively that John reacted in response to the provocation of Linda. This argument falls short of the meaning of "sufficient provocation" in three respects. First, when buying the gun John acted calmly, free of any extreme emotions. Second, John walked about the area a considerable period of time before approaching Linda's residence. He did not act immediately or soon after the provocation. Even if we assumed that initially John was angered, he had sufficient time to cool off. He did not lose self control. Sudden anger or heat of passion and provocation must concur. *State v. Nevares*, 36 N.M. 41 (1932). Finally, "And words alone, however scurrilous or insulting, will not furnish the adequate provocation required for this purpose." *Nevares, supra*, at 44-5.

The Committee Commentary shows that *Nevares* was considered in arriving at the definition of "sufficient provocation." The "words alone" concept does not fall within the terms "any action, conduct or circumstances which arouse anger" as set forth in U.J.I. Crim. 2.20, supra. We conclude that the telephone conversation did not constitute "sufficient provocation." Absent "sufficient provocation," there was no evidence to support submission of voluntary manslaughter to the jury. John is discharged on this count of the criminal information.

* * * *

Defendant's conviction of voluntary manslaughter is reversed. Defendant's conviction of aggravated burglary is affirmed.

NOTES FROM THE JUDGE:

1. Does the *result* of Castro's appeal make any sense, in light of the *purpose* of the "crime" of voluntary manslaughter?

2. In *People v. Rios*, 23 Cal. 4th 450 (2000), Rios was convicted of voluntary manslaughter. On appeal, defense counsel argued that the jury should have been instructed that they could convict of voluntary manslaughter only if the prosecutor proved that defendant was reasonably provoked to a heat of passion. The court disagreed:

> Provocation and imperfect self-defense cannot be elements of voluntary manslaughter when murder and voluntary manslaughter are under joint consideration. Were it otherwise, the prosecution would face irreconcilable requirements, where provocation or imperfect self-defense was at issue, to

obtain an appropriate conviction. On the one hand, the People would have to prove, beyond reasonable doubt, the *absence* of these factors in order to establish the greater offense [murder], but on the other hand, would have to prove their *presence* beyond reasonable doubt to establish the lesser one. A fact finder doubtful that provocation or imperfect self-defense was lacking, but also not persuaded beyond reasonable doubt that either was present, could convict the defendant of *neither* murder *nor* voluntary manslaughter, even though it found the defendant had killed intentionally, without justification or excuse. Such a result would turn the law of criminal homicide on its head.

3. If a voluntary manslaughter instruction permits the jury to reduce murder to a lower crime, defense counsel should want the judge to give such an instruction, right? Well, not always. Maybe defense counsel thinks, "The prosecution's case against me for murder isn't too strong, so I have a good shot at an acquittal. But maybe the jurors who want to convict me for murder and the jurors who want to acquit will cut a deal, and convict me of voluntary manslaughter — if the judge gives them that option. I'd rather take my chance on a total acquittal (or maybe a hung jury). So I won't ask the judge to instruct the jury on voluntary manslaughter." Legitimate strategy — or cynical manipulation of the system? The latter, held the Court in *People v. Barton*, 12 Cal. 4th 186 (1995):

> We conclude that a defendant may not invoke tactical considerations to deprive the jury of the opportunity to consider whether the defendant is guilty of a lesser offense included within the crime charged. A trial court should instruct the jury on any lesser included offense supported by the evidence, regardless of the defendant's opposition. Thus, the trial court in this case acted properly when, over defendant's objection, it instructed the jury on voluntary manslaughter. * * * *

> Our courts are not gambling halls but forums for the discovery of truth. Truth may lie neither with the defendant's protestations of innocence nor with the prosecution's assertion that the defendant is guilty of the offense charged, but at a point between these two extremes: the evidence may show that the defendant is guilty of some intermediate offense included within, but lesser than, the crime charged. A trial court's failure to inform the jury of its option to find the defendant guilty of the lesser offense would impair the jury's truth-ascertainment function. Consequently, neither the prosecution nor the defense should be allowed, based on their trial strategy, to preclude the jury from considering guilt of a lesser offense included in the crime charged. To permit this would force the jury to make an "all or nothing" choice between conviction of the crime charged or complete acquittal, thereby denying the jury the opportunity to decide whether the defendant is guilty of a lesser included offense established by the evidence.

> Defendant's proposed rule permitting the defense, upon request, to bar the trial court from instructing the jury on lesser included offenses supported by the evidence would, as just stated, not only impair the jury's search for truth, but would also be unfair to the prosecution. Sometimes the prosecution's evidence that a defendant has committed the crime charged

may be relatively weak, whereas the evidence of a lesser included offense may be much stronger. In that case, a prosecutor need not, and generally does not, separately charge a defendant with the lesser included offense. If instructions on a lesser included offense could be barred at the defendant's request, the prosecutor would be denied the opportunity to argue to the jury that the defendant, even if not guilty of the crime charged, is at least guilty of the lesser included offense.

When, however, the question is whether the trial court must, on its own initiative, instruct the jury on defenses not asserted by the defendant, different considerations arise. Failure to so instruct will not deprive the jury of the opportunity to consider the full range of criminal offenses established by the evidence. Nor is the prosecution denied the opportunity to seek conviction on all offenses included within the crime charged. Moreover, to require trial courts to ferret out all defenses that might possibly be shown by the evidence, even when inconsistent with the defendant's theory at trial, would not only place an undue burden on the trial courts but would also create a potential of prejudice to the defendant. Appellate insistence upon *sua sponte* instructions which are inconsistent with defense trial theory or not clearly demanded by the evidence would hamper defense attorneys and put trial judges under pressure to glean legal theories and winnow the evidence for remotely tenable and sophistical instructions.

SELLS v. STATE
New Mexico Supreme Court
98 N.M. 786, 653 P.2d 162 (1982)

FEDERICI, JUSTICE.

Joseph Sells petitioned this Court on a writ of certiorari to review the judgment of the Court of Appeals, which affirmed the conviction of the defendant for the crime of murder in the second degree with a firearm enhancement. Mr. Sells was charged with the deliberate first degree murder of his wife, Barbara Sells. The jury was instructed on first and second degree murder and on involuntary manslaughter. Mr. Sells' requested instruction on voluntary manslaughter was refused. The issue we decide on certiorari is whether the trial court erred in refusing to instruct on voluntary manslaughter. We hold that it did, and reverse.

It is necessary at the outset to set forth the facts and circumstances in this case that warranted the giving of the instruction on voluntary manslaughter. The evidence adduced at trial showed that there had been a series of heated arguments between Mr. Sells and his wife. The arguments occurred during the night and into the early morning when the fatal shot was fired about 5:00 a.m. The arguments occurred at several bars and finally at the family residence at Farmington, New Mexico. Both Mr. Sells and Mrs. Sells had been drinking heavily during the night and morning the shot was fired.

The arguments concerned Mrs. Sells' boyfriend. Mr. Sells was unaware of his wife's infidelity and sexual relationship with her boyfriend until the revelations were made to him that night and morning. Witnesses stated that Mr. Sells was dazed, shocked and stared at the ceiling after the revelations. The Sells' daughter testified that her father was unaware of Mrs. Sells' boyfriend before the revelations were made. Other witnesses staying at the family residence heard Mrs. Sells say to Mr. Sells, the morning the shot was fired, that she enjoyed her sexual relationship with her boyfriend. The extent of Mrs. Sells' relationship with her boyfriend became apparent to Mr. Sells as he realized that Mrs. Sells' recent trip to Phoenix, Arizona, was to be with her boyfriend. Also, it became apparent that an unusually large long-distance telephone bill involved Mrs. Sells and her boyfriend.

A scuffle or struggle occurred between the parties just before the shot was fired. Mr. Sells shot Mrs. Sells fatally a short time afterwards as she sat at the kitchen table. Mr. Sells testified that he did not believe the .22 caliber handgun that fired the fatal shot was loaded. He also testified that he did not remember shooting his wife.

Mr. Sells argued before the trial court and in the Court of Appeals that voluntary manslaughter was a necessarily included lesser offense of first degree murder, requiring, at least, a submission of a jury instruction to that effect. The trial court did not instruct the jury on voluntary manslaughter. The Court of Appeals affirmed the trial court, stating that it was bound by this Court's decision of *State v. Farris*, 95 N.M. 96 (1980), to the extent that words alone, no matter how scurrilous, cannot provide adequate provocation to support a voluntary manslaughter instruction.

This interpretation of *Farris* is too restrictive. Such a reading of *Farris* does not allow sufficient flexibility under relevant facts, and would prohibit submission of the jury instruction on voluntary manslaughter in appropriate cases. We note that both § 30-2-3(A), N.M.S.A. 1978, which defines voluntary manslaughter, and N.M.U.J.I. Crim. 2.22, N.M.S.A. 1978 (Repl.Pamp.1982), which defines sufficient provocation, permit the instruction of voluntary manslaughter based upon broad concepts. Section 30-2-3(A) reads: "Voluntary manslaughter consists of manslaughter committed upon a sudden quarrel or in the heat of passion." N.M.U.J.I. Crim. 2.22 defines sufficient provocation as: "Any action, conduct or circumstances which arouse anger, rage, fear, sudden resentment, terror or other extreme emotions . . ."

Provocation "must be 'such as would affect the ability to reason and to cause a temporary loss of self control in an ordinary person of average disposition.'" *State v. Reynolds*, 98 N.M. 527 (1982). The provocation must concur with sudden anger or heat of passion and an ordinary person would not have cooled off before acting. Id.

In this case, Mr. Sells' contention is that there was sufficient provocation to properly warrant a voluntary manslaughter instruction. We agree. We believe there was credible evidence introduced at trial that tended to show that Mr. Sells could have been sufficiently provoked by action, conduct or circumstances which aroused in him anger, rage, sudden resentment, or other extreme emotions, all of which could have contributed in precipitating his actions. His wife had revealed to him that she had a lover, someone that apparently Mr. Sells knew. Mr. Sells was unaware of the clandestine relationship between his wife and her boyfriend until she revealed it to him. Mr. Sells appeared dazed or shocked.

These facts, together with other facts already mentioned above, indicate that in the totality of the circumstances, the instruction of voluntary manslaughter should have been given to the jury.

We have no quarrel with the statement that words alone, however scurrilous or insulting, will not furnish adequate provocation to require submission of a voluntary manslaughter instruction. *State v. Farris, supra*; *State v. Castro*, 92 N.M. 585 (1979); *State v. Nevares*, 36 N.M. 41 (1932). However, if there is evidence to raise the inference that by reason of actions and circumstances the defendant was sufficiently provoked, as defined in § 30-2-3(A) or in N.M.J.U.I. Crim. 2.22, then the jury should be given the voluntary manslaughter instruction.

The fact that words were used in this case is not dispositive. It is well recognized that informational words, as distinguished from mere insulting words, may constitute adequate provocation. 2 Wharton's Criminal Law, § 156 (14 ed. 1979). Accordingly, "a sudden disclosure of an event (the event being recognized by the law as adequate) may be the equivalent of the event presently occurring." *Id.* at 249. See also W. LaFave, A. Scott, Jr., *Criminal Law*, § 76 (1972). Thus, the substance of the informational words spoken, the meaning conveyed by those informational words, the ensuing arguments and other actions of the parties, when taken together, could amount to provocation.

The defendant is entitled to an instruction on voluntary manslaughter as a lesser included offense of murder in the first degree if there is evidence to support, or tending to support, such an instruction. *State v. Robinson*, 94 N.M. 693, (1980). In this case the record reflects that there was such evidence. Defendant was entitled to have the trial court instruct the jury on voluntary manslaughter.

Generally, it is for the jury to determine whether there is sufficient provocation under an appropriate instruction on voluntary manslaughter. *State v. Ulibarri*, 67 N.M. 336 (1960).

Various results have been reached in prior cases decided by this Court and the Court of Appeals, in the application of the term "provocation." Each case must be read and interpreted in the light of the facts in that particular case. * * * * To the extent that *State v. Farris, supra*, or other cases decided by this Court or the Court of Appeals are inconsistent with the views announced in this case, they are hereby expressly overruled.

The trial court erred in refusing to instruct the jury on voluntary manslaughter. The Court of Appeals and the trial court are reversed and this cause is remanded to the trial court for granting of a new trial to the defendant.

NOTES FROM THE JUDGE:

(1) Does *Sells* change any of the rules set down in *Nevares* or *Castro*? If so, how do these rules bear on the question of whether Brenda's testimony would justify a verdict of voluntary manslaughter?

(2) Does *Sells* hold that "informational words" may *always* be adequate provocation?

(3) In *Gonzales v. State*, 689 S.W.2d 900 (Texas Ct.Crim.App.1985), Gonzales killed Malva Forbes, a woman he was living with, during a stormy argument in which Ms. Forbes had said, "You goddamn son-of-a-bitch Mexican, I hate you." Gonzales was convicted of murder, and he appealed, arguing that the "person of ordinary temper" standard for voluntary manslaughter used in Texas should not be strictly applied to him. The court disagreed:

> Appellant seems to contend that because he is an Hispanic farm worker who was living with a Caucasian woman on a low income he should be granted more latitude in the degree of insult, etc., sufficient to enrage him. Yet appellant fails to recognize that the standard of the reasonable man, the person of ordinary temper, is employed precisely to avoid different applications of the law of manslaughter to defendants of different races, creed, color, sex or social status. * * * *

> As Associate Justice Miller opined in *Hart v. United States*: "While sympathy might at first glance suggest a more lenient rule for persons of low mentality or unstable emotions, the result would be disastrous in the uncertainty of its application. The rule suggested by appellant would become a refuge for ill-tempered, irresponsible citizens; it would put a premium upon lack of self-control and would penalize the reasonable man, the average man, the prudent man, because of the restraint which he practices in his dealings with his fellows." *Hart v. United States*, 130 F.2d 456, 458 (D.C.cir. 1942).

(4) In Nancy S. Kim, *The Cultural Defense and the Problem of Cultural Preemption: A Framework for Analysis*, 27 New Mexico L.Rev. 101 (1997), the author "advocates the formal adoption of an evidentiary framework which would permit cultural evidence to be admitted to explain the defendant's state of mind at the time of the offense." She discusses cases involving a Japanese woman who allegedly followed a Japanese custom (oya-ko-shinju) by drowning her 2 children (and trying to drown herself) after learning of her husband's adultery, a Laotian man who allegedly followed a Laotian custom of "marriage by capture" (zij poj niam) by kidnapping and raping a Laotian woman, and a Chinese man who allegedly followed a Chinese custom of seeking revenge to avoid "loss of face" by shooting and killing a man who had beaten him a year earlier. All these incidents occurred in America.

Questions: Should evidence of these customs be (1) admissible? (2) a complete defense? (3) in the 1st and 3rd cases, a reason to reduce a murder charge to voluntary manslaughter?

(5) In *Commonwealth v. Halbert*, 410 Mass. 534, 573 N.E.2d 975 (1991), Halbert testified that he killed the victim because of the victim's homosexual advances towards Halbert, and he argued that this testimony required the trial judge to instruct the jury on voluntary manslaughter. The Supreme Judicial Court disagreed:

> The defendant suggests that he was provoked by the victim's homosexual advance, which consisted of the victim's putting his hand on the

defendant's knee and asking, "Josh, what do you want to do?" The defendant offered evidence that he was sexually abused as a child and that he was the victim of a homosexual "gang" rape shortly before the night of the murder. While the defendant's history of sexual abuse is tragic, it has no bearing on the question whether the victim's conduct satisfied the objective test of provocation. The issue is: would the victim's nonthreatening physical gesture and verbal invitation have provoked a reasonable person into a homicidal rage?

The victim's question ("Josh, what do you want to do?") was neither insulting nor hostile; it was at most a salacious invitation. Clearly, neither the question nor the accompanying physical gesture (the victim's placing his hand on the defendant's knee) would have been likely to produce in an ordinary person such a state of passion, anger, fear, fright, or nervous excitement as would eclipse his capacity for reflection or restraint. Because the evidence was insufficient to support a finding of reasonable provocation, the judge did not err in refusing to instruct the jury on voluntary manslaughter.

See also Robert Mison, Comment, *Homophobia in Manslaughter: The Homosexual Advance As Insufficient Provocation*, 80 Calif.L.Rev. 133, 136 (1992), where the author states that "judges should hold, as a matter of law, that a homosexual advance alone is not sufficient to incite a 'reasonable man' to kill." Compare, however, Joshua Dressler, *When "Heterosexual" Men Kill "Homosexual" Men: Reflections on Provocation Law, Sexual Advances, and the "Reasonable Man" Standard*, 85 J.Crim.Law & Criminology 726 (1995), where the author disagrees: "Mison's position seems right at first glance, but is wrong on deeper reflection."

(6) In *Canipe v. Commonwealth*, 25 Va.App. 629, 491 S.E.2d 747 (1997), Canipe inadvertently "cut off" another driver, who responded by passing Canipe, moving in front of him, and slowing down, whereupon Canipe pulled in front of the other driver and slowed down. After both drivers pulled into a parking lot, the other driver got out of his car and angrily approached Canipe, who then drove into the other driver, killing him. The court upheld Canipe's murder conviction, rejecting his argument that the jury should have been instructed on voluntary manslaughter: "Although appellant and the victim had minutes earlier been enmeshed in a fit of 'road rage' spurred by each other's aggressive driving, such conduct alone does not render a reasonable person 'deaf to the voice of reason.'"

STATE v. MUNOZ
New Mexico Court of Appeals
827 P.2d 1303 (1992)

APODACA, JUDGE.

Defendant appeals from his convictions under three counts for separate criminal offenses. A jury found defendant guilty of murder in the second degree of J.A. Hatfield (Hatfield), attempted murder in the second degree of Lila Hatfield, and attempted murder in the first degree of Ralph Hernandez.

Only one of the issues raised by defendant merits publication, so only that part of the opinion discussing that issue will be formal and published. The issue meriting publication is whether the trial court erred in refusing defendant's requested jury instruction on the lesser-included-offense of voluntary manslaughter in connection with the death of Hatfield. We hold that defendant's testimony provided a factual basis for such an instruction and thus conclude that the trial court committed reversible error in denying defendant's requested instruction. The second-degree murder conviction under count 1 is therefore reversed and the case is remanded for a new trial on that count. For the reasons stated in the unpublished portions of this opinion, we affirm the other two convictions with respect to all other issues raised by defendant.

Background

During the late night or early morning of March 15-16, 1989, defendant went to the home of Hatfield and Lila Hatfield, his wife, where he shot and killed Hatfield. As defendant was leaving the Hatfield residence, he ran over Lila Hatfield with his pickup truck, severely injuring her. Defendant then shot Ralph Hernandez in both legs and left him in a secluded place. In addition to the criminal offenses for which he was convicted, defendant was charged with aggravated burglary for his entry into the Hatfield residence and aggravated assault for allegedly assaulting his wife, Donna Munoz, with a firearm.

Defendant testified at trial, admitting that he committed the acts in question. However, his defense theory was that he was unable to form the specific intent required, resulting from certain events that occurred from March 13 through March 16. In support of this defense, he introduced the testimony of several expert witnesses who testified that, during the events, defendant was suffering from a brief reactive psychosis. The jury found defendant not guilty of the aggravated burglary and aggravated assault.

Discussion

The critical difference between murder and voluntary manslaughter is the existence of legally sufficient provocation. SCRA 1986, 14-220 [a standard jury instruction]. A homicide is murder if done without what the law considers to be sufficient provocation. However, if the homicide occurs as a result of what the law deems as sufficient provocation, the homicide is considered voluntary manslaughter. *Id.* A trial court must instruct the jury on voluntary manslaughter if the defense requests such an instruction and the instruction is warranted under the facts of the case.

SCRA 1986, 14-222 [also a standard jury instruction], defines sufficient provocation as "any action, conduct or circumstances which arouse anger, rage, fear, sudden resentment, terror or other extreme emotions." This rule also provides that "the provocation must be such as would affect the ability to reason and to cause a temporary loss of self control in an ordinary person of average disposition." *Id.* The required provocation is insufficient "if an ordinary person would have cooled off before acting." *Id.* Whether a particular set of circumstances is sufficient provocation is generally a question for the jury to decide. *Sells v. State*, 98 N.M. 786 (1982). Thus, our task as a reviewing court is to determine whether the jury could have determined that defendant's actions were the result of legally sufficient provocation based on the evidence presented.

Defendant testified at length concerning the events of March 13 through 16. What follows is a summary of his testimony. Defendant and Donna Munoz were married in 1980. He was eighteen years old at the time, she was fifteen years old. She had run away from home a few months earlier. She told defendant that she was running away because Hatfield, who was her stepfather, had attempted to touch her sexually. Throughout the marriage, Donna Munoz continually maintained that Hatfield had only tried to touch her but had not succeeded.

During the evening hours of March 15, 1989, Donna Munoz told defendant that she wanted to talk to him. They left their son, Christopher, in the spare bedroom, watching television, and went into the living room. There, Donna Munoz spoke generally about her family and specifically about events that had occurred when she was nine years old, Hatfield, as well as her uncle, Ralph Hernandez, and her brother, Fabian McClean, had sexually molested her. The acts of molestation occurred on many occasions, and included anal and vaginal intercourse, as well as oral sex, for which the men gave her money. She told defendant that she had informed other family members of these occurrences, including her mother. They had responded by telling her to be quiet about the molestations so that the family could stay together. As she revealed these events to defendant, Donna Munoz was screaming and crying hysterically.

Becoming extremely upset as he heard these disclosures, defendant picked up his rifle and went to his in-laws' house, located a few miles away. He testified that he went there because he wanted to talk to Hatfield. He took his rifle with him because he was afraid of Hatfield. He had been to the house before and knew that Hatfield kept guns there in the spare bedroom. Upon arriving at the Hatfield residence, defendant entered the house uninvited, went into the bedroom, and awakened Hatfield and Lila Hatfield. He told them of his wife's revelations and that they had ruined his and his wife's lives. Hatfield denied everything, but Lila Hatfield admitted that her daughter had come to her for help and that she had refused her plea. At that point, Hatfield gave Lila Hatfield a "go-to-hell look" and said he wanted a cigarette. Defendant said no, that he wanted to talk. Hatfield stood up and walked toward defendant. Defendant loaded his rifle. Both men were yelling. Hatfield, who appeared to be very angry, stared into defendant's eyes, then stepped back and started walking out of the bedroom. Defendant testified that, as he was losing Hatfield in the dark, the gun went off.

Based on these facts, defendant requested an instruction on the lesser-included offense of voluntary manslaughter in connection with the resulting death of Hatfield. The trial court refused the instruction, holding that *State v. Manus*, 93 N.M. 95 (1979), required that, to establish voluntary manslaughter, a defendant must show that he was provoked by the victim. The trial court stated that there was sufficient evidence by which a jury could find provocation. Nevertheless, it concluded that defendant was not entitled to the instruction because the provocation in this appeal came, not from the victim, but from the disclosures made by Donna Munoz to defendant. We disagree with the trial court's view of the law.

It is settled law that the victim must be the source of the provocation. *State v. Manus.* In applying this rule, however, it is important to distinguish between the actual provocation, which in this case consisted of Hatfield's sexual molestations of Donna Munoz, and the manner in which defendant learned of the provocation, which consisted of Donna Munoz's disclosures. To establish manslaughter, both of these must occur before the killing. As the facts of this appeal illustrate, the provocation and the disclosure of the events constituting the provocation may occur at different times. However, as our supreme court has observed, "a sudden disclosure of an event (the event being recognized by the law as adequate) may be the equivalent of the event presently occurring." *Sells v. State*, 98 N.M. at 788. See also F. Lee Bailey & Henry B. Rothblatt, 1 *Crimes of Violence: Homicide and Assault*, § 565 (1973); Wayne R. La Fave & Austin W. Scott, Jr., 2 *Substantive Criminal Law* § 7.10(b)(1986). Thus, we believe the trial court erred in determining that, as a matter of law, Hatfield had done nothing that was legally sufficient to provoke defendant.

The state does not argue that Hatfield's sexual abuse of Donna Munoz would not be a legally sufficient provocation, nor does it contend that the trial court correctly applied the holding of *Manus*. Instead, the state argues that defendant's testimony demonstrates that defendant killed Hatfield because he thought Hatfield was going to get a gun. Thus, the state maintains, defendant's own actions caused the true provocation — Hatfield's attempt to get a gun. We disagree.

We recognize that a defendant cannot pose a threat to the victim and then rely on the victim's response as a legal provocation. In the present case, however, defendant's provocation argument was based on Hatfield's alleged sexual mistreatment of defendant's wife, rather than on the possibility Hatfield was going to get a gun. We thus hold that defendant was entitled to have the jury instructed on voluntary manslaughter in connection with the death of Hatfield.

Conclusion

Based on our discussion and the unpublished portions of this opinion, we (1) reverse and remand for a new trial on count 1, involving the death of J.A. Hatfield; and (2) affirm defendant's convictions for the attempted second-degree murder of Lila Hatfield and the attempted first-degree murder of Ralph Hernandez.

NOTES FROM THE JUDGE:

(1) By my calculations, the alleged sexual molestation of Donna had ended about 10 years before Munoz killed Hatfield. Suppose it had ended 20 years earlier? 30 years earlier? Should there be any "statute of limitations" on Munoz's right to be provoked by what Hatfield allegedly did?

(2) Suppose Hatfield had already been convicted of sexually molesting Donna, served time in prison for the offense, and had been released, having fully paid his "debt to society"? Should that have had any effect on Munoz's right to claim

voluntary manslaughter? Should it matter whether or not Munoz *knew* that Hatfield had been convicted and served his prison term?

(3) Suppose that it turned out that Donna had lied to Munoz, and no sexual molestation had occurred at all? Should that have any effect on Munoz's right to claim voluntary manslaughter?

(4) In all the cases in this Chapter, it seems that the murder charge was based on intent to kill. What if it had instead been based on "depraved heart" (extreme recklessness)? Could defendant seek to lower the charge to voluntary manslaughter? Yes, held the court in *People v. Lasko*, 23 Cal. 4th 101 (2000):

> Under the Attorney General's approach, one who shoots and kills another in the heat of passion and with the intent to kill is guilty only of voluntary manslaughter, yet one who shoots and kills another in the heat of passion and with conscious disregard for life but with the intent merely to injure, a less culpable mental state than intent to kill, is guilty of murder. This cannot be, and is not, the law.

PROBLEM A

This problem raises issues covered in many of the ten chapters you have just read. Try to write out an answer to this problem (as if it were an exam question). When you are done, take a look at the sample answer at the end of the book. Don't peek!

Memo to: My law clerk

From: Deputy District Attorney Pat Pickle

Re: *People v. Dill*

Dave Dill has been charged with murder of Bill Brine and Carl Cuke. Attached is a transcript of the police interrogation of Dill. Based on that, do we have substantial evidence of murder on either charge? Our jurisdiction follows the common law rules on crimes, as modified by the statutes and cases in the first ten chapters of your casebook. If any of the facts are unclear, say what they are and why it matters.

Transcript of Interrogation of Dave Dill

Q: [Advice of *Miranda* rights, which Dill waived.] What happened last night, Dave?

A: My brother Al gave me a new watch. I had seen this brand in stores, and it sold for $50. I needed some money, so I decided to try to sell it to Brine for $50. I knew Brine was always looking for a bargain, so I planned to tell him that the watch was an expensive import worth $200, but I was willing to sell it for $50 because it was stolen. I would also tell him that I would give him back the money if he didn't like the watch.

Q: Did you then go Brine's house?

A: Yes. I first called him and told him I had a watch he might want to buy, and he said to come over. I went there that afternoon and rang the bell, and he let me in.

His buddy Cuke was with him. I told Brine the story I had planned to tell him about the watch. He said he would buy it, and he gave me the $50. I gave him the watch. He then looked at it closely and said that it was *his* watch, and my brother Al had stolen it from him. I got mad and said Al would never do a thing like that. Brine pulled out a gun and pointed it at me. Cuke then grabbed me. I tried to push him off, and Brine fired the gun. The bullet hit Cuke in the chest, and he went down. Brine dropped the gun and started to leave. I was still mad, so I picked up a bookend and threw it at him. It weighed a couple of pounds, and it hit him in the head. He went down too. Both of them died.

Part IV

Causation

Chapter 11

CAUSATION

With crimes so defined as to require not merely conduct but also a specified result of conduct, the defendant's conduct must be the "legal" or "proximate" cause of the result. For one thing, it must be determined that the defendant's conduct was the cause in fact of the result, which usually (but not always) means that but for the conduct the result would not have occurred. In addition, even when cause in fact is established, it must be determined that any variation between the result intended (with intent crimes) or hazarded (with reckless or negligent crimes) and the result actually achieved is not so extraordinary that it would be unfair to hold the defendant responsible for the actual result.

LaFave & Scott, *Criminal Law* (West)

Suppose Tom fires a gun at X, Dick fires at Y, and Harry fires at Z. Each shooter intends to kill his target. Tom succeeds, but Dick fails — he is a lousy shot and misses. Harry succeeds, but not as he had planned: his shot wounds Z in the arm, and Z is so frightened that he runs into the street, where Z's old enemy Bart sees him and intentionally runs him down, killing him.

How much should we punish these defendants? They each have the same *mens rea* — intent to kill — and they each committed the same *actus reus* — shooting a gun at the victim. Therefore, it seems that they are equally culpable and merit the same punishment. But our murder statute requires not just a mental state and an act, but also *a certain harm*: the death of a human being. Dick's victim is not dead, so we *cannot* punish Dick as much as we punish Tom — even though he seems to deserve it (though we might punish Dick for *attempted* murder).

What about Harry? He too is just as culpable as Tom, and — since his intended victim is dead — the murder statute would not seem to prevent us from punishing Harry as much as we punish Tom. Harry got just what he wanted: his intended target is dead. Is there any reason why we *shouldn't* punish Harry as much as Tom?

Even if Harry "deserves" as much punishment as Tom, perhaps he is saved by the *language* of our murder statute, which probably says that one is guilty of murder only if his act "caused" the death of a human being. Does this help Harry? Well, Harry did "cause" Z's death, in the sense that "but for" Harry's shooting Z, Z would not have run into the street where Bart found him and was able to run him down. (We might call this "actual" cause.)

Is there another sense in which we might read the word "cause" — like "proximate" cause (whatever that means)? *Should* we read it in any other sense?

Why? That is the central issue in this Chapter.

PROBLEM 11

To: My law clerk

From: Tom E. Gunn, Deputy District Attorney

Re: *People v. Bill Sykes*

I am in the middle of trial in this case. Defendant is charged with robbery and second degree murder. I just finished putting on my case, and defense counsel has moved for a directed verdict of acquittal on the murder charge, arguing that there is insufficient evidence of causation. He cited the attached cases. Also attached is the transcript of the testimony of our key witness.

Please let me know what arguments I can make against the motion, and whether I am likely to win.

Transcript of Testimony of Phil Lerrup

Q. Please state your occupation.

A. I own and run a gas station out on Long Island.

Q. What happened there on the morning of June 4?

A. I was filling up a car at one of the pumps, when the defendant drove up to another pump. My employee, Hal Hill, went to take care of him. I saw the defendant pull out a handgun and point it at Hal, and Hal raised his hands. Defendant said something, and Hal went over to the cashbox, then went back to defendant's car and gave him the money. Defendant then drove off, but as he did, he fired a shot at Hal. The bullet missed Hal, but it hit the gas pump next to him. The pump exploded and splashed some burning gasoline on Hal. Hal screamed and ran out into the street, which is a busy boulevard. A car hit Hal, though it braked first and wasn't going too fast. Hal fell down. I ran out to him and put out the fire on him with my jacket. He said, "Thanks. I think I'm OK, but my neck hurts." I thought of putting some flares around him and calling an ambulance, but I decided to carry him off the street so the cars could pass. When I picked him up, I heard his neck crack.

NOTE FROM TOM:

Expert medical witnesses presented uncontradicted testimony that Hill died of a broken neck, and that it was unlikely that he would have died if Lerrup had not picked him up and had instead called for medical assistance.

New York Penal Law

Section 125.25: Murder in the Second Degree

A person is guilty of murder in the second degree when:

1. With intent to cause the death of another person, he causes the death of such person or of a third person * * * *

2. Under circumstances evincing a depraved indifference to human life, he recklessly engages in conduct which creates a grave risk of death to another person, and thereby causes the death of another person; or

3. Acting either alone or with one or more other persons, he commits or attempts to commit robbery, burglary, kidnapping, arson, rape in the first degree, sodomy in the first degree, sexual abuse in the first degree, aggravated sexual abuse, escape in the first degree, or escape in the second degree, and, in the course of and in furtherance of such crime or of immediate flight therefrom, he, or another participant, if there be any, causes the death of a person other than one of the participants * * * *

Note: Compare Model Penal Code § 2.03, re causation, in the Appendix.

PEOPLE v. KIBBE
New York Court of Appeals
35 N.Y.2d 407, 321 N.E.2d 773 (1974)

GABRIELLE, JUDGE.

Subdivision 2 of § 125.25 of the Penal Law, c.40, provides, in pertinent part, that "a person is guilty of murder" when "under circumstances evincing a depraved indifference to human life, he recklessly engages in conduct which creates a grave risk of death to another person, and thereby causes the death of another person."

The factual setting of the bizarre events of a cold winter night of December 30, 1970, as developed by the testimony, including the voluntary statements of the defendants, reveal the following: During the early evening the defendants were drinking in a Rochester tavern along with the victim, George Stafford. The bartender testified that Stafford was displaying and "flashing" one hundred dollar bills, was thoroughly intoxicated and was finally "shut off" because of his inebriated condition.

At some time between 8:15 and 8:30 p.m., Stafford inquired if someone would give him a ride to Canandaigua, New York, and the defendants, who, according to their statements, had already decided to steal Stafford's money, agreed to drive him there in Kibbe's automobile. The three men left the bar and proceeded to another bar where Stafford was denied service due to his condition. The defendants and Stafford then walked across the street to a third bar where they were served, and each had another drink or two. After they left the third bar, the three men entered Kibbe's automobile and began the trip toward Canandaigua. Krall drove the car while Kibbe demanded that Stafford turn over any money he had. In the course of an exchange, Kibbe slapped Stafford several times, took his money, then compelled him to lower his trousers and to take off his shoes to be certain that Stafford had given up all his money; and when they were satisfied that Stafford had no more money on his person, the defendants forced Stafford to exit the Kibbe vehicle.

As he was thrust from the car, Stafford fell onto the shoulder of the rural two-lane highway on which they had been traveling. His trousers were still down around his ankles, his shirt was rolled up towards his chest, he was shoeless and he had also been stripped of any outer clothing. Before the defendants pulled away, Kibbe placed Stafford's shoes and jacket on the shoulder of the highway. Although Stafford's eyeglasses were in the Kibbe vehicle, the defendants, either through inadvertence or perhaps by specific design, did not give them to Stafford before they drove away.

It was some time between 9:30 and 9:40 p.m. when Kibbe and Krall abandoned Stafford on the side of the road. The temperature was near zero, and, although it was not snowing at the time, visibility was occasionally obscured by heavy winds which intermittently blew previously fallen snow into the air and across the highway; and there was snow on both sides of the road as a result of previous plowing operations. The structure nearest the point where Stafford was forced from the defendants' car was a gasoline service station situated nearly one half of a mile away on the other side of the highway. There was no artificial illumination on this segment of the rural highway.

At approximately 10:00 p.m., Michael W. Blake, a college student, was operating his pickup truck in the northbound lane of the highway in question. Two cars, which were approaching from the opposite direction, flashed their headlights at Blake's vehicle. Immediately after he had passed the second car, Blake saw Stafford sitting in the road in the middle of the northbound lane with his hands up in the air. Blake stated that he was operating his truck at a speed of approximately 50 miles per hour, and that he "didn't have time to react" before his vehicle struck Stafford. After he brought his truck to a stop and returned to try to be of assistance to Stafford, Blake observed that the man's trousers were down around his ankles and his shirt was pulled up around his chest. A deputy sheriff called to the accident scene also confirmed the fact that the victim's trousers were around his ankles, and that Stafford was wearing no shoes or jacket.

At the trial, the Medical Examiner of Monroe County testified that death had occurred fairly rapidly from massive head injuries. In addition, he found proof of a high degree of intoxication with a .25%, by weight, of alcohol concentration in the blood.

For their acts, the defendants were convicted of murder, robbery in the second degree and grand larceny in the third degree. However, the defendants basically challenge only their convictions of murder, claiming that the People failed to establish beyond a reasonable doubt that their acts "caused the death of another," as required by the statute (Penal Law § 125.25, subd.2). As framed by the Appellate Division, the only serious question raised by these appeals "is whether the death was caused by the defendants' acts".

In answering this question, we are required to determine whether the defendants may be convicted of murder for the occurrences which have been described. They contend that the actions of Blake, the driver of the pickup truck, constituted both an intervening and superseding cause which relieves them of criminal responsibility for Stafford's death.

There is, of course, no statutory provision regarding the effect of an intervening cause of injury as it relates to the criminal responsibility of one who acts in motion the machinery which ultimately results in the victim's death; and there is surprisingly little case law dealing with the subject. Moreover, analogies to causation in civil cases are neither controlling nor dispositive, since, as this court has previously stated: "A long distance separates the negligence which renders one criminally liable from that which establishes civil liability" (*People v. Rosenheimer*, 209 N.Y. 115, 123); and this is due in large measure to the fact that the standard or measure of persuasion by which the prosecution must convince the trier of all the essential elements of the crime charged, is beyond a reasonable doubt. *In re Winship*, 397 U.S. 358.

Thus, actions which may serve as a predicate for civil liability may not be sufficient to constitute a basis for the imposition of criminal sanctions because of the different purposes of these two branches of law. Stated another way, the defendants should not be found guilty unless their conduct "was a cause of death sufficiently direct as to meet the requirements of the *criminal*, and not the *tort*, law." *Commonwealth v. Root*, 403 Pa. 571. However, to be a sufficiently direct cause of death so as to warrant the imposition of a criminal penalty therefor, it is not necessary that the ultimate harm be intended by the actor. It will suffice if it can be said beyond a reasonable doubt, as indeed it can be here said, that the ultimate harm is something which should have been foreseen as being reasonably related to the acts of the accused. 1 Wharton, Criminal Law Procedure, § 169.

In *People v. Kane*, 213 N.Y. 260, the defendant inflicted two serious pistol shot wounds on the body of a pregnant woman. The wounds caused a miscarriage; the miscarriage caused septic peritonitis, and the septic peritonitis, thus induced, caused the woman's death on the third day after she was shot. Over the defendant's insistence that there was no causal connection between the wounds and the death and, in fact, that the death was due to the intervention of an outside agency, namely, the negligent and improper medical treatment at the hospital, this court affirmed the conviction "even though the medical treatment may also have had some causative influence" (p. 277).

We subscribe to the requirement that the defendants' actions must be *a sufficiently direct cause* of the ensuing death before there can be any imposition of criminal liability, and recognize, of course, that this standard is greater than that required to serve as a basis for tort liability. Applying these criteria to the defendants' actions, we conclude that their activities on the evening of December 30, 1970 were a sufficiently direct cause of the death of George Stafford so as to warrant the imposition of criminal sanctions.

In engaging in what may properly be described as a despicable course of action, Kibbe and Krall left a helplessly intoxicated man without his eyeglasses in a position from which, because of these attending circumstances, he could not extricate himself and whose condition was such that he could not even protect himself from the elements. The defendants do not dispute the fact that their conduct evinced a depraved indifference to human life which created a grave risk of death, but rather they argue that it was just as likely that Stafford would be miraculously rescued by a good Samaritan. We cannot accept such an argument. There can be little doubt but that Stafford would have frozen to death in his state of undress had he remained on the shoulder of the road. The only alternative left to him was the highway, which in his condition, for one reason or another, clearly foreboded the probability of his resulting death.

Under the conditions surrounding Blake's operation of his truck (i.e., the fact that he had his low beams on as the two cars approached; that there was no artificial lighting on the highway; and that there was insufficient time in which to react to Stafford's presence in his lane), we do not think it may be said that any supervening wrongful act occurred to relieve the defendants from the directly foreseeable consequences of their actions. In short, we will not disturb the jury's determination that the prosecution proved beyond a reasonable doubt that their actions came clearly within the statute (Penal Law § 125.25, subd. 2) and "caused the death of another person."

We also reject the defendants' present claim of error regarding the trial court's charge. Neither of the defendants took exception or made any request with respect to the charge regarding the cause of death.[1]

The orders of the Appellate Division should be affirmed.

NOTES FROM TOM:

(1) *Kibbe* holds that where the defendant's act is a "direct cause" of the victim's death and the "intervening cause" is not a "supervening cause," the defendant is responsible for the death. I think this might help us - if I just understood what these terms mean. Can you define them for me, and tell me how to use them in my argument to the judge?

(2) *Kibbe* is about "proximate" cause, not "actual" cause. Cases about "actual" cause are rare. One such case is *State v. Guerrero*, 896 P.2d 14 (Ore.Ct.App.1995), where defendant was convicted of fleeing the scene of an accident and ordered to pay the costs of the victim's funeral because the death resulted from the crime. The appellate court reversed this order, because there was no evidence that the flight had any causal connection to the death, i.e., that had defendant stayed and assisted the victim, the victim would have survived.

(3) *Brackett v. Peters*, 11 F.3d 78 (7th Cir. 1993), involved the following facts:

> Brackett, age 21 at the time, had raped and severely beaten an 85-year-old widow, Mrs. Winslow, for whom he had previously done yard work. She was admitted to the hospital with a broken arm, a broken rib, and

---

[1] Ed. - In a later habeas corpus proceeding, the United States Supreme Court held that the trial court's failure to instruct the jury on causation did not violate the defendant's constitutional right to due process of law. *Henderson v. Kibbe*, 431 U.S. 145 (1977).

extensive bruises. During her stay in the hospital, which lasted several weeks, she — described as "feisty" before the rape and beating - became depressed, resisted efforts to feed her, and became progressively weaker. Transferred to a nursing home, she continued to deteriorate, even though her physical injuries were healing. Her appetite was very poor. Her doctor ordered a nasal gastric feeding tube for her but the tube could not be inserted, in part because facial injuries inflicted by Brackett made insertion of the tube too painful. About ten days after her admission to the nursing home, she died while a nurse was feeding her some pureed food through a feeder syringe. An autopsy revealed that a large quantity of food, some six or seven ounces, had become lodged in Mrs. Winslow's trachea, asphyxiating her.

The court held Brackett responsible for Mrs. Winslow's death:

> The question is whether Brackett's assault on Mrs. Winslow could be found to be a cause of her death. If so, Brackett is guilty of felony murder; if not, not.
>
> So far as bears on this case, an act is a cause of an event if two conditions are satisfied: the event would not have occurred without the act; the act made the event more likely. The first condition is necessary to distinguish the attempted from the completed crime, the second to rule out cases in which, while the event in question would not have occurred but for the act, the act did not create the kind of dangerous condition that would make such events more likely to occur.
>
> Suppose, for example, that Mrs. Winslow had been killed by a fire at the nursing home. She would not have been in the nursing home (in all likelihood), so would not have been killed, but for Brackett's assault. But as there would have been no greater danger of fire in a nursing home than in her own home, in our hypothetical case the assault would not have placed her in a situation of danger and therefore would not be considered a cause of her death.
>
> Even with this qualification, which excludes from the concept of legally relevant causation certain purely adventitious "causes," every event has multiple causes. Mrs. Winslow's age was undoubtedly a cause of her death; a younger woman would have been much less likely to experience so rapid and complete a deterioration as a result of the assault. The autopsy revealed some signs of senility, and senility is a common cause of depression, loss of appetite, and general weakening — all additional causes of Mrs. Winslow's death, in the dual sense, which we have explained is the relevant sense, that had any of these conditions been absent she probably would not have died from the rape and beating *and* that each of the conditions made her death from the assault more likely.
>
> None of them was related to the death merely fortuitously, as in our example of the nursing-home fire, which would be deemed "a supervening act disconnected from any act of the defendant," so that the defendant would not be liable for the death.

The immediate cause of Mrs. Winslow's death was the action of the nurse in depositing food into Mrs. Winslow's trachea. Brackett's lawyer argues that the nurse was grossly negligent, but this is far from plain — Mrs. Winslow appears to have exhibited no signs of distress until she keeled over dead — and even if it is true all that it would mean is that the nurse's negligence was still another cause of Mrs. Winslow's death. An event is, as we have emphasized, typically the consequence of multiple causes. But a murderer does not avoid conviction by pointing out that his act was only one of many causes that concurred to bring about his victim's death. It is enough if his act was one of the causes — enough therefore if Brackett's assault made Mrs. Winslow's death more likely and if, but for the assault, she would not have died as soon as she did.

A rational finder of fact could find these conditions satisfied. The proposition that raping and beating an 85-year-old woman creates a risk of death requires no discussion, but we must also consider the first part of the dual test of cause, and thus ask whether she would have died anyway when she did. That is unlikely. Death was the last link in a continuous series of events that began with the assault. She died a month later, never having returned home. Her condition deteriorated from the start of her hospital-ization, and when she was transferred to the nursing home her doctor already believed her to be near death. Of course she was very old and the autopsy revealed a condition of senile atrophy that must have existed before the assault. But judging from the description of her as "feisty" her senility could not have been so far advanced that death was imminent. It is more than unlikely that had she not been assaulted on October 21, 1981, she still would have entered the hospital the next day and died a month later. The assault appears to have precipitated her rapid decline. Of course there are dangers in inferring consequence from sequence. But they are slight when as in this case the event not only follows the act closely in time but is the kind of event frequently produced by the kind of act, and no persuasive evidence of an alternative causal sequence is presented. Illinois, inciden-tally, has abolished the archaic "year and a day" rule, a rule designed to cut off criminal liability when the inference of causation is attenuated by time.

Brackett's lawyer fastens on the statement in the state trial judge's otherwise uninformative opinion that the judge was rejecting the state's theory of "psychological murder." The theory had been advanced in a press conference called by the prosecutor. We are unable to determine exactly what the theory was or even whether it was pursued at the trial. Brackett's lawyer describes it as follows: the assault caused Mrs. Winslow to become clinically depressed, clinically depressed people (we know) are prone to suicide, Mrs. Winslow committed suicide by refusing to eat, and suicide is one of those "supervening acts disconnected from any act of the defendant" which cut off liability for causing death. If this is "psychological murder," we are puzzled by the trial judge's rejection of it. We think — to take a hypothetical case somewhat clearer than this case — that if a person, desiring the death of another whom he knew to suffer from depression, stole his intended victim's anti-depression medicine hoping to precipitate the victim's suicide, and his hope was fulfilled, this would be murder. The victim's depressive state would no more be a "supervening act" than any other vulnerability of the victim; in criminal law as in tort law, the injurer takes his victim as he finds him. It would be only a shade removed from a case of death by fright, but well removed from a case in which the defendant, not desiring the victim's death, made it more likely, for example by teaching him to play Russian roulette, as distinct from playing it with him. Well removed too from a case of assisted suicide, where the victim desires his death. In our hypothetical case the victim presumably was taking anti-depression medicine because he did *not* want to commit suicide, a recognized risk of depression. The fact that a psychiatric condition, whether or not by precipitating suicide, is one of the causes of a victim's death does not excuse his murderer. Otherwise it would be open season on sufferers from mental illness.

Courts worry, naturally, about problems of evidence and inference in settings where cruel, deceptive, or even simply inconsiderate behavior might be claimed with more or less plausibility to have driven a susceptible person to suicide, or, as here, to loss of the "will to live." But we do not think that there is or should be a *categorical* bar to the imposition of criminal liability in such cases. It has long been the rule in tort law (the "thin-skull" or "eggshell-skull" rule) not only that the tortfeasor takes his victim as he finds him, but also that psychological vulnerability is on the same footing with physical. If for example the victim is predisposed to schizophrenia, and the tortfeasor inflicts a minor injury which precipitates the schizophrenia, he is liable for the entire consequences even though they were both highly unlikely and unforeseen. * * * *

The eggshell-skull principle does not quite fit a case of intentional murder, for the murderer must intend his victim's death and ordinarily this will presuppose some awareness of the likely consequences of his act. It is not murder to kill a person by a slight blow harmless to an ordinary person if you do not know the person is unusually vulnerable; there is even a presumption in Illinois that one who beats another with his bare fists does not intend to kill him. But felony murder is different, and it is time to remind the reader that this a felony-murder case. No intent to kill, as in our hypothetical "psychological murder" case, is required; and though the Illinois cases do require that death be a "foreseeable" consequence of the felony, all they mean is that the death must be caused by the felony; for remember that "cause" in law means not just but-for cause but also an enhancement of the likelihood (what in law is often called "foreseeability") that the class of events would occur. (Some courts do not require proof of such enhancement in a felony-murder case. But the Illinois courts do.) Here the only issue is whether a rational finder of fact could conclude that the felonies which Brackett committed caused the death of his victim; the answer, we have seen, is yes.

We have emphasized analogies from tort law because the doctrine of causation is more developed there than in criminal law. The reason is that tort law, which has compensatory as well as deterrent functions, focuses on injury, while criminal law, which emphasizes deterrence and incapacitation, focuses on the dangerousness of the defendant's conduct. There is no tort liability without proof of injury, but there are plenty of crimes that are punishable though no injury resulted — many attempts and conspiracies, for example. A victim's eggshell skull may require a refined adjustment in damages to reflect the likelihood that the victim would because of his vulnerability have been injured sooner or later nontortiously. But a criminal assailant is punishable as a first-degree murderer "no matter how feeble the spark" of life that his blow extinguished. Uncompleted crimes are often punished severely; and when injury or death ensues from deliberate wrongdoing, even if (as in the case of felony murder) it is not an intended consequence, the criminal law comes down heavily on the defendant without worrying overmuch about the precise amount of harm inflicted.

(4) In *Commonwealth v. Casanova*, 429 Mass. 293 (1999), Casanova shot a man in the neck, paralyzing him and limiting his ability to breathe. This led to adult respiratory distress syndrome, and he died of this — *six years* after the shooting. Defense counsel conceded that Massachusetts had abolished the "year-and-a-day" rule, but argued that there should be some longer cut-off period (but shorter than six years, of course). The Supreme Judicial Court disagreed:

> At common law, a defendant could not be prosecuted for murder unless his victim died within a year and a day of the act inflicting injury. 4 H. Broom, Commentaries on the Laws of England 235-236 (1869) ("no person shall be adjudged by any act whatever to have killed another, if that other does not die within a year and a day after the stroke received, or cause of death administered"). Otherwise, the loss of life would be attributed to natural causes rather than the distant act inflicting injury. This requirement envisioned that the death must be shown to be sufficiently connected with the act. See 1 W.R. LaFave & A.W. Scott, Jr., Substantive Criminal Law § 3.12(i), at 421 (1986) ("the difficulty in proving that the blow caused the death after so long an interval was obviously the basis of the rule").

> In 1980, after a complete review of the history, rationale, and current status of the rule, we abolished it, deeming it "anachronistic upon a consideration of the advances of medical and related science in solving etiological problems as well as in sustaining or prolonging life in the face of trauma or disease." *Commonwealth v. Lewis*, 381 Mass. 411, 413-414 (1980).

> The defendant contends that this court should replace the year and a day rule with some other limiting rule. He contends that to have a potential prosecution hanging over his head indefinitely deprives him of due process and that, when death occurs so long after the injury, the trial would turn into a costly, time consuming, and confusing battle of the experts. In support of the need for a definite time period beyond which prosecution for murder is barred, the defendant cites our statement in *Lewis* that such "a task of adjustment is characteristically for the Legislature, but if not undertaken by that branch, may fall to the courts" The Legislature has not acted to alter our conclusion and we have not been convinced that any new

knowledge or fresh arguments require our further intervention.

Our research indicates that in no jurisdiction has a court abrogated the year and a day rule and subsequently imposed a new time limit on murder prosecutions. * * * *

A primary factor making the year and a day rule obsolete is the advance of medical knowledge and techniques. Medicine can now sustain the critically afflicted for months and even years beyond what might have been imagined only decades ago. Parallel progress has also been made in the development of diagnostic skills, so that problems of medical causation are more readily resolved. Modern pathologists are able to determine the cause of death with greater accuracy than was possible in earlier times and thus causation, even in complex cases, is a less difficult problem in modern day prosecutions. Although the defendant objects to the likely necessity of reliance on expert testimony in instances where death does not closely follow the act, neither this reliance on experts nor the presence of difficult issues of causation present unfamiliar problems for modern day courts. Accordingly, the abrogation of the rule does not make the determination of guilt so inherently unreliable or undeterminable as to deprive a defendant of procedural due process.

Nor is it unjust that the perpetrator is exposed over an indefinite time to the possibility of a murder prosecution. It follows that the abrogation of the year and a day rule does not work a deprivation of substantive due process. There is no statute of limitations applicable to murder. The possibility of a murder prosecution does hang over a potential defendant's head differently here than it does in cases where death immediately follows the precipitating act but the suspect evades detection or capture. But we fail to see why this difference should work a denial of due process in one case but not the other.

As in any criminal trial, proof of causation beyond a reasonable doubt is as much as any defendant may claim as a matter of right. Further, it is true as a general matter that, as the period between assault and the victim's death is prolonged, proof of causation may be more difficult. This greater difficulty affects the ability of the prosecution to prove its case. And jurors may bring a natural skepticism to the claim that an act distant in time was the proximate cause of death.

The year and a day rule functioned as a rule of judicial economy based on an assessment of the likely ability to prove causation beyond a reasonable doubt. The decision to abrogate the rule was based on the notion that science had advanced to the point that the previous assessment was no longer appropriate. Institution of a new time period between injury and death beyond which a defendant may not be prosecuted for murder is appropriate only if there is a time past which there is no significant number of cases in which the prosecution could satisfy its burden of proof. We have no basis for estimating what such a time may be, if, indeed, one exists at all. Although it will undoubtedly be difficult in many cases for the prosecution to prove causation where death is remote in time from the allegedly precipitating injury, in cases where this link can be proved, such as where a slow-acting poison is used or where a person purposely infects another with a virus such as HIV, prosecution should not be barred by some arbitrary time limit. It would be incongruous if developments in medical science that allow a victim's life to be prolonged were permitted to be used to bar prosecution of an assailant, where scientific evidence is presented to establish beyond a reasonable doubt that the defendant's acts proximately caused the victim's death. Nor should the availability of modern life-sustaining equipment and procedures ever raise the specter of the choice between terminating life-support systems or allowing the defendant to escape a murder charge.

PEOPLE v. STEWART
New York Court of Appeals
40 N.Y.2d 692, 358 N.E.2d 487 (1976)

WACHTLER, JUDGE.

The defendant was charged with stabbing and killing Daniel Smith. There is no doubt that the defendant stabbed Smith and that Smith later died at a hospital. However at trial one of the principal issues was whether the stab wound caused the death, or whether death was caused solely by medical malpractice at the hospital or by other intervening effective medical cause. The jury, after being charged to consider several alternative counts of assault and homicide, found the defendant guilty of manslaughter in the first degree. On this appeal, the defendant urges that the evidence was only sufficient to establish assault because the People failed, as a matter of law, to prove that the stab wound caused Smith's death beyond a reasonable doubt.

The stabbing occurred when the defendant arrived unexpectedly at his former girlfriend's Brooklyn apartment on the evening of October 8, 1971. He found Daniel Smith there and ordered him to leave at knife point. When Smith suggested that they talk it over, the defendant rejected the idea and stabbed him in the stomach. Smith was then taken to a Brooklyn hospital where he was operated on later that evening. The following day the defendant was arrested and charged with assault. On November 8, 1971 Smith died in the hospital and the defendant was charged with murder.

At the trial, the People called Dr. Dominck Di Maio, the Deputy Chief Medical Examiner for the Borough of Brooklyn, to establish the cause of death. Di Maio had not been present during the operation performed on October 8; but he had reviewed the reports of the surgeons and the anesthesiologist and had also performed an autopsy on November 10, 1971. Since neither the surgeons nor the anesthesiologist testified at the trial, the only evidence regarding the cause of death came from Di Maio and the reports of the operation, both of which were introduced into evidence.

Di Maio stated that when Smith entered the hospital, he had a single knife wound in the abdomen, which had punctured the stomach. Prior to the operation he was given "a substance which is commonly called Curare," which paralyzes the chest muscles, making it impossible for the patient to breathe on his own. As a result, the anesthesiologist had to "breathe" for him by squeezing a bag of oxygen into the lungs, a procedure called ventilation. During the initial stages of the operation, the surgeons discovered that Smith also had an incarcerated hernia. After they had sutured the wounds and completed the operation on the stomach, the surgeons proceeded to correct the hernia. During this phase of the operation "it was noted that the body was turning blue and there was no pulse, which means the person went into cardiac arrest." Smith then suffered a loss of oxygen to the brain and massive brain damage. He died a month later without ever regaining consciousness.

At the time of death, the stomach wound had completely healed. Nevertheless at the trial, and in his autopsy report, Di Maio stated that in his opinion death was caused by "a stab wound of the abdomen, stomach, cardiac arrest during surgical correction of the stab wound and another operation which was indicated during the surgical procedure with sepsis, which means infection, and kidney shut down." Thus Smith's death was immediately caused by heart failure, with resulting massive brain damage, which occurred during the operation, and Di Maio concluded that the stab wound was ultimately responsible for this. But the heart failure had occurred after the surgeons had successfully closed the stomach wound inflicted by the defendant, and while they were correcting the hernia which, concededly, was not in any way related to the defendant's act.

Di Maio was asked whether this phase of the operation was also made necessary by the defendant's act. He had initially stated in conclusory terms that when the surgeons discovered that Smith had the hernia they "felt it should be operated upon or it would possibly endanger his life." But later, more equivocally, he observed that "They saw that and they, I suppose, believed it might be a good thing to take care of that at the same time." When asked whether it was a "correct medical decision," he said that it was because it is always proper "if you are in the belly, and you see something that may aggravate or may complicate the condition you are operating for, you should do something about it." Besides, he noted, the hernia might have become gangrenous and "If it did occur, they would have to go in again, and they would risk his life." However when he was asked for his opinion as to whether the patient would have survived the operation if the surgeons had simply treated the stomach wound without "attending to the additional hernia operation," he answered "the chances are he would.

Dr. Di Maio was also asked to explain exactly what had caused the cardiac arrest. Here he recognized several possibilities. It could have been caused by the shock of the stab wound or by the shock or physical strain of either or both of the operations. But it also could have been caused by something that occurred in the operating room. He initially stated that since he had not participated in the operation he did not feel that he should make any judgment on this. This reluctance was also prompted by the fact that "There is an anesthesia report which I have read, and there is a surgeon's report, which I have read, and they are in direct contradiction."

The anesthesiologist's report stated that Smith had experienced a "broncho spasm" which, Di Maio explained, could have blocked the air passage making it impossible for the anesthesiologist to ventilate the patient. The surgeons' report on the other hand stated that when they noticed the patient's color change, they asked the anesthesiologist "about the status of the patient, and he said he had difficulty ventilating the patient. It was the opinion of all three surgeons at the table that the anesthesiologist was in complete unawareness of what happened to the patient. When we investigated the situation first, the diaphragm was not moving and the patient was not being assisted with ventilation." Finally Di Maio concluded "Now these are the two contradictions. If the anesthesiologist is correct, *and I have to assume so*, there was a bronchial spasm, the diaphragm couldn't move because he couldn't get the air beyond the obstruction." Italics supplied. However, on cross-examination he conceded that if the anesthesiologist was not doing his job so that the patient "wasn't getting any ventilation" or oxygen, he could suffer cardiac arrest, and that alone could be "the competent producing cause of death."

At the conclusion of the trial, the court submitted various counts to the jury including common-law murder, manslaughter in the first degree[1] and assault in the first degree.[2] As indicated they found the defendant guilty of manslaughter in the first degree, on the theory that he assaulted Daniel Smith to inflict serious physical injury and, without intending to do so, caused his death.

The Appellate Division affirmed by a bare majority.

We have recently observed that there is "no statutory provision regarding the effect of an intervening cause of injury as it relates to the criminal responsibility of one who sets in motion the machinery which ultimately results in the victim's death; and there is surprisingly little case law dealing with the subject" (*People v. Kibbe*, 35 N.Y.2d 407, 412). The concept of causation, although frequently considered and discussed in civil cases, is rarely encountered in criminal law (see, e.g., Ryu, *Causation in Criminal Law*, 106 U.Pa.L.Rev. 773). It has been suggested that the criminal concepts involved are less complex than the civil (Hall, *General Principles of Criminal Law* (2d ed.), p. 254), but the burden of proof is more demanding and analogies are "neither controlling nor dispositive" (*People v. Kibbe*, supra, p. 412). In criminal cases, questions of causation only arise when the crime charged involves not only conduct — and usually intent — but also proof that a specific harm has resulted (see La Fave and Hall, *Criminal Law*, p. 247). Typically, the cases in which the problems arise involve homicide.

One accused of homicide, of course, cannot be convicted unless it is shown that he "caused the death of a person" (Penal Law § 125.00). No matter what degree of homicide is charged, this is always an essential element which the People must prove beyond a reasonable doubt (*People v. Brengard*, 265 N.Y. 100). This means that the prosecutor must, at least, prove that the defendant's conduct was an actual

---

[1] On this count the court charged the jury under subdivision 1 of § 125.20 of the Penal Law which states: "A person is guilty of manslaughter in the first degree when * * * (w)ith intent to cause serious physical injury to another person, he causes the death of such person."

[2] On this count the charge was pursuant to subdivision 1 of § 120.10 of the Penal Law which states: "A person is guilty of assault in the first degree when * * * (w)ith intent to cause serious physical injury to another person, he causes such injury to such person * * * by means of a deadly weapon or a dangerous instrument."

cause of death, in the sense that it forged a link in the chain of causes which actually brought about the death (see, e.g., Perkins, *Criminal Law*, 687). But something more is required before his conduct will be recognized as a legal cause of death warranting criminal sanctions. The requirement here is that "the defendant's actions must be a *sufficiently direct cause* of the ensuing death before there can be any imposition of criminal liability" (*People v. Kibbe, supra*, at p. 413). Thus an "obscure or merely probable connection between an assault and death will, as in every case of alleged crime, require acquittal of the charge of any degree of homicide" (*People v. Brengard, supra*, p. 108).

We have held that "direct" does not mean "immediate." The defendant may be held to have caused the death even though it does not immediately follow the injury (see, e.g., *Cox v. People*, 80 N.Y. 500). Neither does "direct" mean "unaided," for the defendant will be held liable for the death although other factors, entering after the injury, have contributed to the fatal result. Thus if "felonious assault is operative as a cause of death, the causal co-operation of erroneous surgical or medical treatment does not relieve the assailant from liability for homicide" (*People v. Kane*, 213 N.Y. 260, 270). But if "the death is solely attributable to the secondary agency, and not at all induced by the primary one its intervention constitutes a defense (*Kane, supra*, at p. 270).

In the *Kane* case, the defendant shot a pregnant woman, Anna Klein, inflicting two "serious pistol-shot wounds" — one bullet lodged in the back three inches from the spine, and the other fractured a rib and lodged in one of the lungs. The wounds caused a miscarriage; the miscarriage caused septic peritonitis and that lead to death. The defendant argued that the miscarriage and the blood poisoning had been caused by improper medical treatment. We held that there was no testimony that the miscarriage or the septic condition "was or could have been developed" as the defendant claimed. On the other hand the evidence that was introduced was "sufficient to warrant the finding that the wounds inflicted by the defendant operated as causes of death even though the medical treatment may also have had some causative influence" (*Kane, supra*, at p. 277).

In *Kane* however we observed that if one of the interns at the hospital "had carelessly killed Anna Klein by the negligent administration of a deadly poison, the defendant would not have been liable for her death" (*Kane, supra*, at pp. 270-271). Thus despite the fact that the defendant had inflicted serious wounds, he could not have been convicted if the death was solely attributable to grossly negligent treatment. This often presents a delicate question. Later in the *Kane* opinion, we cited with approval a case (*Commonwealth v. Eisenhower*, 181 Pa. 470) in which the defendant was held liable for homicide although there was evidence that a surgeon operating on the wound forgot to remove a drainage tube which later found its way into the spinal cord "and thus caused death." The Pennsylvania court said that even if this had occurred "the prisoner cannot escape by showing that death was the result of an accident occurring in an operation which his felonious act made necessary."

One of the problems in the case now before us is that there is some question as to whether the operation on the hernia was made necessary by the defendant's act. According to the testimony it was "medically correct," arguably necessary, clearly incidental — but the hernia itself was absolutely unrelated to the stab wound. Dr. Di Maio conceded that the chances were that if it had not been performed, the patient would have survived. This type of necessity is obviously of a different order than is normally required to fix responsibility for homicide. It is, we believe, a factor we must consider in determining whether the causal relationship is sufficiently direct.

The other difficulty in the case is that it was never determined what actually caused the cardiac arrest. Dr. Di Maio acknowledged several possibilities which individually or combined could have created the condition. Most of the factors cited would indicate that the defendant's act was responsible either because it created a physical strain or shock or created the need for an operation which had the same effect. But Dr. Di Maio conceded that there was some evidence that the anesthesiologist failed to provide oxygen to the patient and that this alone could have been the cause of death. In our view if this occurred it was a grave neglect, perhaps gross negligence, but in any event sufficient to break whatever tenuous causal relationship existed at the time of this incidental operation. There is of course no showing that this was in fact the cause of death but on this record it cannot be ruled out as a possibility, certainly not beyond a reasonable doubt.

Finally, it should be noted that this is not a case where two or more witnesses gave conflicting testimony which simply created a credibility question for the jury. Here all the evidence on this point came from a single prosecution witness who offered irreconcilable testimony pointing in both directions to guilt and innocence on the homicide charge. There was then no basis for the jury to find that the injury inflicted by the defendant caused the death of Daniel Smith, beyond a reasonable doubt.

Accordingly, the order of the Appellate Division should be modified by reducing the conviction from manslaughter in the first degree to assault in the first degree (Penal Law § 120.10, subd. 1) and the defendant should be resentenced.

NOTES FROM TOM:

(1) Precisely what facts did the court rely on in holding that the evidence of causation was insufficient? Why? Do we have similar facts in our case?

(2) From the fact that Stewart stabbed Smith, we can infer that he intended that Smith should die. Smith did die. Stewart apparently got what he wanted, so he should be punished for homicide. Why should it matter what happened in the hospital - particularly since Stewart wasn't even there and didn't even know about it? What is this proximate cause nonsense all about, anyway?

(3) In *People v. Vaughn*, 579 N.Y.S.2d 839 (Erie County, 1991), Vaughn stabbed Amelia Robinson in the abdomen, causing severe internal bleeding. Seventy days later, after several operations and infections, her physicians determined that she was beyond medical help and would surely die within 3 to 5 days. Then, while Ms. Robinson was being kept alive by a life support system, a nurse "turned off the ventilator and the drips because somebody had to have the balls to do it." Ms. Robinson then died. Vaughn claimed that his indictment for manslaughter should be dismissed, because the nurse's action was a supervening cause which broke the

chain of causation between his act and Ms. Robinson's death. The court rejected his claim, even assuming that the nurse's act was "malicious."

Has not the law now evolved to that point, where it ought to recognize the injustice to both the victim and to society that results if we continue to require of a jury a finding of superceding causation and to release the perpetrator from a homicide charge upon their finding that an unauthorized "angel of mercy" stepped forward and removed artificial life supports from a mortally wounded crime victim? This Court believes it has. Whether that person should also be deemed to have committed murder (or better, to have committed some yet to be defined crime) should no longer provide escape to the initial perpetrator whose vicious act propelled the victim to certain and extended death and which act, at the time of the victim's release from artificial life supports, continued to be a substantial contribution to that death. What is, therefore, both legally and logically compelling to this Court is that the Defendant Evelyn Vaughn's alleged criminal conduct was the direct competent producing cause of Amelia Robinson's ultimate fate - to lie mortally wounded, irretrievably dying, her moment of death being stayed only by artificial life supports.

(4) In *People v. Velez*, 602 N.Y.S.2d 758 (Bronx County, 1993), Velez shot a cabdriver in the head. While recovering in a hospital, the victim became depressed at his slow progress, pulled out his feeding tubes, and died from lack of nourishment. Citing *Kibbe*, *Stewart*, and *Vaughn*, the court upheld defendant's murder conviction, finding that the gunshot wound was a "sufficiently direct cause" of the victim's death.

This Court concludes that the People have met their burden of proving causation. The victim acted voluntarily in refusing nourishment and medical treatment. However, his inability to ingest food orally was directly caused by the gunshot wound he suffered. The gunshot wound created the difficulty swallowing and the difficulty swallowing prevented him from ingesting food orally. The gunshot wound set in motion a chain of events resulting in hospitalization, difficult swallowing, and forced feeding, the cessation of which resulted in death. The gunshot wound forged a causative link between the initial injury and death and was a sufficiently direct and contributing event which eventually resulted in death. The suicide does not operate as an intervening act that excuses criminal liability because death was not solely attributable to this secondary agency. Death was caused by both the gunshot wound and the malnutrition. Perhaps criminal liability would be excused if the victim had recovered sufficiently to be discharged from the hospital and committed suicide at a more remote time to the initial injury. However, that is not the situation here and this Court is not called upon to answer that question. Here, the People established causation beyond a reasonable doubt.

PEOPLE v. FLORES

New York Supreme Court*, Westchester County

124 Misc.2d 478, 476 N.Y.S.2d 478 (1984)

McMahon, Justice.

The defendant has moved after the close of the People's case for a trial order of dismissal (CPL 290.10(1)). Decision was reserved until the entire case was completed. Defendant stands charged with the crimes of murder in the second degree (2 counts); manslaughter in the second degree; assault in the first degree; robbery in the first degree; burglary in the first degree; grand larceny in the third degree; criminal possession of stolen property in the first degree and second degree; and criminal possession of a weapon in the fourth degree.

These crimes stem from a robbery committed on September 14, 1982 at 12 Kensington Oval and a high-speed chase which occurred during the defendant's immediate flight therefrom.

Here, defendant argues that the People have failed to establish legally sufficient proof that defendant in any way caused the tragic death of Police Officer Gary Pagano and serious physical injury to Sgt. Eric Halbekath (now Lieutenant). The People, while conceding there is no authority directly supporting their position, seek to expand the scope of the felony murder statute and hold the defendant liable for the death and serious injury of the police officers simply because they were pursuing the defendant in his immediate and evasive flight from a robbery.

Penal Law § 125.25(3) provides in part "that a person is guilty of murder in the second degree when in acting alone or with one or more persons, he commits or attempts to commit (a) robbery and in the immediate flight therefrom, he or another participant, if there be any, *causes* the death of a person other than one of the participants." (emphasis added). In effect, the People seek to expand the felony murder statute so as to eliminate the material element of causation. To this, we cannot subscribe. Penal Law § 125.00.

Before a court can submit a charge to the jury, the People must first bring forward legally sufficient trial evidence as to each and every material element of the crime. Where proof falls below this level, then as a matter of law, the court should dismiss the count. CPL 290.10(1).

Alternatively, the People argue that sufficient proof in the nature of circumstantial evidence has been established prima facially. We turn briefly to a discussion of the facts:

Defendant and his accomplice were observed leaving the scene of a robbery at 12 Kensington Oval in a red Dodge van. Information concerning the incident, including the description of the getaway van, was related to police. Officer Pagano received this information while on patrol with Sgt. Eric Halbekath in New Rochelle, and shortly thereafter observed a van fitting this description heading

---

* [Ed. In New York, the Court of Appeals — not the Supreme Court — is the highest court in the state.]

toward the southbound entrance ramp of Interstate 95. The van failed to pull over, entered the highway and a high-speed chase ensued with speeds approaching 90 MPH or more. Defendant eluded his pursuers by blocking, weaving and speeding. Clearly, defendant's manifest intent was to put as much distance as possible between himself and the police car.

Two witnesses also traveling southbound observed a portion of the chase. Each observed the vehicles pass out of sight because of their speed and the fact that the interstate gradually began to curve to the right. At a point within the curve, just inside the Bronx, the witnesses observed a large cloud of dust rise up. Traversing this distance, which took upwards of ten seconds and 1/4 to 1/2 mile, the witnesses came upon the accident involving the police car and an abandoned truck illegally parked on the right and shoulder of the roadway. Police Officer Pagano was killed and Sgt. Halbekath was seriously injured.

The People's reliance on a circumstantial theory of causation is unsupportable, since there is no proof of any physical interaction between the fleeing van and the police car in the ten seconds immediately prior to the accident. No witness saw the crash and there is no evidence of any contact between these vehicles.

In terms of the felony murder statute, these facts, if believed, clearly establish that defendant committed a robbery, and that Police Officer Pagano was killed and Sgt. Halbekath seriously injured while pursuing defendant in the immediate flight therefrom. The remaining element and integral nexus is that of causation.

What act, if any, on defendant's part can fairly be said to have caused the resulting death and injury so as to warrant the imposition of criminal liability? What legal standard applies?

The issue of causation was addressed by the Court of Appeals in *People v. Kibbe*, 35 N.Y.2d 407.[2] There, they held that before criminal liability may be imposed, a defendant's action must be found to be "a sufficiently direct cause of the ensuing death." *Kibbe*, 35 N.Y.2d at page 412. In so holding, they recognized this standard is greater than that required to serve as a basis of tort liability.

For an act to be a sufficiently direct cause, it is not necessary that the ultimate harm be intended by the actor. It will suffice if it can be said, prima facially, that the ultimate harm is something which should have been foreseen as being reasonably related to the acts of the accused. *Kibbe* at page 412.

In other words, to establish legally sufficient trial evidence, the People must show that a defendant committed some act which is a proximate cause of death (irrespective of his intent), and upon evaluating that act, it must be said that death was a reasonably foreseeable and nonaccidental consequence.

From the evidence presented, it can fairly be said that defendant brought into motion a chain of events which eventually led to the death of Police Officer Pagano. High-speed chases by their very nature are inherently dangerous and, accordingly,

---

[2] While this case of homicide was prosecuted under a theory of depraved indifference to human life (P.L. 125.25(2)) the analysis of the proximate causation element is directly relevant with respect to felony murder.

it is reasonably foreseeable that a death could result. This conclusion, however, is supportable only if causation is shown.

Taking the evidence in its best light to the People, as we must on a motion to dismiss, we find that the defendant eluded his pursuers solely by means of defensive tactics, i.e., blocking, weaving and speeding. Accordingly, no affirmative acts on defendant's part can be said to be a "sufficiently direct cause" of the accident being mindful that there was no contact between vehicles.

In addition, there are a number of factors which may be considered as interrupting or superseding the chain of events which defendant set in motion. Among these factors are the condition of the roadway, the condition of the police vehicle and the reasonableness of the pursuit. We consider the reasonableness of pursuit highly significant in light of the Vehicle and Traffic Law § 1104.

That statute, *inter alia*, provides that a driver of an emergency vehicle, when involved in an emergency operation (such as hot pursuit) may "exceed the maximum speed limits so long as he does not endanger life or property." Further, the statute admonishes emergency drivers that they "will not be relieved from the duty to drive with due regard for the safety of all persons, nor shall (this statute) protect the driver from the consequences of his reckless disregard for the safety of others."

Testimony of the expert witness for the People in accident reconstruction, Officer Stephen Coulon, established that in the few seconds before the accident, the police officer never applied his brakes. The vehicle bounced off the center divider yawing and skidding sideways diagonally to the right and striking the abandoned truck on the right shoulder. The precise position of the truck at that point was not foreseeable and was a cause of great damage.

As to the condition of the vehicle and the road surface, the People's expert witness testified that the police vehicle had a partially bald left front tire and the road surface had a "drag factor" of slightly less than average. Since the road surface was dry on the date of the accident, both of these conditions, in the opinion of the expert, had little or no effect on the accident. However, Officer Coulon conceded the tire was below required State standards and maintenance records for the police vehicle reflected a recent complaint the car pulled to the left. This was allegedly corrected.

On these facts, taken in the light most favorable to the People, we hold that prima facie proof with respect to causation by the defendant has not been established. Accordingly, counts one through four of the indictment dealing with felony murder and related crimes are dismissed.

NOTES FROM TOM:

I have trouble squaring this case with *Stewart*. Wasn't what Officer Pagano did (and what the person who illegally parked the truck did) pretty similar to what the doctors did in *Stewart*?

PEOPLE v. RAKUSZ
Supreme Court of New York, New York County
127 Misc.2d 1, 484 N.Y.S.2d 784 (1985)

CRANE, JUSTICE:

This is one of the few non-homicide cases presenting an issue of causation. Defendant is charged under Penal Law § 120.05(3), with assault, second degree: "A person is guilty of assault in the second degree when: * * * 3. With intent to prevent a police officer from performing a lawful duty, he causes physical injury to such police officer."

The Grand Jury testimony pertinent to this charge was that Police Officer Hipple attempted to arrest defendant as a coconspirator in a drug bust. When the officer announced that defendant was under arrest, defendant ran. Hipple pursued, grabbed defendant and struggled with him. During the struggle defendant reached into his jacket pocket. Hipple pulled defendant's arm out of the pocket. Thinking that defendant had a gun, Hipple put his own hand into defendant's jacket pocket cutting himself on a serrated kitchen knife resting there.

Other than his resisting arrest, there is nothing defendant himself did to cut the officer with the knife. Therefore, I asked the parties to address the issue of causation. No case drawn to my attention resolves this issue. The case these facts most closely approach is *People v. Wheeler*, 317 N.Y.S.2d 111 (1971).[1] There, the defendant attempted to escape from custody. The officer tried to recapture him but fell to the ground injuring his wrist and knee. If the facts ended there Wheeler would be comparable to the case at bar. But, in Wheeler the pursuit continued, and in the struggle defendant's feet struck the officer causing further injuries. At bar, none of defendant Rakusz's actions directly injured Hipple in a similar fashion.

Thus, we must assess whether defendant's attempt to put his hand in his pocket - indeed his success in doing so — to which Officer Hipple reacted by placing his own hand in that pocket, was a cause of injury for which defendant is criminally responsible.

In the murder context, it has been said that the defendant's conduct must be an actual cause "in the sense that it forged a link in the chain of causes which actually brought about the death." *People v. Stewart*, 40 N.Y.2d 692, 697. It has also been held that the defendant's conduct must be a sufficiently direct cause for criminal liability to attach; that this is a greater standard than exists for mere tort liability; and that the ultimate harm must have been foreseeable. *People v. Kibbe*, 35 N.Y.2d 407.

In the case at bar, defendant's actions were not the direct cause of injury because the officer's own action in going into the defendant's pocket, though reactive to defendant's efforts in that direction, was the direct, intervening cause of his own injury. Yet, by requiring a cause to be direct, the law does not rule out such

---

[1] That court affirmed a conviction after trial for assault, second degree, and rejected an argument that the People had failed to prove causation beyond a reasonable doubt.

interventions. Most recently illustrating this principle, the Court of Appeals upheld convictions where defendants' criminal conduct brought on cardiac problems resulting in death. *Matter of Anthony M.*, 63 N.Y.2d 270. Judge Kaye, writing for the court on this point, rejected arguments that causation was inadequately established:

> For criminal liability to attach, a defendant's actions must have been an actual contributory cause of death. A defendant's acts need not be the sole cause of death; where the necessary causative link is established, other causes, such as a victim's preexisting condition, will not relieve the defendant of responsibility for homicide. By the same token, death need not follow on the heels of injury. Even an intervening, independent agency will not exonerate defendant unless "the death is solely attributable to the secondary agency, and not at all induced by the primary one," but that is not to say that a victim who evidences no immediate decline cannot just as surely have been set by defendant's acts on a certain course to death. To establish a causal connection, conclusions which are only "contingent, speculative, or merely possible" will not suffice, but neither is absolute certainty and the exclusion of every other possibility required. [*Id.* at 280-281]

See also *People v. Lozano*, 434 N.Y.S.2d 588 (Sup.Ct., N.Y.County, 1980) (sustaining the sufficiency of an indictment for felony murder of a fireman who suffered a fatal heart attack while responding to a fire that defendant had set in his mother's apartment).

Another approach to the problem of divining whether an effect has been caused by a defendant was suggested by Professor Paul K. Ryu in "Causation in Criminal Law," 106 U.Pa.L.Rev. 773 (1958). It was his thesis that the purpose of the legal provision governing the particular crime ought to determine what test to apply in assessing causation. Clearly, Penal Law § 120.05(3) was intended as a deterrent to those who would interfere with the performance by police officers of their lawful duties and as a special protection to these guardians of public safety. *People v. Praetz*, 445 N.Y.S.2d 50 (1981).

Returning our attention to the case at bar, we can now answer whether defendant is prima facie criminally responsible for Police Officer Hipple's physical injury. Defendant did nothing directly with the instrument that inflicted the injury. If he had, there would obviously have been causation. On the opposite end of the spectrum, defendant could scarcely be held criminally responsible had the injury occurred during a frisk after the defendant had been subdued and cuffed. This would in no way have occurred in the course of his resisting arrest and would be a result beyond the protective policy of Penal Law § 120.05(3). Indeed, it would have been a result uninfluenced by any action initiated by defendant.

The facts at bar fall between these extremes. Defendant, during his resistance, attempted to place his hand in his pocket. I conclude that it was foreseeable that Officer Hipple would try to prevent him from extracting a weapon from that pocket. Among the foreseeable ways in which Officer Hipple would bend his efforts was that the officer would place his own hand in the pocket during the struggle. Therefore, it cannot be said that Officer Hipple's intervening conduct, instigated as it was by defendant's action, was the sole cause of his injury so as to relieve defendant of criminal responsibility.

The motion to dismiss the assault count of Indictment No. 3815/84 is denied.

NOTES FROM TOM:

(1) The court mentioned *People v. Lozano*, 434 N.Y.S.2d 588 (Sup.Ct., N.Y.County, 1980). There, Lozano committed arson by starting a fire in his mother's apartment. Fireman Donald Bub collapsed and died while stretching a fire hose.

> Dr. Josette J. Montas of the office of the Chief Medical Examiner testified as to the autopsy performed on the deceased. There was no unusual medical finding other than in the area of the heart. The heart was enlarged and there was evidence of arteriosclerosis of the coronary arteries which are the blood vessels to the heart. This "hardening of the arteries" indicated to the doctor that Fireman Bub had progressive heart disease over a period of time, although there was no scarring which would be evidence of a prior heart attack. In addition, there was a relatively fresh occlusion of the lumen of the right coronary artery and evidence of hemorrhage which was the immediate cause of the heart attack. Further, there was some carbon monoxide in the victim's system. The conclusion as to the cause of death was occlusive coronary arteriosclerosis and thrombosis together with smoke inhalation. The Medical Examiner testified that while there was no way of ascertaining whether Fireman Bub would have had a fatal heart attack had he been otherwise engaged, even resting at home at the time, it was also Dr. Montas' opinion that the exertion expended by Bub and his inhalation of carbon monoxide could be said "with a reasonable degree of medical certainty" to have contributed to the occurrence and severity of the heart attack.

The court held that there was sufficient evidence to find Lozano guilty of felony murder:

> That Fireman Bub had a previous weakened heart is of no legal consequence. The fact that a victim is particularly vulnerable does not exempt the perpetrator from responsibility. Firemen are in a constant state of vulnerability. They are subject to death from flames, smoke, falling beams, collapsing walls, and failing ropes. That a heart should fail is manifestly foreseeable. That Fireman Bub might have met a similar fate from natural or accidental fires does not insulate the arsonist against homicide liability for the fire deliberately ignited. The evidence before the grand jury establishes a direct spatiotemporal nexus between the fire and the death sufficient to warrant holding the defendant for a trial by jury on the charge of murder.

(2) Can *Rakusz* be reconciled with *Stewart* and *Flores*?

PEOPLE v. GALLE
New York Court of Appeals
77 N.Y.2d 953, 573 N.E.2d 569 (1991)

Defendant was convicted of criminally negligent homicide (Penal Law § 125.10),[*] based upon his having twice injected his girlfriend with cocaine on the night she died from a drug overdose. On appeal, he contends that his conviction should be reversed and the indictment against him dismissed on the ground that the evidence introduced at his trial was legally insufficient to support the jury's guilty verdict. We cannot agree.

The proof adduced at trial demonstrated that, on the night in question, defendant injected the decedent with her first two doses of cocaine, knowing full well that she planned to continue taking injections that evening until their relatively substantial supply of that drug had been exhausted. Although the decedent subsequently administered her own injections, including the one which immediately preceded her death, an expert witness called by the People testified that each of the injections, including the two given to the decedent by defendant, was a contributing cause of her death.

Viewing this evidence in a light most favorable to the People, we conclude that the jury could have reasonably found that defendant's actions were a "sufficiently direct cause" of death to subject him to criminal liability. *People v. Kibbe*, 35 N.Y.2d 407. Contrary to defendant's contention, the "ultimate harm" here was something which he should have, under the circumstances, plainly "foreseen as being reasonably related to his acts." *People v. Kibbe*, 35 N.Y.2d 407, 412; *People v. Stewart*, 40 N.Y.2d 692, 697.

We likewise disagree with defendant's assertion that the People failed to prove, as a matter of law, that he acted with criminal negligence. Viewing the evidence, as we must, in a light most favorable to the prosecution, we conclude that the jury could have rationally found that defendant, by intravenously administering cocaine to the decedent when he knew that she intended to continue taking injections of that drug throughout the night, had created "a substantial and unjustifiable risk" that his actions would contribute to her death, and that this "risk was of such nature and degree that defendant's failure to perceive it constituted a gross deviation from the standard of care that a reasonable person would observe in the situation" Penal Law § 15.05[4]; § 125.10.

PEOPLE v. DUFFY
New York Court of Appeals
79 N.Y.2d 611 (1992)

TITONE, JUDGE.

This appeal calls upon us to address two related questions: whether a person may be convicted of second degree manslaughter for engaging in reckless conduct

---

[*] Defendant was also convicted of criminal injection of a narcotic drug (Penal Law § 220.46).

which results in another person's committing suicide and, if so, whether the conduct of the defendant in this case was a sufficiently direct cause of the victim's death to support his conviction. For the reasons that follow, we conclude that both these questions should be answered in the affirmative.

I.

According to the evidence adduced below, Jason Schuhle — a 17-year-old youth — met defendant on a street in the Village of McGraw, New York, during the early morning hours of August 6, 1988. Schuhle — who, at the time, was extremely distraught over having recently broken-up with his girlfriend — immediately imparted to defendant his desire to kill himself. At defendant's invitation, Schuhle then accompanied him back to defendant's apartment. There, for approximately the next half hour or so, Schuhle — who had been drinking heavily — continued to express suicidal thoughts and repeatedly importuned defendant to shoot him. In response to these entreaties, defendant provided Schuhle with some more alcohol and challenged him several times to jump headfirst off the porch of his second-story apartment. Finally, defendant — who later explained to the police that he was "tired" of hearing Schuhle complain about wanting to die — told Schuhle that he had a gun which he could use to kill himself. Defendant then retrieved a British .303 caliber Enfield rifle from his gun cabinet, and handed it to Schuhle, along with a number of bullets. He then urged Schuhle to "put the gun in his mouth and blow his head off." Moments later, Schuhle loaded the rifle, pointed the barrel at himself and pulled the trigger. He later died as a result of the massive injuries he suffered.

Defendant was thereafter indicted for two counts of manslaughter in the second degree. The first count alleged that he had intentionally caused or aided Schuhle in committing suicide (see Penal Law § 125.15[3]), and the second alleged that he had recklessly caused Schuhle's death (see Penal Law § 125.15[1]). After a jury trial, defendant was acquitted of the first count but convicted of the second.

On appeal, however, the Appellate Division reversed and dismissed the indictment. * * * *

II.

At the outset, we note that the conduct with which defendant was charged clearly fell within the scope of 6125.15(1)'s proscription against recklessly causing the death of another person. As the People aptly observe, a person who, knowing that another is contemplating immediate suicide, deliberately prods that person to go forward and furnishes the means of bringing about death may certainly be said to have "consciously disregarded a substantial and unjustifiable risk" that his actions would result in the death of that person (see Penal Law § 15.05[3]; § 125.15[1]). * * * *

III.

Having concluded that a person may be convicted of second degree manslaughter for having engaged in reckless conduct which results in another person's committing suicide, we now turn to the question whether defendant's conduct here was a "sufficiently direct cause" of Schuhle's death to subject him to criminal liability. Defendant, stressing the fact that it was Schuhle — not he — who loaded the rifle and pulled the trigger, urges us to answer this question in the negative. We find defendant's argument to be unpersuasive.

Generally speaking, a person will not be held criminally accountable for engaging in conduct which results in another person's death unless it can be demonstrated that his actions were "an actual contributory cause of death, in the sense that they 'forged a link in the chain of causes which actually brought about the death" '. *People v. Stewart*, 40 N.Y.2d 692, 697. The proof adduced below, when viewed in a light most favorable to the People, indicates that defendant gave Schuhle a rifle and a number of rounds of ammunition knowing full well that Schuhle had been drinking heavily and was in an extremely depressed and suicidal state, and that he then began taunting Schuhle to "put the gun in his mouth and blow his head off." In light of this evidence, we must disagree with defendant that Schuhle's act of loading the rifle and using it to kill himself constituted an intervening cause which — as a matter of law — relieved defendant of criminal responsibility. The jury could rationally have concluded that the risk of Schuhle's taking these actions was something which defendant should have, under the circumstances, plainly foreseen. *People v. Kibbe*, 35 N.Y.2d 407, 412. There is therefore no basis, on this Court's review, to disturb the jury's verdict.

Accordingly, the order of the Appellate Division should be reversed and the case remitted to that court for consideration of the facts.

NOTES FROM TOM:

1. In *Galle* and in *Duffy*, the victim did something *after* the defendant's act which was extremely reckless and was a causal factor leading to the victim's death. Didn't *Stewart* hold that subsequent extreme recklessness (or gross negligence) lets the defendant off the hook? Aren't these two cases inconsistent with *Stewart*?

2. In *Bonhart v. U.S.*, 691 A.2d 160 (D.C. 1997), Bonhart set fire to Della's home to punish Della for failing to pay a drug debt. Della escaped, but returned to try to rescue his dog, whereupon Della was burned to death. The court held that Bonhart was responsible for Della's death:

> Even if the government proves that the commission of the felony actually caused the killing, a legal cause defense is available if an extraordinary intervening event supersedes the defendant's act and becomes the sole legal cause of the result. If this extraordinary event is the victim's own response to the circumstances that the defendant created, the victim's reaction must be an abnormal one in order to supersede the defendant's act. Therefore, the question here is whether Della's response was abnormal if he reentered his burning apartment building to save his dog's life.
>
> This question admits of only one answer, because the impulse to protect one's personal property from a fire is generally recognized to be normal and ordinary rather than abnormal and extraordinary. Experience teaches us that even if one's dwelling is burning, it is quite common for a person to

reenter it to try to rescue property. This normal human instinct to rescue can be especially pronounced when an animal's life is at stake.* * * *

We conclude that even if Della voluntarily and deliberately reentered the building, this course of conduct is so natural and commonplace a reaction that it cannot constitute a legal cause of Della's death superseding Bonhart's felonious act of setting the fire.

PEOPLE v. MATOS
New York Court of Appeals
83 N.Y.2d 509 (1994)

CIPARICK, J.

The issue to be considered in this appeal is under what circumstances a fleeing felon's actions cause another's death for purposes of Penal Law § 125.25 (3), the felony murder statute.

There was evidence at trial that, in the early morning hours of October 17, 1989, defendant, Eddic Matos, and two accomplices broke into a McDonald's restaurant on Seventh Avenue and 40th Street in Manhattan by shattering the glass door with a sledgehammer. Once inside, Matos and his accomplices rounded up the employees at gunpoint. A maintenance worker, however, managed to escape and then returned to the restaurant with three police officers. As they approached the restaurant, they saw Matos run toward the back of the restaurant. The officers ran into the restaurant in time to see Matos climb up a ladder that led to the roof. Police Officer Dwyer hurriedly climbed up the ladder right behind Matos. About 10 seconds later, another officer, Sergeant Flanagan, proceeded up the ladder to the roof and later discovered Dwyer lying on his back about 25 feet down an airshaft. It took emergency services personnel about 45 minutes to rescue Dwyer from the airshaft, but he was later pronounced dead at Bellevue Hospital.

The Appellate Division affirmed the conviction of murder in the second degree, burglary in the second degree and attempted robbery. The Court concluded that the elements of felony murder were established. A Judge of this Court granted leave to appeal and we now affirm.

It is well established that in order for criminal responsibility to attach, a defendant's actions must have been an actual contributory cause of death (People v. Stewart, 40 NY2d 692, 697). It must be shown that the defendant sets in motion the events which ultimately result in the victim's death *(People v. Kibbe*, 35 NY2d 407). However, the defendant's acts need not be the sole cause of death.

Here, defendant's conduct set in motion and legally caused the death of Police Officer Dwyer. Had defendant not first committed an armed violent felony and then attempted to escape by way of the roof, the officer would not have pursued him onto the roof, thereafter plunging to his death in the airshaft.

The trial court stressed to the jury that "but for" causation was only one step in determining cause in the criminal context, an aspect defendant-appellant does not dispute. Additionally, the jury was told that it must also find that defendant's conduct was a sufficiently direct cause of the ensuing death before it could impose criminal responsibility. The defendant's conduct qualifies as a sufficiently direct cause when the ultimate harm should have been reasonably foreseen *(People v. Kibbe*, 35 NY2d, at 412, *supra)*.

The accused need not commit the final, fatal act to be culpable for causing death. In *Kibbe*, the fatal act was inflicted by a passing truck driver who struck and killed the victim. The defendants were held to have caused his death, for the event was a directly foreseeable consequence of their own earlier act of abandoning the victim on the shoulder of a highway. In *People v. Kern* (75 NY2d 638), the "Howard Beach" defendants were held to have caused their victim's death even though he was actually killed by the intervening act of a passing motorist.

In *People v. Hernandez* (82 NY2d 309), this Court held that the defendants initiated or participated in the chain of events that led to an officer's death by attempting to rob an undercover officer in a failed drug transaction. Since, in initiating a gun battle, they should have foreseen that someone's bullet might go astray, their conduct was a sufficiently direct cause of a backup officer's death even though the shot which killed him was fired by another officer. The Court held that "immediate flight and attempts to thwart apprehension are patently within the furtherance of the cofelons' criminal objective." The Court further noted that foreseeability does not mean that the result must be the most likely event.

In the instant case, the jury was correctly given the issue as to whether it was foreseeable that upon defendant's attempt to escape by way of the roof, he would be pursued by an officer. In those circumstances it should also be foreseeable that someone might fall while in hot pursuit across urban roofs in the middle of the night.

Accordingly, the order of the Appellate Division should be affirmed.

What is a "defense" to a criminal charge? A "defense" is commonly understood to mean the same thing as an "affirmative defense" in a civil case: it *assumes* (but does not *concede*) that all the allegations of the complaint (or indictment or information) are true, but makes *new* allegations which — if believed — would show that the defendant is nevertheless not liable or guilty. "Even if everything you say about me is true, I'm still not guilty, because _____ ."

Thus, if an indictment alleges that Dan committed murder by intentionally killing Vic, Dan might assert the defense of self-defense: "Even if I *did* intentionally kill him, I did it to prevent Vic from killing me."

Note that if Dan claims an *alibi* ("Someone killed Vic, but *it wasn't me* — I was in another city"), that is *not* a "defense," as it does *not* assume that all of the allegations in the indictment are true. Dan is merely presenting evidence that tends to *negate* one of the prosecution's allegations — the one that says that Dan killed Vic. The same is true if Dan claims that he killed Vic accidentally (i.e., he negates the allegation that he had an intent to kill). This is "negation evidence."

Is this difference between a "defense" and "negation evidence" mere semantics, or does it matter?

It matters. Generally, the defendant has the burden of producing evidence and/or the burden of proof as to any *defense*, while the prosecution retains the burden of proving all allegations in the indictment or information.

So, if Dan claims an alibi, the judge will instruct the jury that the prosecution has the burden of disproving the alibi — beyond a reasonable doubt. Why? Because the indictment alleged that Dan was the killer, and the prosecution therefore has the burden of proving beyond a reasonable doubt that Dan was the killer — and the fact that Dan presents evidence that he was *not* the killer does not change this. So, if a prosecution witness testifies that she saw Dan kill Vic, and Dan testifies that he wasn't there, the jury should not convict unless they decide "beyond a reasonable doubt" that the prosecution witness — and not Dan — is telling the truth.

On the other hand, to allege the elements of murder, the indictment *need not* allege that Dan did *not* act in self-defense, was *not* insane, did *not* act under duress, etc. — and the prosecution has no obligation to prove these negatives. If Dan wants to claim one of these things, he'll have to raise it as a *defense* and introduce evidence supporting that defense. And then — in some jurisdictions — the judge will instruct the jury that *Dan* has the burden of proving that defense (usually by "a preponderance of the evidence"). In other jurisdictions, the judge will instruct the jury that the prosecution has the burden of disproving the defense beyond a reasonable doubt.

What "defenses" are recognized by the law? That is the subject of this Part.

Chapter 12

INSANITY, INCOMPETENCE, AND DIMINISHED CAPACITY

In a majority of the jurisdictions in this country, what is most often referred to as the *M'Naughten* rule has long been accepted as the test to be applied for the defense of insanity. Under *M'Naughten*, an accused is not criminally responsible if, at the time of committing the act, he was laboring under such a defect of reason, from disease of the mind, as not to know the nature and quality of the act he was doing, or if he did know it that he did not know he was doing what was wrong.

LaFave & Scott, *Criminal Law* (West).

Under the Model Penal Code test [also known as the American Law Institute, or ALI, test], followed in a substantial minority of the states, a person is not responsible for criminal conduct if, as a result of mental disease or defect . . . he lacks substantial capacity either to appreciate the criminality (wrongfulness) of his conduct or to conform his conduct to the requirements of law.

LaFave & Scott, *Criminal Law* (West).

Incompetency at Time of Criminal Proceedings. If a defendant is suffering from a mental disease or defect which renders him unable to understand the proceedings against him or to assist in his defense, he may not be tried, convicted, or sentenced so long as that condition persists. Rather, he is ordinarily committed to a mental institution until such time as he recovers.

LaFave & Scott, *Criminal Law* (West).

Insanity is a "defense" under the above description of defenses. It is not "negation evidence." Suppose Dan is charged with larceny of Vic's hat, and he claims that because of his mental illness, he believed that the hat was his own, and therefore he had no intent to steal. This would not be a *defense*, but it would be *negation evidence* — it negates the prosecution's evidence of the *mens rea* required for larceny (intent to steal). But if Dan claims that he knew he was taking Vic's hat but did so because his mental illness led him to believe that the devil ordered him to steal the hat, he is not negating any element of the crime charged. If we hear Dan's claim, we must hear it as a defense or not at all. And the only defense that might apply here is the insanity defense.

Why allow *any* insanity defense? We should answer this question before we can decide *which* test for insanity to adopt.

Everyone has problems. Every criminal defendant can point to some deficiency in intelligence, personality, or moral training that contributed to ("caused"?) his crime. Most can point to a history of poverty, poor education, and broken homes. Many have been beaten by family members, abused drugs, or suffered psychological abuse.

Should these problems excuse criminal conduct? Most people would say, "No. I sympathize with these defendants, but they have to learn to control their behavior anyway. Otherwise, we just have anarchy. And many people with similar problems *don't* commit crimes."

But isn't this true of the "insane"? Mentally ill people *can* control their behavior — to some extent. They respond to discipline imposed by hospital administrators ("No dessert unless you stop yelling"). And most mentally ill people do *not* commit crimes.

So what is different about insanity? Why do we allow an *insanity* defense, and *not* allow a defense of "persistent poverty," "chronic stupidity," or "impoverished moral upbringing"? Consider this question as you read the cases in this Chapter. If you can think of *reasons* to allow an insanity defense, do these reasons dictate *which people should qualify* for the insanity defense, i.e., how we should *define* "insanity"? You might get some help by taking another look at the *purposes of punishment* discussed at the end of Chapter 1, and thinking about how they apply to the question of whether and how to allow an insanity defense.

While reading this Chapter, there are a couple of peculiarities to watch out for.

First, do not confuse the *insanity defense* with *incompetency to stand trial*. The purposes of these two rules are very different, and therefore the test for each is different. These are discussed in the statutes and cases in this Chapter (and in the above quotations from LaFave & Scott).

Second, the insanity defense is raised in an unusual way and — if successful — leads to an unusual result. To raise self defense, duress, or any other defense discussed in the Part, the defendant need only plead "not guilty." If the jury accepts this defense, the defendant is free to go home. To raise an insanity defense, however, the defendant must plead "not guilty by reason of insanity." If the jury accepts this defense, the defendant is then sent to a mental hospital, where he must stay until he is well and no longer dangerous. This is not as pleasant as going home, but perhaps it is better than prison — or maybe at least better than having the moral stigma of a criminal conviction.

Suppose the defendant has *both* a conventional defense (or negation evidence) *and* an insanity defense. May be assert *both*? Yes. He may, if he wishes, plead *both* "not guilty" and "not guilty by reason of insanity." But if both of these issues are raised in a single trial, the jury might reject a valid conventional defense (or valid negation evidence) and accept the insanity defense — simply to ensure that the defendant is locked up. They might not want to return a mentally ill person to the streets. To stop the jury from doing this, we give the defendant a *bifurcated trial*.

Phase #1 is the "guilt" phase, where the prosecution must prove all elements of the crime and the defendant may raise any defense other than insanity and may present any negation evidence. If the jury acquits at the end of Phase #1, the case is *over*: there is no Phase #2. But if the jury convicts at the end of Phase #1, then Phase #2 — the "insanity" phase — is held. (And in a death penalty case, there might even be a Phase #3 — the *penalty* Phase — resulting in a *trifurcated* trial.)

In Phase #1, the prosecution must prove, of course, whatever *mens rea* is required for the crime charged. May an ingenious defense attorney present evidence *negating* this *mens rea* by showing that — because of his mental illness — the defendant could not form the required mental state? If we allow this and the jury accepts this negation evidence, then the defendant might be convicted of a lesser crime (i.e., he has a "diminished capacity"), and he might even be *acquitted* — he will go home, and not face Phase #2 and the possibility of being forced into a mental institution! Does this result defeat the whole point of the insanity defense and the bifurcated trial: to ensure that defendants who are both mentally ill and dangerous are put in a mental hospital until they are well? This Chapter will consider that problem too.

PROBLEM 12

To: My law clerk

From: Wally Flower

Re: *People v. Loco*

My client, Louie Loco, has been charged with larceny, robbery, and first degree murder. I had a psychiatrist, Dr. Sigmund Meshuga, interview Louie. After he finished, I met with Dr. Meshuga. Attached is a transcript of our meeting. Also attached is a transcript of the police interrogation of Louie, during the evening after the robbery. Please read these and the attached authorities, and advise me as to how we get the best disposition for Louie. If there are any additional questions I should ask Dr. Meshuga, please advise.

Transcript of Meeting With Psychiatrist

F: Did Louie tell you what he did?

M: Yes, in our first interview. He said that a voice in his head told him that the Bank of America was owned by the Devil, and that all the money in the bank belonged to Louie. The voice commanded him to go and take back his money, and to shoot whoever was keeping his money. He felt that he had to obey the voice, so he then went to a Bank of America branch in San Diego, with a gun. He ordered the teller to give him all her cash, and she did. He then shot her and ran out of the bank with the money. The teller died.

F: Did you check Louie's medical history?

M: Yes. He's had a long history of mental illness, and has spent considerable time in mental hospitals. Other doctors have diagnosed him as paranoid schizophrenic, subject to delusions and prone to violence. I agree.

F: Did he rob the bank because he needed the money?

M: I don't think so. Patients with delusions, like Louie, usually don't base their decisions on such practical things.

F: Was Louie able to premeditate the killing?

M: No, not in any real sense. He was in a different world, mentally. He knew killing was against the law, but he couldn't premeditate, and he didn't premeditate.

F: Was he insane?

M: Yes, he was.

F: Did you interview Louie a second time?

M: Yes, about a month after the first interview. In the second interview, he couldn't remember a thing about the incident at the bank. I think he's now blocked it out. With some extensive treatment, we might be able to help him remember.

F: Did you consult any other psychiatrists about this case?

M: Yes. I spoke to Dr. Young and Dr. Attler. Both totally agree with my diagnosis. I doubt that any reputable psychiatrist would disagree.

Transcript of Police Interrogation of Louie Loco

T: [Advice of *Miranda* rights, which Loco waived]. Louie, I'm Detective Richard Tracy. Why did you rob the bank?

L: I had been thinking about money, because I had lost my job and was behind in my rent. That morning, a voice in my head told me that the Devil owned the Bank of America, and they had my money. The voice ordered me to go get my money and shoot the people who had it.

T: Had you ever heard this voice before?

L: Yes, lots of times. Once I even saw it, when I was smoking marijuana. It was a pookah.

T: A what?

L: A pookah. It looks like a big rabbit. No one could see it, except me.

T: What did you do after the voice told you to get the money?

L: I went to the downtown San Diego branch of the bank and looked it over. I saw that they had only one guard, who was half-asleep. I went home and got my gun. I came back and held up the bank.

T: Did you know it was wrong to shoot the teller?

L: Sure. Everyone knows it's wrong to kill people. But I had no choice.

T: When did you decide to shoot the teller?

L: I guess when I was at home that morning, when the voice told me to. But I didn't really think about it. I just kind of acted automatically after I heard the voice. The teller gave me a nasty look after she gave me the money. Then I shot her.

T: What happened next?

L: I ran out of the bank. When I got to the sidewalk, I got into a crowd of people and blended into them. I ditched the gun in a trash can, and I took the money home. I guess someone saw me, because the police arrested me an hour later.

California Penal Code

Section 25. Diminished Capacity; Insanity

(a) The defense of diminished capacity is hereby abolished. In a criminal action, as well as any juvenile court proceeding, evidence concerning an accused person's intoxication, trauma, mental illness, disease, or defect shall not be admissible to show or negate capacity to form the particular purpose, intent, motive, malice aforethought, knowledge, or other mental state required for the commission of the crime charged.

(b) In any criminal proceeding, including any juvenile court proceeding, in which a plea of not guilty by reason of insanity is entered, this defense shall be found by the trier of fact only when the accused person proves by a preponderance of the evidence that he or she was incapable of knowing or understanding the nature and quality of his or her act and of distinguishing right from wrong at the time of the commission of the offense.

(c) Notwithstanding the foregoing, evidence of diminished capacity or of a mental disorder may be considered by the court only at the time of sentencing or other disposition or commitment.

(d) The provisions of this section shall not be amended by the Legislature except by statute passed in each house by rollcall vote entered in the journal, two-thirds of the membership concurring, or by a statute that becomes effective only when approved by the electors.

[Enacted by initiative in 1982]

Section 28. Evidence of Mental Disease; Defense of Diminished Capacity

(a) Evidence of mental disease, mental defect, or mental disorder shall not be admitted to show or negate the capacity to form any mental state, including, but not limited to, purpose, intent, knowledge, premeditation, deliberation, or malice aforethought, with which the accused committed the act. Evidence of mental disease, mental defect, or mental disorder is admissible solely on the issue of whether or not the accused actually formed a required specific intent, premeditated, deliberated, or harbored malice aforethought, when a specific intent crime is charged.

(b) As a matter of public policy there shall be no defense of diminished capacity, diminished responsibility, or irresistible impulse in a criminal action or juvenile adjudication hearing.

* * * *

[Enacted by the Legislature in 1981]

Section 29. Expert Testimony About Mental Illness

In the guilt phase of a criminal action, any expert testifying about a defendant's mental illness, mental disorder, or mental defect shall not testify as to whether the defendant had or did not have the required mental states, which include, but are not limited to, purpose, intent, knowledge, or malice aforethought, for the crimes charged. The question as to whether the defendant had or did not have the required mental states shall be decided by the trier of fact.

[Enacted by the Legislature in 1981, and reenacted by a two-thirds vote of the Legislature in 1984]

Section 1026. Procedure on Plea of Not Guilty Because Insane

(a) When a defendant pleads not guilty by reason of insanity, and also joins with it another plea or pleas, the defendant shall first be tried as if only such other plea or pleas had been entered, and in that trial the defendant shall be conclusively presumed to have been sane at the time the offense is alleged to have been committed. If the jury shall find the defendant guilty, or if the defendant pleads only not guilty by reason of insanity, then the question whether the defendant was sane or insane at the time the offense was committed shall be promptly tried, either before the same jury or before a new jury in the discretion of the court. In that trial, the jury shall return a verdict either that the defendant was sane at the time the offense was committed or was insane at the time the offense was committed. If the verdict or finding is that the defendant was sane at the time the offense was committed, the court shall sentence the defendant as provided by law. If the verdict of finding be that the defendant was insane at the time the offense was committed, the court, unless it shall appear to the court that the sanity of the defendant has been recovered fully, shall direct that the defendant be confined in a state hospital for the care and treatment of the mentally disordered. * * * *

[Enacted by the Legislature in 1927 (with subsequent minor amendments)]

Section 1026.1. Release From State Hospital or Other Treatment Facility

A person committed to a state hospital or other treatment facility under the provisions of § 1026 shall be released . . . only under one or more of the following circumstances:

(a) Pursuant to the provisions of § 1026.2 [which permits the court to release the person upon finding that sanity has been restored and that the person would no longer be a danger to the health and safety of others, including himself or herself].

(b) Upon expiration of the maximum term [of imprisonment for the crime(s) the person was found guilty of committing], [unless the director of the facility petitions and convinces the court that the defendant represents a substantial danger of physical harm to others].

[Enacted by the Legislature in 1980, amended in 1984]

Section 1367. Mentally Incompetent Person; Effect of Incompetency

(a) A person cannot be tried or adjudged to punishment while such person is mentally incompetent. A defendant is mentally incompetent for purposes of this chapter if, as a result of mental disorder or developmental disability, the defendant is unable to understand the nature of the criminal proceedings or to assist counsel in the conduct of a defense in a rational manner. * * * *

[Enacted by the Legislature in 1872, with subsequent minor amendments.]

NOTES:

(1) Sections 1368-1375.5 give the defendant the right to a jury trial on the issue of his competency to stand trial, provide that — if found incompetent — he shall be sent to a treatment facility until he is competent (but no longer than the maximum term for the most serious charge against him), and that he receive a credit for time served in the treatment facility against any sentence later imposed on him in the case.

(2) Compare these statutes to Model Penal Code §§ 4.01 through 4.08, in the Appendix.

PEOPLE v. WOLFF
California Supreme Court
61 Cal.2d 795, 394 P.2d 959 (1964)

SCHAUER, J.

Defendant appeals from a judgment imposing a sentence of life imprisonment (with recommendation that he be placed in a hospital for the criminally insane). After he pleaded not guilty by reason of insanity to a charge of murder, the jury found that he was legally sane at the time of the commission of the offense, and the court determined the killing to be murder in the first degree.

Defendant contends that the evidence is insufficient to support the verdict of sanity, that the court gave conflicting instructions on the presumptions of sanity and of the continuance of prior "permanent" insanity, and that his crime should have been determined to be second degree rather than first degree murder. Upon a comprehensive view of all the evidence, we have concluded that the first two of these contentions are without merit, but that the judgment should be reduced to murder of the second degree.

Defendant, a 15-year-old boy at the time of the crime, was charged with the murder of his mother. The juvenile court found him to be "not a fit subject for consideration" under the Juvenile Court Law, and remanded him to the superior court for further proceedings in the criminal action. To the information accusing him of murder, defendant entered the single plea of "not guilty by reason of insanity," thereby admitting commission of the basic act which, if not qualified under the special plea, constitutes the offense charged. Pen. Code § 1016.

After considering reports of three alienists appointed to examine defendant (Pen. Code § 1027) the court declared a doubt as to his mental capacity to stand trial (§ 1368 et seq.). At a hearing on that issue, however, the court found defendant to be "mentally ill but not to the degree that would preclude him from cooperation with his counsel in the preparation and presentation of his defense." The plea of not guilty by reason of insanity was then tried to a jury and resulted in a verdict that defendant was legally sane at the time of the commission of the jurisdictional act of killing.

Defendant's motion for new trial on the ground of insufficiency of the evidence was heard and denied, and by stipulation the question of the degree of the crime was submitted to the court on the basis of the evidence introduced at the trial and the report of the probation officer. The court determined the crime to be murder in the first degree; sentenced defendant to life imprisonment; and to the judgment added, "Placement in hospital for criminally insane recommended."

The California M'Naughton Rule

On the issue of insanity, the jury were instructed in terms of the California rule; i.e., the so-called *M'Naughton* rule, as that rule has been developed by statute and decision in California. In hereinafter discussing and ruling upon the sufficiency of the evidence to support the finding (a) that defendant was legally sane and (b) that the murder was of the first degree, the liberality of the California rule, and the sometimes dual materiality (where the crime is divided into degrees) of evidence admitted thereunder, will become apparent.

The original *M'Naughton* language from which the California rule has been evolved is set out in the margin.[1] Under that language, a mentally ill defendant could be found sane even though his "knowledge" of the nature or wrongfulness of his act was merely a capacity to verbalize the "right" (i.e., socially expected) answers to questions put to him relating to that act, without such "knowledge" having any affective meaning for him as a principle of conduct. Such a narrow, literal reading of the *M'Naughton* formula has been repeatedly and justly condemned. 2 Stephen, *History of the Criminal Law of England* (1883) pp.170-171; Weihofen, *Mental Disorder as a Criminal Defense* (1954) pp. 76-77; Hall, *General Principles of Criminal Law* (2d ed. 1960) pp. 481, 494, 520; Diamond, *Criminal Responsibility of the Mentally Ill* (1961); Glueck, *Law and Psychiatry* (1962) p. 49, fn. 14. Rather, it is urged by many that the word "know" as used in the formula be given "a wider definition so that it means the kind of knowing that is relevant, i.e., realization or appreciation of the wrongness of seriously harming a human being" (Hall, op. cit. supra, at p. 520).

---

[1] "To establish a defence on the ground of insanity, it must be clearly proved that, at the time of committing the act, the party accused was labouring under such a defect of reason, from disease of the mind, as not to know the nature and quality of the act he was doing; or, if he did know it, that he did not know he was doing what was wrong." *Queen v. M'Naughton* (1843) 4 St.Tr. (N.S.) 847, 931; *M'Naughton's Case* (1843) 10 Clark & F. 200, 210, 8 Eng. Reprint 718, 722; see *People v. Coffman* (1864) 24 Cal. 230, 235.

If the word "know" were given this broader interpretation, so as to require knowledge "fused with affect" and assimilated by the whole personality - so that, for example, the killer was capable of identifying with his prospective victim - much of the criticism of the knowledge test would be met." [Weihofen, op. cit. supra, at p. 77.]

The California courts have not been unresponsive to such proposals for liberalization of the original language of the *M'Naughton* rule; in evolving our own rule to meet statutory requirements, apply humane concepts, and at the same time protect society, we have reformulated the test with a variety of specifications to achieve this end. See, e.g., *People v. Willard* (1907) 150 Cal. 543, 554 ["if he understands the nature and character of his action and its consequences"]; *People v. Oxnam* (1915) 170 Cal. 211, 213 ["If appellant had sufficient mental capacity to appreciate the character and quality of his act, knew and understood that it was a violation of the rights of another, if he had the capacity thus to appreciate the character and comprehend the possible or probable consequence of his act"]; *People v. Wells* (1949) 33 Cal.2d 330 ["to know the nature of his act and appreciate that it was wrongful and could subject him to punishment"].

Guided by such decisions, our trial courts place a commendably broad interpretation upon the *M'Naughton* "knowledge" test: in the case at bench, for example, the jury were given the now standard instruction (CALJIC No. 801 Rev.) that

Insanity, as the word is used in these instructions, means a diseased and deranged condition of mind which renders a person incapable of knowing or *understanding* the nature and quality of his act, or to distinguish right from wrong in relation to that act. The test of sanity is this: First, did the defendant have sufficient mental capacity to know *and understand* what he was doing, and second, did he know *and understand* that it was wrong *and a violation of the rights of another*? To be sane and thus responsible to the law for the act committed, the defendant must be able to know *and understand* the nature and quality of his act *and* to distinguish between right and wrong at the time of the commission of the offense. [Italics added.][2]

Nevertheless, *amicus curiae* contends that the California rule is unconstitutional, in that it assertedly deprived defendant of due process and equal protection of the law. Similar arguments as to the *M'Naughton* rule were rejected by the United States Supreme Court in *Leland v. Oregon* (1952) 343 U.S. 790, 800-801. Quoting the high court to the effect that "The science of psychiatry has made tremendous strides since that test was laid down in *M'Naghton's Case*, but the progress of science has not reached a point where its learning would compel us to require the states to eliminate the right and wrong test from their criminal law," *amicus curiae* urges that now, 12 years after *Leland*, scientific knowledge has reached that point. But the extent and nature of advances in psychiatric knowledge during the past decade are not shown, and we are not persuaded that they have

---

[2] The jury were also instructed (CALJIC No. 806) that "irresistible impulse" is not a defense "If a person is conscious of, knows *and appreciates* the nature and wrongfulness of his act." Italics added.

been of such a revolutionary scope as to undermine the holding in *Leland*.[4]

Moreover, as the United States Supreme Court further observed in *Leland*, "choice of a test of legal sanity involves not only scientific knowledge but questions of basic policy as to the extent to which that knowledge should determine criminal responsibility. This whole problem has evoked wide disagreement among those who have studied it." While attacking the *M'Naughton* rule (and not differentiating the California rule), *amicus curiae* does not offer a more workable test in its stead, and in any event fails to demonstrate that the issue is now a judicial rather than a legislative one. As we have repeatedly stated in recent years, the *M'Naughton* test (of course, as evolved and applied in the California rule) has become "an integral part of the legislative scheme for the appraisal of criminal responsibility in California and any change therein should come from the Legislature." *People v. Darling* (1962) 58 Cal.2d 15, 23.

The Sufficiency of the Evidence of Sanity

Turning now to defendant's more specific contentions, it is first urged that "As a matter of law, defendant was legally insane at the time of the commission of the offense." In support of this proposition, defendant stresses the fact that each of the four psychiatrists who testified at the trial stated (1) that in his medical opinion, defendant suffers from a permanent form of one of the group of mental disorders generically known as "schizophrenia" and (2) that defendant was also legally insane at the time he murdered his mother. Much confusion has been engendered in this and similar cases by failure to distinguish between these two branches of the testimony and by uncritical acceptance of both as equally "expert." The bases of the psychiatrists' "legal" opinion will be explored hereinafter; on the purely medical question, these witnesses agreed (and in this litigation no one disputes their findings) that defendant's illness is characterized by a "disintegration of the personality" and a "complete disassociation between intellect and emotion," that defendant "is not capable of conceptual thinking" but only of "concrete" thinking, and that although his memory is not impaired his judgment is affected "to a considerable degree."

---

[4] The brief of amicus curiae, a society for the advancement of forensic psychiatry, tends to leave the reader with the impression that psychiatric diagnoses are as reliable and predictable as those of the classic branches of medicine, and that the general unanimity of the psychiatrists in the case at bench is the rule rather than the exception. For a documented discussion that dispels this impression and reveals the other side of the psychiatric coin, see Hakeem, *A Critique of the Psychiatric Approach to Crime and Correction* (1958) 23 Law & Contemp. Prob. 650; see also Szasz, *Psychiatry, Ethics, and the Criminal Law* (1958) 58 Colum.L.Rev. 183; Hall, *Psychiatry and Criminal Responsibility* (1956) 65 Yale L.J. 761; *Werthan, Psychoauthoritarianism and the Law* (1955) 22 U.Chi.L.Rev. 336. Indeed, the trend if anything is away from dogmatic certainty and agreement: as recently pointed out by a psychiatrist experienced in the treatment of offenders, "The intelligent public has the right to know that, today, psychiatry is in ferment — many concepts, held for decades to be firmly established, are being increasingly challenged, and fundamental divergences are developing among its leading exponents on almost every issue of psychiatric diagnosis, therapy, and prophylactic recommendation. This holds true to an even greater degree for legal psychiatry. The popular picture painted by its propagandists is sometimes totally unrealistic and irresponsible. Attempts to present a united front to outsiders neither further the cause of psychiatry nor are they socially and scientifically justifiable." Schmideberg, *The Promise of Psychiatry: Hopes and Disillusionment* (1962) 57 Nw.U.L.Rev. 19, 21.

However impressive this seeming unanimity of expert opinion may at first appear (and we give it due consideration not only on the issue of sanity, but also in a subsequent portion of this opinion wherein we discuss the degree of the crime), our inquiry on this, just as on other factual issues, is necessarily limited at the appellate level to a determination whether there is substantial evidence in the record to support the jury's verdict of sanity (and the trial court's finding as to the degree of the murder) under the law of this state. It is only in the rare case when "the evidence is uncontradicted and entirely to the effect that the accused is insane" (*In re Dennis* (1959) 51 Cal.2d 666, 674) that a unanimity of expert testimony could authorize upsetting a jury finding to the contrary. While the jury may not draw inferences inconsistent with incontestably established facts, nevertheless if there is substantial evidence from which the jury could infer that the defendant was legally sane at the time of the offense, such a finding must be sustained in the face of any conflicting evidence, expert or otherwise.

The question of what may constitute substantial evidence of legal sanity cannot be answered by a simple formula applicable to all situations. To begin with, in *In re Dennis* (1959) 51 Cal.2d 666, we disapproved an implication in *People v. Chamberlain* (1936) 7 Cal.2d 257, to the effect that the presumption of sanity alone might be sufficient in the face of uncontradicted evidence of insanity introduced by the defendant. The court in *Chamberlain* also stressed such factors as "The personal appearance, mannerisms and actions of the defendant before the jurors during the trial, and the character of his testimony and manner of giving it;" but evidence of that nature would seem to be of doubtful sufficiency in a case where, as here, defendant's mental illness is not of a type characterized by continual maniacal activity or obvious physical symptoms.

Beyond this point, however, it is settled that "the conduct and declarations of the defendant occurring within a reasonable time before or after the commission of the alleged act are admissible in proof of his mental condition at the time of the offense." *People v. David* (1939) 12 Cal.2d 639, 649. In the present case, such evidence was introduced, both of defendant's conduct and of his declarations.

Conduct of Defendant as Evidence of Legal Sanity

Among the kinds of conduct of a defendant which our courts have held to constitute evidence of legal sanity are the following: "an ability on the part of the accused to devise and execute a deliberate plan" *(People v. David* (1939), 12 Cal.2d 639, 647); "the manner in which the crime was conceived, planned and executed" *(People v. Darling* (1962), 58 Cal.2d 15, 21); the fact that witnesses "observed no change in his manner and that he appeared to be normal" *(People v. Caetano* (1947) 29 Cal.2d 616, 620); the fact that "the defendant walked steadily and calmly, spoke clearly and coherently and appeared to be fully conscious of what he was doing" *(People v. Van Winkle* (1953) 41 Cal.2d 525, 529); and the fact that shortly after committing the crime the defendant "was cooperative and not abusive or combative" *(People v. Dennis* (1960), 177 Cal.App.2d 655, 658), that "questions put to him were answered by him quickly and promptly" *(People v. Loomis* (1915) 170 Cal. 347, 349), and that "he appeared rational, spoke coherently, was oriented as to time, place and those persons who were present" *(People v. Fraters* (1956) 146 Cal.App.2d 305, 306).

In the case at bench, there was evidence that in the year preceding the commission of the crime defendant "spent a lot of time thinking about sex." He made a list of the names and addresses of seven girls in his community whom he did not know personally, but whom he planned to anesthetize by ether and then either rape or photograph nude. One night about three weeks before the murder, he took a container of ether and attempted to enter the home of one of these girls through the chimney, but he became wedged in and had to be rescued. In the ensuing weeks, defendant apparently deliberated on ways and means of accomplishing his objective and decided that he would have to bring the girls to his house to achieve his sexual purposes, and that it would therefore be necessary to get his mother (and possibly his brother) out of the way first.

The attack on defendant's mother took place on Monday, May 15, 1961. On the preceding Friday or Saturday, defendant obtained an axe handle from the family garage and hid it under the mattress of his bed. At about 10 p.m. on Sunday, he took the axe handle from its hiding place and approached his mother from behind, raising the weapon to strike her. She sensed his presence and asked him what he was doing; he answered that it was "nothing," and returned to his room and hid the handle under his mattress again. The following morning, defendant arose and put the customary signal (a magazine) in the front window to inform his father that he had not overslept. Defendant ate the breakfast that his mother prepared, then went to his room and obtained the axe handle from under the mattress. He returned to the kitchen, approached his mother from behind, and struck her on the back of the head. She turned around screaming and he struck her several more blows. They fell to the floor, fighting. She called out her neighbor's name, and defendant began choking her. She bit him on the hand and crawled away. He got up to turn off the water running in the sink, and she fled through the dining room. He gave chase, caught her in the front room, and choked her to death with his hands. Defendant then took off his shirt and hung it by the fire, washed the blood off his face and hands, read a few lines from a Bible or prayer book lying upon the dining room table, and walked down to the police station to turn himself in. Defendant told the desk officer, "I have something I wish to report. I just killed my mother with an axe handle." The officer testified that defendant spoke in a quiet voice and that "His conversation was quite coherent in what he was saying and he answered everything I asked him right to a T."

Defendant's counsel repeatedly characterizes as "bizarre" defendant's plan to rape or photograph nude the seven girls on his list. Certainly in common parlance it may be termed "bizarre;" likewise to a mature person of good morals, it would appear highly unreasonable. But many a youth has committed - or planned - acts which were bizarre and unreasonable. This defendant was immature and lacked experience and judgment in sexual matters. But it does not follow therefrom that the jury were precluded as a matter of law from finding defendant legally sane at the time of the murder. From the evidence set forth hereinabove, the jury could infer that defendant had a motive for his actions (gratification of his sexual desires), that he planned the attack on his mother for some time (obtaining the axe handle from the garage several days in advance; abortive attempt to strike his mother with it on the evening before the crime), that he knew that what he was doing was wrong (initial concealment of the handle underneath his mattress; excuse offered when his mother saw him with the weapon on the evening before the crime; renewed concealment of the handle under the mattress), that he persisted in the fatal attack (pursuit of his fleeing mother into the front room; actual infliction of death by strangling rather than bludgeoning), that he was conscious of having committed a crime (prompt surrender to the police), and that he was calm and coherent (testimony of desk officer and others).

We need not determine whether such conduct would alone constitute substantial evidence from which the jury could find defendant legally sane at the time of the murder, for as will next be shown, the record contains further evidence on this issue.

Declarations of Defendant as Evidence of Legal Sanity

Oral declarations made by a defendant during the period of time material to his offense may constitute evidence of legal sanity. In *People v. Darling* (1962), 58 Cal.2d 15, 21, we referred *inter alia* to statements made by a defendant relating to his "reason for first committing the homicide and later surrendering himself," and held that "such evidence firmly establishes that defendant was aware at all times that his actions were wrong and improper."

In the case at bench, defendant was questioned by Officers Stenberg and Hamilton shortly after he came to the police station and voluntarily announced that he had just killed his mother. The interrogation was transcribed and shown to defendant; he changed the wording of a few of his answers, then affixed his signature and the date on each page. When asked by Officer Hamilton why he had turned himself in, defendant replied, "Well, for the act I had just committed." Defendant then related the events leading up to and culminating in the murder, describing his conduct in the detail set forth hereinabove. With respect to the issue of his state of mind at the time of the crime, the following language is both relevant and material: When asked how long he had thought of killing his mother, defendant replied,

A: I can't be clear on that. About a week ago, I would suppose, the very beginning of the thoughts. First I thought of giving her the ether. Then Thursday and Friday I thought of it again.

Q: Of killing your mother?

A: Not of killing. Well, yes, I think so. Then Saturday and Sunday the same." After stating that he struck her the first blow on the back of the head, defendant was asked:

Q: Did you consider at the time that this one blow would render her unconscious, or kill her?

A: I wasn't sure. I was hoping it would render her unconscious.

Q: Was it your thought at this time to kill her?

A: I am not sure of that. Probably kill her, I think.

Defendant described the struggle in which he and his mother fell to the floor, and was asked:

Q: Then what happened?

A: She moved over by the stove, and she just laid still. She was breathing, breathing heavily. I said "I shouldn't be doing this" - not those exact words, but something to that effect, and laid down beside her, because we were on the floor.

Q: Were you tired?

A: Yes.

After defendant had choked her to death, he said, "God loves you, He loves me, He loves my dad, and I love you and my dad. It is a circle, sort of, and it is horrible you have done all that good and then I come along and destroy it."

Detective Stenberg thereafter interrupted Officer Hamilton's interrogation, and asked the following questions:

Q: You knew the wrongfulness of killing your mother?

A: I did. I was thinking of it. I was aware of it.

Q: You were aware of the wrongfulness. Also had you thought what might happen to you?

A: That is a question. No.

Q: Your thought has been in your mind for three weeks of killing her?

A: Yes, or of just knocking her out.

Q: Well, didn't you feel you would be prosecuted for the wrongfulness of this act?

A: I was aware of it, but not thinking of it.

Q: Can you give a reason or purpose for this act of killing your mother? Have you thought out why you wanted to hurt her?

A: There is a reason why we didn't get along. There is also the reason of sexual intercourse with one of these other girls, and I had to get her out of the way.

Q: Did you think you had to get her out of the way permanently?

A: I sort of figured it would have to be that way, but I am not quite sure.

Thus, contrary to the misunderstanding of counsel and *amicus curiae*, Officer Stenberg's question ("You knew the wrongfulness of killing your mother?") related unequivocally to defendant's knowledge at the time of the commission of the murder; and defendant's equally unequivocal answer ("I did. I was thinking of it. I was aware of it.") related to the same period of time. This admission, coupled with defendant's uncontradicted course of conduct and other statements set forth hereinabove, constitutes substantial evidence from which the jury could find defendant legally sane at the time of the matricide.

It is contended that the foregoing evidence of defendant's conduct and declarations is equally consistent with the type of mental illness (i.e., a form of "schizophrenia") from which, according to the psychiatric witnesses, defendant is said to be suffering. But this consistency establishes only that defendant is suffering from the diagnosed mental illness - a point that the prosecution readily concedes; it does not compel the conclusion that on the very different issue of legal sanity the evidence is insufficient as a matter of law to support the verdict. To hold otherwise would be in effect to substitute a trial by "experts" for a trial by jury, for it would require that the jurors accept the psychiatric testimony as conclusive on an issue — the legal sanity of the defendant — which under our present law is exclusively within the province of the trier of fact to determine.

To guard against misunderstanding of our rules, it is pertinent to observe that we do not reject expert testimony simply or solely because it may also answer the ultimate question the jury is called upon to decide; but, strictly speaking, a psychiatrist is not an "expert" at all when it comes to determining whether the defendant is legally responsible under the terms of the California rule. Thus Dr. Alfred K. Baur, psychiatrist and Chief of Staff of the Veteran's Administration Hospital at Salem, Virginia, has recently warned that the question of a defendant's "insanity" (which he defines as legal irresponsibility) should not even be asked of members of his profession:

> As psychiatrists, we can testify as to our findings regarding the "mental condition" of the person in question; but, to ask the psychiatric witness, "Doctor, in your opinion is this person insane (or sane)?" is the same as asking an expert witness in a criminal trial, "In your opinion, is the accused guilty or not guilty?" Yet, many lawyers ask psychiatrists to state opinions on the sanity of the accused and, unfortunately, many psychiatrists perpetuate the problem by accepting the role of oracle and answering the question, even thinking it properly within their functions. [Baur, *Legal Responsibility and Mental Illness* (1962) 57 Nw.L.Rev. 12, 13; for similar views, see *Address of Dr.Karl Menninger to the Judicial Conference of the 10th Circuit* (1962) 32 F.R.D. 566, 571; Glueck, *Law and Psychiatry* (1962) pp. 65-67.]

In the light of the authorities which have been brought to our attention, it thus appears that a psychiatrist's conclusion as to the legal insanity of a schizophrenic is inherently no more than tentative. As Dr. Manfred S. Guttmacher observes,

> In the most malignant type of psychosis, schizophrenia, the decision is often extremely difficult and the psychiatrist, conscientiously attempting to assay the individual's capacity to distinguish right and wrong will be able to do little more than conjecture. Much, indeed, is known about the schizophrenic disorders at a descriptive level and valid generalizations about the symptomatology can be made. But our methods of examination do not permit us to particularize convincingly in regard to the individual patient. [Guttmacher, *Principal Difficulties with the Present Criteria of Responsibility and Possible Alternatives*, in Model Pen. Code, Tent. Draft No. 4 (1955) p. 171.]

In this uncertain state of knowledge, the fact that the four psychiatrists in the case at bench happened each to diagnose defendant's medical condition as "schizophrenia"[13] did not preclude the jury from weighing, as they were required to do,

---

[13] Even on this diagnosis there was not complete unanimity: Dr. Smith testified that defendant's

these witnesses' further opinion that defendant was legally insane at the time of the murder.

To the extent, moreover, that the psychiatric witnesses in the case at bench were asked their opinion as to defendant's legal sanity, a close examination of their responses discloses still further grounds in support of the verdict. * * * *

The final psychiatric witness, Dr. Skrdla, testified on direct examination that at the time of the killing defendant "knew that he had committed a wrong act, at least morally wrong, and possibly legally wrong, because, according to the story he gave me, he washed the blood from himself and changed his clothes, and, a few minutes after the murder, went to the police station to report it. This would indicate that he recognized that his act was wrong." On cross-examination, Dr. Skrdla testified that when defendant killed his mother "he probably did know the difference between right and wrong," but that he was one of those schizophrenics who "because of their emotional problems, their own conflicts, are not able to prevent themselves from going ahead and acting on whatever ideas or compulsions they may have." The doctor agreed that the fact that defendant hid the axe handle under his mattress would indicate that "he didn't want to be caught with that axe handle before he was able to go ahead with the plan" and that "He had appreciation of the fact, perhaps, that it wasn't entirely right, however, he still planned to do it." Dr. Skrdla termed the killing "an automatic act," and explained that "once defendant attempted to get his mother out of the way, he went on as was described and couldn't stop until she was in fact dead."

The doctrine of "irresistible impulse" as a defense to crime is, of course, not the law of California; to the contrary, the basic behavioral concept of our social order is free will. *People v. Nash* (1959), 52 Cal.2d 36, 45-46.

Finally, to accept defendant's thesis would be tantamount to creating by judicial fiat a new defense plea of "not guilty by reason of schizophrenia." To do so (assuming arguendo that it were within our power) would be bad law and apparently still worse medicine. It would require the jurors to accept as beyond dispute or question the opinions of the psychiatric witnesses as to the defendant's legal sanity. But it is doubtful that any reputable psychiatrist today would claim such infallibility; clearly the four who testified in the case at bench did not do so. Thus, Dr. Daryl D. Smith agreed with counsel's assertion with respect to schizophrenia that "there is quite a bit of divergence of psychiatric opinion relative to this disease." Indeed, it is often acknowledged that the causes and cure of schizophrenia are unknown (e.g., Diamond, *From M'Naughton to Currens, and Beyond* (1962) 50 Cal.L.Rev. 189, 195; Weihofen, *Mental Disorder as a Criminal Defense* (1954) p. 16), and that "schizophrenia" is not even a single disease as such but merely a label or term of convenience encompassing a variety of more or less related symptoms or conditions of mental disorder; thus in the case at bench Dr. J. M. Nielsen agreed that

---

schizophrenia is of the paranoic type, while Dr. Maculans was equally firm in stating that "In my opinion he is not" of the paranoic type. Similarly, Dr. Maculans found the incident of defendant's attempting to enter a girl's house through the chimney to be "very significant," whereas Dr. Nielsen said of the same incident, "You don't have to be a schizophrenic to do that. You can be a psychopath or you can be anything else. It could be due to normal instincts with extremely poor judgment."

"schizophrenia" is "just a psychiatric classification, simply an abstract definition as applied to the behavior pattern."

Such a classification covers a broad spectrum of mental conditions. As Dr. Alfred K. Baur emphasizes,

> Some people are sophisticated enough to know that schizophrenia is one of the "major psychoses" and contributes to many in the "insane" category. But it is very difficult to get across to lay people the idea that a person diagnosed schizophrenic may be quite competent, responsible, and not dangerous, and, in fact, a valuable member of society, albeit at times a personally unhappy one. The same can be said of every psychiatric diagnosis or so-called mental illness. [Baur, *Legal Responsibility and Mental Illness* (1962) 57 Nw.U.L.Rev. 12, 16-17.]

The argument for defendant, in short, ignores our often-repeated admonition that "'Sound mind' and 'legal sanity' are not synonymous." *People v. Baker* (1954) 42 Cal.2d 550, 568. * * * *

The Degree of Murder

From what has been said, it follows that there was no substantial error in the trial on the issue raised by the plea of not guilty by reason of insanity and that the evidence adequately supports the jury's verdict. But another and more substantial problem remains to be considered: the contention that the evidence is insufficient to support the trial court's finding that the murder was of the first, rather than the second, degree.

This problem, however, is by no means new to us. In dealing with it we recognize that every relevant and tenable presumption is to be indulged in favor of sustaining the judgment of the trial court; but when a proper case appears, we do not hesitate to modify the judgment to murder of the second degree and affirm it as modified.

As hereinabove mentioned, by stipulation of the parties the question of the degree of the crime was submitted to the court on the basis of the evidence introduced at the trial on the plea of not guilty by reason of insanity, as augmented by the report of the probation officer. To confidently resolve the issue, it is essential that we identify the elements which (insofar as relevant to the facts of this case) should as a matter of law be given weight as characterizing, distinguishing, or differentiating, the two degrees of murder.

In *People v. Holt* (1944) 25 Cal.2d 59, 83, we said * * * "Dividing intentional homicides into murder and voluntary manslaughter was a recognition of the infirmity of human nature. Again dividing the offense of murder into two degrees is a further recognition of that infirmity and of difference in the quantum of personal turpitude of the offenders. The victim of manslaughter or second degree murder is just as dead as is the victim of first degree murder. The law has fixed standards by which such personal depravity of the offender, i.e., the character of the particular homicide, is to be measured. When the homicide is perpetrated by means of poison, or lying in wait, or torture, or in the perpetration of or attempt to perpetrate the enumerated felonies, the standard is definite and no difficulty in fixing the degree ensues. But when it is claimed that the homicide is by 'any other kind of willful, deliberate, and premeditated killing,' there is necessity for an appraisal which involves something more than the ascertainment of objective facts. This appraisal is primarily a jury [or trial court] function and within a wide field of discretion its determination is final. But as is true as to all factual issues resolved by a jury [or trial court], the evidence upon which the determination is made is subject to review on the question of its legal sufficiency to support the verdict. To the extent that the character of a particular homicide is established by the facts in evidence the jury is bound, as are we, to apply the standards fixed by law."

In the case at bench, there is no question that the defendant had the intent to kill; but the mental infirmity of this defendant presents a very serious factual problem as to the quantum of his personal turpitude and depravity as inherently related to the degree of the murder.

In the case now at bench, in the light of defendant's youth and undisputed mental illness, all as shown under the California *M'Naughton* rule on the trial of the plea of not guilty by reason of insanity, and properly considered by the trial judge in the proceeding to determine the degree of the offense, the true test must include consideration of the somewhat limited extent to which this defendant could maturely and meaningfully reflect upon the gravity of his contemplated act.

Certainly in the case now at bench the defendant had ample time for any normal person to maturely and appreciatively reflect upon his contemplated act and to arrive at a cold, deliberated and premeditated conclusion. He did this in a sense — and apparently to the full extent of which he was capable. But, indisputably on the record, this defendant was not and is not a fully normal or mature, mentally well person. He knew the difference between right and wrong; he knew that the intended act was wrong and nevertheless carried it out. But the extent of his understanding, reflection upon it and its consequences, with realization of the enormity of the evil, appears to have been materially — as relevant to appraising the quantum of his moral turpitude and depravity - vague and detached. We think that our analysis in *Holt* of the minimum essential elements of first degree murder, especially in respect to the quantum of reflection, comprehension, and turpitude of the offender, fits precisely this case: that the use by the Legislature of "wilful, deliberate, and premeditated" in conjunction indicates its intent to require as an essential element of first degree murder (of that category) substantially more reflection; i.e., more understanding and comprehension of the character of the act than the mere amount of thought necessary to form the intention to kill. It bears repeating (*People v. Holt* (1944) *supra*, 25 Cal.2d 59, 89) that "Dividing intentional homicides into murder and voluntary manslaughter was a recognition of the infirmity of human nature. Again dividing the offense of murder into two degrees is a further recognition of that infirmity and of difference in the quantum of personal turpitude of the offenders. The difference is basically in the offenders."

Upon the facts, upon the law, and for all of the reasons hereinabove stated, we are satisfied that the evidence fails to support the finding that the murder by this defendant, in the circumstances of his undisputed mental illness, was of the first degree, but that it amply sustains conviction of second degree murder. The fact that we reduce the degree of the penal judgment from first to second degree murder is not to be understood as suggesting that this defendant's confinement should be in an institution maintaining any lower degree of security than for persons convicted of murder of the first degree. To the contrary, we approve of the trial court's recommendation that defendant be placed in a hospital for the criminally insane of a high security character, such as the California Medical Facility at Vacaville where he is presently confined.

For all of the reasons above stated, the judgment is modified by reducing the degree of the crime to murder of the second degree and, as so modified, is affirmed. The cause is remanded to the trial court with directions to arraign and pronounce judgment on defendant in accordance with the foregoing ruling.

NOTES FROM WALLY:

(1) If all experts testified that the defendant is insane, where did the court find substantial evidence that he is sane? Doesn't this court have a rather low opinion of psychiatric experts?

(2) How does our evidence regarding Louie compare to the evidence in *Wolff*?

PEOPLE v. DREW
California Supreme Court
22 Cal.3d 333, 583 P.2d 1318 (1978)

TOBRINER, JUSTICE.

For over a century California has followed the *M'Naghten* test[2] to define the defenses of insanity and idiocy. The deficiencies of that test have long been apparent, and judicial attempts to reinterpret or evade the limitations of *M'Naghten* have proven inadequate. We shall explain why we have concluded that we should discard the *M'Naghten* language, and update the California test of mental incapacity as a criminal defense by adopting the test proposed by the American Law Institute[3] and followed by the federal judiciary and the courts of 15 states.

Understandably, in view of our past adherence to *M'Naghten*, neither the psychiatrists who examined defendant nor the jury evaluated defendant's capacity in terms of the ALI test. Since the evidentiary record indicates that defendant, a former mental patient with a history of irrational assaultive behavior, lacked the capacity to conform his conduct to legal requirements, we conclude that the court's

---

[2] "To establish a defence on the ground of insanity, it must be clearly proved that, at the time of the committing the act, the party accused was labouring under such a defect of reason, from disease of the mind, as not to know the nature and quality of the act he was doing; or, if he did know it, that he did not know he was doing what was wrong." *M'Naghten's Case* (1843) 10 Clark & Fin. 200, 210 (8 Eng.Rep. 718, 722).

[3] "A person is not responsible for criminal conduct if at the time of such conduct as a result of mental disease or defect he lacks substantial capacity either to appreciate the criminality (wrongfulness) of his conduct or to conform his conduct to the requirements of law." Model Pen.Code, Proposed Official Draft (1962) § 4.01, subpart (1).

failure to instruct the jury under the ALI test was prejudicial, and therefore reverse the conviction.

Defendant Drew also contends that Evidence Code § 522, which requires a defendant to prove insanity by a preponderance of the evidence, is unconstitutional. Controlling precedent in the United States Supreme Court (see *Patterson v. New York* (1977) 432 U.S. 197), and in this court (see *People v. Miller* (1972) 7 Cal.3d 562) mandates the rejection of this contention. Finally, Drew argues that the record is insufficient to sustain the jury finding of sanity. We conclude, however, that a jury instructed under the *M'Naghten* rule could reasonably find that defendant failed to prove by a preponderance of the evidence that he was unaware of the wrongfulness of his conduct. Thus Drew is not entitled to an order directing the trial court to find him insane, but only to a new trial on the issue of sanity in which the jury is instructed under the ALI test.

1. *Statement of Facts.*

Defendant Drew, a 22-year-old man, was drinking in a bar in Brawley during the early morning of October 26, 1975. He left $5 on the bar to pay for drinks and went to the men's room. When he returned, the money was missing. Drew accused one Truman Sylling, a customer at the bar, of taking the money. A heated argument ensued, and the bartender phoned for police assistance. Officers Guerrero and Bonsell arrived at the bar. When Guerrero attempted to question Sylling, Drew interfered to continue the argument. Bonsell then asked Drew to step outside. Drew refused. Bonsell took Drew by the hand, and he and Officer Schulke, who had just arrived at the bar, attempted to escort Drew outside. Drew broke away from the officers and struck Bonsell in the face. Bonsell struck his head against the edge of the bar and fell to the floor. Drew fell on top of him and attempted to bite him, but was restrained by Guerrero and Schulke. Drew continued to resist violently until he was finally placed in a cell at the police station.

Charged with battery on a peace officer (Pen.Code § 243), obstructing an officer (Pen.Code § 148), and disturbing the peace (Pen.Code § 415), Drew pled not guilty and not guilty by reason of insanity.

At the guilt trial, Drew testified on his own behalf; he denied striking Bonsell and maintained that the officer's injuries were accidental. Bonsell's testimony, however, was corroborated by Guerrero and Sylling. The jury found Drew guilty as charged.

Two court-appointed psychiatrists testified at the sanity trial. Dr. Otto Gericke, former Medical Director at Patton State Hospital, testified that Drew was committed to that hospital for nine months in 1972 after Drew was found incompetent to stand trial on an unspecified charge. He examined him on that occasion; again on February 1, 1976, to determine Drew's competency to stand trial on the instant charge; and a third time on June 6, 1976, on the question of Drew's sanity.

Dr. Gericke described Drew's condition as one of latent schizophrenia, characterized by repeated incidents of assaultive behavior and by conversing with inanimate objects and nonexistent persons; this condition could be controlled by medication, but if left untreated would deteriorate to paranoid schizophrenia.

Relying upon his examinations and Drew's medical history at Patton State Hospital, Dr. Gericke concluded that Drew was unable to appreciate the difference between right and wrong at the time he attacked Officer Bonsell. The second witness, Dr. Ethel Chapman, was a staff psychiatrist at Patton State Hospital. She also examined Drew under court appointment in February and June of 1976, and was acquainted with him from his stay at the hospital in 1972. She concurred with Dr. Gericke's diagnosis of his condition, adding the observation that his symptoms would be aggravated by the ingestion of alcohol, and joined in Dr. Gericke's conclusion that Drew did not understand that his assault upon Officer Bonsell was wrong.

The prosecution presented no evidence at the sanity trial. Nevertheless the jury, instructed that the defendant has the burden of proving insanity under the *M'Naghten* test, found him sane. The court thereupon sentenced Drew to prison on the battery conviction. He appeals from the judgment of conviction.

2. This court should adopt the American Law Institute test, as stated in § 4.01, subpart (1) of the Model Penal Code, to define the defense of insanity.

The trial court instructed the jury that "Legal insanity means a diseased or deranged condition of the mind which makes a person incapable of knowing or understanding the nature and quality of his act, or makes a person incapable of knowing or understanding that his act was wrong." We explain that this instruction, based on the *M'Naghten* test, was erroneous, and on the record before us constitutes prejudicial error requiring reversal of the judgment.

The purpose of a legal test for insanity is to identify those persons who, owing to mental incapacity, should not be held criminally responsible for their conduct. The criminal law rests on a postulate of free will that all persons of sound mind are presumed capable of conforming their behavior to legal requirements and that when any such person freely chooses to violate the law, he may justly be held responsible. See Goldstein, *The Insanity Defense* (1967) pp. 9-10. From the earliest days of the common law, however, the courts have recognized that a few persons lack the mental capacity to conform to the strictures of the law. Thus, in 1582 William Lambart of Lincoln's Inn wrote that "If a mad man or a natural fool, or a lunatic in the time of his lunacy, or a child who apparently had no knowledge of good or evil, do kill a man, this is no felonious act for they cannot be said to have any understanding will." Lambart, *Eirenarcha* (1582) Cat. 21.218. The principle that mental incapacity constitutes a defense to crime is today accepted in all American jurisdictions. See Weihofen, *Mental Disorder as a Criminal Defense* (1954) p. 51.

The California Penal Code codifies the defense of mental incapacity. Section 20 states that "in every crime there must exist a union of act and intent." Section 21 provides as to persons of sound mind "the intent is manifested by the circumstances connected with the offense" and that "All persons are of sound mind who are neither idiots nor lunatics, nor affected with insanity." Finally, § 26 specifies that "All persons are capable of committing crimes except those belonging to the following classes" and includes among those classes "Idiots" and "Lunatics and insane persons."

Although the Legislature has thus provided that "insanity" is a defense to a criminal charge, it has never attempted to define that term. The task of describing the circumstances under which mental incapacity will relieve a defendant of criminal responsibility has become the duty of the judiciary. Since *People v. Coffman* (1864) 24 Cal. 230, 235, the California courts have followed the *M'Naghten* rule to define the defense of insanity.

The curious origin of the *M'Naghten* rule has been frequently recounted. In 1843 Daniel M'Naghten, afflicted with paranoia, attempted to assassinate the Prime Minister of England, and succeeded in killing the Prime Minister's secretary. M'Naghten's acquittal on grounds of insanity so disturbed Queen Victoria that she summoned the House of Lords to obtain the opinion of the judges on the law of insanity. The 15 judges of the common law courts were called in an extraordinary session, "under a not too subtle atmosphere of pressure," to answer five hypothetical questions on the law of criminal responsibility.

In response to two of the questions propounded the judges stated that "to establish a defence on the ground of insanity, it must be clearly proved that, at the time of the committing the act, the party accused was labouring under such a defect of reason, from disease of the mind, as not to know the nature and quality of the act he was doing; or, if he did know it, that he did not know he was doing what was wrong." *M'Naghten's Case*, 10 Clark & Fin. 200, 210 (8 Eng.Rep. 718, 722). Although an advisory opinion, and thus most questionable authority (see 2 Stephen, *History of the Criminal Law of England* (1883) p. 153), this language became the basis for the test of insanity in all American states except New Hampshire.

Despite its widespread acceptance, the deficiencies of *M'Naghten* have long been apparent. Principal among these is the test's exclusive focus upon the cognitive capacity of the defendant, an outgrowth of the then current psychological theory under which the mind was divided into separate independent compartments, one of which could be diseased without affecting the others. As explained by Judge Ely of the Ninth Circuit:

> The *M'Naghten* rules fruitlessly attempt to relieve from punishment only those mentally diseased persons who have no cognitive capacity. This formulation does not comport with modern medical knowledge that an individual is a mentally complex being with varying degrees of awareness. It also fails to attack the problem presented in a case wherein an accused may have understood his actions but was incapable of controlling his behavior. Such a person has been allowed to remain a danger to himself and to society whenever, under *M'Naghten*, he is imprisoned without being afforded such treatment as may produce rehabilitation and is later, potentially recidivistic, released. [*Wade v. United States* (9th Cir. 1970) 426 F.2d 64, 66-67.]

M'Naghten's exclusive emphasis on cognition would be of little consequence if all serious mental illness impaired the capacity of the affected person to know the nature and wrongfulness of his action. Indeed, the early decision of *People v. Hoin* (1882) 62 Cal. 120, 123, in rejecting the defense of "irresistible impulse," rested on this gratuitous but doubtful assumption. Current psychiatric opinion, however, holds that mental illness often leaves the individual's intellectual understanding relatively unimpaired, but so affects his emotions or reason that he is unable to prevent himself from committing the act.

> Insanity does not only, or primarily, affect the cognitive or intellectual faculties, but affects the whole personality of the patient, including both the will and the emotions. An insane person may therefore often know the nature and quality of his act and that it is wrong and forbidden by law, and yet commit it as a result of the mental disease. [Rep. Royal Com. on Capital Punishment, 1949-1953, p. 80.]

The annals of this court are filled with illustrations of the above statement: the deluded defendant in *People v. Gorshen*, 51 Cal.2d 716, who believed he would be possessed by devilish visions unless he killed his foreman; the schizophrenic boy in *People v. Wolff*, 61 Cal.2d 795, who knew that killing his mother was murder but was unable emotionally to control his conduct despite that knowledge; the defendant in *People v. Robles* (1970) 2 Cal.3d 205, suffering from organic brain damage, who mutilated himself and killed others in sudden rages. To ask whether such a person knows or understands that his act is "wrong" is to ask a question irrelevant to the nature of his mental illness or to the degree of his criminal responsibility.

Secondly, "*M'Naghten's* single track emphasis on the cognitive aspect of the personality recognizes no degrees of incapacity. Either the defendant knows right from wrong or he does not. But such a test is grossly unrealistic. As the commentary to the American Law Institute's Model Penal Code observes, 'The law must recognize that when there is no black and white it must content itself with different shades of gray.' " *United States v. Freeman*, 357 F.2d 606, 618-619, quoting ALI, Model Pen.Code, Tent.Drafts, Nos. 1, 2, 3, and 4, p. 158.

In short, *M'Naghten* purports to channel psychiatric testimony into the narrow issue of cognitive capacity, an issue often unrelated to the defendant's illness or crime. The psychiatrist called as a witness faces a dilemma: either he can restrict his testimony to the confines of *M'Naghten*, depriving the trier of fact of a full presentation of the defendant's mental state, or he can testify that the defendant cannot tell "right" from "wrong" when that is not really his opinion because by so testifying he acquires the opportunity to put before the trier of fact the reality of defendant's mental condition. As Justice Frankfurter stated before the Royal Commission on Capital Punishment,

> I think to have rules which cannot rationally be justified except by a process of interpretation which distorts and often practically nullifies them is not a desirable system. The *M'Naghten* Rules are in large measure shams. That is a strong word, but I think the *M'Naghten* Rules are very difficult for conscientious people and not difficult enough for people who say "We'll just juggle them." [Royal Com. on Capital Punishment, supra, p. 102.]

Even if the psychiatrist is able to place before the trier of fact a complete picture of the defendant's mental incapacity, that testimony reaches the trier of fact weakened by cross-examination designed to show that defendant knew right from wrong (see, for example, the cross-examination described in *People v. Wolff*, *supra*, 61 Cal.2d 795, 812-814) and limited by the *M'Naghten* instruction. As a result, conscientious juries have often returned verdicts of sanity despite plain evidence of serious mental illness and unanimous expert testimony that the defendant was insane. See *People v. Wolff*, *supra*, 61 Cal.2d 795, 812.

Conscious of the inadequacies of the *M'Naghten* test, California decisions have modified that test in two significant respects.

First in *People v. Wolff*, we held that the mere capacity to verbalize socially acceptable answers to questions did not prove sanity; the defendant must not only know but also "appreciate" or "understand" the nature and wrongfulness of his act.

Second, in a series of decisions dating from *People v. Wells* (1949) 33 Cal.2d 330 and *People v. Gorshen*, *supra*, 51 Cal.2d 716, we developed the concept of diminished capacity, under which a defendant can introduce evidence of mental incapacity to negate specific intent, malice, or other subjective elements of the charged crime. Recently in *People v. Cantrell* (1973) 8 Cal.3d 672, we expressly held that "irresistible impulse" a concept evolved to supply the volitional element lacking in the *M'Naghten* test can be utilized to prove diminished capacity. But these innovative modifications to the *M'Naghten* Rule fail to cure its basic defects. *Wolff* ameliorates only one of the rigid categories of *M'Naghten*; as Professor Sherry explains: "It still falls short of acknowledging the teaching of psychiatry that mental aberration may not only impair knowledge of wrongfulness but may very well destroy an individual's capacity to control or to restrain himself." Sherry, Penal Code Revision Project Progress Report (1968) 43 State Bar J. 900, 916. The doctrine of diminished capacity, once hailed as a possible replacement for the defense of insanity (see Diamond, Criminal Responsibility of the Mentally Ill (1961) 14 Stan.L.Rev. 59), can now be seen to create its own problems.

The availability of a defense of diminished capacity turns largely on the nature of the crime charged. If the defendant is charged with a general intent crime, he cannot raise a defense of diminished capacity regardless of his impaired mental state. If charged with a specific intent crime, he may be able to reduce the offense to a lesser included general intent crime. If evidence of diminished capacity is used to negate criminal intent in a crime which contains no lesser offense, however, the defendant may secure his outright acquittal and release. The effectiveness of the defense, and the disposition of the defendant, thus turn less on the nature and seriousness of the defendant's mental disability than on the technical structure of the criminal law. A defendant whose criminal activity arises from mental illness or defect usually requires confinement and special treatment. Penal Code §§ 1026 and 1026a provide such confinement and treatment for persons acquitted on grounds of insanity. A successful diminished capacity defense, on the other hand, results either in the release of the defendant or his confinement as an ordinary criminal for a lesser term. Because the diminished capacity defense thus fails to identify the mentally disturbed defendant, it may result in the defendant not receiving the care appropriate to his condition. Such a defendant, who may still suffer from his mental disturbance, may serve his term, be released and thus permitted to become a danger to the public.

In our opinion, the continuing inadequacy of *M'Naghten* as a test of criminal responsibility cannot be cured by further attempts to interpret language dating from a different era of psychological thought, nor by the creation of additional concepts designed to evade the limitations of *M'Naghten*. It is time to recast *M'Naghten* in modern language, taking account of advances in psychological knowledge and changes in legal thought.

The definition of mental incapacity appearing in § 4.01 of the American Law Institute's Model Penal Code represents the distillation of nine years of research, exploration, and debate by the leading legal and medical minds of the country. It specifies that "A person is not responsible for criminal conduct if at the time of such conduct as a result of mental disease or defect he lacks substantial capacity either to appreciate the criminality (wrongfulness) of his conduct or to conform his conduct to the requirements of law."[8]

Adhering to the fundamental concepts of free will and criminal responsibility, the American Law Institute test restates *M'Naghten* in language consonant with the current legal and psychological thought. It has won widespread acceptance, having been adopted by every federal circuit* except for the first circuit and by 15 states.[10]

"In the opinion of most thoughtful observers this proposed test (the ALI test) is a significant improvement over *M'Naughton*." *People v. Kelly* (1973) 10 Cal.3d 565, 581-582 (Mosk, J., concurring). The advantages may be briefly summarized. First, the ALI test adds a volitional element, the ability to conform to legal requirements, which is missing from the M'Naghten test. Second, it avoids the all-or-nothing language of *M'Naghten* and permits a verdict based on lack of substantial capacity. Third, the ALI test is broad enough to permit a psychiatrist to set before the trier of fact a full picture of the defendant's mental impairments and flexible enough to adapt to future changes in psychiatric theory and diagnosis. Fourth, by referring to the defendant's capacity to "appreciate" the wrongfulness of his conduct, the test

---

[8] The American Law Institute takes no position as to whether the term "criminality" or the term "wrongfulness" best expresses the test of criminal responsibility; we prefer the term "criminality." Subpart 2 of the American Law Institute test provides that "the terms 'mental disease or defect' do not include an abnormality manifested only by repeated criminal or otherwise anti-social conduct." This language, designed to deny an insanity defense to psychopaths and sociopaths, is not relevant to the present case. The question whether to adopt subpart 2 of the ALI test is one which we defer to a later occasion.

* Ed. - This all changed after John Hinkley shot and wounded President Reagan. His jury was instructed under the ALI test, and he was found not guilty by reason of insanity. In 1984, Congress responded by directing the federal courts to abandon the ALI test and return to the *M'Naughton* test. See 18 U.S.C.A. § 20.

[10] Alaska: *Schade v. State* (1973) 512 P.2d 907. Connecticut: Conn.Gen.Stats., § 53a-13. Idaho: *State v. White*, 93 Idaho 153. Illinois: Ill.Rev.Stats., ch. 38, § 6-2. Indiana: *Hill v. State* (1969) 252 Ind. 601. Kentucky: *Terry v. Commonwealth* (1963) 371 S.W.2d 862. Maryland: Md.Code, art. 59, § 25. Massachusetts: *Commonwealth v. McHoul* (1967) 352 Mass. 544. Missouri: Rev.Stats.Mo., § 552.030(3)(1). Montana: Mont.Rev.Codes, § 95-501. Ohio: *State v. Staten* (1969) 18 Ohio St.2d 13. Oregon: ORS 161.295(1). Texas: Texas Pen.Code, § 8.01. Vermont: Vt.Stats., tit. 13, § 4801. Wisconsin: *State v. Shoffner* (1966) 31 Wis.2d 412.

confirms our holding in *People v. Wolff* that mere verbal knowledge of right and wrong does not prove sanity. Finally, by establishing a broad test of nonresponsibility, including elements of volition as well as cognition, the test provides the foundation on which we can order and rationalize the convoluted and occasionally inconsistent law of diminished capacity. * * * *

For the foregoing reasons, we now conclude that the California courts should employ the ALI test to define the defense of insanity. * * * *

4. *The record supports the jury's finding that defendant was sane under the M'Naghten test of insanity.*

Defendant Drew argues that even under the *M'Naghten* test the jury's finding of sanity is not supported by substantial evidence. If Drew should prevail in this contention, he would be entitled to an order directing the trial court to find him insane, thus avoiding a retrial of the case under the ALI test.[14] Thus, although we have today rejected the *M'Naghten* rule, we must nevertheless determine whether the jury's verdict based on that rule is supported by the record. We therefore explain our conclusion that on the present record a jury instructed under the *M'Naghten* rule could reasonably reject the opinions of psychiatric witnesses; finding that Drew had thus failed to prove his lack of understanding of the nature or wrongfulness of his act, the jury accordingly could return a verdict of sanity.

Drew relies on the fact that both court-appointed psychiatrists testified that he was unaware of the wrongfulness of his assault. The jurors, however, are not automatically required to render a verdict which conforms to the expert opinion. We explained in *People v. Wolff* that: "However impressive this seeming unanimity of expert opinion may at first appear, our inquiry on this just as on other factual issues is necessarily limited at the appellate level to a determination whether there is substantial evidence in the record to support the jury's verdict of sanity under the law of this state. It is only in the rare case when 'the evidence is uncontradicted and entirely to the effect that the accused is insane' that a unanimity of expert testimony could authorize upsetting a jury finding to the contrary." 61 Cal.2d at 804.

In *People v. Coogler*, 71 Cal.2d 153, 166, we pointed out that "The chief value of an expert's testimony in this field, as in all other fields, rests upon the *material* from which his opinion is fashioned and the *reasoning* by which he progresses from his material to his conclusion." In the present case, the jurors might well note that both experts were unfamiliar with Drew's conduct during the four years following his release from Patton State Hospital, and that their subsequent examinations of him were relatively brief. More significantly, the jurors could note that, although both psychiatrists stated an opinion that Drew did not appreciate the wrongfulness of his act, nothing in their testimony explained the reasoning which led to this opinion. Although the psychiatric testimony described Drew's repeated aggressive acts, and

---

[14] Drew would also be entitled to an order directing the trial court to find him insane if the evidence at the sanity trial demonstrated that he was insane as a matter of law under the ALI test. The defense witnesses, however, failed to direct their testimony to the issues critical in establishing insanity under the ALI test; in consequence the record on appeal is insufficient to prove insanity as a matter of law under that test.

diagnosed his condition as one of latent schizophrenia, neither psychiatrist explained why that behavior and diagnosis would lead to the conclusion that Drew was unable to appreciate the wrongfulness of his aggressive acts.

The prosecution presented no evidence at the sanity trial. Defendant, however, has the burden of proof on the issue of insanity; if neither party presents credible evidence on that issue the jury must find him sane. Thus, the question on appeal is not so much the substantiality of the evidence favoring the jury's finding as whether the evidence contrary to that finding is of such weight and character that the jury could not reasonably reject it. Because the jury could reasonably reject the psychiatric opinion that Drew was insane under the *M'Naghten* test, on the ground that the psychiatrists did not present sufficient material and reasoning to justify that opinion, we conclude that the jury's verdict cannot be overturned as lacking support in the trial record.

Our conclusion that the jury could reasonably find Drew sane under the *M'Naghten* rule, however, is itself a commentary on the inadequacy of that rule. In order to meet his burden of proof under *M'Naghten*, defendant had to prove his lack of cognitive capacity at the moment of the assault. This condition, however, is not a matter which psychiatrists can detect by testing or interview; neither is such cognitive incapacity a characteristic symptom of defendant's illness. The psychiatric account of the history and characteristics of Drew's illness does not bear directly on his ability to understand the difference between right and wrong Because that alleged inability is not a relevant psychiatric fact. In sum, inadequacy of the expert evidence to prove insanity under the *M'Naghten* rule is essentially the result of the fact that *M'Naghten* requires proof of a subjective cognitive state which is largely unrelated to the reality of mental illness.

5. *Disposition of this appeal.*

It is not surprising that, in view of the fact that we had not then endorsed the ALI test of mental incapacity, neither witnesses nor counsel structured their presentation at trial in terms of the ALI test, and the court did not instruct the jury on that standard. The record on appeal, nevertheless adduces substantial evidence of incapacity under the ALI criteria. His pattern of repetitive irrational assaults suggests the likelihood that he is unable to control his behavior to conform to legal requirements. His incapacity to control his behavior, moreover, is psychologically relevant to the diagnosis and treatment of his condition; thus the defense psychiatrists, who observed Drew's behavior and succeeded temporarily in controlling it through medication, might well have been able to state and support an opinion that he was insane under the ALI test. In view of the absence of prosecution evidence on the insanity issue, we conclude that if the case had been tried under the ALI standard and the jury instructed accordingly, it probably would have returned a verdict finding Drew insane. The trial court's failure to employ the ALI test therefore constitutes prejudicial error.

Finally, we recognize that in setting out a legal test to decide whether or not a person is insane we deal in a matter so delicate and obscure that it cannot be captured in a perfect definition. Yet because of the grave, and often life and death consequences that follow from a decision as to the sanity of an offender, we are surely enjoined to spare no effort to frame the best standard that is currently extant. We cannot justify the retention of a test based upon the single factor of cognition that has been abandoned by almost all the experts in the field and that has been rejected by all except one of the federal circuits and by an impressive number of state courts. Nor can we escape our obligation by relegating the problem to the Legislature in face of the fact that the *M'Naghten* test is a court-made test that this court itself has adopted and at times reiterated and at other times amended and variously construed.

We cannot continue to cast human beings in an ancient and discarded psychological mould. We must, at least to the best of our limited ability, accept the reality of the human psyche, as expert opinion depicts it, and bring the law as close as possible to an appraisal of the human being. We must recognize in certain cases his substantial incapacity either to appreciate the criminality of his conduct or to conform his conduct to the requirements of law. In judgment upon the sanity of the fragile and often inadequate human being we cannot be frozen into a stereotyped, rejected formula of the past.

The judgment is reversed and the cause remanded for a new trial on the issue raised by defendant's plea of not guilty by reason of insanity.

BIRD, C. J., MOSK and NEWMAN, JJ., concur.

RICHARDSON, JUSTICE, dissenting.

I respectfully dissent. My objection to the majority's approach may be briefly stated. I believe that a major change in the law of the type contemplated by the majority should be made by the Legislature. Although variously phrased, this has been the consistent, firm, and fixed position of this court for many years for reasons equally as applicable today as when first expressed. * *··

The ALI test is not without its critics. Indeed, in its desire to abandon the modified California test, the majority accepts a proposed new rule which may well create an entirely new set of problems. The Legislature's refusal thus far to adopt the ALI rule may result from its wish to learn from the English experience. As simply one illustration, it should be noted that a 1975 study of the British Home Office, Department of Health and Social Security, entitled *Report of the Committee on Mentally Abnormal Offenders* (hereinafter cited as *Report*) dealt with the specific question of the extent to which mental disorders should constitute defenses to criminal charges. In devising its own proposed test, the committee carefully considered but rejected the ALI test for reasons suggesting that it is not, to use the majority's term, the "best criteria currently extant."

The English committee focused on the ALI's use of the term "Mental disease or defect," and noted that such a vague undefined expression does not help to distinguish between minor and major disorders. The term has been abandoned in Britain for several years. This may be the case in the United States as well.

** Ed. In *Durham v. U.S.* (D.C. Cir., 1954) 214 F.2d 862, the court held that "an accused is not criminally responsible if his unlawful act was the product of mental disease or defect."

Furthermore the *Report* notes that the ALI test, as with the so-called *Durham* rule, leaves the interpretation of "mental disease or defect" with "psychiatrists who give evidence to the court." The *Report* observes that this fact prompted the author of the *Durham* rule, Judge Bazelon, to abandon *Durham* with this comment:

> In the end, after 18 years, I favored the abandonment of the *Durham* rule because in practice it had failed to take the issue of criminal responsibility away from the experts. Psychiatrists continued to testify to the naked conclusion instead of providing information about the accused so that the jury could render the ultimate *moral* judgment about blameworthiness. *Durham* had secured little improvement over *M'Naghten*." [Bazelon, *Psychiatrists and the Adversary Process*, Scientific Am. (June 1974) p. 230]

The committee then opines that the emphasis on capacity "to conform," which appears to be the only attractive portion of the ALI test, presents some very considerable additional problems, saying: "The Model Penal Code (ALI) proposal is open to the same objection as *Durham* in its reference to 'mental disease or defect,' but its second limb raises other problems. In particular the test of capacity to conform has to face a well-known philosophical criticism. How can one tell the difference between an impulse which is irresistible and one which is merely not resisted? Let us imagine two patients whose clinical symptoms appear similar, each of whom has been involved with a friend in an argument. Patient A flies into a rage and stabs his friend: Patient B does not. If A is prosecuted, a psychiatrist may be ready to testify that by reason of his disease of the mind he was deprived of the capacity to conform to the law, and he will no doubt be influenced by the fact that A did not conform to it. Patient B, not having assaulted his friend, is not prosecuted, so that no court hears psychiatric evidence about his capacity to conform: but presumably a psychiatrist would say that he had such a capacity, since he did not strike his friend. Some would seek to find a way out of this argument. There are offenders whose lack of self-control shows itself not only in a single offence, but also in their response to everyday temptations or frustrations. If patient A had a history of frequent and violent loss of temper, or if under observation after the assault he reacted violently to petty frustrations in the ward, such evidence would support the claim that he is less able than most men to control his temper. If, on the other hand, he was known to be extremely self-controlled, a psychiatrist would be justified in assuming that at normal times he was able to control himself and would have to explain the assault in some other way, for example, by showing that the argument developed in such a way as to give him extreme provocation (as the psychiatric witness did in the California case of *People v. Gorshen* ((1959) 51 Cal.2d 716. To this argument, the determinist would reply that the fact remains that the man who was normally able to control himself (i.e., who normally conformed) was not able to control himself on the occasion in question, as is shown by the fact that he did not conform. Also, even the psychopath or schizophrenic who is often aggressive is not *always* aggressive, so that aggression on a particular occasion is not completely explained by the psychopathy or schizophrenia. However this may be, it will generally be agreed that most cases are of the intermediate sort in which neither the circumstances nor the offender's usual behavior provided the obvious explanation; and in such cases it is usually fair to say that the only evidence of incapacity to conform with the law was the act itself." (*Report*, pp. 221-222.)

The majority in its uncritical acceptance has given no analytical consideration to problems of the type which have caused the English to reject the ALI rule. Furthermore, it seems fundamental that any "insanity" test should ideally and to the extent possible avoid the use of ambiguous standards which may be subject to varying interpretations and meanings. The ALI test includes such vague terms as "mental disease or defect," "substantial capacity," "appreciate criminality," and "conform conduct."

Additionally, any proposed test should limit the extent to which psychiatrists, in Judge Bazelon's language, may "testify to the naked conclusion" about criminal responsibility. As stressed in the new English formulation, the proposed test seeks to "(a) avoid the use of medical terms about which there may be disputed interpretations or whose meaning may change with the years; and (b) be such as to allow psychiatrists to state the facts of the defendant's mental condition without being required to pronounce on the extent of his responsibility for his offence. Degrees of responsibility are legal, not medical, concepts." (*Report*, p. 222.)

The ALI test does very little to assist in either critical area. Its primary appeal is that it is different.

Professor Richard Gambino, professor of educational philosophy, Queens College, in a current article entitled *The Murderous Mind: Insanity v. The Law* ((Mar. 18, 1978) Saturday Review, at p. 10, traces the origins of the *M'Naughten* rule, and of various suggested changes in the light of more modern scientific knowledge. Professor Gambino stresses the extreme difficulty in meshing the different disciplines of psychiatry and the law, each possessing as it does its own variant definitions and standards. He emphasizes that

> Psychiatry is a healing art. Its function is to understand and cure, not to define moral or legal responsibility or to accomplish justice. In fact, the profession of psychiatry does not use or recognize the terms "sanity" and "insanity." They are strictly legal terms.

On the point before us, his assessment of the experience with the majority's proposed ALI test is not encouraging. After describing the *M'Naughten* and *Durham* rules and their limitations he concludes, "In 1961, the American Law Institute recommended a new test, which was a merger of the *M'Naghten* and *Durham* rules. Unfortunately, it has served little purpose except to compound the difficulties of both standards."

The formulation of intelligent rules covering the assertion of insanity as a criminal defense is a very complex problem. This fact underscores the wisdom of judicial restraint. Professor Gambino cites two interesting experiments conducted at Stanford University in 1972 which illustrate the disturbing uncertainties which persist 135 years after *M'Naughten*. He reports that "Eight researchers feigned hearing 'voices' and gained admission to 12 different psychiatric hospitals. None of the eight falsified their real life history, except for the voices, nor did any of them have a history of pathological behavior. Yet in 11 of the 12 instances, the researchers were diagnosed as 'schizophrenic,' while in the twelfth, the diagnosis was 'manic depressive.' Although other patients regarded the researchers as normal, no member of the hospitals' staff did. Then, in a follow-up experiment, the staff of a psychiatric hospital were told that one or more fake patients would be sent to them. Although none were actually sent, 41 of 193 patients admitted for treatment in the following period of time were thought to be fakes, in each case by at least one member of the hospital's staff."

While the examples may be extreme, they do caution a judicial "go slowly" approach in this area. Assuming, as we may, the validity of the majority's contention that in the 135 years since *M'Naughten* there have been many psychiatric advances, the Legislature is thoroughly justified in taking a very long and careful, indeed skeptical, look before jettisoning the existing and carefully evolved body of law which now composes the California *M'Naughten* rule as illustrated by *Wolff*.

I have no doubt that further improvements may be made in the techniques used to resolve the difficult issue of insanity as a defense in criminal cases. This goal is much more likely to be achieved, in my opinion, through a fact-finding process which enlists the aid of experts in the relevant disciplines who have given careful and close study to this very troublesome problem. I believe that this is what the Legislature is attempting in its evaluation of the critical medical-legal dialogue. It is a slow process. Undoubtedly, professional disagreements will appear, but as in many comparable areas there may well emerge a responsible consensus which would, by providing guidance to the Legislature, make possible a reasoned improvement over the present California rule. Such a legislative process, as repeatedly described by us, is to me a much sounder approach than that adopted by the majority which, disregarding legislative attention, chooses its own formulation predicated primarily and essentially upon judicial instinct, second-hand sources, and appellate argument.

I would affirm the judgment.

CLARK, and MANUEL, JJ., concur.

NOTES FROM WALLY:

(1) Compare the Court's attitude toward psychiatric witnesses expressed in *Wolff* with that expressed in *Drew*. Were there dramatic improvements in psychiatry between 1964 and 1978 which might explain this difference?

(2) The court is concerned that psychiatrists have difficulty testifying under the *M'Naughten* rule. So what? Is the *purpose* of the insanity defense to make it easy for psychiatrists to testify? Just what is the purpose of the insanity defense, anyway? Put another way, how does the insanity defense *not* diminish the usual purposes of punishment — deterrence, retribution, etc.? Does the *M'Naughten* rule or the ALI test do a better job of this?

(3) Would our client do better under the ALI test than the *M'Naughten* test? How so?

(4) Does it really matter which test (*M'Naughten* or ALI) is adopted? Is this merely an academic tempest in a teapot, or does it actually affect the outcome of cases? At least one jury apparently thought there was a difference. In 1983, a young man named Alex Cabarga was charged in California with a series of very

similar sex offenses which spanned several months in 1982. During the early months, the *Drew*-ALI test was operative. During the later months, the *Skinner-M'Naughten* test was operative.

The jury used two different definitions of sanity in judging Cabarga, depending on whether the crimes were committed before or after the 1982 passage of the Victims' Bill of Rights. Using one definition of sanity [the ALI test], the jury was deadlocked on whether Cabarga was sane when he committed 58 of the crimes. After the longest deliberation in recent judicial memory, the jury found Cabarga was sane during the commission of 35 crimes under a different definition of insanity [the *M'Naughton* test]. For this he was sentenced to 208 years in prison. [San Francisco Chronicle, *This World*, 3/20/88, page 14.]

PEOPLE v. WETMORE
California Supreme Court
22 Cal.3d 318, 583 P.2d 1308 (1978)

TOBRINER, J.

Charged with burglary, defendant argued that psychiatric reports showed that as a result of mental illness he lacked the specific intent required for conviction of that crime. Relying on a dictum in *People v. Wells* (1949) 33 Cal.2d 330, the trial court reasoned that because the reports described defendant's insanity as well as his diminished capacity, such description of defendant's condition in those reports should not be admitted to prove lack of specific intent. The court found defendant guilty of second degree burglary; subsequently, relying on the psychiatric reports, it found him insane.

We hold that the dictum from *Wells* on which the trial court relied must be rejected. The state bears the burden of proving every element of the offense charged; defendant cannot logically or constitutionally be denied the right to present probative evidence rebutting an element of the crime merely because such evidence also suggests insanity.

Defendant's evidence established that he entered an apartment under a delusion that he owned that apartment and thus did not enter with the intent of committing a theft or felony. That evidence demonstrated that defendant lacked the specific intent required for a conviction of burglary; the trial court's refusal to consider the evidence at the guilt phase of the trial therefore constituted prejudicial error.

We reject the suggestion of *amicus* that we sustain the trial court by holding that a defense of diminished capacity cannot be raised whenever, owing to the lack of a lesser included offense, it might result in the defendant's acquittal. A defendant who, because of diminished capacity, does not entertain the specific intent required for a particular crime is entitled to be acquitted of that crime. If he cannot be convicted of a lesser offense and cannot safely be released, the state's remedy is to institute civil commitment proceedings, not to convict him of a specific intent crime which he did not commit.

The only evidence submitted to the trial court in this case was the testimony of Joseph Cacciatore, the victim of the burglary, at the preliminary hearing, and three psychiatric reports. Cacciatore testified that he left his apartment on March 7, 1975. When he returned three days later, he discovered defendant in his apartment. Defendant was wearing Cacciatore's clothes and cooking his food. The lock on the front door had been broken; the apartment lay in a shambles. Cacciatore called the police, who arrested defendant for burglary. Later Cacciatore discovered that a ring, a watch, a credit card, and items of clothing were missing.[1]

The psychiatric reports submitted to the court explain defendant's long history of psychotic illness, including at least 10 occasions of hospital confinement for treatment. According to the reports, defendant, shortly after his last release from Brentwood Veteran's Hospital, found himself with no place to go. He began to believe that he "owned" property, and was "directed" to Cacciatore's apartment. When he found the door unlocked he was sure he owned the apartment. He entered, rearranged the apartment, destroyed some advertising he felt was inappropriate, and put on Cacciatore's clothes. When the police arrived, defendant was shocked and embarrassed, and only then understood that he did not own the apartment.

Defendant pled not guilty to a charge of burglary and requested court appointment of a psychiatrist to advise him whether to enter a plea based on insanity. After receiving the report from Dr. John Woodward, defendant entered a plea of not guilty by reason of insanity. The court then appointed Drs. Michael Colburn and Marshall Cherkas to examine defendant.

When the matter was called for trial, defendant personally and all counsel waived trial by jury and stipulated that the cause be submitted on the transcript of the preliminary hearing, which contained only the testimony of Cacciatore, and the reports of Drs. Colburn and Cherkas. Defense counsel pointed out that burglary requires an entry with specific intent to commit larceny or felony. See Pen. Code § 459. The reports of Drs. Colburn and Cherkas, counsel argued, indicate that defendant entered the apartment under the delusion that he owned the apartment and its contents; he thus had no intent to commit theft or any felony.

In response to counsel's argument, the court acknowledged that defendant might lack the specific intent required to commit the crime of burglary. It stated, however, that under the controlling cases, "if a defendant's mental capacity which would preclude the forming of a specific intent is that of insanity," that mental condition is "not admissible to establish the question of lack of specific intent due to diminished capacity." The court thereupon found defendant guilty of second degree burglary. Turning to the issue of insanity, the court found on the basis of the psychiatric reports that defendant was insane under the *M'Naghten* test then applicable[3] and, hence, not guilty by reason of insanity.

---

[1] At the preliminary hearing defendant appeared wearing one of Cacciatore's shirts. The magistrate directed the sheriff to provide defendant with a county shirt, and admitted Cacciatore's shirt into evidence as an exhibit.

[3] "Insanity, under the California *M'Naughton* test, denotes a mental condition which renders a person incapable of knowing or understanding the nature and quality of his act, or incapable of

At a subsequent hearing the trial court found that defendant had not recovered his sanity. The court therefore ordered defendant committed to Patton State Hospital for treatment. Defendant appeals from the order of commitment.

In holding that defendant's psychiatric evidence could not be utilized to prove that he lacked the specific intent required for the offense of burglary, the trial court followed a dictum laid down in our decision in *People v. Wells, supra,* 33 Cal.2d 330. *Wells,* the seminal decision which established the doctrine of diminished capacity in California law, held that "evidence of diminished mental capacity, whether caused by intoxication, trauma, or disease, can be used to show that a defendant did not have a specific mental state essential to an offense." *People v. Conley* (1966) 64 Cal.2d 310, 316.

In dictum, however, *Wells* stated that since sanity is conclusively presumed at the guilt trial, "evidence tending to show lack of mental capacity to commit the crime because of legal insanity is barred at that stage." The *Wells* opinion later restated that conclusion in different terms: "If the proffered evidence tends to show not merely that he [defendant] did or did not, but rather that because of legal insanity he could not, entertain the specific intent or other essential mental state, then that evidence is inadmissible under the not guilty plea."

As we shall explain, the *Wells* dictum imposes an illogical and unworkable rule which has not been followed in subsequent cases. *Wells* spoke of excluding evidence which tended to prove "lack of mental capacity because of legal insanity." Mental incapacity does not occur "because of legal insanity;" instead both insanity and diminished capacity are legal conclusions derived from evidence of defendant's mental condition. Consequently, if the evidence of a defendant's mental illness indicates that the defendant lacked the specific intent to commit the charged crime, such evidence cannot reasonably be ignored at the guilt trial merely because it might (but might not) also persuade the trier of fact that the defendant is insane.

Wells' distinction between evidence that defendant did not entertain the requisite intent, which is admissible, and evidence that he could not entertain that intent, which is inadmissible, cannot be supported. "As a matter of logic, any proof tending to show that a certain mental condition could not exist is relevant and should be admissible to show that it did not exist. And, of course, proof that something could not exist is the best possible evidence that it did not exist." Louisell & Hazard, *Insanity as a Defense: The Bifurcated Trial* (1961) 49 Cal.L.Rev. 805, 819. Moreover, as Justice Kaus pointed out in *People v. Steele* (1965) 237 Cal.App.2d 182, 190-191, evidence which tends to prove that a defendant could not entertain a certain intent may, when subject to cross-examination, convince the trier of fact that defendant was able to entertain the intent but did not do so on the occasion of the crime. Thus, *Steele* concludes, the trial court cannot refuse to admit such evidence when offered to prove diminished capacity.[4]

---

distinguishing right from wrong in relation to that act." (*People v. Kelly* (1973) 10 Cal.3d 565, 574)

[4] *Amicus curiae* proposed that a defendant who desires to present evidence of diminished capacity be required to lay a foundation that the evidence, if believed, would not establish legal insanity. This proposal encounters two objections. First, as the court observed in *People v. Steele, supra,* evidence which at first viewing appears to prove insanity may, after cross-examination and rebuttal, prove only diminished capacity. Second, insanity is a jury question; the ruling of the trial judge, rendered in the

Numerous cases have repeated the *Wells* dictum barring evidence tending to prove insanity from admission at the guilt trial; yet the courts, in violation of the *Wells* dictum, have consistently relied on such evidence to resolve issues of diminished capacity. A series of decisions of this court, beginning with *People v. Wolff* (1964) 61 Cal.2d 795, illustrates the point. *Wolff*, a 16-year-old boy, was convicted of the first degree murder of his mother. Although four psychiatrists testified at the sanity trial that *Wolff* was insane, the jury nevertheless found him sane. On appeal, we held that substantial evidence supported the finding of sanity, but that the evidence introduced at the sanity phase demonstrated as a matter of law that since *Wolff* did not premeditate, he committed not first, but second degree murder. Our opinion thus treated evidence introduced at the sanity phase for the purpose of establishing defendant's insanity as not merely probative but in fact convincing proof of diminished capacity.

* * * *

The foregoing cases demonstrate that *Wells'* distinction between evidence which tends to prove insanity and evidence probative of diminished capacity cannot stand. Although the cases occasionally reiterate the dictum that evidence of insanity cannot be admitted to prove diminished capacity, the appellate courts nevertheless consistently rely upon such evidence to resolve issues of diminished capacity, to hold that the trial courts err in refusing to consider such evidence at the guilt phase, and to rule that counsel who fail to offer such evidence at the guilt phase are incompetent. In concluding that the *Wells* dictum is erroneous and should no longer be followed, we merely confirm the actual practice of the California courts.[6]

The *Wells* dictum limits the defendant's ability to rebut the element of specific intent by barring evidence at the guilt phase that, owing to mental illness, he lacks the requisite intent if such evidence would also tend to prove insanity. Although defendant can present that evidence later to prove insanity, defendant bears the burden of proof on the issue of sanity. Evid.Code § 522. To deny the defendant the opportunity to present that evidence at a time when the state still bears the burden of proof beyond a reasonable doubt may deny him due process of law.

We therefore hold that evidence of diminished capacity is admissible at the guilt phase whether or not that evidence may also be probative of insanity. The trial court erred when, relying on the *Wells* dictum, it refused to consider evidence of diminished capacity in determining defendant's guilt.

---

context of an objection to the admissibility of evidence at the guilt trial, would not bind the jury at the sanity trial. Consequently, under the proposal of *amicus*, a defendant who presented conclusive evidence that he lacked the capacity to commit a crime could be convicted of that crime because the evidence, although held inadmissible at the guilt phase on the ground that it established insanity, subsequently proved insufficient to convince the jury of his insanity.

[6] Recent court decisions, moreover, suggest that the *Wells* dictum, because it excludes evidence probative of defendant's innocence from the guilt phase, may be unconstitutional. In *Mullaney v. Wilbur* (1975) 421 U.S. 684, the United States Supreme Court implied broadly that the state must prove beyond a reasonable doubt every fact critical to the guilt of the offender or the severity of the offense. Although the court subsequently limited the broad language of *Mullaney in Patterson v. New York* (1977) 432 U.S. 197, *Patterson* explained that the state has at least the constitutional duty to prove beyond a reasonable doubt all traditional elements of the crime.

Amicus Los Angeles City Attorney urges that we sustain the trial court's ruling on a different ground. He contends that a defendant should be permitted to assert the defense of diminished capacity caused by mental disease or defect only to reduce a specific crime to a lesser included offense. Claiming that there is no lesser included offense in burglary, amicus argues that the trial court correctly refused to consider evidence of defendant Wetmore's diminished mental capacity.

* * * *

A defense of diminished capacity arising from mental disease or defect extends to all specific intent crimes, whether or not they encompass lesser included offenses. Clearly, if a crime requires specific intent, a defendant who because of mental disease or defect lacks that intent, cannot commit that crime. The presence or absence of a lesser included offense within the charged crime cannot affect the result. The prosecution must prove all elements of the crime beyond a reasonable doubt; we do not perceive how a defendant who has in his possession evidence which rebuts an element of the crime can logically be denied the right to present that evidence merely because it will result in his acquittal.

Amicus' argument, although legally flawed, addresses a matter of real concern. A defendant whose criminal activity arises from mental disease or defect usually requires confinement and special treatment. Penal Code §§ 1026 and 1026a provide such confinement and treatment for persons found not guilty by reason of insanity. A defendant acquitted because, as a result of diminished capacity, he lacked the specific intent required for the crime cannot be confined pursuant to §§ 1026 and 1026a, yet often he cannot be released without endangering the public safety.

The same danger may arise, however, when a diminished capacity defense does not result in the defendant's acquittal, but in his conviction for a lesser included offense. A defendant convicted of a lesser included misdemeanor, for example, will be confined for a relatively short period in a facility which probably lacks a suitable treatment program, and may later, having served his term, be released to become a public danger. The solution to this problem thus does not lie in barring the defense of diminished capacity when the charged crime lacks a lesser included offense, but in providing for the confinement and treatment of defendants with diminished capacity arising from mental disease or defect.

The Lanterman-Petris-Short Act provides for the civil commitment of any person who, "as a result of mental disorder, [is] a danger to others, or to himself, or gravely disabled." Welf. & Inst. Code § 5150. Recognizing that evidence of such mental disorder may arise at trial, the Legislature provided that a judge of the county where a prisoner is confined may institute evaluation and treatment procedures under the Lanterman-Petris-Short Act. Pen. Code § 4011.6. Thus if evidence adduced in support of a successful diminished capacity defense indicates to the trial judge that the defendant is dangerous, the court is not compelled to foist the defendant upon the public; it may, instead, initiate procedures for civil commitment.

The Attorney General points out that a person who commits a crime against property, such as defendant Wetmore, might not be commitable under the

Lanterman-Petris-Short Act unless he were "gravely disabled." A more serious omission lies in the act's failure to provide for long term commitment of persons dangerous to others; unless found "gravely disabled," a person "who, as a result of mental disorder, presents an imminent threat of substantial physical harm to others" cannot be confined beyond the initial 90-day postcertification treatment period unless "he has threatened, attempted, or actually inflicted physical harm to another during his period of postcertification treatment." Welf. & Inst. Code, § 5304. If the Lanterman-Petris-Short Act does not adequately protect the public against crimes committed by persons with diminished mental capacity, the answer lies either in amendment to that act or in the enactment of legislation that would provide for commitment of persons acquitted by virtue of a successful diminished capacity defense in the same manner as persons acquitted by reason of insanity are presently committed. It does not lie in judicial creation of an illogical — and possibly unconstitutional -rule denying the defense of diminished capacity to persons charged with crimes lacking a lesser included offense.

Before concluding, we think it appropriate to note the effect of this decision, the latest in a line of decisions establishing and refining the concept of diminished capacity, on the California statutes governing the trial and disposition of persons who plead not guilty by reason of insanity. Doubtless when the 1927 Legislature provided for the bifurcated trial, it believed that it had cleanly separated the trial of issues of objective guilt from those involving mental illness or incapacity. The rise of the defense of diminished capacity has obliterated the distinction the Legislature sought to enact. The development of that defense has brought it so close to that of insanity that we doubt that the issue of diminished capacity has currently been placed on the proper side of the judicial ledger. Indeed, when we changed the designation of the defense from diminished "responsibility" to diminished "capacity," we approached more nearly the concept of inability to conform one's conduct to the requirements of law, which is now a facet of the test of insanity. We said in *People v. Anderson*, "Clearly we cannot hold defendant responsible for a crime which requires as one of its elements the presence of a state of mind which he is incapable of achieving because of subjective abnormality or impaired volitional powers." 63 Cal.2d at p.365.

Prior to this appeal we have been confronted with a substantial number of cases that have illustrated the overlap in evidence admissible to prove diminished capacity and evidence admissible to prove insanity; with the present decision the duplication approaches a totality. To require the jury to hear the same evidence twice, once to determine diminished capacity and once to determine insanity, appears a pointless waste of judicial time and resources.

As we did once before, we again suggest that the Legislature reconsider the wisdom of the statutes providing for bifurcated trial. The evidentiary duplication inherent in the present procedure could be eliminated either by a unitary trial or by a new method of bifurcation in which issues of diminished capacity and insanity are tried together at the second phase of the trial The decision to modify or abolish the bifurcated trial remains, of course, a legislative prerogative; our role is limited to noting the impact of judicial developments upon the statutory structure erected by the Legislature, and suggesting the possibility of legislative reconsideration.

In conclusion, the trial court in the present case erroneously refused to consider at the guilt phase evidence which clearly indicated that defendant believed that he owned the apartment and its contents, and thus entered the apartment without specific intent to commit a theft or felony. If the court had considered that evidence, it is reasonably probable that it would not have found defendant guilty of burglary; thus the error was prejudicial. Although defendant might have been subject to civil commitment proceedings even if acquitted of burglary, he would not have been subject to commitment pursuant to Penal Code § 1026 as ordered by the trial court.

The judgment (order of commitment) is reversed and the cause remanded for further proceedings consistent with this opinion.

NOTES FROM WALLY:

(1) As the trial court found Wetmore not guilty by reason of insanity anyway, how did he benefit from the court's ruling?

(2) Since the *Wetmore* decision, Penal Code §§ 25, 28, and 29 were enacted. If you were representing Wetmore today, what would be your strategy?

(3) How can we use Dr. Meshuga's testimony regarding premeditation? What effect do Penal Code § 25 and § 28 have on this? Note the discussion in *Wetmore* about a possible *constitutional* basis for a diminished capacity defense. What do you think about this?

Note Re Diminished Capacity

The history of California's handling of diminished capacity has been turbulent and fascinating.

In Penal Code § 1026, the legislature determined that, where insanity is pleaded, there should be a bifurcated trial: first try the issue of guilt, then the issue of insanity. This was meant (1) to make it easier for the jury to understand the case, (2) to ensure that the defendant would be sent to a mental hospital if his insanity defense succeeded, (3) to give the defendant the opportunity to avoid this fate if — for example — he had a valid alibi defense.

In a series of decisions on diminished capacity, however, the California Supreme Court gradually undermined these purposes. The court held that the defendant *could* raise his mental disease as a defense or mitigation in the guilt phase, and this might reduce his culpability to the point that he could "live with" his sentence (e.g., for manslaughter instead of murder) and not rely on winning the insanity defense in the second phase.

In *People v. Wells*, 33 Cal.2d 330 (1949), defendant was charged with the crime of assault by a life-term prisoner with "malice aforethought." The court held that evidence of his mental abnormality — short of insanity — was admissible to show that he did not act with "malice aforethought." Evidence that showed insanity, however, would be admissible only in the insanity phase of a bifurcated trial:

Thus, if the proffered evidence tends to show not merely that he *did* or *did not*, but rather that because of legal insanity he *could* not, entertain the specific intent or other essential mental state, then that evidence is inadmissible under the not guilty plea and is admissible only on the trial on the plea of not guilty by reason of insanity. [*Id.* at 351.]

After quoting the above language, *Wetmore* called it "an illogical and unworkable rule." (Nevertheless, its essence now appears in California Penal Code § 28(a).)

In *People v. Conley*, 64 Cal.2d 310 (1966), the court held that evidence of the defendant's mental problems was admissible to negate the "malice aforethought" required for murder, citing *Wells*. "A person who intentionally kills may be incapable of harboring malice aforethought because of mental illness . . . and in such a case his killing is voluntary manslaughter." *Id.* at 318. The court overlooked the fact that, according to the modern definition of "malice aforethought" followed by most courts, intent to kill is in fact one of the 4 types of "malice aforethought" which will support a murder conviction.

In *People v. Poddar*, 10 Cal.3d 750 (1974), the court followed *Wells* and *Conley*, holding that the jury should be instructed that evidence of defendant's "depraved heart" mental state could be negated by evidence of his mental problems. "If it is established that an accused, because he suffered a diminished capacity, was unaware of or unable to act in accordance with the law, malice could not properly be found and the maximum offense for which he could be convicted would be voluntary manslaughter." *Id.* at 758. Here again, the court appears to have departed from the definition of "depraved heart" used in most jurisdictions, which have not included awareness of the law or the ability to act in accordance with the law in this definition.

The diminished capacity cases finally culminated in *People v. Wetmore*, where the court went all the way and held that diminished capacity could not only *reduce* the crime, but wipe it out altogether. Thus, the defendant could in effect win an insanity-type defense without automatically being sent to a mental hospital (though he did risk a new suit for civil commitment) — all in the first (or only) phase of the trial! Perhaps this holding logically and inevitably followed from the Court's earlier diminished capacity rulings, but it also threatened to destroy the bifurcated trial system, as the Court itself admitted towards the end of its opinion. (The Court suggested that the Legislature resolve the problem by abolishing the bifurcated trial. In 1982, however, the electorate attempted to resolve the problem in quite a different way: by abolishing diminished capacity!)

This result might have been tolerable while the Court retained the *M'Naughton* test (and a pretty tough version of it at that - rejecting the irresistible impulse addition). In effect, the Court was saying: "We don't want to ease up on the *M'Naughton* test, as the ALI test might lessen the deterrent effect of the threatened punishment. But we do feel somewhat sympathetic to defendants with mental diseases, so we'll have a pretty loose diminished capacity test, to give them a good shot at having first degree murder reduced to second degree, and second degree murder reduced to manslaughter." This trade-off (unstated) seemed to be roughly just.

The Court revoked the trade-off in 1978, in *People v. Drew*, when it adopted the ALI test, with no hint that it was changing the diminished capacity test. (In fact, it decided *Wetmore* at the same time it decided *Drew*!)

In 1978, former San Francisco Supervisor Dan White shot and killed Supervisor Harvey Milk (the city's first gay supervisor) and Mayor George Moscone. White was charged with first degree murder. Using jury instructions based on *Conley* and *Poddar*, and evidence that White's junk food diet had affected his emotional stability (inspiring some wags to label the defense the "Twinkie" defense), White's attorney persuaded the jury to bring in a verdict of voluntary manslaughter. *People v. White*, 117 Cal.App.3d 270 (1981).

In the ensuing uproar over the verdict (including riots by many people in San Francisco's gay community), the California Legislature enacted Penal Code §§ 28 and 29, in 1981.

The following year, an initiative measure (Proposition 8, ambitiously entitled "The Victim's Bill of Rights") was passed by the California electorate. This emanated from a public perception that bleeding-heart judges and weak-kneed legislators were at least partly responsible for a perceived increase in crime. Proposition 8 contained many sections dealing with crime and victims - including elimination of California's state-based exclusionary rule for illegally seized evidence. Penal Code § 25 was also part of this package.

While these actions were certainly meant to diminish the diminished capacity defense in California, do they wipe it out? Particularly troubling is Penal Code § 28(a), which appears to be intended to restore the language of *Wells* which *Wetmore* disapproved. However, in *People v. Cortes*, 192 Cal.App.4th 873 (2011), the court summarized how the courts have interpreted these statutes:

> Sections 28 and 29 in fact leave an expert considerable latitude to express an opinion on the defendant's mental condition at the time of offense, within the confines, of course, of its twin prohibitions: no testimony on the defendant's capacity to have, or actually having, the intent required to commit the charged crime.

> Sections 28 and 29 do not preclude offering as a defense the absence of a mental state that is an element of a charged offense or presenting evidence in support of that defense. They preclude only expert opinion that the element was not present.

> By its terms, section 29 prohibits an expert witness from giving an opinion about the ultimate fact whether a defendant had the required mental state for conviction of a crime. It prohibits no more than that.

In 1990, the California electorate enacted the "Crime Victims Justice Reform Act", which added the following paragraph to Penal Code § 189: "To prove the killing was 'deliberate and premeditated', it shall not be necessary to prove the defendant maturely and meaningfully reflected upon the gravity of his or her act." The preamble to the Act stated that the people "find that the rights of crime victims are too often ignored by our courts and by our State Legislature, that the death penalty is a deterrent to murder, and that comprehensive reforms are needed in order to restore balance and fairness to our criminal justice system." In *People v. Stress*, 205 Cal.App.3d 1259 (1988), the court stated:

> Perhaps in part because of a concern that such formulations [as that set out in *People v. Wolff*] are so vague as to escape understanding, so complex as to prevent workable application, and so ambiguous as to allow for capricious results, the Legislature in 1981 eliminated the judicially created defense of diminished capacity. The next year, the People through Proposition 8 also eliminated the defense. See § 25.

> As a part of the legislation eliminating the defense of diminished capacity, a paragraph was added to § 189 specifically stating that it was unnecessary to prove a defendant maturely and meaningfully reflected on the gravity of his or her act in proving deliberation and premeditation. Mature and meaningful reflection was clearly the California Supreme Court's shorthand way of applying the concept of diminished capacity to the elements of deliberation and premeditation. Essentially the court broadened the elements of premeditation and deliberation by requiring not merely a weighing of considerations and careful thought but by requiring a quality of deliberation and weighing which the court described as mature and meaningful reflection. This broadening of the elements had the practical effect of allowing a defense based on the claim that even though a defendant had carefully planned, and had considered the consequences of an act, he nonetheless was not guilty of first degree murder when, because of mental disease or defect, his reflection was not mature and meaningful. Thus, the phrase mature and meaningful reflection defined the capacity which the defendant could claim was diminished.

> The effect then of the removal of mature and meaningful reflection as part of the elements of deliberation and premeditation is to narrow those elements. We conclude that with the removal of the vague requirement for mature and meaningful reflection, deliberation and premeditation are proved when the trier of facts concludes not merely that the defendant harbored an intent to kill but when that intent was the result of forethought and reflection, and when careful thought and a weighing of considerations are demonstrated. A finding of deliberation and premeditation is not negated by evidence a defendant's mental condition was abnormal or his perception of reality delusional unless those conditions resulted in the failure to plan or weigh considerations for and against the proposed course of action. The mental process necessary for a finding of deliberation and premeditation is not dependent on the motivation for the act. Nor is the necessary mental process lacking when the considerations reflected on by the defendant were the product of mental disease or defect.

In *People v. Bobo*, 221 Cal.App.3d 1432 (1990), defendant was charged with first degree murder of her 3 children. She killed the children because she had a delusion that some men were going to torture and kill her and the children, "that they was going to have a worser death". She claimed that she was not guilty, because her paranoid schizophrenia caused the delusion, which negated both "malice aforethought" and "premeditation." The jury found her guilty, and the Court of Appeal affirmed.

First, the court held that "premeditation" was present, as the defendant had planned the killings for several hours. Defendant argued that her mental illness prevented her from engaging in "mature and meaningful reflection" on her plan, which *People v. Wolff* held was required for "premeditation." The court rejected this argument, because the 1981 amendment to Penal Code § 189 (set out in Chapter 8) eliminated this notion from the definition of "premeditation" — effectively overruling this part of *Wolff*.

Second, the court held that "malice aforethought" was present, simply because defendant intended to kill the children. Defendant argued that her mental illness made her unaware or unable to act in accordance with the law, citing *People v. Conley* and *People v. Poddar*. But the court held that the second paragraph of Penal Code § 188 (set out in Chapter 8) — added by the Legislature in 1981 — repudiated the holdings in *Conley* and *Poddar*.

In *People v. Saille*, 54 Cal.3d 1103 (1992), the California Supreme Court addressed the second issue in *Bobo*, agreeing with how *Bobo* handled it. The Court held that the amendment to § 188 "directly repudiates the expanded definition of malice aforethought in *People v. Conley* and *People v. Poddar* that express and implied malice include an awareness of the obligation to act within the general body of laws regulating society and the capability of acting in accordance with such awareness. After this amendment of § 188, express malice and an intent unlawfully to kill are one and the same." Other than to show insanity, the only way a defendant may use his mental illness is to show that "he did not in fact form the intent unlawfully to kill (i.e., did not have malice aforethought.)"

Where does all this leave *Wetmore* (which was not a murder case)? If the case were to arise today, would it be decided the same way? In *U.S. v. Pohlot*, 827 F.2d 889 (3rd Cir. 1987), the court construed recent federal legislation to mean that Congress intended to disallow any defense of diminished capacity — just as California did. Nevertheless, the court held, this abolition of diminished capacity does not prevent a defendant from presenting evidence of his mental state which tends to disprove the mental state which is a required element of the crime. "Admitting psychiatric evidence to negate *mens rea* does not constitute a defense, but only negates an element of the offense." *Id.* at 897. See also *U.S. v. Cameron*, 907 F.2d 1051 (11th Cir. 1990). Was Wetmore claiming "diminished capacity", or was he simply denying that he had the intent required for the crime charged?

In *In re Christian*, 7 Cal.4th 768 (1994), the court held that California's elimination of diminished capacity did not eliminate the "imperfect self-defense" doctrine, whereby an honest but unreasonable belief that it is necessary to defend oneself may reduce murder to voluntary manslaughter. In *People v. Mejia-Lenares* 135 Cal.App.4th 1437 (2006), the court held that imperfect self-defense cannot be based on a delusion:

> At least in part to ameliorate the law governing criminal responsibility prescribed by the *M'Naghten* rule, two separate and independent, although occasionally overlapping, doctrines emerged: diminished capacity and

imperfect self-defense. Under the doctrine of imperfect self-defense, a defendant can seek to negate malice by introducing evidence that he or she actually, albeit unreasonably, believed it was necessary to defend him-or herself from imminent peril to life or great bodily injury. * * * *

Diminished capacity was eliminated by the Legislature in 1981 and by voter initiative in 1982. However, "diminished actuality" remains a viable concept. While the Legislature, in eliminating the diminished capacity defense, precluded jury consideration of mental disease, defect, or disorder as evidence of a defendant's *capacity* to form a requisite criminal intent, it did not preclude jury consideration of mental condition in deciding whether a defendant *actually* formed the requisite criminal intent. * * * *

In *Christian S.*, the state Supreme Court found no indication in the 1981 amendments to the Penal Code that the Legislature intended to eliminate imperfect self-defense along with diminished capacity, and it rejected the notion that the two concepts are so closely related that when the Legislature eliminated one, it necessarily also eliminated the other. The court explained:

> The two doctrines relate to the concept of malice, but the similarity ends there. Unlike diminished capacity, imperfect self-defense is not rooted in any notion of mental capacity or awareness of the need to act lawfully. To the contrary, a person may be entirely free of any mental disease, defect, or intoxication and may be fully aware of the need to act lawfully - and thus not have a diminished capacity - but actually, although unreasonably, believe in the need for self-defense. Put simply, an awareness of the need to act lawfully does not - in fact or logic - depend on whether the putative victim's belief in the need for self-defense is correct. A person who actually believes in the need for self-defense necessarily believes he is acting lawfully. He is thus aware of the obligation to act lawfully. A defendant could assert one doctrine even though the facts did not support the other. The diminished-capacity defense could be - and often has been - asserted when self-defense was not an issue; and, conversely, imperfect self-defense could be raised when there was no claim of diminished capacity. * * * *

Although *Christian S.* settled the question of the imperfect self-defense doctrine's viability following the elimination of the diminished capacity defense, neither it nor any subsequent Supreme Court opinion suggests this "narrow" doctrine now covers aspects of diminished capacity or diminished actuality not previously included. Thus, imperfect self-defense remains a species of mistake of fact; as such, it cannot be founded on delusion. In our view, a mistake of fact is predicated upon a negligent perception of facts, not, as in the case of a delusion, a perception of facts not grounded in reality. A person acting under a delusion is not negligently interpreting actual facts; instead, he or she is out of touch with reality. That may be insanity, but it is not a mistake as to any fact.* * * *

Persons operating under a delusion theoretically are insane since, because of their delusion, they do not know or understand the nature of their act or, if they do, they do not know that it is wrong. By contrast, persons operating under a mistake of fact are reasonable people who have simply made an unreasonable mistake. To allow a true delusion - a false belief with no foundation in fact - to form the basis of an unreasonable mistake-of-fact defense erroneously mixes the concepts of a normally reasonable person making a genuine but unreasonable mistake of fact (a reasonable person doing an unreasonable thing), and an insane person. Thus, while one who acts on a delusion may argue that he or she did not realize he or she was acting unlawfully as a result of the delusion, he or she may not take a delusional perception and treat it as if it were true for purposes of assessing wrongful intent.

In other words, a defendant is not permitted to argue, "The devil was trying to kill me," and have the jury assess reasonableness, justification, or excuse as if the delusion were true, for purposes of evaluating state of mind.

To hold otherwise would undercut the legislative provisions separating guilt from insanity. Allowing a defendant to use delusion as the basis of unreasonable mistake of fact effectively permits him or her to use insanity as a defense without pleading not guilty by reason of insanity, and thus to do indirectly what he or she could not do directly while also avoiding the long-term commitment that may result from an insanity finding. If a defendant is operating under a delusion as the result of mental disease or defect, then the issue is one of insanity, not factual mistake. To allow a mistake-of-fact defense to be based not on a reasonable person standard but instead on the standard of a crazy person would undermine the defense that is intended to accommodate the problem.

You might find this story of diminished capacity complicated and confusing, but lawyers must often deal with complicated and confusing material. (That's why they get paid so much!) The story might not be over — other cases may resolve some of the difficult issues left hanging by unclear legislation. But lawyers with pending cases cannot wait until appellate courts resolve the big issues. They must use the cases and statutes presently available — and the policies behind those authorities — to make the best arguments they can. Try to do the same with Problem 12.

PEOPLE v. SKINNER
California Supreme Court
39 Cal.3d 765, 704 P.2d 752 (1985)

GRODIN, J.

For over a century prior to the decision in *People v. Drew* (1978) 22 Cal.3d 333, California courts framed this state's definition of insanity, as a defense in criminal cases, upon the two-pronged test adopted by the House of Lords in *M'Naghten's Case* (1843) 8 Eng.Rep. 718, 722: "To establish a defence on the ground of insanity, it must be clearly proved that, at the time of the committing the act, the party accused was labouring under such a defect of reason, from disease of the mind, as not to know the nature and quality of the act he was doing; or, if he did know it, that he did not know he was doing what was wrong."

Over the years the *M'Naghten* test became subject to considerable criticism and was abandoned in a number of jurisdictions. In Drew this court followed suit, adopting the test for mental incapacity proposed by the American Law Institute: "A person is not responsible for criminal conduct if at the time of such conduct as a result of mental disease or defect he lacks substantial capacity either to appreciate the criminality [wrongfulness] of his conduct or to conform his conduct to the requirements of law."

In June 1982 the California electorate adopted an initiative measure, popularly known as Proposition 8, which (among other things) for the first time in this state established a statutory definition of insanity: "In any criminal proceeding . . . in which a plea of not guilty by reason of insanity is entered, this defense shall be found by the trier of fact only when the accused person proves by a preponderance of the evidence that he or she was incapable of knowing or understanding the nature and quality of his or her act and of distinguishing right from wrong at the time of the commission of the offense." Pen. Code § 25, subd.(b).

It is apparent from the language of § 25(b) that it was designed to eliminate the Drew test and to reinstate the prongs of the *M'Naghten* test. However, the section uses the conjunctive "and" instead of the disjunctive "or" to connect the two prongs. Read literally, therefore, § 25(b) would do more than reinstate the *M'Naghten* test. It would strip the insanity defense from an accused who, by reason of mental disease, is incapable of knowing that the act he was doing was wrong. That is, in fact, the interpretation adopted by the trial court in this case.

Defendant claims that the purpose of the electorate in adopting § 25(b) was to restore the *M'Naghten* test as it existed in California prior to this court's decision in *People v. Drew*. If read literally, he argues, § 25(b) would violate both the state and federal Constitutions by imposing criminal responsibility and sanctions on persons who lack the *mens rea* essential to criminal culpability.

The People do not dispute the proposition that the intent of the electorate was to reinstate the pre-*Drew* test of legal insanity. They argue, however, that § 25(b), "amplifies" and "clarifies" the *M'Naghten* test. *Amicus curiae*, the Criminal Justice Legal Foundation, agrees that the intent was not to adopt a stricter test than that applicable prior to *Drew*, but suggest that in fact there is no difference between the two prongs of the *M'Naghten* test — ability to distinguish between right and wrong, and knowledge of the nature and quality of the particular criminal act.

Mindful of the serious constitutional questions that might arise were we to accept a literal construction of the statutory language, and of our obligation wherever possible both to carry out the intent of the electorate and to construe statutes so as to preserve their constitutionality, we shall conclude that § 25(b) was intended to, and does, restore the *M'Naghten* test as it existed in this state before *Drew*. We shall also conclude that under that test there exist two distinct and independent bases upon which a verdict of not guilty by reason of insanity might be returned.

I.

Defendant appeals from a judgment of conviction of second degree murder entered upon his pleas of *nolo contendere* and not guilty by reason of insanity, and a finding by the court, after a jury was waived, that he was sane at the time of the offense. In finding the defendant sane, the judge acknowledged that it was more likely than not that defendant suffered from a mental disease, paranoid schizophrenia, which played a significant part in the killing. The judge stated that under the *Drew* test of legal insanity defendant would qualify as insane, and also found that "under the right-wrong prong of § 25(b), the defendant would qualify as legally insane; but under the other prong, he clearly does not." Concluding that by the use of the conjunctive "and" in § 25(b), the electorate demonstrated an intent to establish a stricter test of legal insanity than the *M'Naghten* test, and to "virtually eliminate" insanity as a defense, the judge found that defendant had not established that he was legally insane.

Probation was denied and defendant was sentenced to a term of 15 years to life in the state prison.

Defendant strangled his wife while he was on a day pass from the Camarillo State Hospital at which he was a patient. Evidence offered at the trial on his plea of not guilty by reason of insanity included the opinion of a clinical and forensic psychologist that defendant suffered from either classical paranoic schizophrenia, or schizo-affective illness with significant paranoid features. A delusional product of this illness was a belief held by defendant that the marriage vow "till death do us part" bestows on a marital partner a God-given right to kill the other partner who has violated or was inclined to violate the marital vows, and that because the vows reflect the direct wishes of God, the killing is with complete moral and criminal impunity. The act is not wrongful because it is sanctified by the will and desire of God.

Although there was also evidence that would have supported a finding that defendant was sane, it was apparently the evidence summarized above upon which the trial judge based his finding that defendant met one, but not both, prongs of the *M'Naghten* test. Defendant knew the nature and quality of his act. He knew that his act was homicidal. He was unable to distinguish right and wrong, however, in that he did not know that this particular killing was wrongful or criminal.

In this context we must determine whether the trial court's conclusion that § 25(b), requires that a defendant meet both prongs of the *M'Naghten* test to establish legal insanity was correct, and if not, whether the court's finding that defendant met the "right-wrong" aspect of the test requires reversal with directions to enter a judgment of not guilty by reason of insanity.

II.

The Insanity Defense in California

"It is fundamental to our system of jurisprudence that a person cannot be convicted for acts performed while insane." *People v. Kelly* (1973) 10 Cal.3d 565,

574. This rule is one aspect of the equally well established and no less fundamental principle that wrongful intent is an essential element of crime, a principle reflected in the first statutory criminal law scheme adopted by our Legislature in 1850.

The test of legal insanity when the Penal Code of 1872 was adopted by the Legislature was the two-prong *M'Naghten* test recognized by this court in *People v. Coffman, supra,* 24 Cal. 230, 235: "The unsoundness of mind, or insanity, that will constitute a defense in a criminal action is well described by Tindal, C.J., in answer to questions propounded by the House of Lords to the Judges. He says, 'that to establish a defense on the ground of insanity, it must be clearly proved that, at the time of committing the act, the party accused was laboring under such a defect of reason, from disease of the mind, as not to know the nature or quality of the act, or if he did know it, that he did not know he was doing what was wrong.' " * * * *

For more than a century after *Coffman* recognized the *M'Naghten* test as applicable in this state, it continued to be used, and although sometimes stated in the conjunctive, was in fact applied so as to permit a finding of insanity if either prong of the test was satisfied. We stated the test in the disjunctive in *Drew* and the instructions given by the trial court in that case did so also.

Because our statutes requiring *mens rea,* and our past formulation of the *M'Naghten* and ALI-*Drew* tests of insanity have afforded adequate defense to mentally ill persons who lack wrongful intent and might otherwise be subject to penal sanctions, we have not been called upon to consider the constitutional implications of the imposition of punishment on persons who act without that intent. Nor has the United States Supreme Court done so, although that court, too, has recognized repeatedly that except in regulatory offenses in which the sanctions are relatively light (*United States v. Dotterweich* (1943) 320 U.S. 277), the existence of wrongful intent is essential to criminal liability. See *United States v. Bailey* (1980) 444 U.S. 394; *Morissette v. United States* (1952) 342 U.S. 246.

Because *mens rea* or wrongful intent is a fundamental aspect of criminal law, the suggestion that a defendant whose mental illness results in inability to appreciate that his act is wrongful could be punished by death or imprisonment raises serious questions of constitutional dimension under both the due process and cruel and unusual punishment provisions of the Constitution. In *Leland v. Oregon* (1952) 343 U.S. 790, the court upheld an Oregon law placing the burden of proving insanity beyond a reasonable doubt on the defendant and affirmed the right of the state to formulate the applicable test of legal insanity. In so doing, however, the court measured the law under due process standards, concluding that the irresistible impulse extension of the traditional insanity test was not "implicit in the concept of ordered liberty." The court thus seemingly accepted the proposition that the insanity defense, in some formulation, is required by due process. See also *Robinson v. California* (1962) 370 U.S. 660, suggesting that punishment for the status of being mentally ill would constitute cruel and unusual punishment. Scholars, too, suggest that abolition of the traditional insanity defense may be constitutionally impermissible if the result would be imposition of punishment on a mentally ill person for acts done without criminal intent. See Robitscher & Haynes, *In Defense of the Insanity Defense* (1982) 31 Emory L.J. 9; Note, *The Proposed*

Federal Insanity Defense: Should the Quality of Mercy Suffer for the Sake of Safety (1984) 22 Am.Crim. L.Rev. 49.

This court suggested a similar view in *People v. Coleman* (1942) 20 Cal.2d 399, 407, where we observed: "Obviously an insane person accused of crime would be inhumanely dealt with if his insanity were considered merely to reduce the degree of his crime or the punishment therefor."[5]

We need not face these difficult constitutional questions, however, if § 25(b) does no more than return to the pre-*Drew* California version of the *M'Naghten* test.

III.

Post-Proposition 8 Return to M'Naghten

If the use of the conjunctive "and" in § 25(b) is not a draftsman's error, a defendant must now establish both that he "was incapable of knowing or understanding the nature and quality of his or her act and of distinguishing right from wrong." We recognize the basic principle of statutory and constitutional construction which mandates that courts, in construing a measure, not undertake to rewrite its unambiguous language. That rule is not applied, however, when it appears clear that a word has been erroneously used, and a judicial correction will best carry out the intent of the adopting body. The inadvertent use of "and" where the purpose or intent of a statute seems clearly to require "or" is a familiar example of a drafting error which may properly be rectified by judicial construction. Whether the use of "and" in § 25(b) is, in fact, a drafting error can only be determined by reference to the purpose of the section and the intent of the electorate in adopting it.

The ballot summaries and arguments are not helpful. The Attorney General's summary of Proposition 8 advises only that the measure included a provision "regarding proof of insanity." The analysis of the Legislative Analyst quotes the conjunctive language and states only that the provision "could increase the difficulty of proving that a person is not guilty by reason of insanity." No reference to the insanity provision appears in the arguments for or against Proposition 8.

These omissions are not without significance, however. As we noted earlier, the insanity defense reflects a fundamental legal principle common to the jurisprudence of this country and to the common law of England[6] that criminal sanctions are imposed only on persons who act with wrongful intent in the commission of a *malum in se* offense. Since 1850 the disjunctive *M'Naghten* test of

---

[5] For a contrary view, see Morris, *Madness and Criminal Law* (Chi. Press 1982) page 76. See also Keilitz and Fulton, *The Insanity Defense* (Nat. Center for State Courts 1984).

[6] This concept of criminal responsibility is not one limited to the laws of this country and of England. In their article on the development of the insanity defense in California, Platt and Diamond trace the defense to Hebrew law, and also find the doctrine of criminal responsibility a recognized part of Greek and Roman philosophy. Platt & Diamond, *The Origins of the "Right and Wrong" Test of Criminal Responsibility and Its Subsequent Development in the United States: An Historical Survey* (1966) 54 Cal.L.Rev. 1227.

insanity has been accepted as the rule by which the minimum cognitive function which constitutes wrongful intent will be measured in this state. As such it is itself among the fundamental principles of our criminal law. Had it been the intent of the drafters of Proposition 8 or of the electorate which adopted it both to abrogate the more expansive ALI-*Drew* test and to abandon that prior fundamental principle of culpability for crime, we would anticipate that this intent would be expressed in some more obvious manner than the substitution of a single conjunctive in a longthy initiative provision.

Applying § 25(b) as a conjunctive test of insanity would erase that fundamental principle. It would return the law to that which preceded *M'Naghten*, a test known variously as the "wild beast test" and as the "good and evil test" under which an accused could be found insane only if he was "totally deprived of his understanding and memory, and doth not know what he is doing, no more than an infant, than a brute, or a wild beast." *Rex v. Arnold* (1724) 16 Howell St. Tr. 695, 765. We find nothing in the language of Proposition 8, or in any other source from which the intent of the electorate may be divined which indicates that such a fundamental, far-reaching change in the law of insanity as that was intended.[8]

We conclude that § 25(b) reinstated the *M'Naghten* test as it was applied in California prior to *Drew* as the test of legal insanity in criminal prosecutions in this state.[9]

IV.

Although the People agree that the purpose of § 25(b) was to return the test of legal insanity in California to the pre-ALI-*Drew* version of the *M'Naghten* test, they argue that reversal of this judgment is not required because both prongs of that test are actually the same. The findings of the trial judge in this case illustrate the fallacy inherent in this argument. It is true that a person who is unaware of the nature and quality of his act by definition cannot know that the act is wrong. In this circumstance the "nature and quality" prong subsumes the "right and wrong" prong.

The reverse does not necessarily follow, however. The expert testimony in this case supported the findings of the trial court that this defendant was aware of the nature and quality of his homicidal act. He knew that he was committing an act of strangulation that would, and was intended to, kill a human being. He was not able to comprehend that the act was wrong because his mental illness caused him to

---

[8] A test of insanity requiring that a defendant meet both prongs of the *M'Naghten* test would not, of course, carry out the intent that was express in Proposition 8 and in the materials supplied to the voters. That intent, insofar as the criminal justice system is concerned, is deterrence of criminal behavior. A person who does not know his act is wrong is not likely to be deterred by the prospect of punishment for wrongful conduct. Nor is there a prospect that one who does not know the nature of his act will be deterred.

[9] In somewhat more colorful language, the Court of Appeal "declined to interpret the statute as enacting a new drooling idiot test in place of the century old *M'Naghten* standard merely because it uses the single, and often misused, conjunctive 'and.' That conjunctive is too thin a reed to support such a massive doctrinal transformation." *People v. Horn*, 158 Cal.App.3d 1014.

believe that the act was not only morally justified but was expected of him. He believed that the homicide was "right."

The People argue further that § 25(b) was intended to "clarify" the meaning of the right/wrong prong of the California *M'Naghten* test by establishing that the "wrong" which the defendant must comprehend is a legal, rather than a moral wrong.

Under this formulation this defendant, who was able to recognize that his act was unlawful, would not escape criminal responsibility even though he believed his act was commanded by God. We fail to see the manner in which § 25(b) conveys this clarification of the *M'Naghten* test.

Moreover, even assuming the validity of this argument, reversal here would be necessary. The trial court did not find that appellant was able to comprehend that his act was considered unlawful or "wrong" even though it was commanded by God. That theory does not appear to have been put forth by the People at trial. Neither appellant, nor the trial court addressed the question of ability to comprehend legal right or wrong.

In any event, past decisions do not support the People's argument that under the California version of the *M'Naghten* test a defendant who could comprehend that his act was unlawful could not be legally insane. * * * * *People v. Coffman*, 24 Cal. 230, is the case in which the *M'Naghten* test was recognized as being applicable in this state. The *Coffman* opinion, in addition to stating the test, considered the standard of proof, quoting as it did so: "Mansfield, Chief Justice, in Billingham's case, 1 *Collinson on Lunacy*, 636: 'To support such a defense (insanity), it ought to be proved that the person was incapable of judging between right and wrong; that at the time he committed the act he did not consider that murder was a crime against the laws of God and nature.'" * * * *

The concept of "wrong" was not limited to legal wrong in *People v. Wolff* (1964) 61 Cal.2d 795. There this court explained that the California version of the *M'Naghten* test had been liberalized by holding that "knowing" in the sense of being able to verbalize the concepts of right and wrong was insufficient to establish legal sanity. Rather, the defendant must "know" in a broader sense — he must appreciate or understand these concepts. Tracing the evolution of the California test we summarized the cases from which the then applicable instruction had been derived. * * * * In none of these cases is it suggested that a defendant whose mental illness caused him to believe that his act was morally correct could not be found insane if he understood that the act was unlawful. * * * *

The applicability of the insanity defense to a person whose mental illness is the cause of an insane delusion such as that suffered by defendant, if that delusion rendered him incapable of appreciating that his act was wrong, was made clear in *People v. Hubert* (1897) 119 Cal. 216. There the trial court had instructed that "defendant 'was laboring under insane delusions which so permeated his reason as to incapacitate him from knowing the difference between right and wrong, as to the acts charged in the information, and his relations with the deceased, and her actions, motives, and intentions toward him, and that he acted in pursuance of such delusions.'" Although we concluded that the court had erred in this and other instructions on insanity which took from the jury the factual issues as to the existence of the delusions, no question was raised as to the applicability of the *M'Naghten* insanity test to insane delusions which render the individual incapable of appreciating the wrongfulness of his conduct.[13]

This response applies the right/wrong prong of the *M'Naghten* test to an insane delusion in the same manner as it is applied to other forms of insanity. The delusion first suggested by the judges results in an inability to appreciate that the act is wrong. The defendant believes he is defending himself. The second delusion, without more, does not suggest that the defendant believes his act is lawful or morally justified.

This understanding of the *M'Naghten* test was further affirmed in *People v. Willard*, 150 Cal. 543, 554, where this court explained: "That insanity may be available as a defense to a crime charged, it must appear that the defendant, when the act was committed, was so deranged and diseased mentally that he was not conscious of the wrongful nature of the act committed. If he has reasoning capacity sufficient to distinguish between right and wrong as to the particular act he is doing, knowledge and consciousness that what he is doing is wrong and criminal and will subject him to punishment, he must be held responsible for his conduct. Although he may be labouring under partial insanity — as, for instance, suffering from some insane delusion or hallucination — still if he understands the nature and character of his action and its consequences — if he has knowledge that it is wrong and criminal, and that if he does the act he will do wrong, such partial insanity or the existence of such delusion or hallucination is not sufficient to relieve him from responsibility for his criminal acts."

Our appreciation of the nature of mental illness has developed greatly since *Hubert* and *Willard* were decided, and the medical community now characterizes some delusional mental illness such as that suffered by defendant as a "schizophrenic disorder,"[14] rather than "monomania" or "partial insanity." The rule expressed in these cases has not changed, however. If the mental illness is manifested in delusions which render the individual incapable either of knowing the nature and character of his act, or of understanding that it is wrong, he is legally insane under the California formulation of the *M'Naghten* test.

Respondent cites no decisional authority of this state for the argument that the

---

[13] Application of the *M'Naghten* test to this type of mental illness was anticipated by the judges who first formulated the test. In response to the fourth question posed by the House of Lords — "If a person, under an insane delusion as to existing facts, commits an offense in consequence thereof, is he thereby excused?" — the judges replied: "The answer must of course depend on the nature of the delusion: but, making the same assumption as we did before, namely that he labors under such partial delusion only, and is not in other respects insane, we think he must be considered in the same situation as to responsibility as if the facts with respect to which the delusion exists were real. For example, if under the influence of his delusion he supposes another man to be in the act of attempting to take away his life, and he kills that man, as he supposes, in self-defence, he would be exempt from punishment. If his delusion was that the deceased had inflicted a serious injury to his character and fortune, and he killed him in revenge for such supposed injury, he would be liable to punishment." *M'Naghten's Case*, 8 Eng. Rep. 718, 723.

[14] American Psychiatric Association, *Diagnostic and Statistical Manual of Mental Disorders* (3d ed. 1980) pages 181-193.

right/wrong prong of the California *M'Naghten* test of insanity does not encompass awareness, or lack thereof, that the defendant's act was inherently, or morally wrong. Reliance is placed instead on a single out-of-state case, *Chase v. State* (Alaska 1962) 369 P.2d 997, overruled on another point in *Fields v. State* (Alaska 1971) 487 P.2d 831, 836. Manifestly, we cannot infer that a 20-year-old decision of the Alaska Supreme Court prompted the drafters of Proposition 8 to believe that the law of California required "clarification."[15] The decision in that case in no way supports a conclusion that the electorate believed such clarification to be necessary or understood the test of legal insanity to be established by § 25(b) would permit a defendant to be found sane who because of mental illness believed that God commanded and expected him to kill another human being and that therefore the killing was morally justified and was not "wrong."

At least two problems appear in this analysis. First, we recognized even before Chase that the test of sanity under the *M'Naghten* formulation is a legal test that does not encompass all of the mental conditions which the medical and psychiatric community recognize as mental disorders. Therefore, there is no inconsistency in recognizing that a person who is legally insane may nonetheless have the mental capacity to understand and appreciate the nature of the physical acts he is performing. Further, as the evidence in this case suggests, it is not uncommon that a person who suffers from one of the various forms of mental illness falling within the category of schizophrenic disorders fully understands the nature and quality of his act, but is unable to appreciate its wrongfulness. One expert, addressing this question in his testimony, explained:

> The act in this particular case is a strangulation and so the appreciation that a person would have to have is that a strangulation could result in death or great bodily harm. The defendant indicated to me in no uncertain terms that he executed this act with the intent of doing great bodily harm, believing of course that he had a right to do but that was his purpose; that was in fact his intent. He admits to that in no uncertain terms. Furthermore, in general, the nature of paranoid schizophrenia is that it does not interfere with the people's cognitive abilities; that is to say, those abilities that relate to the possession of mere knowledge, like the knowledge that strangling someone could kill them is not one of the capacities that is negated by paranoid schizophrenia. With regard to the nature of the act, he knew that he was holding a cord; he knew that what was holding the cord was his hands, what the cord was wrapped around was a neck, that was the neck of a human being.

Courts in a number of jurisdictions which have considered the question have come to the conclusion as we do, that a defendant who is incapable of understanding that his act is morally wrong is not criminally liable merely because he knows the

---

[15] We do not find the reasoning of *Chase* persuasive. The court concluded that if the two prongs of the *M'Naghten* test were disjunctive, "the intellect must be divided into two distinct parts. One part would be rational, so that the nature and quality of the act would be understood; and the other part would be irrational, so there could be no understanding that the act was one generally condemned by the community and therefore wrongful. The apparent implication here would be that one mind could be simultaneously normal and abnormal, sane and insane. That this could be is not supported by established medical or psychiatric principles."

act is unlawful. See *People v. Wood* (1962) 12 N.Y.2d 69; *State v. Kirkham* (1958) 7 Utah 2d 108; cf. *State v. Allen* (1957) 231 S.C. 391, 398; *State v. Carrigan* (1919) 93 N.J.L. 268.

Justice Cardozo, in an opinion for the New York Court of Appeal, eloquently expressed the underlying philosophy: "In the light of all these precedents, it is impossible, we think, to say that there is any decisive adjudication which limits the word 'wrong' in the statutory definition to legal as opposed to moral wrong. The interpretation placed upon the statute by the trial judge may be tested by its consequences. A mother kills her infant child to whom she has been devotedly attached. She knows the nature and quality of the act; she knows that the law condemns it; but she is inspired by an insane delusion that God has appeared to her and ordained the sacrifice. It seems a mockery to say that, within the meaning of the statute, she knows that the act is wrong. If the definition propounded by the trial judge is right, it would be the duty of a jury to hold her responsible for the crime. We find nothing either in the history of the rule, or in its reason or purpose, or in judicial exposition of its meaning, to justify a conclusion so abhorrent. Knowledge that an act is forbidden by law will in most cases permit the inference of knowledge that, according to the accepted standards of mankind, it is also condemned as an offense against good morals. Obedience to the law is itself a moral duty. If, however, there is an insane delusion that God has appeared to the defendant and ordained the commission of a crime, we think it cannot be said of the offender that he knows the act to be wrong." *People v. Schmidt* (1915) 216 N.Y. 324, 338-340.[16]

The trial court found, on clearly sufficient evidence, that defendant could not distinguish right and wrong with regard to his act. No further hearing on the issue of sanity at the time of the act is required. The judgment is reversed and the superior court is directed to enter a judgment of not guilty by reason of insanity and to proceed thereafter pursuant to § 1026.

MOSK, J.

I concur in the excellent analysis of the majority. I write only to relate some relevant background. As Oliver Wendell Holmes observed, "a page of history is worth a volume of logic." *New York Trust Co. v. Eisner* (1921) 256 U.S. 345, 349.

In 1973 I wrote a separate opinion in *People v. Kelly* (1973) 10 Cal.3d 565, urging that the *M'Naughton* test be "disavowed as outmoded and unsupportable in either medical science or law," and that pending legislative action the American Law Institute formulation be adopted by trial courts as the test for insanity. At that time six states had adopted the ALI formulation, as had every federal circuit but one.

---

[16] Justice Cardozo's opinion continued: "It is not enough, to relieve from criminal liability, that the prisoner is morally depraved. It is not enough that he has views of right and wrong at variance with those that find expression in the law. The variance must have its origin in some disease of the mind. The anarchist is not at liberty to break the law because he reasons that all government is wrong. The devotee of a religious cult that enjoins polygamy or human sacrifice as a duty is not thereby relieved from responsibility before the law. In such cases the belief, however false according to our own standards, is not the product of disease. Cases will doubtless arise where criminals will take shelter behind a professed belief that their crime was ordained by God, just as this defendant attempted to shelter himself behind that belief. We can safely leave such fabrications to the common sense of juries."

Within five years a majority of this court had come around to my view in *Kelly* and judicially adopted the ALI test in *People v. Drew* (1978) 22 Cal.3d 333. Despite my invitation in *Kelly*, the Legislature had not taken any action, and it did not do so after *Drew*. I can only surmise that the legislators' disinterest was born of the belief that the test of insanity was a judicial problem, since the *M'Naughton* test had originally been court-created.

Just as trial courts, prosecutors and defense counsel were achieving a reasonable detente with *Drew*, the initiative measure known as Proposition 8 was prepared and submitted to the electorate. It contained the latent ambiguity discussed in the majority opinion. Therein lies one of the problems inherent in attempting to adopt rules of evidence and arcane principles of law by popular vote. It is somewhat comparable to the public deciding by popular vote the appropriate technique for surgeons to employ in brain surgery.

I am convinced that the use of "and" instead of "or" would have been discovered in the traditional legislative process. In an assembly committee, on the floor of the assembly, in a senate committee, on the floor of the senate, in the Governor's veto opportunity, such inadvertence would likely have been detected, or if the choice of words was deliberate, such intent would have been clearly declared. In an initiative measure, however, no revision opportunity is possible and no legislative intent is available; the voter has only the choice of an enigmatic all or nothing.

The analysis of the majority being as reasonable and pragmatic as the circumstances justify, I endorse their opinion.

Bird, C. J., dissenting.

In June of 1982, the voters adopted a ballot measure which radically altered the test for criminal insanity in this state. Pen. Code § 25, subd.(b), added by Initiative Measure, Primary Elec. June 8, 1982, popularly known as Prop. 8. I cannot ignore the fact that they adopted language which unambiguously requires the accused to demonstrate that "he or she was incapable of knowing or understanding the nature and quality of his or her act and of distinguishing right from wrong at the time of the commission of the offense." There is nothing in the statute, in Proposition 8 as a whole, or in the ballot arguments that implies that the electorate intended "and" to be "or." However unwise that choice, it is not within this court's power to ignore the expression of popular will and rewrite the statute.

Since appellant failed to establish his insanity under the test enunciated in Penal Code § 25, subdivision (b), I cannot join the decision of my brethren.

NOTES FROM WALLY:

(1) How does the fact that Louie felt he had to obey "the voice" help us show insanity, under California's test for insanity?

(2) Under the "first prong" of the *M'Naughton* test, how does Louie's state of mind compare to Skinner's?

(3) Under the "second prong" of the *M'Naughton* test, how does Louie's state of mind compare to Skinner's?

(4) I don't quite understand the court's discussion of "insane delusion." Louie was clearly operating under a delusion, and the delusion seems pretty insane to me. Isn't this enough?

(5) The court in *Skinner* discussed the possibility of *abolishing* the insanity defense. Several states have in fact purported to do so. Utah Code § 76-2-305(1) provides: "It is a defense to a prosecution under any statute or ordinance that the defendant, as a result of mental illness, lacked the mental state required as an element of the offense charged. Mental illness is not otherwise a defense." What does this mean? In *State v. Herrera*, 895 P.2d 359 (Utah 1995), the Utah Supreme Court explained the effect of this statute:

> A common example is helpful to illustrate the difference between the prior law and the new law. If A kills B, thinking that he is merely squeezing a grapefruit, A does not have the requisite *mens rea* for murder and would be acquitted under both the prior and the new law. However, if A kills B, thinking that B is an enemy soldier and that the killing is justified as self-defense, then A has the requisite *mens rea* for murder and could be convicted under the new law but not under the prior law, because he knowingly and intentionally took another's life. Under the amended provision, it does not matter whether A understood that the act was wrong. The new law does away with the traditional affirmative insanity defense that the killing was perceived to be justifiable and therefore done with innocent intent.

The court rejected arguments that the new statute was unconstitutional: "One who lacks the requisite state of mind may not be convicted or punished. Utah's *mens rea* model provides this minimum standard of protection to defendants." The court noted that the supreme courts of Idaho and Montana had rejected similar attacks on their abolition statutes.

(6) Another way to abolish the insanity defense is to provide that the jury may find the defendant "guilty but mentally ill." A few states have done this. However, in *People v. Robles*, 288 Ill.App.3d 935, 682 N.E.2d 194 (1997), the court held that an Illinois statute to this effect deprives a defendant of due process of law, because it encourages compromise verdicts. Jurors are unaware that the phrase "but mentally ill" has no practical legal effect in terms of potential punishment and/or psychiatric treatment, and they are seduced into settling on a middle ground between guilty and not guilty, when in fact there is no middle ground. But the Illinois Supreme Court disagreed. *People v. Lantz*, 186 Ill. 2d 243, 712 N.E.2d 314 (1999)

And in *State v. Hornsby*, 326 S.C. 121, 484 S.E.2d 869 (1997), the court rejected a similar argument, upholding a South Carolina statute providing for a "guilty but mentally ill" verdict and noting that courts in several other jurisdictions have done the same.

(7) How important is the insanity defense in the real world? A 1991 study of 9,000 criminal cases in 8 states found that an insanity plea was entered in about 1% of them. 26% of those resulted in acquittals. Most of the acquitted defendants had

been diagnosed with schizophrenia, and 82% of them had been hospitalized for mental illness at least once. 77% of the acquittals were handed down by judges (i.e., the defendant had waived his right to a jury trial). 16% were the result of plea bargains, and only 7% of the acquittals came from juries. "Experts say it is extremely hard to sway jurors with mental illness evidence, even in what is considered an ideal case." Michael Higgins, *Crazy Talk*, Journal of the American Bar Association, December, 1997, p. 34.

(8) The insanity defense tends to divert mentally ill people from the criminal justice system to the medical system. Recently, however, the trend has been running in the opposite direction. Fox Butterfield, *Prisons Replace Hospitals for the Nation's Mentally Ill*, New York Times, 3/5/98, reported that about 200,000 people behind bars nation-wide (10% of all prisoners) suffer from a severe mental illness. Some of these people committed serious crimes, but others are "homeless people charged with minor crimes that are byproducts of their illnesses. Others are picked up with no charges at all, in what the police call mercy arrests, simply for acting strange." Why is this happening?

The trend began in the 1960's, with the mass closings of public mental hospitals. At the time, new antipsychotic drugs made medicating patients in the community seem a humane alternative to long-term hospitalization. * * * *

But the drugs work only when they are taken, and when they work, patients are tempted to stop, because of the unpleasant side effects. As states lagged in opening a promised network of clinics and halfway houses to monitor patients, obtaining treatment became harder. Health insurers restricted coverage, for-profit hospitals turned away the psychotic, and new laws made it more difficult to commit disturbed people. Thousands fell through the cracks.

Coincidentally, with voters willing to spend freely to fight rising crime rates, states were building more jails and prisons. Jails became the only institutions left open to the mentally ill 24 hours a day. * * * *

"The inmates we see in jail today are the same people I used to see in psychiatric hospitals," said Dr. Eugene Kunzman, the former medical director of the mental health program at the Los Angeles jail.

In many states, so many public hospitals have closed, or the laws regulating admission to hospitals have been made so tight, that sometimes the only way to get care is to be arrested. * * * *

Though some people do benefit from regular medication while in jail, others suffer as the stress deepens their depression, intensifies delusions or leads to a psychotic break. * * * *

Advocates for the mentally ill say the clock is being turned back to the 19th century, when it was common in the United States to confine people with mental illness in jails. * * * *

"Criminalization," said Dr. E. Fuller Torrey, a leading researcher of schizophrenia in Washington, D.C., "has been both a personal disaster for the mentally ill, and an institutional disaster for the criminal justice system."

A Note on Intoxication

Unlike insanity, intoxication (from alcohol or narcotics) is not a *defense* to a criminal charge. It might, however, *negate an essential mental element* of the crime charged. The defendant might be too drunk or too high on drugs to form an intent to steal or an intent to kill, or he might be too drunk or too him to "premeditate." But some courts are confused about this:

> It is sometimes stated that intoxication can negative a "specific intent" which the crime in question may require (meaning some intent in addition to the intent to do the physical act which the crime requires), but it cannot negative a crime's "general intent" (meaning an intent to do the physical act — or, perhaps, recklessly doing the physical act — which the crime requires). Some cases therefore have held that voluntary intoxication cannot be a defense to rape even though it blots out the intent to have intercourse, since that intent is a general intent and not a specific intent. But this is wrong on principle, for it intoxication does in fact negative an intention which is a required element of the crime (whether it is called specific intent or general intent), the crime has not been committed. Some cases have held that intoxication cannot be a defense to battery, a crime sometimes said to require only a general intent. This, however, is correct on principle, since battery can be committed not only with an intent to do the physical act of striking the other person (which intoxication can negative) but also, without any such intent to strike, by recklessly striking; and recklessly cannot, by the weight of authority, be negatived by intoxication.
> * * * *
>
> By way of conclusion, it may be said that it is better, when considering the effect of the defendant's voluntary intoxication upon his criminal liability, to stay away from those misleading concepts of general intent and specific intent. Instead one should ask, first, what intent (or knowledge) if any does the crime in question require; and then, if the crime requires some intent (knowledge), did the defendant in fact entertain such an intent (or, did he in fact know what the crime requires him to know.) [LaFave & Scott, *Criminal Law* (West, 2d ed., 1986), pp. 389-390.]

See also Model Penal Code § 2.08, in the Appendix.

In *Montana v. Egelhoff*, 518 U.S. 37 (1996), Egelhoff was charged with two counts of "deliberate homicide," defined in Montana as "purposely" or "knowingly" causing the death of another. He claimed that he was too drunk to be capable of committing the murders. The trial judge instructed the jury not to consider this claim, because a Montana statute provided that a jury could not take into account an accused's "intoxicated condition in determining the existence of a mental statue which is an element of the offense." He was convicted, but the Montana supreme court reversed, finding this statute unconstitutional, as defendant "had a due process right to present and have considered by the jury all relevant evidence to rebut the State's evidence on all elements of the offense charged." The U.S. Supreme Court reversed, holding that the statute was constitutional, because Egelhoff failed to show that his claimed right to have a jury consider his intoxication was a "fundamental principle of justice." The Court noted that at common law, voluntary intoxication was no defense and could not be raised to negate *mens rea*. The modern general rule that it may negate *mens rea* is too recent to be considered so "deeply rooted" as to be "fundamental." The Court (per Justice Scalia) also said:

> It is not surprising that many State have held fast to or resurrected the common-law rule prohibiting consideration of voluntary intoxication in the determination of *mens rea*, because that rule has considerable justification — which alone casts doubt on the proposition that the opposite rule is a "fundamental principle." A large number of crimes, especially violent crimes, are committed by intoxicated offenders; modern studies put the numbers as high as half of all homicides, for example. Disallowing consideration of voluntary intoxication has the effect of increasing the punishment for all unlawful acts committed in that state, and thereby deters drunkenness or irresponsible behavior while drunk. The rule also serves as a specific deterrent, ensuring that those who prove incapable of controlling violent impulses while voluntarily intoxicated go to prison. And finally, the rule comports with and implements society's moral perception that one who has voluntarily impaired his own faculties should be responsible for the consequences.

> There is, in modern times, even more justification for laws such as [the Montana statute] than there used to be. Some recent studies suggest that the connection between drunkenness and crime is as much cultural as pharmacological — that is, that drunks are violent not simply because alcohol makes them that way, but because they are behaving in accord with their leaned belief that drunks are violent. This not only adds additional support to the traditional view that an intoxicated criminal is not deserving of exoneration, but it suggests that juries — who possess the same learned belief as the intoxicated offender — will be too quick to accept the claim that the defendant was biologically incapable of forming the requisite *mens rea*. Treating the matter as one of excluding misleading evidence therefore makes some sense.

Justice Ginsberg concurred. She construed the Montana statute not as a bar to relevant evidence, but as "a measure redefining *mens rea*" — which therefore "encounters no constitutional shoal."

Four justices (O'Connor, Stevens, Souter, and Breyer) dissented. Justice O'Connor wrote:

> The Montana statute places a blanket exclusion on a category of evidence that would allow the accused to negate the offense's mental-state element. * * * * Due process demands that a criminal defendant be afforded a fair opportunity to defend against the State's accusations. Meaningful adversarial testing of the State's case requires that the defendant not be prevented from raising an effective defense, which must include the right to present relevant, probative evidence. * * *

A state legislature certainly has the authority to identify the elements of the offenses it wishes to punish, but once its laws are written, a defendant has the right to insist that the State prove beyond a reasonable doubt every element of an offense charged. Because the Montana legislature has specified that a person commits "deliberate homicide" only if he "purposely or knowingly causes the death of another human being, the prosecution must prove the existence of such mental state in order to convict. * * * * If the defendant may not introduce evidence that might create doubt in the factfinder's mind as to whether that element was met, the prosecution will find its job so much the easier. A subjective mental state is generally proved only circumstantially. If a jury may not consider the defendant's evidence of his mental state, the jury may impute to the defendant the culpability of a mental state he did not possess.

California Penal Code § 22 bars evidence of voluntary intoxication to negate the intent required of certain crimes. In *People v. Martin*, 78 Cal.App.4th 107 (2000), the court rejected a constitutional challenge to the statute, following *Egelhoff*.

Chapter 13

SELF DEFENSE

One who is not the aggressor in an encounter is justified in using a reasonable amount of force against his adversary when he reasonably believes (a) that he is in immediate danger of unlawful bodily harm from his adversary and (b) that the use of such force is necessary to avoid this danger.

LaFave & Scott, *Criminal Law* (West)

One may justifiably use *nondeadly* force against another in self-defense if he reasonably believes that the other is about to inflict unlawful bodily harm (it need not be death or serious bodily harm) upon him (and also believes that it is necessary to use such force to prevent it). * * * * He may justifiably use *deadly* force against the other in self-defense, however, only if he reasonably believes that the other is about to inflict unlawful death or serious bodily harm upon him (and also that it is necessary to use deadly force to prevent it).

LaFave & Scott, *Criminal Law* (West)

Every legal rule is a line. A rule of criminal law sets a line between legal and illegal conduct. The legislature or court that creates the rule assesses the values of competing interests and chooses where to draw the line, in order to best serve both (or all) interests. The line is a compromise, a resolution of the tension between the interests. When the resulting line is fuzzy and it is not clear where it falls in a particular case, the lawyer (or judge) handling the case *must identify those interests* in order to argue (or decide) where the line should fall.

What are the competing interests in self defense? On the one hand, people should be allowed to protect themselves from unjustified attacks. This will tend to protect against death and injury. On the other hand, we do not want people to kill or hurt other people unnecessarily, and we do not want people to take the law into their own hands by taking revenge on attackers after any danger has passed.

As you read the cases in this Chapter, consider where they draw the line and whether they do a good job of balancing these competing interests.

PROBLEM 13

To: My law clerk

From: Appellate Justice Frank N. Stein

Re: *State v. Groves*

Matthew Groves has appealed his conviction for the second degree murder of Ken Krumkey. The prosecution's evidence showed that Krumkey was a Sim City police officer who had obtained a warrant for Groves' arrest for auto theft, that Krumkey went to Groves' house to arrest him, that Groves struck Krumkey on the head with a shovel, and that this blow caused Krumkey's death. It turned out that the arrest warrant was invalid (as the affidavit in support of the warrant did not show probable cause to believe that Groves committed auto theft).

Defendant testified. His lawyer also tried to put on an expert witness, which the trial judge would not allow. The judge also refused defense counsel's request that the jury be instructed on self defense.

Please review the attached transcript and authorities, and advise me as to whether the trial court committed error.

Transcript of Portion of Trial in State v. Groves

Q (by defense counsel): Mr. Groves, what were you doing when you first saw Officer Krumkey?

A. I was working in the garden in front of my house.

Q: What did Officer Krumkey do?

A: He came up to me and said, "You're under arrest, boy." I'm black, and he's white, so I said, "Don't call me 'boy'." He said, "I'll call you what I want to," and he pulled out some handcuffs and shoved me around, real hard. I pushed him back, and he fell down on the grass. His gun fell out of his holster, and he reached out to pick it up. I don't like racist cops, and I hit him on the head with the shovel. I didn't mean to kill him.

Q: Have you had experience with Sim City police officers?

A: Yes. One of them beat me up when I was a kid, and recently one of them stopped me on the street, just because I was black, I think. I've heard similar stories from my friends.

* * * *

Defense Counsel: Your honor, you indicated in chambers that you would not allow me to have Professor Plum testify, so I would now like to make an offer of proof and put it on the record. Professor Plum would testify that he is a noted sociologist who has conducted a study of the relations between the police department and the black community in this city. He would also testify that a large percentage of the police officers have racist attitudes, are afraid of blacks, and tend to use undue violence when arresting them. He would also testify that most blacks in the city are afraid of the police and view them as racist.

The Court: As I indicated, I will sustain the prosecutor's objection to this evidence, on the ground that it is irrelevant.

Defense Counsel: And you also ruled that I cannot put on testimony regarding prior racist acts by Officer Krumkey.

The Court: That is correct. None of those incidents involved this defendant, so they are also irrelevant.

New Jersey Statutes

Section 2C:3-4. Use of Force in Self-Protection

a. *Use of force justifiable for protection of the person.*

Subject to the provisions of this section and of section 2C:3-9, the use of force upon or toward another person is justifiable when the actor reasonably believes that such force is immediately necessary for the purpose of protecting himself against the use of unlawful force by such other person on the present occasion.

b. *Limitations on justifying necessity for use of force.*

(1) The use of force is not justifiable under this section:

(a) To resist an arrest which the actor knows is being made by a peace officer in the performance of his duties, although the arrest is unlawful, unless the peace officer employs unlawful force to effect the arrest; * * *

(2) The use of deadly force is not justifiable under this section unless the actor reasonably believes that such force is necessary to protect himself against death or serious bodily harm; nor is it justifiable if:

(a) The actor, with the purpose of causing death or serious bodily harm, provoked the use of force against himself in the same encounter; or

(b) The actor knows that he can avoid the necessity of using such force with complete safety by retreating or by surrendering possession of a thing to a person asserting a claim of right thereto or by complying with a demand that he abstain from any action which he has no duty to take, except that:

(i) The actor is not obliged to retreat from his dwelling, unless he was the initial aggressor; * * * *

(3) Except as required by paragraphs (1) and (2) of this

subsection, a person employing protective force may estimate the necessity of using force when the force is used, without retreating, surrendering possession, doing any other act which he has no legal duty to do or abstaining from any lawful action.

NOTES FROM JUSTICE STEIN:

(1) This statute was enacted in 1979. It was adapted from (and is similar to) § 3.04 of the Model Penal Code, which appears in the Appendix.

(2) The statute seems to contain all the basic elements of self defense. Please read it carefully and identify each element. Does Groves' testimony show evidence of *each* of those elements?

STATE v. MULVIHILL
New Jersey Supreme Court
57 N.J. 151, 270 A.2d 277 (1970)

FRANCIS, J.

Defendant Mulvihill was charged by indictment with violating N.J.S.A. 2A:90-4 in that he allegedly committed an assault and battery upon a Somerville policeman who was in uniform and acting in the performance of his duty at the time. He was convicted at a jury trial in which the court refused to allow him to defend by asserting self-defense and declined to submit that issue to the jury for determination.

The testimony reveals that Officer Dowling was operating a patrol car along a public street in Somerville, N.J. While doing so, he observed the defendant Mulvihill, a 20-year-old youth, and two other persons standing in front of a pizzeria. He noticed Mulvihill pouring something from a bottle into a paper cup held by one of the other two persons. Since there was a local ordinance prohibiting the drinking of alcoholic beverages on a public street, the officer stopped the car, got out and called to the young men to come over to him. As they did so, Mulvihill threw the paper cup on the sidewalk. Dowling asked him what was in the cup and defendant did not answer.

The testimony as to the events which immediately followed is in conflict. However, for the purpose of determining whether the legal issue of self-defense was available for jury consideration, it is necessary to consider the facts in the light most favorable to the defendant.

According to Mulvihill, when he failed to disclose what he had been drinking, the officer grabbed him and asked to smell his breath. He held his breath and remained silent, whereupon Dowling shook him "back and forth" by the shoulders and said "I should arrest you, you punk." Mulvihill tried to pull away and Dowling "jerked him back around" with the result that both men fell. They arose with Dowling still holding him. When he tried to pull free, Dowling struck defendant on the side of the head with his gun lacerating his scalp. Mulvihill then fell toward Dowling and they both went down again. The officer's right hand was being held by Mulvihill who was trying to keep the gun pointing away from himself, while the officer was endeavoring to direct it at him and saying "Stop or I'll shoot." Mulvihill testified that at this time he was trying to avoid being shot. Then the gun went off, harmlessly, and with his right hand Mulvihill punched the officer in the left side of the face. It was for this blow that he was indicted. In the meantime, other officers appeared and defendant was immobilized.

On the assumption as a matter of law that Mulvihill had been arrested before he struck the allegedly criminal blow, the trial court informed defense counsel that no discussion of or reliance upon self-defense would be permitted in summation, nor would that issue be submitted in the charge for consideration by the jury. The action was taken because the court believed it was required by *State v. Koonce*, 89 N.J. Super. 169 (App. Div. 1965). That belief, of course, was incorrect.

Koonce held that "a private citizen may not use force to resist arrest by one he knows or has good reason to believe is an authorized police officer engaged in the performance of his duties, whether or not the arrest is illegal under the circumstances obtaining." The opinion put to rest the notion that the common law rule existing in some jurisdictions, which permits a citizen to resist, even with reasonable force, an unlawful arrest by a police officer, was applicable in New Jersey. Instead, the Appellate Division adopted the above quoted contrary doctrine, and we think rightly so. Accordingly, in our State when an officer makes an arrest, legal or illegal, it is the duty of the citizen to submit and, in the event the seizure is illegal, to seek recourse in the courts for the invasion of his right of freedom.

However, as the Appellate Division said in reversing the conviction here, it went no further in *Koonce* than to hold that the citizen must submit peaceably to an apparently authorized arrest or other apparently lawful restraint by a police officer, even if it later proves to have been illegal. If the citizen resists the arrest, the officer is not only justified in but has the duty of employing such force as is reasonably necessary to overcome the resistance and accomplish the arrest. Fisher, *Laws of Arrest*, sec. 133 (1967).

But, as the Appellate Division noted, that principle is not dispositive in all cases of an arrestee's right to claim self-defense to a charge of assault and battery on the officer. If, in effectuating the arrest or the temporary detention, the officer employs excessive and unnecessary force, the citizen may respond or counter with the use of reasonable force to protect himself, and if in so doing the officer is injured no criminal offense has been committed. See *State v. Montague*, 55 N.J. 387, 404 (1970); *People v. Curtis*, 70 Cal.2d 347 (1969); *Mullis v. State*, 196 Ga. 569 (1943); 5 Am. Jur. 2d, *Arrest*, sec. 94 (1962).

There is sound reason for a difference in the rights and duties of the citizen in the two situations. Despite his duty to submit quietly without physical resistance to an arrest made by an officer acting in the course of his duty, even though the arrest is illegal, his right to freedom from unreasonable seizure and confinement can be protected, restored and vindicated through legal processes.

However, the rule permitting reasonable resistance to excessive force of the officer, whether the arrest is lawful or unlawful, is designed to protect a person's bodily integrity and health and so permits resort to self-defense. Simply stated, the law recognizes that liberty can be restored through legal processes but life or limb cannot be repaired in a courtroom. And so it holds that the reason for outlawing resistance to an unlawful arrest and requiring disputes over its legality to be resolved in the courts has no controlling application on the right to resist an officer's excessive force.

Two qualifications on the citizen's right to defend against and to repel an officer's excessive force must be noticed. He cannot use greater force in protecting himself against the officer's unlawful force than reasonably appears to be necessary. If he employs such greater force, then he becomes the aggressor and forfeits the right to claim self-defense to a charge of assault and battery on the officer. See Restatement, *Torts* 2d, § 70 (1965). Furthermore, if he knows that if he desists from his physically defensive measures and submits to arrest the officer's unlawfully excessive force would cease, the arrestee must desist or lose his privilege of self-defense.

It has been suggested that the latter qualification is not reasonable because it would require a citizen being subjected to excessive force or attack and defending against it to make a split second determination, amounting to a gamble, as to whether if he terminates his defensive measures, he will suffer further beyond arrest. But application of the rule does not require such action as should follow opportunity for detached reflection. It merely commands that the citizen's conduct be reasonable in the light of all the circumstances apparent to him at the moment. And thus it is a counterprotective measure for the original aggressor officer. Administration of the rule should be no more difficult than those dealing with the duty of an assaulted person to retreat to avoid the attack or the duty not to continue the affray after the original aggressor ceases the assault; once the danger is past, the original victim cannot continue measures that were originally defensive.

Applying the stated principles to the present case, it is plain that the trial court erred in eliminating self-defense from the case as a matter of law. Two bases exist for that conclusion. The jury could have found on the disputed facts that Dowling had informed Mulvihill expressly, or by his course of conduct, that he was under arrest for an ordinance violation offense. If such a finding were made, it would follow that Dowling was justified in using such force in overcoming Mulvihill's resistance as was reasonably necessary to make the arrest effective.

But it was open to the jury to find also that the resistance was such that the officer, in attempting to overcome it, employed unnecessary and excessive force when he drew his gun and struck Mulvihill in the head with it so as to cause a lacerated scalp. They could have found further that this caused Mulvihill reasonably to feel and to fear that an effort was being made to point the gun at him and to fire it. Assuming a finding of such facts and that they preexisted the charged assault and battery on the officer, defendant was entitled to have the issue of self-defense passed upon by the jury.

The judgment of the Appellate Division is affirmed and the cause remanded for new trial.

NOTES FROM JUSTICE STEIN:

(1) In *U.S. v. Branch*, 91 F.3d 699 (5th Cir. 1996), defendants were charged with voluntary manslaughter of federal agents who attempted to execute search and arrest warrants against the Branch Davidians (a religious sect) at their compound near Waco, Texas. The court rejected defendants' claim that the agents used excessive force. "A citizen may not initiate a firefight solely on the ground that the police sent too many well-armed officers to arrest him."

(2) In our case, did Officer Krumkey use or threaten "excessive force?" When, exactly? Does it matter which of his acts we focus upon?

STATE v. BONANO
New Jersey Supreme Court
59 N.J. 515, 284 A.2d 345 (1971)

MOUNTAIN, J.

Defendant was convicted of murder in the second degree.

On the evening of the fatal shooting, defendant, a resident of Camden, had gone to Philadelphia to play cards with friends. Before departing, for some reason which is not explained, he placed a loaded revolver in the belt of his trousers. Failing to find the diversion he sought, he returned sooner than had been anticipated and found his wife gone from home. She was in fact attending a christening party in the neighborhood. Upon her return shortly thereafter, defendant "smacked" her in the face, apparently because she had left the house without his permission. His eleven year old stepdaughter, a witness to the incident, hastened back to the party and informed her uncle Carlos, defendant's brother-in-law, of what had occurred.

Carlos immediately armed himself with a knife from the kitchen and set out for his sister's home. The several statements of the actual encounter that ensued differ somewhat, but it is agreed that defendant was standing in the doorway of his home as Carlos approached the house and commenced to mount the porch steps. There was testimony that at about this point Carlos drew his knife and uttered some imprecation of a threatening nature. Defendant fired the revolver, with which he was still armed, inflicting a wound from which Carlos shortly died.

The ground of appeal which we think most significant relates to the right of a defendant to invoke the plea of self-defense as a justification for a killing, and more particularly the application of the doctrine of retreat as a corollary to this rule.

N.J.S.A. 2A:113-6 provides, in pertinent part, that "[any] person who kills another * * * in his or her own defense, * * * is guiltless and shall be totally acquitted and discharged." At early common law self-defense did not justify homicide. A defendant who slew another to save his own life was nevertheless convicted and forced to seek relief as a supplicant for mercy. "The man who commits homicide by misadventure or in self-defense deserves but needs a pardon." 2 Pollock & Maitland, *History of English Law*, (2d ed. 1898) 479. Later, of course, the right to protect oneself became recognized as a complete defense to a charge of homicide. This appears always to have been the law in New Jersey. But self-defense may be successfully invoked only in those cases where the act of killing is necessary or reasonably appears to be so in order to preserve the defendant's life or to protect him from serious bodily harm. "Self-defense is measured against necessity." *State v. Abbott*, 36 N.J. 63, 69 (1961).

This brings us to a consideration of the question as to whether, and under what circumstances, a man must retreat when confronted by an assailant, before he may justifiably kill another in his own defense. Specifically, was the defendant in this case, standing on the threshold of his own home, required to seek refuge indoors rather than resort to deadly force? The doctrine of retreat may be broadly stated as requiring one who is attacked to withdraw, before employing deadly force in his own defense, where there lies open a safe avenue of escape and he is consciously aware of this fact; he may stand his ground and not retreat, if he employs less than deadly force. The result of an improper resort to deadly force, within the concept of this rule, is to deny the defendant the benefit of a plea of self-defense.

Some other jurisdictions reject the doctrine of retreat, holding that one who is attacked may defend himself, even to the point of killing his assailant, as long as he had a right to be at the place where he was attacked. See, for example, *State v. Blanton*, 111 Ohio App. 111 (Ct.App. 1960); *People v. Washington*, 54 Ill.App.2d 467 (App.Ct. 1965).

This state has, however, heretofore accepted the doctrine of retreat as an expression of the more humane and enlightened rule. *State v. Abbott*, supra. We continue to adhere to this view. "When it comes to a question whether one man shall flee or another shall live, the law decides that the former shall rather flee than that the latter shall die." *Commonwealth v. Drum*, 58 Pa.St. 9, 22 (1868).

While we take the general doctrine of retreat to be settled in this State, the case before us presents an exception to this rule which has not hitherto been squarely presented to this court. Must a man retreat when attacked in his own dwelling house? The well nigh universal rule, with which we are in accord, declares that under such circumstances no duty to retreat arises.

A man is not bound to retreat from his house. He may stand his ground there and kill any person who attempts to commit a felony therein, or who attempts to enter by force for the purpose of committing a felony, or of inflicting great bodily harm upon an inmate. In such a case the owner or any member of the family, or even a lodger in the house, may meet the intruder at the threshold, and prevent him from entering by any means rendered necessary by the exigency, even to the taking of his life, and the homicide will be justifiable. Clark & Marshall, *Law of Crimes* (7th ed.) § 7.03.

At this time, however, we limit our acceptance of this rule to those cases where the defendant is actually in his dwelling house. A porch or other similar physical appurtenance is deemed to come within this concept.

In *State v. Provoid*, 110 N.J. Super. 547, 554 (App. Div. 1970), Judge Goldmann noted that, "As to just what constitutes the limits of a 'dwelling,' the majority of jurisdictions in this country have concluded that the privilege of self defense without retreat extends to anywhere within the 'curtilage' of a man's home." This is, indeed, the majority view, and yet one may question its soundness. See Beale,

Homicide in Self-Defense, 3 Colum. L. Rev. 526, 541-42 (1903). "Curtilage" is not a term that can in all cases be precisely defined. * * * * It may be seriously doubted whether a concept arising in the mediaeval land law furnishes an intelligent guide in determining whether the taking of a life is to be justified. What, also, of a disputed boundary line? Is the justification for a slaying to rest upon the resolution of a title issue? If a defendant can show good title to the ground upon which he stood when he fired the fatal shot, is he to be exonerated, whereas if the land is later determined to be that of his neighbor, is he to be found guilty? Might not the better rule be that a duty to retreat should exist except as to the dwelling house itself, defined, as stated above, to include a porch or other similar appurtenance? This case does not raise the issue and we leave its resolution to another day.

During summation the assistant prosecutor, in commenting upon the alternative courses of action open to defendant at the time of the encounter, said, "What could this defendant have done? Gone in the house and shut the door? Possibly." This statement was clearly capable of leaving in the minds of the jury the thought that the defendant perhaps should have retreated indoors rather than have done what he did. At the conclusion of the court's charge, which had made no mention of retreat, defense counsel asked that the charge be in this respect supplemented. He specifically stated, "I respectfully ask that Your Honor instruct the jury that the man doesn't have to run from his own home."

After some further discussion during which the judge questioned whether the instruction should be given, defense counsel concluded, "I leave it to Your Honor's discretion." Nothing further was done. We think the court's discretion should have been exercised in favor of giving a supplementary instruction on the subject of retreat. Had the jury known that defendant had no legal duty to withdraw indoors, this knowledge would almost certainly have eradicated any doubt unfavorable to defendant that the assistant prosecutor's comment may have engendered.

Furthermore, and quite apart from anything arising from the assistant prosecutor's remark, it would appear from the record that defendant was entitled to a charge to the effect that if the jury believed from the evidence before it that he was standing at his own doorway, that Carlos approached and commenced to mount the steps, that he drew a knife and threatened to kill defendant and that defendant reasonably believed he was in danger of losing his life or suffering serious bodily harm, he was under no duty to retreat but might stand his ground and resist the attack even to the extent of employing deadly force. Since the giving of such an instruction might well have resulted in an acquittal, the failure so to charge requires a reversal.

NOTE FROM JUSTICE STEIN:

I assume that a front lawn or garden is part of the "curtilage" of a house. Should it be considered part of the "dwelling," under the retreat doctrine? "My lawn is my castle" sounds a bit odd.

STATE v. KELLY

New Jersey Supreme Court
97 N.J. 178, 478 A.2d 364 (1984)

WILENTZ, C.J.

The central issue before us is whether expert testimony about the battered-woman's syndrome is admissible to help establish a claim of self-defense in a homicide case. The question is one of first impression in this state. We hold, based on the limited record before us (the State not having had a full opportunity to prove the contrary), that the battered-woman's syndrome is an appropriate subject for expert testimony; that the experts' conclusions, despite the relative newness of the field, are sufficiently reliable under New Jersey's standards for scientific testimony; and that defendant's expert was sufficiently qualified. Accordingly, we reverse and remand for a new trial. If on retrial after a full examination of these issues the evidence continues to support these conclusions, the expert's testimony on the battered-woman's syndrome shall be admitted as relevant to the honesty and reasonableness of defendant's belief that deadly force was necessary to protect her against death or serious bodily harm.

I.

On May 24, 1980, defendant, Gladys Kelly, stabbed her husband, Ernest, with a pair of scissors. He died shortly thereafter at a nearby hospital. The couple had been married for seven years, during which time Ernest had periodically attacked Gladys. According to Ms. Kelly, he assaulted her that afternoon, and she stabbed him in self-defense, fearing that he would kill her if she did not act.

Ms. Kelly was indicted for murder. At trial, she did not deny stabbing her husband, but asserted that her action was in self-defense. To establish the requisite state of mind for her self-defense claim, Ms. Kelly called Dr. Lois Veronen as an expert witness to testify about the battered-woman's syndrome. After hearing a lengthy *voir dire* examination of Dr. Veronen, the trial court ruled that expert testimony concerning the syndrome was inadmissible on the self-defense issue under *State v. Bess*, 53 N.J. 10 (1968). Apparently the court believed that the sole purpose of this testimony was to explain and justify defendant's perception of the danger rather than to show the objective reasonableness of that perception.

Ms. Kelly was convicted of reckless manslaughter. * * * *

II.

The Kellys had a stormy marriage. Some of the details of their relationship, especially the stabbing, are disputed. The following is Ms. Kelly's version of what happened - a version that the jury could have accepted and, if they had, a version that would make the proffered expert testimony not only relevant, but critical.

The day after the marriage, Mr. Kelly got drunk and knocked Ms. Kelly down. Although a period of calm followed the initial attack, the next seven years were accompanied by periodic and frequent beatings, sometimes as often as once a week. During the attacks, which generally occurred when Mr. Kelly was drunk, he threatened to kill Ms. Kelly and to cut off parts of her body if she tried to leave him. Mr. Kelly often moved out of the house after an attack, later returning with a promise that he would change his ways. Until the day of the homicide, only one of the attacks had taken place in public.

The day before the stabbing, Gladys and Ernest went shopping. They did not have enough money to buy food for the entire week, so Ernest said he would give his wife more money the next day. The following morning he left for work. Ms. Kelly next saw her husband late that afternoon at a friend's house. She had gone there with her daughter, Annette, to ask Ernest for money to buy food. He told her to wait until they got home, and shortly thereafter the Kellys left. After walking past several houses, Mr. Kelly, who was drunk, angrily asked "What the hell did you come around here for?" He then grabbed the collar of her dress, and the two fell to the ground. He choked her by pushing his fingers against her throat, punched or hit her face, and bit her leg.

A crowd gathered on the street. Two men from the crowd separated them, just as Gladys felt that she was "passing out" from being choked. Fearing that Annette had been pushed around in the crowd, Gladys then left to look for her. Upon finding Annette, defendant noticed that Annette had defendant's pocketbook. Gladys had dropped it during the fight. Annette had retrieved it and gave her mother the pocketbook.

After finding her daughter, Ms. Kelly then observed Mr. Kelly running toward her with his hands raised. Within seconds he was right next to her. Unsure of whether he had armed himself while she was looking for their daughter, and thinking that he had come back to kill her, she grabbed a pair of scissors from her pocketbook. She tried to scare him away, but instead stabbed him.[1]

III.

The central question in this case is whether the trial court erred in its exclusion of expert testimony on the battered-woman's syndrome. That testimony was intended to explain defendant's state of mind and bolster her claim of self-defense. We shall first examine the nature of the battered-woman's syndrome and then consider the expert testimony proffered in this case and its relevancy.

In the past decade social scientists and the legal community began to examine the forces that generate and perpetuate wife beating and violence in the family.[2]

---

[1] This version of the homicide — with a drunk Mr. Kelly as the aggressor both in pushing Ms. Kelly to the ground and again in rushing at her with his hands in a threatening position after the two had been separated — is sharply disputed by the State. The prosecution presented testimony intended to show that the initial scuffle was started by Gladys; that upon disentanglement, while she was restrained by bystanders, she stated that she intended to kill Ernest; that she then chased after him, and upon catching up with him stabbed him with a pair of scissors taken from her pocketbook.

[2] The works that comprise the basic study of the problem of battered women are all relatively recent. See, e.g., R. Langley & R. Levy, *Wife Beating: The Silent Crisis* (1979); D. Martin, *Battered Wives* (1976); L. Walker, *The Battered Woman* (1979); R. Gelles, *The Violent Home: A Study of Physical Aggression*

What has been revealed is that the problem affects many more people than had been thought and that the victims of the violence are not only the battered family members (almost always either the wife or the children). There are also many other strangers to the family who feel the devastating impact, often in the form of violence, of the psychological damage suffered by the victims.

Due to the high incidence of unreported abuse (the FBI and other law enforcement experts believe that wife abuse is the most unreported crime in the United States), estimates vary of the number of American women who are beaten regularly by their husband, boyfriend, or the dominant male figure in their lives. One recent estimate puts the number of women beaten yearly at over one million. See California Advisory Comm'n on Family Law, *Domestic Violence*, App F at 119 (1st report 1978). The state police statistics show more than 18,000 reported cases of domestic violence in New Jersey during the first nine months of 1983, in 83% of which the victim was female. It is clear that the American home, once assumed to be the cornerstone of our society, is often a violent place.[3]

While common law notions that assigned an inferior status to women, and to wives in particular, no longer represent the state of the law as reflected in statutes and cases, many commentators assert that a bias against battered women still exists, institutionalized in the attitudes of law enforcement agencies unwilling to pursue or uninterested in pursuing wife beating cases.[4] See Comment, *The Battered Wife's Dilemma: Kill or be Killed*, 32 Hastings L.J., 895, 897-911 (1981).

Another problem is the currency enjoyed by stereotypes and myths concerning the characteristics of battered women and their reasons for staying in battering relationships. Some popular misconceptions about battered women include the beliefs that they are masochistic and actually enjoy their beatings, that they purposely provoke their husbands into violent behavior, and, most critically, as we shall soon see, that women who remain in battering relationships are free to leave

---

between Husbands and Wives (1971); *Battered Women: A Psychosociological Study of Domestic Violence* (M. Roy ed. 1977).

Similarly, legislative activity in this field is relatively new; for example, New Jersey's Prevention of Domestic Violence Act, L. 1981, c. 426, N.J.S.A. 2C:25-1 to -16 and the Shelters for Victims of Domestic Violence Act, L. 1979, c. 337, N.J.S.A. 30:14-1 to -17.

In enacting the Prevention of Domestic Violence Act, the New Jersey Legislature recognized the pervasiveness and seriousness of domestic violence:

> The Legislature finds and declares that domestic violence is a serious crime against society; that there are thousands of persons in this State who are regularly beaten, tortured and in some cases even killed by their spouses or cohabitants; that a significant number of women who are assaulted are pregnant; that victims of domestic violence come from all societal and economic backgrounds and ethnic groups; that there is a positive correlation between spouse abuse and child abuse; and that children, even when they are not themselves physically assaulted, suffer deep and lasting emotional effects from exposure to domestic violence. It is therefore, the intent of the Legislature to assure the victims of domestic violence the maximum protection from abuse the law can provide. [N.J.S.A. 2C:25-2].

[3] In her book, *The Battered Woman*, Dr. Lenore Walker cites research by sociologists Straus, Gelles, and Steinmetz finding that in 1976 at least one assault between family members occurred in 28% of all American homes.

[4] In 1976, for example, battered women in California and New York instituted class actions alleging that the police customarily denied women legal protection by refusing to assist battered women or arrest their abusing husbands.

their abusers at any time. See L. Walker, *The Battered Woman*, at 19-31 (1979).

As these cases so tragically suggest, not only do many women suffer physical abuse at the hands of their mates, but a significant number of women kill (or are killed by) their husbands. In 1978, murders between husband and wife or girlfriend and boyfriend constituted 13% of all murders committed in the United States. Undoubtedly some of these arose from battering incidents. Federal Bureau of Investigation, *Crime in the United States 1978* (1978) Men were the victims in 48% of these killings.

As the problem of battered women has begun to receive more attention, sociologists and psychologists have begun to focus on the effects a sustained pattern of physical and psychological abuse can have on a woman. The effects of such abuse are what some scientific observers have termed "the battered-woman's syndrome," a series of common characteristics that appear in women who are abused physically and psychologically over an extended period of time by the dominant male figure in their lives. Dr. Lenore Walker, a prominent writer on the battered-woman's syndrome, defines the battered woman as one who is repeatedly subjected to any forceful physical or psychological behavior by a man in order to coerce her to do something he wants her to do without concern for her rights. Battered women include wives or women in any form of intimate relationships with men. Furthermore, in order to be classified as a battered woman, the couple must go through the battering cycle at least twice. Any woman may find herself in an abusive relationship with a man once. If it occurs a second time, and she remains in the situation, she is defined as a battered woman.

According to Dr. Walker, relationships characterized by physical abuse tend to develop battering cycles. Violent behavior directed at the woman occurs in three distinct and repetitive stages that vary both in duration and intensity depending on the individuals involved.

Phase one of the battering cycle is referred to as the "tension-building stage," during which the battering male engages in minor battering incidents and verbal abuse while the woman, beset by fear and tension, attempts to be as placating and passive as possible in order to stave off more serious violence.

Phase two of the battering cycle is the "acute battering incident." At some point during phase one, the tension between the battered woman and the batterer becomes intolerable and more serious violence inevitable. The triggering event that initiates phase two is most often an internal or external event in the life of the battering male, but provocation for more severe violence is sometimes provided by the woman who can no longer tolerate or control her phase-one anger and anxiety. *Id.* at 59-65.

Phase three of the battering cycle is characterized by extreme contrition and loving behavior on the part of the battering male. During this period the man will often mix his pleas for forgiveness and protestations of devotion with promises to seek professional help, to stop drinking,[5] and to refrain from further violence. For

---

[5] Alcohol is often an important component of violence toward women. Evidence points to a correlation between alcohol and violent acts between family members. In one British study, 44 of 100 cases of wife

some couples, this period of relative calm may last as long as several months, but in a battering relationship the affection and contrition of the man will eventually fade and phase one of the cycle will start anew.

The cyclical nature of battering behavior helps explain why more women simply do not leave their abusers. The loving behavior demonstrated by the batterer during phase three reinforces whatever hopes these women might have for their mate's reform and keeps them bound to the relationship. R. Langley & R. Levy, *Wife Beating: The Silent Crisis* 112-14 (1977).

Some women may even perceive the battering cycle as normal, especially if they grew up in a violent household. *Battered Women, A Psychosociological Study of Domestic Violence* 60 (M. Roy ed. 1977); D. Martin, *Battered Wives*, 60 (1981). Or they may simply not wish to acknowledge the reality of their situation. T. Davidson, *Conjugal Crime*, at 50 (1978) ("The middle-class battered wife's response to her situation tends to be withdrawal, silence and denial").

Other women, however, become so demoralized and degraded by the fact that they cannot predict or control the violence that they sink into a state of psychological paralysis and become unable to take any action at all to improve or alter the situation. There is a tendency in battered women to believe in the omnipotence or strength of their battering husbands and thus to feel that any attempt to resist them is hopeless. L. Walker, supra, at 75.

In addition to these psychological impacts, external social and economic factors often make it difficult for some women to extricate themselves from battering relationships. A woman without independent financial resources who wishes to leave her husband often finds it difficult to do so because of a lack of material and social resources.

Even with the progress of the last decade, women typically make less money and hold less prestigious jobs than men, and are more responsible for child care. Thus, in a violent confrontation where the first reaction might be to flee, women realize soon that there may be no place to go. Moreover, the stigma that attaches to a woman who leaves the family unit without her children undoubtedly acts as a further deterrent to moving out.

In addition, battered women, when they want to leave the relationship, are typically unwilling to reach out and confide in their friends, family, on the police, either out of shame and humiliation, fear of reprisal by their husband, or the feeling they will not be believed.

Dr. Walker and other commentators have identified several common personality traits of the battered woman: low self-esteem, traditional beliefs about the home, the family, and the female sex role, tremendous feelings of guilt that their

---

abuse occurred when the husband was drunk. Gayford, *Wife Battering: A Preliminary Survey of 100 Cases*, British Medical Journal 1:194-197 (1975). Gelles, in *The Violent Home: A Study of Physical Aggression between Husbands and Wives* (1979), found that in 44 families where violence had occurred, drinking accompanied the violence in 21 of the cases. He also posited that alcohol and family violence are more closely related than alcohol and other types of violence.

marriages are failing, and the tendency to accept responsibility for the batterer's actions. L. Walker, supra, at 35-36.

Finally, battered women are often hesitant to leave a battering relationship because, in addition to their hope of reform on the part of their spouse, they harbor a deep concern about the possible response leaving might provoke in their mates. They literally become trapped by their own fear. Case histories are replete with instances in which a battered wife left her husband only to have him pursue her and subject her to an even more brutal attack. D. Martin, supra, at 76-79.

The combination of all these symptoms — resulting from sustained psychological and physical trauma compounded by aggravating social and economic factors — constitutes the battered-woman's syndrome. Only by understanding these unique pressures that force battered women to remain with their mates, despite their long-standing and reasonable fear of severe bodily harm and the isolation that being a battered woman creates, can a battered woman's state of mind be accurately and fairly understood.

The *voir dire* testimony of Dr. Veronen, sought to be introduced by defendant Gladys Kelly, conformed essentially to this outline of the battered-woman's syndrome. Dr. Veronen, after establishing her credentials, described in general terms the component parts of the battered-woman's syndrome and its effects on a woman's physical and mental health. The witness then documented, based on her own considerable experience in counseling, treating, and studying battered women, and her familiarity with the work of others in the field, the feelings of anxiety, self-blame, isolation, and, above all, fear that plagues these women and leaves them prey to a psychological paralysis that hinders their ability to break free or seek help.

Dr. Veronen stated that the problems of battered women are aggravated by a lack of understanding among the general public concerning both the prevalence of violence against women and the nature of battering relationships. She cited several myths concerning battered women that enjoy popular acceptance — primarily that such women are masochistic and enjoy the abuse they receive and that they are free to leave their husbands but choose not to.

Dr. Veronen described the various psychological tests and examinations she had performed in connection with her independent research. These tests and their methodology, including their interpretation, are, according to Dr. Veronen, widely accepted by clinical psychologists. Applying this methodology to defendant (who was subjected to all of the tests, including a five-hour interview), Dr. Veronen concluded that defendant was a battered woman and subject to the battered-woman's syndrome.

In addition, Dr. Veronen was prepared to testify as to how, as a battered woman, Gladys Kelly perceived her situation at the time of the stabbing, and why, in her opinion, defendant did not leave her husband despite the constant beatings she endured.

IV.

Whether expert testimony on the battered-woman's syndrome should be admitted in this case depends on whether it is relevant to defendant's claim of self-defense, and, in any event, on whether the proffer meets the standards for admission of expert testimony in this state. We examine first the law of self-defense and consider whether the expert testimony is relevant.

The present rules governing the use of force in self-defense are set out in the justification section of the Code of Criminal Justice. The use of force against another in self-defense is justifiable "when the actor reasonably believes that such force is immediately necessary for the purpose of protecting himself against the use of unlawful force by such other person on the present occasion." N.J.S.A. 2C:3-4(a). Further limitations exist when deadly force is used in self-defense. The use of such deadly force is not justifiable unless the actor reasonably believes that such force is necessary to protect himself against death or serious bodily harm. N.J.S.A. 2C:3-4(b)(2).

These principles codify decades of prior case law development of the elements of self-defense. We focus here on the critical requirement that the actor reasonably believe deadly force to be necessary to prevent death or serious bodily harm, for the proffer of expert testimony was argued to be relevant on this point.

Self-defense exonerates a person who kills in the reasonable belief that such action was necessary to prevent his or her death or serious injury, even though this belief was later proven mistaken. "Detached reflection cannot be demanded in the presence of an uplifted knife," Justice Holmes aptly said, *Brown v. United States*, 256 U.S. 335 (1921); and the law accordingly requires only a reasonable, not necessarily a correct, judgment.

While it is not imperative that actual necessity exist, a valid plea of self-defense will not lie absent an actual (that is, honest) belief on the part of the defendant in the necessity of using force. While no case in New Jersey has addressed the point directly, the privilege of self-defense does not exist where the defendant's action is not prompted by a belief in its necessity: "He has no defense when he intentionally kills his enemy in complete ignorance of the fact that his enemy, when killed, was about to launch a deadly attack upon him." W. LaFave & A. Scott, *Criminal Law* sec. 53 (1972).[7] The intent of the drafters of the present Code was that a necessity to act should not give rise to a meritorious plea of self-defense where the defendant was unaware of that necessity. Ultimately, of course, it is for the jury to determine if the defendant actually did believe in the necessity of acting with deadly force to prevent an imminent, grave attack.

Honesty alone, however, does not suffice. A defendant claiming the privilege of self-defense must also establish that her belief in the necessity to use force was reasonable. As originally proposed, the new Code of Criminal Justice would have eliminated the reasonableness requirement, allowing self-defense whenever the

---

[7] See also Restatement of Torts 2d, § 63 (1965). Under principles of self-defense as a justification for the torts of assault and battery — which closely parallel criminal self-defense principles -no privilege of self-defense exists for one acting in ignorance of another's intent to inflict harm on him.

defendant honestly believed in the imminent need to act. This proposed change in the law was not accepted by the Legislature. N.J.S.A. 2C:3-4, as finally enacted, retains the requirement that the defendant's belief be reasonable.[8]

Thus, even when the defendant's belief in the need to kill in self-defense is conceded to be sincere, if it is found to have been unreasonable under the circumstances, such a belief cannot be held to constitute complete justification for a homicide.[9] As with the determination of the existence of the defendant's belief, the question of the reasonableness of this belief "is to be determined by the jury, not the defendant, in light of the circumstances existing at the time of the homicide."

It is perhaps worth emphasizing here that for defendant to prevail, the jury need not find beyond a reasonable doubt that the defendant's belief was honest and reasonable. Rather, if any evidence raising the issue of self-defense is adduced, either in the State's or the defendant's case, then the jury must be instructed that the State is required to prove beyond a reasonable doubt that the self-defense claim does not accord with the facts; acquittal is required if there remains a reasonable doubt whether the defendant acted in self-defense.

With the foregoing standards in mind, we turn to an examination of the relevance of the proffered expert testimony to Gladys Kelly's claim of self-defense.

V.

Gladys Kelly claims that she stabbed her husband in self-defense, believing he was about to kill her. The gist of the State's case was that Gladys Kelly was the aggressor, that she consciously intended to kill her husband, and that she certainly was not acting in self-defense.

The credibility of Gladys Kelly is a critical issue in this case. If the jury does not believe Gladys Kelly's account, it cannot find she acted in self-defense. The expert testimony offered was directly relevant to one of the critical elements of that account, namely, what Gladys Kelly believed at the time of the stabbing, and was thus material to establish the honesty of her stated belief that she was in imminent danger of death.[10]

---

[8] The rejected form of § 2C:3-4 was patterned after § 3.04 of the Model Penal Code. The purpose of the proposed Code and M.P.C. provisions was to prevent one who killed in the honest but mistaken and unreasonable belief in the necessity of the action from being convicted of a crime like murder, which is premised on an act motivated by unlawful purpose. See Model Penal Code § 3.04 commentary at 14-15 (Tent. Draft No. 8 1958).

[9] In *State v. Powell*, 84 N.J. 305 (1980), we explicitly recognized that before enactment of the Code the doctrine of imperfect self-defense could reduce murder to manslaughter when the defendant honestly but unreasonably perceived himself in such danger as to require the use of deadly force. However, we expressed no opinion on whether imperfect self-defense was available under the new Code for the purpose of reducing murder to manslaughter. The resolution of that issue is immaterial to the case at bar.

[10] The factual contentions of the parties eliminated any issue concerning the duty to retreat. If the State's version is accepted, defendant is the aggressor; if defendant's version is accepted, the possibility of retreat is excluded by virtue of the nature of the attack that defendant claims took place. We do not understand that the State claims defendant breached that duty under any version of the facts. If, however, the duty becomes an issue on retrial, the trial court will have to determine the relevancy of the

As can be seen from our discussion of the expert testimony, Dr. Veronen would have bolstered Gladys Kelly's credibility. Specifically, by showing that her experience, although concededly difficult to comprehend, was common to that of other women who had been in similarly abusive relationships, Dr. Veronen would have helped the jury understand that Gladys Kelly could have honestly feared that she would suffered serious bodily harm from her husband's attacks, yet still remain with him. This, in turn, would support Ms. Kelly's testimony about her state of mind (that is, that she honestly feared serious bodily harm) at the time of the stabbing.

On the facts in this case, we find that the expert testimony was relevant to Gladys Kelly's state of mind, namely, it was admissible to show she honestly believed she was in imminent danger of death. * * * *

We also find the expert testimony relevant to the reasonableness of defendant's belief that she was in imminent danger of death or serious injury. We do not mean that the expert's testimony could be used to show that it was understandable that a battered woman might believe that her life was in danger when indeed it was not and when a reasonable person would not have so believed, for admission for that purpose would clearly violate the rule set forth in *State v. Bess*, supra, 53 N.J. 10. Expert testimony in that direction would be relevant solely to the honesty of defendant's belief, not its objective reasonableness. Rather, our conclusion is that the expert's testimony, if accepted by the jury, would have aided it in determining whether, under the circumstances, a reasonable person would have believed there was imminent danger to her life.

At the heart of the claim of self-defense was defendant's story that she had been repeatedly subjected to "beatings" over the course of her marriage. While defendant's testimony was somewhat lacking in detail, a juror could infer from the use of the word "beatings," as well as the detail given concerning some of these events (the choking, the biting, the use of fists), that these physical assaults posed a risk of serious injury or death. When that regular pattern of serious physical abuse is combined with defendant's claim that the decedent sometimes threatened to kill her, defendant's statement that on this occasion she thought she might be killed when she saw Mr. Kelly running toward her could be found to reflect a reasonable fear; that is, it could so be found if the jury believed Gladys Kelly's story of the prior beatings, if it believed her story of the prior threats, and, of course, if it believed her story of the events of that particular day.

The crucial issue of fact on which this expert's testimony would bear is why, given such allegedly severe and constant beatings, combined with threats to kill, defendant had not long ago left decedent. Whether raised by the prosecutor as a factual issue or not, our own common knowledge tells us that most of us, including the ordinary juror, would ask himself or herself just such a question. And our knowledge is bolstered by the experts' knowledge, for the experts point out that one of the common myths, apparently believed by most people, is that battered wives are free to leave. To some, this misconception is followed by the observation

---

battered-woman's syndrome to that issue. Without passing on that question, it appears to us to be a different question from whether the syndrome is relevant to defendant's failure to leave her husband in the past.

that the battered wife is masochistic, proven by her refusal to leave despite the severe beatings; to others, however, the fact that the battered wife stays on unquestionably suggests that the "beatings" could not have been too bad for if they had been, she certainly would have left. The expert could clear up these myths, by explaining that one of the common characteristics of a battered wife is her inability to leave despite such constant beatings; her "learned helplessness"; her lack of anywhere to go; her feeling that if she tried to leave, she would be subjected to even more merciless treatment; her belief in the omnipotence of her battering husband; and sometimes her hope that her husband will change his ways.

Unfortunately, in this case the State reinforced the myths about battered women. On cross-examination, when discussing an occasion when Mr. Kelly temporarily moved out of the house, the State repeatedly asked Ms. Kelly: "You wanted him back, didn't you?" The implication was clear: domestic life could not have been too bad if she wanted him back. In its closing argument, the State trivialized the severity of the beatings, saying:

> I'm not going to say they happened or they didn't happen, but life isn't pretty. Life is not a bowl of cherries. We each and every person who takes a breath has problems. Defense counsel says bruised and battered. Is there any one of us who hasn't been battered by life in some manner or means?

Even had the State not taken this approach, however, expert testimony would be essential to rebut the general misconceptions regarding battered women.

The difficulty with the expert's testimony is that it sounds as if an expert is giving knowledge to a jury about something the jury knows as well as anyone else, namely, the reasonableness of a person's fear of imminent serious danger. That is not at all, however, what this testimony is directly aimed at. It is aimed at an area where the purported common knowledge of the jury may be very much mistaken, an area where jurors' logic, drawn from their own experience, may lead to a wholly incorrect conclusion, an area where expert knowledge would enable the jurors to disregard their prior conclusions as being common myths rather than common knowledge. After hearing the expert, instead of saying Gladys Kelly could not have been beaten up so badly for if she had, she certainly would have left, the jury could conclude that her failure to leave was very much part and parcel of her life as a battered wife. The jury could conclude that instead of casting doubt on the accuracy of her testimony about the severity and frequency of prior beatings, her failure to leave actually reinforced her credibility.

Since a retrial is necessary, we think it advisable to indicate the limit of the expert's testimony on this issue of reasonableness. It would not be proper for the expert to express the opinion that defendant's belief on that day was reasonable, not because this is the ultimate issue, but because the area of expert knowledge relates, in this regard, to the reasons for defendant's failure to leave her husband. Either the jury accepts or rejects that explanation and, based on that, credits defendant's stories about the beatings she suffered. No expert is needed, however, once the jury has made up its mind on those issues, to tell the jury the logical conclusion, namely, that a person who had in fact been severely and continuously beaten might very well reasonably fear that the imminent beating she was about to suffer could be either life-threatening or pose a risk of serious injury.

What the expert could state was that defendant had the battered-woman's syndrome, and could explain that syndrome in detail, relating its characteristics to defendant, but only to enable the jury better to determine the honesty and reasonableness of defendant's belief. Depending on its content, the expert's testimony might also enable the jury to find that the battered wife, because of the prior beatings, numerous beatings, as often as once a week, for seven years, from the day they were married to the day he died, is particularly able to predict accurately the likely extent of violence in any attack on her. That conclusion could significantly affect the jury's evaluation of the reasonableness of defendant's fear for her life.[13]

[The court then held that Dr. Veronen's testimony met the requirements of New Jersey Evidence Rule 56(2), which requires that (1) the intended testimony must concern a subject matter that is beyond the ken of the average juror, (2) the field testified to must be at a state of the art such that an expert's testimony could be sufficiently reliable, and (3) the witness must have sufficient expertise to offer the testimony.]

Judgment reversed and remanded for a new trial.

NOTES FROM JUSTICE STEIN:

(1) Did the court create a new defense, or did it hold that an old defense applies to a new (or newly recognized) situation?

(2) In our case, defendant did not offer to prove that Professor Plum ever met Groves or Krumkey or talked to either of them or knows anything personal about them. Therefore, how is the professor's testimony relevant to this case? Aren't the

---

[13] At least two other courts agree that expert testimony about the battered-woman's syndrome is relevant to show the reasonableness as well as the honesty of defendant's fear of serious bodily harm. *Ibn-Tamas v. United States*, 407 A. 2d 626, 634-35 (D.C. 1979) (expert testimony "would have enhanced Mrs. Ibn-Tamas' general credibility in responding to cross-examination designed to show that the testimony about the relationship with her husband was implausible," and also "would have supplied an interpretation of the facts which differed from the ordinary lay perception"); *Hawthorne v. State*, 408 So. 2d 801, 806-07 (Fla. Dist. Ct. App. 1981) (expert testimony would "aid the jury in interpreting the surrounding circumstances as they affected the reasonableness of defendant's belief," because "a jury would not understand why defendant would remain with her husband"); *State v. Allery*, No. 49674-9, slip op. at 8 (Wash. Sup. Ct. May 17, 1984) (court approved use of expert testimony "to effectively present the situation as perceived by the defendant, and the reasonableness of her fear to enable the jury to overcome stereotyped impressions about women who remain in abusive relationships"). But see *Commonwealth v. Light*, 326 A.2d 288 (Pa., 1974) (psychiatric testimony held to be of no help in determining whether fear of serious bodily harm was reasonable).

Defendant's counsel at oral argument made it clear that defendant's basic contention was that her belief in the immediate need to use deadly force was both honest and reasonable; and that the evidence concerning the battered-woman's syndrome was being offered solely on that issue. We therefore are not faced with any claim that a battered woman's honest belief in the need to use deadly force, even if objectively unreasonable, constitutes justification so long as its unreasonableness results from the psychological impact of the beatings. * * * * Nor is there any claim that the battering provocation might have some legal effect beyond the potential reduction of defendant's culpability to manslaughter, or that something other than an "immediate" need for deadly force will suffice. See *State v. Felton*, 110 Wis. 2d 485 (1983) (battered wife stabs sleeping husband).

elements of self defense *personal* (i.e., what did the *defendant* believe, and were *his* beliefs reasonable)?

(3) Courts in many jurisdictions allow expert testimony on the battered woman syndrome. See, e.g. *Hawthorne v. State*, 408 So.2d 801 (Fla.Ct.App., 1982); *State v. Hodges*, 239 Kan. 63, 716 P.2d 563 (1986); *State v. Anaya*, 438 A.2d 892 (Me. 1981); *People v. Wilson*, 194 Mich. App. 599, 487 N.W.2d 822 (Mich.Ct.App. 1992), *State v. Gallegos*, 719 P.2d 1268 (N.M.App. 1986); *People v. Torres*, 128 Misc.2d 129, 488 N.Y.S.2d 358 (1985); *State v. Leidholm*, 334 N.W.2d 811 (N.D. 1983); *Bechtel v. State*, 840 P.2d 1 (Okla.Ct.Crim.App. 1992); *State v. Middleton*, 657 P.2d 1215 (Ore. 1983); *Commonwealth v. Miller*, 430 Pa.Super. 297, 634 A.2d 614; *State v. Kelly*, 685 P.2d 564 (Wash. 1984); Annot., 18 A.L.R.4th 1153 (1994 Supp.).

Some legislatures have followed suit. See, e.g., Calif.Ev.C. § 1107; Ky.Rev.Stat. § 503.050; Mo.Stat. § 563.033.

Nevertheless, several commentators have challenged these views — on both scientific and on policy grounds.

In Robert F. Schopp, Barbara J. Sturgis, & Megan Sullivan, *Battered Woman Syndrome, Expert Testimony, & The Distinction Between Justification & Excuse*, 1994 U.Ill.L.Rev. 45, 47-64, the authors examine in some detail the studies relied on by the court in *Kelly* — particularly those of Dr. Lenore Walker. They report:

> Although expert testimony regarding the battered woman syndrome has been widely admitted as relevant to self-defense, the sources usually cited as support for the syndrome by the admitting courts do not provide strong reason to accept it either as a clinical syndrome or as relevant to self-defense. * * * *

> [Dr. Walker's] method of data gathering created substantial potential for selective or biased self-reporting by the subjects as well as for distortion through interviewer demand or bias in interpretation. * * * * Other criticisms of Walker's study involve the lack of statistical analysis to test the significance of some findings, and the absence of clear theoretical foundations for interpretation of the data. * * * * Perhaps most troubling, however, is the apparent lack of clear support in the data for the conclusions drawn. * * * *

> In summary, Walker's data provided incomplete support for some and actively undermined other of her hypothesized personality characteristics of battered women. * * * *

> Perhaps most importantly from the perspective of the criminal courts, learned helplessness has been the aspect of the battered woman syndrome most frequently cited as central to cases of self-defense by battered women, yet it draws very little support from the available data. The complete body of work provides neither any clear conception of learned helplessness nor any good reason to believe that it regularly occurs in battered women. Some factors that seem intuitively related to learned helplessness, such as decreased self-esteem and problem-solving skills, are supported by some sources but not by others. In addition, the studies consistently report

elevated depression which may account for these factors. The data consistently fails to support other intuitively plausible indicators of learned helplessness, including traditional gender roles and external locus of control. Collectively, the data reviewed supports the proposition that battered women do not suffer learned helplessness, at least as well as it supports the claim that they do.

Another professor has attacked expert testimony re the battered woman's syndrome as "pseudoscientific social science" — a symptom of "syndromic lawyer syndrome." David L. Faigman, *The Syndromic Lawyer Syndrome: A Psychological Theory of Evidentiary Munificence*, 67 Colorado L.Rev. 817 (1996). "The law's gullibility in regard to syndrome evidence is profound; it displays the wishful desire to come to the correct political outcome, rather than any statement about the situation battered women confront. * * * * Anecdotal research is not science, it is literature." *Id.* at 821.

Another professor writes:

As a witness, Dr. [Lenore] Walker's approach is to depict the battered woman as "just like you and me" and to denounce as prejudice or ignorance any hint that battered wives are other than victims of circumstance. There is, she asserts, "nothing special about their personalities." Experience, of course, suggests the opposite: that most women have enough sense to leave a man before he lands the first blow — or, at least immediately thereafter. Dr. Walker disagrees. "Any woman" who meets up with the wrong man "is in danger of becoming a battered woman."

This is either poor social science or empathy caricatured; and may explain why Dr. Walker has been able to find self-defense in cases that the layman would recognize as first-degree murder. * * * *

Reduced to its essence, battered-woman syndrome is not a physician's diagnosis but an advocate's invention. It means: blame the deceased.

Unfortunately, the term has been received judicial recognition. The early decisions did exclude expert testimony on battered-woman syndrome as unscientific. * * * * But as Dr. Walker and others continued to publish, judicial resistance wilted. Most courts now allow expert testimony on battered-woman syndrome . . . and a few have swallowed Dr. Walker's "learned helplessness" adaptation in one gulp. The New Jersey Supreme Court, for example, mimicked Dr. Walker by finding that battered women "become so demoralized and degraded by the fact that they cannot predict or control the violence that they sink into a state of psychological paralysis and become unable to take any action at all to improve or alter the situation."

Of course, such reasoning doesn't explain how women who are that helpless manage to stab their husbands repeatedly in the chest with butcher knives, shoot them at close range, or hire hitmen to do the job. Nor does it explain why, if battered women are capable of such violent actions, they are incapable of nonhomicidal responses such as leaving the house. * * * *

Judges who allow a jury to find self-defense where the victim was asleep, or eating or bathing, or otherwise unoffending when slain ignore long-settled, dearly won legal principles evincing respect for life. [Caplan, "Battered Wives, Battered Justice", National Review, 2/25/91, p. 39]

And even some feminists have criticized "battered woman's syndrome" evidence. Professor Anne M. Coughlin, in *Excusing Women*, 82 Calif.L.Rev. 1, 4-5 (1994), states:

> While many feminist scholars conclude that the courts cannot justly blame an accused woman without considering abuse that she endured at the hands of her husband, several others have expressed uneasiness with the battered woman syndrome defense because it institutionalizes within the criminal law negative stereotypes of women. I agree with this criticism; in particular, the defense is objectionable because it relieves the accused woman of the stigma and pain of criminal punishment only if she embraces another kind of stigma and pain: she must advance an interpretation of her own activity that labels it the irrational product of a "mental health disorder." * * * *

> The defense itself defines the woman as a collection of mental symptoms, motivational deficits, and behavioral abnormalities; indeed, the fundamental premise of the defense is that women lack the psychological capacity to choose lawful means to extricate themselves from abusive mates.

A different problem was raised by James Acker & Hans Toch, *Battered Women, Straw Men, & Expert Testimony. A Commend on State v. Kelly*, 21 Crim.L.Bulletin 125 (1985):

> When the prior bad acts (the repeated beatings) and the bad character ("battering husband") of the deceased are made principal issues, this through the supportive testimony of an expert witness, the classic defense stratagem of "blaming the victim" for his own demise has been interjected before the jury. * * * * The killing of a battering husband could be "justified" in the jurors' minds not because it was necessary that a battered woman act with responsive deadly force when she was threatened with death or serious bodily injury by her mate but because it was a fitting act of retribution directed at a member of a sadistic fraternity who had finally reaped his just deserts.

(4) Suppose the man was *asleep* when the woman killed him. In *State v. Norman*, 89 N.C.App. 384, 366 S.E.2d 586 (1988), the court held that it was error to refuse to instruct the jury on self defense, even though the husband was napping when shot, because the shooting was close in time to his earlier attack on the wife, and the nap was "but a momentary hiatus in a continuing reign of terror." In *People v. Emick* (1984) 103 App.Div.2d 643, 481 N.Y.S.2d 552, and *State v. Leidholm, supra*, those courts too allowed a self defense claim where the man was shot while sleeping.

Other courts have reacted differently. The North Carolina Supreme Court reversed the appellate court decision in *Norman*, holding that the threat to the defendant was not "imminent." 324 N.C. 253, 378 S.E.2d 8 (1989). In *State v. Stewart* (Kansas Supreme Court 1988) 763 P.2d 572, the court held that because the wife shot the husband while he was sleeping, she could not have a reasonable belief of an imminent attack by him, so the trial court erred by giving the jury an instruction on self-defense. The court noted that "no jurisdictions have held that the existence of the battered woman syndrome in and of itself operates as a defense to murder." The fact that the victim was an evil man should not be a defense, as to permit capital punishment by individuals for this reason "would amount to a leap into the abyss of anarchy."

(5) In *People v. Yaklich*, 833 P.2d 758 (1991), the Colorado Court of Appeals held that the trial court should not have instructed the jury on self-defense where the defendant hired two killers to murder her husband in the driveway while the defendant slept in the house. Despite evidence that defendant was a battered woman, the court held that the defendant was too far removed from imminent danger at the time of the killing.

(6) Using the "battered woman syndrome" cases as precedent, the court in *State v. Janes*, 822 P. 2d 1238 (Wash.Ct.App. 1992) allowed evidence of "battered child syndrome." But see *Jahnke v. State*, 682 P.2d 991 (Wyoming, 1984), and J.Q. Wilson, *Sorry I Killed You, But I Had a Bad Childhood*, 17 Cal. Law. 43 (1997).

(7) In *Werner v. State*, 711 S.W.2d 639 (Texas Crim.App., 1986), Werner was visiting his friend Netterville when a man drove his car into Netterville's car and drove away. Werner chased the man and — after a confrontation — shot and killed him. At his murder trial, Werner offered the testimony of a psychiatrist, Dr. Rudolph Roden, who had interviewed Werner and learned that his father had been a concentration camp inmate. The trial court disallowed the evidence, Werner was convicted, and the appellate court affirmed:

> It was proffered that Dr. Roden would testify that beginning in August, 1982, four months after the alleged offense, he began to see the appellant as a patient, and saw him some 18 or 19 times. Dr. Roden learned that the appellant's paternal grandmother was Jewish, his paternal grandfather was Protestant, and after the grandfather's death in 1941 or 1942 appellant's grandmother and his half-Jewish father and other members of the family were placed in concentration camps, that the father and grandmother survived, the other members of the family did not. Dr. Roden also learned the appellant grew up with stories of concentration camps told to him by his father and grandmother, who related seeing people beaten to death who did not fight back. Dr. Roden determined appellant showed "some" of the characteristics of an individual who has the syndrome associated with children of survivors of Nazi concentration camps.

> It was also stated Dr. Roden would testify that the appellant told him of the events that occurred on the night in question. Dr. Roden related that appellant told him the moment he (appellant) pulled the trigger that he wasn't thinking about anything except protecting himself. Dr. Roden would testify, however, "that one does not need to be thinking of an event for another event in one's life to have an effect, a subconscious effect on him;" that the appellant disliked injustice, and one of the greatest injustices was the Holocaust, and that his knowledge thereof shaped his view of self-defense, that the act of the deceased in "running into a car and leaving the

scene was an unjust act in the appellant's view, and he sought to right the wrong by detaining the deceased for the police. Dr. Roden would testify that appellant's background caused him to make the decision to protect himself if his life was threatened, and though at the moment the alleged offense occurred he was not thinking of the Holocaust, it "was his state of mind to defend himself because he comes from a family that did not."

The State objected to the proffered testimony of Dr. Roden on the ground of relevancy, that if self-defense is urged the "test to be made by the jury in applying the standard of an ordinary and prudent person in the Defendant's position at the time of the offense." * * * *

Dr. Roden's testimony was that, although appellant continued to disclaim he was not thinking of the Holocaust at the time of the offense, he showed "some" characteristics of the syndrome associated with children of the survivors of the Holocaust, and the same might have had a subconscious effect on him. All that can be inferred from this evidence is that appellant may have been more susceptible to actions in self-defense. It did not establish that appellant did in fact act under the influence of the Holocaust on the night of the offense. The self-defense statutes permit the use of force only when and to the degree a person "reasonably believes" it immediately necessary. As stated in V.T.C.A., Penal Code, § 1.07(31), a "reasonable belief" is one that would be held by an "ordinary and prudent man in the same circumstances as the actor." Although the test assumes that a defendant may act on appearances as viewed from his standpoint, the test also assumes the "ordinary prudent man test of tort law." * * * *

The evidence excluded only tended to show that possibly appellant was not an ordinary and prudent man with respect to self-defense. This did not entitle appellant to an enlargement of the statutory defense on account of his psychological peculiarities.

JUSTICE TEAGUE dissented:

Although there appears to be a paucity of case law regarding "The Holocaust Syndrome," this in itself should not have been reason for the trial judge to have excluded Dr. Roden's testimony; to the contrary, this is probably the best reason why such testimony should have been admitted in this case. Dr. Roden's testimony was highly relevant on the issue of the condition of the appellant's state of mind at the time he fired the fatal shot, and would have aided the jury, all of whom were probably totally unfamiliar with this type syndrome, in better deciding what the appellant's state or condition of his mind was when he shot the deceased, and how his suffering from "The Holocaust Syndrome" affected the condition of his mind at that time. * * * *

When a relatively large number of persons, having the same symptoms, exhibit a combination or variation of functional psychiatric disorders that leads to purely emotional stress that causes intense mental anguish or emotional trauma, i.e., trauma having no direct physical effect upon the body, psychiatrists put those persons under one or more labels. Today, we have the following labels: "The Battered Wife Syndrome," "The Battered Woman Syndrome," "The Battered Child Syndrome," "The Battered Husband Syndrome," "The Battered Parent Syndrome;" "The Familial Child Sexual Abuse Syndrome," "The Rape Trauma Syndrome," "The Battle Fatigue Syndrome," "The Viet Nam Post-Traumatic Stress Syndrome," "The Policeman's Syndrome," "The Post-Concussive Syndrome," "The Whiplash Syndrome," "The Low-Back Syndrome," "The Lover's Syndrome," "The Love Fear Syndrome," "The Organic Delusional Syndrome," "The Chronic Brain Syndrome," and "The Holocaust Syndrome." [Citations omitted.] Tomorrow, there will probably be additions to the list, such as "The Appellate Court Judge Syndrome." * * * *

In this instance, I find that the subject "The Holocaust Syndrome" was beyond the ken of the average lay person. The jury was entitled to know that when the appellant fired the fatal shot he believed that because of his past experiences, if his life was ever threatened, he would act to protect himself, and that is why he acted in the manner in which he did, i.e., that his state of mind at the time was affected, not only by that which he visually saw on the night in question, but also because of his belief that it was necessary for him to defend himself because he comes from a family who did not defend themselves, thus causing them to perish in the Holocaust. Dr. Roden's proffered testimony as to what effect being a descendant of a survivor of "The Holocaust" had upon the appellant, as to his reasonable belief of danger, was not only relevant and material as to his state of mind, but it was also relevant and material on his defense of self-defense, on which the jury was instructed. * * * *

Although there are obvious differences between the syndrome now known as "The Battered Wife Syndrome" and the syndrome now known as "The Holocaust Syndrome," in principle they have much in common. Today, it is not unusual for our more enlightened trial courts to admit testimony of expert witnesses on "The Battered Wife Syndrome," as relevant to explain the legitimacy of a wife's reactions to threats of danger from her spouse, and to counteract prosecutorial claims that the wife's continued presence in the home means that the homicide was not necessary. It should be obvious to almost anyone that without such testimony it would be difficult, if not impossible, for persons unfamiliar with how "The Battered Wife Syndrome" manifests itself to understand what effect the actions of the former spouse had on the state or condition of the wife's mind when she shot and killed her former spouse. In any event, it simply cannot be logically argued that such testimony would not be of assistance to the trier of fact in determining what the condition of the defendant's mind might have been when the offense was committed.

(8) In *"Rotten Social Background": Should the Criminal Law Recognize a Defense of Severe Environmental Deprivation?*, 3 Law & Inequality 9 (1985), Professor Richard Delgado opines:

An environment of extreme poverty and deprivation creates in individuals a propensity to commit crimes. In some cases, a defendant's impoverished background so greatly determines his or her criminal behavior that we feel it unfair to punish the individual. This sense of unfairness arises from the morality of the criminal law itself, in that "our collective conscience does not allow punishment where it cannot impose blame. And blame is inappropriate when a defendant's criminal behavior is caused by extrinsic factors beyond his or her control. [*Id.* at 54-55.]

(9) Professor (and noted criminal defense attorney) Alan Dershowitz finds these developments disturbing:

The "abuse excuse" — the legal tactic by which criminal defendants claim a history of abuse as an excuse for violent retaliation — is quickly becoming a license to kill and maim. More and more defense lawyers are employing this tactic and more and more jurors are buying it. It is a dangerous trend, with serious and widespread implications for the safety and liberty of every American.

Among the recent excuses that have been accepted by at least some jurors have been "battered woman syndrome," "abused child syndrome," "rape trauma syndrome," and "urban survival syndrome." * * * *

On the surface, the abuse excuse affects only the few handfuls of defendants who raise it, and those who are most immediately impacted by an acquittal or reduced charge. But at a deeper level, the abuse excuse is a symptom of a general abdication of responsibility by individuals, families, groups, and even nations. Its widespread acceptance is dangerous to the very tenets of democracy, which presuppose personal accountability for choices and actions. It also endangers our collective safety by legitimating a sense of vigilantism that reflects our frustration over the apparent inability of law enforcement to reduce the rampant violence that engulfs us. * * * *

The worst consequence of these abuse excuses is that they stigmatize all abuse victims with the violence of the very few who have used their victimization as a justification to kill or maim. The vast majority of abuse victims are neither prone to violence nor to making excuses. Moreover, abuse excuses legitimate a cycle of abuse and further abuse, since most abusers have themselves been victims of abuse. Thus, by taking the abuse excuse to its logical conclusion, virtually no abusers would ever be culpable. * * * *

At bottom, the subtle message of these abuse-excuse defenses is that the real criminal is the dead victim and the defendant performed a public good by dispatching him. The abuse excuse places the *victim* of the killing or maiming on trial — generally in absentia — and if the defense lawyer can persuade the jury that he or she "had it coming," there is a chance that the jury will disregard the established rules of self-defense and take the law into its own hands by acquitting the defendant or reducing the charges. * * * *

The tactic of putting the dead or maimed victim on trial and getting the jury to identify with the defendant can be dangerous. Recall the early days of the civil rights movement, when white juries in the Deep South routinely acquitted white sheriffs, Klansmen, and other assorted killers for murdering both black and white civil rights workers "who had it coming." Everyone loves vigilante justice when the vigilantes are on "our side," but they hate it when the vigilantes are on "their side."

That is why — as a *civil libertarian* and as a *defense attorney* — I am so concerned about the excesses of the abuse excuse. [Dershowitz, *The Abuse Excuse* (Little Brown, 1994), Introduction.]

(10) In *People v. Romero*, 69 Cal.App.4th 846 (1999), Romero was charged with murder, based on a killing committed during an altercation with another young Hispanic male. Romero claimed self-defense. At trial, his counsel offered the testimony of Professor Jankowski, a sociologist who was an expert on street violence and Hispanic culture. The trial court refused to admit this testimony. The appellate court affirmed Romero's conviction:

The roots of this case are planted in a simple street scene. A group of men were crossing the road when Alex Bernal sped around the corner in his vehicle, and had to quickly brake. Words were exchanged, threats were hurled, and moments later Bernal was dying with a knife wound to his heart.

What makes this case unusual is defense counsel's attempt to introduce expert testimony on the sociology of poverty, and the role of honor, paternalism, and street fighters in the Hispanic culture. Although interesting, we conclude the trial court correctly decided this evidence was irrelevant to 1) whether defendant *actually* believed he was in imminent danger of death or great bodily injury; and 2) whether such a belief was *objectively* reasonable. In the words of the trial court, we are not prepared to sanction a "reasonable street fighter standard." The judgment is affirmed. * * * *

According to defense counsel, Professor Jankowski's expertise deals with the sociology of poverty. He would testify that (1) street fighters have a special understanding of what is expected of them; (2) for a street fighter in the Hispanic culture, there is no retreat; (3) the Hispanic culture is based on honor, and honor defines a person; and (4) in this culture a person "would be responsible to take care of someone," i.e., defendant had a strong motivation to protect his younger brother. Stated differently, "He's the eldest male. He would assume a paternalistic role whether he wanted to or not. Something is expected of him."

Given the law, we conclude the testimony of Professor Jankowski was irrelevant to whether defendant actually believed he was in imminent danger of death or great bodily injury, and whether such a belief was *objectively* reasonable. We are unsure what defendant means by his reference to the sociology of poverty, and how it might affect his actual beliefs and the *objective* reasonableness of those beliefs. Similarly, even if we assume street fighters have a special understanding of what is expected of them, and that this is something with which the jurors are not acquainted, why is it relevant? Are street fighters expected to kill every person they fight with, regardless of the circumstances? If so, does this expectation replace or relax the legal requirement that before deadly force may be used a person must actually fear imminent death or great bodily injury? As noted by the trial court, "Then you're creating a separate standard for what you call street fighters." No authority or case law has been cited which supports a separate standard, and we decline to adopt one here.

In the same vein, whether a person should or should not retreat from a "street fight," has no bearing on whether that person may lawfully use deadly force. A decision not to retreat from a physical confrontation and a decision to kill are two separate acts and involve different mental exercises. The laws governing self-defense recognize these distinctions and apply different rules to these legal concepts. While defendant attempted to blur the distinctions between the laws governing self-defense, the trial court correctly did not.

The evidence regarding honor, like evidence of street fighter mentality, is not relevant to whether deadly force was warranted under the circumstances. Is there honor in killing an unarmed man, and assuming that in defendant's mind it was the honorable thing to do, how does this relate to self-defense? Clearly, the question of defendant's honor was irrelevant to whether defendant was in actual fear of death or great bodily injury, and whether his fear was objectively reasonable.

Question: Can this decision be reconciled with cases such as *State v. Kelly*, holding that evidence of "battered woman's syndrome" is admissible in cases in which a woman claims self-defense? If not, which line of reasoning is more persuasive?

(11) If there is a "battered woman's syndrome," must there also be a "batterer" syndrome — and may evidence that a man had such a syndrome be used to identify him as the killer in a "whodunit" case?

During the 1994 criminal prosecution against O.J. Simpson, prosecutor Marcia Clark was prepared to introduce the testimony of Dr. Donald Dutton, a psychologist who had worked with many batterers, to show that because Simpson had battered his wife in the past, it was likely that he was the one who later killed her. Defense attorney Johnnie Cochran then announced that he had retained Dr. Lenore Walker (a leading expert on battered woman's syndrome) to testify that "it cannot be predicted that a particular batterer will turn out to be a killer unless there is evidence of prior escalating life-threatening behavior," and such behavior was not evident in Simpson's case.

As the trial unfolded, neither Dr. Dutton nor Dr. Walker testified before the jury, but Dr. Walker's preliminary decision to testify for an alleged batterer was very upsetting to one commentator, who opined that "reliance on expert testimony on the battered woman's syndrome to explain the behavior of a defendant-batterer is irrelevant and misleading." Griffith, *Battered Woman Syndrome: A Tool For Batterers?*, 64 Fordham L.Rev. 141, 149 (1995). See also Myrna S. Raeder, *The Better Way: The Role of Batterers' Profiles & Expert "Social Framework Back-*

ground in Cases Implicating Domestic Violence, 68 U. Colo. L. Rev. 147, 153 (1997) (describing Dr. Dutton's writings, while concluding that, "Currently, there is no agreement about the profile of batterers").

In *Brunson v. State*, 79 S.W.3d 304 (Ark. 2002), Brunson was charged with murdering his wife. The trial court allowed the prosecution to introduce the testimony of an expert witness, who testified that "she gleaned from Brunson's behavior as a domestic abuser and stalker certain warning signs that placed him within a profile that predicted he would become homicidal." The Arkansas Supreme Court reversed his conviction:

> Brunson contends that Ms. Neiss's testimony led the jury irresistibly and ineluctably to a verdict that he had transformed from stalker to murderer. In doing so, he claims that she gave her opinion on the ultimate issue of the case and invaded the province of the jury. Her testimony further violated Rule 403 of the Arkansas Rules of Evidence, he asserts, in that the testimony was more prejudicial than probative. He contends that her testimony should have been excluded. We agree.

(12) In *State v. Vue*, 606 N.W.2d 719 (MInn.App.2000), Vue and M.V. never married, but lived together as husband and wife. Both were immigrants from the Hmong tribe in Laos. Vue was charged with criminal sexual conduct against M.V.

> At trial, M.V. testified about the clan structure of Hmong society, the hierarchy of leadership within the clan, and the role of Hmong women in choosing a husband. She said it was inappropriate in Hmong culture for individuals with family or clan-related problems to seek help from outside the clan and that she was being treated as an outcast for having reported her husband to the police. She claimed appellant had been threatening and abusive to her throughout their marriage and had forced her to have sex with him hundreds of times. She said she did not report the rapes earlier because of Hmong social pressure and because appellant said he would kill her if she did.

> During a break in the state's case-in-chief, the court held a voir dire examination of the proposed expert witness, a white Minneapolis Park Police officer, and a hearing on the defense motion to exclude his testimony. On direct and cross-examination, the officer described his interest in and personal and professional exposure to Hmong culture.

> The prosecutor said the officer would testify to the following: a general history of the Hmong in America; the clan system and the hierarchy within the clans; assimilation issues facing the Hmong in America; Hmong-Americans' attitudes toward the American criminal justice system; the traditional system for resolving family and clan-related problems; issues with going outside the clan for help; the role and position of women in Hmong culture; and male-female relations in traditional marriages.

> In allowing the testimony, the court compared it to expert testimony on battered woman syndrome, noted it was being offered to promote a complete understanding of the evidence, and found it would be helpful to the jury.

As an example of a conflict between Hmong culture and the American legal system, the officer described a traditional marriage practice in which men "kidnap" young girls. Among other generalized statements, the state's expert testified that Southeast Asian victims are generally reluctant to report crimes. Speaking of Hmong culture, he testified in part:

> Well, as I indicated it is a male-dominated culture, very clearly. It's not the only culture that's male dominated, I might add, but it's very clear in Hmong culture. Women are to be obedient, to be silent, to suffer rather than to tell. Domestic abuse is a very private situation. I'm not even so sure if the abuse is shared with other women. I think it's kept very much internal.

On cross-examination, the officer stated that "male-dominance" was "fairly universal in the Hmong culture." In addition, the defense counsel asked and the expert responded as follows:

> Q: Are you suggesting that what male dominance really means is abuse?
>
> A: I have seen evidence — secondhand, I might add, maybe third-hand, not firsthand or I would have to act as a police officer — of male aggression within the Hmong community to keep the female in her place.
>
> Q: Are you saying that that is a general trait or are you saying that all Hmong traditional males are abusive?
>
> A: I've been around long enough to know that you can never make a statement that says all of anything will happen all of the time. I think there are patterns that can be identified over time and that that pattern is disturbing in the Hmong culture.

The appellate court reversed Vue's conviction:

> The primary issue at trial was whether M.V. consented to the sexual contact with appellant. Both sides addressed her delay in bringing the allegations. The prosecutor offered the testimony of a park policeman to bolster M.V.'s story by "explaining" why a Hmong immigrant who had been raped by her husband would be reluctant to go to the police.
>
> There is little in this record suggesting cultural testimony was necessary. The complainant was a grown woman; she was bilingual and educated; and she had been in the United States for many years. A lay jury would not have had trouble understanding or believing her testimony simply because she was Hmong. It is patronizing to suggest otherwise.
>
> The expert testimony itself confirmed the lack of relevancy to this case and to this victim. The transcription shows the following questions and answers:
>
> Q: Are you saying then that all of the Hmong people in Minnesota are following the same cultural trends?

A: I would not say that all Hmong follow the same cultural trends, but I would say that the Hmong culture that I've observed is slower to change than other cultures that I've observed.

Q: Would you say that language is one reason why, at least in your observations, there has been a slower cultural change?

A: I would strongly agree that, *particularly among older Hmong citizens where English is nonexistent or very difficult at best.* I would say that the isolation that comes from not being able to go to a mall and shop and exchange normal conversation with shopkeepers or other people in society has kept Hmong women, in particular older Hmong women, prisoners in their homes. (Emphasis added.)

Thus, the "expert's" cultural testimony emphasized the barriers on reporting "among older Hmong citizens where English is nonexistent or very difficult at best." This is not our case. * * * *

The "expert" testimony was inherently prejudicial. It went far beyond describing Hmong cultural practices that would help explain the alleged victim's behavior, *if* such testimony was needed. The testimony included generic statements about "male-dominance" in Hmong culture and directly implied a generalized perceived pattern of abuse of Hmong females by Hmong males.

While some of these statements could conceivably be relevant to a complainant's reluctance to come forward, their probative value, if any, is based on generalizations that appellant is part of a "guilty class" of spouse-abusers, and the victim is part of a "victim class" of abused women. By asserting that Hmong men tend to abuse their wives, the expert testimony directly implied to the jury that because defendant was Hmong, he was more likely to have assaulted his wife. It is self-evident that this is highly prejudicial. It is impermissible to link a defendant's ethnicity to the likelihood of his guilt. *See, e.g., United States v. Vue, 13 F.3d 1206, 1212-14 (8th cir. 1994)* (reversing opium-related convictions of Hmong defendants for error in allowing expert to testify that 95% of the opium-smuggling cases in the area were Hmong-related); *see also United States v. Doe, 903 F.2d 16, 20-22 (D.C.cir. 1990)* (holding expert testimony concerning Jamaican immigrants' takeover of local drug trade was unfairly prejudicial in drug trial of Jamaican defendants).

Our criminal code is supposed to be blind to the array of cultures present in the State of Minnesota. The state wants it that way when cultural testimony goes against them. The state conceded at oral argument that it would object, in a statutory rape case or a domestic abuse trial, if defense counsel attempted to introduce expert evidence showing the charged conduct was permissible in the defendant's culture (in Minnesota, intercourse with a young woman under the age of 14 is prohibited, whether consensual or not). For instance, marriage to young women under the age of 14 is acceptable in many cultures, including Hmong. The prosecutor stated she would object to that as irrelevant, if offered by a defense attorney. But here the state urges the *same kind of cultural evidence* be allowed to bolster a case against appellant.

We conclude the prejudicial effect of the expert testimony about Hmong males' tendency to dominate and abuse their wives, and the tendency of Hmong wives not to want to report assaults, far outweighed any probative value. We find the district court abused its discretion in qualifying the expert and admitting his testimony.

STATE v. GARTLAND
New Jersey Supreme Court
149 N.J. 456, 694 A.2d 564 (1997)

PER CURIUM

This appeal concerns the statutory duty to retreat before resorting to the use of deadly force in self-defense. In this case a woman killed her husband in a bedroom of their home. The jury convicted her of reckless manslaughter. She died while her appeal was pending. * * * *

I.

The killing occurred on February 8, 1993. The jury heard evidence of long-standing physical and emotional abuse inflicted by the victim on defendant. Witnesses portrayed John Gartland as a violent and threatening husband obsessed with jealousy.

On the afternoon of the killing, the Gartlands stopped at a tavern in Newark. There, they began to argue. When the Gartlands returned home at about 5:00 p.m., a neighbor heard Mr. Gartland (John) threaten his wife. Other neighbors heard similar abuse and threats.

The argument continued when John could not find the remote control for the television and accused Ellen of hiding it. Angered, he left the home. When he returned, he renewed the argument about the remote control. Ellen asked him to leave her alone and went upstairs to her bedroom. For over ten years, she and her husband had had separate bedrooms.

Previously, John had left her alone in this room. On this evening, he followed her into her bedroom. She told him to go to bed and to leave her alone. He approached her, threatening to strike her. One of them, the parties dispute which, said "I'm going to hurt you" as he approached her.

Ellen took her son's hunting shotgun from her bedroom closet. She pointed it at her husband and told him to stop. He said, "You're not going to do anything to me because you, bitch, I'm going to kill you." He lunged at her with his fists clenched. She pulled the trigger. The shotgun blast hit her husband. He stepped into the hallway and fell.

Ellen dropped the gun, called an operator, and asked for an ambulance, saying that she had just shot her husband. She then called her son as well as John

Gartland's son. She told the responding officers that she had feared for her life. She said that she would never forget the look on his face and that he approached her looking "like a devil."

At trial, the jury had asked twice during its deliberations for clarification of the court's charge on self-defense. On both occasions the trial court repeated its initial instructions. The instruction never specifically apprised the jury that it could consider the seventeen years of spousal abuse suffered by Mrs. Gartland in determining whether she honestly and reasonably believed that deadly force was necessary to protect herself against her husband. The trial court used the Model Jury Charge and told the jury that "a reasonable belief is one which is to be held by a person of ordinary prudence and intelligence situated as Mrs. Gartland was on February 8, 1993."

Prior to the charge, defense counsel objected to the court's intent to charge that Ellen had a duty to retreat before resorting to deadly force. Counsel renewed his objection immediately after the charge. Before the first recharge on self-defense, defense counsel again objected. He noted that because Ellen had been in her own room, one that her husband never occupied, he was not a cohabitant and under the law she had no duty to retreat from her own separate dwelling. The trial court ruled that "under the statute, there was a duty to retreat." The court gave the Model Jury Charge:

> And even if you find the use of deadly force was reasonable, there are limitations on the use of deadly force. If you find that Mrs. Gartland knew that she could avoid the necessity of using deadly force by retreating from that house, providing Mrs. Gartland knew that she could do so with complete safety, then the defense is not available to her.

The jury convicted Mrs. Gartland of reckless manslaughter. Two jurors later contacted the court describing confusion and indecision in their deliberations. After denying a motion for a new trial, the court sentenced Mrs. Gartland to a five-year term with a mandatory three-years imprisonment under the Graves Act.

II.

* * * * The power to entertain a criminal appeal even after death should be sparingly exercised. A conviction should not be set aside unless the record shows palpably that there has been a fundamental miscarriage of justice, an error that cut mortally into the substantive rights of the defendant or impaired a defendant's ability to maintain a defense on the merits. Such caution is required because there is an intrinsic imbalance in the conduct of a criminal appeal on behalf of a deceased defendant. The contest is one-sided. The defendant can no longer be retried for the crime. The State and the victims of the crime cannot win. If the conviction is set aside, the State is realistically deprived of the opportunity to vindicate the public interest in enforcement of the law. On the other hand, important interests of the defendant or society at large may be at stake if an erroneous conviction is left standing. We find those important interests present here.

III.

Did the trial court err in failing to instruct the jury that defendant had no duty to retreat if defendant's bedroom functioned as a separate dwelling and that her husband was an intruder into that separate room within the house that they shared?

A.

As noted, this was the principal objection raised at trial: Traditionally self-defense claims require that a person who can safely retreat from the confrontation avail themselves of that means of escape. However, this requirement has since been modified, and today most courts recognize exceptions to the general retreat principle. The most notable and expansive exception has been the "castle doctrine." The castle doctrine states that if the confrontation takes place in one's home or "castle" then the requirement is suspended. This exception was established to allow individuals to defend their place of habitation. Application of this exception, however, becomes more challenging when the aggressor intruder is a co-occupant of the structure or when both parties have a legal right to occupy the dwelling. Currently, jurisdictions vary as to their willingness to extend the castle doctrine to self-defense situations where both parties legally occupy the home, but the majority of these jurisdictions extend the privilege of non-retreat to apply in these types of situations.

New Jersey is among the minority of jurisdictions that impose a duty of retreat on a woman attacked by her cohabitant spouse. The New Jersey Code of Criminal Justice contains carefully articulated standards for determining when the use of force against another is justified. The drafters of our Code originally approached the concept of justification in terms of the subjective attitudes of the criminal actor. However, in the course of legislative modifications the self-defense provisions of the Code were altered to reestablish objective standards of self-defense: Use of force justifiable for protection of the person. Subject to the provisions of this section and of § 2C:3-9, the use of force upon or toward another person is justifiable when the actor reasonably believes that such force is immediately necessary for the purpose of protecting the actor against the use of unlawful force by such other person on the present occasion. N.J.S.A. § 2C:3-4a.

Those general provisions are qualified in the case of the use of deadly force as that is defined in N.J.S.A. § 2C:3-11. Concerning deadly force, the Code provides: "The use of deadly force is not justifiable under this section unless the actor reasonably believes that such force is necessary to protect [the actor] against death or serious bodily harm . . ." N.J.S.A. § 2C:3-4b(2). Even if deadly force is permissible, the actor still has the duty to retreat from the scene if the actor can do so safely. N.J.S.A. § 2C:3- 4b(2)(b). One exception to this duty to retreat is if the actor is in his or her own home at the time of the attack (the so-called "castle doctrine"), unless the attacker is a cohabitant. N.J.S.A. § 2C:3-4b(2)(b)(i) states that "[the actor] is not obliged to retreat from the dwelling, unless [the actor] was the initial aggressor or is assailed in [the actor's own] dwelling by another person whose dwelling the actor knows it to be . . ." N.J.S.A. § 2C:3- 4c provides special rules for the use of deadly force on an intruder into one's dwelling. For example, under this provision, deadly force may be used against an intruder to counter any level of unlawful force threatened by the intruder.

The Public Defender argues that it is ironic that Ellen Gartland could have used the shotgun against a burglar who intended to do her no serious harm but was precluded from using the same force against the true threat in her life, her husband. Instead, the law requires her to flee from her bedroom, which she had described as the only sanctuary in her chaos-filled home.

B.

The retreat doctrine is one of several related legal doctrines affecting battered women as criminal defendants. See generally Holly Maguigan, *Battered Women and Self-Defense: Myths and Misconceptions in Current Reform Proposals*, 140 U. Pa. L.Rev. 379 (1991). The male pronouns used in the Code reflect a history of self-defense that is derived from a male model.[1]

> Under the common law regime, even if faced with immediate danger of death or great bodily harm, an individual could use only equal force to repel the danger. The doctrine of equal force, developed on a prototype of two males of equal size and strength, held that, if attacked without a deadly weapon, one could not respond with a deadly weapon. This doctrine obviously disadvantaged women, who are generally smaller and lack the same upper-body strength as men. Traditional common law self-defense imposes no duty to retreat, except for co-occupants of the same house. Given that most men are assaulted and killed outside their homes by strangers, while most women are assaulted and killed within their homes by male intimates, this doctrine also disadvantaged women. [Marina Angel, Criminal Law And Women: *Giving The Abused Woman Who Kills A Jury Of Her Peers Who Appreciate Trifles*, 33 Am.Crim. L.Rev. 229, 320 (1996).]

Advocates of women's rights seek change.

> Imposition of the duty to retreat on a battered women who finds herself the target of a unilateral, unprovoked attack in her own home is inherently unfair. During repeated instances of past abuse, she has "retreated," only to be caught, dragged back inside, and severely beaten again. If she manages to escape, other hurdles confront her. Where will she go if she has no money, no transportation, and if her children are left behind in the "care" of an enraged man? One commentator points out the injustice and absurdity of expecting a battered woman to retreat and "just walk away."

> Indeed, battered women seem to be expected to escape from situations in which escape, for anyone else, would clearly be seen to be impossible. In case after case, in which the obligation to retreat was an issue at the trial or on appeal, women have been convicted for killing men who were holding

---

[1] For example, the "true man" doctrine basically provides that "an individual need not retreat, even if he can do so safely, where he has a reasonable belief that he is in imminent danger of death or great bodily harm, is without fault, and is in a place that he has a right to be. The rationale behind this rule comes from a policy against making a person act in a cowardly or humiliating manner." 1 W. LaFave & A. Scott, Substantive Criminal Law, § 5.7(f).

them with one hand and beating them with the other or who had them pinned down on the floor or trapped in a corner or were menacing them with a knife or with a loaded gun. The loophole in the castle doctrine profoundly impacts battered women. If the attacker has as much right to be in the home where the attack occurs, the duty to retreat still applies.

What this exception means for a battered woman is that as long as it is a stranger who attacks her in her home, she has a right to fight back and labors under no duty to retreat. If the attacker is her husband or live-in partner, however, she must retreat. The threat of death or serious bodily injury may be just as real (and, statistically, is more real) when her husband or partner attacks her in her home, but still she must retreat. [Maryanne E. Kampmann, *The Legal Victimization Of Battered Women*, 15 Women's Rts. L. Rep. 101, 112-13 (1993).]

These are grave concerns. When the drafters of our Code of Criminal Justice commenced their work in 1971, the public was not fully aware of the epidemic of domestic violence. Knowledge of the problem, however, was more widespread at the time of the adoption of the Code in 1979. Legislative activity in the field of domestic abuse was already underway. * * * * However, there is no evidence that the Legislature specifically considered the loophole in the castle doctrine. As presently structured, the Code of Criminal Justice requires that a cohabitant who can safely leave the home to avoid violence should do so before resorting to deadly force. We have invariably adhered to the Code's concepts of self-defense. We have insisted, as the Code requires, that the belief of the person wielding deadly force must be a reasonable belief, not simply an honest belief. *State v. Kelly*, 97 N.J. 178, 204. Moreover, we have declined to create new justifications for criminal conduct. *State v. Tate*, 102 N.J. 64 (1986) (holding that Code did not provide defense of medical necessity to illegal possession of drugs). Only when we have been satisfied that the structure of the Code makes a defense available have we allowed it to be asserted.

There is no comparable basis for departing from the language of the Code, specifically, from the Code requirement that an actor may not use deadly force against a cohabitant if an actor may safely retreat. The Legislature and the Executive do not decide cases — the judiciary does not pass laws. One of the categories of legislation that the judiciary has no power to adopt is that of defining crimes and providing for their punishment. Although we find present the statutory duty to retreat, we commend to the Legislature consideration of the application of the retreat doctrine in the case of a spouse battered in her own home. There are arguments to be made on each side of the issue. See majority and dissenting opinions in *State v. Thomas*, 673 N.E.2d 1339 (Ohio 1997) (holding that domestic partner assaulted in her own home has no duty to retreat before using deadly force in self defense).

C.

That leaves for resolution whether John Gartland could be considered a cohabitant of Ellen's bedroom. Put the other way, the question is whether the upstairs bedroom in which Ellen slept was a separate dwelling. It is a close question on this record, but we agree with the courts below that the bedroom was not a separate dwelling.

N.J.S.A. 2C:3-11c defines "dwelling" as "any building or structure, though movable or temporary, or a portion thereof, which is for the time being the actor's home or place of lodging except that, as used in § 2C:3-7 [concerning arrest for burglary of a dwelling], the building or structure need not be the actor's own home or place of lodging." The Commentary to this section concludes that cases such as *State v. Bonano*, 59 N.J. 515, 520 (1971) (holding porches and thresholds within the definition of dwelling), "leave open the question how much further the term 'dwelling' might be extended." Cannel, New Jersey Criminal Code Annotated, Comment 3 on N.J.S.A. 2C:3-11c (1996-97). * * * *

It is true that one building may have separate apartments. However, the idea of a dwelling is that one has an "exclusive right to occupy" a portion of a building. In *State v. Pontery*, 19 N.J. 457 (1955), an estranged couple jointly owned a summer home. The wife went there to be away from her husband. When he and other family members joined her over the weekend, she could not claim that she was under no duty to retreat from the jointly-owned dwelling before inflicting deadly force. In contrast, in *State v. Lamb*, 71 N.J. 545 (1976), the Court exempted a wife from a duty to retreat from her husband's attack within an apartment that she exclusively occupied. He had burst in uninvited through an unlocked door. The Court stated: "In the circumstances of this case the defendant's estranged husband did not have as much right to be in the apartment as the defendant. It was her home. The husband was in fact an intruder and the defendant was under no duty to retreat."

In this case, there is simply no evidence that the door to the bedroom had normally been kept locked or that John Gartland did not generally have access to the room. Defendant merely testified that because of sexual dysfunction, the couple slept in separate rooms. We cannot say that Ellen had the exclusive right to occupy this room. Hence, we agree, on this record, that the court correctly charged the statutory duty to retreat. * * * *

V.

We now turn to consider other aspects of this case that have been neither raised nor argued by the parties, that would have been grounds for retrial in the case of a living defendant.

In a long series of cases, we have held that an essential ingredient to a fair trial is that adequate and understandable instructions be given to the jury. * * * * It is not always enough simply to read the applicable provision of the Criminal Code, define the terminology, and set forth the elements of the crime. An instruction that is appropriate in one case may not be sufficient for another case. Ordinarily, the better practice is to mold the instruction in a manner that explains the law to the jury in the context of the material facts of the case.

The instructions in this case were largely devoid of reference to the specific circumstances of the case. As noted, the trial court instructed the jury that if Mrs. Gartland "knew that she could avoid the necessity of using deadly force by retreating from that house, providing that she could do so with complete safety, then the defense is not available to her." We intend no criticism of the trial court because neither party requested a charge tailored to the facts. However, an abstract charge on the duty to retreat could only have been confusing in the circumstances of this case. Exactly where could she retreat? As we understand the record, there was no other way out of the bedroom other than the doorway where her assailant stood. The charge should have asked whether, armed with a weapon, she could have safely made her way out of the bedroom door without threat of serious bodily injury to herself. * * * * One of the problems in applying the retreat doctrine to the case of a battered woman is that the jurors may confuse the question of leaving the abusive partner with the duty to retreat on the occasion. See Maguigan, supra, 140 U. Pa. L.Rev. at 419 (noting "there is a tendency to blur the definition of the retreat rule with the question of whether the woman could have escaped the relationship"). Among the many myths concerning battered women is the belief "that they are masochistic and actually enjoy their beatings, that they purposely provoke their husbands into violent behavior, and, most critically that women who remain in battering relationships are free to leave their abusers at any time." *Kelly*, supra, 97 N.J. at 192.

The charge on self-defense should also have been tailored to the circumstances of the case. In *State v. Wanrow*, 88 Wash.2d 221 (1977), the Washington Supreme Court recognized that its traditional self-defense standard failed to account for the perspective of abused women. Any limitation of the jury's consideration of the surrounding acts and circumstances to those occurring at or immediately before the killing would be an erroneous statement of the applicable law. The Washington court held that a battered woman was entitled to have the jury consider her actions in the light of her own perceptions of the situation, including those perceptions that were the product of our nation's unfortunate history of sex discrimination. At a minimum, the jury in Ellen Gartland's case should have been asked to consider whether, if it found such to be the case, a reasonable woman who had been the victim of years of domestic violence would have reasonably perceived on this occasion that the use of deadly force was necessary to protect herself from serious bodily injury.

In another context, the failure to relate to the facts of the case the duty to retreat and right of self-defense might not have cut so mortally into a defendant's ability to maintain a defense on the merits. However, the persistent stereotyping of the victims of domestic violence requires special concern. Both partners to the domestic tragedy are now deceased. Although we cannot fully right past wrongs, we can correct errors in the charge that were clearly capable of producing an unjust result.

The judgment of the Appellate Division is reversed and the conviction of manslaughter is set aside.

NOTES FROM JUSTICE STEIN:

(1) *Gartland* was followed by the Florida Supreme Court in *Weiand v. State*, 732 So.2d 1044 (Fla. 1999). See also *State v. Glowacki*, 630 N.W.2d 392 (2001), where the court held:

> Although derived from the same common law defense, self-defense in the home is slightly different from defense of dwelling. We require

reasonable retreat in self-defense outside the home because the law presumes that there is somewhere safer to go — home. But self-defense in the home is based on the premise that the home is "a place critical for the protection of the family." Requiring retreat from the home before acting in self-defense would require one to leave one's safest place. As Justice Cardozo explained in *People v. Tomlins*, "it is not now and never has been the law that a man assailed in his own dwelling is bound to retreat. If assailed there, he may stand his ground and resist the attack. He is under no duty to take to the fields and the highways, a fugitive from his own home. Flight is for sanctuary and shelter, and shelter, if not sanctuary, is in the home." 213 N.Y. 240. The court in *Tomlins* went on to explain that the no retreat from the home rule was the same regardless of whether the aggressor was an intruder or a co-resident.

We agree that when acting in self-defense in the home, a person should not be required to retreat from the home before using reasonable force to defend himself, regardless of whether the aggressor is also rightfully in the home. Thus we adopt the following rule: There is no duty to retreat from one's own home when acting in self-defense in the home, regardless of whether the aggressor is a co-resident. But the lack of a duty to retreat does not abrogate the obligation to act reasonably when using force in self-defense. Therefore, in all situations in which a party claims self-defense, even absent a duty to retreat, the key inquiry will still be into the reasonableness of the use of force and the level of force under the specific circumstances of each case.

(2) In *State v. Brown*, 467 S.E.2d 922 (S.C.1996), the court held that a lawful guest in a home has a duty to retreat when attacked by the homeowner. The court noted that an individual who is attacked on his own premises or a guest who is attacked by an intruder has no duty to retreat prior to defending himself, but that such a duty does exist when the host is the attacker.

(3) In *State v. McClain*, 591 A.2d 652 (N.J.Super., 1991), Ms. McClain shot and killed a man who had physically assaulted her during their relationship, but he hadn't done so recently. He ignored her and seemed to want to break off the relationship. They were not married or even living together and had no children, and she apparently had an independent income. She was convicted of murder.

On appeal, she claimed that the trial judge should have instructed the jury on voluntary manslaughter, based on expert testimony that she suffered from battered woman's syndrome. The court disagreed, holding that evidence of the syndrome "is irrelevant on the question of whether the victim's conduct was adequately provocative because that inquiry requires application of the objective 'reasonable person' test." The court also noted that "evidence that defendant was sexually rejected, teased or repulsed by a paramour is insufficient to constitute adequate provocation."

(4) *Commonwealth v. Fowlin*, 710 A.2d 1130 (Pa. Supreme Court, 1998), involved the following facts:

On December 12, 1993, Fowlin was present in a nightclub in Easton, Pennsylvania. He was armed with a handgun. Three men, two of whom were also armed with handguns, accosted Fowlin in the club, and one of the three sprayed pepper gas in his eyes. At approximately the same time, a second man drew a handgun. Fearing that he was about to be killed, Fowlin drew his own handgun and fired repeatedly in the direction of the attackers. Although he was nearly blinded by the pepper spray, he killed the assailant who had drawn the gun and wounded one of the others. He also wounded a bystander. At the time of the shooting, approximately 200 people were present in the nightclub.

The district attorney declined to prosecute Fowlin for any crime against his attackers, because he had acted in self defense. But the district attorney did charge Fowlin with recklessly endangering and aggravated assault of the bystander. Before the case went to trial, the Pennsylvania Supreme Court blocked the prosecution (by reversing a lower court order denying Fowlin's petition for a writ of *habeas corpus*):

> When one is the victim of an attack, the assailant, not the victim, picks the time, the place, the manner, and the circumstances of the attack. Leisurely assessment of the circumstances and the danger to others is almost never a feature of such an assault, and most often, the best the victim can do is to mount a defense which hopefully will preserve his life. In many cases, the victim has only seconds to act in order to avoid injury or death. In this case, Fowlin was accosted by three men who assaulted him with pepper spray and simultaneously drew a handgun. Fowlin assumed, with reason, that they intended to kill or seriously injure him. He acted instinctively and within our law in defending himself.

> Any victim of crime who justifiably exercises his right of self-preservation may inadvertently injure a bystander. Admittedly, this court could fashion a rule of law which holds the defender criminally liable, but in doing so, we would have furthered no policy of the criminal law. Instead, we would have punished a person who was acting within his instinct for self-preservation and, in an appropriate case, within the boundaries of our law.

Justices Castille and Newman dissented, noting that the Model Penal Code and most other jurisdictions would disagree with the majority:

> The holding of the majority effectively allows an actor to respond in any manner and with whatever amount of force he chooses no matter who he injures, so long as he is justified in acting in self-defense. This is a dangerous precedent. Such blanket authority for the use of self-defense defies logic, especially in contemporary society where possession of lethal weapons and confrontations involving them have become all too common-place. Under the majority's reasoning, one would be justified and could not be found criminally liable for detonating a hand-grenade in a crowded shopping mall in order to defend himself against an attacker. * * * *

> Here, appellant was at a crowded nightclub, drew his gun and fired a series of eleven random shots while blinded by pepper spray. Even if appellant was justified in shooting his attackers in self-defense, the issue of

whether he was criminally responsible for the reckless behavior which caused an innocent bystander to be injured should have gone to the jury.

(5) Suppose a robber or burglar faces a victim who threatens to shoot. May the defendant shoot first to save his own life — and then claim self defense? In *U.S. v. Thomas*, 34 F.3d 44 (2nd Cir., 1994), the court stated:

> One who commits or attempts a robbery armed with deadly force, and kills the intended victim when the victim responds with force to the robbery attempt, may not avail himself of the defense of self-defense. It has long been accepted that one cannot support a claim of self-defense by a self-generated necessity to kill. The right of homicidal self-defense is denied to slayers who incite the fatal attack. In sum, one who is the aggressor in a conflict culminating in death cannot invoke the necessities of self-preservation.

In *People v. Loustaunau*, 181 Cal.App.3d 163 (1986), the court came to same conclusion via a different route:

> When a burglar kills in the commission of a burglary, he cannot claim self-defense, for this would be fundamentally inconsistent with the very purpose of the felony murder rule. * * * * Citing *People v. Flannel* (1979) 25 Cal.3d 668, appellant next contends that an honest but unreasonable belief in self-defense should reduce felony murder to manslaughter. This is incorrect. *Flannel* held that an honest but unreasonable belief in self-defense negates malice aforethought. In felony murder, on the other hand, malice aforethought is not required. The trial court properly limited its *Flannel* instruction to theories of murder other than felony murder.

Chapter 14

DEFENSE OF HABITATION, PREVENTION OF FELONY, PREVENTION OF ESCAPE

One is justified in using reasonable force to protect his property from trespass or theft, when he reasonably believes that his property is in immediate danger of such an unlawful interference and that the use of such force is necessary to avoid that danger. Under the better view, deadly force is never reasonable except where the unlawful interference with property is accompanied by a threat of deadly force (in which case it is proper to use deadly force in self-defense), or where the unlawful interference involves an invasion of an occupied dwelling house under circumstances causing the defender reasonably to believe that the invader intends to commit a felony therein or to do serious bodily harm to its occupants.

LaFave & Scott, *Criminal Law* (West,)

One who reasonably believes that a felony, or a misdemeanor amounting to a breach of the peace, is being committed, or is about to be committed, in his presence may use reasonable force to terminate or prevent it.

LaFave & Scott, *Criminal Law* (West)

A police officer, or a person aiding him, is justified in using reasonable force to make a lawful arrest or to prevent the escape from custody of one already arrested. Deadly force may not be used to arrest or prevent the escape of a misdemeanant, but may be used in the case of a felon if it reasonably appears that the felon will otherwise avoid arrest or escape from custody. * * * *

At common law a police officer or private person may arrest without an arrest warrant for a felony or breach of the peace committed in his presence. In addition, an officer may arrest without a warrant for a felony not in his presence if he has reasonable grounds to believe (a) that a felony has been committed, and (b) that the person to be arrested committed it. A private person, however, is privileged to make such an arrest only if the felony has in fact been committed.

LaFave & Scott, *Criminal Law* (West)

Self defense makes sense. It seems understandable that one should be allowed to use force (even deadly force, in appropriate circumstances) to protect oneself from death or injury. While we want to save lives, there are occasions when a life must be taken — and it is preferable that the taken life be that of the one who threatens to take an innocent life.

But do the defenses mentioned above make sense? Are there interests *other than* your body and life which are *also* worthy of protection by force — including *deadly* force? Should you be allowed to hit (or *shoot*?) someone who someone threatens to steal your car? Does it matter if the theft is by stealth or by threat? What if he is burglarizing your home? Your anger at these intrusions might be understandable, but shouldn't we leave punishment to the courts — and not to your passions — so long as your life isn't threatened (in which case you may use self defense anyway)? Isn't it better to suffer the loss of property or privacy than take a life — even a criminal life?

And suppose a criminal has *already completed* his crime and is now *running away*? You are in no danger. Should you be allowed to shoot him? Why? A police officer who caught the criminal would not be allowed to shoot him, and the court that convicted him would not be allowed to put him to death (except for a capital crime). So why (and when) should the law allow you to shoot him?

Consider these questions as you read this Chapter.

PROBLEM 14

To: My Law Clerk

From: Superior Court Judge Peter Pupik

Re: *People v. Able and Baker*

Alvin Able has been charged with murder of Dave Doink and assaulting Ed Evans with a deadly weapon. Bob Baker has been charged with assaulting Evans with a deadly weapon. We just finished taking evidence in the case, and I am about to instruct the jury. Able's attorney has asked me to instruct the jury about the law of defense of habitation, prevention of a felony, and prevention of escape. Baker's attorney has asked me to instruct the jury on the law of prevention of escape. The prosecutor, however, objects to any instructions on these defenses, arguing that testimony of the defendants - even if believed by the jury - would not permit the jury to acquit.

Here is the testimony of Able, Baker, and Evans. Please read it, along with the attached authorities, and advise me as to whether I should instruct on any of these defenses. Also, if I should instruct the jury on prevention of escape, should I give the same instruction for each defendant?

Incidentally, sale of heroin is a felony, punishable by between 3 and 5 years in state prison. Anyone who intentionally assists ("aids and abets") the seller is, of course, just as guilty as the seller.

Testimony of Al Able

Ms. Bonds (Able's attorney): Please tell the jury what happened when Doink came to your door.

Able: It's about 8 o'clock on a Monday night. I'm home with my wife, Alice, and my 18-year-old son, Andy. Andy's had a bit of a drug problem. I think he's addicted to heroin. He told me that he sometimes buys dope from Doink and Evans. So Doink knocks on the door and Andy answers it. I'm sitting in my chair near the door, and I hear them talking about drugs. I think Doink is selling heroin to Andy, so I get really angry, and I get up and tell Doink to get the hell away from my door. He says "Calm down, old man. I got some stuff to help you relax, if you like." When I hear that, I grab a rifle I keep behind the door and tell Doink to leave. He says, "Out of my way, old man. I'm here to see Andy, not you." And then he starts to walk through the doorway. So I pull the trigger. I didn't mean to kill him, just to scare him off. But he died.

Ms. Bonds: What happened next?

Able: Well, I looked outside, and there's Evans sitting in a car in front of my house, waiting for Doink. He quickly started the engine and started to drive off. Just then a police car drove up, and Officer Baker got out. I yelled, "Stop him. He's a drug dealer." We both fired our weapons at Evans' car. I guess one of us hit a tire or something, because Evans crashed into a lightpost. He was hurt, but I'm glad he wasn't killed too.

Testimony of Bob Baker

Mr. Gomez: Why did you shoot at Evans' car?

Baker: While I was on patrol nearby, I got a radio message that Mrs. Able had made a 911 call saying that a drug dealer was breaking into their house, so I rushed over. I saw this car rushing off, fast, and Mr. Able told me that he was a drug dealer. I yelled at the driver to stop, but he kept going, so I fired.

Testimony of Ed Evans

Ms. Lee (prosecutor): Why did you and Doink go to the house?

Evans: Doink said that Andy owed him some money, and he asked me to give him a ride.

Ms. Lee: Did Doink plan to sell him some drugs?

Evans: No way. Doink said he'd never sell to Andy again, because he didn't pay his debts.

California Penal Code

§ 196. *Justifiable homicide; public officers*

Homicide is justifiable when committed by public officers and those acting by their command in their aid and assistance, either 1. In obedience to any judgment of a competent Court; or,

2. When necessarily committed in overcoming actual resistance to the execution of some legal process, or in the discharge of any other legal duty; or,

3. When necessarily committed in retaking felons who have been rescued or have escaped, or when necessarily committed in arresting persons charged with felony, and who are fleeing from justice or resisting such arrest. [Enacted in 1872.]

§ 197. *Justifiable homicide; any person*

Homicide is also justifiable when committed by any person in any of the following cases:

1. When resisting any attempt to murder any person, or to commit a felony, or to do some great bodily injury upon any person; or,

2. When committed in defense of habitation, property, or person, against one who manifestly intends or endeavors, by violence or surprise, to commit a felony, or against one who manifestly intends and endeavors, in a violent, riotous or tumultuous manner, to enter the habitation of another for the purpose of offering violence to any person therein; or,

3. When committed in the lawful defense of such person, or of a wife or husband, parent, child, master, mistress, or servant of such person, when there is reasonable ground to apprehend a design to commit a felony or to do some great bodily injury, and imminent danger of such design being accomplished; but such person, or the person in whose behalf the defense was made, if he was the assailant or engaged in mutual combat, must really and in good faith have endeavored to decline any further struggle before the homicide was committed; or,

4. When necessarily committed in attempting, by lawful ways and means, to apprehend any person for any felony committed, or in lawfully suppressing any riot, or in lawfully keeping and preserving the peace. [Enacted in 1872, with subsequent amendments.]

§ 198. *Justifiable homicide; sufficiency of fear*

A bare fear of the commission of any of the offenses mentioned in subdivisions 2 and 3 of § 197, to prevent which homicide may be lawfully committed, is not sufficient to justify it. But the circumstances must be sufficient to excite the fears of a reasonable person, and the party killing must have acted under the influence of such fears alone. [Enacted in 1872, with subsequent amendments.]

§ 198.5. *Home protection; use of deadly force; presumption of fear of death or great bodily injury*

Any person using force intended or likely to cause death or great bodily injury within his or her residence shall be presumed to have held a reasonable fear of imminent peril of death or great bodily injury to self, family, or a member of the household when that force is used against another person, not a member of the family or household, who unlawfully and forcibly enters or has unlawfully and forcibly entered the residence and the person using the force knew or had reason to believe that an unlawful and forcible entry occurred. As used in this section, great bodily injury means a significant or substantial physical injury. [Enacted in

1984, as "The Home Protection Bill of Rights."]

§ 199. *Justifiable and excusable homicide; discharge of defendant*

The homicide appearing to be justifiable or excusable, the person indicted must, upon his trial, be fully acquitted and discharged. [Enacted in 1872.]

Note: Compare Model Penal Code § 3.05 through § 3.09, in the Appendix.

PEOPLE v. KILVINGTON
California Supreme Court
104 Cal. 86, 37 Pac. 799 (1894)

The defendant, George Kilvington, was informed against by the district attorney of Santa Clara county for the crime of murder, alleged to have been committed at said county on the 3d day of May, 1892, by the felonious killing of one Henry Schmidt. The defendant was convicted of manslaughter, and adjudged to be punished by imprisonment in the state prison of the state of California, at San Quentin, for the term of seven years.

It appears that the defendant was night watchman in Chinatown, San Jose, and was, as the court instructed the jury, a police officer of the city of San Jose. On the night of the 3d day of May, 1892, he had been at Chinatown with one Henry Burgess, for the purpose of showing the latter through a cannery. On their return from the cannery, about 9 o'clock in the evening, and when on Taylor street, they heard someone cry, "Stop thief!" two or three times, and upon looking around they observed two men running across a vacant lot or open ground fronting on the street northerly and diagonally to their course, in a direction which, if continued, would have taken them across defendant's line of travel 20 feet of more ahead of defendant and his companion. The two men running were not together, but one was in advance, and the other pursuing him, and crying out, "Stop thief!" according to the testimony of the defendant. The night was dark, but the parties were visible at some distance. Defendant ordered the man in advance to stop, and repeated the order two or three times. The order was not obeyed, but the stranger threw up his hands, when, as defendant claims, he saw something in his hands, and he drew his own pistol and fired, killing the man, who at the time was, say, 30 feet distant. The man fell upon his face, and upon examination proved to be one Henry Schmidt, and he had no weapons upon his person. Defendant did not, so far as appears, recognize deceased before firing the fatal shot, and did not consider himself in danger, but, as he testifies, intended to arrest the deceased, and for the purpose of intimidating and stopping him attempted to shoot over his head, but, the deceased being upon higher ground, about two or three feet, the ball entered his neck. Upon this point the defendant testified:

> My object in ordering him to stop was to see why he was running away; what he had done. I thought he was some criminal, some thief, some sneak thief, or something of that kind, that time of night, to see a man running, and another man chasing him, calling, "Stop thief!" I intended to find out - to investigate - and see what it was. I had every cause to believe by the calling of "Stop thief!" that he was a criminal, and my object was to arrest

him. I fired to intimidate him, and I endeavored to shoot over his head. I heard a man call "Stop thief!" and I couldn't tell whether this man had stolen a loaf of bread or robbed a bank.

And in another part of his testimony he said:

> For all I know, this man might have committed a murder, or robbed some one. I don't know what he was guilty of. I could not judge. All I know the man was running after another, hollering, "Stop thief! Stop thief!"

The man in pursuit of the deceased was one William H. Howard. The testimony of the latter was lengthy, but may be epitomized as follows: He was passing the house of one Mrs. Hayford, when the deceased ran out of the back yard, and the witness, thinking he was a criminal, pursued him, crying "Stop!" or "Stop thief!" for some distance, with the result as above stated.

DeHaven, J. (after stating the facts).

There was no conflict in the evidence as to the circumstances under which the defendant killed the deceased, and, in order to determine whether his act was excusable or not, it was necessary for the jury to consider, first, whether the defendant was justified in attempting to arrest the deceased at all; and, if so, whether the act of shooting merely for the purpose of intimidating, and thus causing the deceased to stop, and without any intention of killing or wounding him, was or was not criminal negligence. It was important to the defendant to have these questions, and the law in relation to each, clearly and separately stated to the jury. The court correctly instructed the jury that a peace officer has the right, without a warrant, to arrest any person in the night, when the officer has reasonable ground to believe that such person has committed a felony. Pen. Code § 836; *Burns v. Erben*, 40 N.Y. 463. But the court erred in the manner in which it submitted the question of probable cause to the jury. [The Court held that "probable cause" was an issue of law for the court, not a question of fact for the jury. The trial court should not have given the entire issue of "probable cause" to the jury, but should have told the jury that if it found certain facts to be true, then "probable cause" would or would not be present as a matter of law.]

This brings us to the consideration of the question, did the defendant, in view of the facts as presented to him at the time, have reasonable or probable cause to believe that the deceased had committed a felony? There is a substantial agreement in the decisions of the courts as to what constitutes probable cause or reasonable cause such as will justify one in arresting or prosecuting another upon a criminal charge; and perhaps as clear and comprehensive a statement of the rule as can be found is that of Shaw, C.J., in *Bacon v. Towne*, 4 Cush. 217. "There must be such a state of facts," ' said he, "as would lead a man of ordinary care and prudence to believe, or entertain an honest and strong suspicion, that the person is guilty."

Applying this rule to the facts of this case, we think it must be held that the defendant had reasonable cause to believe that the deceased may have committed a felony. It is true, the deceased was not charged in terms with the commission of a felony, but this was not necessary in order to justify the defendant in entertaining a reasonable suspicion that he was guilty of a felony. It was night. The deceased was fleeing, pursued by a person who was shouting, "Stop thief!" This was, in effect, a charge that the deceased had committed a theft of some kind, and the defendant had just as much reason to suspect or believe that the deceased may have committed robbery or burglary or grand larceny as to suppose that his pursuer only meant by the cry of "Stop thief!" to charge him with petit larceny. The defendant was called upon to act promptly, and, as the language used by the witness Howard was broad enough in its popular sense to import a charge of felony, the defendant was justified in attempting to arrest the deceased. An officer who would refuse to arrest a person fleeing and pursued under the circumstances disclosed in this case, because the charge was not more direct and specific as to the commission of a felony, would be justly censurable for a neglect of official duty.

In considering this question of probable cause upon the part of the defendant to arrest the deceased, we are to look only at the facts and circumstances presented to him at the time he was required to act. The defendant did not recognize the deceased before he fired, and the fact that the latter was an innocent and respectable citizen, and who may have been fleeing from an assailant, cannot be allowed to affect the question we are now discussing. It is only necessary to add upon this point that, in our opinion, the court ought to have instructed the jury that the defendant had the right, under the circumstances established by the evidence, to arrest the deceased, leaving the jury to determine the further question whether the act of shooting the deceased in attempting to effect such arrest was or was not an act of criminal negligence upon the part of the defendant. This latter is purely a question of fact, and its determination must be left to the sound judgment and discretion of the jury, and in the decision of which question the defendant is entitled to the benefit of any reasonable doubt arising upon the evidence.

The court also erred in admitting the evidence of the witnesses Schloss and Weissel tending to show that deceased went down to the place near where he was shot on that particular night on lawful business. This fact was wholly irrelevant. The defendant knew nothing of the matter, and did not recognize the deceased at the time of the shooting. Under such circumstances the evidence was wholly irrelevant, at it threw no light whatever upon the question whether the defendant was justified in attempting to arrest the deceased under the circumstances as actually presented to him; nor did it have any bearing upon the question whether or not the defendant was guilty of criminal negligence in shooting the deceased.

Judgment and order reversed, and cause remanded for a new trial.

NOTES FROM THE JUDGE:

(1) The court assumes that Kilvington was an on-duty police officer when he shot Mr. Howard. Suppose he wasn't, and was acting only as a private citizen trying to apprehend a criminal. How would this have affected the court's analysis?

(2) Suppose that Officer Kilvington realized that he couldn't catch up with Howard, and the only way to stop him was to shoot him. Would the shooting have been proper? Would it matter whether Kilvington thought "Stop thief!" meant that Howard was (1) a petty thief, (2) a house burglar, or (3) an armed robber? And suppose Kilvington believed that "Stop thief!" could have meant *any* of these

things, and he couldn't tell which one was intended?

PEOPLE v. CEBALLOS
California Supreme Court
12 Cal.3d 470 (1974)

BURKE, JUSTICE.

Don Ceballos was found guilty by a jury of assault with a deadly weapon (Pen.Code § 245). Imposition of sentence was suspended and he was placed on probation. He appeals from the judgment, contending primarily that his conduct was not unlawful because the alleged victim was attempting to commit burglary when hit by a trap gun mounted in the garage of defendant's dwelling and that the court erred in instructing the jury. We have concluded that the former argument lacks merit, that the court did not commit prejudicial error in instructing the jury, and that the judgment should be affirmed.

Defendant lived alone in a home in San Anselmo. The regular living quarters were above the garage, but defendant sometimes slept in the garage and had about $2,000 worth of property there. In March 1970 some tools were stolen from defendant's home. On May 12, 1970, he noticed the lock on his garage doors was bent and pry marks were on one of the doors. The next day he mounted a loaded .22 caliber pistol in the garage. The pistol was aimed at the center of the garage doors and was connected by a wire to one of the doors so that the pistol would discharge if the door was opened several inches.

The damage to defendant's lock had been done by a 16-year-old boy named Stephen and a 15-year-old boy named Robert. On the afternoon of May 15, 1970, the boys returned to defendant's house while he was away. Neither boy was armed with a gun or knife. After looking in the windows and seeing no one, Stephen succeeded in removing the lock on the garage doors with a crowbar, and, as he pulled the door outward, he was hit in the face with a bullet from the pistol.

Stephen testified: He intended to go into the garage "for musical equipment" because he had a debt to pay to a friend. His "way of paying that debt would be to take [defendant's] property and sell it" and use the proceeds to pay the debt. He "wasn't going to do it [i.e., steal] for sure, necessarily." He was there "to look around," and "getting in, I don't know if I would have actually stolen."

Defendant, testifying in his own behalf, admitted having set up the trap gun. He stated that after noticing the pry marks on his garage door on May 12, he felt he should "set up some kind of a trap, something to keep the burglar out of my home." When asked why he was trying to keep the burglar out, he replied, "Because somebody was trying to steal my property and I don't want to come home some night and have the thief in there; usually a thief is pretty desperate and they just pick up a weapon, if they don't have one, and do the best they can."

When asked by the police shortly after the shooting why he assembled the trap gun, defendant stated that "he didn't have much and he wanted to protect what he did have."

As heretofore appears, the jury found defendant guilty of assault with a deadly weapon. Pen.Code § 245. An assault is "an unlawful attempt, coupled with a present ability, to commit a violent injury on the person of another." Pen.Code § 240.

Defendant contends that had he been present he would have been justified in shooting Stephen since Stephen was attempting to commit burglary (Pen.Code § 459), that under cases such as *United States v. Gilliam*, 25 Fed.Cas. p. 1319, No. 15, 205a, defendant had a right to do indirectly what he could have done directly, and that therefore any attempt by him to commit a violent injury upon Stephen was not "unlawful" and hence not an assault. The People argue that the rule in *Gilliam* is unsound, that as a matter of law a trap gun constitutes excessive force, and that in any event the circumstances were not in fact such as to warrant the use of deadly force.

The issue of criminal liability under statutes such as Penal Code § 245 where the instrument employed is a trap gun or other deadly mechanical device appears to be one of first impression in this state, but in other jurisdictions courts have considered the question of criminal and civil liability for death or injuries inflicted by such a device.

At common law in England it was held that a trespasser, having knowledge that there are spring guns in a wood, cannot maintain an action for an injury received in consequence of his accidentally stepping on the wire of such gun. *Ilott v. Wilkes* (1820) 3 B.& Ald. 304. That case aroused such a protest in England that it was abrogated seven years later by a statute, which made it a misdemeanor to set spring guns with intent to inflict grievous bodily injury but excluded from its operation a spring gun set between sunset and sunrise in a dwelling house for the protection thereof. 7 & 8 Geo. IV, ch. 18.

In the United States, courts have concluded that a person may be held criminally liable under statutes proscribing homicides and shooting with intent to injure, or civilly liable, if he sets upon his premises a deadly mechanical device and that device kills or injures another. *Katko v. Briney* (Iowa), 183 N.W.2d 657, 660; *State v. Plumlee*, 177 La. 687; *State v. Beckham*, 306 Mo. 566; *State v. Childers*, 133 Ohio St. 508; *Marquis v. Benfer* (Ct. of Civ.App., Tex.) 298 S.W.2d 601; *Pierce v. Commonwealth*, 135 Va. 635). However, an exception to the rule that there may be criminal and civil liability for death or injuries caused by such a device has been recognized where the intrusion is, in fact, such that the person, were he present, would be justified in taking the life or inflicting the bodily harm with his own hands. See *United States v. Gilliam*, *supra*; *Scheuermann v. Scharfenberg*, 163 Ala. 337; *Katko v. Briney*, *supra*; *Gray v. Combs*, 30 Ky. 478; *State v. Plumlee*, *supra*; *State v. Beckham*, *supra*; *State v. Childers*, *supra*; *Marquis v. Benfer*, *supra*; Rest. 2d Torts, § 85; Prosser on Torts (4th ed.) p. 1116; but see Posner, "Killing or Wounding to Protect a Property Interest" (1971), 14 J. Law & Econ. 201, 214-215. The phrase "were he present" does not hypothesize the actual presence of the person (see Rest. 2d Torts, § 85, coms. (a), (c) & (d)), but is used in setting forth in an indirect manner the principle that a person may do indirectly that which he is privileged to do directly.

Allowing persons, at their own risk, to employ deadly mechanical devices imperils the lives of children, firemen and policemen acting within the scope of their employment, and others. Where the actor is present, there is always the possibility he will realize that deadly force is not necessary, but deadly mechanical devices are without mercy or discretion. Such devices "are silent instrumentalities of death. They deal death and destruction to the innocent as well as the criminal intruder without the slightest warning. The taking of human life (or infliction of great bodily injury) by such means is brutally savage and inhuman." See *State v. Plumlee*, supra.

It seems clear that the use of such devices should not be encouraged. Moreover, whatever may be thought in torts, the foregoing rule setting forth an exception to liability for death or injuries inflicted by such devices "is inappropriate in penal law for it is obvious that it does not prescribe a workable standard of conduct; liability depends upon fortuitous results." See Model Penal Code (Tent. Draft No. 8), § 3.06, com. 15. We therefore decline to adopt that rule in criminal cases.

Furthermore, even if that rule were applied here, as we shall see, defendant was not justified in shooting Stephen. Penal Code § 197 provides: "Homicide is . . . justifiable . . . 1. When resisting any attempt to murder any person, or to commit a felony, or to do some great bodily injury upon any person; or, 2. When committed in defense of habitation, property, or person, against one who manifestly intends or endeavors, by violence or surprise, to commit a felony . . ." Since a homicide is justifiable under the circumstances specified in § 197, *a fortiori* an attempt to commit a violent injury upon another under those circumstances is justifiable.

By its terms, subdivision 1 of Penal Code § 197 appears to permit killing to prevent any "felony," but in view of the large number of felonies today and the inclusion of many that do not involve a danger of serious bodily harm, a literal reading of the section is undesirable. *People v. Jones*, 191 Cal.App.2d 478, 481, in rejecting the defendant's theory that her husband was about to commit the felony of beating her (Pen. Code § 273d) and that therefore her killing him to prevent him from doing so was justifiable, stated that Penal Code § 197 "does no more than codify the common law and should be read in light of it." *Jones* read into § 197, subdivision 1, the limitation that the felony be "some atrocious crime attempted to be committed by force." *Jones* further stated, "the punishment provided by a statute is not necessarily an adequate test as to whether life may be taken for in some situations it is too artificial and unrealistic. We must look further into the character of the crime, and the manner of its perpetration. When these do not reasonably create a fear of great bodily harm, as they could not if defendant apprehended only a misdemeanor assault, there is no cause for the exaction of a human life." *Jones* involved subdivision 1 of Penal Code § 197, but subdivision 2 of that section is likewise so limited. The term "violence of surprise" in subdivision 2 is found in common law authorities (see *Flynn v. Commonwealth*, 204 Ky. 572), and, whatever may have been the very early common law, the rule developed at common law that killing or use of deadly force to prevent a felony was justified only if the offense was a forcible and atrocious crime. See *Storey v. State*, supra. "Surprise" means an unexpected attack — which includes force and violence — and the word thus appears redundant.

Examples of forcible and atrocious crimes are murder, mayhem, rape and robbery. See *Storey v. State*, supra. In such crimes "from their atrocity and violence human life (or personal safety from great harm) either is, or is presumed to be, in peril" (see *United States v. Gilliam, supra*).

Burglary has been included in the list of such crimes. See, e.g., *United States v. Gilliam, supra*. However, in view of the wide scope of burglary under Penal Code § 459, as compared with the common law definition of that offense, in our opinion it cannot be said that under all circumstances burglary under § 459 constitutes a forcible and atrocious crime.2

Where the character and manner of the burglary do not reasonably create a fear of great bodily harm, there is no cause for exaction of human life or for the use of deadly force. The character and manner of the burglary could not reasonably create such a fear unless the burglary threatened, or was reasonably believed to threaten, death or serious bodily harm.

In the instant case, the asserted burglary did not threaten death or serious bodily harm, since no one but Stephen and Robert was then on the premises. A defendant is not protected from liability merely by the fact that the intruder's conduct is such as would justify the defendant, were he present, in believing that the intrusion threatened death or serious bodily injury. There is ordinarily the possibility that the defendant, were he present, would realize the true state of affairs and recognize the intruder as one whom he would not be justified in killing or wounding.

We thus conclude that defendant was not justified under Penal Code § 197, subdivisions 1 or 2, in shooting Stephen to prevent him from committing burglary. Our conclusion is in accord with dictum indicating that there may be no privilege to use a deadly mechanical device to prevent a burglary of a dwelling house in which no one is present. See *State v. Green, supra*, 110 S.E. 145, 147; *State v. Barr*, 11 Wash. 481; *Contra*, e.g., *State v. Beckham, supra*; *Scheuermann v. Scharfenberg, supra*; *State v. Moore, supra*.

In support of his position that had he been present he would have been justified in shooting Stephen, defendant cites *Nakashima v. Takase*, 8 Cal.App.2d 35, a case in which the decedent's mother was seeking damages. The defendant, a cafe proprietor, suspected a burglary might be committed, returned to the cafe after dark, and hid inside. The decedent and a companion broke into the cafe intending to commit larceny, and after they entered, the defendant, who was secreted in a position where he could not be seen or heard, shot the decedent without warning. *Nakashima*, in reversing the judgment in the plaintiff's favor, concluded that the defendant's act was a justifiable homicide under Penal Code § 197, subdivision 2. That case manifestly differs on its facts from the present one in that, among other things, here no one except the asserted would-be burglar and his companion was on the premises when the gun was fired. * * * *

We recognize that our position regarding justification for killing under Penal Code § 197, subdivisions 1 and 2, differs from the position of § 143, subdivision (2), of the Restatement Second of Torts, regarding the use of deadly force to prevent a "felony . . . of a type . . . involving the breaking and entry of a dwelling place", but in view of the supreme value of human life, we do not believe deadly force can be justified to prevent all felonies of the foregoing type, including ones in which no person is, or is reasonably believed to be, on the premises except the would-be burglar.

Defendant also argues that had he been present he would have been justified in shooting Stephen under subdivision 4 of Penal Code § 197, which provides, "Homicide is . . . justifiable . . . 4. When necessarily committed in Attempting, by lawful ways and means, to apprehend any person for any felony committed . . ." The argument cannot be upheld. The words "attempting . . . to apprehend' contain the idea of acting for the purpose of apprehending. An attempt to commit a crime includes, *inter alia*, the specific intent to commit a particular crime, and "In statutes and in cases other than criminal prosecutions an 'attempt' ordinarily means an intent combined with an act falling short of the thing intended." Black's Law Dictionary (4th ed.) p. 462. Here no showing was made that defendant's intent in shooting was to apprehend a felon. Rather it appears from his testimony and extrajudicial statement heretofore recited that his intent was to prevent a burglary, to protect his property, and to avoid the possibility that a thief might get into defendant's house and injure him upon his return. * * * *

Defendant also does not, and could not properly contend that the intrusion was in fact such that, were he present, he would be justified under Civil Code § 50 in using deadly force. That section provides, "Any necessary force may be used to protect from wrongful injury the person or property of oneself . . ." This section also should be read in the light of the common law, and at common law in general deadly force could not be used solely for the protection of property. See Model Penal Code § 3.06, com. 8. "The preservation of human life and limb from grievous harm is of more importance to society than the protection of property." *Commonwealth v. Emmons*, 157 Pa.Super. 495. Thus defendant was not warranted under Civil Code § 50 in using deadly force to protect his personal property. * * * *

At common law an exception to the foregoing principle that deadly force could not be used solely for the protection of property was recognized where the property was a dwelling house in some circumstances. See *Simpson v. State, supra,* 59 Ala. 1, 14. "According to the older interpretation of the common law, even extreme force may be used to prevent dispossession (of the dwelling house)." See Model Penal Code, supra, com. 8. Also at common law if another attempted to burn a dwelling the owner was privileged to use deadly force if this seemed necessary to defend his "castle" against the threatened harm. See Perkins on Criminal Law, p. 1023. Further, deadly force was privileged it if was, or reasonably seemed, necessary to protect the dwelling against a burglar. See Perkins on Criminal Law, p. 1023.

Here we are not concerned with dispossession or burning of a dwelling, and, as heretofore concluded, the asserted burglary in this case was not of such a character as to warrant the use of deadly force. * * * *

We conclude that as a matter of law the exception to the rule of liability for injuries inflicted by a deadly mechanical device does not apply under the circumstances here appearing.

* * *

The judgment is affirmed.

NOTES FROM THE JUDGE:

(1) Which defense(s) was the Court analyzing in *Ceballos*? Defense of habitation? Prevention of felony? Both? Neither?

(2) As the Court notes, the statute says "felony" — without any limitation. The Court then holds, in effect, "Well, it may say 'felony', but that doesn't mean *every* felony, so Ceballos must be punished." Is this fair to Ceballos? Shouldn't the Court assume that people read statutes (or consult lawyers who read them) and have a right to rely on what they say?

(3) The court says that, were Ceballos present, he would have seen that "no one but Stephen and Robert were then on the premises." But if Ceballos were there to see it, then Ceballos would be there too — and possibly in danger from the two boys! Is this simply illogical, or is the court supposing that Ceballos might be there spiritually, without corporeal presence?

(4) In *Castles and Carjackers: Proportionality & The Use of Deadly Force In Defense of Dwellings and Vehicles*, 1999 U. Ill. L. Rev. 1, 2 (1999), Professor Stuart Green says:

> The American law of justified homicide reflects a seeming intractable conflict. On the one hand is the traditional rule of self-defense, under which deadly force may be used only in response to a threat of death or serious bodily injury. On the other hand is the doctrine of defense of premises, which permits the use of deadly force when no such threat exists.

Professor Green goes on to examine several possible justifications for the defense of habitation doctrine, concluding that none of them are sufficient, but the aggregation of these justifications might be sufficient.

PEOPLE v. MARTIN
California Court of Appeal, 5th District
168 Cal.App.3d 1111 (1985)

HAMLIN, ASSOCIATE JUSTICE

The People appeal from an order granting defendant's Penal Code § 995 motion to set aside the information charging defendant with involuntary manslaughter (Pen.Code § 192, subd. 2) and alleging the use of a firearm in the commission of that offense (§ 12022.5).

This appeal requires us to decide whether § 197, subdivision 4,[2] justifies

---

[2] Section 197, subdivision 4, provides: "Homicide is also justifiable when committed by any person in any of the following cases: ". . . . 4. When necessarily committed in attempting, by lawful ways and means, to apprehend any person for any felony committed . . ."

defendant's shooting and killing one of the apparently unarmed participants in the nighttime burglary of his son's temporarily unoccupied residence while that participant was fleeing from the scene of the burglary. We conclude that the statute must be construed to justify the homicide. We will affirm the order setting aside the information.

The Facts

After dark on December 22, 1983, two unarmed youths, one 17 and the other 14 years old, broke into the Bakersfield residence of defendant's son to steal marijuana. Defendant, an off-duty deputy sheriff who lived next door and who knew his son and his family were not home at the time, heard his dogs barking and went out to investigate. He saw one of the youths getting ready to enter his son's residence and heard the voice of another already inside the residence. He then reentered his home to get his 12-gauge shotgun and told his wife to call the sheriff's office. When he went back outside with his gun in hand he saw the two burglars fleeing. He pointed his shotgun at them and ordered them to stop. One immediately dropped to the ground. The other kept running, climbed a fence, and was about to get away. Defendant fired one shot at the fleeing felon, which resulted in his death.

Soon after the shooting sheriff's officers arrived at the scene. Defendant gave them the tape-recorded statement set forth in the margin.[3]

Discussion

The magistrate denied defendant's motion at the conclusion of the preliminary hearing to dismiss the charges against him. After the information was filed, defendant moved to dismiss under § 995. The superior court granted this motion.

Since the facts in this case are undisputed, it is apparent that the different conclusions reached by the magistrate and the trial court on whether the homicide was justified are based upon conflicting interpretations of § 197, subdivision 4. It is well established that the applicability of a statute to undisputed facts is a question

---

[3] "I heard my dogs barking on the west side of the house. They had been barking for three or four minutes. I went out to see if I could see anything in the neighborhood going wrong. My boy lives in the house next door, 2211, and he has been burglarized three or four times in the past year or so. When I went out the front door, there was a blackheaded individual with the screen door open working on the front door. I heard a voice from the inside talking to him on the outside. I came in the house, got my shotgun, went back out and the fellow on the outside was just going inside. I went around to the back of the house and I saw the back door's glass had been kicked out or broken out. Came back around and told the wife to call the Sheriff's Office. Went back down the side of the house on the west side of his place; and as I got to the corner, they come running out the back door. Two boys crossed the back lawn and I started hollering, told them to halt, don't move, stay put. One boy, the dark-haired one, tripped on something. The other boy — they had something in their hands — the other boy kept on running a little west, then south. I yelled at him to stop and hold it several times. I got no response. He got to the canal bank, jumped over the fence and was running east down the canal bank and I was still hollering at him to stop and I fired one shot then. Heard no other noise of any kind and the boy that was down with me at the place where I fired the shot hadn't moved yet. He was complaining his foot was cut or something like that. And then the Sheriff's Office started arriving probably three or four minutes later."

of law and this court is not bound by the lower court's conclusion.

At common law, an officer or private person could use deadly force if necessary to capture a fleeing felon. *State v. Rutherford* (1821) 8 N.C. 457; Perkins, *Criminal Law* (1957) 873-874. This remains the law in a substantial number of jurisdictions. In at least one leading criminal law textbook, the common law rule is stated as the general rule, subject to exceptions:

> Ordinarily, an officer or private person, in making an arrest for a felony, may use whatever force is reasonably necessary to overcome a resisting felon or to stop a fleeing felon, even to the extent of taking his life; and, if deadly force is used, the homicide is justifiable.

> The supportive theory is that "felons ought not to be at large, and that the life of a felon has been forfeited; for felonies at common law were punishable with death." Although according to some courts a felony must in fact have been committed, according to others it is sufficient merely that there be reasonable ground for the belief that a felony had been committed. Some courts allow deadly force only if the felony is a dangerous one; others allow deadly force in the case of any felony. [2 Wharton's Criminal Law (Torcia 14th ed. 1979) § 122]

This common law privilege of using deadly force to prevent the escape of a fleeing felon served to deter criminals from attempting to escape. It arose at a time when almost all felonies were punishable by death. The same privilege of using deadly force did not exist to stop one fleeing after commission of a misdemeanor. With the exception of murder under special circumstances, the common law crimes punishable by death[4] no longer are or can be. *Tennessee v. Garner* (1985) 471 U.S. 1, 105 S.Ct. 1694, 85 L.Ed.2d 1.

Similarly, the compelling distinction which in earlier times existed between felonies and misdemeanors is today minor and often arbitrary. Many crimes classified as misdemeanors, or nonexistent, at common law are now felonies. These changes have made the assumption that a "felon" is more dangerous than a misdemeanant untenable.

Admittedly, the significant changes pointed out in *Tennessee v. Garner* have undermined the justification for homicide which § 197, subdivision 4, facially provides. The California Legislature enacted that statute in 1872 and has not seen fit to amend it. We must determine the legislative intent when enacted. We presume that when the statute was enacted the Legislature was familiar with the common law rule, and, when it couches its enactment in common law language, that its intent was to continue those rules in statutory form. This is particularly appropriate in considering the work of the first session of our Legislature: its precedents were necessarily drawn from the common law, as modified in certain respects by the Constitution and legislation of our sister states.

Burglary was a common law felony. 1 Wharton, supra, at p. 81. As such, it was

---

[4] The common law felonies were murder, manslaughter, rape, robbery, mayhem, burglary, arson, larceny and prison break. 1 Wharton, supra, at p. 81.

defined as a breaking and entering of a dwelling house at night with the intent to commit a felony.

Although on its face § 197, subdivision 4, justifies every homicide necessarily committed in attempting to apprehend any person for any felony, our courts have not always so construed it. In the early case, *People v. Lillard* (1912) 18 Cal.App. 343, the court relied on this statutory provision in reversing the defendant's manslaughter conviction. There, the fleeing felon was shot after he had entered a woman's residence and assaulted her with the intent to commit robbery. The court did not find it necessary to characterize that felony as a common law crime or a dangerous crime. The defendant had taken his pistol and joined a crowd in pursuit of the felon as a result of the screams he had heard indicating the fleeing person might have been a thief or a murderer. While in the lead of the crowd and when he noted that the felon refused to stop and was reaching a dark place about 40 feet away, he fired a shot which caused the felon's death. In reversing defendant's conviction the court stated:

> There is and can be no question from the record that a felony had been committed; that the deceased had committed the felony; that the defendant had reason to believe and did believe these facts, and that he pursued the deceased with the intent to capture him, and for no other purpose. Section 197 of our Penal Code provides that homicide is justifiable when necessarily committed in attempting, by lawful ways and means, to apprehend any person for any felony committed. Wharton on Homicide declares the rule, and quotes abundant authority in its support: "Even a private person is justified in killing a fleeing felon who cannot otherwise be taken, if he can prove that the person is actually guilty of the felony." [*Id.* at pp. 345-346.]

The court went on to state that "if officers and citizens are to be punished for an effort to suppress crime and to bring to justice those who commit offenses against the law, it is but offering a premium for crime." *Id.* at p. 346. * * * *

People v. Walker (1973) 32 Cal.App.3d 897, required the court to interpret § 197, subdivision 4, the provision with which we are most concerned in this case. There, the defendant, a private citizen, shot to death a person he believed was fleeing after participating in a nighttime burglary of his next-door neighbor's residence. The trial court submitted to the jury the question of whether the decedent had actually committed a burglary and instructed the jury to consider the decedent's state of intoxication in determining whether he had the specific intent required for the commission of a burglary. The jury found the defendant guilty of involuntary manslaughter.

The appellate court reversed, holding that the defendant was entitled to the instruction that the decedent had committed burglary, a felony. The decedent's diminished capacity was irrelevant in the context of evaluating the defense of justifiable homicide.

Although the reversal was based on an instructional error, the court discussed in dictum that under a justifiable homicide theory it is reasonable to require that the underlying crime be of serious magnitude. "In short, it is reasonable to require that the act be of felony stature, rather than a misdemeanor. It is also reasonable to require a showing of necessity to take a life in order to apprehend." *People v. Walker, supra*, at 902. The court went on to conclude that the term "felony" in § 197, subdivision 4, "refers to the statutory definition of such an offense and nothing more." Id. at 903.

In *People v. Piorkowski* (1974) 41 Cal.App.3d 324, the defendant, while walking along a city street in the afternoon, saw three youths in a drycleaning establishment. One appeared to have climbed over the counter. When defendant returned to that area a few minutes later he saw the same youths walking away from the drycleaning establishment. He asked the proprietor if everything was all right. She then discovered the wallet from her purse was missing. The defendant pursued the youths, caught up with them, drew his holstered pistol, and ordered them to halt. Two did, but one kept going. The defendant pursued, caught him, a struggle ensued, and the youth was shot to death. The jury rejected the defendant's § 197, subdivision 4, defense and convicted him of involuntary manslaughter.

The conviction was affirmed on appeal. The court stated that deadly force may be used to arrest a felon where the "felony committed is one which threatens death or great bodily harm. *Commonwealth v. Chermansky* (1968) 430 Pa. 170; *State v. Nyland* (1955) 47 Wn.2d 240." *People v. Piorkowski, supra*, 41 Cal.App.3d at 329.

The *Piorkowski* court then quoted *People v. Jones* (1961) 191 Cal.App.2d 478, and concluded that:

> The law of this state makes it a felony to commit such offenses as the theft of $50 worth of avocados, olives, artichokes, nuts, etc. (Pen.Code § 487), the conversion of real estate of the value of $50 or more into personal property by severance from the realty of another (Pen.Code § 487b), theft of a dog the value of which exceeds $200 (Pen.Code §§ 487e and 487g), a second conviction for indecent exposure (Pen.Code § 314), or conspiracy to commit any crime (Pen.Code § 182). Needless to say, modern rationale must preclude the holding that a private citizen may use deadly force in attempting to arrest a person for such offenses.

> The evidence disclosed in this case clearly demonstrates that the crime committed by the victim was not of the type which normally threatens death or great bodily harm. Even though the evidence did evince the commission of a burglary by the victim, as defendant asserts, the use of deadly force to effect the arrest was not warranted. We do not have here a burglary of a dwelling at night (common law burglary), such as was the case in *People v. Walker*. Rather, the crime was committed during daylight hours and in a business establishment which was open to the public at the time. No confrontation aided by force was involved. While this factual pattern may constitute "statutory burglary," which is a felony (Pen.Code § 459), clearly there is not the attendant risk to human life which accompanies common law burglary.

> We are of the opinion that the character of the crime and the manner of its perpetration did not warrant the use of deadly force to effect the arrest, i.e., it was not "necessarily committed." [*People v. Piorkowski, supra*, at pp. 329-330.]

Although *Piorkowski* appears to support the People's position, it is distinguishable from the case at bar. First, *Piorkowski* held that under its facts deadly force was not necessary to apprehend the felon as required under § 197, subdivision 4. The defendant there had grabbed the felon and was struggling with him when he shot him. Here, defendant was separated from the victim by a fence some 60 feet away on a dark night. Additionally, defendant was concerned with keeping in custody the burglar he had already caught. Under the undisputed facts, defendant's use of a gun was necessary in order to apprehend the fleeing felon. Second, *Piorkowski* involved a daytime burglary of a business which, unlike our case, was not recognized as a felony at common law. *Piorkowski* even acknowledges this in distinguishing the nighttime residential burglary in *People v. Walker*. *Piorkowski* also pointed out that the definition of felonies has dramatically expanded. While most of the crimes discussed in *Piorkowski* were not felonies at common law, it bears repeating that in this case the victim committed a crime that was a felony at common law.

Shortly after *Piorkowski*, our Supreme Court decided *People v. Ceballos* (1974) 12 Cal.3d 470. In that case two boys attempting a burglary were injured by a trapgun designed to fire when a residential garage door opened. The owner was convicted of assault with a deadly weapon despite his contention that the shooting would have been justified had he been present at the time of injury, and that he had a right to do indirectly (trapgun) what he was entitled to do directly.

Our Supreme Court affirmed the conviction and held that under § 197, subdivisions 1 and 2, the use of deadly force is permitted only in the event a felony constitutes a "forcible and atrocious" crime such as murder, mayhem, rape, robbery, and some, but not all, burglaries.

The defendant in *Ceballos* also argued that if he had been present he would have been justified in shooting the victim under § 197, subdivision 4. The court discussed *People v. Lillard, supra*, and distinguished it because the *Ceballos* defendant made no showing that he had intended to apprehend a felon; rather, he appeared to have intended to prevent a burglary, protect his property, and to avoid the possibility that a thief might get into his house and injure defendant on his return.

Although *Ceballos* deals with a justifiable homicide defense, it does not resolve the instant case. First, the court interpreted and based its decision on § 197, subdivisions 1 and 2. This is significant because, as was pointed out in *Ceballos*, cases are, of course, not authority for propositions not there considered. Second, *Ceballos*, unlike the instant case, involved the use of a trapgun device which is clearly not encouraged. "Such devices 'are silent instrumentalities of death. They deal death and destruction to the innocent as well as the criminal intruder without the slightest warning. The taking of human life . . . by such means is brutally savage and inhuman." ' *Id*. at 477. Third, *Ceballos* discussed *People v. Lillard* with approval and *Lillard* is quite similar to this case.

The next key case is *People v. Quesada* (1980) 113 Cal.App.3d 533.[6] There, the

---

[6] *Jones, Piorkowski*, and *Ceballos* were cited as authority in two later civil cases which stated in dicta that a police officer's right under § 196, subdivision 3, to use deadly force in apprehending felons is limited to those felonies which threaten death or great bodily harm. See *Kortum v. Alkire* (1977) 69

defendant reasonably suspected that a certain person had burglarized his unoccupied home. Hoping to apprehend the suspect, the defendant set up a "buy" two days later. After the "buy," when the suspect turned to leave, the defendant tried to arrest him. The suspect proceeded to drive away so the defendant shot him to death. The defendant contended that the killing was justified under § 197, subdivision 4. The trial judge refused the defendant's requested instruction tailored to take advantage of that statutory provision. The jury returned a guilty verdict on the involuntary manslaughter charge. The appellate court affirmed. * * * *

Although *Quesada* involved a nighttime burglary recognized as a felony at common law, the specific issue before the court was the defendant's right to have the jury instructed to the effect that homicide is justifiable "when necessarily committed in attempting, by lawful ways and means, to apprehend any person who has committed burglary of the first degree." *People v. Quesada, supra,* at 537. Such an instruction made no distinction between apprehension of the person who had committed the burglary while fleeing from the scene and apprehension after the felon had completed his escape. The social need for justification of a homicide committed in the latter circumstance, as in *Quesada,* is virtually nonexistent. In sharp contrast, failure to apprehend when the felon is fleeing the scene of the crime frequently means that the felon remains at large. Later investigation cannot represent a substitute for immediate apprehension. Accordingly, a person may reasonably expect that he is justified in using deadly force to apprehend a felon fleeing the scene of the crime. No such reasonable expectation could exist in attempting apprehension after escape. Other safer and less drastic procedures for apprehension after escape are well known. * * * *

When we apply the unqualified and unrestricted "any felony" language of § 197, subdivision 4, as interpreted by the courts of this state prior to defendant's commission of the homicide in this case, we conclude that the statute is ambiguous. In adopting the words "any felony" to define justifiable homicide under § 197, subdivision 4, the Legislature necessarily intended to include all the common law crimes then recognized, including nighttime burglary of a dwelling house. Admittedly, the crimes classified as felonies have been substantially enlarged since 1872 and there are other unanticipated meanings of the words "any felony" which we have considered above. However, none of the cases reviewed justifies disregarding the presumed intent of the Legislature to include in the definition of "any felony" those crimes which were felonies at common law.

In the circumstances of this case it is appropriate that we follow "the policy of this state to construe a penal statute as favorably to the defendant as its language and the circumstances of its application may reasonably permit; just as in the case of a question of fact, the defendant is entitled to the benefit of every reasonable doubt as to the true interpretation of words or the construction of language used in a statute." *Keeler v. Superior Court,* 2 Cal.3d at 631. Stated another way, "when the language used in a penal law is reasonably susceptible of two constructions, ordinarily that construction which is more favorable to the defendant will be

Cal.App.3d 325, 333; *Long Beach Police Officers Assn. v. City of Long Beach* (1976) 61 Cal.App.3d 364. However, in *Peterson v. Long Beach* (1979) 24 Cal.3d 238, 247, footnote 8, our Supreme Court declined to decide the correctness of this limitation.

adopted." *People v. Moreland* (1978) 81 Cal.App.3d 11, 17.

The approach we adopt to the construction of § 197, subdivision 4, is dictated not only as a matter of fairness in restricting the meaning of a statute to that which should have been foreseen but also to avoid a violation of the first essential of due process of law. As Justice Holmes pointed out in *McBoyle v. United States* (1931) 283 U.S. 25, 27: "Although it is not likely that a criminal will carefully consider the text of the law before he murders or steals, it is reasonable that a fair warning should be given to the world in language that the common world will understand, of what the law intends to do if a certain line is passed. To make the warning fair, so far as possible the line should be clear." In this case we cannot say it is unlikely that defendant considered the text of § 197, subdivision 4, in deciding to fire his gun at the fleeing felon. He was an off-duty police officer who may reasonably be expected to have general knowledge of legislative restrictions on the use of deadly force in apprehending felons. That is an even more compelling reason to interpret the statute in favor of defendant.

The result we reach is not affected by the recent United States Supreme Court decision in *Tennessee v. Garner*. There the court held that a Tennessee statute permitting police to use deadly force to prevent escape of all felony suspects whatever the circumstances, is constitutionally unreasonable. It noted that insofar as the statute authorizes use of such force against apparently unarmed, nondangerous suspects it violates the Fourth Amendment.[7] The court held that deadly force may not be used unless it is necessary to prevent escape and the officer has probable cause to believe that the suspect poses significant threat of death or serious physical injury to the pursuing officer or others.

While *Tennessee v. Garner* necessarily limits the scope of justification for homicide under § 197, subdivision 4, and other similar statutes from the date of that decision (March 27, 1985), the requirements it imposes for justification cannot be applied retroactively to the detriment of one accused of crime. As the court pointed out in *Bouie v. City of Columbia* (1964) 378 U.S. 347:

> When a statute on its face is vague or overbroad, it at least gives a potential defendant some notice, by virtue of this very characteristic, that a question may arise as to its coverage, and that it may be held to cover his contemplated conduct. When a statute on its face is narrow and precise, however, it lulls the potential defendant into a false sense of security, giving him no reason even to suspect that conduct clearly outside the scope of the statute as written will be retroactively brought within it by an act of judicial construction. If the Fourteenth Amendment is violated when a person is required to speculate as to the meaning of penal statutes, or to guess at the statute's meaning and differ as to its application, the violation is that much greater when, because the uncertainty as to the statute's meaning is itself not revealed until the court's decision, a person is not even afforded an opportunity to engage in such speculation before committing the act in question. [*Id.* at 352.]

---

[7] "The right of the people to be secure in their persons . . . against unreasonable searches and seizures, shall not be violated . . ." U.S. Const., 4th Amend.

The due process considerations are the same whether the statutory crime is enlarged or justification for conduct otherwise criminal is restricted by judicial interpretation. There is the same lack of notice and lulling the potential defendant into a false sense of security.

We therefore conclude that the trial court did not err in dismissing the information. The undisputed facts establish that defendant necessarily committed the homicide in attempting by lawful ways and means to apprehend the victim while fleeing from the scene of his nighttime residential burglary. We specifically limit our holding to felons fleeing after commission of a crime which was a felony at common law. Further, our interpretation of § 197, subdivision 4, is applicable only to offenses alleged to have occurred prior to the decision in *Tennessee v. Garner*.

The judgment is affirmed.

NOTE FROM THE JUDGE:

It seems odd that the court discussed a lot of cases, but didn't even cite *Kilvington*. Why not? Isn't *Kilvington* a pretty strong case for the defendant?

Chapter 15

DURESS AND NECESSITY

"Duress" has been described this way:

> A person's unlawful threat (1) which causes the defendant reasonably to believe that the only way to avoid imminent death or serious bodily injury to himself or to another is to engage in conduct which violates the literal terms of the criminal law, and (2) which causes the defendant to engage in that conduct, gives the defendant the defense of duress (sometimes called compulsion or coercion) to the crime in question unless that crime consists of intentionally killing an innocent third person. The rationale of the defense of duress is that, for reasons of social policy, it is better that the defendant, faced with a choice of evils, choose to do the lesser evil (violate the criminal law) in order to avoid the greater evil threatened by the other person.

> LaFave & Scott, *Criminal Law* (West)

"Necessity" has been described as follows:

> The pressure of natural physical forces sometimes confronts a person in an emergency with a choice of two evils; either he may violate the literal terms of the criminal law and thus produce a harmful result, or he may comply with those terms and thus produce a greater or equal or lesser amount of harm. For reasons of social policy, if the harm which will result from compliance with the law is greater than that which will result from violation of it, he is by virtue of the defense of necessity justified in violating it.

> LaFave & Scott, *Criminal Law* (West)

And what is the difference between the two?

> With the defense of necessity, the traditional view has been that the pressure must come from the physical forces of nature (storms, privations) rather than from other human beings. (When the pressure is from human beings, the defense, if applicable, is called duress rather than necessity.) However, the modern cases have tended to blur the distinction between duress and necessity. Most significantly, most but not all of the modern recodification (following the Model Penal Code in this respect) contain a broader choice-of-evils defense which is not limited to any particular source of danger.

LaFave & Scott, Criminal Law (West)

In Chapters 13 (Self Defense) and 14 (Defense of Habitation, etc.), the victim was usually a "bad guy." This in itself might not justify the defendant's attack on him, but usually we are not too troubled when such a person is injured or killed.

This Chapter is different. Here, all the victims are wholly innocent. They had no role in creating the situation that led the defendant to commit the crime. May a defendant *ever* commit a crime — even *murder* — against innocent persons in order to save the defendant or other people from some awful fate? If so, *when*?

Also, as you read this Chapter, consider these questions: what is the difference between necessity and duress — and is this difference important?

PROBLEM 15

To: My law clerk

From: Tiffany Lamp, Esq.

Re: *U.S. v. Karta*

I am in the middle of the trial in this case. My client, Makna Karta, has been indicted for violating 49 U.S.C. § 46504.* The prosecution presented evidence showing that Karta was being escorted by a federal marshal on a commercial flight from Chicago to New York - where he was to be deported back to his home country of Ambia. During the flight, he got away from the marshal and took his gun. He then threatened to shoot the crew unless they allowed him to use the radio to speak to the press on the ground. They complied. He then returned the gun to the marshal and sat down. He gave up quietly when the plane reached New York.

Karta has just finished testifying. The transcript of his testimony is attached. The prosecutor has moved to strike his testimony and have the court instruct the jury to disregard it, on the ground that it does not present any defense cognizable by the law. His brief supporting the motion cites the attached authorities — as well as Model Penal Code § 2.09 and § 3.02 (in the Appendix). Please review them and advise me how to deal with them. Also, I might have a chance to put on further evidence before the judge rules on the motion, so please let me know if there is any other evidence I should look for to help defeat the motion. I think Karta's testimony struck an emotional chord with the jury, so if we can keep the judge from telling the jury to disregard it, we might well win this case.

Transcript of Testimony of Makna Karta

Q: Mr. Karta, why were you on the plane?

---

* This statute provides: "An individual on an aircraft within the special aircraft jurisdiction of the United States who, by assaulting or intimidating a flight crew member or flight attendant of the aircraft, interferes with the performance of the duties of the member or attendant or lessens the ability of the member or attendant to perform those duties, shall be fined under title 18, imprisoned for not more than 20 years, or both. However, if a dangerous weapon is used in assaulting or intimidating the member or attendant, the individual shall be imprisoned for any term of years or for life."

A: My country, Ambia, is ruled by an cruel dictator, Pa Jama. He has murdered thousands of my countrymen. Until a few months ago, I was the leader of an underground movement seeking to depose him and bring democracy to Ambia. When I learned I was about to be arrested and shot, I fled. I found my way into the United States, where I applied for political asylum. This was denied, solely because the present administration in Washington does not want to offend Pa Jama. Ambia is a major supplier of oil to the United States, and the administration fears the wrath of Jama — that he might cut off the oil. No other country would accept me, probably because of pressure from the administration or fear of Jama. I told some reporters all this, but they were not interested in writing about it. So I was being sent back to Ambia. When I landed in Ambia, I would be shot immediately.

Q: Why did you want to send a message from the plane?

A: I felt that it was important to tell the American people about this situation, to save my life and to pressure the government to force some changes in Ambia, to stop the killings and bring about democracy. The message I broadcast was the story I just told. It worked, partly. Many American people wrote to their legislators and the president, and now Congress is holding hearings on what is happening in Ambia. But so far the administration has not changed its mind about deporting me.

UNITED STATES v. HOLMES
U.S. Circuit Court, E.D. Penna
26 Fed. Cases 360 (1842)

The American Ship William Brown left Liverpool on the 13th of March, 1841, bound for Philadelphia, in the United States. She had on board (besides a heavy cargo) 17 of a crew, and 65 passengers, Scotch and Irish emigrants. About 10 o'clock on the night of the 19th of April, when distant 250 miles south east of Cape Race, Newfoundland, the vessel struck an iceberg and began to fill so rapidly that it was evident she must soon go down. The long-boat and jolly-boat were cleared away and lowered. The captain, the second mate, 7 of the crew, and 1 passenger got into the jolly boat. The first mate, 8 seamen, of whom the prisoner was one (these 9 being the entire remainder of the crew), and 32 passengers, in all 41 persons, got indiscriminately into the long boat . . . . The remainder of the passengers, 31 persons, were obliged to remain on board the ship. In an hour and a half from the time when the ship struck, she went down, carrying with her every person who had not escaped to one or the other of the small boats. Thirty-one passengers thus perished . . . . On the following morning (Tuesday), the captain, being about to part company with the long-boat, gave its crew several directions, and, among other counsel, advised them to obey all the orders of the mate, as they would obey his, the captain's. This the crew promised that they would do. The long-boat was believed to be in general good condition; but she had not been in the water since leaving Liverpool, now thirty-five days; and as soon as she was launched, began to leak. She continued to leak the whole time; but the passengers had buckets, and tins, and, by bailing, were able to reduce the water, so as to make her hold her own. The plug was about an inch and a half in diameter. It came out more than once, and finally, got lost; but its place was supplied by different expedients.

It appeared by the depositions of the captain and of the second mate . . . that on

Tuesday morning, when the two boats parted company, the long-boat and all on board were in great jeopardy. The gunwale was within from 5 to 12 inches of the water. "From the experience" which they had had, they thought "the long-boat was too unmanageable to be saved." If she had been what, in marine phrase, is called a "leaky boat," she must have gone down. Even without a leak, she would not have supported one-half her company, had there been a "moderate blow." "She would have swamped very quickly." The people were half naked and were "all crowded up together like sheep in a pen." "A very little irregularity in the stowage would have capsized the long boat." "If she had struck any piece of ice, she would inevitably have gone down. There was great peril of ice for any boat." (Captain's and second mate's depositions.) Without going into more detail, the evidence of both these officers went to show that, loaded as the long-boat was on Tuesday morning, the chances of living were much against her. But the captain thought, that even if lightened to the extent to which she afterwards was, "it would have been impossible to row her to land and that the chances of her being picked up were ninety-nine to one against her." It appeared, further, that on Monday night, when the passengers on the ship (then settling towards her head and clearly going down) were shrieking and calling on the captain to take them off on his boat, the mate on the long-boat said to them: "Poor souls! you're only going down before we do." And, further, that on the following morning, before the boats parted company, the mate, in the long-boat, told the captain, in the jolly-boat, that the long-boat was unmanageable, and, that unless the captain would take some of the long-boat's passengers, it would be necessary to cast lots and throw some overboard. "I know what you mean," or, as stated by one witness, "I know what you'll have to do," said the captain. "Don't speak of that now. Let it be the last resort." There was little or no wind at this time, but pieces of ice were floating about.

Notwithstanding all this, the long-boat, loaded as she is above described to have been, did survive throughout the night of Monday, the day of Tuesday, and until 10 o'clock of Tuesday night, full twenty-four hours after the ship struck the iceberg. The crew rowed, turn about, at intervals, and the passengers bailed. On Tuesday morning, after the long boat and jolly-boat parted, it began to rain, and continued to rain throughout the day and night of Tuesday. At night the wind began to freshen, the sea grew heavier, and once, or oftener, the waves splashed over the boat's bow so as to wet, all over, the passengers who were seated there. Pieces of ice were still floating around, and, during the day, icebergs had been seen. About 10 o'clock of Tuesday night, the prisoner and the rest of the crew began to throw over some of the passengers, and did not cease until they had thrown over 14 male passengers. These, with the exception of two married men and a small boy, constituted all the male passengers aboard. Not one of the crew was cast over . . .

It was among the facts of this case that, during these solemn and distressful hours, scarce a remark appeared to have been made in regard to what was going to be done, nor, while it was being done, as to the necessity for doing it. None of the crew of the long-boat were present at the trial, to testify, and, with the exception of one small boy, all the witnesses from the long-boat were women, mostly quite young. It is probable that, by Tuesday night (the weather being cold, the persons on the boat partially naked, and the rain falling heavily), the witnesses had become considerably overpowered by exhaustion and cold, having been 24 hours in the boat. None of them spoke in a manner entirely explicit and satisfactory in regard to the most important point, viz. the degree and imminence of the jeopardy at 10 o'clock on Tuesday night, when the throwing over began. As has been stated, few words were spoken. It appeared, only, that, about 10 o'clock of Tuesday night, it being then dark, the rain falling rather heavily, the sea somewhat freshening, and the boat having considerable water in it, the mate, who had been bailing for some time, gave it up, exclaiming: "This work won't do. Help me, God. Men, go to work." Some of the passengers cried out, about the same time: "The boat is sinking. The plug's out. God have mercy on our poor souls." Holmes and the crew did not proceed upon this order; and after a little while, the mate exclaimed again: "Men, you must go to work, or we shall all perish." They then went to work; and, as has been already stated, threw out, before they ended, 14 male passengers, and also 2 women.[5] The mate directed the crew "not to part man and wife, and not to throw over any women." There was no other principle of selection. There was no evidence of combination among the crew. No lots were cast, nor had the passengers, at any time, been either informed or consulted as to what was now done. Holmes was one of the persons who assisted in throwing the passengers over. The first man thrown over was one Riley, whom Holmes and the others told to stand up, which he did. They then threw him over, and afterwards Duffy, who, in vain, besought them to spare him, for the sake of his wife and children, who were on shore. They then seized a third man, but, his wife being aboard, he was spared. Coming to Charles Conlin, the man exclaimed: "Holmes, dear, sure you won't put me out?" "Yes, Charley," said Holmes, "you must go, too." And so he was thrown over. Next was Francis Askin, for the manslaughter of whom the prisoner was indicted. When laid hold of, he offered Holmes five sovereigns to spare his life till morning, "when," said he, "if God don't send us some help, we'll draw lots, and if the lot falls on me, I'll go over like a man." Holmes said, "I don't want your money, Frank," and put him overboard. When one McAvoy was seized, he asked for five minutes to say his prayers, and, at the interposition of a negro, the cook, was allowed time to say them before he was cast overboard. It appeared, also, that when Askin was put out, he had struggled violently, yet the boat had not sunk. Two men, very stiff with cold, who had hidden themselves, were thrown over after daylight on Wednesday morning, when, clearly, there was no necessity for it. . . . On Wednesday morning, while yet in the boat, some of the witnesses had told the crew that they (i.e. the crew) should be made to die the death they had given to the others. The boat had provisions for six or seven days, close allowance: that is to say, 75 pounds of bread, 6 gallons of water, 8 or 10 pounds of meat, and a small bag of oatmeal. The mate had a chart, quadrant and compass. The weather was cold, and the passengers, being half clothed, much benumbed. On Wednesday morning the weather cleared, and early in the morning the long-boat was picked up by the ship "Crescent." All the persons who had not been thrown overboard were thus saved.

---

[5] It was a matter of doubt whether these women (two sisters of Frank Askin, an Irish youth, spoken of further on) had been thrown over, or whether their sacrifice was an act of self-devotion and affection to their brother. When Holmes seized him, his sisters entreated for his life. and said that if he was thrown over they wished to be thrown over too; that they wished to die the death of their brother." "Give me only a dress to put around me," said one of the sisters, after her brother had been thrown out, "and I care not now to live longer."

On the other hand, the character of the prisoner stood forth, in many points, in manly and interesting relief. A Finn by birth, he had followed the sea from youth, and his frame and countenance would have made an artist's model for decision and strength. He had been the last man of the crew to leave the sinking ship. His efforts to save the passengers, at the time the ship struck, had been conspicuous, and, but that they were in discharge of duty, would have been called self-forgetful and most generous . . . . As a sailor, his captain and the second mate testified that he had ever been obedient to orders, faithful to his duty, and efficient in the performance of it - "remarkably so," said the second mate. "He was kind and obliging in every respect," said the captain, "to the passengers, to his shipmates, and to everybody. Never heard one speak against him. He was always obedient to officers. I never had a better man on board ship. He was a first-rate man." While on the long-boat, in order to protect the women, he had parted with all his clothes, except his shirt and pantaloons; and his conduct and language to the women were kind. After Askin had been thrown out, some one asked if any more were to be thrown over. "No," said Holmes, "no more shall be thrown over. If any more are lost, we will all be lost together." Of both passengers and crew, he finally became the only one whose energies and whose hopes did not sink into prostration. He was the first to descry the vessel which took them up, and by his exertions, the ship was made to see, and, finally, to save, them . . .

The prisoner was indicted under the act of April 30, 1790, "for the punishment of certain crimes against the United States" (1 Stat. 115), an act which ordains (§ 12) that if any seaman shall commit manslaughter upon the high seas, on conviction, he shall be imprisoned not exceeding three years, and fined not exceeding one thousand dollars. The indictment charged that Holmes — First, with force "unlawfully and feloniously" did make an assault, and cast and throw Askin from a vessel into the high seas, by means of which, Askin, in and with the waters thereof, then and there was suffocated and drowned; second, in the same way, on board the long-boat of the ship William Brown, did make an assault, and cast, etc. The trial of the prisoner came on upon the 13th of April, 1842, a few days before the anniversary of the calamitous events referred to. The case was replete with incidents of deep romance, and of pathetic interest . . .

* * *

Baldwin, Circuit Justice, charging the jury, alluded to the touching character of the case:

> Cases of this kind are viewed with tenderness, and punished in mercy, we must yet bear in mind that man, in taking away the life of a fellow being, assumes an awful responsibility to God, and to society; and that the administrators of public justice do themselves assume that responsibility if, when called on to pass judicially upon the act, they yield to the indulgence of misapplied humanity. It is one thing to give a favourable interpretation to evidence in order to mitigate an offence. It is a different thing, when we are asked, not to extenuate, but to justify, the act. In the former case, as I have said, our decision may in some degree be swayed by feelings of humanity; while, in the latter, it is the law of necessity alone which can

disarm the vindicatory justice of the country. Where, indeed, a case does arise, embraced by this "law of necessity," the penal laws pass over such case in silence; for law is made to meet but the ordinary exigencies of life. But the case does not become "a case of necessity," unless all ordinary means of self preservation have been exhausted. The peril must be instant, overwhelming, leaving no alternative but to lose our own life, or to take the life of another person. An illustration of this principle occurs in the ordinary case of self-defense against lawless violence, aiming at the destruction of life, or designing to inflict grievous injury to the person; and within this range may fall the taking of life under other circumstances where the act is indispensably requisite to self existence. For example, suppose that two persons who owe no duty to one another that is not mutual should, by accident, not attributable to either, be placed in a situation where both cannot survive. Neither is bound to save the other's life by sacrificing his own, nor would either commit a crime in saving his own life in a struggle for the only means of safety. Of this description of cases are those which have been cited to you by counsel, from writers on natural law, cases which we rather leave to your imagination than attempt minutely to describe. And I again state that when this great "law of necessity" does apply, and is not improperly exercised, the taking of life is divested of unlawfulness.

But in applying this law, we must look, not only to the jeopardy in which the parties are, but also to the relations in which they stand. The slayer must be under no obligation to make his own safety secondary to the safety of others. A familiar application of this principle presents itself in the obligations which rest upon the owners of stages, steamboats, and other vehicles of transportation. In consideration of the payment of fare, the owners of the vehicle are bound to transport the passengers to the place of contemplated destination. Having, in all emergencies, the conduct of the journey, and the control of the passengers, the owners rest under every obligation for care, skill, and general capacity; and if, from defect of any of these requisites, grievous injury is done to the passenger, the persons employed are liable. The passenger owes no duty but submission. He is under no obligation to protect and keep the conductor in safety, nor is the passenger bound to labour, except in cases of emergency, where his services are required by unanticipated and uncommon danger. Such is the relation which exists on shipboard. The passenger stands in a position different from that of the officers and seamen. It is the sailor who must encounter the hardships and perils of the voyage. Nor can this relation be changed when the ship is lost by tempest or other danger of the sea, and all on board have betaken themselves, for safety, to the small boats; for imminence of danger can not absolve from duty. The sailor is bound, as before, to undergo whatever hazard is necessary to preserve the boat and the passengers. Should the emergency become so extreme as to call for the sacrifice of life, there can be no reason why the law does not still remain the same. The passenger, not being bound either to labour or to incur the risk of life, cannot be bound to sacrifice his existence to preserve the sailor's. The captain, indeed, and a sufficient number of seamen to navigate the boat, must be preserved; for, except these abide in the ship, all will perish.

But if there be more seamen than are necessary to manage the boat, the supernumerary sailors have no right, for their safety, to sacrifice the passengers. The sailors and passengers, in fact, cannot be regarded as in equal positions. The sailor (to use the language of a distinguished writer) owes more benevolence to another than to himself. He is bound to set a greater value on the life of others than on his own. And while we admit that sailor and sailor may lawfully struggle with each other for the plank which can save but one, we think that, if the passenger is on the plank, even "the law of necessity" justifies not the sailor who takes it from him. This rule may be deemed a harsh one towards the sailor, who may have thus far done his duty, but when the danger is so extreme, that the only hope is in sacrificing either a sailor or a passenger, any alternative is hard; and would it not be the hardest of any to sacrifice a passenger in order to save a supernumerary sailor?

But, in addition, if the source of the danger have been obvious, and destruction ascertained to be certainly about to arrive, though at a future time, there should be consultation, and some mode of selection fixed, by which those in equal relations may have equal chance for their life. By what mode, then, should selection be made? The question is not without difficulty; nor do we know of any rule prescribed, either by statute or by common law, or even by speculative writers on the law of nature. In fact, no rule of general application can be prescribed for contingencies which are wholly unforeseen. There is, however, one condition of extremity for which all writers have prescribed the same rule. When the ship is in no danger of sinking, but all sustenance is exhausted, and a sacrifice of one person is necessary to appease the hunger of others, the selection is made by lot. This mode is resorted to as the fairest mode, and, in some sort, as an appeal to God, for selection of the victim. This manner, obviously, was regarded by the mate, in parting with the captain, as the one which it was proper to adopt, in case the long-boat could not live with all who were on board on Tuesday morning. The same manner, as would appear from the response given to the mate, had already suggested itself to the captain. For ourselves, we can conceive of no mode so consonant both to humanity and to justice; and the occasion, we think, must be peculiar which will dispense with its exercise. If, indeed, the peril be instant and overwhelming, leaving no chance of means, and no moment for deliberation, then, of course, there is no power to consult, to cast lots, or in any such way to decide; but even where the final disaster is thus sudden, if it have been foreseen as certainly about to arrive, if no new cause of danger have arisen to bring on the closing catastrophe, if time have existed to cast lots, and to select the victims, then, as we have said, sortition should be adopted. In no other than this or some like way are those having equal rights put upon an equal footing, and in no other way is it possible to guard against partiality and oppression, violence and conflict. What scene, indeed, more horrible, can imagination draw than a struggle between sailor and sailor, passenger and passenger, or, it may be, a mixed affray, in which, promiscuously, all destroy one another? This, too, in circumstances which have allowed time to decide, with justice, whose life should be calmly surrendered.

When the selection has been made by lots, the victim yields of course to his fate, or, if he resist, force may be employed to coerce submission. Whether or not "a case of necessity" has arisen, or whether the law under which death has been inflicted have been so exercised as to hold the executioner harmless, cannot depend on his own opinion; for no man may pass upon his own conduct when it concerns the rights, and especially, when it affects the lives of others. We have already stated to you that, by the law of the land, homicide is sometimes justifiable; and the law defines the occasion in which it is so. The transaction must, therefore, be justified to the law; and the person accused rests under obligation to satisfy those who judicially scrutinize his case that it really transcended ordinary rules. In fact, any other principle would be followed by pernicious results, and, moreover, would not be practicable in application. Opinion or belief may be assumed, whether it exist or not; and if this mere opinion of the sailors will justify them in making a sacrifice of the passengers, of course, the mere opinion of the passengers would, in turn, justify these in making a sacrifice of the sailors. The passengers may have confidence in their own capacity to manage and preserve the boat, or the effort of either sailors or passengers to save the boat, may be clearly unavailing; and what, then, in a struggle against force and numbers, becomes of the safety of the seamen? Hard as is a seaman's life, would it not become yet more perilous if the passengers, who may outnumber them tenfold, should be allowed to judge when the dangers of the sea will justify a sacrifice of life? We are, therefore, satisfied, that, in requiring proof, which shall be satisfactory to you, of the existence of the necessity, we are fixing the rule which is, not merely the only one which is practicable, but, moreover, the only one which will secure the safety of the sailors themselves.

The court said, briefly, that the principles which had been laid down by them, as applicable to the crew, applied to the mate likewise, and that his order (on which much stress had been laid), if an unlawful order, would be no justification to the seamen, for that even seamen are not justified, in law, by obedience to commands which are unlawful. The court added that the case was one which involved questions of gravest consideration and, as the facts, in some sort, were without precedent, that the court preferred to state the law, in the shape of such general principles as would comprehend the case, under any view which the jury might take of the evidence. After a few remarks upon the evidence, the case was given to the jury, who, about 16 hours afterwards, and after having once returned to the bar, unable to agree, with some difficulty, found a verdict of guilty. The prisoner was, however, recommended to the mercy of the court . . .

When the prisoner was brought up for sentence, the learned judge said to him, that many circumstances in the affair were of a character to commend him to regard, yet, that the case was one in which some punishment was demanded; that it was in the power of the court to inflict the penalty of an imprisonment for a term of three years, and a fine of $1,000, but, in view of all the circumstances, and, especially as the prisoner had been already confined in gaol several months, that the court would make the punishment more lenient. The convict was then sentenced to undergo an imprisonment in the Eastern Penitentiary of Pennsylvania, (solitary confinement) at hard labour, for the term of six months, and to pay a fine of $20.

Note from Tiffany: If the jury in *Holmes* followed the judge's instruction, why do you think they convicted Holmes? Which element of the necessity defense (as explained by the judge) was missing?

THE QUEEN v. DUDLEY & STEPHENS
England, Queen's Bench
14 Q.B. 273 (1884)

Indictment for the murder of Richard Parker on the high seas within the jurisdiction of the Admiralty.

At the trial before Huddleston, B., at the Devon and Cornwall Winter Assizes, November 7, 1884, the jury, at the suggestion of the learned judge, found the facts of the case in a special verdict which stated "that on July 5, 1884, the prisoners, Thomas Dudley and Edward Stephens, with one Brooks, all able-bodied English seamen, and the deceased also an English boy, between seventeen and eighteen years of age, the crew of an English yacht, a registered English vessel, were cast away in a storm on the high seas 1,600 miles from the Cape of Good Hope, and were compelled to put into an open boat belonging to the said yacht. That in this boat they had no supply of water and no supply of food, except two 1-pound tins of turnips, and for three days, they had nothing else to subsist upon. That on the fourth day they caught a small turtle, upon which they subsisted for a few days, and this was the only food they had up to the twentieth day when the act now in question was committed. That on the twelfth day, the remains of the turtle were entirely consumed, and for the next eight days, they had nothing to eat. That they had no fresh water, except such rain as they from time to time caught in their oilskin capes. That the boat was drifting on the ocean, and was probably more than 1,000 miles away from land. That on the eighteenth day, when they had been seven days without food and five without water, the prisoners spoke to Brooks as to what should be done if no succour came, and suggested that some one should be sacrificed to save the rest, but Brooks dissented, and the boy, to whom they were understood to refer, was not consulted. That on the 24th of July, the day before the act now in question, the prisoner Dudley proposed to Stephens and Brooks that lots should be cast who should be put to death to save the rest, but Brooks refused to consent, and it was not put to the boy, and in point of fact, there was no drawing of lots. That on that day, the prisoners spoke of their having families, and suggested it would be better to kill the boy that their lives should be saved, and Dudley proposed that if there was no vessel in sight by the morrow morning, the boy should be killed. That next day, the 25th of July, no vessel appearing, Dudley told Brooks that he had better go and have a sleep, and made signs to Stephens and Brooks that the boy had better be killed. The prisoner Stephens agreed to the act, but Brooks dissented from it. That the boy was then lying at the bottom of the boat quite helpless, and extremely weakened by famine and by drinking sea water, and unable to make any resistance, nor did he ever assent to his being killed. The prisoner Dudley offered a prayer asking forgiveness for them all if either of them should be tempted to commit a rash act, and that their souls might be saved. That Dudley, with the assent of Stephens, went to the boy, and telling him that his time was come, put a knife into his throat and killed him then and there; that the three men fed upon the body and blood of the boy for four days; that on the fourth day after the act had been committed, the boat was picked up by a passing vessel, and the prisoners were rescued, still alive, but in the lowest state of prostration. That they were carried to the port of Falmouth, and committed for trial at Exeter. That if the men had not fed upon the body of the boy they would probably not have survived to be so picked up and rescued, but would within the four days have died of famine. That the boy, being in a much weaker condition, was likely to have died before them. That, at the time of the act in question, there was no sail in sight, nor any reasonable prospect of relief. That, under these circumstances, there appeared to the prisoners every probability that, unless they then fed or very soon fed upon the boy or one of themselves, they would die of starvation. That there was no appreciable chance of saving life except by killing some one for the others to eat. That, assuming any necessity to kill anybody, there was no greater necessity for killing the boy than any of the other three men. But, whether upon the whole matter by the jurors found the killing of Richard Parker by Dudley and Stephens be felony and murder, the jurors are ignorant, and pray the advice of the Court thereupon, and if upon the whole matter the Court shall be of opinion that the killing of Richard Parker be felony and murder, then the jurors say that Dudley and Stephens were each guilty of felony and murder as alleged in the indictment."

On the application of the Crown, the case was ordered to be argued before a Court consisting of five judges.

Sir H. James, A.G., arguing for the Crown: With regard to the substantial question in the case — whether the prisoners in killing Parker were guilty of murder - the law is that, where a private person acting upon his own judgment takes the life of a fellow creature, his act can only be justified on the ground of self-defence — self-defence against the acts of the person whose life is taken. This principle has been extended to include the case of a man killing another to prevent him from committing some great crime upon a third person. But the principle has no application to this case, for the prisoners were not protecting themselves against any act of Parker. If he had had food in his possession and they had taken it from him, they would have been guilty of theft; and if they killed him to obtain this food, they would have been guilty of murder.

A. Collins, Q.C., arguing for the prisoners: The facts found on the special verdict shew that the prisoners were not guilty of murder, at the time when they killer Parker, but killed him under the pressure of necessity. Necessity will excuse an act which would otherwise be a crime. The law as to compulsion by necessity is further explained in Stephen's History of the Criminal Law, and an opinion is expressed that in the case often put by casuists, of two drowning men on a plank large enough to support one only, and one thrusting the other off, the survivor could not be subjected to legal punishment. In the American case of *The United States v. Holmes*, the proposition that a passenger on board a vessel may be thrown overboard to save the others is sanctioned. Lord Bacon gives the instance of two shipwrecked persons clinging to the same plank and one of them thrusting the other from it, finding that it will not support both, and says that this homicide is excusable through unavoidable necessity and upon the great universal principle of self-preservation, which prompts every man to save his own life in preference to that of another, where one of them must inevitably perish. It is true that Hale's Pleas of the Crown states distinctly that hunger is no excuse for theft, but that is on the ground that there can be no such extreme necessity in this country. In the present case, the prisoners were in circumstances where no assistance could be given. The essence of the crime of murder is intention, and here the intention of the prisoners was only to preserve their lives.

LORD COLERIDGE, C.J.

The two prisoners, Thomas Dudley and Edwin Stephens, were indicted for the murder of Richard Parker on the high seas on the 25th of July in the present year. They were tried before my Brother Huddleston at Exeter on the 6th of November, and, under the direction of my learned Brother, the jury returned a special verdict, the legal effect of which has been argued before us, and on which we are now to pronounce judgment.

From these facts, stated with the cold precision of a special verdict, it appears sufficiently that the prisoners were subject to terrible temptation, to sufferings which might break down the bodily power of the strongest man, and try the conscience of the best. Other details yet more harrowing, facts still more loathsome and appalling, were presented to the jury, and are to be found recorded in my learned Brother's notes. But nevertheless, this is clear, that the prisoners put to death a weak and unoffending boy upon the chance of preserving their own lives by feeding upon his flesh and blood after he was killed, and with the certainty of depriving *him* of any possible chance of survival. The verdict finds in terms that "if the men had not fed upon the body of the boy they would *probably* not have survived," and that "the boy being in a much weaker condition was *likely* to have died before them." They might possibly have been picked up next day by a passing ship; they might possibly not have been picked up at all; in either case it is obvious that the killing of the boy would have been an unnecessary and profitless act. It is found by the verdict that the boy was incapable of resistance, and, in fact, made none; and it is not even suggested that his death was due to any violence on his part attempted against, or even so much as feared by, those who killed him. * * * *

There remains to be considered the real question in the case — whether killing under the circumstances set forth in the verdict be or be not murder. The contention that it could be anything else was, to the minds of us all, both new and strange, and we stopped the Attorney General in his negative argument in order that we might hear what could be said in support of a proposition which appeared to us to be at once dangerous, immoral, and opposed to all legal principle and analogy. * * * *

Is there, then, any authority for the proposition which has been presented to us? Decided cases there are none. * * * * The American case cited by my Brother Stephen in his Digest, from Wharton on Homicide, in which it was decided, correctly indeed, that sailors had no right to throw passengers overboard to save themselves, but on the somewhat strange ground that the proper mode of determining who was to be sacrificed was to vote upon the subject by ballot, can hardly, as my Brother Stephen says, be an authority satisfactory to a court in this country. * * * *

The one real authority of former time is Lord Bacon, who, in his commentary on the maxim, "necessitas inducit privilegium quoad jura privata," lays down the law as follows. "Necessity carrieth a privilege in itself. Necessity is of three sorts - necessity of conservation of life, necessity of obedience, and necessity of the act of God or of a stranger. First of conservation of life; if a man steal viands to satisfy his present hunger, this is no felony nor larceny. So if divers be in danger of drowning by the casting away of some boat or barge, and one of them get to some plank, or on the boat's side to keep himself above water, and another to save his life thrust him from it, whereby he is drowned, this is neither se defendendo nor by misadventure, but justifiable." On this it is to be observed that Lord Bacon's proposition that stealing to satisfy hunger is no larceny is hardly supported by Staundforde, whom he cites for it, and is expressly contradicted by Lord Hale in the passage already cited. And for the proposition as to the plank or boat, it is said to be derived from the canonists. At any rate he cites no authority for it, and it must stand upon his own. Lord Bacon was great even as a lawyer; but it is permissible to much smaller men, relying, upon principle and on the authority of others, the equals and even the superiors of Lord Bacon as lawyers, to question the soundness of his dictum. There are many conceivable states of things in which it might possibly be true, but if Lord Bacon meant to lay down the broad proposition that a man may save his life by killing, if necessary, an innocent and unoffending neighbour, it certainly is not law at the present day. * * * *

Now, except for the purpose of testing how far the conservation of a man's own life is in all cases and under all circumstances, an absolute, unqualified, and paramount duty, we exclude from our consideration all the incidents of war. We are dealing with a case of private homicide, not one imposed upon men in the service of their Sovereign and in the defence of their country. Now it is admitted that the deliberate killing of this unoffending and unresisting boy was clearly murder, unless the killing can be justified by some well-recognised excuse admitted by the law. It is further admitted that there was in this case no such excuse, unless the killing was justified by what has been called "necessity." But the temptation to the act which existed here was not what the law has ever called necessity. Nor is this to be regretted. Though law and morality are not the same, and many things may be immoral which are not necessarily illegal, yet the absolute divorce of law from morality would be of fatal consequence; and such divorce would follow if the temptation to murder in this case were to be held by law an absolute defence of it.

It is not so. To preserve one's life is generally speaking a duty, but it may be the plainest and the highest duty to sacrifice it. War is full of instances in which it is a man's duty not to live, but to die. The duty, in case of shipwreck, of a captain to his crew, of the crew to the passengers, of soldiers to women and children, as in the noble case of the *Birkenhead*; these duties impose on men the moral necessity, not of the preservation, but of the sacrifice of their lives for others, from which in no country, least of all, it is to be hoped, in England, will men ever shrink, as indeed, they have not shrunk.

It is not correct, therefore, to say that there is any absolute or unqualified necessity to preserve one's life. "Necesse est ut eam, non ut vivam," is a saying of a Roman officer quoted by Lord Bacon himself with high eulogy in the very chapter on necessity to which so much reference has been made. It would be a very easy and cheap display of commonplace learning to quote from Greek and Latin authors, from Horace, from Juvenal, from Cicero, from Euripides, passage after passage, in which the duty of dying for others has been laid down in glowing and emphatic language as resulting from the principles of heathen ethics; it is enough in a Christian country to remind ourselves of the Great Example whom we profess to follow. It is not needful to point out the awful danger of admitting the principle which has been contended for. Who is to be the judge of this sort of necessity? By what measure is the comparative value of lives to be measured? Is it to be strength, or intellect or what? It is plain that the principle leaves to him who is to profit by it to determine the necessity which will justify him in deliberately taking another's life to save his own. In this case the weakest, the youngest, the most unresisting, was chosen. Was it more necessary to kill him than one of the grown men? The answer must be "No" -

So spake the Fiend, and with necessity,

The tyrant's plea, excused his devilish deeds.

It is not suggested that in this particular case the deeds were "devilish," but it is quite plain that such a principle once admitted might be made the legal cloak for unbridled passion and atrocious crime. There is no safe path for judges to tread but to ascertain the law to the best of their ability and to declare it according to their judgment; and if in any case the law appears to be too severe on individuals, to leave it to the sovereign to exercise that prerogative of mercy which the Constitution has intrusted to the hands fittest to dispense it.

It must not be supposed that in refusing to admit temptation to be an excuse for crime it is forgotten how terrible the temptation was; how awful the suffering; how hard in such trials to keep the judgment straight and the conduct pure. We are often compelled to set up standards we cannot reach ourselves, and to lay down rules which we could not ourselves satisfy. But a man has no right to declare temptation to be an excuse, though he might himself have yielded to it, nor allow compassion for the criminal to change or weaken in any manner the legal definition of the crime. It is therefore our duty to declare that the prisoners' act in this case was murder, that the facts as stated in the verdict are no legal justification of the homicide; and to say that in our unanimous opinion the prisoners are upon this special verdict guilty of murder.[15]

The Court then proceeded to pass sentence of death upon the prisoners.[16]

NOTES FROM TIFFANY:

(1) For the story behind this case and the context in which it arose, see Neil Hanson, *The Custom of the Sea* (John Wiley & Sons, 2000).

---

[15] My brother Grove has furnished me with the following suggestion, too late to be embodied in the judgment but well worth preserving: "If the two accused men were justified in killing Parker, then if not rescued in time, two of the three survivors would be justified in killing the third, and of the two who remained, the stronger would be justified in killing the weaker, so that three men might be justifiably killed to give the fourth a chance of surviving."

[16] This sentence was afterwards commuted by the Crown to six months' imprisonment.

(2) Assume that, unless one of the four were killed and eaten, all four would certainly die. Did the court hold that there is *no* permissible way to select which one to kill — that all four have a duty to die? If so, does this make sense?

(3) Suppose the boy had *consented* to being killed, to save the others. Should this "method of selection" be a valid defense?

(4) Assuming that *some* method of selection is valid, which one? Select the weakest, as he is less likely to survive anyway? Select the oldest, as he has less years of life remaining? Select the heaviest, as he will feed the other three for a longer period? Select the one who does not have a family depending on him for support (the method apparently used by the defendants)? Select the one whose occupation contributes the least to society? Examine all of these factors, and assign points to each? Draw lots? If all of these seem rational, may the defendants choose *any* of them?

UNITED STATES v. CONTENTO-PACHON
U.S. Court of Appeals, 9th Circuit
723 F.2d 691 (1984)

BOOCHEVER, CIRCUIT JUDGE.

This case presents an appeal from a conviction for unlawful possession with intent to distribute a narcotic controlled substance in violation of 21 U.S.C. § 841(a)(1). At trial, the defendant attempted to offer evidence of duress and necessity defenses. The district court excluded this evidence on the ground that it was insufficient to support the defenses. We reverse because there was sufficient evidence of duress to present a triable issue of fact.

The defendant-appellant, Juan Manuel Contento-Pachon, is a native of Bogota, Colombia and was employed there as a taxicab driver. He asserts that one of his passengers, Jorge, offered him a job as the driver of a privately-owned car. Contento-Pachon expressed an interest in the job and agreed to meet Jorge and the owner of the car the next day. Instead of a driving job, Jorge proposed that Contento-Pachon swallow cocaine-filled balloons and transport them to the United States. Contento-Pachon agreed to consider the proposition. He was told not to mention the proposition to anyone, otherwise he would "get into serious trouble." Contento-Pachon testified that he did not contact the police because he believes that the Bogota police are corrupt and that they are paid off by drug traffickers.

Approximately one week later, Contento-Pachon told Jorge that he would not carry the cocaine. In response, Jorge mentioned facts about Contento-Pachon's personal life, including private details which Contento-Pachon had never mentioned to Jorge. Jorge told Contento-Pachon that his failure to cooperate would result in the death of his wife and three year-old child. The following day the pair met again. Contento-Pachon's life and the lives of his family were again threatened. At this point, Contento-Pachon agreed to take the cocaine into the United States.

The pair met two more times. At the last meeting, Contento-Pachon swallowed

129 balloons of cocaine. He was informed that he would be watched at all times during the trip, and that if he failed to follow Jorge's instruction he and his family would be killed. After leaving Bogota, Contento-Pachon's plane landed in Panama. Contento-Pachon asserts that he did not notify the authorities there because he felt that the Panamanian police were as corrupt as those in Bogota. Also, he felt that any such action on his part would place his family in jeopardy. When he arrived at the customs inspection point in Los Angeles, Contento-Pachon consented to have his stomach x-rayed. The x-rays revealed a foreign substance which was later determined to be cocaine.

At Contento-Pachon's trial, the government moved to exclude the defenses of duress and necessity. The motion was granted. We reverse.

A. *Duress*

There are three elements of the duress defense: (1) an immediate threat of death or serious bodily injury, (2) a well-grounded fear that the threat will be carried out, and (3) no reasonable opportunity to escape the threatened harm. Sometimes a fourth element is required: the defendant must submit to proper authorities after attaining a position of safety. *United States v. Peltier*, 693 F.2d 96 (9th cir. 1982).

Factfinding is usually a function of the jury, and the trial court rarely rules on a defense as a matter of law. If the evidence is insufficient as a matter of law to support a duress defense, however, the trial court should exclude that evidence.

The trial court found Contento-Pachon's offer of proof insufficient to support a duress defense because he failed to offer proof of two elements: immediacy and inescapability.[1] We examine the elements of duress.

Immediacy: The element of immediacy requires that there be some evidence that the threat of injury was present, immediate, or impending. "A veiled threat of future unspecified harm" will not satisfy this requirement. *Rhode Island Recreation Center v. Aetna Casualty and Surety Co.*, 177 F.2d 603, 605 (1st cir. 1949). The district court found that the initial threats were not immediate because "they were conditioned on defendant's failure to cooperate in the future and did not place defendant and his family in immediate danger."

Evidence presented on this issue indicated that the defendant was dealing with a man who was deeply involved in the exportation of illegal substances. Large sums of money were at stake and, consequently, Contento-Pachon had reason to believe that Jorge would carry out his threats. Jorge had gone to the trouble to discover that Contento-Pachon was married, that he had a child, the names of his wife and child, and the location of his residence. These were not vague threats of possible future harm. According to the defendant, if he had refused to cooperate, the consequences would have been immediate and harsh. Contento-Pachon contends that he was being watched by one of Jorge's accomplices at all times during the airplane trip. As a consequence, the force of the threats continued to restrain him.

---

[1] We believe that a triable issue was presented as to the third element, that the fear be well-grounded, based on the same facts that lead us to the conclusion as to the immediacy of the threats.

Contento-Pachon's contention that he was operating under the threat of immediate harm was supported by sufficient evidence to present a triable issue of fact.

Escapability: The defendant must show that he had no reasonable opportunity to escape. See *United States v. Gordon*, 526 F.2d 406, 407 (9th cir. 1975). The district court found that because Contento-Pachon was not physically restrained prior to the time he swallowed the balloons, he could have sought help from the police or fled. Contento-Pachon explained that he did not report the threats because he feared that the police were corrupt. The trier of fact should decide whether one in Contento-Pachon's position might believe that some of the Bogota police were paid informants for drug traffickers and that reporting the matter to the police did not represent a reasonable opportunity of escape.

If he chose not to go to the police, Contento-Pachon's alternative was to flee. We reiterate that the opportunity to escape must be reasonable. To flee, Contento-Pachon, along with his wife and three year-old child, would have been forced to pack his possessions, leave his job, and travel to a place beyond the reaches of the drug traffickers. A juror might find that this was not a reasonable avenue of escape. Thus, Contento-Pachon presented a triable issue on the element of escapability.

Surrender to Authorities: As noted above, the duress defense is composed of at least three elements. The government argues that the defense also requires that a defendant offer evidence that he intended to turn himself in to the authorities upon reaching a position of safety. Although it has not been expressly limited, this fourth element seems to be required only in prison escape cases. *United States v. Peltier*, 693 F.2d 96, (9th cir. 1982). Under other circumstances, the defense has been defined to include only three elements. *United States v. Shapiro*, 669 F.2d 593 (9th cir. 1982) (sale of drugs); *United States v. Atencio*, 586 F.2d 744 (9th cir. 1978) (failure to appear for trial); and *United States v. Wood*, 566 F.2d 1108 (9th Cir. 1977) (carrying a knife in a federal prison). The Supreme Court in *United States v. Bailey*, 444 U.S. 394 (1980), noted that "escape from federal custody is a continuing offense and an escapee can be held liable for failure to return to custody as well as for his initial departure." This factor would not be present in most crimes other than escape.

In cases not involving escape from prison there seems little difference between the third basic requirement that there be no reasonable opportunity to escape the threatened harm and the obligation to turn oneself in to authorities on reaching a point of safety. Once a defendant has reached a position where he can safely turn himself in to the authorities he will likewise have a reasonable opportunity to escape the threatened harm.

That is true in this case. Contento-Pachon claims that he was being watched at all times. According to him, at the first opportunity to cooperate with authorities without alerting the observer, he consented to the x-ray. We hold that a defendant who has acted under a well-grounded fear of immediate harm with no opportunity to escape may assert the duress defense, if there is a triable issue of fact whether he took the opportunity to escape the threatened harm by submitting to authorities at the first reasonable opportunity.

B. *Necessity*

The defense of necessity is available when a person is faced with a choice of two evils and must then decide whether to commit a crime or an alternative act that constitutes a greater evil. Contento-Pachon has attempted to justify his violation of 21 U.S.C. § 841(a)(1) by showing that the alternative, the death of his family, was a greater evil. Traditionally, in order for the necessity defense to apply, the coercion must have had its source in the physical forces of nature. The duress defense was applicable when the defendant's acts were coerced by a human force. W. LaFave & A. Scott, *Handbook on Criminal Law* § 50 at 383 (1972). This distinction served to separate the two similar defenses. But modern courts have tended to blur the distinction between duress and necessity.

It has been suggested that, "the major difference between duress and necessity is that the former negates the existence of the requisite mens rea for the crime in question, whereas under the latter theory there is no actus reus." *United States v. Micklus*, 581 F.2d 612, 615 (7th cir. 1978). The theory of necessity is that the defendant's free will was properly exercised to achieve the greater good and not that his free will was overcome by an outside force as with duress.

The defense of necessity is usually invoked when the defendant acted in the interest of the general welfare. For example, defendants have asserted the defense as a justification for (1) bringing laetrile into the United States for the treatment of cancer patients, *Richardson*, 588 F.2d at 1239; (2) unlawfully entering a naval base to protest the Trident missile system, *United States v. May*, 622 F.2d 1000, (9th Cir.); (3) burning Selective Service System records to protest United States military action, *United States v. Simpson*, 460 F.2d 515, (9th cir. 1972).

Contento-Pachon's acts were allegedly coerced by human, not physical forces. In addition, he did not act to promote the general welfare. Therefore, the necessity defense was not available to him. Contento-Pachon mischaracterized evidence of duress as evidence of necessity. The district court correctly disallowed his use of the necessity defense.

II. *Conclusion*

Contento-Pachon presented credible evidence that he acted under an immediate and well-grounded threat of serious bodily injury, with no opportunity to escape. Because the trier of fact should have been allowed to consider the credibility of the proffered evidence,[2] we reverse. The district court correctly excluded Contento-Pachon's necessity defense.

Reversed and remanded.

---

[2] The dissent takes the position that the trial court made findings adverse to the duress defense which were supported by the record. That would be an appropriate test if the case had been tried by the judge without a jury. We acknowledge that the record in this case will support a finding of guilty. The problem is that there has been evidence tendered which, if found credible by the jury, would justify a determination that Contento-Pachon acted under duress. A defendant has the right to have a jury resolve the disputed factual issues.

COYLE, DISTRICT JUDGE (dissenting in part and concurring in part):

In order to establish a defense of duress, the trial court in this case required Contento-Pachon to show (1) that he or his family was under an immediate threat of death or serious bodily injury; (2) that he had a well grounded fear that the threat would be carried out; and (3) that he had no reasonable opportunity to escape the threat. Applying this three-part test, the trial court found that the defendant's offer of proof was insufficient to support a defense of duress.

The government argues that this holding should be affirmed and I agree. The government also contends that the defense of duress includes a fourth element: that a defendant demonstrate that he submitted to proper authorities after attaining a position of safety. This is not an unreasonable requirement and I believe it should be applied. I do not agree with the majority's conclusion that the fourth element of the duress defense is only required in prison escape cases. Cases applying the fourth element have not so expressly limited its application. See, e.g., *United States v. Peltier*, 693 F.2d 96 (9th cir. 1982); *United States v. Campbell*, 609 F.2d 922 (8th cir. 1979); *United States v. Michelson*, 559 F.2d 567 (9th cir. 1977). The distinction which the majority attempts to draw between prison escape cases and non-prison escape cases is not persuasive. The force of threats which allegedly excused the defendant's failure to submit to proper authorities upon his arrival in Los Angeles are no more present, immediate, or impending than the force of threats or fear of retaliation faced by a "snitch" upon his return to prison after an escape.

In granting the government's motion *in limine* excluding the defense of duress, the trial court specifically found Contento-Pachon had failed to present sufficient evidence to establish the necessary elements of immediacy and inescapability. In its order the district court stated:

> The first threat made to defendant and his family about three weeks before the flight was not immediate; the threat was conditioned upon defendant's failure to cooperate in the future and did not place the defendant and his family in immediate danger or harm. Moreover, after the initial threat and until he went to the house where he ingested the balloons containing cocaine, defendant and his family were not physically restrained and could have sought help from the police or fled. No such efforts were attempted by defendant. Thus, defendant's own offer of proof negates two necessary elements of the defense of duress.

In cases where the defendant's duress has been raised, the courts have indicated that the element of immediacy is of crucial importance. See, e.g., *United States v. Atencio*, 586 F.2d 744 (9th cir. 1978); *United States v. Patrick*, 542 F.2d 381 (7th cir. 1976). The trial court found that the threats made against the defendant and his family lacked the requisite element of immediacy. This finding is adequately supported by the record. The defendant was outside the presence of the drug dealers on numerous occasions for varying lengths of time. There is no evidence that his family was ever directly threatened or even had knowledge of the threats allegedly directed against the defendant.

Moreover, the trial court found that the defendant and his family enjoyed an adequate and reasonable opportunity to avoid or escape the threats of the drug dealers in the weeks before his flight. Until he went to the house where he ingested the balloons containing cocaine, defendant and his family were not physically restrained or prevented from seeking help. The record supports the trial court's findings that the defendant and his family could have sought assistance from the authorities or have fled. Cases considering the defense of duress have established that where there was a reasonable legal alternative to violating the law, a chance to refuse to do the criminal act and also to avoid the threatened danger, the defense will fail. Duress is permitted as a defense only when a criminal act was committed because there was no other opportunity to avoid the threatened danger. *United States v. Hernandez*, 608 F.2d 741 (9th cir. 1979).

The district court is vested with broad discretion whether to admit or exclude proffered evidence and its rulings will not be overturned on review without a clear showing of abuse of discretion. * * * * Because the district court's decision granting the government's motion *in limine* is fully and adequately supported by the record, I cannot agree that the district court abused its discretion and I therefore respectfully dissent. I agree with the majority, however, that the district court properly excluded Contento-Pachon's necessity defense.

NOTES FROM TIFFANY:

(1) The majority found that defendant presented enough evidence to show duress, but not necessity. Why? What is the difference between the two defenses? How does this difference apply to our case?

(2) Compare *Contento-Pachon* with the following cases. Can they be reconciled?

In *Williams v. State*, 646 A.2d 1101 (Md.App.1994), defendant was charged with attempted robbery and housebreaking. He claimed duress, testifying that in the past he had picked up drugs for a drug dealer (Eubanks), and three men threatened to kill defendant unless he took them to Eubanks' "stash house." Noting that the Model Penal Code makes duress unavailable when defendant "recklessly placed himself in a situation in which it was probable that he would be subjected to duress," the court held that the trial court properly rejected the defense, as "This was a situation that would not have occurred but for Williams's association with the drug organization."

In *U.S. v. Gomez*, 81 F.3d 846 (9th Cir. 1996), defendant was charged with being a felon in possession of a firearm. Defendant alleged that a drug dealer had asked him to kill several people, defendant had reported this to federal authorities, who then obtained an indictment against the dealer for solicitation to commit murder — the indictment including defendant's name. The dealer then threatened to kill defendant, who asked federal agents and the local sheriff's department for protection. Both refused, so defendant armed himself with a shotgun. The trial court rejected this defense, but the Court of Appeals reversed, holding that this was a proper "justification" defense rather than a necessity or duress defense (though the three are "closely related"). The court held that, if defendant's allegations were true, he had no reasonable legal alternative.

In *People v. Metters*, 61 Cal.App.4th 1489 (1998) (review granted on another issue by California Supreme Court, 6/10/98), Metters robbed a cashier at a Wendy's restaurant. He presented evidence of the following:

> On the day of the holdup, appellant was abducted by drug dealers to whom he owed money. He was permitted to make telephone calls to attempt to raise the money. He contacted his aunt, who brought $50 to the dealers. They took the $50 and agreed to free appellant after warning him that he and his family would be killed unless he repaid the rest of the money that night. Appellant committed the robbery in order to prevent the dealers from killing him and his family.

> "As a backdrop," the offer of proof included facts predating the date of the robbery. In February 1994, appellant was shot at by the same drug dealers. He contacted the police and attempted to have his parole revoked because he feared for his life. Appellant met with his parole agent, who placed him on a waiting list for a halfway house in another part of Oakland. He lost this placement when he was erroneously transported to San Quentin State Prison on a parole hold. Upon his release, appellant was forced to return to his old neighborhood until another placement became available. * * * *

> Oakland Police Sergeant Sharon Banks testified that she had interviewed appellant on February 28, 1994, shortly after the previous shooting incident had occurred. During their interview, appellant told her someone had shot at him. Appellant also informed Banks that he was in trouble because he owed drug dealers $500 for crack. He requested that Banks [have his parole terminated] for drug possession so he could be sent back to prison. She passed this information along to his parole agent. Banks took no further action because appellant did not request an investigation of the shooting, did not request police protection, and did not provide her with sufficient facts to commence an investigation.

> California Department of Corrections Parole Agent Ramon DeCastro testified appellant met with him earlier in 1994 to request assistance with housing and employment. Appellant told him he wanted to get out of his current living environment. DeCastro arranged for appellant to be placed on a waiting list for a halfway house. Appellant obtained a job at the Old Spaghetti Factory in Oakland. Appellant lost his placement on the waiting list when he was transported to San Quentin State Prison on a parole hold. Later, appellant was released because there was no evidence of parole violations. Although DeCastro received information concerning appellant's conversation with Sergeant Banks, he did not recall appellant contacting him to discuss the shooting incident or his request to return to prison.

> Appellant's supervisor at the Old Spaghetti Factory testified that appellant was employed there sometime during April through June 1994, that he earned $5.45 per hour for 15-20 hours of work per week, and that he was paid every other Sunday. The company does not give salary advances to its employees.

Appellant's aunt, Mary Metters, testified that she lived near an area where illicit drugs were sold. She had "heard" of a number of instances where drug dealers retaliated against people who reported them to the police. On the date of the robbery, appellant telephoned her and asked her to bring $50 to a specified location. He told her that he "owed some guys some money" and that "he was being held against his will." She delivered the money to appellant between 4 and 5 p.m. Appellant's aunt did not contact the police because she feared retaliation. If she thought appellant's life was in danger, appellant's aunt would have given him whatever money she "had to give." Although she did not recall the exact amount of money she had on deposit at the bank that day, appellant's aunt testified "It could have been in the area between $200 or $300." * * * *

According to appellant, he had owed $500 to drug dealers for approximately three or four years. At approximately 10:30 a.m. on the morning of the Wendy's robbery, these drug dealers kidnapped him at gunpoint. They held him for four hours while he arranged for his aunt to bring him $50 to partially pay the debt. At approximately 8 p.m., they agreed to release him as long as he returned with $200 within one hour. On direct examination, appellant testified that the drug dealers told him to "get the rest of the money however I could get it, do whatever I had to do. " He later explained that the drug dealers told him "to go out and get the money, they didn't care what I had to do to get it. If I had to rob somebody, rob somebody, do whatever I had to do to get the money." If appellant didn't return with the money, the dealers threatened to "do a drive-by" at appellant's aunt's house.

Appellant had resigned from his job with the Old Spaghetti Factory shortly before the Wendy's incident, and believed he had no legitimate way of obtaining the money. He did not seek police assistance because appellant did not think they could protect his family even if they could protect him. Appellant explained that he did not believe the police had protected him successfully in the past.

On cross-examination, appellant admitted that upon his release by the drug dealers, he did not attempt to warn his family of the threatened "drive- by," nor did he approach his aunt to borrow additional funds. Appellant testified that he decided to commit a robbery to protect himself and his family. He admitted committing the Wendy's robbery, but claimed he did not intend to permanent deprive Wendy's of the stolen money. On cross-examination, appellant acknowledged that he had no intent to return the stolen money to Wendy's. Following his arrest appellant did not report the threatened "drive- by" to the police, nor did he take subsequent steps to warn his family of the threat.

The court held that the trial court properly refused to give the jury an instruction on duress:

A threat, no matter how serious or extreme, loses its immediacy if the aggressor is not present and capable of carrying out the threatened harm at the time of the crime. Thus, absent that temporal propinquity between the threat and the crime, the defense of duress will not act legally to negate criminal intent.

Applying this principle to the case at hand, we conclude that appellant's offer of proof failed to satisfy the immediacy requirement as a matter of law. The proffered evidence clearly indicates that the drug dealers posed no threat of immediate harm. Although the drug dealers had kidnapped and threatened appellant at gunpoint earlier that day, when appellant robbed Wendy's he was no longer in the custody of the drug dealers, and the drug dealers were not physically present at the scene of the crime. Thus, appellant failed to demonstrate the existence of a "present and active aggressor threatening immediate danger" at the time the robbery was committed.

To hold otherwise would excuse the commission of a crime against an entirely innocent person on the basis of a future danger capable of being averted by innocent methods. The law cannot countenance such an anomalous result.

For a similar holding, see *McCrae v. U.S.*, 980 A.2d 1082 (D.C.Ct.App. 2009).

In *Budoo v. U.S.*, 677 A.2d 51 (D.C.App. 1996), defendant was convicted of criminal contempt for refusing to testify against suspects charged with murder. He claimed necessity, asserting that he feared retaliation from the murder suspects. The court disagreed, because he had refused to accept a reasonable alternative: the government's offer of entry into a witness protection program.

(3) In *United States v. Willis*, 38 F.3d 170 (5th cir. 1994), Kathy Willis was convicted of carrying a gun during a drug transaction. She claimed duress, testifying that her boyfriend Perez had put the gun in her purse, and she feared that he would have beaten her if she had protested. Her attorney attempted to introduce expert testimony of battered woman syndrome, but the trial court sustained the prosecution's objection, and she was convicted. The appellate court affirmed.

We hold that such evidence is not relevant. This is because in order for a duress defense to criminal liability to succeed, the coercive force of the threat must be sufficient such that a person of ordinary firmness would succumb. Model Penal Code § 2.09. Additionally, there must be no reasonable legal alternative to violating the law. These requirements set out an objective test. To consider battered woman's syndrome evidence in applying that test, however, would be to turn the objective inquiry that duress has always required into a subjective one. The question would no longer be whether a person of ordinary firmness could have resisted. Instead, the question would change to whether this individual woman, in light of the psychological condition from which she suffers, could have resisted. In addition to being contrary to settled duress law, we conclude that such a change would be unwise. Accordingly, while evidence that a defendant is suffering from the battered woman's syndrome provokes our sympathy, it is not relevant, for purposes of determining criminal responsibility, to whether the defendant acted under duress.

But see Beth I.Z. Boland, *Battered Women Who Act Under Duress*, 28 New England L.Rev. 603 (1994) and Laurie Dore, *Downward Adjustment & The Slippery Slope: The Use of Duress in Defense of Battered Offenders*, 56 Ohio State L.J. 665 (1995).

Compare *State v. VanNatta*, 149 Or.App.587, 945 P.2d 1062 (1997), where the court refused to allow defendant to support his duress defense with evidence of his "submissive character." "Whether defendant was a timid individual easily coerced is not relevant to whether, at the time of the robbery, defendant was subjected to a physical force of such a degree as to overcome earnest resistance."

(4) In *United States v. Bailey*, 444 U.S. 394 (1980), defendants were charged with violating 18 U.S.C. § 751, escape from prison. They admitted that they had escaped, but claimed that they did so because guards had beat them and threatened them with death. They requested the trial court to instruct the jury on both necessity and duress, but the court refused. They were convicted, but the Court of Appeals reversed. Supreme Court reversed the Court of Appeals, holding that, even if a defendant's initial escape was justified, he must also justify remaining out of custody, because escape is a "continuing offense" (i.e., defendant commits the offense not just by leaving the prison, but also by staying out). Therefore, to have the jury instructed on duress or necessity, "he must proffer evidence of a bona fide effort to surrender or return to custody as soon as the claimed duress or necessity had lost its coercive force" — which defendants had failed to do. The court noted that, "To hold otherwise would indeed quickly reduce the overcrowding in prisons . . ."

The Court had some difficulty deciding whether to "pigeon-hole" the case as a necessity or a duress case:

> Common law historically distinguished between the defenses of duress and necessity. Duress was said to excuse criminal conduct where the actor was under an unlawful threat of imminent death or serious bodily injury, which threat caused the actor to engage in conduct violating the literal terms of the criminal law. While the defense of duress covered the situation where the coercion had its source in the actions of other human beings, the defense of necessity, or choice of evils, traditionally covered the situation where physical forces beyond the actor's control rendered illegal conduct the lesser of two evils. Thus, where A destroyed a dike because B threatened to kill him if he did not, A would argue that he acted under duress, whereas if A destroyed the dike in order to protect more valuable property from flooding, A could claim a defense of necessity.

> Modern cases have tended to blur the distinction between duress and necessity. In the court below, the majority discarded the labels "duress" and "necessity," choosing instead to examine the policies underlying the traditional defenses. In particular, the majority felt that the defenses were designed to spare a person from punishment if he acted "under threats or conditions that a person of ordinary firmness would have been unable to resist," or if he reasonably believed that criminal action "was necessary to avoid a harm more serious than that sought to be prevented by the statute defining the offense." The Model Penal Code redefines the defenses along

similar lines. See Model Penal Code § 2.09 (duress) and § 3.02 (choice of evils).

We need not speculate now, however, on the precise contours of whatever defenses of duress or necessity are available against charges brought under § 751(a). Under any definition of these defenses one principle remains constant: if there was a reasonable, legal alternative to violating the law, "a chance both to refuse to do the criminal act and also to avoid the threatened harm," the defenses will fail. LaFave & Scott 379. Clearly, in the context of prison escape, the escapee is not entitled to claim a defense of duress or necessity unless and until he demonstrates that, given the imminence of the threat, violation of § 751 was his only reasonable alternative.

(5) In *State v. Harvill*, 234 P.3d 1166 (Wash. 2010), Harvill was charged with sale of cocaine to Nolte. Harvill claimed duress, because he feared that Holte would kill him if he did not sell the cocaine. Harvill testified that Nolte said, "You better get me some cocaine," and his tone was aggressive. While Nolte never said "or else", Harvill knew that Nolte had earlier smashed another man's head with a beer bottle, had stabbed another man, and that Nolte used steroids. The trial court held that this evidence was insufficient to justify instructing the jury on duress, because the threat was only implicit, and not explicit. The Washington Supreme Court reversed:

> Properly defining "threat" to include both explicit and implicit threats serves the purpose of the duress statute. The statute is concerned with the lesser of two evils. Faced with danger to his or another's safety, the defendant is excused for choosing the lesser evil of perpetrating a crime, unless the crime involves killing an innocent person, which is never the lesser of two evils. The defendant forfeits his excuse if by his own fault he necessitates his Hobson's choice. This purpose applies with equal force to direct threats, arising from overtly threatening words or physical intimidation, and to indirect threats, arising from other conduct and circumstances. So long as the defendant's perception of the implicit threat is reasonable under the circumstances, he is put to the choice between two evils through no fault of his own and should be allowed to argue the defense.

(6) Is duress a defense to murder? Not in California, held the court in *People v. Anderson*, 28 Cal. 4th 767 (2002):

> The basic rationale behind allowing the defense of duress for other crimes "is that, for reasons of social policy, it is better that the defendant, faced with a choice of evils, choose to do the lesser evil (violate the criminal law) in order to avoid the greater evil threatened by the other person." (LaFave, Criminal Law, *supra*, § 5.3, p. 467.) This rationale, however, is strained when a defendant is confronted with taking the life of an innocent third person in the face of a threat on his own life. When the defendant commits murder under duress, the resulting harm — i.e. the death of an innocent person-is at least as great as the threatened harm — i.e. the death of the defendant. We might add that, when confronted with an apparent kill-an-innocent-person-or-be-killed situation, a person can always choose to resist. As a practical matter, death will rarely, if ever, inevitably result from a choice not to kill. The law should require people to choose to resist

rather than kill an innocent person. A state may, of course, modify the common law rule by statute. The Model Penal Code, for example, does not exclude murder from the duress defense.

But may such an "imperfect" duress (where defendant honestly believes he will be killed by X unless he kills V) reduce a murder to voluntary manslaughter? No, held the court in *People v. Son*, 79 Cal.App.4th 224 (2000):

> Although recognizing honest and *reasonable* duress as a complete defense to some crimes, the Legislature has determined that such "perfect" duress does not warrant absolving a defendant from culpability for murder. For those same policy reasons, honest but *unreasonable* duress ("imperfect" duress) does not negate malice for purposes of reducing a defendant's culpability from murder to voluntary manslaughter.

ANDREWS v. PEOPLE
Colorado Supreme Court
800 P.2d 607 (1990)

JUSTICE ERICKSON delivered the Opinion of the Court.

The defendant-petitioners were tried and convicted by a jury in the Jefferson County Court of obstructing a roadway without a legal privilege to do so, and of disobeying the request of a peace officer to move to prevent the obstruction of the roadway in violation of §§ 18-9-107(1)(a) & (b), 8B C.R.S. (1986). An appeal was taken to the Jefferson County District Court, which affirmed the convictions. We granted certiorari to determine whether the trial court erred in ruling that the defendants' offer of proof was insufficient as a matter of law to provide the necessary foundation for invoking the choice of evils defense. We affirm.

I.

On August 9, 1987, several hundred people blocked the roadway to the east entrance of the Rocky Flats nuclear weapons plant in Jefferson County. The protest was intended to halt the manufacture of plutonium triggers by preventing the entry of workers and materials into the federal facility. The ultimate goal of the protest was to close down the Rocky Flats facility and force its conversion to a non-nuclear civilian use.

The defendants were charged and pled not guilty to violating §§ 18-9-107(1)(a) & (b). Prior to trial, the defendants jointly served notice of their intent to employ the choice of evils defense set forth in § 18-1-702, 8B C.R.S. The choice of evils defense was created by statute and may only be invoked when an offer of proof is made that establishes the requisite statutory foundation. The defendants' offer of proof consisted of fifteen affidavits from experts in the fields of sociology, international law, public health, and nuclear weapons production.[1] Defense counsel advised the

---

[1] The following persons provided affidavits supporting the offer of proof: Elise Boulding, Adjunct Professor of Sociology at the University of Colorado at Boulder; George A. Johnson, practicing attorney;

court that the affiants were willing to testify as expert witnesses at trial. The trial court ruled that the offer of proof was insufficient as a matter of law to establish the statutory foundation required for the choice of evils defense.

At trial, the defendants did not deny they were obstructing traffic and disobeyed the request of the State Patrol officers to move. The jury found all the defendants guilty of obstructing a highway or other passage area, and convicted most of the defendants of disobeying a reasonable request of a peace officer. The sentences imposed ranged from four to sixteen hours of community service, and fines of $40 to $100.

On appeal, the district court affirmed the trial court's decision on the defendants' failure to lay a proper foundation for the choice of evils defense. We agree.

II.

Section 18-1-702, 8B, defines and limits the choice of evils defense: (1) Conduct which would otherwise constitute an offense is justifiable and not criminal when it is *necessary* as an *emergency measure to avoid an imminent public or private injury which is about to occur* and which is of sufficient gravity that, according to ordinary standards of intelligence and morality, the desirability and urgency of avoiding the injury clearly outweigh the desirability of avoiding the injury sought to be prevented by the statute defining the offense in issue. (2) When evidence relating to the defense of justification under this section is offered by the defendant, before it is submitted for the consideration of the jury, *the court shall first rule as a matter of law whether the claimed facts and circumstances would, if established, constitute a justification.* Emphasis added.

The statutory codification of the choice of evils defense has its roots in the common law doctrine of necessity.[2] The choice of evils defense thus does not arise from a "choice" of several courses of action, but rather is based on a real emergency involving specific and imminent grave injury that presents the

---

Carl J. Johnson, former Director of the Jefferson County Department of Health; Arthur Kinoy, Professor of Law at Rutgers University School of Law; Robert C. Aldridge, Aerospace Engineer with a nuclear weapons design background; Joseph Goldfield, Engineering Consultant in the fields of energy conservation, environmental engineering, air pollution control and industrial hygiene engineering; Francis A. Boyle, Professor of Law at the University of Illinois; Walter L. Gerash, practicing attorney; John Candler Cobb, Professor Emeritus of Preventive Medicine and Community Health at the University of Colorado Health Sciences Center; Howard Zinn, Professor of Political Science at Boston University; Daniel Ellsberg, lecturer, writer, and political activist; Richard Anderson Falk, Professor of International Law and Practice at Princeton University; Paul Wehr, Associate Professor and Chair of Sociology, University of Colorado at Boulder; Ved P. Nanda, Professor of Law and Director of the International Legal Studies Program at the University of Denver College of Law; Haywood Burns, Dean of the City University of New York School of Law at Queens College.

[2] The Colorado statute was derived from § 3.02 of the Model Penal Code and § 65.00(2) of the New York Penal Code. Illustrations of the intended application of the choice of evils defense include blasting buildings to prevent a major fire from spreading, appropriating foodstuffs in time of famine, or forcibly restraining a person infected with a highly contagious and dangerous disease. Comment to § 40-1-801, 3 C.R.S. (1971 Supp.).

defendant with no alternatives other than the one taken.[3] See *United States v. Dorrell*, 758 F.2d 427, 431 (9th cir. 1985).

In Colorado, the choice of evils defense has been upheld as an affirmative defense to prison escapes when the inmate faced a choice between escape and imminent death or homosexual rape. See *People v. Strock*, 623 P.2d 42 (Colo., 1981). We have narrowly construed the statute and have required that threats of murder or homosexual rape must be specific with imminent threats of injury to the inmate that provide no reasonable alternative under the circumstances but escape. *People v. McKnight*, 626 P.2d 678, 681 (Colo.1981).[4]

III.

Before a defendant can present a choice of evils defense to the jury, § 18-1-702 requires that the trial court make an initial determination of whether the allegations of facts by the defendant, if proved, would constitute legal justification for the prohibited conduct. *Strock*, 623 P.2d at 46.

A.

The choice of evils statute requires that the defendant establish that the crime committed was necessary to prevent an imminent injury. A sufficient offer of proof must therefore establish: (1) all other potentially viable and reasonable alternative actions were pursued, or shown to be futile, (2) the action taken had a direct causal connection with the harm sought to be prevented, and that the action taken would bring about the abatement of the harm, and, (3) the action taken was an emergency measure pursued to avoid a specific, definite, and imminent injury about to occur.

The defendants claim that they had previously sought to stop production at the Rocky Flats facility by public demonstrations and lobbying, and that the use of conventional methods of demonstration and protest had been inadequate. Neither the offer of proof nor the fifteen supporting affidavits contain facts that, if proved, would show the defendants tried other potentially viable and reasonable alternatives[8], or that any other alternatives would be futile.[9] *Dorrell*, 758 F.2d at 431 (mere impatience with the political process does not constitute necessity);

The defendants claim the demonstration did affect public attitudes, and resulted

---

[3] No state has enacted legislation that makes the choice of evils defense available as a justification for behavior that attempts to bring about social and political change outside the democratic governmental process. A Pennsylvania appellate court did permit the use of the choice of evils defense for civil disobedience in two cases, but the Pennsylvania Supreme Court reversed the court of appeals in both cases. *Commonwealth v. Berrigan*, 472 A.2d 1099 (1984), rev'd 501 A.2d 226 (1985); *Commonwealth v. Capitolo*, 471 A.2d 462 (1984), rev'd, 498 A.2d 806 (1985).

[4] The inmate must also effect the escape without violence, and must immediately report to the proper authorities when he reaches a position of safety. *People v. McKnight*, 626 P.2d at 681.

[8] In fact, the supporting affidavits state in numerous places, "There are conventional means available to citizens of the State of Colorado and of the United States to protest and attempt to change environmental hazards and other evils." The affidavits then proceed to list numerous alternatives.

[9] An offer of proof is also insufficient if it merely alleges other persons have attempted to pursue reasonable alternatives, or that the action taken was a more effective alternative. *Dorrell*, 758 F.2d at 431.

in basic policy changes being made with regard to the continued maintenance and operation of the Rocky Flats facility. The defendants did not, however, allege facts that, if proved, would establish that the protest brought about the termination or prevention of the harm they were protesting. *Dorrell*, 758 F.2d at 433 (vandalism of military base not sufficient to lead to the termination of the MX missile program); *United States v. May*, 622 F.2d 1000, 1008 (9th cir. 1980) (illegal entry onto naval base not sufficient to eliminate the Trident missile program); *United States v. Simpson*, 460 F.2d 515, 518 (9th cir. 1972) (burning the file room of local draft board not sufficient to end the Vietnam War); *Commonwealth v. Averill*, 12 Mass.App. 260 (1981) (publicity of defendant's arrest not sufficient to abate an immediate peril).[10]

Finally, the defendants assert that the evils presented by the Rocky Flats facility in terms of the threat to the environment and in terms of enhancing the risk of nuclear war were imminent in the context of the magnitude and nature of the evil. Although the defendants' affidavits articulate the radiation hazards and the dangers of nuclear war associated with the operation of Rocky Flats, these dangers are long-term and speculative, and thus insufficient to demonstrate that a specific, definite, and imminent injury is about to occur as required by § 18-1-702. *May*, 622 F.2d at 1009 (harm must be direct and to the defendant; a possible future harm to members of the society is not sufficient).

The judgment of the district court is affirmed.

QUINN, J., dissenting.

I respectfully dissent. The majority, in my view, has construed the statutory choice of evils defense in § 18-1-702, 8B C.R.S., in a manner not intended by the statutory text and in derogation of the defendants' right to a jury trial on that defense.

It is appropriate at the outset to clarify what this case is not about. This case does not turn on whether the Rocky Flats nuclear weapons plant was operating contrary to law. I assume, and have no reason to believe otherwise, that the plant was operating in accord with both federal and state law when the defendants' conduct occurred. Nor is the question before us whether the defendants should be acquitted as a matter of law for the class 3 misdemeanors of obstructing a highway and disobeying the police officer's order to move from that location. See § 18-9-107(1), 8B C.R.S. Rather, the sole question raised by this case is whether the defendants were entitled to present evidence to the jury on the statutory affirmative defense of choice of evils so that the jury could consider that defense during its deliberations. In my opinion, the defendants were entitled to no less, and the trial court erred in striking the choice of evils defense from this case.

---

[10] The offer of proof and affidavits also fail to distinguish between the effect of criminal actions and the effect of legal actions taken by the protestors and other parties. The demonstration consisted not only of protestors who blocked the roadway, but also of protestors who engaged in only legal activity. The offer of proof and the affidavits address the effectiveness of the demonstration as a whole and thus can not adequately lay the foundation that it was the criminal element of the protest which precipitated the claimed effects.

I.

There is a significant procedural difference between the choice of evils defense and other affirmative defenses. Before evidence relating to the choice of evils defense is presented to the jury, the trial court must first rule as a matter of law whether "the claimed facts and circumstances would, if established, constitute a justification" for the conduct charged against the defendant. § 18-1-702(2), 8B C.R.S. What this provision means is that the defendant in an *in limine* hearing must demonstrate, by offer of proof, affidavit, or otherwise, that there is "some credible evidence" on each element of the choice of evils defense. If the defendant does so, then the trial court must permit the defendant to submit evidence on the affirmative defense to the jury and to permit the jury to consider that defense in its deliberations. As in the case of other affirmative defenses, the trial court must view the evidence in the light most favorable to the defendant in passing on these questions.

When I analyze the evidence under the aforementioned standard, I am satisfied that some credible evidence exists on each element of the choice of evils defense and that, therefore, the choice of evils defense should have been submitted to the jury for its consideration.

II.

The first element of the choice of evils defense requires that a defendant's conduct be "necessary as an emergency measure to avoid an imminent public or private injury." The majority holds that the "necessity" element requires that a defendant's choice be based on a real emergency involving "specific and imminent grave injury," that all other potentially viable and reasonable alternatives have been pursued, and that the action taken have such a direct causal connection to the harm sought to be prevented as to bring about the abatement of that harm. The statutory text does not require that there be no alternatives other than the one taken by the defendant. Furthermore, the statute does not speak to whether there must be a direct causal connection between the defendant's conduct and the harm sought to be prevented. Nor does it require that the conduct actually succeed in abating the public or private injury. The stringent three-part standard on which the majority relies was adopted by this court in *People v. McKnight*, 626 P.2d 678, 681 (Colo.1981), which involved a prison escape and was developed in the interest of limiting any right of escape to truly exigent circumstances. We deal in the instant case, however, with an entirely different situation — a nonviolent citizen protest — and I believe *McKnight* is ill-suited to provide the controlling standard for resolving the question before us.

The rationale behind the choice of evils defense is grounded in the concept of necessity and can be simply stated: a defendant should not be punished when his or her conduct in violating the law prevents more evil than the violation causes. See Model Penal Code § 3.02, comment at 9-10 (1985). The concept of necessity does not demand one and only one response to the exclusion of all others. Necessity is often a matter of degree, involving competing values and alternatives, and its presence depends on both the likelihood and the gravity of the harm sought to be prevented. If the harm is an appreciable one and the possible consequences grave, then the presence of necessity should not be resolved solely on the basis of the mathematical probability of the harm actually occurring. Although an allegation of generalized or speculative injury will not support a claim of necessity, the fact that the harm is not about to occur "immediately" is not to say that the harm may not be "imminent." Imminent danger is relative, and not absolute, and is measured more by the nature of consequences than by the lapse of time. The law does not fix the distance of time between the justifiable defense and the mischief, for all cases, by the clock or the calendar. The chronological part of the doctrine of defense, like the rest of it, is a matter of reasonableness; and reasonableness depends upon circumstances.

We live in an environment in which one serious mistake in dealing with nuclear weapons and their production can be disastrous. Albert Einstein summed it up best when he wrote: "Our world faces a crisis as yet unperceived by those possessing the power to make right decisions for good and evil. The unleashed power of the atom has changed everything save our modes of thinking and thus we drift toward unparalleled catastrophe. A new type of thinking is essential if mankind is to survive and move toward higher levels." R. Lapp, "The Einstein Letter That Started It All," New York Times, August 2, 1964, § E (Magazine) at 54.

A.

The majority views the dangers articulated in the affidavits submitted by the defendants as "long-term and speculative" and thus "insufficient to demonstrate that a specific, definite, and imminent injury is about to occur." This analysis, in my view, misses the mark. The peril of radiotoxic pollution need not arise from a single event, such as the calamity of a nuclear war, but can result from an on-going process over a prolonged period of time. The fact that the catastrophic consequences of a potential danger might not be immediate is not to say that the magnitude and probability of harm are not increasing at every point on the time line. The question of whether a danger is sufficiently imminent to merit action is not resolved simply by viewing the most serious consequences as long-term. Levitin, *Putting the Government on Trial: The Necessity Defense and Social Change*, 33 Wayne L.Rev. 1221, 1230 (1987).

The affidavits submitted by the defendants provide ample evidence that the chain of causation arising from radiotoxic pollution emanating from the Rocky Flats plant started in the past, has continued for many years, and still exists today. Carl J. Johnson, M.D., formerly the Director of the Jefferson County Department of Health, stated in his affidavit that the Rocky Flats plant had a major impact on the health of its employees and Denver area residents and continues to present a threat to the public health of the region.[1] Joseph Goldfield, a chemical and

---

[1] An abbreviated list of the harm described by Dr. Johnson includes the following: compared to all white males in Colorado, Rocky Flats nuclear workers have an eight-fold incidence of brain tumors and three-fold incidence of malignant melanoma; a Department of Energy (DOE) follow-up study of white males at Rocky Flats in 1987 of Dr. Johnson's earlier study found a 7.7-fold excess of lymphatic sarcoma, 3.3 times more esophageal cancer than expected, 80% more gastric cancer, 3.7 times more prostatic cancer; exposures to the surrounding population began in 1953 and peaked in 1957 when an explosion blew out all 600 plus industrial filters in the main smokestack; a 1969-71 study found concentrations of

environmental engineer, also submitted an affidavit on the hazard created by the Rocky Flats plant.[2] It was Goldfield's opinion, based on a review of documents submitted by Rockwell International and the Department of Energy to the Colorado Department of Health, that the Rocky Flats fluidized bed incinerator, which was designed to dispose of materials contaminated with low levels of plutonium, presents significant hazards, from both the possibility of an explosion and from normal emissions of radiotoxic materials, to Rocky Flats workers and the surrounding Denver metropolitan population. John Candler Cobb, Professor Emeritus of Preventative Medicine and Community Health at the University of Colorado Health Sciences Center, submitted an affidavit in which he stated that he conducted an investigation for the Environmental Protection Agency concerning human plutonium burdens in people who have lived near Rocky Flats from 1975 until 1982. It was his opinion that, on the day of the defendants' demonstration and afterwards, the Rocky Flats plant presented and continues to present a clear and imminent danger to Colorado front range citizens from both past actual releases of radioactive materials and from potential future accidents, both large and small. The inevitability of human error, in his view, constitutes a major factor in the risk of nuclear accidents. Cobb's affidavit further stated that, due to poor planning two decades ago, plutonium is currently blowing from the southeast corner of Rocky Flats.

The sworn statements of these qualified and respected experts certainly qualify as "some credible evidence" that, for purposes of the choice of evils defense, the danger from the Rocky Flats plant was imminent at the time of the defendants' conduct.

B.

The majority also concludes that the defendants did not "allege facts that, if proved, would establish that the protest brought about the termination or prevention of the harm they were protesting." This analysis injects a novel element of "sufficiency" into the necessity calculus and results in limiting the choice of evils defense only to those defendants who succeed in their efforts in preventing the injury against which their actions are directed.

Citizen protests, such as the one in this case, are often part of a broader movement to extricate the government from a policy or a course of conduct that is perceived to be inimical to the public welfare. While an individual protest may not

---

plutonium in the Denver area drinking water 7,000 to 40,000 times the background level of world-wide fallout; a DOE monitoring station near Rocky Flats recorded the highest air concentrations of plutonium reported in the world for every month measured; leukemia rates for children in Jefferson County were below the U.S. rate in the five year period before 1953, but increased to about twice the U.S. rate after 1957; a study performed in 1979-81 found an increase in age-adjusted cancer incidence in the Denver metro area of 15%, which was 61% greater than the national trend.

[2] Mr. Goldfield stated that potential failure exists in the incinerator design, exemplified by three fires which occurred during testing of the incinerator with non-radioactive materials. If such fires had occurred during incineration of radioactive materials, it is possible that emission of radioactive materials into the atmosphere would have occurred. If such fire occurred and an explosion resulted after six months of operation, the incinerator would have released an amount of plutonium into the atmosphere 28 trillion times as great as the DOE prediction of the yearly emission rate of the incinerator.

be sufficient in itself to terminate the perceived harm, the combined effect of several protests well might effectuate a significant change in or termination of the policy or conduct against which a particular protest is directed. Levitin, 33 Wayne L.Rev. at 1234-37. The defendants' assertion that their action, in combination with the actions of others, might accelerate a political process ultimately leading to the elimination of the perceived harm should not be rejected out of hand. On the contrary, the issue of necessity should turn on whether the evidence, when viewed in a light most favorable to the defendants, will support a finding that defendants' conduct was reasonably calculated to have a significant impact on the perceived danger which the defendants sought to prevent.

The affidavits submitted by the defendants satisfied this standard. Eight experts from such diverse fields as the law, the social and political sciences, and aerospace engineering offered opinions that the defendants' conduct was reasonably calculated to prevent the evil of environmental pollution from radiotoxic substances. Haywood Burns, Dean of the City University of New York School of Law, offered the opinion that the protest "appears to be reasonably calculated to have an ultimate impact on the Rocky Flats plant which seeks to be permitted to contaminate and threaten with contamination the soil, air and groundwater of people who live in the area." Professor Elise Boulding, an expert in the social sciences, offered the opinion that "the demonstration was reasonably calculated to prevent or mitigate the evils of pollution hazards to the surrounding population." Robert C. Aldridge, an aerospace engineer, offered the opinion that the defendants reasonably believed that a causal connection exists between citizen intervention and prevention of the harm.

C.

The majority also holds that the defendants failed to offer "facts that, if proven, would show the defendants tried other potentially viable and reasonable alternatives, or that any other alternatives would be futile." In addition to lacking support in the statutory text, this requirement virtually eliminates the availability of the choice of evils defense in challenges to governmental policies. In the real world, it is impossible to predict what effect alternative actions would have had. The existence of alternatives is merely an argument that the jury should consider relevant to the issue of necessity, but it should rarely absolutely preclude the use of the defense. For example, a court may consider bringing an action before a regulatory agency a viable legal alternative, when in fact it is futile, if that agency has been "captured" by the regulated industry. It would be misleading for the court to call such an action an alternative. Moreover, many industries have unregulated elements. To suggest that there are always legal alternatives available in political protest cases is to assert that there can never be a necessity defense in such cases. Levitin, 32 Wayne L.Rev. at 1233. In contrast to the majority, I view the existence of alternatives as merely one factor, and not necessarily conclusive, in considering whether the defendants' action was necessary.

The affidavits submitted by the defendants provide "some credible evidence" that resorting to other alternatives would be futile. George A. Johnson, attorney at law, and Arthur Kinoy, Professor of Law at Rutgers University School of Law, stated in their affidavits that, although conventional means exist, none of the conventional methods have brought about results eliminating the serious dangers of radiotoxic pollution. Robert C. Aldridge, an aerospace engineer, stated in his affidavit that "no reasonable traditional alternatives are available to stop or prevent the harm" and that "a history of futile attempts to use accepted means makes any anticipated results from such means alone illusory." Frances A. Boyle, Professor of Law at the University of Illinois, echoed the same theme. Howard Zinn, Professor of Political Science at Boston University, stated in his affidavit that "conventional means alone are insufficient to effect such substantive changes." Finally, Daniel Ellsberg, an economist and political activist, presented an affidavit in which he stated that in the domain of nuclear policy, the "'normal' legal processes of democracy, by themselves, have not functioned adequately — or even been permitted to operate, in terms of openness and public awareness — to protect American citizens and other humans from vast, in some cases unprecedented and unlimited, risks of harm." Such opinion evidence clearly rises to the level of "some credible evidence" on the futility of other alternatives to the defendants' conduct.

III.

The second element of the choice of evils defense is that the public or private injury was about to occur because of a situation occasioned or developed through no conduct of the defendant. Clearly, the injury that the defendants sought to prevent was not "occasioned or developed" by any conduct on their part, but rather had its source in the pollution emanating from the Rocky Flats plant. It cannot reasonably be disputed, therefore, that the defendants' offer of proof satisfied the second element of the choice of evils defense.

IV.

The choice of evils defense also requires that the public or private injury sought to be prevented be of sufficient gravity that, according to ordinary standards of intelligence and morality, the desirability and urgency of avoiding the public or private injury clearly outweigh the desirability of avoiding the injury sought to be prevented by the statute which the defendants were accused of violating. This requirement echoes the principle that the defendants' conduct must promote "some value higher than the value of literal compliance with the law." G. Williams, *The Criminal Law*, § 229 (2nd ed. 1970). The majority does not address this element, as it concludes that the defendants failed to satisfy the other elements of the choice of evils defense. Since I believe the defendants have satisfied the other elements of the statutory defense, I will address the issue of competing values.

The choice of evils defense contemplates an objective standard in determining whether the injury sought to be prevented clearly outweighs the injury caused by the defendants' violation of the criminal law. See Model Penal Code § 3.02, comment at 12; G. Williams, *The Criminal Law*, § 239 (while "necessity is subjective as to its facts, it is objective as to its values"). Section 18-1-702(2), however, does not specify the manner in which the balancing of values is to be resolved. In light of this statutory silence, it is appropriate to look to the law governing the respective functions of the court and jury in resolving that question.

The issue of competing values is for the jury as long as there is evidence which, when viewed in the light most favorable to the defendant, is sufficient to permit a reasonable trier of fact to conclude that the relative value of a defendant's conduct, according to ordinary standards of intelligence and morality, outweighs the value underlying the statutory proscription violated by the defendant. See Arnolds and Garland, *The Defense of Necessity in Criminal Law: The Right to Choose the Lesser Evil*, J.Crim.Law & Criminology 289, 296 (1974). This standard is nothing more than a recognition of the fact that one's choice of value does not occur under ideal conditions where right and wrong are obvious, but under circumstances where the right most often must be wrenched from less than ideal alternatives. In most cases, therefore, the issue of whether the value of a defendant's action preponderates over the value of obeying the statutory proscription will be a question for the jury to resolve.

In the present case, the affidavits submitted on behalf of the defendants satisfied the threshold of "some credible evidence" on the issue of competing values. The particular injury pertinent to the choice of evils defense in this case was the prevention of radiotoxic pollution from explosion or from normal emissions from the Rocky Flats plant. In contrast, the injury caused by the defendants' conduct consisted of obstructing a highway and disobeying a lawful order of a police officer to remove themselves from that particular location.

The defendants' conduct in this case did not rest upon considerations pertaining to the morality and advisability of the statutory proscriptions which they were accused of violating, but instead was directed to the completely separate concern over what they perceived to be an imminent public injury. The jury might conclude under these circumstances, or might not for that matter, that the balance of values in this case weighed in favor of the defendants. The jury, after all, is the safety valve which, by its own inherent structure, permits society to accommodate itself to its own internal stresses and strains.

I would reverse the judgment of conviction and remand the case for a new trial.

NOTES FROM TIFFANY:

(1) The trial court held that Andrews' "offer of proof" was insufficient. What does this mean? What effect does it have?

(2) Justice Quinn's dissent notes that necessity differs from other defenses in that the defendant's proposed evidence must be screened by the judge before it is heard by the jury. Why? What is so special about necessity?

(3) The Rocky Flats nuclear facility was presumably operating under federal licenses, federal contracts, federal money, and federal legislation. Therefore, Congress probably heard all the arguments presented by opponents of the facility, and nevertheless decided that it was in the nation's interests to have such a facility. Isn't this *enough by itself* to require a rejection of a necessity defense here? If "the people" — through their elected representatives — vote to approve some controversial program, should individuals be allowed to break the law in an effort to end the program? And suppose we allow the jury to hear defendants' evidence and defendants succeed in persuading the jury that Rocky Flats is dangerous and

should be terminated. Should 12 people be allowed to overrule our national Congress?

Consider *City of St. Louis v. Klocker*, 637 S.W.2d 174 (Mo.Ct.App., 1982), where defendants were charged with blocking access to an abortion clinic. Defendants claimed necessity: they were trying to save the lives of unborn children. In rejecting the defense, the court noted that abortions in some circumstances had been declared legal by the Missouri Legislature.

> The legislature's decision prevails if and when it makes specific value choices. * * * * Our legislature has made its value judgment in this area and has concluded the interests defendants seek to vindicate are outweighed by the right to privacy defendants seek to invade.

(4) If you were the judge and agreed with Andrews' position on nuclear issues, should that influence your decision as to whether to allow the defense? Suppose some other defendant (such as Klocker) takes a position you do *not* agree with. Would your sense of fairness require you to allow him to present his defense too? Don't *Andrews* and *Klocker* have to be decided the same way?

(5) How would *Andrews* apply to a situation where a defendant was protesting *the very law which he was violating*? Suppose, for example, the law required blacks to sit in the back of the bus, and a black defendant protested this law by sitting in the front of the bus. In *United States v. Schoon*, 971 F.2d 193 (9th Cir., 1991), defendants invaded an IRS office in Tucson, chanting "keep American's tax dollars out of El Salvador" and splashing simulated blood on the office. The trial court rejected their necessity defense and convicted them of obstructing IRS activities. The Court of Appeals affirmed, drawing a distinction between "direct" and "indirect" civil disobedience.

> This case involves indirect civil disobedience because these protestors were not challenging the laws under which they were charged. In contrast, the civil rights lunch counter sit-ins, for example, constituted direct civil disobedience because the protestors were challenging the rule that prevented them from sitting at lunch counters. Similarly, if a city council passed an ordinance requiring immediate infusion of a suspected carcinogen into the drinking water, physically blocking the delivery of the substance would constitute direct civil disobedience: protestors would be preventing the execution of a law in a specific instance in which a particularized harm — contamination of the water supply - would otherwise follow.

An interesting distinction. Does it follow that the "direct" protester *does* have a valid necessity defense? Doesn't he have an alternative legal remedy: challenging the law in court? And if his challenge fails, isn't he pretty much in the same position as the "indirect" protester?

(6) The court in *Schoon* went on to discuss the relation between the necessity defense and validly enacted legislation.

> In some sense, the necessity defense allows us to act as individual legislatures, amending a particular criminal provision or crafting a one-

time exception to it, subject to court review, when a real legislature would formally do the same under those circumstances. For example, by allowing prisoners who escape a burning jail to claim the justification of necessity, we assume the lawmaker, confronting this problem, would have allowed for an exception to the law proscribing prison escapes. * * * *

However, the mere existence of a constitutional law or governmental policy cannot constitute a legally cognizable harm. See *Comment, Political Protest and the Illinois Defense of Necessity*, 54 U.Chi.L.Rev. 1070, 1083 (1987) ("In a society based on democratic decision making, this is how values are ranked - a protester cannot simply assert that her view of what is best should trump the decision of the majority of elected representatives.") * * * *

The protest in this case was in the form of indirect civil disobedience, aimed at reversal of the government's El Salvador policy. That policy does not violate the Constitution, and appellants have never suggested as much. There is no evidence that the procedure by which the policy was adopted was in any way improper; nor is there any evidence that appellants were prevented systematically from participating in the democratic processes through which the policy was chosen. The most immediate harm the appellants sought to avert was the existence of the government's El Salvador policy, which is not in itself a legally cognizable harm.

And finally, the court went beyond the facts of the case before it to enunciate a broad rule: "Indirect protests of congressional policies can never meet all the requirements of the necessity doctrine. Therefore, we hold that the necessity defense is not available in such cases."

Never, or hardly ever? Can you imagine an instance of "indirect" civil disobedience which *should* permit a necessity defense?

STATE v. THAYER
Vermont Supreme Court
14 A.3d 213 (2010)

BURGESS, J.

In this interlocutory appeal, defendant challenges the trial court's denial of her right to present a necessity defense to the jury. Defendant is charged with knowingly and unlawfully cultivating more than twenty-five marijuana plants in violation of 18 V.S.A. § 4230(a)(4). Before trial, defendant moved for a jury instruction on the defense of necessity, asserting she used marijuana medicinally for her son, whose wasting symptoms are recognized under the state's therapeutic use of cannabis act. The trial court denied defendant's motion, holding (1) that she failed to establish a prima facie case on each of the elements required for a necessity defense, and (2) that the legislative law precluded the necessity defense in this case through its "deliberate choice as to the values at issue concerning the legal growth of marijuana." We granted defendant's request for interlocutory review of the trial court's ruling, and affirm.

The trial court accepted the following facts as true. In the summer of 2003, defendant, a Master Gardener, began growing marijuana on her property to treat her ailing son TT, who was battling leukemia. After several bone-marrow transplants and repeated bouts of chemotherapy, TT used marijuana to ease his nausea, improve his appetite, and eventually return to school. Although TT passed away in May 2005, defendant noted how effectively marijuana alleviated his symptoms. She continued growing marijuana to treat her youngest son, MT, who was experiencing wasting symptoms, including chronic nausea and loss of appetite, due to scarred kidneys resulting from a medical emergency when he was an infant. Marijuana greatly improved his condition.

Each summer since 2003, defendant grew marijuana outside of her home. In the spring, defendant would normally seed fifty-to-one-hundred plants indoors and select the most vigorous of those seedlings to plant outdoors in June. To ensure an adequate supply of marijuana, each season she grew fifty-to-seventy percent more plants than she needed to compensate for natural crop losses.

On August 2, 2007, following a tip from Vermont's Marijuana Eradication Reduction Team, police seized thirty semi-mature marijuana plants growing in defendant's backyard. Defendant conceded that neither she nor her son were registered with the state, as required by statute, as patients or caregivers authorized to grow and use medicinal marijuana. The pending felony drug charge resulted.

Defendant argues the trial court erred in denying her request to present the affirmative defense of necessity. * * * * The immediate inquiry is not whether the necessity defense would have been persuasive, but whether the trial court erred in denying the jury the opportunity to consider the defense at all. Defendant needed only to make a prima facie presentation from which a "reasonable juror could find that the requirements of the necessity defense were satisfied" to be entitled to her requested instruction.

In determining whether a reasonable juror could find that the elements of necessity were satisfied, we first examine the four requirements of the defense:

 (1) there must be a situation of emergency arising without fault on the part of the actor concerned;

 (2) this emergency must be so imminent and compelling as to raise a reasonable expectation of harm, either directly to the actor or upon those he was protecting;

 (3) this emergency must present no reasonable opportunity to avoid the injury without doing the criminal act; and

 (4) the injury impending from the emergency must be of sufficient seriousness to outmeasure the criminal wrong.

In the instant case, the trial court ruled correctly that defendant's proffer was insufficient to establish the third element of her defense: that she had no reasonable alternative except to violate the law.

The third element of the necessity defense requires defendant to show that her emergency presented no reasonable opportunity to avoid the injury without doing the criminal act. This element is governed by defendant's belief, and that belief must be reasonable. Defendant must therefore present enough evidence to raise a question of fact as to whether she reasonably believed she had no opportunity to alleviate her son's symptoms without committing the outlawed act of growing more than twenty-five marijuana plants. Since, before defendant's arrest, Vermont had legalized medicinal use of marijuana under certain circumstances and then expanded its exemption from criminal penalties, a brief look at the law's provisions lends guidance as to the reasonableness of defendant's conduct.

Three years before defendant's arrest, in May 2004, Vermont passed Public Act 135, "An Act Relating to Marijuana Use by Persons with Severe Illness." Although the Act legalized therapeutic use of marijuana, the Legislature crafted its permission narrowly. Individuals wishing to grow marijuana must be "registered patients" with a qualifying medical condition, or assume the role of "registered caregiver" to grow for another qualified patient. 18 V.S.A. § 4472(6) & (7). The Act provided that marijuana grown for symptom relief may be cultivated only in a "secure indoor facility." § 4472(8). It limited possession to "no more than one mature plant, two immature plants, and two ounces of usable marijuana." § 4472(4) (2005). The Legislature did not alter its pre-existing penalties for more ambitious marijuana possession, including jail terms of up to five and ten years for cultivating more than ten and more than twenty-five plants, respectively. § 4230(a)(3)-(a)(4). In 2007, the Legislature amended the Act to increase the cultivation limit to two mature plants and seven immature plants per grower, again leaving the felony penalties in place. Vermont law has thus required registered legal growers of medicinal marijuana to do so indoors, with a maximum of nine plants, since May 2004.

Defendant posits that her belief in the necessity of unlawful outdoor marijuana cultivation was reasonable because she needed to maintain a constant supply for her son. According to the proffer, defendant was "dismayed" to learn, in July 2007, of the indoor growing requirement of Vermont's amended medicinal marijuana law, which was, in her opinion, its "worst provision." In the four years during which defendant grew marijuana, she refused to grow indoors and failed to observe either the three or seven plant maximum. She insists that thirty plants were necessary to ensure an adequate supply of marijuana to compensate for "the constant risks of loss to frost, drought, too much rain, deer, woodchucks, moles, grouse, mold and disease" and argues that these outdoor growing problems necessitated planting substantially more marijuana than she would actually harvest. Defendant asserts that she was attempting to comply with Vermont's medicinal marijuana law just before her arrest, but lacked sufficient time after the 2007 amendments to research indoor growing or to build indoor growing facilities. Defendant's argument fails for two reasons.

First, defendant proffered nothing to actually demonstrate that indoor cultivation was impossible or impractical for her, or that it would not have cured the need to grow more marijuana than authorized by the statute.[FN1] Indeed, she makes no

---

[FN1] In his dissent, Chief Justice Reiber submits that this reference to a lack of proof fails to credit defendant's filings with the trial court. We disagree. As the dissent points out, defendant did submit that the limit on outdoor planting "was particularly challenging," that indoor cultivation would take "two

claim that she would still have had to grow more marijuana plants than the law allowed if growing indoors, safe from the uncertainties of nature. Moreover, defendant's assertion that she had no time to create a compliant indoor facility for growing marijuana is not reasonable, given over three years in which to do so. Vermont's therapeutic marijuana law has required indoor growing since its original passage in 2004, and defendant admits to growing medicinal marijuana outdoors before and after this regulated legalization. Defendant had no evident intent to move her operation indoors before the amendment in 2007 and instead monitored the legislative process hoping outdoor cultivation would be authorized. On that record, it cannot be said that a reasonable juror could find that she had not had enough time in which to grow marijuana indoors before her arrest. That the exemption from prosecution was not applicable to her son's wasting condition until the 2007 amendment is of no moment since, according to defendant's explanation, it was the outdoor cultivation, rather than the child's illness, that necessitated her cultivation of marijuana in felony quantities for more than three years, eventually leading to her arrest and the instant charge.

Second, to the extent defendant justifies the violation based on her disagreement or disapproval of the law's provisions, this argument falls outside the scope of the necessity defense. The necessity defense is generally not available to excuse criminal activity by those who disagree with the policies of the government. The Legislature enacted marijuana prohibitions, and enacted and amended the law to allow medicinal use of marijuana. While its specific provisions may have "dismayed" defendant and seemed to her "grossly inadequate and seemingly arbitrary," she is nonetheless bound — like the rest of us — to abide by the law. An emergency necessity to commit an act otherwise deemed a crime does not turn upon the rationality of the legislative choice. There is no basis for the necessity defense outside of its essential common law elements. The element of having no reasonable alternative to the violation was not evident from defendant's submissions to the trial court.

Thus, assuming the truth of defendant's proffer, it was insufficient to establish this predicate third prong of the necessity defense. Since defendant's evidence failed to raise legitimate factual issues relating to the defense of necessity, the jury needed no instruction on the defense. Given defendant's failure to meet the prima facie showing requirement for her claimed necessity, our analysis ends without considering defendant's proffer in support of the remaining elements or the court's reliance upon legislative preclusion of the common law defense by virtue of the enactment of the medicinal marijuana exemption. We affirm the trial court's conclusion that defendant is not entitled to a necessity defense and remand the case for further proceedings.

Affirmed and remanded.

---

separate grow spaces" within the house, that "research was needed on both the equipment and techniques necessary" to grow indoors and the space would "need to be secure." Taking these recitations as true, but without further elaboration by defendant, none can lead to a reasonable conclusion that such presumed difficulties could not possibly or practically be resolved, or that they left defendant with no choice but to violate the law.

REIBER, C.J., dissenting.

Defendant's oldest son was diagnosed with leukemia in 2002, endured chemotherapy, radiation, and five bone-marrow transplants, and died in 2005. During the course of his illness, he grew and used marijuana to ease the side effects of cancer treatments. Meanwhile, defendant's younger son had a medical emergency when he was an infant. This left his kidneys scarred and led to chronic fatigue and severe nausea. Despite following all medical advice, he remained extremely ill. When he began using marijuana, however, he, like his older brother, experienced an increased appetite and, in turn, improved energy and vigor. Although marijuana is not a cure, it has relieved his worst symptoms. The State does not dispute that the son's already declining kidneys "will fail completely," and his chronic wasting disease will prove fatal. * * * *

The necessity defense may be precluded pretrial only where the facts in defendant's offer of proof, taken as true, cannot sustain the defense. Here, defendant need only present sufficient evidence to raise a question of fact for the jury as to whether it was "reasonably conceived by her to have been a necessity" to grow marijuana plants. If a reasonable juror could conclude that each element of the necessity defense was present, the trial court's decision must be overturned. Although deficiencies in defendant's evidence may appear at trial, defendant proffered sufficient proof on each element, and, as a result, the trial court's foreclosure of such evidence constituted reversible error.

The necessity defense has four prongs:

(1) there must be a situation of emergency arising without fault on the part of the actor concerned;

(2) this emergency must be so imminent and compelling as to raise a reasonable expectation of harm, either directly to the actor or upon those he was protecting;

(3) this emergency must present no reasonable opportunity to avoid the injury without doing the criminal act; and

(4) the injury impending from the emergency must be of sufficient seriousness to outmeasure the criminal wrong.

The issue of whether the trial court properly excluded the necessity defense is a pure question of law. Defendant made the following offer of proof regarding the required elements of the necessity defense.

With respect to the first prong, requiring the situation to be an emergency, defendant asserted in her submission to the trial court that her son has a progressive disease with symptoms of wasting and that conventional medical approaches and dietary modifications have not worked.[FN2] Defendant offered her son's physician to testify about the progression of his disease and its severe consequences, including the prognosis that he will eventually experience kidney failure. The trial court held that this situation was not an "emergency," but failed to

---

[FN2] The first prong of the defense requires that the emergency not be the fault of the defendant claiming necessity. Here, it is undisputed that the son's disease is not the fault of defendant.

explain why this was so. If the serious illness of a child, which ultimately leads to death, is not an emergency, what is? Because defendant offered reasonable proof that this was a critical health issue for her child, the jury should have had the opportunity to determine whether it reached the level of an emergency.

Defendant also offered proof concerning her belief of the imminence of the harm, the second prong. The trial court stated that because the harms sought to be avoided were long-term, the danger was not imminent enough to warrant defendant's actions. * * * *

Here defendant proffered ample proof that the outcome of her son's chronic kidney disease, without treatment, was anything but speculative or uncertain. Her son was already experiencing severe nausea, weight loss, and declining vigor. He was increasingly less able to build his strength and resist the disease. The emergency's imminence need raise only a reasonable expectation of harm. Here, a juror could reasonably conclude that defendant had a reasonable belief that her son would die if she did not provide him with the only effective treatment she and her doctor had found — marijuana.

Defendant also proffered sufficient proof regarding the third prong, which the majority latches onto as being dispositive of the issue. The majority today holds that no reasonable juror could find that defendant reasonably believed that there were no other options in treating her son's disease. The problem with the majority's conclusion is that it involves making a credibility assessment, one that properly lies with the jury. The majority states that it is unreasonable to believe that defendant did not have time to create a compliant indoor growing facility in the three years that the medical-marijuana law was in place. The Court, however, must take as true defendant's offer of proof when making a determination regarding what a reasonable juror could find. The majority wrongly makes a determination as to the reasonableness of defendant's justification and suggests that defendant proffered nothing to actually demonstrate that indoor cultivation was impossible or impractical for her. This is a mischaracterization. In fact, the trial court had a memorandum before it in which defendant stated that "the limit on the number of plants was particularly challenging from a technical standpoint." She elaborated that "essentially two separate grow spaces would have to be created in the house," research was needed on both the equipment and techniques necessary to grow the plants indoors, the facility would need to be secure, and her son would need to have "continued access to a secure, safe supply of marijuana." The trial court had to take defendant's statements about the difficulty of building the indoor facility as true when asking whether a reasonable juror could have found that defendant reasonably believed alternatives were not available.

Further, the trial court's suggestion that "there were not only legal means of medical treatment which could have reasonably been attempted, but there was also a legal means of cultivating marijuana" is faulty. This is not the issue. Defendant, by raising the necessity defense, concedes that she broke the law. The bare fact that there are legal means of medical treatment and cultivation of marijuana is of no consequence. The issue is whether she acted reasonably in determining that none of those legal means was of use in preventing her son's further decline. Here, taking defendant's proffer as true, a reasonable juror could conclude that a mother with an ill child acted reasonably in deciding that all other avenues for saving the child's life were foreclosed. That question, therefore, should have gone to the jury.

Finally, with respect to the fourth prong — that the injury resulting from the emergency must be of sufficient seriousness to outmeasure the crime — defendant's proffer satisfied this requirement. At the heart of the necessity defense is a difficult value judgment. A violation of a criminal statute is no small matter, but neither is a child's illness, particularly when, as here, that illness is life-threatening. Defendant proffers that she was placed in the hapless position of having to choose between following the law and saving — or at least prolonging — the life of her child. A reasonable juror could conclude that the life of a child outmeasured the seriousness of committing the crime of cultivation of marijuana. For that reason, the question was for the jury.

It is telling that many of our previous decisions denying the necessity defense are nothing like the present case. Most involve driving under the influence (DUI), while many out-of-state decisions involve civil disobedience. Where a defendant argued that it was necessary to trespass on a test-firing facility to prevent the testing of guns, in turn to prevent the deaths of civilians in El Salvador, we denied the defense because the defendant could not have believed that his actions would have a direct causal effect. *State v. Cram* 157 Vt. at 471. Where a defendant did not tag a deer because he was afraid the tag would become dislodged — in effect, committing the crime to avoid committing the crime — we held that each of the elements of the necessity defense was missing. *State v. Sullivan*, 154 Vt. 437 (1990). Where a defendant claimed that it was necessary to take the wheel from his seventeen-year-old nephew who had stalled the vehicle in the middle of the road, we held that the defense was not available because the defendant's own conduct — his self-induced intoxication requiring his nephew to drive — created the emergency. *State v. Squires*, 147 Vt. at 431. Where a defendant claimed necessity for DUI because his child was missing earlier in the day, we held that no emergency existed at the time he was arrested because the defendant had already found his son. *State v. Dapo*, 143 Vt. 610 (1983). In each of these cases, we held that the proffering party failed to make out a prima facie case on at least one of the elements and was thus not entitled to an instruction on the necessity defense. Courts, however, do not always deny a necessity defense jury instruction, even in DUI cases. See *State v. Shotton*, 142 Vt. 558. In *Shotton*, the defendant was arrested for DUI, but claimed necessity because she was badly injured and was seeking medical assistance. She said that she had been drinking and her husband assaulted her and pushed her down a flight of stairs. She further testified that no one was home but her husband, her telephone was disconnected, and the neighbors' homes were a short walk away, but she did not want to walk and risk finding no one home at those houses. She stated that she was driving to the hospital when she was pulled over. We explicitly noted that:

> The jury should have had the opportunity to weigh the reasonableness and credibility of all the evidence, and to decide if it was sufficient to establish the defense of necessity. It was the function of the jury to determine first whether defendant was driving while under the influence of intoxicating liquor, and if she was, then to determine whether she was justified in doing so because of necessity. By refusing to charge the jury on the second issue, the trial court committed reversible error.

While it is true that the defendant in *Shotton* had other avenues available to her — for example, she could have walked to a neighbor's house to use the phone, even if no one was home — we held that it is up to the jury to decide issues of reasonableness and credibility. We recognized that, although the jury could have chosen to believe the State over the defendant, the trial court nevertheless committed reversible error by refusing to instruct the jury on the necessity defense. The same principle applies in this case. Defendant should have had the opportunity to present the necessity defense to the jury to determine issues of reasonableness and credibility.

Although the necessity defense has often been used in cases where a defendant disagrees with government policies and trespasses, pickets, or otherwise displays disagreement in illegal ways, this is not a civil disobedience case. The majority claims that defendant justified breaking the law "based on her disagreement or disapproval of the law's provisions." The majority analogizes this case to a civil disobedience one, citing *Planned Parenthood of Mid-Iowa v. Maki* for the proposition that the defense cannot be used to "excuse criminal activity by those who disagree with the policies of the government." 478 N.W.2d 637, 640 (Iowa 1991). I agree that, typically, disagreement with government policy does not make criminal actions noncriminal. See *United States v. Dorrell*, 758 F.2d 427 (9th cir. 1985) (necessity defense not available to justify defendants entering air force base and spray-painting government property to avert nuclear war and world starvation); *People v. Garziano*, 230 Cal.App.3d 241 (1991) (necessity defense not available to justify criminal conduct at abortion protest aimed at interfering with pregnant woman's constitutionally protected decision to terminate pregnancy); *State v. Dansinger*, 521 A.2d 685 (Me.1987) (necessity defense not available to justify defendants trespassing on air national guard property to protest nuclear arms race); *State v. Prince*, 71 Ohio App.3d 694 (1991) (necessity defense not available to justify unlawful activity in protest of CIA's on-campus recruiting efforts). Nevertheless, that is not the underlying tension of this case.

Although defendant conceded in her memorandum to the trial court that she was "dismayed" by many of the statutory provisions in the medical-marijuana law, being dismayed with the law was not her motive for growing marijuana in illegal quantities. Nowhere in the record does defendant state that her purpose in growing marijuana was to protest the provisions of Vermont's medical-marijuana law. Rather, it was her son's illness that she felt necessitated breaking the law. Defendant was not growing marijuana to achieve political ends — thus, the reasoning for barring civil disobedience defendants from using the necessity defense is inapplicable.

The trial court also erred in concluding that the necessity defense was legislatively precluded here. We have previously held that the necessity defense is not applicable if it has been precluded by the Legislature. *State v. Cram*, 157 Vt. at 469; see also *United States v. Oakland Cannabis Buyers' Coop.*, 532 U.S. 483, 491 (2001) ("Under any conception of legal necessity, one principle is clear: The defense cannot succeed when the legislature itself has made a determination of values." But see *People v. Mower*, 28 Cal.4th 457 (2002) (refusing to follow *Oakland Cannabis* because it involved interpretation of federal law, not state law).[FN3] Nevertheless, here the Legislature did not preclude the necessity defense.

The Legislature has made a determination of values in this arena. It has determined that marijuana has therapeutic uses. See 18 V.S.A. §§ 4471–4474d (permitting patients with certain debilitating medical conditions to use marijuana for symptom relief, subject to various qualifications). Specifically, the Legislature has recognized that marijuana can be used to "alleviate the symptoms or effects of a debilitating medical condition." § 4472(10) (defining "use for symptom relief"). It has created a review board whose duties include "reviewing studies, data, and any other information relevant to the use of marijuana for symptom relief." § 4473(b)(5)(B). In enacting its therapeutic use of cannabis act, the Legislature created a distinction between the medical and nonmedical use of marijuana. While protecting registered patients and caregivers from a measure of criminal prosecution, see 18 V.S.A. § 4474b, it did nothing to alter existing criminal penalties for marijuana possession and specifically enumerated restrictions on even the legal use of the drug, see 18 V.S.A. § 4474c (listing "prohibitions, restrictions, and limitations regarding the use of marijuana for symptom relief" including use "for purposes other than symptom relief"). Thus, the Legislature recognized and permitted the limited medical use of marijuana for seriously ill people.

The trial court incorrectly concluded that the Legislature must have intended to preclude the necessity defense because it "has twice made a deliberate choice as to the values at issue concerning the legal growth of marijuana and has decided not to include an exception for the defense of necessity." The trial court's reasoning does not withstand analysis. In Vermont, the necessity defense emanates from the common law. We presume that the Legislature has not overruled common law doctrines unless it does so explicitly. Here, as the trial court noted, the medical-marijuana statute says nothing about the necessity defense. But, contrary to the trial court's ruling, the legal significance of this omission is that the common-law defense has not been overruled and is therefore still available to defendant.

The trial court further stated that, although it sympathized with defendant's situation, it was "bound to apply the law as enacted and not as it could have been enacted." This is, however, the precise purpose of the necessity defense. See *United States v. Schoon*, 971 F.2d 193, 196–97 (9th cir. 1991) (holding that necessity defense allows court to recognize "one-time exception" to a statute). The question, then, is whether the Legislature would formally make an exception for a mother like defendant who is trying to save her son's life by growing medical marijuana. Given the purpose underlying the law, as expressed by the Legislature, I cannot say that

---

[FN3] The United States Supreme Court in *Oakland Cannabis* held that the necessity defense was unavailable to defendants who manufactured or distributed marijuana. This left open the question of whether defendants who merely used marijuana could employ the necessity defense. In dicta, however, the majority went further and said that nothing in the Controlled Substances Act, nor in the Court's analysis, suggested that there should be a distinction between prohibitions on manufacturing and distributing and the other prohibitions in the Controlled Substances Act. The concurring Justices reiterated that the holding applied only to manufacturing and distribution and "whether the defense might be available to a seriously ill patient for whom there is no alternative means of avoiding starvation or extraordinary suffering is a difficult issue that is not presented here." *Id.* at 501 (Stevens, J., concurring).

the Legislature intended to preclude the necessity defense here, and I would therefore send this issue to the jury.

One of the many sad ironies of today's decision stems from the fact that the majority's analysis rests entirely on defendant's failure to follow the precise contours of a relatively recent statute that aimed to decriminalize certain uses of medical marijuana. Had defendant been arrested before Vermont's medical-marijuana law went into effect, I imagine that the majority would reach a different decision today, as there would be no rationale for preventing defendant from presenting the necessity defense to the jury. Now, after the Legislature has clearly shifted its position to allow some use of medical marijuana, the majority concludes that defendant cannot avail herself of the necessity defense since she has not followed the mandates of that law. The irony is that a statute that aimed to decriminalize certain uses of medical marijuana has effectively criminalized defendant's actions in this case.

Ultimately, this is a case in which the necessity defense should be heard by a jury. Indeed, it is a case where defendant's actions cannot be explained in any way other than through a presentation of the necessity defense. I worry that today's ruling will lead to a trial where defendant's actions will be viewed in a vacuum and where she will be treated as a run-of-the-mill drug possessor, when, in fact, according to defendant, she is a loving mother who simply wishes to provide her son with the best medical treatment available to avoid losing him like she lost her first son. Ascertaining the ultimate truth or falsity of defendant's necessity defense is the principal mission of the jury, and the trial court should have squarely presented the defense to the jury so that they could confront it, consider it, and resolve its truth or falsity by their verdict. I therefore respectfully dissent.

I am authorized to state that Justice JOHNSON joins this dissent.

NOTES FROM TIFFANY:

(1) In *Commonwealth v. Hutchins*, 410 Mass. 726 (1991), Hutchins was charged with cultivation of marijuana. He offered to prove the following facts:

> The defendant is a forty-seven year old man who has been diagnosed as having scleroderma accompanied by Raynaud's phenomenon, related to his service in the Navy. Scleroderma is a chronic disease that results in the buildup of scar tissue throughout the body. The cause of scleroderma is not known and no effective treatment or cure has been discovered. In the most severe cases, scleroderma may result in death. The defendant's medical history includes episodes of fatigue, hypertension, loss of appetite, weight loss of up to twenty-five pounds, diarrhea, nausea, vomiting, reflux of food and stomach acid into the mouth, reduced motility and constriction of the esophagus, extreme difficulty and pain in swallowing, and swollen, painful joints and extreme sensitivity to the cold in his hands and feet. He also suffers from severe depression, related at least in part to his disease, and was briefly hospitalized after attempting suicide. As a result of his illness, the defendant has been unable to work since1978.

According to the offer of proof, the defendant's medical condition has been unsuccessfully treated with numerous medications and therapies by physicians of the Veterans Administration. The constriction of his esophagus has been treated by dilation and in 1974 was so severe that his treating physician advised him to have his esophagus surgically removed and replaced with a piece of his own intestine. The defendant has informed his treating physicians that since 1975, with some success, he has used marihuana, in lieu of antidepressants and surgery, to alleviate certain symptoms of his illness including nausea, loss of appetite, difficulty in eating, drinking or swallowing, loss of motility of the esophagus, spasticity, hypertension, and anxiety. Two of his treating physicians state that, although they are unable to "confirm [the defendant's] claim that his use of marihuana has caused his remarkable remission, it does appear that his use of marihuana does alleviate the previously mentioned symptoms." These two physicians also state that "there appears to be a sufficient basis to conduct a scientific and medical investigation into the possible use of marihuana to treat the disease of scleroderma." A research study of its therapeutic potential and medical uses indicates that the use of marihuana, indeed, may be effective to treat loss of appetite, nausea, vomiting, and weight loss and may relieve severe anxiety and depression. One of the defendant's other treating physicians, however, does not find that marihuana "had any effect in [the defendant's] case" and that he is "unaware of any published or unpublished evidence of a beneficial effect of marihuana in this condition."

Through correspondence with his physicians, the Veterans Administration, and members of the Massachusetts Legislature and the United States Congress, the defendant has made numerous, albeit unsuccessful, attempts lawfully to obtain either a prescription for marihuana or permission to participate in a research study on the use of marihuana to treat scleroderma. The Massachusetts Legislature has considered a bill providing for the use of marihuana in therapeutic research on more than one occasion, but no such statute has been enacted in the Commonwealth. The Veterans Administration has determined that presently there is no research study on the use of marihuana to treat scleroderma and therefore will not dispense marihuana for the defendant's treatment.

The court held that these facts — even if proved — would be insufficient to permit a jury to acquit him because of "medical necessity":

In our view, the alleviation of the defendant's medical symptoms, the importance to the defendant of which we do not underestimate, would not clearly and significantly outweigh the potential harm to the public were we to declare that the defendant's cultivation of marihuana and its use for his medicinal purposes may not be punishable. We cannot dismiss the reasonably possible negative impact of such a judicial declaration on the enforcement of our drug laws, including but not limited to those dealing with marihuana, nor can we ignore the government's overriding interest in the regulation of such substances.

Justice Liacos dissented:

> While I recognize that the public has a strong interest in the enforcement of drug laws and in the strict regulation of narcotics, I do not believe that the interest would be significantly harmed by permitting a jury to consider whether the defendant cultivated and used marihuana in order to alleviate agonizing and painful symptoms caused by an illness. The court seems to suggest that we should not condone the use of marihuana, regardless of a particular individual's reasons for using the drug. Although the court appears to recognize the defense by taking this position, it fails to give sufficient consideration to the rationale behind the common law defense of necessity. That rationale is based on the recognition that, under very limited circumstances, the value protected by the law is, as a matter of public policy, eclipsed by a superseding value which makes it inappropriate and unjust to apply the usual criminal rule.

> The superseding value in a case such as the present one is the humanitarian and compassionate value in allowing an individual to seek relief from agonizing symptoms caused by a progressive and incurable illness in circumstances which risk no harm to any other individual. In my view, the harm to an individual in having to endure such symptoms may well outweigh society's generalized interest in prohibiting him or her from using the marihuana in such circumstances. On a proper offer of proof I would recognize the availability of a necessity defense when marihuana is used for medical purposes. *Accord: Jenks v. State*, 582 So.2d 676 (Fla.Dist.Ct.App.1991); *State v. Bachman*, 61 Haw. 71 (1979); *State v. Hastings*, 118 Idaho 854 (1990); *State v. Diana*, 24 Wash.App. 908 (1979). *
> * * *

(2) In *Commonwealth v. Leno*, 415 Mass. 835 (1993), defendants were charged with distribution of hypodermic needles without a prescription.

> Leno started a needle exchange program in Lynn in September, 1990, after realizing that "in my own back yard, people were dying of AIDS, and this particular service was not offered to them." Leno testified that he believed that by providing clean needles to addicts he was helping to stem the spread of AIDS, he was helping addicts, especially the homeless, to reach recovery, and that he was not helping addicts continue their habit. *
> * * *

> The two defendants legally purchased new sterile needles over-the-counter in Vermont. The defendants were at a specific location on Union Street in Lynn from 5 P.M. to 7 P.M. every Wednesday evening in 1991 until they were arrested June 19. They accepted dirty needles in exchange for clean needles; they exchanged between 150 and 200 needles each night, for fifty to sixty people. The defendants did not charge for the service or for the materials. * * * *

> The defendants offered expert testimony on AIDS and needle exchange programs. Doctor Ernest Drucker of the Montefiore Medical Center in the Bronx, who is also a professor of epidemiology at Einstein College of

Medicine and an authority on the treatment of drug users and the relationship between intravenous drug use and AIDS, stated that: the sharing of needles by infected drug users transmits the AIDS virus; the mortality rate of persons diagnosed with human immunodeficiency virus (HIV) ten years ago is very high, in that fewer than five per cent still are alive; there is no cure for AIDS; studies of needle exchange programs revealed no evidence that such programs cause people who are not drug addicts to become addicts, but that evidence indicates that needle exchange programs bring some addicts into drug and AIDS treatment programs who would not otherwise be there; he could not think of any harmful effects caused by needle exchange programs, and no studies found harmful effects; needle exchange programs save lives; and AIDS accounts for three times as many deaths as all other drug-related causes, such as overdosing, combined. * * * *

The court held that the trial court had properly refused to instruct the jury on the necessity defense.

The defendants' argument is that, in their view, the prescription requirement for possession and distribution of hypodermic needles and syringes is both ineffective and dangerous. The Legislature, however, has determined that it wants to control the distribution of drug-related paraphernalia and their use in the consumption of illicit drugs. That public policy is entitled to deference by courts. Whether a statute is wise or effective is not within the province of courts. * * * *

Citizens who disagree with the Legislature's determination of policy are not without remedies. The popular initiative is coextensive with the Legislature's law-making power under Part II, c.1, § 1. See also Mass. Const. Pt. I, art. 19 (the right of people to petition the Legislature). Thus, the defendants did not meet the requirement that there be no legal alternative to abate the danger.

The defendants argue that the increasing number of AIDS cases constitutes a societal problem of great proportions, and that their actions were an effective means of reducing the magnitude of that problem; they assert that their possession, transportation and distribution of hypodermic needles eventually will produce an over-all reduction in the spread of HIV and in the future incidence of AIDS. The defendants' argument raises the issue of jury nullification, not the defense of necessity. We decline to require an instruction on jury nullification. We recognize that jurors may return verdicts which do not comport with the judge's instructions. We do not accept the premise that jurors have a right to nullify the law on which they are instructed by the judge, or that the judge must inform them of their power.

Compare *People v. Bordowitz*, 588 N.Y.S.2d 507 (Crim.Ct. N.Y.City, 1991), where defendants were charged with possession of a hypodermic instrument. After a non-jury trial, the court issued a written verdict:

The defendants contend that they were engaged in a needle exchange program justified by the exigencies created by the AIDS epidemic. By providing clean needles to drug addicts, coupled with health care counseling, the defendants argue they were helping to prevent the spread of HIV infection, thereby saving lives. They claim that their actions fall squarely within the provisions of the "necessity" justification defense. * * * *

This court finds it was reasonable for the defendants to believe their action necessary as an emergency measure to avert an imminent public injury. Without doubt, AIDS has created an imminent crisis in New York City. There is no dispute that use of clean needles by addicts prevents the spread of HIV infection. The defendants presented significant expert medical and public health witnesses who testified that needle exchange programs have proven successful as a means of providing addicts with clean needles which addicts will use.

The witnesses further testified that addicts are either aware of or can be educated to the fact that needle sharing spreads the virus. Although studies in this area are limited, defense witnesses claimed the available evidence suggests addicts will not continue to share needles if they know they have a source for clean ones. Moreover, the witnesses testified that there is no reason to believe needle exchange programs encourage people to use drugs.

Most significantly, when coupled with AIDS education and counseling, a needle exchange program serves as a means for convincing addicts to avoid other risk-related behavior, to get medical care and ultimately to discontinue use of drugs.

Others may not agree with this approach. The People's witness (Dr. Brown) suggests that not enough is known about the long term effects of a needle exchange program on the community and that, in any event, such a program is merely a band-aid solution. Without fundamental societal changes such as providing increased job opportunities and better education, AIDS will remain just one of a myriad of problems facing the poorer communities of this city.

There is much validity to Dr. Brown's contentions. However, the issue before this court is not to choose between the different policy options offered by the witnesses, nor is it necessary for defendants' efforts to be proven successful. Rather, the court must find whether it was reasonable for the defendants, relying on competent medical evidence, to engage in the conduct at issue. While defendants' actions alone would not end the epidemic, it is reasonable to believe their actions served to avert further risks of infection for some individuals. This court is satisfied that the nature of the crisis facing this City, coupled with the medical evidence offered, warranted defendants' action.

Obviously, the defendants themselves did not create the crisis. Although some might argue that addicts have brought this scourge upon themselves, that would not preclude the defendants from trying to help the addicts or to help prevent the spread of the disease by the addicts to unsuspecting sex partners or unborn children.

This court is also satisfied that the harm the defendants sought to avoid was greater than the harm in violating the statute. Hundreds of thousands of lives are at stake in the AIDS epidemic. The crime of possessing a hypodermic needle was enacted as a weapon in the war on drugs. Although law enforcement officials believe the statute essential in this fight, available evidence suggests it has had limited success. As the testimony revealed, only eleven states have statutes similar to New York's law. Despite these statutes, these states — and New York in particular — have among the highest rates of addiction and there are still plenty of dirty needles available. The defendants did not violate the drug possession laws. Rather, they violated a law that has been of limited, if any, success in preventing illegal drug use.

The distinction, in broadest terms, during this age of the AIDS crisis is death by using dirty needles versus drug addiction by using clean needles. The defendants' actions sought to avoid the greater harm.

It is equally apparent that there were no meaningful available options. As the evidence revealed, insufficient drug programs exist for the number of addicts in New York and there is no reason to believe more treatment slots will come into existence in the near future. Moreover, many addicts are not willing or able to face the need for full scale treatment and withdrawal from drugs. Providing counseling or bleach kits only would not be as direct or successful an approach. Defendants' action was not hastily considered and occurred only after the city shut its own needle exchange program.

No legislative or executive action precludes the necessity defense in this case. The hypodermic possession statute and the related public health law provision were enacted to fight drug usage well before the onset of the AIDS crisis. The state legislature has yet to consider whether to revise the hypodermic possession statute in the wake of the epidemic. Although efforts to repeal or amend the law have not been successful, without a specific vote based on consideration of the AIDS epidemic, this court cannot find legislative action to have precluded the defense in this case.

Moreover, as one of the defendants testified, the government has given mixed signals on whether it approves or disapproves the idea of a needle exchange program (Williams). The City Department of Health ran its program for over a year despite a vote by the City Council disapproving the concept. The city ended its program without, apparently, any clear reason being given. Police action against the defendants has, at best, been sporadic. Thus, neither legislative nor executive action precludes the defense. * * * *

For the reasons set forth in this decision, with respect to the one count of criminally possessing a hypodermic needle, this court finds each of the defendants not guilty.

(3) In *In re Eichorn*, 69 Cal.App.4th 382 (1998), Eichorn was convicted of violating a Santa Ana city ordinance barring camping in public parks. He offered a necessity defense:

> Eichorn had offered to prove that on the night of the violation every shelter bed within the city that was available to a homeless single man with no children was occupied, and that he was involuntarily homeless, i.e., he had done everything he could to alleviate his condition. Due to circumstances beyond his control, defendant, a 14-year resident of Santa Ana, had been unable to find work as a manual laborer that paid enough to allow him to find an alternative place to sleep.

The trial court refused to allow this evidence, because it failed to show that Eichorn violated the ordinance in order to avoid a significant evil. "What do you mean ' bodily harm?' Like tired eyelids or blood? If he didn't sleep here, he'd lose sleep and this would be a horrible physical thing to impose on him?"

The appellate court reversed Eichorn's conviction:

> At a minimum, reasonable minds could differ whether defendant acted to prevent a "significant evil." Sleep is a physiological need, not an option for humans. It is common knowledge that loss of sleep produces a host of physical and mental problems (mood irritability, energy drain and low motivation, slow reaction time, inability to concentrate and process information). Certainly, no one would suggest that a groggy truck driver who stops his rig on the side of a road rather than risk falling asleep at the wheel does not act to prevent a significant evil, i.e., harm to himself and others.

> The court must instruct if the evidence could result in a finding defendant's criminal act was justified by necessity. Eichorn's offer of proof was sufficient. There was substantial if not uncontradicted evidence that defendant slept in the civic center because his alternatives were inadequate and economic forces were primarily to blame for his predicament. Thus, whether denominated a denial of his right to jury trial or of his due process right to present a defense the court's error was clear, fundamental, and struck at the heart of the trial process.

> The court suggested defendant had adequate alternatives to sleeping in a public place in Santa Ana ("The court is aware firsthand that other buildings, nearby churches have rear stairs, rear doors. Couldn't your client have found a nice little warm, covered stairwell, on private property, to sleep? How about other private property, backyards, trees, under a tree in a condemned home? Is it a reasonable alternative walking a mile or so to a nearby city without a camping ordinance? Stroll on a nice sunny day, find a cushy spot in Tustin, in a city park and make his home there.") For guidance of the court at any retrial, neither trespassing on private property nor walking to a different city was an adequate alternative. Simply put, Santa Ana may not "solve" its social problems by foisting them onto nearby localities; an individual who has no reasonable alternative to sleeping in a public place in Santa Ana need not travel in search of streets and other

public places where he can catch his 40 winks.

Compare *Hoagland v. State*, 126 Nev. Adv. Rep. 37 (2010), where defendant was charged with driving under the influence of intoxicating liquor (DUI):

> Hoagland was sleeping in his truck in an "employee parking" stall at the Salvation Army in Las Vegas. A security officer for the Salvation Army approached the truck and informed Hoagland that he could not sleep on the property and requested that Hoagland move his truck to another location. Hoagland was living out of his truck and believed that if he did not move his truck, it would be towed and impounded with all of his belongings.

> Hoagland, attempting to comply with the request, backed into another parked vehicle. Although he never left the parking lot, Hoagland drove to the other side of the building only to return within minutes to the scene of the accident. The security officer called the Las Vegas Metropolitan Police Department (Metro), blocked the driveway exiting the parking lot, and ordered Hoagland to park his truck. When the Metro officer arrived, he conducted a field sobriety test, which Hoagland failed. Hoagland was subsequently arrested and charged with driving and/or being in actual physical control of a vehicle while under the influence of intoxicating liquor.

> During his opening statement at trial, Hoagland asserted the defense of necessity. He informed the jury that he had no other choice, under the circumstances, but to operate his truck while intoxicated. * * * * Hoagland made an offer of proof: that prior to the security officer's request that he move his truck, he had no intention of driving while intoxicated; he had no means to drive his truck because his keys were with another party and were only given to him after he was instructed to move his truck; and he feared that if his truck was impounded, he would lose his shelter and personal possessions and would be unable to pay the impound fees. Therefore, according to Hoagland, it was necessary for him to move his truck while intoxicated.

The trial court held that this offer of proof was insufficient to justify instructing the jury on necessity. The Nevada Supreme Court agreed:

> While we have not formulated the elements of the necessity defense to DUI, authority from other jurisdictions consistently include one element - whether the defendant presented sufficient evidence to show that he did not substantially contribute to the emergency or create the situation.

> Hoagland's offer of proof shows that he parked his truck in a prohibited parking stall at the Salvation Army. Hoagland's actions of parking in a prohibited stall created the situation requiring him to operate his truck while under the influence. As a result, Hoagland's offer of proof does not satisfy the element that the defendant did not substantially contribute to the situation. Therefore, we conclude that the district court was not required to instruct the jury on the necessity defense.

(4) In the late 1980's, an Israeli Commission issued a report concerning the use of "physical pressure" by Israeli General Security Service (GSS) agents while

interrogating persons (usually Arabs) suspected of Hostile Terrorist Activity (HTA). The Commission also addressed the agents' practice of falsely testifying (at subsequent criminal trials of some of the suspects) that no torture was used. The Commission noted that the interrogation was used primarily to obtain information regarding plans for terrorist acts in the future, and thus the agents were trying to obtain only true information (rather than false confessions) and that this was designed to save innocent lives (rather than to obtain convictions). The Commission found that the interrogation methods were justified by the necessity doctrine, but the perjury was improper. An American law professor commented:

> It is not surprising that the Commission found no authoritative judicial discussion — in Israel or elsewhere — of the significance of the necessity defense in the special context of activities designed to foil terrorist acts. Simply put, the necessity defense is not an appropriate rubric under which to consider the problems faced by the GSS. This is so for several reasons.

> The necessity defense is by its very nature an *emergency* measure: it is not suited to situations which recur over long periods of time. This is especially so when the claimant to the benefits of the defense is a state agency for its members.

> A state agency faced with systemic problems over a long period of time has options available to it other than civil disobedience — other than the deliberate decision to violate the law repeatedly. These options may not be completely satisfactory, but they are democratic options: namely, to seek a change in the law, an exemption from the law's strictures, or a change in its own responsibilities. A legislature or court — or populace — faced with "weighing the two evils against each other," at least has the authority and legitimacy to make the choice. An individual law enforcement agent or agency does not — and for good reasons.

> Even if the mere *public* disclosure of the problem would be dangerous to the security of the state — always a matter of degree, especially in an open democracy like Israel where the problem will inevitably surface as it did here — there are *secret* options which are far more democratic than the ones employed here. Among these are special cabinet committees or judicial panels authorized to approve special measures under extraordinary circumstances.

> Perhaps I am especially skeptical of the claims of "necessity" as an American. If that defense were available in my country, it would be quickly employed by the likes of Colonel Oliver North, to justify his lying to Congress, and by former President Richard M. Nixon, to justify the break-in at the Democratic National Committee and its subsequent cover-up. Indeed, in my country, the defense of necessity is being used — abused — by all manner of illegal protestors ranging from Abbie Hoffman to Amy Carter to anti-abortion protestors.

> Moving back to Israel, what if Palestinian rock-throwers raised the defense of their "honor or property?" Would the courts be forced to choose — on an entirely political basis — between conflicting claims? Or what if a

suspected terrorist decides to resist the "physical pressures" of his interrogators by physical countermeasures designed to protect his honor or person — i.e., what if he fights back? Could he defend himself against assault charges by invoking "necessity"?

The point of the necessity defense is to provide a kind of "interstitial legislation," to fill "lacunae" left by legislative and judicial incompleteness. It is not a substitute legislative or judicial process for weighing policy options by state agencies faced with long-term systemic problems.

To demonstrate the inappropriateness and subjectivity of the necessity defense to the problems faced by the GSS, it is interesting to ask why the Commission so quickly and forcefully rejected its application to the systematic lying engaged in by the agents? This is what the Commission says: "Here the investigator cannot rely on the defense of necessity, since perjury is a grave criminal offence and manifestly illegal, above which flies the black flag saying "forbidden."

So held! *Ipse dixit!* But why? The GSS interrogators believed that lying was *as necessary* to their work as applying physical pressure. Both are grave criminal offenses and are manifestly illegal. The difference surely cannot be that the immediate victims of the illegal physical pressure are suspected Arab terrorists, whereas the immediate victims of the perjury are the judges! [Alan Dershowitz, *Is It Necessary to Apply "Physical Pressure" to Terrorists — And To Lie About It?*, 23 Israel Law Revew 192 (1989)].

Chapter 16

ENTRAPMENT

There are currently two major approaches to the defense of entrapment . . . . The majority view is usually referred to as the "subjective approach" . . . . A two-step test is used under the subjective approach: the first inquiry is whether or not the offense was induced by a government agent; and the second is whether or not the defendant was predisposed to commit the type of offense charged. * * * * The emphasis under the subjective approach is clearly upon the defendant's propensity to commit the offense rather than on the officer's misconduct.

The objective approach focuses upon the inducements used by the government agents. This means that entrapment has been established if the offense was induced or encouraged by "employing methods of persuasion or inducement which create a substantial risk that such an offense will be committed by persons other than those who are ready to commit it."

LaFave & Scott, *Criminal Law* (West)

Which definition of entrapment is better? Before deciding, perhaps you should consider why there should be *any* defense of entrapment.

Jim (a private citizen) urges his friend Dan to use cocaine: "It will make you feel good." Dan declines: "I've never done drugs, and I don't plan to start now." Jim persists, and eventually Dan succumbs to temptation, "just this once."

Has Dan committed the crime of "use of cocaine"? It would seem so. Dan had the requisite *mens rea*, and he committed the necessary *actus reus*. Jim's pressure does not negate any element of the charged crime. Jim has "pressured" Dan, but his pressure didn't rise to the level of *duress*. Dan might not be as culpable as regular cocaine users, but that fact should be considered only when sentencing him. *Jim* might be guilty of some crime (solicitation of — or perhaps being an accomplice to — use of cocaine), but that fact seems irrelevant to *Dan's* criminal liability.

Suppose, however, we keep all the facts the same, except one: Jim was no mere private citizen, but instead was an undercover police officer. *Now* does Dan have a possible defense? Why? Some might say that Jim or his superiors are not very good police officers — they should not be spending taxpayers' money tempting people to commit crimes, when so many "real" criminals are running around uncaught. Others might say that Jim performed a valuable public service — now, anyone thinking of following his "friend's" suggestion that he commit a crime must worry that his "friend" is in fact a cop.

An interesting debate, which might be resolved when the police chief's contract is up for renewal or at the next mayoral election. But what does it have to do with Dan's criminal liability? Why should Dan have *any* "entrapment" argument? Why should he be relieved of criminal liability merely because — unbeknownst to Dan — his tempter was a cop?

A satisfactory answer to this question (if there is one) might help us decide *which test* for entrapment best serves the legitimate purposes (if there are any) of the defense of entrapment.

PROBLEM 16

To: My Law Clerk

From: Superior Court Judge Leonard Handelman

Sue Snow, Norman Nome, and Jack Frost are each on trial for possession of stolen property. Each has moved for dismissal of the charges, on the grounds of entrapment and denial of due process. Though these are separate cases, I held a joint hearing on the motions, because they stemmed from the same operation set up by the Anchorage Police Department. Attached is the transcript of key testimony at that hearing. Please review it and the attached authorities and advise me as to whether I should grant any of the motions.

Transcript of Testimony of Sergeant Preston

Q: Sergeant Preston, how did you happen to meet defendant Snow?

A: We had reports from some oil companies about thefts of equipment, so we set up a "sting store". We rented a storefront and called it "Constable Supply Company." Snow came in one day and looked around, and I started talking to her. She said she worked at Avaricious Oil Company. I told her that I would pay good prices for any tools she brought in, and I didn't care where she got them, and I gave her a wink. The next day, she came in with a set of tools worth about $100. She wanted to sell them for $200. I paid her the $200 and she left.

Q: Sergeant Preston, in fact you took those tools home and used them to work on your own snowmobile, isn't that right?

A: Well, I guess I did, but I brought most of them back to the police department when I was done.

Q: How did you happen to meet defendant Frost?

A: He came in looking to buy a special kind of drill called a "double-diamond drill". I didn't have one in the store. He said he needed it badly for a job he was doing. I said I would try to get him one.

Q: How did you meet defendant Nome?

A: After Frost left, Nome came in looking for work. He said that he had just lost his job and was broke and needed to feed his family. I told him that I didn't have a job for him, but I needed a double-diamond drill, and I would pay him $400 if he brought one in. I told him Spill Oil Company had some, and that Slick's watchman usually took a nap at about 10 p.m. The next day, Nome came in with one of the drills. He thanked me for my tip, and I paid him $400 for the drill.

Q: Did you see Frost again?

A: Yes. He came in again a few days later, saying that he still needed a double-diamond drill. I said, "I just got one, but it's hot." He said, "I'd better not. I don't want any trouble." I said, "There won't be trouble. The police don't care about this kind of thing. These drills are really hard to get. If you don't buy this one, I'll sell it to someone else, and there might not be another one around for months. It's worth $400, but I'll sell it to you for $300." He paid me the $300 and left with the drill.

Alaska Statutes, § 11.81.450: ENTRAPMENT.

In any prosecution for an offense, it is an affirmative defense that, in order to obtain evidence of the commission of an offense, a public law enforcement official or a person working in cooperation with the official induced the defendant to commit the offense by persuasion or inducement as would be effective to persuade an average person, other than one who is ready and willing, to commit the offense. Inducement or persuasion which would induce only a person engaged in an habitual course of unlawful conduct for gain or profit does not constitute entrapment. [Enacted in 1978]

Note: Compare Model Penal Code § 2.13, in the Appendix.

GROSSMAN v. STATE
Supreme Court of Alaska
457 P.2d 226 (1969)

CONNOR, JUSTICE.

This appeal raises the question of whether the evidence before the court below required a finding of entrapment as a matter of law.

Appellant was indicted for selling morphine to an undercover agent of the Alaska State Police. She pleaded not guilty, was tried by a jury, and was convicted and sentenced upon a verdict of guilty. At the close of the prosecution's case, her counsel moved for a judgment of acquittal on the ground that the evidence required a finding of entrapment as a matter of law. The motion was denied and the issue of entrapment was submitted to the jury, which found against appellant. * * * * *

Although some authorities regard the defense of entrapment as a relatively simple concept, outstanding jurists have had difficulty in stating a workable or rational set of rules for its application. The doctrine of entrapment has occupied an identifiable position in our law for over 50 years, having evolved from earlier decisions covering unconscionable deceit or activity by the police.[5]

---

[5] Examples from the earlier cases are *United States v. Healy*, 202 F. 349 (D.Mont.1913), in which the

It is plain enough that the underlying basis of entrapment is found in public policy, as discerned and announced by the courts. As Judge Learned Hand perceptively observed in *United States v. Becker*, 62 F.2d 1007, 1009 (2d Cir. 1933),

> The whole doctrine derives from a spontaneous moral revulsion against using the powers of government to beguile innocent, though ductile, persons into lapses which they might otherwise resist.

A similar notion was expressed in *Butts v. United States*, 273 F. 35, 38 (8th Cir., 1921), where the court said,

> It is unconscionable, contrary to public policy, and to the established law of the land to punish a man for the commission of an offense of the like of which he had never been guilty, either in thought or in deed, and evidently never would have been guilty of if the officers of the law had not inspired, incited, persuaded and lured him to attempt to commit it.

It is in the attempt to state more precise standards that trouble has been encountered. In *Sorrells v. United States*, 287 U.S. 435, the majority opinion viewed entrapment as an implied statutory condition that one who has been entrapped shall not be convicted of violating the statute. It held that the defense of entrapment should be treated as a matter of law when the facts are substantially undisputed, but as a question of fact for the jury when the evidence is more conflicting. The court stated that the officers of government may afford opportunities to commit crime, may employ artifice and stratagems to catch persons engaged in criminal enterprise, but they cannot implant in the mind of an innocent person the disposition to commit the alleged offense and induce its commission in order that they may prosecute.

The court emphasized that entrapment applies only when the criminal conduct is "the product of the creative activity" of the government agents. It held that the determination in each case should focus on whether the particular defendant was predisposed to commit the crime or was an otherwise innocent person who would not have erred except for the persuasion of the government's agents. This permits a searching inquiry into the conduct and motivations of both the officers and the defendant, including the past conduct of the defendant in committing similar crimes, and the general activities and character of the defendant.

In a separate opinion by Mr. Justice Roberts, who was joined by Brandeis and Stone, JJ., it was urged that entrapment in all cases should be determined by the trial court as a matter of law. He did not regard entrapment as a true defense, but as an analogue of the principle in civil actions that the courts will refuse their aid in perpetrating or consummating an illegal scheme. He saw entrapment as based on public policy which protects the purity of government and its processes, and not as an implied statutory condition to be attributed to congressional intent.

Because the effect of the *Sorrells* decision was to focus inquiry upon the particular mental and character traits of the defendant, it has been labeled by some

---

defendant was charged with selling liquor to an Indian who was disguised to mislead the accused as to his race; and *United States v. Whittier*, 28 F.Cas. 591 (C.C.E.D.Mo.1878), where the government connived with the victim to lure the defendant into a violation of the postal laws.

as a "subjective" test. The outlines of the *Sorrells* approach were stated by Judge Learned Hand in United *States v. Becker*, 62 F.2d 1007 (2d Cir. 1933). There is little that could be added to his summary to express the state of the law under *Sorrells* today. In his analysis, the inquiry turns on whether the government instigation of a crime is excusable. He observed,

> The only excuses that courts have suggested so far as we can find, are these: an existing course of similar criminal conduct; the accused's already formed design to commit the crime or similar crimes; his willingness to do so, as evinced by ready complaisance. The decisions are plentiful, but the judges generally content themselves with deciding the case upon the evidence before them; we have been unable to extract from them any definite doctrine, and it seems unprofitable once more to merely catalogue the citations. However, it has been uniformly held that when the accused is continuously engaged in the proscribed conduct, it is permissible to provoke him to a particular violation which will be no more than an instance in a uniform series.

The majority opinion in *Sorrells* was reaffirmed in *Sherman v. United States*, 356 U.S. 369 (1958). But four members of the court, speaking through Mr. Justice Frankfurter, took issue with the majority and with the majority in the *Sorrells* case. They proposed an objective test of whether the police activity falls below standards of fair and honorable administration of justice. The standards of honorable administration of justice would depend upon the effect of the officer's inducements upon an average person, and not upon the particular defendant in each case. The determination would not be made by the jury. The standards themselves would be evolved gradually in accumulative precedents. The effect would be to check police activity in a manner similar to the exclusionary rules that apply to search and seizure, custodial interrogation, and confessions.

The minority opinion in *Sherman* dealt with both the policy behind the law of entrapment and the way in which that policy can best be effectuated:

> The courts refuse to convict an entrapped defendant, not because his conduct falls outside the proscription of the statute, but because, even if his guilt be admitted, the methods employed on behalf of the Government to bring about conviction cannot be countenanced. * * * * Insofar as they are used as instrumentalities in the administration of criminal justice, the federal courts have an obligation to set their face against enforcement of the law by lawless means or means that violate rationally vindicated standards of justice, and to refuse to sustain such methods by effectuating them. They do this in the exercise of a recognized jurisdiction to formulate and apply proper standards for the enforcement of the federal criminal law in the federal courts. [356 U.S. at 380]

The minority then stated that the better way to further this policy is to focus the determination upon the character of the police conduct rather than upon the defendant's predisposition. To rest the determination on the origin of intent is irrelevant because,

> In every case of this kind the intention that the particular crime be committed originates with the police, and without their inducement the crime would not have occurred. [356 U.S. at 382]

The result of that logic is that the inquiry becomes limited to one of predisposition, and the defendant is then put on trial for his past offenses and character. This results in prejudice, especially if the question is presented to a jury. Moreover, the result will differ on whether the defendant has previously committed a crime or has no record.

> Appeals to sympathy, friendship, the possibility of exorbitant gain, and so forth, can no more be tolerated when directed against a past offender than against an ordinary law-abiding citizen. Past crimes do not forever outlaw the criminal and open him to police practices, aimed at securing his repeated conviction, from which the ordinary citizen is protected. The whole ameliorative hopes of modern penology and prison administration strongly counsel against such a view. [356 U.S. at 383]

The scholarly examinations of the defense of entrapment have also revealed the inadequacies of the subjective test.[8] To speak of entrapment as an implied statutory condition, and then to focus inquiry on the origin of intent, the implantation of criminal design, and the predisposition of the defendant does not make much sense. If entrapment is a substantive condition of guilt, then it ought to apply when private persons induce the commission of an offense. But no court has ever been willing to make such an application of the *Sorrells* doctrine. An external standard, if it can be achieved, is certainly preferable to a doctrine founded in theoretical riddles.

We feel that the proper solution is the objective test, which focuses the determination upon the particular conduct of the police in the case presented. Inducements should be limited to those measures which, objectively considered, are likely to provoke to the commission of crime only those persons, and not others, who are ready and willing to commit a criminal offense.

The objective test can be stated as follows: unlawful entrapment occurs when a public law enforcement official, or a person working in cooperation with him, in order to obtain evidence of the commission of an offense, induces another person to commit such an offense by persuasion or inducement which would be effective to persuade an average person, other than one who is ready and willing, to commit such an offense. Conversely, instigations which would induce only a person engaged in an habitual course of unlawful conduct for gain or profit do not constitute entrapment.[9]

Examples of what might constitute prohibited activity, depending upon an

---

[8] The American Law Institute in its proposed Model Penal Code has recommended that an objective test should be employed. Model Penal Code § 2.13 (Proposed Official Draft, 1962). [Ed.: Model Penal Code § 2.13 appears in the Appendix.]

[9] DeFeo, *Entrapment As A Defense To Criminal Responsibility: Its History, Theory and Application*, 1 U.S.F.L.Rev. 243 (1967), criticizes the objective test because he believes that it permits only police activity which would tempt a chronic violator, but would require that a number of situational offenders be set free who commit consensual offenses. We do not intend such a result, nor do we state the test of entrapment in those terms.

evaluation of the facts in each case, are extreme pleas of desperate illness, appeals based primarily on sympathy, pity, or close personal friendship, and offers of inordinate sums of money. While the line between what is permitted and not must be drawn somewhat as a matter of degree, this is no different from many determinations which the courts must make in the case before them. For example, an officer should be able to offer money in reasonable amounts at a prevailing price level in an unlawful traffic. But offers of profit which are grossly disproportionate to what is reasonably expectable in that traffic should not be permitted when those offers would have the effect of overwhelming the self-control of a normal person.

In applying the objective test we do not mean that the course of conduct between the officer and the defendant should be ignored. The transactions leading up to the offense, the interaction between the officer and the defendant, and the defendant's response to the inducements of the officer are all to be considered in judging what the effect of the officer's conduct would be on a normal person.

In short, we do not intend that entrapment should become a ready escape hatch for those who are engaged in a course of criminal enterprise. But, under standards of civilized justice, there must be some control on the kind of police conduct which can be permitted in the manufacture of crime.

While we do not need to consider in this case all of the procedural changes which flow from our decision, it is obvious that the issue of entrapment can be litigated either before or during trial and should be determined by the court and not the jury.

We now turn to the case before us.

At her trial appellant presented no evidence on her own behalf. The state's evidence consisted largely of the testimony of Joseph P. Turner about the events leading up to the sale of morphine and the circumstances of the sale itself. His testimony was along the following lines.

Officer Turner was assigned to the Anchorage area during November of 1967 to investigate and report on criminal activities in Anchorage. On December 2, 1967, at about 5:30 a.m., he went to the Woods' Barbecue, an establishment run by the appellant. On that occasion he had a conversation with her during which she said that she was using pills to stay awake and that if he needed any she could get him some. He declined this offer but said that he could use some "pot." They discussed the price and he ordered a matchbox of it. He returned at about 10:30 a.m. that day, at which time she said she would get the marijuana. Subsequently she did get the marijuana for him.

Officer Turner throughout his dealings with the appellant made it his policy to gain her confidence and attempt to befriend her. He saw her almost daily from the date of their first meeting until December 18, 1967, the date of the offense charged. On one occasion, the night of December 4, he took appellant to various bars in the Anchorage area. At another time he helped her with her grocery shopping. His policy of friendship toward appellant was so successful that she asked Turner to help her run the bar on December 8.

The officer testified to other dealings with the appellant leading up to the sale of morphine. On December 3, while at the Woods' Barbecue, he asked the appellant about the possibilities of getting "dexies" (amphetamines). She said that she would take care of it for him, and he ordered about a dozen. On December 8 he delivered some pills for her and collected payment from the recipient for her. In the early morning of December 12 she told him that when the "squares" left the premises of the Woods' Barbecue there would be a party. Apparently he did not stay for the party. On December 16 appellant asked Turner to watch the bar for her while she took someone home. She said that if anyone came by for pills while she was gone to tell them she would have some on Monday.

On December 13 officer Turner again went to the bar, and on this occasion he asked appellant about the possibility of getting some "hard stuff" for a friend in Fairbanks who needed a new contact. By "hard stuff" the officer said that he meant heroin or morphine. Officer Turner stated that between the time of this initial request and the sale, he repeated his request a number of times. He specifically mentioned a telephone call he made to the appellant on December 15 when he asked if she had received the morphine yet. On December 18 she told the officer that she had received the shipment. She then took him to her trailer and sold him part of the shipment amounting to ten "fixes." She told him also that she had given some of the shipment to a friend to dispose of on her behalf. It was for the sale to officer Turner that appellant was arrested and prosecuted.

Although, in the present case, Turner dated the defendant on one occasion, there is no evidence of a romantic relationship between them. Nor does it appear that the brief friendship between them was close. After appellant evinced an interest in supplying marijuana and dexedrine pills to Turner, he was justified in continuing his contacts with her and in asking to purchase morphine.

Under the objective test we have announced today, the issue of entrapment is to be ruled on by the trial court. Therefore, it was error for the court below to submit the question to the jury. Although on the face of the record appellant's claim seems rather weak, we feel that the trial judge who heard and saw the witness would be better able to weigh the evidence. Accordingly, the case is remanded to the superior court for determination of the issue of entrapment by the trial judge. If the trial judge should conclude, as the jury was allowed to conclude, that the claim of entrapment was not sustained, the conviction shall stand. If the trial judge reaches a different result, the indictment should be dismissed.

Reversed and remanded.

NOTES FROM JUDGE HANDELMAN:

(1) Suppose Turner were not working for the police, but was merely a private citizen interested in ferreting out crime. Could Grossman then use an entrapment defense? Why (not)?

(2) Under *Grossman's* "objective" test for entrapment, am I to ask myself whether the "average person" would made a deal with Preston? Who is the "average person?"

(3) The court in *Grossman* seemed to believe that its "objective" test would *expand* the entrapment defense. Does it?

(4) Why should the issue of entrapment be decided by the trial judge instead of by the jury? Doesn't the jury decide factual question of guilt or innocence?

(5) In *U.S. v. Hollingsworth*, 9 F.3d 593 (7th cir. 1993), the court explored and explained "the animating idea behind the doctrine of entrapment", and on how the "predisposition" requirement fits into it:

> The federal government shall not use its resources to increase the criminal population by inducing people to commit crimes who otherwise would not do so. The reason that this is a matter of judicial concern rather than of unreviewable prosecutorial discretion is not that the courts want to economize on the costs of running the criminal justice system — the responsibility for the efficient allocation of resources to criminal prosecution is lodged elsewhere in our governmental system — but because the proper use of the criminal law in a liberal society is to regulate potentially harmful conduct for the protection of society, rather than to purify minds and to perfect character. A person who would not commit a crime unless induced to do so by the government is not a threat to society and the criminal law has no proper concern with him, however evil his thoughts or deficient his character. The moral law is different; Eve's plea of entrapment by the serpent was rejected. The criminal law of a secular polity has a more limited domain.
>
> A person who will commit a particular type of crime without being induced to do so by government agents — who in other words is predisposed to commit this type of crime although, for want of a suitable opportunity, he would not have committed it when he did had it not been for the government's inducement - is a threat to society. The likelihood that he has committed this type of crime sometime in the past or that he will do so sometime in the future is great, and by arranging for him to commit it now, in circumstances that enable the government to apprehend and convict him, the government punishes and prevents real crimes at lower cost than would be possible if the circumstances had been allowed to develop without government intervention.

In *Soriano v. State*, 248 P.3d 381 (Okla.Crim.App. 2011), the court stated:

> Trickery and deceit are natural and inherent parts of any sting operation. The government agents and informants directly involved in such stings are often misrepresenting their true identities, and they are always misrepresenting their true intentions, i.e., they are purporting to be willing participants in a crime, when they are actually trying to "catch" the target in the commission of that crime, in order to apprehend, prosecute, or perhaps use that target in a future sting. Hence the entrapment question is more about what kind of person the government has set out to catch, and whether that person was already ready and willing (i.e., "predisposed") to commit the crime at issue when he or she was first approached, than it is about whether the government tricked or deceived that target. The public policy behind the entrapment defense is meant to discourage the government from corrupting the innocent (otherwise law-abiding citizens) in its legitimate quest to apprehend and prosecute the wicked (those who are

already violating or already ready and willing to violate the law at issue).

(6) The *Sorrells-Sherman* "predisposition" test for entrapment is alive and well in our federal courts. Or is it? In *Jacobson v. United States*, 503 U.S. 540 (1992), a 56-year old Nebraska farmer was charged with knowing receipt of child pornography through the mails. Postal inspectors had found his name on a mailing list of a bookstore that had sent him similar materials before such receipt became illegal. Inspectors sent him a letter supposedly from "The American Hedonist Society," a fictitious organization, inviting him to join. He did, returning a "sexual attitude questionnaire" indicating an interest in "pre-teen sex." Inspectors then sent him information from another fictitious organization supporting "sexual freedom and freedom of choice," which purported to lobby for the repeal of "age of consent" laws. Then an inspector calling himself "Carl Long" wrote to Jacobson and asked what kind of materials he liked, and defendant responded "I like good looking young guys (in their late teens and early 20's) doing their thing together." Inspectors then sent him a catalog of child pornography from another fictitious company. Jacobson ordered "Boys Who Love Boys." Inspectors mailed it, Jacobson received it, and inspectors arrested him. The trial court properly instructed the jury on the "predisposition" test of entrapment, but the jury convicted him. The Supreme Court reversed, holding that Jacobson had been entrapped "as a matter of law."

Artifice and stratagem may be employed to catch those engaged in criminal enterprises. In their zeal to enforce the law, however, Government agents may not originate a criminal design, implant in an innocent person's mind the disposition to commit a criminal act, and then induce commission of the crime so that the Government may prosecute. Where the Government has induced an individual to break the law and the defense of entrapment is at issue, as it was in this case, the prosecution must prove beyond reasonable doubt that the defendant was disposed to commit the criminal act prior to first being approached by Government agents.

Thus, an agent deployed to stop the traffic in illegal drugs may offer the opportunity to buy or sell drugs, and, if the offer is accepted, make an arrest on the spot or later. In such a typical case, or in a more elaborate "sting" operation involving government-sponsored fencing where the defendant is simply provided with the opportunity to commit a crime, the entrapment defense is of little use because the ready commission of the criminal act amply demonstrates the defendant's predisposition. Had the agents in this case simply offered petitioner the opportunity to order child pornography through the mails, and petitioner — who must be presumed to know the law — had promptly availed himself of this criminal opportunity, it is unlikely that his entrapment defense would have warranted a jury instruction.

But that is not what happened here. By the time petitioner finally placed his order, he had already been the target of 26 months of repeated mailings and communications from Government agents and fictitious organizations. Therefore, although he had become predisposed to break the law by May 1987, it is our view that the Government did not prove that this predisposition was independent and not the product of the attention that the

Government had directed at petitioner since January 1985. * * * *

Rational jurors could not say beyond a reasonable doubt that petitioner possessed the requisite predisposition prior to the Government's investigation and that it existed independent of the Government's many and varied approaches to petitioner. * * * *

When the Government's quest for convictions leads to the apprehension of an otherwise law-abiding citizen who, if left to his own devices, likely would have never run afoul of the law, the courts should intervene.

JUSTICE O'CONNOR and 3 other Justices dissented:

Today, the Court holds that Government conduct may be considered to create a predisposition to commit a crime, even before any Government action to induce the commission of the crime. In my view, this holding changes entrapment doctrine. Generally, the inquiry is whether a suspect is predisposed before the Government induces the commission of the crime, not before the Government makes initial contact with him. There is no dispute here that the Government's questionnaires and letters were not sufficient to establish inducement; they did not even suggest that Mr. Jacobson should engage in any illegal activity. If all the Government had done was to send these materials, Mr. Jacobson's entrapment defense would fail. Yet the Court holds that the Government must prove not only that a suspect was predisposed to commit the crime before the opportunity to commit it arose, but also before the Government came on the scene.

The rule that preliminary Government contact can create a predisposition has the potential to be misread by lower courts as well as criminal investigators as requiring that the Government must have sufficient evidence of a defendant's predisposition before it ever seeks to contact him. Surely the Court cannot intend to impose such a requirement, for it would mean that the Government must have a reasonable suspicion of criminal activity before it begins an investigation, a condition that we have never before imposed. The Court denies that its new rule will affect run-of-the-mill sting operations, and one hopes that it means what it says. Nonetheless, after this case, every defendant will claim that something the Government agent did before soliciting the crime "created" a predisposition that was not there before. For example, a bribe taker will claim that the description of the amount of money available was so enticing that it implanted a disposition to accept the bribe later offered. A drug buyer will claim that the description of the drug's purity and effects was so tempting that it created the urge to try it for the first time. In short, the Court's opinion could be read to prohibit the Government from advertising the seductions of criminal activity as part of its sting operation, for fear of creating a predisposition in its suspects. That limitation would be especially likely to hamper sting operations such as this one, which mimic the advertising done by genuine purveyors of pornography. No doubt the Court would protest that its opinion does not stand for so broad a proposition, but the apparent lack of a principled basis for distinguishing these scenarios exposes a flaw in the more limited rule the Court today adopts.

How would *Jacobson* have been analyzed and decided by the Alaska Supreme Court, under its "objective" test for entrapment?

(7) In *U.S. v. Gendron*, 18 F.3d 955 (1st Cir. 1994), Judge (now Justice) Breyer stated:

> The Supreme Court saw in the entrapment defense not so much a sanction used to control police conduct, but rather a protection of the ordinary law-abiding citizen against government overreaching. Consequently, it saw no need to permit a defendant to take advantage of that defense unless he himself was such a citizen. The upshot is that we must find out just who that "innocent person" is. Who is the "otherwise law-abiding citizen" who would not "otherwise" have committed the crime?
>
> The question's difficulty lies in the word "otherwise." That word requires us to abstract from present circumstances. We cannot simply ask whether, without the government's present activity, the defendant would likely have committed the crime when he did. After all, without the government's having presented that opportunity, the defendant, no matter how "predisposed," would likely not have acted then. Nor can we simply ask whether the defendant would have acted similarly at some other time had he faced similar circumstances, since his present behavior virtually compels an affirmative answer to the question phrased in this way.
>
> The right way to ask the question, it seems to us, is to abstract from — to assume away — the present circumstances insofar as they reveal government overreaching. That is to say, we should ask how the defendant likely would have reacted to an ordinary opportunity to commit the crime. By using the word "ordinary," we mean an opportunity that lacked those special features of the government's conduct that made of it an "inducement," or an "overreaching." Was the defendant "predisposed" to respond affirmatively to a proper, not to an improper, lure?
>
> This way of looking at the matter seems to flow from the way in which the Supreme Court has resolved the clash between "objective" and "subjective" views of entrapment — at least if one looks at that resolution as simply denying the defense to one whom it is not designed to help, namely the kind of defendant who (without a "sting") might well be out committing crimes of the sort that a "sting" seeks to stop. Further, our effort to define "predisposition" through reference to the nature of the government conduct reflects the fact that, despite partial descriptions that focus primarily upon the defendant's state of mind, government misconduct lies at the heart of the entrapment defense. Were that not so — were the issue simply the defendant's state of mind — the law would permit an innocent minded defendant to raise an entrapment claim when a private person "induced" him (through similar "overreaching" conduct) to commit a crime. But the law does not authorize the defense in those circumstances, however "outrageous" the private person's conduct.
>
> Finally, this way of phrasing the question prevents one from concluding automatically, simply from the fact that the defendant committed the

crime, that he was "predisposed" to commit it. At the same time, if the answer to the question so phrased is affirmative, the defendant would seem to be the sort of person (and his conduct in this instance is the sort of conduct) that the criminal statute intends to punish. He is, in other words, someone who would likely commit the crime under the circumstances and for the reasons normally associated with that crime, and who therefore poses the sort of threat to society that the statute seeks to control, and which the government, through the "sting," seeks to stop.

PASCU v. STATE
Supreme Court of Alaska
577 P.2d 1064 (1978)

BURKE, JUSTICE.

This appeal concerns the defense of entrapment.

On November 25, 1975, Gordon Pascu sold one half ounce of heroin to Phillip Geiger and James Blair. Geiger and Blair were police agents.[1] Pascu, as a result of that transaction, was indicted for sale of a narcotic drug, in violation of AS 17.10.010.

Following his indictment, Pascu's attorney sought a pre-trial hearing on his claim of entrapment. That request was granted, and the hearing was held before the Honorable Jay A. Rabinowitz, justice of the Supreme Court of Alaska, sitting, by assignment, as judge of the Superior Court. After the presentation of Pascu's evidence, the state requested a ruling on the sufficiency of his showing of entrapment before calling its own witnesses. Justice Rabinowitz ruled that such evidence was not sufficient to establish the defense. Following his later conviction before another judge and the entry of a final judgment, Pascu appealed.

I.

On appeal, Pascu first contends that Justice Rabinowitz erred in denying his claim of entrapment. We agree and reverse his conviction on that ground.

In *Grossman v. State*, 457 P.2d 226, 227 (Alaska 1969), we noted that "the underlying basis of (the defense of) entrapment is found in public policy," quoting Judge Learned Hand's remarks in *United States v. Becker*, 62 F.2d 1007, 1009 (2d Cir. 1933), "The whole doctrine derives from a spontaneous moral revulsion against

---

[1] Geiger was apparently a modern version of the legendary bounty hunter. After being indicted on multiple counts for sale and possession of narcotic drugs, Geiger entered into an agreement with the Fairbanks District Attorney's office. By the terms of the agreement, Geiger was given sixty days to obtain evidence against no less than six other individuals, with which those individuals could be charged with narcotics violations. In return, it was agreed that all but one of the charges against Geiger would be dismissed. On the remaining charge, he agreed to plead guilty in return for a recommendation of leniency. In further consideration of Geiger's services, the state agreed to dismiss all but one of several similar charges pending against his girlfriend, Kathy Blair. James Blair was not actually a party to the agreement. However, the record clearly demonstrates that he was working with Geiger and under the supervision of the police. Thus, he too must be considered a police agent.

using the powers of government to beguile innocent, though ductile, persons into lapses which they might otherwise resist." Adopting an "objective test," we held, in *Grossman*, that permissible inducements on the part of law enforcement officials "should be limited to those measures which, objectively considered, are likely to provoke to the commission of crime only those persons, and not others, who are ready and willing to commit a criminal offense." 457 P.2d at 229. We described the objective test as follows:

> Unlawful entrapment occurs when a public law enforcement official, or a person working in cooperation with him, in order to obtain evidence of the commission of an offense, induces another person to commit such an offense by persuasion or inducement which would be effective to persuade an average person, other than one who is ready and willing, to commit such an offense. Conversely, instigations which would induce only a person engaged in an habitual course of unlawful conduct for gain or profit do not constitute entrapment.

Since announcing our decision in *Grossman*, we have come to realize that there are certain difficulties in applying the foregoing standard. An "average person" probably cannot be induced to commit a serious crime except under circumstances so extreme as to amount to duress. Yet it is clear that entrapment may occur where the degree of inducement falls short of actual duress. What is prohibited, by *Grossman*, is unreasonable or unconscionable efforts on the part of the police to induce one to commit a crime so that he may be arrested and prosecuted for the offense. In determining whether entrapment has occurred, the trial court must focus "upon the particular conduct of the police in the case presented." The question is really whether that conduct falls below an acceptable standard for the fair and honorable administration of justice.

With these basic principles in mind, we turn to the facts in the instant case.[4]

Pascu, a heroin addict, testified that he had known Blair for four or five years, and that they were good friends. On November 25, 1975, Blair contacted him and asked Pascu to buy heroin for him. According to Pascu, Blair "said that he was sick and that he needed a fix."[5] At that time Blair appeared to Pascu to be undergoing narcotics withdrawal. Blair also told Pascu that he had a friend who was "very sick, sicker than he was." Pascu refused Blair's plea for help. He testified that he told Blair that he was "pretty much in the same boat," in that he was trying to stop using heroin himself, "was feeling sick too,"[6] and that he didn't think he should obtain

---

[4] Of course the "facts" at this point in time and derived entirely from the evidence presented by the defense, since the state has not yet presented its evidence on the issue of entrapment. If and when the state has the opportunity to present contrary evidence, the true facts may prove to be entirely different. The resolution of any conflicts in the evidence will be a matter for the trial court.

[5] "Sick" is a term used by those in the drug culture to describe one suffering withdrawal symptoms. A "fix" is a shot of heroin. To "get well" means to "shoot enough heroin to take away the withdrawal to get high."

[6] Earlier Pascu testified that he was "trying very hard" to stop using drugs and was suffering from withdrawal.

heroin for Blair.[7] When asked what Blair's reaction was, Pascu testified, "He was quite upset. He was very agitated because he said he'd had a whole day of looking for heroin, and not being able to find any, and that he had been sick when he woke up."

According to Pascu, Blair continued with his efforts to persuade Pascu to obtain heroin for him, doing so "a number of times;" he reminded Pascu that they had been friends for a long time and that he had done similar favors for Pascu in the past when Pascu had been "sick."[8] Pascu testified:

> I explained to him that I was trying to clean up, and that I didn't want to put myself up front, and expose myself to heroin; that it would be pretty hard for me to stay away from it. And he again asked me, and he reminded me that we'd been friends for a number of years, and that he had done me a lot of favors in the past, and he thought it was very cold-blooded of me not to not to at least try to get him something. And he did this two or three more times.

Blair also offered Pascu a share of the heroin, sufficient to alleviate Pascu's own withdrawal pains:

> Blair said that I looked sick, and he said I could probably use a hit of dope, and that he would give me a hit of dope, if I would do that. And then he went on to say that he would give me enough to get down, and enough for tomorrow morning, which was the next day. It would be worth roughly $200.[9]

Eventually, Pascu yielded and entered into the transaction leading to his indictment and conviction.

We hold that the evidence presented was sufficient to establish the defense of entrapment, and that Justice Rabinowitz erred in ruling to the contrary. We believe such evidence, viewed objectively, shows a degree of inducement going well beyond the limits of permissible police conduct described in *Grossman v. State*. Thus, Pascu's conviction must be reversed.

It is quite clear from the record before us that Blair played heavily on his close personal friendship with Pascu, making repeated appeals to Pascu's sense of obligation and sympathy. In addition, Blair took advantage of Pascu's own addiction and withdrawal pains by offering to give him enough heroin to "make him well."[10]

---

[7] Pascu indicated that he feared that if he exposed himself to heroin he would not be able to resist the temptation to resume use of the drug.

[8] Pascu explained that when he had been "sick," Blair had supplied him with the heroin he needed to relieve his withdrawal symptoms.

[9] Although Pascu indicated that he could also have made a $300 monetary profit in the transaction, there was no evidence that Blair actually offered him any such amount.

[10] We think this case is clearly distinguishable from *McKay v. State*, 489 P.2d 145 (Alaska 1971). There we held that entrapment had not been established by evidence that an undercover police officer represented himself to be a "big man in narcotics," offered the defendant a fifty-fifty split of the profits in a marijuana sale worth $10,000, and said he had a friend who was addicted and needed heroin badly. Unlike Pascu and Blair, the officer and the defendant in that case were not close friends. Noting that

We are firmly convinced that law enforcement officials can, and often must, employ deceptive measures in order to detect and apprehend those engaged in criminal conduct, particularly in the area of narcotics. Thus, it is quite proper for the police to provide the opportunity for one engaged in criminal activities to ply his trade. See, e.g., *McKay v. State, supra* note 10. However, we also subscribe to the view that officials cannot "implant in the mind of an innocent person the disposition to commit the alleged offense and induce its commission in order that they may prosecute." *Sorrells v. United States*, 287 U.S. 435 (1932).[11] "Under standards of civilized justice, there must be some control on the kind of police conduct which can be permitted in the manufacture of crime." *Grossman v. State, supra.*

In order to allow the state an opportunity to present its evidence on the issue of entrapment, this matter is remanded to the superior court. After hearing such evidence as may be presented, the superior court shall resolve any factual conflicts that may arise as a result of that evidence, and thereafter redetermine the issue of entrapment.[12]

* * * *

Reversed and remanded.

Matthews, Justice, concurring.

I agree with the majority that the average man standard of *Grossman v. State* requires modification and that what is sought to be prevented by the defense of entrapment is unreasonable or unconscionable police conduct. I would particularize this somewhat by adding that in drug sales it is neither unconscionable nor unreasonable for a police agent to behave as an ordinary buyer. The police should be allowed to provide stimuli to induce a drug sale which are like those which a seller normally encounters. It may not be unusual for a buyer of illegal drugs to claim, or for a seller to require a buyer to claim, dire physical need for drugs. If that is the case, a police agent ought to be able to feign a drug need. In such cases the inquiry should be whether the persuasion employed by the police is significantly greater than that generally encountered for similar transactions. This approach has been employed in a number of California cases;[1] its advantage is that it does not permit drug sellers to insulate themselves from conviction by the device of requiring all their customers to grovel briefly before a sale is made.

---

after mentioning his "strung-out friend" the officer did not emphasize that fact further, and the fact that drug sales commonly involve large profits, we rejected the defendant's claim of entrapment, concluding that there was "a strong inference that he was ready and willing to engage in the drug transactions wholly independent of the officer's pleas to his humanitarian and pecuniary motives." The evidence in this case just as strongly suggests an opposite inference.

[11] In *Grossman*, we rejected the subjective test enunciated in *Sorrells*. Thus, *Sorrells* is quoted here simply to describe what we consider to be impermissible police conduct.

[12] The accused must carry the burden of establishing the defense of entrapment by a preponderance of the evidence. *Batson v. State*, 568 P.2d 973, 978 (Alaska 1977).

[1] E.g., *People v. Braddock*, 41 Cal.2d 794 (1953); *People v. Woolwine*, 258 Cal.App.2d 385 (1968). [Ed. - More recently, the California Supreme court has adopted the "objective" test set out in *Grossman*. See *People v. Barraza*, 23 Cal.3d 675, 689-691 (1979).]

In this case, there was but one short conversation which lead to the sale. The trial judge had the opportunity to judge the demeanor of the witnesses, and he was not required to believe all that he heard. For these reasons, I am not persuaded that we are justified in ruling as a matter of law that the defense of entrapment was made out. However, in light of the modified standard expressed in this opinion, I would remand to the superior court for a rehearing.

DIMOND, JUSTICE PRO TEM, concurring.

I agree with the majority in holding that the evidence presented was sufficient to establish the defense of entrapment. But I am hesitant to accept the court's statement that "We are firmly convinced that law enforcement officials can, and often must, employ deceptive measures in order to detect and apprehend those engaged in criminal conduct, particularly in the area of narcotics."

In the course of pursuing those engaged in traffic in drugs, it is a wide-spread and almost standard procedure for the police to utilize the services of one against whom criminal charges may be brought or are pending. In exchange for immunity against prosecution, and at times with some monetary inducement, such a person buys drugs from those who are able to procure and sell them and then informs against those persons in subsequent criminal prosecutions.

This procedure may be of value in obtaining convictions for drug related offenses. But the means of achieving this is of dubious justification. The difficulty I have with this type of law enforcement is that it is based almost wholly on lies and deceit.

I believe it is essential to have objective morality and ethics in law, because this is essential to the "civilized justice" that the majority refers to. If I am correct, then it is repugnant to that concept to justify the apprehension of criminals on the basis that the end justifies the means i.e., that it is proper to utilize the tools of lies and deceit to effect criminal justice. In my opinion, this means of obtaining a desired end is distasteful and objectionable, because it eventually undermines, rather than enhances, the high standards of conduct in the administration of justice required of law enforcement agencies and the courts of this state.

NOTES FROM JUDGE HANDELMAN:

(1) Now I'm thoroughly confused. Did *Pascu* change the "average person" test? What is the test for entrapment in Alaska now? How does it apply to our case?

(2) If the "average person" test were applied to Pascu, was he entrapped?

(3) I found Justice Dimond's concurring opinion intriguing. What effect would his position — if adopted — have on the enforcement of narcotics laws and the investigation of organized crime?

(4) In *U.S. v. Thickston*, 110 F.3d 1394 (9th Cir. 1997), the court held that five factors may be considered to show predisposition: (1) the defendant's character and reputation, (2) whether the government initially suggested the criminal activity, (3) whether the defendant engaged in the activity for profit, (4) whether the defendant showed any reluctance, and (5) the nature of the government's inducement.

(5) In *State v. Dawson*, 681 So.2d 1206 (Fla.App. 1996), the court held that Dawson was not entrapped into stealing the closed bag or piece of luggage which police officers had intentionally left unattended in the passenger area of an airport as part of an undercover police operation designed to catch luggage thieves. Leaving a closed bag unattended did not operate as an "inducement" to open the bag and steal it.

Can *Dawson* be reconciled with *State v. Powell*, 726 P.2d 266 (Hawaii, 1986)? The facts:

> The incidence of thefts and robberies in the vicinity of the intersection of Wilikina Drive and Kamehameha Highway in Wahiawa prompted a police decision to institute a series of "drunk decoy" operations in the area of the reported crimes. And between November of 1984 and March of 1985 officers of the Honolulu Police Department organized such operations on eleven occasions and arrested nineteen individuals. Laverne Powell was arrested on March 21, 1985 when she pilfered a wallet containing nine dollars.

> The victim on this occasion was a police officer feigning drunkenness. As he lay on his side in a fetal position with a paper bag containing a beer bottle in his hand, a wallet protruded from a rear pocket of his jeans. That the wallet contained money was rendered obvious by the partial exposure of currency. Several other officers stationed themselves at nearby vantage points and awaited possible criminal activity. Shortly after 11:00 p.m., Laverne Powell walked by the officer posing as a helpless drunkard. She then turned back, approached the apparently vulnerable victim, and stole the wallet planted on his person. Two officers who witnessed the theft sprang from cover and apprehended Ms. Powell as she left the scene. The Grand Jury returned an indictment charging Laverne Powell with Theft in the First Degree.

The Hawaii Supreme Court held that this constituted entrapment as a matter of law:

> The State argues a reversal of the court's ruling is in order because the police were "looking to interrupt ongoing criminal activity" and employed means "reasonably tailored to apprehend those involved in stealing from intoxicated persons." But we are convinced from a review of the record that the police "employed methods of inducement which created a substantial risk that theft would be committed by persons other than those who were ready to commit it." HRS § 702-237(1)(b).

> That the police were concerned with reports of "thefts and robberies in the area" is not to be disputed. Nor can the decision to organize covert operations be faulted. Criminal activity is such that stealth and strategy are necessary weapons in the arsenal of the police officer. Yet the reported thefts and robberies did not involve sleeping drunks or thefts of the same nature as the instant case. We would be hard put to contradict the circuit court's further finding that the "drunk decoy" operations were expressly designed to ensnare anyone who would commit theft when "bait money" is

placed in plain view and within easy reach.

The stealth and strategy employed here resulted in the apprehension of nineteen persons, including Laverne Powell, for "rolling drunks." Undeniably, the function of law enforcement is the prevention of crime and the apprehension of criminals. Yet, what was reported previously as happening in the vicinity were thefts of a different nature, including robberies. Manifestly, the law enforcement function does not include the manufacturing of crime. Under the circumstances, we would have to agree with the circuit court that the "drunk decoy" operation created a substantial risk that thief would be committed by persons other than those who were ready to commit it.

Can *Powell* be reconciled with *People v. Watson*, 22 Cal.4th 220 (2000)? Watson was charged with stealing a car.

One March evening in 1997, Bakersfield police officers conducted a vehicle theft "sting" operation. They staged an arrest of a plainclothes police officer driving a black 1980 Chevrolet Monte Carlo that belonged to the police department. The arresting officers activated the emergency lights and siren of their marked patrol car and stopped the Monte Carlo. The Monte Carlo's driver drove into a parking lot and parked. While a group of spectators watched, a uniformed police officer approached the Monte Carlo, ordered the driver out, patted him down, handcuffed him, placed him in the backseat of the patrol car, and drove away, leaving the Monte Carlo behind. The police left the Monte Carlo unlocked with the keys in the ignition to make it easier to take. They wanted to "give the impression the driver was arrested and the vehicle was left there."

A couple of hours later, police arrested defendant after he drove the Monte Carlo from the parking lot. He told the arresting officer that his niece had informed him of the earlier apparent arrest and told him to "come and take" the car. He did just that, intending to use it to "roll," i.e., to drive it. * * * *

The California Supreme Court held that this evidence did not justify a jury instruction on entrapment:

Merely providing people in general an opportunity to commit a crime is not an improper enticement or otherwise entrapment. The rule is clear that ruses, stings, and decoys are permissible stratagems in the enforcement of criminal law, and they become invalid only when badgering or importuning takes place to an extent and degree that is likely to induce an otherwise law-abiding person to commit a crime.

The sting operation in this case presents no evidence of entrapment, both because the police did not specifically intend it as a communication to defendant personally, and because it did not actually *guarantee* anything, but merely conveyed the idea detection was unlikely. The police did nothing more than present to the general community a tempting opportunity to take the Monte Carlo. Some persons, obviously including defendant, might have found the temptation hard to resist. But a person who steals when given the opportunity is an opportunistic thief, not a normally law-abiding person. Specifically, normally law-abiding persons do not take a car not belonging to them merely because it is unlocked with the keys in the ignition and it appears they will not be caught. Defendant presented no evidence of any personal contact whatever between police and himself; certainly he could not show that the police cajoled him, gave him any enticement or guarantee, or even knew or cared who he was.

In his concurring opinion, Justice Mosk argues that "next we may anticipate arranging for a homeowner to leave his front door open all night to attract a burglar. Or a bank to leave a signed check on the counter to attract a forger. Or leaving a loaded gun on a park bench to attract a potential robber." A big difference exists, however, between the police risking their own property in tightly controlled circumstances and asking the public to do the same (or, in the loaded gun hypothetical, to invite violence) in uncontrolled circumstances. Moreover, the police might reasonably believe that sting operations like this *deter*, not encourage, crime. For example, once word of this case circulated in the community, future would-be car thieves might hesitate before taking advantage of what appears to be an easy target.

JUSTICE MOSK concurred:

I cannot resist expressing my reservations about the morality of the conduct by the police.

It is a primary function of a law enforcement agency not only to investigate the commission of crimes but also to prevent their commission in the first place, certainly not to encourage them. Members of the public are persuaded to lock their motor vehicles and to remove the keys therefrom. The police acted to the contrary here and thus deliberately encouraged commission of a crime. The defendant, so motivated, accommodated them.

If leaving the keys in an open motor vehicle is sound law enforcement, then next we may anticipate arranging for a homeowner to leave his front door open all night to attract a burglar. Or a bank to leave a signed check on the counter to attract a forger. Or leaving a loaded gun on a park bench to attract a potential robber. Police may thus apprehend more criminals. But there will be more crimes.

In a strange rebuttal, the majority opinion refers to the police "risking their own property." The fact, of course, is that police possess and use *public property* and must act with that in mind.

My preference is for law enforcement agencies to take steps to make the commission of crimes impossible, or at least more difficult, rather than simpler. Admittedly there are potential criminals in our midst, and weak-willed persons who will take advantage of criminal opportunity. I would prefer discouraging them rather than devising techniques to make their task easier.

(6) In *U.S. v. Staufer*, 38 F.3d 1103 (9th Cir., 1994), the court found "sentencing entrapment" where, although Staufer was predisposed to selling drugs in small quantities, he was not predisposed to sell the large quantity of LSD undercover DEA agents induced him to sell. Therefore, Staufer was entitled to a downward departure from his sentence for possession with intent to distribute LSD.

In *U.S. v. Cannon*, 886 F.Supp. 705 (D.N.D. 1995), the court held that the government engaged in impermissible "sentencing entrapment." While defendants had requested that undercover government agents supply them with handguns, the agents brought machine guns as well, for no legitimate purpose other than to increase the defendants' sentences. Possession of the machine gun carried a 30 year mandatory sentence, while the handgun offenses carried only five years.

ANCHORAGE v. FLANAGAN
Court of Appeals of Alaska
649 P.2d 957 (1982)

BRYNER, CHIEF JUDGE

In this case, we are called upon to review an order entered by the district court dismissing, on grounds of entrapment, a criminal complaint filed by the Municipality of Anchorage. * * * *

The essential facts are not in dispute. During the month of January, 1981, John H. Chandler worked on a voluntary basis as a reserve officer for the Anchorage Police Department. While reading a local advertising tabloid, Chandler spotted an advertisement for the "North Star Dating Service." He mentioned the ad to members of the Anchorage Police Department's vice squad, with whom he occasionally worked, and was encouraged to call the dating service. Chandler placed a call on January 31, 1981. The call was answered by a woman who gave Chandler directions to the dating service and told him that he could receive a "body massage" for the price of forty dollars.

In order to ascertain whether the North Star Dating Service was involved in prostitution, Chandler, with the approval of vice squad officers, agreed to go to that establishment and pose as a prospective customer. Chandler followed the directions he had been given to reach the dating service; upon arrival, he knocked at the door. Lynda Flanagan answered the door and asked Chandler to enter. Flanagan asked Chandler if he was the person who had just called, and when Chandler responded that he was, Flanagan led him to a bedroom.

In the bedroom, Chandler asked Flanagan a number of questions about her willingness to perform specific sexual acts in return for payment of money. Although Flanagan initially indicated some suspicion that Chandler might be an undercover police officer, she eventually told him that she would perform a body massage for forty dollars, fellatio for fifty dollars, and a combination of fellatio and sexual intercourse for sixty dollars.

Chandler told Flanagan that he wanted her to perform both fellatio and sexual intercourse, and he paid her sixty dollars. He was then directed by Flanagan to take off his clothes and lie down on the bed; Flanagan also disrobed. Once Chandler was undressed and on the bed, Flanagan gave him a brief back massage after which she asked him to turn over. Chandler complied with this request, and when he did so, Flanagan stroked his penis several times with her hand. After a period of several seconds, Flanagan prepared to engage in fellatio with Chandler. At this point, Chandler stopped Flanagan and placed her under arrest. She was charged with assignation for the purpose of prostitution, a misdemeanor under Anchorage Municipal Code § 8.14.020.

Flanagan filed a pretrial motion to dismiss the complaint against her on the ground of entrapment. In the motion, she argued that Chandler had waited an impermissibly long period of time before performing an arrest and that Chandler's willingness to engage in sexual contact with Flanagan before arresting her was unconscionable conduct, amounting to entrapment under Alaska law.

After conducting an evidentiary hearing, the district court granted Flanagan's motion to dismiss. In granting the motion, the court relied primarily on a portion of the holding in *Pascu v. State*, 577 P.2d 1064 (Alaska 1978). We conclude that the district court's application of the *Pascu* standard of entrapment to the particular factual circumstances of this case was mistaken. Flanagan at no time asserted, nor did the district court find, that Chandler's conduct before he disrobed and permitted Flanagan to engage in sexual contact with him was improper. Indeed, it would be difficult to claim entrapment based solely on Chandler's adoption of an undercover role and his involvement in a conversation with Flanagan in the course of which he arranged to obtain sexual favors in return for the payment of money. As the court in *Pascu* noted:

> It is quite proper for the police to provide the opportunity for one engaged in criminal activities to ply his trade. [577 P.2d at 1068][2]

Thus, the district court's finding of entrapment in this case was, of necessity, predicated exclusively upon the fact that Chandler delayed his arrest of Flanagan until after sexual contact between them had been initiated.

We do not believe, however, that the defense of entrapment, as provided for in *Pascu*, can properly be invoked as to the challenged conduct on the part of Chandler. We reach this conclusion because we find that those aspects of Chandler's conduct which have been challenged were not causally related to Flanagan's commission of the crime charged.

The entrapment doctrine has traditionally been regarded as a safeguard against the use of unfair inducement by law enforcement officers to instigate commission of crimes by individuals who would otherwise be innocent of wrongdoing. This view of the defense of entrapment was espoused by the Alaska Supreme Court in *Grossman v. State*, 457 P.2d 226, 227 (Alaska 1969): "It is plain enough that the

---

[2] See also *United States v. Becker*, 62 F.2d 1007, 1008 (2d Cir. 1933), in which Judge Learned Hand wrote:

> It has been uniformly held that when the accused is continuously engaged in the proscribed conduct, it is permissible to provoke him to a particular violation which will be no more than an instance in a uniform series.

underlying basis of entrapment is found in public policy, as discerned and announced by the courts." * * * *

This view of the entrapment defense presupposes the existence of some form of active inducement that leads to the commission of an offense by the accused.

The need for a causal link between police conduct and the commission of a crime by the accused as a precondition to invocation of the entrapment defense was recently noted by the Michigan Court of Appeals. In *People v. Moore*, 73 Mich.App. 514 (1977), the court, applying an objective standard of entrapment, concluded that drug use by an undercover police officer in the presence of the defendant prior to the defendant's sale of drugs to the officer did not constitute entrapment. In so holding, the court in *Moore* relied on a finding that the officer's conduct was independent of and causally unconnected to the defendant's sale of drugs:

> We cannot find a causal connection between the acts of the officer and those of the defendant that could be properly characterized as inducement or incitement. The acts were independent of each other, so do not warrant invocation of the entrapment sanction.

In this case, even assuming that the mere acquiescence by Chandler to Flanagan's sexual contact with him could be construed as a form of police conduct inducing or instigating commission of an offense, it is manifest that this conduct was independent of and unconnected to Flanagan's commission of the offense of assignation. In no realistic sense could it be said that Flanagan's decision to commit the crime of assignation was prompted by, or causally related to the questioned conduct on Chandler's part. In fact, Flanagan accepted Chandler's money and agreed to commit an act of prostitution, thus in effect committing the crime charged,[3] prior to Chandler's acquiescence to sexual contact.

The district court apparently recognized the absence of any causal nexus between the challenged conduct of Chandler and the commission of assignation by Flanagan. Nevertheless, the court interpreted our supreme court's decision in *Pascu v. State* as dispensing with any requirement of police inducement or persuasion as a prerequisite to the defense of entrapment.

Pascu undeniably expanded the scope of the entrapment defense by abandoning the objective, "average person" standard of entrapment previously adopted by the court in *Grossman v. State*, 457 P.2d at 229. However, we do not think that *Pascu* can correctly be read to have abandoned the need for police conduct involving inducement, persuasion or instigation as an essential component of the entrapment defense. * * * *

In this case, the district court chose to emphasize the language of *Pascu*, in which the Alaska Supreme Court stated:

---

[3] This is true regardless of whether or not the offense of assignation for the purpose of prostitution is considered to be a continuing offense. Even if Flanagan's touching of Chandler is deemed to be an act in furtherance of the initial assignation, thus rendering the offense a continuing one, evidence of such continuing conduct is not necessary to prove assignation. Under the terms of AMC 8.14.020 and 8.14.010(a), all acts necessary to establish the crime of assignation were completed when Flanagan made an engagement with Chandler for an act of prostitution.

In determining whether entrapment has occurred, the trial court must focus "upon the particular conduct of the police in the case presented." The question is really whether that conduct falls below an acceptable standard for the fair and honorable administration of justice. [577 P.2d at 1067]

Applying that part of the *Pascu* standard, the district court concluded that Chandler's conduct fell "below an acceptable standard for the fair and honorable administration of justice," and that it therefore constituted entrapment.

In our view, however, this language of the *Pascu* decision cannot properly be read in isolation; it must be read in the context of the paragraph in which it appears:

> Since announcing our decision in *Grossman*, we have come to realize that there are certain difficulties in applying (the "average person") standard. An "average person" probably cannot be induced to commit a serious crime except under circumstances so extreme as to amount to duress. Yet it is clear that entrapment may occur where the degree of inducement falls short of actual duress. What is prohibited, by *Grossman*, is unreasonable or unconscionable efforts on the part of the police to induce one to commit a crime so that he may be arrested and prosecuted for the offense. In determining whether entrapment has occurred, the trial court must focus "upon the particular conduct of the police in the case presented." The question is really whether that conduct falls below an acceptable standard for the fair and honorable administration of justice. [577 P.2d at 1066-67]

Upon a reading of the entirety of this paragraph, it becomes apparent that the supreme court, in deciding *Pascu*, did not intend to expand the entrapment defense by opening up all police conduct in criminal cases — without regard to whether the conduct induced or was otherwise causally related to commission by the accused of the offense charged — to general judicial scrutiny for the purpose of determining "whether that conduct falls below an acceptable standard for the fair and honorable administration of justice." Repeated references by the supreme court to police inducement furnish a strong indication of its intent to limit scrutiny of police conduct to cases within the traditional scope of the entrapment doctrine: those cases in which commission of an offense was apparently the direct result of inducement by law enforcement officials.

Because the police conduct that served as the basis for Flanagan's claim of entrapment in this case cannot realistically be viewed as having induced or instigated Flanagan's commission of the offense of assignation for the purpose of prostitution, and because this conduct appears to have had no other causal connection to the crime with which Flanagan was charged, we hold that the defense of entrapment was inapplicable and could not properly be invoked as the basis for dismissal of the complaint.

Flanagan has alternatively maintained that the district court's order of dismissal must be upheld on the ground that Chandler's conduct violated her constitutional right to due process. U.S. Constitution, Amendments V and XIV; Alaska Constitution, Art. I. § 7. The question whether police conduct that does not constitute entrapment can be held to violate due process absent a violation of an independent constitutional right of the accused was the subject of passing but inconclusive reference by the United States Supreme Court in *United States v. Russell*, 411 U.S. 423, 431-32 (1973). The Alaska Supreme Court has noted *Russell's* reference to the possibility of a due process defense based on police misconduct. However, the court has neither adopted nor rejected the theory. See *Evans v. State*, 550 P.2d 830, 844-45 (Alaska 1976).

A number of cases have expressly applied the due process theory. However, these cases have invariably dealt with situations involving extensive and elaborate efforts by law enforcement officers to induce criminal activity or manufacture crime; they have uniformly arisen in jurisdictions that adhere to the subjective theory of entrapment and have involved situations where the defendant was foreclosed from raising entrapment as a result of affirmative evidence of his subjective predisposition to commit the offense charged. See *United States v. Twigg*, 588 F.2d 373 (3d Cir., 1978); *People v. Isaacson*, 44 N.Y.2d 511 (1980). Such cases might well fall within the broader, objectively based standard of entrapment applicable in Alaska under *Pascu v. State*.

However, in the present case, we need not decide whether dismissal of a criminal charge on due process grounds might be compelled under appropriate circumstances. It is sufficient to observe that the circumstances of the present case involve conduct falling short of a due process violation. Any case involving a potentially tenable due process claim would require the existence of outrageous police conduct, shocking the universal sense of justice and violating the concept of fundamental fairness. We do not think that Chandler's conduct approaches this level of seriousness.

Our conclusion in this regard is bolstered by the recent decision in *State v. Putnam*, 31 Wash.App. 156 (1982). In *Putnam*, the Washington Court of Appeals rejected the assertion of a due process defense in a case involving use of an undercover civilian agent who actively worked as a prostitute over a period of several months while infiltrating an illicit enterprise engaged in the business of prostitution. While the investigation in *Putnam* resulted in felony convictions, the investigative tactics employed by police in that case were far more repugnant than those in the present case. Although Chandler's conduct toward Flanagan might be considered questionable, we do not think that this conduct — even in the context of an investigation involving a relatively minor misdemeanor charge — can accurately be characterized as outrageous; nor do we think that Chandler's conduct toward Flanagan could fairly be said to shock the universal sense of justice. Accordingly, we find no violation of Flanagan's due process right to fundamental fairness.

The order of the district court dismissing the complaint in this case is reversed, and this case is remanded for further proceedings.

NOTES FROM JUDGE HANDELMAN:

1. In *Commonwealth v. Chon*, 983 A.2d 784 (Pa. Super. 2009), Chon was charged with prostitution. The trial court granted her motion to dismiss due to "outrageous government conduct" — not entrapment. The appellate court affirmed the dismissal:

The Pennsylvania State Police commenced a prostitution investigation at Shiatsu Spa based upon a complaint by a citizen. It appears that after receiving a massage, the citizen was offered manual sexual stimulation by "Coco," but he was not able to afford the additional fee. Instead, he reported the conversation with "Coco" to the state police, who, after concluding he was an "acceptable informant," provided him with the fees for sexual contact.

On June 8, 2006, the citizen volunteered his services to the police and was provided with $100 in pre-recorded money and equipped with a transmitter to visit Shiatsu Spa as a customer. The monies provided to the citizen were used to purchase sexual acts at the Spa, in the amount of sixty ($60) dollars, and to compensate the citizen for his "time", in the amount of forty ($40) dollars. The state police investigator provided instructions to the citizen, including taking "universal precautions regarding sexual contact with any employees." The citizen, in response, indicated that he had brought condoms. The citizen was also searched prior to entering the premises, and, according to the investigating trooper, no concealed weapons were uncovered. Thereafter, he entered Shiatsu Spa, received manual sexual stimulation for sixty ($60) dollars and was permitted to fondle "Gina's" breasts. Testimony also revealed that after the activities inside Shiatsu Spa, the citizen was debriefed. The tape of the incident reveals both banter and laughter between the citizen and the police.

Law enforcement directed three additional visits to Shiatsu Spa after June 8th under similar circumstances, with the exception that the amount of money provided to the citizen was greater, and the sexual conduct escalated. On June 13, 2006, the citizen was provided one hundred ($100) dollars for sex and forty ($40) dollars for his "time." On this occasion, he had both oral sex and sexual intercourse in various positions with "Coco." Other sexual contact between the two is described in the Affidavit of Probable Cause for the Search Warrant.

On July 19, 2006, the citizen was provided with one hundred ($100) dollars for sex and forty dollars for his "time." On this occasion, he had both oral sex and sexual intercourse in various positions with "Coco."

Finally, on July 26, 2006, the citizen was provided one hundred ($100) dollars for sex and sixty ($60) dollars for his "time." On this occasion, "Gina" began performing oral sex on him, but was interrupted on two occasions by a phone call. The two then continued with oral sex and also had sexual intercourse. * * * *

In *United States v. Cuervelo*, 949 F.2d 559 (2d cir. 1991), the Second Circuit remanded to the district court for an evidentiary hearing to determine whether the conduct of an undercover DEA agent who developed a romantic and sexual relationship with the defendant engaged in outrageous government conduct. The court adopted the following criteria:

> In order to make out a successful outrageousness claim in these circumstances, at a minimum, the defendant must show the following:

(1) That the government consciously set out to use sex as a weapon in its investigatory arsenal, or acquiesced in such conduct for its own purposes upon learning that such a relationship existed;

(2) That the government agent initiated a sexual relationship, or allowed it to continue to exist, to achieve governmental ends; and

(3) That the sexual relationship took place during or close to the period covered by the indictment and was entwined with the events charged therein. * * * *

The application of *Cuervelo* criteria to the within case leaves no doubt that the police used sex as a weapon in its investigatory arsenal, that they permitted the sex to continue even after having enough evidence for an arrest, and that the sexual conduct was entwined with the investigation. The police conduct is made more egregious because they permitted or acquiesced in the most intimate of sexual encounters. They did so even though it was unnecessary to their investigation, and they learned very little by doing so. The mere agreement to perform sexual acts for money would have satisfied the statute

We conclude that the decision to send the citizen into Shiatsu Spa on four occasions for a smorgasbord of sexual activity violates principles of fundamental fairness. Neither prostitution activity inside Shiatsu Spa nor the police decision-making is to be condoned. We expect more from the police, and demand that they conduct their investigations and utilize their resources without resorting to such embarrassing investigative techniques. No adequate supervisory guidance was provided, no standards existed for this type of investigation, and some of the behavior by the participants was sophomoric.

A decision by the courts to place restraints on police tactics is reserved for very limited circumstances. For example, if this case involved international terrorism or a threat to the safety of our citizens, then the police conduct would not be as easily challenged. But it does not, this case involves prostitution. Additionally, very few would question placing the brakes on a similar prostitution investigation if the agent of the police had entered the business on ten (10) occasions, or had engaged in some form of brutality. Likewise, due process would seemingly not be outraged with limited sexual interaction. However, a strong presumption should exist against trading in the currency of intimate relations. Here, the totality of the circumstances, which include the quantity of visits to Shiatsu Spa, the nature and extent of the sexual conduct, the payment of the citizen for his "time," the nature of the investigation, the lack of standards for conducting this type of investigation and the lack of focused supervision, leads to the conclusion that due process requires dismissal of the prosecution. * * * *

We reject the holdings in factually similar cases from other state jurisdictions that the Commonwealth relies upon in the instant case for the proposition that the investigatory conduct used herein was not outrageous. For example, in *State v. Tookes*, 67 Haw. 608 (1985), a "civilian volunteer" assisted the Honolulu police in a prostitution investigation by using money provided by the police to have sexual intercourse with the defendant prostitutes. The police instructed the volunteer to "engage in sexual intercourse if necessary to obtain evidence sufficient for a conviction." Although the *Tookes* Court questioned whether the investigating officers' methods were consistent with ethical standards, it nevertheless concluded that the conduct did not violate the defendant's due process rights. The *Tookes* court's analysis did not include consideration of any criteria such as those in *Cuervelo*. Rather, the *Tookes* court relied on, *inter alia, Municipality of Anchorage v. Flanagan*, 649 P.2d 957 (Alaska Ct.App.1982), which was, in actuality, factually distinguishable insofar as the police officer who was involved in an undercover prostitution sting on a dating service stopped the target prostitute before she started performing fellatio. Accordingly, the extent of the sexual contact in *Flanagan* was easily distinguishable from that in *Tookes*, which involved repeated instances of sexual intercourse. Accordingly, we find the *Tookes* court's reliance on *Flanagan* flawed. But more importantly, these older cases did not consider the prudent criteria developed in later cases such as *Cuervelo*, which we adopt herein.

2. In *State v. Burkland*, 775 N.W.2d 372 (Minn.App. 2009), the appellate court reversed a conviction for prostitution:

> After receiving a tip that prostitution was occurring at Peaceful Image Tanning and Bodyworks, the Minneapolis Police Department conducted an undercover investigation in which an officer, in plain clothes and with a recording device hidden in his clothing, posed as a customer. Upon entering the establishment, the undercover officer was greeted by appellant Betsy Lou Burkland with whom he arranged a one-hour massage for $70. Burkland took the officer to a room, asked him to disrobe, and left the room while he did so. After she returned and began the massage, Burkland offered to perform the massage topless for an additional $30. The officer accepted the offer.

> The massage lasted for approximately one hour, during which Burkland and the officer engaged in small talk. The conversation included a discussion about the recent arrest of women who were engaged in prostitution. And then Burkland then discussed the benefits of massage and the stigma attached to it, stating that "it's actually a thing with a happy ending, it does release, release endorphins in your brain." After discussing the establishment's hours, the collapse of the Interstate 35W bridge, and the weather, Burkland directed the officer to turn onto his back and continued the massage. Shortly thereafter, the officer asked, "Do you think I can touch your breasts now?" Burkland replied, "Um hmm." The officer massaged Burkland's bare breasts as she put oil on her hand and rubbed the officer's penis. The officer then asked, "Do you include the release with the 100 dollars?" Burkland responded, "Yeah." The officer then asked for additional sexual services if he put on a condom, which Burkland declined to perform. The officer testified that the word "condom" was the signal for other officers to enter and make the arrest. The officer also testified that "manual

release" is a term used during massage to indicate that the masseuse will "give you a hand job until you have an orgasm." * * * *

In both *State v. Morris*, 272 N.W.2d 35 (Minn.1978) and *State v. Crist, 281 N.W.2d 657, 658 (Minn.1979)*, the actions taken by undercover officers were held not to constitute outrageous government conduct because the officer's conduct was in response to the defendant's demand, and the demand was a means used by the defendant to avoid police detection. That is not what occurred in this case. Here, the officer initiated the sexual contact when he asked to touch Burkland's breasts and proceeded to do so. He permitted Burkland to rub his penis while continuing to massage Burkland's bare breasts and inquired whether a "release" was included in the $100 cost. Thus, the facts of the case are distinguishable from those in Morris and Crist in several important respects. First, there is no evidence in the record, nor did the officer contend, that Burkland's conduct was necessary to dispel a suspicion that he was a police officer. Second, Burkland made no demands of the officer to detect whether he was a police officer. Third, there is no evidence that the officer considered it necessary for the collection of evidence to initiate sexual contact by asking to touch Burkland's breasts or permitting her to rub his penis in order to gain her confidence. Police investigation is important in prosecuting and reducing the incidence of prostitution. But the officer could have successfully sought the necessary agreement to engage in sexual contact for hire by inquiring about the charge for the "release" at almost any point throughout the almost hour-long massage without ever initiating sexual contact by touching Burkland's breast. Thus, unlike the facts of *Morris* and *Crist*, the officer's initiation of sexual contact and assent to the escalation of that contact was unnecessary to any reasonable investigation and offensive to due process.

3. What is the basis for a rule quashing a criminal prosecution because the police engaged in "outrageous government conduct"? And how does this differ from entrapment? Consider the follow case, *Vaden v. State*.

VADEN v. STATE
Supreme Court of Alaska
768 P.2d 1102 (1989)

COMPTON, JUSTICE.

This petition arises out of convictions of two hunting guides, Douglas Vaden and Floyd Saltz, Jr., following undercover operations by the State of Alaska. The primary issue we address is whether allegedly illegal conduct by the undercover agents warrants reversal of the convictions. * * * *

I. *Factual and Procedural Background*

A. *Vaden*

In November 1983, a horse wrangler employed by Douglas B. Vaden during the fall 1983 hunting season informed Fish and Wildlife Protection officers of illegal hunting methods allegedly used by Vaden while guiding a foreign hunter. In the spring of 1984, John Snell, an undercover agent for the Alaska Department of Fish & Game * * * posing as a hunter, contracted for guiding services from Vaden. Snell was instructed on how to conduct himself on the hunt.[2]

During the hunt, Snell shot and killed four foxes from Vaden's aircraft. The season on foxes was closed at that time. Vaden provided Snell with the shotgun used to shoot the foxes, and maneuvered the aircraft so Snell could shoot the foxes. The fox carcasses were then transported to Anchorage by Vaden. Vaden was convicted, as an accomplice, * * * on four counts of taking foxes from an aircraft (5 AAC 92.080(5)) and four counts of taking foxes during closed season (5 AAC 88.160(2)). * * * * He was also convicted in his own right on three counts of possession and transportation of illegally taken game (5 AAC 92.140(c)). He was acquitted on several other counts, including solicitation of the agent's takings.

Vaden appealed his convictions, contending that no illegal acts were committed by Snell and thus no criminal liability could attach to Vaden for "aiding and abetting" or transportation of illegally taken game, and alternatively, if crimes had been committed by Snell, such law enforcement tactics amounted to entrapment as a matter of law and violated due process. The court of appeals upheld Vaden's convictions. * * * *

B. *Saltz*

In October 1984, undercover agent Thomas Pagel, posing as a client, accompanied licensed assistant guide Floyd Saltz into the bush.

Initially Pagel had contracted for a fishing trip. Pagel apparently expressed a desire to hunt on the trip also and questioned Saltz about hunting. Pagel testified that Saltz responded by saying "you could not kill a caribou the same day you were airborne but that once you got in the bush you did basically what the hell you wanted to."

On October 6, the pair flew out to Talarik Creek. Pagel testified that Saltz told

---

[2] "Instructions to Hunters:

　　1. During your scheduled guide hunt you are considered an agent of the State, this however, does not permit you to take game contrary to State statutes or regulations.

　　2. Your assignment during all phases of your guided hunt is to observe, record and determine the method of operation used by the guide in providing his guide service to a client.

　　3. You are to follow all instructions provided to you by your guide.

　　4. You are not to take any game without first being instructed to do so by your guide.

　　5. Do not at any time or under any circumstances induce a guide to commit any crime.

　　6. All game taken on your hunt is the property of the State.

him the area was limited to flyfishing only and gave him a fly rod. A short time later, Saltz decided the fishing was slow and gave Pagel a baited spinning rod. The pair then caught about thirty trout on spinning gear. Pagel also testified that after the trout stopped biting the pair began catching Northern Pike. According to Pagel, Saltz caught 20 to 30 pike, killed them and threw them into the lake.

On October 7, Saltz flew Pagel into an area with little air traffic for a caribou hunt. Saltz handed Pagel a rifle and pointed out which bull caribou to shoot. Pagel shot and killed the bull. Saltz also pointed out a cow caribou for Pagel to shoot. However, Pagel gave Saltz the rifle and Saltz shot the cow. They did not salvage the meat from the cow. Saltz allegedly shot at another bull, but it is not clear whether it was killed.

After the two took pictures of the bull Pagel shot, they started to skin it. While working on the hindquarters, Saltz told Pagel the meat was not worth salvaging because the caribou "smelled as if it was in rut." Pagel indicated he wanted the antlers and Saltz salvaged them. The pair left the meat. Saltz testified to a different version of facts. He claimed Pagel initiated the fishing violations. He also claimed Pagel was left alone and shot the caribou while Saltz was not present, and that it was Pagel's idea to leave the meat behind.

The offenses with which Saltz was charged grew out of three basic incidents: (1) Pagel's killing and wasting of a bull caribou the same day he was airborne, (2) Saltz's killing and wasting of a cow caribou the same day he was airborne, and (3) both parties' use of illegal fishing gear and waste of fish. Saltz's pretrial motions to dismiss were denied by the trial court. At trial, the jury believed Pagel's version and convicted Saltz on all 16 counts alleged against him, including soliciting the violations.[9]

Saltz appealed, arguing inter alia that his convictions must be reversed because of Pagel's illegal acts. * * * *

---

[9] Specifically, the counts were:

Count I: Soliciting taking bull caribou same-day airborne

Count II: Soliciting taking cow caribou same-day airborne

Count III: Soliciting waste of bull caribou

Count IV: Aid taking bull caribou same-day airborne

Count V: Taking cow caribou same-day airborne

Count VI: Attempt take bull caribou same-day airborne

Count VII: Aid waste bull caribou

Count VIII: Wasting cow caribou

Count IX: Guide aiding taking bull caribou same-day airborne Count X: Guide aiding waste of bull caribou

Count XI: Transportation of illegally-taken game

Count XII: Solicit fishing with illegal gear

Count XIII: Using illegal fishing gear

Count XIV: Aid use of illegal fishing gear

Count XV: Waste of fish

Count XVI: Guide aiding illegal fishing.

II. *Discussion*

A. *Legality of the Undercover Agent's Activities*

* * * * [Appellants] argue that for these convictions to be sustained, someone must have committed an illegal act. We agree with the court of appeals that the agents committed the offenses. * * * *

C. *The Actions of Snell and Pagel Do Not Constitute Entrapment.*

* * * *

The availability of the entrapment defense in a particular case is a question for the trial court. The defendant must show, by a preponderance of the evidence, that the police employed tactics of "persuasion or inducement such as would be effective to persuade the average person . . . to commit the offense." AS 11.81.450. Here there is no indication in the record that Pagel employed such tactics. On the basis of the record, the trial judge could reasonably conclude that Saltz failed to establish entrapment by a preponderance of the evidence. Therefore, we affirm the court of appeals on this issue.

D. *The Conduct of the Undercover Agents Did Not Violate Due Process.*

Both Vaden and Saltz challenge their convictions on due process grounds. They rely on dictum of the United States Supreme Court in *United States v. Russell*, 411 U.S. 423 (1973). In *Russell*, the Supreme Court indicated that at some point government involvement in detecting criminal activity could rise to a level of outrageousness "shocking to the universal sense of justice." 411 U.S. at 432. Under this approach, illegal conduct of the government is not a per se bar to prosecution; the test is whether the government's conduct is outrageous enough to warrant dismissal of the charges. The court of appeals divided over whether the due process defense was incorporated into our entrapment defense. Generally, police conduct that is outrageous or below the level of "an acceptable standard for the fair and honorable administration of justice" will be encompassed by the entrapment defense. *Pascu*, 577 P.2d at 1067. There may be other times when police conduct is so unacceptable that it rises to a "demonstrable level of outrageousness" that warrants dismissal.

Both Vaden and Saltz cite numerous cases in which federal and state courts found government conduct to be outrageous enough to bar prosecution. The majority of these cases involve government conduct in drug sales or manufacture. They support the proposition that at some point government conduct can be outrageous enough to warrant a dismissal. See, e.g., *United States v. Twigg*, 588 F.2d 373 (3rd cir. 1978); *State v. Hohensee*, 650 S.W.2d 268 (Mo.App.1982).

Hohensee presents a more egregious set of facts than the instant case. Hohensee was convicted as an accomplice to a burglary. The actual burglary was carried out by two paid informants and a police officer. Hohensee merely acted as a lookout. In reversing Hohensee's conviction, the court held that sponsoring the break in was outrageous conduct on the part of the government and barred prosecution. The court observed that Hohensee's only conduct was standing watch as lookout one-half block from the building burglarized.

In the instant case, we conclude that the government's conduct is not outrageous enough to bar prosecution. However, we reject the implication in the opinion of the court of appeals that outrageous government conduct is subsumed within the entrapment defense. It alone may justify judicial intervention.

In searching for a standard by which government conduct, or misconduct, is to be measured, we find persuasive the reasoning of the Ninth Circuit Court of Appeals in *United States v. Williams*, 791 F.2d 1383 (9th Cir., 1986). There the court suggested that in general, to be outrageous enough to bar prosecution "the government must have 'engineered and directed the criminal enterprise from start to finish.'"[13] *Id.* at 1386.

In neither Vaden's nor Saltz's case did the government "engineer and direct the criminal enterprise from start to finish." *Williams* at 1386. In Vaden's case, the state had information that Vaden had used illegal hunting practices the previous fall.[14] Vaden was in control of the aircraft when Snell shot the foxes. Vaden maneuvered the aircraft to provide Snell with a platform from which to shoot. Vaden also provided the shotgun used to shoot the foxes. This was not a government engineered crime from start to finish. Nor was Vaden merely standing watch while the government agents perpetuated the crime, as in *Hohensee*. Instead, Vaden was an active participant.

In Saltz's case, the jury found that he "engineered" the crimes. His convictions demonstrate that the jury believed he provided the rifle and pointed out the bull caribou Pagel should shoot. The jury also believed that he indicated the meat was bad and suggested that they salvage only the antlers. The government did not engineer Saltz's criminal conduct from start to finish, either. The jury implicitly found he was a willing instigator of the crimes. * * * *

---

[13] The court also said that outrageous conduct barring prosecution would be found when the government's involvement was "*malum in se*." In the instant case, the government involvement was not *malum in se.* "*Malum in se*" is defined as follows:

> A wrong in itself; an act or case involving illegality from the very nature of the transaction, upon principles of natural, moral, and public law. An act is said to be *malum in se* when it is inherently and essentially evil, that is, immoral in its nature and injurious in its consequences, without any regard to the fact of its being noticed or punished by the law of the state. Such are most or all of the offenses cognizable at common law (without the denouncement of a statute); as murder, larceny, etc. [Black's Law Dictionary 865 (5th ed. 1979)]

Acts merely prohibited and not rising to the level of *malum in se* are *malum prohibitum*, which is defined as follows:

> A wrong prohibited; a thing which is wrong because prohibited; an act which is not inherently immoral, but becomes so because its commission is expressly forbidden by positive law; an act involving an illegality resulting from positive law. [*Ibid.*]

Because fish and game violations are not inherently evil or immoral and are proscribed only by statute, they are *malum prohibitum* and not *malum in se.*

[14] Vaden was targeted for investigation based on information supplied by an employee who allegedly had observed illegal hunting practices during fall hunts in 1983.

We are not persuaded by Vaden and Saltz's argument that the charges in this case be dismissed solely because the government agents engaged in illegal hunting and fishing activity. In the plurality opinion in *U.S. v. Hampton*, the Supreme Court suggested that the correct remedy when police go outside the scope of their duties is to "prosecute the police," not "free the equally culpable defendant." 425 U.S. at 490. This remedy has been used in other states to curb offensive conduct. See, e.g., *Reigan v. People*, 120 Colo. 472 (1949) (prosecution of game wardens for conspiracy for entrapping 18 and 19-year olds to unlawfully trap beaver).

III. *Conclusion*

For the above reasons we affirm the convictions of Vaden and Saltz.

BURKE, JUSTICE, dissenting.

The danger to Alaska's resources posed by persons willing to assist others in the violation of state fish and game laws is both obvious and substantial. There must, however, be limits upon the degree of police involvement in criminal activity which will be tolerated. When the police or their agents commit criminal acts in order to charge others as accessories to those same acts, in my view the line is crossed.

The convictions in the cases now before us could not have been obtained had law enforcement officers not broken the law. Accordingly, the situation differs markedly from that found in the "outrageous conduct" cases cited by my colleagues. Here, the state seeks to obtain convictions because of the illegal conduct of its own agents, rather than in spite of such conduct. The state does not ask this court merely to close its eyes to the officers' illegal acts. On the contrary, it asks that we recognize such acts as an acceptable means of providing an element essential to conviction of these defendants. Notably, the court cites no case in which an officer of the law has been permitted to commit a crime as principal, for the sole purpose of securing the conviction of another as an accomplice; nor does it cite any case in which the police have been allowed to break the law in order to imbue some object with contraband status, so that it may later be used to support a charge of illegal possession or transportation. There is, however, case law to the contrary.

In *State v. Hohensee*, 650 S.W.2d 268 (Mo.App.1982), state police retained the services of one undercover police officer, Roberts, and two known burglars, Bressie and Yarberry, who were instructed to burglarize a building. The purpose of the plan was to secure the conviction, on a theory of accomplice liability, of a fourth burglar who had agreed to stand lookout for the other three. The court held that the government's involvement in the break-in was outrageous and that due process barred the conviction of the defendant for burglary. Distinguishing the case from those in which convictions had been sustained notwithstanding some police involvement in the criminal enterprise carried out by the defendants, the court noted:

> In those cases the defendant himself participated in the illegal entry. If the conduct of Bressie, Yarberry and Officer Roberts, each acting as a salaried agent of the police department, is subtracted from the break-in, what remains of that midnight enterprise is a lone figure, sitting in a

parking lot 1/2 block away. It is true that defendant had criminal intent but his conduct, standing alone, represented no more of a threat to society than that of a stargazer, similarly situated, contemplating Polaris. It is difficult to conceive a situation where the government's involvement could be greater or the defendant's could be less, and the conduct of the latter still be a likely subject for prosecution.

The break-in was accomplished by the government agents, whether or not defendant was in the vicinity. If the government agents had not been there, doing their illegal acts, defendant's conduct would not be illegal.

The instant case is on all fours with *Hohensee*. Here, as in that case, the criminal act which serves as the basis for both the accomplice liability and the illegal transportation charges was supplied by government agents. When such illegal conduct is subtracted from the equation, the conduct of the defendants, however evil the intent which accompanied it, does not amount to a crime. Accordingly, their convictions should be quashed as was the conviction in *Hohensee*.

The majority apparently assumes that game offenses, being "malum prohibitum" rather than "malum in se," cannot be deemed sufficiently outrageous to trigger due process concerns. This notion, however, was implicitly rejected by the Ninth Circuit Court of Appeals in *United States v. Stenberg*, 803 F.2d 422 (9th Cir., 1986).

In *Stenberg*, United States Fish and Wildlife Service agents carried out two hunts virtually identical to those involved in the cases at bar. The charges based upon these hunts, at least as to the outrageous conduct defense, were not directly at issue on appeal. * * * * The Court of Appeals refused to dismiss the defendants' numerous other convictions for independent wildlife crimes on the basis of outrageous conduct. The court reasoned that the defendants' involvement in "a continuing series of similar crimes during the government conduct at issue" precluded them from raising the defense. *Id.* at 429. The court was careful to note, however:

> But for the evidence of that additional unlawful activity, we might well have reached a different result. The killing of wildlife, on more than one occasion, by an FWS agent raises significant questions as to the extent to which government agents may commit serious crimes in order to prevent others from committing similar offenses. Here, the government agent was not a passive participant or simply a purchaser or transmitter of contraband otherwise destined for the market place. To the contrary, he himself was the perpetrator of the most serious offenses involved - the actual killing of protected wildlife. Under different circumstances, such active criminal behavior by a government agent might well result in our upholding a defense of outrageous government conduct. [*Id.* at 430-31.

Again, the reasoning contained in the quoted portion of Stenberg would seem perfectly applicable in the case at bar. Indeed, the conduct by fish and game agents in this case is identical to that described in *Stenberg*. There has been no showing that the defendants in this case were "involved in a continuing series of similar crimes during the government conduct at issue"; at least none which comes close to the level of criminal activity engaged in by the defendants in *Stenberg*.[4] Accordingly, dismissal based upon the outrageous conduct defense is appropriate.

* * * *

I would uphold those of Saltz' convictions which were based upon his independent criminal acts. However, I would reverse those convictions, for both Saltz and Vaden, which could not have been established but for the illegal acts of the government agents in this case, i.e., the accomplice liability and transportation of illegally taken game charges. In my view, these convictions fall squarely within the parameters of the due process/outrageous conduct defense as discussed and applied in *Hohensee* and *Stenberg*. * * * *

NOTE FROM JUDGE HANDELMAN:

How is a "due process" defense different from entrapment?

In *U.S. v. Ornelas-Rodriguez*, 12 F.3d 1339 (5th cir. 1994), the court held that a police officer's sexual relationship with a key witness against defendant was not outrageous government conduct requiring dismissal of the indictment, because the witness testified that she would have assisted the government even without the sex.

Compare *State v. Williams*, 623 So.2d 462 (Fla.Sup.Ct.1993), where the court held that police manufacture of crack cocaine (from confiscated powder cocaine) for use in a reverse sting operation constitutes outrageous conduct that precludes prosecution of the buyer. The court distinguished cases rejecting due process attacks on police stings where they sold drugs to defendants: "The delivery of a controlled substance in a reverse-sting operation is worlds apart from the manufacture of a dangerous controlled substance." The court noted that some of the crack cocaine had escaped into the community, and that the police had conducted the reverse sting operation near a high school.

In *State v. Lively*, 921 P.2d 1035 (1996), the Washington Supreme Court held that the conduct of the police in using an informant to attend Alcoholics Anonymous and Narcotics Anonymous meetings and to attempt to lure recovering addicts to commit illegal acts was so outrageous as to violate the due process rights of a recovering addict prosecuted for cocaine trafficking.

But compare *U.S. v. Young*, 78 F.3d 758 (5th cir. 1996), where a recovering drug addict held not to have been *entrapped* into selling drugs merely because the government informant who approached him about participating in a controlled drug buy happened to be a friend whom the addict had met at a drug treatment center.

---

[4] There was absolutely no showing on the record that Vaden was engaged in "similar crimes during the government conduct at issue" here. Saltz' contemporaneous fishing and wildlife violations (e.g., personal commission of fishing and wildlife offenses) arguably qualify as sufficient to trigger the *Stenberg* rule, and I would agree that Saltz should be precluded from arguing for dismissal of these collateral offenses. As to those offenses based solely upon the agents' illegal conduct, however, i.e., accomplice liability and illegal transportation, I see no reason to preclude the challenge.

And in *U.S. v. Diggs*, 8 F.3d 1520 (10th cir. 1993), a reverse sting operation induced Diggs ("a prominent Wichita attorney") to take possession of four ounces of cocaine from an undercover seller. The court held that this was not "outrageous conduct" and therefore did not violate the due process clause, because Diggs had previously been involved in drug trafficking with the seller, and the government merely interposed itself in defendant's ongoing criminal activity.

Can these cases be reconciled? Put another way, is this "due process" test really a workable test? Judge Easterbrook believes this "outrageousness" test is too vague to be any real test at all:

> Any line we draw would be unprincipled and therefore not judicial in nature. More likely there would be no line; judges would vote their lower intestines. Such a meandering, personal approach is the antithesis of justice under law, and we ought not indulge it. Inability to describe in general terms just what makes tactics too outrageous to tolerate suggests that there is no definition — and "I know it when I see it" is not a rule of any kind, let alone a command of the Due Process Clause. [Concurring opinion in *U.S. v. Miller* 891 F.2d 1265, 1271 (7th cir. 1989).]

Part VI
Anticipatory Offenses

Most crimes require not just a *mens rea* and an *actus reus*, but also a specified harm. Murder requires the death of a human being. Larceny requires property to be stolen.

But suppose there is no harm. Defendant asks someone to help rob a bank, but that person declines. Or defendant shoots with intent to kill, but misses. Or two defendants plan to rob a bank, but they are arrested before they can go through with their plan. No harm, no foul? Or are there some good reasons to punish these people anyway? If so, should they be punished *less* than those who complete the intended crime, or the same?

Is there a *danger* in punishing people for incomplete (or "anticipatory," or "inchoate") crimes? We don't want to punish people for "thought crimes," do we? At the same time, shouldn't we protect ourselves from people who really do mean to complete their crimes but — for one reason or another — just happened to fail this time (but might not fail next time)? Is there a way to construct our rules re "anticipatory" crimes to meet *both* of these needs, i.e., might we draw our lines to resolve the tension between these interests?

These are some of the issues posed by this Part.

Chapter 17

SOLICITATION

For the crime of solicitation to be completed, it is only necessary that the actor with intent that another person commit a crime, have enticed, advised, incited, ordered or otherwise encouraged that person to commit a crime. The crime solicited need not be committed.

LaFave & Scott, *Criminal Law* (West)

Take a close look at the above definition: the *actus reus* of solicitation is asking someone to do something. Isn't this *speech*? And isn't freedom of speech protected by the First Amendment of the United States Constitution? Even if not all talking is protected by the First Amendment, shouldn't we be pretty careful before we criminalize mere talking?

PROBLEM 17

To: My law clerk

From: Clarence Barrow

Re: *People v. Green*

My client, Olive Green, has been charged with solicitation to commit arson, in violation of California Penal Code § 653f. At her preliminary hearing, the key witness against her was Felicia Finkess. I would like to file a motion to dismiss the charges, based on an argument that Finkess' testimony does not show probable cause to believe Green committed solicitation. Please read the attached transcript and authorities and advise me as to whether my motion is likely to succeed.

Transcript of Testimony of Felicia Finkess

Q: Did you hear Ms. Green speak at a meeting of the Protectors of the Environment last May?

A: Yes. I was a member of PE, and Olive was our vice-president. There were about 20 of us at our monthly meeting in Oakland. Olive got up and spoke to us about how the Castor Oil Corporation had just begun drilling for oil on national forest land in Oregon. She said that we had to do something to stop it. She said, "We should go burn down Castor's drilling platform, to demonstrate that these big oil companies can't go on raping the environment whenever they like. If anyone would like to help me with this, please see me after the meeting."

Q: Did anyone talk to her about this after the meeting?

A: Yes. I happened to be standing near Olive after the meeting, and Tom Torch came up to her. Tom said, "Forget the drilling platform. It's made mostly of steel and won't burn too well. Castor is building a wooden bridge across a stream in the forest. Let's burn down the bridge. I can leave for Oregon a week from tomorrow." Olive said, "Great idea. We can use my car."

Q: Did they go to Oregon?

A: Olive didn't. Like most members of our group, she is all talk and little action. Olive has suggested violent action against oil companies and industrial polluters to our members in the past. She and others would start to make plans to do it, but they have never followed through. Torch, however, was a new member, and that was his first meeting. He did go to Oregon the following week, alone, and he was arrested while pouring some gasoline on the bridge.

California Penal Code

Section 653f. Solicitation

(a) Every person who, with the intent that the crime be committed, solicits another to offer, accept, or join in the offer or acceptance of a bribe, or to commit or join in the commission of carjacking, robbery, burglary, grand theft, receiving stolen property, extortion, perjury, subornation of perjury, forgery, kidnapping, arson or assault with a deadly weapon or instrument or by means of force likely to produce great bodily injury, or, by the use of force or a threat of force, to prevent or dissuade any person who is or may become a witness from attending upon, or testifying at, any trial, proceeding, or inquiry authorized by law, shall be punished by imprisonment in a county jail for not more than one year or in the state prison, or by a fine of not more than ten thousand dollars ($ 10,000), or the amount which could have been assessed for commission of the offense itself, whichever is greater, or by both the fine and imprisonment.

(b) Every person who, with the intent that the crime be committed, solicits another to commit or join in the commission of murder shall be punished by imprisonment in the state prison for three, six, or nine years.

* * * *

(f) An offense charged in violation of subdivision (a), (b), or (c) shall be proven by the testimony of two witnesses, or of one witness and corroborating circumstances.
* * * *

(*Note:* Compare this statute to Model Penal Code § 5.02 and § 5.04, in the Appendix.)

Section 450. Definitions.

In this chapter, the following terms have the following meanings:

(a) "Structure" means any building, or commercial or public tent, bridge, tunnel, or powerplant.

(b) "Forest land" means any brush covered land, cut-over land, forest, grasslands, or woods.

(c) "Property" means real property or personal property, other than a structure or forest land. * * * *

(e) "Maliciously" imports a wish to vex, defraud, annoy, or injure another person, or an intent to do a wrongful act, established either by proof or presumption of law.

Section 451. Arson.

A person is guilty of arson when he or she willfully and maliciously sets fire to or burns or causes to be burned of who aids, counsels or procures the burning of, any structure, forest land or property. * * * *

Oregon Revised Statutes

Section 164.305. Definitions for ORS 164.305 to 164.377

As used in ORS 164.305 to 164.365, except as the context requires otherwise:

* * * *

(2) "Protected property" means any structure, place or thing customarily occupied by people, including "public buildings" as defined by ORS 479.010 and "forestland" as defined by ORS 477.001.

(3) "Property of another" means property in which anyone other than the actor has a legal or equitable interest that the actor has no right to defeat or impair, even though the actor may also have such an interest in the property.

Section 164.315. Second Degree Arson.

(1) A person commits the crime of arson in the second degree if, by starting a fire or causing an explosion, the person intentionally damages:

(a) Any building of another that is not protected property; or

(b) Any property of another and the damages to the property exceed $750.

* * * *

Section 164.325. First Degree Arson.

(1) A person commits the crime of arson in the first degree if, by starting a fire or causing an explosion, the person intentionally damages:

(a) Protected property of another;

(b) Any property, whether the property of the person or the property of another person, and such act recklessly places another person in danger of physical injury or protected property of another in danger of damage.

* * * *

(2) Arson in the first degree is a Class A felony.

Section 164.335. Reckless Burning.

(1) A person commits the crime of reckless burning if the person recklessly damages property of another by fire or explosion.

(2) Reckless burning is a Class A misdemeanor

PEOPLE v. BURT
California Supreme Court
45 Cal.2d 311 (1955)

TRAYNOR, JUSTICE.

Defendant was charged by information with violating § 653f of the Penal Code, in that he solicited the prosecutrix to commit and join in the commission of the crime of extortion. After a trial by the court sitting without a jury, defendant was found guilty. His motion for a new trial was denied, but the proceedings were suspended and he was placed on probation. He appeals.

The evidence presented at the trial established that defendant solicited the prosecutrix in Los Angeles to get acquainted with men at hotels in the Los Angeles area and to persuade them to accompany her to Tijuana, Mexico, to engage in sexual intercourse, and to join with defendant's associate in committing acts in Mexico that would constitute extortion, as defined in § 518 of the Penal Code.[1] The prosecutrix reported the solicitations to the police and the scheme was never carried out.

The basic question raised on appeal is whether it is a punishable offense in California to solicit a person to commit or join in the commission outside of California of any of the crimes mentioned in § 653f of the Penal Code.[2] Defendant contends that, to punish him for soliciting in this state, the performance of acts outside this state that would amount to "extortion," as that word is defined in § 518 of the Penal Code, is to punish him for acts to be done outside this state and thus without the jurisdiction of the California courts.

---

[1] "Extortion is the obtaining of property from another, with his consent, or the obtaining of an official act of a public officer, induced by a wrongful use of force of fear, or under color of official right."

[2] "Every person who solicits another to offer or join in the offer or acceptance of a bribe, or to commit or join in the commission of murder, robbery, burglary, grand theft, receiving stolen property, extortion, rape by force and violence, perjury, subornation of perjury, forgery, or kidnapping, is punishable by imprisonment in the county jail not longer than one year or in the state prison not longer than five years, or by a fine of not more than five thousand dollars. Such offense must be proved by the testimony of two witnesses, or of one witness and corroborating circumstances."

In support of this contention, defendant invokes *People v. Buffum*, 40 Cal.2d 709. In that case the court stated: "The object of defendants' agreement, as alleged in the indictment, was 'to violate § 274, Penal Code of the State of California.' No other unlawful purpose was stated, and defendants, of course, cannot be punished for conspiracy unless the doing of the things agreed upon would amount to a violation of § 274. The statute makes no reference to the place of performance of an abortion, and we must assume that the Legislature did not intend to regulate conduct taking place outside the borders of the state. Similarly, § 182 of the Penal Code, standing alone, should not be read as applying to a conspiracy to commit a crime in another jurisdiction."

In the present case, however, we are not concerned with a statute prohibiting a conspiracy "to commit any crime," however petty, or to commit the numerous other acts listed in § 182. Two or more persons may conspire to commit an act in another state that would not be a crime there but would be a crime if committed in this state, or that would not be a crime here but would be a crime in the other state.

Section 653f, however, prohibits the solicitation of only twelve of the most serious crimes, all of which are felonies under the law of this state and at common law and are crimes under the law of all civilized nations. Since the Legislature is not ordinarily concerned with regulating conduct in other jurisdictions, *People v. Buffum, supra,* and since § 182 suggests no answer to the many difficult questions that would otherwise arise from the conflict in California law and the law of other states, that section may reasonably be interpreted as limited to conspiracies to commit crimes in this state. It does not follow, however, that when the Legislature has singled out the solicitation of the most serious of crimes, it likewise intended to punish their solicitation only when they were to be committed in this state.

Legislative concern with the proscribed soliciting is demonstrated not only by the gravity of the crimes specified, but by the fact that the crime, unlike conspiracy, does not require the commission of any overt act. It is complete when the solicitation is made, and it is immaterial that the object of the solicitation is never consummated, or that no steps are taken toward its consummation.

Section 653f is concerned not only with the prevention of the harm that would result should the inducements prove successful, but with protecting inhabitants of this state from being exposed to inducements to commit or join in the commission of the crimes specified, and the evils it seeks to prevent are present whether the object of the solicitation is to be accomplished within or without this state. Thus, in the present case, defendant used the prospects of large monetary rewards to attempt to induce the prosecutrix to commit acts of prostitution and extortion, with residents of this state as intended victims. Such solicitation is inimical to the public welfare and to the safety and morals of the inhabitants of this state, regardless of where the solicited acts are to be performed, and a construction of § 653f that limits its operation to solicitation of acts that are to be consummated within this state would defeat, rather than effect, the object of that statute. See Pen.Code § 4.

Defendant contends, however, that since he was charged with soliciting 'the crime of extortion' he could not properly be convicted unless it was proved that the acts solicited would constitute the crime of extortion at the place where they were to be performed, and that the prosecution therefore failed to sustain its burden of proof, since it offered no evidence to prove that the acts solicited would constitute the crime of extortion under the laws of Mexico. Since it is the solicitation in this state alone that is punishable, and since it is immaterial where the acts solicited are to be performed, the law of other states governing such acts is likewise immaterial, and proof of the law of Mexico was therefore unnecessary.

Defendant contends finally that a reversal is required because his solicitations were not proved by the testimony of two witnesses or by that of one witness and corroborating circumstances, as required by § 653f of the Penal Code. Defendant's solicitations were proved by the testimony of the prosecutrix and by that of a police officer who overheard them by means of a listening device installed, with her permission, in the prosecutrix' home. Furthermore, a tape recording of the conversation overheard by the police officer was introduced in evidence, and defendant admitted in his own testimony that he had participated in the conversation that the officer had recorded and had solicited the prosecutrix in the manner described above.

Defendant explained, however, that he had made the solicitations without any intent to carry out the extortion scheme but merely as an excuse to become acquainted with the prosecutrix, whom he wished to know "socially." The slight variation between the testimony of the prosecutrix and the police officer[3] as to the details of carrying out the proposed extortion is of no significance, for the tape recording shows that the two variations were in fact suggested by defendant as alternative means by which the extortion could be effected. Thus, in the light of the well-established rule that the corroborative evidence need not be strong nor sufficient in itself, without the aid of other evidence, to establish the fact in issue, we must conclude that the testimony of the prosecutrix and of the police officer and the recording of defendant's conversation with the prosecutrix are more than adequate to satisfy the requirements of § 653f. Moreover, the admissions in defendant's own testimony supply sufficient corroborative evidence.

The order granting probation and the order denying defendant's motion for a new trial are affirmed.

NOTES FROM CLARENCE:

1. In *Burt*, the court had no evidence before it that Mexico's definition of "extortion" differed from California's. In our case, can we show a difference between Oregon's and California's definition of "arson?" Under *Burt*, does this matter? Should it matter?

2. *People v. Buffum* — discussed in *Burt* — was overruled in *People v. Morante*, 20 Cal.4th 403 (1999):

> *Buffum* has been criticized in a number of treatises. One author stated that the *Buffum* case "stands as an excellent example of the triumph of the rote of the territorial principle over the pragmatic needs of law enforce-

---

[3] The police officer testified that defendant's associate in Mexico, who was to impersonate a Mexican police officer, would threaten to arrest the intended victim as a means of effecting the extortion, whereas the prosecutrix testified that defendant's associate would threaten to arrest her.

ment." (George, *Extraterritorial Application of Penal Legislation* (1966) 64 Mich. L.Rev. 609, 625-627 [also stating that Model Pen. Code, § 1.03(1)(d) implicitly repudiated the rule of *Buffum* by permitting prosecution of conspiracies in state or attempts to commit crimes out of state].) Another commentator challenged the assumption made in *Buffum* that the Legislature did not intend to regulate conduct taking place outside state borders and criticized the *Burt* decision for distinguishing rather than discrediting *Buffum*. (Currie, *Justice Traynor and the Conflict of Laws* (1961) 13 Stan.L.Rev. 719, 745-748.) * * * *

The *Buffum* decision is inconsistent with the principles that define the crime of conspiracy and the rationale for punishing the commission of that offense, does not conform to the legislative intent expressed in sections 27, subdivision (a)(1), and 778a, subdivision (a), regarding the scope of California's jurisdiction, is not mandated by other doctrines or provisions constraining state jurisdiction over criminal conduct that may involve more than one jurisdiction, and does not accommodate considerations of public policy that have assumed greater importance in recent years. * * * *

In addition, if the state may seek the prosecution and punishment of an agreement and overt act (coupled with the requisite intent) amounting to conspiracy *regardless* whether the crime that is the object of the conspiracy is completed, it is not apparent why we should interpret these statutes to require, at the same time, that the location of the intended crime be within the state. The agreement and overt act comprising the criminal offense have taken place within the state. It is that conduct (and intent), arising entirely within the state, that the statutes sanction criminally. We logically cannot hold that those elements of the offense are sufficient to attach criminal liability to the conspirators when they intend to accomplish the criminal objective — even if they do not meet that objective, within the state — but are not sufficient, and must be accompanied by an attempt within the state to commit the crime, when the conspirators intend to consummate the criminal objective outside the state.

IN RE ELIZABETH G.
California Court of Appeal
53 Cal.App.3d 725 (1975)

REGAN, ACTING P.J.

Elizabeth G., a minor, appeals from an order of the Juvenile Court of San Joaquin County finding her to be a ward of the court pursuant to § 602 of the Welfare and Institutions Code, in that she violated § 647, subdivision (b), of the Penal Code (unlawful solicitation to engage in an act of prostitution).

On the evening of February 12, 1975, Officers Mazzuola and Hughes of the Stockton Police Department, while working the vice detail, received information from an anonymous source that two females were working as prostitutes and were taking appointments over the phone. At about 9:45 p.m. on that evening, Officer

Mazzuola called the number furnished by the source.

A female answered the phone and the officer asked for either Theresa or Sherry, and the person responded that "that was them." Mazzuola asked the female if they could get together, and she replied in the affirmative. Another female then came on the line and wanted to know what he wanted. Officer Mazzuola told the second person he had a friend and wanted to know if they could all get together that evening. This second person also agreed. One of the girls then told the officer they would need a ride and would have to be picked up. Mazzuola asked if he should get a motel room first, and the two girls indicated that he should. The officer was also told to pick them up in a short time at the corner of 8th and Ophir.

The officers arrived at the meeting place and shortly thereafter the minor and another girl walked up to the car. One of the girls asked Mazzuola if he was "Tony" (the name he used on the phone), and he stated that he was. The girls then got into the car, and the foursome proceeded to the Regal 8 Motel. En route, the girls questioned the officers as to whether or not they were policemen, and the officers assured the girls they were not. Mazzuola also asked how much it was going to cost, and the minor replied that they did not want to talk about it until they were in their rooms.

All four went into the same motel room, where Officer Mazzuola voiced a preference for the other girl. Officer Hughes and the minor then left and went into the room next door.

Mazzuola told the minor's companion he wanted a "half-and half," and was told that it would cost him $20. He gave her a $20 bill, and she started walking toward the bathroom. She told him, however, that she wanted him to undress first, so she would know he was not a policeman. Mazzuola then produced his badge and I.D., advised her he was a policeman and that she was under arrest for prostitution. At that point, she ran toward the door in the other room and tried to warn the minor. Officer Mazzuola pulled her from the door and warned her to be quiet.

In the adjacent room, Officer Hughes had his wallet out and was in the process of giving the minor a $20 bill, when they heard a commotion and a door slam in the adjoining room. The minor then stated that she had changed her mind and wanted to leave.

Immediately thereafter, Hughes identified himself as a police officer and advised the minor she was under arrest for prostitution. At the police station, she was advised of her constitutional rights. She stated that she had been turning "tricks" for the past several months and that it had been her intention to turn a trick that evening; that she was trying to earn additional money to help out her family.

The minor contends that there is insufficient evidence to sustain a finding that she violated § 647, subdivision (b), of the Penal Code since no money was offered or received by her, and, in fact, no price was ever agreed upon. She argues the solicitation, if any, was made by the officers, and the record shows only "suspicion," which is not evidence. There is no merit to this contention.

Our review of the record discloses substantial evidence in support of the trial court's findings.

For example, the minor indicated during the ride to the motel that the price would be discussed when they got to their room. While in the room, she stated the price would depend on what Hughes wanted. The minor was responsive to the phone call, which was made pursuant to information received by the officers indicating she was working as a prostitute and taking appointments over the phone. Coupled with the circumstances of the events, the fact that no money actually changed hands is irrelevant to the charge of soliciting. In addition, after having been advised of her constitutional rights, the minor admitted to past acts of prostitution. She also admitted it had been her intention to turn a trick that very night. We hold the evidence to be clearly sufficient to support the court's finding that the minor solicited an act of prostitution.

The order appealed from is affirmed.

NOTE FROM CLARENCE:

Is a "solicitation" equivalent to an *offer* in contract law? Did Elizabeth's words or conduct constitute an offer?

PEOPLE v. LEFFEL
California Court of Appeal
54 Cal.App.3d 569 (1976)

FRANSON, J.

This case presents a question of first impression: Does Penal Code § 647, subdivision (b), which defines "disorderly conduct" as including "[every] person . . . [who] solicits . . . any act of prostitution," apply to a "customer" of a prostitute, or is the statute limited in its application to solicitation by the prostitute?

Appellant was arrested and charged with disorderly conduct in violation of Penal Code § 647, subdivision (b). At the arraignment he demurred to the complaint on the grounds, among others, that the facts alleged failed to state a public offense and that the court had no jurisdiction because the complaint violated his right to due process. Appellant also moved to dismiss the charge. At the hearing on the demurrer, it was agreed between appellant and the district attorney that appellant was not a prostitute and had not engaged in an act of prostitution.

The municipal court overruled the demurrer and denied the motion to dismiss. Appellant then filed a petition for writ of prohibition in the Fresno County Superior Court asking that court to restrain the municipal court from taking any further action in the case other than to order a dismissal of the action. After a hearing on the petition, the superior court denied a peremptory writ because "it takes two to tango." Appellant timely filed a notice of appeal.

Penal Code § 647 provides in part: "*Every person* who commits any of the following acts shall be guilty of disorderly conduct, a misdemeanor: * * * (b) Who solicits or who engages in any act of prostitution. As used in this subdivision, 'prostitution' includes any lewd act between persons for money or other consideration." (Italics added.)

While quantitatively the words "every person" would include the customer as well as the prostitute, male or female, appellant nonetheless contends that by reason of the legislative history of § 647 and prior judicial interpretation of the meaning of the words "soliciting for prostitution" the statute applies only to solicitation by a prostitute and not by a customer.

Assuming a degree of uncertainty in the language, "every person," we are not helped by the legislative history of the statute. Section 647, subdivision (b), was revised in 1961 primarily because then § 647, subdivision (10), which declared every "common prostitute" to be a vagrant, punished status rather than acts, and because of its probable unconstitutional vagueness. See Sherry, *Vagrants, Rogues and Vagabonds — Old Concepts in Need of Revision* (1960) 48 Cal.L.Rev. 557; see also *In re Newbern* (1960) 53 Cal.2d 786, 797. The revision proposed by Professor Sherry and ultimately adopted by the Legislature was based on A.B. 2712 (1959). This proposed bill provided that it was a misdemeanor if any person "for pecuniary profit, solicits or engages in any act of prostitution." Professor Sherry's suggested revision deleted the phrase, "for pecuniary profit," as redundant. Sherry, 48 Cal.L.Rev. at 570. The legislative committee that approved his revision, quoted his comments, and expressed its full concurrence.

Appellant argues that, because customers do not realize the pecuniary profit from an act of prostitution, the Legislature did not intend to include them within the scope of § 647, subdivision (b). Although the term "prostitution" connotes commercial sexual conduct, the deletion of "for pecuniary profit," does not ipso facto exclude customers from the scope of the statute. It reasonably can be argued that by use of the term, "prostitution," the Legislature intended only to prohibit commercial sexual acts, rather than "free love." This being so, it follows that the words, "for pecuniary profit," were deleted simply because they were unnecessary to the legislative purpose. Thus, the legislative history to § 647, subdivision (b), contains no clear expression of its intended scope insofar as the customer is concerned.

Appellant cites *In re Carey* (1922) 57 Cal.App. 297 for the proposition that, as a matter of law, only a prostitute can solicit an act of prostitution. In *Carey*, a woman convicted of violating a city ordinance making it unlawful for any person to solicit for the purpose of prostitution challenged her sentence on the ground that the state statute under which she was sentenced was discriminatory in that it applied only to women. In language which in part would be considered anachronistic by today's standards, the court said:

> It is true that the statute provides that every woman carrying on the business of prostitution may be committed to the farm; but the statute would have meant exactly the same had it in terms applied to every person. The fact that the fallen woman carries on the business of commercialized vice justifies whatever discriminations may be found in the statute. The act of her partner in vice, while equally as nefarious, is neither commercialized nor continuous. It is proper enough to send him to jail for his offense, but it is doubtful if the scheme of impounding him for purposes of reformation

would commend itself to the lawgiver. The conditions surrounding the two classes of offenders are so unlike that different methods of treatment are fully justified.

The specific charge against the petitioner is that of soliciting for prostitution. The ordinance, it is true, applies to "every person." But a man can no more commit the offense of soliciting for prostitution than that of carrying on the business of prostitution. The words "soliciting for prostitution" have a well understood and distinct meaning. They are held to mean the act of a fallen woman in hailing passers-by and soliciting them to patronize her business.

Carey is not persuasive authority in the present case, for several reasons.

First, the issue in *Carey* was not whether the customer was punishable under the ordinance, but whether the state act prescribing the punishment was discriminatory since it applied only to women. The court merely decided that different methods of treatment were fully justified, depending on whether it was the customer or the prostitute who violated the law. Thus, the language to the effect that "soliciting for prostitution" can only mean the act of the female prostitute in soliciting patrons for her business is dictum and not binding as precedent.

Moreover, *Carey* recognized that the customer's act was a crime, although not subject to punishment under the challenged ordinance.

Second, the language in *Carey* indicates that the ordinance was designed to punish the female prostitute solely because of her status as a prostitute, rather than for a specific act of prostitution. Penal Code § 647, subdivision (b), is clearly designed to punish specific acts, without reference to the status or sex of the perpetrator.

Third, because of the preemption by state law in the area of criminal sexual activities, § 647, subdivision (b), should be interpreted by reference to its own language and not on the basis of a half-century-old judicial interpretation of a local ordinance. Nothing in the history of § 647, subdivision (b), suggests that the Legislature had the *In re Carey* definition of solicitation in mind when it revised the statute in 1961.

Because of the absence of extrinsic interpretive aids, we must return to the language of the statute to ascertain the legislative intent.

The words "every person . . . who solicits . . . any act of prostitution," are clear and unambiguous. "Every" means "each and all within the range of contemplated possibilities." Webster's New Internat. Dict. (3d ed. 1961) Unabridged, p. 788. "Solicit" means "to entreat or importune: to approach with a request or plea." *Supra* at p. 2169. "Prostitution" means "the act or practice of indulging in promiscuous sexual relations especially for payment." *Supra* at p. 1822. Thus, the ordinary meaning of the statute is that all persons, customers as well as prostitutes, who solicit an act of prostitution are guilty of disorderly conduct.

Furthermore, this interpretation is consistent with the legislative purpose and policy behind the statute. See Pen.Code § 4.

The legislative purpose in proscribing solicitation for prostitution is to eliminate prostitution and its attendant evils. Subjecting the customer to prosecution will further the legislative purpose — probably more so than any other legislative remedy.

We construe the statute to apply to the customer as well as the prostitute.

The order denying the petition for writ of prohibition is affirmed.

NOTE FROM CLARENCE:

How does the court's definition of "solicit" apply to the facts of the prior case, *Elizabeth G.*? What *is* the proper definition of "solicit" in California?

PEOPLE v. RUBIN
California Court of Appeal
96 Cal.App.3d 968 (1979)

FLEMING, ASSOCIATE JUSTICE.

On March 16, 1978, Irving Rubin, a national director of the Jewish Defense League, held a press conference in Los Angeles, California, to protest a planned demonstration and march by the American Nazi Party, to take place in Skokie, Illinois, on April 20, and to announce the organization of a counter demonstration to stop the march. During the press conference, Rubin held up five $100 bills and offered the following reward:

> We are offering five hundred dollars, that I have in my hand, to any member of the community, be he Gentile or Jewish, who kills, maims, or seriously injures a member of the American Nazi Party. This offer is being made on the East Coast, on the West Coast. And if they bring us the ears, we'll make it a thousand dollars. The fact of the matter is, that we're deadly serious. This is not said in jest, we are deadly serious.

A criminal complaint was filed, Rubin was held to answer by the examining magistrate, and an information charged Rubin with solicitation of murder, in violation of Penal Code § 653f. At a hearing to set aside the information, the trial court found probable cause for Rubin's commitment for trial, in that his statements could be interpreted as solicitation to murder; but the court also concluded that the statements were protected as free speech under the First Amendment, in that although they solicited murder, their form and content indicated a desire to attract national media exposure and evidenced a lack of serious intent to solicit the commission of crime. The court ordered the information set aside, and the People have appealed.

Two issues are presented. First, whether the information should have been dismissed for lack of evidence of intent to solicit murder. Second, whether defendant's advocacy of crime is constitutionally protected speech and thus immune from prosecution as criminal solicitation.

I. *Probable Cause Supports The Information*

Both the examining magistrate and the superior court found probable cause to believe Rubin had committed a public offense, and the trial court, apart from First Amendment grounds, denied the motion to set aside the information. Such a motion does not tender the issue of the guilt or innocence of the accused or the quantum of evidence necessary to sustain a conviction. Rather it presents the question whether the magistrate could entertain a reasonable suspicion that defendant had committed a crime.

Defendant argues there was no substantial evidence of his specific intent to solicit the crime of murder, that his only specific intent had been to stimulate action in defense of the Jewish community, that by reason of the lack of evidence of specific intent to solicit murder, probable cause to support the accusation did not exist as a matter of law. The trial court rejected this argument, concluding that Rubin's intent was susceptible to several interpretations, one of which was intent to solicit murder. Solicitation of murder to prevent a march through Skokie, said the judge, would constitute a crime.

We agree with this conclusion of the trial judge, in that under the standard of probable cause defendant's statements could be interpreted as a solicitation of murder. "Solicitation consists of the asking of another to commit one of the specified crimes with intent that the crime be committed." *People v. Gordon* (1975) 47 Cal.App.3d 465, 472. Defendant's true state of mind, his intent in offering a $500 reward to anyone "who kills, maims, or seriously injures a member of the American Nazi Party," presents a question of fact to be determined by the trier of fact on the basis of evidence produced at a trial. Neither the superior court nor this court is entitled to resolve that question as a matter of law.

Accordingly, apart from First Amendment grounds, the information charging the crime of solicitation of murder is valid and is supported by probable cause.

II. *Solicitation of Crime as Protected Advocacy*

The superior court, after concluding that probable cause existed to support the charge of solicitation of murder, went on to further conclude that Rubin's statements were protected as free speech by the First Amendment. The court arrived at this latter conclusion by deducing from the form and content of Rubin's statements that he had not seriously and truly intended to solicit murder, but had merely sought to attract national media attention. Rubin's statements, in the court's view, constituted no more than political hyperbole, and, as such, were protected against abridgement by the First Amendment. Accordingly, the court set aside the information.

Patently, the trial court reached its decision by weighing the quality of Rubin's intent, determining it was not a truly serious intent, and thence concluding that the offer of reward for murder was advocacy rather than solicitation. The court arrived at this result even though Rubin himself at his press conference said he was not speaking in jest and was "deadly serious," and even though the specific intent with which an act is done presents an issue of fact. In our view, the trial court erred in undertaking to evaluate the quality of Rubin's intent.

We start with the demonstrable fact of Rubin's advocacy of violence in the form of murder, mayhem, and serious bodily injury. These acts are crimes, and their solicitation is a crime. Taken at face value, Rubin's statements invite political assassination. But we must also take into account a demonstrable proposition of law — under the First Amendment to the Constitution free speech may include advocacy of the use of force and violence. This latter proposition is not absolute, and advocacy of crime may be limited under various tests, including those of clear and present danger, of probable danger, of incitement, and of balance. T. Emerson, *The System of Freedom of Expression* (New York, 1970) pp. 16, 404-405, 717. Accordingly, solicitation of murder is not written off the books as a crime, but under certain circumstances its prosecution may be circumscribed by a constitutional freedom to advocate murder.

The paradoxical issue before us is the extent to which a summons to crime is protectable as free speech. All tests for protected speech purport to distinguish abstract advocacy of indeterminate measures from concrete solicitation of specific and determinate acts. In a given case, the issue is whether the summons is constitutionally protected advocacy of resort to crime in general, or whether it is incitement to specific crime prosecutable as criminal solicitation.

In past years, free speech cases have presented two contrasting images: one, the classroom professor lecturing his students on the need to resort to terrorism to overthrow an oppressive government (constitutionally protected speech; *cf. Sweezy v. New Hampshire* (1957) 354 U.S. 234); the other, the street demonstrator in the town square urging a mob to burn down city hall and lynch the chief of police (unprotected criminal incitement to violence; *cf. Feiner v. New York* (1951) 340 U.S. 315).

But in these days of the global village and the big trumpet, the line between advocacy and solicitation has become blurred; and when advocacy of crime is combined with the staging of a media event, the prototype images tend to merge. The classroom becomes a broadcasting studio, the mob in the town square becomes a myriad of unknown viewers and listeners throughout the broadcast area, and the critical distinction between abstract advocacy of crime in general and concrete solicitation of crime in particular breaks down. When, as here, political assassination is urged upon a greatly enlarged audience, the incitement to crime may possess a far greater capacity for civil disruption than the oral harangue of a mob in the town square, for the unseen audience of unknown listeners may contain another Oswald, or Ruby, or Sirhan, or Ray, or Bremer, or Moore, or Fromm, who may respond literally to the invitation of the speaker, regardless of the speaker's true intent. The threat to civil order presented by advocacy of assassination must be realistically evaluated in the light of its potential for deadly mischief.

One other general comment is appropriate. The leading cases evaluating the character of speech as lawful advocacy or as criminal threat/solicitation have all been determined after trial of the general issue to verdict and judgment. *Schenck v. United States* (1919) 249 U.S. 47; *Dennis v. United States* (1951) 341 U.S. 494; *Yates v. United States* (1957) 354 U.S. 298; *Watts v. United States* (1969) 394 U.S. 705; *Brandenburg v. Ohio* (1969) 395 U.S. 444; *Hess v. Indiana* (1973) 414 U.S. 105; *United States v. Kelner* (1976) 534 F.2d 1020. In these cases, the quality of the defendant's specific intent to threaten or solicit crime had been evaluated by a factual determination. At bench, we have not yet reached that stage, and the quality of Rubin's specific intent has not been passed upon by a trier of fact.

In considering the motion to set aside the information on First Amendment grounds, the trial court's function was not to evaluate Rubin's specific intent, but rather to analyze the words and circumstances of his offer of reward to anyone "who kills, maims, or seriously injures a member of the American Nazi Party" and determine whether the offer constituted constitutionally protected speech as a matter of law. At that stage of the proceeding, once probable cause had been found, Rubin's specific intent to solicit murder became largely immaterial.

Speech is protected or not in the context of its expression and surroundings, and, if protected, the constitutional protection takes hold, regardless of the purity or malignancy of the speaker's motives. If Rubin's speech were constitutionally protected, his intent would be immaterial and could be as murderous as he pleased. However, the controlling factors for First Amendment purposes are not specific intent, but the words and attendant circumstances of the offer, which determine whether or not the offer is constitutionally protected speech, even though on its face it solicits the commission of crime. If these words in their setting are protected speech, Rubin cannot be held to answer the charge of solicitation of murder, and the trial court's dismissal was correct. *Dennis v. United States* (1951) 341 U.S. 494, 513. But if the words in their circumstances are not protected speech, the issue turns on Rubin's specific intent, the cause presents an issue of fact for resolution by the trier of fact, and its dismissal was improper.

Thus, on this appeal we are not concerned with Rubin's specific intent. Rather we must evaluate Rubin's words in the light of their attendant circumstances to determine whether mere general advocacy of crime was involved, or whether Rubin's offer of reward taken at face value could reasonably be construed as soliciting the commission of crime and was therefore unshielded by the First Amendment. *Cf.* aircraft hijack and bomb threat cases: *United States v. Irving* (5th Cir. 1975) 509 F.2d 1325, false information about a future indefinite hijacking attempt not protected as free speech; *United States v. Rutherford* (2d Cir. 1964) 332 F.2d 444, intent to destroy airplane is immaterial in offense of bomb threat.

The facts and circumstances which differentiate advocacy of crime from solicitation of crime are those which differentiate advocacy of abstract doctrine from advocacy of incitement to unlawful action (*Yates v. United States* (1957) 354 U.S. 298). Their application may be seen in *Brandenburg v. Ohio* (1969) 395 U.S. 444, a conviction under Ohio's criminal syndicalism law of a leader of the Ku Klux Klan for advocating the general propriety of crime at a rally held for media reporters, during which a cross had been burned and statements made derogatory to Negroes and Jews. In reversing the conviction, the court declared that "the constitutional guarantees of free speech and free press do not permit a State to forbid or proscribe advocacy of the use of force or of law violation, except where such advocacy is directed to inciting or producing imminent lawless action and is likely to incite or produce such action." Mere abstract teaching of the moral propriety of resort to force and violence, said the court, is not the same as preparing and steeling a group for violent action.

A similar case is *Watts v. United States* (1969) 394 U.S. 705, a prosecution for threat against the President by a participant in a public discussion group, who had said that if inducted into the Army and made to carry a rifle, "the first man I want to get in my sights is L.B.J." In reversing the conviction, the court declared that threat must be distinguished from constitutionally protected speech, that the prosecution must prove a true threat rather than the kind of political hyperbole that occurred here. A recent informative case dealing with threat is *United States v. Kelner* (2 Cir. 1976) 534 F.2d 1020, where defendant, a member of the Jewish Defense League, was convicted of transmitting over television a threat to assassinate Yasser Arafat. On appeal, the court rejected the claim of freedom of expression, declined to identify the assassination threat as political hyperbole, and declared it the function of the jury to evaluate the intent behind the threat.

Although these cases deal primarily with threats to assassinate rather than solicitation of assassination, they delineate the factors that differentiate advocacy of crime as abstract doctrine from advocacy of crime as incitement to concrete action.

In *Brandenburg v. Ohio* (1969) 395 U.S. 444, 447, the Supreme Court suggested evaluation of the language of advocacy in the light of two considerations: (1) its incitement to imminent lawless action; (2) its likelihood of producing such action. This particular formula parallels the test delineated by Justice Holmes on behalf of the Supreme Court in *Schenck v. United States* (1919) 249 U.S. 47, in which, after saying that the most stringent protection of free speech would not protect a man in falsely shouting fire in a theatre and causing a panic, he refers to the test of clear and present danger and declares that protection of free speech is a question of *proximity* and *degree*. We consider the application of these factors to the cause at bench.

Proximity: Incitement to Imminent Lawless Action.

Since murder is lawless action and an offer of reward for murder is, assuredly, an incitement, imminence is the critical element here in the factor of proximity. Imminence, a function of time, refers to an event which threatens to happen momentarily, is about to happen, or is at the point of happening. But time is a relative dimension and imminence a relative term, and the imminence of an event is related to its nature. A total eclipse of the sun next year is said to be imminent. An April shower thirty minutes away is not.

The event which concerns us here was the scheduled Nazi Party demonstration and march to be held in Skokie in five weeks, an event which had already attracted national attention. We think that in terms of political assassination the demonstration could be said to have been proximate and imminent, just as a Papal visit to Belfast, a Soviet chief of state's visit to Rome, a Presidential campaign trip to Dallas, and a Presidential inauguration in Washington, can each be said to be proximate and imminent, even though occurrence may be some weeks away. The concurring opinion of Judge Mulligan in *United States v. Kelner, supra,* 534 F.2d 1020, makes this point.

> For example, if the threat here had been made in the same setting but had been phrased, "We plan to kill Arafat a week from today unless he pays

us $1,000,000," I would hold that the threat is still well within § 875(c) and not protected under the First Amendment, although the threatened homicide is not immediate, imminent or unconditional under the test proposed by Judge Oakes. We have already held that a threat to assassinate the President some two weeks later is within a comparable statute, 18 U.S.C. § 871. *United States v. Compton*, 428 F.2d 18 (2d Cir. 1970).

United States v. Compton, supra, involved a threat on April 14 to assassinate the President toward the end of April or the beginning of May.

Additionally, the seriousness of the threatened crime, i.e. the nature of the lawless action solicited, bears some relationship to its imminence. Generally speaking, the more serious the crime the greater its time span. Murder, the most serious crime of all, carries the longest time span of any crime, as shown by the lack of any time limitation on its prosecution (Pen.Code § 799), and a threat of murder can be imminent at a time when a threat of trespass is not.

We think solicitation of murder in connection with a public event of this notoriety, even though five weeks away, can qualify as incitement to imminent lawless action.

Degree: Likelihood of Producing Action.

Here we are concerned with the practicality and feasibility of the solicitation - was it likely to incite or produce violence? We cannot, of course, answer this question with assurance, for the effect of emotional appeals for political violence on the actions of inherently unstable personalities remains obscure. But we think it a reasonable inference that serious reportage by respectable news media of a reward for murder tends in some degree to give respectability to what otherwise would remain an underground solicitation of limited credibility addressed to a limited audience, and thereby tends to increase the risk and likelihood of violence. Undoubtedly, the prosecution's case would be stronger if a specific Nazi Party member had been named as the target for assassination and if the demonstration had been one scheduled to take place in Los Angeles rather than in Skokie. Yet murder remains a crime, whether or not a specified victim is identified as the target (*People v. Aranda* (1938) 12 Cal.2d 307, 310), and solicitation in California of murder in Illinois is nonetheless solicitation of murder. *People v. Ayers* (1975) 51 Cal.App.3d 370.

The solicitation to murder here was not made in a jesting or conditional manner, nor was it the outcome of an improvised piece of braggadocio. Its words and circumstances suggest the possibility it might incite or produce the violence sought. Rubin himself referred to earlier bloodshed in St. Louis, and he predicted bloodshed in Skokie unless the permit for the demonstration were revoked. Some of the comments of the court in *United States v. Kelner, supra* 534 F.2d 1020, are germane.

> We believe that important national interests similar to those in *Watts* exist here, more specifically, the governmental interest of reducing the climate of violence to which true threats of injury necessarily contribute. As a part of the Government's constitutional responsibility to insure domestic tranquility, it is properly concerned in an era of ever-increasing acts of

violence and terrorism, coupled with technological opportunities to carry out threats of injury with prohibiting as criminal conduct specific threats of physical injury to others, whether directed toward our own or another nation's leaders or members of the public. [*Id.* at p. 1026.]

From the words and circumstances of Rubin's offer we conclude there was sufficient likelihood of his solicitation being interpreted as a call to arms, as a preparation and steelment of his group to violent action as a systematic promotion of future bloodshed in the streets, rather than as a communication of ideas through reasoned public discussion, to remove it from the category of protected speech and require Rubin to answer the charges against him. The order setting aside the information is reversed.

ROTH, PRESIDING JUSTICE, dissenting.

On March 16, 1978, respondent, a national director of the Jewish Defense League, held a press conference wherein he stated, *inter alia*:

> This is a nationwide offer. We absolutely feel desperate in the sense that, as I've said before, in the last nine months the Nazis have gained a tremendous amount of notoriety. They are building a national movement. They've got money behind them, and we're fearful if we allow it to grow. We begged the Jewish community many years ago, that if we don't stop the Nazis now, in several years they'll be marching through our community. And the Jewish community didn't listen and so we were right. And this is the end result.

> We sincerely mean what we say, that we're going after the Nazis. We're not going to relax, we're not going to let up, we're going to declare all out war on people who want to advocate our destruction.

> April 20. And the Nazis plan to march through Skokie, Illinois, which is 70% Jewish, 7,000 survivors of the holocaust. They plan to bring big shields with gigantic swastikas on them; they plan to state that, we missed you 30 years ago, and we're going to try it again. As I said before, it will cause a tremendous grief to the people who are living there, specifically, the survivors of the holocaust. And we feel it's a desecration of our God, and we feel it's a desecration of the Jewish people to allow it to happen in the name of freedom of speech. We're deadly serious, that we'll even go to jail, that we'll risk spending time in jail, if we have to, in order to stop the Nazis, because we think we've learned from history.

> This was announced the other day in Chicago, when our national director stated that we're there, and we're coming there, and we're going to stop the Nazi march at all cost. And it's a nationwide thing, and we're bringing people as far away as Montreal, Canada. And you can expect a major turnout of Jewish activists, of Jewish militants who are willing to go into the streets and fight Nazis.

> *Questioner*: I need to get one thing clarified before I go off here, ah the $500 reward . . .

Rubin: Right.

Questioner: Ah that is not just blanket for any Jew or Gentile who maims or seriously injures any member of the Nazi party. Is that for anybody who does this in defense of the Jewish . . .

Rubin: *That's in defense of the Jewish or Gentile community*. (Emphasis added.)

Questioner: So it would be incorrect to say just a blanket offer.

Rubin: You could say it's a blanket offer, providing that they could prove that it was in the defense of the community.

Questioner: Don't you think that you're really opening the door?

Rubin: No. No. It doesn't enter my mind at all. I want people to know, that if they go out there and they take the consequences of being arrested, in either the attack of an American Nazi or whatever, that there are people who are grateful. That there are people who are right behind them 100%; and if money is a motivating factor, which it seems to be in America, that seems to be the bottom line, yeah. That's where we're at.

We wish to announce two events. On April twentieth, a number of Neo-Nazis perhaps, a hundred fifty, perhaps two hundred, will march into the Jewish area in Skokie, Illinois. We the Jewish Defense League of the West Coast and East Coast will amass at least five thousand to six thousand people in that area, to literally stop the Neo-Nazi movement. We're not going there under the intention to be pacifists. They like to have a nice non-violent quiet protest. We're going there to take names and bury them if we have to.

We're not going to allow Neo-Nazis to come into Skokie and advocate the Judacide of the Jewish people there. We're not going to allow them, with stench of the crematoria still existing in that city, with seven thousand survivors with numbers on their arms. We're not gonna allow them to be insulted, intimidated again by Nazis. We believe if we would have done it thirty years ago there might have been a different story. Many more Jews would have been alive today.

And we're going there and we're sponsoring the way of people. If they don't have the money, we're providing them a round-trip ticket from Chicago, Los Angeles. It'll cost us. We now have a travel agent who is going to eliminate his commission, and it'll cost us between a hundred and sixty, a hundred seventy dollars per person. If the individual cannot afford his way, we the Jewish Defense League will be sponsoring him, providing he meets our qualifications. The qualifications are: that he is of sound mind and he is of sound body. And I mean that he is able-willing, ready, and able to handle himself or herself in the streets.

Questioner: Are you really . . .

Rubin: And that means. We also have an added feature. We are offering five hundred dollars, that I have in my hand, to any member of the community, be he Gentile or Jewish, who kills, maims, or seriously injures a member of the American Nazi Party. This offer is being made on the East Coast, on the West Coast. And if they bring us the ears, we'll make it a thousand dollars. The fact of the matter is, that we're deadly serious. This is not said in jest, we are deadly serious. In the defense of the Jewish community, should any Nazi even dream of attacking a Jew like they did.

Based upon the foregoing, a complaint was issued on April 3, 1978, charging respondent with violation of Penal Code § 653f, and he was held to answer at a preliminary hearing conducted June 9, 1978.

In addition to the excerpts of the speech quoted above, the record makes clear the following facts: Respondent could not call a meeting at the Press Club; he had to be there by invitation; he did not address a rally of sympathizers for the purpose of stirring them into a frenzy of excitement; he was addressing media representatives seeking to learn what were the plans of the Jewish Defense League in counter-demonstration to a Nazi march in Skokie, Illinois, an event calendared five weeks in the future. In exploitation of that opportunity, respondent, in a speech of approximately 800 words, made the hyperbolized solicitation referred to by the majority, and that included *infra*, to attract attention to a sensitive and explosive national issue and to generate news on a national scale, and thus dramatize the obscene insult the Nazis sought to impose on the Jews of Skokie. Rubin, although not gifted with the eloquence of Elie Weisel, did make clear the sole thrust of his speech, to wit: that the Jewish Defense League wanted the world to know that Skokie had been selected by the Nazis with ruthless calculation because it was a small city with a 70 percent Jewish population comprising in that percentage seven thousand Jews who had indelible numbers on their arms identifying them as surviving victims of Nazi concentration camps, and that the Nazis were about to march in Skokie to remind those survivors and also their co-religionists living in Skokie or elsewhere, that Jews, with or without indelible numbers, were marked for extinction.

As posed by the district attorney in his brief, the language relied upon, taken out of context as is the language of the majority, as the basis of a violation of Penal Code § 653f was in pertinent part as follows:

Q: I need to get one thing clarified before I go off here, ah the $500 reward.

R: Right.

Q: Ah that is not just blanket for any Jew or Gentile who maims or seriously injures any member of the Nazi party. Is that for anybody who does this in defense of the Jewish.

R: That's in defense of the Jewish or Gentile community.

Q: So it would be incorrect to say just a blanket offer.

R: You could say it's a blanket offer, providing that they could prove that it was in the defense of the community.

Q: Of the Jewish community?

R: Or Gentile community. It makes no difference. It makes no difference to us.

Addressing himself to the First Amendment question, the trial judge, with the case of *Watts v. United States*, 394 U.S. 705 undoubtedly in mind, determined as a matter of law that Rubin's alleged solicitation in violation of § 653f was not and could not be construed to be a true "solicitation" when listened to or read in the context of Rubin's speech, and was constitutionally protected.

In *Watts*, a case construing a United States statute and facts strikingly similar to those at bench, the court said:

> Certainly the statute under which petitioner was convicted is constitutional on its face. The Nation undoubtedly has a valid, even an overwhelming, interest in protecting the safety of its Chief Executive and in allowing him to perform his duties without interference from threats of physical violence. *Nevertheless, a statute such as this one, which makes criminal a form of pure speech, must be interpreted with the commands of the First Amendment clearly in mind. What is a threat Must be distinguished from what is Constitutionally protected speech.* But whatever the "willfulness" requirement implies, *the statute initially requires* the Government to *prove a true "threat."* We do not believe that the kind of political hyperbole indulged in by petitioner fits within that statutory term. For *we must* interpret the *language* Congress chose "*against the background* of a *profound* national commitment to the principle that debate on public issues should be *uninhibited, robust, and wide-open,* and that it may well include vehement, caustic, and sometimes unpleasantly sharp attacks on government and public officials." *New York Times Co. v. Sullivan*, 376 U.S. 254, 270 (1964). The language of the political arena, like the language used in labor disputes, see *Linn v. United Plant Guard Workers of America*, 383 U.S. 53, 58 (1966), is often vituperative, abusive, and inexact. We agree with petitioner that his only offense here was "*a kind of very crude offensive method of stating a political opposition to the President.*" Taken in context, and regarding the expressly conditional nature of the statement and the reaction of the listeners, *we do not see how it could be interpreted otherwise.* [Emphasis added]

At bench the trial judge, concluding his analysis of the facts, said in pertinent part:

> I have read your points and authorities viewing the defendant's statement in its proper context I must agree with the comments that appear in the Amicus brief, where they state: "Amicus contend that the form and contents of Rubin's communication were used solely to attract nationwide media exposure. The contents *evidence a lack of any serious intentions to solicit the commission of a crime.* His remarks constitute political hyperbole and were merely a crude, offensive method of stating political opposition to the Nationalist Socialist Party." I feel in reading all of the statements made on March 16th, the language used by Mr. Rubin falls within the language protected by the First Amendment. [Emphasis added.]

The motion to dismiss was thereupon granted. This appeal by the People followed.

In *Watts*, the court deals with a threat in violation of a United States statute admitted to be constitutional. At bench we deal with a solicitation prosecuted under a state statute also conceded to be constitutional.

Tested by the requisites enunciated in *Watts*, the solicitation at bench was not a true "solicitation" any more than was the "threat" in *Watts* a true threat.[6]

United States v. Kelner (2d Cir., 1976) 534 F.2d 1020 illustrates a true "threat" or "solicitation" as distinguished from the one at bench. The *Kelner* court concedes that determination of threat or solicitation is a matter of law and states at p. 1027:

> The purpose and effect of the *Watts* constitutionally-limited definition of the term "threat" is to insure that only unequivocal, unconditional and specific expressions of intention immediately to inflict injury may be punished.

Kelner then proceeds to show that the facts before it as to a threat were "unequivocal, unconditional and specific expressions of intention immediately to inflict injury" and discusses intent, general and specific, to show the certainty, immediacy and the lack of the conditional nature of all the facts and circumstances before it. In *Kelner*, the stated pertinent facts are:

> Miller was assigned to cover the JDL press conference. When he and his film crew arrived at the JDL headquarters, the conference had already started. Appellant, Kelner, was seated in military fatigues behind a desk with a .38 caliber "police special" in front of him. To Kelner's right another man was dressed in military fatigues. Miller heard one of the several reporters at the conference ask Kelner whether he was talking about an assassination plot, and heard Kelner answer in the affirmative. The WPIX crew quickly filmed general shots of the press conference without sound for use as a "lead-in" on the news and then began filming an actual interview of Kelner by Miller.

> *Kelner*: We have people who have been trained and who are out now and who intend to make sure that Arafat and his lieutenants do not leave this country alive.

> *Miller*: How do you plan to do that? You're going to kill him?

> *Kelner*: I'm talking about justice. I'm talking about equal rights under the law, a law that may not exist, but should exist.

> *Miller*: Are you saying that you plan to kill them?

---

[6] "'They always holler at us to get an education. And now I have already received my draft classification as 1-A and I have got to report for my physical this Monday coming. I am not going. If they ever make me carry a rifle the first man I want to get in my sights is L.B.J. They are not going to make me kill my black brothers.' On the basis of this statement, the jury found that petitioner had committed a felony by knowingly and willfully threatening the President. The United States Court of Appeals for the District of Columbia Circuit affirmed by a two-to-one vote. We reverse." *Watts v. United States*, 394 U.S. 705, 706.

Kelner: We are planning to assassinate Mr. Arafat. Just as if any other mur-
just the way any other murder is treated.

Miller: Do you have the people picked out for this? Have you planned it
out? Have you started this operation?

Kelner: Everything is planned in detail.

Miller: Do you think it will come off?

Kelner: It's going to come off.

Miller: Can you elaborate on where or when or how you plan to take care
of this?"

The alleged solicitation at bench considered in the context of the speech was
hyperbole with respect to a vital and explosive public issue, conditioned on the
defense of the Jewish and Gentile community with respect to an event planned five
weeks in the future and two thousand miles removed from Los Angeles; the
language of the solicitation had no immediacy and was uncertain, vague and
general.

The trial court's conclusion as a matter of law that Rubin's remarks were not a
"true" solicitation in violation of Penal Code § 653f but were embraced in the First
Amendment as permitted speech, in my opinion follows the law thus enunciated.

I would affirm.

NOTES FROM CLARENCE:

(1) I had some trouble understanding the majority opinion. When the case goes to
the jury, if the jury believes that Rubin intended his words to be taken seriously,
might they nevertheless acquit him? On what ground?

(2) The majority relies in part on *U.S. v. Kelner*, while the dissent tries to
distinguish *Kelner*. Which is right?

(3) Irv Rubin later had a change of heart about violence. "Not only did it give
Gentiles the idea that we were violent, it also turned off many Jews and closed
thousands of doors to us. We became the black sheep of the family." In 1985, a
booby trap exploded at the Santa Ana offices of the Arab-American Anti-
Discrimination Committee, killing its western regional director, Alex Odeh.
Federal authorities suspected the Jewish Defense League. In a statement he now
says he regrets, Rubin declared, "I have no tears for Mr. Odeh. He got exactly
what he deserves." This was the turning point for Rubin and the JDL. Donations
from the Jewish community dried up, and JDL membership dwindled to a few
thousand. Rubin then began to turn the JDL into "a kinder, gentler JDL, a group
devoted more to debate and defense than to militancy and malevolence." A rabbi
confirmed the change in Rubin, noting that he now wears 3-piece suits. Los
Angeles Times, July 23, 1990, Section E.

PEOPLE v. BOTTGER
California Court of Appeal
142 Cal.App.3d 974 (1983)

WOOLPERT, ASSOCIATE JUSTICE.

The importance of formula jury instructions becomes most obvious when there are none applicable to the principal issue in a criminal case. Because counsel and the court must innovate, the resulting instructions ensure a technical review on appeal. This is such an appeal. The editors of California Jury Instructions, Criminal (CALJIC) have not yet offered instructions and use notes on soliciting the commission of certain felonies.

Defendant John L. Bottger was convicted by a jury of solicitation for murder. Pen.Code § 653f, subd. (b). On this appeal, he urges there were two instructional errors.

In April 1981, defendant was in Sparks, Nevada, living out of his truck and picking up occasional odd jobs. During that time he met Morris Wade. The two men passed the time drinking and talking. In one conversation, defendant told Wade about his relationship with Martha, a married woman in Fresno. Defendant remarked that Martha's husband Billy was "in the way" and that he wished Billy were dead. He then offered Wade $5,000 to kill Billy. When Wade expressed doubt that defendant would get anyone to murder Billy for that amount of money, defendant said he would talk to Martha about it. He subsequently offered Wade $20,000 upon receipt of the proceeds from Billy's life insurance policy. Defendant also commented that killing Billy would be better than having Martha get a divorce, because defendant would ultimately gain control over all the insurance and property, rather than only half of the property.

Unbeknownst to defendant, Wade often served as an informant for various law enforcement agencies. Wade contacted an employee in the Criminal Investigation Division of the Internal Revenue Service in Reno and was ultimately referred to Walt Kubas, a special agent for the California Department of Justice. They agreed that Wade would introduce Kubas to defendant as an assistant capable of carrying out the arrangement to kill Billy.

After Kubas was introduced to defendant, defendant began discussing the proposed murder plan. He described items of property, such as a gun collection and MG Roadster, which he expected to find at Billy's house and said Kubas could take whatever he thought he could resell. Although defendant acknowledged he did not have money to pay Kubas, he confirmed that he would be willing to pay him $20,000 when he received the proceeds from Billy's insurance policy or the sale of Martha's mother's house. Defendant further specified he needed to be sure Martha would be out of town when the murder occurred and wanted the murder to look as if it had been committed during a burglary.

Kubas, Wade, and defendant then drove to Fresno. There defendant bought a map on which he wrote Billy's address and drew directions to the house. Kubas and defendant drove to Billy's residence and discussed how Kubas could enter the house without being observed.

To make it appear that he was executing the plan in a realistic, professional manner, and to get physical evidence of defendant's intent, Kubas insisted that defendant sign a promissory note for $20,000. Defendant was reluctant to sign a note, but finally signed one written by Kubas which stated, "I, John Bottger, owe Walt $20,000. $20,000 payable by January 1st, 1982, for services rendered."

Once the note was signed, Kubas took defendant to the bus station and bought him a ticket back to Nevada. They parted after agreeing defendant would call Kubas that Sunday at 5 p.m. and confirm that Martha was not at the Fresno residence before Kubas executed the plan. Defendant never called Kubas on the appointed day.

On the following Wednesday, Kubas approached defendant at a truck stop in Sparks and said, "I think you forgot something." Defendant replied that he had overslept, and asked whether everything had gone smoothly. When Kubas answered, "Yes, he's deader than a door nail," defendant smiled but said nothing. Defendant was then arrested.

Although defendant had been drinking during the ride to Fresno, Kubas said there was no doubt that defendant was sober. Kubas further stated he never saw defendant indicate that he wanted to cancel the plan.

The Defense

Defendant agreed he had discussed plans to murder Billy, went to Fresno, and signed a promissory note. However, he claimed Wade initiated the plan to kill Billy and persisted in discussing it until defendant capitulated and allowed him to proceed with the scheme. He maintained he never intended to have Billy killed, although he admitted telling Kubas he wished Billy were dead. He had second thoughts about the plan while the men were on their way to Fresno.

Because Wade had told defendant that he knew people in the Mafia, defendant was afraid to cancel the plans. Defendant also felt threatened when Kubas told him there would be no backing out. Since Wade and Kubas were so involved in the scheme, defendant decided to cooperate and never expressed his reservations about proceeding with it. Furthermore, he felt his excessive drinking had interfered with his mental processes.

Defendant acknowledged the arrangement to call Kubas on Sunday evening, but testified he was to call Kubas to tell him to carry out the plan; if he did not call, the deal was off. Thus, when Kubas confronted him at the truck stop and asked him why he had not called, defendant told him he had not made the phone call because he had cancelled the plan.

I. *Was It Error To Instruct The Jury On Implied Malice?*

A. *Was There Invited Error?*

In instructing the jury, the trial court gave a tailor-made instruction based on Penal Code § 653f, subdivision (b), which recited the classic elements of solicitation for murder, including specific intent that another person be murdered. The court then added part of the CALJIC instructions on murder, including definitions of both express and implied malice in the language of CALJIC No. 8.11.[1] In other instructions, the court emphasized that a necessary element of the offense is the defendant's specific intent that a murder be committed.

Defendant contends the trial court erred by instructing the jury on implied malice. He argues that by giving those instructions, the court may have led the jury to believe it could imply malice and find defendant guilty without determining defendant had the specific intent to kill.

B. *The Instructions On Implied Malice.*

In contending it was error to give instructions on implied malice where specific intent must be found, defendant analogizes solicitation for murder to cases involving attempted murder or assault with intent to commit murder, in which the jury must find the defendant had a specific intent to kill. Courts have found error in such cases when jurors were given instructions on implied malice. *People v. Collie* (1981) 30 Cal.3d 43, 61-62; *People v. Murtishaw* (1981) 29 Cal.3d 733, 764-765, mod. 29 Cal.3d 836a. In *Murtishaw*, the Supreme Court stated,

> Once a defendant intends to kill, any malice he may harbor is necessarily express malice. Implied malice, as defined in CALJIC No. 8.11, cannot coexist with a specific intent to kill. To instruct on implied malice in that setting, therefore, may confuse the jury by suggesting that they can convict without finding a specific intent to kill. [*Id.* at 764-765.]

Because solicitation for murder also requires a finding of specific intent to kill or express malice, defendant maintains the reasoning in *Collie* and *Murtishaw*

---

[1] The court instructed the jury in relevant part as follows: "Every person who solicits another to commit or join in the commission of the murder is guilty of the crime charged in the Information.

In order to prove the commission of such crime, each of the following elements must be proved: That a person solicited another person to commit murder or joined in the commission of a murder of another person, that at the time of the solicitation, such person had the specific intent that another person be murdered.

Murder is defined as the unlawful killing of a human being with malice aforethought. Malice may be either expressed or implied. Malice is expressed when there is manifested an attempt unlawfully to kill a human being. Malice is implied when the killing results from an act involving a high degree of probability that it will result in death which act is done for a base, anti-social purpose and with a wanton disregard for human life by which is meant (an awareness) of a duty imposed by law not to commit such act followed by the commission of the act forbidden or the act despite that awareness.

In the crime of solicitation to commit murder, of which the defendant is accused in the Information, a necessary element is the existence in the mind of the defendant of the specific intent that a murder be committed."

compels the conclusion that in this case it was error to instruct on implied malice. The jurors may have felt they could convict defendant without finding he had intended that Billy be killed. Instead, the jury might have found implied malice by concluding that defendant's participation in arranging to murder Billy exhibited a wanton disregard for life or created a situation with a high degree of probability it would result in death.

The People argue specific intent to kill is not a necessary element of solicitation to murder. They contend the instruction on malice is significant only to the extent it is used to define the crime of murder, and is not relevant to the issue of defendant's intent. Since no murder or attempted murder was committed, the People argue no finding of malice was required. We disagree.

The crime of solicitation to commit murder occurs when the solicitor purposely seeks to have someone killed and tries to engage someone to do the killing. This simplified concept becomes unduly complicated if the court is not careful to define "murder" with emphasis on the solicitor's specific intent. The solicitee's expected state of mind and action in carrying out the request is irrelevant.

"Solicitation is complete when the solicitation is made, and it is immaterial that the object of the solicitation is never consummated, or that no steps are taken toward its consummation." *People v. Burt* (1955) 45 Cal.2d 311, 314. It is immaterial that the solicitee may be an undercover agent whose only intent is to arrest the solicitor. *People v. Adami* (1973) 36 Cal.App.3d 452, 457. For the same reason, it is irrelevant that the solicitee may be so intoxicated he could not be convicted of anything higher than voluntary manslaughter, or that he is an incompetent who could not be convicted of any crime.

The solicitation may develop into an attempt, then murder. The differences in these crimes relate to the people involved and the progression of the activity toward the criminal objective. When attempted murder is charged, the definition of the term "murder" remains narrow: "The wrongdoer must specifically contemplate taking life, and though his act is such as, were it successful, would be murder, if in truth he does not mean to kill, he does not become guilty of an attempt to commit murder." *People v. Miller* (1935) 2 Cal.2d 527, 533.

In *People v. Murtishaw, supra*, 29 Cal.3d 733, 762-765, the court analyzed the crime of assault with intent to commit *murder* and held the mental element must be limited to an intent to *kill*. We see no reason to interpret "murder" more broadly in a solicitation case. Solicitation instructions must be similarly limited to exclude reference to implied malice.

We distinguish conspiracy to commit murder cases in which the various degrees of homicide may be considered by the jury in appropriate circumstances. The conspiracy statute makes the punishment depend upon the nature and degree of the substantive offense. *People v. Horn* (1974) 12 Cal.3d 290, 297. Penal Code § 653f, subdivision (b), is not comparable.

C. *Was There Prejudicial Error?*

As the instructions on implied malice were inappropriate and potentially confusing, we now determine whether they were prejudicial. We have reviewed the opening statements and closing arguments. No reference was made to implied malice. * * * * We find the instructional error nonprejudicial. It is not reasonably probable that a result more favorable to defendant would have been reached in the absence of the portion of the instructions relating to implied malice.

The judgment is affirmed.

NOTES FROM CLARENCE:

1. Suppose the defendant sends a letter to X asking X to commit murder, but the letter was intercepted by police before it reaches X. Solicitation? *Attempted* solicitation? No crime? In *People v. Saephanh*, 80 Cal.App.4th 451 (2000), the court held that California Penal Code § 653f requires the second option:

> We agree with appellant that solicitation requires a completed communication.

> Respondent insists that even if solicitation requires a completed communication, Vicki Lawrence, the correctional officer, received the letter. In our view, this argument evades the issue of whether appellant "solicited another." Appellant did not ask Vicki Lawrence to kill anyone, or do anything for that matter. She was not a person solicited.

> Section 653f has the twofold purpose of protecting the inhabitants of California from being exposed to inducement to commit or join in the commission of crimes and preventing solicitations from resulting in the commission of the crimes solicited. Uncommunicated soliciting messages do not expose others to inducements to commit crimes. Nor is there a likelihood that an uncommunicated message would result in the commission of crimes. Thus, letters posted but not delivered do not give rise to the dangers from which section 653f seeks to protect society.

> However, messages urging commission of a crime which are received expose individuals to invitation to crime and create a risk of criminal activity. Criminalizing completed solicitations furthers the policies of protecting individuals from exposure to inducements to commit crimes and preventing commission of the crimes solicited. Thus, a conviction for a violation of section 653f requires proof that the person solicited received the soliciting communication. One cannot "solicit another" without a completed communication. The communication is only completed when it is received by its intended recipient.

> Appellant did not ask Vicki Lawrence to kill Cassandra's fetus and appellant was unsuccessful in asking Saechao to do so because his letter was intercepted. Appellant did not "solicit another" to commit murder within the meaning of section 653f, subdivision (b). Thus, his conviction for solicitation of murder cannot stand.

Appellant next contends he is guilty of no crime. He asserts attempted solicitation is not a crime in California because there is no reference to attempt in section 653f. He cites other criminal and noncriminal statutes containing attempt language and suggests the absence of such language in section 653f is a clear manifestation of legislative intent attempted solicitation is not a crime.

We disagree. "Every person who attempts to commit *any crime*, but fails, or is prevented or intercepted in its perpetration, shall be punished where no provision is made by law for the punishment of those attempts . . ." California Penal Code § 664. Solicitation is a crime, and thus falls within section 664, which applies to the attempted commission of any crime. The plain language of section 664 makes clear the Legislature is aware of specific provisions regarding attempt in the context of some crimes, and it expressly applies to those crimes which do not address attempt. Attempted solicitation of murder is a crime in California.

Appellant insists that attempted solicitation cannot be a crime because, according to appellant, solicitation is an attempt crime in itself — attempted conspiracy. * * * * It does not necessarily follow that every solicitation is an attempted conspiracy. The crime of solicitation is complete when the solicitation is made, i.e., when the soliciting message is received by its intended recipient. It is immaterial that the object of the solicitation is never consummated, or that no steps are taken towards its completion. Pursuant to the plain language of sections 653f and 664, attempted solicitation of murder is a crime.

The court noted that the Model Penal Code "criminalizes uncommunicated solicitations."

2. In *People v. Terrell*, 339 Ill.App.3d 786, 792 N.E.2d 357 (2003), Terrell planned to kill Harp. He asked Wilkins to drive him to the place where Terrell would perform the killing. Terrell was convicted of soliciting Wilkins to commit murder. The state argued that Wilkins would have been guilty of murder as an accomplice to Terrell's murder of Harp, so by asking Wilkins to help, Terrell had solicited murder. The appellate court disagreed:

The defendant argues that the State failed to prove him guilty of solicitation of murder beyond a reasonable doubt because he did not request, encourage, or command Wilkins to commit the murder; rather, he argues that he intended to kill Harp himself and that he asked Wilkins only to drive him and Harp to the site where he planned to kill her. We agree. * * * *

The solicitation statute in Illinois provides, "A person commits solicitation of murder when, with the intent that the offense of first-degree murder be committed, he commands, encourages, or requests another *to commit that offense*." (Emphasis added.) 720 ILCS 5/8-1.1(a). The defendant contends that requesting another person to assist him in committing a murder by driving him and the intended victim to the site where he planned to kill her himself does not fall within this statutory definition. The State, by contrast, contends that because the act that the defendant requested Wilkins to perform would have made Wilkins guilty of murder on an accountability theory had he performed it, the defendant's request was in fact a request "to commit" the murder. * * * *

The dearth of case law addressing analogous facts demonstrates the rarity of the scenario presented by this case. It is quite likely that the legislature, when drafting the solicitation statute, did not even consider whether conduct such as that here at issue should fall within its purview. However, even assuming that the lack of language expressly prohibiting conduct such as the defendant's is the result of legislative oversight, we may not ignore the plain language of the statute.

Moreover, we believe there are valid reasons to distinguish between requests to aid and abet in the commission of a crime and requests that another actually commit the crime or procure a third person to do so. * * * * One purpose of the solicitation statute is to punish the actions of those who might otherwise be able to hide behind their hireling(s). Clearly, such concerns are not raised in a situation where, as here, a defendant merely solicits assistance in carrying out a crime he intends to commit himself.

3. Illinois punishes solicitation to murder with 15 to 30 years imprisonment, while it punishes conspiracy to commit murder with only 3 to 7 years imprisonment. Does this make sense? Doesn't every conspiracy begin with one person asking another to commit a crime with him, i.e., a solicitation? Since conspiracy occurs where the solicitee accepts the solicitation, isn't conspiracy more dangerous than solicitation?

In *People v. Kauten*, 324 Ill.App.3d 588 (2001). the court held that this scheme does not violate a constitutional bar against "disproportionate" sentencing:

Although defendant argues that a greater threat to the public is posed in a conspiracy where two or more persons are involved and that there is a greater likelihood the offense will be committed, the offense of solicitation addresses at least an equally dangerous evil. The person who solicits another by command, encouragement, or request to commit murder generally represents a more sophisticated and planned criminal intent by an actor who attempts to shield himself through his hireling. Imposition of a severe penalty for criminal solicitation may be an important means by which the leadership of a criminal movement may be suppressed.

We agree with the State that solicitation poses special dangers not inherent in conspiracy, one of which is that the instigator will be a sophisticated operator, such as a gang leader, who will hide behind his hireling(s). Laws against solicitation target those at the top of the proverbial totem pole. Thus, these laws play a distinctive and important role in suppressing organized crime. 2 W. LaFave & A. Scott, Substantive Criminal Law § 6.1(b), at 6 (1986).

Furthermore, solicitation cannot be considered the mere equal of conspiracy, as often a solicitation is the proximate cause of a conspiracy. A conspiracy takes place among those who already intend to bring about a crime, but a solicitation is an effort to recruit one who has not yet formed criminal intentions and to implant such intentions in his or her mind. A person who is afraid or unable to commit murder on his or her own may solicit the help of another (or many others) who would otherwise lack the incentive to commit murder. What neither would attempt individually may come about by their cooperation. Thus, many a solicitation creates a conspiracy where none existed before.

Chapter 18

ATTEMPT

The crime of attempt . . . consists of: (1) an intent to do an act or to bring about certain consequences which would in law amount to a crime; and (2) and act in furtherance of that intent which, as it is most commonly put, goes beyond mere preparation.

LaFave & Scott, *Criminal Law* (West)

Attempt raises some fascinating questions.

Generally, the punishment for attempt is about *half* the punishment for the completed crime. Why *only* half? The attemptor has the same intent as the completor, but has failed due to some happenstance — so isn't the *culpability* of the two identical? Why *as much as* half? The attemptor has *failed*, and has hurt no one. Why punish the attemptor *at all*?

Suppose Dan shoots at a wooden dummy, thinking it is his worst enemy Vic. Should Dan be relieved of an attempted murder prosecution because it is "impossible" to kill a human being by shooting into a wooden dummy? Why?

Suppose Dan plans to kill Vic, buys a gun, and waits for Vic at his home. Before Vic arrives, a police officer arrests Dan. Has Dan committed attempted murder?

Suppose — instead of being arrested — Dan simply changes his mind and goes away. Has Dan nevertheless *already* committed attempted murder? Note that if Dan steals an apple and immediately changes his mind and gives it back, he doesn't "take back" the crime of larceny. All the elements of larceny came together at one moment, so the crime was committed. Should Dan be able to "take back" the crime of attempt by changing his mind?

The Problem and cases in this Chapter raise these issues.

PROBLEM 18

To: My law clerk

From: Dan Webster

Re: *U.S. v. Sutton*

My client, Willie Sutton, was just convicted of attempted bank robbery (in violation of 18 U.S.C. § 2113) and attempted murder of an FBI agent (in violation of 18 U.S.C. § 1114). At trial, the key witness against him was FBI agent Edgar Heever, whose testimony is attached. I'd like to appeal on the ground that Heever's testimony does not constitute substantial evidence of defendant's guilt. Please read the attached authorities and let me know if I have much of a chance.

Partial Transcript in *U.S. v. Sutton*

Q. Agent Heever, how did you first learn of Mr. Sutton's plan to rob the bank?

A. Fred Fink has been a paid informant for us for years. Last May, Fink called me and said that Sutton had asked him to help rob the Continental Illinois branch bank in downtown Chicago. Sutton said they would drive to the "drive-in teller" window at 10 a.m. when the bank opened, pull a gun on the teller, take the money in her till, and drive away. Sutton needed Fink's help to watch out for security guards and police while Sutton was focusing on the teller. Fink had told Sutton he would help, though he had no intention of doing so. Fink said that Sutton was going to pick him up the next morning at 9:30.

Q. Did you observe Sutton's actions next morning?

A. Yes. I went to Fink's house. Sutton arrived in his car at about 9:30 a.m. He went to Fink's door and knocked several times, but no one answered. Sutton got back in his car and drove off. I followed him. He drove back to his own house. Before he could get out of his car, I went over to him and said, "Hold it. FBI." He pulled out a handgun and pointed it at me and pulled the trigger. I heard a click, but the gun didn't fire. I arrested him and took the gun. Our ballistics expert checked it out, and he reported that the gun had a defective firing mechanism and would not fire.

Q. So Sutton never did get to the bank?

A. Correct. In fact, if he had gone to the drive-in window at that branch, he would have found it closed, because the driveway was being remodeled. There was no money there. It wasn't reopened until a week later.

Title 18, United States Statutes

Section 1114. Protection of Officers and Employees of the United States.

Whoever kills or attempts to kill any officer or employee of the United States or of any agency in any branch of the United States Government (including any member of the uniformed services) while such officer or employee is engaged in or on account of the performance of official duties, or any person assisting such an officer or employee in the performance of such duties or on account of that assistance, . . . shall be punished (1) in the case of murder, as provided under section 1111; (2) in the case of manslaughter, as provided under section 1112; or (3) in the case of attempted murder or manslaughter, as provided in section 1113.

Section 2113. Bank Robbery and Incidental Crimes.

(a) Whoever, by force and violence, or by intimidation, takes, or attempts to take, from the person or presence of another, or obtains or attempts to obtain by extortion any property or money or any other thing of value belonging to, or in the care, custody, control, management, or possession of, any bank, credit union, or any savings and loan association . . . shall be fined under this title or imprisoned not more than twenty years, or both.

Note: Compare Model Penal Code § 5.01, in the Appendix.

UNITED STATES v. ROMAN
U.S. District Court, Southern District of New York
356 F.Supp. 434 (1973)
(affirmed at 484 F.2d 1271 (2d Cir. 1973), cert. denied, 415 U.S. 978 (1974))

FREDERICK VAN PELT BRYAN, DISTRICT JUDGE:

Defendants Heng Roman (Heng) and Lee Koo (Koo) were tried before me without a jury on a two-count indictment charging them in count I with conspiracy to violate the narcotics laws, 21 U.S.C. §§ 846, 963, and in count II with possession of 2.5 kilograms of heroin, in the Southern District of New York on November 20, 1972, with intent to distribute, 21 U.S.C. §§ 812, 841(a)(1), 841(b)(1)(A). At the conclusion of the four-day trial, I found both defendants guilty on the conspiracy count (count I), and reserved decision on the substantive count (count II). I now find both defendants guilty of an attempt to commit the crime charged in the substantive count.

The facts relating to the substantive count are as follows: John T. Smith, the informer in this case, after several preliminary meetings with Heng, met with both defendants on November 7, 1972 at the Strand Hotel in Singapore. The ensuing discussion concerned the importation and sale of substantial amounts of narcotics in the United States. On November 12th or 13th, the defendants picked up Smith's suitcase at his hotel. The following evening they showed it to Smith at Heng's house. Smith saw that it contained white powder, which Heng said was 2.5 kilograms of heroin. Subsequent laboratory analysis confirmed that it was indeed heroin, over 96% pure.

The next day Heng drove Smith to the airport, with the suitcase in the trunk of the car, with the heroin in it. At the airport, Smith, without Heng's knowledge, gave the suitcase to an agent of the Bureau of Narcotics and Dangerous Drugs (BNDD). The heroin it contained, which is the subject of count II, was removed, and thereafter remained in the custody of law enforcement officers. Smith then flew to New York. Subsequently, the heroin was brought to New York by the BNDD and was produced at the trial.

After Smith arrived in New York City, he contacted BNDD agents here. On November 20, 1972, he picked up the suitcase, which by then contained only soap powder packaged as the heroin had been, at the BNDD office here and placed it in a locker in Pennsylvania Station. Later that evening, by prearrangement made with defendants in Singapore, Smith met them at the Hotel McAlpin in Manhattan and showed Heng the key to the locker.[1]

That evening, November 20th, and the following day, the 21st, the defendants

---

[1] The following day, Smith showed Heng the suitcase in the locker but did not open the suitcase.

offered to sell the 2.5 kilograms of heroin to agents of the BNDD who were posing as buyers. The agents sought to purchase simultaneously an additional 25 kilograms which Heng claimed to have under defendants' control on the West Coast. Heng insisted the initial transaction be limited to the 2.5 kilograms. When it became apparent that an impasse in the negotiations had developed, the agents arrested both defendants. * * * *

Although defendants are not guilty of possession with intent to distribute, as charged in count II, they are guilty of an attempt to commit that crime. 21 U.S.C. § 846.[3] I find them guilty of attempted possession with intent to distribute.

"Attempt", as used in § 846, is not defined. Indeed, there is no comprehensive statutory definition of attempt in federal law. It is not necessary here, however, to deal with the complex question of when conduct crosses the line between "mere preparation" and "attempt," only the latter being a crime. For here we have a situation where the defendants' actions would have constituted the completed crime if the surrounding circumstances were as they believed them to be.[5] Under such circumstances, their actions constitute an attempt. *People v. Siu*, 126 Cal.App. 2d 41 (1954) (defendant guilty of attempted possession of narcotics where he obtained possession of talcum believing it to be narcotics); *O'Sullivan v. Peters*, [1951] S.R. 54 (South Australia, 1951) (defendant who placed bet on horse which had previously been scratched held guilty of attempt of bet on horse race); *Regina v. Ring*, 17 Cox C.C. 491 (England, 1892) (reaching into empty pocket constitutes attempt to steal from pocket); *People v. Moran*, 123 N.Y. 254 (1890) (same); *People v. Fiegelman*, 33 Cal. App. 2d 100 (1939) (same); *United States v. Thomas*, 13 U.S.C.M.A. 278 (1962) (defendants who had nonconsensual sexual intercourse with a woman who was dead, although they believed her to be alive, held guilty of attempted rape); *State v.Damms*, 9 Wis. 2d 183 (1960) (defendant guilty of attempted murder where he pointed gun at another, believing it to be loaded when in fact it was not loaded, and pulled trigger). *Cf.* Model Penal Code § 5.01(1) (P.O.D. 1962) ("A person is guilty of an attempt to commit a crime if, acting with the kind of culpability otherwise required for commission of the crime, he [inter alia] purposefully engages in conduct which would constitute the crime if the attendant circumstances were as he believes them to be . . .").

The defendants contend that since it was impossible for them to possess the 2.5 kilograms of heroin, which at the time charged was in the hands of the BNDD, they cannot be found guilty of attempted possession. This argument does not help the defendants.[6]

"Legal impossibility" denotes conduct where the goal of the actor is not criminal, although he believes it to be. "Factual impossibility" denotes conduct

---

[3] Sec. 846. *Attempt and conspiracy*: Any person who attempts or conspires to commit any offense defined in this subchapter is punishable by imprisonment or fine or both which may not exceed the maximum punishment prescribed for the offense, the commission of which was the object of the attempt or conspiracy.

[5] There is no doubt here, and I so find, that the defendants had the requisite *mens rea*; that is, that their actions were knowing and intentional, and with the purpose of distributing the heroin.

[6] The defendants do not contend that the commission of the completed offense was also impossible because Smith was not really their ally. The result would be the same, however.

where the objective is proscribed by the criminal law, but a circumstance unknown to the actor prevents him from bringing it about. "Inherent impossibility" is where the means chosen are totally ineffective to bring about the desired result, e.g., voodoo. See LaFave & Scott, *supra*, at 445.

Defendants claim their defense is one of legal impossibility. Although the categorization of a case as involving one type of impossibility or another is often difficult, see, e.g., Hughes, *One Further Footnote on Attempting the Impossible*, 42 N.Y.U.L. Rev. 1005 (1967), the case at hand plainly involves factual not legal impossibility.

The commentators and the cases generally divide the impossibility defense into two categories: legal versus factual impossibility. See W. LaFave & A. Scott, *Handbook on Criminal Law* 438-45 (2d ed. 1972); G. Williams, *Criminal Law: The General Part* 633-37 (2d ed. 1961); J. Hall, *General Principles of Criminal Law* 586-99 (2d ed. 1960); *Ventimiglia v. United States*, 242 F. 2d 620, 625-626 (4th Cir. 1957); *United States v. Thomas*, 13 U.S.C.M.A. 278 (1962); *State v. Moretti*, 52 N.J. 182 (1968). Sometimes a third category, "inherent impossibility," is also referred to. See LaFave & Scott, supra, at 439, 445-46.

There are apparently no federal cases in point, but "All courts are in agreement that what is usually referred to as 'factual impossibility' is no defense to a charge of attempt." LaFave & Scott, *supra*, at 440. Moreover, in light of the absence of controlling contrary federal case law,[7] I hold that however this impossibility may be characterized, since the defendants' objective here was criminal, impossibility is no defense. This is in accord with the proposed revision of the federal criminal code (see *Study Draft of a New Federal Criminal Code* § 1001; accord, N.Y. Penal L. § 110.10 (McKinney 1967)), and with the Model Penal Code (see Tentative Draft No. 10, at 32-38 (1960); Wechsler, Jones & Korn, *The Treatment of Inchoate Crime in the Model Penal Code of the American Law Institute*; *Attempt, Solicitation, and Conspiracy*, 61 Colum. Rev. 571, 578-85 (1961)).

The defendants next contend that their conduct was not sufficiently proximate to the completed crime to constitute an attempt. They rely on the well-known dissenting opinion of Justice Holmes in *Hyde v. United States*, 225 U.S. 347, 387 (1921) and Judge Learned Hand's definition in *United States v. Coplon*, 185 F.2d 629, 633 (2d cir. 1950). However, where the conduct would constitute the completed crime if the circumstances were as the defendants believed them to be, the "dangerous proximity" test of Justice Holmes does not apply. See Model Penal Code § 5.01(1). Moreover, the defendants plainly went far beyond "mere preparation."

Accordingly, I find both defendants guilty on count II.

---

[7] In *Osborn v. United States*, 385 U.S. 323, 333 (1966) the Supreme Court indicated there might be some doubt about the "continuing validity" of the doctrine of impossibility in the law of criminal attempt.

NOTES FROM DAN:

(1) I am not sure I understand this distinction between "legal" and "factual" impossibility. Carefully read the language used by the court to explain this distinction. According to the court, was *Roman* a case of "legal" impossibility or "factual" impossibility?

(2) How does this distinction apply to our case?

UNITED STATES v. BERRIGAN
U.S. Court of Appeals, 3rd Circuit
482 F.2d 171 (1973)

ALDISERT, CIRCUIT JUDGE.

Father Philip Berrigan and Sister Elizabeth McAlister appeal from judgments of conviction on seven counts of violating 18 U.S.C. § 1791,[1] as augmented by 28 C.F.R. § 6.1,[2] for sending seven letters into and out of Lewisburg Federal Penitentiary "without the knowledge and consent of the warden." Counts IV-X.

Appellants were originally indicted, along with six others, for conspiracy to kidnap Presidential Advisor Henry Kissinger, to destroy the underground heating system in Washington, D.C., and to unlawfully interfere with the Selective Service System by engaging in "draft board raids" (Count I); for unlawfully sending through the mails a letter containing a threat to kidnap Mr. Kissinger (18 U.S.C § 876) (Counts II and III); and for smuggling or attempting to smuggle letters into and out of a federal prison without the knowledge and consent of the warden (Counts IV to X). The jury was unable to agree upon a verdict on Counts I, II and III. Appellants urge that we reverse the convictions on Counts IV to X, or, alternatively, grant a new trial. Appellants have advanced numerous contentions which we will consider seriatim.

* * * *

III.

Appellants' contentions that the judgments of conviction on Counts V through X must be reversed because the government failed to prove all elements of the crime presents a very serious and difficult question. In these counts they were charged

---

[1] 18 U.S.C. § 1791 provides:

Whoever, contrary to any rule or regulation promulgated by the Attorney General, introduces or attempts to introduce into or upon the grounds of any Federal penal or correctional institution or takes or attempts to take or send therefrom anything whatsoever, shall be imprisoned not more than ten years.

[2] 28 C.F.R. § 6.1 provides:

The introduction or attempt to introduce into or upon the grounds of any federal penal or correctional institution or the taking or attempt to take or send therefrom anything whatsoever without the knowledge and consent of the warden or superintendent of such federal penal or correctional institution is prohibited.

with and convicted of attempts to violate § 1791. Unlike the circumstances attending Father Berrigan's dispatch of the Count IV letter, which occurred prior to any knowledge on the part of the warden, it is undisputed that the prison officials had prior knowledge of letters embraced by these convictions.[17]

A.

We begin with the proposition that the Constitution requires proof beyond a reasonable doubt of all elements of an offense in order to sustain a conviction. *In re Winship*, 397 U.S. 358 (1970). One of the elements of a violation of § 1791 is the absence of "knowledge and consent of the warden or superintendent of (the) federal penal or correctional institution." 28 C.F.R. § 6.1. From this, the defense reasons that if the warden knows of the smuggling, the purpose of the law is satisfied and no crime can exist. The district court rejected this argument holding that

> such an interpretation of the statute is unjustified and inaccurate. The intent of the parties to bypass prison channels and smuggle the letters, combined with action toward that goal is sufficient to complete a punishable offense. The intent of the party committing the offense to deprive the warden of knowledge of such smuggling seems to this court to be the gravamen of the offense.

In support of its conclusion that intent to commit the offense plus some overt act constituted the crime, irrespective of legal impossibility to commit the crime, the district court relied on New York Penal Law, McKinney's Consolidated Laws c. 40, § 110.10; *United States v. Thomas*, 13 U.S.C.M.A. 278 (1962); Hall, *General Principles of Criminal Law*, 586 (2d Ed. 1960); Perkins, *Criminal Law*, 489 (1957); and the Model Penal Code, § 501.

The first difficulty we have in accepting this analysis is that it utilized criminal codes which contain provisions having no counterpart in existing federal criminal law. Federal criminal law is purely statutory; there is no federal common law of crimes. *Levy v. Parker, supra,* 478 F.2d at 796.

The Model Penal Code provides that a person is guilty of an attempt if acting with the kind of culpability otherwise required for commission of the crime he: (a) purposely engages in conduct which would constitute the crime if the attendant circumstances were as he believes them to be.

The proponents of the code report that "the purpose of paragraph 1(a) is to eliminate legal impossibility as a defense to an attempt charge."[18] Absent such

---

[17] On cross-examination, Robert L. Hendricks, Associate Warden of Lewisburg, was asked:

Q. Now, did you know that Douglas was carrying letters in and out while he was on study-release, in and out of the penitentiary -unauthorized letters?

A. After we intercepted the first letter, from that point on I knew that he was.

Hendricks reaffirmed this statement several times during his testimony, eventually admitting that after June 3, 1970, he knew Douglas was carrying letters in and out of the prison. All of the letters involved in Counts V to X were exchanged after June 3.

[18] Wechsler, Jones & Korn, *The Treatment of Inchoate Crimes In The Model Penal Code Of The*

statutory language, courts have held that a person accepting goods which he believed were stolen, but were not actually stolen goods, was not guilty of an attempt to receive stolen goods;[19] that an individual who offered a bribe to a person whom he believed to be a juror, but who was not a juror, could not be said to have attempted to bribe a juror;[20] and, that a hunter who shot a stuffed deer, believing it to be alive, had not attempted to kill a deer out of season.[21] Faced with these holdings, the Model Penal Code proponents suggested that courts were exonerating defendants in situations where attempt liability most certainly should be imposed." Hence, they felt necessity for the statute.

The National Commission on Reform of Criminal Laws, also recognizing this apparent void in the existing federal criminal code, has proposed a general attempt statute, applicable to every federal offense. Its proposal closely resembles that of the Model Penal Code: "Factual or legal impossibility of committing the crime is not a defense if the crime could have been committed had the attendant circumstances been as the actor believed them to be." Section 1001(1). Other measures presently before Congress contain similar provisions.[*]

Indeed, we are informed that elimination of impossibility as a defense to a charge of criminal attempt, as suggested by the Model Penal Code and the proposed federal legislation, is consistent with "the overwhelming modern view," and with criminal provisions in such diverse parts as Canada, India and New Zealand.[23]

Nevertheless, the brute fact remains that present federal criminal statutes do not contain this provision. And for this court to uphold these convictions in the absence of such statutory authority would be to impose criminal liability upon mere intent, where the will is to be taken for the deed, "or, as expressed in the Latin formula appearing in the Year Books, *Voluntas reputabitur pro facto.*"[24]

Professor Williams asserts that "it should need no demonstration that a person who commits or attempts to commit what is not a crime in law cannot be convicted of attempting to commit a crime, and it makes no difference that he thinks it is a crime."[25] Professor Hall[26] is equally insistent that to make such conduct a criminal

---

American Law Institute: Attempt, Solicitation, And Conspiracy, 61 Colum.L.Rev. 572, 578 (1961).

[19] See, e.g., *People v. Jaffe*, 185 N.Y. 497 (1906), where the court said that the following actions do not constitute attempts: voting with the belief that one is under the permissible age when in fact he is not under age; having sexual intercourse with a female with the belief that she is under the age of consent when in fact she is not under the age of consent. The holding of the *Jaffe* case was approved in *People v. Jelke*, 1 N.Y.2d 321 (1956), where the court likened the situation to "selling oil stock and being surprised to discover that oil was actually in the ground where the accused vendor had represented but not believed it to be."

[20] *State v. Taylor*, 345 Mo. 325 (1939); *State v. Porter*, 125 Mont. 503 (1952). Similarly, attempted bribery may not be based upon an offer of a bribe to an official who cannot render the requested service. *State v. Butler*, 178 Mo. 272 (1903).

[21] *State v. Guffey*, 262 S.W.2d 152 (Mo.Ct.App.1953).

[*] Ed. — None of these was enacted. So far, there is no federal general attempt statute.

[23] Wechsler, Jones & Korn, *supra* note 18, at 578-579.

[24] Sayre, *Criminal Attempts*, 41 Harv.L.Rev. 821 (1928).

[25] G. Williams, *Criminal Law, The General Part*, 633 (2d Ed. 1961).

[26] J. Hall, *General Principles of Criminal Law*, 586 (2d Ed. 1960).

attempt would violate the principle of legality.[27]

Moreover, whatever be the approach taken in those jurisdictions utilizing the common law of crimes, except as modified by statute, e.g., Pennsylvania, the interstices of federal criminal law cannot be filled by resort to common law precedents. It cannot be overemphasized that conduct intended to be prohibited by federal law must be explicitly prohibited by statutory authority.

B.

It becomes necessary, therefore, to turn to the rudiments of the law of attempt. "Some words of definition are necessary. For convenience of usage the following terms shall be used as indicated: *act* — the defendant's physical bodily movements; *circumstances or attendant circumstances* — the external, objective situation which the substantive law may require be present in addition to the defendant's act before he can be convicted of the substantive crime; *conduct* — the act combined with the circumstances regarded by the substantive law as relevant; *consequences or result* — an additional occurrence caused by the defendant's act."[28]

We reduce the law of attempt to these basic components because it is a subject that has long attracted the attention of the commentators and legal historians producing a wealth of legal literature. The problems have been called "much-mooted," "intricate and difficult," "one of the most interesting and difficult problems of the criminal law," reflecting "ambivalence as to how far the governing criteria should focus on the dangerousness of the actor's conduct," and exerting "a fascination for legal scholars far beyond their significance in terms of the number of litigated issues." [Citations]

Emanating from the many thoughtful observations and the multitude of case law are the following teachings. (1) We must not generalize in the law of attempt. (2) There is a basic distinction between early common law decisions and those beginning in the latter Eighteenth Century. (3) There is a distinction between the holdings in common law jurisdictions and those which have codified the law of attempt. (4) One of the most sophisticated areas of the troublesome law of attempt is that which must command our attention here — legal impossibility of criminal attempt.

Indeed, even a decision to analyze impossibility on the basis of what is generally described as the two categories of factual impossibility and legal impossibility

---

[27] We have recently emphasized as "the fundament of American law the principle 'that no person can be criminally punished except by judicial process and unless the acts for which he was punished were clearly forbidden. The codification of definite rules in the law of crimes is considered by many in Western democratic societies as a fundamental requirement of liberal democracy. They take their stand on the principle that no one shall be punished for anything that is not expressly forbidden by law. *Nullum crimen, nulla poena, sine lege*. They regard that principle as their great charter of liberty.' A. Denning, *Freedom Under Law* 41 (1949)." *Levy v. Parker, supra*, 478 F.2d at 791.

[28] Enker, *Impossibility In Criminal Attempts - Legality And The Legal Process*, 53 Minn.L.Rev. 665 (1969). For a similar analysis, see Sayre, supra note 24, at 838: "Every attempt involves three factors: (1) some act on the part of the defendant, (2) the particular consequence which the defendant intended or which formed the object of his act, and (3) the actual consequences which in fact ensued."

presents serious problems unless conceptual distinctions between the two labels are recognized and respected. Generally speaking factual impossibility is said to occur when extraneous circumstances unknown to the actor or beyond his control prevent consummation of the intended crime. The classic example is the man who puts his hand in the coat pocket of another with the intent to steal his wallet and finds the pocket empty. *Regina v. Collins*, 9 Cox Crim.Cas. 497 (1864). Generally, the cases which have imposed criminal liability for attempt where factual circumstances precluded commission of the intended crime have emphasized, as a primary requisite, proof of an intent to commit a specific crime.

Legal impossibility is said to occur where the intended acts, even if completed, would not amount to a crime. Thus, legal impossibility would apply to those circumstances where (1) the motive, desire and expectation is to perform an act in violation of the law; (2) there is intention to perform a physical act; (3) there is a performance of the intended physical act; and (4) the consequence resulting from the intended act does not amount to a crime.[35]

Were intent to break the law the sole criterion to be considered in determining criminal responsibility — and this was the approach utilized by the district court — we could sustain the conviction of appellants on Counts V to X. Clearly, it can be said that Father Berrigan intended to send letters to Sister McAlister, and vice versa. Normally, of course, the exchange of letters is not a federal offense. Where one of the senders is in prison, however, the sending may or may not be a criminal offense. If the letter is sent within normal channels with the consent and knowledge of the warden it is not a criminal offense. Therefore, an attempt to send a letter through normal channels cannot be considered an attempt to violate the law, because none of the intended consequences is in fact criminal. If the letter is sent without the knowledge and consent of the warden, it is a criminal offense and so is the attempt because both the intended consequence and the actual consequence are in fact criminal. Here, we are faced with a third situation where there is a motivation,

---

[35] Intent as used in this connection must be distinguished from motive, desire and expectation. If C by reason of his hatred of A plans to kill him, but mistaking B for A shoots B, his motive, desire and expectation are to kill A but his intent is to kill B. If a married man forcibly has intercourse with a woman whom he believes to be his wife's twin sister, but who in fact is his wife, he is not guilty of rape, because his intent was to have intercourse with the woman he attacked, who was in fact his wife. If A takes an umbrella which he believes to belong to B, but which in fact is his own, he does not have the intent to steal, his intent being to take the umbrella he grasps in his hand, which is his own umbrella. If a man, mistaking a dummy in female dress for a woman, tries to ravish it, he does not have the intent to commit rape since the ravishment of an inanimate object cannot be rape. If a man mistakes a stump for his enemy and shoots at it, notwithstanding his desire and expectation to shoot his enemy, his intent is to shoot the object aimed at, which is the stump.

Wharton puts the following case: "Lady Eldon, when traveling with her husband on the Continent, bought what she supposed to be a quantity of French lace, which she hid, concealing it from Lord Eldon in one of the pockets of the coach. The package was brought to light by a custom officer at Dover. The lace turned out to be an English manufactured article, of little value, and of course, not subject to duty. Lady Eldon had bought it at a price vastly above its value, believing it to be genuine." Wharton opined that Lady Eldon had the intent to smuggle this lace into England and was guilty of an attempt to smuggle. 1 *Wharton, Criminal Law*, 304 n. 9 (12th Ed. 1932). Professor Keedy suggests: "The fallacy of this argument is found in the fact that the particular lace which Lady Eldon intended to bring into England was not subject to duty and therefore, although there was the wish to smuggle, there was not the intent to do so." Keedy, *Criminal Attempts at Common Law*, 102 U. of Pa.L.Rev. 464 476-477 (1954).

desire and expectation of sending a letter without the knowledge and consent, and the intended act is performed, but unknown to the sender, the transmittal is accomplished with the knowledge and consent of the warden.

Applying the principles of the law of attempt to the instant case, the writing of the letters, and their copying and transmittal by the courier, Boyd Douglas, constituted the act. This much the government proved. What the government did not prove — and could not prove because it was a legal impossibility - was the "external, objective situation which the substantive law may require to be present," to-wit, absence of knowledge and consent of the warden. Thus, the government failed to prove the "*circumstances or attendant circumstances*" vital to the offense. Without such proof, the *consequence* or *result* did not constitute an offense that violated the federal statute.[36] The warden and the government were aware of the existence of the letters. The courier acted with the consent of the warden. Although there was no entrapment, *United States v. Russell*, 411 U.S. 423 (1973) the public authorities were privy to the Act which gave rise to these charges.

There are many supporters of the view that irrespective of the absence of a necessary element of the offense prohibited by statute — the "external, objective situation which the substantive law may require be present" — criminal responsibility should attach "if the attendant circumstances were as (the actor) believes them to be." The bills presently before the Congress contain such a provision. But the efforts of the distinguished scholars who drafted these proposals must be kept in perspective; they are recommending changes to fill an apparent void in existing law. They suggest a statutory change which would remove one of the elements of the offense which still must be proved under the present federal statutory law of crimes.

We are also aware that in those jurisdictions which permit the development of elements of the criminal law by the common law tradition of judicial decision, the courts have been willing to change the law through the centuries from an absolute defense of factual impossibility, to a jurisprudential environment which, though extremely complicated and confused, seems to be watering down, if not eliminating, the defense of factual impossibility. But as we have heretofore indicated, we will not fall into the trap of equating legal with factual impossibility in the law of criminal attempt.[39]

---

[36] When we analyze the *consequence* or *result* of the *act* and *conduct* in this case, we find no barefaced public injuries present, which by the Eighteenth Century weakened the original absolutism of this defense at common law. Emphasizing that the contents of the letters are not germane to this issue, we do not recognize any serious danger to the public welfare to have resulted from these acts.

[39] Indeed, though it is not before us, we do evidence some concern that the proposed changes in the federal criminal code seem to fashion a new crime where the critical element to be proved is *mens rea simpliciter*. We detect the total lack of objective guidelines in the presentation of such proof or a defense. While *mens rea* is certainly within one's control it is not subject to direct proof; it is proved by circumstantial evidence only. More important, it is not subject to direct refutation. It is the subject of inference and speculation. We perceive the danger of potential abuse where the circumstances admit to very little objective measurement. More important, we are unwilling as a court to legislate by judicial fiat a crime consistent only with thought processes, as this is reminiscent of the German law of the Nazi period "that anything is punishable if it is deserving of punishment according" to the fundamental conceptions of a penal law and sound popular feeling." H.L.A. Hart, Law, *Liberty and Morality*, 12 (1963).

In sum, we distinguish between the federal system, where criminal law is solely statutory, and jurisdictions patterned upon the common law. "It is commonplace that federal courts are courts of limited jurisdiction, and that there are no common law offenses against the United States. "The legislative authority of the Union must first make an act a crime, affix a punishment to it, and declare the Court that shall have jurisdiction of the offence." *United States v. Hudson*, 3 L.Ed. 259, 7 Cranch. 32, 34. "It is axiomatic that statutes creating and defining crimes cannot be extended by intendment, and that no act, however wrongful, can be punished under such a statute unless clearly within its terms." *Todd v. United States*, 158 U.S. 278, 282.

We distinguish between the defense of factual impossibility, which is not involved here, *United States v. Osborn*, 385 U.S. 323 (1966), and legal impossibility, which is. Even were we to concede that factual impossibility of success may not prevent an attempt, there can be no crime of attempt where there is a legal impossibility to commit a crime. Simply stated, attempting to do that which is not a crime is not attempting to commit a crime. Congress has not yet enacted a law that provides that intent plus act plus conduct constitutes the offense of attempt irrespective of legal impossibility. Until such time as such legislative changes in the law take place, this court will not fashion a new non-statutory law of criminal attempt.

Accordingly, the convictions on Counts V-X may not stand.

* * * *

The judgment of conviction of Philip Berrigan on Count IV will be affirmed. The judgments of convictions of Philip Berrigan and Elizabeth McAlister on Counts V through X will be reversed.

NOTES FROM DAN:

(1) I am having some trouble reconciling this decision with *Roman*. Roman mistakenly believed that an element of a substantive crime was present (i.e., that he possessed heroin), and Berrigan mistakenly believed that an element of a substantive crime was present (i.e., that he was smuggling in the letters without the warden's knowledge). Yet Roman was convicted and Berrigan got off. Can you explain the distinction?

(2) What *purpose* of the law of attempt is served by letting Berrigan off here? Didn't his conduct show that he is the kind of guy who will send letters into a prison without the warden's consent, when he gets the chance?

(3) The court says that punishing Berrigan for attempt here would be punishing him for his thoughts, like the Nazis did to people. Sounds pretty scary. If Berrigan can succeed with this argument, can the defendant in *our* case also succeed?

(4) In *U.S. v. Duran*, 884 F.Supp. 577 (D.C.D.C. 1995), Duran was charged with attempted assassination of the President. Duran fired several shots at a White House visitor who resembled President Bill Clinton, believing the visitor to be the President. Duran argued that it was "legally impossible" to assassinate the President by shooting at a person who was *not* the President. The court disagreed:

Aside from the Third Circuit in *Berrigan*, every Circuit that has considered the defense of impossibility has rejected it — a fact of critical importance which defense counsel conveniently ignored in representing that "it is without question that 'a person who commits or attempts to commit what is not a crime in law cannot be convicted of attempting to commit a crime."' * * * * The Court flatly rejects the *Berrigan* approach urged by the Defendant. * * * * Rather, the Court finds that the better approach is that espoused by the majority of the Circuits that have addressed the impossibility defense, to wit, that a defendant may be convicted of attempt where his objective conduct, taken as a whole, corroborates the requisite criminal intent. In essence, this view mirrors the dual elements of the crime of attempt: that the defendant had the specific intent to commit the substantive crime and that he took a substantial step towards commission of that crime.

See also *U.S. v. Gregory*, 315 F.3d 637 (6th Cir. 2003).

In *U.S. v. Farner*, 251 F.3d. 510 (5th Cir. 2001), Farner was convicted of attempting to induce a minor to have sex. Farner had exchanged e-mails with "Cindy", whom he believed to be a 14-year old girl. "Cindy was, in fact, an adult Federal Bureau of Investigation agent named Kathy Crawford, participating in an undercover sting operation." Farner claimed legal impossibility, while the government contended that only factual impossibility was involved. The appellate court affirmed the conviction:

The illusory distinction between the two defenses is evident in the instant case. Thus, Farner says this is a case of legal impossibility because Kathy Crawford was an adult, and the statute does not address attempted sexual activity between adults. On the other hand, the district court viewed the impossibility as factual, because the defendant unquestionably intended to engage in the conduct proscribed by law but failed only because of circumstances unknown to him. We think the latter view is correct.

In any event, this circuit has properly eschewed the semantical thicket of the impossibility defense in criminal attempt cases and has instead required proof of two elements: first, that the defendant acted with the kind of culpability otherwise required for the commission of the underlying substantive offense, and, second, that the defendant had engaged in conduct which constitutes a substantial step toward commission of the crime. The substantial step must be conduct which strongly corroborates the firmness of defendant's criminal attempt. The Model Penal Code endorses this approach. *See* Model Penal Code § 5.01 (1985). In this case, the district court correctly concluded from the stipulated evidence, beyond a reasonable doubt, that Farner intended to engage in sexual acts with a 14-year-old girl and that he took substantial steps toward committing the crime.

Compare *Wilson v. State*, 85 Miss. 687, 38 So. 46 (1905), Wilson received a check for $2.50. The words "two and 50/100 dollars" were written in the body of the check, and the numbers "$2 50/100" were written in the upper right-hand corner of the check. Wilson added a number "1" before the *numbers* — making it "$12 50/100" —

but he did not alter or add to the *words* on the check. His conviction for *attempted forgery* was reversed:

> This was not forgery, because it was an immaterial part of the paper, and because it could not possibly have injured anybody. In order to constitute the crime, there must not only be the intent to commit it, but also an act of alteration done to a material part, so that injury might result.

> An instrument void on its face is not the subject of forgery, and in order to be so subject, it must have been capable of working injury if it had been genuine, and the marginal numbers and figures are not part of the instrument, and their alteration is not forgery.

> This being true, can the conviction of an attempt to commit forgery be sustained in the case before us? We think not. No purpose appears to change anything on the paper except the figures in the margin, and this could not have done any hurt. Our statute confines the crime of forgery to instances where "any person may be affected, bound, or in any way injured in his person or property." This is not such a case, and section 974 forbids convicting of an attempt "when it shall appear that the crime intended or the offense attempted was perpetrated." In this record the innocuous prefix of the figure "1" on the margin was fully accomplished, and no other effort appears, and, if genuine, could have done no harm; and so the appellant is guiltless, in law, of the crime of which he was convicted.

Can *Wilson* be reconciled with *Duran*? (Did Wilson have the "specific intent" to commit "forgery" — as that crime is defined by Mississippi?)

(5) Consider how impossibility relates to the law of *mistake* — which you studied in Chapter 1.

Example #1: Dan takes Vic's hat, which Dan mistakenly believes is Dan's. Dan is not guilty of larceny — he made a "mistake of fact" which negates the requisite intent to steal. If, however, Dan knew the hat was Vic's but mistakenly believed that the law did not punish stealing, he *is* guilty — he made a "mistake of law" which negates *no* element of the crime of larceny.

Example #2: Dan takes a hat which is Dan's but which he mistakenly believes is Vic's. Should he be guilty of *attempted* larceny? In Example #1, Dan's "mistake of fact" was relevant to *negate* the *mens rea* needed for the crime. In Example #2, should his "mistake of fact" likewise be relevant to *create* the *mens rea* needed for the crime?

Suppose, instead, Dan knows the hat is his, but mistakenly believes that taking your own hat is a crime. Should we find that he is *not* guilty of attempted larceny because he made a "mistake of law"? We ignored Dan's mistake of law in Example #1, so shouldn't we also do so here?

When analyzing attempt issues, does it make more sense to use the law of *mistake* than to speak of "factual impossibility" and "legal impossibility"?

Should we use the law of mistake this way? Will it further or hinder the *purposes* that underlay the law of attempt?

(6) To be convicted of attempt, defendant must have had the "specific intent to commit the substantive crime." What does this mean, and how is it proved? In *Smallwood v. State*, 343 Md. 97, 680 A.2d 512 (1996), Smallwood had been informed that he was infected with the HIV virus, and was advised not to have sex with anyone unless he wore a condom. He and an accomplice approached a woman exiting her car, then ordered her at gunpoint to drive to an automated teller machine and withdraw $300, which she did. Smallwood then raped her, without using a condom. The woman survived. Smallwood was convicted of robbery, rape, and attempted murder. He appealed the attempted murder conviction, claiming that there was insufficient evidence that he specifically intended to kill the woman. The intermediate appellate court rejected this argument, because "It is a reasonable inference that one intends the natural and probable consequence of his act." But Maryland's highest court reversed the attempted murder conviction:

> HIV is a retrovirus that attacks the human immune system, weakening it, and ultimately destroying the body's capacity to ward off disease. The virus may reside latently in the body for periods as long as ten years or more, during which time the infected person will manifest no symptoms of illness and function normally. HIV typically spreads via genital fluids or blood transmitted from one person to another through sexual contact, the sharing of needles in intravenous drug use, blood transfusions, infiltration into wounds, or from mother to child during pregnancy or birth. AIDS, in turn, is the condition that eventually results from an immune system gravely impaired by HIV. Medical studies have indicated that most people who carry the virus will progress to AIDS. AIDS patients by definition are profoundly immunocompromised; that is, they are prone to any number of diseases and opportunistic infections that a person with a healthy immune system might otherwise resist. AIDS is thus the acute clinical phase of immune dysfunction. AIDS is invariably fatal. In this case, we must determine what legal inferences may be drawn when an individual infected with the HIV virus knowingly exposes another to the risk of HIV-infection, and the resulting risk of death by AIDS. * * * *

> The required intent in the crimes of assault with intent to murder and attempted murder is the specific intent to murder, i.e., the specific intent to kill under circumstances that would not legally justify or excuse the killing or mitigate it to manslaughter. * * * *

> An intent to kill may be proved by circumstantial evidence. Since intent is subjective and, without the cooperation of the accused, cannot be directly and objectively proven, its presence must be shown by established facts which permit a proper inference of its existence. Therefore, the trier of fact may infer the existence of the required intent from surrounding circumstances such as "the accused's acts, conduct and words. Under the proper circumstances, an intent to kill may be inferred from the use of a deadly weapon directed at a vital part of the human body.

> In *State v. Raines*, 326 Md. 582, 591 (1992), we upheld the use of such an inference. Raines and a friend were traveling on a highway when the defendant fired a pistol into the driver's side window of a tractor trailer in

an adjacent lane. The shot killed the driver of the tractor trailer, and Raines was convicted of first degree murder. The evidence in the case showed that Raines shot at the driver's window of the truck, knowing that the truck driver was immediately behind the window. We concluded that "Raines's actions in directing the gun at the window, and therefore at the driver's head on the other side of the window, permitted an inference that Raines shot the gun with the intent to kill."

The State argues that our analysis in *Raines* rested upon two elements: (1) Raines knew that his weapon was deadly, and (2) Raines knew that he was firing it at someone's head. The State argues that Smallwood similarly knew that HIV infection ultimately leads to death, and that he knew that he would be exposing his victims to the risk of HIV transmission by engaging in unprotected sex with them. Therefore, the State argues, a permissible inference can be drawn that Smallwood intended to kill each of his three victims. The State's analysis, however, ignores several factors.

First, we must consider the magnitude of the risk to which the victim is knowingly exposed. The inference drawn in *Raines* rests upon the rule that "it is permissible to infer that one intends the natural and probable consequences of his act." Before an intent to kill may be inferred based solely upon the defendant's exposure of a victim to a risk of death, it must be shown that the victim's death would have been a natural and probable result of the defendant's conduct. It is for this reason that a trier of fact may infer that a defendant possessed an intent to kill when firing a deadly weapon at a vital part of the human body. When a deadly weapon has been fired at a vital part of a victim's body, the risk of killing the victim is so high that it becomes reasonable to assume that the defendant intended the victim to die as a natural and probable consequence of the defendant's actions.

Death by AIDS is clearly one natural possible consequence of exposing someone to a risk of HIV infection, even on a single occasion. It is less clear that death by AIDS from that single exposure is a sufficiently probable result to provide the sole support for an inference that the person causing the exposure intended to kill the person who was exposed. While the risk to which Smallwood exposed his victims when he forced them to engage in unprotected sexual activity must not be minimized, the State has presented no evidence from which it can reasonably be concluded that death by AIDS is a probable result of Smallwood's actions to the same extent that death is the probable result of firing a deadly weapon at a vital part of someone's body. Without such evidence, it cannot fairly be concluded that death by AIDS was sufficiently probable to support an inference that Smallwood intended to kill his victims in the absence of other evidence indicative of an intent to kill.

In this case, we find no additional evidence from which to infer an intent to kill. Smallwood's actions are wholly explained by an intent to commit rape and armed robbery, the crimes for which he has already pled guilty. For this reason, his actions fail to provide evidence that he also had an intent to kill. As one commentator noted, in discussing a criminal case involving similar circumstances, "because virus transmission occurs simultaneously with the act of rape, that act alone would not provide evidence of intent to transmit the virus. Some additional evidence, such as an explicit statement, would be necessary to demonstrate the actor's specific intent." Note, *Criminal Liability for Transmission of AIDS: Some Evidentiary Problems*, 10 Crim. Just. J. 69, 78 (1994). Smallwood's knowledge of his HIV-infected status provides the only evidence in this case supporting a conclusion that he intended anything beyond the rapes and robberies for which he has been convicted.

The cases cited by the State demonstrate the sort of additional evidence needed to support an inference that Smallwood intended to kill his victims. The defendants in these cases have either made explicit statements demonstrating an intent to infect their victims or have taken specific actions demonstrating such an intent and tending to exclude other possible intents. In *State v. Hinkhouse*, 139 Or.App. 446, 912 P.2d 921 (1996), for example, the defendant engaged in unprotected sex with a number of women while knowing that he was HIV positive. The defendant had also actively concealed his HIV-positive status from these women, had lied to several of them by stating that he was not HIV-positive, and had refused the women's requests that he wear condoms. There was also evidence that he had told at least one of his sexual partners that "if he were HIV-positive, he would spread the virus to other people." The Oregon Court of Appeals found this evidence to be sufficient to demonstrate an intent to kill, and upheld the defendant's convictions for attempted murder.

In *State v. Caine*, 652 So.2d 611 (La.App.), a conviction for attempted second degree murder was upheld where the defendant had jabbed a used syringe into a victim's arm while shouting "I'll give you AIDS." The defendant in *Weeks v. State*, 834 S.W.2d 559 (Tex.App.1992), made similar statements, and was convicted of attempted murder after he spat on a prison guard. In that case, the defendant knew that he was HIV-positive, and the appellate court found that "the record reflects that Weeks thought he could kill the guard by spitting his HIV-infected saliva at him." There was also evidence that at the time of the spitting incident, Weeks had stated that he was "going to take someone with him when he went,' that he was 'medical now,' and that he was 'HIV-4.'" * * * *

In contrast with these cases, the State in this case would allow the trier of fact to infer an intent to kill based solely upon the fact that Smallwood exposed his victims to the risk that they might contract HIV. Without evidence showing that such a result is sufficiently probable to support this inference, we conclude that Smallwood's conviction for attempted murder must be reversed.

Questions: If the victim had died of AIDS, would Smallwood be guilty of murder? If so, why not convict him of *attempted* murder if she does *not* die? Isn't he *just as dangerous* as someone who intended to kill?

(7) Is there such a crime as "attempted voluntary manslaughter"? Yes, held the court in *Dandova v. State*, 72 P.3d 325 (Alaska App. 2003):

> The rationale of allowing a heat of passion defense is that a person who commits murder in response to serious provocation is less blameworthy, and assumedly less of a danger to society, than a typical murderer. This same rationale applies equally to a person who attempts (but fails) to kill in response to serious provocation.

> Moreover, if the heat of passion defense did not apply to defendants charged with attempted murder, this would create severe and illogical disparities in sentencing. A defendant who, acting in the heat of passion, intentionally killed another person would face conviction for manslaughter and a sentence of up to 20 years' imprisonment. But a similarly situated defendant, likewise acting in the heat of passion, who *tried* to kill another person but failed would face conviction for attempted murder and a sentence of up to 99 years' imprisonment. It is inconceivable that, between these two defendants, the legislature intended to impose a five-fold penalty on the unsuccessful assailant.

(8) Suppose the defendant robs a store and, during his getaway, runs into a bystander, who is seriously injured. May the defendant be convicted of "attempted felony murder," or is such a crime logically impossible? In *Amlotte v. State*, 456 So.2d 448 (1984), the Florida Supreme Court held that such a crime was indeed possible:

> We find that whenever an individual perpetrates or attempts to perpetrate an enumerated felony, and during the commission of the felony the individual commits, aids, or abets a specific overt act which could, but does not, cause the death of another, that individual will have committed the crime of attempted felony murder. Because the attempt occurs during the commission of a felony, the law, as under the felony murder doctrine, presumes the existence of the specific intent required to prove attempt.

JUSTICE OVERTON dissented:

> The majority opinion has made it impossible to distinguish those crimes for which there can be an attempt from those crimes for which there cannot be an attempt. A conviction for the offense of attempt has always required proof of the intent to commit the underlying crime. By recognizing the crime of attempt with regard to felony murder, a crime in which the intent to kill is presumed, the Court has created a crime which necessitates the finding of an intent to commit a crime which requires no proof of intent. This holding creates a crime requiring one to intend to do an unintended act, which is a logical absurdity and certainly an inadequate conceptual basis for something that needs to be as clear and understandable as do the elements of a felony crime.

> In my view, the crime of felony murder is based upon a legal fiction which implies malice aforethought from the actor's intent to commit the underlying felony. Thus, whenever a person is killed during the commission of a felony, the felon is said to have had the intent to bring about the death even

if the killing was unintended. This doctrine has been extended to impute intent for deaths caused by the acts of co-felons during the perpetration of certain felonies. Further extension of the felony murder doctrine so as to make intent irrelevant for purposes of the attempt crime is illogical and without basis in law.

In *State v. Gray*, 654 So.2d 552 (1995), the Florida Supreme Court adopted Justice Overton's position and overruled *Amlotto*: "The legal fictions required to support the intent for felony murder are simply too great" to support the crime of "attempted felony murder." See also *State v. Lea*, 485 S.E.2d 874 (N.C. 1997).

UNITED STATES v. MANDUJANO
U.S. Court of Appeals, Fifth Circuit
499 F.2d 370 (1974), cert. denied, 419 U.S. 1114 (1975).

RIVES, CIRCUIT JUDGE:

Mandujano appeals from the judgment of conviction and fifteen-year sentence imposed by the district court, based upon the jury's verdict finding him guilty of attempted distribution of heroin in violation of 21 U.S.C. § 846. We affirm.

I.

The government's case rested almost entirely upon the testimony of Alfonso H. Cavalier, Jr., a San Antonio police officer assigned to the Office of Drug Abuse Law Enforcement. Agent Cavalier testified that, at the time the case arose, he was working in an undercover capacity and represented himself as a narcotics trafficker. At about 1:30 P.M. on the afternoon of March 29, 1973, pursuant to information Cavalier had received, he and a government informer went to the Tally-Ho Lounge, a bar located on Guadalupe Street in San Antonio. Once inside the bar, the informant introduced Cavalier to Roy Mandujano.

After some general conversation, Mandujano asked the informant if he was looking for "stuff." Cavalier said, "Yes." Mandujano then questioned Cavalier about his involvement in narcotics. Cavalier answered Mandujano's questions, and told Mandujano he was looking for an ounce sample of heroin to determine the quality of the material. Mandujano replied that he had good brown Mexican heroin for $650 an ounce, but that if Cavalier wanted any of it he would have to wait until later in the afternoon when the regular man made his deliveries. Cavalier said that he was from out of town and did not want to wait that long. Mandujano offered to locate another source, and made four telephone calls in an apparent effort to do so. The phone calls appeared to be unsuccessful, for Mandujano told Cavalier he wasn't having any luck contacting anybody. Cavalier stated that he could not wait any longer.

Then Mandujano said he had a good contact, a man who kept narcotics around his home, but that if he went to see this man, he would need the money "out front." To reassure Cavalier that he would not simply abscond with the money, Mandujano stated, "You are in my place of business. My wife is here. You can sit with my wife.

I am not going to jeopardize her or my business for $650." Cavalier counted out $650.00 to Mandujano, and Mandujano left the premises of the Tally-Ho Lounge at about 3:30 P.M.

About an hour later, he returned and explained that he had been unable to locate his contact. He gave back the $650 and told Cavalier he could still wait until the regular man came around. Cavalier left, but arranged to call back at 6:00 P.M. When Cavalier called at 6:00 and again at 6:30, he was told that Mandujano was not available. Cavalier testified that he did not later attempt to contact Mandujano, because, "Based on the information that I had received, it would be unsafe for either my informant or myself to return to this area."

* * * *

II.

Section 846 of Title 21, entitled "Attempt and conspiracy," provides that,

> Any person who attempts or conspires to commit any offense defined in this subchapter is punishable by imprisonment or fine or both which may not exceed the maximum punishment prescribed for the offense, the commission of which was the object of the attempt or conspiracy.

The theory of the government in this case is straightforward: Mandujano's acts constituted an attempt to distribute heroin; actual distribution of heroin would violate § 841(a)(1) of Title 21;[2] therefore, Mandujano's attempt to distribute heroin comes within the terms of § 846 as an attempt to commit an offense defined in the subchapter.

Mandujano urges that his conduct as described by agent Cavalier did not rise to the level of an attempt to distribute heroin under § 846. He claims that at most he was attempting to acquire a controlled substance, not to distribute it; that it is impossible for a person to attempt to distribute heroin which he does not possess or control;[3] that his acts were only preparation, as distinguished from an attempt; and that the evidence was insufficient to support the jury's verdict.

Apparently there is no legislative history indicating exactly what Congress meant when it used the word "attempt" in § 846. There are two reported federal cases which discuss the question of what constitutes an attempt under this section. In *United States v. Noreikis* (7 Cir. 1973) 481 F.2d 1177, where the defendants possessed the various chemicals necessary to synthesize Dimethyltryptamine (DMT), a controlled substance, the court held that the preparations had progressed to the level of an attempt to manufacture a controlled substance. In its discussion, the court commented that,

---

[2] "(a) Except as authorized by this subchapter, it shall be unlawful for any person knowingly or intentionally — (1) to manufacture, distribute, or dispense, or possess with intent to manufacture, distribute, or dispense, a controlled substance."

[3] In opening argument, the United States Attorney stated: "There is a stipulation that has been entered into by the Government stating categorically that no heroin exchanged hands in this case."

While it seems to be well settled that mere preparation is not sufficient to constitute an attempt to commit a crime, 22 C.J.S. *Criminal Law* 75(2)b,, it seems equally clear that the semantical distinction between preparation and attempt is one incapable of being formulated in a hard and fast rule. The procuring of the instrument of the crime might be preparation in one factual situation and not in another. The matter is sometimes equated with the commission of an overt act, the "doing something directly moving toward, and bringing him nearer, the crime he intends to commit." 22 C.J.S., supra at 231. [481 F.2d at 1181.]

In *United States v. Roman* (S.D.N.Y.1973) 356 F.Supp. 434, where the defendants' actions would have constituted possession of heroin with intent to distribute in violation of § 841 if federal agents had not substituted soap powder for the heroin involved in the case, the court held that the defendants' acts were an attempt to possess with intent to distribute. The district court in its opinion acknowledged that:

> "Attempt," as used in § 846, is not defined. Indeed, there is no comprehensive statutory definition of attempt in federal law.

The court concluded, however, that it was not necessary in the circumstances of the case to deal with the "complex question of when conduct crosses the line between mere preparation and attempt." 356 F.Supp. at 437.

The courts in many jurisdictions have tried to elaborate on the distinction between mere preparation and attempt. See the Comment at 39-48 of Tent. Draft No. 10, (1960) of the Model Penal Code.[5] In cases involving statutes other than § 846, the federal courts have confronted this issue on a number of occasions.

* * * *

Gregg v. United States (8 Cir. 1940) 113 F.2d 687, involved in part a conviction for an attempt to import intoxicating liquor into Kansas. The court in this case acknowledges with apparent approval the definition of attempt urged by appellant Gregg:

> He calls attention to the fact that an attempt is an endeavor to do an act carried beyond mere preparation, but falling short of execution, and that it must be a step in the direct movement towards the commission of the crime

---

[5] This comment to the Model Penal Code catalogues a number of formulations which have been adopted or suggested, including the following: (a) The physical proximity doctrine — the overt act required for an attempt must be proximate to the completed crime, or directly tending toward the completion of the crime, or must amount to the commencement of the consummation. (b) The dangerous proximity doctrine — a test given impetus by Mr. Justice Holmes whereby the greater the gravity and probability of the offense, and the nearer the act to the crime, the stronger is the case for calling the act an attempt. (c) The indispensable element test — a variation of the proximity tests which emphasizes any indispensable aspect of the criminal endeavor over which the actor has not yet acquired control. (d) The probable desistance test — the conduct constitutes an attempt if, in the ordinary and natural course of events, without interruption from an outside source, it will result in the crime intended.

(e) The abnormal step approach — an attempt is a step toward crime which goes beyond the point where the normal citizen would think better of his conduct and desist. (f) The *res ipsa loquitur* or unequivocality test — an attempt is committed when the actor's conduct manifests an intent to commit a crime.

after preparations have been made. The act must "carry the project forward within dangerous proximity to the criminal end to be attained." Cardozo, J., in *People v. Werblow*, 241 N.Y. 55.

The court held, however, that Gregg's conduct went beyond "mere preparation":

The transportation of goods into a state is essentially a continuing act not confined in its scope to the single instant of passage across a territorial boundary. In our view the appellant advanced beyond the stage of mere preparation when he loaded the liquor into his car and began his journey toward Kansas. From that moment he was engaged in an attempt to transport liquor into Kansas within the clear intent of the statute. [113 F.2d at 691]

In *United States v. Coplon* (2 Cir. 1950) 185 F.2d 629, where the defendant was arrested before passing to a citizen of a foreign nation classified government documents contained in defendant's purse, Judge Learned Hand surveyed the law and addressed the issue of what would constitute an attempt:

Because the arrest in this way interrupted the consummation of the crime one point upon the appeal is that her conduct still remained in the zone of "preparation," and that the evidence did not prove an "attempt. This argument it will be most convenient to answer at the outset. A neat doctrine by which to test when a person, intending to commit a crime which he fails to carry out, has "attempted" to commit it, would be that he has done all that it is within his power to do, but has been prevented by intervention from outside; in short, that he has passed beyond any *locus poenitentiae*. Apparently that was the original notion, and may still be law in England; but it is certainly not now generally the law in the United States, for there are many decisions which hold that the accused has passed beyond "preparation," although he has been interrupted before he has taken the last of his intended steps. The decisions are too numerous to cite, and would not help much anyway, for there is, and obviously can be, no definite line; but Judge Cullen's discussion in *People v. Sullivan*, 173 N.Y. 122, and Mr. Justice Holmes' in two Massachusetts decisions (*Commonwealth v. Kennedy*, 170 Mass. 18; *Commonwealth v. Peaslee*, 177 Mass. 267) are particularly enlightening. In the second of the Massachusetts opinions, Holmes, J., said: "Preparation is not an attempt. But some preparations may amount to an attempt. It is a question of degree. If the preparation comes very near to the accomplishment of the act, the intent to complete it renders the crime so probable that the act will be a misdemeanor, although there is still a *locus poenitentiae*, the need of a further exertion of the will to complete the crime." * * * * [185 F.2d at 632, 633]

In *Mims v. United States* (5 Cir. 1967) 375 F.2d 135, 148, we noted that, "Much ink has been spilt in an attempt to arrive at a satisfactory standard for telling where preparations ends and attempt begins," and that the question had not been decided by this Court. The Court in *Mims* did note that the following test from *People v. Buffum*, 40 Cal.2d 709 has been "frequently approved": "Preparation alone is not enough, there must be some appreciable fragment of the crime committed, it must be in such progress that it will be consummated unless interrupted by circumstances independent of the will of the attempter, and the act must not be equivocal in nature."

Although the foregoing cases give somewhat varying verbal formulations, careful examination reveals fundamental agreement about what conduct will constitute a criminal attempt. First, the defendant must have been acting with the kind of culpability otherwise required for the commission of the crime which he is charged with attempting.

Second, the defendant must have engaged in conduct which constitutes a substantial step toward commission of the crime. A substantial step must be conduct strongly corroborative of the firmness of the defendant's criminal intent.

The use of the word "conduct" indicates that omission or possession, as well as positive acts, may in certain cases provide a basis for liability. * * * *

The requirement that the conduct be strongly corroborative of the firmness of the defendant's criminal intent also relates to the requirement that the conduct be more than "mere preparation. . . ."[6]

III.

The district court charged the jury in relevant part as follows:

> Now, the essential elements required in order to prove or to establish the offense charged in the indictment, which is, again, that the defendant knowingly and intentionally attempted to distribute a controlled substance, must first be a specific intent to commit the crime, and next that the accused wilfully made the attempt, and that a direct but ineffectual overt act was done toward its commission, and that such overt act was knowingly and intentionally done in furtherance of the attempt. In determining whether or not such an act was done, it is necessary to distinguish between mere preparation on the one hand and the actual commencement of the doing of the criminal deed on the other. Mere preparation, which may consist of planning the offense or of devising, obtaining or arranging a means for its commission, is not sufficient to constitute an attempt, but the acts of a person who intends to commit a crime will constitute an attempt

---

[6] Our definition is generally consistent with and our language is in fact close to the definitions proposed by the National Commission on Reform of Federal Criminal Laws and the American Law Institute's Model Penal Code. Section 1001 of the proposed federal criminal code provides as follows:

> (1) Offense. A person is guilty of criminal attempt if, acting with the kind been committed had the attendant circumstances of a crime, he intentionally engages in conduct which, in fact, constitutes a substantial step toward commission of the crime. A substantial step is any conduct which is strongly corroborative of the firmness of the actor's intent to complete the commission of the crime. Factual or legal impossibility of committing the crime is not a defense if the crime could have been committed had the attendant circumstances been as the actor believed them to be. * * * *

Proposed § 1001 is generally consistent with, and probably taken in part from, § 5.01 of the Model Penal Code (Proposed Official Draft 1962). Also, see the recently adopted tests for attempt in the following states, among others: Colorado - § 40-2-101, Colorado Crim.Code; Georgia - § 26-1001, Tit. 26; Hawaii - Tit. 37, Hawaii Rev.Stat.; Illinois - Art. 8-4, Ill.Crim.Code; Kansas - § 21-3301, ch. 180; Kentucky - § 50, Ky. Penal Code; Oregon - § 54, Ore.Crim.Code of 1971.

where they, themselves, clearly indicate a certain unambiguous intent to wilfully commit that specific crime and in themselves are an immediate step in the present execution of the criminal design, the progress of which would be completed unless interrupted by some circumstances not intended in the original design.

These instructions, to which the defendant did not object, are compatible with our view of what constitutes an attempt under § 846.

After the jury brought in a verdict of guilty, the trial court propounded a series of four questions to the jury:

(1) Do you find beyond a reasonable doubt that on the 29th day of March, 1973, Roy Mandujano, the defendant herein, knowingly, wilfully and intentionally placed several telephone calls in order to obtain a source of heroin in accordance with his negotiations with Officer Cavalier which were to result in the distribution of approximately one ounce of heroin from the defendant Roy Mandujano to Officer Cavalier?'

(2) Do you find beyond a reasonable doubt that the telephone calls inquired about in question no. (1) constituted overt acs in furtherance of the offense alleged in the indictment?

(3) Do you find beyond a reasonable doubt that on the 29th day of March, 1973, Roy Mandujano, the defendant herein, knowingly, wilfully and intentionally requested and received prior payment in the amount of $650 for approximately one ounce of heroin that was to be distributed by the defendant Roy Mandujano to Officer Cavalier?

(4) Do you find beyond a reasonable doubt that the request and receipt of a prior payment inquired about in question #3 constituted an overt act in furtherance of the offense alleged in the indictment?

Neither the government nor the defendant objected to this novel procedure. After deliberating, the jury answered "No" to question #1 and "Yes" to questions #3 and #4. The jury's answers indicate that its thinking was consistent with the charge of the trial court.

The evidence was sufficient to support a verdict of guilty under § 846. Agent Cavalier testified that at Mandujano's request, he gave him $650 for one ounce of heroin, which Mandujano said he could get from a "good contact." From this, plus Mandujano's comments and conduct before and after the transfer of the $650, as described in Part I of this opinion, the jury could have found that Mandujano was acting knowingly and intentionally and that he engaged in conduct — the request for and the receipt of the $650 — which in fact constituted a substantial step toward distribution of heroin. From interrogatory (4), it is clear that the jury considered Mandujano's request and receipt of the prior payment a substantial step toward the commission of the offense. Certainly, in the circumstances of this case, the jury could have found the transfer of money strongly corroborative of the firmness of Mandujano's intent to complete the crime. Of course, proof that Mandujano's "good contact" actually existed, and had heroin for sale, would have further strengthened the government's case; however, such proof was not essential.

* * * *

For the reasons stated in this opinion, the judgment is affirmed.

NOTES FROM DAN:

(1) According to the court, what exactly is the test for when the defendant's acts move beyond "mere preparation" and become an "attempt?"

(2) What is the purpose of the test? In other words, if the defendant plans to commit a crime, why *shouldn't* we consider his "mere preparation" an attempt?

(3) How does the court's test apply to our case?

(4) The court said that "A substantial step must be conduct strongly corroborative of the firmness of the defendant's criminal intent." What does this mean? In *U.S. v. Bilderbeck*, 163 F.3d 971 (6th Cir. 1999), the court stated:

> A defendant may be found to have taken a "substantial step" for the purpose of an attempt conviction though he or she has failed to gain possession of drugs or "sham" drugs. Because of the problems of proving intent in attempt cases and the danger of convicting for mere thoughts, desires, or motives, we require that the substantial step consist of objective acts that mark the defendant's conduct as criminal in nature. The defendant's objective conduct, taken as a whole, must unequivocally corroborate the required subjective intent to purchase or sell actual narcotics.

> The key word is *"objective "*: the "substantial step" requirement is an objective requirement, not a subjective one. In other words, under the "substantial step" analysis, an appellate court evaluates whether any reasonable person could find that the acts committed would corroborate the firmness of a defendant's criminal intent, assuming that the defendant did, in fact, intend to commit the crime. The requirement does not mandate that the activity constituting a substantial step must be *sufficient* to prove that the defendant had the subjective, specific intent to commit a crime. The intent may need to be proven separately.

> This point is best illustrated by a hypothetical. A penniless young man, while walking through a city park, is asked to purchase drugs. To further his own misguided pursuit of personal amusement, the man engages in active negotiations with the drug dealer to purchase drugs, fully knowing that he could never consummate the sale. These negotiations, even though they would not establish the man's subjective intent to buy the drugs, no doubt do constitute a "substantial step" towards the commission of a crime of possession, for these negotiations would, objectively, corroborate the firmness of a defendant's criminal intent.

> This, of course, does not mean that the young man in our hypothetical is guilty of an attempt crime — the government must still fulfill its burden to establish that he had the *specific intent* to purchase the drugs. The young man would, no doubt, argue that the fact he was (1) penniless and (2) prone to amusing himself in unconventional ways served as strong evidence that

594 CASES AND PROBLEMS IN CRIMINAL LAW CH. 18

he did not, in fact, intend to possess the drugs. The point is, however, that these two inquiries are, ultimately, separate ones. A defendant cannot argue that overt acts on his part did not constitute a "substantial step," even though a reasonable person would believe that they were strongly corroborative of the firmness of an actor's criminal intent, on the ground that his acts did not *prove* his subjective intent. The acts alleged need only corroborate (*i.e.*, confirm) his intent; they are not the *sole evidence* on which the government can rely to establish that a defendant specifically intended to commit a crime.

Therefore, we hold that when a defendant engages in active negotiations to purchase drugs, he has committed the "substantial step" towards the crime of possession required to convict him of attempted possession. We simply cannot contemplate a situation where a defendant's active negotiations to purchase drugs would not strongly corroborate the firmness of his intent to possess narcotics, assuming he had such an intent. This does *not* mean that any defendant who engages in active negotiations to purchase narcotics has committed an attempt crime; as we pointed out in our earlier hypothetical, the government must still prove a defendant's *intent* to possess narcotics.

(5) In *People v. Lehnert*, 163 P.3d 1111 (Colorado Supreme Court 2007), defendant was convicted of attempted murder.

The owner of a gun shop contacted the Denver Police Department and reported that a suspicious woman had attempted to buy gunpowder from him but refused to say why she wanted it. He declined to sell the gunpowder to her and instead notified the police. Through the license plate number he gave them, the police were able to identify the defendant.

Days later a friend of the defendant contacted the police, reporting that the defendant told her she was planning to kill two "pigs," using two pipe bombs. One of the officers was a male correctional officer at the Denver Women's Correctional Facility, where the defendant had been an inmate, and the other was a female officer named "Shelly." The friend testified that the defendant had borrowed a drill and made holes in the end caps of the bomb, and had asked for wooden clothespins to serve as a switch and a soldering iron to connect two small wires, saying that she only needed a few more parts to complete the bomb. The friend also testified that the defendant told her that she had learned how to construct bombs while in prison and had written instructions at her home. In addition, she testified that Lehnert had not only found out extensive family information and the home address of the correctional officer, but also had driven past his house numerous times.

The defendant's friend became concerned that the defendant was actually going to carry out the killings, and she called the police. In addition to telling the police about the defendant's statements and actions, she also told them that she had found in her home a business card for a second gun shop. By inquiring at the second gun shop, the police learned that the defendant had managed to purchase two boxes of shotgun shells.

A search warrant was issued for the defendant's apartment, where police discovered doorbell wire, electrical tape, a nine-volt battery, two metal pipes (which had been scored, weakening them and increasing their destructive potential), two metal end caps (with drilled out center holes), latex gloves, screwdrivers, wire cutters, safety glasses, magnets, two boxes of shotgun shells full of gunpowder, flashlight bulbs (sometimes used as an ignition device for a pipe bomb), and directions to the victim's house In addition, the police found materials for making false identification cards, the defendant's driver's license, falsified birth certificates, an application for a new social security card, and a falsified high school transcript.

A police detective testified that the materials recovered from the defendant's apartment were explosive parts, capable of being assembled to make a bomb. The detective further testified that the defendant possessed everything required for a pipe bomb except a completed switch and that a switch could probably be made from the wire found at the scene or from a clothespin, which the defendant had tried to acquire from her friend.

On appeal, the court held that this evidence was sufficient to show attempted murder:

A person commits criminal attempt in this jurisdiction if, acting with the kind of culpability otherwise required for commission of a particular crime, he engages in conduct constituting a substantial step toward the commission of that crime. *See* § 18-2-101(1), C.R.S. (2006). The statute immediately makes clear that by "substantial step" it means any conduct that is strongly corroborative of the actor's criminal objective. * * * *

Prior to the enactment of a general criminal attempt statute, the sporadic treatment of attempt by this court focused largely on the dangerousness of the actor's conduct in terms of its proximity to, or the likelihood that it would result in, a completed crime. Emphasizing that neither preparation alone nor a "mere intention" to commit a crime could constitute criminal attempt, we described an attempt as "any overt act done with the intent to commit the crime, and which, except for the interference of some cause preventing the carrying out of the intent, would have resulted in the commission of the crime." By also making clear, however, that the overt act required for an attempt need not be the last proximate act necessary to consummate the crime, we implicitly acknowledged that acts in preparation for the last proximate act, at some point attain to criminality themselves. The question of an overt act's proximity to, or remoteness from, completion of the crime therefore remained, without detailed guidance, a matter for individual determination under the facts of each case.

By contrast, the statutory requirement of a "substantial step" signaled a clear shift of focus from the act itself to the dangerousness of the actor, as a person manifesting a firm disposition to commit a crime. *See* Model Penal Code § 5.01 cmt. 1 (1985). While some conduct, in the form of an act, omission, or possession, is still necessary to avoid criminalizing bad intentions alone; and the notion of "mere preparation" continues to be a useful way of describing conduct falling short of a "substantial step;" the ultimate inquiry under the statutory definition concerns the extent to which the actor's conduct is strongly corroborative of the firmness of his criminal purpose, rather than the proximity of his conduct to consummation of the crime. Even more directly than the Model Penal Code formulation, which makes strong corroboration of criminal purpose a necessary but not sufficient condition of a substantial step, *see* Model Penal Code § 5.01(2) (1985) (not a substantial step "unless" strongly corroborative), the statute adopted by this jurisdiction in 1971 actually *equates* a substantial step with "any conduct that is strongly corroborative of the firmness of his purpose to complete the commission of the offense." § 8-2-101(1).

The question whether particular conduct constitutes a substantial step, of course, remains a matter of degree and can no more be resolved by a mechanical rule, or litmus test, than could the question whether the actor's conduct was too remote or failed to progress beyond mere preparation. The requirement that the defendant's conduct amount to a "substantial step," statutorily defined as it now is, however, provides the fact-finder with a much more specific and predictable basis for determining criminality. Rather than leaving to the fact-finder (as well as the court evaluating the sufficiency of evidence) the task of resolving the policy choices inherent in deciding when acts of preparation have become criminal, the statutory requirement of a substantial step simply calls for a determination whether the actor's conduct strongly corroborates a sufficiently firm intent on his part to commit the specific crime he is charged with attempting.

By actually defining a "substantial step" as "any conduct . . . which is strongly corroborative of the firmness of the actor's purpose," the Colorado statute has no need to further enumerate particular circumstances in which strongly corroborative conduct may constitute a substantial step. Conduct strongly corroborative of the firmness of the actor's criminal purpose is sufficient in itself. Drawn as they are largely from decisional law, however, the acts enumerated in the former statute and Model Penal Code, such as searching out a contemplated victim, reconnoitering the place contemplated for commission of a crime, and possessing materials specially designed for unlawful use and without lawful purpose, remain useful examples of conduct considered capable of strongly corroborating criminal purpose, and in those instances where they do, of being sufficient to establish criminal attempt.

There was evidence at the defendant's trial from which the jury could find that she repeatedly articulated her intent to kill two law enforcement officers with pipe bombs. Unlike many prosecutions for attempt, it was therefore unnecessary for the jury to be able to infer the defendant's criminal intent or purpose from her conduct. The jury need only have been able to find that the defendant committed acts that were strongly corroborative of the firmness of that purpose.

There was also evidence from which the jury could reasonably find that the defendant was determined to make the pipe bombs she needed to implement her plan and that she made substantial efforts and overcame hurdles to do so. Over many days she not only managed to acquire almost all of the materials required to create a bomb but also feloniously altered them to suit her criminal purpose, conduct for which she was separately convicted of possessing explosive or incendiary parts. When rebuffed in her attempt to acquire gunpowder directly from one gun shop, for example, she found a way to do so indirectly from another gun shop. There was testimony from which the jury could believe that she had eventually succeeded in acquiring all but a few necessary materials and that she had already acquired the drawings and written instructions necessary for final assembly.

Beyond the tenacity exhibited by the defendant in actually fabricating the bombs, her friend testified that she also had gathered significant personal information about one of her intended victims, including his address and information about his children and the car his family drove. There was evidence that she had reconnoitered his house and neighborhood more than once, reportedly being forced to leave on one occasion after being noticed. Finally there was evidence from which the jury could believe that she was simultaneously producing forged documents, which would permit her to assume false identities for purposes including the purchase of additional weapons.

The complexity of some criminal schemes, and the extent and uniqueness of the preparatory acts required to implement them without detection, lend themselves, by their very nature, to corroborating the actor's firmness of purpose. Regardless of the fact that the defendant was arrested before producing operational bombs or placing them within striking range of her victims in this case, there was in fact an abundance of evidence of her determined and sustained efforts to implement her plan, which could be found by reasonable jurors to be strongly corroborative of the firmness of her purpose to commit murder. Nothing more was required.

UNITED STATES v. JOYCE
U.S. Court of Appeals, 8th Circuit
693 F.2d 838 (1982)

GIBSON, SENIOR CIRCUIT JUDGE.

Michael Dennis Joyce was convicted after a jury trial on one count of attempting to possess cocaine with the intent to distribute in violation of 21 U.S.C. §§ 841(a)(1) and 846 (Count I), and one count of traveling in interstate commerce to facilitate an unlawful activity in violation of 18 U.S.C. § 1952 (Count II). The trial court sentenced Joyce to a term of ten years imprisonment on Count I and a term of five years probation on Count II, to be served consecutively. A timely appeal was filed. Though Joyce raises several issues on appeal, we are primarily concerned here with his claim that the evidence presented at trial was insufficient to sustain his conviction. For the reasons set forth herein, we reverse Joyce's conviction on each count.

I.

The facts as presented to the jury in this case are undisputed and based entirely upon the uncontradicted testimony of the government's only two witnesses: Robert Jones, a St. Louis police officer assigned to the Drug Enforcement Administration Task Force, and James Gebbie, a government informant.

During 1980, the St. Louis Metropolitan Police Department conducted what has been termed a "reverse sting operation," in which undercover police officers posed as drug sellers actively soliciting major drug transactions with reputed drug dealers. As part of that operation, government informant James Gebbie, who testified to having prior drug dealings with Joyce, contacted Joyce by telephone in September and early October, 1980, to inform Joyce about the prospective availability of drugs for purchase in St. Louis. Joyce told Gebbie to call back when Gebbie found out more definite information.

On October 20, 1980 Gebbie again called Joyce, this time informing Joyce that cocaine was available for purchase in St. Louis. Joyce indicated that he had twenty-two thousand dollars and would be in St. Louis the following day, October 21, 1980. Gebbie and Joyce agreed that twenty-two thousand dollars would be more than sufficient to purchase a pound of cocaine.

On October 21, 1980, Joyce flew from Oklahoma City, Oklahoma to St. Louis, Missouri, where he met Gebbie and undercover officer Robert Jones, who was posing as a cocaine seller. Jones and Gebbie took Joyce to a room in a local St. Louis hotel, where Joyce immediately asked to see the cocaine. Jones told Joyce that the cocaine was not in the hotel room, but could be easily obtained by Jones if Joyce was interested in dealing rather than merely talking. After Joyce professed his interest in dealing, Jones recited prices for various quantities of cocaine and Joyce said that he could "handle" a pound of cocaine for twenty thousand dollars. Officer Jones then went to his office and obtained the cocaine.

When officer Jones returned to the hotel room, he handed Joyce a duct-tape wrapped plastic package said to contain a kilogram of cocaine. Without unwrapping the tape, Joyce immediately returned the package, stating that he could not see the cocaine. Jones then unwrapped about half of the tape covering the plastic package and handed the package back to Joyce. Joyce again returned the package to Jones and asked Jones to open up the package so that Joyce could examine the cocaine more closely. Jones answered that he would only open the plastic package if and when Joyce showed the money that he intended to use to purchase the cocaine. Joyce then replied that he would not produce his money until Jones first opened up the plastic package. After Jones persisted in asking Joyce to produce his money, Joyce again refused, stating that he would not deal with officer Jones no matter how good the cocaine was. Realizing that Joyce was not going to show his money or purchase the cocaine, Jones told Joyce to leave and Joyce left, with no apparent intention of returning at a later time to purchase any cocaine.

As Joyce left the hotel, he was arrested by DEA agents. A search warrant was thereafter obtained and used to search Joyce's luggage revealing twenty-two thousand dollars in cash.

II.

The issue before us is whether the evidence, taken in its entirety and viewed most favorably to the government, is sufficient to prove beyond a reasonable doubt that Joyce attempted to purchase cocaine with the intent to distribute. To resolve this issue we must determine whether Joyce's conduct crossed that shadowy line dividing acts of "mere preparation" to commit a crime and acts constituting an "attempt."

The government argues that Joyce's attempt to possess cocaine was established by evidence that he traveled from Oklahoma City to St. Louis with twenty-two thousand dollars pursuant to a previously discussed drug purchase arrangement, that he expressed an initial willingness to deal with Jones, and that he agreed with Jones on the price for a pound of cocaine. Furthermore, the government adds, Joyce would have purchased the cocaine had it not been for the disagreement between Joyce and Jones resulting from Jones' refusal to open the plastic bag containing the purported cocaine until Joyce first showed his money. The government points out that Jones was acting in compliance with DEA guidelines which prohibit illegal drugs from going into the physical possession of persons under investigation.

Joyce, on the other hand, contends that his conduct did not rise to the level of an attempt to possess cocaine because while he admittedly possessed sufficient money to purchase the cocaine at the agreed upon price, he ultimately refused either to purchase the cocaine or to produce his money. He thus had abandoned any designs he might have had of obtaining cocaine and distributing it before taking the necessary and overt steps of producing the money and obtaining the cocaine.

Although there is no comprehensive statutory definition of attempt in federal law, federal courts have rather uniformly adopted the standard set forth in § 5.01 of the American Law Institute's Model Penal Code (Proposed Official Draft 1962) that the requisite elements of attempt are (1) an intent to engage in criminal conduct, and (2) conduct constituting a "substantial step" towards the commission of the substantive offense which strongly corroborates the actor's criminal intent. *United States v. Mandujano*, 499 F.2d 370, 376-77 (5th cir. 1974).

While we adopt this standard here, we are also mindful of Judge Learned Hand's candid, yet poignant, observation that a verbal formulation aimed at dividing mere preparation from attempt is, in itself, not particularly useful. *United States v. Coplon*, 185 F.2d 629, 633 (2nd cir. 1950). Indeed, whether conduct represents a "substantial step" toward the commission of the criminal design is, in Justice Holmes' words, "a question of degree," necessarily depending on the factual circumstances peculiar to each case. *Commonwealth v. Peaslee*, 177 Mass. 267, 272 (1901). However, as the Tenth Circuit analyzed in *United States v. Monholland*, 607 F.2d 1311, 1318 (10th cir. 1979):

> The cases universally hold that mere intention to commit a specified crime does not amount to an attempt. It is essential that the defendant, with the intent of committing the particular crime, do some overt act adapted to, approximating, and which in the ordinary and likely course of things will result in the commission of the particular crime.

With this in mind, we conclude that even assuming Joyce went to St. Louis intending to purchase cocaine, there was clearly insufficient evidence to establish that he engaged in conduct constituting a "substantial step" toward the commission of the crime of possession of cocaine with the intent to distribute. Whatever intention Joyce had to procure cocaine was abandoned prior to the commission of a necessary and substantial step to effectuate the purchase of cocaine.

The attempt, of course, need not be successful, but generally the abortion of the attempt occurs because of events beyond the control of the attemptor. As the court recognized in *Monholland*, 607 F.2d 1311, 1319, "the attemptor's act must have passed the preparation stage so that if it is not interrupted extraneously, it will result in a crime."

Here it is undisputed that Joyce, despite having both the opportunity and ability to purchase the cocaine at the agreed upon price, unambiguously refused either to produce his money or to purchase the cocaine. This effectively negated the government's effort to consummate the sale.

This case is comparable to the case of *People v. Miller*, 2 Cal.2d 527 (1935) where the defendant announced his intention to kill another, obtained a .22 caliber rifle, pursued his intended victim into an open field carrying the .22 caliber rifle, and after loading the rifle apparently changed his mind and voluntarily surrendered the rifle to a third person standing nearby. The Supreme Court of California concluded that the defendant's conduct did not rise to the level of an attempted murder.

Similarly in *Wooldridge v. United States*, 237 F. 775 (9th cir. 1916), the defendant, pursuant to a previous arrangement, met a sixteen-year-old girl in a closed store, presumably intending to have intercourse with her. However, after receiving some advice from a friend who was at the store, the defendant decided not to carry through with his criminal intent and left the store without ever approaching the girl. The Ninth Circuit reversed the defendant's conviction for attempted rape, holding that while the defendant may have gone to the store with the intent of having intercourse with the girl, he never committed an overt act toward the commission of the intended crime.

Thus, in these two cases and in the instant case, the defendant had the opportunity and ability to commit the completed offense, yet refused to engage in conduct constituting a "substantial step" toward commission of the completed offense. The government, however, urges that Joyce's initially expressed interest in purchasing a pound of cocaine from Jones at the stated price and his momentary possession of the wrapped package said to contain a kilogram of cocaine constituted a substantial step toward possession of cocaine with the intent to distribute.[3]

We disagree. While Joyce professed a desire to purchase cocaine during his preliminary discussions with Jones, Joyce never attempted to carry through with that desire by producing the money necessary to purchase and hence ultimately

---

[3] It should be noted that Joyce's momentary possession of the wrapped and sealed package containing a kilogram of cocaine is not the same possession that Joyce was charged with attempting. Joyce was indicted and tried for attempting to purchase and hence possess a pound of cocaine with the intent to distribute, not with attempting momentarily to possess a kilogram package of cocaine belonging to officer Jones.

possess the cocaine. And, although Jones gave Joyce the sealed and wrapped package said to contain a kilogram of cocaine, Joyce did not open the package but immediately returned the package to Jones who in turn refused to open the package because Joyce refused to produce the money necessary to effectuate the purchase of a pound of cocaine.

Thus, all we have here is a preliminary discussion regarding the purchase of cocaine which broke down before Joyce had committed any "overt act adapted to, approximating, and which in the ordinary and likely course of things (would) result in the commission of the (crime of possessing cocaine with the intent to distribute)" *Monholland*, 607 F.2d 1311, 1318.[4]

We also find unpersuasive the government's claim that Joyce would have purchased the cocaine had it not been for Jones' refusal to open the package of cocaine. We simply fail to see why Joyce's motive for refusing to commit a "substantial step" toward possession of the cocaine is particularly relevant. Joyce's motive for refusing to purchase the cocaine here is no different than had he refused to purchase because he disagreed with Jones as to the price for which the cocaine was offered. And, while we may agree with the government's suggestion that Joyce, who was presumably "street-wise," may have been tipped off that Jones was a DEA undercover agent when Jones refused to open the package, we fail to see how an increased awareness of the risk of apprehension converts what would otherwise be "mere preparation" into an attempt.

Finally, the government makes the rather novel suggestion that because Joyce was only one act away from the completed offense of possession of cocaine with the intent to distribute, he must, therefore, be guilty of attempting to commit the completed offense. First, Joyce was two acts, not one act, away from the completed offense. Before Joyce could have committed the offense of possessing cocaine with the intent to distribute he had to first produce the money necessary to effect the purchase of the cocaine and second take actual physical possession of, or exercise dominion and control over, the cocaine. He obviously could not distribute the cocaine before obtaining either actual or constructive possession of it. *United States v. Batimana*, 623 F.2d 1366 (9th Cir.). Nevertheless, whether conduct may be characterized as being one act or two acts away from the completed offense is not particularly helpful in determining if an attempt has been committed. For example, the defendant in *Miller* who while carrying a rifle pursued his intended victim into the open field was only one overt act away from committing the completed offense of murder; all he had left to do was shoot the intended victim.[5] However, the defendant in *Miller*, as Joyce here, had not yet committed an overt act strongly corroborative of the firmness of his criminal purpose. Thus, in *Miller* and in this

---

[4] In *Monholland*, the Tenth Circuit considered whether a defendant's preliminary discussion with an undercover officer regarding the price at which the defendant could purchase dynamite similar to the sample held by the undercover officer constituted an attempt to receive in interstate commerce an explosive. The court concluded that defendant's preliminary discussion did not constitute an overt act aimed toward commission of the crime defendant was charged with attempting.

[5] If the defendant in *Miller* had shot and missed the intended victim he would have committed an attempted murder. See R.M. Perkins, *Perkins on Criminal Law*, 558 (1969). Similarly, in this case, if Joyce had given Jones the money necessary to purchase the cocaine but Jones refused to give Joyce the cocaine, Joyce would have committed an attempt to possess cocaine with the intent to distribute.

case the conduct which remained to be done, whether characterized as one act or two acts, was the very conduct which separated mere preparation from a substantial step toward commission of the completed offense.

The outright reversal of Count I carries with it the reversal of Count II as mere preparation for any illegal activity that was abandoned prior to the completion of the attempt charged.

* * * *

Judgment reversed.

NOTES FROM DAN:

(1) The court said that Joyce's motive for discontinuing his purchase was irrelevant. Why? Isn't it relevant to the *purpose* of punishing people for attempts?

(2) I have some trouble reconciling this holding with *Mandujano*. Can you help me out?

(3) The court said that it was following the test set out in § 5.01 of the Model Penal Code. It appears in the Appendix. Please read it carefully. Did the court properly apply this test to the facts?

(4) Suppose D offers X money to murder V. D has committed the crime of solicitation to murder. Does this also constitute a "substantial step" towards murder — making D guilty of *attempted murder* too? See *People v. Superior Court (Decker)*, 41 Cal.4th 1 (2007).

(5) How does "renunciation" fit into the law of attempt? If the defendant has "renounced," does this mean he has not committed a "substantial step" — or does it mean that he is allowed to "take back" a crime already committed? In *United States v. Shelton*, 30 F.3d 702 (6th cir. 1994), the court stated:

> Shelton relies on the Model Penal Code § 5.01(4) and Tenn.Code Ann. § 39-12-104, both of which recognize an affirmative defense of abandonment under circumstances manifesting a complete and voluntary renunciation of criminal purpose. According to the Model Penal Code, renunciation is not voluntary "if it is motivated, in whole or in part, by circumstances . . . that increase the probability of detection or apprehension or that make more difficult the accomplishment of the criminal purpose." Likewise, renunciation is not complete "if it is motivated by a decision to postpone the criminal conduct until a more advantageous time or to transfer the criminal effort to another but similar objective or victim." Model Penal Code § 5.01(4). The Model Penal Code relies on two related considerations as justifications for recognizing the defense. First, allowance of the defense recognizes that the actor's conduct no longer poses a danger to society. Second, the availability of the defense provides actors with a "motive for desisting from their criminal designs, thereby diminishing the risk that the substantive crime will be committed." Model Penal Code § 5.01, comment 8.

We decline to follow the approach of the Model Penal Code and Tennessee law, and hold that withdrawal, abandonment and renunciation, however characterized, do not provide a defense to an attempt crime. As noted, the attempt crime is complete with proof of intent together with acts constituting a substantial step toward commission of the substantive offense. When a defendant withdraws prior to forming the necessary intent or taking a substantial step toward the commission of the offense, the essential elements of the crime cannot be proved. At this point, the question whether a defendant has withdrawn is synonymous with whether he has committed the offense. After a defendant has evidenced the necessary intent and has committed an act constituting a substantial step toward the commission of the offense, he has committed the crime of attempt, and can withdraw only from the commission of the substantive offense. We are not persuaded that the availability of a withdrawal defense would provide an incentive or motive to desist from the commission of an offense, especially since the success of the defense presupposes a criminal trial at which the issue would be submitted to the jury for decision. A remote chance of acquittal would appear to have an even more remote chance of deterring conduct. We recognize, of course, that attempt crimes pose unique issues. However, the interest of defendants in not being convicted for mere "thoughts, desires or motives" is adequately addressed by the government's burden of proving that the defendant took a substantial step toward the commission of the substantive offense.

(6) If you think Problem 18 is a bit fanciful, consider the following item from the San Francisco Chronicle of March 24, 1993:

A little preparation is useful when baking a cake, going camping, or robbing a bank. That was the lesson learned by three strangers who visited Tomales, a crossroads hamlet in western Marin County on Monday afternoon. They did not realize that the Tomales Branch of the Novato National Bank closed for the day after the lunch hour. Townspeople watched as three men - their faces concealed by masks - alighted from a silver sedan and rattled the doors of the bank. One carried a pump-action shotgun. When the doors did not open, they jumped back in the car and fled on Highway 1. "Apparently they did not case the place," said Marin County Sheriff's Detective Jess Carroll. There are no suspects.

Question: Did the "three strangers" commit attempted bank robbery?

(7) There are quite a few federal cases dealing with attempted bank robbery. Here is a sampling. They leave me somewhat puzzled as to what the "rule" is. Can you reconcile them?

Rumfelt v. U.S., 445 F.2d 134 (7th cir. 1971)

Facts: "Alto Pass, Illinois, is a small town. Among the buildings are a small grocery store and a small bank (Farmers State Bank) which are located adjacent to each other on the main street. On February 29, 1968, witness John D. Aldrich left the grocery store about 1 p.m. intending to drive his automobile truck which had been parked in front of the store. As he neared his truck, he saw a masked man with rifle in hand standing beside an automobile parked near the truck and in front of the bank. Aldrich testified the masked man pointed the rifle at him and said 'get in the bank.' They both walked toward the bank and Aldrich attempted to open the door but discovered it was locked. Aldrich told the masked man he could not get into the bank and the masked man who was standing a short distance behind him came up to the building and looked in the window. He then told Aldrich to get out of town, and Aldrich got into his truck and left town."

Holding: Conviction upheld.

> We feel that enough evidence was submitted for the jury to find that an attempt under the statute had been made in the present case. We do not deem fatal the fact that defendant never actually entered the Farmers State Bank. An actual entry is not required under the statute. Rather the heart of the crime is the intent to steal. Clearly, the jury could find that such an intent existed here and that the requisite overt acts had been committed toward that end. The presence of defendant in front of the bank clad in a mask, along with his use of a carbine to intimidate a hostage, and the use of that hostage in an effort to get inside of the bank were all facts which would support that finding.

U.S. v. SNELL, 627 F.2d 186 (9th cir. 1980)

Facts: "Snell and two co-conspirators planned to kidnap a bank manager and his wife, hold the wife hostage while accompanying the manager to the bank to obtain $150,000, and then kill the manager. Pursuant to that plan the three went to the manager's home and then to the bank where, from the parking lot, they observed the manager and identified his car. The other two co-conspirators also waited near the manager's house in the evening to observe him returning home. After observing the manager's routine at his home and office, the three assembled false identifications, rubber gloves, hand guns, mace, ropes, and adhesive tape and went to the bank manager's house to carry out their plan. Spotting a Highway Patrol vehicle near the house, they postponed execution of the plan. The following day they returned to the house, again armed. Snell and one co-conspirator carried false police identification. They knocked on the door and identified themselves as policemen, but their plan to force an entry and kidnap the wife was frustrated by a Great Dane that accompanied her to the door. When one of the co-conspirators was picked up on unrelated charges and revealed the plan to the police, Snell and the third co-conspirator were arrested."

Holding: Conviction upheld.

> A conviction for attempt requires proof of culpable intent and conduct constituting a substantial step toward commission of the crime that strongly corroborates that intent. *U.S. v. Mandujano*, 499 F.2d 370, 373-79 (5th Cir. 1974). The evidence here established the existence of both elements. Snell's intent was demonstrated by the plan that he devised with his co-conspirators. His intent was corroborated in a number of ways: assemblage and possession of the materials necessary to commit the crime, reconnoitering the location of the crime and the habits of the victim, and the actions taken to effectuate the plan that were frustrated only by the

fortuity of a police car on one occasion and the presence of a Great Dane at the intended victim's house on another.

U.S. v. Buffington, 815 F.2d 1292 (9th cir. 1987)

Facts: An informant told police that three men planned to rob a Bay View Bank (a bank in a shopping center), and one would dress as a woman. A police officer saw one of the men at the shopping center, driving slowly. Five days later, he saw three men driving slowly at the shopping center. They parked 150 feet from the bank, and one man entered a drugstore. Then, by coincidence, a power outage occurred, and bank employees locked the doors of the bank. The three men left. When arrested, they had guns and one was wearing 4 jackets. Because the prosecutor refused to disclose the informant's report to the defendant, the trial court did not consider the informant's information. Nevertheless, the trial court convicted.

Holding: Conviction reversed.

A reasonable jury could find at least the substantially unequivocal intent to rob someone or some institution. The circumstances fall short of showing the intent to rob a federal bank. If intent to rob existed at all, it could easily have been directed against the Payless market, or the nearby state bank.

Of course, circumstantial evidence is fully admissible in criminal cases, including bank robbery cases. It is permissible to infer intent from a defendant's conduct and the surrounding circumstances. For example, in *Rumfelt v. U.S.*, 445 F.2d 134 (7th Cir.), the Seventh Circuit sustained a conviction of attempted bank robbery where intent to rob was shown by circumstantial evidence. In *Rumfelt*, the court noted that actual entry into the bank was not required to find that an attempt occurred. The defendant's presence in front of a bank while wearing a ski mask, and his use of a rifle to intimidate a passerby into trying to open the door to the bank for him were sufficient to infer an intent to steal. That is not comparable to this case.

Other cases that have permitted the inference of an intent to rob a bank have involved testimony by informants or co-conspirators. Evidence of the defendants' intent here has no such background upon which to rely. There was no admissible testimony concerning defendants' intent by an informant or co-conspirator. No defendant came within 50 yards of the bank. The suggestion that they were "casing" something could be true, but is supported by little more than speculation. The evidence is focused no more on Bay View than on other nearby institutions. Even viewing the evidence in as favorable a light to the government as we may, the evidence presented to the jury could reasonably generate no more than suspicion, and is certainly not sufficient for a rational trier of fact to find intent to commit bank robbery beyond a reasonable doubt.

Moreover, even if sufficient intent to rob were shown, the conduct fell short of constituting a substantial step toward the commission of a robbery. For conduct to be "strongly corroborative of the firmness of the defendant's criminal intent," preparation alone is not enough, there must be some appreciable fragment of the crime committed, it must be in such progress that it will be consummated unless interrupted by circumstances independent of the will of the attempter, and the act must not be equivocal in nature. *U.S. v. Mandujano*, 499 F.2d 370, 376 (5th cir. 1974). Thus, while conduct need not be incompatible with innocence to be punishable as an attempt, the conduct must be necessary to the consummation of the crime and of such nature that a reasonable observer, viewing it in context, could conclude beyond a reasonable doubt that it was undertaken in accordance with a design to violate the statute.

Knowing all that we have learned — which the jury did not have before I it — we could well believe that the defendants intended to do what the informant claimed they had planned; but their actual conduct did not cross the boundary between preparation and attempt. Appellants were afterwards found to be armed and may have appeared to be reconnoitering Bay View Federal, but none made any move toward the bank.

The government argues the generality that movement toward a bank is not required to show attempt, citing *U.S. v. Snell*, 627 F.2d 186 (9th cir. 1980). But that case is distinguishable upon several grounds. * * * * The court in *Snell* observed that Snell's entry into the home was "factually precedent but so far as the total scheme is concerned is analytically little different than entry into the bank itself." There is no comparable entry, nor movement toward the bank in this case. The conduct in *Snell* was unequivocal; that here is entirely tentative and unfocused. Fortified by their information from the informant, the police concluded that, standing by their car 150 feet away, the defendants were "casing" the bank; but resort to that knowledge cannot be utilized because the prosecution had eschewed its use. Not only did appellants not take a single step toward the bank, they displayed no weapons and no indication that they were about to make an entry. Standing alone, their conduct did not constitute that requisite "appreciable fragment" of a bank robbery, nor a step toward commission of the crime of such substantiality that, unless frustrated, the crime would have occurred.

U.S. v. Still, 850 F.2d 607 (9th cir. 1988)

Facts: "On August 7, 1985, at about 10:30 a.m., a lay witness saw the defendant putting on a long blonde wig while sitting in a van with the motor running, parked in the Roseville Square Shopping Center. The van was parked approximately 200 feet away from the Security Pacific Bank. The witness notified the police, who arrived in a marked patrol car shortly thereafter. Upon arrival of the police, the defendant put the van in reverse, and drove off. The police caught up with the defendant, who had fled to a nearby camper/trailer. He was arrested for possession of stolen property and taken to the Roseville Police Department. Following his arrest, the defendant allegedly volunteered the following statements: 'You did a good job. You caught me five minutes before I was going to rob a bank. That's what I was putting the wig on for. The van is stolen. How much do you get for auto theft around here?' After waiving his *Miranda* rights, the defendant told the police that he was planning to rob a bank when the marked police vehicle came up to the van he was in. He planned to drive up to the drive-in window of the bank and place a phony bomb, along with a demand note, on the window. The defendant did not specify, by name, the bank he was planning to rob. He described it as a large, two-story building, made of brown or reddish brick. The defendant stated that Security Pacific sounded like the name of the bank he intended to rob. Of the thirty-nine banks within five miles of the Roseville Square Shopping Center, only Security Pacific fits the defendant's description of the bank he was planning to rob. The defendant told the police that his statements were just "frosting on the cake" because all of the evidence that they needed was located in the van. Inside the van, the police found a hoax bomb which looked like a real bomb, a red pouch with a demand note taped to it, a long blonde wig, a police scanner programmed to the Roseville Police Department, and a notebook containing drafts of demand notes and the radio frequency of the Rocklin Police Department."

Holding: Conviction reversed.

A conviction for an attempt requires proof of both "culpable intent" and "conduct constituting a substantial step toward commission of the crime that is in pursuit of that intent." *U.S. v. Buffington*, 815 F.2d at 1301. A "substantial step" is "conduct strongly corroborative of the firmness of the defendant's criminal intent." *U.S. v. Mandujano*, 499 F.2d 370, 376 (5th cir. 1974). "Culpable intent" can be inferred from a particular defendant's conduct and from the surrounding circumstances. * * * *

In this case, Still's intent to rob the Security Pacific National Bank was clearly established in his statements to the police after his arrest. Without prompting, the defendant stated: "You did a good job. You caught me five minutes before I was going to rob a bank. That's what I was putting the wig on for." After waiving his rights, the defendant stated he intended to use the drive-up window of the bank and place a phony explosive device, along with a note, on that window, to rob a bank. Although the defendant did not state the name of the bank he was planning to rob, he did describe it. Within a five mile area, his description of a large, two-story bank, constructed of brown or reddish color brick fits only the Security Pacific Bank. Additionally, when asked by the police if it was Security Pacific that the defendant intended to rob, he said that Security Pacific sounded like the name of the bank he was going to rob. These statements permit an inference of an unequivocal intent to rob the Security Pacific Bank. Therefore, the first aspect of an attempt, a culpable intent, was established beyond a reasonable doubt.

To establish the second aspect of an attempt, "a substantial step," more than mere preparation must be shown. "There must be some appreciable fragment of the crime committed, it must be in such progress that it will be consummated unless interrupted by circumstances independent of the will of the attempter, and the act must not be equivocal in nature." *U.S. v. Buffington, supra.*

In *Buffington*, the court concluded that the defendants' conduct did not cross the line between preparation and attempt. Although the defendants had assembled the disguises and materials necessary to commit the robbery, drove by the bank twice while staring into it, and left their vehicle, armed, and stood with their attention focused on the bank, the court emphasized that none of them made any move toward the bank. Thus, standing alone, the defendants' conduct was too tentative and unfocused to constitute either the requisite "appreciable fragment" of a bank robbery, or a step toward the commission of the crime of such substantiality that, unless frustrated, the crime would have occurred.

The *Buffington* court stopped short of expressly requiring some actual movement toward the bank to show a substantial step toward an attempt. They cited *U.S. v. Snell* with approval, where this circuit upheld a conviction for attempted robbery without actual movement toward the bank, reasoning that the defendants' entry into the victim's home was analytically similar to entry into a bank.

Our facts do not establish either actual movement toward the bank or actions that are analytically similar to such movement. Before he was apprehended by the police, Still was seen sitting in his van, with the motor running, wearing a long blonde wig, parked approximately 200 feet away from the Security Pacific National Bank. Considering that the *Buffington* defendants' actions went further in manifesting a substantial step than did Still's actions, *Buffington* compels the conclusion that proof of a substantial step toward the attempt was not established beyond a reasonable doubt.

U.S. v. Moore, 921 F.2d 207 (9th cir. 1990)

Facts: "An informant, Krossman, told the FBI that Moore and others planned to rob a bank in Milwaukie, Oregon. The FBI provided Krossman with a 'stolen' car that the others expected to use in the robbery. FBI agents waited in a van near the bank and arrested Moore and another man as they walked toward the bank. Moore wore a ski mask. He carried gloves, two pillowcases in his pocket, and a loaded gun concealed in the waistband of his trousers."

Holding: Conviction upheld.

> The record provides ample evidence both of Moore's culpable intent and of conduct constituting a substantial step toward bank robbery.

(8) Many attempt statutes are called "general attempt" statutes, providing, for example, that "any attempt to commit any crime in this Code shall be punishable by one half the punishment for that crime."

And many statutory crimes are in fact "specific attempt" crimes, such as "possession of burglary tools" and "possession of cocaine with intent to sell." These crimes cause no actual harm, but do pose the potential for harm. Would application of the general attempt statute to burglary (i.e., "attempted burglary") or sale of cocaine (i.e., "attempted sale of cocaine") reach the same result? Not necessarily. Possession of burglary tools alone might not constitute the "substantial step" needed for attempted burglary, and possession of cocaine with intent to sell might not by itself be enough for the "substantial step" needed for attempted sale of cocaine.

Note that a general attempt statute might be applied to a "specific attempt" crime! Thus, one might be prosecuted for "attempted possession of burglary tools" or "attempted possession of cocaine with intent to sell". Does such a prosecution stretch the purposes of punishing attempt too far?

Chapter 19

CONSPIRACY

Although the crime of conspiracy is somewhat vague, which is one of many reasons why it is often asserted that the prosecution has a distinct advantage in conspiracy cases, it may be said to require: (1) an agreement between two or more persons, which constitutes the act; and (2) an intent thereby to achieve a certain objective which, under the common law definition, is the doing of either an unlawful act or a lawful act by unlawful means. The crime of conspiracy serves (like other anticipatory offenses) as a means to proceed against persons who have sufficiently manifested their disposition to criminality, and also as a device for acting against the special and continuing dangers incident to group activity. * * * *

In addition to the agreement and the intent requirements, some jurisdictions also require a showing of an "overt act" in furtherance of the agreement.

LaFave & Scott, *Criminal Law* (West)

There are several notable features of the crime we call "conspiracy."

First, conspiracy — like solicitation and attempt — is not a "stand alone" crime. Conspiracy must be attached to another crime. Thus, one may not be prosecuted for "conspiracy," but may be prosecuted for "conspiracy to commit _____." The crime in the blank space might be any crime: murder, robbery, sale of cocaine, overparking, etc.

Second — while this might not be apparent at first glance — conspiracy does require both a *mens rea* and an *actus reus*. The *mens rea* is the intent to commit the crime in the blank space. The *actus reus* is *the agreement* to commit the crime in the blank space — plus, in some jurisdictions, an "overt act" towards commission of the crime. Like solicitation and attempt, conspiracy is an "anticipatory" (or "inchoate") crime, so no actual harm is required (unlike murder, robbery, etc.).

Third, we punish conspiracy even if the crime in the blank space is in fact completed, And then we punish the defendants for the complete crime too! This is not true of solicitation and attempt. Why? Is there something different about conspiracy that justifies this "double punishment"?

Fourth, why punish conspiracy *at all*? If Dan intends to rob a bank and joins with Don in a plan to do so, hasn't Dan committed a "substantial step" towards robbing the bank — which would make him guilty of *attempted* bank robbery? Isn't the separate crime of conspiracy *unnecessary*?

SECTION A   THE AGREEMENT

The agreement is all-important in conspiracy, for one must look to the nature of the agreement to decide several critical issues, such as whether the requisite mental state is also present, whether the requisite plurality is present, and whether there is more than one conspiracy. As courts have so often said, the agreement is the "essence" or "gist" of the crime of conspiracy.

LaFave & Scott, *Criminal Law* (West)

What is an "agreement"? Is it the same as a *contract*? You learned in your contracts course that, to have a valid contract, there must be an offer, an acceptance, and consideration. And the terms of the offer must be sufficiently "certain." Suppose Dan says to Don, "Let's rob a Wells Fargo bank," and Don replies, "Sure." A contract? We have an offer and acceptance, but where is the consideration? And are the terms sufficiently certain? Aren't the time, place, and manner of the robbery missing — as well as how the loot will be divided?

If no contract, should that mean that there is no agreement — and therefore no conspiracy? Would this approach serve the purposes of the law of conspiracy?

The rules you learned in your contracts course are not easy to apply, but at least they give us some guidance as to when we have a contract. If an "agreement" is not the same as a "contract," then *what are* the essential ingredients of an "agreement"? How uncertain may it be? Do we want to punish people for vague "deals" they might never perform?

And how does the prosecution *prove* that there was in fact an agreement? If the defendants confess to what they said to each other, that makes it easy. But suppose they don't. May the prosecutor reason *backwards*? "I have evidence that they committed the crime together. Therefore, it logically follows that they must have *earlier agreed* to do so. That's my case for conspiracy, your honor." Should this be sufficient evidence of an agreement?

PROBLEM 19A

To: My law clerk

From: Assistant United States Attorney Penny Loafer

Re: *United States v. Dork*

Dan Dork has been indicted for conspiracy to commit bank robbery. Two witnesses testified before the grand jury, George Guardino and Fred Fink. Guardino will testify at trial, but Fink has disappeared and I am not sure we will be able to find him in time for him to testify at trial.

I have two questions for you: based on the attached authorities, (1) is Fink's testimony sufficient to support a conviction? and, (2) is Guardino's testimony sufficient to support a conviction,

Transcript of Grand Jury Testimony

Q: Mr. Fink, what does Mr. Custer look like?

A: He is a tall, white man.

Q: What occurred at your meeting with Custer on the morning of May 4?

A: Custer asked me to help him rob the First National Bank the next day, by driving the getaway car. He said that we also needed a lookout inside the bank, and he planned to ask Dork to do this. I told him that Dork was afraid of guns, and he wouldn't help if any guns were involved. Custer said he did intend to use a gun, but would tell Dork that he would not bring a gun, but simply say to the teller that he had a gun. Later on, Dork came over, and that is exactly what Custer told him. Dork nodded his head and left. Custer then took out his gun and cleaned and loaded it.

Q: Did you agree to drive the getaway car?

A: Yes, but I didn't really plan to do it. Custer is pretty violent, so I was afraid to turn him down. I guess Custer drove his own car to the bank. I dropped by the bank to see what would happen. Custer saw me, but didn't say anything. I saw the robbery and the shooting.

* * * *

Q: Mr. Guardino, what is your occupation?

A: I have been a guard at the First National Bank for 15 years. First National's deposits are insured by the federal government.

Q: What happened in the bank on May 5?

A: I saw two men come in the front door, a short white man and a tall white man.

Q: Is this a photo of one of the men?

A: Yes, this is the short man. [Witness identifies photo of Dork.] I now understand that his name is Dan Dork.

Q: What did they do?

A: Dork stood by the door, looking around the bank and out the door. The other man went to a teller's window, pulled out a gun, and demanded that she fill a bag with money. She did, and he took the bag and walked out the front door. Dork then walked out the front door too.

Q: In your experience, Mr. Guardino, do bank robbers sometimes use associates as lookouts?

A: Yes, quite often. They usually stand by the door, so they can look out for trouble both in the bank and outside, just as Dork did.

United States Code, Title 18

Section 371. Conspiracy to Commit Offense or to Defraud United States

If two or more persons conspire either to commit any offense against the United States, or to defraud the United States, or any agency thereof in any manner or for any purpose, and one or more of such persons do any act to effect the object of the conspiracy, each shall be fined under this title or imprisoned not more than five years, or both. If, however, the offense, the commission of which is the object of the conspiracy, is a misdemeanor only, the punishment for such conspiracy shall not exceed the maximum punishment provided for such misdemeanor.

(Note: Compare this statute to Model Penal Code § 5.03, in the Appendix.)

Section 2113. Bank Robbery and Incidental Crimes.

(a) Whoever, by force and violence, or by intimidation, takes, or attempts to take, from the person or presence of another, or obtains or attempts to obtain by extortion any property or money or any other thing of value belonging to, or in the care, custody, control, management, or possession of, any bank, credit union, or any savings and loan association . . . shall be fined under this title or imprisoned not more than twenty years, or both. * * * *

(f) As used in this section the term "bank" means any member bank of the Federal Reserve System, and any bank, banking association, trust company, savings bank, or other banking institution organized or operating under the laws of the United States, * * * * and any institution the deposits of which are insured by the Federal Deposit Insurance Corporation.

UNITED STATES v. ROSENBLATT
U.S. Court of Appeals, 2nd Circuit
554 F.2d 36 (1977)

MESKILL, CIRCUIT JUDGE:

The material facts of this unusual conspiracy case are not in dispute. Morris D. Brooks, the appellant's alleged co-conspirator, made false entries in the accounts payable records at the Manhattan Postal Service headquarters where he worked and thereby obtained eight checks totaling over $180,000. The checks were drawn on the United States Treasury and were payable to individuals having no claim to payment from the Postal Service.

Brooks was caught and indicted for conspiracy to defraud the United States, 18 U.S.C. § 371. He was also charged with eight counts of falsifying postal records in violation of 18 U.S.C. § 2073. After pleading guilty to conspiracy and to one count of making false entries, he testified against the appellant. Brooks was sentenced to five years imprisonment, but execution of the sentence was suspended, and he was placed on probation for five years.

Appellant, Rabbi Elyakim G. Rosenblatt, was the Dean of the Rabbinical

College of Queens. At Brooks' request, he "laundered" the eight checks through the college's bank account, and kept roughly ten percent of the face value of the checks for his services. Rosenblatt was indicted, along with Brooks, for conspiracy to defraud the United States. After pleading not guilty, he was tried and convicted by a jury and sentenced to six months imprisonment and a fine of $8,000.

Our difficulty with Rosenblatt's conviction arises from the lack of any agreement between him and Brooks concerning the type of fraud in which they were engaged. It is clear that Brooks was defrauding the United States by obtaining payment for government checks which he had caused to be printed without authorization. The government stipulated, however, that Rosenblatt did not know the truth about Brooks' activities. Brooks led him to believe that the checks were valid. He told Rosenblatt that the purpose of the laundering operation was to help some payees evade taxes and to help other payees conceal kickbacks on government contracts. In other words, both men agreed to defraud the United States, but neither agreed on the type of fraud.

On this appeal, Rosenblatt argues that under 18 U.S.C. § 371 a conspiracy to defraud the United States must be grounded upon agreement on some common scheme or plan.[1] He maintains that proof of an agreement to defraud, without further qualification as to the nature of the fraud, is insufficient to support a conviction under § 371. We agree and reverse the conviction.

The Lack of Agreement.

A conspiracy is an "agreement *among* the conspirators." *United States v. Falcone*, 311 U.S. 205, 210 (1940) (emphasis added). A "meeting of minds" is required. *Krulewitch v. United States*, 336 U.S. 440, 448 (1949) (Jackson, J., concurring). "Unless at least two people commit the act of agreeing, no one does. When one of two persons merely pretends to agree, the other party, whatever he may believe, is in fact not conspiring with anyone." *Developments in the Law — Criminal Conspiracy*, 72 Harv.L.Rev. 920, 926 (1959) [hereinafter cited as *Developments*]; see *Sears v. United States*, 343 F.2d 139 (5th Cir. 1965)(no conspiracy with government informant who secretly intends to frustrate the conspiracy); *Delaney v. State*, 164 Tenn. 432 (1932) (no conspiracy with person who feigns agreement.)[2]

The law of conspiracy requires agreement as to the "object" of the conspiracy. This does not mean that the conspirators must be shown to have agreed on the details of their criminal enterprise, but it does mean that the "essential nature of the plan" must be shown. *Blumenthal v. United States*, 332 U.S. 539, 557 (1947).

---

[1] Rosenblatt duly raised this issue in his pre-trial motion to dismiss the indictment, at the close of the government's case, at the end of the entire case and in a motion to set aside the jury's verdict.

[2] Many jurisdictions have adopted the Model Penal Code's "unilateral" formulation of conspiracy. Under that formulation, conspiracy is defined in terms of one person's agreeing with another, rather than in terms of an agreement among or between two or more people. See Wechsler, Jones & Korn, *The Treatment of Inchoate Crimes in the Model Penal Code of the American Law Institute: Attempt, Solicitation, and Conspiracy - Part II*, 61 Colum. L. Rev. 957, 965-66 (1961); Note, *Conspiracy: Statutory Reform Since the Model Penal Code*, 75 Colum.L.Rev. 1122, 1135-45 (1975). The federal definition retains the traditional, common law, "bilateral" formulation.

The problem of identifying the "essential nature" of the conspirators' plan often arises in cases in which knowledge is in issue. An examination of those cases sheds some light on the degree of specificity that is required as to the agreement. In *Ingram v. United States*, 360 U.S. 672 (1959), two individuals who had assisted in the operation of a lottery that was illegal under state law were convicted of conspiracy to evade federal wagering taxes for which their employers were liable. The Supreme Court reversed because there had been no evidence that the individuals knew of the tax liability. Absent such knowledge, tax evasion could not have been one of the objectives of their conspiracy, and the convictions could not stand. In contrast, the convictions of the employers for conspiracy to evade taxes were upheld.

Similarly, in *United States v. Gallishaw*, 428 F.2d 760 (2d Cir. 1970), the defendant was convicted after a trial judge charged the jury that he could be convicted of conspiracy to rob a bank if he had rented a machine gun to another individual "with the knowledge that there was a conspiracy to do something wrong and to use the gun to violate the law." This Court reversed. We said that "at the very least" the government was required to show "that he knew that a bank was to be robbed." We explained that the defendant "had to know what kind of criminal conduct was in fact contemplated." Id. at 763 n.1; *cf. United States v. Calabro*, 467 F.2d 973, 982 (2d Cir. 1972) (supplier of false identification must have known that it would be used in a transaction involving forged bonds in order to be guilty as an aider and abettor; generalized suspicion of illegal use would not suffice). Thus, it is clear that a general agreement to engage in unspecified criminal conduct is insufficient to identify the essential nature of the conspiratorial plan.

Proof of the essential nature of the plan is required because "the gist of the offense remains the agreement, and it is therefore essential to determine what kind of agreement or understanding existed as to each defendant." *United States v. Borelli*, 336 F.2d 376, 384 (2d Cir. 1964). The importance of making this determination cannot be overstated. "Agreement is the essential evil at which the crime of conspiracy is directed" and it "remains the essential element of the crime." *Iannelli v. United States*, 420 U.S. 770, 777 n.10 (1975). "Nobody is liable in conspiracy except for the fair import of the concerted purpose or agreement as he understands it." *United States v. Peoni*, 100 F.2d 401, 403 (2d cir. 1938).

A conspirator's liability for substantive crimes committed by his co-conspirators depends on whether the crimes were committed "in furtherance of the unlawful agreement or conspiracy." *Pinkerton v. United States*, 328 U.S. 640, 645 (1946). Similarly, the admissibility against a defendant of a co-conspirator's declaration depends on whether the declaration was made "during the course and in furtherance of the conspiracy." Fed. R. Evid. 801(d)(2)(E). This determination can be made only after the scope of the agreement has been defined. The question of whether single or multiple conspiracies have been pled or proved depends on the nature of the agreement. *United States v. Dardi*, 330 F.2d 316, 327 (2d Cir.). Because overt acts are acts "to effect the *object* of the conspiracy," 18 U.S.C. § 371 (emphasis added), they are defined by reference to the conspiratorial agreement. *United States v. Bayer*, 331 U.S. 532, 542 (1947). In addition, when questions arise concerning matters such as venue, *Hyde v. United States*, 225 U.S. 347 (1912), or the statute of limitations, *Grunewald v. United States*, 353 U.S. 391, 396-97 (1957), which depend on the formation of the agreement or the occurrence of overt acts, it becomes "crucial" to determine the scope of the conspiratorial agreement. See *Bridges v. United States*, 346 U.S. 209, 224 (1953) (statute of limitations). Finally, the punishment that may be imposed under § 371, for a conspiracy to commit an offense against the United States, depends on whether the "object" of the conspiracy is a felony or a misdemeanor. In order to make this determination, specificity with respect to the "object" of the conspiracy is essential.

It is clear that, under the general rules of conspiracy, Rosenblatt could not have been validly convicted of conspiracy to make false entries on postal records, 18 U.S.C. § 2073, the substantive crime with which Brooks was charged, because he had no knowledge of such a plan; he neither intended nor agreed to commit that offense, or any other offense of which Brooks might have been guilty, e.g., 18 U.S.C. § 641 (embezzlement of public money). The only offenses that Rosenblatt "agreed"[3] to aid and abet were tax evasion, 26 U.S.C. § 7201, and taking kickbacks on government contracts, 18 U.S.C. § 874,[4] but since no one else agreed to commit those offenses, a conviction for conspiracy to commit them could not stand.

* * * *

Accordingly, Rosenblatt's conviction is reversed, and the case is remanded with instructions to dismiss the indictment.

NOTES FROM PENNY:

(1) Didn't Dork and Custer have different understandings of their plan? If so, can we distinguish *Rosenblatt* in some way?

(2) In *United States v. Stavroulakis*, 952 F.2d 686 (2nd cir. 1992), Stavroulakis was convicted of conspiring with Giziakis to violate the "money laundering" statute by attempting to conceal the source of money derived from unlawful activity. Stavroulakis thought the money came from *narcotics*, while Giziakis thought it came from *gambling*. Citing *Rosenblatt*, Stavroulakis argued that he and Giziakis did not agree to the same thing. The court rejected this contention:

> In *Rosenblatt*, we noted that there was no charge or proof that the conspirators intended to commit the same type of fraud on the United States, i.e., Brooks' fraud involved unlawfully obtaining checks, whereas Rosenblatt's fraud involved, for the most part, tax evasion. Thus, there

---

[3] When the word "agree" is surrounded by quotation marks, we are using it in the unilateral sense. See note 2, supra.

[4] By concealing the existence of a check being used in a kickback transaction, Rosenblatt could have been guilty of aiding and abetting the individuals who were taking the kickbacks in violation of 18 U.S.C. § 874. By agreeing to assist, Rosenblatt could have been guilty of conspiracy to commit that offense.

Brooks' "kickback" explanation of the need for laundering two of the checks was an obvious fabrication. Rosenblatt was told that the two payees of the government checks had contracts with the government on which they were getting kickbacks. This makes no sense, for a kickback on a government contract would be unlikely to be paid (1) with a government check, or (2) to the person with the government contract.

could have been no meeting of the minds between the conspirators. Here, defendants were charged with conspiring to commit an offense against the United States. And, in sharp contrast to *Rosenblatt*, the evidence here was overwhelming that Stavroulakis and Giziakis agreed to commit the same offense, albeit with Giziakis having been duped as to an inconsequential detail.

(3) In footnote 2, the court suggested that if it had chosen to follow the Model Penal Code definition of conspiracy (which it calls a "unilateral" formulation), it would have upheld Rabbi Rosenblatt's conviction. How so? What does "unilateral" mean? Take a look at the Model Penal Code section, in the Appendix.

(4) In *U.S. v. Palmer*, 203 F.3d 55 (1st Cir. 1999):

> Defendant was charged with four counts of conspiring with Talbot Curtin to rob three convenience stores in southern New Hampshire. * * * *

> Palmer's defense is straight forward: there was no evidence of any meeting of the minds to rob the stores listed in the conspiracy counts. Curtin insisted that they rob only stores that were serviced by a woman and had no customers at the time of the robbery. Defendant argues that if there was any agreement it was that the stores named in the conspiracy counts were not to be robbed because at the time they were surveilled, they did not meet Curtin's conditions for committing a robbery.

> Logical as this contention may seem, it founders on the rocks of legal precedent holding that a condition imposed by the conspirators upon the carrying out of a conspiracy does not negate the conspiracy.

> The evidence as to Count One was that on February 4, 1998, defendant drove Curtin to the described Mobil station convenience store. The conspirators had agreed to rob the store if there was only a female clerk on the premises. Curtin was to enter the store and take the money if this condition was met. The store was not robbed because the person in charge was a male.

> The same circumstances prevailed as to Count Two. On February 4, 1998 — the same day — defendant drove Curtin to the Shell station described in the count with the intent that Curtin would rob it, if his predetermined conditions were met. Once again, Curtin found a male running the store. It was, therefore, not robbed.

> Count Four is a reprise of Count One, the only difference being the date of the alleged conspiracy — February 7, 1998 — three days later.

> The Count Five conspiracy has a slightly different factual twist. Defendant drove Curtin to Jeannotte's Market, the store described in the count. Curtin decided, based on the number of cars parked in front of the store, that there were too many people present for the robbery to be carried out.

> In answer to a question during his interrogation by the police, defendant said that it upset him that Curtin insisted on robbing only stores clerked by

a woman. "Because I feel that if you're going to do a robbery that [sic] what's the difference male or female? It's to be, end result is the same. You're stealing money."

The gist of conspiracy is an agreement to disobey or to disregard the law. The government must prove an intent to agree and an intent to commit the substantive offense. A conspiracy may be established through circumstantial evidence, and the government need only demonstrate a tacit understanding between the conspirators to prove its case. Because the essence of a conspiracy is an agreement, a failure to achieve the objective, even if factually impossible, is not a defense.

Judge Posner in *United States v. Podolsky*, 798 F.2d 177 (7th cir. 1986), pointed out:

> Every conspiracy is conditional to some extent, for no one agrees to go through with an agreement no matter what. Conditions, express or implied, do not make a contract unenforceable; they merely define the circumstances in which a party can avoid having to perform his contractual obligation; they presuppose rather than nullify the obligation.

The doctrine that a condition made by the conspirators cannot nullify the underlying conspiracy is recognized and applied across the federal circuits. And defendant has cited no cases to the contrary.

The test for conditional conspiratorial liability should focus on the likelihood that the condition precedent will be fulfilled. Liability should attach if the defendant reasonably believed that the conditions would obtain. In this case, one factor suggesting such reasonable belief is the fact that the conditions *were* met in two other cases, and when they were met, the defendants carried out the robberies.

First, defendant himself did not think it should make any difference whether the stores to be robbed were serviced by a woman or a man. If he were the one committing the robbery instead of his partner, he might not have followed Curtin's "woman only" rule. In this connection it is to be noted that in Curtin's statement to the police, he claimed that defendant actually committed the robberies and that he (Curtin) drove the getaway vehicle.

Moreover, whether or not Curtin's rule was followed could depend upon how badly the conspirators needed drugs. In the parlance of the streets, the conspirators were a couple of "junkies" hooked on heroin and crack-cocaine. They conspired to rob the stores to feed their habits. They did not follow normal patterns of behavior. The conditions were self-imposed and could be ignored by either one of the conspirators or both at their whim or caprice. The condition was not a bar to the robbers, it was a self-imposed restraint that could easily be negated.

UNITED STATES v. ESCOBAR DeBRIGHT
U.S. Court of Appeals, 9th Circuit
742 F.2d 1196 (1984)

REINHARDT, CIRCUIT JUDGE:

Hilda Escobar de Bright was charged on counts of conspiring to import heroin (Count One), illegally importing heroin (Count Two), conspiring to possess heroin with intent to distribute (Count Three), and illegally possessing heroin with intent to distribute (Count Four). She was convicted on all four counts and sentenced to concurrent six-year sentences. In Counts One and Three, Escobar de Bright was charged with conspiring with Ernesto Ayala-Zarate, Hector Ayala-Zarate, Ana Maria Zarate de Ayala, and others to import heroin in violation of 21 U.S.C. §§ 952(a), 960(a)(1) and to possess heroin with intent to distribute in violation of 21 U.S.C. § 841(a)(1).

In April 1981, Ernesto Ayala-Zarate contacted Manny Banda, a paid informant for the Drug Enforcement Administration, about the purchase of heroin. Apparently, in that and a later conversation, Ernesto gave Banda the defendant's telephone number — one time so that Banda might approach Ernesto's brother, Hector, who is Escobar de Bright's son-in-law, and one time so that Banda might contact the defendant and solicit her assistance in importing heroin from Mexico. Banda arranged to meet the defendant and, after meeting her, persuaded her to drive immediately to Mexico. At trial, the defendant testified that she drove to Mexico only because she felt threatened by Banda and that she did not know that he planned to import heroin. After entering Mexico, she drove back across the border where her 17-year old son, Francisco, entered the automobile. Her car was later stopped by United States Customs Patrol officers. The officers searched Francisco and discovered four ounces of heroin.

Subsequently, Escobar de Bright and Ernesto and Hector Ayala-Zarate were named in the four count indictment. The jury found the defendant guilty on all four counts.

The defendant challenges her conspiracy conviction. She claims that the district court erred in refusing to instruct the jury that she could not be found guilty of conspiracy if the jury determined that she "conspired" only with the government agent, Manny Banda. In response, the government argues that the jury instructions fully informed the jury of the law of conspiracy. We agree with the defendant.

"A defendant is entitled to an instruction concerning his theory of the case if it is supported by law and has some foundation in the evidence." *United States v. Winn*, 577 F.2d 86, 90 (9th Cir. 1978) (emphasis added). * * * * We have emphasized that failure to give such a requested instruction is reversible error.

In *Sears v. United States*, 343 F.2d 139, 142 (5th Cir. 1965), the Fifth Circuit Court of Appeals established the rule that, "as it takes two to conspire, there can be no indictable conspiracy with a government informer who secretly intends to frustrate the conspiracy." The Fifth Circuit held that, because the jury could have concluded from the evidence that the defendant conspired only with the government agent, the district court erred in failing to instruct the jury that it could find the defendant guilty of conspiracy only if it determined that he acted with the knowledge that persons other than the government agent were also involved in the illegal scheme. Accordingly, the Fifth Circuit reversed the defendant's conviction. * * * *

Strong considerations support the adoption of the *Sears* rule. A conspiracy is defined as an agreement between two or more people to commit an unlawful act. See, e.g., *Iannelli v. United States*, 420 U.S. 770, 777 (1975). There is neither a true agreement nor a meeting of minds when an individual "conspires" to violate the law with only one other person and that person is a government agent. The principle was explained concisely a quarter of a century ago:

> Since the act of agreeing is a group act, unless at least two people commit it, no one does. *When one of two persons merely pretends to agree, the other party, whatever he may believe, is in fact not conspiring with anyone.* Although he may possess the requisite criminal intent, there has been no criminal act. [*Developments in the Law — Criminal Conspiracy*, 72 Harv. L. Rev. 920, 926 (1959) (emphasis added)]

In short, the formal requirements of the crime of conspiracy have not been met unless an individual conspires with at least one bona fide co-conspirator.

The rationale behind making conspiracy a crime also supports the *Sears* rule. Criminal conspiracy is an offense separate from the actual criminal act because of the perception "that collective action toward an antisocial end involves a greater risk to society than individual action toward the same end." *Developments, supra*, at 923-24; see W. LaFave & A. Scott, *Criminal Law* at 459-60 (1972). In part, this view is based on the perception that group activity increases the likelihood of success of the criminal act and of future criminal activity by members of the group, and is difficult for law enforcement officers to detect:

> For two or more to confederate and combine together to commit or cause to be committed a breach of the criminal laws, is an offense of the gravest character, sometimes quite outweighing, in injury to the public, the mere commission of the contemplated crime. It involves deliberate plotting to subvert the laws, educating and preparing the conspirators for further and habitual criminal practices. And it is characterized by secrecy, rendering it difficult of detection, requiring more time for its discovery, and adding to the importance of punishing it when discovered. [*United States v. Rabinowich*, 238 U.S. 78, 88 (1915)]

Such dangers, however, are non-existent when a person "conspires" only with a government agent. There is no continuing criminal enterprise and ordinarily no inculcation of criminal knowledge and practices. Preventive intervention by law enforcement officers also is not a significant problem in such circumstances. The agent, as part of the "conspiracy," is quite capable of monitoring the situation in order to prevent the completion of the contemplated criminal plan; in short, no cloak of secrecy surrounds any agreement to commit the criminal acts.

Finally, the *Sears* rule responds to the same concern that underlies the entrapment defense: the legitimate law enforcement function of crime prevention "does not include the manufacturing of crime." *Sherman v. United States*, 356 U.S. 369, 372 (1958). Allowing a government agent to form a conspiracy with only one other party would create the potential for law enforcement officers to "manufacture" conspiracies when none would exist absent the government's presence.

We find the reasons underlying the *Sears* rule to be compelling and therefore adopt it here. Our inquiry, however, is not finished. Because we have decided that the defendant's requested instruction was supported by law, we now must decide whether there was "some foundation in the evidence" to support giving a *Sears* instruction in this case.

Here, the defendant's testimony is sufficient to support the giving of the requested instruction. Escobar de Bright testified that she did not know why Banda wanted her to go to Mexico but that, because she feared for her own and her son's safety, she felt coerced by him into going; the concern for her safety was based at least in part, she said, on her belief that Banda "might be wearing a gun." She also testified that Banda "commanded" her son, Francisco, to go to Mexico. This testimony provides some support for Escobar de Bright's theory that she "conspired" only with the government agent Banda and did so only after he threatened her.[7]

In addition, there is testimony suggesting that Escobar de Bright would not have conspired with members of either of the Ayala-Zarate families. For example, her husband, Lorring G. Bright, testified that there was "bad blood" between Hector Ayala-Zarate and himself. In fact, Bright testified that he had previously shot Hector Ayala-Zarate. He also testified that his wife did not "get along" with Hector and that she often argued with Hector about her daughter (Hector's wife) and granddaughter. The defendant also testified to that effect. Finally, both the defendant and her husband testified that they had never met or spoken with another alleged co-conspirator, Anna Maria Zarate de Ayala; in addition, there is no evidence suggesting that either of them had ever met Ernesto Ayala-Zarate.

We conclude that there was "some foundation in the evidence" to support the defendant's theory that she conspired only with a government agent. After carefully considering the instructions as a whole, we also must conclude that the jury could have followed those instructions and convicted the defendants of conspiracy even if it concluded that she had conspired only with the government agent. Accordingly, the district court erred in failing to give the jury the defendant's instruction. * * * *

The conspiracy convictions under Counts One and Three of the indictment are reversed and remanded.

---

[7] Despite her testimony, the defendant did not request any instruction as to a defense of duress or coercion.

NOTES FROM PENNY:

(1) If Escobar deBright *believed* that Banda was *not* a government agent, *why shouldn't* she be punished for conspiracy? Didn't she pose a threat to society that the law of conspiracy is meant to deter?

(2) If — as the court holds — the fact that Banda was a government agent means that defendant could not conspire with him, is there *another* "common law" crime she has committed?

(3) How does this opinion affect our case against Dork? Can we distinguish it?

(4) Under the common law, if all other co-conspirators were acquitted, the one remaining alleged co-conspirator must also be acquitted. Some states still follow this "rule of consistency." See, e.g., *Heckstall v. State*, 120 Md.App. 621 (1998). But not all. In *People v. Palmer*, 24 Cal.4th 856 (2001), the court held:

> We conclude that the rule of consistency is a vestige of the past with no continuing validity. Many reasons may explain apparently inconsistent verdicts: lenience, compromise, differing evidence as to different defendants, or, possibly, that two juries simply viewed similar evidence differently. If substantial evidence supports a jury verdict as to one defendant, that verdict may stand despite an apparently inconsistent verdict as to another defendant. * * * *

> The general rationale behind the rule has been that one may not conspire with himself. It does take at least two to conspire. But to go from this irrefutable proposition to a rule requiring reversal of the inconsistent verdict is a precipitous leap. We conclude that we may accept inconsistent verdicts. Consistent verdicts are unrequired in joint trials for conspiracy: where all but one of the charged conspirators are acquitted, the verdict against the one can stand.

> Our criminal justice system, which permits a conviction only if the jury unanimously finds beyond a reasonable doubt that a defendant is guilty of the particular charge, gives the defendant the benefit of the doubt. Moreover, a jury clearly has the unreviewable *power*, if not the right, to acquit whatever the evidence. An inevitable result of this system, and one that society accepts in its quest to avoid convicting the innocent, is that some criminal defendants who are guilty will be found not guilty. This circumstance does not, however, mean that if one person receives lenient treatment from the system, all must. It is always possible for a jury to exercise lenity and acquit some of the defendants while convicting others who are in fact no more guilty, and when this happens the convicted defendants have no remedy. Such incongruities are built into the American system of criminal justice and can have no weight in our decision whether to reverse the denial of a new trial to the present defendants. Here, for example, Palmer's jury may have shown sympathy or lenience because he was 15 years old at the time of the crimes. The other jury may have felt no such sympathy for the 29-year-old Price. Price's verdict must stand or fall on its own merit, not in comparison to Palmer's.

UNITED STATES v. BROWN
U.S. Court of Appeals, 2nd Circuit
776 F.2d 397 (1985)

FRIENDLY, CIRCUIT JUDGE:

This is another case where the federal narcotics laws have been invoked with respect to the New York City Police Department's Operation Pressure Point in Harlem. Here Officer William Grimball, acting under cover as an addict, procured a "joint" of heroin, and a backup team promptly pounced on those thought to have been involved in the sale.

The indictment, in the District Court for the Southern District of New York, contained two counts. Count One charged appellant Ronald Brown and a codefendant, Gregory Valentine, with conspiring to distribute and to possess with intent to distribute heroin in violation of 21 U.S.C. § 846. Count Two charged them with distribution of heroin in violation of 21 U.S.C. §§ 812, 841(a)(1), 841(b)(1)(A), and 18 U.S.C. § 2. After a three day trial, the jury convicted Brown on Count One but was unable to reach a verdict on Count Two. After denying motions for entry of judgment of acquittal or a new trial, the judge suspended imposition of sentence on Count One and placed Brown on three years' probation.

Officer Grimball was the Government's principal witness. He testified that early in the evening of October 9, 1984, he approached Gregory Valentine on the corner of 115th Street and Eighth Avenue and asked him for a joint of "D".[2] Valentine asked Grimball whom he knew around the street. Grimball asked if Valentine knew Scott. He did not. Brown "came up" and Valentine said, "He wants a joint, but I don't know him." Brown looked at Grimball and said, "He looks okay to me." Valentine then said, "Okay. But I am going to leave it somewhere and you [meaning Officer Grimball] can pick it up." Brown interjected,"You don't have to do that. Just go and get it for him. He looks all right to me." After looking again at Grimball, Brown said, "He looks all right to me" and "I will wait right here."

Valentine then said, "Okay. Come on with me around to the hotel." Grimball followed him to 300 West 116th Street, where Valentine instructed him, "Sit on the black car and give me a few minutes to go up and get it." Valentine requested and received $40, which had been prerecorded, and then said, "You are going to take care of me for doing this for you, throw some dollars my way?," to which Grimball responded, "Yeah."

Valentine then entered the hotel and shortly returned. The two went back to 115th Street and Eighth Avenue, where Valentine placed a cigarette box on the hood of a blue car. Grimball picked up the cigarette box and found a glassine envelope containing white powder, stipulated to be heroin. Grimball placed $5 of prerecorded buy money in the cigarette box, which he replaced on the hood. Valentine picked up the box and removed the $5. Grimball returned to his car and made a radio transmission to the backup field team that "the buy had went down"

---

[2] The officer explained that a "joint" is a street term for a Harlem quarter, or $40 worth of heroin, and that "D" is a street term for heroin.

and informed them of the locations of the persons involved. Brown and Valentine were arrested. Valentine was found to possess two glassine envelopes of heroin and the $5 of prerecorded money. Brown was in possession of $31 of his own money; no drugs or contraband were found on him. The $40 of marked buy money was not recovered, and no arrests were made at the hotel.

The Government sought to qualify Officer Grimball as an expert on the bases that he had made over 30 street buys of small quantities of cocaine in Harlem, had received two 8-1/2 hours seminars at the Organized Crime Control Bureau "in respect to street value of drugs, safety, integrity," had once been assigned to the Manhattan North Narcotics Division where he had informal seminars with undercover detectives experienced in making street buys in Harlem target area, and had participated in "ghost operations," where he as undercover would be placed "on the set" and would observe an experienced undercover detective in an actual buy operation.

The judge having ruled him to be qualified as an expert, he testified that the typical drug buy in the Harlem area involved two to five people. As a result of frequent police sweeps, Harlem drug dealers were becoming so cautious that they employed "people who act as steerers and the steerer's responsibility is basically to determine whether of not you are actually an addict or a user of heroin and they are also used to screen you to see if there is any possibility of you being a cop looking for a bulge or some indication that would give them that you are not actually an addict. And a lot of the responsibility relies [sic] on them to determine whether or not the drug buy is going to go down or not."

Officer Grimball was then allowed, over a general objection, to testify that based on his experience as an undercover agent he would describe the role that Ronald Brown played in the transaction as that of a steerer. When asked why, he testified, again over a general objection, "Because I believe that if it wasn't for his approval, the buy would not have gone down."

We deal first with appellant's contention that all the testimony given by Grimball as an expert should have been excluded because Grimball was unqualified. In reviewing the district court's decision to treat Grimball as an expert, we note that the trial judge has broad discretion in the matter of the admission or exclusion of expert evidence, and his action is to be sustained unless manifestly erroneous. The decision that Grimball possessed sufficient knowledge and experience was by no means manifestly erroneous. * * * * While Grimball was scarcely a Chief Superintendent Maigret, he knew a good deal more about street narcotics deal in Harlem that did the jurors, who would consequently be "assisted" by his description of the terms and practices generally used in such sales. For that reason we cannot characterize as "manifestly erroneous" the judge's conclusion that testimony from Grimball that street drug sales in Harlem generally involved the use of a steerer, at least after the inauguration of Operation Pressure Point, would "assist the trier of the fact to understand the evidence or to determine a fact in issue." * * * *

In considering the sufficiency of the evidence, we begin with some preliminary observations. One is that, in testing sufficiency, "the relevant question is whether, after viewing the evidence in the light most favorable to the prosecution, *any* rational trier of fact could have found the essential elements of the crime beyond a reasonable doubt." *Jackson v. Virginia*, 443 U.S. 307, 319 (1979). * * * * *Jackson's* emphasis on "any," while surely not going so far as to excise "rational," must be taken as an admonition to appellate judges not to reverse convictions because they would not have found the elements of the crime to have been proved beyond a reasonable doubt when other rational beings might do so.

The second observation is that since the jury convicted on the conspiracy count alone, the evidence must permit a reasonable juror to be convinced beyond a reasonable doubt not simply that Brown had aided and abetted the drug sale but that he had agreed to do so. *United States v. Borelli*, 336 F.2d 376, 384 (2nd cir. 1964). On the other hand, the jury's failure to agree on the aiding and abetting charge does not operate against the Government; even an acquittal on that count would not have done so. *Dunn v. United States*, 284 U.S. 390 (1932) (Holmes, J.). * * * *8

A review of the evidence against Brown convinces us that it was sufficient, even without Grimball's characterization of Brown as a steerer, although barely so. Although Brown's mere presence at the scene of the crime and his knowledge that a crime was being committed would not have been sufficient to establish Brown's knowing participation in the conspiracy, the proof went considerably beyond that. Brown was not simply standing around while the exchanges between Officer Grimball and Valentine occurred. He came on the scene shortly after these began and Valentine immediately explained the situation to him. Brown then conferred his seal of approval on Grimball, a most unlikely event unless there was an established relationship between Brown and Valentine. Finally, Brown took upon himself the serious responsibility of telling Valentine to desist from his plan to reduce the risks by not handing the heroin directly to Grimball. A rational mind could take this a bespeaking the authority to command, or at least to persuade. Brown's remark, "Just go and get it for him," permits inferences that Brown knew where the heroin was to be gotten, that he knew that Valentine knew this, and that Brown and Valentine had engaged in such a transaction before.

The mere fact that these inferences were not ineluctable does not mean that they were insufficient to convince a reasonable juror beyond a reasonable doubt. Moreover, as we said in *United States v. Geaney*, 417 F.2d 1116, 1121 (2nd Cir. 1969), "pieces of evidence must be viewed not in isolation but in conjunction." When we add to the inferences that can be reasonably drawn from the facts to which Grimball testified the portion of his expert testimony about the use of steerers in street sales of narcotics, which was clearly unobjectionable once Grimball's qualifications were established, we conclude that the Government offered sufficient evidence, apart from Grimball's opinion that Brown was a steerer, for a reasonable juror to be satisfied beyond a reasonable doubt not only that Brown has acted as a

---

8 This scarcely seems to be the case for reconsidering these and many other holdings to the same effect, as the dissent appears to propose in note 2, even if we had the power to do so. Here the jury did not acquit on the substantive count but simply disagreed. Even the dissent in Dunn did not assert that this kind of inconsistency would impair a verdict. Moreover, there was no true inconsistency here. The line between conspiring and aiding and abetting is thin; this jury could rationally be satisfied of the former although, particularly in view of the lack of evidence directly linking Brown with the narcotics, it could not reach a verdict as to the latter.

steerer but that he had agreed to do so.[10]

Affirmed.

OAKES, CIRCUIT JUDGE (dissenting):

While it is true that this is another $40 narcotics case, it is also a conspiracy case, and by the majority's own admission one resting on "barely" sufficient evidence. But evidence of what? An agreement — a "continuous and conscious union of wills upon a common undertaking," in the words of Note, *Developments in the Law — Criminal Conspiracy*, 72 Harv. L. Rev. 920, 926 (1959)? Not unless an inference that Brown agreed to act as a "steerer" may be drawn from the fact that he said to Valentine (three times) that Grimball "looks okay [all right] to me," as well as "just go and get it for him." And the only way that inference may be drawn so as to prove guilt beyond a reasonable doubt is, in my view, with assistance from the "expert" testimony of the ubiquitous Officer Grimball.

It could not be drawn from Brown's possession, constructive or otherwise, of narcotics or narcotics paraphernalia, his sharing in the proceeds of the street sale, his conversations with others, or even some hearsay evidence as to his "prior arrangements" with Valentine of "an established working relationship between Brown and Valentine," which are inferences that the majority believes may reasonably be drawn and which it draws so as to distinguish *United States v. Tyler*, 758 F.2d 66 (2d Cir. 1985). There is not a shred of evidence of Brown's "stake in the outcome," *United States v. Falcone*, 109 F.2d 579, 580 (2d Cir.), aff'd, 311 U.S. 205 (1940); indeed, Brown was apprehended after leaving the area of the crime with only thirty-one of his own dollars in his pocket, and no drugs or other contraband. He did not even stay around for another Valentine sale, though the majority infers, speculatively, that Brown and Valentine had engaged in "such a transaction before."

When, as the majority concedes, numerous other inferences could be drawn from the few words of conversation in which Brown is said to have engaged, I cannot believe that there is proof of conspiracy, or Brown's membership in it,

---

[10] We do not read *United States v. Tyler*, 758 F.2d 66 (2 Cir. 1985), as being to the contrary. The court read the evidence as showing "no more than Tyler helped a willing buyer find a willing seller." Since there was no basis for inferring a prior contact between Tyler, the introducer, and Bennett, the seller, Tyler could properly be convicted only as an aider or abettor, not as a conspirator. Here a jury could reasonably infer prior arrangements or an established working relationship between Brown and Valentine.

Chief Judge Motley's opinion in *United States v. Jones*, 605 F. Supp. 513, also relied upon by Brown, is readily distinguishable. There was insufficient evidence for a jury to conclude beyond a reasonable doubt that Jones, the counterpart of Brown in that case, even knew that a narcotics transaction was going on. By contrast, Brown's conversation with Valentine in the presence of Grimball establishes that he knew precisely what the transaction was.

Finally, the facts in *United States v. Cepeda*, 768 F.2d 1515 (2 Cir. 1985) (Oakes, J.), relied upon by the dissent, are not analogous to the situation here. In *Cepeda*, there was no evidence that there had been a sale, or that anyone other than the defendant was involved in the transaction. Thus, two elements of the charged conspiracy were called into question - the agreement with other persons and the intent to distribute. Here, there is no question that a sale occurred, and it is clear that Brown and at least one other person, Valentine, participated in the transaction. Thus, the only further inference required for a conviction — that Brown's participation was pursuant to an agreement with Valentine, with someone else, or with both — is much stronger.

beyond a reasonable doubt, unless one gives the Court's emphasis on the word "any" — "any rational trier of fact" — such weight that the word "rational" receives little or no significance at all. Until now, as we said in *United States v. Cepeda*, 768 F.2d 1515 (2d Cir. 1985), "the court has insisted on proof, whether or not by circumstantial evidence, of a specific agreement to deal."

This case may be unique. It, like *Cepeda*, supports Justice Jackson's reference to the history of the law of conspiracy as exemplifying, in Cardozo's phrase, the "tendency of a principle to expand itself to the limits of its logic." *Krulewitch v. United States*, 336 U.S. 440, 445 (1949) (Jackson, J., concurring) But it also illustrates Cardozo's phrase at work in two other respects — the use of "expert" testimony to prove guilt and the proposition that inconsistent verdicts on different counts are immaterial. Both are carried here to their threads in the case of the street sale to Officer Grimball seems to me, again to borrow a phrase from Justice Jackson's *Krulewitch* concurrence, to "constitute a serious threat to fairness in our administration of justice." *Id.* at 446. If today we uphold a conspiracy to sell narcotics on the street, on this kind and amount of evidence, what conspiracies might we approve tomorrow? The majority opinion will come back to haunt us, I fear.

On the use of Officer Grimball's expert testimony, I note the following. A "steerer" is presumably one who leads buyers of narcotics to suppliers. Brown's alleged role, however, was either to instruct Valentine, who received a $5 tip for his role as "steerer" to the hotel supplier (although Grimball did testify that suppliers as well as steerers occasionally ask for "tips"), or to serve as an evaluator of a buyer's bona fides. In light of Grimball's limited undercover experience, his broader definition of a "steerer" so as to encompass Brown's role, whatever that role was, lacks the ring of expertise. * * * * And without his "expert" testimony as to Brown's role, I do not believe that the evidence was sufficient to sustain a conviction, and therefore its admission was not harmless error.

As for the rule that "each count in an indictment is regarded as if it was a separate indictment," *Dunn v. United States*, 284 U.S. 390, 393 (1932) so that acquittal on a substantive count is not fatal to a conviction for conspiracy, the verdicts in this case carry the rule to the ultimate extreme. Here the only overt act attributed in the indictment to Brown was the same conversation with Valentine that grounded the substantive charge of aiding and abetting, a charge on which Brown was acquitted. The case appears to me to be the very kind of compromise verdict foreseen by Judge Learned Hand in *Steckler v. United States*, 7 F.2d 59 (2d Cir. 1925), and by Justice Holmes in *Dunn*, 284 U.S. at 394. It may be that, in a given case, see e.g., *Tyler*, 758 F.2d at 71-72, evidence may support a conviction on an aiding and abetting count without supporting a conviction on a conspiracy count. But it is hard to see how, in the case of a completed sale, there can be a conviction of conspiracy but not of aiding and abetting, especially when there is no evidence of a "stake in the outcome."

Although, according to the majority, the admission of "expert" testimony is "rather offensive," the evidence was "sufficient, although barely so," and the verdict is both inconsistent and very probably a compromise, the court permits this conspiracy conviction to stand. I fear that it thereby promotes the crime of conspiracy — "that darling of the modern prosecutor's nursery," *Harrison v. United States*, 7 F.2d 259, 263 (2d Cir. 1925) (L. Hand, J.) — to a role beyond that contemplated even by Sgt. Hawkins of Pleas of the Crown fame. See Note, *Developments in the Law — Criminal Conspiracy, supra*, at 923 & n.14; P. Winfield, *The Chief Sources of English Legal History* 325-26 (1925). Precisely because this is another $40 narcotics case, I would draw the line. This case effectively permits prosecution of everyone connected with a street sale of narcotics to be prosecuted on two counts - a conspiracy as well as a substantive charge. And evidence showing no more than that a defendant was probably aware that a narcotics deal was about to occur will support a conspiracy conviction, our previous cases to the contrary notwithstanding.

Accordingly, I dissent.

NOTES FROM PENNY:

1. Can defense counsel distinguish *Brown* from our case?

2. In *U.S. v. Iriarte-Ortega*, 113 F.3d 1022 (9th Cir. 1997), defendant drove a truck full of marijuana into the United States. He was convicted of conspiring with a driver of another truck to import marijuana. On appeal, he argued that the evidence was insufficient to show that he made an agreement with the other driver. The appellate court disagreed:

> Coordination between conspirators is strong circumstantial proof of agreement; as the degree of coordination between conspirators rises, the likelihood that their actions were driven by an agreement increases. Moreover, a jury may infer the existence of an agreement if there be concert of action, all the parties working together understandingly, with a single design for the accomplishment of a common purpose.

> In this case, a jury could reasonably have inferred a conspiratorial agreement from the defendants' long list of coordinated actions. Two pickup trucks of identical make and model — one gray with a white camper shell, one white with a gray shell — met behind a house south of the border. They drove from behind the house to a location near the border, where they stopped and waited together. Someone placed a ramp across a ditch positioned to prevent vehicles from crossing, and the trucks proceeded into the United States, the white truck preceding the gray truck by about a minute. The trucks took a dirt road to Highway 80 eastbound; proceeded north on Carrizo road; and turned onto Interstate 8 westbound. They contained roughly equal amounts of marijuana in packages as uniform as McDonald's french fries. The interchangeable camper shells were secured with matching hardware.

> Iriarte seems to argue that it was all just a big coincidence, but the jury was entitled to conclude otherwise. Indeed, it's hard to see what other conclusion a rational jury might have reached. There was, therefore, more than sufficient evidence to support Iriarte's conspiracy conviction.

3. In *U.S. v. Garcia*, 151 F.3d 1243 (9th Cir. 1998), at a party, a fight broke out between members of two rival gangs — the Crips and the Bloods. At some point, guns were fired. Garcia (a Blood) was convicted of conspiracy to assault with a dangerous weapon. The court found no evidence that Garcia agreed with any other Blood to fire a weapon. But was his gang membership enough to show an *implied* agreement to shoot? The court stated:

> Given that circumstantial evidence fails to suggest the existence of an agreement, we are left only with gang membership as proof that Garcia conspired with fellow Bloods to shoot the three named individuals. The government points to expert testimony at the trial by a local gang unit detective, who stated that generally gang members have a "basic agreement" to back one another up in fights, an agreement which requires no advance planning or coordination. This testimony, which at most establishes one of the characteristics of gangs but not a specific objective of a particular gang — let alone a specific agreement on the part of its members to accomplish an illegal objective — is insufficient to provide proof of a conspiracy to commit assault or other illegal acts.

> Recent authority in this circuit establishes that "membership in a gang cannot serve as proof of intent, or of the facilitation, advice, aid, promotion, encouragement or instigation needed to establish aiding and abetting." *Mitchell v. Prunty*, 107 F.3d 1337, 1342 (9th cir. 1997), *overruled in part on other grounds, Santamaria v. Horsley, 133 F.3d 1242 (9th cir. 1998)*. In overturning the state conviction of a gang member that rested on the theory that the defendant aided and abetted a murder by "fanning the fires of gang warfare," the *Mitchell* opinion expressed concern that allowing a conviction on this basis would "smack of guilt by association." The same concern is implicated when a conspiracy conviction is based on evidence that an individual is affiliated with a gang which has a general rivalry with other gangs, and that this rivalry sometimes escalates into violent confrontations.

> The *Mitchell* court reasoned that the conviction in that case necessarily rested on the faulty assumption that gang members typically act in a concerted fashion. Such an assumption would be particularly inappropriate here. Acts of provocation such as "talking smack" or bumping into rival gang members certainly does not prove a high level of planning or coordination. Rather, it may be fairly typical behavior in a situation in which individuals who belong to rival gangs attend the same events. At most, it indicates that members of a particular gang may be looking for trouble, or ready to fight. It does not demonstrate a coordinated effort with a specific illegal objective in mind. The fact that gang members attend a function armed with weapons may prove that they are prepared for violence, but without other evidence it does not establish that they have made plans to initiate it. And the fact that more than one member of the Bloods was shooting at rival gang members also does not prove a prearrangement — the Crips, too, were able to pull out their guns almost immediately, suggesting that readiness for a gunfight requires no prior agreement. Such readiness may be a sad commentary on the state of mind

of many of the nation's youth, but it is not indicative of a criminal conspiracy.

Finally, as the *Mitchell* panel warned, allowing gang membership to serve as evidence of aiding and abetting "would invite absurd results. Any gang member could be held liable for any other gang member's act at any time so long as the act was predicated on 'the common purpose of "fighting the enemy." Similarly, allowing a general agreement among gang members to back each other up to serve as sufficient evidence of a conspiracy would mean that any time more than one gang member was involved in a fight it would constitute an act in furtherance of the conspiracy and all gang members could be held criminally responsible — whether they participated in or had knowledge of the particular criminal act, and whether or not they were present when the act occurred. Indeed, were we to accept "fighting the enemy" as an illegal objective, all gang members would probably be subject to felony prosecutions sooner rather than later, even though they had never personally committed an improper act. This is contrary to fundamental principles of our justice system. There can be no conviction for guilt by association.

Because of these concerns, evidence of gang membership cannot itself prove that an individual has entered a criminal agreement to attack members of rival gangs.

SECTION B   THE INTENT

Although the crime of conspiracy is "predominantly mental in composition," there has nonetheless always existed considerable confusion and uncertainty about precisely what mental state is required for this crime. * * * * At the outset, it is useful to note that there are really two intents required for the crime of conspiracy. Every conspiracy involves an agreement, so it must be established that the several parties intended to agree. But such an intent is "without moral content," and thus it is also necessary to determine what objective the parties intended to achieve by their agreement. Only if there is a common purpose to attain an objective covered by the law of conspiracy is there liability.

LaFave & Scott, *Criminal Law* (West)

The *agreement* is the *actus reus* of conspiracy. The *mens rea* is the intent to commit the crime agreed upon. Usually, this poses no problem: once the agreement is proved, the terms of the agreement will often establish the intent to commit the crime. If the prosecutor proves that Dan said to Don, "Let's rob the Wells Fargo bank" and Don replied "OK", this is evidence not only of their agreement, but also of their intent to rob a bank.

But sometimes proving the intent of each party is not so easy.

Suppose Dan fires a gun at Vic's head, killing him. At Dan's murder trial, Dan does not testify, and there is no evidence that Dan told anyone anything regarding his intent. May the jury infer that Dan *intended* to kill Vic? Of course. It is "hornbook law" that one intends the natural and probable consequences of his acts. Everyone knows that firing a gun at someone's head is likely to kill, and it is fair to infer that Dan knew this too.

But suppose that Dan bought the gun at Guy's Gun Shoppe, and Dan said to Guy, "I plan to use this gun to kill Vic." There seems to be an agreement, of sorts, as a sale is an agreement ("You pay me $50, and give you the gun.") We know what *Dan* intended (to use the gun to kill Vic), but what did *Guy* intend? Assuming Guy knew that Dan was serious (and not just kidding around), the "natural and probable consequence" of Guy's act is the death of Vic. Therefore, it is fair to infer that Guy *intended* that Vic be killed. Or is it? Suppose Guy testifies, "I'm in the business of selling guns, not killing people. Sure, I knew that Dan would use the gun to kill Vic, but that was no concern of mine. I had nothing against Vic. All I *intended* was to get the 50 bucks!" Guy is greedy and callous, but is he guilty of conspiracy to commit murder? And if Guy is guilty, what about Sue, who sold Dan gas for his car, after Dan told her, "Fill 'er up, Sue. I'm driving over to kill Vic"? Or Sam, who runs a hot-dog stand — "Two dogs with mustard, Sam. I need lots of energy to kill Vic!" Should the law of conspiracy be used to punish merchants who supply a criminal's needs?

PROBLEM 19B

To: My law clerk

From: Deputy District Attorney Nancy Nicely

I am trying to build up a case against Dan Dip, who is a local kingpin in the numbers racket and cocaine trade in San Francisco. (His numbers game involves taking bets on the last 3 numbers of the total number of stocks sold on the New York Stock Exchange the day before. This is considered an illegal lottery.) I need people who will testify against him, but people are afraid to do so out of fear of retaliation. I think I can pressure Alice Ames, Bart Boyle, and Carl Cole to testify if can bring some charges against *them*, and then drop or reduce the charges in exchange for their testifying against Dip. Based on the attached police report, I would like to charge Ames with conspiracy to run a lottery, Boyle with conspiracy to sell cocaine, and Cole with conspiracy to commit first degree murder. I will not, however, file charges against these people unless the law supports such charges. Please read the attached police report and authorities, and let me know if I have a legitimate case against any of these people for conspiracy.

Police Report

I have been investigating the activities of Dan Dip, whom we suspect is heavily involved in the numbers game and selling cocaine, and is a suspect in the murder of Ed Egan. Yesterday, I followed Dip and interviewed some people he contacted.

In the morning, Dip went into Ames Stationary Store. After he left, I spoke to Ames. She said that, "Dip just bought some pencils and small notepads which he uses to record bets and give receipts in his numbers game. He comes in about once a week to buy this stuff, and spends between $10 and $20 each time. I like him. Sometimes I place a bet with him, and I've given him the names of a couple of my friends who might be interested in placing bets."

Dip later went into Boyle's Toy Store. When he left, Boyle told me that "Dip just bought 100 balloons, for $18.00. He puts cocaine in them, to sell to his customers. He comes in here every week or so, and he accounts for about half of my balloon sales. Because he buys so many, I give him a 10% discount."

In the afternoon, Dip went into Cole's Liquor Store. After he left, Cole told me: "Dip comes in here once in a while, to buy some beer. He's a coke dealer, but he's usually very calm and pleasant. Today, however, he was really acting nervous. He bought a bottle of whiskey, but before he paid me for it, he said, 'That bastard Egan sold me some lousy dope. I'll make him suffer for it, once this booze helps me get some nerve up.' As he was saying this, he was holding a switch-blade knife in his hands and rubbing it. He then paid me and left."

I then lost Dip's trail. I later discovered that Egan was killed that afternoon at his apartment by a single stab wound in the chest. Some neighbors saw a man who looked like Dip running from the building. They said he was staggering like he was drunk.

SAM SNOOP, S.F.P.D.

California Penal Code

Section 182.

If two or more persons conspire:

1. To commit any crime. * * * * 5. To commit any act injurious to the public health, to public morals, or to pervert or obstruct justice, or the due administration of the laws. * * * *

They are punishable as follows: * * * *

When they conspire to commit any . . . felony, they shall be punishable in the same manner and to the same extent as is provided for the punishment of that felony. * * * * When they conspire to do any of the other acts described in this section, they shall be punishable by imprisonment in the county jail for not more than one year, or in the state prison, or by a fine not exceeding $10,000, or by both that imprisonment and fine.

Section 184.

No agreement amounts to a conspiracy, unless some act, besides such agreement, be done within this state to effect the object thereof, by one or more of the parties to such agreement and the trial of cases of conspiracy may be had in any county in which any such act be done.

Section 321.

Every person who sells, gives, or in any manner whatever, furnishes or transfers to or for any other person any ticket, chance, share, or interest . . . in . . . any lottery, is guilty of a misdemeanor.

California Health & Safety Code

Section 11352.

[E]very person who transports, imports into this state, sells, furnishes, administers, or gives away . . . any controlled substance [which includes cocaine] shall be punished by imprisonment in the state prison for three, four, or five years.

PEOPLE v. LAURIA
California Court of Appeal
251 Cal.App.2d 471 (1967)

FLEMING. J.

In an investigation of call-girl activity, the police focused their attention on three prostitutes actively plying their trade on call, each of whom was using Lauria's telephone answering service, presumably for business purposes.

On January 8, 1965, Stella Weeks, a policewoman, signed up for telephone service with Lauria's answering service. Mrs. Weeks, in the course of her conversation with Lauria's office manager, hinted broadly that she was a prostitute concerned with the secrecy of her activities and their concealment from the police. She was assured that the operation of the service was discreet and "about as safe as you can get." It was arranged that Mrs. Weeks need not leave her address with the answering service, but could pick up her calls and pay her bills in person.

On February 11, Mrs. Weeks talked to Lauria on the telephone and told him her business was modeling and she had been referred to the answering service by Terry, one of the three prostitutes under investigation. She complained that because of the operation of the service she had lost two valuable customers, referred to as tricks. Lauria defended his service and said that her friends had probably lied to her about having left calls for her. But he did not respond to Mrs. Weeks' hints that she needed customers in order to make money, other than to invite her to his house for a personal visit in order to get better acquainted. In the course of his talk he said "his business was taking messages."

On February 15, Mrs. Weeks talked on the telephone to Lauria's office manager and again complained of two lost calls, which she described as a $50 and a $100 trick. On investigation the office manager could find nothing wrong, but she said she would alert the switchboard operators about slip-ups on calls.

On April 1, Lauria and the three prostitutes were arrested. Lauria complained to the police that this attention was undeserved, stating that Hollywood Call Board had 60 to 70 prostitutes on its board while his own service had only 9 or 10, that he kept separate records for known or suspected prostitutes for the convenience of himself and the police. When asked if his records were available to police who might come to the office to investigate call girls, Lauria replied that they were whenever the police had a specific name. However, his service didn't "arbitrarily tell the police about prostitutes on our board. As long as they pay their bills we tolerate them." In a subsequent voluntary appearance before the grand jury Lauria testified he had always cooperated with the police. But he admitted he knew some of his customers were prostitutes, and he knew Terry was a prostitute because he had personally used her services, and he knew she was paying for 500 calls a month.

Lauria and the three prostitutes were indicted for conspiracy to commit prostitution, and nine overt acts were specified. Subsequently the trial court set aside the indictment as having been brought without reasonable or probable cause. Penal Code § 995. The People have appealed, claiming that a sufficient showing of an unlawful agreement to further prostitution was made.

To establish agreement, the People need show no more than a tacit, mutual understanding between coconspirators to accomplish an unlawful act. Here the People attempted to establish a conspiracy by showing that Lauria, well aware that his codefendants were prostitutes who received business calls from customers through his telephone answering service, continued to furnish them with such service. This approach attempts to equate knowledge of another's criminal activity with conspiracy to further such criminal activity, and poses the question of the criminal responsibility of a furnisher of goods or services who knows his product is being used to assist the operation of an illegal business. Under what circumstances does a supplier become a part of a conspiracy to further an illegal enterprise by furnishing goods or services which he knows are to be used by the buyer for criminal purposes?

The two leading cases on this point face in opposite directions. In *United States v. Falcone*, 311 U.S. 205, the sellers of large quantities of sugar, yeast, and cans were absolved from participation in a moonshining conspiracy among distillers who bought from them, while in *Direct Sales Co. v. United States*, 319 U.S. 703, a wholesaler of drugs was convicted of conspiracy to violate the federal narcotic laws by selling drugs in quantity to a codefendant physician who was supplying them to addicts. The distinction between these two cases appears primarily based on the proposition that distributors of such dangerous products as drugs are required to exercise greater discrimination in the conduct of their business than are distributors of innocuous substances like sugar and yeast.

In the earlier case, *Falcone*, the sellers' knowledge of the illegal use of the goods was insufficient by itself to make the sellers participants in a conspiracy with the distillers who bought from them. Such knowledge fell short of proof of a conspiracy, and evidence on the volume of sales was too vague to support a jury finding that respondents knew of the conspiracy from the size of the sales alone.

In the later case of *Direct Sales*, the conviction of a drug wholesaler for conspiracy to violate federal narcotic laws was affirmed on a showing that it had actively promoted the sale of morphine sulphate in quantity and had sold codefendant physician, who practiced in a small town in South Carolina, more than

300 times his normal requirements of the drug, even though it had been repeatedly warned of the dangers of unrestricted sales of the drug. The court contrasted the restricted goods involved in *Direct Sales* with the articles of free commerce involved in *Falcone*: "All articles of commerce may be put to illegal ends," said the court.

> But all do not have inherently the same susceptibility to harmful and illegal use. This difference is important for two purposes. One is for making certain that the seller knows the buyer's intended illegal use. The other is to show that by the sale he intends to further, promote, and cooperate in it. This intent, when given effect by overt act, is the gist of conspiracy. While it is not identical with mere knowledge that another purposes unlawful action, it is not unrelated to such knowledge. The step from knowledge to intent and agreement may be taken. There is more than suspicion, more than knowledge, acquiescence, carelessness, indifference, lack of concern. There is informed and interested cooperation, stimulation, instigation. And there is also a "stake in the venture" which, even if it may not be essential, is not irrelevant to the question of conspiracy. [319 U.S. at 710-713.]

While *Falcone* and *Direct Sales* may not be entirely consistent with each other in their full implications, they do provide us with a framework for the criminal liability of a supplier of lawful goods or services put to unlawful use. Both the element of knowledge of the illegal use of the goods or services and the element of intent to further that use must be present in order to make the supplier a participant in a criminal conspiracy.

Proof of knowledge is ordinarily a question of fact and requires no extended discussion in the present case. The knowledge of the supplier was sufficiently established when Lauria admitted he knew some of his customers were prostitutes and admitted he knew that Terry, an active subscriber to his service, was a prostitute. In the face of these admissions he could scarcely claim to have relied on the normal assumption an operator of a business or service is entitled to make, that his customers are behaving themselves in the eyes of the law. Because Lauria knew in fact that some of his customers were prostitutes, it is a legitimate inference he knew they were subscribing to his answering service for illegal business purposes and were using his service to make assignations for prostitution. On this record we think the prosecution is entitled to claim positive knowledge by Lauria of the use of his service to facilitate the business of prostitution.

The more perplexing issue in the case is the sufficiency of proof of intent to further the criminal enterprise. The element of intent may be proved either by direct evidence, or by evidence of circumstances from which an intent to further a criminal enterprise by supplying lawful goods or services may be inferred. Direct evidence of participation, such as advice from the supplier of legal goods or services to the user of those goods or services on their use for illegal purposes, such evidence as appeared in a companion case we decide today, *People v. Roy*, 251 Cal.App.2d 459, provides the simplest case. When the intent to further and promote the criminal enterprise comes from the lips of the supplier himself, ambiguities of inference from circumstance need not trouble us. But in cases where direct proof of complicity is lacking, intent to further the conspiracy must be derived from the sale itself and its surrounding circumstances in order to establish the supplier's express or tacit agreement to join the conspiracy.

In the case at bench the prosecution argues that since Lauria knew his customers were using his service for illegal purposes but nevertheless continued to furnish it to them, he must have intended to assist them in carrying out their illegal activities. Thus through a union of knowledge and intent he became a participant in a criminal conspiracy. Essentially, the People argue that knowledge alone of the continuing use of his telephone facilities for criminal purposes provided a sufficient basis from which his intent to participate in those criminal activities could be inferred.

In examining precedents in this field we find that sometimes, but not always, the criminal intent of the supplier may be inferred from his knowledge of the unlawful use made of the product he supplies. Some consideration of characteristic patterns may be helpful.

1. Intent may be inferred from knowledge, when the purveyor of legal goods for illegal use has acquired a stake in the venture. *United States v. Falcone*, 109 F.2d 579, 581. For example, in *Regina v. Thomas*, [1957] 2 All Eng. 181, 342, a prosecution for living off the earnings of prostitution, the evidence showed that the accused, knowing the woman to be a convicted prostitute, agreed to let her have the use of his room between the hours of 9 p.m. and 2 a.m. for a charge of L3 a night. The Court of Criminal Appeal refused an appeal from the conviction, holding that when the accused rented a room at a grossly inflated rent to a prostitute for the purpose of carrying on her trade, a jury could find he was living on the earnings of prostitution.

In the present case, no proof was offered of inflated charges for the telephone answering services furnished the codefendants.

2. Intent may be inferred from knowledge, when no legitimate use for the goods or services exists. The leading California case is *People v. McLaughlin*, 111 Cal.App.2d 781, in which the court upheld a conviction of the suppliers of horse-racing information by wire for conspiracy to promote bookmaking, when it had been established that wire-service information had no other use than to supply information needed by bookmakers to conduct illegal gambling operations.

In *Rex v. Delaval* (1763) 97 Eng.Rep. 913, the charge was unlawful conspiracy to remove a girl from the control of Bates, a musician to whom she was bound as an apprentice, and place her in the hands of Sir Francis Delaval for the purpose of prostitution. Lord Mansfield not only upheld the charges against Bates and Sir Francis, but also against Fraine, the attorney who drew up the indentures of apprenticeship transferring custody of the girl from Bates to Sir Francis. Fraine, said Lord Mansfield, must have known that Sir Francis had no facilities for teaching music to apprentices so that it was impossible for him to have been ignorant of the real intent of the transaction.

In *Shaw v. Director of Public Prosecutions*, [1962] A.C. 220, the defendant was convicted of conspiracy to corrupt public morals and of living on the earnings of prostitution, when he published a directory consisting almost entirely of advertisements of the names, addresses, and specialized talents of prostitutes. Publication of such a directory, said the court, could have no legitimate use and serve no other purpose than to advertise the professional services of the prostitutes whose advertisements appeared in the directory. The publisher could be deemed a participant in the profits from the business activities of his principal advertisers.

Other services of a comparable nature come to mind: the manufacturer of crooked dice and marked cards who sells his product to gambling casinos; the tipster who furnishes information on the movement of law enforcement officers to known lawbreakers. (*Cf. Jackson v. State of Texas* (1957) 164 Tex.Crim.Rep. 276, where the furnisher of signaling equipment used to warn gamblers of the police was convicted of aiding the equipping of a gambling place.) In such cases the supplier must necessarily have an intent to further the illegal enterprise since there is no known honest use for his goods.

However, there is nothing in the furnishing of telephone answering service which would necessarily imply assistance in the performance of illegal activities. Nor is any inference to be derived from the use of an answering service by women, either in any particular volume of calls, or outside normal working hours. Night-club entertainers, registered nurses, faith healers, public stenographers, photographic models, and free lance substitute employees, provide examples of women in legitimate occupations whose employment might cause them to receive a volume of telephone calls at irregular hours.

3. Intent may be inferred from knowledge, when the volume of business with the buyer is grossly disproportionate to any legitimate demand, or when sales for illegal use amount to a high proportion of the seller's total business. In such cases an intent to participate in the illegal enterprise may be inferred from the quantity of the business done. For example, in *Direct Sales*, the sale of narcotics to a rural physician in quantities 300 times greater than he would have normal use for provided potent evidence of an intent to further the illegal activity. In the same case the court also found significant the fact that the wholesaler had attracted as customers a disproportionately large group of physicians who had been convicted of violating the Harrison Act. In *Shaw v. Director of Public Prosecutions*, [1962] A.C. 220, almost the entire business of the directory came from prostitutes.

No evidence of any unusual volume of business with prostitutes was presented by the prosecution against Lauria.

Inflated charges, the sale of goods with no legitimate use, sales in inflated amounts, each may provide a fact of sufficient moment from which the intent of the seller to participate in the criminal enterprise may be inferred. In such instances participation by the supplier of legal goods to the illegal enterprise may be inferred because in one way or another the supplier has acquired a special interest in the operation of the illegal enterprise. His intent to participate in the crime of which he had knowledge may be inferred from the existence of his special interest.

Yet there are cases in which it cannot reasonably be said that the supplier has a stake in the venture or has acquired a special interest in the enterprise, but in which he has been held liable as a participant on the basis of knowledge alone. Some suggestion of this appears in *Direct Sales*, where both the knowledge of the illegal use of the drugs and the intent of the supplier to aid that use were inferred. In *Regina v. Bainbridge* (1959) 3 All Eng. 200, a supplier of oxygen cutting equipment to one known to intend to use it to break into a bank was convicted as an accessory to the crime. In *Sykes v. Director of Public Prosecutions* [1962] A.C. 528, one having knowledge of the theft of 100 pistols, 4 submachine guns, and 1,960 rounds of ammunition was convicted of misprision of felony for failure to disclose the theft to the public authorities.

It seems apparent from these cases that a supplier who furnishes equipment which he knows will be used to commit a serious crime may be deemed from that knowledge alone to have intended to produce the result. Such proof may justify an inference that the furnisher intended to aid the execution of the crime and that he thereby became a participant. For instance, we think the operator of a telephone answering service with positive knowledge that his service was being used to facilitate the extortion of ransom, the distribution of heroin, or the passing of counterfeit money who continued to furnish the service with knowledge of its use, might be chargeable on knowledge alone with participation in a scheme to extort money, to distribute narcotics, or to pass counterfeit money. The same result would follow the seller of gasoline who knew the buyer was using his product to make Molotov cocktails for terroristic use.

Logically, the same reasoning could be extended to crimes of every description. Yet we do not believe an inference of intent drawn from knowledge of criminal use properly applies to the less serious crimes classified as misdemeanors. The duty to take positive action to dissociate oneself from activities helpful to violations of the criminal law is far stronger and more compelling for felonies than it is for misdemeanors or petty offenses. In this respect, as in others, the distinction between felonies and misdemeanors, between more serious and less serious crime, retains continuing vitality. In historically the most serious felony, treason, an individual with knowledge of the treason can be prosecuted for concealing and failing to disclose it. Calif. Pen. Code § 38; 18 U.S.C. § 2382. In other felonies, both at common law and under the criminal laws of the United States, an individual knowing of the commission of a felony is criminally liable for concealing it and failing to make it known to proper authority. 4 Blackstone 121; *Sykes v. Director of Public Prosecutions* [1962] A.C. 528; 18 U.S.C. § 4. But this crime, known as misprision of felony, has always been limited to knowledge and concealment of felony and has never extended to misdemeanor. A similar limitation is found in the criminal liability of an accessory, which is restricted to aid in the escape of a principal who has committed or been charged with a felony. Calif. Pen. Code § 32.

We believe the distinction between the obligations arising from knowledge of a felony and those arising from knowledge of a misdemeanor continues to reflect basic human feelings about the duties owed by individuals to society. Heinous crime must be stamped out, and its suppression is the responsibility of all. Venial crime and crime not evil in itself present less of a danger to society, and perhaps the benefits of their suppression through the modern equivalent of the posse, the hue and cry, the informant, and the citizen's arrest, are outweighed by the disruption to everyday life brought about by amateur law enforcement and private officiousness in relatively inconsequential dialects which do not threaten our basic security.

The subject has been summarized in an English text on the criminal law:

Failure to reveal a felony to the authorities is now authoritatively determined to be misprision of felony, which is a common-law misdemeanor; misprision of treason is punishable with imprisonment for life. No offence is committed in failing to disclose a misdemeanor. To require everyone, without distinction, as to the nature and degree of the offence, to become an accuser, would be productive of inconvenience in exposing numbers to penal prosecutions, multiplying criminal charges, and engendering private dissension. It may sometimes be more convenient that offences should be passed over, than that all should indiscriminately be made the subject of prosecution; and a law would be considered to be harsh and impolitic, if not unjust, which compelled every party injured by a criminal act, and, still more so, to compel everyone who happened to know that another had been so injured, to make a public disclosure of the circumstances. Here, therefore, there is reason for limiting the law against mere misprisions to the concealment of such crimes as are of an aggravated complexion. [*Criminal Law*, Glanville Williams (2d ed.) p. 423.]

With respect to misdemeanors, we conclude that positive knowledge of the supplier that his products or services are being used for criminal purposes does not, without more, establish an intent of the supplier to participate in the misdemeanors. With respect to felonies, we do not decide the converse, *viz*, that in all cases of felony knowledge of criminal use alone may justify an inference of the supplier's intent to participate in the crime. The implications of *Falcone* make the matter uncertain with respect to those felonies which are merely prohibited wrongs. See also *Holman v. Johnson* (1775) 98 Eng.Rep. 1120 (sale and delivery of tea at Dunkirk known to be destined for smuggling into England not an illegal contract). But decision on this point is not compelled, and we leave the matter open.

From this analysis of precedent we deduce the following rule: the intent of a supplier who knows of the criminal use to which his supplies are put to participate in the criminal activity connected with the use of his supplies may be established by (1) direct evidence that he intends to participate, or (2) through an inference that he intends to participate based on, (a) his special interest in the activity, or (b) the aggravated nature of the crime itself.

When we review Lauria's activities in the light of this analysis, we find no proof that Lauria took any direct action to further, encourage, or direct the call-girl activities of his codefendants, and we find an absence of circumstance from which his special interest in their activities could be inferred. Neither excessive charges for standardized services, nor the furnishing of services without a legitimate use, nor an unusual quantity of business with callgirls, are present. The offense which he is charged with furthering is a misdemeanor, a category of crime which has never been made a required subject of positive disclosure to public authority. Under these circumstances, although proof of Lauria's knowledge of the criminal activities of his patrons was sufficient to charge him with that fact, there was insufficient evidence that he intended to further their criminal activities, and hence insufficient proof of his participation in a criminal conspiracy with his codefendants to further prostitution. Since the conspiracy centered around the activities of Lauria's telephone answering service, the charges against his codefendants likewise fail for want of proof.

In absolving Lauria of complicity in a criminal conspiracy, we do not wish to imply that the public authorities are without remedies to combat modern manifestations of the world's oldest profession. Licensing of telephone answering services under the police power, together with the revocation of licenses for the toleration of prostitution, is a possible civil remedy. The furnishing of telephone answering service in aid of prostitution could be made a crime. *Cf.* Pen. Code § 316, which makes it a misdemeanor to let an apartment with knowledge of its use for prostitution. Other solutions will doubtless occur to vigilant public authorities if the problem of call-girl activity needs further suppression.

The order is affirmed.

NOTES FROM NANCY:

(1) Suppose D shoots V with a gun, *knowing* that this will kill V. Isn't it fair to say that D thereby *intended* that V die? If so, then I do not understand why the *Lauria* opinion is so long and complicated. Lauria clearly *knew* that his service was being used for an illegal purpose, so he must have *intended* that to happen, and he made *agreements* with the prostitutes which allowed this to happen. Why shouldn't this be enough to hold him for conspiracy?

(2) Exactly which element of the definition of conspiracy was at issue in *Lauria*? How do each of the factors listed by the court relate to this element?

UNITED STATES v. BLANKENSHIP
U.S. Court of Appeals, 7th Circuit
970 F.2d 283 (1992)

Easterbrook, Circuit Judge.

Courts do not enforce bargains among the producers of illegal drugs, or between these producers and their customers. Extra-judicial remedies tend to be violent, which makes drug running a crime of the young and vigorous. Substitutes for both legal processes and brutality are possible, however; family ties may suffice.

Nancy Nietupski, a grandmother in her early 60s, ran a methamphetamine ring through her extended family. She started on the west coast, working with her nephew William Zahm. Later she moved to her sister's farm in Illinois. While sister Violet Blankenship supplied a base of operations, nephew Robert Blankenship helped distribute the drug and collect debts.

Nietupski initially bought methamphetamine from outside sources. When these proved unreliable, Zahm helped her enter the manufacturing end of the business. "Cooking" methamphetamine is messy, and there is a risk of explosion when volatile chemicals such as acetone reach high temperatures. Nietupski and Zahm moved their laboratory frequently, to reduce the risk of detection. In February 1989 Zahm leased from Thomas Lawrence a house trailer in which to set up shop for a day. Nietupski told Lawrence what Zahm planned to make and offered $1,000 or one ounce of methamphetamine; Lawrence preferred the cash and took $100 as a down payment. He covered the floor of the trailer with plastic for protection.

Zahm postponed the operation when he could not find a heating control. A few days later Lawrence got cold feet, telling Marvin Bland (one of Nietupski's assistants) that he wanted the chemicals and equipment removed. Bland complied.

Zahm soon joined William Worker to set up a new methamphetamine ring. Agents of the DEA infiltrated the Zahm-Worker clique. Zahm cut his losses by turning against his aunt, whose operations collapsed. Eighteen persons from the Nietupski ring were indicted. Robert Blankenship, Thomas Lawrence, and six others were in one group, all charged in a single count with conspiring to manufacture and distribute methamphetamine. 21 U.S.C. § 846. Of the six, three pleaded guilty and three were acquitted. Blankenship and Lawrence, convicted by the jury, received identical sentences of 120 months' imprisonment plus five years' supervised release. * * * *

Lawrence has filed two appeals, one from his sentence and the second from an order denying his motion under Fed.R.Crim.P. 33 for a new trial. * * * *

Conspiracy is agreement to violate the law. Unless Lawrence willingly joined the Nietupski venture, he did not commit the crime of conspiracy. What evidence was there that Lawrence knew, let alone joined? Nietupski and Zahm told Lawrence what they planned to do in his trailer; Zahm and Lawrence sampled some of the product scraped off the apparatus; for $1,000 he furnished the space, covered the floor with plastic, supplied refreshments, and let Zahm take a shower to wash some acid off his legs. If providing assistance to a criminal organization were the same thing as conspiracy, then Lawrence would be guilty. Yet there is a difference between supplying goods to a syndicate and joining it, just as there is a difference between selling goods and being an employee of the buyer. Cargill sells malt and barley to Anheuser Busch, knowing that they will be made into beer, without being part of Busch; by parallel reasoning, someone who sells sugar to a bootlegger knowing the use that will be made of that staple is not thereby a conspirator, *United States v. Falcone*, 311 U.S. 205 (1940), and someone who buys one load of marijuana has not conspired with the sellers, *United States v. Baker*, 905 F.2d 1100, 1106-07 (7th cir. 1990).

Falcone illustrates the doctrine that "mere" sellers and buyers are not automatically conspirators. If it were otherwise, companies that sold cellular phones to teenage punks who have no use for them other than to set up drug deals would be in trouble, and many legitimate businesses would be required to monitor their customers' activities. *Cf. People v. Lauria*, 251 Cal.App.2d 471 (1967) (answering service furnished to prostitute). Yet this does not get us very far, for no rule says that a supplier cannot join a conspiracy through which the product is put to an unlawful end. *Direct Sales Co. v. United States*, 319 U.S. 703 (1943), makes that point in holding that the jury may infer that a pharmaceutical house selling huge quantities of morphine to a physician over a seven-year span conspired with the physician to distribute the drug illegally.

Where does the "mere" sale end, the conspiracy begin? One may draw a line, as *Falcone* and *Direct Sales* did, between knowledge of other persons' crimes and intent to join them, but this restates the elements of the offense without telling us when an inference of intent to join is permissible. Selling a camera to a spy does not make one a traitor - but selling camera and film, developing the prints, enlarging the detail in the critical areas, and collecting half of the payment for the secret information would assuredly land one in prison. Stating polar cases is easy, but locating the line of demarcation is hard. Courts have a tendency in these situations to draw up a list of relevant factors, without describing necessary or sufficient conditions. Lists have burgeoned since *Falcone*. See Wayne R. LaFave & Austin W. Scott, Jr., 2 *Substantive Criminal Law* § 6.4(e)(3) (1986) (culling nine factors from the cases and implying that others might be pertinent).

When writing for the court of appeals in *Falcone*, 109 F.2d 579 (2d cir. 1940), Learned Hand concluded that a supplier joins a venture only if his fortunes rise or fall with the venture's, so that he gains by its success. Judge Hand offered a similar definition of aiding and abetting in *United States v. Peoni*, 100 F.2d 401 (2d cir. 1938), and we adopted his approach in *United States v. Pino-Perez*, 870 F.2d 1230, 1235 (7th cir. 1989). On this view, the sale of a staple commodity such as sugar or telephone service does not enlist the seller in the criminal venture; in a competitive market the vendor could sell to someone else at the market price, and the buyer could turn to other sources. Anonymous transactions are the norm in markets and do not create criminal liability; when the seller has knowledge but the terms remain the same, there is no reason to infer participation in the enterprise any more than in the Cargill-Busch case we have given. Although the Supreme Court did not discuss this approach in *Falcone*, we have been favorably disposed in *Pino-Perez* and, e.g., *United States v. Giovannetti*, 919 F.2d 1223, 1227 (7th cir. 1990). See also Model Penal Code § 2.06(3)(a) and commentary at 315-16 (1985) (supplier culpable only if he has "the purpose of promoting or facilitating" the crime).

Trailers do not rent for $1,000 per week — not in legitimate markets, anyway. By charging a premium price, Lawrence seemingly threw in his lot with the Nietupski operation and may be convicted under Judge Hand's approach. Yet the price cannot be the end of things. What does the $1,000 represent: a piece of the action, or only a premium for the risks? Lawrence bore two. One was that the chemicals would damage his trailer. Although he took precautions by spreading plastic on the floor, an explosion would have spattered chemicals on the walls and ceiling. Lawrence would have charged for taking this risk even if the manufacture of methamphetamine were entirely legal. The other risk was the hazard of criminal liability, a cost of doing business. One who covers his own costs and no more does not share in the venture's success. Using a price calculated by reference to the risk of criminal conviction as support for that conviction would be circular. Reduce the risk of conviction, and you reduce the price. Either way, the price responds to the legal system rather than to the potential profits of the Nietupski gang and does not establish a desire to promote its success. Repeat business, as in *Direct Sales*, might show such a desire, but Lawrence did not carry through with the initial transaction and never realized even the $1,000. *Giovannetti* and other cases from this court speak reverentially of Judge Hand but actually ask a different, and more functional, question. It is whether the imposition of liability on transactions of the class depicted by the case would deter crime without adding unduly to the costs of legitimate transactions. So, we observed in *Giovannetti*, "a stationer who sells an address book to a woman whom he knows to be a prostitute is not an aider and abettor. Perkins & Boyce, *Criminal Law* 747 (3d ed. 1982). He can hardly be said to be seeking by his action to make her venture succeed, since the transaction has very little to do with that success and his livelihood will not be affected appreciably by whether her venture succeeds or fails. And, what may well be the same point seen from another angle, punishing him would not reduce the amount of prostitution — the prostitute, at an infinitesimal cost in added inconvenience, would simply shop for address books among stationers who did not know her trade." 919 F.2d at 1227. Treating the stationer as an accomplice would, however, raise the costs of legitimate business, for it would either turn sellers into snoops (lest they sell to the wrong customers) or lead them to hire blind clerks (lest they learn too much about their customers); either way, the costs of business would rise, and honest customers would pay more.

If the product is itself contraband — for example, the methamphetamine Nietupski bought in California early on — the analysis differs but the result is the same: an isolated sale is not the same thing as enlisting in the venture. A sale of methamphetamine is a substantive crime. Because the substance is illegal, the seller knows that the buyer will put the drug to an illegal use, yet this does not make the sale a second, inchoate offense. To treat it as a second crime of aiding and abetting (or conspiring with) the buyer is to multiply the criminal punishment and so distort the penalty system the legislature adopted — for what is the point of setting at five years the maximum penalty for selling a given quantity of methamphetamine if every sale violates a second law and doubles the penalty? As we held in *Pino-Perez*, a long course of sales may permit a finding of conspiracy or aiding and abetting, for such conduct is both more dangerous (it is harder to ferret out crime when the criminals have a closed circle of suppliers) and more likely that the vendor's welfare is bound up with that of the organization to which he sells. *Direct Sales*, 319 U.S. at 713. So too with "fronting" of drugs, a credit arrangement in which the parties to the sale share the profits.

Sometimes a single transaction extends over a substantial period and is the equivalent of enduring supply. *Giovannetti* involved premises leased for the purpose of illegal gambling (a "wire room"). Periodic payments of rent link the landlord with the criminal enterprise. Because a lessor almost inevitably knows his tenant's business, the imposition of a criminal penalty is likely to deter but not to raise the costs of legitimate transactions. A bookie needs a wire room; if the law deters landlords from providing space for these operations, it will substantially cut down on crime.

Does *Giovannetti* describe Lawrence's situation? Not quite; Lawrence negotiated for one payment, not a stream of rentals. What is more, it remains necessary to identify just what crime a long-term supplier such as a landlord commits. We supposed in *Giovannetti* that the crime was aiding and abetting the operation of the wire room at the leased premises, just as the Supreme Court concluded in *Direct Sales* that the crime was a conspiracy between Direct Sales Company and John V. Tate to distribute the narcotics Dr. Tate ordered. Suppose the bookie operated not one wire room but 50, one in each ward of Chicago; suppose Dr. Tate bought morphine sulfate from nine distributors in addition to Direct Sales. Would the owner be criminally responsible for all 50 wire rooms, or Direct Sales for the quantities procured from its competitors? A landlord's offense is not the greater if his customer operates additional wire rooms, and a seller of opiates should not be subjected to additional punishment if it cuts down on supplies, forcing its customer to shop elsewhere.

Some states have statutes forbidding "criminal facilitation," an apt description of Lawrence's acts. E.g., N.Y.Penal Code § 115.05.* Lawrence agreed to facilitate the manufacture of methamphetamine, but the United States Code lacks a facilitation statute. It does forbid aiding and abetting substantive offenses. Although Zahm did not complete the "cook," 21 U.S.C. § 846 forbids attempted violations of other drug laws. Yet the prosecutor did not charge Lawrence with assisting this offense — or with assisting a conspiracy to make methamphetamine on his premises. Instead the prosecutor not only selected the conspiracy component of § 846 but also lumped Lawrence with a single, overarching conspiracy, the entire Nictupski venture. Neither joining nor abetting this whole conspiracy is an appropriate description of Lawrence's fling.

In charging Lawrence with joining the Nietupski conspiracy, the prosecutor sought to hold him responsible for that organization's entire activities, just as if the landlord were to be punished for all 50 wire rooms, or Direct Sales for the drugs Dr. Tate had to scrounge from its rivals. Members of conspiracies may be punished for all of the crimes within the scope of the venture. *Pinkerton v. United States*, 328 U.S. 640 (1946). The Sentencing Guidelines, when coupled with the sky-high punishments authorized for drug crimes, produce the same vicarious liability without the bother of obtaining convictions. In a drug case the court must impose a sentence computed by reference to all "acts and omissions that were part of the same course of conduct or common scheme or plan as the offense of conviction". U.S.S.G. § 1B1.3(a)(2). When the "offense of conviction" is a conspiracy, this means counting the full sales of the criminal enterprise throughout its duration. Thus Robert Blankenship, who was a cog of the Nietupski organization from the time his aunt moved to Illinois, and Thomas Lawrence, who obtained $100 by opening his trailer to a single failed "cook," received identical sentences — ten years in prison without possibility of parole.

Neither *Direct Sales* nor any of this court's cases permits a supplier to a criminal organization to be sentenced for all of that organization's sins when he facilitated only one. If the United States Code contained a facilitation statute along the lines of New York's, Lawrence would receive a sentence proportioned to his own iniquity rather than that of Nietupski and her henchmen. So too if the Code penalized abetting criminal attempts. But it does not, and if the only options are conspiracy, with full responsibility for all of the venture's other crimes, and no crime, then no crime comes much closer to describing Lawrence's responsibility. Although the guidelines permit a reduction of four levels for marginal figures such as Lawrence, a sentence based on the sales of the full organization, less 30% (the effect of a four-level reduction), still vastly overstates the culpability of persons who supply goods and services to criminals.

---

* "A person is guilty of criminal facilitation in the second degree when, believing it probable that he is rendering aid to a person who intends to commit a class A felony, he engages in conduct which provides such person with means or opportunity for the commission thereof and which in fact aids such person to commit such class A felony. Criminal facilitation in the second degree is a class C felony." Note the difference in degree between the principal and the facilitator, appropriate to the different roles but not achievable when conspiracy or aiding and abetting supplies the theory of responsibility.

Let us be clear: we do not hold that in reforming criminal sentences Congress altered the definition of conspiracy. We come to the same conclusion as the Supreme Court did in *Falcone*. Lawrence knew what Zahm wanted to do in the trailer, but there is a gulf between knowledge and conspiracy. There is no evidence that Lawrence recognized, let alone that he joined and promoted, the full scope of the Nietupski organization's activities. He may have joined, or abetted, a more limited agreement to manufacture a quantity of methamphetamine, but he was not charged with that offense. Lawrence facilitated an attempted crime, and probably conspired to do this, but he did not subscribe to the broader agreement on which his conviction depends.

On Lawrence's appeal, the judgment is reversed. On Blankenship's appeal, the judgment is affirmed.

NOTES FROM NANCY:

1. In *U.S. v. Yang*, 281 F.3d 534 (6th Cir. 2002), defendant conspired to steal information that he believed were trade secrets, but were not. Charged with conspiracy to steal trade secrets, he claimed impossibility:

> The Yangs' conspiracy to steal the trade secrets was completed when, with the intent to steal the trade secrets, they agreed to meet with Lee in the hotel room and they took an overt act towards the completion of the crime, that is, when the Yangs went to the hotel room. The fact that the information they conspired to obtain was not what they believed it to be does not matter because the objective of the Yangs' agreement was to steal trade secrets, and they took an overt step toward achieving that objective. Conspiracy is nothing more than the parties to the conspiracy coming to a mutual understanding to try to accomplish a common and unlawful plan, where at least one of the conspirators knowingly commits an overt act in pursuit of the conspiracy's objective. It is the mutual understanding or agreement itself that is criminal, and whether the object of the scheme actually is, as the parties believe it to be, unlawful is irrelevant.

2. In *People v. Iniguez*, 96 Cal.App.4th 75 (2002), the court held that "conspiracy to commit *attempted* murder" (to which D had pleaded guilty) was not possible. Such a crime is "a conclusive legal falsehood. This is because the crime of attempted murder requires a specific intent to actually commit the murder, while the agreement underlying the pleaded conspiracy contemplated no more than an ineffectual act. No one can simultaneously intend to do and not do the same act, here the actual commission of a murder. Defendant has pleaded guilty to a nonexistent offense."

3. Recall the several types of homicide you studied earlier: first degree murder, second degree murder, voluntary manslaughter, and involuntary manslaughter. Is it possible to conspire to commit *any one* of these?

In *People v. Swain*, 12 Cal.4th 593 (1996), defendants were charged with conspiracy to commit murder. The trial court instructed the jury that it could convict if it found an agreement to commit "implied malice" — California's extreme recklessness ("depraved heart") form of murder. The California Supreme Court reversed, holding that only "express malice" (intent to kill) may constitute the intent needed for conspiracy to murder. The court stated:

> Conspiracy is a specific intent crime. The specific intent required divides logically into two elements: (a) the intent to agree, or conspire, and (b) the intent to commit the offense which is the object of the conspiracy. To sustain a conviction for conspiracy to commit a particular offense, the prosecution must show not only that the conspirators intended to agree *but also that they intended to commit the elements of that offense.*

One of the elements of murder, of course, is the death of a human being. Therefore, to conspire to commit murder, one must intend the death of a human being. One who commits depraved heart murder does *not* intend the death of a human being. Thus, when he conspires with another to commit an extremely dangerous act, he does not conspire to commit murder.

In *People v. Cortez*, 18 Cal.4th 1223 (1998), the court held that a trial court should not instruct the jury on conspiracy to commit *second* degree murder — because every conspiracy to commit murder must be conspiracy to commit *first* degree murder:

> Conspiracy is a specific intent crime requiring both an intent to agree or conspire and a further intent to commit the target crime or object of the conspiracy. Murder that is premeditated and deliberated is murder of the first degree. "Premeditated" means "considered beforehand," and "deliberate" means "formed or arrived at or determined upon as a result of careful thought and weighing of considerations for and against the proposed course of action." *People v. Perez* (1992) 2 Cal.4th 1117. The process of premeditation and deliberation does not require any extended period of time. The true test is not the duration of time as much as it is the extent of the reflection. Thoughts may follow each other with great rapidity and cold, calculated judgment may be arrived at quickly.
>
> Consequently, it logically follows that where two or more persons conspire to commit murder — i.e., intend to agree or conspire, further intend to commit the target offense of murder, and perform one or more overt acts in furtherance of the planned murder — each has acted with a state of mind functionally indistinguishable from the mental state of premeditating the target offense of murder. The mental state required for conviction of *conspiracy* to commit murder necessarily establishes premeditation and deliberation of the target offense of murder — hence all murder conspiracies are conspiracies to commit first degree murder, so to speak. More accurately stated, conspiracy to commit murder is a unitary offense *punishable* in every instance in the same manner as is first degree murder under the provisions of Penal Code section 182.

JUSTICE KENNARD dissented:

> Nor is the majority correct that as a factual matter it is impossible for two or more persons to conspire without deliberation and premeditation. By creating the separate crimes of (1) first degree murder for killings in

which the killer acts not only with the intent to kill but with premeditation and deliberation, and (2) second degree murder for killings in which the killer acts with the intent to kill but *without* premeditation and deliberation, the Legislature has recognized that the intent to kill can exist without premeditation and deliberation. Contrary to the majority, there is no logical reason why a sudden intent to kill that is neither "considered beforehand" nor "formed or arrived at or determined upon as a result of careful thought and weighing of considerations for and against the proposed course of action "cannot arise in two persons just as it can arise in one.

Conspiracies do not require formal expressions of agreement or advance planning. For example, with a shout of "let's get him," two friends who have been drinking all night in a bar can, without premeditation and deliberation, impulsively form and share the intent to kill when their sworn enemy walks in. Similarly, a sudden and unexpected encounter on disputed turf between groups from two different gangs can similarly lead to a spontaneous and unreflective agreement to kill. Juries are capable of distinguishing between first degree murder conspiracies requiring premeditation and deliberation and second degree murder conspiracies requiring only intent to kill. For this reason, the federal courts recognize murder conspiracies of varying degrees. (*U.S. v. Croft* (9th Cir. 1997) 124 F.3d 1109, 1122-1123 [holding that federal law recognizes conspiracy to commit second degree murder when conspirators act with intent to kill but without premeditation and deliberation]; *United States v. Chagra* (5th Cir. 1986) 807 F.2d 398, 400-402 [same].)

The majority responded:

With due respect, we believe Justice Kennard misconstrues our analysis when suggesting we are concluding "conspiracy to murder is a unitary crime requiring proof of only intent to kill, the mental state of second degree murder, but subject to the punishment for first degree murder." We are not concluding conspiracy to commit murder "requires only intent to kill" — we are instead merely recognizing that the mental state required for conviction of conspiracy to commit express malice murder *necessarily equates with and establishes* the mental state of deliberate and premeditated first degree murder. It is inconceivable that two persons can harbor the mental state required to conspire to commit express malice murder, and, we might add, additionally commit an overt act or acts in furtherance thereof as required for conviction of the crime of conspiracy, without being deemed to have willfully "premeditated and deliberated" the commission of that murder.

In *Evanchyk v. Stewart*, 47 P.3d 1114 (Ariz. 2002), the court held: "Any agreement with another to kill a third person constitutes premeditation, the mental state that exists under Arizona law whenever the intention to kill 'precedes the killing by a length of time to permit reflection." '

4. Can one be convicted of conspiracy to commit a *non-intentional* (i.e., reckless or negligent) crime — or is this "legally impossible"? See *U.S. v. Sdoulam*, 398 F.3d 981 (8th Cir. 2005).

SECTION C   SCOPE OF THE CONSPIRACY

The agreement which is an essential element of every conspiracy has two dimensions: the persons privy thereto, and the objectives encompassed therein. Even when it is clear that every defendant is a conspirator, it may be extremely important to determine precisely what the object dimension and party dimension of the agreement are, for that in turn will decide the critical question of whether more than one conspiracy exists. * * * *

The general rule that hearsay is not admissible in a criminal prosecution is marked by many exceptions. One of these is the co-conspirator exception: any act or declaration by one co-conspirator committed during and in furtherance of the conspiracy is admissible against each co-conspirator. The rationale most often given for this exception is that each of the conspirators is the agent of all the others.

LaFave & Scott, *Criminal Law* (West)

In contract law, we rarely care whether the parties had one big contract or several small contracts. Either way, the parties are bound by their contracts and liable if they breach them.

But in conspiracy law, it is often vitally important whether the parties have made one big agreement or several small agreements. Why? Well, for one thing, each agreement constitutes a separate conspiracy, and each conspiracy is a separate crime — and each conspiracy may be separately punished. Therefore, if the prosecutor has a choice between charging several small conspiracies and one large conspiracy, she should prefer the former — the more conspiracies, the more crimes, so the greater the total sentence.

But in the cases in this Chapter, the prosecutor is usually trying to do *just the opposite!* The prosecutor is trying to persuade the court that there is *one large* conspiracy rather than *several small* ones. And the defense attorney is arguing that there are several small conspiracies! Each side puts a lot of time and energy into this dispute. See if you can figure out *why*.

Here's a hint. The law of *partnership* tells us that partners act for each other — so long as those acts were committed "in furtherance of the partnership." If Jack is a partner in the law firm of Jack & Jill, and Jack offers you a job as a law clerk for the firm, Jill is bound by Jack's offer. And if Jill commits legal malpractice while representing a client, Jack is liable to the client.

If we view *conspirators* as "partners in crime," these same rules apply to them. They are responsible for each other's acts — so long as they were committed "in furtherance of the conspiracy." The bigger the conspiracy, the more acts — including substantive crimes — are committed in furtherance of that conspiracy. So if Dan steals a car to use in carrying out the planned Dan-Don bank robbery, Don is guilty of larceny of the car!

This issue also arises in the law of evidence (which you probably haven't studied yet). The *hearsay* rule provides that an out-of-court statement is not admissible in evidence. Thus, at Dan's trial, Wanda may not testify that "I heard Otto say that he saw Dan shoot Vic." Admitting this testimony is not fair to Dan, as he cannot cross-examine Otto. But there are exceptions to the hearsay rule. If Wanda testifies, "I heard Dan say that he killed Vic," this testimony is admissible as an "admission of a party," because Dan may simply take the stand and deny or explain the statement.

The law of partnership applies to the hearsay rules: an admission of one partner is also an admission of the other partner. Suppose Jack (of the law firm of Jack & Jill) offered to hire you as a law clerk, you accepted, and now Jack changes his mind. You sue *Jill*. May Wanda (the firm secretary) testify that "Jack told me he had hired a new clerk, so I should put a new law clerk on the payroll"? Yes. This is hearsay, but it is admissible as an "admission of a party" — Jill. *Jack spoke for Jill* in furtherance of the partnership, so Jill (through Jack) has spoken an *admission* that the firm has hired you.

If co-conspirators are partners in crime, then this same reasoning applies to *their* hearsay statements. So the bigger the conspiracy, the more hearsay statements will be admissible against the co-conspirators.

These are difficult issues. But why should they be controlled by *conspiracy* law? Shouldn't the question of whether Don is guilty of Dan's crimes be determined by the purposes of punishment (discussed at the end of Chapter 1)? And shouldn't the question of what hearsay statements are admissible against Dan be determined by the principles regarding what evidence is reliable and when it is fair to deprive a party of the right to cross-examine? Consider these questions as you read this Section.

PROBLEM 19C

To: My law clerk

From: Assistant U.S. Attorney Peggy Soo

Re: *United States v. Allen*

Ellen Allen has been indicted for sale of cocaine, in violation of 21 U.S.C § 841.

Attached is the grand jury testimony of Frank Fink, which includes his recounting of some statements made by Betty Bates, Carl Cates, and David Dates. I am pretty sure that, at trial, defense counsel will argue that Fink's testimony regarding these statements is inadmissible hearsay. It is hearsay, but I think it is admissible anyway. Please read the attached authorities and advise me as to the best arguments I can make to get this testimony in, and whether they are likely to succeed.

Grand Jury Testimony of Frank Fink

Q: How did you come to know Allen?

A: Each of us rented a separate apartment in the same apartment building, while we were going to school at the state university here in the city.

Q: Did you have a conversation with Betty Bates?

A: Yes. One day, Bates knocked on my door. She said, "I just knocked on Allen's door and there was no answer. Do you know where she is? I buy cocaine from her every week, and I'm here for my weekly supply. I'll get sick if I don't get it."

Q: Did you have a conversation with Carl Cates?

A: Yes. Cates was Allen's boyfriend. He lived in the apartment with her. One day, I passed him in the hall. He was carrying some ledger books. He asked me where the trash incinerator was. I told him, and I asked him what he was doing. He said, "Ellen is graduating from the university, so we're moving to another city where she will be going to law school. She has stopped selling coke, and these are her account books. I'm burning them, to make sure that her past doesn't catch up to her."

Q: Did you have a conversation with David Dates?

A: Yes. I saw Dates on campus one day, and he asked me to lend him $100. I asked him why, and he said, "I'm putting myself through college by selling a little cocaine now and then. I get my supply from Big George, who is a big-time dealer. He sells to several small-time dealers, like me and Ellen Allen. I need $100 to buy some coke from George. I'll pay you back next week." I did not lend him the money.

McDONALD v. UNITED STATES
U.S. Court of Appeals, 8th Circuit
89 F.2d 128 (1937)

Faris, Circuit Judge.

Appellant was indicted jointly with ten others for the violation of § 408c, title 18, U.S.C.A., for that he had conspired with such other ten to kidnap, transport interstate and hold for ransom, one Edward George Bremer. Appellant was tried jointly with two other of his co-indictees. He was found guilty and his punishment fixed at imprisonment in a penitentiary for the term of fifteen years. He has appealed.

Specifically, the overt acts charged against appellant were (as the indictment set out and the evidence showed) that he had on September 2, 5, 9, and 10, 1934, at Miami, Florida, and Havana, Cuba, knowingly done acts to further the exchange and had exchanged some $92,000 of marked money, which had been paid as a ransom, or reward to his coconspirators for the release of Edward George Bremer, in exchange for unmarked money.

Bremer, the person kidnapped, had been seized by certain of the conspirators jointly indicted with appellant (who was not personally present) at St. Paul, Minnesota, on January 17, 1934, and had been thence transported by them to Bensenville, in the State of Illinois; had at the latter place been detained as a prisoner for some two weeks, pending negotiations for his release upon payment of ransom money, and had been thence transported back to the State of Minnesota, to a point near Rochester in that state, whereat he was released on payment to the actual kidnapers, or to some of them, of the sum of $200,000 in cash, which was "marked" (so called), or the numbers, denominations, and banks of issue listed. The release of Bremer, and the payment of the ransom, in marked money occurred on

February 6, 1934; while, as already said, the overt acts charged against appellant occurred on and between September 2 and September 10, 1934.

The first mention in the evidence of appellant's connection with the case (as one living in Detroit, Michigan, who, as soon as he could go to Cuba, would for a commission of 25% exchange the ransom money for unmarked money) occurred late in June, 1934. Appellant, from his own statement, was at that time a resident of Detroit; his principal business consisted of "gambling activities in Chicago, Detroit and Havana, Cuba." He had for some ten years, in connection with such "activities," been on occasions a visitor in Havana and as a result of such visits he "managed to control gambling in Havana."

The money paid for the release of Bremer consisted wholly of small bills, namely, fives and tens. Appellant's coindictees had so stipulated in divers ransom notes to the kin and friends of Bremer. They also insisted that it should not be "hot," that is, marked; otherwise they would not accept it, or release Bremer. But as the record discloses, they did accept it, expecting that it would be marked, and of course, it was marked. They relied on their ability to discover markings on it; but either their ability failed them or their cupidity overcame them. The whole sum largely intact, till July, 1934, was traced from one point to another in the hands of divers of the actual kidnapers to various States, till some $92,000 of it was found to have been exchanged by appellant, at Havana, Cuba, for large bills of unmarked money, in the early days of September, 1934.

[Appellant argues that he] could not be legally prosecuted or found guilty of a conspiracy under § 408c to violate the provisions of § 408a, because the conspiracy, if any, was fully consummated and had ended upon the payment of the ransom money and the release of Bremer, on February 6, 1934, and so the acts of appellant, if any, in and about the exchange of marked ransom money for unmarked money, occurring subsequent to February 6, 1934, are not within the denouncement of the statute on which appellant was tried and convicted.

Section 408a, title 18, U.S.C., defines and denounces as a crime the transportation across a state line or a national boundary of a person who has been kidnapped and is being held for ransom. Section 408c, title 18, U.S.C., denounces as a crime and punishes the entering by two or more persons "into an agreement, confederation, or conspiracy to violate the provisions of sections 408a and 408b of this title" and the doing of "any overt act toward carrying out such unlawful agreement, confederation, or conspiracy." As said already, appellant was indicted and convicted for violating the conspiracy clause of § 408c, which in substance we quote above.

The sections referred to, define two crimes: First, the transportation in interstate commerce of a person who has been kidnapped and is being held for ransom; and, second, a conspiracy to commit the crime first above mentioned. We are here directly concerned only with the conspiracy.

Certain rules which apply to the crime of conspiracy have become so well settled as not to require exposition or citation of authority. These are: (a) that a person may be convicted of a conspiracy to commit a defined substantive offense against the law, even though such latter offense be actually and entirely consummated; (b) that a person who knowingly enters into a conspiracy after its formation, but before it is ended, is equally as guilty as are those who were in it at its formation; and (c) that a criminal conspiracy once formed continues until the object of it has been accomplished unless abandoned short of an overt act, or broken up by the arrest of the participants.

Though appellant himself did no overt act till the early days of September, 1934, the evidence warranted the jury in finding that he came into the conspiracy as early as June, 1934, and at a time when the ransom money except as to a small part thereof had not been divided or "cut up" among the conspirators, because of their fear that a division of it till it had been exchanged would lead to detection and their arrest and conviction. As said, a settled rule of law admonishes us that a criminal conspiracy, once formed, continues till the object, for which it was formed, has been accomplished. What was the object to be attained by the capture and detention of Bremer? Clearly, it was not for the mere pleasure of his company at the "hide-out" over in Illinois, or in moonlight joy rides back and forward across the Illinois, Wisconsin, and Minnesota boundaries. But as in almost all cases which fall under the ban of the statute, the seizure and detention of Bremer was for the purpose, therefore with the object, of illicit gain. Such gain, in order to be usable for the sustenance, pleasures, and vices of the conspirators, had to be in a form to be used by them without danger of detection and arrest. The record is replete with facts and circumstances showing that the ransom money was listed or marked, that the conspirators expected it to be marked, and after it came into their hands, knew it was marked and so knowingly engaged appellant to exchange it for unmarked money.

The phase of the rule of law here involved, namely that a continuing conspiracy ends only upon the accomplishment of the object thereof, is settled as a rule of decision. No general rule of law can be accurately laid down touching when accomplishment has been achieved. It follows that the latter question therefore is one well-nigh wholly of fact to be resolved by common sense and human observation and experience, and largely each category must be weighed in its own facts.

But if a court should be so hardy as to attempt to formulate a general rule as to when a continuing criminal conspiracy, having for its object illicit gain, is at an end, it might well run somewhat thus: Whenever the unlawful object of the conspiracy has reached that stage of consummation, whereat the several conspirators having taken in spendable form their several agreed parts of the spoils, may go their several ways, without the necessity of further acts or consultation, about the conspiracy, with each other or among themselves, the conspiracy has ended.

It is obvious that the view thus taken disposes of appellant's contention that the trial court erred in admitting in evidence acts done and conversations and statements had and made by appellant's co-indictees, as also physical exhibits and documents coming into existence subsequent to the payment of the ransom money and the release of Bremer. For, as already indicated, nothing is better settled as a rule of law than that while the conspiracy continues the acts and statements of one conspirator are binding on all.

The case should be affirmed, and this we order.

NOTES FROM PEGGY:

1. I think *McDonald* might have some bearing on the admissibility of Fink's testimony as to Cates' statement.

2. In *U.S. v. Jimenez Recio*, 537 U.S. 270 (2003), defendants joined a conspiracy to sell drugs after (unbeknownst to defendants) federal agents had seized the drugs. The trial court held that, under 9th Circuit rulings, defendants were not guilty of conspiracy to sell drugs, because the conspiracy had already terminated. The Supreme Court reversed:

> The Ninth Circuit held that a conspiracy continues "until there is affirmative evidence of abandonment, withdrawal, disavowal or defeat of the object of the conspiracy." The critical portion of this statement is the last segment, that a conspiracy ends once there has been "defeat of its object." The Circuit's holdings make clear that the phrase means that the conspiracy ends through "defeat" when the Government intervenes, making the conspiracy's goals impossible to achieve, even if the conspirators do not know that the Government has intervened and are totally unaware that the conspiracy is bound to fail. In our view, this statement of the law is incorrect. A conspiracy does not automatically terminate simply because the Government, unbeknownst to some of the conspirators, has "defeated" the conspiracy's "object."

> The Ninth Circuit's rule is inconsistent with our own understanding of basic conspiracy law. The Court has repeatedly said that the essence of a conspiracy is an agreement to commit an unlawful act. That agreement is a distinct evil, which may exist and be punished whether or not the substantive crime ensues. The conspiracy poses a threat to the public over and above the threat of the commission of the relevant substantive crime — both because the combination in crime makes more likely the commission of other crimes and because it decreases the probability that the individuals involved will depart from their path of criminality. Where police have frustrated a conspiracy's specific objective but conspirators (unaware of that fact) have neither abandoned the conspiracy nor withdrawn, these special conspiracy-related dangers remain. Cf. 2 W. LaFave & A. Scott, Substantive Criminal Law § 6.5, p. 85 (1986) ("impossibility" does not terminate conspiracy because "criminal combinations are dangerous apart from the danger of attaining the particular objective"). So too remains the essence of the conspiracy — the agreement to commit the crime. That being so, the Government's defeat of the conspiracy's objective will not necessarily and automatically terminate the conspiracy. * * * *

> The American Law Institute's Model Penal Code § 5.03, p. 384 (1985), would find that a conspiracy "terminates when the crime or crimes that are its object are committed" or when the relevant "agreement is abandoned." It would not find "impossibility" a basis for termination.

UNITED STATES v. BRUNO
U.S. Court of Appeals, 2nd Circuit
105 F.2d 921 (1939), reversed on other grounds, 308 U.S. 287 (1939)

PER CURIAM

Bruno and Iacono were indicted along with 86 others for a conspiracy to import, sell and possess narcotics; some were acquitted; others, besides these two, were convicted, but they alone appealed. They complain (1) that if the evidence proved anything, it proved a series of separate conspiracies, and not a single one, as alleged in the indictment.

The point was made at the conclusion of the prosecution's case: the defendants then moved to dismiss the indictment on the ground that several conspiracies had been proved, and not the one alleged. The evidence allowed the jury to find that there had existed over a substantial period of time a conspiracy embracing a great number of persons, whose object was to smuggle narcotics into the Port of New York and distribute them to addicts both in this city and in Texas and Louisiana. This required the cooperation of four groups of persons; the smugglers who imported the drugs; the middlemen who paid the smugglers and distributed to retailers; and two groups of retailers - one in New York and one in Texas and Louisiana - who supplied the addicts.

The defendants assert that there were, therefore, at least three separate conspiracies; one between the smugglers and the middlemen, and one between the middlemen and each group of retailers. The evidence did not disclose any cooperation or communication between the smugglers and either group of retailers, or between the two groups of retailers themselves; however, the smugglers knew that the middlemen must sell to retailers, and the retailers knew that the middlemen must buy of importers of one sort or another. Thus the conspirators at one end of the chain knew that the unlawful business would not, and could not, stop with their buyers; and those at the other end knew that it had not begun with their sellers. That being true, a jury might have found that all the accused were embarked upon a venture, in all parts of which each was a participant, and an abettor in the sense that the success of that part with which he was immediately concerned, was dependent upon the success of the whole.

It might still be argued that there were two conspiracies; one including the smugglers, the middlemen and the New York group, and the other, the smugglers, the middlemen and the Texas & Louisiana group, for there was apparently no privity between the two groups of retailers. That too would be fallacious. Clearly, *quoad* the smugglers, there was but one conspiracy, for it was of no moment to them whether the middlemen sold to one or more groups of retailers, provided they had a market somewhere. So too of any retailer; he knew that he was a necessary link in a scheme of distribution, and the others, whom he knew to be convenient to its execution, were as much parts of a single undertaking or enterprise as two salesmen in the same shop. We think therefore that there was only one conspiracy. * * * *

Judgment reversed as to Iacono. Judgment affirmed as to Bruno.

NOTES FROM PEGGY:

(1) Why did the defendants argue that there were 3 conspiracies rather than one? If accepted, wouldn't this subject them to punishment for 3 crimes rather than one?

(2) Does *Bruno* have any affect on the issue of Dates' statement? Consider *United States v. Borelli*, 336 F.2d 376 (2nd cir. 1964), where the court had the following comments on *Bruno's* approach:

"As applied to the long term operation of an illegal business, the common pictorial distinction between 'chain' and 'spoke' conspiracies can obscure as much as it clarifies. The chain metaphor is indeed apt in that the links of a narcotics conspiracy are inextricably related to one another, from grower, through exporter and importer, to wholesaler, middleman, and retailer, each depending for his own success on the performance of all the others. But this simple picture tends to obscure that the links at either end are likely to consist of a number of persons who may have no reason to know that others are performing a role similar to theirs — in other words the extreme links of a chain conspiracy may have elements of the spoke conspiracy.[2]

Moreover, whatever the value of the chain concept where the problem is to trace a single operation from the start through its various phases to its successful conclusion, it becomes confusing when, over a long period of time, certain links continue to play the same role but with new counterparts, as where importers who regard their partnership as a single continuing one, having successfully distributed one cargo through X distributing organization, turn, years later, to moving another cargo obtained from a different source through Y. Thus, however reasonable the so-called presumption of continuity may be as to all the participants of a conspiracy which intends a single act, such as the robbing of a bank, or even as to the core of a conspiracy to import and resell narcotics, its force is diminished as to the outer links - buyers indifferent to their sources of supply and turning from one source to another, and suppliers equally indifferent to the identity of their customers.

The basic difficulty arises in applying the seventeenth century notion of conspiracy, where the gravamen of the offense was the making of an agreement to commit a readily identifiable crime or series of crimes, such as murder or robbery (see *Developments in the Law — Criminal Conspiracy*, 72 Harv.L.Rev. 922, 923 (1959)), to what in substance is the conduct of an illegal business over a period of years. There has been a tendency in such cases "to deal with the crime of conspiracy as though it were a group of men rather than an act" of agreement. See 72 Harv.L.Rev. 922, 934. Although it is usual and often necessary in conspiracy cases for the agreement to be proved by inference from acts, the gist of the offense remains the agreement, and it is therefore essential to determine what kind of agreement or understanding existed as to each defendant. It is a great deal harder

---

[2] Thus, in the oft-cited *Bruno* case, although it is clear enough that "*quoad* the smugglers, there was but one conspiracy, for it was of no moment to them whether the middlemen sold to one or more groups of retailers, provided they had a market somewhere," 105 F.2d at 923, it is not so clear why the New York and Texas groups of retailers were not in a "spoke" relation with the smugglers and the middleman, so that there would be two conspiracies unless the evidence permitted the inference that each group of retailers must have known the operation to be so large as to require the other as an outlet.

to tell just what agreement can reasonably be inferred from the purchase, even the repeated purchase, of contraband, than from the furnishing of dynamite to prospective bank robbers or the exchange of worthless property for securities to be subsequently distributed. Purchase or sale of contraband may, of course, warrant the inference of an agreement going well beyond the particular transaction. A seller of narcotics in bulk surely knows that the purchasers will undertake to resell the goods over an uncertain period of time, and the circumstances may also warrant the inference that a supplier or a purchaser indicated a willingness to repeat. But a sale or a purchase scarcely constitutes a sufficient basis for inferring agreement to cooperate with the opposite parties for whatever period they continue to deal in this type of contraband, unless some such understanding is evidenced by other conduct which accompanies or supplements the transaction."

KRULEWITCH v. UNITED STATES
U.S. Supreme Court
336 U.S. 440 (1949)

MR. JUSTICE BLACK delivered the opinion of the Court.

A federal district court indictment charged in three counts that petitioner and a woman defendant had (1) induced and persuaded another woman to go on October 20, 1941, from New York City to Miami, Florida, for the purpose of prostitution, in violation of 18 U.S.C. § 399; (2) transported or caused her to be transported from New York to Miami for that purpose, in violation of 18 U.S.C. § 398; and (3) conspired to commit those offenses in violation of 18 U.S.C. § 88. Tried alone, the petitioner was convicted on all three counts of the indictment. The Court of Appeals affirmed. We granted certiorari, limiting our review to consideration of alleged error in admission of certain hearsay testimony against petitioner over his timely and repeated objections.

The challenged testimony was elicited by the Government from its complaining witness, the person whom petitioner and the woman defendant allegedly induced to go from New York to Florida for the purpose of prostitution. The testimony narrated the following purported conversation between the complaining witness and petitioner's alleged coconspirator, the woman defendant.

"She asked me, she says, 'You didn't talk yet?' And I says, 'No.' And she says, 'Well, don't,' she says, 'until we get you a lawyer.' And then she says, 'Be very careful what you say.' And I can't put it in exact words. But she said, 'It would be better for us two girls to take the blame than Kay (the defendant) because he couldn't stand it, he couldn't stand to take it." '

The time of the alleged conversation was more than a month and a half after October 20, 1941, the date the complaining witness had gone to Miami. Whatever original conspiracy may have existed between petitioner and his alleged coconspirator to cause the complaining witness to go to Florida in October, 1941, no longer existed when the reported conversation took place in December, 1941. For on this latter date the trip to Florida had not only been made - the complaining witness had left Florida, had returned to New York, and had resumed her residence there. Furthermore, at the time the conversation took place, the complaining witness, the alleged coconspirator, and the petitioner had been arrested. They apparently were charged in a United States District Court of Florida with the offense of which petitioner was here convicted.

It is beyond doubt that the central aim of the alleged conspiracy - transportation of the complaining witness to Florida for prostitution - had either never existed or had long since ended in success or failure when and if the alleged coconspirator made the statement attributed to her. The statement plainly implied that petitioner was guilty of the crime for which he was on trial. It was made in petitioner's absence and the Government made no effort whatever to show that it was made with his authority. The testimony thus stands as an unsworn, out-of-court declaration of petitioner's guilt.

This hearsay declaration, attributed to a coconspirator, was not made pursuant to and in furtherance of objectives of the conspiracy charged in the indictment, because if made, it was after those objectives either had failed or had been achieved. Under these circumstances, the hearsay declaration attributed to the alleged coconspirator was not admissible on the theory that it was made in furtherance of the alleged criminal transportation undertaking. *Fiswick v. United States*, 329 U.S. 211, 216-217.

Although the Government recognizes that the chief objective of the conspiracy - transportation for prostitution purposes — had ended in success or failure before the reported conversation took place, it nevertheless argues for admissibility of the hearsay declaration as one in furtherance of a continuing subsidiary objective of the conspiracy.

Its argument runs this way. Conspirators about to commit crimes always expressly or implicitly agree to collaborate with each other to conceal facts in order to prevent detection, conviction and punishment. Thus the argument is that even after the central criminal objectives of a conspiracy have succeeded or failed, an implicit subsidiary phase of the conspiracy always survives, the phase which has concealment as its sole objective. The Court of Appeals adopted this view. It viewed the alleged hearsay declaration as one in furtherance of this continuing subsidiary phase of the conspiracy, as part of "the implied agreement to conceal." It consequently held the declaration properly admitted.

We cannot accept the Government's contention. There are many logical and practical reasons that could be advanced against a special evidentiary rule that permits out-of-court statements of one conspirator to be used against another. But however cogent these reasons, it is firmly established that where made in furtherance of the objectives of a going conspiracy, such statements are admissible as exceptions to the hearsay rule. This prerequisite to admissibility, that hearsay statements by some conspirators to be admissible against others must be made in furtherance of the conspiracy charged, has been scrupulously observed by federal courts.

The Government now asks us to expand this narrow exception to the hearsay rule and hold admissible a declaration, not made in furtherance of the alleged criminal transportation conspiracy charged, but made in furtherance of an alleged implied but uncharged conspiracy aimed at preventing detection and punishment. * * * * The rule contended for by the Government could have far-reaching results. For under this rule plausible arguments could generally be made in conspiracy cases that most out-of-court statements offered in evidence tended to shield coconspirators. We are not persuaded to adopt the Government's implicit conspiracy theory which in all criminal conspiracy cases would create automatically a further breach of the general rule against the admission of hearsay evidence. * * * *

Reversed.

MR. JUSTICE JACKSON, concurring in the judgment and opinion of the Court.

This case illustrates a present drift in the federal law of conspiracy which warrants some further comment because it is characteristic of the long evolution of that elastic, sprawling and pervasive offense. Its history exemplifies the "tendency of a principle to expand itself to the limit of its logic."[1] The unavailing protest of courts against the growing habit to indict for conspiracy in lieu of prosecuting for the substantive offense itself, or in addition thereto, suggests that loose practice as to this offense constitutes a serious threat to fairness in our administration of justice.

The modern crime of conspiracy is so vague that it almost defies definition. Despite certain elementary and essential elements, it also, chameleon-like, takes on a special coloration from each of the many independent offenses on which it may be overlaid. It is always "predominantly mental in composition" because it consists primarily of a meeting of minds and an intent.

An English author — Wright, *The Law of Criminal Conspiracies and Agreements*, p. 11 — gives up with the remark: "but no intelligible definition of 'conspiracy' has yet been established."

Carson offers the following resume of American cases: "It would appear that a conspiracy must be a combination of two or more persons by some concerted action to accomplish some criminal object; or some object not criminal by criminal means; or, some object not criminal by means which are not criminal, but where mischief to the public is involved; or, where neither the object nor the means are criminal, or even unlawful, but where injury and oppression to individuals are the result." *The Law of Criminal Conspiracies and Agreements, as Found in The American Cases*, p. 123.

The crime comes down to us wrapped in vague but unpleasant connotations. It sounds historical undertones of treachery, secret plotting and violence on a scale that menaces social stability and the security of the state itself. "Privy conspiracy" ranks with sedition and rebellion in the Litany's prayer for deliverance. Conspiratorial movements do indeed lie back of the political assassination, the coup d'etat, the putsch, the revolution, and seizures of power in modern times, as they have in all history.

---

[1] The phrase is Judge Cardozo's — *The Nature of the Judicial Process*, p. 51.

On conspiracy principles, German courts, on May 30, 1924, adjudged the Nazi Party to be a criminal organization. It also held in 1928 that the Leadership Corps of the Communist Party was a criminal organization and in 1930 entered judgment of criminality against the Union of Red Front Fighters of the Communist Party.

But the conspiracy concept also is superimposed upon many concerted crimes having no political motivation. It is not intended to question that the basic conspiracy principle has some place in modern criminal law, because to unite, back of a criminal purpose, the strength, opportunities and resources of many is obviously more dangerous and more difficult to police than the efforts of a lone wrongdoer. It also may be trivialized, as here, where the conspiracy consists of the concert of a loathsome panderer and a prostitute to go from New York to Florida to ply their trade, and it would appear that a simple Mann Act prosecution would vindicate the majesty of federal law. However, even when appropriately invoked, the looseness and pliability of the doctrine present inherent dangers which should be in the background of judicial thought wherever it is sought to extend the doctrine to meet the exigencies of a particular case.

Conspiracy in federal law aggravates the degree of crime over that of unconcerted offending. The act of confederating to commit a misdemeanor, followed by even an innocent overt act in its execution, is a felony and is such even if the misdemeanor is never consummated.

A recent tendency has appeared in this Court to expand this elastic offense and to facilitate its proof. In *Pinkerton v. United States*, 328 U.S. 640, it sustained a conviction of a substantive crime where there was no proof of participation in or knowledge of it, upon the novel and dubious theory that conspiracy is equivalent in law to aiding and abetting.

Further, the Court has dispensed with even the necessity to infer any definite agreement, although that is the gist of the offense. "It is elementary that an unlawful conspiracy may be and often is formed without simultaneous action or agreement on the part of the conspirators." *United States v. Masonite Corp.*, 316 U.S. 265, 275. One might go on from the reports of this and lower courts and put together their decisions condoning absence of proof to demonstrate that the minimum of proof required to establish conspiracy is extremely low, and we may expect our pronouncements in civil cases to be followed in criminal ones also.

Of course, it is for prosecutors rather than courts to determine when to use a scatter-gun to bring down the defendant, but there are procedural advantages from using it which add to the danger of unguarded extension of the concept.

An accused, under the Sixth Amendment, has the right to trial "by an impartial jury of the State and district wherein the crime shall have been committed." The leverage of a conspiracy charge lifts this limitation from the prosecution and reduces its protection to a phantom, for the crime is considered so vagrant as to have been committed in any district where any one of the conspirators did any one of the acts, however innocent, intended to accomplish its object. The Government may, and often does, compel one to defend at a great distance from any place he ever did any act because some accused confederate did some trivial and by itself innocent act in the chosen district. Circumstances may even enable the prosecution to fix the place of trial in Washington, D.C., where a defendant may lawfully be put to trial before a jury partly or even wholly made up of employees of the Government that accuses him.

When the trial starts, the accused feels the full impact of the conspiracy strategy. Strictly, the prosecution should first establish prima facie the conspiracy and identify the conspirators, after which evidence of acts and declarations of each in the course of its execution are admissible against all. But the order of proof of so sprawling a charge is difficult for a judge to control. As a practical matter, the accused often is confronted with a hodgepodge of acts and statements by others which he may never have authorized or intended or even known about, but which help to persuade the jury of existence of the conspiracy itself. In other words, a conspiracy often is proved by evidence that is admissible only upon assumption that conspiracy existed. The naive assumption that prejudicial effects can be overcome by instructions to the jury all practicing lawyers know to be unmitigated fiction.

The trial of a conspiracy charge doubtless imposes a heavy burden on the prosecution, but it is an especially difficult situation for the defendant. The hazard from loose application of rules of evidence is aggravated where the Government institutes mass trials.[20]

A codefendant in a conspiracy trial occupies an uneasy seat. There generally will be evidence of wrong-doing by somebody. It is difficult for the individual to make his own case stand on its own merits in the minds of jurors who are ready to believe that birds of a feather are flocked together. If he is silent, he is taken to admit it and if, as often happens, codefendants can be prodded into accusing or contradicting each other, they convict each other. There are many practical difficulties in defending against a charge of conspiracy which I will not enumerate.

Against this inadequately sketched background, I think the decision of this case in the court below introduced an ominous expansion of the accepted law of conspiracy. The prosecution was allowed to incriminate the defendant by means of the prostitute's recital of a conversation with defendant's alleged coconspirator, who was not on trial. The conversation was said to have taken place after the substantive offense was accomplished, after the defendant, the coconspirator and the witness had all been arrested, and after the witness and the other two had a falling out. The Court of Appeals sustained its admission upon grounds stated as follows:

> We think that implicit in a conspiracy to violate the law is an agreement among the conspirators to conceal the violation after as well as before the illegal plan is consummated. Thus the conspiracy continues, at least for purposes of concealment, even after its primary aims have been accom-

---

[20] An example is afforded by *Allen v. United States*, 4 F.2d 688. At the height of the prohibition frenzy, seventy-five defendants were tried on charges of conspiracy. A newspaper reporter testified to going to a drinking place where he talked with a woman, behind the bar, whose name he could not give. There was not the slightest identification of her nor showing that she knew or was known by any defendant. But it was held that being back of the bar showed her to be a coconspirator and, hence, her statements were admissible against all. He was allowed to relate incriminating statements made by her.

plished. The statements of the coconspirator here were made in an effort to protect the appellant by concealing his role in the conspiracy. Consequently, they fell within the implied agreement to conceal and were admissible as evidence against the appellant.

I suppose no person planning a crime would accept as a collaborator one on whom he thought he could not rely for help if he were caught, but I doubt that this fact warrants an inference of conspiracy for that purpose. Of course, if an understanding for continuous aid had been proven, it would be embraced in the conspiracy by evidence and there would be no need to imply such an agreement. Only where there is no convincing evidence of such an understanding is there need for one to be implied.

It is difficult to see any logical limit to the "implied conspiracy," either as to duration or means, nor does it appear that one could overcome the implication by express and credible evidence that no such understanding existed, nor any way in which an accused against whom the presumption is once raised can terminate the imputed agency of his associates to incriminate him. Conspirators, long after the contemplated offense is complete, after perhaps they have fallen out and become enemies, may still incriminate each other by deliberately harmful, but unsworn declarations, or unintentionally by casual conversations out of court. On the theory that the law will impute to the confederates a continuing conspiracy to defeat justice, one conceivably could be bound by another's unauthorized and unknown commission of perjury, bribery of a juror or witness, or even putting an incorrigible witness with damaging information out of the way.

Moreover, the assumption of an indefinitely continuing offense would result in an indeterminate extension of the statute of limitations. If the law implies an agreement to cooperate in defeating prosecution, it must imply that it continues as long as prosecution is a possibility, and prosecution is a possibility as long as the conspiracy to defeat it is implied to continue.

There is, of course, strong temptation to relax rigid standards when it seems the only way to sustain convictions of evildoers. But statutes authorize prosecution for substantive crimes for most evil-doing without the dangers to the liberty of the individual and the integrity of the judicial process that are inherent in conspiracy charges. We should disapprove the doctrine of implied or constructive crime in its entirety and in every manifestation. And I think there should be no straining to uphold any conspiracy conviction where prosecution for the substantive offense is adequate and the purpose served by adding the conspiracy charge seems chiefly to get procedural advantages to ease the way to conviction.

MR. JUSTICE FRANKFURTER and MR. JUSTICE MURPHY join in this opinion.

NOTES FROM PEGGY:

(1) How can *Krulewitch* be reconciled with *McDonald*?

(2) Mr. Justice Jackson had some prior experience with conspiracy. In 1946, he took a break from his Supreme Court duties to serve as Chief Prosecutor at the

first Nuremberg trial, where defendants Herman Goering, Rudolph Hess, and 20 more top Nazi officials were tried before a tribunal of British, American, French, and Russian judges. Each defendant was alleged to have committed different war crimes, so the only way to convict all of them for all crimes was to charge them with a single conspiracy. It didn't work, partly because the French and Russian judges did not really understand the concept of conspiracy, which does not exist in the continental legal system. Ten of the 22 defendants were sentenced to death, and 9 others received long prison terms — due to their own acts, not to conspiracy. Telford Taylor, *Anatomy of the Nuremberg Trials* (1992).

(3) How may a co-conspirator *withdraw* from the conspiracy? In *U.S. v. Grimmett*, 236 F.3d 452 (8th Cir. 2001), the court stated:

> Federal drug conspiracy crimes are subject to the five-year statute of limitations found in 18 U.S.C. § 3282. The limitations period begins when a conspirator withdraws from a continuing conspiracy. But it is not easy to withdraw from a criminal conspiracy.

> Mere cessation of activity is not enough to start the running of the statute; there must also be affirmative action, either the making of a clean breast to the authorities, or communication of the abandonment in a manner reasonably calculated to reach co-conspirators. * * * *

> A conspirator's confession — the making of a "clean breast" — qualifies as an affirmative act because it tends both to defeat the purposes of the ongoing conspiracy and to evidence the confessing conspirator's bona fide intent to withdraw. But the confession is not, by itself, enough to start the limitations period. The issue is still withdrawal, and even a full confession may be followed by conduct demonstrating the conspirator's continuing support of or acquiescence in the conspiracy. In that event, the statute of limitations will *not* begin to run until the conspiracy runs its course.

UNITED STATES v. PEREZ
U.S. Court of Appeals, Fifth Circuit
489 F.2d 51 (1973)

BROWN, CHIEF JUDGE

The facts of this case, in a purely legalistic sense, need no embellishment in a literary sense to classify this as a piece of prose that could well be called a second "American tragedy." It would be an American tragedy, not only because the events took place here, but because it is just another instance in which large numbers of Americans get willingly involved in enterprises which reflect a lack of compunction, possibly even a proclivity, to enter into the proverbial "get-rich-quick scheme" evidencing not only a disregard for law but, sadly, also a deafness to conscience. As we undertake our profound but prosaic role of adjudicating these cases, what we see is not pleasant. It reveals a wreckage of promising professional careers, evidence of deliberate and unabashed attempts to prey upon financially pressed expectant mothers for gain and the seemingly all too eager participation by a large cast of characters in a patently illegal undertaking.

The Scheme

A recital of the facts must precede resolution of the issues raised on appeal. The Louisiana-wide get-rich quick scheme involved the staging of fraudulent automobile accidents for the purpose of creating false personal injury claims. These claims would be submitted to the insurance carriers for the respective vehicles involved in the wrecks with the aid and contrivance of certain physicians and lawyers.

As the scheme evolved, the participants even coined their own terminology which, though alien to the uninitiated, became known to all those who participated. This glossary of modern day crookedness was quite descriptive. Certain participants were known as "recruiters". The recruiters' function, not unnaturally, was to recruit others who assumed titles commensurate with their organizational function. There were the "hitters", whose function it was to drive the "hitter" vehicle in each collision which supposedly was to be liable for causing the accident. Then there was the "target" vehicles. The occupants of the "target" were known as the "driver" and the "riders." It was determined at the outset that pregnant women made exceptionally good riders as they could claim pregnancy-related injuries, which would be both hard to disprove and easily settleable with the insurance carriers. Throughout the scheme, there was an effort made on the part of the participants to use vehicles and drivers which were covered by high limits of liability insurance.

According to a pre-arranged timetable, the "hitter" vehicle would strike the "target" vehicle either broadside or in the rear end. The occupants of the "target" vehicle — the driver and riders — and occasionally some of those in the "hitter" vehicle, feigning injuries, would be sent to a particular doctor and lawyer who would facilitate phony claims by creating a medical history for treatment of non-existent injuries and making a demand on the appropriate insurance company.

The key to immediate financial gain in each staged collision was advances paid by the attorneys to the "riders" for whom allegedly false claims were being submitted. These advances were paid in the form either of cash payments or loans from local financial institutions, co-signed by the attorney handling the claim. Of the usual advance ranging from $250 to $500, part was retained by the rider-claimant with the rest being distributed among the organizers, recruiters, and others who assisted with various aspects of staging the wreck. When the claim was ultimately settled with the insurance carrier, the proceeds would be applied to (i) repay the advancing attorney or in such cases, to liquidate the guaranteed bank loan and (ii) to pay the inflated doctor's bill, not infrequently, with kickbacks going to both the organizers and the participating attorneys in addition to their usual shares.

The feature of this case which brought it into federal court was that, in the course of asserting and negotiating for settlement the fraudulent claims of the voluntary victims, the United States mails were used.

On April 3, 1967, the Grand Jury returned a thirteen-count indictment against the appellants and nine others charging them all with conspiracy to violate the mail fraud statute (18 U.S.C.A. § 371), and selected defendants with the additional offense of violating the mail fraud statute (18 U.S.C.A. § 1341). [At trial, appellants were convicted of conspiracy to violate the mail fraud statute.]

Single Or Multiple Conspiracies

All appellants assert that a variance existed between the indictment charging a single conspiracy involving multiple defendants and the proof which, at best they claim, revealed plural conspiracies involving multiple parties which, admittedly, overlapped upon one another in personnel.

The necessity for distinguishing between evidence which tends to show a single overall conspiracy and that which tends to show several separate conspiracies, a frustrating and challenging task indeed, has been faced by this court before. *United States v. Morado*, 5 cir. 1972, 454 F.2d 167. The necessity for drawing this distinction derives from our interest, clearly our duty, in jealously protecting those accused from the possible transference of guilt of others accused, at least in the eyes and minds of a jury, which so often is claimed to be encountered where en masse prosecutions are undertaken for a conglomeration of separate offenses. The object of such an inquiry must be, in the first instance, to ascertain whether (i) such a variance between the indictment and the proof actually exists and, if it does, (ii) to determine whether substantial rights of an accused are in fact affected by the variance. To conclude in the negative on element (i), of course, would obviate inquiry on (ii).

The theory of the government's case, as expressed in count XIII of the indictment, was that all defendants were co-conspirators in a single common scheme to cause the mails to be used in furtherance of a scheme or artifice to defraud insurance companies through the staging of automobile collisions prior to January 1, 1967 and continuously thereafter until the date of the return of the indictment.

Kenneth DeMary testified that he was approached in October of 1965 by his friend and former employee Mayo Perez, with the idea of making "fast money" by staging fraudulent automobile collisions and collecting from the insurance carriers for alleged damages suffered. This testimony indicated that it was Kenneth's acquaintance with various attorneys around the state of Louisiana with whom he could arrange the handling of fraudulent claims which induced Perez to seek his participation. Larry DeMary testified that shortly thereafter his brother (Kenneth DeMary) and Mayo Perez came to him and asked that he join them in the proposed scheme. When he agreed, the trio staged the first of a long series of fraudulent collisions near Bossier City, Louisiana on November 3, 1965.

Hub - Spokes - Wheel?

With the law's sometime misleading quest for manageable analogy, the government contends that the agreement reached between Kenneth DeMary, Larry DeMary and Mayo Perez constituted them as the "hub" members of a conspiracy which remained operative for many months thereafter until the return of the indictment. The structure of the conspiracy charged, if portrayed schematically, would resemble a "wheel."[7] At the "hub" of the wheel would be the three initial conspirators.[8] The "spokes" would be the participants of the individual staged accidents proved. The government maintains that the lawyers, doctors, recruiters, and passengers who comprised these "spokes" would, at times, enter the conspiracy by participating in an accident as initially planned and expected, thereby adopting the common objective of the conspiracy as their own. Each spoke, under the government's theory, thus, was engaged in a similar relationship with one or more of the hub figures.

If Not A Spoke — Hub — Wheel, A Chain

Structural analysis can be carried a step further, by viewing each individual spoke as a "chain" type of conspiracy. The "chain" conspiracy is characterized by different activities carried on with regard to the same subject such that each conspirator, in a chain-like manner, performs a separate function which serves as a step or phase in the accomplishment of the overall contrivance. Here the end product in each chain was the defrauding of insurance companies through the creation of false personal injury claims with a resultant use of the mails. Viewed strictly in terms of their degree of involvement,[9] from the periphery of the wheel inward to the "hub", the "chain" or "spoke" participants would appear in the order of rider — driver (of target) — hitter — recruiters — doctors — lawyers — hub figures.

What Appellants Accept

Appellants, with regard to the staging of each individual wreck, do not vigorously argue that knowledge and awareness of one conspirator, relative to the existence and general activities of the other conspirators, could not have been inferred. Using the test of *United States v. Bruno*, 2 Cir., 1938, 105 F.2d 921, each conspirator, once he knew he was to be involved in a staged collision, should have been aware of the others.[10] As such, the riders must have known that their phony

---

[7] See, Note, *Federal Treatment of Multiple Conspiracies*, 57 Columbia Law Review 387, which distinguishes the "wheel" type conspiracy from the "chain" type.

[8] The principal "hub" figures here would be Kenneth and Larry DeMary. Mayo Perez would be a lesser "hub" figure since he participated in fewer of the accidents. At the trial, the government also attempted to establish Earl DeMary as a "hub" figure for his part in organizing the January 5 accident, but the trial court struck the counts of the indictment relating to this accident on grounds that it probably was a separate and distinct conspiracy and, as such, not a part of the overall conspiracy.

[9] Here we view the spoke participants in terms of their degree of involvement, rather than necessarily viewing them according to the succession of functions or steps performed, as previously discussed under the section of this opinion headed "The Scheme".

[10] In *Bruno*, narcotics were smuggled into New York and ultimately sold in Texas and Louisiana as well as in New York. Four independent groups were involved: the smugglers, the middlemen, and two groups of retailers. The importers' hope of profitable sale was dependent on the existence of a selling outlet. Similarly, the retailers could not stay in business without a continuing source of supply. The Court held that the conspirators at one end of the chain knew that the unlawful business would not, and could not, stop with their buyers; and those at the other end knew it had not begun with their sellers. Thus, in a "chain" conspiracy prosecution, the requisite element - knowledge of the existence of remote links — may be inferred solely from the nature of the enterprise.

claims were processed by insurance companies. Likewise, to each participant in the chain, the knowledge can be inferred that much more was required to complete the overall goal of obtaining funds on false pretenses than the sole function that they were performing.

Thus, appellants do not contend that the finding of a "chain" conspiracy as to each alleged auto wreck could not be properly reached by a jury. Nor do appellants contend that the jury could not properly find that perhaps some of these individual chain conspiracies were connected, since the participants overlapped to a degree and the activities performed were similar. It has been held that where the additional element of overlapping membership exists, there is considerable authority that a single overall conspiracy may be found, *United States v. Morado, supra*, and that there is sufficient evidence to allow the jury to consider the issue of whether there was a single conspiracy, or multiple conspiracies. *Jolley v. United States*, 5 Cir., 1956, 232 F.2d 83.

Not One, But Many Wheels - Or A Wheel Without A Rim

Though conceding an occasional overlapping of membership between the several spokes, appellants argue that here there existed several separate conspiracies. Appellants contend that subsequent to the first collision collaborated on between Kenneth and Larry DeMary in Bossier City on November 3, 1965, the two brothers proceeded to set up separate and distinct operations with no control exerted by either over the other's sphere of operation. Likewise they argue that Mayo Perez, also one of the initial collaborators, became the "hub" figure in another separate and distinct conspiracy. Again employing a structural analysis, appellants strenuously argue that the "wheel" which the government attempted to prove was deficient in that it lacked a "rim" of connexity. Absent, they contend, was a common objective and awareness of the other "spokes" existence which acts to bind the spokes together into one overall conspiracy.[11]

As supportive of their proposition, appellants point to the trial court's dismissal of counts I through IV of the indictment which were based on the January 5, 1966 collision which the trial Judge viewed as a separate and distinct conspiracy. Appellants contend that, just as the trial court disallowed the January 5, 1966 accident to be grouped by the government within an overall conspiracy in count XIII of the indictment, it should have further disallowed the grouping of the separate operations of Kenneth and Larry DeMary under the heading of one overall conspiracy.

---

[11] The importance in a wheel type conspiracy of such knowledge by individual spokes of the existence of other spokes was emphasized in *Federal Treatment of Multiple Conspiracies, supra* at 388-393. As there articulated, the test seems to be one of "interdependence." As there pointed out, although this test can be applied to the functional levels of a "chain" conspiracy with relative ease (see note 10, *supra*), its application to the spokes in a "wheel" conspiracy depends on whether the combined efforts of the spokes, as with the functions in a "chain", are required to insure the success of the venture.

As for us, the problem is difficult enough without trying to compress it into figurative analogies. Conspiracies are as complex as the versatility of human nature and federal protection against them is not to be measured by spokes, hubs, wheels, rims, chains, or any one or all of today's galaxy of mechanical molecular or atomic forms.

In asserting that a variance between the indictment and the proof here existed, and furthermore, that it is fatal, appellants primarily rely on the Supreme Court's decision in *Kotteakos v. United States*, 1946, 328 U.S. 750. In that case, one where the indictment charged but one overall conspiracy, the government's proof at trial, by its own admission, showed that there were eight separate conspiracies involving some thirty-two persons. The key figure in the scheme, which involved the obtaining of government loans by making fraudulent representations, was a man named Brown, who was a part of, and directed each of the eight conspiracies. Brown was the only element common to the eight otherwise completely separate undertakings, no other person taking part in, nor having knowledge of the other conspiracies. Though each of the conspiracies had similar illegal objects, none depended upon, was aided by, or had any interest in the success of the others.[12] The Supreme Court reversed the convictions. * * * *

We are unpersuaded that anything resembling the impairment of substantial rights so evident in *Kotteakos* took place here. A review of the record has convinced us that the evidence adduced, both direct and circumstantial, was adequate to warrant the inference that all the participants had entered into this concerted program. To conspire is to agree — the presence of an agreement is the primary requirement for the establishment of a conspiracy, the commission of an overt act in furtherance being attendant. Since conspiracy is a crime which by its nature tends to be secret, the agreement is seldom susceptible of direct proof.

Thus, the existence of a conspiracy is usually proved in one or more of three ways - by circumstantial evidence, by the testimony of a co-conspirator who has turned state's evidence,[15] or by evidence of out-of-court declarations or acts of a co-conspirator[16] or of the defendant himself. If the totality of these types of evidence is adequate to show a concert of action, all the parties working together understandingly, with a single design for the accomplishment of a common purpose, then the conspiracy may be found. This is not to be confused with situations where separate conspiracies exist and certain parties are common to each.[17]

"Every agreement has two dimensions: the persons privy thereto, and the objectives encompassed therein." Note, *Federal Treatment of Multiple Conspiracies, supra*. With respect to the first dimension, there is no requirement that every defendant must participate in every transaction in order to find a single conspiracy. While the conspiracy may have a small group of core conspirators, other parties who knowingly participate with these core conspirators and others to achieve a common goal may be members of an overall conspiracy. With respect to

---

[12] The only connection between the separate conspiracies was that each group had dealt independently with Brown as their agent.

[15] The testimony of a co-conspirator as to facts within his knowledge involves no hearsay problem, since the statements are given on the stand and are open to cross-examination.

[16] The general rule with regard to the admission of hearsay evidence as to the statements of a co-conspirator may be stated -any act or declaration by one co-conspirator committed in furtherance of the conspiracy and during its pendency, is admissible against each co-conspirator, provided that a foundation for its admission is laid by independent proof of the conspiracy.

[17] As was the case in *Kotteakos v. United States, supra*.

the objectives of the conspiracy, it can be said that the prohibited activity must be committed in furtherance of a common objective. Implicit within this second dimension, though, is the requisite that, not only must the objectives of all charged under one conspiracy be common, but there must be one objective, or set of objectives, or an overall objective to be achieved by multiple actions.[18]

In essence, the question is what is the nature of the agreement. If there is one overall agreement among the various parties to perform different functions in order to carry out the objectives of the conspiracy, then it is one conspiracy. If that agreement contemplates bringing to pass a continuous result that will not continue without the continuous cooperation of the conspirators to keep it up, then such agreement constitutes a single conspiracy. *United States v. Palermo*, 7 Cir., 1969, 410 F.2d 468. And the same is true as to an agreement that contemplates that the activity will be repeated sometimes with, sometimes not, the same actors.

Here, there was direct, positive testimony, if credited, from which the jury could find that each of the defendants were participants in one overall conspiracy. With hardly any exception, the testimony squared with the common sense of the scheme. The dictates of self-preservation and longevity necessitated that the scheme rapidly expand beyond the relatively small geographical area represented by Lake Charles, Louisiana and its environs. Hence the alleged separate operations of Kenneth and Larry DeMary in different areas of the state.[19] As the geographical area increased, it became necessary to vary the pattern of doctors and lawyers on each individual collision.[20] Avoidance of detection also necessitated constant changing of passengers and claimants.[21] There was evidence, direct and circumstantial, that the DeMary brothers were in constant communication throughout the life of the scheme.

---

[18] While this sounds like an exercise in semantics, the Supreme Court in *Kotteakos* concluded that while each of the eight separate schemes proved had as its objective the obtaining of fraudulent loans, each scheme to obtain a loan was an end in itself, and thus arose from a separate agreement.

[19] Testimony at trial revealed that Larry DeMary had a hand in planning and staging approximately 10 fraudulent collisions. Kenneth DeMary, on the other hand, planned and staged approximately 25 or 30 fraudulent collisions. Of the total, there is evidence that at least four staged collisions were jointly planned and organized by the two brothers.

Appellants argue that subsequent to the first staged collision jointly planned by the brothers in Bossier City, Louisiana on November 3, 1965, they proceeded to dissolve any common plan, which arguably may have existed between them, and set up separate operations. They contend that Larry began staging accidents in the Lake Charles area, while Kenneth pursued a similar, but separate, course in other areas of the state, primarily the northern part of Louisiana in and around Shreveport. While there is some indication that the brothers concentrated the bulk of their activities with some regard for geographical separation, we are convinced that the jury could conclude that the totality of their activities remained one overall conspiracy. We are aided in arriving at this conclusion, among other things, by the evidence that, subsequent to the November 3, 1965 collision, the DeMary brothers collaborated together on at least three more staged collisions. These occurred on January 6, April 25, and June 29 of 1966.

[20] The varying pattern of participation in the proved collisions by the appellant professionals also detracts heavily from the separate conspiracy argument advanced by appellants. An indication of this variation occurred in the May 25, 1966 staged collision organized by Kenneth DeMary in Shreveport where appellant attorneys Shaheen and Hennigan of Lake Charles represented the claimants from the "target" vehicle.

[21] No two staged collisions involved identical personnel, although there was considerable overlapping of personnel between staged collisions.

That here we have a single scheme which envisioned a series of staged collisions, rather than it being a series of "one shot" efforts, is evident by examining the sources of profitability for the convicted participants. The DeMary brothers and the convicted professionals, as well as the recruiters, could only benefit by direct participation in repeated staged collisions.[22] Each participated in as many of the staged collisions as prudence dictated.[23] This was the only way to make the scheme pay for these active participants and, as such, it can be said that the scheme inherently envisioned multiple collisions.

Not insignificant in pointing out the unitary nature of the scheme were the facts surrounding the collision staged on March 28, 1966 in Shreveport. Here, reimbursement of advances made by the appellant attorneys prior to learning of the non-existence of an insurance policy under which to make claims was contingent upon future staged collisions. There was testimony that these advances were subsequently repaid in this manner.

The record reflects careful planning and cooperation on the part of each of the persons involved in the conspiracy. We agree with the Seventh Circuit in *United States v. Palermo, supra,* at 470, where they wrote that — it would be "a perversion of natural thought and of natural language to call such continuous cooperation a cinematographic series of distinct conspiracies, rather than to call it a single one." In any event, in an instance such as the one presented by this case, with overlapping membership and activities all directed toward a common goal, most courts have found, as we do here, sufficient evidence to uphold a jury verdict reflecting a single conspiracy. *United States v. Borelli,* 2 Cir., 1964, 336 F.2d 376.

Non Spokes, Non Hubs, Non Rings, Non Wheels, Non Chains Should Stop The Law In Its Appointed Rounds

This thing seems terribly complex but it really is not. The scheme simply would not have gotten off the ground — involving, as it did, the professional people of doctors and lawyers as the key to ultimate success — were this to be a one shot operation. For rewards high enough to compensate for the awesome risks of loss of professional status, the ring leaders knew that there had to be a series of phony accidents. Nor were the riders, drivers, targets or hitters unaware of this. All knew that each occurrence was but a part of a plan by which phony accidents would be staged, necessarily at times and intervals, temporally and geographically separated to allay intense suspicions. Even the most innocuous of "riders" — indeed even a pregnant one — was aware in the execution of his/her part that the

---

[22] In an attempt to show the existence of multiple conspiracies appellants argue that each participant only benefited personally from the staged accidents in which he performed some function. While this is true, we do not think it exculpates any of those who were convicted. Although several of the appellants here at times served in the dual capacity of "rider," a role which might be characterized as passive — but still illegal — each did more. Each also handled an active role. Whether an organizer, hitter, rider, driver, recruiter, or professional, their roles actively furthered the scheme to defraud the insurance companies, and we think they were properly subject to being charged under one overall conspiracy. Not only was there ample evidence from which the jury could find that they performed the various functions charged, but there was likewise such evidence that they performed them on repeated occasions.

[23] Caution demanded that the conspirators avoid leaving a "trail" of identical doctors and lawyers.

enterprise was a crooked one in which each stood to gain.

From an operational sense this was not a series of little concoctions to set up a particular collision. It was rather a grand scheme for all to obtain some reward for his/her participation each according to the part played and the risk undertaken.

It only confounds the law to try to characterize this in the figure of spokes, wheels, hubs, rims or chains. See note 11, *supra*. It was one big, and hopefully profitable, enterprise, which looked toward successful frequent but none-the-less discreet repetitions, and in which each participant was neither innocent nor unrewarded.

We affirm the judgment of the trial court as respects all appellants on all counts under which they were convicted.

NOTES FROM PEGGY:

(1) How did the court distinguish *Kotteakos v. U.S.*?

(2) Recall Justice Jackson's statement in *Krulewitch* that "In *Pinkerton v. U.S.*, 328 U.S. 640 (1946), [the Court] sustained a conviction of a substantive crime where there was no proof of participation in or knowledge of it, upon the novel and dubious theory that conspiracy is equivalent in law to aiding and abetting." Putting this together with the holding in *Perez* that there was one large conspiracy here, does this mean that "the most innocuous of 'riders' - indeed even a pregnant one" is guilty of each of the hundreds of crimes of mail fraud and grand theft committed here? If it *does* mean this, then is there something faulty with the court's reasoning? On this score, you might compare *Perez* with *U.S. v. Blankenship* (in Section B of this Chapter).

(3) The *Pinkerton* rule was summarized in *State v. Coltherst*, 820 A.2d 1024 (Conn. 2003), where the court rejected an argument that the rule violated defendant's right to due process of law:

> Under the *Pinkerton* doctrine, a conspirator may be held liable for criminal offenses committed by a coconspirator that are within the scope of the conspiracy, are in furtherance of it, and are reasonably foreseeable as a necessary or natural consequence of the conspiracy. The rationale for the principle is that, when the conspirator has played a necessary part in setting in motion a discrete course of criminal conduct, he should be held responsible, within appropriate limits, for the crimes committed as a natural and probable result of that course of conduct. * * * *

> The defendant in the present case also claims that the application of *Pinkerton* under the facts of this case violates due process because it relieves the state of the burden of proving an element of the crime, namely, intent to kill. Again, we disagree. The defendant does not dispute the notion that *Pinkerton* constitutionally may reach *conduct* in which the defendant did not engage. We fail to see why a constitutional flaw appears when *Pinkerton* applies to the *intent* that accompanies that conduct. Both the intent and the conduct are essential elements of the crime and are subject to the principles of *In re Winship*, 397 U.S. 358, 364 (1970), that due process

requires the state to prove every element of the offense charged beyond a reasonable doubt. The United States Supreme Court in *Pinkerton* itself acknowledged that *Pinkerton* rests on the same principles as those governing accessory liability, which allow conduct to be imputed to a defendant. Our research has uncovered no case in which any court has suggested that accessory liability offends due process. We fail to see, therefore, why the imputation of intent under *Pinkerton* would do so. * * * *

We conclude that the *Pinkerton* doctrine constitutionally may be, and, as a matter of state policy, should be, applied in cases in which the defendant did not have the level of intent required by the substantive offense with which he was charged. The rationale for the doctrine is to deter collective criminal agreement and to protect the public from its inherent dangers by holding conspirators responsible for the natural and probable — not just the intended — results of their conspiracy.

(4) *Perez* involved a pretty well organized criminal scheme. Suppose it is *more loosely* organized. Suppose that some drug importers sell drugs in large quantities to various drug dealers on an irregular basis, and these dealers resell on an irregular basis to various "small timers" who use some and occasionally sell some to other users. Each person knows, in a general sense, the nature of the system, and each benefits somewhat from the size of the system, as it enables the big guys to dispose of large quantities of drugs in an efficient way. Are all of these people involved in one big conspiracy, as in *Perez*? The court in *U.S. v. Townsend*, 924 F.2d 1385 (7th cir. 1991), considered this issue:

As will be seen, the evidence clearly demonstrated that all but one of the defendants conspired with *someone* to distribute drugs. Why, then, do we care whether there was one conspiracy or many; what does it matter whether the defendants conspired as one large group or several smaller groups? There are at least three reasons.

First, alleging a single conspiracy enables the government to join a group of defendants together for trial, and joint trials almost always prejudice the rights of individual defendants to some degree. Some trade-off between prejudice and efficiency is, of course, necessary for the judicial system to function; otherwise the slow pace of our court system would go from a crawl to paralysis. Nevertheless, defendants are tried together only in cases where the prejudice to the defendant does not deprive him of a fundamentally fair trial and where a joint trial contributes significantly to the efficiency of the judicial system.

Second, and particularly apposite to this case, by alleging a single conspiracy, the government may invoke the coconspirator exception to the hearsay rule (Fed.R.Evid. 801(d)(2)(E)) to admit evidence against defendants that would otherwise be inadmissible. Statements of any of the defendants can be used to establish not only the existence of a conspiracy but also to establish that a particular defendant was a member of the conspiracy. The appellants jointly contested the government's use of coconspirator statements to prove each defendant's membership in a conspiracy. The appellants' challenge underscores the potency of the coconspirator exception and the need to ensure that it is invoked only against those who have actually conspired with the declarant.

And third, coconspirators are liable for the substantive crimes committed by members of the conspiracy that are in furtherance of the conspiracy. *Pinkerton v. U.S.*, 328 U.S. 640, 647 (1946). A finding that a defendant joined a conspiracy therefore exposes that defendant to much more than criminal liability for joining the conspiracy; he or she also faces liability for the substantive crimes of the conspiracy. A related consideration arises in drug cases. The type of drug with which one is involved does not change the nature of crime; 21 U.S.C. § 841(a) applies to all illicit drugs. Nevertheless, the penalties incurred vary dramatically with the type of drug involved in the offense. See 21 U.S.C. § 841(b). One convicted, as were the appellants in this case, of a conspiracy to distribute a variety of drugs can be sentenced to the highest range applicable to the drugs in which the conspiracy dealt even if the evidence suggests that a defendant had nothing to do with that drug. See 21 U.S.C. § 846. * * * *

The crime of conspiracy focuses on agreements, not groups. * * * * To join a conspiracy, then, is to join an agreement, rather than a group. It follows that to be a conspirator you must know of the agreement, and must intend to join it. Defendants, while conceding that the evidence may have shown that several agreements to distribute drugs existed among various subgroups, contend that the government presented no evidence that any of those dealing with Apolinar Marquez knew of, or intended to join, a larger agreement between Marquez and others to distribute drugs. * * * *

Typically we say that if the evidence indicates that a defendant must have known that his actions were benefiting a larger conspiracy, he may be said to have agreed to join that conspiracy. Seizing upon this logic, the government submits that by dealing with Apolinar Marquez, who was known by each defendant to be a large-scale drug dealer, each defendant supported, and therefore conspired with, the others with whom Marquez dealt. Taken to its extreme, the government's logic suggests that anyone selling or buying drugs from any one of these defendants also could have been convicted as a coconspirator. Anyone who does so must know, so its reasoning goes, that he's dealing with someone connected to a large drug conspiracy; each benefits from dealing with the conspiracy; therefore each participant is a member of the conspiracy.[3]

We think the government's argument stretches the boundaries of conspiracy law to the breaking point. We recognize that, by their very

---

[3] See Appellee's Brief at 20: "Here, each defendant knew or had reason to know that others were involved in an overall narcotics distribution scheme, and had reason to believe that his benefit from membership in the scheme depended on the success of the scheme as a whole; thus, each participated." As written, this argument begs the question of whether each defendant agreed to join the conspiracy; it posits that the reason each defendant participated in the conspiracy was to ensure that he benefited from participating in the conspiracy. In context, however, we think our characterization of the government's argument is accurate.

nature, drug conspiracies are loosely-knit ensembles. Where drug distribution conspiracies are charged, we can often infer that "the smugglers knew that the middlemen must sell to retailers, and the retailers knew that the middlemen must buy of importers of one sort or another." *U.S. v. Bruno*, 105 F.2d 921 (2d Cir.), rev'd on other grounds, 308 U.S. 287 (1939). But the liability of members of the distribution chain is predicated upon the notion that participants at different levels in the chain know that the success of those at each level hinges upon the success of the others and therefore cooperate for their mutual benefit. Only if "the conspirators at one end of the chain knew that the unlawful business would not, and could not, stop with their buyers; and those at the other end knew that it had not begun with their sellers," id., will the inference of knowledge and benefit be valid.

One may question, however, whether "the links of a narcotics conspiracy are inextricably related to one another, from grower, through exporter and importer, to wholesaler, middleman, and retailer, each depending for his own success on the performance of all the others." *U.S. v. Borelli*, 336 F.2d 376, 383 (2d cir. 1964). The suppliers in a "chain" are not necessarily interested in the success of a particular retailer, or group of retailers, down the line. If the chain is characterized by sporadic dealings between independent dealers, what do suppliers care if the middlemen are able to unload the stuff further? As Judge Friendly noted in *Borelli*, however reasonable the so-called presumption of continuity may be as to all the participants of a conspiracy which intends a single act, such as the robbing of a bank, or even as to the core of a conspiracy to import or resell narcotics, its force is diminished as to the outer links — buyers indifferent to their sources of supply and turning from one source to another, and suppliers equally indifferent to the identity of their customers. We reiterated this point in *U.S. v. Cerro*, 775 F.2d 908 (7th cir. 1985), where we observed that "the viability of wholesale drug trafficking does not depend on the adherence of any single dealer. Lop off one dealer, and the wholesaler can hire another in his place."

The chain paradigm is also flawed because it does little to establish any relationship between parties tied horizontally rather than vertically - i.e. those working at the same level of distribution - when they are charged with conspiring together. To evaluate these relationships we often invoke another conspiratorial paradigm — the wheel — comprised of a group of conspirators playing similar roles — the "spokes" — each related to the activities of a single "hub" conspirator or group. Again, however, mere knowledge of the hub's activities, or those of the other spokes, is not enough to tie the conspiracy together. In *Blumenthal v. U.S.*, 332 U.S. 539 (1947), for example, the Court distinguished the multiple conspiracies of *Kotteakos* from the single "wheel" conspiracy it was addressing:

Except for the common figure, no conspirator was interested in whether any loan except his own went through. And none aided in any way, by agreement or otherwise, in procuring another's loan. The conspiracies therefore were distinct and disconnected, not parts of a larger general scheme. Here the contrary is true.

Neither of these paradigms suffices, then, to show mutual support or interest among the component parts of the organizational construct. They don't eliminate the need to inquire directly into whether the defendants had a mutual interest in achieving the goal of the conspiracy and their relevance is therefore questionable. The fact that we can squeeze a group into a hypothetical organizational chart says little about whether a single agreement exists between the members of the group. An enterprise can have many divisions, programs, activities, contracts; they are not all a single agreement just because a handful of top officers is in charge of the entire firm and some of the lower-level employees may work on more than one program or contract.

It is easy to say, as we have in the past, that to be liable as coconspirators, defendants must be mutually dependent on one another, or must render mutual support. But "it is a great deal harder to tell just what agreement can reasonably be inferred from the purchase, even the repeated purchase, of contraband." *Borelli*, 336 F.2d at 384. By definition, market transactions — whether in legal or illegal markets — benefit both parties, but we do not assume, *ab initio*, that they carry with them the excess baggage of conspiracy. The agreement between the parties may not transcend the scope of the transaction itself. For example, in the absence of other evidence we would not presume that one who purchases drugs from a dealer who also runs an automobile "chop shop" intends to join the car theft ring, even if he knows about it. Neither activity necessarily, or even logically, advances the other. The analysis doesn't change when the other party confines his criminal activities to one market. For example, if a thief plans to rob two banks, with a different accomplice on each occasion, we do not presume, from this fact alone, that the three bank robbers have conspired together, even if each accomplice knows that his partner is also planning a robbery with someone else. See Note, *Developments in the Law — Conspiracy*, 72 Harv.L.Rev. 920, 933 (1959).

By the same token, when dealer A sells drugs to dealer B, we don't presume that A has agreed to work for the benefit of everyone else with whom B deals, or that A benefits from B's other deals. If A knows of, and benefits from, B's subsequent distribution, we may infer a limited agreement to distribute between A and B. See, e.g., *U. S. v. Roth*, 777 F.2d 1200, 1205 (7th cir. 1985) ("while the ultimate consumer is not himself a conspirator, the middleman is"). But agreement to join other endeavors and distributors "cannot be drawn merely from knowledge the buyer will use the goods illegally." *Direct Sales Co. v. U.S.*, 319 U.S. 703, 709 (1943). The scope of a conspiracy is determined by the scope of the agreement, and if the jury is to infer an agreement to join a conspiracy that transcends the scope of a more limited conspiracy, there must be some additional evidence to justify taking the inference further:

A seller of narcotics in bulk surely knows that the purchasers will undertake to resell the goods over an uncertain period of time, and the circumstances may also warrant the inference that a supplier or a purchaser indicated a willingness to repeat. But a sale or a purchase scarcely constitutes a sufficient basis for inferring agreement to cooperate with the opposite parties *for whatever period they continue to deal in this type of contraband, unless some such understanding is evidenced by other conduct which accompanies or supplements the transaction.* [*Borelli*, 336 F.2d at 384 (emphasis added).]

To sustain a conspiracy conviction, then, there must be "more than suspicion, more than knowledge, acquiescence, carelessness, indifference, or lack of concern." *Direct Sales*, 319 U.S. at 713. Drug dealers are no more likely to be confederates than are criminals who engage in disparate activities; this is true even if A knows that B deals with others as well. * * * *

Granted, one crime might aid the commission of another, but the point is that we cannot infer that both parties agreed to work together to achieve that result from the fact that they engaged together in some other crime. One may know of, and assist (even intentionally), a substantive crime without joining a conspiracy to commit the crime - witness the landlord who rents to an illegal gambling den, see *U.S. v. Giovanetti*, 919 F.2d 1223 (7th cir. 1990), and the retailer who sells sugar to one he knows will use it to make bootleg whiskey, see *U.S. v. Falcone*, 311 U.S. 205 (1940). We cannot, then, reasonably assume that everyone with whom a drug dealer does business benefits, directly or indirectly, from his other drug deals. In fact, any inference should probably run in the other direction. There is — hard though it may be to believe — a finite supply of drugs. Those in the market to sell or buy large quantities (for distribution) are just as likely, if not more, to be competitors as collaborators. * * * *

To be sure, the landlord in our example might be liable under civil forfeiture provisions, and, along with the retailer, might be liable for aiding and abetting the substantive offenses, but we do not subject them to additional liability as conspirators simply because they aided the conspiracy and derived a benefit from doing so. "Aiding, abetting, and counseling are not terms which presuppose the existence of an agreement. Those terms have a broader application, making the defendant a principal when he consciously shares in a criminal act, regardless of the existence of a conspiracy." *Pereira v. U.S.*, 347 U.S. 1, 11 (1954).

The reason for the distinction is simple. We punish conspiracy because joint action is, generally, more dangerous than individual action. "What makes the joint action of a group of n persons more fearsome than the individual actions of those n persons is the division of labor and the mutual psychological support that collaboration affords." L.Katz, *Bad Acts and Guilty Minds: Conundrums of the Criminal Law* (1987). Both the conspiracy and the market transaction are agreements, but only conspiracy poses the added danger of group action. True, aiding and abetting presupposes the existence of more than one actor, but aiders and abettors are already punished as principals. To justify imposing additional criminal liability,[4] there must be some additional evidence that their actions are intended to bring about the object of the conspiracy. Conspiracies, which are really "agreements to agree" on the multitude of decisions and acts necessary to successfully pull off a crime, pose an additional risk that the object of the conspiracy will be achieved, and so warrant additional penalties.

For this reason, evidence of a buyer-seller relationship, standing alone, is insufficient to support a conspiracy conviction. A sale, by definition, requires two parties; their combination for that limited purpose does not increase the likelihood that the sale will take place, so conspiracy liability would be inappropriate. (By contrast, when an agreement requires something more than the simple exchange of drugs for money, such as obtaining drugs for distribution — adding liability to that carried by the substantive offense may be appropriate.) The buy-sell transaction is simply not probative of an agreement to join together to accomplish a criminal objective beyond that already being accomplished by the transaction. The relationship of buyer and seller absent any prior or contemporaneous understanding beyond the mere sales agreement does not prove a conspiracy. In such circumstances, the buyer's purpose is to buy; the seller's purpose is to sell. There is no joint objective. The mere purchase or sale of drugs (even in large quantities) does not demonstrate an agreement to join a drug distribution conspiracy any more than a purchase of 100 tons of steel to build a skyscraper shows that the buyer has "joined" the corporate enterprise of the manufacturer. The analogy to the corporate arena is apt. What distinguishes a conspiratorial agreement from an isolated transaction also distinguishes a decision to incorporate from one to let a contract. In the jargon of economists, business combinations — whether corporations, partnerships, joint ventures, or other variations — exist because they lower the transaction costs of legitimate profit-seeking endeavors. Conspiracies exist for the same reason - to lower the transaction costs of committing crimes. Rather than having "to discover who it is that one wishes to deal with, to inform people that one wishes to deal and on what terms, to conduct negotiations leading up to a bargain, to draw up the contract, to undertake the inspection needed to make sure that the terms of the contract are being observed, and so on," in order to accomplish a goal - whether legitimate or illegitimate — corporations and conspiracies "will emerge to organize what would otherwise be market transactions." See Coase, *The Firm, The Market, and The Law* at 6-7 (1988). Conspiracies aren't necessary to the commission of crime; a single person can commit a crime without any assistance at all, or with the limited assistance of others who do not know of his goal or who have no stake in the success of his venture. But conspiracies are often convenient to the commission of crime, because they

---

[4] The general rule is that conspiracy does not merge with the substantive offense; both may be punished independently. In addition, a conspirator faces the disadvantages at trial noted earlier in this opinion.

yield the benefits of group activity that make it more likely that the crime born of a conspiratorial agreement will actually occur than the crime that is the product of individual effort.

A conspiracy "is a partnership in criminal purposes," *U.S. v. Kissel*, 218 U.S. 601, 608 (1910), and conspirators, like partners, are mutual agents. Conspiracies, like all business ventures, are typically distinguished by cooperative relationships between the parties that facilitate achievement of the goal. See, e.g., *Direct Sales*, 319 U.S. at 713 (evidence of "informed and interested cooperation" permitted the jury to take "the inferential step from knowledge to intent and agreement"). True, any business combination conceivably could be viewed as a nexus of separate transactions. See L.Katz, *supra*, at 264-68 (cautioning that cooperation may exist in the absence of agreement). The reverse, however, is unlikely to be true; higher transaction costs will distinguish most market transactions from cooperative ventures. Evidence that the parties must negotiate the terms of every transaction, seek to maximize their gains at the expense of others, or engage in other forms of opportunistic behavior at the expense of the group, suggests that transaction costs among the group are high and counsel against a finding of conspiracy between its members.

(4) *Townsend* questions whether people involved in drugs are part of a large conspiracy with importers, dealers, and users up and down the line. But isn't there always at least a *simple two-person conspiracy* between each user and his dealer? Under contract law, a sale is an agreement. So when a user buys drugs, he enters into an agreement. As the agreement is the gist of conspiracy, there's your conspiracy, right? Check out the next case.

UNITED STATES v. LECHUGA
U.S. Court of Appeals, 7th Circuit
994 F.2d 346 (1993)

POSNER, CIRCUIT JUDGE.

An indictment charged Humberto Lechuga with having in his possession more than 500 grams of cocaine, with the intention of distributing the cocaine; and also with having conspired with Evelio Pinto and unnamed others to distribute the cocaine. 21 U.S.C. § 841(a)(1), § 846. The jury convicted Lechuga on both counts, and the judge sentenced him to 75 months in prison.

A government undercover agent named Carr had arranged to buy 500 grams of cocaine from Pinto. To obtain the cocaine for the sale, Pinto got in touch with Sam Pagan, who had previously sold Pinto cocaine that Pagan had obtained from Lechuga. Pagan relayed Pinto's order to Lechuga, who designated an apartment building where Pagan was to receive the cocaine from Lechuga for transfer to Pinto and to pay Lechuga for it, presumably with money that Pagan would collect from Pinto at the time of the transfer. Accompanied by Pinto and Carr, Pagan went to the building designated by Lechuga and emerged carrying two packages. One contained the 500 grams (1.1 lbs.) that Pinto had ordered. The other contained 3 ounces. The reason for the second package was that on a previous three-cornered deal involving Lechuga, Pagan, and Pinto, Lechuga had delivered 3 ounces less than Pinto had ordered and paid for. So now Lechuga was making up for the short delivery. As soon as Pagan handed over the packages of cocaine to Pinto, the two were arrested. Lechuga was arrested later.

Lechuga's main argument is that the mere fact that he sold Pinto a quantity of cocaine too large for Pinto's personal use, and therefore must have known that Pinto was planning to resell it, is insufficient to prove a conspiracy between Pinto and him. Before today, it was widely assumed that a conviction for participation in a drug conspiracy could be affirmed with no more evidence than that the defendant had sold in a quantity too large to be intended for his buyer's personal consumption. Today we resolve the conflict in our cases by holding that large quantities of controlled substances, without more, cannot sustain a conspiracy conviction. What is necessary and sufficient is proof of an agreement to commit a crime other than the crime that consists of the sale itself.

To understand the problems created by an allegation of a conspiracy between a seller on the one hand and a buyer for resale on the other, we must take a step back and ask why uncompleted conspiracies are punished, even though the conspiracy here was completed — the cocaine was delivered to Pinto before he was arrested. It is not a good answer to say that they are punished on the same theory as attempts are punished; for given a law of attempts we must ask why uncompleted conspiracies are also punished. The full answer may include historical accident but there is also a functional reason. Because crimes are difficult to deter by mere threat of punishment, society tries to prevent them and one way to do this is by identifying and incapacitating people who are likely to commit crimes. The risk to civil liberties that would be created by a purely preventive theory of criminal punishment is so great, however, that society insists on definite proof of dangerousness. An attempt is one form of satisfactory proof. A person who goes so far in the preparation of a criminal act as to be guilty of an attempt has given definite proof that he is likely to commit such an act. And likewise a person who agrees to commit a crime, even if he takes no additional preparatory steps and as a result does not come close enough to committing the crime to be guilty of an attempt.

All this makes good sense when we are speaking of the punishment of uncompleted conspiracies, but what of the punishment of a completed one? Lechuga delivered cocaine in violation of federal criminal law; why should he also be punished for agreeing to deliver it? The stock answer is that a conspiracy has more potential for doing harm than a single individual does. It is not a bad answer, as the facts of this case indicate. Lechuga might have been frightened to deal face to face with Pinto, whom he had short-changed, as it were, on their previous transaction; or he might have been wary about delivering the cocaine to Pinto and Pinto's customer in person, since then he would be outnumbered two to one and honor among thieves is more an aspiration than a presumption.

This is the point at which sale for resale rather than for consumption becomes relevant. Contrast two modes of distribution. In one, a bulk dealer like Lechuga sells his inventory directly to the ultimate consumer. So if he has a kilogram of cocaine to sell he breaks it up into numerous small packages (for example, into 500 2-gram packages) and hawks it on street corners. The process of breaking bulk and selling at retail is time- consuming. That will limit the scale of our hypothetical Lechuga's operations. If all drug dealers were constrained to sell at retail the drug trade would be smaller than it is, just as the legitimate drug trade would be smaller than it is if manufacturers of legitimate drugs were forbidden to sell through pharmacists or other retailers and therefore had to sell directly to the consuming public if at all.

This is an argument for treating any sale of drugs for resale as a conspiracy. It is only a short step to the conclusion that any sale of drugs in a quantity greater than appropriate for individual consumption is presumptively a sale for resale, though the presumption could be rebutted, for example by evidence that the bulk purchaser was planning to throw a huge party at which he would serve his guests cocaine. Many of the objections to this approach are superficial, for example that the federal statute forbidding the sale of, and possession with intent to sell, drugs already imposes heavier penalties the larger the quantity sold or possessed. 21 U.S.C. § 841(b). The quantity goes to the severity of the sentence, not the existence of the crime. The issue of inferring the crime of conspiracy from the sale of or the agreement to sell a quantity so large that it is almost certainly intended for resale by the buyer rather than for his personal consumption is distinct. Nor is it an objection that to deem the seller (Lechuga) and the buyer (Pinto) members of a conspiracy to distribute drugs would imply that someone who rented Pinto the premises from which he conducted his business of reselling drugs to the ultimate consumers would be a conspirator with Pinto in the sale of drugs, though even if the landlord knew the purpose to which his tenant was putting the premises he would be at most an aider and abettor of Pinto's illegal business. *U.S. v. Giovannetti*, 919 F.2d 1223, 1227 (7th cir. 1990). Someone who provides an input into another's business usually cares only about selling the input, not about furthering the other's business. It is different when the buyer is the seller's distributor, without whom the seller cannot reach the market for his product.

Yet there is still a serious objection to concluding that a sale for resale leagues the seller and the buyer in a conspiracy (which can be inferred from the quantity involved in the sale — but that is not the problem). The objection is that while dangerousness may be the justification for punishing conspiracies separately from attempts and completed crimes, proof of dangerousness cannot be substituted for proof of conspiracy. The conspiracy itself must be proved.

We must therefore ask what a conspiracy is. A criminal conspiracy, the cases say, is an agreement to commit a crime. E.g., *Iannelli v. U.S.*, 420 U.S. 770, 777 (1975); *U.S. v. Blankenship*, 970 F.2d 283, 285 (7th cir. 1992). The definition is incomplete, as we shall see. Nevertheless it is a beginning, for there cannot be conspiracy without agreement. What is an "agreement"? The term is like "contract" but is at once broader and narrower. It is broader because it embraces agreements that might for one reason or another, including illegality, not be legally enforceable. It is true that we sometimes speak of an "unenforceable contract" without a sense of semantic strain. But, at least to lawyers, the term "contract" ordinarily signifies an agreement that might in principle be enforced in a court of law, or in some substitute tribunal, such as a panel of arbitrators, agreed to by the parties in advance. Yet some legally enforceable contracts do not involve a "real" agreement in the sense of a meeting of the minds but are enforced because the parties uttered words or engaged in acts that the law deems sufficient to create a legally enforceable contract. In this respect the term "agreement" is narrower than the term "contract."

This shows that to know what a "contract" is you must be a lawyer; but "agreement" is a lay term, and while it may be difficult to define, it usually is easy to identify. There was an agreement between Lechuga and Pinto — an agreement on Lechuga's part to sell, and on Pinto's to buy, a specified amount of a specified product at a specified time and place and for a specified price. Was there therefore a conspiracy? Our cases hold, as do many in other circuits, that there would not be a conspiracy if Pinto were buying for his own consumption. See, e.g., *U.S. v. Moran*, 984 F.2d 1299, 1302 (1st cir. 1993). Evidently, while proof of an agreement is necessary for a finding of conspiracy, it is not sufficient.

The rationale for the own-consumption exception is that when a crime requires the joint action of two people to commit (prostitution, adultery, incest, bigamy, and dueling are other examples), a charge of conspiracy involves no additional element unless someone else is involved besides the two persons whose agreement is the sine qua non of the substantive crime. The rationale could be questioned, on the ground that it is at most a reason for requiring that the sentences for the conspiracy and the completed crime run concurrently (though even this is unnecessary if the legislature intends cumulative punishment, *Missouri v. Hunter*, 459 U.S. 359, 368 (1983)), or perhaps that the punishment for the conspiracy be capped at the punishment for the completed crime on the theory that the punishment prescribed for the specific offense is the best evidence of what the legislature thought a proper sanction for the defendant's conduct. Considerations such as these have persuaded the Supreme Court to demote the rule that forbids punishing as conspirators the minimum number of offenders necessary for a joint-action crime from a strict rule ("Wharton's Rule") to a principle of statutory interpretation. *Iannelli v. U.S.*, 420 U.S. at 785-86.

There is another way to understand the own-consumption exception, however — a way that shows that, at least in some of its manifestations, as in this case, it is not an exception at all, but an instantiation of the rule that makes conspiracies criminal. A conspiracy is not merely an agreement. It is an agreement with a particular kind of object — an agreement to commit a crime. When the sale of some commodity, such as illegal drugs, is the substantive crime, the sale agreement itself cannot be the conspiracy, for it has no separate criminal object. What is required for conspiracy in such a case is an agreement to commit some other crime beyond the crime constituted by the agreement itself. We shall see that there was such an agreement here (as there had been in *Iannelli*) — the agreement between Lechuga and Pagan to cooperate in the sale of drugs to Pinto. The object of the agreement was to commit the crime of selling drugs to Pinto. But insofar as there was an agreement between Lechuga and Pinto merely on the one side to sell and on the other to buy, there was no conspiracy between them no matter what Pinto intended to do with the drugs after he bought them. Lechuga would not, merely by selling to Pinto, have been agreeing with Pinto to some further sale. A person who sells a gun knowing that the buyer intends to murder someone may or may not be an aider or abettor of the murder, but he is not a conspirator, because he and his buyer do not have an agreement to murder anyone.

There might have been a separate agreement between Lechuga and Pinto. Suppose Lechuga had told Pinto that he needed a good distributor on the south side of Chicago and wanted to enter into a long-term relationship with Pinto to that end. Then it would be as if Lechuga had hired Pinto to assist him in reaching his market. It should not make a difference whether an illegal agreement takes the form of an illegal simulacrum of an employment contract or of a "relational" contract, implying something more than a series of spot dealings at arm's length between dealers who have no interest in the success of each other's enterprise. Vertical integration is not a condition of conspiracy. And of course the initiative might in our hypothetical case have come from Pinto rather than from Lechuga without affecting the analysis. Even the number of sales, a factor stressed in some cases, would be significant only insofar as it cast light on the existence of a continuing relation, implying an agreement with an objective beyond a simple purchase and sale and thus an agreement separate from the sale itself — the latter being an agreement, all right, but not a conspiracy. What made "prolonged cooperation" a factor in inferring conspiracy in *Direct Sales Co. v. U.S.*, 319 U.S. 703, 713 (1943), was that it showed that the defendant not only knew that it was selling drugs to someone for use in an illicit enterprise but had "joined both mind and hand with him to make its accomplishment possible." Prolonged cooperation is neither the meaning of conspiracy nor an essential element, but it is one type of evidence of an agreement that goes beyond what is implicit in any consensual undertaking, such as a spot sale.

A more difficult case would be that of an agreement between A and B for A to make a spot sale of drugs to B in the future — an agreement with a separate criminal object, that of making an illegal sale, but an agreement that seems only adventitiously distinct from the sale itself. No agreement of any kind between Lechuga and Pinto separate from the sale of cocaine to Pinto was proved, however, so Lechuga's conviction for conspiracy cannot be affirmed on the basis of the agreement with Pinto.

It does not follow that the conviction must be reversed. The indictment charged a conspiracy with others besides just Pinto, and the evidence showed that Lechuga had in fact conspired with Pagan; therefore the conviction of conspiracy must be upheld after all. * * * *

The critical issue is whether, on the one hand, the relationship between Lechuga and Pagan is properly characterized as that of a spot seller and a spot buyer; or, on the other hand, whether the sale was from Lechuga to Pinto with Pagan functioning as a go-between, facilitator, sales agent, and general helper. If, knowing that Lechuga was a drug dealer, Pagan assisted him in distributing drugs to at least one dealer farther down the chain of distribution, namely Pinto, then Lechuga and Pagan were coconspirators. *U.S. v. Townsend*, 924 F.2d 1385, 1400-01 (7th cir. 1991). If Lechuga and Pagan had the same simple seller-buyer relationship as Lechuga and Pinto, then, for the reasons explained earlier, there was no conspiracy between them.

We must take a closer look at the facts concerning their relationship. Pagan was asked on direct examination what his purpose had been in seeking to meet Lechuga. He answered that it had been to "get in some kind of drug deals." He was then asked, "What did you want to do with drugs with Lechuga?" Answer: "Just sell it." It is apparent that he wanted to sell drugs on Lechuga's behalf, for when the two had first met he had told Lechuga, "I know this guy, he's looking for some amount of drugs, and he [Lechuga] had it." In other words, Pagan had a customer (although his testimony is not entirely clear on this point, apparently it was Pinto) for a particular amount of drugs, and he wanted Lechuga to supply him with the necessary amount. This is hardly consistent with Lechuga's being a spot seller unaware of what activities Pagan, or any subsequent occupier of a place in the chain of distribution, might undertake. Lechuga knew precisely what Pagan was going to do with the drugs he sold him. Pagan told Lechuga what he was going to do with them.

This was in February 1988. In May, Pinto told Pagan that he had a friend who wanted cocaine, so Pagan "called Lechuga," and told him the amount he needed. The inference is inescapable that Pagan told Lechuga that Pinto would require an extra three ounces to make up for a previous short delivery by Lechuga and Pagan. For Pagan testified that the reason Pinto was to get an extra three ounces was that "We had another deal with him [Pinto] and he claimed that we were short, so I request from Lechuga again the three ounces." The "we" is obviously Lechuga and Pagan. A rational jury could infer from the testimony we have summarized that Lechuga and Pagan were dealing jointly with Pinto, with Pagan's role that of a sales agent. Therefore the jury's finding of conspiracy is adequately supported by the evidence. * * * *

Affirmed.

KANNE, CIRCUIT JUDGE, concurring.

I join in the result reached in Judge Posner's opinion — affirmance of Lechuga's conspiracy conviction. I do not believe, however, that the inclusion of dicta that proposes an absolute rule that a conspiracy conviction can never be supported solely on the basis of a single "large quantity" sale of drugs is necessary or correct. The single sale conspiracy rule is an aside that has not achieved a consensus on this court. I write separately to express my disagreement with this proposed broad rule, the analytical framework for which is grounded in the context of the hand-to-hand drug transaction.

In my view, such a rule cannot reasonably be extended to apply to those multi-million dollar drug transactions found in real life, such as a single sale of a sea-going shipload of marijuana, *U.S. v. Kramer*, 955 F.2d 479 (7th Cir.) (individual deliveries of 15,000, 20,000, 30,000, 14,000, 147,000, 152,000, and 130,000 pounds), or cocaine, *U.S. v. Gonzalez*, 933 F.2d 417 (7th cir. 1991) (individual deliveries of 1,148 and 2,265 kilograms), or a cargo aircraft load of cocaine, *U.S. v. Markowski*, 582 F.Supp. 1276 (N.D.Ind.1984) (importation of 864 kilograms valued at $27,000,000), or a tractor trailer load of marijuana, *U.S. v. Canino*, 949 F.2d 928 (7th cir. 1991) (individual deliveries of 27,000 and 18,000 pounds). That the foregoing examples involve successive deliveries does not detract from the size and complex nature of each individual transaction.

Even when single sales of drugs are not carried out on such an extraordinary scale, our cases illustrate that major dealers frequently traffick in "large quantities" of drugs. E.g., *U.S. v. Liefer*, 778 F.2d 1236 (7th cir. 1985) (individual deliveries of 2,500 and 7,000 pounds of marijuana for distribution); *U.S. v. Wables*, 731 F.2d 440 (7th cir. 1984) (storage of 2,500 pounds of marijuana for distribution). It is unfortunate, but true, that demand exists for such distributable quantities.

Today the court suggests a prophylactic rule that the sale of "large quantities" of narcotics, without more, cannot sustain a conspiracy conviction. Presumably this rule would apply to a single sale that requires massive coordination of air, sea, and ground transportation, regardless if the buyer is a known large-scale distributor and regardless if the quantity is so large that it is certainly intended for resale. If the rule is adopted, a jury will be precluded from reasonably inferring that a seller of large quantities of drugs agreed to their distribution by others down the line, notwithstanding his interest (and stake) in the retailer's successful distribution.

Ironically, a majority, if not every member, of the court appears to recognize a drug dealer's interest in successful distribution. Judge Posner concedes that "someone who provides an input into another's business usually cares only about selling the input, not about furthering the other's business. It is different when the buyer is the seller's distributor, without whom the seller cannot reach the market for his product." Judge Cudahy acknowledges as much: "Of course, any wholesaler hopes that his customers will be successful. The more the retailers sell, the more they will buy from the wholesaler." Still, a majority insists on a rule that knowledge and a stake in the venture sufficient to prove participation in a conspiracy can never be inferred from evidence of a single large quantity sale.

When one sells an amount of drugs too large for personal consumption to a distributor, I am not willing to foreclose a jury's finding that the seller "joined both mind and hand" with the buyer to make further distribution possible. *Direct Sales Co. v. U.S.*, 319 U.S. 703, 713 (1943). After all, the large sale transaction is the *sine qua non* of subsequent distribution. Conspiracy can be inferred from prolonged cooperation with another's unlawful purpose, (though we affirm Lechuga's conviction on the evidence of only two transactions) but not, apparently, from a transaction involving an extraordinarily large quantity of drugs. Neither Judge Posner nor Judge Cudahy offers an explanation as to why the first inference is more reasonable and should carry more weight than the second. Surely it cannot be said that "prolonged cooperation" makes it more likely that a seller knew of and agreed to a buyer's distribution of drugs but evidence of an extremely large sale to the distributor does not. Both, it seems to me, could be sufficient to allow "the step from knowledge to intent and agreement to be taken."

It is true that many drug sales — the hand-to-hand variety — are relatively small and simple transactions, thus preventing a rational factfinder from inferring that the seller joined a drug distribution conspiracy. It is just as true, on the other hand, that there are individual sales of such size and scale that a rational factfinder could properly draw the inference that the seller had joined a conspiracy to distribute the drugs involved.

As I see it, a rule that treats every sale of narcotics in a conspiracy case as if it were a simple spot sale belies the nature and reality of today's wholesale drug trade. Rather than needlessly adopt an absolute standard that cannot be applied intelligibly as the size and complexity of the drug sale increases, we should, I believe, allow the factfinder to assess the nature of the transaction in the first instance and to draw such reasonable inferences of conspiratorial membership as the evidence may warrant.

CUDAHY, CIRCUIT JUDGE, concurring in part and dissenting in part.

* * * *

If there is no conspiracy involving Pinto, how can there be one involving Pagan? For Pagan acted here on behalf of Pinto — in effect as Pinto's agent for the purchase of cocaine. If there is no conspiracy with the principal, Pinto (as the majority finds), how can there be one with the agent? * * * *

One possibility on the facts of this case is that Lechuga joined an ongoing conspiracy between Pagan and Pinto. But although Lechuga presumably knew that Pagan would resell or reconvey the cocaine, he did not know to whom or in what manner. Lechuga did not know the "scope" of the putative Pagan-Pinto conspiracy. Knowledge of a buyer's illegal objectives does not establish an agreement to help him carry out those objectives. As we noted in *Townsend*:

> The suppliers in a "chain" are not necessarily interested in the success of a particular retailer, or group of retailers, down the line. If the chain is characterized by sporadic dealings between independent dealers, what do suppliers care if the middlemen are able to unload the stuff further? [924 F.2d at 1391.]

Of course, any wholesaler hopes that his customers will be successful. The more the retailers sell, the more they will buy from the wholesaler. But proving participation in a conspiracy requires "substantial" evidence. This presumably means that proof of more than an abstract desire for more business is required.

An appropriate standard of proof of conspiracy helps ensure that vicarious responsibility will not be improperly assessed. Coconspirators are liable for crimes committed by other members of the conspiracy in furtherance of the conspiracy. *Pinkerton v. U.S.*, 328 U.S. 640, 647 (1946). To hold that a defendant joined a conspiracy therefore exposes that person to much more than criminal liability for joining the conspiracy itself: he also faces conviction for the substantive crimes committed by other members of the conspiracy. In *Townsend* we also stated: "To join a conspiracy is to join an agreement. To be a conspirator you must know of the agreement and intend to join it." *Id.* at 1390. Here Lechuga had no adequate knowledge of any agreement between Pagan and Pinto (whose very identity was unknown to Lechuga). Although Lechuga supplied cocaine to the Pagan-Pinto distribution chain through two apparently arm's-length sales to Pagan, Lechuga was wholly unaware of what activities Pagan, or any subsequent occupier of a place in the chain of distribution, might undertake. The relationship of Lechuga to Pagan is simply that of seller to buyer or to buyer's agent. The sale was consummated by Pagan taking delivery on Pinto's behalf. For his part, Pinto gave an order to Pagan and Pagan saw that it was filled. None of this in any way changed the simple seller-buyer relationship between Lechuga and Pagan. And, as we have said repeatedly (but unfortunately not consistently) elsewhere, a buyer-seller relationship, standing alone, is insufficient to prove participation in a conspiracy. See *Townsend*, 924 F.2d at 1394. * * * *

All this discussion raises the crucial question: If a sale for resale is not enough evidence of a conspiracy, what is? Although no exhaustive catalog is possible, examples are not difficult to find. Clearly, "prolonged cooperation" between buyer and seller is sufficient evidence of a conspiracy to distribute drugs. *Direct Sales*, 319 U.S. at 713. So too might be evidence that the putative buyer is really working as the seller's agent. Such evidence would, in many circumstances, destroy the presumption that the parties are dealing at arm's length and would show an agreement to distribute. Sales on consignment may also establish a conspiracy since they indicate an ongoing relationship of the sort that "lowers the transaction costs of committing crimes," *Townsend*, 924 F.2d at 1394, and also show that the seller has a "stake in the success of the buyer's enterprise." *Id.* at 1397. Evidence that the parties had standardized their transactions with one another might also lead to an inference that they were engaged in a cooperative effort.

In sum, the evidence shows nothing more than a typical buyer seller relationship between Lechuga and Pagan. Further, Lechuga did not have the requisite knowledge of Pagan's arrangements with Pinto to be said to have joined that purported conspiracy. Accordingly, Lechuga's conviction for conspiracy must be reversed. I, therefore, respectfully dissent in the matters indicated.

NOTES FROM PEGGY:

In *U.S. v. Caldwell*, 589 F.3d 1323 (10th Cir. 2009), Herrera sold marijuana to Caldwell, who resold to street dealers, who resold to users. Herrera also sold marijuana to Anderson, who resold to street dealers, who resold to users. All three were convicted of being part of a single, "tripartite" conspiracy. The conviction was reversed:

> We are told by the government that the relationship between Caldwell, Anderson, and Herrera was a "vertical conspiracy." A vertical conspiracy, or "chain-and-link" conspiracy, involves a series of consecutive buyer-seller relationships. The classic vertical conspiracy involves Supplier A selling contraband to Supplier B, who then sells the contraband to Supplier C. But drug distribution organizations often do not fit neatly into the concept of vertical conspiracy.
>
> In the present case, Caldwell and Anderson were equal-level purchasers rather than links in a vertical chain. After Herrera became their joint supplier, neither Caldwell nor Anderson bought or sold marijuana to the other. Instead, each independently sold marijuana to third parties. Thus, their relationship does not evince the characteristics of a vertical conspiracy. Were we to categorize this alleged conspiracy, it would fit more neatly into the concept of a "hub-and-spoke" conspiracy, in which several separate players all interact with a common central actor, here Herrera. See, e.g., *Kotteakos v. United States*, 328 U.S. 750 (1946). However, because

any conspiracy requires a showing of interdependence, we prefer to eschew rigid labels and instead engage in the general, yet fact-specific, inquiry of whether there is evidence of interdependence among all alleged coconspirators.

When multiple individuals are involved in the sale of illegal drugs, they are engaged in an inherently illicit enterprise. Consequently, the degree of specificity with which the government must prove interdependence among them may be lower in the drug context than in the context of other types of conspiracies. But even in the drug context, we must scrupulously safeguard each defendant individually, as far as possible, from loss of identity in the mass.

It is essential that the evidence demonstrate a mutual benefit before we proceed to determine that several drug dealers who interact with one another are involved in a single conspiracy. It is not enough that a group of people separately intend to distribute drugs in a single area, nor even that their activities occasionally or sporadically place them in contact with each other. People in the same industry in the same locale (even competitors) can occasionally be expected to interact with each other without thereby becoming coconspirators. What is needed is proof that they intended to act together for their shared mutual benefit within the scope of the conspiracy charged.

For example, we determined in *Powell* that several drug dealers who shared a common supplier and sold to the same customers and wholesalers in a cooperative matter could be found to have engaged in a single conspiracy. 982 F.2d at 1431. However, sharing a common supplier, without more, does not demonstrate that two drug dealers are acting together for their shared mutual benefit. Accordingly, in the case at bar, the fact that Caldwell and Anderson both bought from Herrera is insufficient to establish interdependence among the three.

UNITED STATES v. COLE
U.S. Court of Appeals, 11th Circuit
704 F.2d 554 (1983)

GODBOLD, CHIEF JUDGE:

All appellants were convicted in a bench trial of conspiracy to violate the Travel Act, 18 U.S.C. § 371 & § 1952. Holley, Hawkins, and Hensley were also convicted of substantive violations of the Travel Act, 18 U.S.C. § 1952. Cole and Holley were convicted of violating the Mann Act, 18 U.S.C. § 2421. The convictions all arose from operation of an interstate prostitution enterprise. The convictions of all appellants are affirmed.

Appellants, along with Kenneth Hart and Jerry Owens, were active members of the Tampa (Florida) Chapter of the Outlaw Motorcycle Club. To join the Outlaws one must be male, own a Harley-Davidson motorcycle, and embrace the Outlaw lifestyle.

The Tampa Outlaws are an insular group with members living at or near their clubhouse, occupying themselves primarily with their motorcycles, touring, and "partying." Gainful employment among the Outlaws is rare. Women closely associated with the Outlaws are termed "patched old ladies" and sport insignia, sometimes tattoos, proclaiming them "Property of the Outlaws." These women are treated as "property" by the Outlaws. At a given time an individual woman is typically associated with a particular Outlaw. But she may be sold, traded, or given to another. Unlike the males, the women are expected to work — sometimes as waitresses, dancers, barmaids — often as prostitutes. An "old lady's" duties to the man with whom she is associated include giving him her money and following orders without question. Mostly the women are compliant in all this; if not, compliance may be enforced with physical violence.

In the spring of 1979, Mary Carley was living at the Outlaw clubhouse in Tampa with Kenneth Hart as his "old lady" and supplying Hart's income by working locally as a prostitute. But local work became difficult. She was out on bond from a firearms charge, and the local police were cracking down on prostitution. Through Lori, another "old lady," she and Hart learned of the Club Caprice, a brothel in Meridian, Mississippi. Lori, Carley and Hart telephoned the club owner and arranged jobs there for Carley and Lori.

The two women went to Meridian and began work at the club. Lori was fired soon after for misconduct. Carley continued to work there but didn't like working alone. She called Hart and asked him to send some other "old ladies" to join her. Soon afterwards two more Outlaw women arrived from Tampa. Carley worked intermittently at the Club Caprice for more than a year, joined at different times by various Outlaw women including those associated with Hawkins, Cole, Hensley, and Owens. During that year she was traded by Hart and became Holley's "old lady." At times some of the men came to Meridian to see the women, and phone calls were exchanged between the women in Meridian and the men in Florida.

At times Carley and the other women would return to Tampa. When this occurred Carley would personally deliver her prostitution proceeds to her "old man." Other times Hart, and later Holley, would telephone Carley asking for money, and she would wire the money via Western Union. She also instructed other Outlaw women on how to send money back to the men and on occasions accompanied them to the Meridian Western Union office.

At trial Carley was the government's primary witness. Much of her testimony was corroborated by the owner of the Club Caprice and to a lesser extent by Outlaw member Owens. Documentary evidence from Western Union confirmed that the Outlaw women wired money from Meridian across state lines to Hawkins, Holley, Hensley, Cole, Owens, and Hart.[3] *

---

[3] Western Union documents show the following interstate wire transfers made from Meridian:

Date	To	From	Amount
8/4/79	Hart	Mary Money *	$1000
8/10/79	Hart	Mary Money *	300
8/14/79	Hart	Gloria Hedges	850

Most of the wire transfers were made to Tampa. The Hedges-Hart transfer was to Detroit, Michigan where Hart and other Outlaws were attending a funeral. The remainder went to other Florida locations where the men were attending bike runs.

Appellants contend the indictment, which charged a single conspiracy involving multiple defendants, varies fatally from the proof which at best, they say, revealed several conspiracies. They urge that no unifying agreement was proved and each man-woman pair should be viewed as a conspiracy unto itself.

In determining whether there is a common design, the nature and effect of the scheme is not to be judged by dismembering it, but rather by looking at it as a whole. The conspiracy here is similar to that in *U.S. v. Clemones*, 582 F.2d 1373 (5th cir. 1978) (a prostitution ring composed of a changing cast of pimps and their prostitutes); and that in *U.S. v. Perez*, 489 F.2d 51 (5th cir. 1973) (different teams of people staged automobile collisions in various parts of Louisiana for the common purpose of defrauding insurers).

Various Outlaw women were dispatched by the men to Meridian at different times to work in the Club Caprice as prostitutes. While there, each woman wired money back to her associated male. Some man-woman pairs changed membership; other pairs floated in and out of the ongoing operation. The intermittent nature of the enterprise was shaped by the desires and financial needs of the participants. That the appellants did not share the money received with each other does not negate the existence of a single conspiracy, where as here a mutually beneficial

Date	To	From	Amount
3/3/80	Holley	Mary Saxton *	350
3/7/80	Holley	Mary Saxton *	160
3/7/80	Owens	Helen Owens	200
3/10/80	Cole	Karen King	120
3/15/80	Owens	Helen Owens	170
3/22/80	Owens	Helen Owens	150
3/24/80	Holley	Mary Saxton *	350
4/2/80	Holley	Mary Saxton *	500
4/9/80	Holley	Mary Saxton *	400
4/11/80	Hawkins	Leah Eiring	1200
4/18/80	Holley	Mary Saxton *	200
4/20/80	Hawkins	Leah Eiring	500
4/26/80	Holley	Mary Saxton *	100
5/27/80	Hawkins	Leah Eiring	600
5/30/80	Holley	Mary Saxton *	175
5/30/80	Hensley	Brenda Lupton	180
6/2/80	Holley	Mary Saxton *	150
6/5/80	Hensley	Brenda Lupton	270
6/5/80	Hawkins	Leah Eiring	500

* Carley was also known as Mary Money and Mary Saxton

scheme is shown. An agreement to conspire may be inferred from the acts of the parties and other circumstantial evidence. While association alone will not support an inference of a conspiracy, the association of the appellants may be considered as a factor. Viewing the evidence in the light most favorable to the government, there was sufficient evidence of one overall conspiracy that each appellant joined.

Affirmed.

NOTES FROM PEGGY:

(1) As a prosecutor, I think I like this case. What does it demonstrate regarding how much (or how little) evidence is needed to show that someone — such as Cole — is part of a conspiracy? Take a good look at footnote 3.

(2) The court cites *Perez*. Is this case really like *Perez*, or is *Perez* distinguishable?

(3) How would the court that decided *Townsend* decide *Cole*?

(4) In 1970, Congress decided that traditional conspiracy laws were not adequate to deal with the problem of organized crime, so Congress enacted the Racketeer Influenced & Corrupt Organizations statute — commonly called by its acronym, "RICO" — codified at 18 U.S.C. §§ 1961-1968. Very briefly summarized, RICO criminalizes the use of proceeds of "racketeering activity" (gambling, extortion, drug dealing, and a host of other crimes) to control other businesses — even legitimate businesses. See *U.S. v. Turkette*, 452 U.S. 576 (1981) and *U.S. v. Salerno*, 868 F.2d 524 (2nd Cir., 1988). It provides stiff civil and criminal penalties for violations, and — far from superceding traditional conspiracy laws — it forbids conspiring to violate RICO! (Is this a "conspiracy to form a conspiracy"?) See *U.S. v. Neapolitan*, 791 F.2d 489 (1986)). While supposedly directed at organized crime, the RICO statutes were broadly written and have been broadly interpreted and applied to defendants who have no connection to what we usually consider "organized crime."

Some states have adopted their own "baby RICO" statutes. See, e.g., California Penal Code §§ 186.21 et.seq. (dealing with "criminal street gangs").

Part VII

Accomplices

Chapter 20

ACCOMPLICE LIABILITY

It may generally be said that one is liable as an accomplice to the crime of another if he (a) gave assistance or encouragement or failed to perform a legal duty to prevent it (b) with the intent thereby to promote or facilitate commission of the crime.

LaFave & Scott, *Criminal Law* (West)

If Dan intentionally helps Don commit a crime, then Dan should be punished. But several difficult questions may arise.

How do we know that Dan *intended* that his acts help Don commit the crime? How do we know that Dan *knew* that Don was about to commit a crime? If Dan does not tell us his intent (e.g., through a confession), may his *acts* alone be evidence sufficient to show his *intent*?

Even if Dan *knew* that Don meant to commit a crime (and perhaps even *wanted* Don to commit the crime), *what acts* on Dan constitute sufficient help? And if Dan helps in only a minor way, should he be punished as much as Don?

And finally, the most controversial question: If Dan knowingly helps Don commit Crime #1, and during that crime Don commits Crime #2, should Dan be found guilty of *both* crimes — even though Dan did not intend that Don commit Crime #2? (Note how similar this question is to that raised by the *Pinkerton* rule, discussed in Chapter 19.)

PROBLEM 20

To: My law clerk

From: Judge Solomon King

Re: *State v. Marks, Stolz, and Derby*

Milly Marks, Sally Stolz, and Dolly Derby have been charged with larceny and battery. The only witness for the prosecution was Marshall Fields, the store manager of Zaks Department Store, in Miami. After the prosecution rested, Marks and Stolz each moved for a directed verdict of acquittal. Based on the attached authorities, how should I rule?

Transcript of Testimony of Marshall Fields

Q: Mr. Fields, did you see the defendants in your store on July 8?

A: Yes, I saw three elderly women come in together, and they are the defendants.

Q: What did they do?

A: They went to the dress department and looked at the dresses. Dolly took a red dress from the rack and went into a dressing room. Milly and Sally stood near the dressing room. A few minutes later, Dolly came out, wearing the red dress from the rack. Dolly handed her handbag to Milly, and the three of them walked past the cash registers and out the front door. I followed them with Gus, a security guard. Gus stopped Dolly and asked if she had a receipt for payment for the dress. Dolly swung her umbrella at Gus, hitting him in the head. I grabbed Dolly, and she quieted down. I looked in the handbag Milly was carrying, and I saw the yellow dress that Dolly had worn when she came into the store. Sally then said, "Before we came in, Dolly told me that she was going to steal a dress."

Florida Statutes

Section 777.011. Principal in First Degree.

Whoever commits any criminal offense against the state, whether felony or misdemeanor, or aids, abets, counsels, hires, or otherwise procures such offense to be committed, and such offense is committed or is attempted to be committed, is a principal in the first degree and may be charged, convicted, and punished as such, whether he is or is not actually or constructively present at the commission of such offense.

Section 777.03. Accessory After the Fact.

(1)(a) Any person not standing in the relation of husband or wife, parent or grandparent, child or grandchild, brother or sister, by consanguinity or affinity to the offender, who maintains or assists the principal or **an** accessory before the fact, or gives the offender any other aid, knowing that the offender had committed a **crime and such crime was a third-degree** felony**,** or **had** been **an** accessory thereto before the fact, with **the** intent that the offender avoids or escapes detection, arrest, trial or punishment, is an accessory after the fact. * * * *

Note: Compare these statutes with Model Penal Code § 2.06, in the Appendix.

HAMPTON v. STATE
Florida District Court of Appeal
336 So.2d 378 (1976)

RAWLS, ACTING CHIEF JUDGE.

Appellant, George Hampton, was found guilty by a jury of assault with intent to commit robbery and, under a charge of assault with intent to commit murder in the first degree, guilty of the lesser and included offense of assault with intent to commit murder in the second degree. By way of this appeal, appellant complains of the insufficiency of the evidence.

It is undisputed that the appellant (accompanied by his brother, Leonard, and one Hillman Arnold) arrived at Fred Coles' Store for the purpose of robbing Coles. Appellant, armed with a rifle, positioned himself outside of the store to act as a lookout while Leonard and Hillman entered the store, confronted Coles with a shotgun, and demanded Coles turn over to them the proceeds from the cash register. When Coles pointed to the empty cash drawer and stated that there was no money, Leonard fired the shotgun and wounded Coles, who retaliated with a shot that felled Hillman. Leonard threw the shotgun at Coles and ran out the door, leaving Hillman on the floor. Before escaping with Leonard, appellant fired a rifle shot through the window into a table near Coles.

There is no doubt that appellant was a willing participant in the attempted robbery. The evidence sustains the judgment of appellant's guilt of assault with intent to commit robbery. He was present aiding and abetting agents who threatened Coles with a shotgun intending to take money from him forcibly.[2]

Next, we consider appellant's contention that the evidence is insufficient to sustain his conviction of assault with intent to commit murder in the second degree. It has always been the law of this state that where several persons combine to commit an unlawful act, each is criminally responsible for the actions of his associates committed in furtherance or prosecution of a common design. The key is whether the extra criminal act done by one's confederate is in furtherance or prosecution of the initial common criminal design. This is a factual question which must be resolved on a case-by-case basis.

Of significance in this case is the fact that the shooting of Coles occurred during the course of a robbery. The legislature has decreed that one who kills another during the course of a robbery is guilty of murder in the first degree.[6] All that is necessary to establish the requisite intent to kill is to show that the killing occurred during the course of a robbery.

In *Pope v. State*, 84 Fla. 428 (1922) the Florida Supreme Court specifically and in detail addressed itself to the question of whether an accomplice is guilty pursuant to Florida Statute 776.011 of murder in the first degree when a confederate kills a person during the course of a robbery.[9] The facts in Pope are in several respects strikingly similar to the instant case. Pope and one Rawlins, the perpetrator of the actual murder, planned together the robbery. Their agreement was that Rawlins would take a gun (given to him by Pope) and go to the Palace Theater and rob the manager, Mr. Hickman. Pope was to wait several blocks away from the scene in a

---

[2] Florida Statutes 784.06 and 776.011 (1973).

[6] Florida Statute 782.04(1)(a)(2).

[9] While appellant was charged with the substantive crime of assault with intent to commit murder pursuant to Florida Statute 784.06, it has long been the law of this state that it is immaterial whether the indictment or information alleges that the defendant committed the crime or was merely aiding and abetting in its commission, as long as the proof establishes that he was guilty of either one of the acts prescribed by the statute. *State v. Roby*, 246 So.2d 566 (Fla.1971).

getaway car with the engine running. The twosome did not contemplate the murder of Hickman, and there was evidence adduced at trial that Rawlins' gun, during the course of the robbery, accidentally discharged resulting in Hickman's death. While the robbery murder was taking place, Pope was waiting several blocks away in the getaway car. In holding that Pope, as a principal to the robbery, was guilty of murder in the first degree, the Florida Supreme Court stated:

> It was an "unlawful killing" while committing a robbery that had been planned, and such a result should reasonably have been contemplated as probable, because the pistol was furnished and carried to the scene of the robbery. And whether the shooting was actually contemplated or intended or not, it grew out of the unlawful conspiracy and preparation to rob, and the principals in the robbery are guilty of the resulting homicide in the degree defined by the statute.

The Supreme Court has placed to rest the question of whether an accomplice in a robbery is guilty of murder in the first degree if his confederate kills a person during the course of the robbery. The only remaining question is whether an accomplice in a robbery is guilty of assault with intent to commit murder if the shooting victim is fortunate enough to live. An excellent discussion on this question has been undertaken by our sister court of appeal in Michigan in *People v. Poplar*.[10]

In *Poplar*, appellant Poplar was charged with breaking and entering and with assault with intent to commit murder. Appellant and his two confederates planned the breaking and entering of a warehouse. Pursuant to these plans, the two confederates entered the warehouse, while Poplar positioned himself across the street to act as lookout. Upon being discovered, one of Poplar's confederates shot the warehouse watchman in the face, wounding him. In upholding Poplar's conviction of both breaking and entering and assault with intent to commit murder, the Michigan court stated:

> There was no evidence that defendant harbored any intent to commit murder. Therefore, knowledge of the intent of Hill to kill the deceased is a necessary element to constitute him [defendant] a principal. This, however, may be established either by direct or circumstantial evidence from which knowledge of the intent may be inferred. Whether the crime committed was fairly within the scope of the common unlawful enterprise is a question of fact for the jury. In our opinion the jury could reasonably infer from the defendant's knowledge of the fact that a shotgun was in the car that he was aware of the fact that his companions might use the gun if they were discovered committing the burglary or in making their escape. If the jury drew that inference, then it could properly conclude that the use of the gun was fairly within the scope of the common unlawful enterprise and that the defendant was criminally responsible for the use by his confederates of the gun in effectuating their escape.

The facts of this case clearly show that appellant was a willing participant in a robbery in which he and his brother both employed and used firearms to accomplish

---

[10] *People v. Poplar*, 20 Mich.App. 132 (1969). See also *Walton v. State*, 57 Ala.App. 317 (1975), and *Johnson v. State*, 9 Md.App. 37 (1970).

their common mission. Sufficient evidence was presented to the jury from which they could infer that appellant knew Leonard might use his shotgun in attempting to accomplish the planned robbery and, in so doing, kill or wound an innocent citizen. In drawing this inference, it was proper for the jury to conclude that the use of the shotgun by Leonard resulting in Coles' wounds was fairly within the common unlawful enterprise and that the appellant was criminally responsible for the use by his confederates of the gun in effectuating their planned robbery. Appellant's conviction of assault with intent to commit second degree murder is affirmed.

NOTES FROM JUDGE KING:

(1) What purpose of criminal punishment is served by punishing Hampton for Leonard's crime of shooting Coles?

(2) Recall what you learned about the *Pinkerton* rule in Chapter 19. Is that rule any different from the *"Hampton"* rule?

In *U.S. v. Alvarez*, 755 F.2d 830 (11th Cir., 1985), five suspects (Simon, Alvarez, Portal, Concepcion, and Hernandez) agreed to sell two kilograms of cocaine at a motel to Rios and D'Atri, who were in fact undercover agents of the Bureau of Alcohol, Tobacco, & Firearms. As other agents broke into the motel to arrest the suspects, two of the suspects — Simon and Alvarez — began to shoot. Simon shot and killed Agent Rios. All five suspects were convicted of conspiracy to distribute cocaine. They were also convicted of murder. On appeal, Portal, Concepcion, and Hernandez argued that they should not be held responsible for the murder committed by Simon, because it was not a foreseeable consequence of the conspiracy to sell cocaine. The court disagreed:

> We find ample evidence to support the jury's conclusion that the murder was a reasonably foreseeable consequence of the drug conspiracy alleged in the indictment. In making this determination, we rely on two critical factors. First, the evidence clearly established that the drug conspiracy was designed to effectuate the sale of a large quantity of cocaine. The conspirators agreed to sell Agents Rios and D'Atri three kilograms of cocaine for a total price of $147,000. The transaction that led to the murder involved the sale of one kilogram of cocaine for $49,000. In short, the drug conspiracy was no nickel-and-dime operation; under any standards, the amount of drugs and money involved was quite substantial.

> Second, based on the amount of drugs and money involved, the jury was entitled to infer that, at the time the cocaine sale was arranged, the conspirators must have been aware of the likelihood (1) that at least some of their number would be carrying weapons, and (2) that deadly force would be used, if necessary, to protect the conspirators' interests. We have previously acknowledged the "nexus" between weapons and drugs, and we have also recognized that weapons have become "tools of the trade" for those involved in the distribution of illicit drugs. Experience on the trial and appellate benches has taught that substantial dealers in narcotics keep firearms on their premises as tools of the trade almost to the same extent as they keep scales, glassine bags, cutting equipment, and other narcotic

equipment. * * * * In light of these observations, and in view of the amount of drugs and money involved in the instant case, the jury's inference was both reasonable and proper.

In our opinion, these two critical factors provided ample support for the jury's conclusion that the murder was a reasonably foreseeable consequence of the drug conspiracy alleged in the indictment. In addition, we note the evidence at trial indicating that at least two of the conspirators were extremely nervous about the possibility of a rip-off or a drug bust. During a lull in the negotiations, Alvarez observed, "In this business, you have to be careful. It's a dangerous business. You have to watch out for rip-offs and Federal agents." Alvarez also stated that he would never go back to prison, and that he would rather be dead than go back to prison. Alvarez' statements clearly implied that he contemplated the use of deadly force, if necessary, to avoid a rip-off or apprehension by Federal agents. The evidence also indicated that, immediately prior to the shoot-out, Simon looked nervously out the window while fidgeting with a leather pouch that was suspected to contain a weapon. The jury properly could take this additional evidence into account in reaching its conclusion about the foreseeability of the murder.

Because we find that the evidence in this case was more than sufficient to allow a reasonable jury to conclude that the murder was a reasonably foreseeable consequence of the drug conspiracy alleged in the indictment, we hold that the court did not err by submitting the *Pinkerton* issue to the jury.

The three appellants also contend that, even if the murder was reasonably foreseeable, their murder convictions nevertheless should be reversed. The appellants argue that the murder was sufficiently distinct from the intended purposes of the drug conspiracy, and that their individual roles in the conspiracy were sufficiently minor, that they should not be held responsible for the murder. We are not persuaded.

It is well established that, under the *Pinkerton* doctrine, a co-conspirator is vicariously liable for the acts of another co-conspirator even though he may not have directly participated in those acts, his role in the crime was minor, or the evidence against a co-defendant more damaging. * * * * Thus, in a typical *Pinkerton* case, the court need not inquire into the individual culpability of a particular conspirator, so long as the substantive crime was a reasonably foreseeable consequence of the conspiracy.[24]

---

[24] A typical *Pinkerton* case falls into one of two categories. The first and most common category includes cases in which the substantive crime that is the subject of the *Pinkerton* charge is also one of the primary goals of the alleged conspiracy. See, e.g., *U.S. v. Luis-Gonzalez*, 719 F.2d 1539 (11th cir. 1983) (conspiracy to possess with intent to distribute marijuana; substantive crime of possession of marijuana). The second category includes cases in which the substantive crime is not a primary goal of the alleged conspiracy, but directly facilitates the achievement of one of the primary goals. See, e.g., *Shockley v. U.S.*, 166 F.2d 704 (9th Cir., 1948) (conspiracy to escape by violent means from federal penitentiary; substantive crime of first degree murder of prison guard). In either of these two categories, *Pinkerton*

We acknowledge that the instant case is not a typical *Pinkerton* case. Here, the murder of Agent Rios was not within the originally intended scope of the conspiracy, but instead occurred as a result of an unintended turn of events. We have not found, nor has the government cited, any authority for the proposition that all conspirators, regardless of individual culpability, may be held responsible under *Pinkerton* for reasonably foreseeable but originally unintended substantive crimes. Furthermore, we are mindful of the potential due process limitations on the *Pinkerton* doctrine in cases involving attenuated relationships between the conspirator and the substantive crime.[26]

Nevertheless, these considerations do not require us to reverse the murder convictions of Portal, Concepcion, and Hernandez, for we cannot accept the three appellants' assessment of their individual culpability. All three were more than "minor" participants in the drug conspiracy. Portal served as a look-out in front of the Hurricane Motel during part of the negotiations that led to the shoot-out, and the evidence indicated that he was armed. Concepcion introduced the agents to Alvarez, the apparent leader of the conspiracy, and was present when the shoot-out started. Finally, Hernandez, the manager of the motel, allowed the drug transactions to take place on the premises and acted as a translator during part of the negotiations that led to the shoot-out.

In addition, all three appellants had actual knowledge of at least some of the circumstances and events leading up to the murder. The evidence that Portal was carrying a weapon demonstrated that he anticipated the possible use of deadly force to protect the conspirators' interests. Moreover, both Concepcion and Hernandez were present when Alvarez stated that he would rather be dead than go back to prison, indicating that they, too, were aware that deadly force might be used to prevent apprehension by Federal agents.

We find the individual culpability of Portal, Concepcion, and Hernandez sufficient to support their murder convictions under *Pinkerton*, despite the fact that the murder was not within the originally intended scope of the conspiracy. In addition, based on the same evidence, we conclude that the relationship between the three appellants and the murder was not so

---

liability can be imposed on all conspirators because the substantive crime is squarely within the intended scope of the conspiracy.

[26] We also note the observations of Judge Mansfield of the Second Circuit who, in discussing the analogous issue of aider-and-abettor liability, stated:

It seems to me to place an undue strain on the concept to reason that, once a general conspiracy is shown, a minor or subordinate member who commits some act in furtherance of it thereby becomes an aider and abettor of parallel conduct of which he was unaware on the part of another member whose existence is unknown to him, merely because he should have reasonably foreseen that his conduct might assist others to commit such acts. Although such a foreseeability test might provide a basis for tort liability, the relationship strikes me as too attenuated to support a criminal conviction on the theory of aiding and abetting. [*U.S. v. Blitz*, 533 F.2d 1329, 1346-47 (2d Cir.) (Mansfield, J., dissenting).]

Judge Mansfield acknowledged that the conviction in *Blitz* could have been upheld under the *Pinkerton* doctrine, but he strongly intimated that he would have disagreed with such a result as well.

attenuated as to run afoul of the potential due process limitations on the *Pinkerton* doctrine. We therefore hold that *Pinkerton* liability for the murder of Agent Rios properly was imposed on the three appellants, and we decline to reverse their murder convictions on this ground.[27]

Question: Would the three appellants have been guilty of the murder under the "*Hampton*" rule, i.e., as accomplices to the crime of distribution of cocaine, they were responsible for all foreseeable crimes committed in furtherance of distribution of cocaine?

(3) LaFave & Scott, *Criminal Law*, criticize the *Pinkerton* rule, and they criticize the "*Hampton*" rule on much the same ground:

> The "natural and probable consequence" rule of accomplice liability, if viewed as a broad generalization, is inconsistent with more fundamental principles of our system of criminal law. It would permit liability to be predicated upon negligence even when the crime involved requires a different state of mind. Such is not possible as to one who has personally committed a crime, and should likewise not be the case as to those who have given aid or counsel.

See also *Sharma v. State*, 56 P.3d 868 (Nev. 2002),

(4) The close similarity between *Hampton* and *Pinkerton* got me to thinking about the similarity between accomplices and co-conspirators. Are they the same?

ESTRADA v. STATE
Florida District Court of Appeal
400 So.2d 562 (1981)

PER CURIAM

The judgment of conviction and sentence for aggravated assault which is under review by this appeal is affirmed, upon a holding that: * * * * the state's circumstantial evidence relevant to the defendant's intent to participate in the subject aggravated assault as an aider and abetter was, sufficient to withstand a motion for judgment of acquittal, as it established that the defendant: (a) was the driver of the get-away car in a gas station holdup; (b) drove the said car into the gas station prior to the holdup and hid the car behind a wall on the gas station property so that the car could not be seen from the street or from inside the building on the gas station property; (c) waited while his two companions in the car got out and committed a robbery with a firearm upon the attendant at the gas station; and, (d) hastily fled the scene in the car with his two companions after the robbery was committed, and was caught shortly thereafter with the fruits and instrumentalities of the robbery plainly visible to all in the car. See e.g., *Lynch v.*

---

[27] Although our decision today extends the *Pinkerton* doctrine to cases involving reasonably foreseeable but originally unintended substantive crimes, we emphasize that we do so only within narrow confines. Our holding is limited to conspirators who played more than a "minor" role in the conspiracy, or who had actual knowledge of at least some of the circumstances and events culminating in the reasonably foreseeable but originally unintended substantive crime.

State, 293 So.2d 44 (Fla. 1974); *Amato v. State*, 296 So.2d 609, 610 (Fla. 3d DCA 1974).

Affirmed.

G.C. v. STATE
Florida District Court of Appeal
407 So.2d 639 (1981)

FERGUSON, JUDGE.

G.C., a juvenile, was adjudicated delinquent as an aider and abettor to attempted burglary.

Accepting all of the evidence in a light most favorable to the state, at best there is proof that (1) G.C. knew that Delgado was going to burglarize an apartment, (2) G.C. followed Delgado to the scene of the crime, (3) G.C. stood back at least fifteen feet and watched Delgado remove jalousie glasses from the window of the apartment. The evidence before the court is less than that necessary to prove that G.C. aided and abetted in the attempted burglary.

In order for one person to be guilty of a crime physically committed by another under § 777.011, Florida Statutes (1979), it is necessary that he not only have a conscious intent that the criminal act shall be done, but further requires that pursuant to that intent, he do some act or say some word which was intended to and which did incite cause, encourage, assist or induce another person to actually commit the crime. *Ryals v. State*, 112 Fla. 4 (1933).

The state implores that the necessary elements of intent and act may be inferred - because G.C. knew that Delgado was going to commit a crime and was present during Delgado's attempt, it is established beyond and to the exclusion of any reasonable doubt that G.C. was a "lookout". Where two or more inferences must be drawn from the direct evidence, then pyramided to prove the offense, the evidence lacks the conclusive nature necessary to support a conviction. *Gustine v. State*, 86 Fla. 24 (1923). Presence at the scene, without more, is not sufficient to establish either intent to participate or act of participation. *J.H. v. State*, 370 So.2d 1219 (Fla. 3d DCA 1979). Mere knowledge that an offense is being committed is not equivalent to participation with criminal intent. See, e.g., *United States v. Martin*, 533 F.2d 268 (5th Cir. 1976). Knowledge that a crime is going to be committed and presence at the scene, without more, is generally insufficient to establish aiding and abetting. See, e.g., *Nye & Nissen v. United States*, 336 U.S. 613, 619 (1949).

Reversed with instructions to discharge the juvenile.

GAINS v. STATE

Florida District Court of Appeal

417 So.2d 719 (1982)

McCord, J.

In this consolidated appeal Michael Gains, Lonnie Williams, and Joseph Edward Williams, a/k/a Milton Kearney, appeal from their respective convictions, after a jury trial, of two counts of armed robbery. We affirm as to Gains and Lonnie Williams and reverse as to Joseph Williams.

Joseph Williams urges error in the trial court's denial of his motion for judgment of acquittal on the two armed robbery counts.

This appeal rises out of a criminal episode which occurred on October 1, 1980, at the Florida First National Bank on Merrill Road in Jacksonville, Florida. At approximately 11 a.m. on that date, three males, Michael Gains, Lonnie Williams, and a third juvenile entered into the bank and, while brandishing pistols, took approximately $1,065 of the bank's money from the custody of one bank teller, Betty Jean Cook, and something over $26,000 of the bank's money from a second teller, Bonnie Thompson. Thompson and Cook were working at different bank teller windows at the time of the robbery. The testimony of the various witnesses reveals that Lonnie Williams and the juvenile took the money from Cook and that the juvenile and Michael Gains took the bank money from Thompson. While the robbery was in progress, a mailman, John R. Osterhout, unfortunately entered the bank on personal banking business. Lonnie Williams put a gun to his head, forced him to the floor, and took his wallet and its contents.

As the three robbers left the bank, they walked slowly across the parking lot and calmly got into a car. This car had been parked far away from the bank at the end of the parking lot facing outward. While in the parking lot, the three men were not seen to be carrying guns, the masks worn during the robbery, or money. The driver, Joseph Williams, had not been inside the bank and sat casually in the car as the others got in. The car pulled slowly out of the lot, stopping because of traffic and obeying traffic signals.

Meanwhile, a customer at one of the bank's drive-in windows noticed the commotion inside the bank. She followed the car as it left the parking lot and entered into a residential neighborhood, still obeying traffic signals and not speeding. This witness waved down a police car which immediately gave chase.

When the police tailing the appellants first observed their car, it was not violating any traffic laws. As the police pulled closer, the officer noted that the passengers, Gains, Lonnie Williams, and the juvenile, did something unusual:

> They saw me coming down Townsend Boulevard and they turned and starting talking to the driver. At that point, when they'd made a complete turn onto Townsend Boulevard, the two in the back and Lonnie Williams in the front all laid down inside the vehicle as they approached my patrol car, which at that time I was still northbound coming up on them.

At this point, the officer turned on his lights and pulled in front of the car. The driver initially eluded the officer by driving up into a yard, and a chase ensued. This officer never lost sight of the vehicle during the two-minute chase which was concluded when the car being pursued crashed into another car at the intersection of Lone Star and Samontee. During the chase, Lonnie Williams fired his pistol at the officer approximately 15 times, and on several occasions reached into the back seat as if getting aid or ammunition.

Since Joseph Williams' argument regarding the insufficiency of the evidence stands in a somewhat different stead than the other arguments offered by him and the other appellants, we find it appropriate to address this argument first. In the commission of the crime, both the actor and the one who aids and abets him are principals in the first degree and may be charged and convicted of the crime. Section 777.011, Fla.Stat. It is not necessary that the aider or abettor be physically present aiding and abetting his partner or partners in the crime. However, he must be sufficiently near or so situated as to aid or encourage or to render assistance to the actual perpetrator. *Pope v. State*, 84 Fla. 428 (1923).

The guilt of an aider or abettor, of course, can be established by circumstantial evidence; however, that evidence must be both consistent with guilt and inconsistent with any reasonable hypothesis of innocence. *Williams v. State*, 206 So.2d 446 (Fla. 4th DCA 1968). Here, it is apparent that Joseph Williams was not an active participant in the armed robbery. Rather, the prosecution's theory implicitly rests on the assumption that he was the "wheelman" for the crime. The evidence that, as the driver of the car, he was a knowing participant in the crime is circumstantial, and thus more is needed than a suspicion or belief that under the circumstances, he knew what was occurring. The mere fact that he fled from the scene after the crime "does not exclude the reasonable inference that he had no knowledge of the crime until it actually occurred, and thus that he did not intend to assist in its commission." *J.H. v. State*, 370 So.2d 1219, 1220 (Fla. 3d DCA 1979).

Applying these standards to the facts elicited by the prosecution, we find that Joseph Williams' conviction cannot be sustained on the basis of circumstantial evidence. Considered in a light most favorable to the state's case, the evidence merely places Joseph Williams in the automobile outside the scene of the crime. There is no evidence that he had seen his companions carrying guns or that he had heard them discussing the crime prior to its inception. There is no evidence that he could see into the bank and thereby have ascertained the apparent intentions of his companions. There is no showing that he acted as a lookout for the trio. Further, he drove out of the parking lot at normal speeds while obeying traffic signals. He did not attempt to elude the police until, as we can fairly infer from the evidence, his companions informed him of something. Moreover, upon being apprehended, he did nothing to resist arrest. Thus, the evidence in this case just as reasonably supports the inference that, although Joseph Williams may have been in the general vicinity of the crime, he had no knowledge of his companion's intentions and attempted to flee only upon being apprised of their actions while in the bank.

The State relies upon *Enmund v. State*, 399 So.2d 1362 (Fla. 1981), to support the conviction of Joseph Williams. *Enmund v. State* was a robbery-murder case which construed § 782.04, Florida Statutes (1973). The court ruled that there was no direct evidence that Enmund was present with the accomplices at the back door where the robbery and murder took place; that the only evidence of the degree of his participation was the jury's likely inference that he was the person in the car by the side of the road near the scene of the crime; that the jury could have concluded that he was there, a few hundred feet away, waiting to help the robbers escape with the money. The court, therefore, held there was sufficient evidence that Enmund was a principal in the second degree, constructively present aiding and abetting the commission of the crime of robbery and, therefore, guilty of murder in the first degree under § 782.04(1)(a).

Unlike the case *sub judice*, there was evidence in *Enmund v. State* that Enmund had been at the scene of the crime on an earlier occasion and had commented on the large amount of money carried by the victim. Also, as contrasted to the circumstance that Joseph Williams was parked in the parking lot of a bank in the late morning business hours, Enmund was parked on the side of a rural highway in early morning hours near the scene of the robbery-murder, a scene, as above stated, which he had visited earlier and had commented on the victim's money. Also, unlike the evidence in the present case, there was evidence that the Enmund car drove from the scene "pretty fast" with one or two passengers lying across the back seat.

The evidence adduced at trial *sub judice* fails to exclude a reasonable hypothesis of innocence and is thus inadequate to convict Joseph Williams as an aider and abettor to the armed robberies. He should have been charged, if at all, as an accessory after-the-fact. See, e.g., *Ferguson v. State*, 321 So.2d 139 (Fla. 4th DCA 1975). Since the evidence was not sufficient, his convictions for the armed robberies are reversed. Moreover, because the retrial of a defendant whose conviction has been reversed for insufficiency of the evidence would violate the double jeopardy clause of the United States Constitution, which is fully applicable to state criminal proceedings, we have no choice but to direct that he be discharged from further custody for this alleged crime.

Joseph Williams' conviction is reversed and the case is remanded with directions that he be discharged from custody.

NOTES FROM JUDGE KING:

1. How can this decision be reconciled with *Estrada*?

2. If the principal actor is convicted of voluntary manslaughter, may his accomplice be convicted of murder? Yes, held the court in *People v. McCoy*, 25 Cal.4th 1111 (2001):

> Resolution of this question requires a close examination of the nature of aiding and abetting liability. "All persons concerned in the commission of a crime whether they directly commit the act constituting the offense, or aid and abet in its commission, are principals in any crime so committed." Pen. Code § 31. Thus, a person who aids and abets a crime is guilty of that crime even if someone else committed some or all of the criminal acts. Because aiders and abettors may be criminally liable for acts not their own, cases have described their liability as "vicarious." This description is accurate as far as it goes. But, as we explain, the aider and abettor's guilt for the

intended crime is not entirely vicarious. Rather, that guilt is based on a combination of the direct perpetrator's acts and the aider and abettor's *own* acts and *own* mental state.

It is important to bear in mind that an aider and abettor's liability for criminal conduct is of two kinds. First, an aider and abettor with the necessary mental state is guilty of the intended crime. Second, under the natural and probable consequences doctrine, an aider and abettor is guilty not only of the intended crime, but also for any other offense that was a natural and probable consequence of the crime aided and abetted. Thus, for example, if a person aids and abets only an intended assault, but a murder results, that person may be guilty of that murder, even if unintended, if it is a natural and probable consequence of the intended assault.

In this case, however, the trial court did not instruct the jury on the natural and probable consequences doctrine. It instructed only on an aider and abettor's guilt of the intended crimes. Accordingly, only an aider and abettor's guilt of the intended crime is relevant here. Nothing we say in this opinion necessarily applies to an aider and abettor's guilt of an unintended crime under the natural and probable consequences doctrine.

Except for strict liability offenses, every crime has two components: (1) an act or omission, sometimes called the actus reus; and (2) a necessary mental state, sometimes called the mens rea. This principle applies to aiding and abetting liability as well as direct liability. An aider and abettor must do something *and* have a certain mental state.

We have described the mental state required of an aider and abettor as different from the mental state necessary for conviction as the actual perpetrator. The difference, however, does not mean that the mental state of an aider and abettor is less culpable than that of the actual perpetrator. On the contrary, outside of the natural and probable consequences doctrine, an aider and abettor's mental state must be at least that required of the direct perpetrator. To prove that a defendant is an accomplice the prosecution must show that the defendant acted with knowledge of the criminal purpose of the perpetrator *and* with an intent or purpose either of committing, or of encouraging or facilitating commission of, the offense. When the offense charged is a specific intent crime, the accomplice must share the specific intent of the perpetrator'; this occurs when the accomplice knows the full extent of the perpetrator's criminal purpose and gives aid or encouragement with the intent or purpose of facilitating the perpetrator's commission of the crime. What this means here, when the charged offense and the intended offense — murder or attempted murder — are the same, i.e., when guilt does not depend on the natural and probable consequences doctrine, is that the aider and abettor must know and share the murderous intent of the actual perpetrator.

Aider and abettor liability is thus vicarious only in the sense that the aider and abettor is liable for another's actions as well as that person's own actions. When a person chooses to become a part of the criminal activity of another, she says in essence, "your acts are my acts." Dressler, *Reassessing the Theoretical Underpinnings of Accomplice Liability: New Solutions to an Old Problem* (1985) 37 Hastings L.J. 91, 111. But that person's *own* acts are also her acts for which she is also liable. Moreover, that person's mental state is her own; she is liable for her mens rea, not the other person's.

As stated in another work by Professor Dressler, "many commentators have concluded that there is no conceptual obstacle to convicting a secondary party of a more serious offense than is proved against the primary party. As they reason, once it is proved that 'the principal has caused an *actus reus*, the liability of each of the secondary parties should be assessed according to his own *mens rea*. That is, although joint participants in a crime are tied to a single and common *actus reus*, the individual *mentes reae* or levels of guilt of the joint participants are permitted to float free and are not tied to each other in any way. If their *mentes reae* are different, their independent levels of guilt will necessarily be different as well." Dressler, Understanding Criminal Law (2d ed. 1995) § 30.06[C], p. 450.

Professor Dressler explained how this concept operates with homicide. "An accomplice may be convicted of first-degree murder, even though the primary party is convicted of second-degree murder or of voluntary manslaughter. This outcome follows, for example, if the secondary party, premeditatedly, soberly and calmly, assists in a homicide, while the primary party kills unpremeditatedly, drunkenly, or in provocation. Likewise, it is possible for a primary party negligently to kill another (and, thus, be guilty of involuntary manslaughter), while the secondary party is guilty of murder, because he encouraged the primary actor's negligent conduct, with the intent that it result in the victim's death." Dressler, Understanding Criminal Law, *supra*, § 30.06[C], p. 450. * * * *

The statement that an aider and abettor may not be guilty of a greater offense than the direct perpetrator, although sometimes true in individual cases, is not universally correct. Aider and abettor liability is premised on the combined acts of all the principals, but on the aider and abettor's own mens rea. If the mens rea of the aider and abettor is more culpable than the actual perpetrator's, the aider and abettor may be guilty of a more serious crime than the actual perpetrator. * * * *

As another example, assume someone, let us call him Iago, falsely tells another person, whom we will call Othello, that Othello's wife, Desdemona, was having an affair, hoping that Othello would kill her in a fit of jealousy. Othello does so without Iago's further involvement. In that case, depending on the exact circumstances of the killing, Othello might be guilty of manslaughter, rather than murder, on a heat of passion theory. Othello's guilt of manslaughter, however, should not limit Iago's guilt if his own culpability were greater. Iago should be liable for his own acts as well Othello's, which he induced and encouraged. But Iago's criminal liability, as Othello's, would be based on his own personal mens rea. If, as our hypothetical suggests, Iago acted with malice, he would be guilty of murder even if Othello, who did the actual killing, was not.

We thus conclude that when a person, with the mental state necessary for an aider and abettor, helps or induces another to kill, that person's guilt is determined by the combined acts of all the participants as well as that person's own mens rea. If that person's mens rea is more culpable than another's, that person's guilt may be greater even if the other might be deemed the actual perpetrator.

Similarly, in *State v. Stills*, 125 N.M. 66 (1998), the court held that an accomplice may be convicted of voluntary manslaughter where the principal actor committed murder:

Sufficient provocation is viewed from a defendant's perspective.

The notion that the accomplice may be convicted, on an accomplice liability theory, only for those crimes as to which he personally has the requisite mental state, is applicable in a variety of circumstances. It means, for example, that one may not be held as an accomplice to the crime of assault with intent to kill if that intent was not shared by the accomplice. But this limitation has proved most significant in the homicide area, where the precise state of mind of the defendant has great significance in determining the degree of the offense. To determine the kind of homicide of which the accomplice is guilty, it is necessary to look to his state of mind; it may have been different from the state of mind of the principal and they thus may be guilty of different offenses. Thus, because first degree murder requires a deliberate and premeditated killing, an accomplice is not guilty of this degree of murder unless he acted with premeditation and deliberation.

And, because a killing in a heat of passion is manslaughter and not murder, an accomplice who aids while in such a state is guilty only of manslaughter even though the killer is himself guilty of murder. Likewise, it is equally possible that the killer is guilty only of manslaughter because of his heat of passion but that the accomplice, aiding in a state of cool blood, is guilty of murder.

Question: Under the *Hampton* approach, if the principal actor's premeditation is the "natural and probable consequence" of the plan to kill, isn't the accomplice guilty of first degree murder even if the accomplice was "adequately provoked to a heat of passion"?

CABLE v. STATE
Florida District Court of Appeal
436 So.2d 160 (1983)

GRIMES, JUDGE.

This is an appeal from a conviction of aggravated assault.

Detective Richard Swann, an undercover narcotics officer, met an informant at about 5:00 p.m. on June 16, 1981. The informant introduced Swann to appellant, and Swann told appellant that he wanted to buy some cocaine. Appellant's first efforts to acquire the cocaine were unsuccessful, so he told Swann to return later. At about 8:00 p.m., Swann picked appellant up, and they went to several places searching for drugs. Appellant then directed Swann to return to a gameroom that they had earlier visited to see if he could find someone with cocaine. Before arriving at the gameroom, appellant directed Swann to turn in to see several men who were in the parking lot of a convenience store. One of the men in the parking lot was appellant's brother William. After talking awhile, they decided to return to the gameroom.

Once at the gameroom, Swann noticed several others present, including a man named H. P. Brock. While the men talked, appellant drove off in William's car. He returned shortly and then told Swann to come outside. He took Swann to the side of the building away from the parking lot and told him that he could not find any cocaine that night. Suddenly, Swann turned and found William Cable advancing towards him with a large pair of hedge clippers. William Cable placed the clippers at Swann's throat and threatened to kill him. Appellant remained behind Swann, and Brock stood by as well. William Cable demanded Swann's wallet. As Swann gave it to him, Brock held the clippers. After searching Swann's wallet, William Cable ordered the officer against a car and patted him down. They also made Swann remove his shoes to see if he was carrying a weapon. After satisfying themselves that Swann was not a police officer, the men told him that if he would return the following night, they would sell him narcotics. Swann left without further incident. Appellant, his brother, and Brock were eventually arrested. The state charged appellant with aggravated assault.

Unquestionably, William Cable committed an aggravated assault on Officer Swann. See *Gilbert v. State*, 347 So.2d 1087 (Fla. 3d DCA 1977); § 784.021(1), Fla. Stat. (1981). We now must decide whether appellant's activities were sufficient to make him a principal in the first degree pursuant to § 777.011, Florida Statutes (1981). Section 777.011 provides in pertinent part:

> *Principal in first degree.* — Whoever commits any criminal offense against the state, whether felony or misdemeanor, or aids, abets, counsels, hires, or otherwise procures such offense to be committed, and such offense is committed or is attempted to be committed, is a principal in the first degree and may be charged, convicted, and punished as such, whether he is or is not actually or constructively present at the commission of such offense.

Before one can be convicted as an aider or abettor, there must be proof of his intent to participate in the crime. *Shockey v. State*, 338 So.2d 33 (Fla. 3d DCA 1976). The state must also show that the accused has done or said something which causes, encourages, assists, or induces the other person to actually commit the crime. *G.C. v. State*, 407 So.2d 639 (Fla. 3d DCA 1981).

In most cases of this type, the crime perpetrated by others is an end in itself, and the state simply seeks to prove that the defendant aided in the commission of that crime. Here, appellant actively tried to commit a crime, and the question is whether he can be convicted as a principal for the commission of a second crime carried out in furtherance of a scheme to commit the first one. Obviously, appellant and his brother and Brock were attempting to consummate a drug sale. At some point, they became suspicious that Swann was an undercover agent. Appellant asked Swann to come outside ostensibly to talk with him about the sale of the cocaine. When Swann was sufficiently removed from the premises, appellant's brother accosted him with some hedge clippers. While appellant did not handle the clippers, he was present at all times. His brother's acts did not appear spontaneous, and they were entirely consistent with the preservation of the common drug scheme. The jury was entitled to conclude that appellant was a principal in the commission of the aggravated assault.

Affirmed.

NOTES FROM JUDGE KING:

How can this decision be reconciled with *G.C.* and *Gains*? Was there substantial evidence that the defendant *knew* that William would attack Swann, and that defendant actually *helped* William to do so?

RODRIGUEZ v. STATE
Florida Court of Appeal
571 So.2d 1356 (1990)

CAMPBELL, ACTING CHIEF JUDGE.

Appellant, Heriberto Rodriguez, appeals his conviction and sentence for first degree felony murder. We must reverse and remand for a new trial because the trial judge committed reversible error when she failed to give appellant's requested independent act jury instruction. The instruction would have informed the jury that if it found that appellant's co-defendant committed the murder as an independent act, not during the course of or in furtherance of the attempted robbery, it would have to find appellant not guilty of first degree felony murder.

The evidence presented during appellant's trial showed that on March 14, 1988, at approximately 9:00 p.m., appellant parked his car in the vicinity of a Shell service station and store. His passenger, Victor Ballester, exited appellant's vehicle, went into the Shell station, confronted the attendant on duty and demanded money. The attendant refused to give Ballester the money and Ballester walked to the door of the station as if he were leaving. After a lapse of approximately four seconds, Ballester returned to the counter, placed a revolver to the head of the attendant and executed him on the spot. After the shooting, Ballester, without making any effort to take money or other property from the station or the body of the attendant, exited the station, apparently rejoined appellant in his vehicle and left the scene.

On March 19, 1988, appellant told his father that he had participated in an attempt to rob a store, but did not know about the killing until long after appellant and Ballester left the scene. Appellant expressed fear of Ballester and went to Puerto Rico to seek safety from him. On March 20, 1988, appellant's father drove to the Hillsborough County Sheriff Office in appellant's car and repeated appellant's story to the sheriff's personnel. Appellant was contacted in Puerto Rico and told his brother-in-law, a Tampa Police Department officer, that he did not know that a person had been shot until some time after the attempted robbery. Appellant stated that he was only the driver of his vehicle at the time of the attempted robbery, had not gotten out of his car and had seen nothing of the attempted robbery or the shooting. Arrangements were made for appellant's voluntary surrender to authorities. Appellant has continued to repeat the same version of the events that he told his father and brother-in-law.

The Shell station had a number of non-audio video tape cameras as part of a surveillance security system. The cameras were operational and recorded the attempted robbery and the shooting of the attendant in sequential pictures that indicated the date and timing of the events in seconds.

The video tape sequence of the attempted robbery and shooting was shown to the jury at trial. Twice during its deliberations, the jury requested and was allowed to view again the video tape sequences. As depicted in the video, only Ballester was seen when he first arrived at the store on March 14, 1988, at 20:55:06 (six seconds after 8:55 p.m.). The tape shows Ballester entering the store at 20:55:18, and no longer present in the store at 20:55:44. During the course of the events shown on the tape, Ballester is seen to approach the attendant, turn as if to leave the scene after apparently being stymied in the attempt at robbery, return to the attendant holding a weapon and then shoot the attendant. It was undisputed at trial that appellant never knew Ballester intended to shoot anyone. It was also undisputed that nothing was taken from the store and that appellant never witnessed any of the events that took place as he was parked in his car some distance away from the store and out of the line of vision.

Appellant's entire defense to the felony murder charge was that the murder was an independent act on the part of Ballester and not committed in the course of or in furtherance of the attempted robbery.

In closing arguments, appellant's counsel focused on the murder as an independent act because it was committed after the attempted robbery had failed and, since the entire scene had been filmed by the three visible surveillance cameras, it was arguably not done as an attempt to eliminate the witness. Appellant's counsel argued that the video tape showed that the murder was a spiteful act in the nature of an execution committed by Ballester as an afterthought to the attempted robbery.

The jury here had for its consideration a video tape of the entire sequence of events from which it could determine as a matter of fact whether in its opinion the attempted robbery had terminated before the murder, thus rendering the murder of the attendant a separate, independent act. Where there is any evidence introduced at trial which supports the theory of the defense, the defendant is entitled to have the jury instructed on the law applicable to his theory of defense.

It is settled law in this state that the felony murder rule and the law relating to principals combine to make a felon liable for the acts of murder committed by his co-felons in the furtherance of their joint felony. However, where there is evidence from which a jury could determine that the acts of the co-felons resulting in murder were independent of the joint felony, a defendant is entitled to an instruction that if the murder was such an independent act, not committed in furtherance of or in the course of the joint felony, the jury should find the defendant not guilty of felony murder. *Bryant v. State*, 412 So.2d 347 (Fla.1982). There was such evidence in this case from which the jury could have determined that the murder of the attendant was an independent act of Ballester, unrelated to the attempted robbery. The jury should have been so instructed.

We therefore reverse and remand for a new trial.

NOTES FROM JUDGE KING:

(1) *Why did* Ballester shoot the attendant? When a robber says "Your money or your life" and the victim rejects the first alternative, the robber might deliver on the second in order to maintain his credibility as a robber. By this reasoning, isn't this shooting "in furtherance" of the robbery?

(2) The court says that because the surveillance cameras were visible, the shooting "was arguably not done as an attempt to eliminate the witness." Does this depend on whether Ballester *saw* the cameras and *understood* what they were doing?

(3) How can this case be reconciled with *Hampton*?

RODRIGUEZ v. STATE
Florida Court of Appeal, 1993
617 So.2d 1101

FRANK, JUDGE

Heriberto Rodriguez, charged with first degree felony murder, was found guilty and sentenced to a life term. In his first appearance here, we reversed his conviction because of the trial court's erroneous refusal of his request for a jury instruction, i.e., that the victim's death stemmed from the independent act of a co-felon. Hence, we remanded the matter for a new trial, *Rodriguez v. State*, 571 So.2d 1356 (Fla. 2d DCA 1990) (*Rodriguez I*), and he was again found guilty of first degree felony murder.

The facts adduced on remand are essentially the same as those set forth in *Rodriguez I*.

At the remanded proceeding, the trial court instructed the jury on Rodriguez's liability for the lethal acts of his co-felon:

> If you find that the killing of Alain Dubrose was an independent act on the part of Victor Raymond Ballester and was not committed during the course of and in furtherance of the crime of attempted robbery, then you must find the Defendant, Heriberto Rodriguez, not guilty of murder in the first degree. "During the course of attempted robbery" means that the act occurred prior to, contemporaneous with or subsequent to the attempted robbery and that the act and attempted robbery constitute a continuous series of events.

Rodriguez argues the latter instruction effectively constituted "a judicial command" to the jury to return a verdict of guilty. We disagree. No aspect of the instruction relieved the state of its burden to prove a causal connection between the homicide and the attempted robbery. Without emphasizing Rodriguez's participation in the shooting, the trial court's instruction informed the jury that the state's burden included proving that the death of Alain Dubrose "occurred as a consequence of and while Heriberto Rodriguez was attempting to commit a robbery." We subscribe to the view that the term "during the course of attempted robbery" embodies the period when, as here, there is flight from the scene of the crime.

Because we have found no error in the instructions given the jury, we affirm.

NOTES FROM JUDGE KING:

Assuming that the jury dutifully followed the judge's instruction, why do you think they convicted Rodriguez?

UNITED STATES v. ORTEGA
U.S. Court of Appeals, 7th Circuit
44 F.3d 505 (1995)

POSNER, CHIEF JUDGE.

The defendant, Agustin Ortega, was sentenced to 63 months in prison following his conviction by a jury of aiding and abetting the possession of heroin with intent to distribute it. He had also been charged with conspiracy to distribute heroin but that charge was dismissed after the jury hung on it. There was no inconsistency in the jury's verdict, since while a conspirator is almost always also an aider and abettor, an aider and abettor is often not a conspirator. You can assist an enterprise and want it to succeed without being a party to the agreement under which the enterprise was created or is being operated.

The charges against Ortega arose out of a deal that Jesus Villasenor and Mario Gomez (who was Ortega's nephew) made to sell heroin to a pair of individuals who, unbeknownst to them, were an FBI agent and an FBI informant. The deal was struck at a restaurant and afterward the parties repaired to Villasenor's van, which was parked outside. Ortega was sitting in the van, behind the driver's seat. Villasenor went to the rear of the van and poked around, looking for something. Then he asked (in Spanish, as was the entire conversation among the parties), "Where is it?," and Ortega pointed to an area on the floor of the van and said, "Over there." Villasenor went to the place indicated and came up with a plastic bag, which he opened. The informant tasted it, and pronounced it heroin. The bag emitted a pungent odor and Ortega remarked - depending on the translation — either, "The damn aroma comes from that thing," or, "It still fuckin' smells like that's what it is." There was also testimony that after the informant declared the substance in the bag to be heroin, Ortega commented, "the best."

The evidence was not sufficient to convict Ortega of possession of heroin beyond a reasonable doubt. Possession, including constructive possession, implies a right -

not necessarily a legal right, but a right recognized by the relevant community, which may be an illegal community - to control. There is a sense in which, when Ortega was alone in the van with the heroin, he had "control" over it. He could have picked up the bag of heroin and run. But the power to make off with someone else's property is not equivalent to a right to the property. There is no evidence that the heroin was Ortega's in that sense. The heroin was Villasenor's. It is no answer that if only Ortega knew where it was, only Ortega could possess it. You can be the only person to know where something is, yet not own the thing; it may be inaccessible to you, and even if accessible may be the rightful possession of another. We doubt very much whether by the usages and customs of the heroin trade Ortega could have played finders keepers with Villasenor and expected to live to tell about it.

But if Ortega did not possess the heroin, Villasenor did; and the question then becomes whether Ortega aided and abetted Villasenor's possession. 18 U.S.C. § 2(a). If the evidence that Ortega said "the best" is credited, the answer is clearly yes. The canonical definition of aiding and abetting a federal offense, stated by Judge Learned Hand in *United States v. Peoni*, 100 F.2d 401, 402 (2d cir. 1938), requires not only that the defendant have aided his principal to commit a crime but also that he have wanted the principal to succeed in committing it. Obviously this rules out inadvertent assistance, but it also — and plausibly when we consider that the aider and abettor can be punished as severely as the principal, 18 U.S.C. § 2(a); U.S.S.G. § 2X1.1 — rules out cases in which the defendant was a mere accomplice after the fact, who did not assist the principal to commit the crime and therefore could not have been supposed to be acting out of a desire that the crime be committed. * * * *

If Ortega pronounced the heroin "the best," this makes him an aider and abettor. He was speaking to a customer and warranting the quality of the seller's product. He was assisting the sale in circumstances that made clear that he wanted it to succeed. But the evidence that Ortega, rather than the informant or the FBI agent, said "the best" is so weak that we hesitate to base our decision on the assumption that he did say it. If he did not, he still assisted the sale by pointing to the bag of heroin, and he did so knowingly. His remarks (quite apart from "the best") showed that he knew the bag contained heroin, as his reply brief concedes; and he must also have known — or so at least a reasonable jury could have found — that Villasenor wanted the heroin in order to make a sale.

Even so, if the evidence that Ortega said "the best" is discounted there is no evidence that he wanted the sale to succeed. He might have pointed to the bag because Villasenor asked him where it was and he knew, not because he wanted Villasenor to succeed in selling the heroin in it. The jury, recall, could not agree on a verdict on the conspiracy charge. Presumably it failed because there was very little evidence that Ortega, who happened to be an uncle of Gomez, Villasenor's partner in the sale of the heroin, was a member of the Villasenor-Gomez conspiracy. One of the alternative possibilities is that he was someone along for the ride who rendered one-time assistance by watching over the heroin (the van's door was broken, and as a result could not be locked, and there had been a previous theft) while Villasenor and Gomez were in the restaurant negotiating with the FBI agent and the informant. If we knew that Ortega was to be paid, as corrupt policemen are paid to look the other way when a drug deal is about to come off, it would be plain enough that he wanted the deal to succeed, as that would greatly enhance the probability of his actually being paid; and all the elements of the traditional test for aiding and abetting would then be satisfied. Likewise as we have said if he joined actively in the selling by talking up the quality of the product, showing that he wanted the sale to go through.

But what if he merely rendered assistance, without being compensated or otherwise identifying with the goals of the principal? We do not think it should make a difference, provided the assistance is deliberate and material. One who, knowing the criminal nature of another's act, deliberately renders what he knows to be active aid in the carrying out of the act is, we think, an aider and abettor even if there is no evidence that he wants the act to succeed — even if he is acting in a spirit of mischief. The law rarely has regard for underlying motives. *Peoni's* formula for aiding and abetting, if read literally, implies that the defendant must to be convicted have some actual desire for his principal to succeed. But in the actual administration of the law it has always been enough that the defendant, knowing what the principal was trying to do, rendered assistance that he believed would (whether or not he cared that it would) make the principal's success more likely — in other words did what he could do or what he was asked to do to help make success more likely. No more is required to make the defendant guilty of joining the principal's venture and adopting its aims for his own within the meaning of *Peoni* and the cases that follow it.

Affirmed.

Part VIII
Rape

Chapter 21

RAPE

Consent of the victim is a defense only when it negatives an element of the offense or precludes infliction of the harm to be prevented by the law defining the offense. * * * *

Generally, it may be said that consent by the victim is not a defense in a criminal prosecution. The explanation most commonly given for this rule is that a criminal offense is a wrong affecting the general public, at least indirectly, and consequently cannot be licensed by the individual directly harmed. Thus, it is no defense to a charge of murder that the victim, upon learning of the defendant's homicidal intentions, furnished the defendant with the gun and ammunition. * * * *

Certain crimes, however, are defined in terms of the victim's lack of consent, and as to these the consent of the victim is obviously a bar to conviction. Rape, for example, is typically defined as the "unlawful carnal knowledge of a woman without her consent," and thus consent by the woman to sexual intercourse negatives an element of the offense.

LaFave & Scott, *Criminal Law* (West)

Rape is a sensitive but important topic. Many of its most difficult issues are more appropriately considered when studying the law of *evidence*. (Is expert testimony regarding "rape trauma syndrome" admissible to show why the alleged victim did not promptly report the incident? Is evidence of an alleged victim's prior sexual behavior admissible to support the defendant's claim that the alleged victim consented to sex with the defendant? Is evidence of the defendant's prior assaults admissible to show that he raped this alleged victim?) Often, the main issue in a rape case is "whodunnit" — it is undisputed that the woman was raped by a stranger, but the defendant denies that he was the rapist, and the prosecutor must produce convincing evidence that the man on trial is the man who did it. The accuracy of eyewitness identification and scientific evidence loom as the key issues in such a trial.

But rape does raise "criminal law" issues — primarily involving the problem of *consent*.

Consent issues arise only rarely in other crimes. In the above quote, LaFave & Scott give an example of consent in a homicide prosecution, but it seems rather far-fetched (although something similar might arise in "assisted suicide" prosecutions).

In rape trials, however, consent issues arise rather frequently, especially in "date-rape" cases. Consensual sex is a common and complex human activity, and the expression of consent is often implied, non-verbal, or otherwise less clear than it might be. This raises some troubling problems. Should a man be barred from proceeding with sex unless the woman's consent is "perfectly clear"? Should he be barred if her words and behavior are ambiguous? If she does not resist as much as she might have, has she impliedly consented — or has the man used "force" to compel her to have sex? (Are these two questions — consent and force — merely two ways of asking the *same* question, or are they *different* questions? Can sex be based on *both* consent and force?)

From whose point of view should we consider consent: the woman's or the man's? What if he is acting from certain assumptions (based on his upbringing, his prior experience with other women, etc.) and she is acting from a different set of assumptions? What if he is *mistaken* about whether she meant to consent, but his mistake is a reasonable one? An unreasonable but honest one? Recall what you learned about "mistake of fact" in Chapter 1.

When considering these questions, keep in mind that rape is a felony, calling for many years of imprisonment. If the defendant "shouldn't" have believed that the woman consented, does it follow that we should punish him as a felon? On the other hand, would an acquittal "send a message" that society approves of his misbehavior?

PROBLEM 21

To: My law clerk

From: Justice Molly Ballew, Maryland Court of Special Appeals

Re: *Carson v. State*

Clark Carson was convicted of one count of second degree rape, under Maryland Code, Article 27, § 463. He was sentenced to 3 years imprisonment. He now appeals his conviction, claiming that the evidence is insufficient to support the jury's verdict. Three people testified at his trial: Lois Lake, Carson, and Katherine Kingsfield. Attached are transcripts of all of their testimony and some authorities on rape. Please read them over and advise me as to whether to vote to affirm or reverse the conviction.

Testimony of Lois Lake

Q (by Prosecutor): How did you come to know Defendant Carson?

A: We are both first year students at State University Law School, and we are in several classes together.

Q: Did you see him during the evening of March 7?

A: Yes. I was at a law school party, and he came up to me and started talking to me. I mentioned that I was having some difficulty in my torts class, and he hugged me and said, "Come on up to my apartment, and I'll show you my torts outline." I said, "OK, but no funny business, because I have a boyfriend, Darth."

Q: Then what happened?

A: We went in my car to his apartment, near the law school. We sat on the bed and read over his torts outline, when Clark started to kiss me. I pushed him away and said, "Let's keep this Platonic, or at least Socratic, OK?" He said, "I can't keep my mind on torts with you on my bed. I just have to make love to you." I said, "I'm leaving." I looked for my purse, but couldn't find it. He looked at me real mean and said, "You'll get your purse after we do it." There was a pocket knife on the table, and he was looking at it as he spoke to me. I became really afraid that he was going to hurt me. To calm him down, I sat back down on the bed, picked up the outline, and said to him quietly, "Calm down, Clark. Let's just look at the elements of assault." It didn't work. He pulled me down and got on top of me. He took off our clothes and had intercourse with me.

Q: Did you want to have intercourse with him?

A: No, of course not. I never told him that I wanted to. After he got inside of me, I tried to push him off, but he was too heavy.

Q: What happened next?

A: Well, after he was done, we got dressed. He gave me my purse and said, "I'll see you in class." I said, "You've got no class at all!" I took my car keys out of the purse and drove home.

* * * *

Q (Cross-examination): At this law school party, did you approach Mr. Carson and complain to him about your boyfriend?

A: Never. As I said, he approached me.

Q: Had you been drinking?

A: No. Just some lemonade.

Q: Is your boyfriend Darth a jealous type?

A: I suppose you could say that.

Testimony of Clark Carson

Q: Did you see Ms. Lake at the law school party?

A: Yes, she came up to me and started complaining about her boyfriend, Darth. She said she was tired of him and wanted to dump him, but she was afraid of him because he was very jealous and sometimes was violent. She had a few drinks and maybe was a little tipsy, and she started crying. I kind of hugged her to comfort her, and she grabbed me and said, "Let's go to your place, now." We went to my apartment in her car, and we made love.

Q: Did she ever say that she did not want to have sex with you?

A: Well, after we got to my apartment, I started kissing and petting her, and she said, "No, I don't really want to do this. Let me go home." I didn't believe her, so I picked her up and carried her to the bed and took off her clothes and made love to her. She didn't protest any more, and she seemed to like it.

Q: What happened after you made love?

A: She said, "Maybe I shouldn't have done that. If Darth ever finds out, he'll kill me." Then she left. When I saw her the next day at law school, she was very upset. She told me, "Darth phoned me this morning. A friend of his told Darth that he saw us leaving the party together last night. Darth is really angry. I don't know what to tell him." Then class started and I didn't speak to her anymore. That afternoon, the police arrested me for rape.

Testimony of Katherine Kingsfield

Q: What is your occupation?

A: I am a law professor at State University Law School.

Q: On March 7, did you see Ms. Lake and Mr. Carson at a law school party?

A: Yes. I was having a nice time chatting with Mr. Carson about demurrers, when Ms. Lake came up to him and said she wanted to talk to him. I could see that she was a little bit drunk. They started talking. I couldn't hear what they were saying, but I saw her start crying and then he hugged her. Then they left the party together.

Maryland Code, Article 27

§ 3-302. *Construction of subtitle*

In this subtitle an undefined word or phrase that describes an element of common-law rape retains its judicially determined meaning, except to the extent it is expressly or impliedly changed in this subtitle.

§ 3-303. *Rape in the first degree*

(a)   Prohibited. — A person may not:

     (1)   engage in vaginal intercourse with another by force, or the threat of force, without the consent of the other; and

     (2)

         (i)   employ or display a dangerous weapon, or a physical object that the victim reasonably believes is a dangerous weapon;

         (ii)   suffocate, strangle, disfigure, or inflict serious physical injury on the victim or another in the course of committing the crime;

         (iii)   threaten, or place the victim in fear, that the victim, or an individual known to the victim, imminently will be subject to death, suffocation, strangulation, disfigurement, serious physical injury, or kidnapping;

(iv)   commit the crime while aided and abetted by another; or

(v)   commit the crime in connection with a burglary in the first, second, or third degree.

(b)   Violation of § 3-503(a)(2) of this title. — A person may not violate subsection (a) of this section while also violating § 3-503(a)(2) of this title involving a victim who is a child under the age of 16 years.

(c)   Age considerations. — A person 18 years of age or older may not violate subsection (a) of this section involving a victim who is a child under the age of 13 years.

(d)   Penalties. —

(1)   Except as provided in paragraphs (2), (3), and (4) of this subsection, a person who violates subsection (a) of this section is guilty of the felony of rape in the first degree and on conviction is subject to imprisonment not exceeding life.

(2)   A person who violates subsection (b) of this section is guilty of the felony of rape in the first degree and on conviction is subject to imprisonment not exceeding life without the possibility of parole.

(3)   A person who violates subsection (a) or (b) of this section is guilty of the felony of rape in the first degree and on conviction is subject to imprisonment not exceeding life without the possibility of parole if the defendant was previously convicted of violating this section or § 3-305 of this subtitle.

(4)

(i)   Subject to subparagraph (iv) of this paragraph, a person 18 years of age or older who violates subsection (c) of this section is guilty of the felony of rape in the first degree and on conviction is subject to imprisonment for not less than 25 years and not exceeding life without the possibility of parole.

(ii)   A court may not suspend any part of the mandatory minimum sentence of 25 years.

(iii)   The person is not eligible for parole during the mandatory minimum sentence.

(iv)   If the State fails to comply with subsection (e) of this section, the mandatory minimum sentence shall not apply.

(e)   Required notice. — If the State intends to seek a sentence of imprisonment for life without the possibility of parole under subsection (d)(2), (3), or (4) of this section, or imprisonment for not less than 25 years under subsection (d)(4) of this section, the State shall notify the person in writing of the State's intention at least 30 days before trial.

§ 3-304. *Rape in the second degree*

    (a)   Prohibited. — A person may not engage in vaginal intercourse with another:

        (1)   by force, or the threat of force, without the consent of the other;

        (2)   if the victim is a mentally defective individual, a mentally incapacitated individual, or a physically helpless individual, and the person performing the act knows or reasonably should know that the victim is a mentally defective individual, a mentally incapacitated individual, or a physically helpless individual; or

        (3)   if the victim is under the age of 14 years, and the person performing the act is at least 4 years older than the victim.

    (b)   Age considerations. — A person 18 years of age or older may not violate subsection (a)(1) or (2) of this section involving a child under the age of 13 years.

    (c)   Penalty. —

        (1)   Except as provided in paragraph (2) of this subsection, a person who violates subsection (a) of this section is guilty of the felony of rape in the second degree and on conviction is subject to imprisonment not exceeding 20 years.

        (2)

            (i)   Subject to subparagraph (iv) of this paragraph, a person 18 years of age or older who violates subsection (b) of this section is guilty of the felony of rape in the second degree and on conviction is subject to imprisonment for not less than 15 years and not exceeding life.

            (ii)   A court may not suspend any part of the mandatory minimum sentence of 15 years.

            (iii)   The person is not eligible for parole during the mandatory minimum sentence.

            (iv)   If the State fails to comply with subsection (d) of this section, the mandatory minimum shall not apply.

    (d)   Required notice. — If the State intends to seek a sentence of imprisonment for not less than 15 years under subsection (c)(2) of this section, the State shall notify the person in writing of the State's intention at least 30 days before trial.

Note: Compare Model Penal Code §§ 2.11, 213.0-213.6, in Appendix II.

GOLDBERG v. STATE
Court of Special Appeals* of Maryland
395 A.2d 1213 (1979)

MELVIN, JUDGE.

On October 18, 1977, Randy Jay Goldberg, the appellant, was found guilty by a jury in the Circuit Court for Baltimore County, of rape in the second degree (Art. 27, § 463(a)(1)). The appellant was sentenced to a five year term, of which the first two years were to be served in a work release program at the jail and the remaining three years on probation.

On appeal, the appellant contends that the evidence was insufficient to sustain his conviction.

I.

The eighteen year old prosecuting witness was a high school senior who worked part-time as a sales clerk in the Merry-Go-Round clothing store at Towson Plaza. Around 1:00 P.M., on August 10, 1977, she was at work when the appellant, aged twenty-five, entered the store. The prosecuting witness started out trying to sell the appellant clothing, but ended up being sold a story by the appellant that he was a free-lance agent and thought she was an excellent prospect to become a successful model. They arranged to meet at 5 o'clock when she got off from work.

When the appellant returned for her at 5:00 P.M., she asked him for "any ID to show me if you are who you say you are." He showed her his driving license with his picture on it. This satisfied her: "Well, I figured that he wouldn't, if he was planning to harm me in any way, wouldn't give his name like that, and I figured that, you know, he was who he said he was. I believed him". Despite some cautioning from her employer, she drove off with the appellant at 5:10 P.M. in a silver-grey Cadillac El Dorado. The appellant was actually a student at Catonsville Community College and the car belonged to his mother. Appellant told her he was taking her to "a temporary studio" in the Pikesville area. When the "studio" was found to be closed, they drove to a condominium building on Slade Avenue. Upon arrival there, she stayed in the car while appellant went inside. Shortly, he returned to the car and told her he had contacted a friend who said they could use his house for his "studio." When they arrived at the friend's house, she helped appellant find a door that was open. The door led to the kitchen, which she described as "very dirty" and she "didn't, you know, understand why we were coming here." From the kitchen, they walked into the bedroom which by contrast she described as being "really made up really nice" with "a queen sized bed, real big bed, with a red velvet bedspread, and a big backboard on the back." She was "pretty impressed by the room."

Soon after they entered the bedroom, appellant "motioned" her to sit beside him on the bed. Instead, she sat on a chair at the foot of the bed. Appellant then said it

---

* Maryland's intermediate appellate court.

was hot in the room and took his shirt off. When asked her reaction to appellant's removing his shirt she responded: "He told me he was hot, so I figured he was hot." She then stood up and appellant "came over to me and he started unbuttoning my blouse. He said this is what I want you to do." She pulled her blouse together and said "no." Asked to describe what happened next she said:

> He just kept on smooth-talking me and saying I won't hurt you. This is what I do to all the models that I interview. And he, you know, started *motioning* me to take my blouse off and everything, and then I went through the same thing with every piece of clothing. It was like, you know, kept on trying to tell me to take it off, and I didn't want to. And he kept on trying to convince me that he was still trying to convince me that this was this modeling job, and I knew that it wasn't any more. [Emphasis added.]

She said she removed her clothes because she "was really scared of him." "There was nothing I could do." When asked what caused her fright she said: "Because he was he was so much bigger than I was, and, you know, I was in a room alone with him, and there was nothing, no buildings around us, or anything, and I mean wouldn't helped if I wouldn't help me if I didn't. It was like being trapped or something." On cross-examination she said she was "afraid" she was "going to be killed."

After her clothes were removed, the appellant "pushed" her down on the bed and tried "to move (her legs) in different ways, and (she) kept pulling them together, and telling him that (she) didn't want to do it, and just wanted to go home." He kept telling her that he wouldn't hurt her "and just to relax." But she was "just really scared" and she was "shaking and my voice was really shaking" and she "kept on telling him (she) wanted to go home, and that "(she) didn't want to do this;" that she "didn't want to be a model, and (she) didn't want to do it any more. Just to let (her) alone." When asked, "And what was his reaction?", she testified as follows:

> A. He was just really cool about the whole thing, telling me not to worry, and he wouldn't hurt me, and to relax.

> Q. All right. Now, after you were on the bed, and he was moving your legs around, what, if anything, occurred next?

> A. Well, he kept on trying to make me get in different positions, and kept on telling me to look sexual or something like that. I don't know what the word was.

> Q. All right. And what, if anything, occurred after he said that?

> A. He laid me down and placed his hands on my vagina and told me he was doing that to make me relax. I told him that it didn't make me relax.

> Q. All right. Then what happened after he placed his hands on your vagina?

> A. He went into the other room, and I couldn't see him. He wasn't facing me, and had his back to me, and his hands down by his belt buckle. And I realized what he was doing, and I jumped up and grabbed my clothes and started putting them on. Then he came in and pulled them away from me and said no.

Q. What did he say?

A. He said don't worry. What are you doing that for. I am not going to hurt you, and he kept telling me just to relax, and not to be nervous. And he laid me down on the bed and tried to get me to that stuff again, and I told him I didn't want to do that.

Q. What happened then?

A. And then he put his arms up on my stomach and his torso was in between my legs. He said just take your time; take a deep breath. And then he moved up on me and placed his penis in my vagina.

Q. What were you doing when this occurred?

A. I squeezed my legs together and got really tense, and I just started crying real hard. And I told him not to do that to me.

Q. And what was his response?

A. He didn't say anything. Just stayed there. And then I felt him move.

Q. How long was he on top of you?

A. Not very long.

Q. How long was he moving?

A. I guess for about two minutes, and then I felt him. Just for about two minutes.

Q. Did the Defendant ejaculate to your knowledge?

A. Yes, I think he did.

Q. Now, what, if anything, occurred after the Defendant ejaculated?

A. He got up and he said that if I can't enjoy it, then he can't enjoy it.

The appellant then asked her to go to dinner with him, but she declined, and he drove her to her home where she lived with her parents. On the way home, the appellant gave her his telephone number which she wrote down on a piece of paper. At his request she gave him her telephone number by writing it on a piece of paper with her lipstick. Although she told him she "would never see him again," she said she gave him her correct telephone number because she "didn't want to get him suspicious of me." They had a "general conversation about sex" in which he told her that "girls act like they don't want to, but they really do." She told him that he "had the wrong impression of her;" that she "didn't want him to do that." She further testified, somewhat inconsistently, as follows:

> I told him I didn't want that. I told him I didn't like him doing that to me, and didn't let him. I didn't make him think that I enjoyed all of it, and that I ever wanted to do it again, because I know I would never do it again. Never. I know I would never get near him again. [Emphasis supplied]

The appellant let her off at her home at 6:25 P.M., 1 1/4 hours after she left her place of employment with him at 5:10 P.M. Before the appellant drove off, she told him to "drive home safely. I guess I was being more sarcastic than anything." She estimated that they had been at the house where the alleged rape took place for 30 minutes.

When she arrived inside her house she "walked straight past my parents" to her upstairs room. She said nothing to them because she was "just scared, nervous, just you know, I wanted to go upstairs and just clean myself up and just forget, you know, about it. Just think." After cleaning herself and using a contraceptive, she called her boyfriend on the telephone and talked to him for "about three minutes." She did not tell him "what happened," because she "didn't know how he would take it." She then called her girlfriend and told her that she "had a problem, and that I was raped today." She did not relate the details of the "rape." She told her girlfriend not to tell anybody and not to tell her girlfriend's boyfriend, "but she told him anyways." She contemplated calling the police but said she "didn't know who to call," so she called her girlfriend back and asked what she should do. Shortly thereafter, the girlfriend and the girlfriend's boyfriend came to her house and, after picking up her own boyfriend, the four young people eventually went to the police station where the "rape" was reported at approximately 9:00 P.M. According to the girlfriend, the prosecuting witness did not want to report the matter but "we convinced her into going to the police." After reporting the incident the prosecuting witness was taken to the Greater Baltimore Medical Center for a physical examination. The examining physician's "Impression" was "Recent sexual inter-course," but he found "no evidence of recent trauma" to any part of her body, including the "perineal and genital" areas.

Testifying in his own behalf, the appellant admitted having sexual relations with the prosecuting witness at the time and place alleged, but maintained that it was mutually consensual and that the prosecuting witness did not appear to be frightened at any time.

II.

Prior to 1976, the Maryland rape statute was primarily a sentencing law, fixing the penalties without actually defining the crime. * * * * The common law definition of rape that has been applied in Maryland is: "the act of a man having unlawful carnal knowledge of a female over the age of ten years by force without the consent and against the will of the victim". *Hazel v. State*, 221 Md. 464, 468-469 (1960).

By Chapter 573 of the Laws of 1976, effective July 1, 1976, the Legislature divided the crime of rape into "rape in the first degree" and "rape in the second degree". See Art. 27, § 462 (first degree rape) and § 463 (second degree rape). Section 463 provides, *inter alia*, that,

> A person is guilty of rape in the second degree if the person engages in vaginal intercourse with another person:
>
> (1) By force or threat of force against the will and without the consent of the other person.

Section 462 deals with first degree rape and provides, *inter alia*, that,

A person is guilty of rape in the first degree if the person engages in vaginal intercourse with another person by force against the will and without the consent of the other person and: * * * (3) Threatens or places the victim in fear that the victim . . . will be imminently subjected to death, suffocation, strangulation, disfigurement, serious physical injury, or kidnapping . . .[2]

Section 464E of the new Act provides that,

Undefined words or phrases in this subheading (Sexual Offenses) which describe elements of the common-law crime of rape shall retain their judicially determined meaning except to the extent expressly or by implication changed in this subheading.

The terms "force," "threat of force," "against the will" and "without the consent" are not defined by the 1976 Act. We therefore look to the "judicially determined meaning" of these elements of the common law crime of rape. In doing so, we conclude that the evidence was legally insufficient to sustain the conviction and the judgment will be reversed. We reach this conclusion because on the record before us, viewing the evidence in the light most favorable to the State, we find legally insufficient evidence of the requisite element of "force or threat of force".

There was certainly no "threat of force." On the contrary, the prosecuting witness on numerous occasions in her testimony negated that element. As to actual force, the only arguable evidence is the prosecuting witness' testimony that after she herself had removed all her clothes, the appellant put his hands on her shoulders and "pushed" her down on the bed. This is negated, however, by her further testimony on cross-examination that "he didn't push but guided (her) on the bed". She admitted that she was not "injured or anything" by the encounter. This, of course, is consistent with the findings of the physician who subsequently examined her. Those findings so far as they relate to the use of any actual force were completely negative. But *actual physical* force is not an indispensable element of the crime of rape. As said by the Court of Appeals in *Hazel v. State, supra*, at 469:

Force is an essential element of the crime and to justify a conviction, the evidence must warrant a conclusion either that the victim resisted and her resistance was overcome by force *or that she was prevented from resisting by threats to her safety*. But no particular amount of force, either actual or constructive, is required to constitute rape. Necessarily that fact must depend upon the prevailing circumstances. Force may exist without violence. If the acts and threats of the defendant were reasonably calculated to create in the mind of the victim having regard to the circumstances in which she was placed a real apprehension, due to fear, of

---

[2] In the instant case, the first count of the six count indictment charged rape in the first degree. This count was "withdrawn" by the State before trial. This would seem to be a concession by the State that it lacked legally sufficient evidence that vaginal intercourse occurred because of any threats or acts on the part of the appellant that placed the prosecuting witness "in fear" that she would be "imminently subjected to death" or "serious physical injury". There was no concession, however, of the absence of "force or threat of force" that are essential alternative elements of rape in the second degree. Also, of course, the fact that the first count was withdrawn did not preclude the State from offering proof of first degree rape in its attempt to prove the lesser included offense of second degree rape.

imminent bodily harm, serious enough to impair or overcome her will to resist, then such acts and threats are the equivalent of force. 44 Am.Jur., Rape, § 5 [Emphasis added]

With respect to the presence or absence of the element of consent, it is true, of course, that however reluctantly given, consent to the act at any time prior to penetration deprives the subsequent intercourse of its criminal character. There is, however, a wide difference between consent and a submission to the act. Consent may involve submission, but submission does not necessarily imply consent. Furthermore, submission to a compelling force, or as a result of being put in fear, is not consent.

The authorities are by no means in accord as to what degree of resistance is necessary to establish the absence of consent. However, *the generally accepted doctrine seems to be that a female who was conscious and possessed of her natural, mental and physical powers when the attack took place must have resisted to the extent of her ability at the time, unless it appears that she was overcome by numbers or was so terrified by threats as to overpower her will to resist.* 44 Am.Jur., Rape, § 7. Since resistance is necessarily relative, the presence or absence of it must depend on the facts and circumstances in each case. But the real test, which must be recognized in all cases, is whether the assault was committed without the consent and against the will of the prosecuting witness. [Emphasis added]

The kind of fear which would render resistance by a woman unnecessary to support a conviction of rape includes, but is not necessarily limited to, a fear of death or serious bodily harm, or a fear so extreme as to preclude resistance or a fear which would well nigh render her mind incapable of continuing to resist, or a fear that so overpowers her that she does not dare resist.

Applying these principles to the present case, we hold that the evidence is legally insufficient to warrant a finding by the jury that the prosecutrix exerted the necessary degree of resistance that was overcome by force or that she was prevented from resisting by fear based upon reasonable apprehension of bodily harm.

The State argues that the "totality of the circumstances" caused the prosecutrix's fear of being killed and that the fear was a reasonable fear, thus rendering more resistance than that exerted by her unnecessary. First of all, we find nothing in the record evidencing any real resistance by the prosecutrix to anything the appellant said or did. It is true that she *told* the appellant she "didn't want to do that (stuff)." But the resistance that must be shown involves not merely verbal but *physical* resistance "to the extent of her ability at the time." *Hazel v. State, supra*, at 460. The State points to her testimony that when penetration occurred she "squeezed her legs together and got really tense." Assuming that this was evidence of her reluctance, even unwillingness, to engage in vaginal intercourse, it was not evidence that she resisted "to the extent of her ability" *before* the intercourse occurred.

We are left therefore with the question of whether the prosecutrix's lack of resistance was caused by fear based upon reasonable apprehension of physical harm. We find no legally sufficient evidence warranting an affirmative answer to that question. As we said in *Winegan v. State*, 10 Md.App. 196, 200 (1970):

> Where the victim's story could not be corroborated by wounds, bruises or disordered clothing, the lack of consent could be shown by fear based upon reasonable apprehension. The rule requiring the apprehension be reasonable was first enunciated in Maryland in *Hazel v. State*, 221 Md. 464, 469: "If the acts and threats of the defendant were reasonably calculated to create in the mind of the victim having regard to the circumstances in which she was placed a real apprehension, due to fear, of imminent bodily harm, serious enough to impair or overcome her will to resist, then such acts and threats are the equivalent of force."

On the record before us, we find the evidence legally insufficient to warrant a conclusion that the appellant's words or actions "were reasonably calculated to create in the mind of the victim" a reasonable fear that if she had resisted he would have harmed her, or that, faced with such resistance, he would have used force to overcome it. The prosecutrix swore that the reasons for her fear of being killed if she did not accede to appellant's advances were two-fold: 1) she was alone with the appellant in a house with no buildings close by and no one to help her if she resisted, and 2) the appellant was much larger than she was. In the complete absence of any threatening words or actions by the appellant, these two factors, as a matter of law, are simply not enough to have created a reasonable fear of harm so as to preclude resistance and be "the equivalent of force." *Hazel v. State, supra*, at 469. Without proof of force,[3] actual or constructive, evidenced by words or conduct of the defendant or those acting in consort with him, sexual intercourse is not rape. This is so even though the intercourse may have occurred without the actual consent and against the actual will of the alleged victim. Thus it is that the absence of actual force, unreasonable subjective fear of resisting cannot convert the conduct of the defendant from that which is non-criminal to that which is criminal.

Judgment reversed.

NOTE FROM JUSTICE BALEW:

In Jane Findlater, *Reexamining the Law of Rape*, 86 Mich.L.Rev. 1213, 1219-20 (1988), the author asks regarding *Goldberg*: "What sense can be made of this paradox: the victim was not forced to have sexual intercourse, but she had sexual intercourse against her will and without her consent?"

---

[3] I.e., force beyond what is involved in the very act of intercourse itself. See Perkins on Criminal Law, p. 162 (2nd ed. 1969).

STATE v. RUSK
Court of Appeals*x of Maryland
289 Md. 230, 424 A.2d 720 (1981)

MURPHY, CHIEF JUDGE.

Edward Rusk was found guilty by a jury in the Criminal Court of Baltimore of second degree rape in violation of Maryland Code Art. 27, § 463(a)(1), which provides in pertinent part:

> A person is guilty of rape in the second degree if the person engages in vaginal intercourse with another person: (1) By force or threat of force against the will and without the consent of the other person. . . .

On appeal, the Court of Special Appeals, sitting *en banc*, reversed the conviction; it concluded by an 8-5 majority that in view of the prevailing law as set forth in *Hazel v. State*, 221 Md. 464 (1960), insufficient evidence of Rusk's guilt had been adduced at the trial to permit the case to go to the jury.

At the trial, the 21-year-old prosecuting witness, Pat, testified that on the evening of September 21, 1977, she attended a high school alumnae meeting where she met a girl friend, Terry. After the meeting, Terry and Pat agreed to drive in their respective cars to Fells Point to have a few drinks. On the way, Pat stopped to telephone her mother, who was baby sitting for Pat's two-year-old son; she told her mother that she was going with Terry to Fells Point and would not be late in arriving home.

The women arrived in Fells Point about 9:45 p.m. They went to a bar where each had one drink. After staying approximately one hour, Pat and Terry walked several blocks to a second bar, where each of them had another drink. After about thirty minutes, they walked two blocks to a third bar known as E. J. Buggs. The bar was crowded and a band was playing in the back. Pat ordered another drink and as she and Terry were leaning against the wall, Rusk approached and said "hello" to Terry. Terry, who was then conversing with another individual, momentarily interrupted her conversation and said "Hi, Eddie." Rusk then began talking with Pat and during their conversation both of them acknowledged being separated from their respective spouses and having a child. Pat told Rusk that she had to go home because it was a week-night and she had to wake up with her baby early in the morning.

Rusk asked Pat the direction in which she was driving and after she responded, Rusk requested a ride to his apartment. Although Pat did not know Rusk, she thought that Terry knew him. She thereafter agreed to give him a ride. Pat cautioned Rusk on the way to the car that "I'm just giving a ride home, you know, as a friend, not anything to be, you know, thought of other than a ride;" and he said, "Oh, okay." They left the bar between 12:00 and 12:20 a.m.

Pat testified that on the way to Rusk's apartment, they continued the general conversation that they had started in the bar. After a twenty-minute drive, they arrived at Rusk's apartment in the 3100 block of Guilford Avenue. Pat testified that

---

she was totally unfamiliar with the neighborhood. She parked the car at the curb on the opposite side of the street from Rusk's apartment but left the engine running. Rusk asked Pat to come in, but she refused. He invited her again, and she again declined. She told Rusk that she could not go into his apartment even if she wanted to, because she was separated from her husband and a detective could be observing her movements. Pat said that Rusk was fully aware that she did not want to accompany him to his room. Notwithstanding her repeated refusals, Pat testified that Rusk reached over and turned off the ignition to her car and took her car keys. He got out of the car, walked over to her side, opened the door and said, "Now, will you come up?" Pat explained her subsequent actions:

> At that point, because I was scared, because he had my car keys. I didn't know what to do. I was someplace I didn't even know where I was. It was in the city. I didn't know whether to run. I really didn't think at that point, what to do. Now, I know that I should have blown the horn. I should have run. There were a million things I could have done. I was scared, at that point, and I didn't do any of them.

Pat testified that at this moment she feared that Rusk would rape her. She said: "It was the way he looked at me, and said 'Come on up, come on up;' and when he took the keys, I knew that was wrong."

It was then about 1 a.m. Pat accompanied Rusk across the street into a totally dark house. She followed him up two flights of stairs. She neither saw nor heard anyone in the building. Once they ascended the stairs, Rusk unlocked the door to his one-room apartment, and turned on the light. According to Pat, he told her to sit down. She sat in a chair beside the bed. Rusk sat on the bed. After Rusk talked for a few minutes, he left the room for about one to five minutes. Pat remained seated in the chair. She made no noise and did not attempt to leave. She said that she did not notice a telephone in the room. When Rusk returned, he turned off the light and sat down on the bed. Pat asked if she could leave; she told him that she wanted to go home and "didn't want to come up." She said, "Now, that I came up, can I go?" Rusk, who was still in possession of her car keys, said he wanted her to stay.

Rusk then asked Pat to get on the bed with him. He pulled her by the arms to the bed and began to undress her, removing her blouse and bra. He unzipped her slacks and she took them off after he told her to do so. Pat removed the rest of her clothing, and then removed Rusk's pants because "he asked me to do it." After they were both undressed Rusk started kissing Pat as she was lying on her back. Pat explained what happened next:

> I was still begging him to please let, you know, let me leave. I said, "You can get a lot of other girls down there, for what you want," and he just kept saying, "no"; and then I was really scared, because I can't describe, you know, what was said. It was more the look in his eyes; and I said, at that point I didn't know what to say; and I said, "If I do what you want, will you let me go without killing me?" Because I didn't know, at that point, what he was going to do; and I started to cry; and when I did, he put his hands on my throat, and started lightly to choke me; and I said, "If I do what you want, will you let me go?" And he said, yes, and at that time, I proceeded to do what he wanted me to.

Pat testified that Rusk made her perform oral sex and then vaginal intercourse.

Immediately after the intercourse, Pat asked if she could leave. She testified that Rusk said, "Yes," after which she got up and got dressed and Rusk returned her car keys. She said that Rusk then "walked me to my car, and asked if he could see me again; and I said, 'Yes,' and he asked me for my telephone number; and I said, 'No, I'll see you down Fells Point sometime,' just so I could leave." Pat testified that she "had no intention of meeting him again." She asked him for directions out of the neighborhood and left.

On her way home, Pat stopped at a gas station, went to the ladies room, and then drove "pretty much straight home and pulled up and parked the car." At first she was not going to say anything about the incident. She explained her initial reaction not to report the incident: "I didn't want to go through what I'm going through now [at the trial]." As she sat in her car reflecting on the incident, Pat said she began to "wonder what would happen if I hadn't of done what he wanted me to do. So I thought the right thing to do was to go report it, and I went from there to Hillendale to find a police car." She reported the incident to the police at about 3:15 a.m. Subsequently, Pat took the police to Rusk's apartment, which she located without any great difficulty.

Pat's girlfriend Terry corroborated her testimony concerning the events which occurred up to the time that Pat left the bar with Rusk. Questioned about Pat's alcohol consumption, Terry said she was drinking screwdrivers that night, but normally did not finish a drink. Terry testified about her acquaintanceship with Rusk: "I knew his face, and his first name, but I honestly couldn't tell you apparently I ran into him sometime before. I couldn't tell you how I know him. I don't know him very well at all." Officer Hammett of the Baltimore City Police Department acknowledged receiving Pat's rape complaint at 3:15 a.m. on September 22, 1977. He accompanied her to the 3100 block of Guilford Avenue, where it took Pat several minutes to locate Rusk's apartment.

Officer Hammett entered Rusk's multi-dwelling apartment house, which contained at least six apartments, and arrested Rusk in a room on the second floor.

Hammett testified that Pat was sober, and she was taken to City Hospital for an examination. The examination disclosed that seminal fluid and spermatozoa were detected in Pat's vagina, on her underpants, and on the bed sheets recovered from Rusk's bed.

At the close of the State's case-in-chief, Rusk moved for a judgment of acquittal. In denying the motion, the trial court said:

> There is evidence that there is a taking of automobile keys forcibly, a request that the prosecuting witness accompany the Defendant to the upstairs apartment. She described a look in his eye which put her in fear. Now, you are absolutely correct that there was no weapon, no physical threatening testified to. However, while she was seated on a chair next to the bed, the Defendant excused himself, and came back in five minutes; and then she testifies, he pulled her on to the bed by reaching over and grabbing her wrists, and/or had her or requested, that she disrobe, and assist him in disrobing. Again, she said she was scared, and then she

testified to something to the effect that she said to him, she was begging him to let her leave. She was scared. She started to cry. He started to strangle her softly she said. She asked the Defendant, that if she'd submit, would he not kill her, at which point he indicated that he would not; and she performed oral sex on him, and then had intercourse.

Rusk and two of his friends, Michael Trimp and David Carroll, testified on his behalf. According to Trimp, they went in Carroll's car to Buggs' bar to dance, drink and "try to pick up some ladies." Rusk stayed at the bar, while the others went to get something to eat.

Trimp and Carroll next saw Rusk walking down the street arm-in-arm with a lady whom Trimp was unable to identify. Trimp asked Rusk if he needed a ride home. Rusk responded that the woman he was with was going to drive him home. Trimp testified that at about 2:00-2:30 a.m. he returned to the room he rented with Rusk on Guilford Avenue and found Rusk to be the only person present. Trimp said that as many as twelve people lived in the entire building and that the room he rented with Rusk was referred to as their "pit stop." Both Rusk and Trimp actually resided at places other than the Guilford Avenue room. Trimp testified that there was a telephone in the apartment.

Carroll's testimony corroborated Trimp's. He saw Rusk walking down the street arm-in-arm with a woman. He said "she was kind of like, you know, snuggling up to him like. She was hanging all over him then." Carroll was fairly certain that Pat was the woman who was with Rusk.

Rusk, the 31-year-old defendant, testified that he was in the Buggs Tavern for about thirty minutes when he noticed Pat standing at the bar. Rusk said: "She looked at me, and she smiled. I walked over and said, hi, and started talking to her." He did not remember either knowing or speaking to Terry. When Pat mentioned that she was about to leave, Rusk asked her if she wanted to go home with him. In response, Pat said that she would like to, but could not because she had her car. Rusk then suggested that they take her car. Pat agreed and they left the bar arm-in-arm.

Rusk testified that during the drive to her apartment, he discussed with Pat their similar marital situations and talked about their children. He said that Pat asked him if he was going to rape her. When he inquired why she was asking, Pat said that she had been raped once before. Rusk expressed his sympathy for her. Pat then asked him if he planned to beat her. He inquired why she was asking and Pat explained that her husband used to beat her. Rusk again expressed his sympathy. He testified that at no time did Pat express a fear that she was being followed by her separated husband.

According to Rusk, when they arrived in front of his apartment Pat parked the car and turned the engine off. They sat for several minutes "petting each other." Rusk denied switching off the ignition and removing the keys. He said that they walked to the apartment house and proceeded up the stairs to his room. Rusk testified that Pat came willingly to his room, and that at no time did he make threatening facial expressions. Once inside his room, Rusk left Pat alone for several minutes while he used the bathroom down the hall. Upon his return, he switched the light on but immediately turned it off because Pat, who was seated in the dark in a chair next to the bed, complained it was too bright. Rusk said that he sat on the bed across from Pat and reached out

> and started to put my arms around her, and started kissing her; and we fell back into the bed, and she we were petting, kissing, and she stuck her hand down in my pants and started playing with me; and I undid her blouse, and took off her bra; and then I sat up and I said "Let's take our clothes off"; and she said, "Okay;" and I took my clothes off, and she took her clothes off; and then we proceeded to have intercourse.

Rusk explained that after the intercourse, Pat "got uptight."

> Well, she started to cry. She said that she said, "You guys are all alike," she says, "just out for," you know, one thing." She started talking about I don't know, she was crying and all. I tried to calm her down and all; and I said, "What's the matter?" And she said, that she just wanted to leave; and I said, "Well, okay"; and she walked out to the car. I walked out to the car. She got in the car and left.

Rusk denied placing his hands on Pat's throat or attempting to strangle her. He also denied using force or threats of force to get Pat to have intercourse with him. In reversing Rusk's second degree rape conviction, the Court of Special Appeals, quoting from *Hazel*, 221 Md. at 469, noted that:

> Force is an essential element of the crime of rape and to justify a conviction, the evidence must warrant a conclusion either that the victim resisted and her resistance was overcome by force or that she was prevented from resisting by threats to her safety.

Writing for the majority, Judge Thompson said:

> In all of the victim's testimony we have been unable to see any resistance on her part to the sex acts and certainly can we see no fear as would overcome her attempt to resist or escape as required by *Hazel*. Possession of the keys by the accused may have deterred her vehicular escape, but hardly a departure seeking help in the rooming house or in the street. We must say that "the way he looked" fails utterly to support the fear required by Hazel.

The Court of Special Appeals interpreted *Hazel* as requiring a showing of a reasonable apprehension of fear in instances where the prosecutrix did not resist. It concluded:

> We find the evidence legally insufficient to warrant a conclusion that appellant's words or actions created in the mind of the victim a reasonable fear that if she resisted, he would have harmed her, or that faced with such resistance, he would have used force to overcome it. The prosecutrix stated that she was afraid, and submitted because of "the look in his eyes." After both were undressed and in the bed, and she pleaded to him that she wanted to leave, he started to lightly choke her. At oral argument, it was brought out that the "lightly choking" could have been a heavy caress. We do not believe that "lightly choking" along with all the facts and circum-

stances in the case, were sufficient to cause a reasonable fear which overcame her ability to resist. In the absence of any other evidence showing force used by appellant, we find that the evidence was insufficient to convict appellant of rape.

In argument before us on the merits of the case, the parties agreed that the issue was whether, in light of the principles of *Hazel*, there was evidence before the jury legally sufficient to prove beyond a reasonable doubt that the intercourse was "by force or threat of force against the will and without the consent" of the victim in violation of Art. 27, § 463(a)(1). Of course, due process requirements mandate that a criminal conviction not be obtained if the evidence does not reasonably support a finding of guilt beyond a reasonable doubt. However, as the Supreme Court made clear in *Jackson v. Virginia*, 443 U.S. 307 (1979), the reviewing court does not ask itself whether it believes that the evidence established guilt beyond a reasonable doubt; rather, the applicable standard is "whether, after viewing the evidence in the light most favorable to the prosecution, *any* rational trier of fact could have found the essential elements of the crime beyond a reasonable doubt." 443 U.S. at 319.

The vaginal intercourse once being established, the remaining elements of rape in the second degree under § 463(a)(1) are, as in a prosecution for common law rape (1) force actual or constructive, and (2) lack of consent. The terms in § 463(a)(1) "force," "threat of force," "against the will" and "without the consent" are not defined in the statute, but are to be afforded their "judicially determined meaning" as applied in cases involving common law rape. See Art. 27, § 464E. In this regard, it is well settled that the terms "against the will" and "without the consent" are synonymous in the law of rape.

Hazel, which was decided in 1960, long before the enactment of § 463(a)(1), involved a prosecution for common law rape, there defined as "the act of a man having unlawful carnal knowledge of a female over the age of ten years by force without the consent and against the will of the victim." 221 Md. at 468-69. The evidence in that case disclosed that Hazel followed the prosecutrix into her home while she was unloading groceries from her car. He put his arm around her neck, said he had a gun, and threatened to shoot her baby if she moved. Although the prosecutrix never saw a gun, Hazel kept one hand in his pocket and repeatedly stated that he had a gun. He robbed the prosecutrix, tied her hands, gagged her, and took her into the cellar. The prosecutrix complied with Hazel's commands to lie on the floor and to raise her legs. Hazel proceeded to have intercourse with her while her hands were still tied. The victim testified that she did not struggle because she was afraid for her life. There was evidence that she told the police that Hazel did not use force at any time and was extremely gentle. Hazel claimed that the intercourse was consensual and that he never made any threats. The Court said that the issue before it was whether "the evidence was insufficient to sustain the conviction of rape because the conduct of the prosecutrix was such as to render her failure to resist consent in law." *Id.* at 468. It was in the context of this evidentiary background that the Court set forth the principles of law which controlled the disposition of the case. It recognized that force and lack of consent are distinct elements of the crime of rape. It said:

Force is an essential element of the crime and to justify a conviction, the evidence must warrant a conclusion either that the victim resisted and her resistance was overcome by force or that she was prevented from resisting by threats to her safety. But no particular amount of force, either actual or constructive, is required to constitute rape. Necessarily, that fact must depend upon the prevailing circumstances. As in this case force may exist without violence. If the acts and threats of the defendant were reasonably calculated to create in the mind of the victim, having regard to the circumstances in which she was placed, a real apprehension, due to fear, of imminent bodily harm, serious enough to impair or overcome her will to resist, then such acts and threats are the equivalent of force. [*Id.* at 469]

As to the element of lack of consent, the Court said in *Hazel*:

It is true, of course, that however reluctantly given, consent to the act at any time prior to penetration deprives the subsequent intercourse of its criminal character. There is, however, a wide difference between consent and a submission to the act. Consent may involve submission, but submission does not necessarily imply consent. Furthermore, submission to a compelling force, or as a result of being put in fear, is not consent.

The Court noted that lack of consent is generally established through proof of resistance or by proof that the victim failed to resist because of fear. The degree of fear necessary to obviate the need to prove resistance, and thereby establish lack of consent, was defined in the following manner:

The kind of fear which would render resistance by a woman unnecessary to support a conviction of rape includes, but is not necessarily limited to, a fear of death or serious bodily harm, or a fear so extreme as to preclude resistance, or a fear which would well nigh render her mind incapable of continuing to resist, or a fear that so overpowers her that she does not dare resist. [*Id.* at 470]

Hazel thus made it clear that lack of consent could be established through proof that the victim submitted as a result of fear of imminent death or serious bodily harm. In addition, if the actions and conduct of the defendant were reasonably calculated to induce this fear in the victim's mind, then the element of force is present. *Hazel* recognized, therefore, that the same kind of evidence may be used in establishing both force and non-consent, particularly when a threat rather than actual force is involved.

The Court noted in *Hazel* that the judges who heard the evidence, and who sat as the trier of fact in Hazel's non-jury case, had concluded that, in light of the defendant's acts of violence and threats of serious harm, there existed a genuine and continuing fear of such harm on the victim's part, so that the ensuing act of sexual intercourse under this fear "amounted to a felonious and forcible act of the defendant against the will and consent of the prosecuting witness." In finding the evidence sufficient to sustain the conviction, the Court observed that "the issue of whether the intercourse was accomplished by force and against the will and consent of the victim was one of credibility, properly to be resolved by the trial court." 221 Md. at 470.

Hazel did not expressly determine whether the victim's fear must be "reasonable." Its only reference to reasonableness related to whether "the acts and threats of the defendant were reasonably calculated to create in the mind of the victim a real apprehension, due to fear, of imminent bodily harm." 221 Md. at 469. Manifestly, the Court was there referring to the calculations of the accused, not to the fear of the victim. While *Hazel* made it clear that the victim's fear had to be genuine, it did not pass upon whether a real but unreasonable fear of imminent death or serious bodily harm would suffice. The vast majority of jurisdictions have required that the victim's fear be reasonably grounded in order to obviate the need for either proof of actual force on the part of the assailant or physical resistance on the part of the victim.[3] We think that, generally, this is the correct standard.

As earlier indicated, the Court of Special Appeals held that a showing of a reasonable apprehension of fear was essential under *Hazel* to establish the elements of the offense where the victim did not resist. The Court did not believe, however, that the evidence was legally sufficient to demonstrate the existence of "a reasonable fear" which overcame Pat's ability to resist. In support of the Court's conclusion, Rusk maintains that the evidence showed that Pat voluntarily entered his apartment without being subjected to a "single threat nor a scintilla of force"; that she made no effort to run away nor did she scream for help; that she never exhibited a will to resist; and that her subjective reaction of fear to the situation in which she had voluntarily placed herself was unreasonable and exaggerated. Rusk claims that his acts were not reasonably calculated to overcome a will to resist; that Pat's verbal resistance was not resistance within the contemplation of *Hazel*; that his alleged menacing look did not constitute a threat of force; and that even had he pulled Pat to the bed and lightly choked her, as she claimed, these actions, viewed in the context of the entire incident, no prior threats having been made, would be insufficient to constitute force or a threat of force or render the intercourse non-consensual.

We think the reversal of Rusk's conviction by the Court of Special Appeals was in error, for the fundamental reason so well expressed in the dissenting opinion by Judge Wilner, when he observed that the majority had "trampled upon the first principle of appellate restraint because it had substituted its own view of the evidence (and the inferences that may fairly be drawn from it) for that of the judge and jury and had thereby improperly invaded the province allotted to those tribunals." In view of the evidence adduced at the trial, the reasonableness of Pat's apprehension of fear was plainly a question of fact for the jury to determine. * * * * Applying the constitutional standard of review articulated in *Jackson v. Virginia*, *supra*, *i.e.* whether after considering the evidence in the light most favorable to the prosecution, any rational trier of fact could have found the essential elements of the crime beyond a reasonable doubt, it is readily apparent to us that the trier of fact could rationally find that the elements of force and non-consent had been established and that Rusk was guilty of the offense beyond a reasonable doubt. Of course, it was for the jury to observe the witnesses and their demeanor, and to judge their credibility and weigh their testimony. Quite obviously, the jury disbelieved Rusk

---

[3] Some jurisdictions do not require that the victim's fear be reasonably grounded. See, e.g., *State v. Herfel*, 49 Wis.2d 513 (1971).

and believed Pat's testimony. From her testimony, the jury could have reasonably concluded that the taking of her car keys was intended by Rusk to immobilize her alone, late at night, in a neighborhood with which she was not familiar; that after Pat had repeatedly refused to enter his apartment, Rusk commanded in firm tones that she do so; that Pat was badly frightened and feared that Rusk intended to rape her; that unable to think clearly and believing that she had no other choice in the circumstances, Pat entered Rusk's apartment; that once inside Pat asked permission to leave but Rusk told her to stay; that he then pulled Pat by the arms to the bed and undressed her; that Pat was afraid that Rusk would kill her unless she submitted; that she began to cry and Rusk then put his hands on her throat and began "lightly to choke" her; that Pat asked him if he would let her go without killing her if she complied with his demands; that Rusk gave an affirmative response, after which she finally submitted.

Just where persuasion ends and force begins in cases like the present is essentially a factual issue, to be resolved in light of the controlling legal precepts. That threats of force need not be made in any particular manner in order to put a person in fear of bodily harm is well established. Indeed, conduct, rather than words, may convey the threat. That a victim did not scream out for help or attempt to escape, while bearing on the question of consent, is unnecessary where she is restrained by fear of violence.

Considering all of the evidence in the case, with particular focus upon the actual force applied by Rusk to Pat's neck, we conclude that the jury could rationally find that the essential elements of second degree rape had been established and that Rusk was guilty of that offense beyond a reasonable doubt.

Judgment of the Court of Special Appeals reversed. Case remanded to that court with direction that it affirm the judgment of the Criminal Court of Baltimore.

COLE, JUDGE, dissenting.

I agree with the Court of Special Appeals that the evidence adduced at the trial of Edward Salvatore Rusk was insufficient to convict him of rape. I, therefore, respectfully dissent.

The standard of appellate review in deciding a question of sufficiency, as the majority correctly notes, is whether, after viewing the evidence in the light most favorable to the prosecution, *any* rational trier of fact could have found the essential elements of the crime beyond reasonable doubt. However, it is equally well settled that when one of the essential elements of a crime is not sustained by the evidence, the conviction of the defendant cannot stand as a matter of law.

The majority, in applying this standard, concludes that "in view of the evidence adduced at the trial, the reasonableness of Pat's apprehension of fear was plainly a question of fact for the jury to determine." In so concluding, the majority has skipped over the crucial issue. It seems to me that whether the prosecutrix's fear is reasonable becomes a question only after the court determines that the defendant's conduct under the circumstances was reasonably calculated to give rise to a fear on her part to the extent that she was unable to resist. In other words, the fear must stem from his articulable conduct, and equally, if not more importantly, cannot be inconsistent with her own contemporaneous reaction to that conduct. The conduct of the defendant, in and of itself, must clearly indicate force or the threat of force such as to overpower the prosecutrix's ability to resist or will to resist. In my view, there is no evidence to support the majority's conclusion that the prosecutrix was forced to submit to sexual intercourse, certainly not fellatio.

This Court defined rape in *Hazel v. State*, 221 Md. 464 (1960), as "the act of a man having unlawful carnal knowledge of a female over the age of ten years by force without the consent and against the will of the victim." The Court went on to declare that "force is an essential element of the crime and to justify a conviction, the evidence must warrant a conclusion either that the victim resisted and her resistance was overcome by force or that she was prevented from resisting by threats to her safety." 221 Md. at 469. We noted that "no particular amount of force, either actual or constructive, is required to constitute rape. Necessarily that fact must depend upon the prevailing circumstances." However, we hastened to add that "if the acts and threats of the defendant are reasonably calculated to create in the mind of the victim having regard to the circumstances in which she is placed a real apprehension, due to fear, of imminent bodily harm, serious enough to impair or overcome her will to resist, then such acts and threats are the equivalent of force."

To avoid any confusion about the substantive law to be applied, we further stated in *Hazel* that:

> While the authorities are by no means in accord as to what degree of resistance is necessary to establish the absence of consent, the generally accepted doctrine seems to be that a female who was conscious and possessed of her natural, mental and physical powers when the attack took place must have resisted to the extent of her ability at the time, unless it appears that she was overcome by numbers or so terrified by threats as to overcome her will to resist. [221 Md. at 469-70]

In *Selvage v. State*, 148 Neb. 409 (1947), an 18-year-old woman went to a dance with her brother and later decided to go to a cafe with the defendants and some other acquaintances. They drove to a ball park several blocks away where she and the defendant and another got out. The others in the car drove away. She and the two males walked about a block into the park; she refused their advances for intercourse. She claimed they threw her to the ground, held her while they took turns having sexual intercourse. While this was going on, a car with its lights on drove up and the two young men hurried some distance away from her. She made no outcry, nor attempted to communicate with the people in this car. Later at a different place in the park, she claimed each had intercourse with her again. The three walked back to the cafe, drank coffee, and waited to get a car to take them to the city near her home. When they finally got a car, she testified the two repeated the acts of intercourse with her. She resisted but made no complaint to those riding in the front seat. When she got home she related to her parents what had happened.

The Supreme Court of Nebraska, in holding the evidence insufficient to convict for rape, said:

> Resistance or opposition by mere words is not enough; the resistance must be by acts, and must be reasonably proportionate to the strength and

opportunities of the woman. She must resist the consummation of the act, and her resistance must not be a mere pretense, but must be in good faith, and must persist until the offense is consummated. [27 N.W.2d at 637]

In *Kidd v. State*, 97 Okl.Cr. 415 (1953), the rape took place in a car in an isolated spot. One assailant in that case told the victim that if she did not shut up he would kill her with a beer bottle. "By the time the defendant took over," the court concluded, "this victim was whipped down and demoralized."

These cases make plain that *Hazel* intended to require clear and cognizable evidence of force or the threat of force sufficient to overcome or prevent resistance by the female before there would arise a jury question of whether the prosecutrix had a reasonable apprehension of harm. The majority today departs from this requirement and places its imprimatur on the female's conclusory statements that she was in fear, as sufficient to support a conviction of rape.

It is significant to note that in each of the fourteen reported rape cases decided since *Hazel* in which sufficiency of the evidence was the issue, the appellate courts of this State have adhered to the requirement that evidence of force or the threat of force overcoming or preventing resistance by the female must be demonstrated on the record to sustain a conviction. In *Goldberg v. State*, 41 Md.App. 58, the conviction was reversed by the Court of Special Appeals. Goldberg concerned a student, professing to be a talent agent, who lured a young woman to an apartment upon the pretext of offering her a modeling job. She freely accompanied him, and though she protested verbally, she did not physically resist his advances. The Court of Special Appeals held:

> The prosecutrix swore that the reasons for her fear of being killed if she did not accede to appellant's advances were two-fold: 1) she was alone with the appellant in a house with no buildings close by and no one to help her if she resisted, and 2) the appellant was much larger than she was. In the complete absence of any threatening words or actions by the appellant, these two factors, as a matter of law, are simply not enough to have created a reasonable fear of harm so as to preclude resistance and be "the equivalent of force".

While courts no longer require a female to resist to the utmost or to resist where resistance would be foolhardy, they do require her acquiescence in the act of intercourse to stem from fear generated by something of substance. She may not simply say, "I was really scared," and thereby transform consent or mere unwillingness into submission by force. These words do not transform a seducer into a rapist. She must follow the natural instinct of every proud female to resist, by more than mere words, the violation of her person by a stranger or an unwelcome friend. She must make it plain that she regards such sexual acts as abhorrent and repugnant to her natural sense of pride. She must resist unless the defendant has objectively manifested his intent to use physical force to accomplish his purpose. The law regards rape as a crime of violence. The majority today attenuates this proposition. It declares the innocence of an at best distraught young woman. It does not demonstrate the defendant's guilt of the crime of rape.

My examination of the evidence in a light most favorable to the State reveals no conduct by the defendant reasonably calculated to cause the prosecutrix to be so fearful that she should fail to resist and thus, the element of force is lacking in the State's proof.

Here we have a full grown married woman who meets the defendant in a bar under friendly circumstances. They drink and talk together. She agrees to give him a ride home in her car. When they arrive at his house, located in an area with which she was unfamiliar but which was certainly not isolated, he invites her to come up to his apartment and she refuses. According to her testimony he takes her keys, walks around to her side of the car, and says "Now will you come up?" She answers, "yes." The majority suggests that "from her testimony the jury could have reasonably concluded that the taking of her keys was intended by Rusk to immobilize her alone, late at night, in a neighborhood with which she was unfamiliar." But on what facts does the majority so conclude? There is no evidence descriptive of the tone of his voice; her testimony indicates only the bare statement quoted above. How can the majority extract from this conduct a threat reasonably calculated to create a fear of imminent bodily harm? There was no weapon, no threat to inflict physical injury.

She also testified that she was afraid of "the way he looked," and afraid of his statement, "come on up, come on up." But what can the majority conclude from this statement coupled with a "look" that remained undescribed? There is no evidence whatsoever to suggest that this was anything other than a pattern of conduct consistent with the ordinary seduction of a female acquaintance who at first suggests her disinclination.

After reaching the room, she described what occurred as follows:

> I was still begging him to please let, you know, let me leave. I said, "you can get a lot of other girls down there, for what you want," and he just kept saying, "no," and then I was really scared, because I can't describe, you know, what was said. It was more the look in his eyes; and I said, at that point I didn't know what to say; and I said, "If I do what you want, will you let me go without killing me?" Because I didn't know, at that point, what he was going to do; and I started to cry; and when I did, he put his hands on my throat and started lightly to choke me; and I said "If I do what you want, will you let me go?" And he said, yes, and at that time, I proceeded to do what he wanted me to.

The majority relies on the trial court's statement that the defendant responded affirmatively to her question "If I do what you want, will you let me go without killing me?" The majority further suggests that the jury could infer the defendant's affirmative response. The facts belie such inference, since by the prosecutrix's own testimony the defendant made no response. He said nothing!

She then testified that she started to cry and he "started lightly to choke" her, whatever that means. Obviously, the choking was not of any persuasive significance. During this "choking" she was able to talk. She said "If I do what you want will you let me go?" It was at this point that the defendant said yes.

I find it incredible for the majority to conclude that on these acts, without more, a woman was forced to commit oral sex upon the defendant and then to engage in vaginal intercourse. In the absence of any verbal threat to do her grievous bodily harm or the display of any weapon and threat to use it, I find it difficult to understand how a victim could participate in these sexual activities and not be willing.

What was the nature and extent of her fear anyhow? She herself testified she was "fearful that maybe I had someone following me." She was afraid because she didn't know him and she was afraid he was going to "rape" her. But there are no acts or conduct on the part of the defendant to suggest that these fears were created by the defendant or that he made any objective, identifiable threats to her which would give rise to this woman's failure to flee, summon help, scream, or make physical resistance.

As the defendant well knew, this was not a child. This was a married woman with children, a woman familiar with the social setting in which these two actors met. It was an ordinary city street, not an isolated spot. He had not forced his way into her car; he had not taken advantage of a difference in years or any state of intoxication or mental or physical incapacity on her part. He did not grapple with her. She got out of the car, walked with him across the street and followed him up the stairs to his room. She certainly had to realize that they were not going upstairs to play Scrabble.

Once in the room, she waited while he went to the bathroom where he stayed for five minutes. In his absence, the room was lighted but she did not seek a means of escape. She did not even "try the door" to determine if it was locked. She waited.

Upon his return, he turned off the lights and pulled her on the bed. There is no suggestion or inference to be drawn from her testimony that he yanked her on the bed or in any manner physically abused her by this conduct. As a matter of fact there is no suggestion by her that he bruised or hurt her in any manner, or that the "choking" was intended to be disabling.

He then proceeded to unbutton her blouse and her bra. He did not rip her clothes off or use any greater force than was necessary to unfasten her garments. He did not even complete this procedure but requested that she do it, which she did "because he asked me to." However, she not only removed her clothing but took his clothes off, too.

Then for a while they lay together on the bed kissing, though she says she did not return his kisses. However, without protest she then proceeded to perform oral sex and later submitted to vaginal intercourse. After these activities were completed, she asked to leave. They dressed and he walked her to her car and asked to see her again. She indicated that perhaps they might meet at Fells Point. He gave her directions home and returned to his apartment where the police found him later that morning.

The record does not disclose the basis for this young woman's misgivings about her experience with the defendant. The only substantive fear she had was that she would be late arriving home. The objective facts make it inherently improbable that the defendant's conduct generated any fear for her physical well-being.

In my judgment, the State failed to prove the essential element of force beyond a reasonable doubt and, therefore, the judgment of conviction should be reversed.

NOTES FROM JUSTICE BALLEW:

(1) Who do you think was telling the truth, Pat or Rusk? If an appellate justice believes that Rusk was telling the truth, should that justice vote to affirm Rusk's conviction?

(2) Was *Rusk* a case of "force" or "threat of force"?

(3) The facts of *Rusk* seem very similar to those of *Goldberg*? Can the two cases be reconciled?

(4) Consider the following excerpt from the Commentary to Model Penal Code § 213.1 (defining "rape"), and see if it helps in analyzing our case:

> The law of rape protects the female's freedom of choice and punishes unwanted and coerced intimacy. The male who imposes himself upon the female by force or compulsion obviously violates these interests. To this paradigm case, * * * certain other situations are assimilated in which the female's consent is either non-existent or ineffective. Thus, rape has traditionally included not only intercourse by force or threat, but also sexual imposition on an unconscious or otherwise incapacitated female, intimacy achieved by certain fundamental kinds of deception, and intercourse with a mentally incompetent or underage female.

> The unifying principle among this diversity of conduct is the idea of meaningful consent. If the law regards the female as competent to consent and if she does so, intercourse is not rape. * * * *

> Ancient authorities defined the offense as carnal knowledge of a woman "without her consent," "against her will," or by some similar phrasing. Statutes derived from the common law frequently added a requirement that the intercourse be achieved "forcibly" or "by force." Judicial interpretations of this language, however, have substantially vitiated its content, so that in many jurisdictions non-consent by the female has become the primary point of focus rather than the elements of overreaching in the conduct of the actor.

> There are a number of problems that arise if too much emphasis is placed upon the non-consent of the victim as opposed to the overreaching of the actor. In the first place, overemphasis on non-consent tends to obscure differences among the various circumstances covered by the law of rape. An exclusive focus on non-consent would collect under one label the wholly uninvited and forceful attack by a total stranger, the excessive zeal of a sometime boyfriend, and the clever seducer who dupes his victim into believing that they are husband and wife. In the words of one commentator, such an approach would compress into a single statute a diversity of conduct ranging from "brutal attacks . . . to half won arguments . . . in parked cars." Many older statutes failed to recognize this point and hence did not make provision for grading differentials within the law of rape. Such statutes generally assigned to every case within their coverage the same

draconian penalties deemed appropriate for the most violent and shocking version of the offense. The result under such an approach is that some offenders are subjected to punishment more drastic than any rational grading scheme would allow, while others are windfall beneficiaries of the reluctance of jurors to condemn every offender to possible death or life imprisonment.

A second way in which overemphasis on non-consent can be troublesome relates to problems of proof. Evidentiary considerations aside, consent appears to be a conceptually simple issue. Either the female assented to intercourse, or she did not. Searching for consent in a particular case, however, may reveal depths of ambiguity and contradiction that are scarcely suspected when the question is put in the abstract. Often the woman's attitude may be deeply ambivalent. She may not want intercourse, may fear it, or may desire it but feel compelled to say "no". Her confusion at the time of the act may later resolve into non-consent. Some have expressed the fear that a woman who subconsciously wanted to have sexual intercourse will later feel guilty and "cry rape." It seems plain, on the other hand, that a barrage of conflicting emotions at the time of the assault does not necessarily imply the victim's consent, although it may lead to misperception by the actor. Further ambiguity may be introduced by the fact that the woman may appear to consent because she is frozen by fear and panic, or because she quite rationally decides to "consent" rather than risk being killed or injured.

The point, in any event, is that inquiry into the victim's subjective state of mind and the attacker's perceptions of her state of mind will not yield a clear answer. The deceptively simple notion of consent may obscure a tangled mesh of psychological complexity, ambiguous communication, and unconscious restructuring of the event by the participants. Courts have not been oblivious to this difficulty, but in attempting to resolve it they have often placed disproportionate emphasis upon objective manifestations of non-consent by the woman. It seems plain that some courts have gone too far in this direction, although it is equally plain that one can go too far in the opposite direction.

What is required is that a balanced inquiry be made into the factors that indicate imposition by the male as well as those that indicate non-consent by the victim. It is appropriate in this effort to focus primarily upon the conduct of the male, particularly in the more serious forms of the offense, and to seek objective verification in the actor's conduct of the overreaching and imposition that is the major characteristic of the offense in its most serious form. At the same time, however, the possibility of consent by the victim, even in the face of conduct that may give some evidence of overreaching, cannot be ignored. As intractable as the imposition-consent issue necessarily will be, it cannot be avoided. [*Model Penal Code & Commentaries*, Part II, pp. 301-303 (American Law Institute, 1980)]

(5) Consider Richard A. Posner, *Sex & Reason* (1992), p. 391:

We can expect date rape to be frequent in a society, such as ours, in which sexual mores are not uniform — and apparently it is. The reason is not just differences between the mores of sexually active women on the one hand and of police officers and judges on the other, but differences between the mores of men and of their dates. Suppose, as is in fact the case, that some women in our society believe that the courtship ritual requires them to pretend to resist a man's sexual advances, that others are not coy and when they say no do not intend finally to succumb, and that still others dress and deport themselves in a manner that seems provocative but in fact they adhere to traditional values. Insofar as men find it difficult to distinguish among these groups of women (search costs again), they will make mistakes with respect to the existence of consent. The result will be sexual acts perceived as rape by the victim and reported as rape in victim surveys.

(6) In *State v. M.T.S.*, 609 A.2d 1266 (N.J.Supreme Ct. 1992), the court interpreted the words "physical force" as used in New Jersey's "sexual assault" (formerly "rape") statute:

Because the statute eschews any reference to the victim's will or resistance, the standard defining the role of force in sexual penetration must prevent the possibility that the establishment of the crime will turn on the alleged victim's state of mind or responsive behavior. We conclude, therefore, that any act of sexual penetration engaged in by the defendant without the affirmative and freely-given permission of the victim to the specific act of penetration constitutes the offense of sexual assault. Therefore, physical force in excess of that inherent in the act of sexual penetration is not required for such penetration to be unlawful. The definition of "physical force" is satisfied under N.J.S.A. 2C:14-2c(1) if the defendant applies any amount of force against another person in the absence of what a reasonable person would believe to be affirmative and freely-given permission to the act of sexual penetration.

Under the reformed statute, permission to engage in sexual penetration must be affirmative and it must be given freely, but that permission may be inferred either from acts or statements reasonably viewed in light of the surrounding circumstances. Persons need not, of course, expressly announce their consent to engage in intercourse for there to be affirmative permission. Permission to engage in an act of sexual penetration can be and indeed often is indicated through physical actions rather than words. Permission is demonstrated when the evidence, in whatever form, is sufficient to demonstrate that a reasonable person would have believed that the alleged victim had affirmatively and freely given authorization to the act. * * * *

In short, in order to convict under the sexual assault statute in cases such as these, the State must prove beyond a reasonable doubt that there was sexual penetration and that it was accomplished without the affirmative and freely-given permission of the alleged victim. As we have indicated, such proof can be based on evidence of conduct or words in light of surrounding circumstances and must demonstrate beyond a reasonable doubt that a reasonable person would not have believed that there was affirmative and freely-given permission. If there is evidence to suggest that the defendant reasonably believed that such permission had been given, the State must demonstrate either that defendant did not actually believe that affirmative permission had been freely-given or that such a belief was unreasonable under all of the circumstances. Thus, the State bears the burden of proof throughout the case.

In Dripps, *Beyond Rape: An Essay On The Difference Between The Presence Of Force And The Absence Of Consent*, 92 Columbia L.Rev. 1780, 1792, fn. 41 (1992), the author says:

> The New Jersey approach requires affirmative permission to privilege sexual penetration, and mere negligence regarding the absence of permission exposes the accused to liability. By contrast, I favor imposing liability only when the accused knows that the victim has refused. In effect, the *M.T.S.* court adopts a presumption that sex is criminal. The principal justification given for this result is that the legislature has so ordained. Given the court's fast-and-loose approach to the statutory language requiring "force or coercion," that is an unsatisfyingly formalistic explanation.

> The burden of asking permission can be placed on the man, or the burden of expressing refusal can be placed on the woman. Granting that gender prejudice is implicated by either choice, I think the second alternative is superior, because sexual encounters ought not to be lived or analyzed as sequences of particular touchings. In practice couples do not discuss in advance each specific sex act that one or another might initiate, and there is no strong reason why the law should attempt to compel them to do so. Suppose, for example, the victim in the *M.T.S.* case had begun to perform fellatio on the defendant without asking permission. Suppose, further, that he has religious or other scruples about oral sex. He protests as soon as he knows what she is doing, and she stops as soon as he protests. Still, under the court's opinion, she is guilty of sexual assault. If uncertainty and spontaneity can enhance the pleasures of lovemaking, people of either sex might prefer not being asked - so long as they can be sure that behavior they don't like will be stopped on demand. The interest in freedom from wrong guesses by one's bedmates is not so great as to call the criminal law into play.

> Finally, whether the defendant must ask first or only respect the expressed refusal of his partner, predicating felony liability on simple negligence offends the principle of culpability.

Professor Dripps' comments raise two questions.

First, is he fairly reading *M.T.S.*? Did the court "compel" couples to "discuss in advance each specific sex act that one or another might initiate"?

Second, most states require that, to sustain a defense of self-defense, the defendant prove that his beliefs (that he was facing an imminent attack, that a deadly response was necessary to repel the attack, etc.) were reasonable. Don't these requirements "predicate felony liability on simple negligence"? If so, do they too "offend the principle of culpability"?

(7) *In re John Z.*, 29 Cal.4th 756 (2003), addressed the question of "whether the crime of forcible rape is committed if the female victim consents to an initial penetration by her male companion, and then withdraws her consent during an act of intercourse, but the male continues against her will." The court held that "a withdrawal of consent effectively nullifies any earlier consent and subjects the male to forcible rape charges if he persists in what has become nonconsensual intercourse." The court overruled a prior California decision holding the contrary:

> *People v. Vela* held that where the victim consents to intercourse at the time of penetration but thereafter withdraws her consent, any use of force by her assailant past that point is not rape. The court in *Vela* found "scant authority" on point, relying on two out-of-state cases which had held that if consent is given prior to penetration, no rape occurs despite the withdrawal of consent during intercourse itself. See *Battle v. State* (1980) 287 Md. 675; *State v. Way* (1979) 297 N.C. 293. According to *Vela*, these cases held that "the presence or absence of consent at the moment of initial penetration appears to be the crucial point in the crime of rape."

> *Vela* agreed with these cases, reasoning that "the essence of the crime of rape is the outrage to the person and feelings of the female resulting from the nonconsensual violation of her womanhood. When a female willingly consents to an act of sexual intercourse, the penetration by the male cannot constitute a violation of her womanhood nor cause outrage to her person and feelings. If she withdraws consent during the act of sexual intercourse and the male forcibly continues the act without interruption, the female may certainly feel outrage because of the force applied or because the male ignores her wishes, but the sense of outrage to her person and feelings could hardly be of the same magnitude as that resulting from an initial nonconsensual violation of her womanhood. It would seem, therefore, that the essential guilt of rape is lacking in the withdrawn consent scenario."

> With due respect to *Vela* and the two sister state cases on which it relied, we find their reasoning unsound. First, contrary to *Vela*'s assumption, we have no way of accurately measuring the level of outrage the victim suffers from being subjected to continued forcible intercourse following withdrawal of her consent. We must assume the sense of outrage is substantial. More importantly, California Penal Code § 261(a)(2), defines rape as "an act of sexual intercourse accomplished with a person not the spouse of the perpetrator where it is accomplished against a person's will by means of force, violence, duress, menace, or fear of immediate and unlawful bodily injury on the person or another." Nothing in § 261 conditions the act of rape on the degree of outrage of the victim. Section 263 states that "the essential guilt of rape consists in the outrage to the person and feelings of the victim of the rape. Any sexual penetration, however slight, is sufficient to complete the crime." But no California case has held that the victim's outrage is an element of the crime of rape. * * * *

[There are] several cases from other states either criticizing *Vela* or reaching a contrary conclusion. See *State v. Crims* (Minn.Ct.App. 1995) 540 N.W.2d 860, 865; *State v. Jones* (S.D. 1994) 521 N.W.2d 662, 672; *State v. Siering* (1994) 35 Conn.App. 173; *State v. Robinson* (Me. 1985) 496 A.2d 1067, 1071; see also *McGill v. State* (Alaska Ct.App. 2001) 18 P.3d 77, 84 [*Vela*'s view that sexual assault statute is based on considerations of " 'outrage' " to victim's " 'womanhood' " represents "archaic and outmoded social conventions"]; Note, *Post-Penetration Rape-Increasing the Penalty* (1991) 31 Santa Clara L.Rev. 779, 804-808 [criticizing *Vela* and advocating legislation to punish forcible and nonconsensual postpenetration intercourse as second degree rape].)

While outrage of the victim may be the cause for criminalizing and severely punishing forcible rape, outrage by the victim is not an element of forcible rape. Pursuant to § 261, (a)(2) forcible rape occurs when the act of sexual intercourse is accomplished against the will of the victim by force or threat of bodily injury and it is immaterial at what point the victim withdraws her consent, so long as that withdrawal is communicated to the male and he thereafter ignores it. * * * *

Vela appears to assume that, to constitute rape, the victim's objections must be raised, or a defendant's use of force must be applied, *before* intercourse commences, but that argument is clearly flawed. One can readily imagine situations in which the defendant is able to obtain penetration before the victim can express an objection or attempt to resist. Surely, if the defendant thereafter ignores the victim's objections and forcibly continues the act, he has committed "an act of sexual intercourse accomplished against a person's will by means of force" § 261(a)(2).

Defendant, candidly acknowledging *Vela*'s flawed reasoning, contends that, in cases involving an initial consent to intercourse, the male should be permitted a "reasonable amount of time" in which to withdraw, once the female raises an objection to further intercourse. As defendant argues, "By essence of the act of sexual intercourse, a male's primal urge to reproduce is aroused. It is therefore unreasonable for a female and the law to expect a male to cease having sexual intercourse immediately upon her withdrawal of consent. It is only natural, fair and just that a male be given a reasonable amount of time in which to quell his primal urge."

We disagree with defendant's argument. Aside from the apparent lack of supporting authority for defendant's "primal urge" theory, the principal problem with his argument is that it is contrary to the language of § 261(a)(2): Nothing in the language of § 261 or the case law suggests that the defendant is entitled to persist in intercourse once his victim withdraws her consent.

(8) *Boro v. Superior Court*, 163 Cal.App.3d 1224 (1985) raised some different issues:

Ms. R., the rape victim, was employed as a clerk at the Holiday Inn in South San Francisco when, on March 30, 1984, at about 8:45 a.m., she received a telephone call from a person who identified himself as "Dr.

Stevens" and said that he worked at Peninsula Hospital.

"Dr. Stevens" told Ms. R. that he had the results of her blood test and that she had contracted a dangerous, highly infectious and perhaps fatal disease; that she could be sued as a result; that the disease came from using public toilets; and that she would have to tell him the identity of all her friends who would then have to be contacted in the interest of controlling the spread of the disease.

"Dr. Stevens" further explained that there were only two ways to treat the disease. The first was a painful surgical procedure-graphically described- costing $9,000, and requiring her uninsured hospitalization for six weeks. A second alternative, "Dr. Stevens" explained, was to have sexual intercourse with an anonymous donor who had been injected with a serum which would cure the disease. The latter, nonsurgical procedure would only cost $4,500. When the victim replied that she lacked sufficient funds the "doctor" suggested that $1,000 would suffice as a down payment. The victim thereupon agreed to the nonsurgical alternative and consented to intercourse with the mysterious donor, believing "it was the only choice I had."

After discussing her intentions with her work supervisor, the victim proceeded to the Hyatt Hotel in Burlingame as instructed, and contacted "Dr. Stevens" by telephone. The latter became furious when he learned Ms. R. had informed her employer of the plan, and threatened to terminate his treatment, finally instructing her to inform her employer she had decided not to go through with the treatment. Ms. R. did so, then went to her bank, withdrew $1,000 and, as instructed, checked into another hotel and called "Dr. Stevens" to give him her room number.

About a half hour later the defendant "donor" arrived at her room. When Ms. R. had undressed, the "donor," petitioner, after urging her to relax, had sexual intercourse with her.

At the time of penetration, it was Ms. R.'s belief that she would die unless she consented to sexual intercourse with the defendant: as she testified, "My life felt threatened, and for that reason and that reason alone did I do it."

Petitioner was apprehended when the police arrived at the hotel room, having been called by Ms. R.'s supervisor. Petitioner was identified as "Dr. Stevens" at a police voice lineup by another potential victim of the same scheme.

Upon the basis of the evidence just recounted, petitioner was charged with five crimes, as follows: Count I: § 261(2) — rape: accomplished against a person's will by means of force or fear of immediate and unlawful bodily injury on the person or another. Count II: § 261(4) — rape "where a person is at the time unconscious of the nature of the act, and this is known to the accused." Count III: § 266 — procuring a female to have illicit carnal connection with a man "by any false pretenses, false representation, or other fraudulent means." Count IV: §§ 664/487 — attempted grand theft. Count V: § 459 — burglary (entry into the hotel room with intent to commit theft). Counts I and III were dismissed.

[Petitioner argues that the evidence is insufficient to support Count II.]

The People's position is stated concisely: "We contend, quite simply, that at the time of the intercourse Ms. R., the victim, was 'unconscious of the nature of the act': because of petitioner's misrepresentation she believed it was in the nature of a medical treatment and not a simple, ordinary act of sexual intercourse." Petitioner, on the other hand, stresses that the victim was plainly aware of the *nature* of the act in which she voluntarily engaged, so that her motivation in doing so (since it did not fall within the proscription of § 261(2)) is irrelevant.

Our research discloses sparse California authority on the subject. A victim need not be totally and physically unconscious in order that § 261(4) apply. In *People v. Minkowski* (1962) 204 Cal.App.2d 832, the defendant was a physician who "treated" several victims for menstrual cramps. Each victim testified that she was treated in a position with her back to the doctor, bent over a table, with feet apart, in a dressing gown. And in each case the "treatment" consisted of the defendant first inserting a metal instrument, then substituting an instrument which "felt different"-the victims not realizing that the second instrument was in fact the doctor's penis. The precise issue before us was never tendered in *People v. Minkowski* because the petitioner there *conceded* the sufficiency of evidence to support the element of consciousness.

The decision is useful to this analysis, however, because it exactly illustrates certain traditional rules in the area of our inquiry. Thus, as a leading authority has written, "if deception causes a misunderstanding as to the fact itself (fraud in the *factum*) there is no legally-recognized consent because what happened is not that for which consent was given; whereas consent induced by fraud is as effective as any other consent, so far as direct and immediate legal consequences are concerned, if the deception relates not to the thing done but merely to some collateral matter (fraud in the inducement)." Perkins & Boyce, Criminal Law (3d ed. 1982) ch. 9, § 3, p. 1079.

The victims in *Minkowski* consented, not to sexual intercourse, but to an act of an altogether different nature, penetration by medical instrument. The consent was to a pathological, and not a carnal, act, and the mistake was, therefore, in the *factum* and not merely in the inducement.

Another relatively common situation in the literature on this subject-discussed in detail by Perkins is the fraudulent obtaining of intercourse by impersonating a spouse. As Professor Perkins observes, the courts are not in accord as to whether the crime of rape is thereby committed. "The disagreement is not in regard to the underlying principle but only as to its application. Some courts have taken the position that such a misdeed is fraud in the inducement on the theory that the woman consents to exactly what is done (sexual intercourse) and hence there is no rape; other courts, with better reason it would seem, hold such a misdeed to be rape on the theory that it involves fraud in the *factum* since the woman's consent is to an innocent act of marital intercourse while what is actually perpetrated upon her is an act of adultery. Her innocence seems never to have been questioned in such a case and the reason she is not guilty of adultery is because she did not consent to adulterous intercourse. Statutory changes in the law of rape have received attention earlier and need not be repeated here." Perkins & Boyce, Criminal Law (3d ed. 1982) ch. 9, § 3, pp. 1080-1081.

In California, of course, we have by statute adopted the majority view that such fraud is in the *factum*, not the inducement, and have thus held it to vitiate consent. It is otherwise, however, with respect to the conceptually much murkier statutory offense with which we here deal, and the language of which has remained essentially unchanged since its enactment (§ 261(4)).

The language itself could not be plainer. It defines rape to be "an act of sexual intercourse" with a nonspouse, accomplished where the victim is "at the time unconscious of the nature of the act." § 261(4).) Nor, as we have just seen, can we entertain the slightest doubt that the Legislature well understood how to draft a statute to encompass fraud in the *factum* (§ 261 (5)) and how to specify certain fraud in the inducement as vitiating consent. Moreover, courts of this state have previously confronted the general rule that fraud in the inducement does not vitiate consent. * * * *

Finally, the Attorney General cites *People v. Howard* (1981) 117 Cal.App.3d 53. There, the court dealt with § 288a(f) and § 286(f) making criminal oral copulation or sodomy between adults where one person is "unconscious of the nature of the act." But in *Howard*, the victim was a 19-year-old with the mental capacity of a 6-to-8-year-old, who "simply did not understand the nature of the act in which he participated."

Whether or not we agree with the *Howard* court's analysis, we note that here, in contrast, there is not a shred of evidence on the record before us to suggest that as the result of mental retardation Ms. R. lacked the capacity to appreciate the nature of the sex act in which she engaged. On the contrary, her testimony was clear that she precisely understood the "nature of the act," but, motivated by a fear of disease, and death, succumbed to petitioner's fraudulent blandishments.

To so conclude is not to vitiate the heartless cruelty of petitioner's scheme, but to say that it comprised crimes of a different order than a violation of § 261(4).

These issues are discussed more fully in Patricia F. Falk, *Rape by Fraud and Rape by Coercion*, 64 Brooklyn L.Rev. 39 (1998).

(9) For further readings on the law of rape, see, e.g., Susan Estrich, *Real Rape: How The Legal System Victimizes Women Who Say No* (1987); Susan Brownmiller, *Against Our Will: Men Women & Rape* (1975); Diana E.H. Russell, *The Politics of Rape: The Victim's Perspective* (1975); Stephen Scholhofer, *Taking Sexual Autonomy Seriously: Rape Law & Beyond*, 11 Law & Philospophy 35 (1992); Randy

Thornhill & Craig Palmer, *Why Men Rape, Why Women Suffer: Rape, Evolution, & the Social Sciences* (1999).

(10) Do men have a biological predisposition towards rape — or is the thought simply too horrible to contemplate? This question is extensively explored in Owen Jones, *Sex, Culture, and the Biology of Rape: Toward Explanation and Prevention*, 87 California L.Rev. 827 (1999). Professor Jones challenges writers who claim that rape is merely "learned" behavior caused by cultural factors (a patriarchal society that demeans women, etc.) and notes:

> While we may wish, for example, that patterns of human rape were unaffected by evolved brain architecture and predispositions, we cannot suppose that explanation follows inclination, and that facts follow preferences. Thus, while it obviously would be unsound to conclude that rape is acceptable simply because other species rape too, it is equally invalid to conclude that there are no biobehavioral influences on rape, simply because it may be offensive or undesirable that there be such influences. * * * *

> Law works best when its predicates are sound, not when these predicates are based in myth. Flawed behavioral models bring flawed remedial plans.

See also, however, Cheryl Brown Travis, *Evolution, Gender, & Rape* (2002).

Appendix I

CUMULATIVE PROBLEMS

PROBLEM B

This problem raises issues covered in Chapters 11 through 21. Try to write out an answer to this problem (as if it were an exam question). When you are done, take a look at the sample answer at the end of the book.

Memo to: My law clerk

From: Appellate Justice Jose Canusi

Re: *People v. Ames & Burns*

The transcript of the trial in this case shows the following evidence.

Art Ames and Bill Burns were walking down the street one day. Vic Vance was standing in a doorway. Ames and Burns went over to Vance. Ames put a cigarette in his mouth and asked Vance for a match. As Vance was reaching for a match, Burns pulled out a knife, held it next to Vance's throat, and said, "Your wallet or your life." Vance pulled out his wallet and handed it to Burns. Burns took the wallet, dropped the knife, and ran down the street. Ames started to walk away.

Vance picked up the knife, looked at Ames, took a step toward Ames, and raised the knife. Ames pulled out a gun and shot Vance once in the shoulder. Vance was badly hurt, but he did not die.

Charles Copp, a police officer, saw Burns running down the street. He pulled out his gun and pointed it at Burns, and yelled, "Stop." Burns pulled out his own gun, turned around and fired it at Copp. The bullet hit Copp in the thigh. Bleeding badly, Copp hobbled into his police car, which was parked nearby. He drove off, intending to go to a hospital 5 blocks away. After driving two blocks, however, he passed out from shock and loss of blood. His car then ran into a lamppost, and the impact killed Copp. Expert witnesses testified that if Copp had stayed at the scene of the shooting and radioed for help instead of trying to drive to the hospital, he would have received adequate medical aid in plenty of time to save his leg and his life.

Based on the above evidence, Ames and Burns were each convicted of (1) attempted murder of Vance, and (2) murder of Copp. Each appeals, claiming that the evidence was not sufficient to permit the jury to convict each of them for each crime. Should our court affirm or reverse all or some of the convictions? Note: Our jurisdiction follows the common law of crimes, as modified by the statutes and cases in your casebook.

SAMPLE ANSWER TO PROBLEM A

I. Did D murder <u>B</u>?

D killed B, a human being, but did he do so with "<u>malice</u>"? There are 4 possible ways of finding malice.

First, "malice" may consist of an <u>intent to kill</u>. D used no <u>words</u> showing an intent to kill, and a bookend is not a deadly weapon. Also, we have no evidence regarding how far away B was and how hard threw the bookend or of the relative weight and ages of the men, which might indicate how hard D could throw or how vulnerable B was. Also, if D had intended to kill, he might have picked up and used the gun which B had dropped, but he didn't. On the other hand, the fact that the bookend killed B might furnish evidence that D was close enough and threw it hard enough to kill him. But because this might have just been a "lucky" shot, I conclude that there is not sufficient evidence of intent to kill.

The same evidence might be used in an effort to show another form of "malice": <u>intent to commit serious bodily injury</u>, which requires intent to cause an injury close to death. If D intended to hit B on the head, though not to kill him, this might cause brain damage, which is an injury close to death. But, for the reasons discussed above, I conclude that the evidence is insufficient to show this intent.

The 3rd way of showing malice is <u>depraved heart</u>, or extreme recklessness. The key factor for this issue is the degree of risk raised by D's act. The risk of death raised by throwing a 2-pound bookend at someone <u>might</u> be as high as the classic case of extreme recklessness - throwing a large stone off a roof onto a sidewalk - but we cannot tell if the risk is this high without knowing how far B was from D and how hard D threw it. So I conclude that there is insufficient evidence of extreme recklessness here.

The 4th way of showing malice is through the <u>felony murder doctrine</u>.

One possible felony D committed is <u>false pretenses</u>. But to qualify for felony-murder, a felony must be inherently dangerous, when viewed in the abstract. Our jurisdiction has held that grand larceny is not inherently dangerous, as it does not usually raise a danger to life. As false pretenses is no more dangerous to life than grand larceny, I conclude that it does not qualify for the felony murder rule.

Did D commit <u>burglary</u>? As D did not break in and this was not at night, D did not commit common law burglary. But our modern statute requires only a trespassory entry with intent to commit a felony or steal. Here, D might have had the intent to commit a felony — false pretenses — when he entered. If so, De trespassed, as even though B invited D in, B's consent contains an implied exception where D intends to steal.

So we must examine whether, when D entered, he intended to commit false pretenses.

Did he intend a <u>misrepresentation</u>? D's statement that the watch was stolen might not have been false, if his brother in fact stole it from B. D's statement that he would give back the money related to the future, which does not qualify in our jurisdiction. Also, it is not clear that this statement is false. But D's statement that the watch was an import worth $200 qualifies, as it was false and related to the present.

This misrepresentation would be material — likely to cause B to pass title to the money - as D knew that B liked bargains, and this statement said that the watch was worth 4 times the price D was charging.

The fact that the watch was in fact worth the $50 B paid does not negate D's intent to steal, as he intended his misrepresentation to cause B to pass title to the $50.

So I conclude that when D entered, he intended to commit false pretenses, a felony, and therefore he did commit burglary.

Burglary is listed in our first degree murder statute. As the killing of B occurred during the burglary, D is guilty of first degree murder of B.

II. Did D murder C?

There is no evidence that D intended to kill or cause serious bodily injury to C, or that D was extremely reckless regarding C.

Regarding felony murder, C was killed during D's burglary, but he was shot by B, who did not shoot "to perpetrate" the burglary. Therefore, the killing did not occur in perpetration of the felony, so D is not guilty of felony murder of C.

SAMPLE ANSWER TO PROBLEM B

I. Ames

A. Attempted murder of Vance?

To uphold conviction of attempted murder, there must be substantial evidence of both intent to kill (other forms of "malice aforethought" will not do) and acts beyond preparation.

Was there substantial evidence of intent to kill? A used a deadly weapon (a gun), but shooting V in the shoulder would not be using it in a deadly way if A intended only to hit V in the shoulder. But as we have no evidence that A had such a narrow intent, it was reasonable for the jury to infer that A intended to kill.

Acts beyond preparation would seem to be present. Firing the gun was a "substantial step" in the direction of murder. Some cases in our jurisdiction have also suggested that the act must also be "unequivocal." If this is required, there might be a problem here, as a shot in the shoulder does not "unequivocally" show an intent to kill. But I conclude that the "substantial step" should be sufficient to convict, as it serves the purpose of the "acts beyond preparation" requirement - to separate dreamers from doers. Here, Ames was clearly a doer, not a dreamer.

A reasonable jury could find on this evidence that the crime was not committed in self-defense. Self-defense has several requirements.

First, A could reasonably believe that a deadly attack was imminent, as V was moving toward him with an uplifted knife.

Second, A would have to retreat, if he knew he could do so in complete safety. It appears that A could have simply run away from V without being hurt, but perhaps A did not know this.

Third, A may not use self-defense against lawful force by V, but it appears that V's attack was unlawful, as the robbery was over and V could therefore not justify the attack with prevention of a felony, and he could not use prevention of escape, as A was not in V's custody.

Fourth, it appears that A will lose self-defense because his force (shooting V) was excessive: A could have done something less than shooting V to stop V from attacking, such as threatening to shoot V or by shooting V in the leg.

As a reasonable jury could find on this evidence the presence of the basic elements of attempted murder and could reject self-defense, A's conviction for attempted murder of V should be affirmed.

B. Murder of Copp?

As A did not attack C, A might be found guilty of murder of C only vicariously, for the acts of B. Therefore, to find A guilty there must be substantial evidence both that (1) B is guilty of murder of C, and (2) A was a co-conspirator or accomplice to the robbery, and the shooting of C was in furtherance of the robbery.

Was there substantial evidence that B was guilty of murder of C? Malice aforethought is clearly present. In fact, all 4 types of malice might be present. B's use of deadly weapon to shoot C in thigh might be use in deadly way, allowing the jury to infer an intent to kill, and even if B intended only to hit thigh, this might be intent to cause serious bodily injury, if a bullet in the thigh would cause an injury close to death. In any event, shooting C in a part of the body near vital organs is extremely reckless, so depraved heart would work, and B was escaping from a robbery, so felony murder would work.

But was the shooting a proximate cause of C's death? An intervening force which is a response to the injury directly caused by the defendant is not a supervening cause which breaks the causal chain, unless this intervening force was abnormal or unforeseeable. Here, C's decision to drive to a hospital was a response to the shooting. I do not think it was abnormal or unforeseeable, as the hospital was only a few blocks away, it is not too unusual for a victim to go a short distance to medical aid rather than wait for it to come to him. C might reasonably have thought it would take too long for an ambulance to reach him. Therefore, I conclude that his response was not abnormal or unforeseeable, so it did not break the causal chain, and there is sufficient evidence to convict B of murder of C.

Is the evidence sufficient to show that A aided and abetted B in the robbery? A did commit an act which helped B. A got V's attention by asking V for a match, which helped B pull the knife and get it to V's throat before V could get away. But did A intend this act to help B? This is possible, but it is equally possible that A simply needed a light for his cigarette. According to a case we read [*Gains*], where a man drove a getaway car but there was no direct evidence that he knew of the robbery, where the possibilities are about equal this is not enough to support a verdict that he was an accomplice. Here, in addition, A did not run away with B or share in the loot. Therefore, I conclude that there is not enough evidence to show that he was an accomplice to the robbery, so the rule that makes an accomplice guilty of crimes committed by other principals in furtherance of the main crime does not apply here. (If it did, A would be guilty of B's murder of C, because that was in furtherance of the object of the robbery, to get away with the loot). For the same reason, the evidence is not sufficient to show that A conspired with B to commit robbery, so the rule that holds co-conspirators guilty of crimes committed in furtherance of the conspiracy [*Pinkerton*] does not apply here. A is not guilty of murder of C, so this part of the judgment should be reversed.

II. Bill

A. Attempted murder of Vic?

As discussed above, A was not B's accomplice, and A and B were not co-conspirators. (Even if they *did* have this relationship, I doubt that A's crime was in furtherance of or a natural consequence of the robbery. V knew that A did not have V's wallet, and he seems to have attacked A just to retaliate.) Therefore, even if A is guilty of attempted murder of V, B is not, and this part of the judgment should be reversed.

B. Murder of Copp?

As discussed above, there is substantial evidence to hold B guilty of murder of C, so this conviction should be affirmed.

Appendix II

MODEL PENAL CODE (SELECTED SECTIONS)

PART I.
GENERAL PROVISIONS

ARTICLE I.
PRELIMINARY
* * * *

Section 1.12: **Proof Beyond a Reasonable Doubt; Affirmative Defenses; Burden of Proving Fact When Not an Element of an Offense; Presumptions.**

(1) No person may be convicted of an offense unless each element of such offense is proved beyond a reasonable doubt. In the absence of such proof, the innocence of the defendant is assumed.

(2) Subsection (1) of this Section does not:

    (a) require the disproof of an affirmative defense unless and until there is evidence supporting such defense; or

    (b) apply to any defense that the Code or another statute plainly requires the defendant to prove by a preponderance of evidence.

(3) A ground of defense is affirmative, within the meaning of Subsection (2)(a) of this Section, when:

    (a) it arises under a section of the Code that so provides; or

    (b) it relates to an offense defined by a statute other than the Code and such statute so provides; or

    (c) it involves a matter of excuse or justification peculiarly within the knowledge of the defendant on that he can fairly be required to adduce supporting evidence.

(4) When the application of the Code depends upon the finding of a fact that is not an element of an offense, unless the Code otherwise provides:

    (a) the burden of proving the fact is on the prosecution or defendant, depending on whose interest or contention will be furthered if the finding should be made; and

    (b) the fact must be proved to the satisfaction of the Court or jury, as the case may be.

(5)   When the Code establishes a presumption with respect to any fact that is an element of an offense, it has the following consequences:

    (a)   when there is evidence of the facts that give rise to the presumption, the issue of the existence of the presumed fact must be submitted to the jury, unless the Court is satisfied that the evidence as a whole clearly negatives the presumed fact; and

    (b)   when the issue of the existence of the presumed fact is submitted to the jury, the Court shall charge that while the presumed fact must, on all the evidence, be proved beyond a reasonable doubt, the law declares that the jury may regard the facts giving rise to the presumption as sufficient evidence of the presumed fact.

(6)   A presumption not established by the Code or inconsistent with it has the consequences otherwise accorded it by law.

* * * *

ARTICLE 2.
GENERAL PRINCIPLES OF LIABILITY

Section 2.01:   Requirement of Voluntary Act; Omission as Basis of Liability; Possession as an Act.

(1)   A person is not guilty of an offense unless his liability is based on conduct that includes a voluntary act or the omission to perform an act of that he is physically capable.

(2)   The following are not voluntary acts within the meaning of this Section:

    (a)   a reflex or convulsion;

    (b)   a bodily movement during unconsciousness or sleep;

    (c)   conduct during hypnosis or resulting from hypnotic suggestion;

    (d)   a bodily movement that otherwise is not a product of the effort or determination of the actor, either conscious or habitual.

(3)   Liability for the commission of an offense may not be based on an omission unaccompanied by action unless:

    (a)   the omission is expressly made sufficient by the law defining the offense; or

    (b)   a duty to perform the omitted act is otherwise imposed by law.

(4)   Possession is an act, within the meaning of this Section, if the possessor knowingly procured or received the thing possessed or was aware of his control thereof for a sufficient period to have been able to terminate his possession.

Section 2.02:   **General Requirements of Culpability.**

(1)   *Minimum Requirements of Culpability.* Except as provided in Section 2.05, a person is not guilty of an offense unless he acted purposely, knowingly, recklessly or negligently, as the law may require, with respect to each material element of the offense.

(2)   *Kinds of Culpability Defined.*

    (a)   Purposely.

       A person acts purposely with respect to a material element of an offense when:

       (i)   if the element involves the nature of his conduct or a result thereof, it is his conscious object to engage in conduct of that nature or to cause such a result; and

       (ii)   if the element involves the attendant circumstances, he is aware of the existence of such circumstances or he believes or hopes that they exist.

    (b)   Knowingly.

       A person acts knowingly with respect to a material element of an offense when:

       (i)   if the element involves the nature of his conduct or the attendant circumstances, he is aware that his conduct is of that nature or that such circumstances exist; and

       (ii)   if the element involves a result of his conduct, he is aware that it is practically certain that his conduct will cause such a result.

    (c)   Recklessly.

       A person acts recklessly with respect to a material element of an offense when he consciously disregards a substantial and unjustifiable risk that the material element exists or will result from his conduct. The risk must be of such a nature and degree that, considering the nature and purpose of the actor's conduct and the circumstances known to him, its disregard involves a gross deviation from the standard of conduct that a law-abiding person would observe in the actor's situation.

    (d)   Negligently.

       A person acts negligently with respect to a material element of an offense when he should be aware of a substantial and unjustifiable risk that the material element exists or will result from his conduct. The risk must be of such a nature and degree that the actor's failure to perceive it, considering the nature and purpose of his conduct and the circumstances known to him, involves a gross deviation from the standard of care that a reasonable person would observe in the actor's situation.

(3)   *Culpability Required Unless Otherwise Provided.* When the culpability sufficient to establish a material element of an offense is not prescribed by law, such element is established if a person acts purposely, knowingly or recklessly with respect thereto.

(4)   *Prescribed Culpability Requirement Applies to All Material Elements.* When the law defining an offense prescribes the kind of culpability that is sufficient for the commission of an offense, without distinguishing among the material elements thereof, such provision shall apply to all the material elements of the offense, unless a contrary purpose plainly appears.

(5)   *Substitutes for Negligence, Recklessness and Knowledge.* When the law provides that negligence suffices to establish an element of an offense, such element also is established if a person acts purposely, knowingly or recklessly. When recklessness suffices to establish an element, such element also is established if a person acts purposely or knowingly. When acting knowingly suffices to establish an element, such element also is established if a person acts purposely.

(6)   *Requirement of Purpose Satisfied if Purpose Is Conditional.* When a particular purpose is an element of an offense, the element is established although such purpose is conditional, unless the condition negatives the injury or evil sought to be prevented by the law defining the offense.

(7)   *Requirement of Knowledge Satisfied by Knowledge of High Probability.* When knowledge of the existence of a particular fact is an element of an offense, such knowledge is established if a person is aware of a high probability of its existence, unless he actually believes that it does not exist.

(8)   *Requirement of Wilfulness Satisfied by Acting Knowingly.* A requirement that an offense be committed wilfully is satisfied if a person acts knowingly with respect to the material elements of the offense, unless a purpose to impose further requirements appears.

(9)   *Culpability as to Illegality of Conduct.* Neither knowledge nor recklessness or negligence as to whether conduct constitutes an offense or as to the existence, meaning or application of the law determining the elements of an offense is an element of such offense, unless the definition of the offense or the Code so provides.

(10)   *Culpability as Determinant of Grade of Offense.* When the grade or degree of an offense depends on whether the offense is committed purposely, knowingly, recklessly or negligently, its grade or degree shall be the lowest for that the determinative kind of culpability is established with respect to any material element of the offense.

Section 2.03: Causal Relationship Between Conduct and Result; Divergence Between Result Designed or Contemplated and Actual Result or Between Probable and Actual Result.

(1) Conduct is the cause of a result when:

 (a) it is an antecedent but for that the result in question would not have occurred; and

 (b) the relationship between the conduct and result satisfies any additional causal requirements imposed by the Code or by the law defining the offense.

(2) When purposely or knowingly causing a particular result is an element of an offense, the element is not established if the actual result is not within the purpose or the contemplation of the actor unless:

 (a) the actual result differs from that designed or contemplated, as the case may be, only in the respect that a different person or different property is injured or affected or that the injury or injury designed or contemplated would have been more serious or more extensive than that caused; or

 (b) the actual result involves the same kind of injury or injury as that designed or contemplated and is not too remote or accidental in its occurrence to have a [just] bearing on the actor's liability or on the gravity of his offense.

(3) When recklessly or negligently causing a particular result is an element of an offense, the element is not established if the actual result is not within the risk of that the actor is aware or, in the case of negligence, of that he should be aware unless:

 (a) the actual result differs from the probable result only in the respect that a different person or different property is injured or affected or that the probable injury or injury would have been more serious or more extensive than that caused; or

 (b) the actual result involves the same kind of injury or injury as the probable result and is not too remote or accidental in its occurrence to have a [just] bearing on the actor's liability or on the gravity of his offense.

(4) When causing a particular result is a material element of an offense for that absolute liability is imposed by law, the element is not established unless the actual result is a probable consequence of the actor's conduct.

* * * *

Section 2.04: Ignorance or Mistake.

(1) Ignorance or mistake as to a matter of fact or law is a defense if:

(a)   the ignorance or mistake negatives the purpose, knowledge, belief, recklessness or negligence required to establish a material element of the offense; or

(b)   the law provides that the state of mind established by such ignorance or mistake constitutes a defense.

(2)   Although ignorance or mistake would otherwise afford a defense to the offense charged, the defense is not available if the defendant would be guilty of another offense had the situation been as he supposed. In such case, however, the ignorance or mistake of the defendant shall reduce the grade and degree of the offense of that he may be convicted to those of the offense of that he would be guilty had the situation been as he supposed.

(3)   A belief that conduct does not legally constitute an offense is a defense to a prosecution for that offense based upon such conduct when:

(a)   the statute or other enactment defining the offense is not known to the actor and has not been published or otherwise reasonably made available prior to the conduct alleged; or

(b)   he acts in reasonable reliance upon an official statement of the law, afterward determined to be invalid or erroneous, contained in (i) a statute or other enactment; (ii) a judicial decision, opinion or judgment; (iii) an administrative order or grant of permission; or (iv) an official interpretation of the public officer or body charged by law with responsibility for the interpretation, administration or enforcement of the law defining the offense.

(4)   The defendant must prove a defense arising under Subsection (3) of this Section by a preponderance of evidence.

* * * *

Section 2.06:   Liability for Conduct of Another; Complicity.

(1)   A person is guilty of an offense if it is committed by his own conduct or by the conduct of another person for that he is legally accountable, or both.

(2)   A person is legally accountable for the conduct of another person when:

(a)   acting with the kind of culpability that is sufficient for the commission of the offense, he causes an innocent or irresponsible person to engage in such conduct; or

(b)   he is made accountable for the conduct of such other person by the Code or by the law defining the offense; or

(c)   he is an accomplice of such other person in the commission of the offense.

(3)   A person is an accomplice of another person in the commission of an offense if:

      (a)   with the purpose of promoting or facilitating the commission of the offense, he

          (i)   solicits such other person to commit it; or

          (ii)   aids or agrees or attempts to aid such other person in planning or committing it; or

          (iii)   having a legal duty to prevent the commission of the offense, fails to make proper effort so to do; or

      (b)   his conduct is expressly declared by law to establish his complicity.

(4)   When causing a particular result is an element of an offense, an accomplice in the conduct causing such result is an accomplice in the commission of that offense, if he acts with the kind of culpability, if any, with respect to that result that is sufficient for the commission of the offense.

(5)   A person who is legally incapable of committing a particular offense himself may be guilty thereof if it is committed by the conduct of another person for that he is legally accountable, unless such liability is inconsistent with the purpose of the provision establishing his incapacity.

(6)   Unless otherwise provided by the Code or by the law defining the offense, a person is not an accomplice in an offense committed by another person if:

      (a)   he is a victim of that offense; or

      (b)   the offense is so defined that his conduct is inevitably incident to its commission; or

      (c)   he terminates his complicity prior to the commission of the offense and

          (i)   wholly deprives it of effectiveness in the commission of the offense; or

          (ii)   gives timely warning to the law enforcement authorities or otherwise makes proper effort to prevent the commission of the offense.

(7)   An accomplice may be convicted on proof of the commission of the offense and of his complicity therein, though the person claimed to have committed the offense has not been prosecuted or convicted or has been convicted of a different offense or degree of offense or has an immunity to prosecution or conviction or has been acquitted.

* * * *

Section 2.08:   Intoxication.

(1)   Except as provided in Subsection (4) of this Section, intoxication of the actor is not a defense unless it negatives an element of the offense.

(2) When recklessness establishes an element of the offense, if the actor, due to self-induced intoxication, is unaware of a risk of that he would have been aware had he been sober, such unawareness is immaterial.

(3) Intoxication does not, in itself, constitute mental disease within the meaning of Section 4.01.

(4) Intoxication that (a) is not self-induced or (b) is pathological is an affirmative defense if by reason of such intoxication the actor at the time of his conduct lacks substantial capacity either to appreciate its criminality [wrongfulness] or to conform his conduct to the requirements of law.

(5) Definitions. In this Section unless a different meaning plainly is required:

   (a) "intoxication" means a disturbance of mental or physical capacities resulting from the introduction of substances into the body;

   (b) "self-induced intoxication" means intoxication caused by substances that the actor knowingly introduces into his body, the tendency of that to cause intoxication he knows or ought to know, unless he introduces them pursuant to medical advice or under such circumstances as would afford a defense to a charge of crime;

   (c) "pathological intoxication" means intoxication grossly excessive in degree, given the amount of the intoxicant, to that the actor does not know he is susceptible.

Section 2.09: **Duress.**

(1) It is an affirmative defense that the actor engaged in the conduct charged to constitute an offense because he was coerced to do so by the use of, or a threat to use, unlawful force against his person or the person of another, that a person of reasonable firmness in his situation would have been unable to resist.

(2) The defense provided by this Section is unavailable if the actor recklessly placed himself in a situation in that it was probable that he would be subjected to duress. The defense is also unavailable if he was negligent in placing himself in such a situation, whenever negligence suffices to establish culpability for the offense charged.

(3) It is not a defense that a woman acted on the command of her husband, unless she acted under such coercion as would establish a defense under this Section. [The presumption that a woman, acting in the presence of her husband, is coerced is abolished.]

(4) When the conduct of the actor would otherwise be justifiable under Section 3.02, this Section does not preclude such defense.

* * * *

Section 2.11:   **Consent.**

(1)   *In General.* The consent of the victim to conduct charged to constitute an offense or to the result thereof is a defense if such consent negatives an element of the offense or precludes the infliction of the injury or evil sought to be prevented by the law defining the offense.

(2)   *Consent to Bodily Injury.* When conduct is charged to constitute an offense because it causes or threatens bodily injury, consent to such conduct or to the infliction of such injury is a defense if:

(a)   the bodily injury consented to or threatened by the conduct consented to is not serious; or

(b)   the conduct and the injury are reasonably foreseeable hazards of joint participation in a lawful athletic contest or competitive sport; or

(c)   the consent establishes a justification for the conduct under Article 3 of the Code.

(3)   *Ineffective Consent.* Unless otherwise provided by the Code or by the law defining the offense, assent does not constitute consent if:

(a)   it is given by a person who is legally incompetent to authorize the conduct charged to constitute the offense; or

(b)   it is given by a person who by reason of youth, mental disease or defect or intoxication is manifestly unable or known by the actor to be unable to make a reasonable judgment as to the nature or injuryfulness of the conduct charged to constitute the offense; or

(c)   it is given by a person whose improvident consent is sought to be prevented by the law defining the offense; or

(d)   it is induced by force, duress or deception of a kind sought to be prevented by the law defining the offense.

* * * *

Section 2.13:   **Entrapment.**

(1)   A public law enforcement official or a person acting in cooperation with such an official perpetrates an entrapment if for the purpose of obtaining evidence of the commission of an offense, he induces or encourages another person to engage in conduct constituting such offense by either:

(a)   making knowingly false representations designed to induce the belief that such conduct is not prohibited; or

(b)   employing methods of persuasion or inducement that create a substantial risk that such an offense will be committed by persons other than those who are ready to commit it.

(2)   Except as provided in Subsection (3) of this Section, a person prosecuted for an offense shall be acquitted if he proves by a preponderance of evidence that his conduct occurred in response to an entrapment. The issue of entrapment shall be tried by the Court in the absence of the jury.

(3)   The defense afforded by this Section is unavailable when causing or threatening bodily injury is an element of the offense charged and the prosecution is based on conduct causing or threatening such injury to a person other than the person perpetrating the entrapment.

ARTICLE 3.
GENERAL PRINCIPLES OF JUSTIFICATION

Section 3.01: Justification an Affirmative Defense; Civil Remedies Unaffected.

(1)   In any prosecution based on conduct that is justifiable under this Article, justification is an affirmative defense.

(2)   The fact that conduct is justifiable under this Article does not abolish or impair any remedy for such conduct that is available in any civil action.

Section 3.02:   Justification Generally: Choice of Evils.

(1)   Conduct that the actor believes to be necessary to avoid a injury or evil to himself or to another is justifiable, provided that:

(a)   the injury or evil sought to be avoided by such conduct is greater than that sought to be prevented by the law defining the offense charged; and

(b)   neither the Code nor other law defining the offense provides exceptions or defenses dealing with the specific situation involved; and

(c)   a legislative purpose to exclude the justification claimed does not otherwise plainly appear.

(2)   When the actor was reckless or negligent in bringing about the situation requiring a choice of injurys or evils or in appraising the necessity for his conduct, the justification afforded by this Section is unavailable in a prosecution for any offense for that recklessness or negligence, as the case may be, suffices to establish culpability.

* * * *

Section 3.04:   Use of Force in Self-Protection.

(1)   *Use of Force Justifiable for Protection of the Person.* Subject to the provisions of this Section and of Section 3.09, the use of force upon or toward another person is justifiable when the actor believes that such

force is immediately necessary for the purpose of protecting himself against the use of unlawful force by such other person on the present occasion.

(2) *Limitations on Justifying Necessity for Use of Force.*

    (a)   The use of force is not justifiable under this Section:

        (i)   to resist an arrest that the actor knows is being made by a peace officer, although the arrest is unlawful; or

        (ii)   to resist force used by the occupier or possessor of property or by another person on his behalf, where the actor knows that the person using the force is doing so under a claim of right to protect the property, except that this limitation shall not apply if:

            (1)   the actor is a public officer acting in the performance of his duties or a person lawfully assisting him therein or a person making or assisting in a lawful arrest; or

            (2)   the actor has been unlawfully dispossessed of the property and is making a re-entry or recaption justified by Section 3.06; or

            (3)   the actor believes that such force is necessary to protect himself against death or serious bodily injury.

    (b)   The use of deadly force is not justifiable under this Section unless the actor believes that such force is necessary to protect himself against death, serious bodily injury, kidnapping or sexual intercourse compelled by force or threat; nor is it justifiable if:

        (i)   the actor, with the purpose of causing death or serious bodily injury, provoked the use of force against himself in the same encounter; or

        (ii)   the actor knows that he can avoid the necessity of using such force with complete safety by retreating or by surrendering possession of a thing to a person asserting a claim of right thereto or by complying with a demand that he abstain from any action that he has no duty to take, except that:

            (1)   the actor is not obliged to retreat from his dwelling or place of work, unless he was the initial aggressor or is assailed in his place of work by another person whose place of work the actor knows it to be; and

            (2)   a public officer justified in using force in the performance of his duties or a person justified in using force in his assistance or a person justified in using force in making an arrest or preventing an escape is not obliged to desist from efforts to perform such duty, effect such arrest or prevent such escape because of

resistance or threatened resistance by or on behalf of the person against whom such action is directed.

(c) Except as required by paragraphs (a) and (b) of this Subsection, a person employing protective force may estimate the necessity thereof under the circumstances as he believes them to be when the force is used, without retreating, surrendering possession, doing any other act that he has no legal duty to do or abstaining from any lawful action.

(3) *Use of Confinement as Protective Force.* The justification afforded by this Section extends to the use of confinement as protective force only if the actor takes all reasonable measures to terminate the confinement as soon as he knows that he safely can, unless the person confined has been arrested on a charge of crime.

Section 3.05:   Use of Force for the Protection of Other Persons.

(1) Subject to the provisions of this Section and of Section 3.09, the use of force upon or toward the person of another is justifiable to protect a third person when:

(a) the actor would be justified under Section 3.04 in using such force to protect himself against the injury he believes to be threatened to the person whom he seeks to protect; and

(b) under the circumstances as the actor believes them to be, the person whom he seeks to protect would be justified in using such protective force; and

(c) the actor believes that his intervention is necessary for the protection of such other person.

(2) Notwithstanding Subsection (1) of this Section:

(a) when the actor would be obliged under Section 3.04 to retreat, to surrender the possession of a thing or to comply with a demand before using force in self-protection, he is not obliged to do so before using force for the protection of another person, unless he knows that he can thereby secure the complete safety of such other person; and

(b) when the person whom the actor seeks to protect would be obliged under Section 3.04 to retreat, to surrender the possession of a thing or to comply with a demand if he knew that he could obtain complete safety by so doing, the actor is obliged to try to cause him to do so before using force in his protection if the actor knows that he can obtain complete safety in that way; and

(c) neither the actor nor the person whom he seeks to protect is obliged to retreat when in the other's dwelling or place of work to any greater extent than in his own.

Section 3.06:   Use of Force for the Protection of Property.

(1) *Use of Force Justifiable for Protection of Property.* Subject to the provisions of this Section and of Section 3.09, the use of force upon or toward the person of another is justifiable when the actor believes that such force is immediately necessary:

   (a) to prevent or terminate an unlawful entry or other trespass upon land or a trespass against or the unlawful carrying away of tangible, movable property, provided that such land or movable property is, or is believed by the actor to be, in his possession or in the possession of another person for whose protection he acts; or

   (b) to effect an entry or re-entry upon land or to retake tangible movable property, provided that the actor believes that he or the person by whose authority he acts or a person from whom he or such other person derives title was unlawfully dispossessed of such land or movable property and is entitled to possession, and provided, further, that:

   (i) the force is used immediately or on fresh pursuit after such dispossession; or

   (ii) the actor believes that the person against whom he uses force has no claim of right to the possession of the property and, in the case of land, the circumstances, as the actor believes them to be, are of such urgency that it would be an exceptional hardship to postpone the entry or re-entry until a court order is obtained.

(2) *Meaning of Possession.* For the purposes of Subsection (1) of this Section:

   (a) a person who has parted with the custody of property to another who refuses to restore it to him is no longer in possession, unless the property is movable and was and still is located on land in his possession;

   (b) a person who has been dispossessed of land does not regain possession thereof merely by setting foot thereon;

   (c) a person who has a license to use or occupy real property is deemed to be in possession thereof except against the licensor acting under claim of right.

(3) *Limitations on Justifiable Use of Force.*

   (a) Request to Desist. The use of force is justifiable under this Section only if the actor first requests the person against whom such force is used to desist from his interference with the property, unless the actor believes that:

   (i) such request would be useless; or

   (ii) it would be dangerous to himself or another person to make the request; or

(iii) substantial injury will be done to the physical condition of the property that is sought to be protected before the request can effectively be made.

(b) Exclusion of Trespasser. The use of force to prevent or terminate a trespass is not justifiable under this Section if the actor knows that the exclusion of the trespasser will expose him to substantial danger of serious bodily injury.

(c) Resistance of Lawful Re-entry or Recaption. The use of force to prevent an entry or re-entry upon land or the recaption of movable property is not justifiable under this Section, although the actor believes that such re-entry or recaption is unlawful, if:

(i) the re-entry or recaption is made by or on behalf of a person who was actually dispossessed of the property; and

(ii) it is otherwise justifiable under paragraph (1)(b) of this Section.

(d) Use of Deadly Force. The use of deadly force is not justifiable under this Section unless the actor believes that:

(i) the person against whom the force is used is attempting to dispossess him of his dwelling otherwise than under a claim of right to its possession; or

(ii) the person against whom the force is used is attempting to commit or consummate arson, burglary, robbery or other felonious theft or property destruction and either:

(1) has employed or threatened deadly force against or in the presence of the actor; or

(2) the use of force other than deadly force to prevent the commission or the consummation of the crime would expose the actor or another in his presence to substantial danger of serious bodily injury.

(4) *Use of Confinement as Protective Force.* The justification afforded by this Section extends to the use of confinement as protective force only if the actor takes all reasonable measures to terminate the confinement as soon as he knows that he can do so with safety to the property, unless the person confined has been arrested on a charge of crime.

(5) *Use of Device to Protect Property.* The justification afforded by this Section extends to the use of a device for the purpose of protecting property only if:

(a) the device is not designed to cause or known to create a substantial risk of causing death or serious bodily injury; and

(b) the use of the particular device to protect the property from entry or trespass is reasonable under the circumstances, as the actor believes them to be; and

   (c)   the device is one customarily used for such a purpose or reasonable care is taken to make known to probable intruders the fact that it is used.

(6)   *Use of Force to Pass Wrongful Obstructor.* The use of force to pass a person whom the actor believes to be purposely or knowingly and unjustifiably obstructing the actor from going to a place to that he may lawfully go is justifiable, provided that.

   (a)   the actor believes that the person against whom he uses force has no claim of right to obstruct the actor; and

   (b)   the actor is not being obstructed from entry or movement on land that he knows to be in the possession or custody of the person obstructing him, or in the possession or custody of another person by whose authority the obstructor acts, unless the circumstances, as the actor believes them to be, are of such urgency that it would not be reasonable to postpone the entry or movement on such land until a court order is obtained; and

   (c)   the force used is not greater than would be justifiable if the person obstructing the actor were using force against him to prevent his passage.

Section 3.07:   Use of Force in Law Enforcement.

(1)   Use of Force Justifiable to Effect an Arrest. Subject to the provisions of this Section and of Section 3.09, the use of force upon or toward the person of another is justifiable when the actor is making or assisting in making an arrest and the actor believes that such force is immediately necessary to effect a lawful arrest.

(2)   Limitations on the Use of Force.

   (a)   The use of force is not justifiable under this Section unless:

      (i)   the actor makes known the purpose of the arrest or believes that it is otherwise known by or cannot reasonably be made known to the person to be arrested; and

      (ii)   when the arrest is made under a warrant, the warrant is valid or believed by the actor to be valid.

   (b)   The use of deadly force is not justifiable under this Section unless:

      (i)   the arrest is for a felony; and

      (ii)   the person effecting the arrest is authorized to act as a peace officer or is assisting a person whom he believes to be authorized to act as a peace officer; and

      (iii)   the actor believes that the force employed creates no substantial risk of injury to innocent persons; and

      (iv)   the actor believes that:

(1)   the crime for that the arrest is made involved conduct including the use or threatened use of deadly force; or

(2)   there is a substantial risk that the person to be arrested will cause death or serious bodily injury if his apprehension is delayed.

(3)   Use of Force to Prevent Escape from Custody. The use of force to prevent the escape of an arrested person from custody is justifiable when the force could justifiably have been employed to effect the arrest under that the person is in custody, except that a guard or other person authorized to act as a peace officer is justified in using any force, including deadly force, that he believes to be immediately necessary to prevent the escape of a person from a jail, prison, or other institution for the detention of persons charged with or convicted of a crime.

(4)   Use of Force by Private Person Assisting an Unlawful Arrest.

(a)   A private person who is summoned by a peace officer to assist in effecting an unlawful arrest, is justified in using any force that he would be justified in using if the arrest were lawful, provided that he does not believe the arrest is unlawful.

(b)   A private person who assists another private person in effecting an unlawful arrest, or who, not being summoned, assists a peace officer in effecting an unlawful arrest, is justified in using any force that he would be justified in using if the arrest were lawful, provided that (i) he believes the arrest is lawful, and (ii) the arrest would be lawful if the facts were as he believes them to be.

(5)   Use of Force to Prevent Suicide or the Commission of a Crime.

(a)   The use of force upon or toward the person of another is justifiable when the actor believes that such force is immediately necessary to prevent such other person from committing suicide, inflicting serious bodily injury upon himself, committing or consummating the commission of a crime involving or threatening bodily injury, damage to or loss of property or a breach of the peace, except that:

    (i)   any limitations imposed by the other provisions of this Article on the justifiable use of force in self-protection, for the protection of others, the protection of property, the effectuation of an arrest or the prevention of an escape from custody shall apply notwithstanding the criminality of the conduct against that such force is used; and

    (ii)   the use of deadly force is not in any event justifiable under this Subsection unless:

    (1)   the actor believes that there is a substantial risk that the person whom he seeks to prevent from committing a crime will cause death or serious bodily injury to another unless the commission or the consummation of the crime is prevented and that the use of such force presents no substantial risk of injury to innocent persons; or

    (2)   the actor believes that the use of such force is necessary to suppress a riot or mutiny after the rioters or mutineers have been ordered to disperse and warned, in any particular manner that the law may require, that such force will be used if they do not obey.

    (b)   The justification afforded by this Subsection extends to the use of confinement as preventive force only if the actor takes all reasonable measures to terminate the confinement as soon as he knows that he safely can, unless the person confined has been arrested on a charge of crime.

Section 3.08: Use of Force by Persons with Special Responsibility for Care, Discipline or Safety of Others.

The use of force upon or toward the person of another is justifiable if:

    (1)   the actor is the parent or guardian or other person similarly responsible for the general care and supervision of a minor or a person acting at the request of such parent, guardian or other responsible person and:

        (a)   the force is used for the purpose of safeguarding or promoting the welfare of the minor, including the prevention or punishment of his misconduct; and

        (b)   the force used is not designed to cause or known to create a substantial risk of causing death, serious bodily injury, disfigurement, extreme pain or mental distress or gross degradation; or

    (2)   the actor is a teacher or a person otherwise entrusted with the care or supervision for a special purpose of a minor and:

(a)   the actor believes that the force used is necessary to further such special purpose, including the maintenance of reasonable discipline in a school, class or other group, and that the use of such force is consistent with the welfare of the minor; and

(b)   the degree of force, if it had been used by the parent or guardian of the minor, would not be unjustifiable under Subsection (1)(b) of this Section; or

(3)   the actor is the guardian or other person similarly responsible for the general care and supervision of an incompetent person; and:

(a)   the force is used for the purpose of safeguarding or promoting the welfare of the incompetent person, including the prevention of his misconduct, or, when such incompetent person is in a hospital or other institution for his care and custody, for the maintenance of reasonable discipline in such institution; and

(b)   the force used is not designed to cause or known to create a substantial risk of causing death, serious bodily injury, disfigurement, extreme or unnecessary pain, mental distress, or humiliation; or

(4)   the actor is a doctor or other therapist or a person assisting him at his direction, and:

(a)   the force is used for the purpose of administering a recognized form of treatment that the actor believes to be adapted to promoting the physical or mental health of the patient; and

(b)   the treatment is administered with the consent of the patient or, if the patient is a minor or an incompetent person, with the consent of his parent or guardian or other person legally competent to consent in his behalf, or the treatment is administered in an emergency when the actor believes that no one competent to consent can be consulted and that a reasonable person, wishing to safeguard the welfare of the patient, would consent; or

(5)   the actor is a warden or other authorized official of a correctional institution, and:

(a)   he believes that the force used is necessary for the purpose of enforcing the lawful rules or procedures of the institution, unless his belief in the lawfulness of the rule or procedure sought to be enforced is erroneous and his error is due to ignorance or mistake as to the provisions of the Code, any other provision of the criminal law or the law governing the administration of the institution; and

(b)   the nature or degree of force used is not forbidden by Article 303 or 304 of the Code; and

(c)   if deadly force is used, its use is otherwise justifiable under this Article; or

(6)   the actor is a person responsible for the safety of a vessel or an aircraft or a person acting at his direction, and

    (a)   he believes that the force used is necessary to prevent interference with the operation of the vessel or aircraft or obstruction of the execution of a lawful order, unless his belief in the lawfulness of the order is erroneous and his error is due to ignorance or mistake as to the law defining his authority; and

    (b)   if deadly force is used, its use is otherwise justifiable under this Article; or

(7)   the actor is a person who is authorized or required by law to maintain order or decorum in a vehicle, train or other carrier or in a place where others are assembled, and:

    (a)   he believes that the force used is necessary for such purpose; and

    (b)   the force used is not designed to cause or known to create a substantial risk of causing death, bodily injury, or extreme mental distress.

Section 3.09:   Mistake of Law as to Unlawfulness of Force or Legality of Arrest; Reckless or Negligent Use of Otherwise Justifiable Force; Reckless or Negligent Injury or Risk of Injury to Innocent Persons.

(1)   The justification afforded by Sections 3.04 to 3.07, inclusive, is unavailable when:

    (a)   the actor's belief in the unlawfulness of the force or conduct against that he employs protective force or his belief in the lawfulness of an arrest that he endeavors to effect by force is erroneous; and

    (b)   his error is due to ignorance or mistake as to the provisions of the Code, any other provision of the criminal law or the law governing the legality of an arrest or search.

(2)   When the actor believes that the use of force upon or toward the person of another is necessary for any of the purposes for that such belief would establish a justification under Sections 3.03 to 3.08 but the actor is reckless or negligent in having such belief or in acquiring or failing to acquire any knowledge or belief that is material to the justifiability of his use of force, the justification afforded by those Sections is unavailable in a prosecution for an offense for that recklessness or negligence, as the case may be, suffices to establish culpability.

(3)   When the actor is justified under Sections 3.03 to 3.08 in using force upon or toward the person of another but he recklessly or negligently injures or creates a risk of injury to innocent persons, the justification afforded by those Sections is unavailable in a prosecution for such recklessness or negligence towards innocent persons.

* * * *

Section 3.11: Definitions.

In this Article, unless a different meaning plainly is required:

(1) "unlawful force" means force, including confinement, that is employed without the consent of the person against whom it is directed and the employment of that constitutes an offense or actionable tort or would constitute such offense or tort except for a defense (such as the absence of intent, negligence, or mental capacity; duress; youth; or diplomatic status) not amounting to a privilege to use the force. Assent constitutes consent, within the meaning of this Section, whether or not it otherwise is legally effective, except assent to the infliction of death or serious bodily injury.

(2) "deadly force" means force that the actor uses with the purpose of causing or that he knows to create a substantial risk of causing death or serious bodily injury. Purposely firing a firearm in the direction of another person or at a vehicle in that another person is believed to be constitutes deadly force. A threat to cause death or serious bodily injury, by the production of a weapon or otherwise, so long as the actor's purpose is limited to creating an apprehension that he will use deadly force if necessary, does not constitute deadly force;

(3) "dwelling" means any building or structure, though movable or temporary, or a portion thereof, that is for the time being the actor's home or place of lodging.

ARTICLE 4.
RESPONSIBILITY

Section 4.01: Mental Disease or Defect Excluding Responsibility.

(1) A person is not responsible for criminal conduct if at the time of such conduct as a result of mental disease or defect he lacks substantial capacity either to appreciate the criminality [wrongfulness] of his conduct or to conform his conduct to the requirements of law.

(2) As used in this Article, the terms "mental disease or defect" do not include an abnormality manifested only by repeated criminal or otherwise anti-social conduct.

Section 4.02: Evidence of Mental Disease or Defect Admissible When Relevant to Element of the Offense; [Mental Disease or Defect Impairing Capacity as Ground for Mitigation of Punishment in Capital Cases].

(1)   Evidence that the defendant suffered from a mental disease or defect is admissible whenever it is relevant to prove that the defendant did or did not have a state of mind that is an element of the offense.

[(2)   Whenever the jury or the Court is authorized to determine or to recommend whether or not the defendant shall be sentenced to death or imprisonment upon conviction, evidence that the capacity of the defendant to appreciate the criminality [wrongfulness] of his conduct or to conform his conduct to the requirements of law was impaired as a result of mental disease or defect is admissible in favor of sentence of imprisonment.]

Note: The bracketed provision (2) applies only in those jurisdictions that have the death penalty.

Section   4.03: Mental   Disease   or   Defect   Excluding Responsibility Is Affirmative Defense; Requirement of Notice; Form of Verdict and Judgment When Finding of Irresponsibility Is Made.

(1)   Mental disease or defect excluding responsibility is an affirmative defense.

(2)   Evidence of mental disease or defect excluding responsibility is not admissible unless the defendant, at the time of entering his plea of not guilty or within ten days thereafter or at such later time as the Court may for good cause permit, files a written notice of his purpose to rely on such defense.

(3)   When the defendant is acquitted on the ground of mental disease or defect excluding responsibility, the verdict and the judgment shall so state.

Section 4.04: Mental Disease or Defect Excluding Fitness to Proceed.

No person who as a result of mental disease or defect lacks capacity to understand the proceedings against him or to assist in his own defense shall be tried, convicted or sentenced for the commission of an offense so long as such incapacity endures.

Section 4.05: Psychiatric Examination of Defendant with Respect to Mental Disease or Defect.

(1)   Whenever the defendant has filed a notice of intention to rely on the defense of mental disease or defect excluding responsibility, or there is reason to doubt his fitness to proceed, or reason to believe that mental disease or defect of the defendant will otherwise become an issue in the

cause, the Court shall appoint at least one qualified psychiatrist or shall request the Superintendent of the _____ Hospital to designate at least one qualified psychiatrist, that designation may be or include himself, to examine and report upon the mental condition of the defendant. The Court may order the defendant to be committed to a hospital or other suitable facility for the purpose of the examination for a period of not exceeding sixty days or such longer period as the Court determines to be necessary for the purpose and may direct that a qualified psychiatrist retained by the defendant be permitted to witness and participate in the examination.

(2)   In such examination any method may be employed that is accepted by the medical profession for the examination of those alleged to be suffering from mental disease or defect.

(3)   The report of the examination shall include the following: (a) a description of the nature of the examination; (b) a diagnosis of the mental condition of the defendant; (c) if the defendant suffers from a mental disease or defect, an opinion as to his capacity to understand the proceedings against him and to assist in his own defense; (d) when a notice of intention to rely on the defense of irresponsibility has been filed, an opinion as to the extent, if any, to that the capacity of the defendant to appreciate the criminality [wrongfulness] of his conduct or to conform his conduct to the requirements of law was impaired at the time of the criminal conduct charged; and (e) when directed by the Court, an opinion as to the capacity of the defendant to have a particular state of mind that is an element of the offense charged.

If the examination can not be conducted by reason of the unwillingness of the defendant to participate therein, the report shall so state and shall include, if possible, an opinion as to whether such unwillingness of the defendant was the result of mental disease or defect.

The report of the examination shall be filed [in triplicate] with the clerk of the Court, who shall cause copies to be delivered to the district attorney and to counsel for the defendant.

Section 4.06: Determination of Fitness to Proceed; Effect of Finding of Unfitness; Proceedings if Fitness is Regained [; Post-Commitment Hearing].

(1)   When the defendant's fitness to proceed is drawn in question, the issue shall be determined by the Court. If neither the prosecuting attorney nor counsel for the defendant contests the finding of the report filed pursuant to Section 4.05, the Court may make the determination on the basis of such report. If the finding is contested, the Court shall hold a hearing on the issue. If the report is received in evidence upon such hearing, the party who contests the finding thereof shall have the right to summon and to cross- examine the psychiatrists who joined in the report and to offer evidence upon the issue.

(2)   If the Court determines that the defendant lacks fitness to proceed, the proceeding against him shall be suspended, except as provided in Subsection (3) [Subsections (3) and (4)] of this Section, and the Court shall commit him to the custody of the Commissioner of Mental Hygiene [Public Health or Correction] to be placed in an appropriate institution of the Department of Mental Hygiene [Public Health or Correction] for so long as such unfitness shall endure. When the Court, on its own motion or upon the application of the Commissioner of Mental Hygiene [Public Health or Correction] or the prosecuting attorney, determines, after a hearing if a hearing is requested, that the defendant has regained fitness to proceed, the proceeding shall be resumed. If, however, the Court is of the view that so much time has elapsed since the commitment of the defendant that it would be unjust to resume the criminal proceeding, the Court may dismiss the charge and may order the defendant to be discharged or, subject to the law governing the civil commitment of persons suffering from mental disease or defect, order the defendant to be committed to an appropriate institution of the Department of Mental Hygiene [Public Health].

(3)   The fact that the defendant is unfit to proceed does not preclude any legal objection to the prosecution that is susceptible of fair determination prior to trial and without the personal participation of the defendant.

[Alternative: (3) At any time within ninety days after commitment as provided in Subsection (2) of this Section, or at any later time with permission of the Court granted for good cause, the defendant or his counsel or the Commissioner of Mental Hygiene [Public Health or Correction] may apply for a special post-commitment hearing. If the application is made by or on behalf of a defendant not represented by counsel, he shall be afforded a reasonable opportunity to obtain counsel, and if he lacks funds to do so, counsel shall be assigned by the Court. The application shall be granted only if the counsel for the defendant satisfies the Court by affidavit or otherwise that as an attorney he has reasonable grounds for a good faith belief that his client has, on the facts and the law, a defense to the charge other than mental disease or defect excluding responsibility.]

[(4) If the motion for a special post-commitment hearing is granted, the hearing shall be by the Court without a jury. No evidence shall be offered at the hearing by either party on the issue of mental disease or defect as a defense to, or in mitigation of, the crime charged. After hearing, the Court may in an appropriate case quash the indictment or other charge, or find it to be defective or insufficient, or determine that it is not proved beyond a reasonable doubt by the evidence, or otherwise terminate the proceedings on the evidence or the law. In any such case, unless all defects in the proceedings are promptly cured, the Court shall terminate the commitment ordered under Subsection (2) of this Section and order the defendant to be discharged or, subject to the law governing the civil commitment of persons suffering from mental disease or defect, order the defendant to be committed to an appropriate institution of the Department of Mental Hygiene [Public Health].]

Section 4.07: **Determination of Irresponsibility on Basis of Report; Access to Defendant by Psychiatrist of His Own Choice; Form of Expert Testimony When Issue of Responsibility Is Tried.**

(1)   If the report filed pursuant to Section 4.05 finds that the defendant at the time of the criminal conduct charged suffered from a mental disease or defect that substantially impaired his capacity to appreciate the criminality [wrongfulness] of his conduct or to conform his conduct to the requirements of law, and the Court, after a hearing if a hearing is requested by the prosecuting attorney or the defendant, is satisfied that such impairment was sufficient to exclude responsibility, the Court on motion of the defendant shall enter judgment of acquittal on the ground of mental disease or defect excluding responsibility.

(2)   When, notwithstanding the report filed pursuant to Section 4.05, the defendant wishes to be examined by a qualified psychiatrist or other expert of his own choice, such examiner shall be permitted to have reasonable access to the defendant for the purposes of such examination.

(3)   Upon the trial, the psychiatrists who reported pursuant to Section 4.05 may be called as witnesses by the prosecution, the defendant or the Court. If the issue is being tried before a jury, the jury may be informed that the psychiatrists were designated by the Court or by the Superintendent of the _____ Hospital at the request of the Court, as the case may be. If called by the Court, the witness shall be subject to cross-examination by the prosecution and by the defendant. Both the prosecution and the defendant may summon any other qualified psychiatrist or other expert to testify, but no one who has not examined the defendant shall be competent to testify to an expert opinion with respect to the mental condition or responsibility of the defendant, as distinguished from the validity of the procedure followed by, or the general scientific propositions stated by, another witness.

(4)   When a psychiatrist or other expert who has examined the defendant testifies concerning his mental condition, he shall be permitted to make a statement as to the nature of his examination, his diagnosis of the mental condition of the defendant at the time of the commission of the offense charged and his opinion as to the extent, if any, to that the capacity of the defendant to appreciate the criminality [wrongfulness] of his conduct or to conform his conduct to the requirements of law or to have a particular state of mind that is an element of the offense charged was impaired as a result of mental disease or defect at that time. He shall be permitted to make any explanation reasonably serving to clarify his diagnosis and opinion and may be cross-examined as to any matter bearing on his competency or credibility or the validity of his diagnosis or opinion.

Section 4.08: Legal Effect of Acquittal on the Ground of Mental Disease or Defect Excluding Responsibility; Commitment; Release or Discharge.

(1)   When a defendant is acquitted on the ground of mental disease or defect excluding responsibility, the Court shall order him to be committed to the custody of the Commissioner of Mental Hygiene [Public Health] to be placed in an appropriate institution for custody, care and treatment.

(2)   If the Commissioner of Mental Hygiene [Public Health] is of the view that a person committed to his custody, pursuant to Subsection(1) of this Section, may be discharged or released on condition without danger to himself or to others, he shall make application for the discharge or release of such person in a report to the Court by that such person was committed and shall transmit a copy of such application and report to the prosecuting attorney of the county [parish] from that the defendant was committed. The Court shall thereupon appoint at least two qualified psychiatrists to examine such person and to report within sixty days, or such longer period as the Court determines to be necessary for the purpose, their opinion as to his mental condition. To facilitate such examination and the proceedings thereon, the Court may cause such person to be confined in any institution located near the place where the Court sits, that may hereafter be designated by the Commissioner of Mental Hygiene [Public Health] as suitable for the temporary detention of irresponsible persons.

(3)   If the Court is satisfied by the report filed pursuant to Subsection (2) of this Section and such testimony of the reporting psychiatrists as the Court deems necessary that the committed person may be discharged or released on condition without danger to himself or others, the Court shall order his discharge or his release on such conditions as the Court determines to be necessary. If the Court is not so satisfied, it shall promptly order a hearing to determine whether such person may safely be discharged or released. Any such hearing shall be deemed a civil proceeding and the burden shall be upon the committed person to prove that he may safely be discharged or released. According to the determination of the Court upon the hearing, the committed person shall thereupon be discharged or released on such conditions as the Court determines to be necessary, or shall be recommitted to the custody of the Commissioner of Mental Hygiene [Public Health], subject to discharge or release only in accordance with the procedure prescribed above for a first hearing.

(4)   If, within [five] years after the conditional release of a committed person, the Court shall determine, after hearing evidence, that the conditions of release have not been fulfilled and that for the safety of such person or for the safety of others his conditional release should be revoked, the Court shall forthwith order him to be recommitted to the Commissioner of Mental Hygiene [Public Health], subject to discharge or release only in accordance with the procedure prescribed above for a first hearing.

(5)   A committed person may make application for his discharge or release to the Court by that he was committed, and the procedure to be followed upon such application shall be the same as that prescribed above in the case of an application by the Commissioner of Mental Hygiene [Public Health]. However, no such application by a committed person need be considered until he has been confined for a period of not less than [six months] from the date of the order of commitment, and if the determination of the Court be adverse to the application, such person shall not be permitted to file a further application until [one year] has elapsed from the date of any preceding hearing on an application for his release or discharge.

* * * *

Section 4.10: Immaturity Excluding Criminal Convictions; Transfer of Proceedings to Juvenile Court.

(1)   A person shall not be tried for or convicted of an offense if:

(a)   at the time of the conduct charged to constitute the offense he was less than sixteen years of age [, in that case the Juvenile Court shall have exclusive jurisdiction [FN*]]; or

(b)   at the time of the conduct charged to constitute the offense he was sixteen or seventeen years of age, unless:

(i)   the Juvenile Court has no jurisdiction over him, or,

(ii)   the Juvenile Court has entered an order waiving jurisdiction and consenting to the institution of criminal proceedings against him.

(2)   No court shall have jurisdiction to try or convict a person of an offense if criminal proceedings against him are barred by Subsection (1) of this Section. When it appears that a person charged with the commission of an offense may be of such an age that criminal proceedings may be barred under Subsection (1) of this Section, the Court shall hold a hearing thereon, and the burden shall be on the prosecution to establish to the satisfaction of the Court that the criminal proceeding is not barred upon such grounds. If the Court determines that the proceeding is barred, custody of the person charged shall be surrendered to the Juvenile Court, and the case, including all papers and processes relating thereto, shall be transferred.

ARTICLE 5.
INCHOATE CRIMES

Section 5.01: Criminal Attempt.

(1)   *Definition of Attempt.* A person is guilty of an attempt to commit a crime if, acting with the kind of culpability otherwise required for commission of the crime, he:

(a)   purposely engages in conduct that would constitute the crime if the attendant circumstances were as he believes them to be; or

(b)   when causing a particular result is an element of the crime, does or omits to do anything with the purpose of causing or with the belief that it will cause such result without further conduct on his part; or

(c)   purposely does or omits to do anything that, under the circumstances as he believes them to be, is an act or omission constituting a substantial step in a course of conduct planned to culminate in his commission of the crime.

(2)   *Conduct That May Be Held Substantial Step Under Subsection (1)(c).* Conduct shall not be held to constitute a substantial step under Subsection (1)(c) of this Section unless it is strongly corroborative of the actor's criminal purpose. Without negativing the sufficiency of other conduct, the following, if strongly corroborative of the actor's criminal purpose, shall not be held insufficient as a matter of law:

(a)   lying in wait, searching for or following the contemplated victim of the crime;

(b)   enticing or seeking to entice the contemplated victim of the crime to go to the place contemplated for its commission;

(c)   reconnoitering the place contemplated for the commission of the crime;

(d)   unlawful entry of a structure, vehicle or enclosure in that it is contemplated that the crime will be committed;

(e)   possession of materials to be employed in the commission of the crime, that are specially designed for such unlawful use or that can serve no lawful purpose of the actor under the circumstances;

(f)   possession, collection or fabrication of materials to be employed in the commission of the crime, at or near the place contemplated for its commission, where such possession, collection or fabrication serves no lawful purpose of the actor under the circumstances;

(g)   soliciting an innocent agent to engage in conduct constituting an element of the crime.

(3)   *Conduct Designed to Aid Another in Commission of a Crime.* A person who engages in conduct designed to aid another to commit a crime that would establish his complicity under Section 2.06 if the crime were committed by such other person, is guilty of an attempt to commit the crime, although the crime is not committed or attempted by such other person.

(4)   *Renunciation of Criminal Purpose.* When the actor's conduct would otherwise constitute an attempt under Subsection (1)(b) or (1)(c) of this Section, it is an affirmative defense that he abandoned his effort to commit the crime or otherwise prevented its commission, under circumstances

manifesting a complete and voluntary renunciation of his criminal purpose. The establishment of such defense does not, however, affect the liability of an accomplice who did not join in such abandonment or prevention.

Within the meaning of this Article, renunciation of criminal purpose is not voluntary if it is motivated, in whole or in part, by circumstances, not present or apparent at the inception of the actor's course of conduct, that increase the probability of detection or apprehension or that make more difficult the accomplishment of the criminal purpose. Renunciation is not complete if it is motivated by a decision to postpone the criminal conduct until a more advantageous time or to transfer the criminal effort to another but similar objective or victim.

Section 5.02: Criminal Solicitation.

(1) *Definition of Solicitation.* A person is guilty of solicitation to commit a crime if with the purpose of promoting or facilitating its commission he commands, encourages or requests another person to engage in specific conduct that would constitute such crime or an attempt to commit such crime or that would establish his complicity in its commission or attempted commission.

(2) *Uncommunicated Solicitation.* It is immaterial under Subsection (1) of this Section that the actor fails to communicate with the person he solicits to commit a crime if his conduct was designed to effect such communication.

(3) *Renunciation of Criminal Purpose.* It is an affirmative defense that the actor, after soliciting another person to commit a crime, persuaded him not to do so or otherwise prevented the commission of the crime, under circumstances manifesting a complete and voluntary renunciation of his criminal purpose.

Section 5.03: Criminal Conspiracy.

(1) *Definition of Conspiracy.* A person is guilty of conspiracy with another person or persons to commit a crime if with the purpose of promoting or facilitating its commission he:

(a) agrees with such other person or persons that they or one or more of them will engage in conduct that constitutes such crime or an attempt or solicitation to commit such crime; or

(b) agrees to aid such other person or persons in the planning or commission of such crime or of an attempt or solicitation to commit such crime.

(2) *Scope of Conspiratorial Relationship.* If a person guilty of conspiracy, as defined by Subsection (1) of this Section, knows that a person with whom he conspires to commit a crime has conspired with another person or persons to commit the same crime, he is guilty of conspiring with such

other person or persons, whether or not he knows their identity, to commit such crime.

(3) *Conspiracy With Multiple Criminal Objectives.* If a person conspires to commit a number of crimes, he is guilty of only one conspiracy so long as such multiple crimes are the object of the same agreement or continuous conspiratorial relationship.

(4) *Joinder and Venue in Conspiracy Prosecutions.*

(a) Subject to the provisions of paragraph (b) of this Subsection, two or more persons charged with criminal conspiracy may be prosecuted jointly if:

(i) they are charged with conspiring with one another; or

(ii) the conspiracies alleged, whether they have the same or different parties, are so related that they constitute different aspects of a scheme of organized criminal conduct.

(b) In any joint prosecution under paragraph (a) of this Subsection:

(i) no defendant shall be charged with a conspiracy in any county [parish or district] other than one in that he entered into such conspiracy or in that an overt act pursuant to such conspiracy was done by him or by a person with whom he conspired; and

(ii) neither the liability of any defendant nor the admissibility against him of evidence of acts or declarations of another shall be enlarged by such joinder; and

(iii) the Court shall order a severance or take a special verdict as to any defendant who so requests, if it deems it necessary or appropriate to promote the fair determination of his guilt or innocence, and shall take any other proper measures to protect the fairness of the trial.

(5) *Overt Act.* No person may be convicted of conspiracy to commit a crime, other than a felony of the first or second degree, unless an overt act in pursuance of such conspiracy is alleged and proved to have been done by him or by a person with whom he conspired.

(6) *Renunciation of Criminal Purpose.* It is an affirmative defense that the actor, after conspiring to commit a crime, thwarted the success of the conspiracy, under circumstances manifesting a complete and voluntary renunciation of his criminal purpose.

(7) *Duration of Conspiracy.* For purposes of Section 1.06(4):

(a) conspiracy is a continuing course of conduct that terminates when the crime or crimes that are its object are committed or the agreement that they be committed is abandoned by the defendant and by those with whom he conspired; and

(b)   such abandonment is presumed if neither the defendant nor anyone with whom he conspired does any overt act in pursuance of the conspiracy during the applicable period of limitation; and

(c)   if an individual abandons the agreement, the conspiracy is terminated as to him only if and when he advises those with whom he conspired of his abandonment or he informs the law enforcement authorities of the existence of the conspiracy and of his participation therein.

Section 5.04:   Incapacity, Irresponsibility or Immunity of Party to Solicitation or Conspiracy.

(1)   Except as provided in Subsection (2) of this Section, it is immaterial to the liability of a person who solicits or conspires with another to commit a crime that:

(a)   he or the person whom he solicits or with whom he conspires does not occupy a particular position or have a particular characteristic that is an element of such crime, if he believes that one of them does; or

(b)   the person whom he solicits or with whom he conspires is irresponsible or has an immunity to prosecution or conviction for the commission of the crime.

(2)   It is a defense to a charge of solicitation or conspiracy to commit a crime that if the criminal object were achieved, the actor would not be guilty of a crime under the law defining the offense or as an accomplice under Section 2.06(5) or 2.06(6)(a) or (b).

Section 5.05:   Grading of Criminal Attempt, Solicitation and Conspiracy; Mitigation in Cases of Lesser Danger; Multiple Convictions Barred.

(1)   *Grading.* Except as otherwise provided in this Section, attempt, solicitation and conspiracy are crimes of the same grade and degree as the most serious offense that is attempted or solicited or is an object of the conspiracy. An attempt, solicitation or conspiracy to commit a [capital crime or a] felony of the first degree is a felony of the second degree.

(2)   *Mitigation.* If the particular conduct charged to constitute a criminal attempt, solicitation or conspiracy is so inherently unlikely to result or culminate in the commission of a crime that neither such conduct nor the actor presents a public danger warranting the grading of such offense under this Section, the Court shall exercise its power under Section 6.12 to enter judgment and impose sentence for a crime of lower grade or degree or, in extreme cases, may dismiss the prosecution.

(3)   *Multiple Convictions.* A person may not be convicted of more than one offense defined by this Article for conduct designed to commit or to culminate in the commission of the same crime.

* * * *

PART II.
DEFINITION OF SPECIFIC CRIMES.
OFFENSES INVOLVING DANGER TO THE PERSON.

ARTICLE 210.
CRIMINAL HOMICIDE

Section 210.0:   **Definitions.**

In Articles 210-213, unless a different meaning plainly is required:

   (1)   "human being" means a person who has been born and is alive;

   (2)   "bodily injury" means physical pain, illness or any impairment of physical condition;

   (3)   "serious bodily injury" means bodily injury that creates a substantial risk of death or that causes serious, permanent disfigurement, or protracted loss or impairment of the function of any bodily member or organ;

   (4)   "deadly weapon" means any firearm, or other weapon, device, instrument, material or substance, whether animate or inanimate, that in the manner it is used or is intended to be used is known to be capable of producing death or serious bodily injury.

Section 210.1:   **Criminal Homicide.**

   (1)   A person is guilty of criminal homicide if he purposely, knowingly, recklessly or negligently causes the death of another human being.

   (2)   Criminal homicide is murder, manslaughter or negligent homicide.

Section 210.2:   **Murder.**

   (1)   Except as provided in Section 210.3(1)(b), criminal homicide constitutes murder when:

      (a)   it is committed purposely or knowingly; or

      (b)   it is committed recklessly under circumstances manifesting extreme indifference to the value of human life. Such recklessness and indifference are presumed if the actor is engaged or is an accomplice in the commission of, or an attempt to commit, or flight after committing or attempting to commit robbery, rape or deviate sexual intercourse by force or threat of force, arson, burglary, kidnapping or felonious escape.

   (2)   Murder is a felony of the first degree [but a person convicted of murder may be sentenced to death, as provided in Section 210.6].

Section 210.3:   Manslaughter.

(1)   Criminal homicide constitutes manslaughter when:

    (a)   it is committed recklessly; or

    (b)   a homicide that would otherwise be murder is committed under the influence of extreme mental or emotional disturbance for that there is reasonable explanation or excuse. The reasonableness of such explanation or excuse shall be determined from the viewpoint of a person in the actor's situation under the circumstances as he believes them to be.

(2)   Manslaughter is a felony of the second degree.

Section 210.4:   Negligent Homicide.

(1)   Criminal homicide constitutes negligent homicide when it is committed negligently.

(2)   Negligent homicide is a felony of the third degree.

Section 210.5:   Causing or Aiding Suicide.

(1)   Causing Suicide as Criminal Homicide. A person may be convicted of criminal homicide for causing another to commit suicide only if he purposely causes such suicide by force, duress or deception.

(2)   Aiding or Soliciting Suicide as an Independent Offense. A person who purposely aids or solicits another to commit suicide is guilty of a felony of the second degree if his conduct causes such suicide or an attempted suicide, and otherwise of a misdemeanor.

* * * *

ARTICLE 213.
SEXUAL OFFENSES

Section 213.0:   Definitions.

(1)   the definitions given in Section 210.0 apply;

(2)   "Sexual intercourse" includes intercourse per os or per anus, with some penetration however slight; emission is not required;

(3)   "Deviate sexual intercourse" means sexual intercourse per os or per anus between human beings who are not husband and wife, and any form of sexual intercourse with an animal.

Section 213.1:   Rape and Related Offenses.

(1)   *Rape.* A male who has sexual intercourse with a female not his wife is guilty of rape if:

(a)   he compels her to submit by force or by threat of imminent death, serious bodily injury, extreme pain or kidnapping, to be inflicted on anyone; or

(b)   he has substantially impaired her power to appraise or control her conduct by administering or employing without her knowledge drugs, intoxicants or other means for the purpose of preventing resistance; or

(c)   the female is unconscious; or

(d)   the female is less than 10 years old.

Rape is a felony of the second degree unless (i) in the course thereof the actor inflicts serious bodily injury upon anyone, or (ii) the victim was not a voluntary social companion of the actor upon the occasion of the crime and had not previously permitted him sexual liberties, in that cases the offense is a felony of the first degree.

(2)   Gross Sexual Imposition. A male who has sexual intercourse with a female not his wife commits a felony of the third degree if:

(a)   he compels her to submit by any threat that would prevent resistance by a woman of ordinary resolution; or

(b)   he knows that she suffers from a mental disease or defect that renders her incapable of appraising the nature of her conduct; or

(c)   he knows that she is unaware that a sexual act is being committed upon her or that she submits because she mistakenly supposes that he is her husband.

Section 213.2: Deviate Sexual Intercourse by Force or Imposition.

(1)   *By Force or Its Equivalent.* A person who engages in deviate sexual intercourse with another person, or who causes another to engage in deviate sexual intercourse, commits a felony of the second degree if:

(a)   he compels the other person to participate by force or by threat of imminent death, serious bodily injury, extreme pain or kidnapping, to be inflicted on anyone; or

(b)   he has substantially impaired the other person's power to appraise or control his conduct, by administering or employing without the knowledge of the other person drugs, intoxicants or other means for the purpose of preventing resistance; or

(c)   the other person is unconscious; or

(d)   the other person is less than 10 years old.

(2)   *By Other Imposition.* A person who engages in deviate sexual intercourse with another person, or who causes another to engage in deviate sexual intercourse, commits a felony of the third degree if:

(a)   he compels the other person to participate by any threat that would prevent resistance by a person of ordinary resolution; or

(b)   he knows that the other person suffers from a mental disease or defect that renders him incapable of appraising the nature of his conduct; or

(c)   he knows that the other person submits because he is unaware that a sexual act is being committed upon him.

Section 213.3:   Corruption of Minors and Seduction.

(1)   *Offense Defined.* A male who has sexual intercourse with a female not his wife, or any person who engages in deviate sexual intercourse or causes another to engage in deviate sexual intercourse, is guilty of an offense if:

(a)   the other person is less than [16] years old and the actor is at least [4] years older than the other person; or

(b)   the other person is less than 21 years old and the actor is his guardian or otherwise responsible for general supervision of his welfare; or

(c)   the other person is in custody of law or detained in a hospital or other institution and the actor has supervisory or disciplinary authority over him; or

(d)   the other person is a female who is induced to participate by a promise of marriage that the actor does not mean to perform.

(2)   *Grading.* An offense under paragraph (a) of Subsection (1) is a felony of the third degree. Otherwise an offense under this section is a misdemeanor.

Section 213.4:   Sexual Assault.

A person who has sexual contact with another not his spouse, or causes such other to have sexual contact with him, is guilty of sexual assault, a misdemeanor, if:

(1)   he knows that the contact is offensive to the other person; or

(2)   he knows that the other person suffers from a mental disease or defect that renders him or her incapable of appraising the nature of his or her conduct; or

(3)   he knows that the other person is unaware that a sexual act is being committed; or

(4)   the other person is less than 10 years old; or

(5)   he has substantially impaired the other person's power to appraise or control his or her conduct, by administering or employing without the other's knowledge drugs, intoxicants or other means for the purpose of preventing resistance; or

(6) the other person is less than [16] years old and the actor is at least [4] years older than the other person; or

(7) the other person is less than 21 years old and the actor is his guardian or otherwise responsible for general supervision of his welfare; or

(8) the other person is in custody of law or detained in a hospital or other institution and the actor has supervisory or disciplinary authority over him.

Sexual contact is any touching of the sexual or other intimate parts of the person for the purpose of arousing or gratifying sexual desire.

* * * *

Section 213.6:   **Provisions Generally Applicable to Article 213.**

(1) *Mistake as to Age.* Whenever in this Article the criminality of conduct depends on a child's being below the age of 10, it is no defense that the actor did not know the child's age, or reasonably believed the child to be older than 10. When criminality depends on the child's being below a critical age other than 10, it is a defense for the actor to prove by a preponderance of the evidence that he reasonably believed the child to be above the critical age.

(2) *Spouse Relationships.* Whenever in this Article the definition of an offense excludes conduct with a spouse, the exclusion shall be deemed to extend to persons living as man and wife, regardless of the legal status of their relationship. The exclusion shall be inoperative as respects spouses living apart under a decree of judicial separation. Where the definition of an offense excludes conduct with a spouse or conduct by a woman, this shall not preclude conviction of a spouse or woman as accomplice in a sexual act that he or she causes another person, not within the exclusion, to perform.

(3) *Sexually Promiscuous Complainants.* It is a defense to prosecution under Section 213.3 and paragraphs (6), (7) and (8) of Section 213.4 for the actor to prove by a preponderance of the evidence that the alleged victim had, prior to the time of the offense charged, engaged promiscuously in sexual relations with others.

(4) *Prompt Complaint.* No prosecution may be instituted or maintained under this Article unless the alleged offense was brought to the notice of public authority within [3] months of its occurrence or, where the alleged victim was less than [16] years old or otherwise incompetent to make complaint, within [3] months after a parent, guardian or other competent person specially interested in the victim learns of the offense.

(5) *Testimony of Complainants.* No person shall be convicted of any felony under this Article upon the uncorroborated testimony of the alleged victim. Corroboration may be circumstantial. In any prosecution before a jury for an offense under this Article, the jury shall be instructed to evaluate the testimony of a victim or complaining witness with special care

in view of the emotional involvement of the witness and the difficulty of determining the truth with respect to alleged sexual activities carried out in private.

OFFENSES AGAINST PROPERTY.

* * * *

ARTICLE 221.
BURGLARY & OTHER CRIMINAL INTRUSION

Section 221.0: Definitions.

In this Article, unless a different meaning plainly is required:

(1) "occupied structure" means any structure, vehicle or place adapted for overnight accommodation of persons, or for carrying on business therein, whether or not a person is actually present.

(2) "night" means the period between thirty minutes past sunset and thirty minutes before sunrise.

Section 221.1: Burglary.

(1) *Burglary Defined.* A person is guilty of burglary if he enters a building or occupied structure, or separately secured or occupied portion thereof, with purpose to commit a crime therein, unless the premises are at the time open to the public or the actor is licensed or privileged to enter. It is an affirmative defense to prosecution for burglary that the building or structure was abandoned.

(2) *Grading.* Burglary is a felony of the second degree if it is perpetrated in the dwelling of another at night, or if, in the course of committing the offense, the actor:

    (a) purposely, knowingly or recklessly inflicts or attempts to inflict bodily injury on anyone; or

    (b) is armed with explosives or a deadly weapon.

Otherwise, burglary is a felony of the third degree. An act shall be deemed "in the course of committing" an offense if it occurs in an attempt to commit the offense or in flight after the attempt or commission.

(3) *Multiple Convictions.* A person may not be convicted both for burglary and for the offense that it was his purpose to commit after the burglarious entry or for an attempt to commit that offense, unless the additional offense constitutes a felony of the first or second degree.

* * * *

ARTICLE 222.
ROBBERY

Section 222.1:   Robbery.

(1) *Robbery Defined.* A person is guilty of robbery if, in the course of committing a theft, he:

  (a)   inflicts serious bodily injury upon another; or

  (b)   threatens another with or purposely puts him in fear of immediate serious bodily injury; or

  (c)   commits or threatens immediately to commit any felony of the first or second degree.

An act shall be deemed "in the course of committing a theft" if it occurs in an attempt to commit theft or in flight after the attempt or commission.

(2) *Grading.* Robbery is a felony of the second degree, except that it is a felony of the first degree if in the course of committing the theft the actor attempts to kill anyone, or purposely inflicts or attempts to inflict serious bodily injury.

ARTICLE 223.
THEFT & RELATED OFFENSES

Section 223.0:   Definitions.

In this Article, unless a different meaning plainly is required:

(1)   "deprive" means: (a) to withhold property of another permanently or for so extended a period as to appropriate a major portion of its economic value, or with intent to restore only upon payment of reward or other compensation; or (b) to dispose of the property so as to make it unlikely that the owner will recover it.

(2)   "financial institution" means a bank, insurance company, credit union, building and loan association, investment trust or other organization held out to the public as a place of deposit of funds or medium of savings or collective investment.

(3)   "government" means the United States, any State, county, municipality, or other political unit, or any department, agency or subdivision of any of the foregoing, or any corporation or other association carrying out the functions of government.

(4)   "movable property" means property the location of that can be changed, including things growing on, affixed to, or found in land, and documents although the rights represented thereby have no physical location. "Immovable property" is all other property.

(5)   "obtain" means: (a) in relation to property, to bring about a transfer or purported transfer of a legal interest in the property, whether to the obtainer or another; or (b) in relation to labor or service, to secure performance thereof.

(6)   "property" means anything of value, including real estate, tangible and intangible personal property, contract rights, choses-in-action and other interests in or claims to wealth, admission or transportation tickets, captured or domestic animals, food and drink, electric or other power.

(7)   "property of another" includes property in that any person other than the actor has an interest that the actor is not privileged to infringe, regardless of the fact that the actor also has an interest in the property and regardless of the fact that the other person might be precluded from civil recovery because the property was used in an unlawful transaction or was subject to forfeiture as contraband. Property in possession of the actor shall not be deemed property of another who has only a security interest therein, even if legal title is in the creditor pursuant to a conditional sales contract or other security agreement.

Section 223.1: Consolidation of Theft Offenses; Grading; Provisions Applicable to Theft Generally.

(1)   *Consolidation of Theft Offenses.* Conduct denominated theft in this Article constitutes a single offense. An accusation of theft may be supported by evidence that it was committed in any manner that would be theft under this Article, notwithstanding the specification of a different manner in the indictment or information, subject only to the power of the Court to ensure fair trial by granting a continuance or other appropriate relief where the conduct of the defense would be prejudiced by lack of fair notice or by surprise.

(2)   *Grading of Theft Offenses.*

(a)   Theft constitutes a felony of the third degree if the amount involved exceeds $500, or if the property stolen is a firearm, automobile, airplane, motorcycle, motor boat, or other motor-propelled vehicle, or in the case of theft by receiving stolen property, if the receiver is in the business of buying or selling stolen property.

(b)   Theft not within the preceding paragraph constitutes a misdemeanor, except that if the property was not taken from the person or by threat, or in breach of a fiduciary obligation, and the actor proves by a preponderance of the evidence that the amount involved was less than $50, the offense constitutes a petty misdemeanor.

(c)   The amount involved in a theft shall be deemed to be the highest value, by any reasonable standard, of the property or services that the actor stole or attempted to steal. Amounts involved in thefts committed pursuant to one scheme or course of conduct, whether from the same person or several persons, may be aggregated in determining the grade of the offense.

(3)   *Claim of Right.* It is an affirmative defense to prosecution for theft that the actor:

    (a)   was unaware that the property or service was that of another; or

    (b)   acted under an honest claim of right to the property or service involved or that he had a right to acquire or dispose of it as he did; or

    (c)   took property exposed for sale, intending to purchase and pay for it promptly, or reasonably believing that the owner, if present, would have consented.

(4)   *Theft from Spouse.* It is no defense that theft was from the actor's spouse, except that misappropriation of household and personal effects, or other property normally accessible to both spouses, is theft only if it occurs after the parties have ceased living together.

Section 223.2:   Theft by Unlawful Taking or Disposition.

(1)   *Movable Property.* A person is guilty of theft if he unlawfully takes, or exercises unlawful control over, movable property of another with purpose to deprive him thereof.

(2)   *Immovable Property.* A person is guilty of theft if he unlawfully transfers immovable property of another or any interest therein with purpose to benefit himself or another not entitled thereto.

Section 223.3:   Theft by Deception.

A person is guilty of theft if he purposely obtains property of another by deception. A person deceives if he purposely:

(1)   creates or reinforces a false impression, including false impressions as to law, value, intention or other state of mind; but deception as to a person's intention to perform a promise shall not be inferred from the fact alone that he did not subsequently perform the promise; or

(2)   prevents another from acquiring information that would affect his judgment of a transaction; or

(3)   fails to correct a false impression that the deceiver previously created or reinforced, or that the deceiver knows to be influencing another to whom he stands in a fiduciary or confidential relationship; or

(4)   fails to disclose a known lien, adverse claim or other legal impediment to the enjoyment of property that he transfers or encumbers in consideration for the property obtained, whether such impediment is or is not valid, or is or is not a matter of official record.

The term "deceive" does not, however, include falsity as to matters having no pecuniary significance, or puffing by statements unlikely to deceive ordinary persons in the group addressed.

Section 223.4:   **Theft by Extortion.**

A person is guilty of theft if he purposely obtains property of another by threatening to:

(1)   inflict bodily injury on anyone or commit any other criminal offense; or

(2)   accuse anyone of a criminal offense; or

(3)   expose any secret tending to subject any person to hatred, contempt or ridicule, or to impair his credit or business repute; or

(4)   take or withhold action as an official, or cause an official to take or withhold action; or

(5)   bring about or continue a strike, boycott or other collective unofficial action, if the property is not demanded or received for the benefit of the group in whose interest the actor purports to act; or

(6)   testify or provide information or withhold testimony or information with respect to another's legal claim or defense; or

(7)   inflict any other injury that would not benefit the actor.

It is an affirmative defense to prosecution based on paragraphs (2), (3) or (4) that the property obtained by threat of accusation, exposure, lawsuit or other invocation of official action was honestly claimed as restitution or indemnification for injury done in the circumstances to that such accusation, exposure, lawsuit or other official action relates, or as compensation for property or lawful services.

* * * *

Section 223.7:   **Theft of Services.**

(1)   A person is guilty of theft if he purposely obtains services that he knows are available only for compensation, by deception or threat, or by false token or other means to avoid payment for the service. "Services" includes labor, professional service, transportation, telephone or other public service, accommodation in hotels, restaurants or elsewhere, admission to exhibitions, use of vehicles or other movable property. Where compensation for service is ordinarily paid immediately upon the rendering of such service, as in the case of hotels and restaurants, refusal to pay or absconding without payment or offer to pay gives rise to a presumption that the service was obtained by deception as to intention to pay.

(2)   A person commits theft if, having control over the disposition of services of others, to that he is not entitled, he knowingly diverts such services to his own benefit or to the benefit of another not entitled thereto.

Section 223.8: Theft by Failure to Make Required Disposition of Funds Received.

A person who purposely obtains property upon agreement, or subject to a known legal obligation, to make specified payment or other disposition, whether from such property or its proceeds or from his own property to be reserved in equivalent amount, is guilty of theft if he deals with the property obtained as his own and fails to make the required payment or disposition. The foregoing applies notwithstanding that it may be impossible to identify particular property as belonging to the victim at the time of the actor's failure to make the required payment or disposition. An officer or employee of the government or of a financial institution is presumed: (i) to know any legal obligation relevant to his criminal liability under this Section, and (ii) to have dealt with the property as his own if he fails to pay or account upon lawful demand, or if an audit reveals a shortage or falsification of accounts.

Section 223.9: Unauthorized Use of Automobiles and Other Vehicles.

A person commits a misdemeanor if he operates another's automobile, airplane, motorcycle, motorboat, or other motor-propelled vehicle without consent of the owner. It is an affirmative defense to prosecution under this Section that the actor reasonably believed that the owner would have consented to the operation had he known of it.